THE BOOK OF
COSTUME

VOLUME I

THE
BOOK
OF
COSTUME

BY
MILLIA DAVENPORT

VOLUME I

CROWN PUBLISHERS, INC.
NEW YORK

To Hark—my greatest help and hindrance

CONTENTS

Volume I

Introduction

YEARS OF WORK, research and study in the field of costume have led me to three conclusions about books on costume which I do not think are valid for me alone.

1. Books illustrated by the author are usually to be deplored, and many of them are terrible.

2. The best book is the one with the most pictures, all of them contemporary documents; the best text is based on the words of contemporaries—friends, enemies, or travelers.

3. The physical location or source of every picture, and the number of every manuscript should be given, if possible, as a help in finding colored reproductions, further information, or more illustrations from a series.

The ideal book of costume, to my way of thinking, would provide so many pictures (all documents, arranged chronologically, and in color) that the story would tell itself without words.

This book was originally planned, when commissioned more than seven years ago, as a "Dictionary of Costume" in one volume, with compressed chart-outlines of the development of dress, by civilization or century. Because of difficulties in obtaining pictures, the book lay in abeyance through the war. During these years, I found time to read more source books than research for the theater had previously permitted. I had long known that plays have a stubborn will of their own. Now I discovered that this is true also of books. The proposed dictionary had become, after the first Christian centuries, a documented survey of European and American dress and ways, calling for a very large number of illustrations.

The Book of Costume is now a chronological survey of dress through the ages. Each segment-civilization or century has been given an historical summary and an outline of changes in its dress. These are followed by a picture section, which is subdivided by centuries and by countries, as regional differentiations become well established. When a great culture is segregated by time, it has been massed under one heading, for example: Egypt, under which will be found neighboring peoples and aliens as seen by the Egyptians. The order in which countries are presented changes with the fluctuations of their influence on dress. Basic comments will be found under the leading country, and differentiations defined under the dress of others. By XIXc., when all fashion is basically French, illustrations are again massed by chronology alone.

It became clear that bibliographical and documentary material and acknowledgments might clutter and disturb the text. An Appendix was established to hold such material, which will be found there, either under general chapter headings, or under the number of relevant illustrations. The Appendix also gives primary sources; manuscripts, with indications about their availability in reprint or facsimile; early engraved books and series of plates on costume; present-day authorities, and more recently published books to which we are indebted for facts and pictures (since they are apt to be well illustrated, comprehensive, and to lead to collateral material). When space allowed, the words of original authorities are quoted in the text. Limitations of space have occasionally made it necessary to withdraw them to the Appendix, under the illustration number. For reasons which are explained in the Appendix, no bibliography of books on costume has been attempted, but a few books with documentary illustrations or special usefulness have been indicated there.

In the Index, three sorts of material will be found: names and the location of biographies of artists; of named subjects shown in illustrations; and material immediately relative to costume. A complete index would obviously be more unwieldy than useful. Our costume index has selected outstanding examples in illustration and important references in text, from the many thousands of possibilities in our two volumes.

It is almost impossible to redraw (even with the most laudable intention of clarification) without falsifying another age in terms of one's own. Illustrations redrawn at several removes from Racinet (where they were not very good to begin with, although largely taken from Willemin, an excellent book of its kind) seem to me inexcusable in the age of photo-engraving. The amount of collateral information you absorb, as you get facts from documentary illustrations, more than repays the extra effort which may be required in research. Where we have used redrawings, it is usually because the original has disappeared, has deteriorated since the record was made, or is difficult or impossible to photograph. Since there can never be enough pictures, they must be threaded together on a text, and texts are even more suspect than redrawings. All clues to the original authority for a statement are apt to have been sieved out, many books back.

The best and often the only really good information about dress comes from books which are not concerned primarily—or at all—with costume: old histories, books of Antiquaries; compilations of photographs and prints works on archaeology; histories of civilizations and their arts; catalogs and volumes sponsored by museums, libraries, universities, learned societies, and organizations like the Roxburghe Club, Walpole Society and Society of travel, diaries, memoirs and account books, even novels; and art books, sponsored by such publishers as Georg Hirth, Belvedere, Hyperion, Pantheon, Phaidon, and éd. Tel and Belles-lettres; volumes like those of D'Allemagne and Max von Boehn, dealing with textiles, accessories, toys and games, etc.; and periodicals devoted to the arts and antiquities.

Many disparate dates, spellings and attributions appear, as one collects data from even the most scrupulous museum sources. Each eminent authority has his own pet chronology, opinions and preferred way of spelling. These things are constantly being altered in the light of further research. Art objects change hands, not to mention the dislocations of war. I have not made desperate attempts to reconcile these inconsistencies, and have chosen many middle roads. Because a Pharaoh was familiar in my childhood as Sesostris is no reason why we should insist on using the Greek form of his name when many modern Egyptologists prefer Sen-Wosret. On the other hand, I have used the familiar Nefret-ity in place of more meticulous modern spellings.

I hope I have given enough quotations from sources to show in how many ways it was possible not so long ago for one man to spell the same word, even his own name, in the space of one paragraph. Changes in orthography, sometimes within less than a century, are so interesting that I have attempted, here and there, to preserve them within the limitations of type-faces available in the U.S.A., and by circumventing the diligence of proofreaders.

Many alternative and equally correct spellings for certain words in costume use will be found, even in the abridged Oxford Dictionary. The most anglicized of half a dozen or more forms is apt to be a long way from the original, which was probably French. Words change their spelling, and even their meaning, with time, country and use. I try to hold to a spelling which retains some of the significance of its origin without being archaic; but I make deliberate use of others (to which you will constantly be exposed in other books), if only to draw them to your attention.

People, events and new usages are taken up, along the way, as they present themselves in relation to illustrations. Once in a while, we have lingered over a family like the Pastons, whose rise from Saxon bondsmen is part of England's story; a family of bourgeois bankers, like the Medici, turned merchant princes, patrons of arts and letters; a court like Louis XIV's, which formed manners and taste; a sainted ecclesiastic in contrast to a hideously worldly one, at a time when French society was rent by its opinions of the Church, and divided *paniers* were called *jansénistes;* or a Cavalier like Buckingham, in contrast to the Protestant general who became his father-in-law. These things were not premeditated; but there are all sorts of disproportions which are not necessarily accidental. There is apt, for instance, to be more biographical material about obscure painters than about familiar ones. There may be more about helmets than about the rest of the equipment, just because I am a theatrical designer who has learned how much the right helmet helps, when you have to concoct extra soldiers from nearly nothing.

The end of the American Civil War, when clothing began to be mass-produced, and international exhibitions multiplied, seemed like a logical stopping place. The following eighty-odd years would require at least another volume, and a great deal of time and travel. I think it is very much needed, and I should like to do it, if ever I get my garden in shape, and my courage back; and we are still alive, and interested in such matters.

Acknowledgments

IT IS NOT possible to collect thousands of pictures and information about them without receiving more kindness and help than one can ever acknowledge.

I have worked so long at the Metropolitan Museum that I must be under obligation to almost everybody on its payroll. Mr. Horace H. F. Jayne, its Vice-Director, made available the Museum's collection of negatives just when the low point of discouragement about photographs from Europe had been reached, and the book had kept me from going to Hollywood to do *Macbeth* for Orson Welles. In the order in which the Museum lists its departments in the Bulletin, I must thank Mr. Ambrose Lansing, Curator of Egyptology; Miss Gisela Richter and her Associate in Greek and Roman Art, Miss Christine Alexander; Mr. William H. Forsyth and Miss Margaret B. Freeman, in Mediaeval Art; Mrs. A. Ten Eyck Gardner, Miss Margaretta M. Salinger, and Miss Margaret Scherer, in the Department of Paintings. Mr. William J. Ivins, Jr., Curator Emeritus, and Mr. A. Hyatt Mayor, present Curator of the Print Department, and the staff have shown so much interest, made so many suggestions, and answered so many cries for help from the country that I must thank them all, Miss Alice Newlin, Miss Olivia H. Paine, and Miss Janet S. Byrne in particular. My greatest regret is that the physical mass of my material, which was filed in the country, made it impossible for me to avail myself of the extraordinarily kind offer of Mr. Stephen V. Grancsay, Curator of the Arms and Armor Department, to go over all of that material in the illustrations. The Executive Director of the Costume Institute, Miss Polaire Weissman, was very helpful, as was Miss Marian P. Bolles of the Textile Collection. For a year, the Photograph Collection, whose Curator, Miss Alice Franklin, had gone to Barnard with me, was practically my office, while I selected material and consulted about its suitability for reproduction with Mr. Alexander, the ablest photostat man I ever met, now unfortunately lost to the Museum. Nobody could have been friendlier than Miss Franklin's entire staff have been for many years. I spent pleasant months in the Lending and the Lantern Slide Collections, both under Mrs. Ruth J. Terrill, and then put Mr. Edward J. Milla, who is responsible for the Museum's fine photographs, and his assistants to a great deal of trouble. Literally thousands of orders were filled by Miss Evelyn B. Grier's Information and Sales service. Mr. Walter Hauser's staff in the Library showed much helpful interest.

I am greatly indebted to Dr. Guido Schoenberger of the Institute of Fine Arts of New York University for being given access to the Institute's collection of lantern slide negatives, and to the help of Mr. Russell and other members of the staff. As we met at the files, Dr. Karl Lehmann-Hartleben of N.Y.U. was good enough to indicate material which I should otherwise have missed, and give me information about the content of other photographs.

The wonderful resources of the Frick Art Reference Library were made available by Miss Ethelwyn Manning and her assistant, Miss Hanna Johnson; and research by Miss M. Steinbach and Miss V. Seery was a godsend when I had to stay for long periods in the country.

The principal source of manuscript material and XVIIc. costume plates was, of course, the Pierpont Morgan Library, under Miss Belle da Costa Greene, and endless courtesies were extended by Miss Meta Harssen.

Near-by Cooper Union was always a great help. I am particularly obliged to Mr. Calvin Hathaway, the Director of the Museum for the Arts of Decoration, the late Miss Elizabeth Haines, and Miss Edna Donnell. Mr. Richard E. Morse and Mrs. E. Volkov, in the Museum's delightful little library, were tireless in looking up details for us, as were the staff of the main library, and the library of the Art School, many of whom I met only by telephone.

At the New York Public Library, Mr. Karl Kup and Mr. A. M. Trotter in the Print Collection; Mr. Percy Clapp in the Rare Book Room; Miss Eleanor Mitchell and her successor, Miss Muriel Baldwin, in Arts and Architecture; Mr. George Freedley and his successor, Mrs. E. P. Barrett, in the Theater Section; the staff of the Genealogy Room, who clarified so many relationships by telephone; Mr. Robert Kingery, the Readers' Adviser; Miss Romana Javitz of the Picture Collection; and perhaps most of all, the many services of the Reference Department under Mr. Paul North Rice, must be thanked for their assistance.

At the Hispanic Society, Miss Ruth M. Anderson was generous with time and information.

We are under great obligation to Mr. John D. Cooney, Curator of Egyptology at the Brooklyn Museum, and to his assistant, my old friend Mrs. Elizabeth Riefstahl, for the loan of illustrations from the precious out-of-print catalogue of the exhibition of "Pagan and Christian Egypt" in 1941. The Museum is also the source of many photographs of actual costumes.

Very special thanks indeed are given to Miss Gertrude Townsend, Curator of Textiles in the Boston Museum of Fine Arts, and to her assistant in charge of Costume, Mrs. Jean Reed. They put off vacations in order to show me a glimpse of the wonders of the Elizabeth Day McCormick Collection of Costume, which was still being accessioned. In beginning the photography of the collection (which will take a lifetime to complete), they were good enough to select objects in which I had shown special interest, and accompanied each with detailed descriptions, in case there were lacunae in the notes I took during two and a half frantic days at the Museum, in the midst of a collection which cannot possibly be seen in so short a time as a month. I am also obliged to the Director, Mr. G. H. Edgell, and to Mr. Henry P. Rossiter, the Curator of Prints.

Mrs. Fern Rusk Shapley and her assistant, Miss Caroline L. Huddle, at the National Gallery of Art in Washington, D.C., have answered many questions, as have Miss Louisa Dresser of the Worcester Art Museum; Mr. James W. Foster, Director of the Maryland Historical Society; Mr. James L. Cogar, Curator of Colonial Williamsburg; Mr. Heinrich Schwarz, of the Museum of the Rhode Island School of Design; Mr. David Wilder, Librarian of Hamilton College; the Secretary of the Elizabethan Club, and Miss Anna S. Pratt, Reference Librarian, at Yale University; Miss Carolyn Scoon of the New York Historical Society; Mrs. Alexander Quarrier Smith; and Sir Osbert Sitwell.

Special questions have been answered by Mr. Benjamin Parry, head of the United States Weather Bureau in New York, and Mr. Merrill Barnard of the Washington headquarters; by the Very Rev. Msgr. Thomas J. McMahon, S.T.D.; by Prof. Edgar Wind of Smith College; by Henri Marceau, Curator of the John G. Johnson Collection in Philadelphia; by Mr. Francis Thompson, Librarian and Keeper of the Collections of the Duke of Devonshire; by the Directors of the Victoria and Albert, and of the South Kensington Museums; and by Monsieur J. Porcher, Curator of the Manuscript Collection of the Bibliothèque nationale.

Not nearly enough residents of New York State have ever heard about the wonders of their State Library. No matter how far back in the woods you may find yourself, practically any book you may require will be sent down within three days after application to your nearest branch library. I am obliged to Mr. Charles F. Gosnell, the State Librarian, and to Miss Powell and Miss Halstead of the excellent library at Nyack, for many weeks' use of books which no city library would ever circulate, such as the five volumes of the superb Clark edition of Anthony Wood.

I cannot begin to thank another old and dear friend, M. Jacques E. J. Manuel, for his help in gathering material in Paris. While directing a motion picture, he was still able to slash red tape and shortages which made it difficult to get permission to photograph material in French government collections. My aunt, Miss Millia Crotty, also procured pictures in Paris, and Mrs. Don Blatchley was helpful in London.

During the years when my old friend and brother in Local 829, Hermann Rosse, was detained with the rest of his family in Occupied Holland, his daughter and son-in-law, Jannelise and Paul Galdone, enabled me to avoid visitors and telephones by letting me work in the chauffeur's quarters in the garage-stable which has since become their own home.

I am much obliged for the loan of books or photographs, to Henry Varnum Poor, Marion Hargrove, Aline Bernstein, and to Lee Simonson, whose enthusiasm has been very heartening.

Mr. William D. Allen, formerly of Cooper Union Museum, has given invaluable last-minute help in editorial and historical checking.

I believe that permission to use illustrations was refused in two cases only, and that another unanswered series of letters can be laid to the dislocations of war. I am grateful to all the private owners and institutions, authors and publishers, who have been gracious in granting permissions for use.

THE BOOK OF
COSTUME

The Ancient Orient

THE BABYLONIANS were merchants, traders by land and sea, and farmers; a population of mixed races, with relatively little caste system, under a king who was also a priest. Education was general; common also to women, who occupied a position of respect. The cultural level was high, providing libraries, astronomical observatories, dated legal documents and contracts on clay tablets. There was little stone available between the Tigris and the Euphrates, so clay brick was used for building; glazed tiles, colored fresco. Cylindrical seals of precious and semi-precious stones were minutely engraved with the aid of crystal lenses ground on a wheel.

During the *Early Sumerian Dynasties* c. 3000-2500 B.C., the chief cities were Nippur, Tello, Susa, Lagash, Kish. The influence of Babylonian art was felt as far as Syria and Egypt.

BABYLONIAN COSTUME

Male clothing consisted of a *cape*, a rectangle around the body, over shoulders, and a *kaunakes,* a long shaggy skirt, probably closed in front. It was made of hanks of wool fastened in horizontal lines like coarse fringe, on cloth; or perhaps twisted locks of wool, still fastened to the hide. Sometimes it covered the left shoulder. The women wore a form of *kaunakes,* but more enveloping, and the female cape was worn over the shoulder or caught at the center front.

Gods, and priests, or noblemen as priests, shaved their hair. Other men wore their hair long, looped and braided into the *catogan*. Women also used the *catogan,* but more elaborately arranged, with bands and knobbed pins. Male and female feet were bare, but on arms and legs they wore beads of lapis, carnelian, onyx, agate. In addition, they wore gold and bronze bracelets, earrings, and ornaments. Pins and hairpins were used.

Men wore hats.

During the *Agade Dynasty,* there was the rise to power of the Semitic servant class (*Akkad*).

Sargon (a Semite) subdued Babylonia, Elam, Syria, Palestine. Art was marked by the finest cylinder seals. Culture flourished to the greatest extent, reaching the Mediterranean during the Arabian-Semitic *Ur Dynasty* c. 2700 B.C. Its chief cities were Ur, Lagash, Kish, Nina (later Nineveh).

The *kaunakes* led to a garment often fringed, worn over the left shoulder, under the right arm, which eventually became a short-sleeved shirt. Kings and nobles wore high turbans; others wore round hats with cylindrical brims.

During the *Babylonian Dynasty,* Babylonia was invaded and eventually divided, North Babylonia going to the South Arabians, South Babylonia to the Elamites. About 2250 B.C., Hammurabi shook off the Elamites, consolidated the monarchy to the Mediterranean; Syria and Canaan became dependencies. An excellent code of laws was formulated. The new city of Babylon became the capital; Susa, Larsa and Nineveh flourished.

The *Kassite Dynasty* c. 1786 B.C., contemporaneous with the Hyksos (Egypt), was marked by the loss of West Asia and the independence of Palestine and Syria.

About 1700 B.C., the horse appeared from the East in Babylonia, Greece, Egypt.

The Assyrians, living since Sargon's time in the Tigris valley, and coming of the same stock, increased their power as that of Babylonia weakened. The kingship of Assyria was assumed by the high priests of Assur. There was correspondence, and relationships, with Egypt (Amenophis IV to Deltaic Dynasty when Egypt became Assyria's vassal). The kings became generals; the population completely militarized, ruthlessly aggressive and cruel. The great culture of Babylonia was entirely and uncritically taken over. The personal portraits of Egyptians never appear in the stylized bas-reliefs of the Assyrians (in which one king might be any other). But details, such as those of the costumes of aliens, are much more accurately observed in Assyrian than in Egyptian art. The Assyrian code of laws differed from the Babylonian, and their women were veiled.

ASSYRIAN COSTUME DETAILS

Costume was dyed madder red, indigo blue, saffron yellow (combined in a dull green), snail purple; priests wore bleached linen.

The basic garment was the shirt, worn by everybody. The female shirt was long, with or without rolled belt, accompanied by a mantle worn over the head. The male shirt was short, with a belt often rolled. Common soldiers wore the short shirt with a wide protective belt. Kings and personages wore a long shirt—embroidered, brocaded, tasseled, fringed in a manner commensurate with rank.

Other garments of important personages were like the shirt in respect to material and decoration. The king's cloak, originally like that of *Aamu-Ribu* (see Egyptian, Semitic Nomads), followed the same mutations of cut and eventually became a tabard.

Scarves were worn by all important persons and the wearer's position was indicated by the number, disposition, and width of fringe of the scarves. Scarves were worn by kings to the Second Assyrian Empire only.

Priests' costumes were of two sorts: *spiral,* of which another variety was worn by kings, and *cloaked* or *aproned,* of bleached linen. The *spiral* was a triangular fringed garment, rolled spirally around the body over the shirt, with the point brought over the right shoulder to the belt. The king's *spiral* was a fringed rectangle, wound around the body in an ascending spiral and ending in a pointed piece brought over the right shoulder while a rectangular piece was brought around the left arm.

The High Priest's apron was worn around the back of the body, fastened with hanging tasseled cords, and was ankle-length, exposing the hem of the short shirt in front. He also wore a cloak.

The king's headdress was a truncated conical *tiara* of white felt, with a spiked top; and purple *infulae,* two narrow tabs hanging almost to the waist in back. It was duplicated in gold for use in war. Bullocks' horns were added around this headdress for the priest or for the king as priest.

Women and common men went barefoot, as did soldiers in early days. Soldiers later were superbly shod. Kings and personages wore sandals enclosing the heel, beautifully made yet relatively plain in comparison with the costume.

Jewelry consisted of arm bands, bracelets, necklaces, and weapons of gold.

The conical helmet of peaked Assyrian form eventually assumed the Graeco-Carian crest. It was made of copper, then bronze, and finally of iron. The king's helmet was a gold replica of his tiara.

The shield was oblong or round, and convexly pointed, made of bronze.

The archer's shirt was short so that the body, left relatively unprotected, had freedom in the use of the bow. The archer also wore a wrist-band with a protective, often decorative, boss.

The officer's shirt was a cuirasse of bronze plates fastened on a short leather shirt. The leaders had long shirts of plates of mail, very like Egyptian (Tomb of Ken-Amun). The belt was wide and protective. There were crossed straps on the breast, with a protective metal plate at the intersection.

Kings and officers wore fringed scarves, indicative of rank, and fringed and tasseled aprons. The end of the scarf was drawn through the belt.

Soldiers originally went barefoot; then they were given excellent high leggings and boots, which often were worn over long, apparently quilted stockings. No spurs were used.

Their arms were a bow with case, arrows in quiver, spears, glaives, and daggers in sheath.

THE ASSYRIAN EMPIRE

Four great emperors from Shalmaneser I in 1310 B.C. to Shalmaneser II 856-881 B.C. helped to build the *First Assyrian Empire.* Under the first Shalmaneser the Assyrians took the place formerly held by their nominal masters, though Babylon itself was conquered by a later king. Tiglath-pileser I, 1129 B.C., conquered Armenia and Cappadocia. Assur-nasir-pal II, 883-858 B.C., and Shalmaneser II also extended the Empire. Both kings built palaces at Nimrud. This was a period of coalitions, revolts, plagues, ruthless militarized life, and strong, simple sculpture.

The *Second Assyrian Empire* began under a series of professional soldiers but the usurper Tiglath-pileser III, 745 B.C., consolidated and co-ordinated the Empire, perfected the army. Art was at a low ebb. Sculpture was definitely inferior, though in reliefs at Balawat there is some useful military detail. But later, under Sargon, sculpture shows meticulous realism (Khorsabad). In fact, the following two-thirds of the century is the great period of Assyrian sculpture.

During the reign of Sargon's son, Sennacherib, 705-681 B.C., Babylon was destroyed as the result of a revolt, and a palace was built at Nineveh. Under Sennacherib's grandson, Assur-bani-pal, 668-626 B.C., the Empire began to fall apart. Egypt was lost, there were struggles with Elam and Babylonia, and Assyria was left exhausted, prey to the invading Scythians and Medes, whose court costume was affected by Assyrian fashions.

With the Aryan Scythians and Persians appears an entirely new costume: the fitted sleeved coat, opening down the front, long trousers, and boots —the basis of our own costume today. The dress (and diet based on fermented milk) of the present-day Siberians is almost identical with that of the Scythians.

The garments of the Greeks and Egyptians, as well as those we have just been considering, were made from, or evolved out of the use of, draped rectangles of woven materials.

The tailoring of our own clothes was influenced by the invading Indo-Germanic peoples of the cold Eastern plateau, cattle-raising nomads in search of pasture, mounted warriors who brought with them the horse, "the ass of the East," and who dressed in the skins and hides of their beasts. The comparatively intricate cut of their garments was determined first by the resemblance, and then by the disparities, between the patterns of the skins of different animals, and of man.

Thus came about pattern, cut, piecing, and tailoring. With these people went their tailored garments which will be found on Celt and German, as on Persian and Parthian; Scythian and Sarmathian of the steppes; Dacians, Lydians, and Phrygians; spreading amongst the gentry of Cyprus and Cappadocia and Asia Minor; and given by the Greeks to the mythical Amazons.

Persian (Achaemenian) Empire

Cyrus, 558-528 B.C., Aryan king of Semitic Elam, conquered his Median sovereign and capital, Ecbatana; became king of Persia; united Medes and Persians into the greatest empire yet seen; defeated the coalition of Sparta, Lydia, Babylon, and Egypt.

The Median national costume, very different from the Persian, was adopted for court wear. Silk and cotton cloth, instead of leather and fur, became known to the Persians. There were six great Persian families in addition to that of the king; but Medians and other peoples, subjugated by relatively humane warfare, were allowed to retain power and serve in important Empire posts as officers of court, in the colonies as satraps, and in the army. The court served as training school and proving ground for all of noble birth.

The superb army, under a number of great warrior-kings, included every able-bodied citizen. Its tactics were based on a massive offensive hail of arrows. The bow, native weapon of the Iranians, was drawn from behind light standing shields, by kneeling men, unhampered by defensive armor except metal helmets; meanwhile their cavalry darted into, broke up, and pursued the enemy. Only the leaders were strongly armed. The short lances and daggers which Persian soldiers carried in addition to the bow were of little Marathon, the Persian ranks were penetrated by the heavily armed *hoplite*.

The peasantry were strong and manly, brought up in a healthy climate, and habituated to all hardships, Herodotus tells us, adding that "of all mankind" they "were the readiest to adopt foreign customs, good or bad." The art forms of use in hand-to-hand battle, when, as finally at

Babylonia and Assyria were taken over by the Persians, and produced for them by craftsmen of many races.

During the Luristan period, the Medes wore a *kilt,* wrapped around the hips, lapped on the right side; and a *shirt* which went halfway down the thigh, or, in the case of kings and attendants, down to the ankles. It had a diagonal closing across the breast, quarter sleeves, and it was belted, with bands of braid or thin gold strips (Scythic) at the borders, and in suspender lines.

Later, the Medes used the *kandys,* a long, flowing cloth gown, looped up to a belt at the sides; with or without voluminous sleeves, widening from shoulder to cuff, much as the garment itself widened from shoulder to hem.

Headcoverings included Median caps or *kyrbasia* (the modern *bashlik*), like the Phrygian bonnet. There was a soft, high crown which fell forward; and usually there were flaps at the neck and at either side which could be fastened under the chin. One form, without these flaps, had a hanging cord. Another headcovering was the *padom,* a hood worn by the royal entourage, surrounding the face and often concealing the chin, falling in flaps which covered the back and chest. Courtiers and satraps were allowed to wear round spreading caps. Blue and white cord designated the royal family (Cyrus).

The king wore the *kidaris,* a ribbed tiara, or embroidered hat. His kandys was purple, crimson, or saffron, with a white stripe down the center front. The king also carried a staff.

The garments of the priests, regarded as "magicians" (of whom the king was chief), varied in cut with rank and duties. They were white or purple.

The High Priest wore a purple girdled kandys, a shaped cape which also was purple, a spreading cylindrical hat, and a staff with a gold knob head.

Lesser priests wore a plain white shirt with a belt (*kosti*) which was the only ornament allowed.

The cape was a folded rectangle with tasseled corners and a triangular collar.

Persian Costume

Persian costume was originally of leather, and later of cloth. The nobility used polychrome fabrics brocaded and embroidered in lines, stars, animal and floral motifs, edged with gold. They affected the costume of the nobility of Phrygia, Lydia, Cappadocia, Lycia, and Cyprus.

The male wore a coat that was open down the front, had a fitted waist, and long tight sleeves sewn into the armholes. At first it was kneelength, later calf-length. Trousers were wide but close at the ankle. High boots and leggings were worn over the trousers. The nobility had shoes with edged tops and three straps over the instep; or colored slippers.

The *overcoat* was a sleeved kandys, often fur-collared. It was slung over the shoulder by cord, the sleeves hanging unused except on great occasions.

For *headcovering,* the king wore a modified Assyrian tiara which had assumed the flaps of the Median cap. It was conical, spiralled in two colors; or a truncated cone, swathed with a turban. Hair and beard were worn in Assyrian cut. Nobles wore the *kulah,* a high cylindrical felt hat; or the *kyrbasia* (bashlik) either with flaps or as a round felt hat with cord but no flaps.

Women wore the same garments as the men, with the addition of a long veil. The female coat was longer than the male's. It had a closed front, with a slit for the head, and wide sleeves for court wear or narrow sleeves for ordinary dress.

Soldiers wore Persian national costume, but the use of Median court dress was granted by Darius to his bodyguard, the 10,000 Immortals. Persian arms are listed in the *Zend Avesta.* Ring-mail originated in Persia between the ninth and eighth centuries B.C.

During the Achaemenian period, helmets were leather or metal, some with movable sections very like mediaeval helmets. The *padom,* with chin protectors and flaps covering the back and chest, was worn by the royal entourage. The *"Phrygian" bonnet,* a segmented conical casque, was worn particularly by heavily armed Parthian and Sarmathian cavalry. Sarmathians shown on the Trajan Column wear short, pointed conical caps with cheek plates and splints covering the neck.

Armor consisted of a cuirasse made of metal scales, or rings of bronze, iron, or gold, on leather; arm and leg plates; a shield, rectangular, round, or rondache (violin-shaped), made of wicker or leather.

Arms consisted of a sword, fifteen to sixteen inches long; javelin; knife; club; bow; quiver with thirty brass-headed arrows; and a sling with thirty stones.

During the reign of Darius I, 521-485 B.C., there was considerable infiltration of Greek culture at court. The art was imperial rather than national, and craftsmen generally were foreigners. Darius adopted the crenellated tiara, long used in Assyria and Asia Minor.

The turning point of the Persian Empire came during the rule of Xerxes I, 485-465 B.C. There was a war with Greece in which the Persian archers were defeated by the Greek phalanx. Macedonia started its ascendancy a century later.

THE SELEUCID EMPIRE

Alexander the Great, 331-323 B.C., adopted the Persian dress and ceremonial in newly-united Persia and Macedonia. The brilliant Greek court, and the city colonies in conquered lands, spread Greek culture throughout Asia. The reaction against Hellenic culture began during the Parthian period, when Mithridates (124-88 B.C.) was king and nomadic Scythians gradually were establishing themselves as great proprietors and serf owners in Parthia.

There were notable changes in style during the Seleucid and Parthian periods. *Trousers* were wide at the top and very tight at the ankle; they were strapped under the foot, and also under the crotch for riding. The *coat* was knee-length and had narrow sleeves. The king's *mantle* was knee-length, and an *apron* came into general use. The king's *mitre* was a cylindrical Assyrian battlemented crown from which longer and wider infulae fluttered. His *hood* was a lighter, smaller, and shorter kyrbasia, with the point of its crown more vertical and the flaps hanging loose. Scarves of ribbons in fluttering bows on the chest, sash, infulae, and shoes were worn through the Sassanian period. Sovereigns also took to wearing knots of hair on the top of their heads.

Under Ardashir I, 226 A.D., and Shapur I, the Iranians were welded into one nation (the Sassanian Neo-Persian Empire) in the old Achaemenian tradition. There was a return to old Persian styles, and Median fashions disappeared except for the Median bandeau. High tiaras and jewelry—necklaces, beads, and earrings—were popular. Hair was worn bushy. Revers and rounded aprons were worn on coats, and trousers were wide and fluttering. The kulah (either round or conical, sometimes with flaps) carried a bandeau. The kyrbasia disappeared. Women wore a smaller veil and bandeau with a knot at the back of the head.

During the Sassanian period, heavy cavalry and horse were armed remarkably like the mediaeval knight and steed. The helm was conical with a ribbon floating from the crest; visor and mail-coif extended to the shoulders. The cuirasse was made of ring- and scale-mail combined; ring-mail encased the legs and feet. The head, chest, and shoulders of the horse also were mailed.

The struggle between Rome and Persia gradually weakened both until Persia fell victim in 641 A.D. to the Arab (Islamic) conquest.

1. Sumerian, Agade Dyn. Relief Tablet. c. III mill. B.C. Tello. (Louvre.)

King Or-Nina and Family. Kaunakes worn by seated and standing figures, one shown with a basket on his head.

2. Sumerian 2800 B.C. Votive Mace Head. Lagash (Tello) (British Museum.)

Enannatum 1, patesi of Lagash. Wearing the

sheep's wool kaunakes of the early Sumerian.

3. Sumerian e. III mill. B.C. (Berlin Museum.)

Goddess of Vegetation. In horned headdress, and cape garment.

4. Sumerian c. 2800 B.C. Marble statue. (British Mus.)

Priestess. Hair elaborately clubbed up in a catogan with a band; fringed cape.

Courtesy of British Museum (2), (4); the Louvre (1)

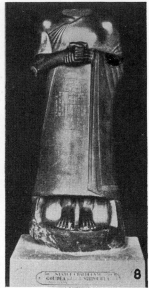

5-7. Elamite 2000 B.C. Ivory statue. Susa. (Louvre.)

Elamite lady. Cape garment, under right arm, caught on left shoulder; fringed scarf over bare shoulder; collar, bracelets.

8, 9. Sumerian mid-III mill. B.C. Statue. Summer Palace, Tello. (Louvre.)

Goudea. Patesi (high priest) of Lagash: showing arrangement of cape. The headdress is also shown on a number of other statues of Goudea, which exist together with elaborate accounts of his greatness as a builder, and plans and specifications for his palace.

10. Babylonian II mill. B.C. Koudourrou of King. Susa. (Louvre.)

King Hammurabi as judge. Spiral garments; tiara.

11. Babylonian e. XIIc. B.C. Koudourrou of King. Susa. (Louvre.)

Goddess Nanaï on throne, King Melishpak II, and his daughter. With symbols of sun, moon, and planet Venus (Goddess Ishtar).

12. Babylonian e. I mill. B.C. Relief. Susa. (Louvre.)

Lady of rank spinning, fanned by servant. Elaborate catogan of type worn since archaic times. Simple garments, heavy belts, borders, bracelets; bare feet. (See Ill. 273.)

About a hundred years ago, the excavations of the Englishman, Layard, (*Discoveries at Nineveh*), and of the Frenchman, Botta (*Monuments at Nineveh*), brought to light the first great Assyrian remains and laid the foundations for the great collections of the British Museum and the Louvre, respectively, the third important collection being that at Constantinople.

The engraved illustrations in their books give information on artifacts which in some cases no longer remain in clear form for recording by photography.

As the titles of the books indicate, each thought that what he was excavating was Nineveh, whereas Layard's was actually Nimrud, and that of Botta (who had turned away from Quyunjig, the actual Nineveh) was Sargon's Khorsabad.

13-16. 1st Assyrian Emp. 885-856 B.C. Reliefs, Nimrud (Calah). (British Museum.)

Assur-nasir-pal; young male attendants; priest dressed as a winged god. The priest, carrying a pail and pine-cone, is about to anoint the king with the "juice of the Enurta," in a fertility rite. He wears the priest's headdress with bullock horns; the priest's apron, fastened by knotted cords; and fringed scarf of rank, over short fringed shirt.

The young male attendants with fly whisks may or may not be eunuchs, as was formerly believed. One is offering the king a libation; the other carries dagger, bow and quiver.

The king wears a spiked tiara with infulae; and royal cloak over long shirt. These personages wear fine but simple sandals (which the Greeks criticized as being disparately plain). They have richly embroidered and fringed garments and jewelry—earrings, necklaces, arm-bands and bracelets with medallions.

17. 1st Assyrian Emp. 885-856 B.C. Alabastrine limestone statue Nimrud (Calah). (Louvre.)

Assur-nasir-pal. In spiral garments of a priest of the Temple of the War-God Enurta, without headdress, carrying crook-shaped sceptre, long dagger. This is the only perfect example of Assyrian sculpture in the round, not relief.

From Layard: Discoveries at Nineveh.

18

19

18. 2nd Assyrian Empire 705-680 B.C. Relief. Kuyunjik (Nineveh) s.w. palace, passage LI. (British Museum.)

Sennacherib's horses: being led by men with carefully arranged hair and beards. Simple shirts, with fringed scarves, indicative of rank, are tucked into wide belts which have handsome webbed fastenings. Sandals enclose heel.

19. 1st Assyrian Empire 824-810 B.C. Limestone relief, Nabu Temple, Nimrud. (British Museum.)

Shamshi-Adad V, husband of Semiramis, brother of Sardanapalus: king with divine emblems. Above to king's right:—sun, moon, planet Venus (goddess Ishtar). He wears the king's tiara with infulae, set on typically curled Assyrian hair; beard. Simple shirt, with heavily fringed hem, indicative of rank; mystic cross on breast.

20. 2nd Assyrian Emp. 705-680 B.C. Reliefs, Kuyunjik.

Flight of the inhabitants of Lachish from Senna-cherib's soldiers. Soldier: in Graeco-Carian helmet, long spear, round shield, dagger; short shirt with wide protective belt and crossed straps with plate at intersection; high quilted or knitted stockings, gartered, under strapped boots. Officer: cuirasse of metal plates, fringed scarf of rank, and wide baldric; mace and dagger. Canaanite peasant women, with mantles like veils over their heads, carrying their belongings, and followed by their captive men, in short shirts with thick belts, and high laced buskins; their hair cropped shorter than that of Assyrians.

21. Assyrian Empire. Relief, Nimrud.

King before the walls of a besieged city. King as an archer, with little defense; tiara, probably in metal (as helmet) distinguishes monarch; wide protective belt and baldric, over long shirt and tasseled apron. Shield-bearer, in shirt of mail, carrying rectangular wicker shield, which could be set up for archer's protection; conical helmet; heavy wide belt. Attendants (eunuchs) carrying quiver, baton, umbrella. Soldier with mace, dagger, bow and arrows pursuing child and three women in long patterned shirts, and thick rolled belts. Other soldiers in loin cloths or shirts, and helmets; daggers, spears, bows.

From Layard: Discoveries at Nineveh.

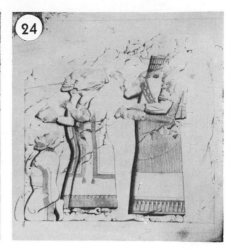

22. 2nd Assyrian Emp. 722-705 B.C. Reliefs, Khorsabad.

Sargon II and his Vizier. Traces of color, red, ochre and black, still remain.

Sargon, in spiked tiara with infulae; magnificent hair and beard; cruciform earrings; fringed mantle brocaded in rosettes; over brocaded shirt; sword with lion's heads; arm bands, bracelets; baton of rank; laced sandals covering heel; ring on big toe.

Vizier: bareheaded; rich bandeau with infulae; earrings, necklace, bracelets, arm-band; scarf with very wide fringe, indicating his importance.

23, 24. Same provenance as 22.

Hebrew tribute bearers (23) *and prisoners* (24): with small "prayer curls" in front of ear.

The costume of Semitic noblemen assumed many Assyrian characteristics, during the Assyrian domination, while retaining specific Semitic characteristics. All these figures wear a long fringed linen shirt, the belt of which, when worn, is quite different from that of an Assyrian. They also wear a characteristic shorter woolen garment: either the caftan, a sleeved coat, open down the front, the edges of which are caught together in front by elaborate clasps and cord; or a tabard-like garment, open at the sides. These garments carried purple tassels at the corners to commemorate the 4 statutes of Jehovah. Some wear tasselled "stocking" caps; the others a wound headcloth, over hair which differs from the Assyrians in length and arrangement.

25. Hittite VIIIc. B.C. (Berlin Museum.)

Grave stela of a queen in the time of King Barrekub: the fibula which she wears pinned to her gown above the left breast will have a long life in Semitic use, as will the distaff (see Ill. 273).

26. 2nd Assyrian Emp. 655 B.C. Relief, Kuyunjik. (British Museum.)

Assur-bani-pal and his queen celebrating the death of Te-Umman. The only Assyrian sculpture showing a female. Similar furniture, fillets and jewelry, patterned and fringed garments with weighted corners, and fine shoes, can be found in Etruria and N. Italy in VI-V c. use.

27. Persian Achaemenian Vc. (British Museum.)

Silver figurine of a man in dress previously seen on reliefs.

From Botta and Flandin: Monuments de Nineveh (22-24).

28-32. Achaemenian, Artaxerxes II. 404-359 B.C. Persep-
olis, Apadena Stair.

28. Men in alternating Persian and Median dress.
The Median robe has a dagger of Scythic type, with
characteristic wide guard, thrust into belt; bow cases
not of Scythic type. Shoes with three lacings. Fluted,
flat-topped headdresses. The Persian garments are of
the nomad type, with short swords ingeniously slung
and held in place by a strap under the crotch. Round-
topped felt bonnets (*bashlik*), without lappets, some
with a forward rake. Some overcoats with collars and
ribbon ties slung over the shoulders without using
sleeves (like XVc. Magyar *huszars,* see XIXc. hussar
costume). Shoes tie around ankles. Hair in Assyrian

curls, but bushier shape; beards more natural. Necklaces of the twisted torque variety brought by the
nomad people (see Frankish guard, Ill. 283). *Engraving by Flandin.* 29. Photograph of the relief, detail
near the one shown in 28. 30. Anatolians bringing
tribute; cups of Scythic round-bottomed type, bowls
of kumyss, and Scythic bracelets. Conical segmented
felt hats, brought by Central Asiatic nomads, but
gowns and tassels of Semitic type. 31. Bactrian with
camel: wider breeches, from Sacian conquerors; Assyrian bandeau instead of *kyrbasia* (*bashlik*). 32.
Others, in nomad costume: conical hats with flaps;
short swords, slung out of the way for riding; shoes
tied at ankle; carry Scythic bracelets.

Archer of the Persian Guard: dark-skinned Elamite, dressed in the Median court costume granted by Darius to his body-guard, the 10,000 Immortals. 1,000 of these carried lances with knobs of gold; 9,000, of whom this is one, knobs of silver. He wears a blue band around his hair. There is a re-peated design of little fortresses in blue and purple on a white ground, all over the top and bottom of his *kandys,* the cen-ter of which, like the circularly cut under-section of the sleeve, is in unembroidered yellow material, edged with blue and purple braid. Purple stock-ings; yellow shoes; bow and quiver covered with panther skin. Other archers are dressed in similar combinations of olive green, maroon, blue, yel-low and white, as:—yellow with white and blue dots, pur-ple sleeves and mid-section, edged with blue and purple braid, purple stockings, yellow shoes.

34. Darius 521-485 B.C. (Berlin Museum.)
Anatolian guards.

35. Persian 383-388 A.D. Silver Plate, repousse, en-graved, partly gilded. (Hermitage Museum, Lenin-grad.)

Shapur III dispatching a lion: fluttering ribboned effects show on *infulae* sash; wide trousers, caught up at the crotch, bows on shoes. Crown set on bushy hair with puffed knot on top (since Ardashir I); each ruler now makes additions and modifications in head-dress.

36. Persian IXc. A.D. Post-Sassanian. Silver Plate, re-pousse, engraved, partly gilded. (Hermitage Mu-seum, Leningrad.)

Bahram Gur hunting lions: grandson of Shapur III, and a Vc. king of legendary beauty, called the

'Wild Ass" for his strength and valor; combatted Christianity, warred with Rome, but he was actually just the weak aristocrat he appears here, wearing the headdress with eagle wings, adopted by him.

37. Persian XIIIc. A.D. Galen Manuscript, Seljuk School. (Staatsbibliothek, Vienna.)

Andromachus and the boy bitten by the snake: manuscript leaf filled with the new ideas to which Europe was exposed by the Crusades: the turban; band about the upper arm; ideas of design and manu-script illumination, using leaves, flowers, and birds, which profoundly affected European manuscript style. Venice was a "boom town" during the Cru-sades; East and West met there in trade; and it was by way of Venice that "pantaloons" entered Euro-pean dress.

EGYPTIAN COSTUME

Egyptian costume was based on two elements: the wrapped loin cloth of men, and the sewed *kalasiris* (a sheath which developed into a shirt) of women; by the New Kingdom, it became incorporated into male costume as well. Increasingly finer materials were used, and were worn, from the Middle Kingdom, in increasingly numerous combinations and superimpositions of garments of different lengths, and different weights: such as a long pleated skirt of gauzy linen over a short plain one of heavy material.

From the earliest times a mantle was occasionally worn; it became an important part of both male and female costume by the New Kingdom, arranged around the body or tied about the buttocks, ends arranged at center front.

Female entertainers and slaves frequently wore nothing but jewelry.

The strong lay position in Egyptian religion lost out to the professional priesthood, which had become extremely powerful by the Eighteenth Dynasty. As lay costume became more elaborate and colorful, the priesthood retained the simple white loin cloth (linen, never wool) and leopard skin of earlier days; the priestly functions of the king increased, and the spotted animal skin became, late, a granted honorific.

A notably cleanly people, the Egyptians of both sexes clipped or shaved their heads, and the men their beards, which for ceremonious occasions they replaced with wigs of wool or hair, and artificial beards. Common people wore their own hair.

Materials: Egyptians dressed almost entirely in white linen. Linen more than half again as fine as today's handkerchief has been found in First Dynasty tombs, c. 3000 B.C. Fringed ends are knotted into tassels on loin cloths of the Fifth Dynasty. Linen was stiffened and pleated with exquisite art in horizontal and vertical patterns; herring-bone pleating is used by the Fifth Dynasty. Some line patterns may have been produced by weaving cords into the fabric. Cords are used to give elaborate bands, lines, and zigzags by the Eleventh Dynasty (c. 2000 B.C.). Long furry loops are woven into cloth by the Eighteenth Dynasty.

The few sheep native to Egypt had dark, goat-like hair; fleecy sheep began to appear from the East during the New Kingdom. Herodotus says Egyptians had wool mantles in his time (Vc. B.C), but wool was considered unclean, and not to be worn in temples by priests and worshippers. There was little silk and cotton until the late dynasties.

The Egyptians, expert leather-workers, used the spotted patterns of hides, and imitated them in paint; they cut leather into netted patterns. Leopard skins were worn by kings and priests.

Defensive mail armor was imported during the Eighteeth Dynasty; until that time, defensive garments were quilted, or covered with feathers, symbolic of divine guardianship.*

Color: Egyptian garments were largely white, because of the difficulties in dyeing linen permanently without mordants, with which Pliny says the Egyptians had become familiar by Ic. A.D.

Cloths were dipped in safflower for yellows and orange reds; native woad for blue; combinations of these for dull green; madder for a fugitive red; kermes (cochineal) for a more permanent red.

Color was most used in the earliest, and in the latest periods, and in the dress of royalty, gods, and the dead; entertainers' costumes were often yellow. Dark blue was the color of mourning.

Color was applied in many ways; netted or zig-zag patterns of bead strings were sewed and caught into the fabric as it was woven. Feathers or their imitations were applied. Cut-leather nettings appear to have been used, together with patterned hides, and their painted imitations, which became stylized into rosettes. Woven patterns and embroidery were introduced from the East during the Eighteenth Dynasty, together with wool, which could be dyed satisfactorily.

Jewelry: A great deal of the color of Egyptian costume was furnished by its wonderful jewelry which included collars, necklaces, arm and leg bands, bracelets, earrings, fillets, diadems, and rings. Colored pebbles were replaced by beautiful glazed beads during the Old Kingdom. Semi-precious stones (turquoise, lapis-lazuli, carnelian), glass, and faience were used in beads, inlay, and pendants. Gold was worked in granular and fili-gree techniques on scarabs and seals.

Flowers were dearly loved. They were worn in necklaces and headdresses or carried in the hand. Eventually they were stylized in jewelry.

Fans of papyrus and feathers were used.

Cosmetics: Eyebrows were blackened, blue eye-shadow came into use, nails were hennaed, and lips were colored.

Symbols of Pharaoh were a *crook* (originally

---

* I am much indebted to Elizabeth Riefstahl: *Patterned Textiles in Pharaonic Egypt;* Brooklyn Museum, 1944; 56 pages, 8″ x 11″, and 56 excellent photographs. Since no one interested in the subject will fail to get it, I use Riefstahl page references for statements which are verified in eight pages of scholarly notes. Mrs. Riefstahl is in charge of the Wilbour Library of Egyptology at Brooklyn Museum, an institution which is rich in Coptic textiles.

the boomerang), a *flail* with three lashes, and a tall, animal-headed *staff*. Two staffs or scepters, the straight *was* and the wavy *tsam,* were carried by dignitaries to signify support of heaven. Crowns signified the district ruled. The red crown of Lower Egypt, and the white tiara or *atef* of Upper Egypt were worn together by kings of both regions. Crowns were often decorated with the *uraeus* (a rearing viper), a common symbol of royalty, and with the *Ankh cross* as a sign of life.

Gods (as priests) were depicted with the *as,* a lock of hair hanging on one side as worn by the young prince-god Horus, and with a tail which hung from the girdle or the headdress.

The costume of royalty of one dynasty would become that of nobility, and in turn the "best" clothes of lower classes in later dynasties. The short, pleated, gold-trimmed loin cloth of kings became an assumed or granted honorific, as did the lock of hair, animal tail, and spotted animal skin. This skin, taken from gentlemen by priests, was later reassumed by gentlemen.

EGYPTIAN COSTUME DETAILS

The geographical situation of Egypt brought her into contact with African, Aegean, and Asiatic civilizations. Representations of the costumes of these aliens—nomads, allies, subject peoples, mercenaries, and slaves—appear plentifully in Egyptian wall paintings, almost synchronously with the peoples themselves in Egypt.

A large number of these illustrations is included here for two reasons. Enmeshed though it is in Egyptian life, alien dress is seldom shown in works on Egyptian costume. It is from Asia that most of our ideas of textile design, our long tight sleeves, and trousers have evolved.

THE OLD KINGDOM

The First through the Eighth Dynasties center around Memphis. First Dynasty sculpture was noble, serene, and naturalistic. Jewelry: characterized by fine goldsmith's work and by blue and green glazed beads. The Second and Third Dynasties saw the beginning of conventionalization in sculpture, and in architecture the use of glazed tiles and brick mastaba tombs (Sakkara).

The Fourth to Sixth Dynasties, 2830-2530 B.C.* was the period of Cheops and the Pyramid Kings. The pyramids—Gizeh, Abusir, and Sakkara—illustrate its grand conventionalized style in architecture, and it is the best period in sculpture.

Men wore the loin cloth or kilt, ends tucked in belt and hanging down in front. The dress of nobles and of common men differed little, except in fineness of materials. Linen and other woven fabrics, including rushes, were used, with leather for reinforcement at the seat. Sailors wore cord looped in front into a bow as loin cloth. The

* Meyer's chronology.

king's loin cloth, which was finely pleated and rounded off, showed gold trimming on the right side and was worn with a lion's tail hanging from the belt. Noblemen wore capes made either of cloth rectangles or leopard skins, drawn under the left arm and knotted on the right shoulder. Nobility were distinguished also by a strip of white stuff, worn hanging over the shoulder. The governor and the chief justice wore a long skirt, suspended at breast height from shoulder bands.

By the Fifth Dynasty, a triangular erection rose at the front of the starched or pleated loin cloth. Nobility copied the king's short, old-style, gold-trimmed loin cloth, without lion tail but with a beautiful catch on the belt; Fifth and Sixth Dynasties: loin cloth was longer, wider, gathered in front. Leopard skin was frequently stylized in fabric with simulated head and claws.

Women's dress, to the Eighteenth Dynasty, consisted of the *kalasiris,* a form-fitting sheath extending from the breast to the ankles, made of thick, flexible materials (possibly knitted), attached either by single or double shoulder straps or else by a wide collar of beads. This garment, worn by all classes of women, was generally yellow or red or occasionally white, with multicolored decoration in bead netting or feathers. Working women wore a shorter skirt, and often were nude above the waist.

From the Fifth to the Eighteenth Dynasty men and women both wore their hair clipped rather than shaved. Wigs replaced natural hair; short and woolly, in little curls all over the head, or simple and straight to the breast, separated or shortened over the shoulders. The size of all wigs gradually increased, but women's were always larger than men's except in the Thirteenth Dynasty.

THE MIDDLE KINGDOM

From the Ninth to the Seventeenth Dynasty, Memphis gradually declined. Thebes rose as the civilization's center.

In the Twelfth Dynasty (Heraclite Kings), 2130 B.C., the workmanship of sculpture was vigorous and fine, particularly in the characteristic low reliefs of the period. This was also the finest period in architecture; tombs with wall paintings (Beni-Hassan). Jewelry of inlay, cloisonné and gold filigree.

The male loin cloth lengthened into a skirt, which was frequently multiplied, i.e., a short thick underskirt combined with a longer, stiffened, transparent overskirt. There was usually a border around the hem, which dipped in front. These skirts, often overlapping, were worn high under the armpits as late as the Eighteenth Dynasty. Men's attire was almost universally white, with gold reserved for king and nobility. A cloak or shoulder cape gathered at the center-front was common. Sandals, which the master might need, were carried by a servant who followed him.

Women's clothes were green, white, or multi-colored, but beyond this there was little change in female attire down to the Eighteenth Dynasty.

Toward the end of the Twelfth Dynasty, Asiatic nomads began to appear in patterned, woven and painted wool and leather clothes. The ensuing long period of Asiatic invasions was artistically sterile; little change in dress to Eighteenth Dynasty.

The New Empire

The period from the Eighteenth to Twentieth Dynasty was one of great expansion and conquest, plunder and tribute. Egypt ruled the East. The Hyksos Shepherd Kings were overthrown and a succession of great kings—Amenophis I, Thutmosis I, Thutmosis III (greatest of the Pharaohs), and others to Tutankhamun in 1350 B.C.—extended Egypt's power and dominion.

Woven and embroidered patterns in color, found in Egyptian tombs of the Eighteenth Dynasty, were the work of captive Syrian weavers.*

Coats of mail were brought in tribute from Syria, and fleecy sheep were imported from Asia.

It was in 1320 B.C. during the Nineteenth Dynasty, founded by Rameses I, that the great hall of Karnak and a magnificent painted tomb in the Valley of the Kings were completed by Seti I, Rameses' son. During the later years of this dynasty and well into the Twentieth Dynasty—1180 B.C.—revolts, unrest, strikes, tomb-robbing, and starvation plagued the people. Rameses III finally effected peace and some revival of the old glory.

New Empire Characteristics

Magnificent architecture characterized the extensive tomb and temple building, although this activity began to degenerate during the Nineteenth Dynasty. Wall painting was natural, lively, and charming in its careful detail. Beads used as jewelry were not simply glazed but rather were made of glass, and gold was used extravagantly.

During the New Empire and after, simplicity in costume was gone. Wealth and luxury made for increasingly greater use of color and pattern so that, by the Nineteenth Dynasty, embroidery was common. Garments were full, with vertical pleats. The *kalasiris,* now worn by men as well as women, in varying lengths and widths, was either sleeveless, supported by a shoulder strap; or with a short sleeve on the left arm only, sometimes with a hole cut for the head. Often the *kalasiris* in this period was worn in bolero-jacket length.

There was considerable variety in skirts. The thin, pleated outer skirt gradually became less important than the underskirt. By the end of the Eighteenth Dynasty, this outer skirt characteristically was tucked back and up, often covering only the rear of the body and revealing a long

fringed underskirt which was also tucked up and puffed. During the Nineteenth Dynasty this underskirt was fully pleated and longer, but less puffed, and until the Twentieth Dynasty there were apron arrangements in front. By the end of the Twentieth Dynasty the outer skirt had disappeared. At this time an apron was added to the front of the old-style nobleman's short skirt.

The mantle, made of wool or pleated linen, was either an oblong or a wide oval with a hole for the head, thus forming a covering for the shoulders. It was often gathered up at the center of the chest, giving the appearance of pleated sleeves.

The kalasiris of women was worn covering the left shoulder with little deviation until time of Twentieth Dynasty, when left sleeves were added. Often two kalasiris were worn, the lower one being heavier and plainer. The mantle had an embroidered edge, and was gathered and caught at center front thus giving the appearance of sleeves.

Men's and women's wigs were commonly wide and short, although occasionally they were long, perhaps covering the whole upper body and ending in a fringe of curls. By the end of the Eighteenth Dynasty ladies sometimes dispensed with wigs and set their headdresses directly on the shaved head, which in many cases had been deliberately deformed from childhood.

The XXI-XXV Deltaic Dynasties

During the period from 1100 B.C. to 668 B.C., Libyan mercenaries gradually rose in power as the Egyptians became less warlike. Egyptian influence abroad weakened. Syria was repeatedly lost and then regained. Assyria captured Memphis in 668 B.C. and made the Pharaohs their vassals.

Trade, extended by the Phoenicians (Carthage) to the western shore of the Mediterranean, had brought new ideas to the rich delta of Egypt. Religion had gained in power over the masses. Egypt became less warlike and more interested in culture and the sciences.

After fighting off the Scythians, Egypt succumbed to the Assyrians in 664 B.C.

By the Twenty-fifth Dynasty, the taste for archaic simplicity began to revive. Fifth Dynasty round wigs and loin cloths in plain colors reappeared.

Later History

Then followed the Persian period, the conquest by Alexander the Great, and the spread of Greek culture in the Ptolemaic period, circa 323 B.C., after thousands of years of Egyptian antipathy to the Greeks. It was at this time that Alexandria was founded. Although Greek influence became strong in the Delta region, it did not affect Upper Egypt. Egyptian decline persisted through the Roman Period (beginning 30 B.C.), and the Coptic Period, to the Moslem conquest in 640 A.D.

---

* *Riefstahl,* p. 31.

THE EGYPTIAN ARMY; ADVERSARIES AND MERCENARIES

The Egyptians were faced by a series of enemies, many of whom appeared later in the Egyptian army as slave or mercenary troops, often fighting against their own kind. (For the Nubian and Ethiopian types, see Ills. 60, 62, 77.)

Libya, to Egypt's west, was her most dreaded neighbor from the Eleventh through the Twentieth Dynasties. The nomad Ribu, Tehennu, etc., were probably indigenous Berbers.

The *Libyans* wore their hair divided, sometimes partly shaved above the ear, with a long braided lock falling in front of the ear at one side and curling up at the end. Two feathers were worn in hair typically, but in illustrations of battles on Tombs of Seti I, Merneptah, and Rameses III the feathers are often shown on captive leaders only. The third distinguishing Libyan characteristic is tattooing of arms, wrists, thighs, shanks, and instep in dotted and crosshatched patterns.

Loin cloths took two forms: either the straight or wrapped kilt, or the belt with an ornamented, tasseled pendant strip in front.

A wrap of fabric or painted ox-hide with large patterns was worn, carried around the body under one arm and caught up or tied to cover the other shoulder. Selvage edges were left open, and like the hem, were richly bordered.

Warriors, led by a standard bearer, carried boomerangs, lassos, spears, javelins, double-headed axes, maces, bows and arrows, and shields which might be oblong, ovoid, or pear-shaped.

The "Sea People," "Island People," "Barbarians," "whom the miserable Libyans had led thither" (reigns of Seti I and Merneptah) were legion.

The *Shardana* (Sardinians?), *Shakarusha,* and *Turusha* (Tyrrhenians), of the first wave, were Mediterranean coast peoples who wore armor of the Mycenaean type. Armor of the Mycenaean type was also worn by the Lycian members of the Hittite confederacy against Rameses II, and the other "Sea People" who, with the *Purasati,* came from the north to trouble Rameses III.

The *Shardana* had lighter skin and hair than the Egyptians. Notable is the helmet they wore, which is different from any other. The helmet was "white" (tinned bronze?) and had horns and a knob, usually on a projection. This helmet was often fastened under the chin, and while it sometimes had hinged ear flaps, it never had feathers like the helmets of the other "Sea People." The *Shardana* were sometimes bearded; hair trimmed so short that it never showed under the helmet.

The *Shardana* wore a cuirasse of overlapping plates of mail which were usually arranged in an inverted "V" pattern, and a kilt like that of the Keftiu, dipping to a "V" in front. There were several lines of decoration parallel to the hem, and another line down the center front, where, as also at the sides and hips, three small tassels often hung. They carried a good-sized round shield without a boss, long spears, and pointed swords.

By the time of Rameses III, the Shardana enemies of Seti I fought with the Egyptian forces.

The *Shakarusha* and the *Purasati* (Philistines), who were always beardless, wore a feather headdress of the Mycenaean-Lycian type. This headdress consisted of a wide, decorated band about the forehead, and a spreading crown of feathers from the center of which, at later periods, rose a Carian crest. The feathers were mounted on a close-fitting, apparently quilted, cap which covered the whole head and usually tied under the chin. These peoples wore the same type of kilt and carried the same weapons as the Shardana.

The *Turusha* (Tyrrhenians), shown with Rameses III hunting lions between campaigns, wore a feather headdress entirely different in shape from that of the Shakarusha. The Turusha headdress, instead of being set on the brow in a spreading tiara, raked back from the forehead in a diminishing rather than spreading form. The Turusha wore their beards narrow and trimmed square at the end. They wore the same kilt and carried the same arms as the Shakarusha and the Shardana. The Turusha wore a circular medallion hanging around the neck.

The *Hittites* were shown with distinctively beaked noses and receding foreheads. They wore headdresses of a baggy, hanging, conical cap variety, or else they wore simple helmets which frequently were furnished with one horn set with a backward rake. Their shields were either oblong or of the Amazonian violin shape, and were made of basket-work. Their garments ranged from a wrapped one like that of the nomad Semite, to a long, sleeved gown, like the Cappadocian, which was elaborately colored in vertical red and blue stripes and was often worn over a yellow undergarment. The *Kheta* (Syrians) also carried an oblong shield. They wore the long gown, caped and girdled, of the Retennu, frequently in a quilted, defensive form. The *Canaanite* soldiers had simple low helmets, horizontally laminated mail, battle axes, spears, and javelins.

The Egyptians wore defensive armor: helmet, shirt and shield; never greaves. The helmet was a metal or quilted cap, often tasseled at the crown but never crested. The shirt, quilted or made of metal plates, had either one or two sleeves shorter than elbow-length. The shield, oblong with rounded top or flat-iron shaped, made of wood covered with patterned ox-hide (see Ill. 47), was carried by the heavily armed infantry.

Egyptian offensive arms were bows and arrows, the quiver being slung horizontally across the back and reached from under the arm; spears and javelins up to six feet long; swords from two and one-half to three feet long and daggers, all double edged for cut and thrust; falchions and axes of many varieties; clubs; maces; slings; boomerangs.

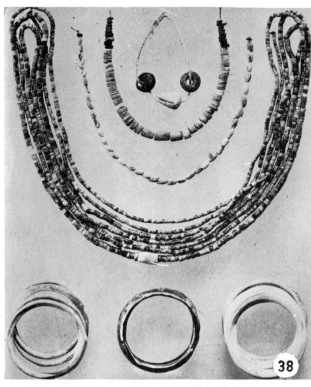

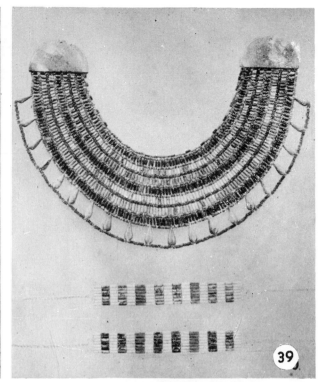

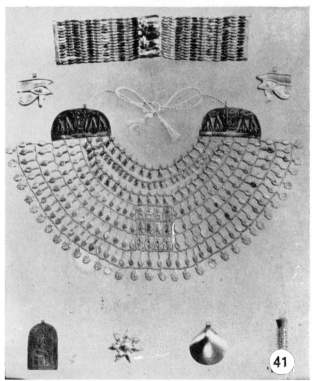

38. Early Egyptian Jewelry, before 4000 B.C.

Top: Badarian period: strings of shell and stone beads. Bottom sides: Pre-Dynastic period, c. 3500 B.C.: shell bracelets. Bottom center: II Dynasty, c. 2800 B.C.: hollow, gold bracelet of Kha'sekhemwy.

39. XII Dyn. 2000-1788 B.C.

Funerary jewelry: broad collar of faience; neutralized greens, variegated beiges, colors of utmost distinction and elegance. Anklets of carnelian and faience. Similar jewelry worn during Old Kingdom.

40, 41. Early XVIII Dyn. 1501-1447 B.C. Thutmosis III.

Headdress of a court lady at a period of great wealth and luxury: gold inlaid with carnelian and glass. The flowers the Egyptians loved are used here in a stylized form, covering the wig.

Jewelry of a court lady: lavish use of gold in jewelry, with inlay of semi-precious stones and glass. The eye has an amuletic significance, connected with the god Horus.

Courtesy of Metropolitan Museum

42. XII Dyn. from Lisht, Tomb of Inhotep. Cedarwood statue.

Sen-Wosret I.

43. XII Dyn. from Lisht, North Pyramid. Limestone statue.

A Priest: horizontal pleating as decoration of a dignitary.

44. XII Dyn. reign of Sen-Wosret I. c. 1950 B.C. Limestone statue.

The Steward Au: artificial beard, fine pleating.

45. XII-XIII Dyn. from Thebes. Wood statue.

The Vizir Yuy: long, skirt-like loin cloth, dipping in front, worn high; probably pleated horizontally to give a design often seen on important personages.

46. XII Dyn. 2000-1788 B.C. Basalt statuette.

Khnum-hotpe (inscribed with a prayer that the god Ptah-Sokar pray for his soul); wrap covering shoulder.

47. XII Dyn. 2000-1788 B.C. from Assiut.

Models of arms and armor (see Ills. 63, 66, 67), painted imitation of patterned hide.

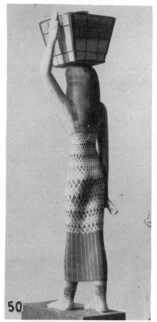

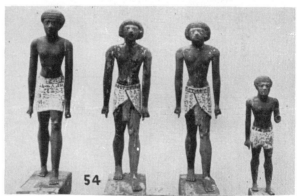

48. V Dyn. c. 2500 B.C. Wood statue from Mitry tomb at Sakkara.

The Official Mitry: fine pleating at one end of kilt; fine catch of belt.

49, 50. XI Dyn. Thebes, Tomb of Mehenkwetre. Funerary model, painted wood.

Peasant girl bearing offerings of meats and a live duck; wig and hem blue; feather decoration and jewelry blue, green, beige, and henna; similar garments were covered with zig-zag patterns in beads (example in Louvre).

51. XII Dyn., from Meir. Wooden statue.

Senba, Superintendent of the Palace: kilt stiffened into a trapezoid.

Courtesy of Metropolitan Museum

52. VI-XII Dyn. Painted Limestone. Stela.

Stiffened triangular point of kilt.

53. VI Dyn. Gizeh, Tomb of Kaemonkh. Wall Painting.

Cattle boats; there are fascinating representations of slaves, busy at every possible occupation, throughout Egyptian art, but their costume remains a comfortable loin-cloth. The hides of these spotted oxen give pattern to Egyptian shields and quivers.

54. XI-XII Dyn., from Assiut. Wooden statues, inscribed.

Four men.

Other peoples as seen by the Egyptians

55-57. XII Dyn. Beni-Hasan, Tomb of Khnum-hotpe. Wall painting.

55. Two nomads: red and blue. Garment wider at top, probably made of painted skins.

56. Semite with donkey: rosy red and deep pink pattern.

57. Group of Semite women: patterned in blue, henna, green and red. Shoes with contrasting tops. Men also wore similar garments of same length.

SEMITIC NOMADS IN EGYPT

In contrast to the simple, short, mainly white garments of the Egyptians, those of the Semitic nomads, the *Aamu*, who began to appear in Egypt in the Twelfth Dynasty, were long, brightly patterned in elaborations of vertical stripes or spots, and decorated with fringe and tassels. The shape of the garments shows that they had been developed out of hides; the Libyans continued to dress in leather until Roman times.*

Men: loin cloth, longer than worn by Egyptians of the period.

Men and Women: wrap, worn long by women, in varying lengths by men. Rectangular, widening at the top; when not of leather, which naturally has that form, small triangles could be sewn on the selvage at the top. Wrap went around body under right arm and fastened on left shoulder, the selvage edges on the left side remaining open.

The *Ribu*, an Aamu tribe, wore a garment developed out of this, with a further refinement of a slit for the right arm, and a hole left for the head. The decorative selvage edges on the left side were caught together at the waist. The *Tehennu*, a maritime Aamu tribe, wore a similar garment with a sleeve on the right arm; it tied on the left shoulder in long ears, and was belted. The *Cheli*, a tribe of the interior, wore a garment of the same type, which tied under the left arm, and had a turned-over collar which covered the right shoulder. (See Ills. 78, 79-86).

NORTHERN SEMITES

Cappadocians (Retennu-Tehennu): The garments of the peoples of the colder Upper Euphrates covered the body more completely than those of the South Syrians.

The costume was based on a fitted shirt (see Ill. 58), shown on armed soldiers; and longer, on persons of rank, with or without spiral scarf about the skirt, but in the latter case, worn with a cape.

Shirt: long; from halfway down calf to ankle length. A fitted garment with long tight sleeves, perhaps in the case of soldiers made of leather, it was of plain material; but all seams were covered with patterned colored braids, which were used to form a design, frequently cruciform at the neck which closed by a tasseled cord. Tassels also hung at hem from ends of seams. Upper and lower sections of sleeve, frequently divided by a line of braid around the arm, were often made of different materials, by the time of Rameses II.

* Riefstahl, p. 11.

der cape: fitted, pushed up on one shoulder to permit use of arm.

58, 59. XVIII Dyn. 1470-1445 B.C., Thutmosis III. Egyptian wall painting. Thebes, Tomb of Rekh-mi-re.

58. Syrian tribute bearers: fair-haired "white Syrians" (Hittites); one with a clipped beard and shock of hair; garments natural color, trimmed with red and blue braid, blue tassels. 59. Keftiu tribute bearers: The Keftiu were the non-Semitic people who lived at "the Back of Beyond" in "the Land of the Very Green Sea,"—"the land of the Ring" (i.e., of islands of the Mediterranean, and to the N.W. of Egypt, Rhodes, Crete, Cyprus and S.W. Asia Minor). They were never Phoenicians, though their commerce with Egypt passed through Phoenician ports. After the Eighteenth Dynasty the generic word "Keftiu" disappears, and the tribes are referred to specifically, as Lycian, etc.

The prototype of all these Aegean costumes was that of Crete, in which the belt was tighter, the hair more elaborately looped, knotted and horned, though the hair of the Keftiu is sometimes represented in the Egyptian fashion. All wore elaborately colored and patterned sandals, leggings, boots, and loin cloths fringed and tasseled. Animal skins were often tucked into the belt, as here shown. The tribute carried has a definitely Mycenaean character, like the metal beer-warmer held by its handle, and the bulls' heads borne by other figures, not reproduced here. The boots and loin cloths are embroidered in blue, red, yellow, browns and grays. Conical Cretan caps.

60. XVIII Dyn. 1420-1411 B.C. Thebes, Tomb of Tjanuy, No. 74. Wall painting.

Nubian soldiers with standard-bearer: black and white costume, and tails (description, see Ill. 77); nets, probably cut leather.

Spiral: like that of Assyrian priest, worn by men of rank. An elongated triangle, examples of which, 30′ x 30′ long, have been found in Egyptian tombs. On the garments of the Retennu princes it is made of plain material, edged with colored braid, and wound from waist to hips over the long seamed shirt. When it is omitted, a braid-edged cape, of another color, might be worn.

Asiatics to the East: *Retennu;* Assyrian origins. (See Ills. 58, 59, 61).

Spiral: as a complete garment; a square, just large enough to go around the body, to which was seamed an enormously long, narrow triangle, which was wound about the body, leaving the right arm and shoulder bare. These were usually embroidered in bright madder reds, indigo blues, and Tyrian purples; worn with matching *shoul-*

61. XVIII Dyn. 1420-1411 B.C. Thutmosis IV. Thebes, Tomb of Sebkhopte, No. 63. Wall painting.

Syrian tribute bearers: Kheta, whose white costumes the Egyptians rather admired, as they did not the red and blue costumes of other Syrian peoples. Spiral edged with one braid, shirt with another, red and blue, alone or in combination.

62. XVIII Dyn. 1411-1375 B.C. Amenophis III. Thebes, Tomb of unknown nobleman, No. 226. Wall painting.

Foreigners beneath the royal throne: Nubians (Cushites): in white loin cloths, and red sashes edged with white. Syrians: man with fillet on hair; white garment edged in red and green. Asiatic: man with shaved head; white garment, red and green edge; cape, green above, with a red and white edge; henna below, with an edge of henna, green and white.

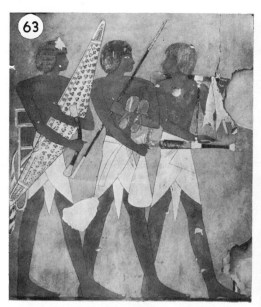

63. XVIII Dyn. c. 1430 B.C. Thebes, from Tomb of Ken-Amun, Chief Steward and Overseer of Cattle. Wall painting.

Attendants of Ken-Amun: carrying his stool, with an animal skin to sit on; sandals, staff and bag of clothing, boomerang, bow and case (made of leopard or painted like it); and a quiver with fur tail, which was carried horizontally across the back, and was reached from under the arm. The shield (see Ill. 47): oblong with rounded top and boss, hide-covered over a wood or wicker frame. Egyptian armor also included quilted caps of helmet or wig shape, quilted cuirasses, spears and javelins, short-straight swords, slings, battle-axes, and maces. Greaves were not worn.

64. XVIII Dyn. c. 1415 B.C. Thebes, Tomb of Zeser-ka-Ra-sonbe, Scribe and Counter of Gold. Wall painting.

Musicians: the first and last in saffron yellow (conventional for entertainers). Two female slaves, naked except belt below waist, and jewelry.

65-68. XVIII Dyn. c. 1430. Thebes, Tomb of Ken-Amun, Chief Steward and Overseer of Cattle. Wall Painting.

65. Dancing girls in funeral procession.

66. New Year's Gifts: bow; whip; dagger. 67. Coat of mail: gold and bronze scales on a heavy cloth backing, blue bordered with red bands. 68. Quivers: covered or painted like hide, and with fur tails.

Courtesy of Metropolitan Museum

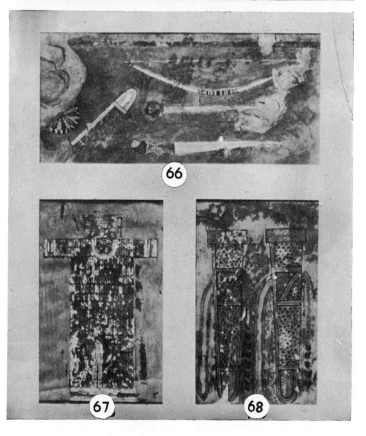

69, 70. XVIII Dyn. c. 1415 B.C. Thebes, Tomb of Menena, Scribe of the Fields of the Lord of Two Lands. Wall painting.

69. Harvest: Overseers and scribes in long and short kalasiris, and one or two loin cloths. Male slaves in loin cloth, one carrying master's "Was" staff with stylized animal head; female slaves in kalasiris held by one shoulder strap. All barefoot, some shaven heads without wigs. 70. Fishing and fowling in the marshes: Gentlemen in long sheer kalasiris,

and heavier loin cloth; shoulder-length bobbed wig. Ladies, kalasiris with left arm covered, heavy wig with long horizontal bottom line. Male slaves, triangular loin cloth. Female slave, naked except for belt below waist.

71. XIX Dyn. after 1350 B.C. Thebes, Tomb of Apuy the Sculptor. Wall painting.

Apuy and his wife receiving an offering: Wife with lotus flower and cone of perfumed fat on her

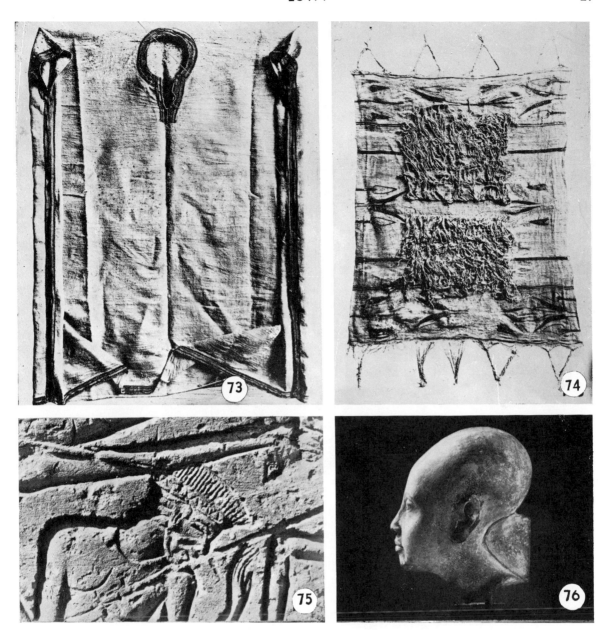

long enveloping wig ending in a fringe of tiny ringlets; pleated cape, equivalent to sleeves; fringed robe. Apuy, like the priest, wears sandals (see Ill. 78) and wears on his cape an eye amulet (see jewelry Ill. 41). The priest wears the simple loin cloth of earlier times, though lengthened and elaborated, and the animal skin.

72. End XVIII Dyn. Amenophis III. 1411-1375 B.C. Thebes, Tomb of Ra-mose No. 55. Wall painting.

Mourners: in gray costumes, although dark blue had been traditional for mourning since the earliest dynasties.

73, 74. XVIII Dyn. Amenophis III-IV. 1405-1352 B.C. Thebes, Tomb of Cha, the Architect. (Turin Museum.)

73. Tunic: edged with colored braid. 74. Fringed cloth, with tapestry-woven lotus pattern, looped on the reverse to give a furry warmth or solidity to the fabric. It is possible that some such technique was responsible for the shaggy garments worn by the Sumerians. Ten pieces of patterned cloth, antedating Tutenkhamun, have been discovered. Of these, two are similar fringed cloths, and a third is one of the seventeen linen tunics found in the tomb of the Architect Cha; no color notes are available.*

75. Egyptian, XIX-XX Dyn. Rameses III. Medinet Habu.

North wall relief: Naval battle with Northerners: head of a dead Philistine.

76. Egyptian, XVIII Dyn. El Amarna. (Neues Museum, Berlin.)

Head of a princess: skull deformed deliberately from birth, and shaved. Many well-known heads of the lovely Nefret-ity show her similarly deformed skull, shaved and without headdress, or with the headdress set directly on the head, without a wig.

* Riefstahl, 21-5.

Courtesy of Metropolitan Museum

77. Egyptian, XVIII Dyn. c. 1350 B.C. Tutankhamun. Tomb of Hoy, viceregent of Nubia. Wall painting. (Neues Museum, Berlin.)

Drawings taken from the papers of Lepsius. Made when the state of preservation of the paintings was more complete than at present.

Nubian tribute (west wall, south side): above Hoy: shields and furniture, covered with hide or painted, often to resemble hide; stools, fixed and folding; chairs; beds with head rests; loaded wheelbarrow.

Top row, r. to l.: Chiefs of Wawat (Lower Nubia), Nubian princes and princess in Egyptian dress, collars and sandals, differenced by leopard skins over shoulders; bands over shoulders and sashes with apron ends, of embroidered red; hoop, and other earrings; cat's tails at sleeves; feathers or ostrich plumes in hair; feather insignia in hands of chiefs. Gifts of rings of gold, animal skins. Ox-drawn chariot with parasol. Followers of princess in patterned ox-hide loin cloths, over sashes, with animal tails fastened

on rear (see Ill. 60), and narrow scarves knotted at neck. Women in many-colored patterned skirts. Children naked, with tufted hair.

Rows 2 & 3: Princes of Cush (Upper Nubia), over whom there had been an Egyptian viceroy since Thutmosis I, 1540 B.C. More Negroid, barefoot, bearing giraffe tails, rings of gold, patterned skins, a giraffe, oxen with horns tipped with hands.

Row 3: The tall men of Trk and the men of Irmi, in loin cloths, sandals, and many bracelets, carrying fans of feathers and gold on long jewelled and gold trimmed staves.

Large figures: Hoy being greeted by his household on his return: wearing kalasiris, tucked up, under overskirt, reduced to a swathing of the back of the figure. Feather fan, insignia of his viceroyalty (originally an actual feather, now probably stylized). Collar, bracelets of massive gold; cone of perfumed fat on head as for a banquet.

78. Egyptian, c. 1350 B.C., Tutankhamun. Tomb of Hoy,
viceregent of Nubia. Wall painting. (Neues Museum,
Berlin.) From Lepsius' papers.

*Tribute of the Princes of Asia, the Retennu and
Syria.*

Large figures: Tutankhamun: with ankh (crux
ansata) in r. hand; flail with 3 lashes, and crook
(symbols of sovereignty) in l. hand. War helmet,
with uraeus (rearing viper, symbol of royalty) and
colored triangular apron of Pharaoh. Collar, bracelets
and arm bands. Pleated collar-sleeves, long pleated
skirt. Hoy: with crook and feather (symbol of viceroyalty), collar, sandals with a beak point, the cords
held from toe and heel by a metal plaque.

Next smaller figures: Hoy, carrying a bowl of
lapis lazuli and a necklace with exaggeratedly enlarged pectoral, "tribute offered by Retennu (Syria)
the vile," as well as carnelian, vases in nets and on
standards, animal skins, offered by the chieftains of
Upper Retennu and ambassadors and "chieftains of
distant lands" (smaller figures) wearing wound costumes of 2 superimposed spirals of different materials,
and followed by slaves in tasseled loin cloths.

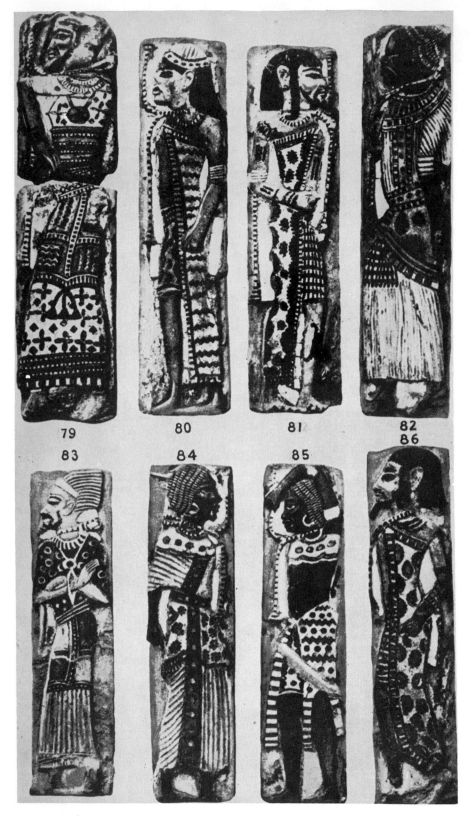

79   80   81   82
                  86
83   84   85

79-86. XX Dyn. c. 1180 B.C. from Medinet Habu. Glazed tiles. (Cairo Museum.)

races. In the case of important Negro personages, where the decorative elements of native costume are superimposed on an Egyptian base, this is very clear. With the Phoenician traders, Semitic patterns and cut, tassels and fringe, travelled west by water to combine with Aegean and Mediterranean native costume. The advance and alteration of an element in costume can be followed like the mutations of an insect, except that among insects fewer fantastic marriages prove fertile than in costume. The descent of many of these patterned, perhaps painted, garments from a pattern of an animal hide, is unmistakable.

79. Philistines: simple helmet fastened under chin; medallion on chest; horizontally laminated cuirasse; Keftiu-type loin cloth, tasseled; over long, patterned, short-sleeved tunic.

80. Differs from Libyan in hair form, fillet, beardlessness, absence of side-lock (which might be on other side). Similar costume, and apparently some tattooing.

81. Libyan: lock of hair in front of ear; tattooed designs on arms, and on lower leg the shuttle of the goddess Neit; straight loin cloth; patterned and bordered upper garment of hide; typical feathers in hair lacking, but unmistakably a Libyan.

82, 84, 85. Negroes: (See Ill. 77.)

83. Shakalousha.

86. Hittite or Syrian, Asiatic in beard trimmed like the Turusha; horizontal stripes of loin cloth; curved lower edge of wrap; lock in front of ear, like prayer-curl rather than Libyan side-lock.

Identification of the costumes of alien peoples is complicated by the mistaken attributions made by the Egyptians themselves, as well as by the mingling, sometimes mistaken, frequently actual, of the costumes of different

87. XVIII Dyn. after 1350 B.C. Thebes, Tomb of Tutankhamun. (Cairo Museum.)

Painted ivory carving from a ceremonial baton:
Syrian in typical narrow-sleeved yellow undergarment, and red and blue overgarment; almost the
identical costume in which the Lords of Lebanon are
shown cutting cedar for tribute to Seti I.

88. Late XVIII Dyn. 1375-50 B.C. Thebes, Valley of the
Kings.

Ostracon (artist's sketch): painted on limestone.
King in the act of spearing a lion; short-sleeved shirt,
slit horizontally across the breast, lower part tied
around the midriff; skirt draped in horizontal pleating, shows the triangular, decorated apron of a king;
red crown of Lower Egypt.

89. XVIII Dyn. Painted Limestone.
Priest presenting an official and his son.

90. XIX Dyn., from Assiut. Limestone.
Ini and Rennut, his wife. Garments more cut and
fitted; wigs, especially of women, enclose whole upper body, and are elaborately dressed. Men now wear
kalasiris with a neck opening, pleated into sleeves;
apron effect of skirt front is probably the mantle tied
around the hips. Kalasiris of women covers left
shoulder.

91. XVIII Dyn. Basalt statue.
General Harmhab, last king of Eighteenth Dynasty. Sleeved kalasiris, short slit at center of throat,
puffed apron arrangement of skirt.

Courtesy of Metropolitan Museum (88-91)

92

93

94

92. XIX Dyn., Rameses II. Thebes, Tomb of Nekht-Amun. Wall painting.

Funeral procession: shaved heads, sign of mourning. Priest with shaved head, in loin cloth and skin.

93. Egyptian, 1292-1225 B.C. Rameses II. Thebes, Tomb of Nefret-ity, Valley of the Queens. Wall painting.

Isis leading Nefret-ity: color is beginning to assume a place in the hitherto white Egyptian dress; strong primary colors and sharp greens, very unlike the grayed and yellowed greens of the earlier dynasties. The worship of Isis increased greatly toward the end of the New Kingdom, and she is shown in the tight garment of earlier days which has persisted as the costume of goddesses; red, with a zig-zag pattern in green and other colored beads. Many symbols related to her headdress of blue cow-horns (sacred to her), set on her blue wig; red disk (universe, phases of the moon), uraeus (rearing viper, of royalty), green staff with stylized jackal's head. Over her shoulder she carries a *menyet,* a necklace composed of a hank of green beads balanced by a gold plaque of equal weight at the other end, which could equally

well be carried and waved, during religious ceremonies.

Nefret-ity: in full white kalasiris, its pleats spreading into a cape; red girdle, gold collar and winged headdress, surmounted by stylized feathers of a queen, worn over blue wig, edged with gold. Uraeus of queen used as earring.

94. XX Dyn., Rameses III, 1198-1167 B.C. Thebes, Tomb of Prince Amenkhopshef. Wall painting.

Isis greets Rameses III and his son: increasing use of color.

Isis: barefoot, in traditional dress; yellow, red, and blue with red and blue sash, blue wig, green collar.

Rameses III: gold headdress; green collar and crossed bands; abbreviated short-sleeved shirt, now a jacket, over heavier white shirt; royal apron, over skirt of red, blue and green feather pattern; sash with one red and one blue end; sandals.

Amenkhopshef: in white, red sash, embroidered, with one red and one blue end, and red, blue and white tassels; gold collar; headdress, blue and gold, with black and white feathers; sandals.

Courtesy of Metropolitan Museum

95 | 96 | 97 | 98

99 | 100

95, 96. Egyptian. Late New Kingdom. 1360 B.C. Wood statuette. (Cairo Museum.)

Official: front and back views.

97, 98. XIX Dyn. c. 1250 B.C. Wood statuette. (Cairo Museum.)

Female: front and back views.

99. c. 210 B.C. Limestone statuette. (Metropolitan Museum.)

Arsinae.

100. Roman - Persian - Egyptian XXVII Dyn. Painted Headpiece of Mummy Case. (Metropolitan Museum.)

Pharaoh: with atef crown, carrying ankh and jackal-headed staff, feather and other patterns. (See Ill. 78.)

Isis and her son, or adopted son, Horus, wearing the crowns of both Upper and Lower Egypt at the same time. Style mixed and impure: old netted bead pattern. (See Ill. 93.)

Courtesy of Metropolitan Museum (99, 100); Cairo Museum (95-98)

101. Egyptian XII Dyn. c. 1900 B.C.

Pectoral of Sit-Hat-Hor Yunet, daughter of Sen-Wosret II: "Tiny pieces of turquoise, carnelian, lapis lazuli, and garnet have been inlaid in cloisons to make a design consisting of two falcons, symbols of the god Horus, which face each other across a cartouche of the king, supported on a figure representing eternity. Not content with decorating only one side, the jeweller engraved details on the solid gold of the reverse side. The pectoral was suspended on a string of drop-shaped beads which repeat the color of the pendant."*

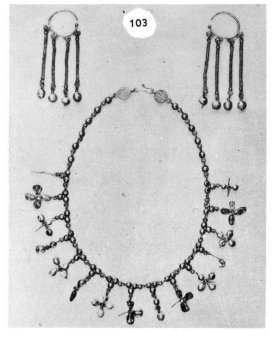

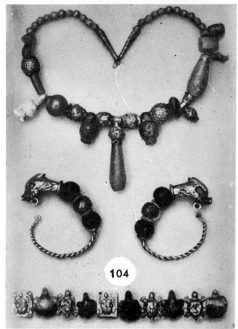

102, 103. Byzantine, Early Christian, prob. VIc. A.D. or earlier.

102. Bracelet of gold, pearls, sapphires, and emerald plasma. 103. Necklace and earrings of gold, pearls and sapphires.

104. Near East and Cyprus. VII-IIIc. B.C.

Necklace, earrings and bracelet.

105. Byzantine (prob. Russian) XI-XIIc. A.D.

Earrings and parts of a necklace in gold, with X-XIIc. cloisonné enameling, a tech-

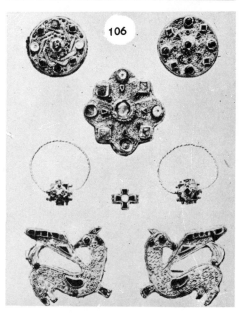

nique of Eastern origin. One earring is still bordered with pearls.

106. Frankish Merovingian VI-VIIIc. A.D.

Costume ornaments from Merovingian graves; brooches, buckle, and earrings of gold and bronze-gilt, inlaid with glass and precious stones.

* Notes by Ambrose Lansing.

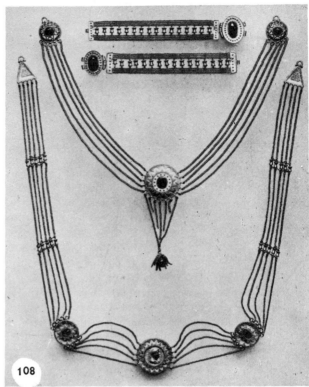

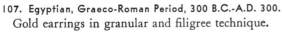

107. Egyptian, Graeco-Roman Period, 300 B.C.-A.D. 300.
Gold earrings in granular and filigree technique.

108. Egyptian, Ptolemy III. 247-222 B.C.
Bracelets, necklace and girdle of gold and precious stones in the Greek style. Braided gold chains connect the medallions, the central one of which is a coin of Ptolemy III.

109. Barbarian. V-VIc. A.D.
Bronze buckles; upper two, Ostrogothic; lower, Visigothic.

110. Barbarian. VII-IXc. A.D.
Gold belt ornaments found in Albania, presumably the work of migrants from Central Asia. Massive; high-lights and deep shadows.

Courtesy of Metropolitan Museum

Coptic Costume

The cultural chaos of Egypt began to coalesce under the influence of Christianity.

The unification brought about by the Coptic church has caused the whole Early Christian period in Egypt, whether Christian or not, to be called "Coptic." It was actually a synthesis of Ancient Egyptian, Roman, Greek, and Near Eastern influences.

The cultural contributions of the early Church were limited to hymns and sermons. The only available vocabulary of art was formed out of old symbols and designs from pagan and classical life. These motifs and mythological figures had become meaningless and purely decorative; they were used freely on Christian dress in Egypt, which was substantially that of the whole Roman empire. In this way, a combination of Near Eastern and Mediterranean patterns passed into the dress of Early Mediaeval Europe.

Christianity made great strides among the lower classes during the desperately poor years of the IIIc. It rose to power in IVc.; Christians were the government workers, scribes and accountants, the surveyors and architects. With the Moslem persecutions, quantities of Christian material were destroyed, future development was inhibited, and "degrading dress" began to be imposed on Christians in IXc. In Xc., they were forced to assume heavy crosses and the black turbans native to one of Islam's most despised enemies; while Jews wore yellow, and Mohammedans, white or red turbans. In 1301, a dark-blue turban, the color of mourning since Ancient Egyptian times, was imposed, and many Christians turned to Islam, rather than wear it.

Coptic burial places furnish actual garments and jewelry of people of every class and sect; mummies are accompanied by portraits painted on wood or linen; there are funerary stelae, and frescos.

For our purposes, the actual garments, and the techniques and colors of their decoration, which formed European dress, are most significant.

There are reserve printed all-over patterns, usually blue. Linen tunics (usually undyed) and wool tunics (sometimes yellow), are both encrusted or inlaid with tapestry-woven borders, square patches, and roundels in colored wools. There is a great variety of purples, orange-yellow, red, blue, green, brown and black. Patterns are geometrical; leaves (grape, laurel, ivy, palm) and fruits, often combined with urns; animals (deer, lions, hare, fish); birds (peacock, eagle, dove and duck); figures and motifs from classical and pagan mythology (Europa and the bull, chariots, hunting and pastoral scenes, Persian figures); and portrait medallions.

111. Coptic. IVc. A.D., from Akhmen. (Metropolitan Museum.)

Tunic: undyed linen; tapestry-woven decoration in purple wool and undyed linen. Cloth woven in loop technique.

112. Coptic. IVc. A.D., from Akhmen. (Metropolitan Museum.)

Tunic: same colors as above sample.

113. Coptic. VI-VIIc. A.D., from Tuna. (Metropolitan Museum.)

Tunic: tapestry-woven in undyed wool, with *clavi* and *orbiculi* in colors on a red ground. Applied woven bands at hem and cuffs, red on brown.

Courtesy of Metropolitan Museum

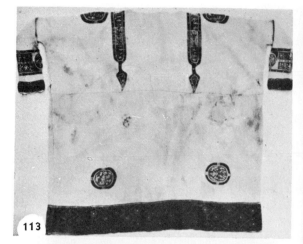

113

114

115

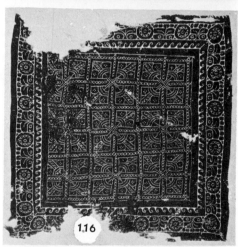

116

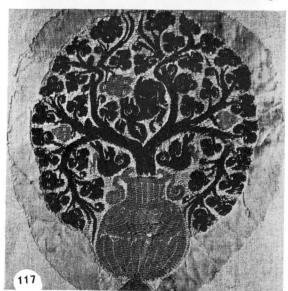

117

118

the Eastern legend of Alexander the Great's journey to Heaven, which was carried over into the Mohammedan period, and passed into mediaeval European use.

115. Coptic. IV-Vc. (Brooklyn Museum.)

Swimming amorino with dolphin: tapestry-woven square in deep purple and undyed linen.

116. Coptic. III-IVc. (Collection of N.Y. Hist. Soc., in Brooklyn Museum.)

Square with geometrical design: tapestry woven purple wool with fine design in undyed linen thread, used on hangings or the cloak, *pallium.*

117. Coptic. IV-Vc. (Brooklyn Museum.)

Vine growing from urn: tapestry weave in wool and linen; deep blue vine with hare and bird in the branches; gadrooned urn and clusters of fruit are red; pale greenish - blue high-light on urn.

118. Coptic. IV-Vc. (Cooper Union Museum.)

Female head in jewelled frame: naturalistic colors with black hair, on red ground; border imitating gold frame set with jewels. Splendid example of late classical portrait heads.

114. Coptic. VII-VIIIc. A.D., (Brooklyn Museum.)

Tunic: yellow wool rep, with tapestry-woven bands in dark blue with touches of pale purple, showing figures in niches. The figure at the neck, between griffons, is probably an illustration from

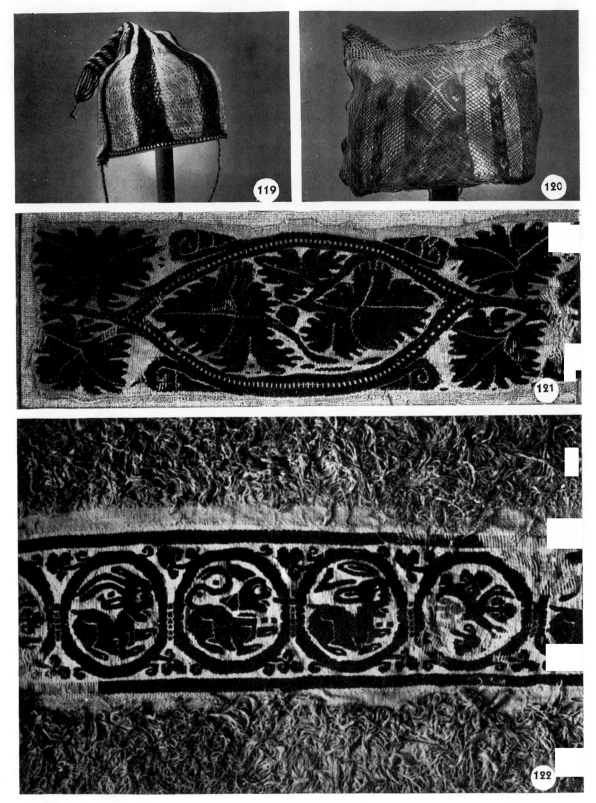

119. Coptic. V-VIc., from Sakkara. (Metropolitan Museum.)
   Cap of red wool and undyed linen network.

120. Coptic. V-VIc., from Akhmen. (Metropolitan Museum.)
   Cap of brownish linen network.

121. Coptic. V-VIc. (Brooklyn Museum.)
   Border with grapevine motif, in purple wool and linen, forming oval cartouches with semi-naturalistic vine leaves and tendrils.

122. Coptic. Vc., said to be from Akhmen. (Brooklyn Museum.)
   Looped linen fabric (see Ill. 74), with tapestry-woven bands of roundels, of vine stems and buds, containing floral and animal motifs.

123. Coptic. VII-VIIIc. (Brooklyn Museum.)

Front of green woolen tunic with tapestry-woven bands.

124. Coptic. V-VIc. (Brooklyn Museum.)

Border; very fine wool tapestry weave. Pale purplish-red ground, with design in red with tan shading outlined in undyed linen thread, combining late Classic and Sassanid motifs, lion, and portrait medallion. Border of undulated vines with pomegranates. A roundel with portrait heads probably from the same garment, is in the Textile Museum of the District of Columbia.

125. Coptic. VIc. (Brooklyn Museum.)

Front of tunic: yellow wool with tapestry-woven bands showing nymphs and sea-monsters, yellow on brown. At neck, in colors, jewelled chain with cross, and, in V formed by chain, a crude, nude female figure in dancing posture, with elaborate headdress and upraised hands holding heart-shaped red objects. Strzygowski speculates as to whether this combination of cross and dancing figures may not be a Gnostic symbol.

126. Greek VIc. 550-530 B.C.
    Athenian black-figured amphora, *The Judgment of Paris*. Hermes escorting the Three Goddesses.

127. Greek IV-IIIc. B.C.
    Tanagra type figurine of painted terra cotta.

128. Coptic IVc. A.D.
    Tapestry-woven decoration in wool on linen.

129. Coptic V-VIc. A.D.
    Tapestry-woven wool: detail of shoulder-band.

Courtesy of Metropolitan Museum (126-128)
Courtesy of Brooklyn Museum (129)

The Greek Sphere

CRETE

CRETE, situated between Egypt, Greece and the mainland of Europe, having very early established an art of immense and unmistakable character, greatly affected Cyprus and the coast of Palestine (where settlements were made by Cretans), Asia Minor, the Greek Islands, Italy, Sardinia and the western Mediterranean as far as Spain.

The Aegean culture falls into three periods, Early, Middle and Late Minoan:

Early Minoan I-III (3400-2100 B.C.): Crete a fertile island without defenses or enemies. Pottery as fine as any then being produced anywhere; spiral patterns, red, black, white. Early Minoan II contemporaneous with Twelfth Dynasty in Egypt.

Middle Minoan I (2100-1900 B.C.): Palace at Cnossos planned.

Middle Minoan II (1900-1700 B.C.): Palace built; frescos, mosaics, high reliefs (to L.M.Ia); gold, silver and bronze work; engraved gems; decorated pottery at its best, red, yellow, white on black. At end of M.M. II, there was a catastrophe, probably connected with Hyksos Dynasty in Egypt, with which country Crete had had age-old relations.

Middle Minoan III (1700-1580 B.C.): The period of Crete's greatest influence and trade. Palaces built in colonies at Mycenae, Tiryns, Troy.*

Middle Minoan IIIa: Palace of Cnossos rebuilt and decorated; baths, magnificent water and drainage system; luxury, gladiatorial sports, bull-fighting by both men and women.

Middle Minoan IIIb: Catastrophe: fire? earthquake? Palace plundered.

Late Minoan I (1580-1450 B.C.): Cnossos rebuilt; cupbearer frescos. Egypt copies Aegean art.

Late Minoan I & II (1450-1375 B.C.): Eighteenth Dynasty in Egypt.

Late Minoan IIb: Cnossos burned, sacked, never recovered.

Late Minoan III (1375-1100 B.C.): Late Mycenaean (Aegean) period. Keftiu tributaries shown on wall paintings in Egypt. (Tombs of Rekhmi-ré and Senmut.) Cnossos partly reoccupied. Introduction of the pottery wheel brought about uniformity; the beginning of the end; horizontal line decoration in white on black. Lifelessness of Crete and whole Aegean.

About 1000 B.C., Cnossos was finally destroyed, probably by invading Dorians. Iron Age of Northern barbarians supplants the Bronze Age.

Cretan religion centered around a mother-goddess with her consort-son. Themes with religious significance were snakes, doves, lions, pillars, bulls, Double-Axe Minotaur Labyrinth.

Cretan costume: the most elaborately cut, fitted, in many cases patterned, in all antiquity.

COSTUME DETAILS (FEMALE)

Up to M.M. period, in the case of common women even later, upper body was bare. Thereafter, they wore a short, tight bodice, possibly made of leather, sleeved, exposing breasts, laced close beneath them. Belt was very tight, wide with rolled edges, or a snake-like roll.

Skirt was bell-shaped, in superimposed tiers, or flounced; sometimes finely pleated. Slanting lines of decoration are seen, from Petsofá examples onward; by M.M. III., flounces follow a convex, dipping hemline; this is universal by L.M., and is paralleled by hemline of men's loin cloths.

Aprons: snake goddesses. Curved front and back sections, over tiered skirts.

Loin cloths, like men's, were worn by women bullfighters. Capes had the high "Medici" collar (Petsofá). Headdress might be horned (Petsofá), a turban, or a high truncated cone (Cnossos).

Hair was worn long; up to L.M., it was covered, then knotted in back, high on the crown, with bound and flowing tail; falling loose at the sides; also clubbed in *catogan*.

Jewelry included diadems, hairpins, buttons and brooches, necklaces, bracelets—of gold, silver, bronze, semi-precious stones, glass beads.

Priestesses and goddesses are depicted with aprons, with snake-like hair and with snakes in their headdresses.

---

* See writings of Evans and Schliemann.

COSTUME DETAILS (MALE)

Cretan men are depicted with the tight "wasp waist" girdled by a belt, possibly of metal riveted on in youth. The loin cloth was worn under a kilt or apron. The kilt, a later development, was decorated characteristically, following a concave hemline, dipping in front, often fringed. Late examples are finished with a triangular beaded netting.

They wore boots of decorated light-colored leather. There were probably sandals and legbands, of white leather, as still worn in Crete.

Male hair was worn longer than that of women; looped, knotted, tied at top or back of head, in top-knot flowing from a metal spiral, or horns, or a *catogan* club at back. Headcoverings were the hood and the wide-brimmed *petasus*. Short hair was worn for mourning.

The cloak was shaped, often fringed.

Priests, like goddesses, wore the apron, which was long up to M.M. III, thereafter reduced to a flap behind. Gods were depicted with the feathered tiara, like the later Lycian headdress.

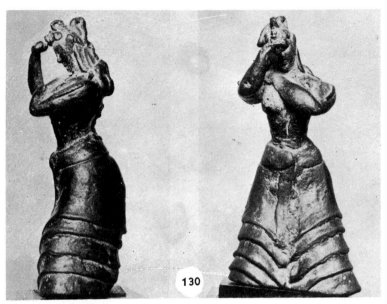

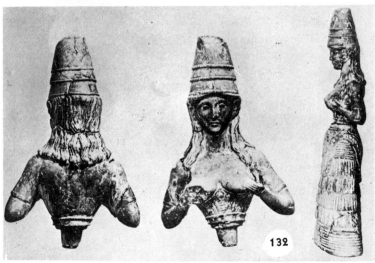

130. Aegean M.M. III. (Berlin Museum.)

Bronze statuette: worshipping woman. Snake-like loops of hair. Bodice cut away to expose breasts, and tightly laced below. Semi-circular wrapped-around skirt, apparently composed of 5 skirts, superimposed and shortening, all dipping at center front (see Ills. 59, 130, 133).

131. Aegean M.M. I., from Petsofa.

Terra cotta statuette: horned *Petsofá* headdress (covering the hair), and standing collar, on a bodice which is probably no more than a piece of leather wrapped around the torso. Snake-like roll of belt, bell-shaped skirt; decoration set at an angle (see Ill. 59).

132. Aegean M.M. III, from the Harbor Town of Cnossos. (Fitzwilliam Museum, Cambridge.)

Three views of a stone statuette of the Mother Goddess which omits the snakes of her underworld aspect. Tiered, truncated conical headdress. Cut-away, fitted, boned and laced bodice. Tight Cretan belt, concave with rolled edges. Patterned apron. Tiered, pleated skirt.

133. Aegean M.M. III, c. 1000-1500 B.C. Cnossos. (Metropolitan Museum.)

Faience figures of a snake goddess, attendant, and part of another. There are no more explicit representations of Cretan goddesses than these. The attendant wears the truncated conical hat. Skirts are now perfectly made, bell-shaped, and tiered with patterned pleating, rather than wrapped around. The Snake Goddess (r.) is costumed in blue-black, purplish-brown, with white and a variety of yellows, the darkest of which is used on the bodice. Her black and white turban is surmounted by a yellow lion (ritual significance). Figure (1); brown tiara; green and brown snakes; beige bodice scrolled in brown; gray apron; milky white skirt lined in purplish brown.

134. Aegean M. Minoan III. XVIc. B.C. (Boston Museum of Fine Arts.)

Cretan Snake Goddess. It is pure sacrilege to have a restoration of a wall painting appear on the same page with the Museum of Fine Arts' tiny snake goddess; it is undoubtedly one of the most enchanting

works of art in existence. It is sad that no photographs can give any idea of the ritual exaltation of this little figure, carved from ivory, and banded in gold, with gold snakes and jutting gold nipples.

135. Aegean L. Minoan III. XIV-XIIIc. B.C., found at Ras-Shamra, Syria. (Louvre.)

Ivory cover from a pyxis. A goddess of fertility and fecundity (ears of wheat, rearing animals); originally received from the Orient, and now taken back by Mycenaean traders. Hair drawn to crown, bound, falling snake-like lock (as in Tiryns fresco). Headdress, modelling of face, and skirts are Mycenaean; she sits on the altar which stands near the Gate of the Lions, Mycenae, where similar fragments have been found. (See Appendix.)

136. Aegean, Late Minoan from Cnossos. (Candia Museum.)

Stucco Relief: Priest-King of Cnossos. Crown, with Lycian plumes, and collar combine the *was* lily, (papyrus) of the Nile Delta, with the iris of Crete, in blue and henna red, which in these frescos are equivalent to silver and gold. Blue roll above red and white belt. Blue Mycenaean loin cloth of modesty, worn with a white apron, lined in red, which has been reduced to a flap behind, by the Late Minoan period. Ridged lines on the right thigh indicate a tiered white sash, related to the tiered skirts of snake-goddesses. Like the silver anklets shown on Oriental figures of antiquity, bracelets and necklaces indicate rank.

The Cupbearer, and other processional figures* in Late Minoan frescos show jutting rumps, like that of the woman in the Tiryns fresco, in kilts similar to those Aegeans in Egyptian wall paintings (See Egypt 1470-45, Rekhmi-Re), falling in a weighted point, from which hangs a triangle of blue-beaded network, finished with lilies and papyrus flowers.

137. Aegean Mainland. Late Minoan III, from Tiryns.

Restoration of a wall painting: The frescos are too badly damaged to give an informative photograph. This redrawing shows clearly the bustled aspect, which is seen in the Berlin Museum's worshipper, and in the VIIIc. dipylons. Hair remains snake-like through all the favorite Cretan methods of dressing it, shown here in combination: clubbed into a *catogan* at the nape; knotted and then flowing from the top of the head; bound in a snake; or falling in wriggling locks. Pattern follows the line of 4 concavities in the hemline, which gives this later skirt a curiously trouser-like look.

138. Aegean, M.M. II, from Hagada-Triada. (Candia Museum.)

Steatite Vase: Young Prince and officer of his guard outside the gate to his house.* Forelock and frontal curls; dirk with knobbed hilt at girdle (tra-

* Evans: Pal. of Minos, sup. pl. XXVII.

138

139

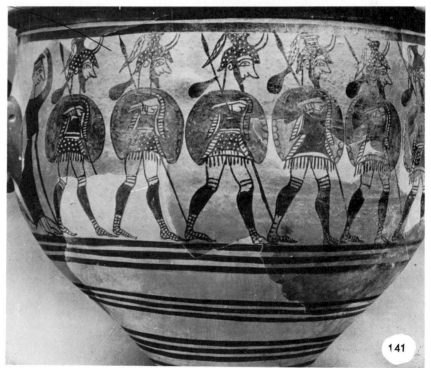

140

141

ditional); collar and bracelets, like officer's torque, indicate rank.

139. Aegean, MM.II., from Hagada-Triada. (Candia Museum.)
The Harvester Vase.

140. Aegean, M.M.III., from Mycenae.
Ivory relief: Warrior.

141. Aegean, Late Minoan III, 1350-1100 B.C. Mycenaean. (Metropolitan Museum.) Vases: Warriors.
Vase: Warriors.

Hagada-Triada was destroyed before Cnossos. The illustrations on this page show the Aegean helmet

with boar's tusks and crest; the exposed ear; hair clubbed at the nape in *catogans,* or knotted high with a falling lock. Shields and spears carried only by officers. Belted wasp-waists, even of naked harvesters. Characteristic dipping hemline of Aegean loin cloth; pattern following this line (on women's skirts, as well); scale decoration; fringe. Capes. High, elaborately patterned shoes and leggings. Compare with women's illustrations, Egyptian wall paintings of Cretans, and XVIIIc. Dipylons.

* Evans

GREECE, HER COLONIES AND NEIGHBORS

PRE-HELLENIC

3400-1375 B.C. *Minoan Period* (Crete).
1375-1100 B.C. *Mycenaean Period* (Aegean).

HELLENIC

Homeric Age: monarchy; position of women freer and more dignified than in IVc. Athens. Archaic architecture: Greek Islands, S. Italy, Syracuse, 1000 B.C. Temple of Olympia. Achaean iron work.

VIIIc. Oligarchy.

VIIc. Tyrants; Temple of Selinus, Sicily and Temple of Assus, Asia Minor (archaic sculpture).

VIc. Return to oligarchy: establishment of Hellenic art. Greek architecture and vase painting at highest point. Sculpture: rigid. Great age of colonization to Aegean, Asia Minor, Italy, Sicily: contacts in Asia Minor with oriental art and costume. Increase in Persian arrogance and Greek apprehension. Greece divided into:

> *Dorians*: inheritors of Mycenaean civilization (Crete and Rhodes); also colonized Lesbos, Halicarnassus and Cos.
> *Ionians:* greatest of the colonizers and traders; most orientalized in art and costume; colonized Samos, Chios, and rich Miletus.
> *Aeolians*: sided with Ionians in Peloponnesian Wars.
> *Spartans:* last monarchy of the old style; preeminent infantry army.

Vc. Internal strife in Greece; Persian invasions; Persians defeated by Greeks.

Persian wars 499-480 B.C. under Spartan leadership; unity, power, increase in trade. Aegina: Temple of Aphaea; sculptures of Trojan War.

Great Age 480-338 B.C. Rise of Athens: political science; painting; poetry; mathematics; astronomy; philosophy. Architecture: Parthenon, Propylaea, Erechtheum, Hall of Eleusinian Mysteries.

Peloponnesian War 431-404 B.C. Athens vs. Dorians and Sparta; decline of Athens, politically and artistically; prose.

Spartan Empire 405-371 B.C.: narrow, selfish oligarchy. Greek art expanded by Alexander's city-colonies; spread through Asia as far as India, and Asia Minor, Syria and Egypt.

Rise of Macedonia to Roman conquest 146 B.C. Artistic development in Italy (painted Etruscan tombs), Sicily (Messina); Greek cities of Asia Minor, Temples of Diana at Ephesus, and Apollo at Miletus, Mausoleum at Halicarnassus, tombs in Lycia.

GREEK COSTUME DETAILS

Greek clothing was formed out of rectangles of material, and consisted of a garment and a wrap. There were two main varieties of the garment, the *Dorian peplos* and the *Ionian chiton*. The wrap, known as the *himation,* or the *chlamys,* was often the sole apparel worn by men, especially in the rude Dorian days and in the revival of earlier styles after the Persian Wars. The Minoan male was much more elaborately dressed than the Dorian invader of Crete.

The Dorian *peplos* was the simpler form, worn by all Greek women to VIc. (but only by women) and revived again after the Persian Wars. It was of wool, dyed indigo, madder or saffron, frequently patterned, especially at the turn of the Vc.; used also as a blanket.

Its upper edge was folded over to hang down on the breast; it was folded around the body, caught together on each shoulder by pins, leaving the arms uncovered, and though open down the right side, was held in place by the girdle over which it bloused. In Corinth and Attica it was sewed together down the side below the waistline.

With time, the garment grew wider, and the overfold deepened so that it was included in the girding, or hung over and concealed the girdle. When not girded, the overfold could be raised over the head in back as a shawl. Spartan girls and women wore the woolen Dorian peplos; married women the himation as well.

The *chiton* (Ionian) was of Phoenician origin; the word has the same root as the Hebrew "kethoneth," our "cotton," and the Roman "tunica." It was worn first by men, later by women also. It was made of thin stuffs; probably crepe-like, similar to materials still woven in Greece; linen; or the gauzy materials from Cos in Asia Minor, patterned in murex purple. It was, therefore, more ample, made of two pieces sewed together, frequently pleated, and long, sometimes trailing.

It was sewed or caught together all the way down the arm, into the equivalent of sleeves, and sewed up the right side. It was worn in many ways: without a girdle, by musicians; and when long, by men; girdled at the waist, by women only, with the girdle worn lowest c. 450 B.C., and raised high under the breasts c. 200-150 B.C.; girded across the breast in various ways by both sexes, and by charioteers.

The chiton was often worn with a short wrap (*chlamydon*), pleated over a band which ran from the right shoulder under the left arm.

There was a short form of this chiton, worn by men at work or sport, which came to Greece from Asia Minor, perhaps originally from Babylon. The chiton was discarded as unmanly, during the return to the old, simple styles, after the Persian wars.

These two garments greatly affected and modified each other. They are found in all sorts of combinations from the Vc. Their colors were: yellow, worn only by women; various greens, purples, red, black, blue-gray, golden brown, as well as white.

There was also an intermediate form of *sleeveless chiton,* worn by Doric men, young girls, country folk; and, caught sometimes on one shoulder only (*exomis*) by athletes; and by workmen, often of sheepskin or leather. Sleeved garments were used, particularly in Asia Minor and Troy, where the Scythian and Persian styles spread, whence they were carried to Ionia. In Greek dress, a long-sleeved garment worn by a woman, in company of other people, indicates a servant or foreigner.

Animal skins were worn (as *aegis*), slit for passage of the wearer's head, with the head of the animal, usually a goat, on the breast. On the aegis of Athene, the hair at the edges developed into a fringe of snakes. The aegis was worn in Crete and early Athens, by women as well as men. Xerxes' Lycian archers wore goat, fox, fawn skins; Arcadians, the bear, wolf, sheep and goat.

The *himation* was a square of wool with weighted corners, slung over the left shoulder, leaving the right arm free; or worn, by married women, with the corner over the head like a shawl. Dorian men wore it as their only garment, as did the Athenians in their return to earlier simplicity; shortened, III-II B.C. A man wearing the himation alone was always adequately dressed, while the chiton, worn alone, was informal. It served also as a blanket. The colors were: gamut of natural wool colors: white, natural, browns, and black; or dyed scarlet, crimson or purple; woven patterns; selvages; embroidery.

The *pharos* was the linen equivalent of himation, worn only by noblemen upon occasions. The *chlamys* was a smaller woolen rectangle, of Macedonian or Italian origin; sometimes bordered, pinned at right shoulder or front: worn with short chiton or alone, by younger, more active men. The *chloene,* like the chlamys, was of coarse wool, worn hooked on one shoulder, running below the other breast; often folded over before fastening; originated in Macedonia or Thessaly. The equivalent female wrap was the *diplax.* The *chlamydon,* a long, narrow chlamys for women, was worn pleated over a band running beneath left breast from right shoulder. The *tribon* was worn by Spartan males over 12; a small, oblong cloak, of Balkan origin, as the only garment,

Footwear was not worn in the house by either sex; women, until late period, barefoot at all times, except goddesses, or for travelling. Sandals were red, black, white. Boots were high laced for hunting, travelling. Buskins, *cothurnus*: to mid-leg; with platform sole, for tragic actors. Common men had feet or legs swathed in skin or cloth. Slippers were Persian influenced, patterned.

Headcoverings consisted of hats worn only when their protection was actually needed for travelling, or by peasants. The *petasus* was a wide brimmed travelling hat, worn also by peasants, shepherds, etc. *Pilos* were caps worn by workmen, shepherds, sailors. The *causia* was a Thessalonian travelling hat for men or women, worn also by actors to indicate an arduous journey. The Tanagra figurines show the Boeotian headcovering and the "Phrygian bonnet" shows the Scythian-Persian influence.

Female headwear included the *ampyx* (diadem); *kekryphalos*: handkerchief, possibly hood or cap; the *kredemnon*: a veil worn over the head, if not covered by himation. It was probably of white linen; dark for mourning; worn to swathe and conceal the face.

Jewelry was of metal rather than jewels; much more worn by women than men. It included pins: stiletto-like, at shoulders of peplos; *fibulae* and brooches; hairpins of ivory, bone, gold; diadems (*ampyx*), and fillets; *sphendome* (sling); and *sakkos,* a completely enveloping form of hair binding; necklaces, earrings, rings.

Male hair was worn very long in the Achaean period, long in Homeric times, and shorter in the days of the Persian wars. Slaves wore short hair which was indicative of servitude. An athlete bound his hair in a *tellex* (cricket), in reference to segmented windings around the hair, which is clubbed at the neck. During the Classical Revival in Europe in late XVIII-early XIXc., both men's and women's hair was clubbed into Etruscan *catogans.* Spartans wore their hair long, carefully dressed.

MYCENAEAN AND GREEK WARRIORS

During the Mycenaean period, warriors fought naked, or with short linen tunic, without cuirasse or breastplates. They did wear a leather belt, protecting the abdomen; a conical helmet, leather edged with boar's tusks, crested in a tuft.

The shield was carried only by leaders. It was large, protecting the whole body: *ancillar,* 8-shaped; or *scutum,* oblong, sometimes notched at the corners, often bent semi-cylindrically to surround the body. Probably of leather, the form of shield related to the shape of an animal hide with legs trimmed off.

Likewise, the sword was carried only by leaders. It was bronze, three feet long, two-edged, was used for thrusting only and therefore at a disadvantage against the Homeric iron cutting blade.

The spear was bronze. The sling with balls, and

the bow and arrows with obsidian or bronze heads were used by common soldiers only.

Archers were not well regarded by the Greeks, but the Mycenaeans were excellent bowmen, down to the time of Xerxes' Lycian mercenaries. Archers are here, as everywhere, at all periods, relatively unprotected by armor which hampers mobility.

In the Homeric period the iron-armed Achaean proved superior to the bronze-armed Mycenaean in single combat. But there was little uniformity in arming.

The breastplate was the *thorex,* a corselet of metal plates fastened on cloth; worn tight over the tunic. It fitted Odysseus "like an onion skin." The helmet was a leather or bronze cap with leather chin-strap; crested, but not yet furnished with side pieces protecting ears and cheeks. The shield was round, iron, with a boss at the center, decorated with designs in concentric circles, slung by baldric. The sword was iron, good for cutting as well as thrusting. The spear had an iron head.

Greek warriors of the Homeric period wore a cloak (*chloene*) of rough wool, caught by pins of animal form, often elaborate; the *aegis,* animal hide over the shoulders, or thrown protectively over the arm; *cnemides,* greaves of shaped hide or bronze, sprung, not strapped around the shank; the *mitre,* a metal belt protecting the abdomen; it was wide in front, tapering toward the back.

The most important division of the Greek army during the Historical period was the *Hoplites,* the heavily armed infantry (of which the best was Spartan). There were also the Archers; the Slingers; the Light Armed Cavalry which used the javelin and the *peltast,* a leather-covered wicker frame shield; and the *Cataphract,* discussed below.

The *Hoplites* used:

Breastplate: front and back plates of metal or leather, with leather shoulder-straps and protective lappets below the waistline; it was not worn by common soldiers (who were given leather cuirasse, metal belt, greaves and helmet) or by archers.

Aegis: skin of goat, sheep, bear, wolf, fox, fawn, worn over head and down back, or over sword-arm. Worn by early Athenian townspeople, Arcadians and Thracians, and eventually by mercenary Lycian archers of Xerxes' army.

Helmet: Corinthian: surrounding face, protecting nose, cheeks, jaw-bone, neck, eye-slits; frequently painted; often crested, horsehair. *Athenian:* not surrounding face; frequently with hinged side-plates; crests, often multiple, adopted from Carians. *Spartan:* cap-shaped, without cheek-plates or crest.

Shield: smaller, round; or rondache with circular cut-outs at sides (like a violin). Handles inside shield instead of strap adopted from Carians, as well as the use of a badge or device on the shield, (which led to the dropping of projecting center boss which interfered with the design).

Greaves: cnemides, bronze; not worn by archers.

Mantle: chlamys, often wound around arm to ward off blows.

Swords: become shorter, 2 foot, double-edged; Spartan's sword had curved blade.

Pike: 8 feet long.

The *Cataphract* was the heavily armed cavalry that developed with the improvement and increasing strength of horses. It had the advantage of armed mobility at a time when the short range of offensive weapons kept fighting at close range. But in this period, this cavalry still lacked the weight and momentum to penetrate the ranks of *Hoplites.* It used a small shield or none.

DETAILS OF COSTUMES OF PELASGIAN, MYCENAEAN AND OTHER SETTLEMENTS

Arcadia, Thrace, Asia Minor, Troy, Phrygia, Lydia, Cappadocia, Lycia, Cyprus, Etruria

Arcadians were small, dark Pelasgians of Mycenaean culture, who lived as shepherds and hunters, landlocked on a high plateau since the Stone Age. They were the most conservative and least Hellenized of Greeks. They fought without greaves or breastplate, protected by large oblong shields, spears and javelins. They wore the aegis of the skin of many animals: bear, wolf, as well as the sheep and goats of their flocks. Arcadia was the principal source of mercenary *peltasts* (lightly armed infantry) of the later Greek army.

Thracians were of two sorts: the Getae of the Danube were red-haired; used iron weapons, round shields with a central boss, and brooches. They were Celts of an entirely different culture from the Bessi of the mountains, who were dark Pelasgians like the Illyrians, and kin to the Trojans and Phrygians. Thracians and *Illyrians* of good family were tattooed to distinguish them from those of low birth. The Greeks considered them very dirty people of horrifyingly low morals. Descent was traced through the female line, and their young girls given complete license. Out of this arose the legends of the Satyrs, (from the Thracian tribe, Satrae) and the girl Bacchantae. Their climate was severe, and, like their Trojan kin and the Cretans, Lycians and early Athenians, they wore the aegis of goat skin; as mercenaries of Xerxes, of fox and fawn skin. They were literate; the greatest lovers of music in all Greece; fine metal workers in the Mycenaean manner; among the earliest coiners.

They wore their hair in a Cretan tuft on the top

of the head, enclosed in a spiral of metal, as did the *Trojans,* who likewise carried the *pelta* (round, Thracian shield) and the short sword. They wore a chiton and the national *zeirai* instead of the Macedonian chlamys.

Troy, fertile, wooded around Mount Ida, was settled by Mycenaean and later Aeolic peoples. Their chief cities were: Ilium (Troy: excavations at Hassarlik), Assus and Alexander Troas.

The *Phrygians* who had crossed from Thrace, colonized Armenia and Cappadocia, taking with them their high buskins and the small, round Thracian shield with boss, *pelta.* In return they received the conical nomad's cap with flaps, and the sleeved, fitted, embroidered garments worn in Asia Minor. They were shepherds and farmers, not sailors or warriors; loved music as did the Thracians, but were not quick-witted or literarily productive.

Lydians, living in a rich and fertile land (cities: Sardis, Magnesia, modern Smyrna, and Ephesus), were busy traders who invented coined money; lively people who first played the games of ball, dice and knuckle-bones; whose daughters earned their doweries by religious prostitution; and whose dances with shield and bow, before the shrine of Cybele (Artemis), played a part in the formation of the myths of the Amazons. They wore several superimposed Graeco-Persian garments, only one of which would be sleeved. Women wore long tight garments, long-sleeved, which might be belted high under the breasts, or not.

Lycians, like the *Philistine** "giants," were of strongly Mycenaean character, and the least Assyrianized of these peoples. Both wore a high tiara of feathers, and coats of plate mail or the goatskin aegis. The Lycians, bowmen like all Mycenaeans, fought as mercenaries with Xerxes. Other Lycians carried two swords, a long spear, and fought within a circle formed of their round shields. Lycian remains: rock tombs and sarcophagi. Philistine: painted tombs, excavations at Gaza.

Cappadocia, inhabited by the Hittite "White Syrians," was made up of salt desert, volcanic mountains and high, cold pasture-land for horses and sheep. There was a peasant population of slaves, of whom there were 6,000 at the Temple of Comana. These later became bond-servants.

Its capital, Pteria (now Boghaz Keui: rock sculptures), was enslaved by the Lydian king, Croesus, and Cappadocia later formed two of the Persian satrapies (illustrations under Egypt, foreigners).

The *Cypriots* were a stubborn, unimaginative people, slow to accept and to relinquish. But because of their rich copper deposits, there was, from the Bronze Age, a steady stream of Phoenician, Egyptian, Mycenaean and Assyrian trade and influence.

The *kefa,* the Cypriot loin cloth, was of Phoenician origin; as was the worship of Astarte (Gk. Aphrodite, R. Venus), goddess of moon (menstruation) and dew (fertilization); elements both male and female. As the androgynous Aphrodite of the Cypriots, her worship spread to Italy, Sicily and Greece (see Ill. 73).

Etruria: was a rich, well-wooded land, peopled by north Italian migrants and about 1000 B.C. by Lydian colonizers. The Etrurians were unaggressive farmers of fertile land, and middlemen who prospered through the passage of the German trade in metals and amber to Greek and Phoenician adventurers. They lived extremely well; beautiful furniture and table settings; ate to the music of flute and trumpet. They played games and had religious dances. Painted tombs giving minute details of their lives, and excellent granular gold filigree work give evidence of artistic development at a late period.

Etruscan costume, intermediate between Greek and Roman, shows strong Oriental influences. Rich patterned designs and borders are notable.

The *male tunic,* like a short tight Greek athlete's chiton, was often the only garment worn by the young and active. It was patterned in braid at neck, hem, edge of short sleeves, and down side closing. Older men wore a longer tunic with pleated chiton beneath.

The *tebenna,* a cape, was a typical Etruscan ceremonial garment, semi-circular like half of a Roman toga. It was the ancestor of the purple-bordered Roman *toga praetexta.* Another semi-circular cloak, worn by active young men, was buttoned or knotted at center-front or shoulder, not oblong and pinned by a brooch like the Greek chlamys. The Etruscans also used a shortened form of the chlamys, which was weighted and bordered; it became the Roman *paludamentum.*

The Etruscan hat besides the wide petasus was the *apex* or *galerius;* leather, conical, of Asiatic origin; its equivalent for women was the *tutulus.*

A *fillet* (*corona Etrusca*) was worn on important occasions.

Shoes had long pointed toes, of Oriental origin; displayed fine workmanship and decoration; were in demand in Greece and Rome, as *calcei repandi.*

The *Female tunic* was long, fitted, slit down in back from its bordered neck; its shoulder-seam was prominent. Early garments were often embroidered all over.

The *Cloak* was usually darker than the gown; patterned all over in sprawling designs; edges banded and weighted.

*See Ill. 75.

Hair was worn looped, bound with the Etruscan fillet. In the early period it was decorated with bells.

Necklaces and earrings were worn.

Women's *shoes*, like those of men, had pointed tips and showed fine workmanship.

Soldiers had body armor of bronze plates and leather, front and back, connected by shoulder straps. They wore belts, helmets (see Helmets, Etruria, Bronze Age), greaves, round shields, double-edged swords, and axes. The development of the Etruscan military costume was like that of the Roman.

HELMETS: ETRURIAN, BRONZE-IRON AGES, AND MIGRATIONS

The Bronze Age, which ran from c. 2000 B.C. in South Germany, to 100 B.C. in countries far removed from the necessary materials, was a culture of Oriental derivation, dependent on tin. Tin was found only in Saxony and Cornwall, where Phoenician traders had sought it, perhaps as early as 1400 B.C. Bronze Age culture reached Italy and France by way of the Danube and Elbe, as southern culture was taken to Denmark by the amber route.

Bronze Age culture and weapons were similar all over Europe. Helmets were conical; sword handles short and narrow; shields round; patterns of bosses, spirals, and concentric circles appeared on jewelry which was equally Eastern in origin: fibulae (like safety pins, at first), torque bracelets and necklets in spirals of wire were used.

The Iron Age, which brought Celtic supremacy, came from the Southeast of Europe and spread northward, from Greece and Etruria, reaching Gaul c. 800 B.C., and Denmark in Ic. A.D., and North Russia, c. 800 A.D.

Smelting of iron seems to have been understood in Etruria, which then included most of Northern Italy, as early as 1200 B.C. Etruria was the meeting place of Phoenician and Greek traders who wished to exchange gold and ivory from the East for tin, iron and amber from the northern countries, and the timber of North Italy. Etruria, at the height of its civilization when it first began to battle the Celts in Xc. was almost extinguished during the second great Celtic invasion of 400 B.C.

The Homeric Achaeans were Celts: tall, fair-haired, and blue-eyed. They brought iron weapons, the round shield with center boss, the habit of cremation, fibulae, and ornament of geometric pattern, instead of spirals and squirming animals. Their civilization slightly preceded the Hallstatt Iron period in Baden and Bavaria, VIII-Vc. B.C., and the Villanova culture in North Italy.

The La Tène period, c. IV-Ic. B.C. brought gold and enamel into Celtic use; its culture spread across the Danube and Balkans to South Russia, to Etruria and Rome, and through Greece to Asia Minor. Glass jewels appeared during the Roman period, Ic. A.D. The great Germanic migrations ran from IV-VIc. A.D.

SCYTHIA, SARMATIA, PARTHIA, ILLYRIA

Scythian and *Sarmatian* costume resembles that in which the Greeks represented the mythical Amazons, from whom Herotodus thought them descended (since the women fought, from horseback, and the men were easy-going and fat). It very much resembles Siberian peasant costume.

Nomadic cattlemen and horsemen, they dressed in leather, hides, furs and felt. They were rich in copper, silver and especially in gold. These metals were worked for them by Assyrian and Greek craftsmen into objects, many examples of which have been found in burial mounds on the steppes —weapons, cauldrons, cups, bridles, toilet articles, and quantities of metal plates and ornaments (which were sewn on their garments and animal-bridles) in all-over and line designs.

Trousers appear almost automatically in the costume of peoples who dress in fur and leather; the pattern of sleeve and trouser is inherent in the shape of the hide.

Men wore high pointed hoods or caps tied on by a cord. Their coats were fur-lined or -bordered, narrow sleeved, fitted, closed in front, often overlapping. The hemline often dipped low in front, and there were vents in the skirts of the coat.

Trousers were frequently stuffed into boots which were soft, high, or tied around the ankle.

Beards were worn and hair generally was longish.

Weapons used were the bow and arrows in a case, a round shield, spear, axe, dagger and sword. These latter were short and with a heart-shaped guard, peculiarly arranged to be slung out of the way in riding.

Articles of jewelry were gold, except for the poorer people who used bronze. There were bracelets, torques, fibulae and ornaments sewn on clothes. Sarmatian jewelry was pierced and interlaced, like the Finnish.

Women wore long gowns, long veils, high pointed hats. They painted their faces.

Parthians wore similar garments and armor, but with the sleeve typically prolonged to hang over the hand. Coats were wider, cut like the short kandys (width increasing from shoulder to hem, not fitted): sometimes several were worn superimposed.

Dacians and *Illyrians* wore the high, truncated conical hat, fez-shaped (see Roman, Traianic examples). Their trousers were narrower, tied at the ankle. Semi-circular, fringed capes were pinned at the right shoulder.

142. **Greek. Attica VIIIc. B.C. (Metropolitan Museum.)**
Geometric dipylon amphora: tasselled cloak (between handles).

143. **Greek VIIIc. B.C. (Metropolitan Museum.)**
Geometric dipylon amphorae: (larger) Procession of two-horse chariots, two-wheeled; line of women,

with long patterned and bustled skirts and flowing hair. (smaller) Round shield with Homeric center boss-crested helmet.

144. **Greek VII-VIc. B.C. (Metropolitan Museum.)**
Fragment of black-figured vase: beard and filleted

hair; long, ungirded chiton; patterned and tasselled himation.

145, 146. Greek Dorian School end VIIc. B.C. (Louvre.)

The Lady of Auxerre. No one knows how this yellowish-gray limestone statue arrived at Auxerre where it was found. It resembles Archaic sculpture from Crete, where it was probably made. The position of the hand indicated prayer (see Berlin Mus.

Aegean, M.M.). She retains the characteristic belt, bustle and hips; skirt fringed and geometrically patterned; snake-like hair represented as an Egyptian wig.

147. Greek VIIIc. B.C. (Metropolitan Museum.)

Geometric dipylon vase: Mycenean wasp-waist and shield with incurved sides; four wheeled chariot.

148. Italian mainland. c. 500 B.C. Italian Prehistoric Bronze Age. (Bologna Museum.)

The Situla of Certosa is "the great landmark of N. Italian Art."

Its information is reinforced by that of the Benvenuti situla (c. 500 B.C., also influenced by Etruscan art), and by the Arnaldi situla. The details of the Certosa situla are "Bolognese when not Etruscan"; the military equipment is "absolutely Etruscan, all well-known types."

The central band shows a religious procession, probably a cremation, which was the form of about one third of Etruscan burials. Women carrying bundles of faggots wear the familiar dark cloaks; the men, the familiar mantle, cross-hatched in blocks or diamonds (see Etruscan, and VIIIc. geometric dipylon amphorae), and the broad-brimmed petasus (*caere, chiusi*).

The lower band shows scenes of daily life. We see servants carrying a stag back from the hunt, slung on a pole, while hunters beat the brush for hare. Other sections show an ox, light plough, slaves dragging a pig, on which sits a bird. There is also an entertainment, in which there is a magnificent bronze divan with 6 ivory legs, and arms of lions eating a man and a rabbit; musicians with lyre and pipes, and a dignified onlooker in cloak and broad hat, dipping wine as he listens and watches the amusements.

149. Ancient Italy. Venetia. Este.

Bronze relief.

150. Prehistoric Italy VIc. B.C., from Abruzzi. (Rome M. delle Terme.)

Italian warrior from Capistrano.

I know relatively little about either of these wonderful costumes, which have turned up at the last minute; I give the reference for one and the location of the other, so that they may be looked up further.

The patterned garments and cuffed shoes of the relief show Etruscan influence, and the plumed headdress may be compared to the Priest-king of Cnossos. The Italiotic helmet of the Hallstatt Bronze period shows one form of combination of the age-old motifs of a standing ridge on the crown of a helmet, and projecting ridges specifically designed for the insertion of plumes; in their infinite permutations between Xc. B.C. and the casques of the Gallic legion, they can be studied in *Léon Coutil: Les Casques Proto-Etrusques, Etrusques et Gaulois, W. Sifter, Gand, 1914; and Franz Freiherr von Lipperheide: Antike helme,* and are utterly fascinating.

The Capistrano warrior's wasp-waist, apron, collar and bracelets, and dagger belted at the breast, can be seen on Ills. 136, 138, 155.

151. Etruscan VIc. B.C. (Louvre.)

Massive cast-bronze statue, found near Viterbo. Helmet protecting sides of face but shaped like the conical Etruscan hat of Phoenician origin. Body armor of metal-studded leather, with shoulder straps and lappeted hem (compare with identical forms in Roman armor usage). Metal greaves and shield; hole through fist originally held spear.

152, 153. Sicilian? VIc. B.C. (Louvre.)

Massive cast-bronze warrior, with inlaid silver eyes. Italiotic workmanship and face, found in Sicily. Short-sleeved leather jacket; cuirasse with circular protective plates, strapped over the shoulders, after the manner of the original breastplate in Rome. Helmet with flattened peaked ridge, and cheek-plates, greaves.

Belt with the Aegean edging.

154-156. Sardinian, Prehistoric, Bronze Age. (Caligari Museum.)

Three figures: warrior; head of tribe; archer in repose. Both warriors wear shallow, horned helmets, slightly peaked in front; narrow tunics, apparently of leather over longer tunics, both with horizontal hems separated by two hanging tabs at the front. Breastplates; greaves, bare feet. Shield with projecting point; bow; two-edged bronze swords. The head of the tribe wears a similar headdress, without horns; cape; same two tunics with paired tabs; staff; dagger on wide band across chest. The first protection added to the hawberk of a XIVc. knight will be a plate on chest, to which dagger and sword are chained.

157. Etruscan c. 500 B.C., from Viterbo. (Metropolitan Museum.)

Terra cotta votive statue: Etruscan warrior, showing strong Greek influence. Almost typical hoplite (heavily-armed infantryman). Bronze Corinthian casque protecting the whole face, carrying the Graeco-Carian horsehair crest; long hair. Moulded bronze cuirasse and greaves. Short athlete's chiton, "tight as an onion-skin," probably of leather, to protect body from chafing. The figure originally carried a shield and spear.

158, 159. Etruscan second half VIc. B.C. Bronze statue. (Metropolitan Museum.)

Woman, front and side views: Long, close-fitting tunic; shoulder-seams stressed in Etruria. Cloak, usually darker than gown (see Et. tomb paintings), patterned all-over, banded and weighted at the corners; laid in pleats. Looped hair exposing the ears: fillet with bells; bead necklace worn high; rosette earrings. Typically elongated point of beautifully made Etruscan shoes.

160. Etruscan Vc. B.C.

Bronze: Reclining youth: patterned chlamydon.

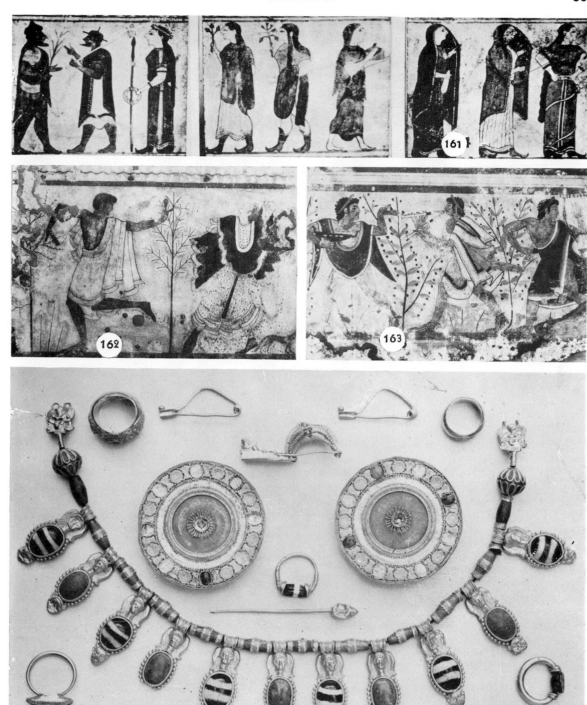

161. Etruscan Vc. Cervetri. Tomba Banditaccia. (British Museum.)

Tomb painting.

162. Etruscan Vc. Corneto, Tarquinia. Grotto del Triclinio.

Tomb painting: mourning dancers.

163. Etruscan Vc. Corneto, Tarquinia. Tomba degli Leopardi.

Tomb painting.

Etruscan tombs are rich in painted scenes of feasts, dances and ceremonies. They show, in color and movement, the fillets, patterned gowns, dark veils, wonderful shoes, the petasus, and fringed and bordered cloaks, about which Etruscan sculpture is so explicit.

164. Etruscan VI-Vc. from Vulci. (Metropolitan Museum.)

Necklace, two round brooches, fibulae, pin, and rings found in an Etruscan tomb. The exaggerated development of the vertical part of the catch (c. fibula), increases until the catch becomes all-important in the T-shaped fibulae of IIIc. A.D. onward. The circular forms of brooches became mediaeval European favorites.

The gold necklace had grayish-green glass beads, and alternating glass pendants of blue striped with white, and grayish flecked with reddish. The disk

fibulae are garnet edged, with glass cabochon centers. Rings of brown and white-banded agate, or of carnelian.

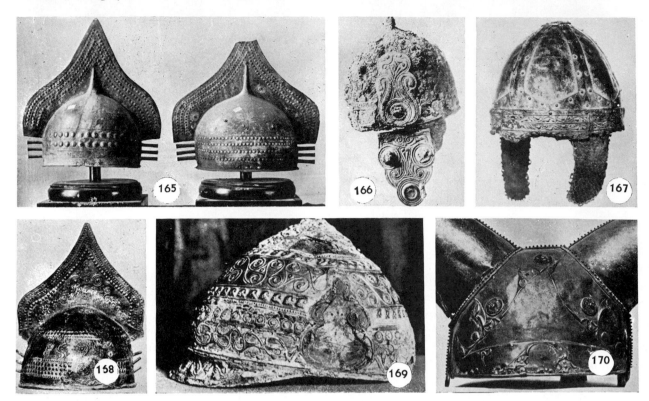

165. Italic end Bronze Age—beg. Hallstatt VII-VIc. B.C. (Tarquinia Municipal Mus.)

Two bronze helmets.

166. Italic La Tene Per. end VI-Vc., B.C., from Umbria. (Berlin Mus.)

Bronze helmet.

167. Celto-Iranian Migrations Frankish VIc. A.D., from Gammertingen (Sigmaringen Hohenzollernsches M.)

Spangelhelm; iron and bronze.

168. Italic XII-VIc. B.C. (Louvre.)

Bronze helmet.

169. Italic La Tene end VI-Vc. B.C., from Normandy. (Louvre.)

The Helmet of Amfreville-sur-Seine: gold and enamel.

170-170b. Bronze Age Celtic Ic. B.C., found in the Thames. (British Museum.)

170. Repoussé bronze and enamel horned helmet. (Detail of 170b.)

170a. Bronze shield; red enamel ornaments.

Orientally inspired Etrurian bronze helmets, and imitative Gallic iron forms, found all over Europe, lead to the conical Norman iron helmet with nasal. They have been classified by Coutil* into twelve groups with many subdivisions between the original Xc. B.C. Etruscan form and the casques worn by Roman Legionaries. The original Etruscan form of

Xc. B.C. was a more angular version of (165-168); crest less elaborate, parallelled crown more narrowly and accurately; had three similar or analagous projections, fore and aft, presumably to hold feathers. Other forms are elaborately crested, with hinged flaps; or round-topped, with narrow crest, no points, but projecting triple bands at the bottom. The helmet (decorated with dots, concentric circles and bird-forms) shows up in Russia, Bavaria, Italy, the Rhine and Seine; and in bronze-studded terra-cotta, as lids for funerary urns at Corneto; they are the prototype of the Etruscan helmet. The crest, reduced to a ridge, with one spike, fore and aft, appears on globular casques with insistently projecting rims in Etruria, VII-IVc. B.C. These pass into Gallic legionary use, often with jugular flaps.

The Umbrian helmet (166), transitional in form between Attic-Ionian casques with uncovered ears and conical Mycenaean helmets, has been found at Paris, in Bavaria and N. Italy. Worn, if not made in Etruria, it appears on Etruscan wall-paintings, and often has an Etruscan inscription inside the brim. Its crown may be round, or of a very high conical form like the Gallic helmet of IIIc. A.D., decorated with

* Coutil: *Les Casques Proto-Etrusques, Etrusques, et Gaulois*, W. Swifter, Gand, 1914.

170 B

170 A

the palmetto leaves used here, but without jugular flaps. The knob may be elaborated into two horns, with a sort of 2-pronged fork between (which, in turn, may become a human figure with raised arms),

from the horned Corinthian and Ionian casques with eyebrows and nasals, of VI-Vc.B.c.

The mastic-enamelled helmet (169) is the richest example of a type which has been found in Finisterre, Weisskirchen, Umbria and Ancona; either cut out around the ears, or with hinged jugular flaps, as this did; Celtic patterns of decoration.

The Celtic helmet (170) in the horned form worn by British chieftains, shows the style of decoration which is continued in VII-IXc. manuscripts (131-3). These remind us of the bright checked and striped garments of the N. W. Celts, which so impressed the Romans. They were worn with flowing hair, long moustaches; chieftain's torques and bracelets in returning spiral forms; animal skin cloaks in war; braccae or bound legs; feet wrapped or bound in hide.

The *spangelhelm* (167), the conical Frankish helmet of VI-IXc. A.D. (of which ten examples exist*), has been found between Finland and Italy. One very similar to our photograph was found at Izère, where a battle was fought in 524 between Burgundians and the King of Orleans. We illustrate a typical example: the band is always elaborate; the outer frame is studded, and usually cross-hatched with geometric design; the inner panel is not always patterned, as it is in this case; and the helmet is always made of combinations of iron with bronze or copper, frequently gold-plated.

* Sir Guy Francis Laking: *A Record of European Armour and Arms through Seven Centuries.*

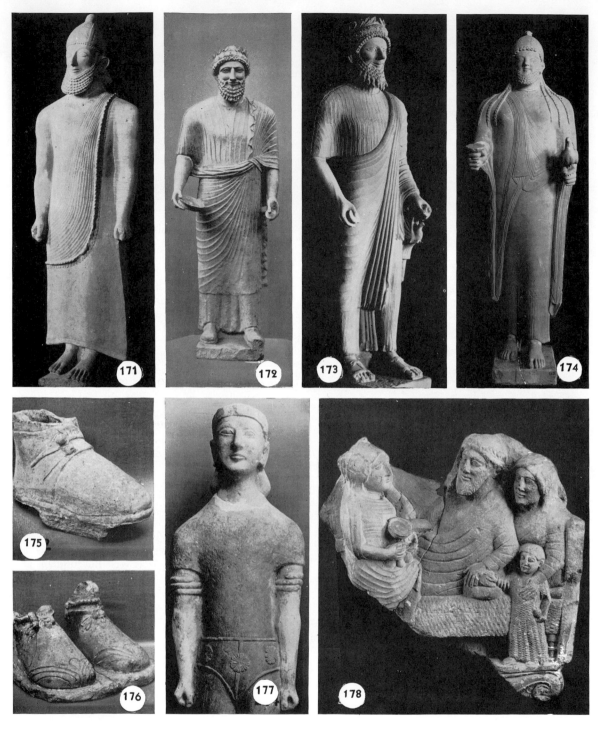

171, 172. Cypriot c. 700-650 B.C. Limestone statues.
Bearded votary; bearded priest or votary.

173. Cypriot c. 500 B.C.
Bearded priest or votary, with bird and incense box. All three in pleated, ungirdled chiton (garment of Oriental derivation) and himation.

174. Cypriot c. 500 B.C.
Bearded Aphrodite: in Assyrian cap, of form still worn by priests in Cyprus. Narrow robe with embroidered hem; traces of red paint indicate embroidered stars around neck. Assyrian influence also shown in hair and beard.

175, 176. Cypriot 700-600 B.C.
Fragments of statue: Feet, elaborate shoes.

177. Cypriot c. 650-500 B.C.
Limestone statuette: Beardless votary: hair clubbed in the *catogan* of nearby Crete (see Aegean); tight leather tunic; protective studded belt; coiled upper-arm bracelets, snake-like (see Aegean).

178. Cypriot Tomb.
Banquet: pleated garments of children (see Ill. 246).

Courtesy of Metropolitan Museum

180. Greek, VIc. B.C.

Lekythos (oil-jar): Battle scene: Persian archer whose conical hat with lappets, patterned garments with sleeves and trousers, form of bow and quiver, indicate origin. Kneeling, typical Greek hoplite.

181. Greek, VIc. 550-540 B.C. Amphora (Exekias).

Arming a warrior: for fighting in the archaic manner, naked except for greaves; spear; helmet with double crest; large shield with device of lion head. Badges on shields were a Carian fashion adopted by Greeks; the boss of the Homeric shield was dropped because of its interference with the design.

182. Greek, 550-540 B.C.

Detail of vase showing warriors.

183. Greek Marble, VIc. B.C.

Maiden, perhaps a Votary, bringing offerings to a Divinity: chiton with finely pleated top; skirt tucked into belt.

179. Greek, Athenian, VIc. B.C. Black figured amphora.

Warrior bearing fallen comrade: crested Corinthian helmet; rondache shield with device of snakes. Fleeing male whose pointed cap with lappets, bow, quiver with hanging tail, all indicate Asiatic influences. Female in Athenian peplos.

184. Greek, Vlc. B.C. Oil jug.

Chlamys pinned over short chiton of active young man. Shield, showing handles which Greeks took from Carian shield, slung over shoulders by cord; helmet painted with legendary beast. Other figure with short sword in scabbard, slung over shoulder on baldric, and chlamys wound, protectively, around arm.

185. Greek, Vlc. 550-500 B.C. Black figured cup

Warriors: crested Corinthian helmets; moulded breastplates with protective flange at bottom; over short pleated chiton; decorated shields; greaves, spears. Adversary in dress of Asia Minor: Phrygian bonnet and sleeved garment, without trousers.

Courtesy of Metropolitan Museum

186. Greek, Athenian, Vlc. 530 B.C. Black figured amphora.

Male: with patterned himation, held by baldric across shoulder sandals. Female with hair caught in high bunch of curls, and wearing patterned himation over Dorian peplos with border.

187. Greek, Athenian, Vlc. B.C. Black figured lekythos.

Women working wool: decorated Dorian peplos of the early narrow sort, sewed up the side in the Athenian way.

188. Greek, Athenian, Vlc. B.C. Black figured amphora.

Hermes, Dionysus and Athena, and an old man: Hermes in typical costume; petasus; sleeveless short chiton of Doric shepherd, bordered; patterned chlamys; winged boots. Athena holds a crested hel-

met; she is dressed in a peplos with wide border and all-over diapered design. Dionysus: dotted short chiton, striped himation. He and the old man have long locks, and like Athena, he wears a wreath.

189. Greek, Athenian, Vlc. B.C. Black figured amphora.

Mercury: in hat, short chiton, chlamys with weighted corners, winged boots and carrying caduceus. Female in peplos, like a bolero, tightly belted; dotted himation with weights in corners; sandals; offering wreath. Man: with filleted long hair; long dotted chiton; decorated himation; spear.

190. Greek, Vlc. B.C. Vases.

Dionysus: in various guises: playing the pipes he wears the sleeved long gown of musician.

191. Greek, Attica, VIc. 500 B.C. Marriage vase.

Marriage bed: women in peplos, sewed up the right side, as was done in Attica. Riders, below, in boldly patterned chlamys.

192. Greek, c. 540 B.C.

Black-figured amphora, attributed to Exekias: Marriage Procession. Narrow, closed and patterned peplos; over-fold reaching almost to girdle.

193. Greek, VIc. B.C. Drinking cup

Warrior in crested helmet, shield and greaves. Woman rider wearing the peaked bonnet with lappets which, with the horse, came to Greece from the Eastern nomads.

194. Greek, c. 550 B.C.

Black-figured pottery aryballas (oil-jug): on lip, battle of pigmies and cranes. On handle: Perseus, Hermes and Satyrs: Hermes' winged boots.

195. Greek Vc. 459-431 B.C. Relief sculpture. Parthenon.

Detail of the procession of the people of Athens: two young girls in wide peplos with deep ungirded overfold, and girded low on hips, characteristic of young girls. Man in himation.

196. Greek Vc. 435 B.C. Relief sculpture. Parthenon, West Frieze.

Young man with horse: sleeveless chiton, girded at waist and again below. Chlamys pinned at center front.

197. Greek Vc. 420 B.C. Sculpture, copy of last original of the School of Phidias. (Nat. Mus., Naples.)

Orpheus, Eurydice and Hermes: Orpheus in chiton girded twice at natural waistline, beneath and above blousing; chiton knotted on right shoulder; petasus slung in back, sandals; Eurydice in garment without overfold, but caught on shoulder like peplos; deep blouse and low girdle; veil over head; sandals. Hermes in cap and high boots, tops dagged and turned down.

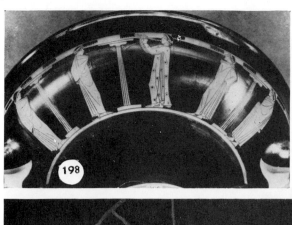

198. Greek, Vc. 480-470 B.C. Red figured pottery. (Metropolitan Museum.)

Youths and piper: in long ungirdled sleeved garment, Asiatic in origin, of Ionian musician. Young men in himation, probably their only garment. Sandals on musician and one youth.

199. Greek, Vc. 460-445 B.C. Red figured vase. (Metropolitan Museum.)

Young people conversing: Dorian male wearing only himation. Females with knotted and filletted hair, pleated white chitons, and bordered himations with weights at corners.

200. Greek, Vc. 490-480 B.C. Red figured pottery. (Metropolitan Museum.)

Man in himation. Woman in finely pleated transparent chiton, caught down the shoulder to form sleeves, and girdled at normal waistline.

201. Greek, Vc. B.C. (Metropolitan Museum.)

Red-figured kylix: Woman Dancing: the chiton has been folded in at the shoulder, and is belted low; its sides swing out in what looks like a sleeve, with the motion of the arm; petasus on the ground.

202. Greek, c. 480 B.C. (Metropolitan Museum.)

Red-figured amphora, attributed to "Providence Painter": Maenad pursued by a Satyr: peplos with border and clearly weighted ends.

203. Greek, Attica, first half Vc. B.C. (Louvre.)

Alabastrum with a white ground. Negro in a sleeved white blouse and trousers, patterned in black stripes and dots, which he certainly brought back from travels in Asia Minor.

204-206. Greek Classical Period.

From various vases:

204. Interior of an Athenian school; instruction in music and the use of arms.

205. Surgical clinic: doctor and patients; bandages, amputations and malformations.

206. Women in the linen room: wide chitons of the second period of decoration, entirely different from that of VIc.; girded low on the hips beneath an overfold like a peplos; one wears a chlamydon.

207. Greek (probably from W. Sicily) early Vc. B.C. Terra cotta statuette.

Maiden: chiton and chloene.

208. Roman copy of Vc. B.C. Greek work, found in Egypt. Bronze statuette.

Woman: in peplos with overfold concealing low, bloused girdling. Hair parted and rolled.

209, 210. Roman copy of Greek statue attributed to Polykleitos, 440-430 B.C. Marble statue.

Wounded Amazon: in sleeveless chiton of an athlete, caught on one shoulder only; girded above and below blousing. Hair parted, rolled back and up.

211. Greek, 450-400 B.C. Bronze mirror stand.

Woman: in peplos with long overfold concealing girdling: Laced shoes. Hair parted and rolled up.

212. Greek, Vc. B.C. Bronze mirror stand.

Woman: in peplos similar to 211, but arranged to form very short sleeves.

213. Greek, Attica, IVc. B.C., from Menidi. (Berlin Mus.)

Mourning girl: sleeves have actually been added to this chiton, but are girded into fitting under the arm.

Courtesy of Metropolitan Museum of Art (207-212); Berlin Museum (213)

214. Greek Vc. B.C.

Replica of a Phidias. *Athena with a collar.* The Athena Parthenos was a colossal statue of gold and ivory, made by Phidias c. 440 B.C. The original statue, which stood within the Parthenon, has been lost. This is one of many copies. The *aegis,* originally a skin tied around the neck by its legs, has become stylized; peplos with a girdle above the overfold. The lost right hand carried a winged victory; the left rested on a carved shield.

215, 216. Greek, IVc., from Gabi, Italy.

By Praxiteles. *Diana:* short chiton, girdled high under the breast, and again, low on the hips; pinning on a diplax or chloene; elaborate fenestrated sandals.

217. Greek, 450 B.C. Red figured vase.

L. to R.: 2nd. figure in bordered chloene, folded over in peplos effect, hooked over chiton. 3rd. in himation draped over chiton. 4th. in peplos, entirely open down right side; overfold included in girdling.

218. Greek, attributed to the Meletos painter, c. 455 B.C. Red figured bell krater, free style.

Nike and youth: the winged goddess of victory wears a chiton with a woven band a foot above the hem, girdled low on the hips. The chiton of the youth, like his chlamys, has woven decorative bands well up into the fabric and is gathered into a neckband. Petasus hanging by cords with slide fastening.

219. Greek, Athenian, attributed to the Persephone painter, c. 440 B.C. Krater, red figured pottery, free style.

The Return of Persephone: led by Mercury, in

217

218

219

220

chiton. Females: in peplos girdled under the over-fold; and in chiton and himation; hair with diadem, fillet, or knotted high.

220. Greek Vc. B.C. Red figured vase.

Girl: in bordered peplos, open down left side, girded beneath overfold; pursued by Poseidon with trident, laurel wreath, and himation.

221. Greek, Athenian, attributed to the Mannheim paint-

er, c. 450 B.C. Orinoche, red figured pottery, early free style.

Amazons starting for battle: showing combination of Eastern nomad and Greek costume: hood with lappets; cuirasse of strips of leather; battle axe; shield; arms and legs with flexible patterned covering; pleated Greek short chiton.

222. Greek, Athenian, attributed to an associate of Poly-gonates, c. 440 B.C. Calyx Krater, red figured pottery.

Kadmus slaying the dragon at the fountain of Ares: Athena with helmet and spear. Kadmus: brimmed hat slung over shoulder, chlamys pinned on right shoulder, short chiton, and high boots. Female figure with bound headdress. Ares: bearded, heavily armed as he is represented to Vc. (later as beardless youth). He wears the Athenian helmet with movable hinged flaps at the sides; body armor with shoulder straps and lappets below waist which developed out of the protective flange at the bottom of the breastplate.

223. Greek, Vc. B.C.

Orpheus among the Thracians: Orpheus in laurel wreath and himation, playing lyre to the music-loving Thracians. Man in nomad hood; outer garment the shape of which was derived from an animal skin, the quarters of which hung over the shoulders; high, laced boots with turned down, dagged tops. Woman, overfolded peplos in thin fabric of chitons.

224. Greek 460 B.C. Column Krater, red figured pottery.

Young warrior arming: Athenian helmet with hinged side flap turned up; body-armor of plate, scales and separate, comfortably flexible lappets protecting abdomen. Elders with staffs, wearing himation. Woman with shield and quiver: bound hair, chiton, himation.

225. Greek, Athenian. Column Krater, attributed to the Pan painter, c. 465 B.C.

Dionysus and a satyr: Dionysus wears a wreath of vine leaves; long pleated chiton, under bordered himation.

226. Greek, Athenian, attributed to the Pan painter, c. 465 B.C. Orinoche, red figured pottery. Early free style.

Ganymede: most beautiful of Greek boys, in bordered himation.

227. Greek, Relief Melian. c. 450 B.C.

Girl playing pipes and young man watching dancer: Girl, knotted hair, bound with fillet; chiton, himation, sandals. Man, himation, sandals.

228. Greek. Melian, first half Vc. Terra cotta relief, c. 450 B.C.

Return of Odysseus: in folded himation, chlamys, knotted animal skins, conical felt cap.

229, 230. Greek, 480 B.C. Temple of Aphaea, Aegina, (Munich, Glyptothek.)

Herakles: in the lion-headed helmet of Aegina; body armor of leather and bronze. One of a set of statues of the Trojan war. 230. Fallen Warrior: of Homeric period, fighting naked except for Athenian helmet, round shield, and greaves.

231. Greek, 480 B.C. (Berlin Altes Museum.)

Painted marble statue: Enthroned goddess: pleated chiton, under chlamydon fastened on a band running under breast from shoulder; long tresses.

232. Roman copy of Greek, c. 450-440 B.C. (Athens Nat. Museum.)

Pentelic marble relief: Demeter, Triptolemus and Persephone: peplos; naked boy with himation; chiton and himation; plain sandals, women; elaborate sandals, males.

233. Greek, Vc. (Delphi Museum.)

Bronze statue: Chariot Driver: chiton of the gir-dled form in which it was worn by charioteers, girt around the shoulders to form manageable sleeves.

234. Greek, c. 455-450 B.C. Island of Paros. (Metropolitan Museum.)

Marble grave relief: Girl feeding pigeons: peplos, sandals.

235. Roman copy of Greek work from Egypt, Vc. (Metropolitan Museum.)

Bronze statuette: Standing woman: back of peplos. (See Ill. 208 for front view.)

236. Greek, Athenian, Vc. B.C. (Metropolitan Mus.)

White lekythos: Hermes conducting a man to Charon's boat (detail): bearded man in workman's hat and animal skin.

237. Greek, V-IVc. B.C. (Metropolitan Museum.)

Arcadian? peasant, the pattern of whose cloak suggests that it is the upper part of a hide; the pin is not far removed from the classic shepherd's thorn; and he wears the hat of a man who is out in all weathers.

238. Late Greek, Tanagra type, IVc. B.C. Terra cotta
    statuette. (Metropolitan Museum.)
    Lady: with lotus leaf fan, hair dressed in high
krobyle above forehead. Gowns and scarves of figures
are in pale colors: rose, violet, lemon, blue, often with
deep border of different color on himation or robe.
239-241. Herculaneum, IV B.C. (Dresden, Albertinium.)
    Female statue: bare heads now draped, like future
Roman matron, mediaeval lady and madonna.
242. Greek, Tanagra type, IV-IIIc. B.C. Terra cotta
    statuette. (Metropolitan Museum.)
    Lady: with typical Tanagra headcovering and
swathing himation.
243. Terra cotta statuettes: a. Tanagra IVc., b. Asia
    Minor IIIc., c. Tanagra IVc. (Metropolitan Museum.)
244. IIIc. or later, (Metropolitan Museum.)
    Statuette: Nike flying.
245. Cyprus, IVc. (Metropolitan Museum.)
    Limestone statuette with traces of red paint: Tem-

ple Boy holding a Bird.
246. Hellenistic (?) (Metropolitan Museum.)
    Limestone: Seated Temple Boy, with a chain of
pendants, holding a hare.
247. Greek, Ic. B.C. (Istambul Museum.)
    Youth: tunic with short sleeves. The cloak of the
Middle Ages is emerging; high strapped boots.
248. Apulia, 350-300 B.C. (Metropolitan Museum.)
    Krater: Conversation Piece.
249. Etruscan, 31 B.C.-14 A.D. (Metropolitan Museum.)
    Relief: Paris and Helen.
    Outlying lands were subjected to the influence of
many neighbors before Greek culture began to spread
over the Mediterranean and Near East in Vc. It first
affected Phoenicia, Cyprus, and S. Russia through
the Black Sea; with Macedonian conquests, it spread
wide, and finally penetrated even Greek-hating Egypt.
    The temple boy from Cyprus (245) wears a Coptic

tunic with *clavi;* the shirt of the other (246) has been affected by Egypt's ancient methods of horizontal pleating, and he wears a necklace of amulets, which goes on into use on Roman children. Eastern trade influences have brought to Etruria the charioteer's

lappeted cap, trousers, and the long-sleeved garment, which he wears girdled in the Greek way. Apulia, on the Adriatic just above the Achilles tendon of the Italian boot, was peopled by indigenous Samnites, and dark pastoral Pelasgians from the Balkans, who brought Thracian Oriental influences.

250. Scythian, late. From Kul-Oba. (Leningrad, Hermitage.)

   Gold plaque: male.

251. Scythian c. 400 B.C., from Kul-Oba. (Leningrad, Hermitage.)

   The Kul-Oba Vase. Man stringing a bow.

252. Scythian c. 400 B.C. Nikopol, S. Russia. Chertomlyk Tomb. (Leningrad, Hermitage.)

   The Chertomlyk or Nikopol Vase; parcel gilt. Scythic figures milking mares.

253. Nomadic.

   Gold torque.

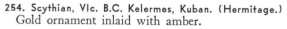

254. Scythian, VIc. B.C. Kelermes, Kuban. (Hermitage.)
Gold ornament inlaid with amber.

255. Scythian, Vc. B.C., said to be from Nikopol, S. Russia. (Metropolitan Museum.)
Gold plate for a sword-sheath: detail of top end. Contest between Greeks and Barbarians: l. to r., Greek, Barbarian, Greek and Persian.

256, 257. Scythian, VI-IIIc. B.C. Melitopol Tumulus of Solokha.
Gold comb: front and reverse. Bareheaded man on foot: typical Scythic garments; coat edged or lined with fur, hem dipping in front; trousers tied at ankle; gold bands and ornaments sewed on garments.

Heavily-armed cavalryman: scale armor (see Roman, Ill. 298); helmet of Greek type; very short Scythic spear; wicker shield of *pelta* form. Heavily-armed foot-soldier: low-peaked helmet, cap form, without flaps; armor of Greek type, edged with the peplum of plates which had evolved out of the spreading metal flange at the bottom of the cuirasse; wicker shield in a variation of the *rondache* form.

258. Sarmatian, Steppes, Siberia. (Hermitage.)
Gold (?) plaque: bird.

259. Scythian and Sarmatian, IIIc. B.C. Craiova. (Bucharest Musee des Antiquites.)
Silver appliqués: animal heads.

Romans and Barbarians

ROMAN COSTUME

Male Roman costume consisted, basically, of a short-sleeved shirt, *tunica,* originally woolen, girded up to knee length; and of an elliptical woolen wrap, the *toga,* typically white, draped about the body from the left shoulder under the right arm. Purple bands, *clavi,* on the tunic indicated the wearer's rank. There were many additional wraps, rectangular, semi-circular or fitted.

Women wore a sleeved, long, girded *tunica,* or *stola;* and an outdoor wrap, *palla,* which might be draped over the head, but did not obviate the necessity for wearing a veil or other head covering. Children were dressed like their elders, in *tunica* and *toga.*

Footwear in the house might be strapped slippers, *soleae;* light shoes, *soccae;* and on the street, leather shoes, *calcei,* strapped, cut-out, and laced sandals, varying in height from ankle to well up the calf. Those of senators were black; patricians and magistrates wore purple.

Jewelry consisted of *fibulae* and brooches, bracelets, earrings, necklaces and the Gallic *torque,* hairpins, fillets, and wreaths.

Popular colors were yellow (worn only by women, however), various greens, gray-blue, red, purple, natural wool colors, browns, blacks, and a great deal of white.

Toga: Outer garment, which was also the badge of the Roman citizen, rich or poor. A slave could not wear it; a freed man was granted permission to assume it; a banished citizen had to give up wearing it.

The *toga* was originally the rectangular Greek *pallium,* but became an ellipse, the draping of which developed infinite complications and subtleties. Folded lengthwise, with one end hanging to the ground in front, the *toga* was draped over the left shoulder, across the back, under the right arm and up across the body (in a mass of folds called the *sinus* which served as pockets), and over the left shoulder or arm, where it was held in place by its own texture, or by an added weight.

The *toga* was of wool, characteristically white, for the citizen. The *toga* of the Emperor was purple; those of artisans, the poor, and of people in mourning or at sacrifices (who wore the *toga* draped over the head) were of the darker colors of natural wool. The *trabea* worn by the equites was a small scarlet-striped *toga.*

The *toga praetexta* had a purple hem. It was worn by senators, certain officials, priests, and by boys up to the age of sixteen, when they assumed the *toga virilis,* the plain white *toga* of the citizen. Senators could not appear in public without the *toga,* which was worn until the end of the IVc. A.D. To appear in the more convenient *paenula* was permitted only to the Prefect of Rome, who in his military capacity had always to be prepared to go anywhere without notice.

The late purple and gold embroidered *toga picta* or *palmata,* worn at triumphs, became the rigidly magnificent garb of those IV-Vc. consuls, whose most arduous duty was to celebrate the circus days. A wide strip of stiff embroidery, wound around the shoulders, simulated the folded bands of the *toga,* and a crescent-shaped apron to match, drawn across the thighs and up to the left arm was a formalization of the *sinus* (the drape of the *toga* under the right arm and across the body in front). (Compare with Diptych of Magnus and XIc Byz. Emperor Nich. Botaniate.)

Pallium: *Palla*: Roman outdoor garment, which could also be used as a bed covering. It was originally Greek, but in Rome it was draped like a Greek *himation,* or held by a *fibula;* not hooked, as in Greece.

It was a rectangle, as wide as from the wearer's shoulder to the floor, and about three times as long, and was worn by men, women and children, civil and military. Women wore the *palla* outdoors, often draped over the head, but always in conjunction with a veil or cap. As today in church, a head covering was customary among women in Rome.

The *pallium* was the characteristic garment of the scholar and philosopher (as the sole garment), the conventional mantle of Christ, and the name of the liturgical garment, though perhaps not the garment itself, derives from it.

Besides the *toga* and *pallium,* the Romans had many other mantles.

Paenula: This was a hooded, bell-shaped weatherproof garment of leather or wool, which was already in use by the Etruscans in IV B.C. It was worn by everybody, civil and military, particularly by centurions. By the time of Tacitus, it was worn by lawyers, and though much condemned and banned, it finally conquered the much less convenient toga even for senatorial use. It was lengthened, closed all the way, except for a slit at the chin, like a poncho, and its name changed to *casula,* from which (cf. Fr. *cagoulle*) we have the liturgical *chasuble.*

The *cucullus* was a Gallo-Roman IIc. hood with a small cape of its own to keep the neck snug, while used in conjunction with some other, more ample, often poncho-like, covering over it.

There were two purely military mantles, *paludamentum* and *saggum.* The paludamentum was the official military mantle of the general in command, or of the Emperor while in the field. It was used particularly in the earlier years, before I A.D. In cut it resembled the *chlamys* or *lacerna,* with two corners truncated to form an elongated primitive semi-circle.

The saggum was Gallic in origin: there it was a folded rectangle of striped cloth, held by a thorn, in place of a fibula. It became the military wrap of the Roman army; opened out it served as a blanket. Generals, as well, wore it in red or purple and L. M. Wilson* says that of 100 cloaked soldiers on Trajan's Column, two-thirds are wearing the saggum, and that of the remaining third, all, except Emperor, generals and 10 centurions, are wearing the paenula. "Putting on the saggum" was the equivalent of declaring war.

Chlamys: The chlamys was a semi-circular cape, hung over the left arm, and fastened by a fibula or clasp at the right shoulder. It can be seen, decorated with the *tablion,* on the Ravenna mosaics, and on the "Diptych of an Empress," and from the Byzantine court it will continue for many centuries as the outer garment of the upper classes of Western Europe.

Lacerna: This garment was the cloak similar to the chlamys, but light and short, which was worn by everybody in the last century of the Republic. Even senators wore it, in place of the toga, although doing so even then caused a scandal. The *abolla* and the red *byrrus* were other chlamys-like cloaks, often hooded.

Tunica - Stola: Wide shirt-like under-garment, the indoor dress of the Roman; worn outdoors, without the toga, only by working people. It was not, like the toga, distinctively Roman. Originally sleeveless and woolen, usually white, it acquired sleeves, and was later made of linen and cotton, as well. Until the late Empire, sleeves below the elbow were considered in poor taste, and were worn by priests only, or by actors and musicians.

The tunic was girded with meticulous care to the exact length which was considered correct for the sex and rank of the wearer: long, for women;

knee-length or a little below, for a man (longer was effeminate); shorter than knee-length and deeply bloused, for a centurion (who, under campaign conditions, might need the protection against cold furnished at night by its full, ungirdled length.) An ungirded tunic was considered slovenly. A workman's tunic might pass under the right arm and have only a right armhole; it could be made of leather or fur-hide.

The stola, the woman's tunica, was worn over the *tunica intima* (which was of similar cut, might or might not have sleeves, and which served as house-dress). The *stola* had sleeves like the men's, or pinned along the shoulder line and tight down the arms; or, after the IVc., very wide. It was girded once, under the breast (which was first held up in place by soft leather bands—equivalent of our brassiere) and was often girded again at the hips. It was frequently lengthened in appearance by the *instita,* an additional piece of stuff, fastened under the lower belt, forming a train in back on the gown of a matron.

The *tunica talaris,* which fell to the feet and had long loose sleeves, was the marriage dress for men, but was looked down upon by the citizens of Rome and did not compete with the short tunic until the IVc. A.D.

By the VIc., the long toga went out of civil use, and developed into the liturgical *alb,* or *surplice.*

As time went on, several tunics were worn, one over another, those beneath being narrower.

Dalmatica: (see Coptic text and plates). An outer garment, originally male, it was introduced c. 190 A.D. from Dalmatia; common in Rome by IIIc. A.D., it was cut like a tunic, but wider, and with wide short sleeves; went on over the head, was worn without girdle, and was characteristically decorated by the *clavus.*

The dalmatic was much worn by the early Christians: St. Cyprien went to his martyrdom dressed in dalmatic and cape; from it developed the liturgical *dalmatic* and *tunicle.*

Purple stripes (*clavi*) running up over each shoulder from hem to hem, on a customarily ungirded dalmatic, indicated the rank of the wearer: wide (*latisclavus*) *for senators;* narrow (*añgusticlavus*) for equites, knights.

With time, the clavus lost distinction, and by the Ic. it was worn by everyone. The *clavi* then became more elaborately decorative in character; broke into spots of decoration, and amalgamated with borders at the hem of the garment, which gradually moved below the knee-length at which it had stayed for 600 years. The dalmatic was, later, patterned all over, even in letters of the Greek alphabet used decoratively.

The original rectangularity of the dalmatic began to be lost by IVc. Diagonal cutting widened the hems of sleeves and shirts. By the Crusades it

---

* L. M. WILSON: *Clothing of Ancient Romans.*

became a gentleman's long, loose-sleeved gown of rich stuff.

From Vc., the dalmatic was more elaborately cut and fitted; also it was shortened. It became part of the coronation robes of the German Emperors, from XIc.; and in a form more nearly approaching the original, it is still part of the English, as it was of the French coronation regalia. It also distinguishes the vestments of a deacon of the modern Roman church.

BASIC EUROPEAN DRESS

During the first five centuries of the Christian era the basic dress of Western Europe was in process of evolution from its Latin, Barbarian and other sources. Dress varied little, during this period, between nations, or, except in length, between sexes. Its foundation was Roman, which remained for a thousand years a potent influence, the vestigial remains of which are still with us in liturgical vestments.

In the IIIc. Eastern influences added sleeves to the Roman tunic, which became the dalmatic. The Roman clavus had gradually lost distinction until, by the Imperial epoch, it was worn by the lowest servants. It was, proudly therefore, as "The servants of God," that the early Christians are shown in the paintings of the Catacombs, wearing the clavus on their wide, ungirdled, sleeved dalmatics.

The trouser, originally the badge of the Barbarian, had been taken up, for garrison wear, in rigorous climates, by the Roman army. During the Ic. Barbarian *bracae* began to filter back towards Rome; they were still an interesting novelty there in the IIIc. In the IV-Vc. they were repeatedly interdicted for wear in the city, but as Barbarians entered into and rose in the Roman service, through the III and IVc. to triumphant positions in the Vc., the Romans succumbed to what Toynbee calls the inverted snobbery of a mania for barbarism.

It was significant to find that among the IVc. illustrations, selected for intrinsic interest, we have, in the colossal statue of Barletta, the Emperor Valentinian I, a Pannonian, a barbarian partly Celtic in origin; in the guard on the Disk of Theodosius (whose daughter, incidentally, married the successor of Alaric), we see a long-haired Frank; and on the Diptych of Stilicho, a Vandal, married to Serena, niece of the Emperor Theodosius (whose son, Arcadius, had married Eudoxia, daughter of the barbarian, Banto). Another trouser became familiar to Rome, from Persia.

Byzantine influences became of paramount importance as the Roman imperial system disintegrated and Constantinople became the capital of the Empire in the IVc.

The long-sleeved *tunica talaris* which the Romans had considered unmanly (actors' or musicians' garb) came into general use in the IVc., as did a linen undergarment.

The clavi changed from simple stripes to decorative ones. In the IVc. they began to shorten, running over the shoulders only, and perhaps up a little from the hem, ending in decorative motifs, *orbiculi*. Decorative roundels and squares were added at shoulder and knees; decorative bands to hems. A widening single band down the center front eventually joined with the shoulder decoration to form a patterned yoke, *superhumeral*, with an analogous border at the hem. (See Coptic, pp. 36-39.)

An embroidered square, the *tablion*, appears on the front and back edges of the semi-circular mantle, chlamys, which (covering the left arm and caught on the right shoulder by a fibula), had replaced the draped Roman toga. The folded bands of the late Roman toga persisted as the embroidered palla around the shoulders and hips of the ceremonial dress of the later Consuls, and in the costume of the XIc. Byzantine emperor Nicholas Botaniate; the palla was also the source of the pallium of episcopal vestments.

Roman footwear, slippers and calcei had developed, by IVc., into the Byzantine shoe.

By VIc the civil dress of Europe became that of the westerners and barbarians, breeched, short-cloaked; and the long hooded garments of earlier centuries were retained by the conservative church.

260. Rome Ic. A.D.

Claudius Family.

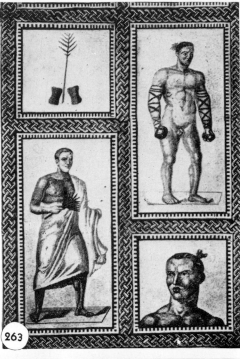

261. Roman. (Rome Conservatori.)

Magistrate: *calcei*: tunic (if two, the lower is longer and sleeved); toga draped in *sinus,* (used as pocket); its banded fold across the shoulder is commemorated in an embroidered band in the 518 A.D. Diptych of Magnus, together with the official handkerchief, *mappula,* which then serves to signal the start of contests in the games (Ludi Circensis).

262. Roman Mid-Ic. A.D. (Rome Mus. delle Terme.)

Augustus: toga draped over head.

263. Roman late. Baths of Caracalla. (Rome Lateran.)

Mosaic: athletes: boxer fighting naked; body oiled;

hair bound up in a knot; hands, in *caestus* strapped around the arms, often held a block of metal. Victor's palms and *tesserae* of bone or ivory, (originally foursided knuckle-bones), on the four sides of which are engraved the name of the athlete, of his patron, the fact that he has passed his trials, and the date.

264. Roman early Pompeii. (Naples National Museum.)

Mosaic: School of Plato: philosophers naked except for pallium and sandals.

265, 266. Roman. (Rome Lateran.)

Sophocles: toga only. Front and side views.

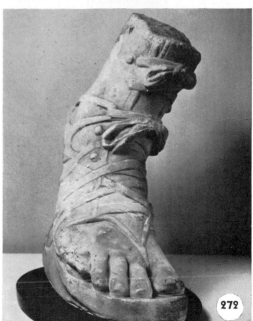

267. Roman adaptation (Greek work).

Marble statue restored as Ceres: *stola* equivalent to *chiton; palla* equivalent to *himation.*

268. Roman (Greek work). Ic. B.C.

Roman boy, of the Julio-Claudia family: bordered and patterned pallium with weighted corners; toga or pallium could be worn in public without tunic, but not tunic without toga.

269. Roman, Empire.

A Camillus: boy assisting at the altar (see also late Greek examples), in tunic and sandals.

270, 271. Roman Ic. B.C.—IIc. A.D.

Bronze: priest sacrificing: wreath, tunic, toga (mourners also wore toga over the head). Front and back views.

272. Roman.

Calcei.

273. Syria. Palmyra Roman Epoch II A.D. (Louvre.)

Funerary portrait. "The wealthy Palmyrene merchants had gorgeously decorated sepulchres built for themselves. The bust of each deceased person was placed over the spot where he was laid and the last word of the epitaph inscribed thereon was 'habal'—alas! The deceased, who is veiled, holds a distaff. She is decked with many jewels—a frontlet, earrings, several rows of necklaces of pearl in particular, fibulas on her left shoulder, large bracelets and rings."*

Strong Persian influences in rosetted border of cloak; and, from a millennium earlier, in both the fibula caught on left breast of garment (independent of mantle) by female aristocrats since the Hittite Queen's (see Ill. 25); and in spinning, which has religious significance (see Ill. 12).

274. Roman. Traianic. e. IIc. A.D. (Louvre.)

Bust of Patrician Woman. Elaborate dressing of Roman Matron's hair.

275. Roman 69-96 A.D.

Funerary portrait: *Cominia Tyche.*

276. 114-116 A.D. Syria. (Dura-Europos, Temple of Zeus.)

Head of Baribonnaea.

Against a gray and buff ground, with dark gray and red lines, Baribonnaea is shown in a Palmyrene headdress and jewels. The stiff *tarboush* is pink, veiled in deep violet, the color of her dress. The tiara is banded above the brow in black, ornamented with a running chevron in yellow (gold), set with pink and green leaves; white band above. The body of the headdress, dotted in yellow, carries a black center band and chevrons, dotted in yellow. The lining of the veil, seen above the ears, is yellow striped in green. Through a red loop on the central band, hangs a chain of braided silver, connected by silver disks and beads, and terminated by elaborate striated pendants.

The gown is almost concealed by five necklaces. From the top, the first, second and fourth strings are of round and cylindrical beads: white, red, black, yellow, and dark gray, the yellow probably representing gold and the white, pearls. The third is a silver braid, carrying a square pendant with a raised edge, and circles which might indicate enamel or stone settings. The fifth braided silver chain is hung with fusiform silver pendants.†

* From Enc. Phot. de l'Art, Louvre
† Information from Dura: Preliminary Report, 1933-5, Yale Univ.

273

274

275

276

277. Syria. 245 A.D. from Dura-Europos (Damascus, New Museum.)

Synagogue frescos. The old pagan gods were losing power; the new proselytising religions of Judaism and Christianity were rising. Rome remained a stronghold of paganism. When Constantine was converted to Christianity and made it the official religion, he decided to move the seat of government to the East, and began to build Constantinople.

The victories of the Ptolemys had sent Jews to Syria, Mesopotamia and Palmyra; Babylonia had become tolerant of Judaism. Dura, lying on the Euphrates, midway between Baghdad and Aleppo, was a largely Semitic city, whose Greek inhabitants realized the unity between Zeus and Artemis, and the Semitic Solar-god and goddess of fertility. Judaism and Christianity were both established there early; the first Synagogue at the end II c. A.D.; the Christian meeting place in 232 A.D. The Synagogue was rebuilt in 245 A.D. by Samuel, the high priest, and other Jews. This unsuspected building came to light during

Yale University's excavations at Dura. The frescos of the Synagogue were removed for their protection from moisture, and placed in an exact replica of the Synagogue in the New Museum at Damascus.

The Jewish prohibition of images began to be liberalized during I c. A.D. to allow illustrations of scenes from sacred books. The Dura Synagogue frescos show battles between Israelites and Philistines; episodes in the lives of Aaron as High Priest; Miriam, Saul and David, with horsemen in Iranian dress; Ahasuerus on Solomon's throne, with Esther and Mordecai; Elijah; and Moses. The exposure of Moses as a baby shows his rescue by Pharaoh's daughter.*

278. Syria. Palmyra. Roman Epoch IIc. A.D.?

Two young military men. Persian trousers tucked into high shoes.

* M. Rostovtzeff: Dura-Europos and its Art, Clarendon Press, Oxford, 1938, Yale University Expedition.

279. Byzantine c. 300 A.D. (Venice St. Marks.)

Two bearded Emperors giving the accolade to two beardless Tetrarchs. Tetrarchs in military costume, moulded cuirasses, elaborate sandals. These porphyry statues (sometimes classed VIIIc.) are dated by Peirce and Tyler, as symbolic representations of the Tetrarchal System, founded 285 A.D. by Diocletian, which was upset after his abdication in 305 A.D.*

280. Byzantine third-quarter IVc., from Barletta, Italy.

Colossal Bronze Statue. Probably the Emperor Valentinian I (364-374), a barbarian (Pannonian) of Celtic-Illyrian origin. The statue, brought from Constantinople in 1204, sank with the ship in the Adriatic; it was later raised, and the arms and legs badly restored in XVc. The diadem of pearls was originally set with stones.

Typical later Roman military costume: moulded lorica lengthened to protect abdomen, shows one of the shoulder straps which secured front and back plates. Costume of Augustus worn with long-sleeved tunic.

281, 282. Byzantine, c. 395 A.D. Monza, Italy (Cathedral Treasure.)

Diptych of Stilicon. Stilicon, the Vandal who defeated Alaric, may be taken as a type of the Barbarian, who by IVc. was rising to the highest military commands and civil honors of the Empire. Then, self-confident, the Barbarians went back to their native names, while the Roman emperors dressed in furs like Scythian warriors. Stilicon's wife, Serena, was the niece of the Emperor Theodosius, whose son Arcadius married Eudoxia, daughter of Banto, another Barbarian. With Stilicon and his wife is their son Eucherius in a Byzantine tunic. Chlamys, caught by a fibula—its *tablion* patterned with horizontal lines. Ser-

ena is a late-Roman matron: two tunics, palla, headdress, girdle and heavy Byzantine pearls and earrings. Stilicon's tunic and chlamys are richly embroidered all over in two patterns, but his fibula is an unjewelled one of metal, conforming strictly to the edict.

---

* From Hayforth Peirce and Royall Tyler: L'Art Byzantin, Librairie de France, Paris, 1932-4, 2 vols., to which I am almost completely indebted for information given under illustrations taken from them.

283. Byzantine 388-394 A.D. (Madrid Academy of History.)

Disk of Theodosius, detail: *one of the Frankish Guards*. The Disk of Theodosius was probably donated by the Viceroy of Spain, where it was found.

The hinged collar, *torque,* which he wears around his neck, was introduced from Gaul; it indicates rank. Torques were used to crown emperors, when a diadem was not available. Decorative patches on the tunic grow larger and more elaborate. Bossed barbarian shield.

284. Byzantine c. 500 A.D. (Florence Bargello.)

Ivory diptych of an Empress. Probably Ariane, daughter of Emperor Leon I. On the tablion of her chlamys is embroidered the portrait (as consul) of her son Leon II, who died emperor at seventeen in 474 A.D. She probably wears this in support of the imperial ambitions of her subsequent husband, in his position as son-in-law of one emperor and step-father of another. Her costume is the ultimate in Byzantine luxury, with feathered diadem, headdress, and collar and borders of fabulous pearls. Shoes such as she wears supplanted sandals in IVc.

285. Byzantine 518 A.D. (Paris Cabinet des Medailles.)

Diptych of Magnus: leaf. Typical costume of a consul celebrating circus day, at the time when the consulate had become a rich man's sinecure, before it was abolished in VIc. Over his tunic, which has bands of embroidery at neck and wrist, is the *toga picta* or *palmata*. The formalized remains of the folded bands of the toga show in the strip of embroidery around the shoulders and down the front. On Magnus' feet are gilded *calcei;* in one hand is the folded handkerchief, *mappa,* with which to signal the start of the games; in the other, the imperial eagle.

286. Byzantine 536-547 A.D. (Ravenna, St. Apollinare-in-Classe.)

Mosaic: St. Michael. Tunic with clavi, orbiculi, roundels on shoulder and cuffs: chlamys has patterned *tablion* and clasps at Byzantine shoulder-closing; beautiful embroidered shoes which continued in European use for centuries.

287. Byzantine before 553 A.D.

Pseudo Sassanian Textile. An attempt (probably Egyptian, but showing Greek influences), to approximate costly Eastern silk in local wool. The mounted archer was an Eastern military invention and the

seated figure of the king also shows costume elements which had filtered westward.

288. Spanish-Hellenistic, second half VIc. A.D. (Seville, Ecija Santa Clara.)

Sarcophagus: Isaac and the Good Shepherd Daniele. Sarcophagus of local limestone, not imported marble, showing Greek influences working in Spain, where, after the Roman withdrawal, the Byzantine armies were confronted by the Visigoths* (whose contributions will in turn be seen—see Visigothic Spanish).

---

* A. Kingsley Porter: Spanish Romanesque Architecture.

289. Italian Vc. A.D. (Naples. San Gennaro, Catacomb 2.)

Grave of Theotecnus. Tombs hewn out of rock were a Jewish method of burial taken over by Christian communities in cities, like Rome and Venice, which were built on porous volcanic rock. Cemetery lots were bought, and excavated in layer on layer of galleries. Pilgrimages were made to these graves of the holy dead, many of them saints, and they were carefully catalogued under Pope Damasus (366-84); many of the catalogues and wall paintings still exist.

Theotecnus wears a tunic decorated on shoulder and cuff; a chlamys caught by a fibula. His wife, tunic, paenula, and scarf over her head. Their two-year-old son wears a long, rather fitted tunic, necklace, jewelled belt, earrings, and head-band.

290. Italian Vc. A.D. (Naples. San Gennaro, Catacomb 2.)

Grave of Cominia, with her daughter Nicatiola, and St. Januarius. All wear tunics with *clavi*, the woman's girdled. Cominia wears a *paenula*, and the embroidered scarf which had supplanted the *pallium*, with the advent of the sleeved dalmatic.

291

292

291, 292. Greek MS. 490 A.D. (Vienna Library.)

These illustrations are from *The Genesis of Vienna* manuscript, the earliest existing Christian book, executed in silver letters and bright color on dark purple vellum.

(291) *Rebecca and Isaac at the court of Abimelech.* Short girdled tunic with short clavi and roundels. Ecclesiastic in chasuble. Beside Pharaoh's throne, soldiers and a man in chlamys with tablion. Women in girdled tunic and palla, under one of which the raised hand is concealed in a gesture which will persist for centuries.

(292) *Joseph interprets Pharaoh's* dream. Joseph in an ungirdled dalmatic short clavi; roundels at shoulder and knee. Both his tunic and Pharaoh's have wide sleeves closing in tightly from elbow toward wrist. Elaborate shoes and the long hose which came into use in VIc.

293

293. Greek MS. V-VIc. (Rome. Vatican Library codex. vat. Pal. Greco 431.)

Joshua Roll. Commander with soldiers and prisoners. Roman armor, trousers, *feminalia;* and high sandals, *calcei.*

294, 295. Byzantine VIc. 547 A.D. Ravenna. San Vitale Choir.

Mosaics: Justinian and followers, including:

294. *Archbishop Maximian and Deacons at the consecration of the church.*

295. *Theodora and her suite at the consecration.*

Justinian, nephew of an illiterate Slavonic peasant who rose, by way of the army, to emperor of the East, was designated by his uncle as his successor, with Theodora as empress—not merely consort. Her father had fed the bears in the ampitheatre; she had been a courtesan. Justinian was unable to marry her until the death of his aunt and the repeal of a law forbidding the marriage of emperors to actresses.

Theodora was small, exquisite, brilliantly intelligent, courageous and imperious; she ruled her very able husband who never remarried after her death from cancer.

Justinian was notable for his compact consolidation of centuries of Roman laws, and for his passionate interest in theology—which led him to built St. Sophia.

In these wonderfully rich mosaics we see Justinian in a white silk tunic embroidered in gold bands and roundels, a purple chlamys, with gold-embroidered *tablion* and the familiar Byzantine closing, from which radiate three lines of decoration.

The dalmatic is still being worn by laymen as well as clergy; from first half IVc. it is the outer garment of deacons, in both liturgical and everyday dress; a fresh garment, although of the same form, must be worn at the mass.

The *pallium*, which came to Rome from the Eastern church, is seen over the Archbishop's chasuble.

The *fibulae* fastening the chlamys of the noblemen; and the *torques* worn by the guards, indicative of rank, have already been seen (see Ill. 283).

The Empress and her suite stand against a basically yellowish-green background, enriched with gold, purple and colors; a scarlet, blue and white curtain is looped up on the right, and a white curtain, patterned in gold, blue-black and red, in the doorway.

The man on the extreme left wears a yellow chlamys with a tablion of the brownish purple which is used throughout. His tunic is white, with a red belt; all the male feet are white, with black tips. The man between him and the Empress is in white and purple.

Theodora's tunic is white, with a deep border in gold; her cloak purple, with human figures in gold embroidery; red appears in her gold and pearl diadem and in the Byzantine collar, dripping with pearls. Gold shoes.

Her attendants wear the palla, both embroidered and decorated, as well as plain; all-over patterned gowns with rich borders, roundels, squares and dalmatic-like vertical bands.

Running right from Empress, the first lady wears a gold-patterned white cloak; purple tunic with gold clavi, patterned in green and red. Next: white cloak, gold squares; white tunic with green and gold figures finished with a dark, pearl-trimmed multi-color band. Next, orange-red cloak with green dots; green gown dotted in red; she holds a fringed white *mappula*. To the extreme right: yellow cloak, green dots; white gown. All the ladies wear scarlet shoes.

THE ROMAN ARMY

The Roman army, which originally fought like the Greek phalanx, passed through three periods of development towards the most disciplined solidarity.

Servian. The army consisted of all citizens 17 to 60 years: there were two main arms, the *equites* (cavalry) and the bodies of heavily armed infantry called *hastati, princeps, triari*. The *equites* were the richest men. They were armed like the Greeks, with only a spear. The shield (*clipeus*) was large, round, oval; it was Argolic Greek, acquired through the Etruscans; in disuse by the time of the Republic. The *hastati, princeps,* and *triari* used a leather helmet and a shield, the oblong Mycenean *ancile*. It was brought by the Romans to the continent of Europe, where the existing circular shield of the Hallstatt Iron period had a projecting boss, *umbo*. The oblong shield assumed this boss and became the *scutum* of the heavily armed soldier, from 334 B.C.; of all Roman soldiers by Caesar's time; and of the Gauls by IVc.

The Republic (Legions). In this period the army saw long service and was paid. Besides the Roman citizens who made up the cavalry and the heavily armed infantry there were also light skirmishers, *velites,* made up of allies, *socii,* and recruits, *auxilia*. The *equites,* or cavalry, used breastplate or cuirasse of scale armor; the spear and the shield. Of the heavily armed infantry, *hastati* and *princeps* used *pilae,* two heavy-throwing spears, seven feet long, one-third iron. About one-third of the *hastati* were without *scutum,* with *hasta,* long spear, and *gaesa,* javelin. *Triari* used the *hasta*. All three bodies used a metal-crested helmet, a leather cuirasse or, in the case of poor men, a nine-inch metal plate worn on the breast. They bore also the *scutum* which was about four feet by two and a half feet, made of wood, hide, and canvas glued or bound with iron and with an iron boss; also the *gladius* which was a two-foot Spanish sword, double edged, worn on the right side on the *cingulum,* belt, or the *balteus,* baldric. The greave, leg armor, was worn on the right leg only. *The socii* (allies) and *velites* (light skirmishers), used the *hasta* and the *spathus,* long sword, toward the end of the Republic. Their tunic was leather with a scalloped bottom; their shield, *parma,* was three feet across, round, light, iron trimmed. Their helmet, *galea,* was leather.

The proportions of these three main bodies were about 300 *equites* to 3,000 heavily armed bodies to 1,200 light skirmishers. The recruits, *auxilia,* were Cretan bowmen, African horsemen, etc.

Empire (Cohorts). The army consisted of recruited Roman citizens and recruited subjects, who were free but not Roman citizens. These could gain citizenship for themselves and family by long service. In this period the *equites* and *velites* disappeared and we have the *legions,* with centurions, standard bearers, etc., infantry, cavalry, Praetorian guard, etc., costume detailed below. The *auxilia* continue with the *spathus,* the long, single-edged sword, and the *hasta*.

The Emperor and the officers like the soldiers were shaved and their hair was clipped. The officers carried no shields. The helmet was crested, or animal-headed. The breastplate, *lorica,* was made of metal scales or moulded in body-form, over a leather protective doublet, the bottom of which was slit into knee-length straps with metal studs which were both protective and decorative. There was the same effect at the armholes, covering shoulder and upper arm. The tunic was wool. Mantles included the scarlet or white *paludamentum,* often fringed and embroidered; *abolla;* red *byrrus;* and *saggum*. The sword was worn in a belt over the *lorica*. The footwear was high-laced sandals or boots, tops often turned down, with animal-head effects.

The *Standard Bearer* had an animal skin on his head instead of a helmet with the paws tied about the neck and the hide hanging down back.

The *Centurion* wore the crested helmet, but the crest varied, sometimes running across the head, ear to ear. He carried also the *vitis,* the official baton, a short plain stick. During the Empire he wore a greave, *ocrea,* on the right leg and the *paenula,* a mantle particularly favored by centurions.

The *Praetorian* used the *lorica squamata,* and *hamata,* and the typical helmet.

The Legionary's helmet was metal, Greek type, protecting the sides of the face, but no longer crested by the time of the Empire. He wore also a cuirasse, the *lorica segmentata,* a corselet of overlapping leather strips, from underarm to waist, usually closed in front, held up by three to six vertical strips over each shoulder, often finished with fringed skirt of leather strips, waist to mid-thigh. During the Empire, his cuirasse was the *lorica squamata* made of metal plates or the *lorica hamata* of chain mail, both on leather or canvas. The tunic was wool, above the knees. He wore also a *focale*, wool muffler; a belt, *cingulum*, with three vertical protective lappets hanging below; a mantle, *saggum*, brown-red wool. There was no leg-wear until the campaigns in Gaul. The *bracae* were the breeches of barbarians adopted for garrison wear; not used in Rome until III-IVc. They used leg-swathings called *fasciae*.

The footwear was called *caligae*, heavy, often hob-nailed boots; or sandals with straps and lacings going well up the leg. Auxiliaries wore native footwear. The sword was the *gladius*, about 20 to 24 inches long, two-edged, worn on the belt or baldric. During the Empire, there was the *spatha*,

the long single-edged sword worn on the left side. The dagger worn on the right side was called the *pugio*.

From 334 B.C. onwards, the shield became the *scutum*, which was oblong, oval, hexagonal, octagonal, about two and a half feet by four feet. It was curved about the body, made of wood, leather covered, with an iron band around the edge and the iron boss, *umbo*, in the center. After IIc. A.D., it was oval. The *clipeus*, the large round leather shield, was used before the Republic; and later, smaller, in iron, it was used by the commander's attendants. The *parma* was the round, light, iron-trimmed shield used by *velites* under the Republic, and by gladiators.

The Legionaries also used the *hasta*, long spear, and the *pila*, the heavy seven-foot, one-third iron spear.

296. Roman 20 B.C. Statue. (Metropolitan Museum.)

Augustus as Commander. Paludamentum; magnificent moulded *lorica* with typically shaped shoulder straps connecting its sections (see also No. 297); pleated leather doublet, its edges cut into fringe, worn between woolen tunic and cuirasse to give additional protection and to prevent chafing.

297. Roman, Traianic. II A.D. Relief Sculpture. (Louvre.)

Praetorians. The feathered Attic crest, often red and black, on the helmets of the Praetorian guards, was removable for wartime use; chin strap outline and studding protects the face. Moulded loricas of handsomely worked metal on ranking officers; doublets elaborately cut into fringes; belt with apron of three protective leather lappets, or a wide protective belt; tunics; boots; oblong shield, decorated, without center boss.

298. Roman II A.D. (Rome, Column of Trajan.)

Battle at walls. Trajan (whose father had risen from the ranks, fighting in Spain) was a soldier whom all soldiers, enemy as well as friends, admired. He was open, simple, solicitous of his men's comfort, and lived and ate as they did. His wonderfully disciplined and organized army fought to secure the northeastern frontier between the Rhine and the Danube. The Column of Trajan, built early in IIc. is a monument to his great Dacian campaign, and shows "Barbarians" of many sorts, both as adversaries, and as Roman auxiliaries.

All the archers, most of the cavalry and much of the infantry is now composed of "Barbarians"; the top leadership was Roman, but more immediately they were commanded by their own tribal leaders, and were allowed to keep their native dress and weapons. The equipment of Roman soldiers began to be standardized in I A.D., but in early II A.D. it is often difficult to distinguish the origins of soldiers shown on triumphal monuments. The dress of the Roman legionaries became affected by barbarian ways, while the barbarians were being Romanized, gaining citizenship, and preparing to become the most powerful men of the Empire.

In the battle for the walled town, we see hairy and bearded barbarians in breeches and sleeved tunics.

Two Asiatic horsemen (perhaps Iranians from the steppes of Southern Russia) wear conical helmets of metal banded leather, and scale-mail which was made to cover the horse as completely as the rider.

299. Roman Traianic 98-114 A.D., from Forum of Trajan. (Rome, Conservatori.)

Captive Barbarian Chief. The prisoner-of-war is Dacian, an Indo-European tribe from what is now Roumania. Cloak is a rectangle, heavily fringed on three sides, folded double, pinned with a fibula on one shoulder and folded up over the other; long bordered tunic with long sleeves; full, horizontally-striped breeches caught with a decorative knot, into shoes which are folded around the foot like a moccasin and laced across an ovally cut-out instep.

300. Danish Early Iron Age 250 B.C.—45 A.D., from Thorsbjerg.

Trousers, stocking feet; cloak materials. In mid-XIXc., remarkable finds were made in Sleswig.* In peat-bogs, situated always between rivers near the sea, and in connection with barrows on adjacent high land, were discovered quantities of objects, in orderly heaps. All had been hastily and deliberately made useless (clay vessels were filled with stones to sink them, and there were traces of fire), whether in some religious ceremony, no one knows.

Iron objects had disintegrated, but the peat had preserved other metals, wood, leather and textiles; a huge boat; clothing; fibulae, buttons and buckles; shields, helmets; weapons and bridles; reed baskets, wood rakes, troughs and spoons; ring-money; lathe-turned awls, knives; nets and pottery.

The clothing at Thorsbjerg consisted of a handsome wool shirt in herring-bone weave, with sleeves of a different diaper-pattern, finished with cuffs of decorative braid; cloaks; and a pair of breeches, with a foot, in a diaper-weave. The breeches have loops to hold a belt, reinforced with a woven braid.

There were also several shirts of fine, linked, iron ring mail, in alternately riveted asd welded rows, bordered in bronze rings. These are of immense importance because it had been supposed that rings were sewed onto canvas until after the period of the Bayeux tapestries; now a considerable amount of linked chain-mail has been found antedating IIIc. A.D.

Dressed corpses have been recovered from other peat-bogs in Denmark, Northwest Germany, and Holland. Roughly summarized: they are dressed in fur, leather, wool in many weaves (some dyed and striped like ticking) trimmed with good-looking fancy braids; later, shirts of linen, over which wool tunics became belted. Conical caps, fitted hoods, and shaped or rectangular capes (the latter, often of striped wool, caught by a fibula) of fur, leather, or wool. Shirts, sleeveless, or with long sleeves which are often of a different weave and finished with a braid, were of hip-to-knee lengths. Trousers, knee-to-ankle length, the shorter ones finished with woven bands, and often worn with leg-wrappings. Extremely good leather shoes, folded about the foot, cut out and slit in handsome decorations (usually diagonal) trimmed in bronze and laced at the ankle.

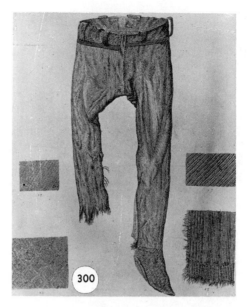

Women, in the grave found near Aarhus, Jutland, wore shorter, sleeved shirts with a slit neck-closing; skirts made of a long piece gathered together into a ruffled top, above a handsome braid girdle going several times around the waist, and ending in tassels of expertly made fringe. Hair was gathered up in back in net hammocks, elaborately patterned; the top tied around the forehead and the lower part over the crown, to hold the net in place.†

Besides fine shoes and decorative braids, the barbarians had wonderful jewelry of gold, silver, bronze and niello, often set with stones; fibulae and buckles, necklets, bracelets, and rings; golden combs.

Sidonius Apollinarius (430-485 A.D.) says that the Franks of the IV-V c. had red hair which they wore knotted high; shaved but carried moustaches; wore tight-fitting knee-length trousers; tunics with sleeves barely covering the shoulders (i.e. a sleeveless shirt, made of a strip of material sewed part-way up the sides, with a hole for the head), made of striped materials; a red *saggum* with a green edging; a wide, studded belt; and hung the sword from a baldric slung across the breast. The Teutonic *braie* (bracchae) were later worn by the Gauls with *pedules* (long socks drawn up to the knee and turned down), which became the national dress of the Franks.

* C. Engelhardt: *Denmark in the Early Iron Age.* Williams and Norgate, London, 1866. Illustrated with scrupulously accurate engravings, such as Ill. 300.

† Other Jutland finds have been made at Borum-Eshoi, Marx-Etzel, Bernuthsfeld, and Oben-Altendorf.

301. Roman Traianic IIc. A.D. (Rome. Column of Trajan.)

*Barbarians who are Roman auxiliaries in uniform, and impossible to identify.** The auxiliaries are less well paid and equipped than the legionaries. They retain their bossed shields; *saggum* caught on shoulder with a *fibula;* breeches reaching to the calves; handsomely-cut shoes finished with patterned bands at the ankle. The figure on the right, next to top, shows the segmented form of *lorica.*

302. Roman Trianic IIc. A.D. (Rome. Column of Trajan.)

Barbarians and Romans before a walled town. Various tribes of the Balkan Peninsula, and possibly southern Russia. Right to left; the three men facing the emperor are Germanic, possibly tribes of the Bastarnae. To the left, the man in a pointed cap is Dacian, or of a related Thracian tribe. Two, with gathered skirts, to the left, wear mittens; they are northern tribesmen, perhaps nomads from the southern steppes of Russia. The two at extreme left are supposedly Sarmatians, of the tribe of the Jazygi; (who at the time occupied what is now Hungary).*

303. 304. Roman. Aurelian. IIc. A.D. (Rome, Arch of Constantine.)

Two Reliefs. (304) Legionaries in breeches; various leather cuirasses segmented or scale-covered; one crested Attic helmet. In back, standard-bearers with animal skins over their heads; praetorians.

(303) Persian soldier in conical helmet, extended in splints to protect the back of the neck; long, segmented cuirasse with segmented shoulder caps.

---

* Prof. Karl Lehmann-Hartleben of New York University has been good enough to identify some of the races represented in these Traianic sculptures, many of which were photographed by him. All identifications are conjectural.

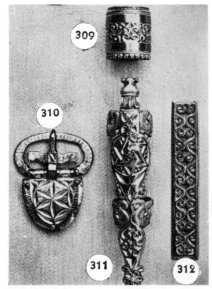

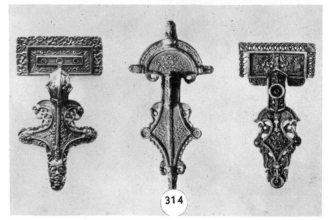

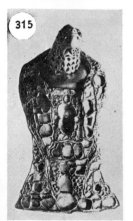

Jewelry of III-VIIIc. Migrations.

305. Pontine S. Russia IIIc. A.D., from N. France.

Gold bracelet: 3 twists of heavy wire, bound in fine wire; finished in approximations of animal heads.

306. Germanic-Celtic-Iranian, La Tene Period, from Trichtingen.

Silver bracelet, ending in sheeps' heads.

307, 308. N. Germany Iron Age from Olleberg.

Gold collar: details.

309-312. Gallo-Roman. France IV-Vc. A.D., from tomb at Vermand.

Buckle and spear-mounts in silver, parcel-gilt and

niello: apparently the insignia of office of a chief of Roman legionary troops; done in the perforated "Kerbschnitt" technique, found along the borders of the Roman Empire: Belgium, N. France, and the Rhineland; it utilized the Scandinavian and Sarmatian coiled animals (magical properties), which can barely be seen on piece 311.

313. Moorish, from excavations. N. Germany.

Silver ornaments and sword shields.

314. Scandinavian Iron Age. c. 500-700 A.D.

Fibulae in silver and bronze: T-shaped fibulae become frog-like in Scandinavia, and are found wherever the Vikings went. The most extremely cut out and interlaced patterns, which went south with the Sarmatians and north with the Finns (both of whom cast them in white-metal and tin), form the basis of the great Celtic manuscript style. Fibulae sometimes reached a length of 15 inches.

315, 316. Roumania V-VIc. A.D., from Petrossa.

315. Vc. Gold fibula: bird: cabochon carbuncles, glass paste.

316. VIc. Gorget: openwork set with garnets, vitreous paste, and lapis-lazuli.

317-326. Frankish VI-VIIIc., A.D., Marne and Rhineland.

Ten rosette-shaped fibulae. The Franks were Teutonic Eastern barbarians, who began their invasion of W. Germany and N. France in IV-V c. They settled in the Frankish kingdoms of Austrasia, Neustria, and Acquitaine, and joined the Romans and Visigoths in fighting the Huns in the Vc. Under Clovis (465-511) they ruled Northern and Central France; in VIIc., they joined the culturally allied Burgundians to the south.

Frankish jewelry includes T-shaped parcel-gilt fibulae, and rosette-shaped fibulae, which are usually of bronze, the face silvered or gilded—and inlaid with glass and stones, cloisonné enamel, or filigreed.

Courtesy of Metropolitan Museum (305, 309-312); Stuttgart Museum (306); Flensburg State Museum (313); Oslo, Stockholm, and Copenhagen Museum (314); Bucharest Museum (315, 316).

317. Marne VIII c.
318. Frankish-Allemanian VII c.
319. Frankish VII c.
320. Marne VII c.
321. VII-VIII c. (rare type).

322. Niederbreisig VI-VII c.
323. VII-VIII c. (rare type).
324. Late VII-e.VIII c.
325. Niederbreisig e.VIII c.
326. Niederbreisig VII-e.VIII (extremely rare).

Courtesy Metropolitan Museum. Gift of J. Pierpont Morgan

The Roman Catholic Church

DEVELOPMENT OF ECCLESIASTICAL VESTMENTS

During the first three Christian centuries the dress of a priest differed from that of a dignified, scholarly layman only in that the Mass had to be celebrated in fresh, clean garments—our "Sunday clothes."

Liturgical dress as we know it was evolved between the IV-IXc. out of elements: Roman, Byzantine, Western. Before the VIIIc. there was little attempt on Rome's part to impose direction on the development of the churches of Gaul and Spain, and from Rome those churches took only the pall, dalmatic, maniple and buskins. The distinctly Roman dalmatic and pall were sent as gifts to honor distinguished prelates of the Western church. But Roman usages were brought to the continent rather by the missionaries to Germany from the British Isles, where Christianity had long been established under Roman rule. By IXc. Roman usage was firmly established in the West and liturgical costume was further defined, to XIIIc. Change between XIII-XVIc. was in the direction of closer fit and richer ornamentation. Since XVIc. it has become progressively less aesthetically satisfying.

The first vestments to appear were the *Pall* and *Stole,* well established by the IV and Vc. as distinguishing marks of bishop and deacon.

The *Paenula,* common to laity and clergy from III-IVc., was separated for liturgical use by the IVc. and, as the *Chasuble,* was retained in its long form by the conservative church, after shorter garments had become the rule in daily life. To XIc. it was worn by all priests, even by acolytes, and later became a Mass vestment.

By the VIc., when gentlemen were wearing the paenula (chasuble) and dalmatic, bishops wore besides these garments the pallium, but deacons wore the dalmatic only and sub-deacons the tunic only. The clergy were tonsured.

In the VIIIc. the *Cope* first appears as a processional garment, worn both by clergy and secular, particularly singers; by Xc. its use is widespread; by XIIc. fixed; by XIIIc. it has replaced the chasuble except at the celebration of the Mass.

The IXc. liturgical garments of a Pope or a Roman deacon, given in *Amalarius: De officis ecclesiastices,* consisted of *amice* (anagolaium), *alb* (tunica alba) girdled with *cingulum, maniple, stole* (orarium), *tunicle* (dalmatica minor), *dalmatic* (dalmatica major), *chasuble* (planeta), *pallium, sandals, pontifical stockings.*

XIc. ecclesiastical costume is still unembroidered, the *clavi* or the folds of handsome woven stuff the only decoration.

Pontifical *gloves* appear in the XIc.: the *mitre* in the Xc., *liturgical shoes* in the XIc.

The *surplice* (super-pellicia) is first mentioned in the XIc. Originally worn over fur garments, by the choir and lower clergy, it replaced the alb, which it resembled, by the XIIIc.

By the XIIc. the mitre and gloves are worn by all Bishops, who are gaining in temporal power and magnificence,* and are, especially in Germany, sometimes assuming a new ornament, the *rationale,* resembling the pallium. The XIIIc. is full of complaints by a scandalized laity, that priests dressed in a way more suitable to knights. The 4th Lateran Council (1215) forbade the clergy to wear green and red clothing, brooches, and copes with sleeves, and exhorted them to wear unextravagant dress, closed down the front.

The red apparel of cardinals had appeared before Innocent IV conferred the cardinals' hat in 1245.

Until the early Middle Ages, prelates of the Church might appear in full regalia, as for the Mass, at a banquet at the palace on a great feast day or in honor of a visiting sovereign.

By XIIc. liturgical color was established and may be roughly charted as follows:

---

* In 1042 the abbot of the Monastery of St. Gall was responsible for providing the Emperor with an army of 60,000 men and was seated at the Emperor's right. Until the XIIc. knighthood might be received from abbots and bishops.

	Priest	Bishop	Arch-Bishop	Cardinal	Pope	Deacon	Other and Lower Orders	Sub-Deacon
CASSOCK Non-liturgical but worn under liturgical.	Black	Black Red or Purple edged	Black Red or Purple edged	Red or Black-edged Red	White	Black	Monks in color of Order	Black
BIRETTA General use; limited liturgical use.	Black	Purple	Purple	Red	White	Black		Black
TIARA					Processional			
SURPLICE (Cotte, rochet) liturgical but not blessed.	Administering sacramental blessing	✔	✔	Proper to all clerics particularly to			Choir and Lower Clergy	✔
COPE Liturgical but not sacerdotal.	✔	Purple	Purple	Red or Purple	Red mantle Morse of precious stones		Early Church Festivals Lay and Choir	
ALMUCE Choir vestment of dignitaries to XVc.; by XIVc. largely superseded by							Choir Vestments of Canons, Since XIVc.	
MOZETTA		Purple	Purple	Red	Ermine-Edged Red Velvet			
LITURGICAL								
AMICE	✔	✔	✔	✔	✔	✔		✔
ALB	✔	✔	✔	✔	✔	✔		✔
CINCTURE	✔	Purple	Purple	Red	White	✔		✔
MANIPLE	✔	✔	✔	✔	✔	✔		particular to
STOLE	✔	✔	✔	✔	✔	✔		
TUNICLE		✔	✔	✔	✔			particular to
DALMATIC		✔	✔	✔	✔	particular to		
CHASUBLE	✔	✔	✔	✔	✔			
SANDALS		Color of Vestments of Day						
STOCKINGS-BUSKINS		‖	‖	‖	‖			
GLOVES		‖	‖	‖	‖			
MITRE		White	White	White	liturgical			
PALLIUM			particular to White	✔	✔			
SUB-CINCTORIUM					✔			
FANION					✔			
PECTORALCROSS		✔	✔	✔	✔			
PONTIFICAL RING		✔	✔	✔	✔			
PASTORAL STAFF		✔	✔	✔				

CHART OF ECCLESIASTICAL VESTMENTS AND COLORS

White (or silver) was used for festivals, consecrations, coronations and such events; red, signifying blood, was used on occasions commemorating the sufferings of Christ, the Apostles, martyrs, etc.; green was used during specified periods (over half of the year) before Lent and after Trinity. Gold brocade could be used instead of any one of these three colors.

Violet and black signified mourning, violet for intercessional and penitential and black for funerals and Masses for the dead.

Hierarchal rank is also indicated by color: white for the Pope, red for cardinals, violet for bishops, black for priests.

ECCLESIASTICAL VESTMENT DETAILS

Alb: liturgical vestment of Catholic Church; derived, with *surplice and rochet,* from the long *tunica alba,* which passed out of Roman civil usage in VIc. It is of white linen, narrow-sleeved, slit for the head to pass through, and girdled to clear the ground. It is worn over the cassock and under the other liturgical garments and ornamented with embroidery or lace.

In the IXc. Rabanus Maurus gives the alb as an integral part of priests' attire; in Spain and Gaul is was often worn instead of the dalmatic, by deacons. In the Xc. it began to be ornamented with embroidered bands at hem, neck and wrists.

During the XIIc. at the day-long services of the Benedictine Monastery at Cluny, albs were worn both by the priests officiating at the altar and by the monks assisting in the stalls.

By the XIIIc. 4-6 brocade or embroidered patches (*apparels, parures* or *orphreys*) at center front and back of hem, wrists, and sometimes at breast and back, began to supplant bands. Spreading from N. France, this became general.

In the XIVc. the alb was reserved for celebration of mass; surplice used otherwise. During the Middle Ages the hem widened to 5 yards, and by XVIc. to more than 7 yards. In the XVI-XVIIc. lace replaced apparels.

The "colored" albs found in church inventories during the Middle Ages were probably carelessly listed dalmatics, or references are to the colors of the embroidery.

Since the XIIc. the alb has gradually been replaced by the *surplice,* originally the vestment proper to the lower orders; except for priests, bishops, deacons and sub-deacons.

Almuce (O. Fr., O. Eng. *Aumuce*): Fur-lined, hooded choir vestment worn from the XIIc. by church canons over the surplices, against cold; by the XVIc. hung over left arm as badge of office. Certain academic and monastic bodies were also granted its use, and by the XIIc. the laity also wore it. Originally open in front and tied at the neck, it became closed and was dropped over the head. As hats began to be worn, the almuce became progressively more cape-like; by the XIVc. it was often shortened at each shoulder for convenience, but hung down in front in two long points, which must not, however be confused with the *stole.* The almuce will sometimes be seen edged with fur tails.

Amice (*Anagolaium*): Liturgical vestment, the first in order to be assumed by a priest vesting himself for the Mass. Developed out of the Roman neckcloth, it is a strip of linen, laid, hood-like, over the head, dropped to the shoulders and tied in position around the upper body with tapes sewed to two corners, forming a collar. Its use is recorded in Rome in the VIIIc. and spread with other Roman usages in the IXc. By the XIIc. the amice, like the alb, was decorated with embroidered apparels, which stiffen it to form an apparent collar. Since the end of the XVIc. there is always a cross at the center of the apparel.

Biretta (*Biretum, Barret-Cap,* cf. *Beret*): Since XVIIc. a ridged cap peculiar to Catholic clergy; of limited liturgical function, worn also outside the Church, as at processionals. It developed out of a close skull-cap (*pileus*), which appeared in XIIIc. and was worn by dignitaries and officials, legal, academic, as well as ecclesiastic, when hoods were the only common head coverings. It had a center tuft, like a modern beret, and, like it, was susceptible of arrangement; out of this developed its present pinched shape. By the XVIc. it was worn by all people of standing, women and men.

In its mediaeval form it is the hat familiar in the portraits by Holbein, and survives in the academic mortarboard.

The ecclesiastical biretta derives from a cap identical in form with the modern beret: it became squarer as it became ampler, and now, completely stiffened, has the excess material at the top seamed into upright folds, forming a cross. Its color: black, purple, red, or white indicates its wearer's rank as priest, bishop, cardinal, pope.

Cassock (*Pellicium*): *Soutane.* Originally the daily wear of everybody, especially the dignified and elderly; and fur-lined, according to the wearer's means, for winter use. It was retained by the church, after the change in lay fashion. It is now the ordinary dress of Roman, and to a more limited extent, of Church of England clergy, upon which vestments, eucharistic and processional, and monastic habit, are super-imposed. Its color: black, purple, red, or black with red pipings, white indicate rank: priest, bishop, cardinal, pope. Monks' cassocks are of the color of the habit of their order.

Chasuble (*Planeta,* Late L. *Casula*: little house): Outermost, and a most important liturgical garment of the Catholic church. The shape varies by period and country. Essentially it is a cape of silk or metal cloth, never linen or cotton, with a hole for the head, shortened at the sides to the shoulder to leave the arms uncovered, and falling down the front and back. Derived from the Roman *paenula,* originally a barbarian garment, adopted by soldiers and low people.

In the IVc. it was considered permissible wear for senators, and its everyday and liturgical uses had been separated, although the cut remained identical. By the VIc. still common to clergy and laity. In his life of St. Germanus of Paris, Fortunatus of Poitiers says that the saint wore tunic and chasuble, but retained only one of each, giving any duplicates to the poor. The portrait of St. Gregory with his layman father shows both wearing dalmatic and chasuble, the saint distinguished by his tonsure and pall.

In 742 A.D. priests in Gaul were ordered to wear the casula instead of the short military saggum. At the end of the Xc. *apparels* common, as border, vertical stripe, or forked cross with arms lifted up.

It was worn by all churchmen, even acolytes, during the XIc. It had become distinctly a Mass vestment, with the establishment of the *cope* as a processional and choral vestment. The chasuble, being a cape sewed up into a pastry-tube shape, was inconvenient. By the VIIc the sides of the tent-like cape are cut away for more convenient celebration of the Mass.

Apparels became wider and more decorative during the mid-XIIIc. In this century the symbolic meaning of the cross began to be emphasized, and the cross with horizontal arms began to appear on the back of the chasuble only, with a vertical strip down the front. In the XIVc. a crucified Christ was added, and in the XVc. a horizontal cross; or vertical apparels, front and back, with short horizontal apparel at base of neck opening in front.

By the XVIc. it had its scapular-like modern form.

The chasuble typical of the Church of England carries the forked cross in front and in back.

Chimere (It. *zimarre*): Liturgical and ceremonial civil vestment of Anglican bishops; developed, together with certain academic robes, out of the *tabard* (*collobium*), the common outer garment of all mediaeval Europe. It is a long sleeveless gown of satin or silk, full across the shoulders in back, and is worn over the *rochet,* the lawn sleeves of which pass through the slits at the sides of the chimere, and were, at a late period, sometimes transferred to the chimere. After the advent of wigs, it was opened down the front to facilitate donning, as were the academic robes.

The various colors in which the chimere is listed during the Middle Ages may have designated academic rank. The chimere is now black or red.

The continental *zimarre* (*simmara*) is a *soutane* with a short cape and short, slit sleeves; and like the soutane is worn by clerics of all ranks, professors, and formerly by Roman senators.

Cope (*Cappa, Pluviale*): liturgical vestment of Catholic and choir vestment of some Anglican churches. Semi-circular cape brocaded or embroidered, fastened across chest by a broad ornamented band, sewed to one edge and hooked or pinned by a jewelled *morse* to the other, and with an embroidered flap, a vestigial hood, hanging down back.

Originally, a protective outer garment, of the same derivation as *chasuble,* open instead of seamed up, common to laity of both sexes and to churchmen.

In VIIIc. the black *Cappa Choralis* (non-liturgical) was worn in outdoor procession by singers, secular and regular clergy; it is the present Dominican winter garment. In 888 in Metz, the laity were forbidden to wear copes. In Xc. the influence of opulent Cluniac ceremonies spread the use of decorative vestment, particularly at high mass for choir-master and choir, who on lesser occasions would wear albs.

By the XIIIc. it was fixed in liturgical use, and substituted, outside the Mass, for the less convenient chasuble. The flap at this period was triangular. The shape and size of the hood evolved with the passage of time. In the XIV-XVc. it was shield-shaped, in the XVIIc. it was rounded at the bottom and by the XVIIIc. the hood was enormously enlarged.

Dalmatic (*Dalmatica Major*): (as a liturgical garment of the Catholic Church). In Rome the dalmatic is now a knee-length, wide-sleeved gown, slit up the sides; outside of Italy it is a poncho-like garment with square flaps hanging from upper arm over shoulder. It is decorated with two vertical stripes over the shoulder to the hem. In Rome these are narrow and are united by two narrow horizontal stripes at the bottom; outside Italy, broad, joined higher up by a broad stripe. The dalmatic of a Bishop is fringed on both sides and sleeves, and that of a Deacon is (properly) fringed on the left side and sleeve only.

Since the IVc. the dalmatic has been distinctly a vestment of the Pope and his Deacons, and always a festal garment, worn (under chasuble, never under cope) during Mass, benedictions, processions, never on penitential days.

In the VIIc. it was wool or linen, fringed at sleeves and side openings. Up to the VIIIc. long tunic, long wide sleeves. In the IXc. shorter and narrower outside Italy; tuft of red fringe began to be set in clavi, especially outside Italy (to the XIIIc).

In the Xc. color came into use, especially outside Italy. The Pope granted it to cardinal-priests and abbots in XIc. When granted to priests, may be worn on specified days only. Changes in the following century: in Italy, it was shorter and narrower; silk began to be used; also it was slit up sides for easier donning, gradually up to sleeves, unless widened by gores.

By the XIIIc. color was the rule (liturgical colors). Its length was 51"-55" outside Italy but to the XIVc. in Italy also. In the XVc. sleeves were opened for convenience, outside Italy.

The dalmatic gradually became shorter, 47" in the XVIc. and 39"-35" by the XVIIIIc. Sleeves were correspondingly narrower.

Maniple (Mappula) liturgical vestment of all orders of Catholic church above sub-deacon. It is a narrow strip of silk, three feet long, decorated with three crosses, now hung or fastened over left forearm. It is one of the four distinctly Roman contributions to liturgical costume, originally a linen handkerchief or cloth derived from the folded consular *mappula,* its use spread from Rome to Ravenna, and thence westward. Originally linen, it lost its useful character, and, like the stole, became silk .

In the IXc. it was already band-like, carried in the left hand, and in the IX-XIc. either carried in left hand or worn on left wrist. By the XIIc. it was worn over the left arm.

Mitre: liturgical headdress of Catholic church, specifically that of bishops, but occasionally worn by abbots and other church dignitaries, by grant of the Pope. Now a high hat composed of two identical stiffened pieces which fold flat against each other when not spread horn-like by being set on the head. From back half depend two narrow fringed strips.

Mitres are of three sorts: *simplex*: white linen or silk, undecorated, except that dependent strips terminate in red fringe; *aurifrigiata*: gold or silver embroidered orphreys on white silk; *pretiosa*: overlayed with gold plates, set with jewels.

The mitre seems to have developed out of the cone-shaped cap of the early Popes. It was established in Rome in the Xc.: conical shape with band around brow. In the XIc. it was frequently granted by the Pope to cardinals in Rome; first granted to an English abbot in 1063, and to some secular dignitaries, and the Roman emperor.

In the XIIc. all western bishops wore it, and it was granted to many abbots; rounder shape; added band running over crown from front to back forced a horned side effect which persisted to the XIIIc. when the mitre had already begun to be turned so that horns were at front and back; decorative embroidery spread from horizontal and vertical bands to triangular spaces outlined by them. Low triangular shape of mitre progressively rises from the XIVc., spreads and becomes arched, XV-XVIc.; the increasingly rich decoration based on horizontal and vertical

bands is supplanted by symmetrical scrolled embroidery.

Mozetta: ceremonial and processional vestment worn by Catholic prelates, in colors designating rank. A short hooded cape, buttoned down front, worn over *rochet*. Also developed out of the cappa, like the cope, it is not a liturgical garment.

Pallium (Omorphion, Pall): vestment worn by Catholic archbishops. It is a woven band of white lambs' wool, "three fingers broad," worn over chasuble. Derived from Roman *pallium,* it was originally a longer strip draped over both shoulders and pinned to the left one; now a strip, decorated with four crosses, made into a circle which is dropped on the shoulders and fastened, front and back, with gold pins, at those points from which hang two tabs, each decorated with a cross. Since the IVc. it was worn by Eastern bishops, and borrowed by Western.

"Teach the faithful, don't amuse them," Pope Celestinus wrote the Bishops of Narbonne and Vienne in 428 A.D., concerning a distinctive costume, *pallium* and *cincture,* concocted by the Gallic bishops. By the late Vc., however, the *pallium* was considered an ornament peculiar to the Pope, and sent by him, at first, to honor distinguished prelates of various ranks.

By the IXc. as a symbol of his delegated authority, the Pope granted it to archbishops. The Anglo-Saxon Chronicle records Robert of Jumièges' return from Rome in 1051 with the pall; his deposition in 1052; the refusal of 2 subsequent Popes to recognize Stigand (see Bayeux Tapestry) as archbishop, until he finally receives the pall in 1058 from Benedict X. After the XIIIc. an archbishop could not exercise his authority before receiving the pall, for which payment had to be made.

Pileolus: non-liturgical skull-cap worn by Catholic prelates under mitre and tiara.

Pastoral Staff (Bishops' Crozier, Archbishops' Cross-Staff): insignia of cardinals, bishops and abbots of the Catholic church. It is a five-foot staff of wood or metal, carried in the right hand, held in the left during benediction.

Heads were originally of four types: *shepherds' crook* (which continued to the XIIc. in Ireland); *knobbed*; *T* (typical of abbots, cont. to the XIIIc.) and in the IXc. *bent crook*, often snake-headed, from which present crozier developed. This became the predominant type in the XIc. and by the XIIIc. supplanted other types. The snake was elaborated into tendrils, with knob below, from which, by the XIV c. a scarf was suspended (now, abbots only).

The *Cross-Staff* of an archbishop does not

necessarily supplant the pastoral staff, both of which are frequently carried together, preceding the archbishop (not carried by him).

Pontifical Ring (Annulus) of bishop of Catholic church, derived from signet, and used since at least the VIIc. It is worn on the middle finger of the right hand (or forefinger, or in the case of the XV-XVIIc. Papal ring given to cardinals, thumb) and being massively set with a large stone, is worn over the glove, or shows through a slit in the glove.

Pectoral Cross of a bishop of the Catholic church has been worn over his vestments only since the XVIc.

Rochet (G. Rock): vestment, not strictly liturgical, of Catholic prelates and also of Anglican bishops. It is a modified alb of fine linen or lawn. In the Catholic church it is now knee-length, having been long in the XIIc.; and has narrow sleeves with a border of lace, embroidery or lining color.

The Anglican rochet, resembling the Catholic of the Middle Ages in its length, differs from it in the size of its sleeves, which increased in size, from the Reformation to the XVIIIc., at which time the huge ruffle-edged sleeves, tied at wrist with black ribbons, were transferred to the *chimere*.

Stole (Orarium): liturgical vestment of Catholic church for Mass, never processional use. It is a long narrow strip of material, usually silk, now decorated by three crosses, at ends and middle, and fringed at hem, and worn over the shoulder in different ways, characteristic of deacon, priest or bishop. It may have descended from the fringed *orarion* given by the IIIc. Emperor Aurelian to be waved in applause at the games.

In the IVc. it was established in the Eastern church, and specified as wear for the deacon who, dressed in white and with the folded stole over his left shoulder as badge of office, would welcome visitors at the guest house. It seems to have been introduced in the VIc. from the East into Gaul and Spain, and from there have gone to conservative Rome by the VIIIc. In 755 A.D. a Western bishop, arriving at the basilica on horseback, changed into fresh garments, with amice and stole. He would have worn a stole even in travelling, as a symbol of his priesthood (as did St. Hugh of Lincoln, as late as the XIIc., but now only the Pope does). It assumed by the IXc. approximately its modern shape: long, narrow, end tabbed, fringed, even finished with bells or tassels. Subsequent changes were straight strips in the XIII-XIVc., and in the XVI-XVIIIc. ends widening to shovel shape, decorated with crosses.

Rationale: Episcopal vestment of Catholic Church =*pallium*, worn over chasuble; now, by a specific few bishops. Rabano Mauro believed all church vestments to be derived from those of the Jewish priesthood. This is probably true only of the *rationale* which first appeared toward the end of the Xc. in a breastplate form almost identical with the *ephod* of the High Priest, and was favored by the German bishops of the Middle Ages. It has had *T* and *Y* forms, and is now a humeral collar composed of front and back sections.

Surplice: *Superpelliceum*: *Cotta*: Liturgical, but not blessed. Originally, as the Latin name shows, worn over fur-lined garments. White linen like the alb, (which, since the XIVc., has been reserved for mass); trimmed with lace or embroidery; great variation in sleeves. Originally long, it began to be shortened in the XIIIc. and by the XVIIc. was very short.

Tunicle (Dalmatica Minor): peculiar to subdeacons at Mass; bishops wear it beneath the dalmatic, but always under chasuble, never under the cope. It is a plainer, narrower-sleeved dalmatic, without clavi, often fringed, originally white, the alterations of which parallel those of the dalmatic. It was the sub-deaconal costume in the VIc. in Rome, and in Spain (where deacons wore alb, not dalmatic).

In the IXc. tunicle not dalmatic, was the liturgical dress of Roman cardinal-priests. From this time through the Middle Ages the tunicle was worn by acolytes. By the XIIc. bishops, hitherto garbed in tunicle or dalmatic, wore both together.

MONASTIC BACKGROUND

399 A.D.: Monasticism introduced into Rome from East; worked West.

IVc.: Cassian and St. Jerome mention cowl as part of monk's dress.

529 A.D.: St. Benedict founded Monte Cassino, which by VIIc. had vast influence. The Benedictines were the only great order in the West, between the decline of the Columbans and the XIc.

590 A.D.: "Monasticism ascended the papal throne in the person of Gregory the Great" (Milman), who sent St. Austin to England where he became Archbishop of Canterbury.

614 A.D.: St. Gall, disciple of the Irish monk Columban, founded the Swiss monastery of St. Gall. The influence of the Columban hermits was immense but short-lived.

English missionaries to the continent:

680-755 A.D.: St. Boniface to Germany.

827 A.D.: Denmark, Sweden.

Xc.: Christianization of Norway begun; missionaries to Slavs.

XIIc.: Christianization of Sweden completed.

IX-Xc.: Degradation of papacy.

910 A.D.: Cluniac reform under Abbot Odo.

XIc.: Decline of Cluny.

XIc.: Religious revival:

    1039 A.D.: Vallombrosa, and its lay brothers.

    1084 A.D.: Carthusians.

    1095 A.D.: Fontevrault, double order, men, women.

    1098 A.D.: Cistercians, with lay brothers.

    All these, like the Benedictines were contemplative, concerned with saving their own souls.

    Canons Regular, Augustinian. Contemplative, plus holy orders.

Crusades, Military orders:

    1023 A.D.: Knights Hospitallers: Militarized later.

    1118 A.D.: Knights Templars.

    1190 A.D.: Teutonic Knights.

XIIc.: Regular and secular clergy under absolute jurisdiction of bishop; some monks free of bishop's jurisdiction. Growing criticism of Church wealth.

XIIIc.: Rise of mendicant* preachers, teachers, universities; decline in XIVc. Like the military orders, active; saving souls and bodies of others. Friars: free of bishops' jurisdiction; no authority but Pope.

    1210: Franciscans (Grey Friars) (Poor Clares, female).

    1216: Dominicans (Black Friars).

    1245: Carmelites (after 1287, White Friars).

    1256: Augustinians (Eremites).

    1535: Jesuits.

MONASTIC ORDERS AND DRESS

Just as the costume of nuns today is essentially that of married women or widows of the Middle Ages in their *barbe,* so all the elements of Monastic costume, habit, cowl, scapular, etc., had been or were still being worn by the laity. Even after these had become specifically monastic garments, the honor of meeting death or being buried in monks' costume might be accorded to lay persons. It must be remembered that a monk was not necessarily a priest; although he might be one, a large proportion of monks were not priests.

Cowl (Cucullus); hooded outer garment, common to both sexes during the Middle Ages, but accepted, from IVc., as essential part of monks' costume. Cowls of both summer and winter weights were prescribed for his followers by St. Benedict. In the ninth century it was forbidden priests as distinctive of monks. The monastic cowl

---

* Francis of Assisi and the earlier mendicants had literally obeyed the command "Sell all that thou hast and give to the poor." The friars, however, soon accumulated the wealth they had condemned in the Bishops, but declared that it belonged not to themselves but the Pope. They obeyed the recommendation to evangelical poverty literally: "Money, the accursed thing, they would only touch with gloves on their hands." G. M. Trevelyan, Eng. in the Age of Wycliffe, Longmans, Green, London, 1904 ed., p. 150, note 3.

and habit are of the same color. The cowl of the Augustinians is still a separate hood; that of the Franciscans small, but attached to the habit; the cowl of the Cistercians, Benedictines, etc., is a great hooded mantle worn as choir dress. It exists, vestigially, on the cope, as the *scutum.*

Scapular: narrow, poncho-like garment now forming an essential part of monastic garb, and worn over the habit. It was a farm-laborer's apron when St. Benedict prescribed it as the work-garment of his monks. A hood, and later, shoulder flaps were often added. The front and back were sometimes connected by straps at the sides, to prevent flapping. By XIIIc. had to be worn by monks even at night.

Benedictines (Black Monks); from first half VIc., monks living in common, and in study, lives of discipline and obedience. They amassed great libraries like Monte Cassino; were early missionaries (today, teachers); did manual work, practicing all the arts and industries; and attended 7 or more services a day. All dressed alike according to the prescription of their founder St. Benedict at Monte Cassino, in "undyed" black wool garments, which came in summer and winter weights:—a sleeved habit; hooded sleeveless cowl (*cuculla,* a slave's garment by law in 382 A.D.), not more than 2 cubits long (cubit-length of arm below elbow, 18" 22"), as a sign of humility; scapular as work-apron; shoes and stockings. Funnel-shaped sleeve of the XIVc. retained in modern habit.

Cluniac: reformed Benedictine, and therefore black-garbed monks, under the customs of Cluny from 910. All the Cluniac Congregations of Europe were under the rule of the Abbot of Cluny, who thus became one of Europe's most powerful figures. The Romanesque Church of Cluny was, until St. Peter's in XVIc., the largest church in Europe, and the richest and most magnificent in its ceremonial.

Carthusians: ascetic monks, living in isolated cells, each with its own garden, and workshop, as established by St. Bruno, 1084, at the Grande Chartreuse. They illuminated manuscripts, carpentered, gardened, ate alone, meeting only at Mass and Sunday dinner. They wore "rude garments" and a hair shirt; now a habit of white serge.

Fontevrault (and other double monasteries from VIIc.): associations of monks and of nuns, under Benedictine rule, living parallel lives in neighboring but separate establishments, both under the rule of the Abbess of the aristocratic nuns, herself a great lady, like St. Etheldreda at Ely; or, at Fontevrault, a member of the French royal family.

Cistercians (White or Grey Monks): association

of monks, each house under the rule of its own Abbot, crystallized c. 1112 at Clarevaux by St. Bernard and a group of noblemen. Dedicated to the Virgin, it was an offshoot of the Benedictines, and rose in importance during the XI-XIIc. decline of Cluny, from which it radically differed in its ideals of functional, unostentatious simplicity. Manual and field labor given a great place; a great number of illiterate lay brothers were admitted as farmers, shepherds and work men; the Cistercians became the greatest of the monastic architects, developed the vaulted style which led to Cathedral Gothic; organized and improved farm, land and mine management; led the English wool trade, and accumulated vast properties; the active life was beginning to gain in importance.

William of Malmesbury (1125-35), writing of the foundation, and regulations of the Cistercians says:

"They wear nothing made with furs or linen, not even that finely spun linen garment which we call staminium (shirt); neither breeches, unless when sent on a journey, which at their return, they wash and restore. They have two tunics with cowls, but no additional garments in winter, though if they see fit, in summer they may lighten their garb. They sleep clad and girded. . . ."

To distinguish themselves from Cluny, they first wore a brown habit; then a gray or white habit, with a brown, or, later, black scapular. The Trappists are an offshoot of the Cistercians.

Augustinians: There are many sorts.

The *Augustine Eremite Friars* started with XIc. hermits, gathered together in mid-XIIIc. into the 4th mendicant preaching order. Luther had been an Augustinian. They dressed in black, and became "barefoot friars" in 1570.

The *Augustinian Canons Regular* are associations of priests, headed by a Prior, not an Abbot. They take vows similar to those of cloistered monks, but live lives of service to a parish. The English Austin "Black Canons" wore a long black cassock, under a white rochet, with a hooded black cloak.

The *Praemonsterian* Order of *Canons Regular,* founded 1120 by St. Norbert, were preachers dressed in white.

The *Gilbertines,* founded in England in mid-XIIc., were a double order; the Canons under the rule of St. Augustine, dressed in black with a white cloak; the women were under Cistercian rule.

The *Trinitarians* were Canons Regular, established in 1198 to recapture prisoners from the infidels; they still do rescue work in Africa. They wore white with a red and blue cross.

Canons Secular: lived similar lives in the same association, without taking vows, and while retaining their own incomes, in addition to re-

ceiving their share of that of the association. By the late XIc. established with enormous success in England. In the XVIc. time of Leo X, English Canons Regular "dressed in violet, like other clergy," said a contemporary account. Now generally dressed in white, sometimes with a scapular, but essentially and characteristically differing from other ecclesiastical dress in the wearing of the *Rochet*.

Franciscans (Friars Minor, Gray Friars): originally a confraternity of mendicants, founded by St. Francis of Assisi, 1209-10, and dressed like the poor and sick among whom they worked with idealism and spiritual fervor. Duns Scotus, Roger Bacon, Bonaventura were Franciscans. They wore a coarse gray habit (now brown), with a small attached hood, and a characteristic cord belt. They might not ride a horse or wear shoes.

Poor Clares: order of Franciscan nuns, founded 1214 by St. Clara. From the earliest times there were nuns, as well, of all the great monastic orders, the Abbesses frequently being the sisters of the founders, as in the case of St. Benedict.

Friars Minor Capuchins: reformed Franciscans (1525), attempting to return to the ideals of the founder. Bearded, bare-foot, and with a conical pointed hood on habit.

Dominicans (Black Friars, Jacobins): originally (1216) mendicant preachers and teachers; (Thomas Aquinas); painters (Fra Angelico); conservatives, in charge of the Inquisition; many houses of nuns. Dominicans dressed only in wool; white tunic, black cloak and hood. By 1220 rochet replaced by scapular.

Carmelites (White Friars after 1287): originally mendicant friars, in whose costume there have been many changes. They now wear a white cloak over a brown habit. Their first costume of girdled tunic, scapular and hood, was of black, brown or gray. The cloak worn over it was composed of vertical stripes, 3 black, 4 white. At this period they were called *fratres barrati* or *de pica* (magpie). By 1287 the white wool cloak was adopted (White Friars).

Jesuits: members of the Society of Jesus, religious order founded by the Spanish St. Ignatius Loyola in 1535. Rigorously chosen, trained and disciplined; teachers and missionaries, under the motto "Ad majoram Dei gloriam." No specific garb was prescribed by the founder: Jesuits are usually dressed like Spanish priests of Loyola's time.

MONASTIC MILITARY ORDERS AND THEIR DRESS

Military religious organizations arose during the Crusades. For whatever purpose they were originally founded, they all degenerated into aristocratic military clubs as they accumulated wealth, from the bequest of the pious at home, or by conquest, plunder, exploitation and trade.

Knights Templars: earliest, and prototype of the military religious orders of the Catholic Church. In 1118 a band of 9, "Poor Knights of the Temple" from Northern France, banded together to protect pilgrims to the Holy Land. At that time they were without rule or habit, except that they were short-haired, rough bearded, and never wore parti-colored garments. They enjoyed immunity from excommunication and received many "rogues and impious men, robbers and committers of sacrilege, murderers, perjurers, and adulterers," who had gone to the Holy Land to plunder, or to save their souls. In 1128 they adopted the rule of St. Benedict, and with it the Cistercian (reformed Benedictine) white wool habit, with a red cross, granted the order mid-XIIc. by Pope Eugenius III. This cross appeared also on their half-white, half-black banner called *Beauséant,* which floated from the great round tent of the Grand Master, who with 7 dignitaries ruled the order. These personages, and those unmarried knights who were under permanent vows, wore the white habit, as, in a closed version, did the chaplains: the brown or black capes of the sergeants and menials were likewise charged with the red cross of the order, the motto of which was *Non Nobis Domine.* The Knights quickly rose in numbers and power. With their fortified Temples all over Europe, leading to Asia, they became the founders of international banking, and the financial districts of London and Paris grew up around their headquarters and bear their name. At the height of their power, jealousy and scandal led to their trial and suppression (1312).

Knights of St. John of Jerusalem (Hospitallers, Rhodes, Malta), were started during the First Crusade to defend pilgrims and nurse the sick. They were established under Augustinian rule, and at first wore any clothing, so long as it was poor.

The first reference to the military side of the Order is in 1200. In 1248, the knights wore a long, wide black tunic with a white cross on the breast; it had supplanted a black *cappa clausa* which proved inconvenient in battle. In 1259, Alexander III gave the infirmarians a black mantle with a white cross, and to the knights a red surcoat with a white cross.

Like the Templars, they were ruled by a Grand Master and 7 dignitaries, including a Marshal for the European knights, and another, the Turcopilier, in charge of the native troops. Unlike the Templars, the knights, whether under vows or lay "subscribers," had to be aristocrats and legitimate. This was not the case with the sergeants and infirmarians. The order was cosmopolitan, predominantly French.

The order, dissolved by Pope Clement in 1314, was reorganized as the Knights of Rhodes, which they took over. They were now a federation of national "langues," not French-controlled. The order turned into the leading sea-power of the Mediterranean while opposing the Turks. In 1523, they removed to Malta. Their membership, disturbed by the Reformation, was effectively ended by the French revolution, although the order is still in existence.

Teutonic Knights: Their order was modelled on the Knights Hospitallers. Like the Hospitallers, it was aristocratic, requiring 16 quarterings; but unlike them, it was intensely German, not cosmopolitan. Its beginnings were made during the 3rd Crusade at the siege of Acre, when a tent, made of their sails, was used as a hospital ministering to German wounded. In 1192, they were regularly established under Augustinian rule, with privileges like those of the Hospitallers and Templars, as a combined hospital and military order, supported by the rich traders of Bremen and Lübeck; ruled by a Grand Master and 5 dignitaries, it had lay members as well, dressed in white with a black cross.

As "missionaries to the Baltic pagans," they conquered and exploited E. Prussia, in XIIIc. They were magnificent, aristocratic and cultured landowners and traders, whose great glory began to fade after their defeat by the Lithuanians at Tannenberg in 1410; in XVIc., they finally withdrew from East Prussia.

The Papal *Knights of the Holy Sepulcher* were supposed to have been founded by Godfrey of Bouillon; in 1496, Pope Alexander VI granted them a red Jerusalem cross with Latin crosses at the angles.

The aristocratic Spanish military orders grew out of an earlier Portuguese one.

St. James of Compostella (of the Sword) was believed to have been instituted by Ramiro II, king of Leon, but it probably dates from Pope Alexander III in 1175. The badge is the red lily-hilted sword of St. James (Santiago).

The *Knights of Alcántara* (1156) and *Calatrava* (1158), organized to fight the Moors in Spain, carry the cross fleury, respectively red and green.

After the fervent crusading days were done, knightly orders continued to develop, but their character was honorary, bestowed by a ruler, rather then ecclesiastical. As we come upon illustrations of their insignia, we will take up the *Garter,* founded in England in mid-XIVc.; the *Annunziata,* established in 1360 by Amadeus VI of Savoy; the *Golden Fleece* of the Burgundian dukes and the later Empire, which was started in 1429-30; and the French orders of *Saint-Michel* (1469, and *Saint-Esprit* (1578.) (See also Heraldry.)

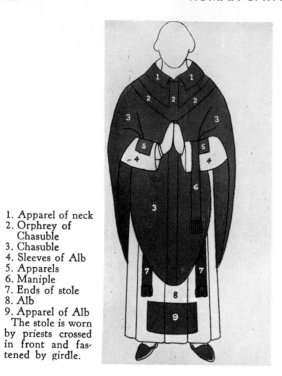

1. Apparel of neck
2. Orphrey of Chasuble
3. Chasuble
4. Sleeves of Alb
5. Apparels
6. Maniple
7. Ends of stole
8. Alb
9. Apparel of Alb
The stole is worn by priests crossed in front and fastened by girdle.

327

1. Apparel of neck
2. Dalmatic or tunicle
3. Orphreys of Dalmatic
4. Sleeves of Alb
5. Apparels
6. Maniple
7. Apparel of Dalmatic
8. Alb
9. Apparel of Alb
The stole is worn by deacons over the left shoulder.

328

329

330

1. Miter of which there are three sorts:
   1 pretiosa
   2 auriphrygiata
   3 simplex
2. Crozier
3. Apparel of neck
4. Chasuble
5. Pallium
6. Orphrey of Chasuble
7. Maniple
8. Dalmatic
9. Tunic
10. Apparels of Alb
11. Gloves
12. Ends of stole worn without crossing
13. Alb
14. Sandals
15. Buskins

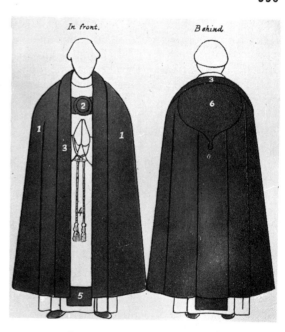

1. Cope
2. Morse
3. Orphrey
4. Alb
5. Apparel
6. Hood
7. Girdle of Alb

327. Priest Vested for Mass.

328. Deacon Vested.

329. Archbishop Vested for Mass.

330. Priest in Cope.

The Dark Ages: Feudal Power

VII-XI Century Background

The unification of costume during the first six centuries was followed, between Justinian and the Crusades, by a period of establishment of regional differentiations which the Crusades in turn helped to amalgamate into European costume. It is helpful to recapitulate the forces, the influence of which will appear in costume.

The Lombard invasion divided Italy into three elements: Byzantine, (Ravenna), Lombard, and the Papacy. Justinian (527-65) failed to unite Western Europe, but did reconquer Italy from the Ostrogoths and gain a foothold on the Spanish pininsula against the Visigoths (cf. VIc. sarcophagus, Xc. and later Visigothic material). The empire he left was a stable one; it declined after his death, but Constantinople, in the VII-VIIIc. withstood Persian and Mohammedan sieges, and was ravaged for the first time in 1204 by Crusaders. The dispersal of its looted treasures spread its civilization over all Western Europe. Greek Byzantium accepted image-worship in the VII-VIIIc., stood at its height in the IX-XIc., and its elements remain clearly in the art and costume of Russia, which accepted Greek Orthodox Christianity after the baptism (Xc.) of its ruler, Vladimir.

The Western church, which was in its infancy in the IVc., expanded with the spread of monasticism in the IV-VIc., from Italy to France, and to the British Isles and Ireland, during the Papacy of Gregory 1 (590-604). Back to the continent and over the world there spread from the two islands the horde of missionaries, Christians since Caesar's time, who formed one of the most notable civilizing forces of history, such as St. Boniface, to Germany, and the Irish monks with their distinctive manuscript style, to the French monasteries already established at Tours and Poitiers, and to St. Gall in Switzerland, founded 614 by the most famous follower of the Irish monk Columban.

The great infiltration of the Goths was over. The Visigoths had come to Spain in 378, and had been its kings, 415-711; Alaric and his Huns at Rome, 410; the Vandals in Africa; the Burgundians and Franks; the Angles, Saxons and Jutes to England from the IVc.; the Ostrogoths in Italy.

In 711 the Saracens had crossed the Mediterranean into Spain and founded the Moorish kingdom of Granada, which endured to 1492.

The Gauls helped to spread the Roman culture with which they had begun to be familiar in Caesar's time. Christianity grew; civilization and rising power seemed its concomitants: Clovis and his Franks were converted on a battlefield in 496; the Burgundians in 517; the Visigoth King by his Frankish wife in 550; the Lombards by the end of the VIIc. The Xc. Norsemen were converted and civilized by the XIc. into the superb Normans, who took England and wrested from the Mohammedans the two Sicilies, where their contact with Mediterranean culture helps to make understandable their spectacular rise.

The VIII-XIc saw the gulf between Latin and Greek cultures widening, and Western Christianity on the defensive, leading to the Crusades. New strength was given the degraded Papacy of the late IXc. to the early Xc., through the Cluniac reforms of Odo, and its connection with the rising power of the new German Empire under Henry III-IV, and the increasing power and dignity of the College of Cardinals.

Within half a century, under the Conqueror's third son, Henry I, London had begun its rise to pre-eminence. Norman merchants from Rouen on the Seine had traded with England in wine and fish for a century, under special privileges; now they flocked to their new capital on the Thames bringing craftsmen of all sorts. They did not attempt to exploit the English, and Norman taste, elegance and dress quickly spread.

Dress of Britons, Gauls and Franks

Our information about the dress of the Gauls and Britons is based on some eye-witness accounts; bas-reliefs on Roman arches, probably somewhat compromised with Roman costume; Gallo-Roman statues showing hooded cloak variants; actual costumes found in Danish peat-bogs; and metal objects fished out of the rivers or dug up.

The Britons, their skin dyed or tattooed blue with woad, loaded their arms with gold bracelets, sometimes weighing as much as 16 oz. each. Fur was available and warm. Cold and the shapes in which fur came led to closer-fitting garments and to tailoring, as against the loose, cool, primarily rectangular Mediterranean costume. The leather work of their sandal-moccasin shoes was admirably sophisticated. Hemp and good woolen materials were woven, even in twilled and diapered designs; they wove patterned, multi-colored braids and tapes, fringes and nets. The colors they loved and the bright woven stripes and checks of their materials impressed Roman observers. There was a woolen trade with the British Isles which by the VIIIc. was sending an especially good cloth to the Continent. Silk was familiar to them, through the Romans, before they knew cotton, a cape of which created a sensation on the streets of Tours in 580.

Their original garments, when made of woven materials, seem to have been less tailored than those of skins; their smocks short and sleeveless. With Roman citizenship or familiarity, this smock grew wider, longer, girded, long-sleeved: became a tunic. Their cloaks were of the many practical varieties, saggum, paenula and poncho-like garments which the Romans had incorporated into their own dress.

The Gallic *breeches* (Lat. *braccae,* Fr. *braie*) had a drawstring at the top, which, by the XII-XIIIc. was threaded through the waist-band to give some points of attachment for longer hose.

Under the Merovingians and the Carolingians a sock-like boot to the calf, or a fabric hose (*chausse*) was drawn up over the breeches. Other forms of breeches were tied at the ankle, or strapped under the foot. Looser varieties of breeches, and longer hose were bound around the leg with puttee-like or cross-gartered bands. Later we see the hose tied below the knee so that the wide top hung down in a cuff: or a knot tied at the top of short hose, made them serve as a sort of fitted boot; worn, by the XIIIc., over longer hose, pulled up in front to fasten at waist-band of breeches.

The Gauls seem to have been extremely shoe-conscious. It is from *gallicae,* the word for their shoes, that the French *galoche* and our word *galoshes* derive. The VI-VIIIc. boot-hose, *pedule,* was considered almost a Frankish uniform. For six hundred years, until the advent of long gowns for men, it is the legs, their decoration, wrappings and footgear, which form the most interesting and varied part of male costume.

Charlemagne (who donned Roman costume on only two occasions in his life) wore a linen shirt under a knee-length tunic, together with bands for his legs, and a small cap. But the shirt, though no longer uncommon, is not yet obligatory male wear, and the head is commonly uncovered (except in travelling or working in the fields) until the end of the Middle Ages, when the lengthening point of the travelling hood, wound around the head to get it out of the way, led to the hat.

There are not many remains of armor between the VIIc. and the Crusades.

Frankish leaders of the Merovingian period are known to have worn helmets and cuirasses. Soldiers had their heads partly shaved, and the rest of the hair dyed red, braided and wound protectively around the head, and held by a leather band. They carried small, round, convex shields; 32″ swords, narrow an ddouble-edged; or the single-edged *francisque,* a sword which could also be thrown; 20″ single-edged dagger; barbed javelin;

long-headed iron-tipped lance; and a battle-axe.

A monk at Saint-Gall, who saw Charlemagne at the end of the IXc., says that he and his men were "literally encased in iron; the emperor wore an iron helmet, his arms were protected by plates of iron, his thighs by scales of the same; the lower part of his legs was protected by greaves, and his horse was clad in armor from head to foot." Charlemagne's soldiers, by his laws, wore armlets, helmets, leg-pieces, and carried shields. The finely tempered long swords of the Iron Age were given names, like Weyland's "Mimung," Charlemagne's "Joieuse," and King Arthur's "Calibran" (Excaliber). (Quoted from Demmin.)

Women's costume for many centuries was based on a tunic, wider than the under tunic (A. S. *cyrtel,* Eng. *kirtle*), which had close sleeves and fell short of the ground and served as house or work dress. This might and later did have a linen shirt beneath. Over the tunic a *mantle* was worn; head was covered by a veil susceptible of arrangement.

By the XIc. gloves and handkerchiefs were in established use, the *fichu* decorated the tunics of both men and women, and men's hair, after Charlemagne, was worn short.

ARMS AND ARMOR

Charts of development of arms and armor of the VII-XVIIc. (illustrations 435-446) have been massed, for convenience, under the chapter: "Knighthood in Flower." Arms and armor of the VII-XIc. are discussed in the captions of illustrations 334, 339, 342, 344, 370-374. Illustrations 165-170, on helmets, may also be consulted.

DEVELOPMENT OF XI-XII CENTURY DRESS

In the XIc. the long garment of the gentry reappears. Called the *bliaud,* the upper tunic is not the Roman tunic, but a cut and fitted gown (by mid-XIc. laced tight at sides or back, and showing the undergarment through the lacings) gored at the sides for additional width in the skirts, and with shaped sleeves. It was worn long by women; and from below the knee to very long by men.

It reflected many oriental influences. The Eastern dalmatic had continued in use in the Carolingian, and in the deliberately Byzantine Ottonian courts, whose contacts with the growing Italian sea power facilitated the passage of Byzantine traders and goods to Germany. The Normans, after recapturing Sicily from the Mohammedans, 1061-91, had carried oriental trends back to the continent and to England, and with the Crusades, all Christendom was brought into contact and trade with the East, so that the *turban,* introduced into Persia only in the Xc., had spread to Europe by the XIc.

The *surcoat,* a sleeveless upper garment, worn both by knights over armor, and by ladies, appears mid-XIIc.

The sleeve of this tunic was typically tight in the upper arm. It either broadened out into a wide funnel, showing the tight sleeve of the under tunic, *chainse,* or continued tight and widened very suddenly and extremely, below elbow, perhaps just above wrist, trailing to the ground and so long that it had to be knotted up, or with a stone tied in the end, might serve as a weapon. By the end of the XIIc. a plain wide sleeve appeared, much longer than the arm, so that it had to be turned back, or hung over the concealed hand.

Decorative bands, orphreys,* heretofore at neck and wrists, moved to horizontal positions around the upper arm, and across the bottom of a shortened and narrowed upper skirt, showing the extremely full skirt (now frequently trailing, and of another, usually lighter color), of the under garment, *chainse,* or kirtle.

While the under tunic often served alone for house wear (in which case it was usually girdled and edged in the older style at wrists, hem and down the front) both garments were now commonly worn, not only by women of the nobility but by those of the class first styled "bourgeoisie" in 1134 by Louis the Fat, and the rapidity of whose rise may be gauged by the fact that in 1374 Charles V ennobled all the bourgeois of Paris. Beneath these two upper garments was worn a linen *chemise,* the tucked or embroidered edge of which showed as the neckline of the upper garments rapidly lowered.

Under the *bliaud* men wore a shirt, frequently long and wide, and breeches, onto the belt of which were laced the hose.

The *cape,* oblong or semi-circular, which had been, for a short time in the XIc., fastened uncomfortably on the left shoulder, is soon fastened in front by a cord running across the chest, where a lady would hold it with two fingers, in a gesture typical of the Middle Ages.

Toward the end of the twelfth century came the introduction of *pelissons,* fur-lined over-garments for men and women. A little later the short Angevin mantle which gave him his nickname was introduced into England by Henry Courtmantel. For travelling, the old paenula and pluviale with capuchon were worn as hoods through the Middle Ages, particularly after the last third of the XIIc., but until the end of the XIVc. men went ordinarily bareheaded.

Berets and *brimmed hats* like the Greek petasus (especially for travelling) were the headwear in the later XIIc.

The pre-invasion English gentleman wore his hair long, a churl's was cropped. The long hair

* Increasing use of decorative orphreys. They were woven on narrow looms by monks and ladies from VII-XVc., while patterned materials had to be imported from the East, before the XIIIc. rise of Italian factories.

of the English was accepted by the Normans, replaced their own high-clipped short hair, and was brought back by them to the continent. Like the beard, it became standard there, although subject to much criticism and attempted regulation. The Normans shaved; beards became fashionable after the conquest. Henry I allowed a bishop to cut off his hair and beard in 1104. By the XIIc., beards were censored; by the XIIIc. they were definitely less common.

Women wore their hair parted and flowing, or braided, or wound about with ribbon, from the early XIIc.; completely uncovered or bound by a fillet for young girls. The veil of married women was smaller, circular, held in place by a circlet or crown.

Girdles were important. By XIIc. two were worn; one wider, at natural waistline; another knotted below. They were woven like orphreys on narrow looms.

Chief articles of jewelry were large high brooches, set with massive stones, fastening the slit bodice at the throat; there were similar stones on crowns and circlets. There were also clasps for the cords of the cape.

As for shoes, pointed toes (invented, William of Malmesbury said, by Foulk of Anjou to hide his ill-formed feet) begin to appear; wooden pattens were devised for bad weather; high boots, often with turned down cuff were not uncommon through the XIIc.

Materials are dotted with small all-over designs. Embroidery is applied in geometric bands. As cut ceases to be purely utilitarian, decoration becomes fanciful, and the three most typical elements of the costume of the Middle Ages appear: *parti-color,* or *mi-parti; dagging,* slitting of edges, from German; *fur.*

The small furs, suitable for lining over-garments, lend themselves also to decorative piecing, and are lavishly used. The Anglo-Saxon Chronicle records, 1074, the gifts of King Malcolm of Scotland and his sister Margaret to Edgar as "great presents and much treasure to him and his men, skins adorned with purple, sable-skin, gray-skin, and ermine-skin pelisses, mantles, gold and silver vessels." Henry I received from the Bishop of Lincoln a fur-lined cloak worth £100.

As the knights' armor became more completely concealing, the necessity of distinguishing one from another was met by the development of armorial bearings, which apparently commenced (early XIIc.) with fur-decorated shields, soon elaborated with the ubiquitous color. The beginnings of armorial bearings are clearly shown on the Bayeux Tapestry, but the first recognizable bearings are the golden "lioncels" on the shield of Geoffrey of Anjou, a wedding gift (1129) of his father-in-law, Henry I of England (see Ill. 396).

331-333. VIIc. Gospels of Durrow. (Trinity College, Dublin.)

Symbols of Sts. Matthew and Mark. Irish priest, in patchwork mantle and multi-colored shoes; tonsured in the Celtic manner, the tonsure of St. John or, mockingly, of Simon Magnus, by which the front hair was shaved from ear to ear. In allusion to this period of tonsure were the first two words of the Druid prophecy about St. Patrick: "Adze-head will come with a crook-head staff, in his house head-holed (*chasuble*)."

332. IXc. 820 A.D. Gospels of MacRegol. (Bodleian Library, Oxford.)

St. John with his symbols: the saint is tonsured according to the method variously called British, Ro- man or St. Peter's, used in France, Spain and Italy until the late Middle Ages, after which it was retained for monks and friars, but reduced in size for clergy. During this period of illumination the folds of what was probably a garment of solid color were indicated as multicolored stripes; a thousand years later, French painters begin to experiment with not dissimilar analyses and syntheses of color. These are typical examples of the crude, raw color and interlaced manuscript style disseminated by the Irish missionaries).

334. VIIIc. 700 A.D. Found at Vendel, Uppland, Sweden. (State Historical Museum, Stockholm.)

Helmet decoration: Warriors wearing coats of ring mail, helmets, swords, lances analogous to the equipment of the Danish and Norman invaders of England.

335. XIII-Xc. (Church of Santa Maria in Valle, Cividale del Friuli.)

Persian-Hellenistic stucco figures. Six female saints wearing under-tunics with tight sleeves, embroidered at the wrist, beneath super-tunics with wide sleeves, the sleeve edges and hems banded with jewelled embroidery. One figure still bears the clavi: her neighbor to the left wears an embroidered mantle. Four wear Byzantine collars and headdresses. The figure at the extreme right carries her hand beneath her mantle, holding it up in the Byzantine manner.

336. 741 A.D. (Rome, S. Maria Antiqua.)

Romanesque wall painting. St. Cyr, in tunic and dalmatic with clavi, and decorated pallium. As in the Gospels of MacRegol, the shadowed folds of a plain colored garment are rendered as multicolored stripes.

337. VIIIc. Celtic-Teutonic-Franco-Byzantine; Illuminated Manuscript. (Treves Capitular Library.)

Saints Michael and Gabriel: in dalmatics with clavi and pallium. Compare with Gospels of Durrow and MacRegol for evidences of the manuscript style brought to the Continent by the Celtic monks.

338

339

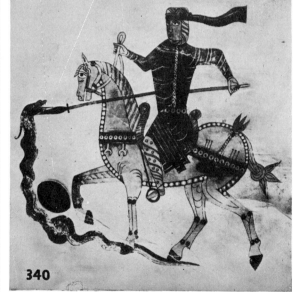

340

338. IX-Xc. Carolingian (Valenciennes Ms. 99, 31x) Apocalipsis Figurata.

The illustrations on this page are from three of the many manuscript versions, between the IX-XIIIc. of the *Commentaria in Apocalypsem* of Beatus of Valcavado (730-798). The only female figure ever shown is the Scarlet Woman, riding upon the Beast. In this example, her tunic still carries the clavii; collar and headdress still very Byzantine.

339. IX-Xc. Carolingian. (Valenciennes Ms. 99, 34x) Apocalipsis Figurata.

Knight on horseback, with a saddle blanket, but without a saddle; first used in Europe in IVc. Before the VIIc. introduction of stirrups, the warrior used his lance as a vaulting pole. Stirrups are dependent from a harness, to which the saddle blanket is strapped. His cape is fastened by a circular brooch, paved with stones, of a type already current for several centuries. Dots probably a method of enlivening the delineation of folds, but the period of small all-over designs on clothing is approaching.

340. Xc. 975 A.D. Spain. (Gerona Cathedral 60) Beatus.

Peaked saddle of oriental type, typical of Middle Ages. Definite stripes now used, horizontally and vertically. Hooded for travelling; patterned leg bandages.

All photographs courtesy of Morgan Library, New York

341. Spanish Visigothic 976 A.D., from Monastery of San Millan de la Cogolla. (Madrid, Escorial Ms. D. I. I.) Codex Aemilianensis.

This manuscript, executed by Velasco and his pupil, Sisebuto, shows the Visigothic Sovereigns of Leon, under whose reign the book was written.

Clundeswith (641-652): who carries in his hand what well may be the *mappa* of a late Roman consul. *Receswith* (649-672): by whom the Visigothic laws were issued, 645 A.D. *Egica* (687-701). *Queen Urracha*: decorated veil. *Sancho I* (955-967). *Ramiro III* (967-982), son and grandson of the traditional founder of the crusading Order of the Knights of St. James of Compostella. *Velasco*: the scribe with his tablets. *Sisebuto*: the bishop, wearing the mitre which came into use during Xc.; pastoral staff. *Sisebuto*: the notary, with his tablets. (See page 145.)

342. XIc. Carolingian. From the Monastery of Fulda. (Rome, Vat. Reg. Lat. 124.)

German work, showing Louis le Debonnaire, the last Carolingian, looking no more forceful than he was: his tunic is treated to give a debased approximation of Roman armor; the shirt set on the low line of the abdomen-protecting moulded lorica; the second belt across the breast. His cape, half a crescent in cut, and tied at the shoulder, is typical of the period. He is wearing Frankish sock-boots, *pedules*. The use of the letters of the Greek alphabet as a decorative background had begun in earlier centuries; words and sentences were used as decorative embroidered bands.

Fulda, founded 744 by a follower of St. Boniface, and endowed by the Carolingians, was the greatest Benedictine monastery in Germany, ranking with Monte Cassino in Italy and St. Gall in Switzerland.

343. End IXc. Carolingian, from Ratisbon. (Munich, Stadbib. Cod. Lat. 14345.)

A tonsured ecclesiastic, in a dalmatic of the original form, tunic, and fine shoes, is being stoned by men in girded tunics (by now definitely shortened to above the knee) and sock-boots over breeches.

344. IXc. (Trier. Stadtbib. s. 31). Apocalypse.

The soldiers' shield is becoming more convex; its boss more prominent. The tunic is above the knee;

346

breeches are cross-gartered or bound, above shoes. The cape, in cut, is between a half-crescent and a semi-circle. Heads are typically bare. The costume of the male saint is now set by tradition: the female saint is dressed as a lady of the period.

345. End IX-mid Xc. (St. Gall Lib. Cod. 250). Pen drawing.

Andromeda, in a short-sleeved super-tunic with embroidered bands and shoes.

The Monastery of St. Gall was founded in 614 by the most famous disciple of Columban, the Irish monk. St. Gall traveled the continent, France, the Vosges, founding the great Swiss monastery.

346. Xc. Ottonian. German. (Conde Museum, Chantilly) Registerum Gregorii.

Otto II enthroned, surrounded by the provinces, Germania, Francia, Italia, Alemania, paying homage. Otto II (955-983) held splendid court at Rome and died there after being crowned Emperor of both Rome and Germany by Pope John XIII, having restored Benedict VII to the Papacy, and secured the election of Peter of Pavia as John XIV, during the decadence of the Papacy. The costumes are deliberately Byzantine, as befitting the heir to the Holy Roman Empire. The band of embroidery on the upper arm will be seen persisting halfway through the XIII c.

347. Xc. 980-990 A.D. Ottonian from Reichenau. (Heidelberg Univ. Lib. Cod. Sal. IXb.)

Enthroned Virgin: *Ecclesia*. In this ms., illuminated in the VIIIc. Benedictine Monastery of Reichenau, she is dressed like a late-Roman matron, with Byzantine superhumeral collar and headdress.

348. Xc. before 920 A.D. (St. Gall, Stiftsbibliothek, Cod. 22). Psalter Aureum.

King David, in a short tunic, with decorative banding at hem, neck and cuff of the tight sleeves. Had the sleeves been wide, their edges would not have been decorated. Breeches, sock-hose and decorated shoes. Fringed cape, tied and clasped on left shoulder.

349-350. End Xc. Ottonian from Reichenau. (Munich State Lib., Cod. Lat. 4453. Gospels of Bamberg Cath. Treasure, Cim. 54.)

349. Provinces of Slavonia, Germania, Gallia and Roma paying homage to Emperor. Byzantine-clad females. Slavonia: white tunic with black and pearl-edged scarlet superhumeral, violet cloak decorated,

like those of all the others, in gold bands set with scarlet circles and edged with pearls. Germania: pale green cloak over bright blue tunic, decorated gold superhumeral. Gallia: plain white tunic, rose overgarment slung like cape. Roma: bright blue undergarment, orange-yellow overgarment; gold-decorated scarlet napkin over hands, Byzantine-fashion, as she offers jewelled tribute.

350. Enthroned Emperor and his suite. Probably Otto III, "The Wonder of the World," who was crowned German King, 983, later King of the Lombards, made his cousin Bruno, Pope Gregory V, and was by him crowned Emperor in 996 at Rome. There the Emperor lived in a court modeled on that of Constantinople, and rather in the style of the preceding century.

The Emperor wears a white under-tunic, a violet tunic richly banded in pearl-edged, gold bands, encrusted with red and blue stones. Pale green mantle simply fastened on right shoulder. Dark green shoes,

351

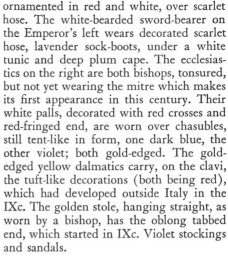

ornamented in red and white, over scarlet hose. The white-bearded sword-bearer on the Emperor's left wears decorated scarlet hose, lavender sock-boots, under a white tunic and deep plum cape. The ecclesiastics on the right are both bishops, tonsured, but not yet wearing the mitre which makes its first appearance in this century. Their white palls, decorated with red crosses and red-fringed end, are worn over chasubles, still tent-like in form, one dark blue, the other violet; both gold-edged. The gold-edged yellow dalmatics carry, on the clavi, the tuft-like decorations (both being red), which had developed outside Italy in the IXc. The golden stole, hanging straight, as worn by a bishop, has the oblong tabbed end, which started in IXc. Violet stockings and sandals.

352

353

351-354. End Xc. Anglo-Saxon. (British Museum). Tenison Prudentius.

Prudentius (348-c. 410), the early Christian poet, was a nobleman and a lawyer who retired to a monastery at 57; of his many books the most influential, "Psychomania," is an allegory of vice and virtue, portraying the Church in its struggle with paganism.

This English Prudentius Ms. shows the circular Anglo-Saxon cloak, both whirling, and lying in folds over the arm. All classes dressed alike. Men wore a linen shirt (A. S. *syrec*); breeches (A. S. *bréc,* "breeks") which were usually of linen also; a girded tunic (A. S. *roc,* German, *roc*-coat) which was of wool, with circular-cut, knee-length skirt; a short mantle, frequently circular, fastened on the right shoulder or in front; and ankle-high shoes.

Women wore an ample outer tunic, with a more fitted garment (A. S. *cyrtel*-kirtle) beneath; a very large mantle, one end of which is shown fastened around the waist; and a veil, the length of which can be seen on the figures of the dancing female in the girded tunic (352). Practically the dress of a Roman matron.

354

355

356

355-356. XIc. 1078-81.

355. *Nicephore Botaniate and his wife, Marie,* protected by Jesus Christ.

356. *Nicephore Botaniate,* Emperor of the Orient, accepting, on the recommendation of the archangel Michael, the works of St. John Chrysostome, presented by that saint.

These engravings were made in 1844 by the Count Auguste de Bastard after a manuscript in the Bibliothèque Royale (now the Bib. Nat. in Paris) No. 79 in the Fonds de Coislin. They show Byzantine costume in its Eastern development from which Russian costume evolved.

The saint is dressed as a bishop of the Eastern church, in *omorphion* (pallium), caught on the left shoulder; *phenonion* (equivalent of chasuble, worn from IVc., usually shortened in front); *epitrachilion* (stole; in Eastern church, a strip with an opening for the head at one end, hanging down in front); *sticharion* (alb), with a *zone* (belt) which is indicated by the blousing, although not shown; and *epimanica* (separate cuffs, allied to the liturgical gloves of the Roman church). A form of dalmatic, caught together but not sewed at the sides, called *saccus,* was worn from the Vc., though not by the saint shown here; a bishop would wear it now. He is tonsured in the short clip which the Eastern church allowed, in place of the shaved Roman tonsure.

The archangel illustrates the change which took place in the Byzantine chlamys with tablion, soon after Justinian. Hitherto flowing, so soft that the left

hand beneath could be used, still covered by it, in the typical Byzantine gesture which we still see at Arles in the XIIc. the chlamys has now become so stiff, of embroidered and jewelled brocade, that it has become necessary to cut the lower edge sharply up to free the left arm, after which the hemline again drops. The shape of the tablion is no longer simply rectangular. His tunic has embroidered superhumeral and hem-band; he wears embroidered Byzantine shoes.

The long brocade tunic which the Emperor wears, standing between these two, is decorated at the knees and center front of the pearl-studded superhumeral, with the conventionalized flower and leaf forms into which the roundels and orbiculi of the IVc. have altered.

As shown with his wife, the Emperor wears, instead of the chlamys, the vestigial *toga palmata* of a late Roman consul; a wide strip of stiff embroidery wound around the body. At the left arm, where it would be hopeless to attempt to drape it, an entirely different piece of soft stuff emerges from its end, to be thrown over the left arm. He carries in one hand the Roman consul's *mappa.*

On the costume of the Empress, nothing remains of the *toga palmata* or *praetexta* but a strip dropping from beneath the Byzantine collar, and the crescent-shaped apron to match—a formalization of the drape of the *sinus* under the right arm and across the body. There is no attempt here to commemorate the draped end hanging over the left arm.

The Emperor and his wife are essentially dressed alike, as Western Europeans will be, after the Crusades, and in materials more luxuriously elaborated, and sleeves more sophisticatedly cut than we will see, even then, in the West. Their sceptres, head-dresses, shoes are typically Byzantine. The band of embroidery across the upper arm passed into Western costume and will be seen until well into the XIIIc.

357. Early XIc. Anglo-Saxon. (London, Victoria and Albert Museum.)

Ivory carving of Virgin, Child and three wise men. The Virgin wears the typical costume of an Anglo-Saxon lady. Over her head the couvre-chef of the married woman or nun, in this case held in place by a circlet. Her mantle, closed in front, might have fastened on the left shoulder in the previous century. Two very full tunics; the upper (A. S. *cyrtel*-kirtle) is the shorter, and its bell-sleeves and hem have a patterned edge. The girdle, which does not show, would, certainly in the previous century, have been a folded, wide strip. The three kings wear the longer tunic with bell sleeves of this century, and their full circular Anglo-Saxon capes fall in stylized folds.

358. XIc. French. St. Pierre. (Moissac.)

Gravestone of Abbot Durand. The amice which the Abbot wears around his neck is at this period just beginning to be decorated. The chasuble with orphreys, is still tent-like, the sides not yet trimmed away. The dalmatic was granted to abbot's use in XIc. Early use of tunicle with dalmatic. Alb has been embroidered since Xc. Long stole. Sandals of early fenestrated type. Pontifical ring on middle finger of right hand. Pastoral staff of an abbot, not in this case bent, but an elaboration of the shepherd's crook.

359. XIc. Spanish. (Burgos, Santo Domingo de Silos.)

Stone relief of *Journey to Emmaus*. Three male figures wearing the longer, more fitted outer garment of this century, over a long, wide under-garment. The sleeves, wider at the wrist, are not typically bell-shaped. Pouch, decorated with cockle shells of Pilgrim is the *gypcière* (from F. *gibier,* the game which the hunter put in the pouch) increasingly important throughout the next two centuries.

360

362

361

360. XIc. Spain, (Burgo de Osma. Cath. Arch., 2. Cod.)

Beatus manuscript. Not only the rider's garments but the background and the bodies of the horses are covered with the small all-over patterns typical of the period.

361-363. XIc. 1028-72 Spain-S. France. (Paris Bib. nat. lat. 8878.)

361. *Beatus of Liébana or St. Sever,* executed by Stephanus Garsia. The only female shown in Beatus manuscripts is the Scarlet Woman. Her undergarment has long, tight sleeves. Over it she wears a short-sleeved, girdled tunic with a fuller skirt than heretofore. The rectangular mantle over her head is caught at center-front by an enormous clasp, and is surmounted by a small circular veil; decorated shoes.

362. The Kings and merchants lament the

fall of Babylon: The small, all-over design of grouped dots is typical of the period. Full circular capes, fastened on either shoulder. Loose breeches and shoes like sock-boots. Hair will remain short until after the Norman conquest of the long-haired English. The crowns and head-coverings worn in Spain during this and the centuries immediately before and after, are full of interest and special character.

363. Soldiers: Their capes, like those of civilians, close either on the right, or on the inconvenient left shoulder. Their kite-shaped shields, derived from the Frankish, are shorter and wider than the Norman, and like them decorated, though not yet heraldic.

363

Photographs courtesy of Morgan Library

364

365

364-65. XIc. 1014. German. (Bamberg, Cathedral Treasure.)

Coronation tunic of Henry II.

Of the 4 coronation ceremonies of the Roman Emperors, the 2 most important were that in which he received the imperial crown from the Pope at Rome, and the German coronation ceremony at Aix-la-Chapelle. This tunic formed part of the German regalia.

The X-XIc. tunic is shorter, often above the knee; neck, cuff, and hem embroidered. The diagonal neck-closing ends in XIIIc.

366-369. XIc. 1023. Italian. (Monte Cassino. Monastery Library.)

Mediaeval Encyclopaedia by Rabanus Maurus (766-856), abbot of Fulda.

366. De monacchis: Benedictine bishop, monk and abbot, dressed according to the directions of St. Benedict, founder of this monastery and order, in hooded sleeveless black wool cowl, over habit; and shoes and stockings. The monk wears a long working scapular; that of the abbot is fastened together at the sides. The bishop's crozier is of a very advanced type; that of the abbot of an earlier sort.

367. De coniugiis: Byzantine influence is still visible in the unbelted women's gowns, and in the placing of decoration on the simple home costumes of these noble Italians.

368-369. De tentoriis: Workmen in tunics, breeches, hose and shoes, dyeing bed-curtains and an unfinished long tunic.

370-374. XIc. Anglo-Norman. (Bayeux Cathedral.)

Bayeux Tapestry. The tapestry was probably commissioned by Odo, bishop of Bayeux (who had fought in the Battle of Hastings, and was William the Conqueror's brother) for the decoration of his cathedral; and was more nearly contemporary than was formerly believed. It is 20″ wide and 231′ long, contains 72 scenes worked in 8 colors. Packed full of information, it shows Halley's comet (which had glowed for 7 nights in 1066), and the earliest representation of a court dwarf in Europe, carefully marked as such above his head. (See Appendix.)

William of Malmesbury describes the English and Normans at the time of the Conquest, only 30 years before his birth:

English: short garments to mid-knee; hair cropped; beards shaven; arms laden with golden bracelets; skin adorned with punctured designs. "They were accustomed to eat until they became surfeited, and

370.

to drink until they were sick. These latter qualities they imparted to their conquerors. As to the rest, they adopted their manners."

Normans: "were and are even now proudly apparelled, delicate in their food but not excessive; a race inured to war, and can hardly live without it; fierce in rushing against the enemy, and where strength fails of success, ready to use stratagem, or to corrupt by bribery. They live in large edifices with economy; envy their equals; wish to excel their superiors; and plunder their subjects, though they defend them from others; they are faithful to their Lords, and though a slight offense renders them perfidious, they weigh treachery by its chance of success, and change their sentiments with money. They are, however, the kindest of nations, and they esteem strangers worthy of equal honor with themselves; they also intermarry with their vassals. They revived, by their arrival, the observances of religion which had everywhere grown lifeless in England. You might see churches rise in every village, and monasteries in the towns and cities built after a style unknown before." William allowed the enemy dead to be properly interred; returned Harold's body to his mother without taking the ransom she offered; and was crowned by Archbishop Aldred, being careful not to use Stigand, who was not canonically an archbishop.

370. Shield bearings. 371. Jazeran armor. 372 (left). Harold being offered the crown by 2 members of the Witan, one of whom carries the official axe. 372 (right). Harold as King, with Stigand the archbishop. 373-374. Warriors.

The details of Stigand's unprincipled 50-year climb to power fill much space in the Anglo-Saxon Chronicle. He appeared in 1020 as Canute's chaplain; got his first bishopric in 1043, and was deposed in 1044 (the year of the great famine) because of his influence over the king's mother; succeeded to the Bishopric of Winchester in 1047 (the year when even the fishes froze). Stigand's rival, Robert of Jumièges, archbishop of Canterbury, came back from Rome with his pall* in 1051, was banished the next year, and Stigand was finally established as archbishop in his place. Then followed 6 years of failure to receive recognition from Rome: Stephen IX died; the new Pope, Benedict X, granted Stigand his pall, but was himself deposed; then papal legates arrived in 1070 to depose Stigand, who died in prison.

Stigand is tonsured, and without mitre, which did not appear until XIIc.; he wears a plain *amice;* his famous *pall;* a chausuble, long in back, cut short in front; *alb* with large sleeves (undecorated until XIIIc.); *stole* with fringed ends: and he holds in his left hand the *maniple* (which, after XIIIc., will be worn over the left arm).

* See Ecc. Cost. for its necessity.

371

Harold's courtiers are shown with high-clipped Norman haircuts, which the Normans abandoned in favor of the longer hair of the Anglo-Saxons, a style which they took back with them to the Continent, where it remained standard for several hundred years.

William's cavalry is shown attacking the *testudo* (tortoise) shield-wall of the English, who fight still as described by Fridegarius at Zülpich in 612 A.D. "In their weapons and their manner of fighting, the bands of Angles, Jutes, and Saxons who overran Britain were more nearly similar to the Franks than to the German tribes who wandered south." The Franks fought at Poictiers as 200 years before, in deep column or wedge.*

Both armies wear conical "Norman" helmets with nosepieces, and hooded *hawberks* (*birnies*) of the chain mail, which had come from Scandinavia. Rings are either sewn on a foundation, or are linked together. There are overlapping scales of jazeran armor (see Norwegian tap., Ill. 411). Other hawberks are of quilted material or leather (small recumbent figures). These hawberks have short wide sleeves; they are of knee-length (in late XI.; lowered to calf, mid-XIIc; shortened again to the knee, mid-XIIIc.); they are slit, front and back, for comfort in riding, and so could have been tied about the leg, trouser fashion, as they seem sometimes to be.

The forearm is protected by the long sleeve of the under-garment, probably quilted against chafing. The legs are covered, and further protected by spiral or cross-gartered leather strips, above a separate shoe.

Archers, on both sides, are unprotected by mail, as they will continue to be until XIIIc.; they shoot from the earlier, low position.

Both armies show 7-foot spears with distinctive pennons, indicating rallying points; javelins; maces (one, with a knobbed head, can be seen flying); and swords with broad blades, stout plain cross-guards, and knobbed pommels. The English use, in addition, the Danish battle-axe.

Shields are of two types: the very long, kite-shaped shield, used by both armies, is slung by shoulder-straps, *gigues,* and held by a loop on the back, *enarmes.* The circular Danish shield, of wood with a center boss and reinforcements of iron is used only by the English.

The shields are decorated in armorial spirit, but the devices cannot be identified as those of any of the known Norman families of the end XIIc.; the same characters reappear carrying differently blazoned shields. Malmesbury (1119) tells of William, Earl of Poitou, "a giddy, unsettled kind of man," who after his return from the Crusades, "wallowed in the sty of vice, and rendered absurdities pleasant by a kind of satirical wit." Among several wonderful anecdotes, he relates that Poitou abducted the wife of a viscount; he was madly in love with her, and placed her figure on his shield, wishing to "bear her in battle in the same manner as she bore him at another time. Being reproved and excommunicated for this by Girard, bishop of Angoulême, and ordered to renounce this illicit love: 'You shall curl with a comb,' said he, 'the hair that has forsaken your forehead, ere I repudiate the countess,' thus taunting a man whose scanty hair required no comb." This is still decorative fantasy, not imposed on future earls of Poitou.

* J. Horace Round: *The Commune of London and other studies,* Archibald Constable & Co., London, 1899.

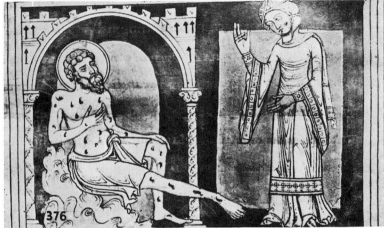

375-378. 1080-1150. German. (Library of St. Peter's Monastery.) Salzburg Antiphonary.

The new costume of women, and the new long gown of gentlemen (as well as the familiar short one) is shown beside the standardized long religious costume of saints, and two liturgical costumes: bishop and deacon.

The mitre of the bishop shows the beginning of the horned effect which it started to assume in the XIIc. He wears an elaborate pall over a chasuble; it has the embroidered edge which did not appear until XIc.; dalmatic, notched, but still sewed together at the sides; stole with the tabbed ends of IX-XIIIc.; alb, with the embroidered cuff which had come in the previous century; and embroidered liturgical shoes.

The deacon is wearing the dalmatic, distinctive vestment of deacons; alb; stole; and maniple, which until the XIIc. was sometimes carried in the left hand, sometimes worn, as it now is, and as he does, on the left arm.

The saints wear the straight tunic, and pallium, instead of the fitted garment and chlamys of the gentlemen, whose sleeves, while cut tight as before, are so long as to wrinkle up the fore-arm.

Job's wife wears the fitted and shortened upper tunic, with a decorative band across the hem, and sleeves widening, funnel-shaped, from a tight upper-arm. The cuff of the tight sleeve of her undertunic is also edged with embroidery, and she, as well as one of the gentlemen, wears the little scarf which appears to be worn at this time only in Germany. Her headdress is the turban which spread so rapidly westward after its introduction from Persia, only a century or two before.

Knighthood in Flower: XII Century

XII-XIV Century Background

THE soaring mediaeval religious impetus built cathedrals; it undertook crusades, which mingled and broadened the peoples of Europe and gave them great events to be celebrated in the Latin which was the common language of all educated people. Under the Templars' protection traders and preaching friars made their way East.

But feudal power, at its height in the Xc., was waning. The placing of the higher clergy among the nobility and the lower among the common people had led to the critical spirit out of which arose the mendicant orders. The struggle between attainment and privilege increased with the growing Universities of Paris, England and Italy, whose Latin-speaking scholars came, even on foot, from many walks of life and countries and wandered from university to university.

By the XIIIc. the centralized monarchical government had won over the feudal. Towns grew and were enfranchised, and the bourgeoisie who inhabited them rose into increasingly consolidated power. Guilds of craftsmen and merchants were formed; trade with Asia increased through the Mediterranean, opened up by travellers like Marco Polo; and the Baltic and North Sea trade was controlled by the Hanseatic League.

In the XIIc. a bourgeoise, no matter how rich her husband might be, was fined for dressing like a noblewoman. By the XIVc. she no longer imitated, she surpassed the noblewoman. This determination to wear what you chose developed the personal in costume; and fantasy and frivolity in dress followed the terror and masochism engendered by the plague of 1348-50, which reduced the population by a half. The resulting scarcity of workmen, who had been oppressed by the feudal nobility, as it simultaneously lost power and required wealth to keep pace with the bourgeoisie, made possible the revolutions of the common people in France and England in the second half of the XIVc.

A woolen mill had been established in Norwich in 1331 by Queen Philippa of Hainault with Flemish weavers, but the raw wool which formed so great a part of England's export trade was woven almost entirely by Flemish mills, and it was to protect this trade that the Hundred Years War was undertaken, as well as because of Edward III's claim to the throne of France, or the danger to the French crown inherent in the feudal Norman coastal possessions.

The slight alterations in costume between the XI-XIIc. have been discussed in the chapter "The Dark Ages."

The costume of Europe in the XIIIc., like its civilization, is French, and increasingly so as the court of Burgundy makes fashion in the XVc. The decline of the feudal nobility is clear by the time of the death of Charles the Bold of Burgundy in 1477.

Heraldry: Its Development

Heraldry is the science of armorial bearings as blazoned on the shield. O. Fr. *blason* originally meant shield. As armor improved in XIIc., shields became smaller; the embroidered design of the surcoat (hence "coat-of-arms," coat-armor), was transferred to the shield, and to the pennon and the trappings of the horse. Blasoning came to mean the bearings on the shield and, eventually, the description of the bearings.

Many factors entered into the development of armorial bearings:

A *Closed Helm* concealed the knights' identity. William the Conqueror had to remove his head-piece after the Battle of Hastings, to convince his men he still lived.

Seals, originally used by kings and great personages, came into universal use by gentry, colleges, guilds, in an age when few could write. The first signature of an English King is that of Richard II (British Mus. Cat. of Seals). These seals often show unblazoned shields, together with badges which, a generation later, are used to blazon shields. By mid-XIIIc. seals became armorial in character, and in 1520 seals and signatures were used together. In 1677 the signature, without seal, became legal on documents.

The *Crusades,* especially the third, were major influences. English, French and German knights had to be identified and rallied under a leader's symbol. Organization, distinguished deeds to be commemorated, brought the use of inherited surnames.

Inherited surnames related to the place of residence, the personal peculiarities, or the prowess of the bearer, his neighbors and tenants, or his office or occupation. Chamberlayne* cites great offices of honor from which surnames came: "Edward Fitz-Theobald long ago made Butler of Ireland, the Duke of Ormond, and his Ancestors, descending from him, took the surname Butler." Chamberlayne's own surname dated from 400 years before his time when Count Tankerville of Normandy was made chamberlain to the king of England. Saxons, Chamberlayne explains, often added "son" to the name or nickname of their father or mother. Saxon names were based on office: Spencer—steward; Kemp—O.E. soldier; place of abode: as Underhill, Atwood or Atwell, often abbreviated later to Wood, Wells; or color or complexion: Fairfax—fairlocks,† Pigot—speckled. With this, much more armorial use of *Canting or Punning Names as*: *Salle*—2 *sal*amanders *sal*ient in *sal*tire. Armorial bearings often gave a more accurate indication of relationship than surnames. The classic example is shown in the arms of the Lullings, originally Lucys, who had retained the canting Lucy coat-of-arms: 3 luces (pikes), after altering their surnames to that of their Yorkshire property.

Tournaments, of the XIIc. onwards: the decorative and social gaining over the utilitarian; magnificent pageants heightened by pennons and banners; streamered crests of knights; crests and armorial trappings of horse, all stemming from the original bearings of the shield. Opponents at tourneys were identified by the spectator's knowledge of blazoning, as football players are now recognized by the numbers on their jerseys. Blazonings began to be collected, codified, and controlled by heralds, and books on heraldry were published. If a gentleman owned a book, it was probably on heraldry; if he owned 10 books, half of them might well be about blazonings, like the library of a XVc. Paston, containing the first English book on heraldry (see English XIVc.)

The armorial shield was in actual use from the XIIc. to 1500. The Bayeux Tapestry, XIc., shows the beginnings of armorial bearings, on 3-foot kite-shaped shields. But these are not yet identifiable as inherited. In the first quarter of the XIIc. Paris armorers provided the English with shields decorated with designs, animals, lions, dragons, etc., but not yet differentiated arms.

The earliest known recognizable bearings were on the shield of Geoffrey of Anjou, 1129 (see illus.), the same golden lioncel used by his grandson, William Longueépée. From this time (when one man might use different arms at different times) to the XIVc., the science of heraldry was in the process of establishment. The rise of the great German tournaments was a major factor. It is stated by a XIVc. authority that the tournaments were open only to those bearing arms since four generations. The XIIIc. English tournaments were also important stimuli. In XIIIc. armorial bearings were hereditary in Spain and Italy, and beginning to be so in Sweden. Shields smaller.

The golden age of heraldry was the period from the XIVc. to 1500.

Coats of arms were established, hereditary; arms differed for sons, bastards, cousins, neighbors. By unwritten law, no two people bore the same arms. Froissart records the rage of Sir John Chandos at finding his arms born by the Marshal of the French King, Lord John de Clermont; because of the truce they had to wait until the next day to settle the matter by arms. Mounted men began to discard shields.

In 1347 we see the first English brass without shield (Wantone) and, in 1360, the last English brass showing shield as part of equipment (Aldeborough). The shield was retained by foot soldiers who did not bear coats-of-arms. To 1500 a lady bore her father's arms on her mantle; her husband's on her kirtle. After that she bore arms impaled; husband's dexter side, father's sinister; if arms appeared on mantle only, or were the same on mantle and kirtle, father's arms were used.

Blazoning developed functionally, out of structural elements of the wooden shield, covered with leather, tanned or furred, braced and reenforced, horizontally, vertically, diagonally with metal strips, edged and supplemented with metal bosses and knobs, all of which lent themselves to decoration. The heraldically undifferentiated crosses on the Crusader's shields, and the first application of bold simple color, followed the shield's structural divisions.

Crests, Wreaths, and Lambrequins. The rise of the tournament on the continent, particularly in Germany in the XIIc., and in England, in the XIIIc., favored the increasing use of the crest, surmounting the helm of the knight and the head of the horse; fans, feathers, birds, beasts, implements and objects of the same character as those used on badges and banners.

The earliest known crest is that on the second seal of Richard II; the lion of England mounted on a fan-shaped crest. But it was in Germany that the crest was most fantastically elaborated, with the back of the moulded leather cap, on which the crest was mounted, ending in flowing, scalloped *lambrequins.* The crest is separated from the coat-of-arms, above which it is set, by a crown, coronet, or rope-like twist of two colors. A lambrequin may fall from the crest to the shield, and the shield may be hung by "supporters," usually animal or plant. Supporters are personal; there may be several, and a person may change them during his lifetime. From James I's time, the coat-of-arms of England has been supported by the

---

* Edward Chamberlayne: The Present State of England, 38th ed., London, MDCCLV.
† A notably dark Fairfax, the Parliamentary general (cf. Eng. XVIIc), was nicknamed "Black Tom."

Scottish unicorn and the English "lion" (actually a leopard since no more than one lion may be blazoned on a shield).

Badges and Banners: The use of badges and war cries* preceded that of armorial bearings. The banner bearing the lord's badge was enormously important as a rallying point†. In the reign of Edward III banners were large, increasing in size, to the 9-yard banner of a king and the 4-yard banner of a knight by the time of Henry VIII. Badges on garments helped to identify followers, who, in the XIVc., were otherwise not dressed alike until the liveries of the XIVc. guilds led to retainer's liveries in the XVc. (when they often remained armorial in character, after the XII-XIVc. passion for applying armorial decoration on everything had passed.) Froissart says that the Flemish soldiers from Alost, Grammont, Courtrai, and Bruges wore liveries to distinguish them from one another: some blue and yellow jackets; a welt of black on a red jacket; white chevron on a blue coat; green and blue; lozenged black and white; quartered red and white; all blue. In 1399, at the entry of Queen Isabella into Paris, 1200 citizens, mounted on horseback, dressed in uniforms of green and crimson, lined both sides of the road.

Richard of Bordeaux, in his tournament at Windsor, had 40 knights and 40 squires, clothed in green with a device of a white falcon.

Great families were as well-known and often referred to by their badges as by their names:

Broom (planta genista), from which the family name: Plantagenet.

Black Bull: Thos. P., Duke of Clarence.

Dun Bull; Blue Boar: Nevill.

White Boar: Humphrey, Duke of Gloucester.

Swan: Lancaster; from de Bohun.

Black Plume: Black Prince (P. of W. feather).

Silver Ostrich Feather: Beaufort.

Golden lion queue fourche: Suffolk.

Rouge Dragon: Wales.

Bear and Ragged Staff: Beauchamp, Earl of Warwick.

White Rose: York.

Red Rose: Lancaster; from Beaufort (Somerset badge in Shapespeare).

Rouge Croix, of St. George: England.

Knots (resembling initial): Bourchier, Stafford, etc.

Silver Crescent: Percys of Northumberland.

Gold Portcullis: Lancaster; from Beaufort (end XVc. Tudor badge).

---

* England: St. George for (e.g.) Guyenne. Percy: Esperance. France: God and Saint Denis; Montjoye Saint Denis; Bertrand du Guesclin: Saint Yves Guesclin.
† Banners also helped to approximate numbers. Froissart approximated the English and French armies opposed at Vironfosse: English: 74 banners, 230 pennons in all, 27,000 men, and King of England, Lord of Kus, Lord of Breda Duke of Gueldres (nephew of King of England) and Sir John Heinault. French: 220 banners, 5,000 knights, 40,000 soldiers, 4 Kings, 6 Dukes, and 26 Earls.

Collars: Heavy chains about the neck were an important part of costume from XIIc., particularly during XIV-XVc. They were, logically, utilized as marks of respect, fealty, and alliance.

There were the collars of orders of knighthood, such as: mid-XIVc. Order of the Garter, with its forms: Garter; collar of knots and roses with an enamelled pendant of St. George mounted (dates from Henry VIII); and the Lesser George pendant, showing St. George within the oval of a purple garter. 1362. Order of the Annunziata, founded by Amadeus VI of Savoy: collar of love-knots and roses. 1429-30. Order of the Golden Fleece, established by Philip of Burgundy: collar of fire-stones and steels; pendant fleece. 1469. Order of Saint-Michel, of Louis XI: linked cockle shells. 1578. Order of the Saint-Esprit, of Henry III of France: collar of HL and fleurs-de-luce; gold and white Maltese cross pendant with an outstretched white dove; often hung on blue ribbon.

There were also personal collars, as: XIIIc. Broom-cod collar of Charles V, sent Richard II by Charles VI, and worn by Henry VI, combined with the SS collar, signifying his claims to both kingdoms. XIVc. SS collar of the House of Lancaster. The most famous English collar, from its inception, while Henry IV was still Bolingbroke, it carried the White Swan of Bohun as its pendant. The SS collar was also worn by women. End XVc. The SS collar of Henry VII; rose or portcullis pendant. XVIc. Legal dignitaries also wear the SS collar; the Lord Chief Justice wears it today. Since 1545, Lord Mayors of London wear the SS collar; not granted them, but bequeathed by former mayors. Various other collars are worn by the mayors, of other cities, as: the triple chain, worn since 1670 by the Lord Mayor of York. Kings-of-Arms and Heralds still wear the SS collar.

The collars of the House of York were: Falcon and Fetterlock. Third quarter of the XVc. Suns and Roses; as pendants, the White Lion of March, the Bull of Clare, the White Boar of Richard II. 1485. Red and White Roses, of Lancaster and York combined into Tudor Rose of Henry VII. XVc. Collar of the White Hart, of Richard II; hart enclosed in park palings.

HERALDIC OFFICERS: "ANCIENTS"

Heralds had existed, as messengers, before armorial bearings; another facet of their work grew out of the XIIc. minstrels, who sang the deeds of victors after combat. Heralds wore the badge of their masters, and while on errands of war and peace, the person of the herald, as his master's proxy, was considered sacred, although the herald himself was a person of no rank whatsoever. As armorial bearings came into use, heraldic officers were concerned with the direction of tournaments, the counting and recognition of those killed in battle,* the funerals of peers and prelates, and questions of precedence. They controlled the use and recording of coats-of-arms, and collected information, in England, on regularly scheduled "visitations" through the counties.

English heraldry surpassed that of any other country, even arms-loving Germany, in its perfection of detail. All the heraldic officers seem to have been established early in the XIIIc. The Norroy King-of-Arms dates from late in the XIIIc. But the first picture of a herald bearing his master's blazon is of Flemish herald Gelré, 1369. The French King-of-Arms, Montjoye, with 10 heralds and poursuivants, was established by Charles IV in 1406, before the incorporation of the English College of Heralds by Henry V. in 1420.

The position of heralds was well established in England by 1420. In 1500 came the institution of ambassadors who took over many functions from heraldic officers; the use of private heraldic officers died out by the middle of the XVIc. and by the end of XVIIc. heraldic "Visitations" ceased.

Space for a striking display of the master's badge was first found on a short, wide mantle (see Gelré, Flemish 1369), such as that of the Blue Mantle poursuivant, until the XVc. introduction of the *tabard*. The wide loose front and back sections of the tabard offered such a suitable background for display that the tabard has remained the distinc-

tive garment of heraldic officers (see Beauchamp, Warwick Pageant), together with the baton of office (a rod or sceptre) and, in England, the SS collar; worn by the King-of-Arms (gold), heralds (silver); not by poursuivants. At coronations only, the Garter King-of-Arms wears a crown.

Heraldic officers were of 3 sorts: Kings-of-Arms, heralds, and poursuivants. Dukes and marquises were served, theoretically, by a herald and a poursuivant; barons and bannerets, by a poursuivant only. Heralds served as assistants and deputies of the Kings-of-Arms, and were named from places as: Leicester, Windsor, or the Hereford Herald of Humphfrey de Bohun, earl of Hereford. It was as Constable of Acquitaine that Sir Chandos kept the Chandos Herald. The names of heralds also signified their master's foreign possessions, as: Agincourt or Guyenne; or their pretensions, as: Jerusalem King-of-Arms.

Poursuivants were apprentice heralds; named from the badges of the house they served, as Vert-Eagle, poursuivant of Richard Nevill, earl of Salisbury; and the Crescent and Esperance, poursuivants of the Percys of Northumberland, the latter named from a Percy war-cry. Private heralds disappeared by the time of Elizabeth.

* After the battle of Crecy, Sir Reginald Cobham and Lord Stafford, with 3 heralds to examine arms and 2 secretaries to write down names, enumerated as dead 11 princes, 1200 knights, and 30,000 common soldiers. (Froissart).

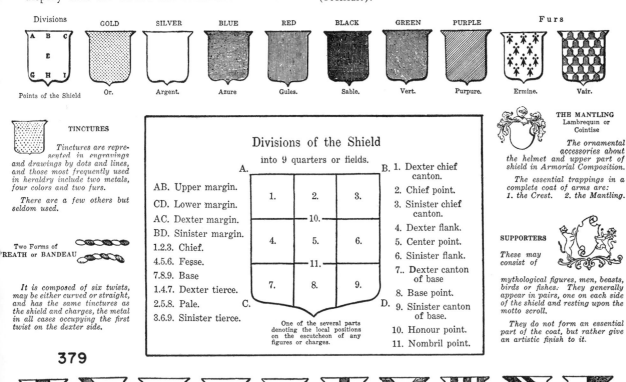

Divisions | GOLD | SILVER | BLUE | RED | BLACK | GREEN | PURPLE | Furs

Points of the Shield | Or. | Argent. | Azure | Gules. | Sable. | Vert. | Purpure. | Ermine. | Vair.

TINCTURES

Tinctures are represented in engravings and drawings by dots and lines, and those most frequently used in heraldry include two metals, four colors and two furs.

There are a few others but seldom used.

Two Forms of WREATH or BANDEAU

It is composed of six twists, may be either curved or straight, and has the same tinctures as the shield and charges, the metal in all cases occupying the first twist on the dexter side.

379

Divisions of the Shield
into 9 quarters or fields.

AB. Upper margin.
CD. Lower margin.
AC. Dexter margin.
BD. Sinister margin.
1.2.3. Chief.
4.5.6. Fesse.
7.8.9. Base
1.4.7. Dexter tierce.
2.5.8. Pale.
3.6.9. Sinister tierce.

B. 1. Dexter chief canton.
2. Chief point.
3. Sinister chief canton.
4. Dexter flank.
5. Center point.
6. Sinister flank.
7. Dexter canton of base.
8. Base point.
9. Sinister canton of base.
10. Honour point.
11. Nombril point.

One of the several parts denoting the local positions on the escutcheon of any figures or charges.

THE MANTLING
Lambrequin or Cointise

The ornamental accessories about the helmet and upper part of shield in Armorial Composition.

The essential trappings in a complete coat of arms are:
1. the Crest. 2. the Mantling.

SUPPORTERS

These may consist of

mythological figures, men, beasts, birds or fishes. They generally appear in pairs, one on each side of the shield and resting upon the motto scroll.

They do not form an essential part of the coat, but rather give an artistic finish to it.

Pale. | Bend. | Fesse. | Bar. | Chevron. | Cross. | Saltire. | Paly. | Bendlet. | Party per pale.

Color is never applied on color, nor metal on metal. The fur *vair* is *argent* and *azure* unless specifically blazoned. *Gules* (red) and *azure* (blue) come from the Persian *gúl* and *lázurd* (lapis-lazuli), and show Arab influence from the Crusades.

The *Ordinaries*, conventional charges commonly found, are shown at bottom, Ill. 379. They are divided by border line *indented*, *engrailed*, etc., shown on Ill. 382.

The *Field* (background) may be semé (powdered or sown with fleurs-de-lys, as in the old arms of France, crosslets, lozenges, etc. Crosses occur in great variety.

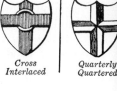

| A Cross Pierced | A Cross Voided | A Cross Surmounted | Couped and Surmounted Voided | Couped Fimbriated | Cross Quartered | Plain Cross Watered | Cross Interlaced | Quarterly Quartered |

THE FILE OR LABEL, Mark of the eldest son

THE CRESCENT, The second son's mark

THE MULLET, The third son's mark

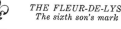
THE MARTLET, The fourth son's mark

THE ANNUET, The fifth son's mark

THE FLEUR-DE-LYS, The sixth son's mark

THE ROSE, The seventh son's mark

THE CROSS MOLINE, The eighth son's mark

THE OCTOFOIL, The ninth son's mark

380

Distinguishing marks applied to the various branches or cadets of a family

MARKS OF CADENCY *to indicate the various branches or cadets of a Coat-of-Arms*

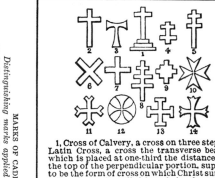

1, Cross of Calvery, a cross on three steps. 2, Latin Cross, a cross the transverse beam of which is placed at one-third the distance from the top of the perpendicular portion, supposed to be the form of cross on which Christ suffered. 3, Tau Cross, (so called from being formed like the Greek letter r, tau), or cross of St. Anthony, one of the most ancient forms of the cross. 4, Cross of Lorraine. 5, Patriarchal Cross. 6, St. Andrew's Cross, the form of cross on which St. Andrew, the national saint of Scotland, is said to have suffered. 7, Greek Cross, or cross of St. George, the national saint of England, the red cross which appears on British flags. 8, Papal Cross. 9, Cross nowy quadrat, that is, having a square expansion in the center. 10, Maltese Cross, formed of four arrow-heads meeting at the points; the badge of the Knights of Malta. 11, Cross fourchée or forked. 12, Cross pattée or formée. 13, Cross potent or Jerusalem Cross. 14, Cross fleury, from the fleur de lis at its ends.

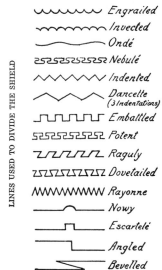

LINES USED TO DIVIDE THE SHIELD

Engrailed
Invected
Ondé
Nebulé
Indented
Dancette (3 Indentations)
Embattled
Potent
Raguly
Dovetailed
Rayonne
Nowy
Escarlelé
Angled
Bevelled

| Cross Pometty | Cross Fleury | Quartered Fleury | Cross Crossed | Cross Nowey | Cross Degraded | Cross Fusilly | Couped and Fitched | Humetty |

Other charges: *Trees, Leaves and Flowers;* naturalistic, and conventionalized (as cinquefoils, fleurs-de-lys, etc.)

Beasts, Birds, and Fish:

Lion; rampant—1 foot on ground; passant—prowling; regardant—looking backward.

Leopard: blazed like lion, but smaller and with face fronting beholder.

Others, often *Canting* (allusive) as: Mauleverer—greyhound, "leverer"; Veel—calves; Griffin—griffon; Shelley—whelk shell; Arundel—martlets, for "hirondel."

Implements: also often canting, as: Malet—mallet; Ferrers—horseshoes; Forester—hunting horn—among which may be remarked the Manche, or conventionalized sleeve.

Roundels, Annulets, Lozenges, etc.

Differenced: to indicate descent, consanguinity, fealty, neighboring place of origin.

This was done in various ways: by changes in color, or in border-line, as engrailed for invected, by additions of:

Label, a horizontal strip across top part of shield, with 3-5 short dependent vertical strips. The label might be decorated in definite ways indicative of order of birth, (marks of cadency). The label was much used by Plantagenet princes (see Monmouth, Clarence; Salzman, Sur. Eng. Hist).

Border, often used by younger sons

Canton, especially England and Low Countries

Escutcheons, of ordinaries, of small charges-semeon a plain field. That is to say, usually a small quartered shield set over a larger quartered shield.

Diminishing, the number of charges; France, not England

Quartering, usually the arms of a queen or great heiress with those of her husband.

OFFICIALS AND ORGANIZATIONS

Religious organizations, colleges, guilds and cities had their coats-of-arms

Archbishops and bishops used their own arms impaled on those of their see (Eng.); sometimes combined, quarterly, or impaled (Continent, and Grand Masters of Hospitallers and Teutonic Knights)

Kings-of-Arms use official arms, as Garter King-of-Arms: argent, St. Georges cross on a chief azure an open crown within the garter, between a lion of England and a fleur-de-lys or.

Voided and Coupled · Cross Potent · Double Fitched · Cross Pomelled · Cross Moline · Cross Masde at each point a Plate · Cross Fusilly · Triparted Fleury · Anseruted

Partitions and Repartitions of the Shield

Parted per Bend · Parted per Pale or Impaled · Parted per Fesse · Parted per Saltire · Parted per Bend Sinister · Parted per Quarter · Parted per Pale Three · Parted Three Fesse · Parted in Three Bendways

Parted in Three Bend Sinister · Parted in Three Mantle · Parted in Three Gusset · Parted in Three Traverse Dexter · Parted in Gyron Bend Sinister Ways · Parted in Pale · Parted in Round Gyrons · Parted per Three Squares · Parted in Four Gyrons

Parted Gyrony of Six · Parted Gyrony of Eight · Parted Champaigne · Parted per Fesse Per Pale · Parted per Pale in Base · Pont Champaigne Concaved · Per Bend Grenelle · Bastille or Embattled · Party per Chevron

Cour · Gore · Gusset · Per Pale and Chevron · Per Pale and Fesse · 381 · Paly of Three Parted per Fesse · Parted per Pale 1st Quarterly · Parted per Pale and Fesse of Six · Paly and Fesse of Nine

Chief · Chief Angled · Chief Chappé · Chief Bevelled · Chief Lowered · Chief Couped · Chief Supported · Chief Surmounted · Chief Corfu

Chief Rebated · Chief Embattled · Chief Potent · Chief Urdée · Chief Nebulé · Chief Engrailed · Chief One Indent · Chief One Label · Chief Arched

Chief Couvert · Chief Wavey · Chief Enmanche · Chief Double Arched · Chief Inverted · Chief Indented · Chief Charged with a Chapournet · Chief Quartered · Chief Point in Point

Chief Rayonne · Chief Vestu · Chief Vestu Sinister · Chasse · Chief Escartelé · Chief with One Embattlement · Chief Bevellways Couped · Chief Inclaved · Chief Nowed

Chief Dovetailed · Ajoure · Bar · Cloet · Barrulet · 382 · Cloetted · Bars Gemel · Barry of Ten · Brettled

383

383. XIIc. 1160-70. English. (Winchester Cath.)
Great Bible of Winchester: Queen. The "manche" of armorial blazoning is descended from the sleeve with a suddenly widened cuff. Queens are represented in very close-fitting gowns, girded very low, in a dipping line, by a knotted sash; mantle always worn.

384-385. 1160-70. (Morgan Library, 619.)
Scenes in the life of David and Samuel. From a folio Bible, executed at St. Swithin's Priory, Winchester, by the artist of the "Great Bible of Winchester," in gradations of cobalt blue; deep, strong vermilion; egg shell colors, from off-white to deep brown; with touches of a dulled light green.

Courtesy of Morgan Library (384-385),

385

The women's costumes show the new sleeve, widening rapidly at the bottom, in a variety of cuts, one of which is so long that it must be turned back (lower l. corner).

The bishop's mitre shows budding horns; amice, as yet, undecorated; chasuble, bordered (since Xc.); pall; dalmatic; embroidered and fringed stole (IX-XIIc. shape); alb. The long garments worn by the saints are the standardized costume allotted to them

since Roman times, and not to be confused with the long fitted garments of the gentry.

The King wears the rich dalmatic which came into regal English use in 1100 with Henry I. His ceremonial garments, like those worn by his gentlemen on state occasions, are longer; the hem of the long-sleeved under-tunic often hangs below that of the short upper tunic, or *hawberk,* in the general elaboration, accompanied by downward movement, which followed the Conquest. The principal hat worn by gentlemen is shaped like the XIc. soldier's *chapel-de-fer,* or the Greek *petasus.*

The most spectacular evidence of the new lavishness is in the use of pieced small furs, ermine and miniver, to line both rectangular and circular capes, which fastened on right shoulder or at center. The Scotch King Malcolm made presents in 1074 of pelisses and mantles of "purple" sable skins, gray skins, and ermine, as well as gold and silver vessels.

There is a parallel growth of interest in all-over patterns on garments (m. fig. in both lower right corners); both are allied with the rise of patterned armorial bearings.

Girdles are knotted at center front, with ends hanging, especially over hawberk and unbloused tunics which permit the effect to be seen.

William of Malmesbury records William II's anxiety, c. 1093, that his clothes should be extravagant, and describes his anger if any were bought at a low price. Men's hair flowed. There were repeated ordinances, forbidding or trying to control the length of the curved points of shoes (which Foulke of Anjou is supposed to have used to hide his deformed feet). "Then the model for young men was to rival women in delicacy of person, to mince their gait, to walk with loose gestures and half-naked, enervated and effeminate. A fierce flame of evil burst forth from what the King conceived to be liberty."

Henry I (1119) was harangued by Serlo, bishop of Sens, on his arrival in Normandy, upon the enormities of the time, one of which was "the bushiness of men's beards, which resembled Saracen's rather than Christian's, and which he supposed they would not clip lest the stumps should prick their mistress' faces; another was their long locks. Henry immediately, to show his submission and repentance, submitted his bushy honor to the bishop, who taking a pair of shears from his trunk, trims his majesty and several of the principal nobility with his own hands." The king returned from Normandy, still wearing his long locks, but his conscience bothered him, he dreamed of strangling by his hair, awoke, and chopped it off. All the knights copied this for a year or so; then went back to vying with women in length of locks, adding false hair if necessary.

Hose and shoes became more elaborate; the decorated shoes of the king are slit up the instep; the tops of loose wrinkled sock-boots are often turned down to show a lining of different color; the hose are now frequently decorated after the manner of the knight's spiral leg-wrappings, which now have feet, not separate shoes. Chain-mail is linked in sophisticated patterns. Chain hose (*chausses*) are used around 1150, as are also quilted or leather puttee-like wrappings, which they supersede in 1190.

The knight's hawberk, now almost invariably of mail, has a shorter, fuller skirt, eliminating the need for slits; the sleeves are typically long, ending in mittens, though occasionally still short, showing the sleeve of the *gambeson* beneath. The *coif-de-mailles* now surrounds the face closely, covering the chin, so that the helm is not always worn. The helm becomes increasingly less conical, and at the end of the century is supplanted by the rounded helm, still with nasal, which has appeared about 1150. The shield, still kite-shaped, is becoming shorter; it can no longer serve as a stretcher; its top is becoming flattened by 1180, and the boss disappears as armorial blazonings come to decorate the shield. The sword-guard has become lighter, and the knobbed ends curve away from the hand to ward the opponent's blade.

386

386. XIIc., before 1170. English. (Canterbury Cathedral.)

Canterbury Psalter. This psalter, written at Christ Church, Canterbury, by the scribe Eadwine, contains interlinear versions of the Psalms in French and Anglo-Saxon; it is the first psalter in French. The chasuble of the tonsured ecclesiastic has a forked cross, and is longer in back, over a checkered dalmatic. The warriors and shepherds are familiar; the vertical slit down the front of the tunic, stressed by bands, is very different from the superhumeral collar we have been seeing.

387. XIIc., 1180-90. English. (Canterbury Cathedral. St. Gabriel's Chapel.)

Wall painting: *Birth and christening of St. John the Baptist.* Ceremonial tunics, longer; longer capes, rectangular and circular, one hooded, all inclined toward center-front closing; decorated hose; studded shoes in sandal designs; sashes, knotted in front and decorated; hat like Greek petasus (see also on Winchester leafs, Ills. 384-85).

388, 389, 391. Early XIIc. French. (Vezelay.)

Vezelay, an abbey church in XIc., was added to in 1125-32, and in 1198-1206. St. Bernard preached the 2nd Crusade and Richard Coeur de Lion assumed the crown there.

These reliefs show many XIIc. developments: tightening upper body, combined with lengthening. The hanging sleeve of the seated figure, if pushed up, would give another typical effect of crinkling. Excessively prolonged sleeves were a fashion of 1100-60.

The tunic shows the characteristic crinkling; probably deliberately pleated; center-front and diagonal closing combined is typical of the century and ends abruptly with the XIIIc. Edges finished with narrow dotted or pierced borders of the early XIIc. Cape edges overlapped and were pinned together with a fibula in Byzantine days and long after; now barely meet and seem to roll away from each other.

Shoes have sandal-like fenestrations; sock-boots of 388 thrust into straps of wonderful, high wooden pattens for protection against mud.

390. XIIc. French. (Arles, St. Trophime, Exterior Portal.)

Procession of men: tunics to mid-calf, with dotted borders; decorated sock-boots; their hands covered in the old Byzantine fashion, which is responsible for the prolonged sleeve of the XIIc. tunic.

392-393. c. 1128. French. (Angouleme, Cathedral of St. Peter, Facade.)

Knights with long, floating veils from conical helmets; hooded shirts, apparently of scale-mail; heavier pike held at lower, horizontal position.

388

389

390

391

394. First half XIIc. French, from St. Etienne Ch. (Toulouse Museum.)

Herodias and Salome: bearded king, center-parted long hair; 2 tunics, tight wrinkled length; one, like cape, decorated with orphreys. Virgin, with long, flowing hair and fillet; trailing clinging tunic; decorated shoes.

395. First half XIIc. French. (Clermont-Ferrand, Notre Dame du Port.)

Psychomania: knights in long tunics; mail hawberks of various patterns; one wears familiar conical helmet; other, the newer chapel-de-fer.

396. XIIc. 1129-51. French. (Mans Museum.)

Limoges enamel memorial plate: *Geoffrey of An-*

jou as lawgiver. The grandfather of "Martel," as Geoffrey was called before he became earl of Anjou at his marriage, having seized a castle and been warned of its owner's rage, said, "he would show the world at large how much an Angevin could excel a Norman in battle, at the same time, with unparallelled insolence, describing the color of his horse and the devices on the arms he meant to use." These devices were still a matter of personal fancy, to be changed at will, but permanency began during Martel's lifetime.

The shield he uses here was given him by Henry I of England, on Geoffrey's marriage to his daughter Matilda, widow of the German emperor, in 1129. It bears the first known recognizable armorial bearings: the three golden lioncels carried by Geoffrey's bastard grandson, William of the Long Sword.

It was Geoffrey's habit of wearing a sprig of broom (*planta genista*) in his cap (see Scotch dress, XIXc.) which gave his descendants the surname of Plantagenet. The shield still protects the entire body; the central boss and functional cross still show. Helm: still

the modified phrygian-conical of the Conquest; but
without the nasal, which was proved to have certain
disadvantages, as when Stephen was captured and
held by the nasal of his helmet at Lincoln in 1139.
Sword; drawn, as lawgiver, is longer and more tapering. Mantle: lined with miniver. Two tunics, both
long and both decorated with gold orphreys. Beard,
long hair.

**397. Mid-XIIc. French. (Chartres Cathedral, Royal
Portal.)**

The Twins: Without hawberk, showing the long
tunic split up the front for convenience. In 1370, Sir
John Chandos, tripping on his long tunic, was unable
to avoid his death-wound. Shield: shorter; top flattened; has lost boss, but decoration is still based on

construction, and is not yet armorial. Hair long, royal
family till mid-XIIc.; then general.

398. Mid-XIIc. French, from N. D. de Corbeil. (Louvre.)

The Queen of Sheba. Dressed in the height of
early mediaeval elegance. Hair: parted in the middle,
hangs in four long tresses, bound in pairs and wound
with colored and golden ribbons. False hair was worn
by both men and women. Cape: long, semi-circular;
orphrey along selvage edge. Upper tunic: bodice
fitted, knitted or smocked. Queens wear two belts:
one at normal waistline; another at hips, covering
seam where full, trailing skirt is gathered onto the
bodice; fastening at center-front by elaborately twisted
and knotted cords, falling below the knees. Kirtle:

398

399

400

401

finely pleated and embroidered, shows above the upper tunic's neckline (considerably lowered, richly decorated, and massively clasped), and at the fitted wrist-length undersleeve. The kirtle sleeve is funnel-shaped, edged with fine pleating.

399. XIIc. French., from Bourges Cathedral. (Berri Mus.)
Queen. Tightly laced bodice, richly bordered, with great brooch; deep, pleated bag-sleeves; finely pleated skirt, widened by fan-shaped, coarsely pleated sections at the sides.

400. XIIc. French., from Bourges Cathedral. (Berri Mus.)
Bishop: unusual mitre, with one horn, worn in front; chasuble with Y-orphreys; decorated stole of modern shape; alb with large apparels above hem, and decorated cuff.

401. Mid-XIIc. French. (Chartres Cathedral.)
Queen of Juda. Hair hidden under small rectangular veil. Fibula on left breast, characteristic of Semitic dress since Hittite times, nearly one and a half millenia before. Upper tunic fitted at the shoulders with three small tucks, caught by buttons; undertunic exquisitely pleated and caught by a smaller fibula. (See Ills. 25, 273.)

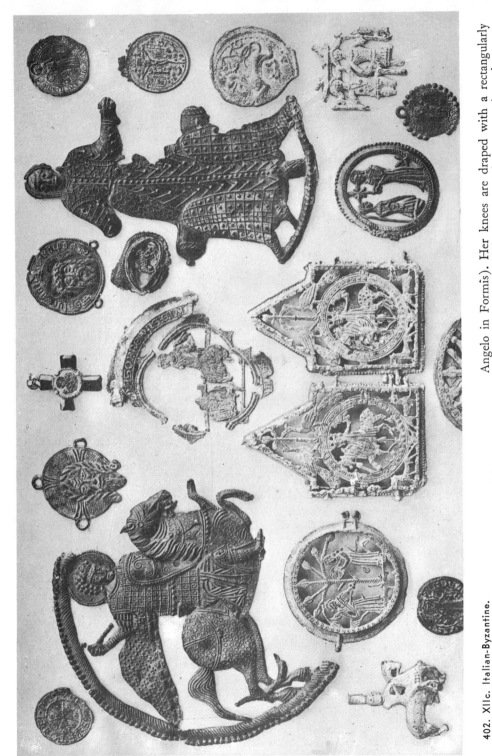

402. XIIc. Italian-Byzantine.

Ornaments; precious metals, and lead. Upper left, Saint George: wearing a practically Roman cuirasse with shoulder-lappets as a hawberk, over long tunic, ring-mail chausses with prick-spurs and knee-plates. Greek anchor cross on small kite-shaped shield.

Upper right, Noblewoman (seated, like Matilda on a sausage-shaped cushion, set on a chair similar to that of the King, St.

Angelo in Formis). Her knees are draped with a rectangularly decorated fabric, possibly to protect her gown, since she wears a gauntlet, on which the claws of the hawk still show. Upper tunic, sleeveless, girdled, decorated with a scale design, is cut deep in the armhole and is split apart below the waist, to show the herring-bone design of the under tunic, which has shaped Byzantine sleeves and a band down the center-front.

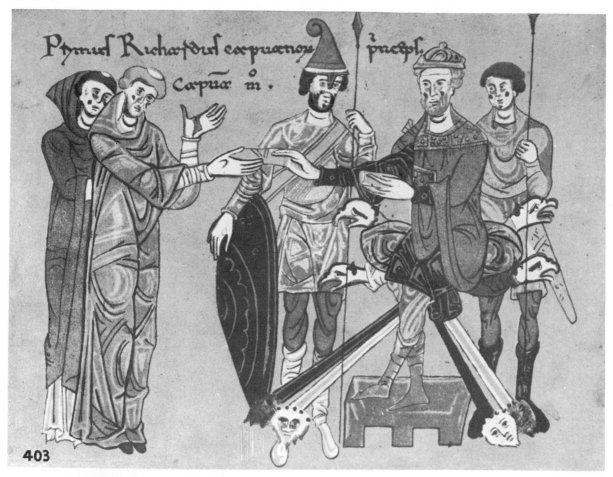

403

404

403. XIIc. Italian. (St. Angelo in Formis.) Miniatures from the Register.

King's costume; impure and muddled Byzantine influences. Mantle has archaic shoulder fastening; tablion of the chlamys is gathered onto a sort of fitted superhumeral yoke. All legwear loose-fitting. The soldier whose shield is neither round nor kite-shaped, wears high, phrygianconical helmet with nasal. Attendant with short wide sword, one monk wear thrown-back cowls.

404. XIIc. Italian. (Morgan Library, Mc. 493.)

Vita Mathildis, by Donizo, her chaplain. Matilda, Countess of Tuscany (1046-1115), was heiress to the greatest estate in Italy, which, deeded by her to the Papacy, formed the largest part of its temporal possessions. Courageous, steadfast and learned, she led her armies into battle on the side of the Guelphs (Papal) against the Ghibellines (Empire), and is known as "The Great Countess." Under her rule, the guilds, out of which the Republic grew, began to be established, and Florence started its rise.

Her wonderful conical hat is set over a veil, the arrangement of which indicates new tendencies; it surrounds the face, and is tucked under another garment at the neck. Her cape, in respect to its asymmetry, and the character of its embroidery, may be compared to those in Ill. 364, 365, 414. The embroidered sleeve of her upper tunic is widely funnel-shaped, but not notably tight in the upper arm. This is, in all its elements, the costume of a very rich and very great lady, less concerned with fashion than with a personal expression of suitable and dignified beauty and comfort.

Donizo, her chaplain, tonsured, wears his every-day tunic and sensible shoes. The bodyguard's shoes show the new tendency to point.

405

406

407

408

405-408. XIIc. 1110-20. German. Stuttgart. (Landesbibliothek.) Stuttgart Passionale.

Three volumes illuminated at the Monastery of Hirsau. 405-406. Martyrdoms: St. Alban's executioner shows the new use of fur (see Ills. 384-85), in a pelisse, with the fabric of the garment serving as lining, and the fur mounted decoratively upon it. St. Alban's collar shows the new interest, both in the vertical line and in the center-front. His has a practical opening-slit; on wider collars the effect of the dependent center block is still often merely decorative. St. Alban's own costume, and those of the torturers

on the other plate, also show lengthening male garments; width introduced at hips by inverted V-shaped insertions; wider sleeves.

Two early Popes: represented in contemporary German dress, with archaic effects.

407. Pope Alexander I, "fifth in line from St. Peter"; outmoded form of mitre, with the daily dress of a dignified German gentleman. Tonsured ecclesiastics with him wear similar, shorter tunics.

408. St. Felix wears a long garment with diagonal neck closing of XIIc; combines features of dalmatic and Imperial regalia.

409

410

411

409. XIIc. German. School of Metz. (Berlin State Museum. Ms. 78A4.)

Foolish virgins: with flowing hair of unmarried women, some with fillets. Their gowns are as Byzantine as those shown in Ills. 414-1417, but an interesting comparison may be made with the costume of Geoffrey (Ill. 396), in respect to the disposition and character of the small decorative motifs, and of the bar, not border, of embroidery across thigh of second figure from the left.

410. XIIc. Swiss. (Engelberg Monastery Library. Cod. 14.)

The lady who has something to confess wears her veil as a turban, with the end passed under the chin, barbette-fashion. Bodice, tight under the arms, widening immediately, to permit bloused effect and side fullness. Very long pleated XIIc cuffs, set below elbow of very tight sleeve. Her urgent friend wears a barbette under her chin (appeared mid-XIIc.), with a fillet. Tight bodice achieved by back lacing. Skirt, long, almost circular; gores added immediately below waist. Sleeves, very tight, with fantastically long pleated hanging bands laid across arm below elbow.

411. XIIc. Norwegian, from Baldishol Church. (Museum of Art and Industry, Oslo.)

Knight in ring-mail such as the Danes had brought to England in IXc., and the Scandinavians to Normandy in the Xc. Long hawberk, with coif-de-mailles which does not protect chin, and long sleeves which do not end in mittens. Conical helm with nasal. Prick spurs, lengthening pointed toes. Kite-shaped shield, decorated, possibly armorial.

412, 413. XIIc. German. Regensburg (Ratisbon). Medical Examination Books.

412. Allegorical: Dress of both sexes shows increasing interest in center-front of top of bodice; as a vertical slit develops below base of neck, width of round collar will be seen to decrease. Decorated girdles close at center-front or side. Skirt of upper tunic is tucked into girdle on one side, giving a diagonal line to hem, showing garment beneath. For the rich, a third tunic appears; if three are worn, edge of uppermost is left plain; middle one of heavy, brocaded stuff, narrow in cut is bordered; lowest is full and plain, usually of linen. Unmarried women: bare, center-parted hair; wives: small draped and twisted veils.

Knights: hoods of mail, not enclosing chin, and frequently separate from short-sleeved hawberks. These, as well as chausses, made of linked mail, in many designs; of overlapping plates; and of studded cuir-bouilli. These are used, in combination, in the armor of one knight. Hawberks have heavy decoratively banded hems; are worn over full, slightly longer tunics. Shields: round, or knee-length and kite-shaped, with rounded or flattened tops. Helmets: conical, phrygian, or rounded. Swords: blade more pointed. Spears. Pennon.

413. Surgical operations: doctors and patients. Unnamed surgeons, dressed in short tunics. Hippocrates and Aesculapius: capes and embroidered hems. Those wearing crowns are referred to as Imperator, indicating founders of schools of medicine.

414-417. Alsatian. 1180. (Strassburg Library.)

Hortus Deliciarum, by the Abbess Herrade de Landsburg (fl. 1167-95), one of the very first encyclopaedias, almost entirely destroyed by fire in 1870.

414. King: standardized Xc. Byzantine costume, but with new fur lining in cape.

Bishop: mitre set in the new way, twisted so that the horns are at front and back, instead of at either side; pall; chasuble; dalmatic, with remnants of fringe decoration on clavi; fringed stole, of new straight shape; alb.

Two monks: one, with oblong mantle, given shape by being looped up at the shoulder; the other, cowled with interesting treatment of side-seam fastening. Men: servants wear shorter garments, closer fitting sleeves, than gentlemen; and do not wear mantles.

415. *Superbia* and knights. The bodice of her full-skirted, trailing gown is laced tight at the sides; her sleeves have the new full cuff falling suddenly from a tight sleeve decorated with the persistent Byzantine upper-arm band. Veil knotted into high turban with flowing ends; it was inevitable, in a century of such impetuous adventureousness in costume, that the susceptibility of the ends of the veil to arrangement should lead to such headdresses as those of the females of the Swiss plate (410). The toes of her decorated shoes show the effect of the new preoccupation with length.

The helms of the knights, all with nasal, show both the phrygian-conical form and the newer rounded top; and their shields, still long and kite-shaped, the new flattened top. Their knee-length hawberks of linked mail, slit in front, though showing increased width toward the hem, have the coif-de-mailles high about the chin, and completely developed fingers, not mittens. The front-knotted sash with its long ends hanging below the bloused tunic has led, especially on the new fitted garments where most effective, to an interest in belts which will increase during several centuries. Here the hanging-knot motif is used

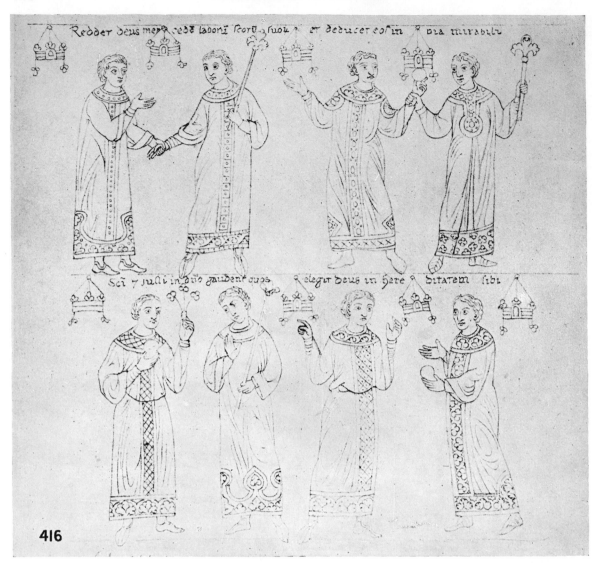

416

417

as the means of fastening a wide flat belt. The under-tunic with trailing, gored fullness is shown in its most extravagantly inconvenient form;* it will have to be slit, and is in Ill. 397.

416-417. Our Lord, in dalmatic and pallium, and 12 male figures in charming variations of standardized Byzantine dress which had perhaps been revived by the Crusades (compare tunic, sleeve in Ill. 355).

* Two centuries later (1370), Sir John Chandos, trip-ping on ice, will entangle his legs in his "large robe which fell to his feet, blazoned with his arms on white sarcenet" (of his surcoat), stumble, and unable to avoid a lance thrust by a French squire, will meet his death. (Froissart)

Scs GEORGIVS

418

Scs Oswaldus

419

418-419. Late XIIc. Swiss. (Morgan Library. M. 645.)

St. George and St. Oswald. Hem of tunic shows early use of "dagging," which started in Germany in the last third of XIIc., and spread rapidly. The use of dagging, particolor, and fur, gives to the costume of the Middle Ages its own particular character. A fur design is used to decorate St. Oswald's hose, and St. George's shoes have the sandal-patterned decoration brought by the revival of Byzantine fashions.

420-421. XIIIc. Norwegian. (British Mus.)

Chessmen of walrus ivory. King, queen, bishop, and foot soldier, as a castle: all rather backward. The bishop's chasuble has not been cut away; his mitre has the vertical band, but shows no impulse to spread into horns.

VISIGOTHIC SPANISH

Spanish civilization had developed out of the comparatively advanced culture of the Visigoths. From 415 until they were overthrown by the Musulman in 1711, the Visigothic sovereigns of Spain were under a disadvantage, particularly after the conversion of Clovis and 3,000 of his Frankish soldiers in a body on a battlefield in 496. The Visigothic kings adhered to the Aryan creed, while ruling a Catholic people. In VIc., King Ricared was converted, and the rulers gained the support of the clergy in their struggle to maintain their dynasty.

They were tolerant, considerably Romanized rulers. Their influence did not, like that of the Ostrogoths

420

421

422

423

upon her marriage to Alfonso VI.

This decorative period, which is that of a great national hero, the Cid, seems to me to be the most undeservedly unexploited in all the history of costume.

422-423. XIIc. 1109 A.D. Visigothic Spanish. (British Museum. Beatus. Add. 11695.)

Four mounted knights and one foot soldier; enumerated, their garments and equipment are identical with those of Western Europe, but in detail there are considerable differences. All the hawberks and chausses are of overlapping metal scales or rings, not of linked chain-mail. The hawberk of the foot soldier, with its shaped sleeve, is extraordinarily long and narrow, and is not slit, as those of the mounted men simply had to be. The Roman lappets at his hem are probably a stylization of the folds of the tunic which shows at the cuff. The chausses have separate feet, with elaborate sandal designs, and prick spurs on the knights; their toes are lengthened and elaborated in the manner of the *solleret* which begins to appear in XIIc. The round shield with boss is very small, apparently a descendant of the two-foot Spanish *caetra* of IIc. B.C. Double-edged Germanic sword with a rounded point. The soldier (423), under his conical ribbed Germanic helmet with nasal, seems to have some misgivings, perhaps about his ferocious pike. The seven-foot Roman *pilum* came from the Iberian *gaesum*, which was originally a Celtic weapon.

Photographs courtesy of the Morgan Library

in Italy, die out with them but is still perceptible in Spanish art. Until the time of Charlemagne, Rome imposed little direction on the development of ritual costume in West Europe; the churches of Spain and Gaul were the last to conform to Roman use, which was brought to the continent principally through the agency of missionaries from the long-Christianized British Isles. Comparison with Bishops of XIIc. will show rate of development during IX-XIIc.

The cultures of racially varied Mohammedan conquerors were too disparate for protracted, massive political effect, but with the Jews as intermediaries, the Mohammedans were princely patrons of learning and art. The Basques, holding off the Mohammedans, helped to seal Spain within its peninsula. Pilgrims to the shrine of St. James of Compostella brought practically her only contacts with Western Europe, until the XIIc. entry into the Spanish court of the cultured French ecclesiastics and knights who formed the entourage of the daughter of the Duke of Burgundy,

424

424-425. XIIc. Visigothic Spanish. (British Museum. Beatus. Add. 11695.)

424. Musicians. 425. The Scarlet Woman.

426. 1126-29 Spanish. (Oviedo Cathedral Archives.) Chartulary of Oviedo.

Ordoño I (850-866), King of Christian N.W. Spain, with his armor-bearer and two bishops, and Queen Mummadonna, between two maids of honor. The bishops, without miter, but with pastoral staffs, wear chasuble with Y orphreys, or pallium of a saint, under pall of bishop.

Nowhere else in this century will we find such sophisticated style as in the arrangement of the veils, and the placing of their plain mass, light or dark, against tunics the border decorations of which are subordinated to or eclipsed by the bold over-all patterns of the fabric out of which the tunics are cut, and in the case of the Visigothic queen, lined as well.

Courtesy of the Morgan Library
(424-26)

427-428. XI-XIIc. Spanish. (Barcelona. Crown Archives. Sp. 4546). Ms. de Fuedo.

Spanish costume shows much more use of elaborately patterned fabric than any other of the same period, although the era of fantasy and parti-colored garments is beginning, among people who long for colored patterns, which they cannot yet make, nor afford to import from the Orient.

Bishop: Mitre banded at the center, which will force top to spread into horns during XIIc. Patterned chasuble with orphreys; shortened in front from XIc.; pall; dalmatic, cut away at sides, is now colored; alb; maniple now fixed in wear over arm; pastoral staff with an early appearance of its scarf.

Gentlemen: parti-colored cloak and sleeveless tunic, slit to show short tunic which serves as sleeves for longer; lengthening hose; fenestrated shoes.

Lady: the way gown is cut away at sides and laced, on one side, over garment of another color, can be seen clearly in XIIIc. Spanish *Book of Chess;* it foreshadows the universal sideless surcoat of XIVc. Turbaned head began to appear in Europe c. Xc.

429. Early XIIc. Spanish. [Burgos]. (Santo Domingo de Silos Cloisters.)

Male figure: cape draped, Byzantine-fashion, over hand, but new in lowering neck-line; and edges barely connected rather than overlapping.

430. Early XIIc. Spanish. [Burgos.] (Santo Domingo de Silos Cloisters.)

Entombment of Christ: knights wearing round-topped helms without nasals over mail hood affording maximum protection to face; scarf, draped about neck (see Ills. 392, 393); knee-length hawberk, short-sleeved, slit up front, over very long wide tunic. No mail chausses or spurs under these long tunics. Shield, almost body length with encircling curve.

431. Second quarter XIIc. Spanish. [Gerona.] (Baget.)

Wooden statue: simple tunic permits display of knotted fastening and long ends of richly studded belt.

432.

433.

434.

432. Third quarter XIIc. Spanish. [Burgos].
(Siones.)
St. Juliana and Devil: center-parted hair
worn in 4 tresses; 2 tunics, fitted; upper
tunic belted; shaped cuff laid on in pleats.

433. 1188 A.D. Spanish. [La Coruna]. (Santiago de Compostella Cathedral.)
Three Apostles: all-over fleurs-de-lys pattern; orphreys on tunic, pallium and scarf.
Upper arm band persists through XIIIc.

434. 1163 A.D. Spanish. [Lerida]. (Solsona
Cathedral.)
Virgin: bare head, long plaits, handsome
orphreys, block of decoration at knee.

Feudal Lords and Kings: XIII Century

XIII CENTURY DEVELOPMENT OF DRESS

THE background of the XIII Century has been given under "Knighthood in Flower."

Nothing is more characteristic of XIIIc. costume, male and female, than the new sleeve, cut in one with the tunic itself. Starting often as low as the waist, it tapers to the wrist; the tunic has lost its fitted bodice and widens below a rather low bloused waistline. The whole effect is of one rather than two garments, even when, with the introduction of the knights' surcoat, similar sleeveless gowns (G. *sorket; sukeni*) are worn by women, and lead to the XIVc. *sideless surcoat,* which again exploits the use of two garments.

A variety of long, loose overcoats for men appears, often hooded, as are the shorter capes, worn with the shorter, fitted tunics (*pourpoints*) which develop for every-day wear, as hose, *chausses,* become longer and better fitting.

Coifs as well as hoods appear, for both men and women; and women's hair is gradually bundled up and braided into arrangements connected with the development of these enclosing head-coverings.

The emphasis on belts gradually moves to the pouches which now depend from them. Shoes are much plainer; the points lengthening with the century.

WOMEN'S DRESS

Tunic; cotte: sleeves tapering from waist to wrist. Garments skimpy around the chest, but no longer fitted; bloused at a low waistline. Whether belted or not, the belly is emphasized; then the garment spreads into skirts which are suddenly gored wide at the hips. Decoration is in horizontal bands; neckline lowered; *sleeveless surcoat* introduced. The use of orphreys, which, like the newer belts, could be woven by the ladies of the castle on a narrow loom, tends to lessen as Italian and Flemish textile factories are established and as Germany uses block-printing to decorate fabrics, antedating its use in book-printing.

Headdress: to the second quarter of the XIIc. ladies veiled, in public; through XIIc. long braids; end XIIc. *wimple* appears; early XIIIc. loose, with fillet (at home); first quarter of XIIIc., fillet widens into pill-box cap; mid-XIIIc. *barbette* appears; hair gathered into net (*crispine*); headdress widens. Young girls wear loose flowing hair.

Cloak: semi-circular; front fastening; often fur-lined.

MEN'S DRESS

Tunics; cyclas or *cyclaton*: sleeves tapering to wrist: use of parti-color; dagged edges; fur-linings.

Overcoats: instead of capes; often hooded. Late XIIc. *pelissons;* fur-lined overgarment. End XIIc. *scapular;* poncho-like; caught but not sewed at the sides; often split up front. First quarter XIIIc. *garde-corps*: long, wide garment; sleeves voluminously gathered at top, and often so long that they were slit along the inseam to allow the arm to be used, while the sleeve of the garde-corps hung free. Second half XIIIc. *guarnache*: poncho-like; caught or sewed at sides; hanging, cape-like, down over shoulders.

Cowls and *Capes*: from third quarter of XIIc. hoods much used; lengthening point in back (*liripipe*); *chape; chapel; gugel; capuchon; aumusse.*

Headcoverings: since XIIc. berets, petasus, brimmed hats turned up in back; fillets. XIIIc. coifs, worn well into XIVc.; hats superimposed.

Accessories: girdles; pouches, *gypcière* (F. *gibier-*game) or *aumonière* (F. for alms). Mid-XIIIc., *fitchets,* vertical slits in outer garment to allow access to pouch, by both men and women. Gloves. Shoes (like women's), plain and increasingly pointed.

Underwear: Shirts. Mid-XIIIc. breeches (under-drawers) shortened; better hose-fastenings.

XIIIc. hose better shaped and longer; lead to shorter, tighter men's tunics, *pourpoints,* for everyday wear.

Improvement in fabrics was one of the factors leading to the wearing of the pourpoint and hose of the XIVc. Silk weaving was established in many Italian and some Flemish cities in the XIIIc. and more flexible materials were locally produced: good scarlet* wool in England; fustian (linen warp, wool weft) in Germany, which was also producing block-printed textiles.

The rise of tailoring was the other factor, starting in Germany, where the first guild of merchant tailors was chartered in 1153. By XIIIc. tailors were subdivided according to the categories of work performed, and women were supplanted by men-tailors. The tailors of Paris rose from 482 in 1292, to 702 in 1300, and were early divided into *tailleurs* (men's tailors) and *couturiers* (who did women's gowns).

Development of Arms and Armor: XII-XIVc.

The XIIIc. knight wore the chain-mail of the XIIc., with protective patches of plate or cuir-bouilli added at knees, over a padded and quilted pourpointed jack (*gambeson, hauketon*) and *cuishes* (covering thighs). With the rise of heraldry a new garment was worn over armor, the *surcoat*—sleeveless, silk or linen, suitable for the display of embroidered or painted armorial bearings.

Details of development of the various elements of armor were:

PLATE: The top of the *helm* was becoming rounded in mid-XIIc. and by the XIIIc. was flattened. The helm often enclosed the head and was supplied with vents for sight and breathing. By the end of this century it rested on the shoulders, chained to the belt and in the XIVc. to a plate on the breast. *Bascinets* were often worn under the helm. By the XIVc. these were visored and edged with mail to protect neck and shoulders. The *chapel-de-fer* was rather like our "tin-hats."

The *shield* was becoming smaller at this time. It was kite-shaped in mid-XIIc., triangular by the end of the century, then its top flattened; and by the middle of the XIIIc. it was heater (flat-iron) shaped. The *sword* becomes slenderer; quillons of the crossguard curved away from the hand. Up to mid-XIIc. it was worn under the hawberk,

drawn through the slit, then over the hawberk on a diagonal belt. By the end of the XIIIc. the sword (and dagger and helm) were chained to the belt; by early XIVc. chained to the plate on the breast. Sir Henry of Flanders was captured by his chained sword by an abbot. *Prick spurs; rowels* begin to appear in XIVc.

Both priests and women might go to war. Froissart tells of the archpriest, Arnault de Cervole, "an expert, hardy knight," who commanded 1600 men; and of the armed Countess of Montfort.

CHAIN: From the latter part of the XIIIc. to late in the XIVc. chain was linked in the manner called banded. A *coif-de-mailles* (*camail*) was worn over a padded arming cap or a steel skull cap. To the end of the XIIIc. this was in one with the hawberk, fastened by a flap (*ventaille*). Thereafter an iron mask was attached and by the XIVc. a mail edge, fastened to the bascinet, protecting neck and shoulders. The *hawberk* had long sleeves ending in gloves and became shorter, exposing the hem of the jack.

Chausses had knee-caps (*poleyns*) of plate or *cuir-bouilli;* laced up the back; prick-spurs (till mid-XIVc.). Metal *greaves* were worn over the chausses by the end of the XIIIc.

PADDED AND QUILTED: An *arming cap* was worn under the helm. The *jack* (*gambeson, hauketon*) was worn under the hawberk; this and the steel cap were the only protection of common soldiers. *Cuishes* protected the thighs.

DECORATIVE: The *surcoat* was sleeveless, of silk or linen, decorated with a coat-of-arms. It was worn over the hawberk. It first appeared at the last quarter of XIIc., knee-length, slit front and back, open under the arm to the waist. It was quite common in the first third of the XIIIc. During that century it became gradually longer and then dangerously long, going down to the calf in early XIVc. It was cut off c. 1350.

Ailettes were tabs, standing on either shoulder, made of leather or parchment, decorated armorially. They appeared in the second half of the XIII century. The helmet had a *crest*.

---

* Scarlet was a material, not a color: a fine elastic wool, particularly suitable for making tights. It was dyed in many colors, of which a red was most successful and common; that red has now taken the name of the fabric.

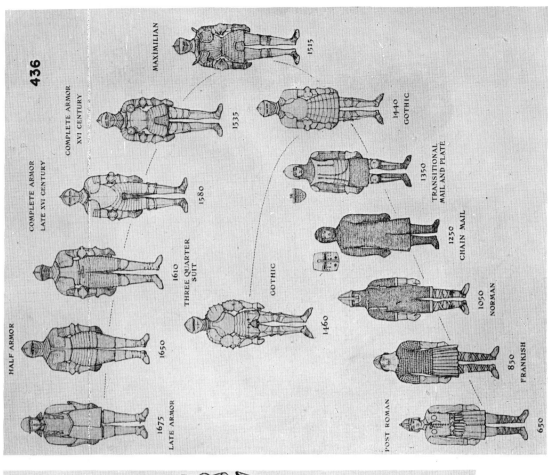

436

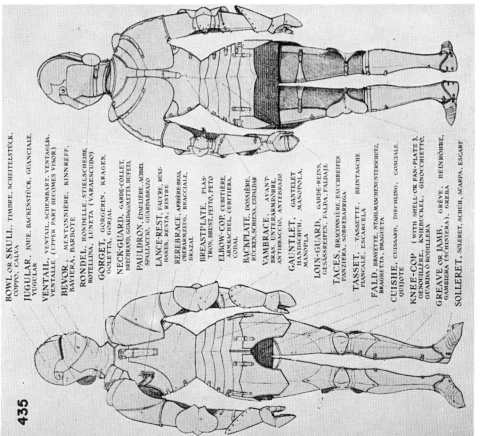

435

BOWL OR SKULL. TIMBRE, SCHEITELSTÜCK.
    COPPO, CALVA

JUGULAR. JOUE, BACKENSTÜCK, GUANCIALE.
    YUGULAR

VENTAIL. VENTAIL, SCHEMBART, VENTAGLIA,
    VENTALLE. (UPPER PART BECOMES VISOR)

BEVOR. MENTONNIÈRE. KINNREFF,
    BAVIERA, BARBOTE

RONDEL. RONDELLE, STIELSCHEIBE,
    ROTELLINA, LUNETA (VARAESCUDO)

GORGET. GORGERIN, KRAGEN,
    GOLETTA, GORJAL

NECK-GUARD. GARDE-COLLET,
    BRECHRAND, GUARDAGOLETTA.BUFETA

PAULDRON. ÉPAULIÈRE, ACHSEL
    SPALLACCIO, GUARDABRAZO

LANCE-REST. FAUCRE, REST-
    HAKEN, RESTA, RISTRE

RERE-BRACE. ARRIÈRE-BRAS,
    OBERARMZEUG, BRACCIALE,
    BRAZAL

ELBOW-COP. CUBITIÈRE,
    ARMKACHEL, CUBITIERA,
    CODAL

BREASTPLATE. PLAS-
    TRON, BRUST,PETTO, PETO

BACKPLATE. DOSSIÈRE,
    RÜCKEN,SCHIENA,ESPALDAR

VAMBRACE. AVANT-
    BRAS, UNTERARMRÖHRE,
    ANTIBRACCIO, ANTEBRAZO

GAUNTLET. GANTELET
    HANDSCHUH, MANOPOLA,
    MANOPLA

LOIN-GUARD. GARDE-REINS,
    GESÄSSREIFEN, FALDA, FALDAJE

TACES. BRACONNIÈRE, BAUCHREIFEN
    PANZIERA, SOBREBARRIGA

TASSET. TASSETTE, BEINTASCHE
    FIANCALE, ESCARCELA

FALD. BRAYETTE, STAHLMASCHENUNTERSCHUTZ,
    BRAGHETTA, BRAGHETA

CUISHE. CUISSARP, DIECHLING, COSCIALE.
    QUIJOTE

KNEE-COP. (WITH SHELL- OR FAN-PLATE),
    GENOUILLÈRE, KNIEBUCKEL, GINOCCHIETTO,
    GUARDA ROHILLERA

GREAVE OR JAMB. GRÈVE, BEINRÖHRE,
    GAMBIERA (SCHINIERA), GREBA

SOLLERET. SOLERET, SCHUH, SCARPA, ESCARPI

435. A complete suit of European armor, second half XVc., showing its various parts and giving their names in English, French, German, Italian and Spanish.

436. European Armor and its development during a thousand years from A.D. 650-1650.

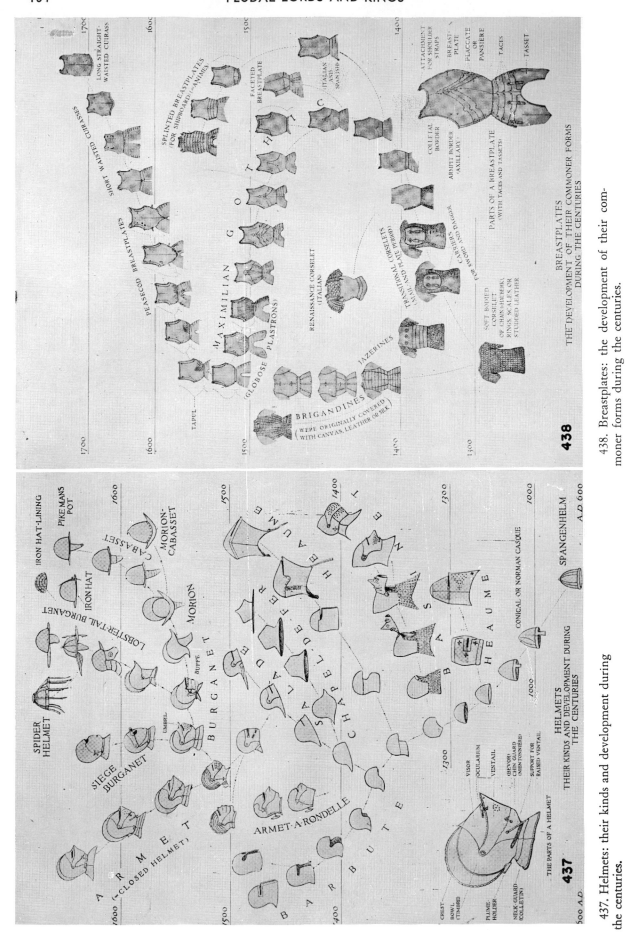

438. Breastplates: the development of their commoner forms during the centuries.

437. Helmets: their kinds and development during the centuries.

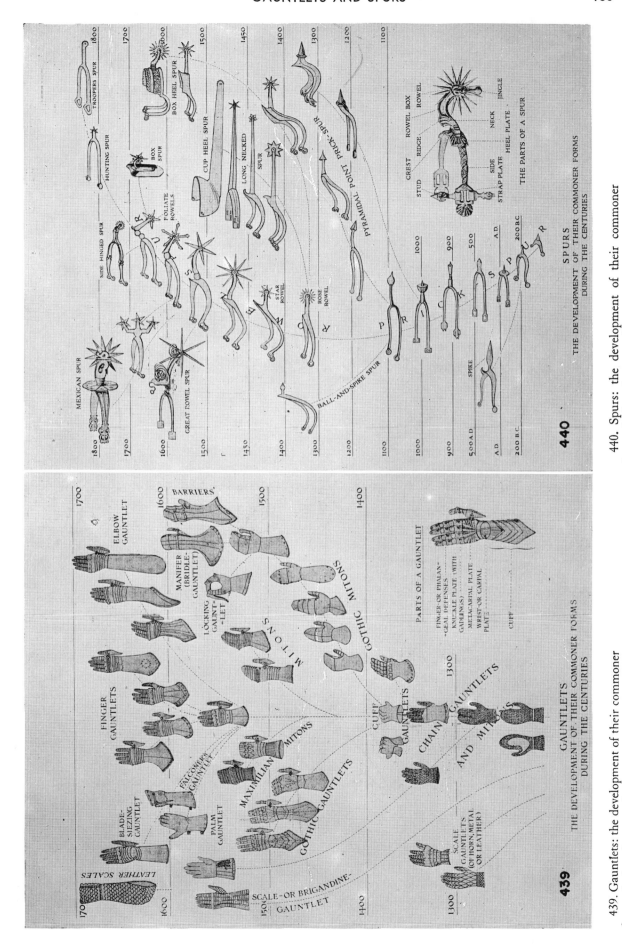

440. Spurs: the development of their commoner forms during the centuries.

439. Gauntlets: the development of their commoner forms during the centuries.

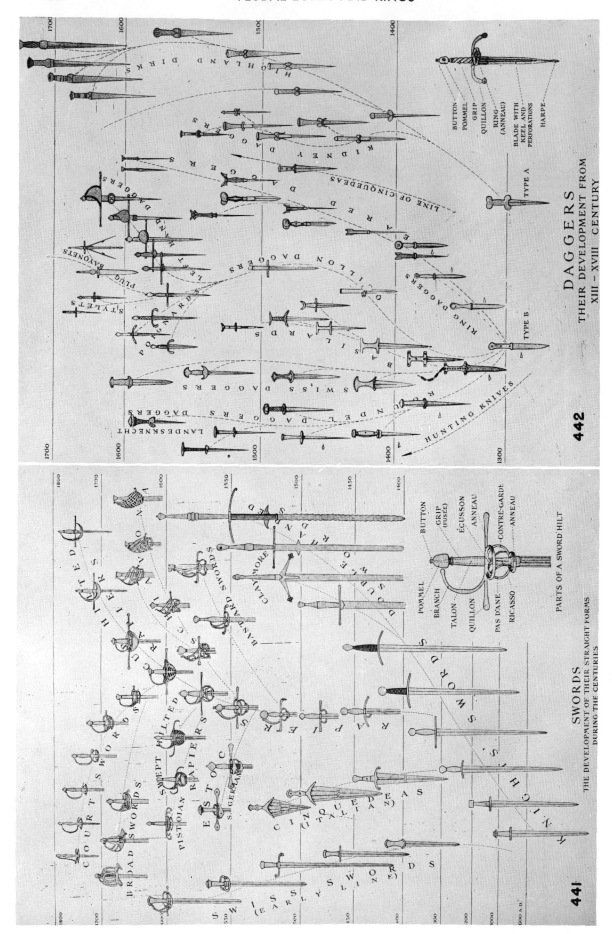

442. Daggers: their development from XIII-XVIIIc.

441. Swords: the development of their straight forms during the centuries.

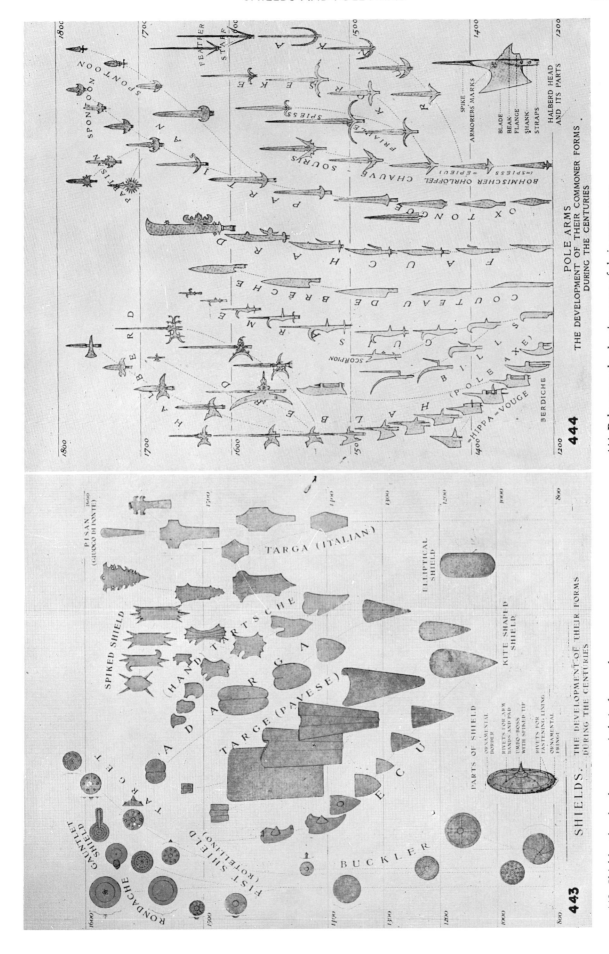

444 POLE ARMS
THE DEVELOPMENT OF THEIR COMMONER FORMS
DURING THE CENTURIES

443 SHIELDS. THE DEVELOPMENT OF THEIR FORMS
DURING THE CENTURIES

444. Pole arms: the development of their commoner forms during the centuries.

443. Shields: the development of their forms during the centuries.

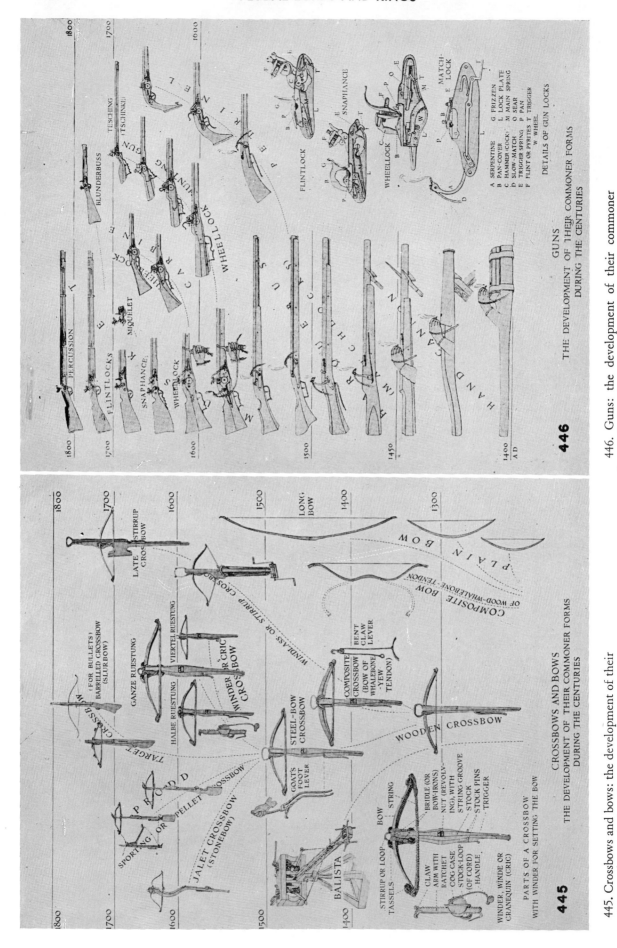

446. Guns: the development of their commoner forms during the centuries.

445. Crossbows and bows: the development of their commoner forms during the centuries.

447

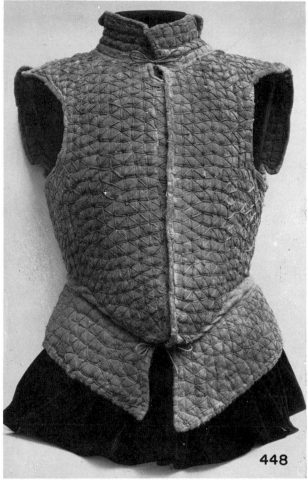

448

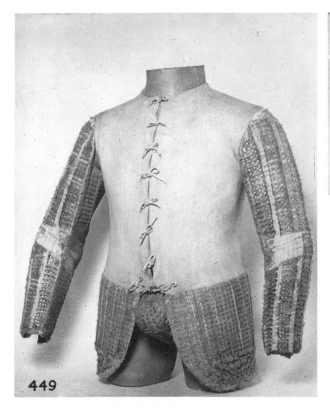

449

450

447. XVc. Spanish.
Brigandine covered with gold-brocaded velvet.

448. XVIc. English.
Jack: plates of iron laced between two folds of canvas.

449. XVIc. 1550. Italian.
Brigandine and brayette: leather, iron plates, brass studs, and silk.

450. XVIc. 1525. German. Maximilian.
Waffenrock; military skirt: quilted gold brocade (see Sir James Scudamore portrait, and Ill. 455).

In contrast to the jazeran, in which plates of leather,

horn, or metal were sewed on top of the fabric of the garment, the riveted brigandine and quilted jack were made of overlapping plates, scales, or bands of metal or horn, sewed between two layers of material, just as some forms of mail appear to have been covered with leather.

Brigandines were highly colored. Examples in the Metropolitan Museum are of red, blue, green, yellow, black, and white velvet, satin, brocade or leather.

In the dangerous days of Cellini, when everybody wished at least to appear protected, the doublet imitated the brigandine in appearance. Commines says that when the confederates marched to Paris in 1465, the troops of Charolois and the Duke of Calabria were in full armor and readiness, but those of Berri and Bretagne were "armed only with very light brigandines, or as some said, with gilt nails sewn upon satin, that they might weigh the lesse."

The brigandine often had protective skirts, or long, studded tassets down the thighs. The Metropolitan Museum Spanish brigandine has a separate gorget; and is covered in gold brocade, in imitation of the etched patterns used on XVIc. armor.

As the use of gunpowder increased, armor had to be made "proof" against it, and "proof marks" even entered into the design of its decoration. Proof armor was unbearably heavy, and armor was largely discarded in favor of leather by XVIIc.

At a time when a large proportion of the populace went armed, the civilian's padded doublets, stuffed trunk-hose, and thick pleated skirts, all developed out of the need to anchor armor firmly in place, prevent it from chafing, or replace its protection in a more comfortable way. A doublet was sometimes sent to the armorer as a pattern; our word "milliner" comes from the fine workmanship of the armorers of Milan.

Armor became ceremonial, rather than useful, during the XVIc. It aped costume in cut, and imitated the patterns of embroidery in its etched and colored decoration, as we see in Burgkmair's illustrations for the "Weisskönig," or in the work of Dürer, both of whom designed and engraved armor.

The tonnelet of Frederick of Saxony's harness is equivalent to a quilted "waffenrock" skirt. Grancsay shows a 1570 corselet with buttoned and tabbed decoration like that of a doublet; he compares Mytens' 1621 portrait of Charles I with the Barberini armor, to illustrate the way in which the breastplates became short-waisted, like the contemporary doublet, and in its decoration, followed the lines of embroidery or guarding of the doublet seams. He reproduces Ambrogio Figini's portrait of Lucio Foppa (Palazzo Brera, Milan), in which the etching of the armor and embroidery on the trunk-hose are identical. He also shows a military hat of metal, turned up on the side like a wide-brimmed beaver, with a socket to hold the plume.

_____
* Grancsay: Mutual Influences of Costume and Armor, from which I have drawn the rest of this material.

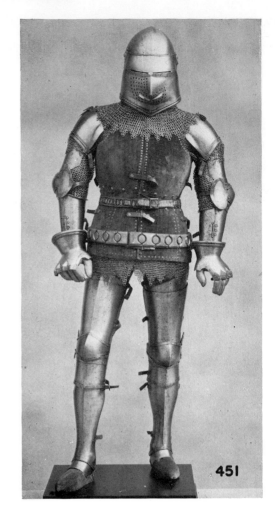

451. XVc. Italian. (Metropolitan Museum.)

Complete suit of Gothic armor (composed): transitional between mail and plate. This armor, unique in age and completeness, comes from one of the two great sources of early armor, the Citadel of Chalcis, near Thebes, taken by the Turks in 1470; the other was Rhodes, which they captured in 1523.

The brigandine, of large, shaped plates, with a fine globose breast and long skirts, was covered by fabric, as armor commonly was in XIV-XVc., to retard rusting, give color, and provide a place for heraldic blasoning; from XVc., color was chemically applied to the metal itself. This brigandine, originally covered with brocaded linen, has been re-covered in velvet with the original bronze rivets. Deep basinet, pointed visor; short-cuffed gauntlets; mail elements bordered with latten (brass).

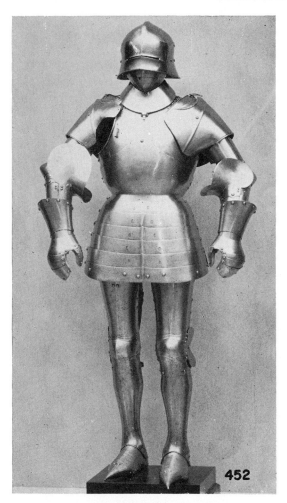

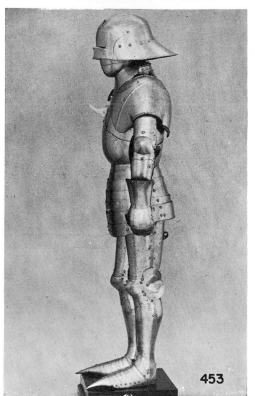

452-453. XVc. c. 1460. Italian. (Metropolitan Museum.)

Gothic armor: front and side views.

The simplest, most beautifully designed of all armor is the Gothic armor of XIV-XVc., which stresses a lean-waisted, athletic elegance of body.

The body, in a globose breastplate, is now well sheathed in plate, which is extended and flanged to deflect blows from the vulnerable shoulders and elbows. Deep skirt of many bands; wide-cuffed mitten gauntlets; salade; lengthening sollerets.

454. XVc. c. 1460. Italian Milanese. (Metropolitan Museum.)

Gothic suit, composed and with minor alterations; authentic elements bear the marks of the Missaglia.

Gothic armor, still beautiful and practical, is beginning to be ridged and fluted on the breast and around the armpits. The helmet, from Chalcis, bears the marks of the Missaglias of Milan, the greatest of all armorers.

The salade has given way to a beautiful fitted helm, prominently ridged and pointed into the "houndskull" form, with a hinged chin-piece which locks at its point. The neck is protected by a mail collar, with the additional protection of a tiny, round shield, set on a stalk, at the most vulnerable spot, in back. This form of casque, called *armet à rondelle*, was used in Italy from 1440 and in Spain, a half century in advance of the rest of Europe; and lasted into the early decades of the XVIc. Sabatons prolonged in 47 lames each, 2½ feet long; such footwear, which had sometimes to be chained up out of the way, is commemorated in the phrase, "to be on a great footing with the world."*

455. XVIc. 1510. German Augsburg. (Metropolitan Museum.)

Harness of Maximilian type, attributed to Frederick of Saxony, (1474-1510); part of a suite of armor (sometimes consisting of as many as 100 pieces) which could be interchanged for field, joust, or court use; preserved in the armory of the Teutonic Knights (of which he was Grand Master, 1498-1510), at Königsberg until the Napoleonic wars. An alternative breastplate in the Historical Museum, Dresden, is etched with the cross of the Order, a device, and Prussian eagles. Steel is forged, embossed, etched, and gilded in the puffed and slashed manner of contemporary dress which is also followed by the sollerets, now 6" wide; visor, of face with mustache. Harness is from the workshop of Koloman Colmar, one of that great dynasty of Augsburg armorers called Helmschmied (see Germ. XVIc., Ch. Weiditz journey to Spain with Colmar's son to deliver armor to Charles V).

456. XVIc. 1527. French or Italian. (Metropolitan Museum.)

Harness of Galiot de Genouilhac, (1465-1546), who served Charles VIII, Louis XII and Francis I, as Master of Artillery. He accompanied Francis to the Field of the Cloth of Gold, and was captured with him and Anne de Montmorency at Pavia by Charles V.

"From the standpoint of practicality it is one of the best harnesses extant." Its helm retains the rondelle at the back of the neck. It is regally etched and gilded with the labors of Hercules, which were also used on his chateau at Assier. It was bought from the Uzès family, into which his daughter had married.

457. VIc. 1549. German Nuremberg. (Metropolitan Museum.)

Harness of Albrecht of Bavaria, nephew by marriage of Charles V. It bears the mark of the Nuremberg guild, and is possibly the work of Kurt Lochner. Albrecht became a member of the Order of the Golden Fleece at 17; the armor is etched with its insignia, the Virgin as its protector, and Peter and Paul, the Princes of the Apostles.

458. XVIc. 1550. French. (Metropolitan Museum.)

Parade armor of Henry II of France. The workmanship for this armor for state processions, made by Italian armorers in the Louvre workshop, had caused it to be attributed to Cellini. The best engravers of XVIc.: Dürer, Hopfer, Hans Burgkmair the Elder, all designed and engraved for

---

* Grancsay.

455

456

457

458

459

armorers, and many original designs like this have been preserved.

459. XVIc. 1550. German. Augsburg.

Armor of Charles V. This suit, for one of the greatest of all patrons of armorers, was made by Mathäus Frauenpreis (Frawenbrys) from the designs of Jörg Sorg of Augsburg, preserved in the Stuttgart Library. It is embossed, etched and gilded with a griffin, and the Columns of Hercules (in allusion to the efforts required by the Spanish conquest of America), and the fire-steels and flints of the Golden Fleece.

The support of puffs and slashed straps (equivalent to folds, in a more comfortable form), was required under the wide taces of the knight; the resulting trunk-hose also gave good leg protection to a foot soldier in a brigandine.

460. XVIc. 1555. Italian.

Harness of Anne of Montmorency, Constable of France. Anne of Brittany's godson and namesake (1493-1567), companion at arms of five kings of France, died of his wounds after the siege of St. Denis. His 50-pound fighting suit shows armor being reduced to its final form: a flexibly articulated breast-plate with long tassets. Its etched decoration includes the clasped hands of peace, which appear on his funeral monument (Louvre). The crest of the armet becomes more pronounced.

460

461

462

461. 1590. English. Greenwich. (Metropolitan Museum.)

Armor of George Clifford, third Earl of Cumberland (1558-1605). Clifford, who "was as merciful as valiant (the best metal bows best) and left an impression of both in all places to which he came,"* succeeded Sir Henry Lee as Queen's Champion in 1590. This beautifully colored black and gold armor is identical with that shown in his portrait by Oliver; every element bears Elizabeth's cypher, and the suit was probably made especially for the occasion at the royal armory at Greenwich. It is etched and gilded with Tudor emblems: fleurs-de-lys and open cinquefoil roses combined with true-lover's knots. The left gauntlet, which is similar but not identical, came from the suit of Prince Henry preserved at Windsor. (See Oliver miniature, Ill. 1202.)

462. XVIIc. 1633. Italian. (Metropolitan Museum of Art.)

Three-quarter suit, probably belonging to Taddeo Barberini, d. 1647. The blazon of bees of the Roman family of Barberini appears on the armor attributed to Pope Urban's nephew. The short waistline of contemporary dress, assumed by armor, and the wide-hipped taces which depend to the boot-tops, would make the upper part of the body look ineffectual, if it were not for the large shoulder-plates, which are stressed by the engraving and gilding, in braid-like embroidered patterns, and the sculpturing, tooling and silver studs of this suit. Burganet with umbril shading the eyes. The gauntlet is a leather glove, with a cuff and plate of metal covering the knuckles.

463

463. XVIIc. c. 1650. French. (Metropolitan Museum of Art.)

Half-suit of armor. Armor is progressively reduced in extent, and loses its fine workmanship, as the need for proof armor outweighs all other considerations; it becomes so heavy that it is abandoned in the XVIIc.

---

* Thomas Fuller, quoted by Grancsay.

464

465

466

464. XIIc. France. (Arles, S. Trophime.)

Gentlemen: hair approaching the rolled form at the nape of the neck, of XIIIc.; small fillets or crowns. Cape edges barely meet at shoulder closing. Width below the hips is obtained by pleated side gores.

465. XIIIc. French. (Paris Bib. Nat.)

Thomas de Roumeis, squire (d. 1264): from his tomb in the nave of the Abbaye de Toussaint, at Chalons in Champagne. As Roger de Gaignières traveled through France, turn of XVI-XVIIc., he was careful to have an enormous number of drawings made of tombs, many of which have since disappeared. The drawings which are particularly rich in examples of bourgeois dress have been reproduced in sets of loose plates by the Bibliothèque Nationale, and a number of them can be found in Piton. (See Appendix.)

Thomas is particularly interesting for the typical diagonal neck-closing of the XIIIc.

466. Second half XIIIc. French. (Florence, Bargello Nat. Museum.)

Bronze knight: floral fillet, over hair rolled at the nape: mail chausses and hawberk: coif about the neck; hanging mitten of the hawberk has become a pendant, decorative as separate mail gauntlets come into use: dagged surcoat.

467. First half XIIIc. French. (Montmorillon Notre Dame.)

The Mystic Marriage of St. Catherine: Saints at the right of the Virgin. Virgin, therefore with flowing hair, under a little pill-box cap. This wonderful dress combines most of the excesses of the late XIIc.-early XIIIc.; narrow upper body laced tight, blousing to stress the belly, jutting suddenly over the hips, and falling in crumpled heaps on the ground, and the most prolonged sleeve possible (see Ill. 389) with a dramatic cuff.

Dates varying from XII-XIIIc. are given by various authorities for these lovely frescos, done in black, white, pearl gray, dark blue, green and brown. The costume would appear to be first half XIIIc.

468. After 1230. French. (Chartres Cathedral.)
Lady: fluted cap and barbette; cape with little rolled-back collar; cape-fastening has broken off statue; small brooch closes slit at front of neck, which is not stressed; exquisite belt.

469. XIIIc. French. Portrait head from tomb. (Walters Art Gallery, Baltimore.)
Noblewoman: stiffened linen cap, and barbette, with fine arrangement of veil.

471

472

470. XIIIc. French. (Bourges Cathedral.)

The Saved in the Last Judgment: middle figure at top: cap, barbette, sleeveless surcoat buttoned on right shoulder; low, bloused waistline below a tight bust, flows into a suddenly wide skirt.

471-472. XIIIc. French. (Chartres, South Portal.)

471. *St. Stephen, St. Martin and St. Laurent*: exquisite ecclesiastical embroideries of a fine period in church vestments. St. Stephen is dressed as a sub-deacon in amice, dalmatic with apparels at hem and cuffs, and with hem and slit sides fringed, alb, and maniple. St. Martin, as bishop of Tours, wears a conical mitre, amice, pall pinned in place over apparel of chasuble at center, dalmatic with 2 rows of fringe, stole, alb, maniple, and pastoral staff.

472. *St. Theodore*: as knight: mittened hawberk with coif dropped back, legs protected by mail *chausses* laced to sole; long surcoat; handsome sword on belt with low waistline; heater-shaped shield, hung over arm by *gigue;* lance with spirally furrowed hand-grip.

473

474

475

473. XIIIc. c. 1240. French, from St. Denis. (Louvre.)

Enamelled memorial plate: *Jean, son(?) of St. Denis*. Royal personage with fleur-de-lys sceptre; simple circular crown with mounting trefoils; cloak with narrow border dotted with jewels; narrow outer tunic with knotted belt (see also Ill. 415) and jewelled border; full under-tunic; slightly conservative, as royal dress is apt to be.

474. XII-XIIIc.* French. (Chartres Cathedral.)

Shepherds: summer, single tunic and covering; stiffening in top of hood, front to back. One bare-legged in boots; the other in loose, wrinkled *chausses*.

475. XIIIc. (Chartres Cathedral. North Portal.)

February warming himself: rectangular cloak fastened over short, hooded scapular; two tunics; drawers, hose without feet, shoes.

* **Houvet,** the director, says XIIc.; others say 1250.

476. XIIIc. before 1260. French. (Morgan Library.)
"Book of Old Testament Illustrations."

There is probably no more complete picture of the life and customs in the middle of the XIIIc. than is provided by these 46 illustrations. Plain people at work or rest; gentlefolk at home or abroad; knights and common soldiers in every sort of armor, and especially in garments worn beneath, or in place of armor, in camp or battle, are drawn in such variety and detail, that new information is revealed at each inspection. An explanatory Latin text was added by an Italian scribe in XIVc. The manuscript became the property of Shah Abbas, the Great King of Persia in 1608, and a description of each scene was added in Persian.

476. The Israelites are repulsed from Hai: The archaic helmets of the Conquest and the round Oriental shields carried by the defenders of Hai, are mediaeval conventions, to indicate warriors of alien race.

Knights: mail *coifs,* tied back from the temples, are worn alone, or under skull-caps, or flat-topped helms; mail *hawberks,* mittened; and *chausses* under plain surcoats. The fallen knight shows dagged sleeves of a quilted garment, worn between hawberk and surcoat. Heater-shaped shields; swords with various pommels and scabbards.

Men-at-arms: *pourpointed* or *gamboised* (quilted and studded) jacks; mittened, short-sleeved or sleeveless; one over another, the uppermost cut like a knight's surcoat, and sometimes dagged at the hem. Lacking the protection of the knight's mailed coif, the men wear a quilted standing collar; coif, covering the ears and tied under the chin, and arming-cap, surmounted by a studded *chapel-de-fer* or steel skull-cap.

Weapons shown, l. to r.: studded mace, staff with metal point, axe, glaive (long blade) falchion (square end, notched below, see No. 478), dagger, cross-bow. Standard: armorial.

477-478. XIIIc. French. (Morgan Library.)

"Book of Old Testament Illustrations." 477. City of Hai captured and its king hanged (from an engine of war). Upper: Knights, armed as in 476, also with lance bearing a pennon, with 2-handed *glaive,* and with heater-shaped shields, one blazoned with 3 cinquefoils. Men-at-arms, as in 476; sappers and miners, with pick, actually using kite-shaped shields of Conquest type, which protect full length of body; crossbow with trigger, and hook for stringing bow hanging from archer's belt. Lower: Knights, the first with his *coif-de-mailles* thrown back, showing padded arming-cap under steel skull-cap; cords at waist of surcoats; sword-belts knotted in front; decorative scabbards, swords. Suppliant populace: 1st standing man in hooded scapular overgarment; *garde-corps* with short, slit sleeves on kneeling figure; *aumonières;* woman in sleeveless surcoat; man in short, hooded scapular on horse; boy in *capuchon.*

478. Bengamites win daughters of Sholoh as wives. Upper: Musician, parti-colored, dagged. Unmarried girls: flowing hair, fillets; effect of one garment, very long, wide and bloused; sleeves cut in one with gown which increases in length. Knights: coifs held back by cord; one with chapel over arming-coif, and collar, instead of coif-de-mailles; knight farthest right has slipped hand out of mail mitten. Weapons: axe, spear, bill, glaive. Lower: Travelling to Jerusalem, and now married; heads covered, some necks swathed; barbes, coifs, and cap; mantles, some fur-lined.

479-480. XIIIc. French. (Morgan
Library.)

"Book of Old Testament Illustrations." 479. Boaz asks the foreman about Ruth.

Upper: gentleman on horseback, cloaked and gloved; on foot, wearing scapular with closed sides. Boaz, straw hat. Ruth, apron and gloves. Woman gleaner, netted hair and capuchon, thrown back. Other gleaners, cuffs unbuttoned, turned back; coifs or linen.

Lower: coifs, straw hats, hoods; hose; man's tunic slit in front, and tucked back out of the way into belt.

480. Ruth, Naomi, and Boaz. Upper: tendency of women's hair to be bundled up; woman's sleeveless surcoat; stockings striped horizontally. Lower: flailer in tunic, linen drawers, long hose. Flailer without tunic shows drawers rolled at waist around cord, to which ends of drawers are knotted.

481

481. XIIIc. French. (Morgan Library.)

"Book of Old Testament Illustrations." David and Goliath. Upper: Foot-soldier, pourpointed hawberk ending in gloves, not mittens, and with standing collar. Padded arming-caps, especially under engraved skull-cap of standard bearer, who wears a short jack caught together under arms. Same bearings on standard and on heater-shaped shield which is hanging on wagon, as do also chapels by their fastenings and pots (which undoubtedly suggested the chapel-de-fer) by their handles. Hair rolled at neck beneath coif. Lower: Goliath, wearing pourpointed *cuisses*, and *greaves* tied about lower leg; shield slung by *guige* and showing strap of *enarmes* on back. Very long lance with fixed cross-bar.

From "Book of Old Testament Illustrations," published in colored facsimiles by The Roxburghe Club, Oxford, 1927, with notes by C. O. Cockerell, M. R. James, and on armor by Charles ffoulkes, to which we are very much indebted.

482

482. Late XIIIc. French. Arras. (Morgan Library M. 730.)

Husband, wife and children: gowns of very simple cut, because of heavy, magnificent material. Arras, by XIVc. was the greatest centre of weaving in Europe; "Arras" another word for tapestries.

483

484

485

486

483-486. First half XIIIc. English.
(British Museum.)
Drawings by Matthew Paris.

483. St. Christopher: holding his tunic up out of the water, discloses the manner of knotting linen drawers at knee (see No. 480.)

484. Archbishop, probably St. Edward of Canterbury, canonized 1247: Mitre pretiosa, horns set front and back (XIIIc.), low shape (until XIVc.); amuce with orphreys; pall narrow, decorated with tiny crosses; dalmatic, rich, diapered, bordered; tunicle, horizontally striped, fringed; alb with apparels; buskins of diapered material; episcopal ring, right hand; maniple over left arm; cross staff of archbishop. No stole or gloves.

485. King: a stalk of fleur-de-lys was supposed to have been used as a sceptre in the coronation ceremonies of the Frankish kings. With the establishment of heraldic devices in the XIIc. the fleur-de-lys was used on the arms of France: azure, semé de fleurs-de-lys or (Old France); changed, third quarter XIVc. to: azur, à trois fleurs-de-lys or (France Modern.) The king, under a green cloak lined with vair, wears a jewelled dalmatic with the horizontal-banded decoration typical of the XIIIc. The tapering sleeves are cut in one with the body and gathered onto a sort of superhumeral collar. Handsome buckled belt with long tongue. Shoes of diapered material, simple in cut.

486. Knight: in mail hawberk with mittens and coif. Palm of mitten shows slit which permitted use of bare hand. The flap of the coif and its method of fastening are clearly indicated. Drawers, *chaussons,* of mail; and chausses covered with metal bosses, laced down back of leg, ending in feet and prick-spurs, buckled on. His long slit surcoat, tied to hawberk under the armhole, bears the same crosses pateés used on his standard, and on the ailettes of either shoulder; with a larger cross superimposed in front. Sword and belt. His closed helm, with cords for fastening, is about to be placed over his coif by his lady.

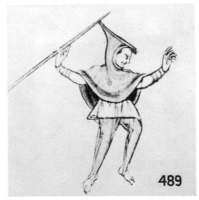

487. Mid-XIIIc. English. (British Museum.)

Matthew Paris: "Life of Offa."

Paris' "Offa" was one of the four old histories which John Stow persuaded Matthew Parker, Archbishop of Canterbury, to publish in 1571. All the servants in Archbishop Parker's house had to spend their unoccupied time with printing, engraving, and bookbinding; Parker had the first Anglo-Saxon typefaces cut. Offa was the VIIIc. king of Mercia to whom Charlemagne offered reciprocal protection for English and French traders, who in mediaeval times, travelled with their goods. English merchants already attended the French fairs, and an English trader was established in Marseilles in VIIIc.

Battle Scene: knights wearing the shorter hawberk, with narrowing mittened sleeves, like tunic of period; closed helms, or rounded helmet with nasal, or sim-

ply coif-de-mailles. Long armorial tabards to match heater-shaped or kite-shaped shields, with flattened tops. Quillons of sword, still straight, but deflect thrusts downward.

488-490. Mid-XIIIc. English. Salisbury. (Belvoir Castle. Duke of Rutland.)

"Rutland Psalter."

Short easy clothes of common men. Man at left has well-fitting hose, caught to his breeches, but they cannot come high enough to be covered by the skirt of his short tunic. The center figure wears hose without feet, very long but very loose, while the right-hand man is fighting in his breeches, without hose, but with shoes (compare breeches in Ills. 479-481.) These two wear hooded capes, *capuchons;* the top of the hood stiffened down the center; one also wears a linen coif tied under the chin.

From O. E. S. Saunders: *English Illumination,* Vol. II (487). From *Rutland Psalter,* Roxburghe Club, 1937 (488-90).

491. XIIIc. c. 1245. English. (Cambridge University Library.)

Matthew Paris: "La Estoire de Seint Aedward li Rei."

Edward the Confessor's marriage to Eadygth (or Edgitha), daughter of Earl Godwin. William of Malmesbury says that Edgitha was a woman "whose bosom was the school of every liberal art, though little skilled in earthly matters; on seeing her, if you were amazed by her erudition, you must absolutely languish for the purity of her mind, and the beauty of her person." The ascetic king never had carnal relations with her or any other woman.

Edgitha, in a horizontally striped gown, receives the fleur-de-lys sceptre. The fleur-de-lys entered regal costume with the XIIc. coronation of Philip Augustus. By the direction of his father, Louis VII, Philip wore a blue dalmatic and blue shoes, patterned in gold

"fleur-de-Loys," which referred both to the father's name and nickname, "Florus." Both Edgitha, under a flowing veil, and Edward wear open-topped crowns with foliated decoration above a low circlet, typical of XIIIc.

The blind earl, who gives his daughter in marriage, wears the new garment, the *garde-corps;* it is buttoned to the throat; its full sleeve is slit to permit free use of the arm in the tight sleeve of the tunic; it has a small cowl which can be drawn up over the beret. Bishop: gloves, maniple, mitre, amice, chasuble, dalmatic and alb, pastoral staff.

492. XIIIc. c. 1230. English. (Cambridge Univ. Lib.)

"Trinity College Apocalypse."

The Scarlet Woman: very Mae West, in comparison with the noble Edgitha above.

493. 1277 A.D. English. (Stoke D'Abernon, Surrey.)

Sir John Daubernoun: the earliest English brass; a knight completely armed in *mail,* with *surcoat;* clean-shaven. *Coif-de-mailles:* protecting chin, neck, shoulders; laced to metal *skull-cap. Surcoat:* long, slit up front, corners cut off diagonally, fringed; over mail *hawberk:* ending in mittens, strapped at wrist; over *haketon* (quilted) or *curie* (leather), protective against chafing; not seen. Mail *chausses:* with ornamented knee-caps, *poleyns,* probably of *cuir-bouilli;* and prick-spurs.

Shield: heater-shaped, charged with his arms in enamel: Azure a chevron or; slung by leather *gigue* ornamented by same crosses and roses as son's (see 1327 A.D.). *Sword:* ornamented pommel, slung in front in sheath fastened on wide *sword-belt,* which is supported in back by attachment to narrow braided *belt* of surcoat; *lance,* with pennon: bearing his arms.

494. XIIIc. Italian. (Bressanone.) Fresco.

Our Lady: In this extremely interesting illustration (which should be compared to Winchester Bible, 1170), the impossible silhouette of the previous centuries' ideal female figure is, as it were, drawn by the white outer garment upon the dark ground of the undertunic which covers a very matter-of-fact female torso. There is also the previous centuries' interest in the horizontal gathering of the material across the bodice. But in this case, the binding which finishes the sides, though furnished with eyelets, is so anchored at the waist and armpits that no lacing (see XI-XIIc. and XIIIc. Sp. "Book of Chess") is necessary, and none is indicated in the drawing: the eyelets are a flexible and decorative equivalent of an orphrey.

495. XIII-XIVc. North Italian. (Baltimore. Walters Art Gallery MS 153.)

Three knights in gloved hawberks, high coifs and chausses, under surcoats, the whole Romanized by the band about the chest and the low belt, simulating the bottom of the moulded lorica. Small, very convex shields protect the shoulder and very large chapels are worn over the coif.

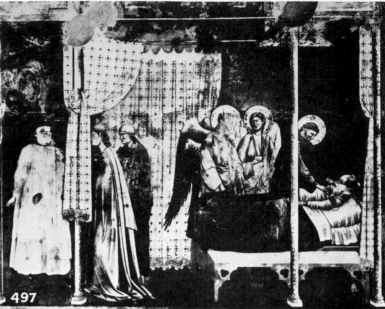

496. XIIIc. 1228. Italian-Byzantine School. (Subiaco S. Benedetto.)

Scenes in the life of St. Gregory: Portrait of St. Francis. Commemorates St. Francis' visit in 1218 to the first headquarters of the order he had founded a decade before. He wears the same clothing as the peasants with whom the Franciscans lived in joyous poverty. The Franciscans (who now wear a brown habit with a white knotted cord), are still, today, called "Gray Friars," from the original color of the habit.

497. XIIIc. Last decade. Italian. (Assisi.)

Master of the St. Cicely Altarpiece, or Giotto di Bondone. St. Francis curing an unbeliever.

Heads bound; or fur caps with drapery falling over the side from the crown, as though the headcloth of the 3rd figure from the left had been banded with fur, and its hanging ends lifted: or coifed, high felt hat.

The long, full tunics of elderly or important men are often fur-lined or hooded. The back-fullness is laid on in formalized pleats from the shoulders, with a hanging, pleated strip, which can be wound around the neck, if the garment has no hood; pocket-slit in the side seam under the pleats.

498. XIIIc. 1295-1300. Italian (Florence, St. Croce.)

Giotto di Bondone. Scenes in the life of St. Francis: The Saint renounces his father.

Looped-up overskirt of woman on left side is typical of the costume of simple Italian women (see XIVc. Giottos). The dignified men in the father's group wear an interesting variety of draped caps and fur hats, over coifs. Fur collars, muffs, with their long garments and overgarments. Group of ecclesiastics on right; children's dresses slit in front, the corner used as a pouch.

500. XIIIc. Spanish. Burgos. (Fogg Museum.)
Sepulchral Monument: Don Diego Garcia:
Spanish cap; notched neck and deep armseye of the Spanish sleeveless surcoat.

499. XIIIc. Spanish. Catalonia. (Solsona Museum.)
Visitation: two women in long patterned tunics and mantillas.

XIIIc. SPANISH COSTUME

Spain, relatively separated from the rest of Europe, had developed its own styles so strongly that much regional character and great richness were retained during the centuries between Spain's XIIc. introduction to the ways of the rest of Europe and her XVIc. position as Europe's first power. We then find all Europe dressed, no longer in the French, but in the Spanish style, which we call "Elizabethan." There are few books on costume in which these most de-veloped and integrated styles do not make a start-lingly sudden appearance; whereas they are, as it could only be, the rich result of a long-simmered stew of the most various elements: Iberian, Greek, Carthaginian, Roman Byzantine, Barbarian, Negro, Jewish, Syrian, Arab, Berber, and European. The permanent union of Léon and Castile had been completed by Alfonso the Wise's father.

Endless information can be extracted from the manuscripts of Alfonso the Wise, the many copies of *The Book of Chess,* and the *Cantigas.*

501-506. XIIIc. Spanish. (Escorial Lib. J. T. 6.)
   "Book of Chess" of Alfonso X the Wise (1221-1284), King of Castile.

501. Alfonso, his secretary beside him, and two Moorish ladies.

502. Young prince (Don Sancho?), with his page, playing with a rich girl, attended by her maid.

503. Two court ladies.

504. Two noblemen.

505. Gentleman playing with a Moor.

506. A gentleman playing with a Jew.

Both men and women wear tunics with the tightest bodices found in this century. These are made possible by a set-in sleeve, so cut as to allow great freedom, which is additionally provided by a wide under-arm lacing, utilitarian elsewhere, but in Spain intensely decorative. Nowhere will the sleevelessness of the surcoat receive more emphasis through cut and use of contrasting bindings than here; and not, elsewhere, until XIVc.

The ladies of the rest of XIIIc. Europe, even though dressed in the sleeveless surcoat, are apt to have the look of wearing one, rather than two garments. These Spanish court ladies, however, have a distinct appearance of wearing three garments. The fitted tunic which the rich girl wears beneath her surcoat, has the set-in sleeve emphasized by embroidery into a yoke; below this, the laced portion of the bodice is made of contrasting, dark material, with the same light material as the sleeves showing through the lacing under the left arm, like a light chemise under a dark corset. As women's hair elsewhere is being braided or netted into widening headdresses, these Castilian ladies, with their stressed vertical lines, wear high, turned-up, patterned hats, with a patterned chin-strap as a barbette, over flowing hair.

On the men's tunics, the sleeve seams are emphasized by braid, as nowhere else in Europe (but not to the point of forming a yoke, as in the case of the court ladies), and are likewise laced over contrasting color. Their belts are rich, patterned rather than studded. Capes are edged with braid, and have flat braid fastenings, rather than the cord between jewelled clasps of the rest of Europe. The three-tined forked effect on the gentleman (right of 504)

is pure Byzantine; the main figure on the Disk of Theodosius, which was found in Spain, wears it. The cape (504, right fig.) has the one-sided collar (see Ill. 515) which is not caught together. But the companion of the young prince, for hunting with his falcon, has an analogous, but more fully developed actual armhole, cut into his cape on the right shoulder, and buttoned firmly into place. Chess and falconry were the chief occupations of the leisure of mediaeval nobles.

The dalmatic, cape, and headdress of the King are patterned with the lions and castles of his arms (Léon and Castile). His shoes are laced up the inside while those of others of the men have the fenestrated character of Roman sandals. The Moorish ladies with the King are barefoot, and wear one very wide, loose, transparent garment, and much jewelry at ears, neck, and headbands; this is the only jewelry worn by anyone in these illustrations.

The Jew wears a wide-sleeved, ungirdled tunic; the Mohammedan, a turban, and a vertically striped and buttoned gown, with the first tailored collar we have seen (outside of Persia), lining of plain material, and a fringed scarf twisted about the waist. His companion wears a surcoat of a Mohammedan brocade trimmed with fringe, and a coif surmounted by a sombrero.

Not only the sombrero, but practically all the decorative motifs used in these costumes, persist in use today in the costume of the Indians of Guatemala. The design of the hat of the court lady to the right is identically used in the weaving of one particular Guatemalan town; the wide-and-narrow braid edging is used in the costumes of Solola; the blocks of color (as on surcoat of rich girl's maid, and gentleman on left, 504) are used all over Guatemala, in fastening together strips from their narrow looms; only the lions and castles have been replaced in Guatemala by the double-headed eagle of Maximilian.

507-512. XIIIc. Spanish. (Escorial Lib., Roy. Mon., T. j. i.)

"Cantigas" of Alfonso the Wise: The story of Count Garcia and the devout knight.

Against Moorish architecture, all the belongings of the knight are covered with a blazoned design as simple and effective as the patterns of Queen Mummadonna and her maids. It is used on the cap of the squire who holds his shield, and the lance with its vertical pendant; on the knight's surcoat and on his horse's caparison. Beneath it, his horse is protected by chain-mail like the others, and like them, by plate on the head. His surcoat has cap sleeves like a XVc. tabard; like the other knights, he has a mittened hawberk, and coif high about the chin; over this the knights wear a variety of small round helmets and closed helms, one of which is crested. The significance of glove as gage appears almost simultaneously with the mitten of mail. The opposing army of infidels wears turbans and carries heart-shaped shields, with tassels instead of the armorial bearings of the Spanish knights.

The courtiers wear the pill-box hat of Spanish gentlemen, in one case brought under the chin like a coif, and the surcoat, very much cut out and bordered in blocks of color which one sees in the *Book of Chess*. The fur-lined capes have an asymmetically raised and stiffened collar on the left shoulder, and the Byzantine forked braid-fastening. Tonsured priest: amice, chasuble, and alb.

513-514. XII-XIIIc. German. (Cathedrals of Mainz and Naumberg.) Reliefs.

513. Men in hats; woman with cap and *barbette;* in background, a hood (German: *gugel,* from *cucullus*); men's hair to shoulders, or parted behind rolled bangs. 514. Men wearing petasus.

515. XIIIc. Swiss. (Chapel, Hocheppen Castle, near Bozen.) Wall painting.

The Foolish Virgins: continuation of the costume we have seen in late XIIc. German and Swiss illustrations; virgins, therefore they are bare-headed, or with small embroidered cap, but long braided or twisted tresses; fitted bodices; tight sleeve ending in immensely prolonged, full band; trailing skirts with

gored fullness. Capes have become very important, sometimes patterned, caught up on one shoulder in a stiffened loop (see Ill. 404) which forms a sort of collar, and is fastened from that to the smooth shoulder with clasp and cord.

516. XIIIc. 1200-32. German. (Morgan Library, M. 710.) "Abbot Berthold Missal."

Salome: underarm lacing of tightly fitted bodice, which draped down, outward, outlining the belly, before the skirt begins to be gored into sudden width. A scapular form of the sleeveless surcoat was often seen in Germany: open down the sides, and projecting in wings over the shoulders.

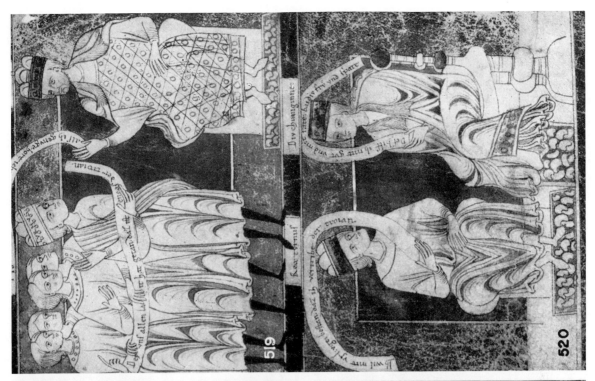

517-520. XIIIc. 1210-20. (Berlin State Library.)

Eneide by Heinrich von Veldeke (c. 1130-89). Askanius shoots Sylvane's brothers; storms and burns their father's city. These German costumes, like those of the rest of Europe, have narrowing sleeves in one with the tunic, even on the hawberks: archers unarmed, except for bows and quivers of arrows, and chapel; hair beginning to be rolled at the nape of the neck.

Sylvane's brothers, surprised in their everyday tunics, have snatched up swords, helms and shields, which like those of the fully armed-knights show the heavily stressed decoration of Germany, the home of tournaments.

The court costumes are of the familiar longer, Byzantine type; crowns same German type as Regensburg illus.; the diapered dalmatic of the seated king is sleeveless like a surcoat; and the fur tippet is a typically German accessory, found nowhere else at this period. Armorial bearings probably originated in pieced patterns of fur, used to cover shields; compare knight (upper corner, l.) with executioner (1100-20, Stuttgart Passionale).

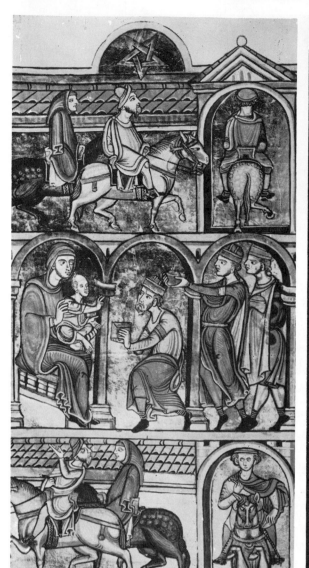

521. XIIIc. 1200-52. German. (Morgan Library, M. 710.)
"Abbot Berthold Missal."
Cowled over-garments with hanging sleeves; capes, caps and felt hats for travelling.

522-523. Early XIIIc. German. (Augsburg Cathedral.)
Stained glass: XIIIc. motifs: diapered, foliated, quatrefoils linked by squares (see Illustrations 528 and 529), horizontal stripes; eyelets; hats shaped like chapel-de-fer.

524. XIIIc. German. Wurzburg. (British Museum.)
"The Wurzburg Psalter."
Petasus for travelling; band around upper arm persists to mid-XIIIc.

525-26. XIIIc. 1210-35. German. (Strassburg Cathedral.)
Ecclesia, Synagogue: the narrow-sleeved XIIc. gown, with its very long wide skirt, is no longer laced tight in the bodice. It widens immediately below the armpit of the sleeve, which is cut in one with tunic, yet still tight under arm. Center-front clasp typical of XIIIc. Foliated crown on flowing hair.

527

526

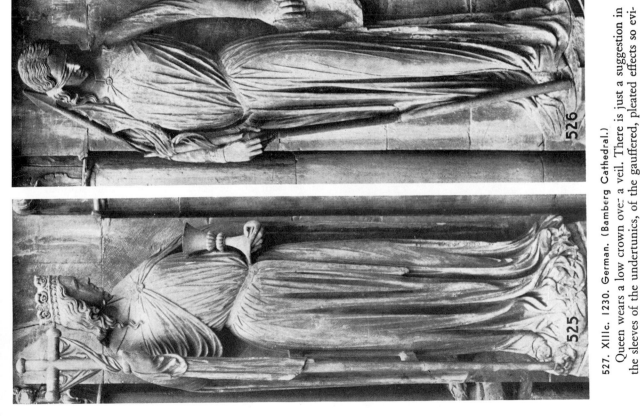

525

527. XIIIc. 1230. German. (Bamberg Cathedral.)
Queen wears a low crown over a veil. There is just a suggestion in
the sleeves of the undertunics, of the gauffered, pleated effects so evi-

dent in French costume second half XIIc. (Chartres, Corbeil). The
angel, a fillet about his head, wears a long tunic of the Byzantine
court type.

528. XIIIc. 1230-40. German. (Pegau, near Leipzig, Klosterkirche.)

Painted monumental effigy: Graf Wiprecht von Groitzsch. The flamboyant character of German decoration becomes increasingly extravagant during XIIIc. It is frequently absurd, sometimes charmingly so, but often brutally heavy and tasteless. German sculpture of XIIIc. was often painted. One of the Prudent Virgins on the North Portal of Magdeburg Cathedral (1210-35) wears a yellow gown horizon-

tally striped in orange-red, a gray-blue cape, and gilded jewelry.

Wiprecht's red cape, blue gown and shield are studded with great glass jewels. The fur tippet he wears is found only in Germany; cape fastens by an almost invisible cord running across breast from beneath jewelled roundlets on the shoulders. The rosette of decoration (see French XIIIc. Chartres; and Ill. 529) has been expanded into a decoration of the whole front of the gown; handsome belt; studded shield; flattened boss, not yet armorial.

529. XIIIc. 1249-80. German. (Naumberg Cathedral.)

Margrave Eckhart II, of Meissen and Uta, his wife: Eckhart wears a coif tied under his chin, over long but not yet controlled hair. The sleeves of his tunic are cut in one with the body and widen into it. Center-front clasp; fringed cape-fastening; wide belt, decorated with studding. Gloves, now very important, hang at sword-handle against shield, a placing characteristic of the period. Elaborately wound scabbard. Uta wears a coronet about her stiffened cap and *barbette* (German, *gebende*). Her cape, fastened from handsome shoulder-clasps, has the rolled collar which has reached Germany from France.

530. XIIIc. German.

Gravestone of Archbishop Siegfried III von Eppenstein.

Mitre aurifrigiata growing higher; pall (which was buried with its wearer); chasuble in a sort of diapered, all-over brocade; dalmatic brocaded in a design of small squares, plain lining; alb with band of the brocade of the dalmatic (a common XII-XIIIc. use) instead of orphreys, in the 4 blocks of decoration, used from XIIIc. on; embroidered liturgical gloves; ring; staff.

Two royal youths with crowns and sceptres. Capes with fringed fastenings; surcoats widely cut out around the armseye, to expose folds made by the excessively tight chest of the tunic, cut in one

with the sleeves of the garment. From the belt of the youth to the right hangs a jewelled pouch with tasselled ends, and a dagger, as well as a longer, broad sword with the wider, straight quillons and wrapped scabbard of XIIIc.

531. XIIIc. 1280. German. (Strassburg Cathedral.)

The King of the World: hair rolled smoothly at nape and above brow in French fashion, surmounted by coronet. His overcoat has short sleeves, slit for the passage of the arm, in the tight sleeve of the tunic; XIIIc. use of buttons to fasten up, or to decorate side-slits, as well as to close neck opening.

The smiling girl with flowing hair and fillet might very well not be wearing a girdle, although in this instance one may exist.

The Rising Bourgeoisie: XIV Century

XIVc. and XVc. Development of Dress

Armor and heraldry affected both male and female civil costume. The devices used on the knight's surcoat were also worn, "parted" (father's on right side, husband's on left) by ladies; and on the garments of retainers. This led to the general use of parti-colored (mi-parti, motley) garments (particularly as the non-armigerous bourgeoisie competed with the aristocracy in costume); and to the eventual rejection of parti-color by the upper classes, and its reduction to livery use alone.

Sumptuary laws multiplied each year during the XIV-XVc., as kings tried fruitlessly to control the manner of living of the steadily rising lower classes. In France, Charles V forbade the long pointed shoes, which the Church had always opposed since they made it difficult or impossible for the wearer to kneel at prayer. All the Edwards tried to control luxury in English food and dress. In 1363, Edward III forbade more than one meal of fish or meat a day to servants; in 1433, James I of Scotland forbade anyone less than a baron from eating pies or meats cooked by the new method of baking in an oven (instead of broiled over a fire). Sumptuary laws fell into disuse or were ignored, were repealed and reimposed. In 1463, Edward IV regulated the dress of all classes, since "the commons of the realm, as well men as women, wear excessive and inordinate apparel, to the great displeasure of God, the enriching of strange realms, and the destruction of this realm."

France led fashion; its influence was most strongly felt by England, with a time-lag of about a quarter century. Costume in Germany, Italy, and Spain, developed more regionally, in ways which later affected French styles. Italian costume exhibited fabrics of great sophistication and luxury. By second half XIVc. French garments became extravagantly short, tight, and padded, or long and dagged. These ways were common in England and Germany by end of XIVc.

As more elastic materials were produced, hose lengthened. The upper garments, to which the hose were laced, were shortened, tightened, and became padded. Belts, elaborate and across the hips in XIVc., tended to disappear in XVc., except over the carefully laid pleats of the long upper garments (new in second half XIVc.)

The lengthening *liripipe* end of the dagged (quainted) hood began to be wrapped around the head to form the turbanned *chaperon*.

Buttons were used in long rows by both male and female, until the advent of the *houppelande*. Gloves were generally worn in XIVc.; indispensable for the gentry by XVc.

Details of Male Dress

In the first quarter of XIVc., long gowns (except for elderly men and ceremonial occasions), and plain hoods had passed out of style.

Pourpoint, gipon, jupon, become the XVc. *doublet:* a padded, close-fitting, low-necked garment, worn under the *cote-hardi.* It had, typically, long tight sleeves. The garment became progressively shorter (eventually supporting the hose, laced to its eyeleted hem), more waisted and padded out at the breast (mid-XIVc.). With the extravagantly padded shoulders, *mahoîtres,* of XVc., padding invaded the upper sleeve as well. By third quarter XIVc., the sleeve often spread over the knuckles. When the sleeve of the *pourpoint* was short, wide, or pendant, the long close sleeve of another short body-garment appeared beneath them. Like the *cote-hardi,* the *pourpoint* assumed the high collar of the *houppelande* at end XIVc.

Gambeson, haketon, (G. *wammes*): body-garment of leather, or of padded and quilted stuff, not decorated; worn under armor, or as indoor garment of knight.

Cote-hardi: low-necked outer garment, laced or buttoned tight (center front opening, mid-XIVc.) with *liripipes* (later, lined *tippets*) hanging from elbow. This garment, too, became progressively shorter, from below knee (first half XIVc.) to just above crotch (end XIVc.). Hem often dagged. By end XIVc., it too, appropriated the collar, sleeves, and pleats of the *houppelande,* which was supplanted by the *jacket, jerkin.*

The new, long outer garments of mid to third quarter XIVc. were the *houppelande* and *housse.* The houppelande: (m. and f.), open down front; high, shaped collar; trailing "sleeves that slod upon the earth" (Richard II), usually funnel-shaped; bag-shaped in first third XVc: hanging, mid-XVc. Usually made of brocade; frequently fur-lined; edges elaborately dagged. The houppelande hung in formalized folds, tacked into place under the belt (the position of which was gradually lowered). Length varied from below knee, to dragging train for great occasions.

Housse: male use; tabard-like; buttoned slit at neck. If belted, only across the front.

Capes: short shoulder-capes of fur; or longer capes with dagged edges; fastened on one shoulder by buttons. Long only for travel, or as worn by peers, or members of knightly orders.

Hoods (G. *gugel*): dagged, with lengthening *liripipe*.

Hats: great variety, in beaver or felt. High conical; topper-shaped; pork-pie; and turned up in back. Arrangements of hood, bound around the head by the *liripipe,* with the dagged edge hanging, developed into the *chaperon* hat of end XVc. Plumes, end XVc. Pins, ornaments, and embroidery.

Hair: parted, exposing the forehead, rolled at the nape to mid-XIVc.; the rolled bottom became bushier. Late in XIVc., appeared the bowl-crop. The hair was combed in radiation from a spot on the crown, and cropped from bangs on the forehead in a continuous line which uncovered the ears. This line dipped in back toward the nape, but in most cases, the neck and head were shaved to a point well above the ears. The hair formed a sort of flat cap on the crown, no larger than a small Spanish beret of our own day.

Leg-wear: *Braies* shortened to drawers. *Hose*: becoming longer, better attached; often parti-colored; soles sewed on feet of hose, to end XVc.; codpiece attached to fork, as body garments shorten.

Shoes: ankle-height; front or inside lacing, or lappets. Simple cut; material often elaborate. Pointed toes, *poulaines* or *crackowes,* supposed to be of Polish origin, end XIVc.-end XVc. Wooden clogs to protect shoes from mud.

Boots: worn by travellers and huntsmen; not otherwise common until XVc.; elaborate, after 1450.

Belt: carrying *gypcière* pouch, writing materials and dagger, *anelace;* losing importance by mid-XVc.

DETAILS OF FEMALE DRESS

Women wore long, close-fitting, laced or buttoned garments.

Kirtle, Fr. *cotte*: close-fitting; tight buttoned sleeves; belted when worn under *cote-hardi,* which was buttoned down front; *liripipes* at elbow.

Sideless Surcoat: (Fr. *surcoat*); (G. *sorket*); very much cut-out armseye, edged with fur (England); with a plaquard or stomacher of fur (France); low neck; back cut wider than front; always prominently buttoned down center-front.

By mid-century women's gowns began to be divided into separately cut bodice and skirt; necks lower; sleeves longer. English robe: high neck; fitted laced back; arranged pleats at girdle.

Towards the end of the century came the *robe, houppelande*: new garment of women, as well as men. Very short-waisted bodice; wide, low, V-neck; wide belt, just under arm and breast; gored skirt, with wide border, often of fur: skirt so long that it had to be held or tucked up, or even carried by an attendant, thus revealing the material of the underskirt. For reasons of economy, luxurious material often appeared as a wide band on the lower part of the underskirt, matching the tight sleeve of the undergarment. Style is always capable of arising out of limitations, as in this case, just as well as out of profusion.

The cloak was now worn only on ceremonial occasions; the hood, by bourgeoisie.

During the first half of XIVc., hair was banded, by *wimples,* under the chin; was set in wide V-arrangements; caught in *crespine* nets. Hair in spirals at ears was replaced by vertical plaits, toward midXIVc. By the third quarter of the century, the wimple was passing and by the end of the century we see the horned headdress, *atours; hennin,* with veil; no hair showing; worn with houppelande. Long hair: brides, children, young girls, the Virgin, queens at their coronation.

A *girdle* was worn with *aumonière;* lady's dagger. Much jewelry and many buttons were used.

XIV CENTURY DEVELOPMENT OF ARMS AND ARMOR

Many of the examples we use to illustrate the main line of development of XIV-XVc. armor are English (in use if not in make) simply because these are the centuries of Crecy, Poitiers and the Black Prince, and of many of the plays of Shakespeare. It is most frequently English information that we require.

The finest armor in Europe, and much of the best worn in England, was of continental manufacture, Italian and German in particular.

Froissart records that Bolingbroke, accused of disloyalty in 1398, the year before he succeeded to the throne, asked Galeazzo Visconti, duke of Milan, to send him four armorers, together with magnificent armor from Lombardy, to wear in his life or death combat with the Earl Marshal, Mowbray, whose equally splendid armor was ordered from Germany.

The XIVc. was a period of superimposition of defenses, leading to the XVc. simplification of complete plate-armor (Eng. *alwite,* Fr. *harnois blanc*). Armor was expensive and good old-fashioned armor was not tossed away; it might even suit your action better. We find it in use, in combination and with additions, long after newer forms had become popular, so long as armor is used at all. The simple chain-mail defense of the XIIIc. lingered through the early XIVc., though defensive portions of leather and plate had already been added, and were constantly being supplemented by articulations at arm, hand and shoulder, at knee, leg and foot, until the sheathing of the entire body in plate was understood; and asymmetric sophistications were developed for special purposes. An articulated sheath of plate with mail gussets, over a leather garment to prevent chafing, was an infinitely more flexible and comfortable arrangement than half-a-dozen, or more, superimposed protections of leather, wadding and studding, and chain.

Mail was provided in a great variety of patterns, as the coif-de-mailles over arming-cap was superseded by the *camail* dependent from the *bascinet*. In battle or tournament, the helm was set over, and supported by the bascinet, until the XVc. when it rested on the plates of the shoulder and was used only in tournaments.

The loose surcoat, dangerously long at the end of the XIIIc.,* was shortened, tightened and dagged during the early XIVc. (and from 1321-46, into various forms of the peculiarly English military garment, the *cyclas*), into the fitted *jupon* of the late XIVc., out of which developed the XVc. *tabard*.

As the jupon (originally a civilian garment), tightened at the waist into the *justaucorps,* the belt at the waistline of the surcoat, as well as the diagonal sword-belt which it had supported, were replaced for both knightly and civil use by an elaborate and precious belt, worn horizontally and low on the hips, where it was held in place by hooks to the jupon; it supported the sword and slender *misericorde* of the knight and the heavier *anelace* of the civilian.

A series of carefully dated records of costume and armor exists, for a period of over 300 years, in the form of English and Continental brasses, commemorative plates of brass or latten, often enamelled, the finest of which were executed in Flanders and brought back to the East coast ports of England through which the Flemish wool-trade passed. Many of the best brasses and most luxurious costumes are those of rich bourgeois, wool-traders, mayors of towns, and their wives. These memorial plates suffered through Cromwell's destruction of the churches, and since then, through vandalism, carelessness, or simple greed for their value as old metal. But the recording of these monuments, through rubbings, became a

gentle but long-lived fad, from the end of the XVIIIc. These were accurately engraved and much published in the mid-XIXc. or the rubbings given to museums, often after the verger had cut up the actual plate to make a new foot-scraper for the church door, so that in many cases, these records are all that remain to us. (See App., XIIIc.)

XIV AND XV CENTURIES IN ENGLAND

The finest of guides to XIVc. England is easily available: Edith Rickert's *Chaucer's World,* Columbia University Press, N. Y., 1948. The great mediaeval scholar, author of the definitive critical text of the *Canterbury Tales,* died in 1938. She had amassed an immense amount of documentary material, uncovered for the first time by her research. This has been classified and combined with contemporary illustrations, to give a picture, painted by those who lived it, of London life, the home, training and education, careers, entertainment, travel, war, the rich and poor, religion, and death and burial, with a bibliography of manuscript and of printed sources. It is my dream of a good book come true.

The *Paston Letters* (ed. J. Gairdner, 3 vols., Archibald Constable & Co., Westminster, 1897) are among the great sources of information about English life in the XVc.

They show the rapid rise into the Norman society of Norfolk of the descendants of Clement, a Saxon bondsman and his bondswoman wife. His son, William, became a respected judge, under Henry VI; his grandson, John, married into county society, became the executor of the will of Sir John Fastolf (prototype of Shakespeare's Falstaff) and (whether by forgery or not), one of his heirs. His two great-grandsons were both knighted, and one became engaged to two ladies "right nigh to the Queen" by birth. Of his great-great grandsons, Sir William married the daughter of the Duke of Rutland, and was the ancestor of the first Earl of Yarmouth; and Clement became a celebrated naval commander, under Henry VIII.

In these letters, we meet most of the families of Norfolk and adjoining counties, whose effigies we use as illustrations: Northwood, Stapleton and Cobham, Felbrigge, Hastings, and Southwell, Say, Calthorpe and Arundel, Eresby, Rous and Warwick, as well as Edmond and Elizabeth Clere, the Pastons' cousins; and the family of the poet Chaucer, connections of the Pastons.

The "Bromholm Psalter" (illustration 534) comes from the nearby Cluniac Abbey to which the letters frequently refer.

There are letters from mothers and sons, about the management of country estates, and the pitched battles which were necessary to retain them; flirtatious Valentine letters; marriage arrangements; letters from wives, asking husbands to bring back dates and yeast, almonds, sugar and

---

* The persistence of old fashions is shown in the death of Sir John Chandos, who, at the end of XIVc. tripped over a long white surcoat, like that commonly worn 100 years before.

salad oil, articles of clothing and lengths of fabric, one of which tactfully concludes: "I would you were at home, liever than a gown, though it were of scarlet"; brothers writing each other to fetch forgotten garments, "iij longe gownys and ij.doblettes, and a jaket of plonket chamlett, and a morey bonet out of my cofyr . . . Sir James has the key," or telling how Sir James (mother's favorite priest) "is evyr choppyng at me, when my modyr is present, with syche wordys as he thynkys wrath me, and also cause my modyr to be dyspleased with me."

We have invaluable wills and inventories of Fastolf, as well as of many Pastons. These give minute instructions for funeral arrangements and tomb-stones; bequests to all the religious establishments, village inhabitants, poor, leperous, and the family; disposing of ten to twenty pages of plate, arras and tapestries, linen, room furniture, wardrobe, armor and books.

They also describe various processions and tournaments, and the costumes of the participants.

The *Paston Letters* show feudal English home life as ordered, mercenary and harsh. Marriages were arranged; property settlements of prime importance. As Scrope complains he was treated by his step-father, Fastolf, wards with property were "bought and sold like beasts." Places were found for children in the households of the great, and daughters were married and got out of the house, as soon as possible. English children were treated with a lack of tenderness which horrified the Venetian ambassador. In Renaissance Italy, chil-dren were not beaten after the age of seven; boys and girls were on the same footing, received the same educations; and the growth of personality was fostered. In feudal society, kings uncovered at the mention of other kings; the greatest lord was some king's "man," as his followers were his "men": all had and knew their places, and were scrupulous to give and receive all due honor, as we see in the headings of these letters of children to parents, and wives to husbands. The brutality of English family life was made bearable by the easiness of external social relationships in England. Erasmus noted the endless kissing which characterized the meetings of English ladies and gentlemen; and we find England in the XVc. notable for its external freedom, courtesy and fine manners.

The letters, which include those of servants, prove a widespread literacy; though the spelling is varied and phonetic, complicated by local pronunciations which still persist in English counties. Great lords and older knights like Fastolf are apt to sign letters written by their clerks; young men had been going to Eton and Cambridge since second quarter XVc. John Paston's library, in 1482, consisted of seventeen books: one, on chess, was produced by Caxton in 1474—the first book printed in England; four romances (one of which he "had off myn ostess at the george," and the other he "hadde neer X yer, and lent it to a dame"); six classics; four on blasoning; one on knighthood and the rules of tournaments and warfare; one of the new statutes of the kingdom.

532-533. XVc. 1477-85. English. (Formerly, Duke of Manchester.)

John Rous of Warwick: "Rows Roll."

Rous, the chaplain and historian of the Warwicks (see also Warwick Pageant, XVc.), in the "Rows Roll" lists the members of the family. These are Thomas, sixth Earl of "Warrewik" (1213-97) and his sister "Margeria," by his death Countess of Warwick; both in the costume of the XIVc. (See Appendix.)

534

535

534. XIVc. c. 1300. English. East
     Anglia. (Oxford Bodleian.)
  "Bromholm Psalter": F o o l
and wise man.
  Fool wears a three-pointed
pink cowl, ending in bells, over
a loose gray tunic; and carries a
fool's bauble with a bladder on
the end, for noisy belaboring.

535. Early XIVc. English. Norfolk.
  "Gorleston Psalter."
  The Church had been criti-
cizing and reforming itself
throughout XIIIc. (see Monastic development). Friars had
gone out from cloisters into active life. Whole categories of the
clergy had become responsible
to a far-off Pope, and were no
longer under the jurisdiction of
a near-by bishop. The people
with whom they mingled knew
and judged them as men. Rising lower classes had more
money and could go on local
pilgrimages. There was an immense amount of gusto and
curiosity, and a good deal less
automatic reverence.
  All this was felt, even by
cloistered monks; geese quack
at   foolish-looking   animals
dressed   like   important   ecclesiastics, and illuminated mis-
sals begin to be very good
fashion plates and embroidery
pattern-books. They were the
only ones available to their contemporaries, and are equally
valuable to us.

536. XIVc. c. 1310. English. Norwich, (Oxford Bodleian, Ms. Douce 366.)

"Ormesby Psalter."

Animal figures: left: fox; hair caught in crespine net, with barbette and circlet; hood thrown back. Right: conical beaver hat, worn over hood with short point. Knight and lady slaying unicorn: Lady: kirtle with XIIIc. sleeve worn under cote-hardi buttoned on right shoulder; crespine and couvre-chef. Knight: chapel over "banded" chain mail furnished with knee and elbow plates; ailettes bearing knight's device on shoulder of surcoat.

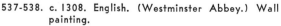

537-538. c. 1308. English. (Westminster Abbey.) Wall painting.

537. Siebert, King of the Saxons, founder of the Abbey, d.616.

538. Edward II (1284-1327) or Edward I.d.1307. Conservatism of the costume of majesty. In the early XIVc. representation of a VIIc. personage, Siebert is given gloves for dignity; an early XIIIc. hair dress;

archaic notes in low, simple crown; bloused tunic with wide orphreys at neck, hem and edges of cape, which is without shoulder clasp or fur lining.

Edward, almost contemporary, is shown against a background semé with lions passant gardant; gloved with great XIVc. elegance; late XIIIc. hairdress; higher, more foliated crown and sceptre than those of Siebert; dressed in costume of majesty of

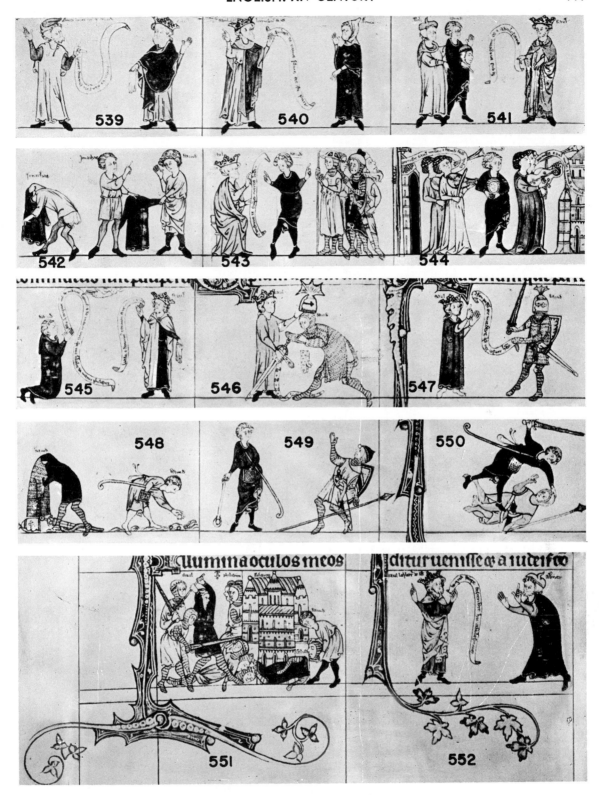

preceding century; narrow orphreys, belt with long tongue hanging at center front over a slit tunic; cape fur lined, clasped on right shoulder.

539-552. 1303-14 A.D. English. (New York Public Library.)

"Tickhill Psalter."

539. Diagonal XIIIc. neck-closing; unused sleeve of overgarment; hat, with crown like point of hood, flopping forward. King's gloves, still an article of great elegance.

540. Saul: cape gathered onto embroidered collar, of Byzantine-regal sort. Abner: guarnache and hood worn over head.

541. Absalom: beret over coif; hood thrown back.

542. Jonathan: doffing tunic, showing shirt and braies tucked into hose.

543. Knights, surcoats below calf.

544. Musicians.

545. King: fine gloves.

546. Knight receiving from king helm with crest, and sword with magnificent belt and fastenings; separate mittens, apparently of flexible plates, hang on cords from sleeves. Slits in hawberk show mail chausses fastened like civilians hose, over braies; laced up back of calf; poleyns at knees.

547. King: familiar over-tunic with hanging sleeve. Knight: wearing accoutrements just given him by king, and shield.

548. King: doffing hawberk, worn over tunic. David: crook and embroidered pouch with tassels (gypcière), into which he gathers stones for sling-shot.

This manuscript, from the Lothian Collection, was written, illuminated, or perhaps merely gilded, by John Tickhill, prior of the Monastery of Worksop, which supplied manuscripts for Augustinian use.

553. 1310 A.D. English. (Trotton, Sussex.)

Margaret, Lady de Camoys: earliest English brass of a lady. Couvre-chef and wimple; enclosing face in manner analagous to coif-de-mailles of knight. Wimple, however, is often tucked into neck of gown.

Side arrangement of hair, with small curl at each temple, under fillet. Tunic (originally semé with enamelled shields); short loose sleeves, over kirtle; long tight buttoned sleeves.

554-555. 1325 A.D. English. (Westley Waterless Church, Cambridgeshire.)

554. Alyne, Lady de Creke, his wife: in carefully composed costume, all garments unified by identical embroidered edging; orphrey-like bands have been superseded by asymmetric, often foliated running designs. *Couvre-chef* and *wimple;* looped plaits of hair. *Mantle:* fur-lined and with embroidered edge, fastened across breast by tasselled cord. *Surcoat:* sleeveless, very long, caught up; embroidered edge and hem. *Kirtle:* long tight buttonless sleeves; hem embroidered to match cape and cote.

555. Sir John de Creke: knight in mixed *mail* and *plate;* surcoat becoming *cyclas;* mustache. *Bascinet:* fluted, pointed, with ornamental *prente,* worn over and laced to *coif-de-mailles,* which is not yet superseded by *camail.*

C y c l a s : shortened surcoat, cut off, *in front* only; slit at sides; tightened at body by lacings which show under arms. Two *pourpoints:* one studded with roses and fringed; one quainted leather. Mail *hawberk:* with short, slit sleeves; hemline pointed down in front; *hauketon:* shows beneath hawberk. *Chausses:* of banded mail, matching rest of mail equipment. *Poleyns:* cuir bouilli.

Plate defences: *rerebraces:* with lion's head *shoulder* and *elbow cops; vambraces:* beneath sleeve of hawberk; hinged around arm; *greaves:* strapped over chausses; *demi-sollerets:* laminated, protect feet; *spurs:* rowell, now not uncommon.

Shield: heater-shaped; charged: Or on a fess gules three lozenges vair; *sword:* knob pommel; scabbard attached to *sword-belt* by metal catches.

Waist-belt of surcoat remains on transitional garment.

556. 1327 A.D. English. (Stoke D'Abrenon, Surrey.) Brass.

Sir John Daubernoun, son of Sir John, 1277: wearing mixed *mail* and *plate; surcoat* becoming *cyclas; camail;* moustache and beard. *Bascinet:* fluted, with dependant *camail,* of banded mail. *Cyclas:* very short front, slit sides, tightened under arms; without waist belt. *Pourpoint:* scalloped, fringed and studded. *Hawberk:* short slit sleeve; hemline curved downward in front. Hauketon, chausses.

Plate defences: *Rerebraces: roundels* protecting shoulder and elbow. *Vambraces:* under sleeve of hawberk; hinged. Poleyns (leather or plate). *Greaves:* strapped over chausses. *Demi-sollerets:* laminated; *prick-spurs. Shield: heater-shaped:* charged like fathers'. *Sword: sword-belt,* worn low; ornamented with crosses and roses of father's gigue.

557-558. 1330 A.D. English. (Minster, Sheppey.) Brass of French Manufacture.

557. Sir John de Northwood: wearing mixed mail and plate; surcoat into cyclas; camail. *Bascinet:* lower and rounder than 1327 Daubernoun, protect-ing ears; camail of banded mail with invected edge. *Cyclas:* short in front; sides and front slit; cut out under arms and bordered like sleeveless surcoat of lady. *Haubergeon:* slit front and sides, and at wrists. *Pourpoint:* quainted and grommeted. *Chausses:* incorrectly restored below knees.

Plate defences: *Rerebraces:* replaced by lengthened *roundel;* roundel on elbow of hawbergeon. *Vambraces:* scale-armor; under hawbergeon. *Mammelière:* on left breast; fastened to haubergeon, or to metal plate beneath (forerunner of breastplate); holding chain which secured helm. *Shield:* larger, very convex; hung on long studded gigue; charged: Ermine a cross engrailed gules. *Sword:* on low *belt;* worn farther to left.

558. Joan de Northwood, 1330: wearing a garment unique in England; occasional in France. *Gorget* "poked up with pins" to looped braids; without couvre-chef. *Surcoat:* sleeveless, lined with vair like hood which can be worn, buttoned over head, or as here, partially unbuttoned, as a cape; embroidered edges. *Kirtle:* embroidery of cuff and coat **match.**

559

560

559. c. 1325-35. English. E. Anglia. (Morgan Library, M. 700.)

"Du Bois Psalter."

Shepherd: hat, held by cord with movable slide, over hood; mittens; shoes with tongue. Small figure: in high flopping hat, over hood with liripipe; hood or collar on garment with funnel-shaped sleeves.

560. XIV-XVc. English. (San Marino, Huntington Library.)

"Ellesmere Chaucer."

The mediaeval excuse for taking a vacation was to go on a pilgrimage. Inns were usually dirty, and as dangerous as the roads, so pilgrims tried to travel in groups, for both fun and protection. The standard of living was at its highest in the monasteries; they served as the luxury hotels of the period. The monks welcomed the distraction of visitors; and educated people looked forward not only to exalted religious satisfactions, but to the cleanliness and good fare, to the intellectual cultivation of the monks, and to interesting and educational sights of beautiful manuscripts being illuminated, cheeses better made, fields and flocks more thriftily managed than anywhere else.

Wife of Bath: wide hat, held by cord like shepherd's; hood; netted hair; skirts and feet thrust into roughly hose-shaped bags; spurs over hose.

561. XIVc. 1326-27. English. (Oxford, Christ Church.)
Walter de Milemete: "de nob., sap., et prud. regum."

Crossbowman: aiming at a fire-box. Archers were for a long time unarmed. He now has plate protection at shoulder and elbow, as well as a chapel-de-fer and bavier. He is gloved; the hook for stringing his bow hangs from his belt.

562. c. 1350. English. (Gresford, Denbigh.)
Freestone memorial slab: a civilian. Guarnache with typical XIVc. lappets; standing collar; fastened over a close hood; shows sleeves of two tunics.

563. 1364 A.D. English. (Norfolk, Lynn Regis.)
Brass of Robert Braunch: compartment. Civilian. The new feathered hat over a hood which is buttoned under the standing collar of a short, loose tunic; this can be left open below the breast, because his long hose must be tied to a doublet.

564-574. 1340 A.D. English. (British Museum.)
"Luttrell Psalter."
Liturgical psalter written and illuminated in East Anglia for Sir Geoffrey Luttrell.

564. Man chasing a goose with his hood and staff; wide tunic tucked into studded belt; loose hose.

565. Lady playing with a squirrel, a common mediaeval pet, wearing a collar and bell. Lady in very long cote-hardi, tippet sleeves; hair in a crespine, under wimple and loose hood.

566-68. Milking ewes. Feed was scarce, and sheep could pick up a living on waste land. Tiny as these sheep were, their fleece made them the most profitable farm animal, as the English wool trade throve from XIIc. English agriculture was almost ruined during the XVc., as more land was enclosed for sheep, and fewer farmers were needed. Cheese-making from ewe's milk was abandoned when sheep became profitable. "They vse to wayne theyr lambes at 12 weekes olde, and to mylke their ewes fiue or syxe weekes," but this was "great hurte to the ewes, and wyll cause them to . . goo barreyne."* The milker's hood can be fastened by its button. One of the women carrying milk wears a similar hood over couvre-chef; aumonière at belt. Her companion has a smocked apron. No perspective in these illustrations.

569. St. James as a pilgrim. Barefoot with staff, and cockle-shell (of a pilgrim to his own shrine at Compostella) fastened to the script which hangs from his shoulder, and on the turned-up, pointed hat worn particularly by pilgrims.

570. Men ploughing. It usually took 8 of these tiny oxen to draw a plough, but as many as 24 are known to have been yoked together, in working clay soil. Ploughman: hat like St. James', turned the other way, over a hood with a small tip; loose tunic, split up side seams; studded belt with hanging

* John ? Fitzherbert: *Book of Husbandry*, 1523.

564

565

566 567 568 569

570

sheath; work gloves; legs protected by bindings. Ox-driver: hood with tabs, which is seen at the neck, in various forms, throughout XIVc.; guarnache over tunic, slit up the front; also gloved.

571   572

potum dabis nobis in lacrimis in

573

Et memores sunt mandatorum ipsius: ipsius: ad faciendum ea

574

571. St. Catherine; dressed as a queen of an earlier period.

572. Bishop: mitre and crozier more elaborate in form; amice, chasuble, dalmatic, alb with apparel, and episcopal ring over glove.

573. Archers: their leader wears a turned-back hat brim with a hood crown. Over the sleeve of his upper tunic, which is open at the side-seams of the skirt, he wears an arm guard; as do the other archers, into whose studded belts are tucked the wide skirts of their tunics, and their spare arrows.

574. Noble ladies travelling in a chariot. Carriages, originally made in Hungary, were a Flemish industry in XIIIc. This chariot, possibly the first in English use, was probably imported; similar ones are seen on the Continent.

Only very rich women or sick people rode in "whirlicotes," (*whirl*-moving, *cote*-house) or "folkwains." It was really much more comfortable to ride, but Elizabeth toured England in uncomfortable state in something not much more refined. When Richard II was married in 1383 to Anne of Bohemia, (who brought the side-saddle to England) whirli-cotes and chariots were forsaken, Stow says, except at coronations.

This chariot has the usual 6-spoked wheel of the period, and no springs at all. Painted coverings, usually of leather, either rolled up or had window openings with curtains. A metal-sheathed box is fastened underneath, and there are rings for fastening luggage or dogs. There are a good many attendants, since the chariot had to be lifted around corners, until the XVIc., when a swivel was added to the front axle. This whirlicote is drawn by 5 horses in line. The first, between shafts, carries a driver with a very long whip; the front horses are between rope traces, caught to the shafts by pegs. The 4th horse is also driven; the lead horse is riderless.

The attendants on horseback all wear hoods with liripipes; over which 2 wear beaver hats. Rider (c.) has a scapular over hood and cote. The lady, who is passing her dog out to an attendant, wears a wimple. The sideless surcoats of the 3 young princesses are still very simple, bound at the edges with another color; veils from crowns set over braided, looped hair.

575-584. 1338-44 A.D. England. (Oxford, Bodleian.)
"Romance of Alexander."

Gentlemen outdoors with king (575); and at *banquet* (576); showing a great variety of cotes-hardi and hoods. Without the hoods (in banquet scene), the cotes show wide bateau-neck and left under-arm fastening; they are parti-colored, motley, and (to left of king at banquet) armorial, as are the hooded capes

front of the skirt, through which to reach the belt (worn over the kirtle) from which hung aumonière, and even dagger. As sideless cotes are worn, and elaborated, the all-over embroidery tends to move to the kirtle (see Ill. 586). Hair is braided and massed over ears.

580. *Court ladies*: ceremonial sideless surcoats, which are of plain material, piped with another color, a line of fur, or braid, but never embroidered all-over; buttons down center-front and forearm of kirtle; hair elaborately braided and looped to a center part, over the forehead.

Windows, without glass, protected by oiled parchment, or shutters of wicker work or battens.

581. *Two ladies and four gentlemen*: all garments finely embroidered; gentlemen's pouches monogrammed; both hoods and cotes embroidered and dagged to match; ankle high, embroidered shoes. Arrangement of buttons and embroidery down front of ladies' cote; looped braids here pinned far back.

Minstrels and their music played an important role in the social life of a mediaeval court. Gaston de Foix gave 500 francs to the minstrels and heralds; and ermine-trimmed gold garments with 200 francs to the minstrels of the Duke of Touraine. (Froissart)

with dagged and slittered edges and long liripipes, which all wear in the outdoor scene above. Tippets and liripipes finish the sleeves of many of the cotes at the elbow, below which the sleeves, whether of cote or doublet, are buttoned to wrist. Buttons are also used down front of a diagonally striped garment. As the belt of the armed knight was lowered, so was that of males out of armor; all are furnished with gypcière and miséricorde, hung at center front.

577. *Musicians*: dressed, as are the servants at the banquet, very much like everyone else, but not invariably carrying a dagger with pouch.

578. *Ladies and gentlemen at games;* and (579) *with a falcon*: the round game presents the back view of the men's cotes and hoods. The cotes of the ladies have the same bateau neck as the men's; long skirts, frequently tucked up to expose the skirt of the kirtle which is frequently banded. Many of these cotes have buttons down the front; are embroidered all over; and have tippets and liripipes, lined with a plain color, at the elbow; and fitchets or latchets at the

PART OF THE CREST

582. *Women at games*: Cotes with tippets at elbow; some sideless, showing plain sleeve of kirtle, shorter skirt of which is exposed by trussed up skirt of cote, and is edged with a wide darker embroidered band, the color of the sleeves, on a lighter colored skirt. Couvre-chef and disordered hair, which had been arranged like that of the ladies in Ill. 580.

583. *Masque*: mummers wearing capes, painted with animals, and with animal-head hoods. Women: parti-colored, plain, and all-over embroidered, with fitchets.

584. *Fools*: in loose motley garments with extreme hoods (see Ill. 534), and sleeves cut with exaggerated point at elbow. The first figure from left has one of these sleeves; the other is so long as to conceal the hand.

585. 1347 A.D. English. (Brass of Flemish workmanship.) (Elsing, Norfolk.)

Sir Hugh Hastings, and contemporary personages: mixed mail and plate defenses; *cyclas* becoming *jupon*; *camail*. *Bascinet*: rounded top, movable vizor, with linked-mail *camail*. *Cyclas-jupon*: full-skirted like cyclas, but cut off all around to jupon length and fitted in body like jupon; charged with arms of shield. *Haubergeon*: hanging mail cuffs. *Hauketon*: wrist, below mail cuff. *Cuishes*: studded leather. *Chausses*: mail, without protective shin-plates; rowell-spurs.

Additional plate defenses were: *Gorget*: metal collar on which helm rested. *Rerebraces*, with roundels. *Vambraces*: over sleeve of hawbergeon. *Poleyns*: of cuir-bouilli with metal spiked plates. *Shield*: very small, charged: Or a manche gules, with labels of three points argent. *Sword* (worn well to left); *sword-belt*, studded. *Helm* (shown on right above figure): flat-topped, perforated movable vizor.

Other personages (some lost) of Hastings brass: several without shields. The first English brass without shield is Wantone, 1347. Several hold lances with pennons; wear metal gorgets and shoulder-plates; spiked poleyns and coutes;

bascinets with pointed vizors. Dexter side: 1. Edward I, crowned, cyclas-jupon, charged France and England quarterly; 2. Thomas Beauchamp, Earl of Warwick; 3. Member of Despencer family (lost); 4. Roger, Lord Gray de Ruthin. Sinister side: 1. Henry Plantagenet, Earl of Lancaster; 2. Lawrence Hastings, Earl of Pembroke, whose shield, Hastings quartering Valence, is one of the earliest examples of quartering of arms of a lesser personage than king; 3. Ralph, Lord Stafford; 4. Almeric, Lord St. Amand, wearing the only *chapel-de-fer* over bascinet shown on any brass.

586. 1349 A.D. English. (Brass of Flemish workmanship.) (St. Margaret's Church, Lynn Regis, Norfolk.)

Margaret de Walsokne: Rich bourgeoise in costume of utmost luxury. Norfolk and Flanders are

587

closely related by the wool trade on which both thrive. Their bourgeoisie rivals the aristocracy, which competes in return. (See Appendix.)

Couvre chef and wimple; looped braids. Mantle: embroidered edge, contrasting lining, cord thrown back. Sideless surcoat: sleeveless, fur-lined; edge embroidered; wide neck, highest at center. Kirtle: tight, buttoned sleeves; cuff detail; magnificent, all-over embroidery.

587. 1360 A.D. English. (Brass of Flemish workmanship.) (Wensley Church, Yorkshire.)

Simon de Wenslagh: Priests vestments. Matching embroidery: amice; chasuble with orphreys; maniple over left arm; stole, fringed; alb with apparels at wrist and hem. The priest, like the ladies, wears the simplest of pointed shoes.

588

589

588-589. 1350-60 English. From St. Stephen's Chapel, Westminster. (British Museum.) Wall paintings.

Sons and daughters of Edward III and Queen Philippa of Hainault. St. Stephen's, built in 1350, was glazed with stained glass designed by John Alemayne (whose name shows him an alien) but manufactured at Chiddingford. In tempera and metal leaf, overpainted in transparent oil; shows perspective.

Sons: camail attached to bascinet, heavily ridged all around; jupon with tightly fitted waist bearing England and France quarterly,* over hawbergeon. Extremities completely protected by laminated, hinged plate and mail gussets; belt, low; carrying sheathed miséricorde, right; sword, left.

Daughters: elaborately composed and unified costume. Foliated crowns over looped plaits of hair, decorated with same floral motifs which serve as buttons down front of cotehardi, which is completely sideless, and exposes body and sleeves of brocade kirtle; fur plastron extended over shoulders, from which hangs mantle, fur lined to waist, and bordered like skirt of cote, with an invected foliation.

* To ingratiate himself with the Irish, among whom St. Edward was a favorite, the English king used, in Ireland, banners bearing Edward's arms: A cross patence or, on a field gules, with four doves argent on the shield or banner as you please, rather than England and France. This was related to Froissart by Henry Castine, who had been sent in advance to try to make gentlemen of the Irish kings. They rode without breeches or stirrups, wrapped only in a cloak, and he had great difficulty in persuading them to wear silken robes, trimmed with squirrel and miniver.

590. 1350-60. English. From St. Stephen's Chapel, Westminster. (British Museum.) Wall painting.

Edward III: King: not robes of majesty; but insignia of kingship assumed over dress of contemporary gentleman. Cloak, fur lined, closing on right
shoulder. Shoulder cape of contemporary gentleman,
done in ermine; remains henceforth as part of insignia of kingship. Very high, foliated crown; gothic
sceptre. Justaucorp, the short fitted cote-hardi of the
XIVc., with bordered liripipe sleeves, same brocade as

tight under-sleeve. Important belt at lowered waistline. Pointed shoes, magnificently embroidered.

Courtiers: high felt and beaver hats, one with
plume (increasingly used). Parti-colored capuchon
with embroidered band and cartridge-pleated edge,
worn over justaucorps and under-tunic of matching
brocade; tiny buttons; diapered shoes. Parti-colored
hose and shoes; magnificently bound swords; tunic
with vertical stripes.

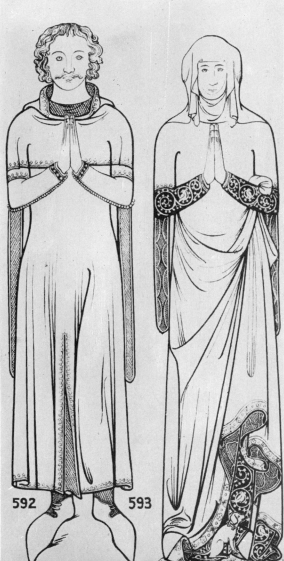

591. c. 1360. English. (Aldborough, Yorkshire.) Brass.

William de Aldeburgh: camail and jupon; mustache. *Bascinet*: high, convex (standard to end of century), covering ears, laced through vervelles to camail of linked mail. *Jupon*: cloth or leather; quainted edge painted or embroidered with arms borne by shield; tightly fitted over body-armor. *Haubergeon*: linked mail. Sleeves and chausses of mail reduced to gussets as plate armor sheathes extremities more efficiently. *Cuishes*: pourpointed leather.

Additional plate protection: *Epaulieres; rerebraces; coutes; vambraces; poleyns; greaves;* articulated *sollerets. Gauntlets*: with articulated metal finger-plates. *Shield*: last brass in which shield is shown as part of equipment. Large, convex, charged: Azure a fess per fess indented and . . . between three crosses botony, or, the dexter cross charged with an annulet for difference. *Sword*: on *baldric*, embroidered with castles; *miséricorde* (from now on, indispensable part of knight's equipment).

592-593. 1364. English. (Flemish workmanship.) (St. Margaret's Church, Lynn Regis, Norfolk.)

Robert and Margaret Braunch: his chaperon and cote-hardi, with liripipe sleeves and center-front slit, are unified by identical linings and a foliated embroidery edge into a typically composed costume; tight buttoned sleeves of under-tunic; shoes with pointed toes, ankle high, closed by parallel lacings. Lady: couvre-chef and wimple; cote-hardi fur lined throughout; over kirtle scrolled with rich embroidery. These brasses (591-94) indicate the wealth which the bourgeoisie attained by XIVc. Sir John Fastolf's will (Paston Letters, 1459) refers to "Sir Philip Braunche, Knight, my brothyr-in-law, that deyde and was slayn in Fraunce," and the Paston's cousin Elizabeth Clere will be married to his grandson.

594. 1376. English. (Flemish workmanship.) (St. Margaret's Church, Lynn Regis, Norfolk.)

Robert Attelath: fur-lined cloak closed on right shoulder by 4 buttons; hood, which could button tight at throat, here worn thrown back. Tunic with contrasting lining closed down entire front and at wrist by grouped buttons. Embroidered sleeve of under-tunic prolonged and spread over knuckles; like Ill. 601, allied to gloves with cuffs. Pointed shoes, notched at ankle and buckled.

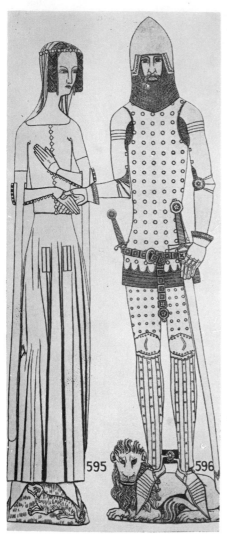

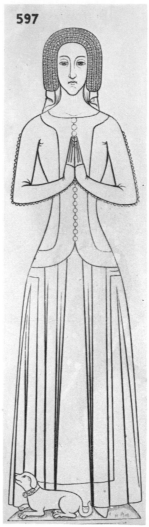

595-596. 1364. English. (Ingham Church, Yorkshire.) Brass.

596. Sir Miles de Stapleton: camail and jupon; mustache, beard. *Bascinet*: laced to *camail* through *vervelles*. *Jupon*: cuir-bouilli; quainted edge; studded. *Haubergeon*: banded mail; gussets of mail at armpit and elbow; mail chausses have disappeared. *Cuishes, poleyns* and *jambes* of studded cuir-bouilli.

Plate defenses: *Epaulieres; rerebraces; coutes; vambraces; sollerets;* articulated. *Gauntlets*: steel *gadlings* on knuckles. *Baldric*: metal plates, linked; carries *sword* and *miséricorde*. No shields.

595. Joan (Ingham), wife of Miles de Stapleton: *Hair*: looped braids; jewelled *fillet;* small *veil*. *Cotehardi*: wide necked: *liripipe* at elbows; buttons at center-front; skirt short; beltless, so provided with *fitchets* to reach *aumonière* hung from belt or kirtle. *Kirtle*: tight buttoned sleeves, spreading over knuckle (compare with gauntlet in Ill. 600: knightly styles influence dress of ladies; wimple was equivalent to coif-de-mailles).

597. c. 1370. English. (Cobham Church, Kent.) Brass.

Maude, Lady Cobham: nebulé headdress, of superimposed gauffered layers, and veil. Sideless cotehardi, buttoned down center-front and with short skirt, bordered at hem and up slit sides. Sleeves of kirtle buttoned from shoulder to spread over knuckles.

598-599. 1384. English. (Southacre, Norfolk.) Brass.

599. *Sir John Harsick:* camail and jupon; shield no longer part of equipment, but still an important method of identification, a little more personal than a calling card today. Froissart, meeting the March Herald, asks: "March, what are the arms of Henry Castide, for I have found him very agreeable . . ."

Helm: with crest, orle, lambrequin (above figures). *Bascinet*: laced to camail of band mail. *Hawbergeon*: jupon; bearing arms of shield: Or a chief indented sable. As epaulieres, rerebraces, coutes, vambraces; and cuishes, jambes and sollerets, curved, hinged, and articulated, enclose the extremities almost completely, the sleeves of the hawbergeon and the chausses exist only vestigially as gussets of mail at elbow and armpit, knee and foot. Rowell spurs; gauntlets with gadlings; belt, elaborate and low; sword worn at left.

598. *Katherine, Lady Harsick* (née Calthorpe): braids looped over fillet; mantle with cords through fermail: kirtle, with sleeves buttoned from shoulder to spreading cuff, and bearing the arms of Geslingthorpe, assumed by Calthorpe: Ermine a manche gules, impaling Harsick.

* Blennerhasset, Bleverhasset, abbreviated to Harsset, etc.

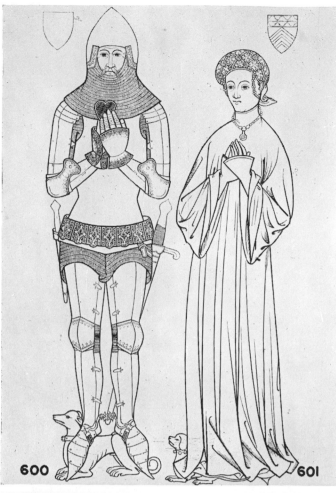

600 601

602

600-601. 1397. English. (Brandsburton Church, Yorkshire.) Brass.

600. *Sir John de Saint Quintin*: camail and jupon. Camail, hawbergeon and gussets of ring mail. Plates, hinged, articulated, buckled, finely chased, covering arms and legs. Gauntlets with cuffs of mail. Magnificent belt; sword borne far to left; miséricorde. Arms blazoned on small shields in corners.

601. *Lora de Saint Quintin*: crespine headdress, padded, covered with jewelled network concealing hair; small veil in back; and looped pearls at ears. Robe: high necked, wide sleeved, ungirdled, very wide skirt, fur lined. Kirtle: sleeves extending over hand.

602. XIVc. 1380-85. English. (London National Gallery.)

Wilton House Diptych.

The most beautiful embroidery in Christendom was done in England during XIII-e.XIVc., and vestments of "English work" were ordered from Italy. The magnificent Sion Cope c. 1300, in the South Kensington Museum, and its accompanying stole and maniple have the coats-of-arms of 124 donors of the vestments worked into the orphreys.

The effigies of Edward III's sons, especially William of Hatfield, at York Minster, show them in beautifully embroidered garments. The actual garments —the "atchievements" of Edward the Black Prince, in war and peace, hang at Canterbury: helmet, gauntlets, shield, and embroidered surcoat laced in back. There is a portrait of Richard II as king, in robes embroidered all-over with R's and roses. The English-made gilt-latten effigy of Richard II and his first wife, Anne of Bohemia, in Westminster Abbey, show both in magnificently embroidered garments. (See Appendix.)

The Wilton House Diptych, against a gold ground, represents (l. to r.) King Edmund: ermine-lined and collared green cloak, blue gown patterned in gold birds collared together by crowns, a blue under-tunic and red shoes. Edward the Confessor: white, with blue under-tunic sleeves prolonged over the hand. John the Baptist: gold lined with pink. Richard II in a red houppelande, covered with the badge of the White Hart in gold, and lined with brown fur. All kings with jewelled brooches.

603. XIVc. c. 1300. Italian. (Bologna, Museo Civico.)
Master of Manni. Pope Boniface VIII.

This huge statue in sheet bronze, of the Pope who died in 1303, shows the tiara, the non-liturgical headwear of the Pope, signifying temporal power. It is white and was originally without crown. One crown was added in XIc. In other statues, Boniface is shown with two crowns, which he was the first to wear. It was not until 1314, under Clement V that the Pope wore 3 crowns on the tiara. A large jewelled morse was originally set at the neck of what I take to be the mozetta. (See Appendix.)

604-606. XIVc. c. 1305. Italian Florentine. (Padua, Madonna dell' Arena.)

Giotto di Bondone. Scenes preceding the Birth of Christ: the Meeting at the Golden Gate (604); Joachim's Dream, detail (605); Betrayal of Christ, detail (606).

604. Females in specifically Italian dress already seen in XIIIc. Giottos: sleeves cut in one with short-waisted bodice; skirt gathered on, and looped under at the hem in front to show underskirt, orange or rose, with gold, pale or bright green.

Italian way of handling the ubiquitous braids, drawn up behind the ears, forming a coronet above forehead, differs from the English fashion of braids looped on either side, in front of the ears. Italian women's heads are relatively uncovered, in comparison with the veils and wimples of France and England. The extravagance of the horned and heart-shaped headdresses of the rest of Europe, will, in Italy, become an extravagance of hair arrangement; the headdress will be a wreath or fillet; this will increase to a stuffed roundlet, and finally to a turban. The veil will always be gauzy. In Italy it is the wo-

men of the lower classes, or the elderly, who cover their hair (black-shawled women, c.). Two of the ladies wear tiny pill-box hats; one of them holds her mantle in place by means of a narrow patterned ribbon which permits her to catch up its trailing side with the same hand. The man at extreme left wears the dress of the peasant of all Europe: coif; belted tunic; loose-fitting, bound sock-boots.

The shepherd in Joachim's Dream (605), and the attendant in the Betrayal of Christ (606), wear the same peasant costume, with the addition of capes with cowls, or a petasus with cord by which it could be worn slung back.

607. c. 1305. Italian. (Same provenance as 604-606.)

Giotto di Bondone. Last Judgment: Group of the Blessed.

A group of monks in cowled habits, coiffed elderly gentlemen, and ladies in robes of the current cut; rich braid trimming at seams, and orphrey-like patches give an effect which is more Byzantine and ecclesiastic than is commonly worn. Hair simple,

often flowing, with coronet braids, crowns, fillets and bands; woman in dark robe wears a gauzy veil pinned, wimple-fashion, to braided hair.

608. c. 1317. Italian, Sienese. (Naples, National Museum.)

Simone Martini. St. Louis of Toulouse Crowning Robert of Anjou.

The saint who had ceded his throne, probably un-

der duress, to his brother, wears the robe of a Franciscan beneath his bishop's garments, all of which bear armorial designs. The new king's dalmatic, likewise, carries his arms in its clavi and orphreys.

609. c. 1328. Italian, Sienese. (Siena, Pal. Pub.)

Simone Martini. Equestrian portrait of Guidoriccio da Fogliana.

The surcote of the proud, victorious general and the caparison of his horse are yellow, with the black diamonds and a running design of green sprigs, *"fogliana,"* of his coat-of-arms. He wears a high-collared, wide-sleeved shirt of mail; legs and knees armed in plate combined with mail.

Beyond the stockade is a mediaeval fortress with moat, ramparts, and towers with projecting galleries; and a military machine of the mangonel type, for hurling stones.

610. XIV.c. Italian, Sienese. (Pisa, Campo Santo.)

Triumph of Death; detail. (Attributed to *Francesco Traini,* also to *A. Orcagna.*)

Rich woven pattern and embroidery characteristic of Italian costume from XIVc. Brocade cote-hardi with short wide sleeves lengthened into liripipes; more richly lined and edged than in other parts of Europe at this period. Close sleeves of the kirtle are likewise of striped or patterned stuffs. Growing importance of the glove; the lady with the falcon wears two, rather than the necessary one gauntlet (see Ills.

629-30). She alone wears a wimple and complete head-covering, made necessary by the sport. The others wear *roundlets,* stuffed turbans in the spirit of the increasingly seen coronets of braids, worn by the central figure. The third wears a simple pleated arrangement, connected with the elaborate male *chaperon* of continental Europe. Chaplet of flowers on rolled hair of man on right.

611. XIVc. Italian, Sienese. (Siena Academy.)
    P. Lorenzetti. Carmelites.
    The early black-and-white "magpie" dress of the Fratres barrati.

614

612. 1331. Italian, Sienese. (Siena, S. Francesco.)

Ambrogio Lorenzetti. Saint Louis of Toulouse before Pope Boniface VIII: detail of crowd.

Italian male headwear: hats worn over hood or integrated into hood; sheer coif; stiffened, turned-up brim with draped crown; and two wide-brimmed, flat-crowned hats. Wide-necked, sleeved tunics; fur lining seen through breast-slit. Patterned materials.

613. XIVc. Italian, Sienese. (Pisa, Campo Santo.)

Francesco Traini, also att. to *A. Orcagna,* or *P. Lorenzetti:** The triumph of Death: Last Judgment and Hell; Thebaid.

Hawking and hunting on horse and mule-back.

For journeys and hunting, women wear wimples and veils; and men, similar arrangements or hoods, gloves (not only for hawking), and high, conical hats with brims turned up in back. The head is always well protected. The king's crown is imposed on his hat, which is worn over a coif below which the hair is rolled. Jewelled brim of female rider, set over veil and wimple, which fill in low neck of brocade gown. Early prevalence in Italy of brocaded and striped materials. Embroidered borders of king's robe, with its cap sleeve. Sophisticatedly cut liripipe end of the short sleeve of the cote-hardi, worn over plain doublet. Follower, in brocade cote-hardi with funnel-shaped sleeve, wears hood of same brocade. Cripples at right: bearded, while gentry are clean-shaven. Tunics: one-piece, or with set-in sleeves. Old hag: head-covering of lower classes.

* In the case of varied attributions, I have tried to use that preferred by the Frick Art Reference Library.

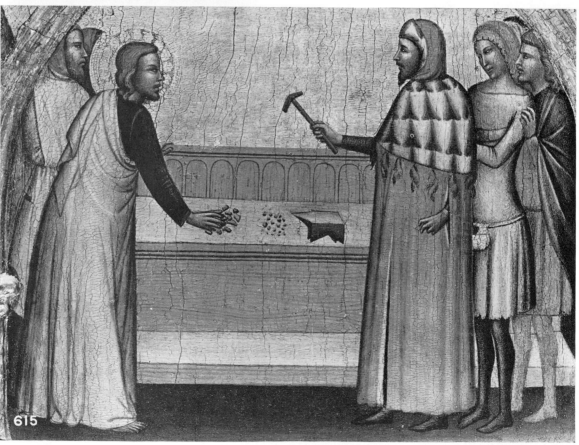

615

616

614. 1330-40. Italian. (Wash., Nat. Gall. of Art.)
Bernardo Daddi. St. Catherine.

Crown over characteristically Italian braids, martyr's palm; brown cloak; gold-embroidered, green cotehardi; both lined with white fur, which shows at the fitchet (emphasized by gold embroidery), behind her right arm.

615. XIVc. Italian. (Wash., Nat. Gall. of Art.)
Allegretto Nuzi (act. 1346-73/74). St. John and the Philosopher Crato.

St. John in blue robe and red mantle, is accompanied by a hooded monastic figure, whose arms are tucked in the front of his scapular; band below hips connects front and back sections of scapular. Crato wears a red cape, lined in white fur; it is slit for the passage of the arms, and is necessarily split up the center-front: hood-facing and shoulder cape of fur, fringed with tails. Accompanying gentlemen in fitted cotes-hardi, with low belts and aumonières.

616. 1337-40. Italian, Sienese. (Siena, Palazzo Pubblico.)
A. Lorenzetti. Results of Good Government: City Life.

Badly damaged, but full of detail of costume, architecture, and street life, which make it worth examining with a magnifying glass.

The gowns of the playful group with the tambourine are worn loose, girdled, or with the skirts gathered onto a low-waisted bodice. With back to us, is a gown brocaded with huge dragon-flies; sleeves are delicately laced across a wide rectangular opening from wrist to elbow in back; lattice-work sandals show clearly below slit which separates short front from longer back section of skirt. A similar skirt (horizontally striped), has corners of back section pinned up on side seams for freer action. Between these two, a diagonally patterned gown has slittered sleeves, and a series of increasingly larger purses, hanging like tassels, from the belt. The stretched-out arm of the man (next to the tambourine player) is slit and laced along the entire seam of the sleeve, which is cut in one with the body. The sleeve of the youth (following the riders, to the left) is baggy at the elbows in the newest fashion.

617. XIVc. 1338-40. Italian. (Siena, Palazzo Pubblico.)

A. Lorenzetti. Good Government: Allegory of Justice.

621

Procession of dignified citizen in long gowns, coifs, and hats with draped crowns (see Traini: Ill. 613). Women in allegorical costume.

618-619. XIVc. Italian. (Siena, Acad. of Fine Arts.)

Bartolo di Fredi. Scenes from the life of the Virgin.

The saints are, by convention, very richly dressed, in brocade garments with fitchets, which are given an archaic Byzantine look by the use of patches and bands of embroidery.

620. XIVc. Italian. (Pisa, Campo Santo.)

Andrea da Firenze. Three Scenes in life of St. Ranieri.

Old gentleman: fur-lined cape; side slits for arms; short gown; contrasting hose and shoes. Child: caped cote-hardi; front closing, tiny ball buttons; separately cut, very flaring skirts. Group of 4 women, right of psaltery player: puffs pulled through slashes at sleeve-top; convex neckline; short, flaring over-garment. Beside her: interesting flapped cap (see XVc.). Girl with pigtail: sleeves buttoned from knuckles to elbow; braid definition of seams and edges.

621. Mid-XIVc. Italian. Florentine. (Assisi, San Martino Chapel.)

Puccio Capanna. Life of St. Francis, detail: Band of Musicians.

The elaborately imaginative dress of this band of street musicians corroborates Machiavelli's statement about Florence in 1350: "The people being conquerors, the nobility was deprived of all participation in government, and in order to regain a portion of it, it became necessary for them not only to seem like the people, but to be like them in mind and mode of living. Hence arose those changes in armorial bearings, and in the titles of families, which the nobility adopted in order that they might seem to be of the people." Under such conditions, there is always a concomitant rise in popular standards.

Parti-color in a very Italian and sophisticated form, enriched with patterned and pleated fabric, braid, and jewelry.

Saint, and singers, r.: characteristic short, clipped bang which accompanied bobbed hair of XIVc. men: this clipped tuft and the ends (carefully rolled by the more elegant) show even when a close coif is worn. For centuries, hair is more beautifully arranged in Italy than anywhere else in Europe.

The yoke of Italian women's dress is reflected in the flute-player's outer garment; a cape-like section, well down on the shoulders, appears to be attached to the cote-hardi. The standing collar, and flaring, stiffened cuff of the cittern-player's matching inner sleeve, are far advanced in sophistication. Fine details of neck-closings: double clasps of stones; turned-back tabs.

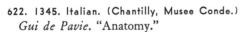

622. 1345. Italian. (Chantilly, Musee Conde.)
Gui de Pavie. "Anatomy."

Slit and hooded, fur-lined gowns with fitchets and liripipe sleeves; row of tiny buttons down outseam of undersleeve.

623-624. c. 1345. Italian. (Morgan Library, M. 735.)
Boniface de Calabria. "Thesauro di cavalli."

Bag sleeve, padded bosom, and high collar of the houppelande affecting the cote-hardi, even of a veterinarian, during first half XIVc.

625-626. 1356. Italian. (San Gemignano, Collegiate.)
Bartolo di Fredi. Old Testament Scenes.

625. Carpenters: aprons, or skirts of tunic tucked up to hold nails. Sock-boots, often without hose. 626. Shepherds: hooded overgarments of comfortable scapular type. Riding hat; plumed, brocade crown; brim turned up in back; cord knotted under chin.

627. XIVc. Italian. (Chantilly, Musee Conde.)

Bartolommeo da Bologna. Allegory.

Knight in surcoat with dagged edges; tight, low-waisted, with the peculiarly full-bellied and portly look of Italian costume of first half XIVc.

Lady mounted astride: veil, which in XIVc. Italy indicated an arduous outdoor trip, a saint or virgin, an elderly woman, or one of the lower classes. Legs protected by rather shapeless, spurred boots, clasped down the outside, and mounting above knee; worn in XIVc. by riders of both sexes. (See Ill. 560.) Embroidered, fur-lined, slit garments with lengthening liripipe sleeve-ends. Pleated, *gugel-like* headdress of woman, developed out of hood thrown across head (see Ill. 628), bound by liripipe end.

628. Late XIVc. Italian, Lombard. (Paris, Bib. Nat. Ms. Lat. 757.)

"Book of Hours for Franciscan use." St. Ursula and the Virgins.

Brocaded or embroidered *cottes,* two of which are high-necked. Turbans and bindings of coronets appear to be affected by the reticulated *kruseler* headdresses of adjacent Germany; looped German braids. Hood with enormously elongated liripipe, thrown over head; the wrapping of this liripipe about the hood, thus worn, led eventually to the extravagant forms of *chaperon.*

629-630. XIVc. Italian. (Florence, Sta. Maria Novella.)

Andrea da Firenze, and assistants. Allegories of doctrine and scenes from the life of Christ; called "Church Militant and Church Triumphant."

629. Worldly temptations: St. Dominic confessing a knight. In these frescos, celebrating the achievements of the Dominicans, the saint wears the hooded, black-and-white habit of his order, together with the scapular which became obligatory in 1220.

There is an infinity of details of the costume of both sexes: prevailing protuberant-bellied look of the long or calf-length garments; this is lost in the shorter, tight-waisted cote-hardi of the bearer, center. Yoked effects on viol player and small female figure (to left of center, bottom) also appear on garments of Italian male musicians. Patterned and embroidered materials, parti-color, dagged edges, fur linings. Hair of women, braided or flowing, relatively uncovered.

630. Lords spiritual and temporal. Throng of dignitaries, hooded and caped in fur. The gentleman in
the short, light costume has been variously identified:
from the French cut of his dress, and his pointed
poulaines as the usurper, Walter de Brienne, Duke
of Athens; and from the garter on his left leg, as an
Englishman, perhaps an ambassador. (The records
of the Order of the Garter, before 1416, have been
lost.) Parti-color and diagonals on hooded cape (center, back to us). Gauzy cape of kneeling lady, whose
headdress has the new, pushed-back look. By mid-
XIVc., beards have begun to reappear; both forked
and pointed.

**631-632. XIVc. Italian.
(Florence.)**

A. Orcagna (?).

632. Tomb of Acciajulo Acciajuoli. The Acciajuoli were a family which, like the Medici, favored the lesser Florentine guilds in their struggle with the major guilds, who were aided by the Albizzi.

Costume of a rich, elderly Florentine, in its perfection. Braid-trimmed cote-hardi, as long and dignified as a gown; magnificently embroidered lining shows at slit front and tongue-shaped, liripipe sleeve. Fitchet behind sword handle. Handsome belt, fine buttons, gloves, and laced, embroidered shoes.

Linen coif; with hood, matching gown, folded and thrown over shoulder. It was often carried thrown across the head; the point, as it lengthened, was used to bind the whole in place, bringing about the draped turbans, *chaperons,* of e.XVc.

631. Tomb of Lorenzo Acciajuoli. Armorial surcoat vanishing. Vambraces and cuishes of leather, metal banded and studded. Hawberk with sleeves to just below the elbow; scalloped metal collar. Pauldrons and poleyns with lions' heads.

631

632

Jupon: dagged border in leaf design. Belt is high and narrow, so breast-chains still secure sword and dagger. Mail gussets between cuishes, jambes, and sabatons; rowelled spurs. Cuffed gauntlets. Fur-lined cape, with embroidered edge, fastened on right shoulder.

633. 1386. Italian. (Florence, Bigallo Coll.)

Niccolo di Pietro Gerini, and assistants. The return of lost children, by the captains of the Misericordia, to their mothers.

Wimples are not worn in Italy, probably because of the climate; more enveloping headwear is seen in N. Italy because of climate and propinquity to continental style (see Ill. 628). The headdress of the Italian woman is based, as it will be for centuries, on the hair itself; it is rolled and twisted with ribbons into coronets, or a roundlet is set over hanging, braided hair on richly dressed women; small caps and veiled heads are seen particularly on poorer women.

633

634

635

636

637

634. XII-XIVc. German. (Metropolitan Museum.)

Fragment of natural linen, block printed in green. Wood-block printed fabrics, in imitation of Italian brocades, often using silver and gold, began to appear in the Rhineland, end XIIc. They apparently antedated block printed initials on manuscripts, which led to the invention of type.

635. XIV-XVc. German. (Victoria & Albert Mus.)

Fragments of block-printed linen: Upper right, Rhenish: eagles, fruit and leaves in dark purple.

636. XIVc. Scandinavian. Herjolfnes, Greenland (Copenhagen, National Museum.)

Brown twill dress. Viking garment found in grave in the Norse colonies. Ungirded gown worn by men; others show slits, *fitchets,* in side seams of front, as in men's and women's gowns in continental Europe; tongue-shaped gore in front is characteristic of Viking gowns.

637. XIVc. German. (Heidelberg University Library, No. 848.)

"Manessa Codex."

The most important record of XIVc. German life and dress is the "Manessa Codex," a collection of the songs of 300 minnesingers, made by Rudiger Manesse (fl.1360-80/4), though dates of 1310 and 1330-40 are sometimes given to the ms.

Dietmar von Ast (d.1171) was a S. German-Austrian lyricist. This illustration was made by the artist referred to as Hand G.

The lady wears a white *barbette* banded under the chin, over long blonde hair; rose surcote with gold collar and blue lining; dark green kirtle with gold cuffs. The trader has a brown petasus with cords to hold it on; blue cape lined with green; red tunic; brown hose. He exhibits belts and gypcières in black, blue and gold; hanging above is a shield and typical German helmet.

638-641. XIVc. German. (Heidelberg, University Library, No. 848.)

"Manessa Codex."

638. *Messenger from Limburg*: the peacock of the crest of the messenger's helm perches in the tree which serves as "supporter" for a shield, blazoned with 3 maces. (e. arms of the City of Limburg). The kneeling messenger wears a green surcote, patterned with white A's (equals amor ?), and lined with red; matching *ailettes* at shoulders; red spurs. The lady holding his helm wears a white *barbette;* blue surcote lined with white fur; gold-edged rose kirtle.

639. *Herr Gösli von Ehenheim*: Battle with swords from horseback. The knight (l.) in gold mail and helm; gold trappings and surcote, lined with pink. The crest of knight and horse is a green parrot with a red beak, sitting on a white nest; flowing pink *lambrequin*. His opponent: diagonal blue and red stripes with gold stars, lined with yellow; gold helm and crest, knobbed in red. Ladies watching from parapet: yellow, pink, and gray surcotes, patterned in white lines and dots; braided, flowing or veiled heads.

640. *Der von Wildonie*: a fast combat with fists, shields, and swords. Helm with knobbed horns and lambrequins. Small shields of hand-combat; other plates show the tiny wrist-shield, no larger than a saucer. Diapered shoes.

641. *Meister Heinrich Frauenlob*: music school. Canting arms; the "woman he loves" is blazoned in white and gold on a green field. Teacher: ermine collar and lining on purple and white robe, dotted in gold. Left to right: parti-colored green and purple cote-hardi; pink with yellow hose and black shoes; red; green and white horizontal stripes, red and white wreath; fiddler in red and purple, lined with white fur; red and green diagonal; parti-colored purple and blue, striped in red and white; pink and white.

Plates in the "Manessa Codex" show every detail of mediaeval life: sappers working underground; the defence of a castle by bowmen, aided by ladies with rocks; harvesters with sickles; Susskind the Jew from Trimberg, his traditionally yellow hat (flat, with an Oriental knobbed steeple-top), painted in gold.

642

643

642-647. XIVc. 1307. German. (Berlin State Library.)

"Codex Baldwinii": Emperor Henry VII's Journey to Rome.

642. Pope Clement makes Henry's brother, Baldwin, Archbishop of Trier: red hats had distinguished cardinals from 1252, but were not worn with liturgical vestments until red biretta was granted cardinals, third quarter XVc., by Paul II. These gloved cardinals wear fur capuchons fringed with tails over fur-lined tabards; the use of the dalmatic at solemn high mass had been granted to the cardinal priests of Trier in 975 by Benedict VII. The mitres of the Pope and the Archbishops all show a concave rake. Pope: amice, chasuble, alb, embroidered gloves and shoes. Archbishops: mitre aurifrigiata, amice, pall, chasuble, dalmatic, alb, maniple and gloves, crozier.

643. Travelling: Baldwin, in a red cap, is dressed like the others (who ride bare-headed) in a capuchon of fur or cloth with slittered edge, the hood generally worn down; over fur-lined tabard; gloves. Knights: in long full surcoats, ungirt and undecorated; over mail hawberk and chausses. Note tiny wrist-shield slung at waist of kneeling messenger.

644. Pennon and banners.

645. Men at arms: cross-bow men and other foot soldiers are now given mail protection. Knights wear a variety of head protections, notably the pig-faced bascinet with pointed vizor, chapel, and rounded bascinets. Mail camail, hawberk and chausses. Small shields.

646. Messenger.

647. Royal ladies at banquet: high gorgets pinned wide to hair (see Ill. 558). Servants all in similar parti-colored garments. Within a century the idea of uniformity, designated by costume, will be well on the way to establishment.

646

647

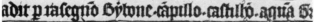

644

645

648

648. XIVc. c.1341. German. (Soest, Staatsar-
        chivs.)

"Das Soester Nequambuch."

Soest in Westphalia was a flourishing
Hanseatic town; its codified laws of the
XIIc. served as a model for the rest of
Germany. Our illustration from a manuscript history of the early days of Soest
shows homage to the archbishop; its costume, being historical, looks back toward
the XIIIc., while that of the "Younger
Titurel," below, looks forward to the XVc.

Bishop: mitra simplex, mantle with
large jewelled morse, cassock, pontifical
gloves. The long, hooded gown of the
chalice-bearer has the XIIIc. horizontal
stripes and hanging sleeve, from which
emerges the narrowing sleeve of the undertunic; it is fur-lined, slit up either side
of the front. The falcon-bearer, hawking
gauntlet on left hand, game pouch,
gypcière, in right hand, wears a fur-lined
tabard over his long tunic.

649. XIVc. Bohemian. Fernberger-Dietrich-
        stein Ms.

"The Younger Titurel," by Albrecht, the
Poet.

The originally close-fitting cote-hardi
feels the influence of the houppelande, to-

649

650

651

652

ward the end of XIVc., and becomes full. It is still belted low in the knightly manner, but has become shorter. The sleeveless form (left) has also taken the standing collar from the houppelande. The cote-hardi of the central figure keeps the band at the upper arm, in fur, as do the high-belted cotes-hardi of the ladies, one of which has ermine liripipes; looped-up braids of last quarter XIVc.

650. 1357. German. Brass of Flemish workmanship. (Stralsund.)

Albert Hovener: luxurious dress of rich bourgeois, shown on one of the finest Flemish brasses. Tabard; fur-lined, hooded, with horizontally banded chaperon-like shoulder caps. Cote-hardi; also fur-lined, long, slit up front, sleeveless, and edged with same in-

vected foliated embroidery as tabard. Doublet; tight buttoned sleeves of brocade cut on diagonal. Shoes; buckled, shaped like sollerets of knight.

651. 1369. German. (Lubeck.) Brass.

Bruno de Warendorp: Chaperon with diapered band and slit edge. Cote-hardi; buttoned body, plain sleeves, to which is gathered, low under a fine belt, a rather long, full slit skirt. Beard.

652. 1394. German. (Paderborn.) Brass.

Bishop Rupert: Mitre, with elaborated edge, rising and becoming convex. Almuce-like tippet edged with fur tails; for choir wear, hung about neck. Wide-sleeved everyday cassock, worn over fur-lined garment with tight sleeves, and another with sleeves prolonged over knuckles and scalloped. Beard.

653. c. 1375. German. (Private coll., Assisi.) Statue (wood, gesso, painted?).

German noblewoman: crown; over gugel (capuchon, cucullus) the corded edge of which is equivalent to the pleating around the face in French examples; mantle, with band border and floral brocade collar showing at left shoulder; robe with full skirt gathered onto fitted bodice under wide, tongued belt (see Ill. 351).

654. 1377. German. (Neckersteinach Chapel.) Brass.

Ritter Hennel Landschaden and Lady: knight of camail-jupon period. Bascinet; camail and hawberk with drooping hem (see Ill. 600); under a jupon which has a quainted edge, and is probably of plate, from breast of which run chains to sword, miséricorde, and (over shoulder) to tilting helm (shown behind figure) with crest of king's head. Other plate defences are decorative in their cut-out shapes rather than in superimposed design, as in Ill. 600: epaulieres, rerebraces, vambraces, cuishes, genouilleres, jambes, sollerets; rowel spurs; gauntlets with articulated fingers.

Lady: zig-zag headdress, G. *kruseler* (kraus equals crinkled, plaited); mantle, with brooch at center front; kirtle.

655. XIVc. 1390. Bohemian. (Prague Cathedral.)

Peter Parler: St. Wenceslas.

The *barbute* worn by the Xc. ruler of Bohemia, who was murdered by his brother, has apparently been affected by the bandings of a bishop's mitre, in token of his canonization after death. Extremely rich belt with anelace, over a laced leather *jupon* with a deeply foliated dagged edge (see No. 631.)

to the hair, the arrangements of which will widen and elaborate with the century. The long, full, ungirded supertunics of the knights have a front slit which shows the lining, and a hood which is beginning to lengthen into a liripipe.

L. to r., on a vermilion bench: Man in light periwinkle blue; man in dark cobalt; woman in mulberry rose with medium blue sleeves. Woman in medium blue, white sleeves; woman in vermilion with light blue sleeves; man in dark cobalt, with vermilion sleeves.

657. XIVc. c. 1390. French. (Poitiers, Palais de Justice.)

Chimney piece: Jeanne de Bourbon, d.1377, wife of Charles V. Classic example of the sideless surcoat of France, with its wide and heavy plastron, made of fur in winter, which is able to support a strip of massive buttons down the center-front. The sleeves of the kirtle are now close-fitting, extended across the knuckles: the kirtle is girdled low, under the surcoat, with a narrow but rich belt. Hair is massed over the ears, in jewelled crespine nets, with crown or coronet.

658. 1362. French. (Paris Bibliotheque Nationale.)

Agnes Eliote, bourgeoise of Mans. (See Appendix.)

659. 1380-90. French. (Paris, Maurice de Rothschild.)

Les très belles heures de Notre Dame of the duke of Berri.

Male bourgeois costume has altered little from that shown in the Old Testament Ills. 476-81, except in richness; the same close white coifs, show the little *dorenlot* bang in front, often curled up over the coif; or the hair is worn combed back, "bobbed" and rolled. Ankle-length, hooded over-garments are richly furred as the bourgeoisie prospers.

The hood has been relegated to bourgeois use; women now wear it, carefully fitted, and with a prominent row of buttons, but it is always worn unbuttoned. The same gowns shown so explicitly in XIVc. English use are worn by these French bourgeoises, on a slightly more bosomy and wide-hipped figure: low-necked, ungirded gowns, fitted or loose, with fitchets in the skirts and liripipes or tippets at the elbows of close sleeves. Rich bourgeoises wear richly furred capes; often appear in sideless surcoats with fur plastrons.

657

656. XIVc. French. N. Eastern. (Morgan Library, M. 805.)

Lancelot du Lac: the first embrace of Lancelot and Guinevere. Ladies in tunics, the under-sleeves of which are decreasing in width on the lower arm and will become entirely close-fitting with the sideless surcoat. The long, ungirded supertunics, by their deepening armholes and lowered necklines, presage the sideless surcoat which begins to appear, second quarter XIVc. The low neck is filled in by the wimple, which is pinned in a V

658

659

661

660-61. c. 1371. Belgian. (Brussels, Bib. Royale, 15652.)

660. *Gelré*: "Wapendichtenen Wapenbock."

Gelré's picture of himself is the earliest representation of a herald bearing his master's arms; in this case: **azure** a lion rampant or, queue fourché, armed and **langued gules**, of Renaud II and III, rulers of Guelderland, which included Nymwegen, Roermonde, Zutphen, Arnhem. Broken chain may signify Gelré's despair and retirement after his master's death.

661. The Emperor Charles IV receiving the homage of different classes of society. Three bishops: mitre, staff, episcopal glove, pontifical ring, morse on cope, dalmatic, alb. Emperor: shortened, tightened surcoat of second half XIVc; knightly girdle, low on

hips, carrying ring dagger (increasingly long); a few inches of mail skirt below belt; rerebraces, vambraces, elbow-cops with mail gussets; greaves; lengthening sollerets; gauntlets of mail and metacarpal plate. Forked beard; hair rolled outward.

King and gentleman behind him in a dagged hem wear long, formal gowns with new fuller sleeve; buttoned, standing collar precedes high fitted collar of houppelande; alternative manner of slinging the obligatory sword, when a belt is not worn.

Two men of lesser estate wear short garments, fullness laid in pleats, held in place by the new, massive, metal-mounted belts. Lesser men wear pointed soles, like poulaines, fastened on hose. Petasus turned up in back; high-crowned hats, round turned-up brims.

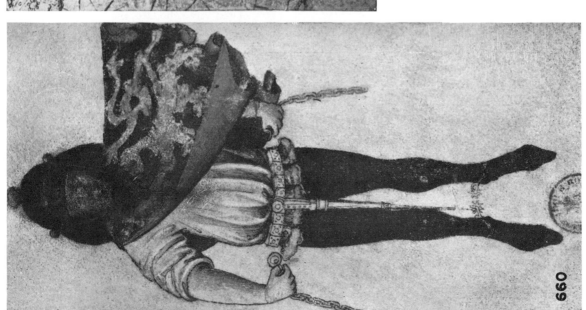

660

18 17   1   9   8   5

20

19   7

21   3

                                                          4

                                                          6

662

16   15   2   10   11   12   13   14

662. 1378-9. French. (Paris, Bib. Nat. Estampes.)

Charles V receiving the homage of Louis II, Duke of Bourbon, for the county of Clermont.

1. Charles V.	12. Mouton de Blainville.
2. Louis of Bourbon.	13. Hugues de Chatillon.
3. Charles, the Dauphin.	14. Jean de Vienne.
4. Louis of Orleans.	15. Edward de Beaujeu.
5. Louis of Anjou.	16. Chaumont.
6. Philip of Burgundy.	17. Gilles de Nedonchel.
7. John, Duke of Berry.	18. Renaud de Trie.
8. John of Artois.	19. John, the Bastard of
9. Pierre d'Orgemont.	Burgundy.
10. Bertrand du Guesclin.	20. Pierre d'Euxy.
11. Louis de Sancerre.	21. La Polpe?

The peers of France, originally 12 feudal lords, were considerably augmented in number during XIVc., as great nobles were honored by the crown. Peers' robes, developed in this century, are closely related to the civilian cloak of the period, buttoned on the right shoulder, as are the cloaks of late XIV-XVc. mayors and men of law. The robes of English peers, of red velvet, hooded and caped with ermine, 2-4 bars on shoulder indicating rank, were cut fuller than the narrow robe of the French peer, which offered a smooth display of armorial bearings.

#9 wears a chaplet of flowers, common in XVc. #1, 5, 7, 8, 19, as sons and brothers of the king, or descendants of St. Louis (the Bourbons), bear

663

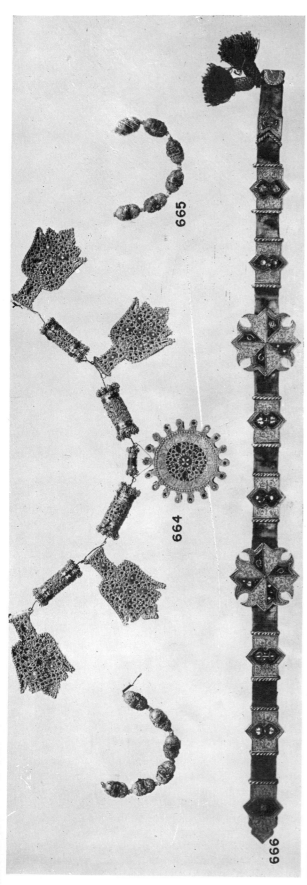

France quarterly, or differenced with a label. #3, 4, the little princes wear robes of the same tabard-like cut as those of the councillors in Ill. 663. That of the little Dauphin bears the canting dolphin and France quarterly. #1, Charles V wears a cape, the hood lined and tabbed with ermine; and gown semé with France ancient; as are also the undertunic and the short-sleeved, ermine-lined, long slit gown of Louis de Bourbon, #2, whose girdle carries a misericorde.

The onlooking commoners are being held back by a huissier in a quilted doublet with studded collar.

663. 1371. French. (Morgan Library, Ms. 717.)

Assembly of the King's Council, Toulouse: in parti-colored tabards, with bars on the shoulders, over parti-colored gowns, of orange, red and brown; and of orange and black. Compare with robes of the 2 little princes, above, and Chaucer's description of the serjeant of law, similarly dressed, with cape instead of tabard.

664-666. XIV-XVc. Spanish. Granada. (Metropolitan Museum.)

Jewelry; so-called "Hispano-Moresque." XIVc. Bracelets and necklace of gold, enamel, and pearls. XVc. Belt: copper-gilt and enamel.

667. XIV-XVc. Spanish. Granada. (Metropolitan Museum.)

Figured silk weaves; so-called "Hispano-Moresque," in red, blue, green, yellow, and white.

Constant friction between Christian and Mohammedan did not keep Christian Europe from eagerly importing Mohammedan-made textiles. Christian and Jewish weavers imitated the costly imported articles. Fine borders, in which woven Koranic prayers to Allah in Cufic and Arabic are conspicuous, were used on robes of Madonnas and saints. Europe backed the gold leaf used in textiles on catgut; the Mohammedan world on very thin paper which was not yet in European use.

668

668-670. XIVc. Spanish. Granada. (The Alhambra.)
Painted ceilings in the Hall of Justice.

668. Heads of the Moorish tribes of Granada.
669. Boar hunt: Christians and Moors.
670. Battle between Moors and Christians.

The painted ceilings of the Alhambra, ascribed to Yousef I, d.1354, give infinite information about life in Granada: architecture, costumes, and pastimes; churches; palaces with courtyards, fountains, and balconies; courtship, games of chess, hawking and hunting with Moorish friends; battles between mounted Moors, and Spanish knights and foot-soldiers.

The Moors, defeated by the Cid in XIIc. had been confined to Granada since XIIIc. Granada, which they ruled until the conquest of the Moors at the end XVc., was the richest and most civilized city in Spain. The intermediaries between the Christians, who made up about half of the population, and the Moors, were the Jews. The Jews were polyglot and learned; during the three centuries in which they had been protected in Spain, the highest aristo-

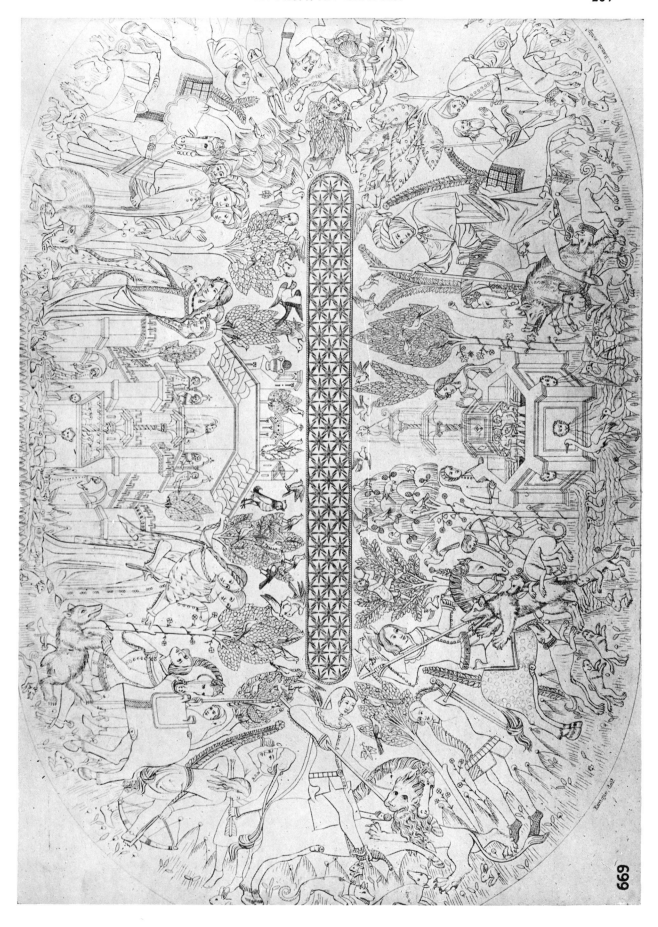

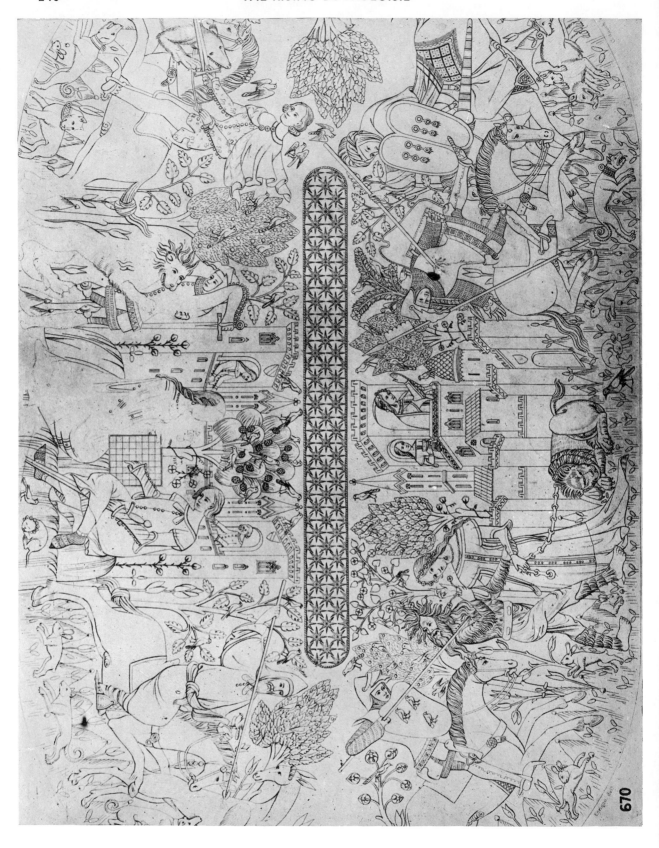

cracy and the princes of the Church had become of partly Jewish stock. I no longer remember which Spanish king was persuaded to sign a decree that all Jews should wear yellow caps; the next morning, his prime minister arrived with three yellow caps, for the king, the minister of finance, and for himself. It was the Jews' position as the hated tax-collectors which led to the first Spanish massacre of the Jews, preached by a priest in 1391.

By mid-XIVc., the Christian men, of high or low degree, will be found to have adopted the dress of men of their stations in France.

The cut of the cote-hardi worn by Spanish women, however, varies from that of the rest of Europe in several important details. (see lady struggling with wild man). Spanish costume was not homogenous, even among the predominantly Spanish aristocracy, in various parts of Spain. But Weiditz, in the XVIc., shows Castilian ladies dressed very much like the Alhambra paintings, and the same sleeveless surcoat still persistent in Barcelona, while Basque dress was as distinct as their tongue.

The surcoat is opened down the entire center-front from neck to hem, and is closed by rows of the ubiquitous buttons; in Spain, however, they are small and are frequently used in groups. There is no plastron on the front. Where a plastron is applied, elsewhere in Europe, it reinforces the front of the surcoat, and permits the use of much heavier and more important buttons, set close together in a row, which must stop when the plastron no longer exists to support their weight.

In the most specifically Spanish form of the sideless surcoat, the sides are cut away, in a different mode from the French-inspired concave sweep from shoulder to hip. From the horizontal line of the hem of the Spanish shoulder-cap, the side is cut away on a diagonal, rather than a curved line; it is edged with a piping or a relatively narrow braid. The Spanish skirt gains width below the hips by diagonal cutting of the side seams, rather than by gathering its material on, below the hips where the much more rigidly reinforced French surcoat will keep it from dragging.

The Renaissance Begins: XV Century

XVc.-Early XVIc. Background and Development of Dress

Protests of clergy, sumptuary laws of kings could not control the extravagance of XIV-XVc. costume, which exploited the superfluous, the fantastic, even the deforming.

The poulaines, forbidden to the French by Charles V, became so elongated that their points were chained to the knees. Edward IV. failed, as had the two preceding Edwards, when he attempted to regulate the dress of all classes in England.

To the already established German modes of dagged and slittered edges were added, by mid-XVc., the fantasy and luxury of the Burgundian court fashions. France, weak under the Valois, invaded with Burgundian aid by the English, had lost its position as the center of European civilization. Philip the Good of Burgundy, having fallen out with the English, concluded the Treaty of Arras with Charles VII, by which Philip was greatly enriched. During the second third XVc., while the French were still involved in the expulsion of the English, the superb court of Burgundy became the greatest in Europe, devoted to learning, the arts, and the fostering of Flemish industry and commerce. The Burgundian possessions were dismembered, after the death in battle of Philip's son, Charles the Bold; and France, under Louis XI, and Charles VIII, began its new rise. In a little more than a century, France, under Louis XIV will again lead fashion.

But at the end of the XVc. the great new influence is that of Italy. The superb civilization attained by her city-states during the XIV-XVc. was spread over Europe, as a result of the Italian campaigns of Charles VIII and his successor. Italy's richly patterned silks and velvets, lavish with metal, were a revelation to her northern neighbors. Ladies in castles had woven decorative bandings on narrow looms; wood-block cutters in Germany had produced printed materials from XII-XIVc., after the demand for manuscripts had led the great German monasteries to mass-production methods of cutting blocks to print the capital letters. Packs of playing cards (showing costume) were produced by German and Italian engravers in second quarter XVc.

Saracen weavers had produced brocades in Granada from early times, and the Norman lords of Sicily had brought Greek weavers to Palermo in the XIIc. The mild Tuscan climate, ideal for silkworm culture, brought these weavers to Lucca in the XIIIc. From there they spread to Florence, Genoa and Venice (where, by the end XIVc magnificent brocades of silk, velvet and metal were produced) and to Bologna and Milan.

The vicissitudes of Italian life under the despots led Italian weavers to emigrate in XIV-XVc., particularly to France and Flanders. They set up, in Paris, Rouen, Lyons and other cities, what were to become the great silk-weaving centers of the XVII-XVIIIc. The revocation of the Edict of Nantes was, in turn, to force Protestant weavers to emigrate to England and Germany at the end of XVIc.

XV Century Italy

Italy, in the XVc., was merely a "geographical expression," made up of the republics of Florence and Venice; Naples, under an Aragon king; Milan, a duchy ruled by the Visconti, and their successors, the Sforza; and a number of lesser states ruled by families which had risen to power during the Age of the Despots in XIIIc.; Ferrara, under the Este; Mantua, under the Gonzaga; Urbino, under the Montfeltro; Rimini, under the Malatesta; Genoa which like Parma and Verona, had many masters, including the Doria; and the Papal States, accretions to the Church's inheritance from Matilda, Countess of Tuscany.

These self-made rulers were inevitably men of immense capacity. Unless their descendants had qualities of their own, they could not expect to maintain their dynasties, as many did for centuries, merely by money and ruthlessness.

In the generation following a *condottiere* com-

mander, risen from the peasantry and married into the aristocracy, it is not surprising to find children of wide interests, great culture, and taste.
This is particularly true of the Este, Montfeltro,
Gonzaga, and the Medici, whose power in Flor-

ence was gained a little later and by other means
than those of the early military despots.

Italy's political and geographical differentiations
fostered the development of a form of dress specific to each.

671-672. XVc. Italian. Tirol. (Cast. del Buon Consiglio.)

Fresco: 12 months of the year, represented by the
appropriate occupations of nobles and peasants.

671. *Taurus*: Ploughing with ox-team and horse,
together; harrowing; sowing fields and garden protected by wattle fence. Farm outbuildings; one with
wattle sides and thatched roof is probably a crib for
storing grain, which requires ventilation.

672. Left. *Gemini*: Walled town and its church.
Ladies and gentlemen eating and courting among
roses. Compare Gemini and Cancer with Ills. 807-10

for the classic houppelande and its Italian variations.
The exaggerated houppelande collar of northern
Europe is usually replaced in Italy, by a long-favored
standing collar. Stuffed and twisted roundlets, such as
the Italians like as headwear, often take the place of
precious chains, around the neck.

672. Right. *Cancer*: Peasants among tile-roofed log
out-buildings. Instead of diagonally strung baldrics,
the Italian male houppelande shows here the use of
two belts, at high waist and at hips, fastened together
by a vertical strap in back, (gentleman, lower right.)

673. 1410-20. N. Italian. (Wash., Nat. Gall. of Art.)

Pisanello. Portrait of a Lady.

Italian version of Burgundian court costume. While the conventional collar is rarely found on Italian gowns, it is used here with great sophistication. The hair, clipped high on the neck, in service to the European idea of hairlessness, is otherwise shown and handled in a specifically Italian way. Instead of being enclosed in the conventional jewelled, reticulated net, it is drawn forward, and bound around in a coronet arrangement with the ends looped back, and ending in a little lock. Hair thus treated, but with the ends brought forward and bound together into a unicorn's horn will be seen in the Italian-influenced S. French frescos of a marketplace. The decorative use of simple pins will also be noted in XVc. Flemish costume. The stuffed roundlet which is set on the hair, is in the twisted Italian form; its decoration in a eyelet-studded, rather than a reticulated pattern. Over her blue and gold velvet gown, she wears filigree beads, and a flat collar of jewelled buttons, instead of the usual linked chain with pendant.

674-678. c. 1400. German-Italian. Tirol. (Castel Roncolo, near Bolzano.) Frescos.

Sleeves spreading over the knuckles, and extremely short male cotes-hardi are seen all over Europe, end XIVc. But the cape-like un-beltedness of the male cote, and the relatively uncovered heads, with roundlets and garments, are Italian, as are the striped patterns, and the sleeves of a different color from the body of the garment.

Courtesy of Frick Art Reference Library

674

675

679-692. XVc. Italian. Lombardy. (Manta Castello.)

These frescos (allegorical) from the north of Italy, near the French border, show French styles relatively unaffected by Italian regionalism. Blazoned surcoats of knights; tilting helm, held by lady in sideless cote-hardi; leaved roundlets, frequently worn with armor, XVc.; and high clipped male hair.

Coryat mentions the rooms hung with painted coat-of-arms in Italy, and in Germany, where even the walls of inns were affected.

676

677

678

693. c. 1420-30. Italian. (Wash., Nat. Gall. of Art.)
Master of the Bambino Vispo. Adoration of the Magi.

694. c. 1405. Italian. (Florence S. Maria Novella.) Fresco.
Student of Spinello Aretino. Episode in the life of St. Gregory.

Physician and friends: little change from the costume of learned, elderly men of XIVc.; in fact, von Marle dates the picture "after 1387."

695. XVc. Italian. (Florence, S. Maria del Carmini.) Fresco.
Masolino da Panicale (?). Raising of Tabitha: detail.

Young men in full, knee-length cotes-hardi of the latter part of first quarter XVc.; with bag sleeves. Brocade gown has sleeve with furlined slit at elbow through which arm can be passed; here the arm

hangs concealed within the sleeve. Turban-like chaperon; Phrygian bonnet (Ills. 804-5); dependent scarf of chaperon little used in Italy.

696-698. 1400-44. Italian. (Siena, Spedale.) Fresco.
Domenico di Bartolo. Hospital Scenes.

696. Nursing children: The heads of women of the lower classes in Italy follow the general European rule, and are covered by a veil or coif, but the coverings are close and exploit the hair; they do not deform or obliterate the natural head, as elsewhere. Turban arrangement of bound hair, center. Italian gowns have a short bodice, with natural round neck; the skirts are often cut separately, and gathered onto the high waist in careful, formal pleats. Shoe soles retained natural shape in Italy.

697. Tending patients: Doctors wear gowns, coifs and caps, of the previous century; but hair is bowl-cropped; no longer rolled at the nape. Hospital beds:

division between parallel bars forms head of one bed, foot of next; no springs; mattress tied like a hammock to end posts. Tasseled and corded velvet cushion on which man, wearing underdrawers, is bleeding. Walls fur-hung against chill.

698. Enlarging the hospital: Cut of doublet of man on ladder; division between body and skirts of garments, of men as well as women, in Italy. Short upper sleeve, with fur cuff, as worn also by children's nurses. Tights still short; worn with drawers. Architect, seen through arch; plain gown with sleeves of brocade. Perspective is now well understood.

699-702. XVc. 1440-50. Italian. (Florence, Academy of Fine Arts.)

Four cassone panels: The wedding of Boccacio Adimari and Lisa Ricasoli.

The same colors are used throughout this picture: black, brown, black or white and gold brocades, plain gold, dark green and a henna red, or vermilion. But three categories of costume are strongly differentiated. The wedding procession is magnificent, pale or somber, dressed entirely in black, white and gold, in combination. The dress of the spectators is intermediate between the muted color of the procession, and the bright clothes of the servants. Both spectators and servants wear parti-colored hose, (which combine 3 colors in one plain and one composed leg.) But the spectators use red in headgear and hose only; their body garments are black, brown, brocade, gold, or dark green, with narrow brown fur, or ermine. The servants' body garments use the brightest colors, sometimes parti-colored, and an additional orange-red appears in their clothing.

Tabard effects appear on the dress of ladies, gentlemen, and servants alike.

The high necklines of the gowns of Italian ladies are emphasized by necklaces worn high about the throat.

In the wedding procession (699-701) (l. to r.), the little page wears a green tabard, lined with white fur, its sleeves slit throughout their length; vermilion doublet and hose. Seated lady: white and gold robe with V-neck of Italian type (see Ill. 709); slit to show black and gold kirtle; white headdress with a small Italian rolled turban. Seated older lady: black gown; white and gold headdress of the current European type. Lady with monstrous black and gold turban: trailing overdress of black, unbelted and slit, tabard-wise, lined with gray; in Italy the long gown is shortened in front, not held up, as elsewhere. Lady leading procession (701): slit pendant oversleeve, stiffened and stylized beyond usability; French headdress.

In the panel of musicians and servants (700) (l. to r.): boy in red doublet, with brown and black hose drawn very imperfectly over white drawers. Servant with dish: black doublet; green and white hose, both parti-colored. With standing dish: vermilion and green tabard; black hose. 1st musician: vermilion hat; gold tunic with wheat (probably a

699

700

badge, see Ill. 706); black and white, and vermilion hose. 2nd musician: hat with orange brim and green crown; dark tunic; green, and black and white hose. 3rd.: orange hat; dark green tunic; vermilion, and black and white hose. 4th.: green cap; vermilion garment; green and white, and black hose.

The spectators at the end of the panel (702) (l. to r.): ermine hat with vermilion crown; brownish-black tabard; black doublet; hose, vermilion, and black and white. Vermilion chaperon; brownish-black doublet, under a brown-furred black garment, belted in gold; black, and black and white hose. Tall black and gold turban; black doublet; vermilion garment, lined and edged with white fur; dark green, and black, white and green hose. Tall green hat;

brown and gold brocade doublet; brown tabard and fur; black and white, and vermilion hose. Creamy-gold chaperon with a long knotted end; dark green tabard lined with greenish white; brown-black doublet; vermilion hose. Man leaving: vermilion chaperon, black tunic and hose.

703. XVc. Italian, Florentine. (Metropolitan Museum.)
Attributed to the *workshop of Filippo Lippi*. Man and woman at a casement.

704. XVc. Italian, Umbrian. (Metropolitan Museum.) Elizabeth Montfeltro, wife of Robert Malatesta, the *Domenico Veneziano*. Portrait of a girl, perhaps great *condottieri* leader.

705. XVc. Before 1450. Italian. (Berlin, Kaiser Friedrich Museum.)

Domenico Veneziano (?) Portrait of a young woman.

706. XVc. 1435-8. Italian Venetian. (The Louvre.)

Antonio Pisanello. Ginevra d'Este.

The bald appearance toward which the European woman of XVc. strived, is compromised in Italy, by interest in the hair itself. Small caps, turbans, and twisted rolls of mixed colors, are always subordinated to hair, flowing, coiled or braided.

The coiffure in Ill. 704, while affected by the head-dresses of N. Europe, allows bound hair to end in little loose tassels (see Ill. 673).

The Italian houppelande avoids a high collar, never stresses a V-neck, is always modest, relatively high-necked, mounting by mid-century to the base of the throat, but consistently sloping down in back.

Pleating, which becomes stylized all over Europe, is particularly fine in Italy, where cartridge pleats are set into plain material at an early date (see Ill. 703). Belt: never of great importance or worn unnaturally high.

Early use in Italy of slit oversleeves, which lend themselves to the Italian preference for differing sleeve and gown. The undersleeve is often of the male doublet form, upper half slightly padded and gathered onto a close undersleeve. There is a still further tendency to differentiate the sleeve from the gown by the use of embroidery, as in Ills. 703, 706.

Red-headed Ginevra (1419-40), of the ruling house of Ferrara, who was probably poisoned by her husband, Sigismondo Malatesta, wears on her gown a sprig of the juniper (purple berries) for which she was named. Cream-colored gown; lavender-brown belt; brown pearl-embellished embroidery on the hanging sleeve. Fur binding, always narrow in Italy, is replaced here by twisted ropes of red, brown, and cream; red inner sleeve; creamy hair ribbons. Her hanging sleeve is embroidered with the *impressa* seen on her brother Lionello's medals: a two-handled crystal vase, banded in pearls, chained from the handles to anchors; the vase is filled with leafless budding branches, which send out roots at the bottom of the vase.

The early interlaced Irish style loosened into scrolls, stylized flowers, and quaint animals in XIVc. Now, we see flowers represented quite literally in XVc. manuscripts, mixed with naturalistic insects as recognizable as the 3 varieties which flutter above Ginevra's head. The missal was also a pattern book; every tendril of a pea-vine, every leg of a caterpillar will be carefully worked in XVIc. embroidery.

707. c. 1460. N. Italian.

Engraved "Tarocchi" card, so called. 50 cards representing all classes of men, arts, sciences, music and astrology; found pasted and written over in a manuscript of St. Gall, completed Nov. 28, 1468; in the style of Ferrara, Tura and Cossa, and are probably Venetian, and not by Mantegna. From the front, the body of the jacket, fitted like a doublet, appears to carry doublet sleeves; jacket sleeves, probably not wearable, hang from shoulder in back. Flaring skirt, gored into high waistline, loosely belted at hips.

708. c. 1460. Italian, Florentine.

Att. to *Maso Finiguerra*.

709

710

Engraved series of the 7 planets: Mercury.

Florentine street scene: At left, a goldsmith's booth, exhibiting flagons, platters and precious belts; an engraver works on a plate; (engraving originated as an offshoot of jeweller's work and was extended to armor). Above, a painter decorates a wall in fresco; assistant grinds colors, which must be available while plaster is still wet. In center foreground a gentleman eats and drinks with a very coarse creature. At right, two learned gentlemen look over books together, while a boy winds a clock; above,

an old man blows a bellows for an organist.

709. c. 1460. Italian, Florentine.
Att. to *Maso Finiguerra*. Engraving: the Fight for the Hose.

Specifically Italian wide skirts, gathered or laid in cartridge pleats onto short bodices with V necks; belt unimportant; emphasis on dependant brocade sleeve or sleeve of doublet type, with the upper fullness sometimes stressed by fur band above elbow. Heart-shaped headdresses, as well as Italian flowing hair and turbans. Clogs on feet of center figure. Cap and costume of a fool.

710. c. 1465-70. Italian, Florentine.
Engraving: an Allegory of Love and Death. French influence strongly shown in costume of center figures.

Woman: high, veiled hennin; flat collar spread in wide V over shoulders, and filled in with gauze; important necklace and belt; tubular cuffed sleeve. Men: high doublet collar; extremely short jacket with padded shoulders and tubular sleeves; horizontal neckline emphasized by chains from shoulder to shoulder. Decorative use of words, already seen in French costume; but the fabrics are Italian, particularly in the use of pattern on gentleman's sleeve.

Tights of gentleman and musician show the new use of pattern in late XVc. (see Ill. 906). Long tights and short jackets require use of codpiece (here tied into place at the top), instead of underdrawers (see Ills. 709, 714). The musician's jacket shows new trends: open front; lacings across shirt, which is also exposed by slashing doublet sleeve below elbow. While his jacket has shortened, its sleeves, ornamental rather than useful, are of the same brocade as the jacket; they retain their old length, but the supremacy of the Italian sleeve over the rest of the garment has begun to wane.

The effect of pointed French shoes is given by stem and sepal-like additions to the toe of the shoe.

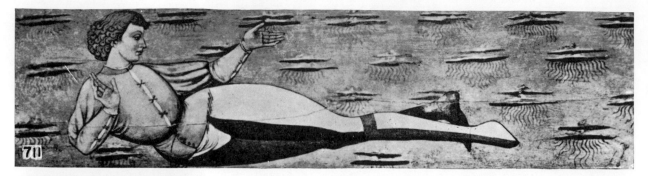

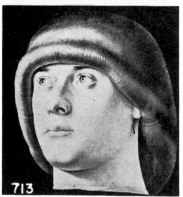

711. c. 1450. Italian, Florentine. (London, Earl of Crawford.)
Cassone panel.

712. Italian, Venetian. (Bergamo, Acad. Carrara.)
Pisanello. Lionello d'Este, (1407-50).

713. c. 1450-60. Italian, Venetian. (Metropolitan Museum, Bache Collection.)
Giovanni Bellini. Portrait of a young man.

714. c. 1445-50. Italian, Florentine. (Florence, Uffizi.)
Florentine youths playing the game of "civetta," a stylized, posturing outdoor game of well-born Florentine youths.

Pisanello was first of all a medalist who has left many records of wonderful hats, haircuts, and collars. He had been on intimate terms with Lionello by 1430, and worked for him again, 1441-8. This portrait is almost identical with Pisanello's medals, celebrating Lionello's 1444 marriage; it shows him in dark red and gold, with pearls, a knot of gold in

back, and the same hair.

Bowl-cropped hair, like d'Este's, became full and fluffy in Italy by the 50's, and developed into the beautifully cared-for, extravagantly designed *zazzara* of the Bellini young man.

The page on the Crawford cassone gives a classic picture of mid-XVc. Florentine youth: bobbed, banged hair; doublet with low standing collar, with bosom, but not upper sleeve, padded and loosely laced like the lower sleeve, to show shirt; red and white parti-colored hose, not yet completely developed, are laced to the firmly buttoned skirt of the doublet; being without cod-piece, they are worn over drawers. (See Ills. 696-698.)

The same garments are worn by the "civetta" players; onlookers in very high turbans and bonnets. Tabard (extreme right) is a Milanese fashion. Bag-sleeves (center back) were particularly worn in Venice. Little Italian boys wore shirts and doublets,

even socks and hose, but nothing resembling drawers.

URBINO AND THE MONTFELTRO FAMILY

The Court of Urbino was small, rich, peaceful, devout, beautifully organized and very learned. It contained one of the finest libraries of the age, and
housed many scholars, among them the mathematician and painter, Piero della Francesca, but none
more learned than the Duke himself. At no court was
the education of the youthful nobility entrusted to
it more scrupulously supervised; the Duke, who
moved unarmed among his people, was equally devoted to their interests, and loved by them.

715, 715A. 1465-66. Italian, Umbrian. (Florence, Uffizi.)
Piero della Francesca. Portraits of Federigo I. di
Montfeltro, Duke of Urbino and Battista Sforza, his
wife.

Donors and their families had long been shown on
wings of altar-pieces, and events in the lives of
princely Italian families pictured in fresco, but this
small wood panel and its companion showing her husband are the first portraits in the modern sense.

Federigo, the great condottieri leader who had lost
the sight of his right eye, and broken his nose, in a
tournament in 1450, wears a red hat like that of
Lodovico Gonzaga, and jacket, its collar stitched in
darker red.

Battista, his second wife, is dressed in black, with
gold brocade sleeves; her blonde hair dressed with
white and gold.

716. XVc. 1445. Italian. (Metropolitan Museum.)
Giovanni di Paolo. Garden of Paradise.

Monks and nuns, prelates and gentlefolk. Left to
right. Upper row: 2 gray friars; a Carthusian talking to a dedicated lady in red; Cistercians in work

clothes; a fashionable young man conversing with an
angel; a hooded Trappist talking to a gentleman; a
youth hand in hand with a female angel.

Middle row: a nun, who looks like a Dominican,
but wears a blue-gray mantle, with an angel; Benedictine nun and Bishop of the same order; an angel
with a pope; a cardinal with a youth.

Lower row: 2 ladies in houppelandes, red and
blue, with monstrous turbans; 2 youths; 2 Dominicans; a Cistercian nun, with another nun, all in
white, and a Franciscan.

FERRARA AND THE ESTE FAMILY

The N. Italian city of Ferrara, despite the violently disordered personal life of some members of
the ruling family of Este, high taxes and a spy system, was, for two centuries, a very efficiently managed and prosperous city, the most modern in Italy,
with the best university of its time. Its citizens felt
secure from mishandling by its well-paid and disciplined army; and, spared from the wars which rent
the rest of Italy, Ferrara flourished under two excellent rulers: Lionel d'Este (1407-50) and his brother,
Borso (1413-71). Borso's court was both magnificent
and cultivated; its painters included Ercole Roberti,
and those "strange . . wild" painters, Turra and
Cossa, who used scenes of Borso's life in their frescos of his Schifanoia Palace. The third brother,
Ercole, was the patron of Ariosto, and the father of
two of the most notable and astute ladies of the Renaissance. The lovely, learned and short-lived Beatrice
d'Este (1475-97), wife of Ludovico (il Moro) Sforza
of Milan was the patron of Leonardo, Bramante and
Castiglione. Her sister, Isabella (1474-1539) established a brilliant court about her when she became

716

marchioness of Mantua; she was the patron of Mantegna, Raphael and Giulio Romano; and sister-in-law of the third great lady of the Renaissance, Elisabetta Gonzaga, duchess of Urbino. The Este of the XVIc. were the patrons of Tasso.

717-719. XVc. 1441-8. Italian.
  Antonio Pisanello.

717. Studies of costume of the Court of Ferrara. (*Milan, Pinacoteca Ambrosiana.*)

718. Woman and two men in long flowered gowns. (*Bayonne, Bonnat Museum.*)

719. St. Anthony and St. George. (*London, Nat. Gall.*)
These illustrations show the culmination of the Italian preoccupation with hair and sleeves. The hair-mass of

717

718

719

Italian women, under the influence of the European ideal of hairlessness, was drawn up and back (see Ill. 706); where it was later bound into or surmounted by swelling turbans. Bowl-cut male hair, a manifestation of the same ideal, takes on height and bulk, in Italy.

On these Ferrara courtiers, the large beaver hats and dagged chaperons of Europe proper are exaggerated, and supplemented by specifically Italian forms of piled-up turbans. The winged, cape-like sleeves of the Ferrara court are emphasized by fantastically heavy fringes of fur, quite different from the flat furs used for linings and narrow bindings, and by multicolored fringes of dagged material They make the superfluity of dagging in German costume (see Ills. 976-79) look almost utilitarian.

The Italian emphasis on sleeves almost obliterates the rest of the houppelande, however full and trailing it may be, on the lady and turbanned gentlemen.

St. George, wearing a plumed Tuscan straw hat, is in silver Gothic armor of second quarter XVc. The mail is almost completely sheathed in plate. The armor shown in the sketch has developed refinements of protection, which have been worked out for the different requirements of right and left sides of the body, in respect to the manipulation of lance and horse. Shoulder plates as large and badly fitted as St. George's appear in other contemporary pictures. His fur-bordered surcoat, embroidered with his cross, is thickly quilted and pleated, after the manner of contemporary dress, and of the *bases* or *waffenrock* skirts of knights. Long rowelled spurs on wide-toed sollerets. (See Appendix.)

720-723. XVc. Italian. Lombard School. (Milan, Casa
Borromeo.)

Casa Borromeo frescos: details.
720. Society games.
721. Ball player.
722. Card player.

723. Card players.
Wonderful North Italian compromises between
the European ideal of baldness under an exaggerated
headdress, and the Italian love of turbans, braids, and
the hair itself; the turban is made of monstrous
braids, or is drawn up, hair-like, over pads.

724

725

726

724-725. XVc. Italian, Florentine. (Metropolitan Mus.)

Sano di Pietro di Menico. Cassone panel: Solomon and the Queen of Sheba.

Conventionally orientalized; especially soldier, Solomon, and conical hat crowns and flat collars of upper classes. Lower classes; contemporary Italian musicians in characteristic parti-color (see Ills. 699-702); camel-leader, in background, shows hose, doublet and haircut.

726. XVc. 1445-53. Italian Sienese. (National Gallery of Art, Washington.)

Giovanni di Paolo. Adoration of the Magi.

(*See also* Color Plate, No. 1: c. 1430. *Sassetta*: Journey of the Magi.)

Loose riding boots, with or without turned-down tops of another color, on figures to left, show seam on inside of calf to ankle where foot of boot is set on. Slit cape-like sleeves, of same length as garments (see Ills. 699-702, 714, 740).

727

728

727. 1430-40. Italian, Florentine. (Cortono, Baptistry.)

Fra Angelico. Altarpiece: Annunciation.

Richly decorated, bloused garments of allegorical or angelic figures.

728. c. 1450-60. Italian, Florentine. (National Gallery of Art, Washington.)

Fra Filippo Lippi. Head of the Madonna.

Veil wound and draped, in combination of fantasy with contemporary usage.

Fra Angelico (1387-1455) entered the Dominican monastery at Fiesole in 1407, was transferred to San Marco in Florence in 1436, and in 1445 went to Rome. Vasari says that he declined an archbishopric offered by the Pope, on the grounds of his own unworthiness, and suggested a more suitable candidate. The utterly saintly painter knelt in prayer before starting work on his fervently devout, unworldly, sexless paintings, with their exquisite gradations of pure color enriched with gold.

Fra Filippo Lippi (1406/12-69) was a very different sort of man and painter. He was warm, human, rich, and much more colloquial than *Fra Angelico.* He was the son of a butcher, orphaned early, and put by his aunt among the Carmelite friars at the age of fourteen. Although a devout man by nature, he was under vows by circumstance rather than vocation. He painted prolifically and profitably, but always under the pressure of having to provide for six marriageable nieces. Vasari says that he was abducted by Barbary pirates during a trip in 1431-37. In 1450 he himself abducted from a convent a beautiful girl inmate, pupil, or novice named Lucrecia Buti, who had been serving as his model for a religious picture. She was the mother of his son, *Filippino Lippi* (1460-1515), a painter at the age of ten, pupil of his father's pupil, Botticelli, and, like his father, one of the greatest painters of his time.

729. 1449. Italian, Florentine. (Rome, Vatican.)

Fra Angelico. St. Lawrence Giving Alms.

The saint, a papal deacon, in a dalmatic with tassels in front and back (a usage which continued through the XVIc.), brocaded in the flames of his martyrdom. The poor: women's heads covered; men's hooded, in manner of earlier period; pouches and wallets; interesting details of shoe fastenings.

729

730-731. XVc. Italian, Florentine. (Metropolitan Mus.)

School of Pesellino. Two cassone panels: Scenes from the story of the Argonauts.

732. XVc. Italian, Florentine. (Metropolitan Museum.)

Cassone panel: Story of Esther.

On cassone panels illustrating biblical and mythological scenes, the costumes are frequently orientalized: this is particularly true of 730, less so of 731, and much less of 732, which, except for the conical hats, shows contemporary dress of second half XVc. (see Ills. 699, 702, 709, 710). These costumes, coming between those in Ills. 699-702, show massive, mounting male hats, in some interesting variations with turned-up brims.

733. XVc. c. 1450. Italian, Florentine. (National Gallery of Art, Washington.)

Master of the Jarves Cassone. Journey of the Queen of Sheba.

734. XVc. c. 1460. Italian, Florentine (National Gallery of Art, Washington.)

Paolo Uccello (?). Battle scene. As in previous cassone panels, we are given, in detail, fortified castles, interiors, and domestic architecture; processions with floats drawn by caparisoned horses; sailing ships, barges, and row-boats. The Jarves Cassone shows a fortified artificial harbor. Except for conical hats and pigtails, and some orientalized men (as usual, soldiers or worthies in long gowns) these are gentlefolk of N. Central Italy in mid-XVc.

Costume originating between the Arno and the Po (cf. Florentine and Ferrarese courts) is characterized by a distinctive use of pattern. The design is not the result of cutting from an all-over patterned brocade; it appears to be embroidered on portions of the costume, particularly on chest and sleeves. This effect could be achieved, in most cases, by the use of specially woven brocades; with borders and analogous, but not literally repeated motifs, which would permit the slight dissimilarities we see in r. and l. sleeves (see Ill. 710).

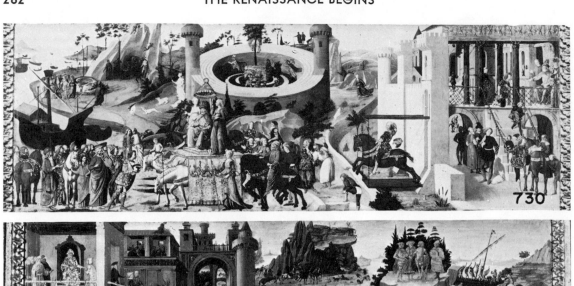

The Medici Family and Florence

The Medicis were an extraordinarily gifted family, under whom their city reached a point where a citizen thanked God "that he was a native of Florence, the greatest city in the world, and lived in the days of the magnificent Medicis." After 500 years we are still in their debt.

Exceptional though they were, they typify the rise that was everywhere taking place. Until mid-XVIc., their history is so mingled with that of Italy's other great families and cities, and of France, that they may well be used as a point of reference.

At the beginning of the XVc. Florence was a republic, of which only the members of its twenty-one guilds were citizens. The leader of its army was always a foreigner; the aristocracy, now ineligible for membership in its governing body, still manoeuvered elections.

Florence had ousted the usurper, Walter of Brienne; it was now the most flourishing commercial city of Europe, pre-eminent in the cloth trade and in banking; its *florin* was the standard gold coin of Europe.

In contests with the seven major guilds, controlled by the aristocratic Albizzi, the minor guilds were repeatedly aided by a family of bourgeois bankers, who added to their popularity by instituting tax-reforms, by their generosity to the plague-ridden populace, and by their commissioning of works of art for the adornment of their city; meanwhile increasing their fortunes by their loans to the King of England, to the princes of the Church, and to the Sforzas of Milan, all powerful allies in an age and country of precarious balance.

The Medicis, as a family, were characterized by the greatest financial and political astuteness; by the most varied intellectual, literary, and scientific interests; by marvellous taste in art and literature; and by a remarkable personal simplicity, kindliness, bonhomie, tact, and commonsense. Their faults were largely those of their age. They were a rather short-lived family, undistinguished for physical beauty, except for fine eyes and hands.

The Medici Palace was called "the hotel of all the Princes of the world"; but however luxuriously they lodged their guests, the life of the family was so simple that the Pope's son, who married Lorenzo's daughter, at first thought that a slight was being put upon him when he moved into the Medici Palace after the wedding, while his retinue continued to be entertained magnificently in another of the family palaces, which had been allotted to him before the wedding.

The high-minded gravity of the first three Medici generations changed, with rising Florentine fortunes, to the joyous lavishness of Lorenzo the Magnificent's time. Temporarily impaired by marriages with arrogant aristocrats, the essential Medici qualities would reappear in the following generation. Intellectual and artistic interests were made the fashion in Florence. This influence could still be felt in the XVIIIc., and was one of the reasons why so many cultivated English aristocrats lived or visited in Florence.

The accomplishments and changes in the Medicis and their city may be briefly summarized:

Under the founding *Giovanni di Bicci* (1360-1428), Florentine life was consciously austere; luxury controlled by sumptuary laws, administered by "foreigners," one of whom describes his difficulties: "When, obeying the orders ye gave me, I went out to seek for the forbidden ornaments of your women, they met me with arguments such as are not to be found in any book of laws. There cometh a woman with the peak of her hood fringed out and twined about her head. My notary sayeth, 'Tell me your name, for you have a peak with fringes.' Then the good woman taketh this peak, which is fastened round her hood with a pin, and, holding it in her hand, she declareth that it is a wreath. Then going further he findeth one wearing many buttons in front of her dress, and he saith unto her, 'Ye are not allowed to wear these buttons.' But she answers, 'These are not buttons but studs, and if ye do not believe me, look—they have no loops, and moreover there are no buttonholes.' Then my notary goeth to another who is wearing ermine, and saith, 'Now what can she say to this? Ye are wearing ermine,' And he prepares to write down her name. But the woman answers 'Do not write me down, for this is not ermine, it is the fur of a suckling.' Saith the notary, 'What is this suckling?' And the woman replies, 'It is an animal.' "

Works of art were commissioned, however, by the guilds, from Ghiberti and Donatello; Giovanni, who built for his city the Foundling Hospital designed by Brunelleschi, was the patron of Masaccio and other painters, and the first to have fresco used to decorate the walls of a private dwelling. He left his sons immensely wealthy, and we are told by Machiavelli: "He never sought the honours of government, yet enjoyed them all. When holding high office, he was courteous to all. Not a man of great eloquence, but of an extraordinary prudence."

Cosimo (Pater Patriae) (1389-1464). Built Medici Palace, 1440 (discarding Brunelleschi's plans as too pretentious), and many public and religious buildings. Art collector; patron of architects, sculptors, and painters, particularly Fra Angelico and Lippi. Scholar; founder of the world's first public library, 1444. Cosimo was influential in having the Council of Ferrara moved to Florence, where he became intimate with the great scholars of the Eastern Church; out of this came his founding of the Platonic Academy, and the financing of expeditions to the Orient to collect rare Greek and Roman manuscripts, many of which were the only copies to survive the fall of Constantinople. Since study of early Church manuscripts showed the supremacy of the bishop of Rome to have been founded on the forged Decretals and Donation of Constantine, Cosimo bears an inadvertent part in bringing on the Reformation. The fall of Constantinople, fatal to the trade of Florence's rival, Venice, consolidated in Florence the refugee scholars and mss. of the East. Florence, long a Guelph city, had been the refuge of Pope Eugenius IV, who took its culture back with him to devastated Rome; his successor, Nicholas V, who founded the Vatican Library, was the former librarian of the Medicis.

Cosimo's conduct of the affairs of the Republic led it to confer on him the title of "Pater Patriae." Machiavelli tells us that: "He was one of the most prudent of men; grave and courteous and of venerable appearance. His early years were full of trouble, exile and personal danger, but by the unwearied generosity of his disposition he triumphed over all his enemies and made himself most popular with the people. Though so rich, yet in his mode of living he was always very simple and without ostentation. None of his time had such an intimate knowledge of government and State affairs. Hence even in a city so given to change, he retained the government for thirty years." And Gibbon says: "Cosimo was the father of a line of princes whose name and age are almost synonymous with the restoration of Learning. His credit was ennobled into fame; his riches were dedicated to the service of mankind; he corresponded at once with Cairo and London; and a cargo of Indian spices and Greek books were often imported in the same vessel."

Piero il Gottoso (the Gouty) (1416-1469). Became head of the family, by the death of Giovanni, who had been trained to the succession because of the life-long ill-health of his older brother; when this permitted, the gentle and scholarly Piero had proved himself a most successful ambassador to the courts of France and Milan, and to Venice. One of the many alterations in the Medici coat-of-arms was that granted Piero by Louis XI: the use of the lily of France, on one of the Medici balls, colored blue.

There appears to be no connection between the three balls on a pawnbroker's sign and the Medici arms, as is so often stated. The red balls of the Medici, on a gold ground, varied in number with the generations: the earliest form was two red balls; nine balls, eight of them red (Giovanni di Bicci); six red, one blue (Piero); five red, one blue (Cosimo). (Details of Medici crests are given in Young's *Medici*, p. 135).

Piero, who commissioned the Gozzoli frescos in the Medici Palace, married Lucrezia Tornabuoni, a poet, and one of the first of the new generations of learned ladies, who later became the glory of the XVIc.

Lorenzo the Magnificent (1449-1492). **Head** of his family at twenty; and probably the **most** variously endowed man the world has seen. **Machia**velli says, "He governed the Republic with **great** judgment, and was recognized as an **equal** by various crowned heads of other countries. Though notably without military ability he yet conducted several wars to a successful conclusion **by** his diplomacy. He was the greatest patron of Literature and Art that any prince has ever been, and he won the people by his liberality and other popular qualities. By his political talents he made Florence the leading state in Italy, and by his other qualities he made her the intellectual, **artis**tic and fashionable center of Italy."

Commercially less astute than his forebears, Lorenzo was a scholar; loved the **company** of learned men; financed trips to collect manuscripts in the Orient, and maintained a staff of copyists for their dissemination; founded the Universities of Pisa for Latin, and Florence for Greek studies; contributing about $15,000,000 to learning. He was a poet, encouraging the use of his native Tuscan instead of Latin; the center of a gay and brilliant literary company, among whom were the fabulous Pico della Mirandola and Politian. He enlivened Florentine life with fire-works, pageants and tournaments; was a sportsman who loved the country and the hunt; was interested in agriculture and husbandry. He founded a free school of sculpture, where he discovered the fifteen-year-old Michelangelo; Botticelli was his court painter; he was the patron of the other great painters of his time, particularly Leonardo, Raphael and Perugino.

He was gay and courteous, charming, simple and helpful; he romped with children and threw snow-balls in the streets. By his marriage to an Orsini, he had three sons, the eldest of whom, Piero, married another arrogant Orsini, and was banished from Florence.

The period of the Medici exile (1494-1512) began with the victorious entry of Charles VIII into Florence at the head of 20,000 men; Italy viewed the potent new weapon, conceived by his father: the standing army. But to the French mass the meeting was even more revealing: here was a great civilization, an undreamed-of refinement of luxury; a standard to be equalled and surpassed. Even fine cookery, which we think of as French, was an Italian art, brought to France by Catherine de' Medici; here the French got their first notions of subtle food.

Without the Medici, Florence was torn by dissension and corruption; her prosperity declined, and in her uncertainty, profligacy increased. Longing for direction and ripe for an attack of bad conscience (for she had a long history of high standards), Florence passionately embraced the precepts of the reforming **Dominican monk,** Savonarola. She became a city of Puritans, plain of garments and way of life; her citizens, among them quantities of her painters, flocked into monasteries. At Savonarola's behest great bonfires were made in the public squares of her "vanities," indecent books and pictures, carnival gear, rouge and gauds, which a Venetian tradesman tried to buy for 20,000 gold florins.

Savonarola's attacks on the vile Borgia Pope led to his eventual torture and martyrdom in 1498. The amiable Cardinal Giovanni became head of the house of Medici; with the death of the unfortunate Pietro, whom they had driven out with his detested Orsini wife, and with some pressure from Pope Julius II, the Florentines recalled the Medici.

Cardinal Giovanni, later Pope Leo X, Lorenzo's second son, was an agreeable epicurean who, though he perhaps did not say, "Since God has given us the Papacy, let us enjoy it," horrified the papal household by wearing hunting costume and riding boots. His Medici entertainments and patronage made Rome gay and brought artists for the embellishment of the city, but he was without his father's real scholarship and taste.

Giuliano, Lorenzo's third son, whose exile had been passed in the cultivated court of Urbino, was a true Medici, talented, attractive and simple. Upon his return as ruler of Florence, he shaved his beard in conformity to the Florentine manner. Leo X, on his accession, transferred the rule of Florence to his nephew, Lorenzo, while offering to make Giuliano Duke of Urbino, at the expense of his former hosts, which he refused. Sent to France as a papal representative, he married there, was made Duke of Nemours, and died soon after.

Lorenzo, Pietro's dissolute son, had the insolence of his Orsini mother, by whom he had been brought up in exile, unaffected by Florentine standards. Bearded, like the foreigner he was, he ruled Florence; was made Duke of Urbino by the machinations of Leo X, who contrived with Francis I, to marry him, at Amboise, to Madeleine de la Tour d'Auvergne. He survived, only by days, her death after childbirth, leaving the baby Catherine, who was to become Queen of France, and a great Medici in her own right.

Giulio, nephew of Lorenzo the Magnificent, who became Pope Clement VII, was a brilliant, learned and adroit Medici, but crafty and cold; his deviousness helped to bring on the Reformation, and was personally disastrous.

As the elder branch of the Medici weakened, at the end of the XVc., the younger, descended from Cosimo's (Pater Patriae) younger brother, began its rise.

Giovanni "Populano" (1467-98), attractive and cultivated, became the third husband of Catherine Sforza, the great Countess of Forli. This brilliantly learned, accomplished, and immensely courageous woman, who led her troops in battle and at one time lived in armor, was the daughter and granddaughter of condottieri commanders, of peasant stock, who had risen to power and great marriages with the Visconti and the House of Savoy. Although her first husband was a Riario, nephew of Pope Sixtus IV, and so an enemy of the Medici, she had been in love with the family, since a visit to them in her childhood.

Giovanni delle Bande Nere (1498-1526), her Medici son, became in his short life the greatest soldier in Italy, the first to realize the importance of the infantry, and to exercise personal attention to the needs of his men. He wore nothing to distinguish him in battle from his black-armored troops (*Bande Nere,* Black Bands), who adored him; and who, from his death until their own, wore mourning for him. Giovanni married his distant cousin, Maria Salvati.

Cosimo I, their son (1519-74), the capable and pitiless Grand Duke of Tuscany, brought his duchy to its greatest prosperity and power. He built the Pitti Palace; his collection of Etruscan art was the world's greatest; he founded the first botanical gardens; established a tapestry manufacture which surpassed those of Flanders; rehabilitated the textile trade; concerned himself with all technological improvements in the utilization of the natural resources of his land, seacoast, and their defense.

Francis I, eldest son of Cosimo I, had a passionate love for art, literature and the sciences, particularly chemistry; he learned to fuse quartz, from which he fabricated vases which still exist; established porcelain manufacture; built the Uffizi; and began the improvements of the port of Leghorn.

Marie de' Medici, Francis' daughter, brought the richest dowry of any Queen of France to her marriage with Henry IV, and died in abject poverty. She was a beautiful, amiable and unintelligent creature, immensely concerned with dress, on which it is probable that no woman ever spent more.

Ferdinand I, second son of Cosimo I, the reluctant cardinal who never took holy orders, was a courageous and generous ruler; he collected Greek and Roman art objects; was the real creator of the port of Leghorn, to which his decree of toleration brought prosperity, in the form of refugees of all races and religions.

The greatest days of Tuscany and the Medicis ended after the first-quarter of the XVIc. though the family continued to rule for another century.

735-738. XVc. 1468-9. Italian. (Florence, Medici-Ric-cardi Palace.)

Benozzo Gozzoli. Frescos: The Journey of the Magi.

735. Youngest of the three kings, on horseback. 736. Detail, with leopards. 737. Detail, children on horseback. 738. Detail, procession and landscape.

Life Magazine, Dec. 24, 1945, furnished complete color reproductions of these frescos. Commissioned by Piero de'Medici, they recalled a magnificent pageant which the 19 year old Gozzoli and 23 year old Piero had seen in 1439, during the meeting of John Paleologus, Emperor of Byzantium, and Pope Eugenius IV. in an attempt to reconcile the Roman and Orthodox churches. As a tactful reinforcement of Pius II.'s renewed efforts to the same end, the Patriarch of Constantinople and the Emperor are represented as two of the three kings, the third being the young Lorenzo de'Medici.

In the foreground of 738, l. to r., we see Piero il Gottoso, shown bareheaded, in reference to his invalidism; his second son, Giuliano, whose love of the hunt is symbolized by the bow which his Negro carried before him; Lorenzo the Elder, ancestor of the cadet line of the Medici, humbly mounted on a mule; and his older brother, Cosimo (Pater Patriae), the trappings of whose horse bear the seven balls of the current Medici arms, together with the peacock feathers which he had chosen as his personal emblem.

The riders are followed by a crowd containing many recognizable portraits of members of the Platonic Academy, bearded Eastern scholars, and clean-shaven Florentine notables; among whom we have Gozzoli's self-portrait, wearing a cap edged with the words, "Opus Benotti."

In Italy the doublet has not assumed the high collar of France; but the V-line in back, (into which the high collar fits) is used here in a specifically Italian way: in front, across the base of the throat, the neckline of the jerkin barely shows the tiny standing collar of the doublet; in back, instead of mounting, the line of the collar of the Italian doublet slides backward, while the neck of the jerkin, cut in the low V, exposes the brocade of the doublet. The Italian jerkin is often sleeveless, even skeletonized (Cosimo P.P.), and the sleeves, when they do exist, are usually split lengthwise to feature the sleeve of the doublet (page, preceding Lorenzo).

735

The commonplace sleeve of the rest of Europe is worn here only by Lorenzo, who is dressed like an elderly European gentleman, rather than an Italian; and by the Negro, whose cartridge-pleated jacket is of one stuff and does not have the backward-slipping Italian neckline.

Lorenzo the Magnificent's costume is that which he wore in his tournament of 1469, studded with rubies and diamonds; his cape-like sleeves, of the same length as the skirts of his jacket, in the Italian way, are split below the elbow only, to show only the fore-arm of his doublet sleeve, in the Medici red and gold. He rides the white charger, which was given him for the tournament by the King of Naples; its trappings bear the seven balls of his father's reign, which will be reduced to six when he rules. His attendants also wear their tournament costumes.

Parti-colored garments and hose are here worn only by servants (handsome jacket of attendant preceding Cosimo P.P.), the Negro, and the hooded walkers.

Mounted astride, on white horses with red and gold trappings, are Piero's three daughters, Nannina, Bianca and Maria, wearing plumed and jewelled red and gold roundlets, golden jackets and sock-boots, scarlet doublets and hose. Not for three generations will the side-saddle be invented.

In 1605-7, Fynes Moryson found Italian women riders, married and virgin, apparelled like men, in close doublet; large breeches open at the knees, Spanish fashion, riding astride like men, but their hair like women, bare and knotted, or with gold net cauls, and feathered hats.

The Duke of Lucca, a ferocious soldier-enemy of the Medici is shown here, reduced to the status of a young sportsman, (carrying behind him the leopard which was his emblem), among the learned and civilized Florentines, one of whom symbolically halts his progress. The dismounting keeper of the other leopard, dressed in green, lets us see the contemporary saddle. In back, to l., a group of pages in wine-purple shows another Italian neckline, pointed both in front and back, disclosing a low-necked V of dark material; this bordered V-front neckline is often carried down into a c. front closing.

739. 1452-66. Italian, Umbrian. (Arezzo, S. Francisco.)
Piero della Francesca. Arrival of the Queen of
Sheba. These austere and noble figures, clad in wonderful browns, greens and blues, with gold, white
and black, show French influence in the slightly
horned veiled headdresses.

741.

740. XVc. Italian. (Sienna, Palazzo Pubblico.)

Att. to *Neroccio di Bartolommeo de' Landi.* Preaching and Miracle of S. Bernardino.

Completely slit outer sleeve gives a tabard-like effect to outer garments, even when pleated and belted. Variation between fabrics of garment and sleeve, and narrowness of fur borders are typically Italian.

MANTUA AND THE GONZAGA FAMILY

Less only than the Medici court were the learned and enlightened courts of the Gonzaga of Mantua, the Este of Ferrara, and the Montfeltro of Urbino.

Coryat, at the end of the XVIc., describes Mantua, and says, "This is the Citie which of all other places in the world I would wish to make my habitation in, and spend the remainder of my dayes." Here it was that "a mountebanke, the first I ever saw, played his part upon a scaffold." Mantegna's relationship with Mantua began even before the 1460's, when he was housed there in the employ of the reigning family.

741. c. 1474. Italian, Venetian. (Mantua, Cast. di Corte.)

Andrea Mantegna. Marquis Lodovico II. Gonzaga, with his wife, Barbara of Brandenburg, and children.

The second marquis of Mantua, Lodovico Gonzaga (1444-78), was also known as Lodovico III, il Turco. The bald man to the left is probably his secretary, Marsilio Andreasi. Behind Lodovico's wife is her favorite son, Gian Francesco (born 1446).

The gray-haired man next to him is Bartolomeo Manfredi, the astrologer of the Gonzaga family. The identity of the man in rich secular costume, standing between Lodovico and the astrologer, is uncertain: some authorities consider him to be the future marquis Frederico I; others, Francesco, the cardinal, second son of Lodovico. The boy-pronotary next to the marquis is his youngest son, Lodovico, who, born in 1459, was already appointed bishop of Mantua in

1468. The girl, holding an apple, may be one of Barbara's younger daughters, Paola or Barbara. The slim youth, before the pillar, is Lodovico's fourth son, Rodolfo, b.1451, killed on the Taro in 1495.

The costume of these men, if compared to French examples from Foucquet onward, show French influences on Italian characteristics. Italian male garments exploit the natural body, where French fashions overwhelm and deform it. They are becoming shorter, though not so short as the French; fuller and squarer, with a padded doublet bosom; but with less padding at the shoulder and upper sleeve of the doublet than in France. The horizontal is played against the vertical at every opportunity; low doublet collar-line, unbroken in front; bateau neck of jacket; natural waistline; width of hem against the columns of neck and legs; simple tubular sleeves; carefully laid cartridge pleats. The tiny cap, and the hair carefully curled from it, are further refinements of the Italian use of these two impulses. Simpler materials are now used; brocades are less spectacular in pattern; subservient to the lines of body and garment. The shoulder line is not confused by humps of padding of the French mahoîtres, nor do the flat edging furs used in Italy flare out the jacket skirt; they follow, enhance, and yet oppose the repeated vertical lines of the fine pleats. Shoes: natural, as is usual in Italy. Gloves: new, not a hawking gauntlet. The costume of the bald secretary at left might be from a Fouquet, except for the bare back of his neck, where a French jacket would have shown a high doublet collar. The simplification and unification of sleeve with the body of the garment is seen in the women's costumes, also; the bodice is gradually taking on importance; the round collar and V plastron are now defined, even when all are of patterned brocade. Female dwarf beside Federigo's wife.

742. c. 1474. Italian, Venetian. (Mantua, Castello di Corte.)

Andrea Mantegna. The meeting of the Marquis Lodovico and Cardinal Francesco Gonzaga.

Lodovico's second son, Francesco, was the first cardinal of the house of Gonzaga. The youth in ecclesiastical costume who holds the cardinal by the hand is Lodovico, the youngest son of the marquis. The little boy who grasps the hand of the young Pronotary Lodovico is Sigismondo, son of Federico and grandson of the marquis. The other boy shown in profile is the oldest son of Federico, Gian Francesco III, afterwards fourth marquis of Mantua and husband of Isabella d'Este the discriminating, if grasping, art patron, and the greatest lady of the Renaissance. The man to the right in front is Fed-

erico, the next heir. The man next to him is supposed to be Mantegna himself. The youth in profile, just visible between Lodovico and the Cardinal is Gian Francesco Gonzaga, son of *il Turco*.

The city in the background is an imaginary picture of the antique Rome, which shows the fortifications and famous classical monuments of architecture.

Many new usages: circular capes thrown back over the shoulder; slashing; and points.

Lodovico and two others wear the high, flat-topped hat which is seen on the elders of the Gonzaga and Montfeltro, and is sometimes called the "ducal mortier." (See Appendix.)

Doublet sleeves of the children and most of the men show the decorative use of knotted points, placed just below shoulder padding. Lodovico's upper doub-

743

let sleeve is cut out in the pattern of its brocade, widely slashed and filled in with plain materials. His tabard-like upper garment is belted in front; tights without a foot are strapped over his shoe. Lodovico's sleeve is of the new detachable sort, laced across the shoulder padding. Federico wears the new Italian cape, circular and folded back over the shoulder, which will become very familiar. Parti-color on one leg of hose.

743. XVc. 1467. Italian. (Metropolitan Museum.)

Fra Carnevale. Birth of the Virgin.

Italian costume, both male and female, is becoming fuller, made of simpler materials, with a larger number of colors used in one garment. Bodice, sleeves and skirt are here shown in different colors. The sleeve is set on a dropped shoulder-line, so that the color of the bodice of the kirtle is also visible. Beads, seen at extreme right, are a new style.

The dirtiest European country was Germany. The Burgundians complained of the filthiness and bad manners of the Count Palatine's retinue; and "German" was synonymous with "dirty" in Italy, the cleanest and most civilized country of Europe. It was in Italy, that the handkerchief (handcouvre-chef, also called "napkin") can be said to have originated in the XVc. (We see it in Ill. 743 hanging from the girdle by a cord, on the fifth figure from the left; similar usage will increase through Tudor and Elizabethan costume.) The first handkerchiefs were large, up to 18″ square, of linen, lawn, or cambric, embroidered in colored or metallic threads, fringed or edged with lace, the corners often finished with an acorn or tassel. Miniature handkerchiefs, worn in the hat-band, were given as favors to their suitors by English ladies. By XVIc. handkerchiefs were in general use in Venice, and appear by the dozen in inventories of the wardrobes of the great all over Europe.

VENICE AND THE DOGES

The city and patricians of Venice resembled no others. Built on piles, over a marsh, and served by over 100 miles of waterways instead of roads, Venice was impregnable but landless; with no natural resources except salt, she was forced to import food and timber. Her situation made her the most logical port of embarkation for the Crusades, the outfitting of which greatly enriched her. After struggling with Genoa for the supremacy of the Mediterranean, she became the world's greatest mercantile marine power. She received special privileges and rights of settlement in Syria and Asia Minor; rigorous government control specified even the dimensions of her ships, which permitted their refitting from stocks at outlying depots, and their conversion into men-of-war; and required them to bring back materials from the Orient for the embellishment of the city.

Her aristocracy were not feudal warriors, but the leading members of her merchant guilds. "Venice was a joint stock company for the exploitation of the East and the patricians were its directory." Her civilization was magnificent but material, without the interest in literature and art of the courts of Florence, Mantua and Urbino; her great painters are those of her decadence: Mantegna and the Bellinis, in the XVc., and the later Carpaccio, Giorgione, Titian, Tintoretto, Veronese and Tiepolo. Canvas, as a painting's surface, was first used in Venice by the Bellinis.

A large part of the population had gradually become disenfranchised, though some fiction of republican government was maintained in the words: "This is your Doge, an it please you," with which the new ruler was presented to the people. The Doges of the Republics of Venice and Genoa were elected for life, as the civil, military and religious heads of their cities. In Genoa, Commines relates, the Dorias, who were gentlemen, could not become Doges, as could the Campoforgosi, who belonged to the same party, "for no gentleman is capable of becoming Doge by their law. . . . The nobility makes Doges, but cannot be made so themselves." The Venetian Doges, though treated with the greatest honor and ceremony, were actually less important than the cabinet, council and senate, whose figure-head they were.

Venetian seizure of the adjoining mainland, at the beginning of the XVc., was the beginning of her downfall. No allies wished to help maintain her trade supremacy; and with the loss of her trade with the East, after the fall of Constantinople, mid-XVc., and the discovery of the route to the Indies around the Cape, Venice was ruined.

Venice became famous for her damask fabrics, particularly velvet brocades; Murano glass; silvered mirrors; mosaic and inlay. Oriental rugs passed into Europe through Venice; her ships, carrying sugar to England, brought away raw wool, which was exchanged in Flanders for finished cloth.

744. XVc. c. 1476. Italian Venetian. (Metropolitan Mus.)
Gentile Bellini. Doge Andrea Vendramin.

745. XVc. Italian Venetian. (Museum of Fine Arts, Boston.)
Att. to Gentile Bellini. Portrait of a Doge.

746

747

748

746. XVc. c. 1470. Italian. (Kaiser Friedrich Museum, Berlin.)

Morone or *Michele da Verona*. Cassone panel: Betrothal of Jason and Medea.

Just such heads, veiled over a little flat hat, with hanging locks in front of the ear, and short-waisted spreading bodices, with more elaborately cut and puffed sleeves, are shown in the Venetian dress drawn

by Dürer in 1494-5. In Venetian use, at that time, two immense buttons closed the skirt in front, and high pattens were worn.

The differentiation in color, seen in gowns in Ill. 743, continues in this Jason and Medea illustration: in the sleeves and their slashings, lengthwise or across the elbow; the plastron; underskirt; lining of overskirt; color of cord belt, cap and veil.

**747. XVc. 1473. Italian. (Perugia, Palazzo del Munici-
pio.)**

B. Caporale or *Fiorenzo di Lorenzo* or *Master of*
1473. Miracle of S. Bernardino.

Very long, or very short garments, showing French
influence: extremely abbreviated jacket and cape;
some high doublet collars; slightly pointing shoes.
Italian: in hair and headwear, some collars, and parti-
color of one leg of hose. Pendant sleeves, here thrown
over the wrist, are sometimes seen knotted in back.

Sleeves are becoming simple, close-fitting and unified with the costume. But the impulse which made
them pre-eminent, earlier in the century, persists:
sometimes in actual separation from the garment
(laced on: see Ill. 742); partly freed, as is Jason's
outer sleeve; caught (angels: see Ill. 749); or barely
tacked on. By the next century, sleeves will become
interchangeable.

The youth in the Miracle of St. Bernardino (ext.
background, c.) wears boots cut into a point high
above the knee and decorated with stitching.

748. XVc. Italian, Sienese. (Met. Mus. of Art.)

Francesco di Giorgio. Chess Players.
Wonderfully dressed clouds of blond hair, with
approximately the costume shown on the Gonzaga
family (741). Inset cartridge pleats.

**749. c. 1470. Italian, Umbrian. (National Gallery of Art,
Washington.)**

Provincial follower of Piero della Francesca. Madonna enthroned with Angels. Slashing and separation of sleeve from garment.

750. 1477. Italian. (Rome, Vatican.)

Melozzo da Forli. Sixtus IV. Nominating Platina
at Librarian of the Vatican.

Implacable enemy of the Medici, Sixtus excommunicated all Tuscany in retaliation for Lorenzo's
"only fault . . . that he had not been murdered" in
the attempt by Sixtus' Riario nephew. Sixtus became "speechless with fury" and died when Lorenzo's
diplomacy deprived him of the support of the Sforzas
in his attacks on Florence and Ferrara. He was, however, an enlightened patron of artists and writers;
his great program of public works included the Sistine Chapel; he founded the Sistine choir, and was
one of the founders of the Vatican Library.

The Pope wears a red skull-cap and cape, ermine-
lined; white rochet and cotta.

R. to l.: a man in dark green; Cardinal Giuliano
della Rovere, later Julius II; Platina kneeling, in a
blue gown with red sleeves; Girolamo Riario, the
Pope's nephew, the Medici's enemy, husband of Cath-

erine Sforza, Countess of Forli (who later married a Medici), and future governor of the Pontifical States, his hands hidden in the sleeves of his blue gown (also a female usage, late XVc. French); Giovanni della Rovere, Prefect of Rome, in a violet gown, was the Pope's favorite nephew, and son-in-law of the Duke of Urbino.

751. c. 1461. Italian, Florentine. (Metropolitan Mus.)

Benozzo Gozzoli. St. Zenobius Resuscitates a Dead Child. Clerics, monks and acolytes; gentlemen, circular sleeve turned up on shoulder in the manner of the new usage of capes.

752. XVc. Italian. (Florence, Uffizi Gallery.)

Pupil of Antonio Pollaiuolo. Study of model in XVc. Florentine costume. Eyelet holes on doublet hem and sleeves for lacing points.

753. 1470. Italian, Venetian. (Ferrara, Palazzo Schifanoia.)

Cosimo Tura and Francesco Cossa. Fresco: Triumph of Minerva: detail.

754. 1468-85. Italian, Florentine. (Pisa, Campo Santo.)

Benozzo Gozzoli and assistants. Fresco: Old Testament Scenes.

Men's and women's work clothes: shirts and drawers; doublet and hose; tucked-up dresses and aprons.

752

754

753

755. 1468-85. Italian, Florentine. (Pisa, Campo Santo.)

Benozzo Gozzoli and assistants.
Old Testament Scenes: detail.

756. 1470. Italian. (Ferrara, Palazzo Schifanoia.)
Cosimo Tura and Francesco Cossa.
Triumph of Minerva: detail.

Lacings of front closing caught by decorative hooks. Fullness of sleeve below shoulder is all that remains of padded sleeve of the doublet type of the first half of the XVc.

757, 758. 1468-85. Italian, Florentine. (Pisa, Campo Santo.)

Benozzo Gozzoli and assistants. Old Testament Scenes.
   757. Construction of the Ark; the Deluge; and Noah Giving Thanks.
   758. Construction of the Tower of Babel.

The padded width of last half XVc. is shown here at its Italian limit, fullness provided by the favorite Italian method of inset cartridge pleats. The idea of hand-covering is increasingly strong; several gentlemen at lower right carry gloves; the youth (second from right, 1st row), thrusts his hands into the bottom of his pendant sleeve, as into a muff.

The separation of sleeve from garment, notably in Flanders and Italy in last half XVc., continues; the sleeve which is being used as a muff is so little a part of the jacket, that the fur lining of the jacket shows around the armseye; the jacket sleeve is merely tucked on in back, under the doublet sleeve. The sleeve of the youth at extreme right is cut in one with the jacket, at the shoulder, but is free of the jacket, under the armpit.

759. XVc. Italian. (Padua, Church of the Eremites.)
Niccolo Pizzolo. St. Christopher.

759

760

The effect of fullness is enhanced by circular capes, wound about, or thrown over the shoulder (see Ill. 751). Fur-lined boots, with turned-down fur cuff and side-buckled closing.

760. XVc. Italian. (Ferrara, Palazzo Schifanoia.)

Cosimo Tura. Triumph of Minerva.

Gloves are not merely carried, but are worn on both hands (gentleman, right). Belts reduced to a cord, knotted in back. Hose, parti-colored, with boot-like pattens on one leg.

761

761. c. 1478. Italian. (Florence, Uffizi.)
Sandro Botticelli. The Return of Spring: detail.

To illustrate Politian's allegorical poem, in celebration of the second and most splendid of the Medici tournaments (that of his younger brother, Giuliano, in 1475), Lorenzo commissioned Botticelli to execute three paintings: The Birth of Venus (Uffizi); Mars and Venus (Nat. Gall., Lond.); and the Return of Spring (from the motto, "Le temps revient," which appeared on the Medici standard, painted by Verrocchio, who had also designed the helmets worn by the brothers in the tournament). For an analysis of the pictures, see Young's: *The Medici,* Chap. VIII.

762. 1480. Italian, Ferrarese. (National Gallery of Art, Washington.)
Ercole Roberti. Giovanni Bentivoglio.

The ruthless but cultivated tyrant of Bologna wears a red cap; red-gold brocade jacket, with white fur.

763. 1483-4. Italian, Florentine. (Nat. Gall. of Art, Wash.)
Sandro Botticelli. Portrait of a Youth.

The blond youth wears a red cap, brown jacket
with separate sleeves.

764-67; 770-75. 1490-1500. Italian. (Metropolitan Mus.)   Panels from the frieze in the Gonzaga Palace,
School of Bramantino.   S. Martino di Guznaja, near Mantua.

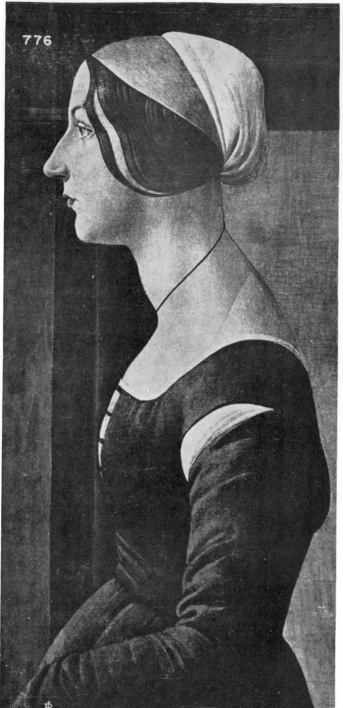

Doge, condottieri, and nobles with the long-flowing hair, the new bonnets and braid-trimmed outer garments with sailor collars, and the lady, the bound chin and tied-on sleeves, of the transition period.

768. XVc. 1487-9. Italian Florentine. (Metropolitan Museum, Bache Coll.)
Domenico Ghirlandaio.

Francesco Sassetti and son Teodoro.

Francesco, of the great Florentine bourgeois banking family, wears a purple cap, red gown, black cord belt and pouch. Teodoro: scarlet cap, gray brocade tunic edged with white fur, green doublet sleeves.

769. XVc. 1480. Italian. (Florence, Church of San Salvatore d'Ognissanti.)
Domenico Ghirlandaio.
St. Jerome.

Portable desk with lectern set on a table covered by one of the Oriental carpets first imported by Venice and spread through their agency throughout Europe in XVI-XVIIc. On its side hang the contemporary spectacles, which folded scissors-fashion to pinch the nose; inkwells, sand, scissors; cardinal's tasselled hat on shelf overhead.

776. XVc. 1489-90. Italian. (Florence, Pitti Gall.)
Sandro Botticelli.
Portrait of a Young Woman.
The Botticelli and Sassetti (Ill. 777) ladies show neckline, lowering and becoming squarer, laced bodices; and separate sleeves, showing shirt beneath. Succession of necklace styles: from the heavy jewelled collar, worn high on throat (see Ill. 715); ropes of pearls: cord caught at throat; coral beads, with Renaissance pearl pendant of Sassetti lady. Hair: loosening and flowing in locks; hair coverings, becoming simplified in arrangement of veils.

777. XVc. 1490. Italian Florentine. (Metropolitan Mus.)
Domenico Ghirlandaio.
Lady of the Sassetti family.
The lady wears a green moiré bodice, with sleeves of plain green silk; dark green lacings through gold catches; and a white fichu collar, in the new neckline of the XVIc. trend.

778. XVc. c. 1480. Italian Ferrarese. (National Gallery of Art, Washington.)
Ercole Roberti.
Ginevra Bentivoglio.
Ginevra wears a brown gown trimmed with gold, jewels and pearls; and a white veil, falling from a horned headdress, and carried under the arm (cf. exposed shirts of others).

779-780. XVc. 1486-90. Italian. (Florence, S. Maria Novella.)
Domenico Ghirlandaio.
779. The Birth of St. John the Baptist.
780. The Visitation (detail: Giovanni degli Albizzi Tornabuoni).

When Ghirlandaio was commissioned by the rich Florentine merchant family of Tornabuoni to redecorate the chapel, after the Orcagna frescos had been ruined by roof leaks, he used as models the painters, poets and leading citizens of Florence, and ladies of the Tornabuoni family. Until Lorenzo's day the Albizzi, leaders of the opposing party of the nobility, had been the most powerful family in Florence, and Giovanna, who had just been married, was the greatest beauty of the city.

The fashionable silhouette is definitely altering to one narrower and more severe. A stiff tabard-like outer garment, cut in a very low V-neck, falls loose over the short-bodiced, full-skirted gown we see on the attendants; the neckline of this under-gown is becoming lower and squarer, frequently exposing a line of the higher neck of the shirt. The greatest characteristic of all European costume, from the end of the XVc. through the first-half of the XVIc., is the increase, elaboration and combination of slashing and puffing, lacing and strapping.

We see lacing under arm (woman reaching for baby), down bodice fronts, and used (underbodice of visiting lady) in combination with strappings, such as catch the inner sleeve at the armseye, and cross the inner and outer elbow.

Many new usages are shown: the nightgown, worn by the invalid; the fan and handkerchief, carried by the great ladies; the use of embroidered edges on the hem of the elderly attendant's gown, and on the neck of the nightgown. Necklaces are now a narrow cord, caught at throat, falling between breasts; or bead necklaces with pearl and jewelled pendants. Lacings are often bead-strung, as across bodice of younger attendant. Hair arrangements have flowing side-locks, no head-covering at all, or a tiny cap or slight veil.
781.XVIc. 1597. Italian-German. (Met. Mus., Print Room.)

Att. to *Jost Amman.*

Venetian Gondola, from the illustrations of the great procession of the Doges, published in Frankfort, 1597.

781

782

Coryat describes the great height of Venice's 3-4 story buildings, made of brick and freestone, with pillars of white stone and Istrian marble; flat roofs, and open galleries hanging from upper stories; painted ceilings equal to those of the Louvre or Tuileries; and with windows of glass; and her checkered pavements, and mosaic walls.

There were no horses in Venice, but 10,000 gondolas—6,000 private and 4,000 for hire. The gondolas, with carved ends, had as many as 15-16 cloth-covered arches, and black leather seats with lace-trimmed white linen curtains below.

782. XVc. 1498. Italian. (Florence, Corsini Palace.)
Unknown artist. Execution of Savonarola in the Piazza della Signoria.

The fervid preacher, who denounced the powerful families of Italy and the corruption of the Papacy, was the virtual ruler of Florence after Lorenzo de' Medici's death. He changed the pleasure-loving city to one of Puritan austerity in dress and manners. Carnival time in 1497 was celebrated by a bonfire of masks and "vanities" for which a Venetian merchant offered 20,000 gold florins. Alexander VI failed to buy off the dangerous man with a Cardinal's hat; then swore he should die "even were he a second John the Baptist." Florentine men began to resent their interrupted marriages. Mobs, incited by Franciscans and Dominicans, arrested, tortured, and burned Savonarola with two of his followers. The calamities which had been foretold by Savonarola for Florence under a Pope named Clement, came true in XVIc.

783. End XVc. Italian. (Milan, Brera Museum.)
Att. to *B. Conti*.

Madonna, SS. Jerome, Gregory and Ambrose, with Lodovico *il Moro* Sforza, Beatrice d'Este, and two sons.

These are the last generations of the 100-year old condottieri dynasty of the Sforza. Beatrice d'Este, the great patron of arts and letters, died before her husband. Lodovico, Leonardo da Vinci's patron, was driven from Milan in 1499, to die a prisoner of the French. One son, Massimiliano, died a pensioner of the French; Francesco Maria was reinstated, but on his death, the duchy went to Charles V.

Spanish styles influence the allied states of Naples, Milan and Florence. Naples is ruled by an Aragon king, and Lodovico had arranged the marriage of his nephew (Bianca Maria's brother), to the granddaughter of the King of Naples. Looped hair, often with a falling lock, as in Spain, is seen in Florence and Milan, and in the highest society, the bound Spanish pigtail appears as well. With this headdress, the forehead is bound by a narrow, flat, black braid with irregular edges; it does not have the thread-like character of the black cord worn around the neck in conjunction with short necklaces of enormous pearls.

784. XVc. c. 1493. Italian Milanese. (National Gallery of Art, Washington.)
Ambrogio de' Predis.
Bianca Maria Sforza.

The auburn-haired sitter, dressed in golden-brown brocade, formerly identified as Lodovico Sforza's

785

wife, Beatrice d'Este, is now generally believed to represent Gian Galeazzo's sister, Bianca Maria, during her engagement (signified by the carnation in her girdle) to the Emperor Maximilian whom she married in 1494.

The long queue, bound in pearls (which we will see in Spanish usage at the turn of the century, in combination with looped hair), is combined with a jewelled headdress and pendant. The pendant bears the Sforza emblems of branches carrying fruit; and the Sforza *spazzola* device, a brush with a ribbon

tied to the handle (which was a great favorite of Lodovico, but had been in use by other members of the family at about the time of his birth); and the motto "Merito et Tempore," which each member of the family interpreted during his lifetime "according to his individual standards and ambitions." (See Appendix.)

785-787. XVc. 1490-95. Italian. (Venice, Academy of Fine Arts.)
Vittore Carpaccio.
The Legend of St. Ursula:

786

785. The English Ambassadors Before King Maurus; 786. The English Ambassadors Return to Their King; 787. The English Ambassadors Before King Maurus: detail.

Commines describes Venice, in 1495, to which he was Ambassador from the King of France: "The houses are very large and lofty, and built of stone; the old ones are all painted; those of about a hundred years standing are faced with white marble from Istria (which is about a hundred miles from Venice), and inlaid with porphyry and serpentine. Within they have, most of them, two chambers at least adorned with gilt ceilings; rich marble chimney pieces, bedsteads of gold color, their portals of the same, and most gloriously furnished. In short, it is the most triumphant city I have ever seen, the most respectful to all ambassadors and strangers, governed with the greatest wisdom, and serving God with the utmost solemnity."

Male costume of the Transition period was strongly affected by these Italian styles. The new diagonal line (shown particularly in the Return of the Ambassadors) is found, not only in the closings and wraparound of the cloaks of the young men, but in long gowns (m. near pillar in crowd before bridge), and in the braid trim of bias-cut cape sleeves (to left and in front of crowd), and in the revers of the cloaks.

The ambassadors' gowns have extremely long sleeves, widening below elbow; the plain high-necked gowns (in line, left of crowd) carry bead girdles. Doublets are excessively short, with sleeves much cut and laced; the lacings diagonal, or grouped horizontally.

Shirts are much exposed, with embroidery or braid holding gathered or smocked fullness. Hose are very long and well made; parti-color of one leg; and division of its decoration at knee. Boots are much worn; soft; slit at back seam; the tops turned down, showing another color, and pinked edges.

Gloves are not carried but worn, with embroidered edges and pointed cuff, weighted by a bead or acorn of precious metal. Doublet points begin to assume precious jewelled tags, aiglettes. Neck chains are heavy and handsome, often carry a pendant. Caps and hats of felt or beaver carry jewelled brooches and feathers; the larger hats, usually of beaver, carry clusters of plumes and a binding scarf.

The hair of the young men is particularly long and flowing; others have long and carefully rolled bobs; or are even clipped (rear: ambassador to Maurus). All are clean shaven.

788

788. End XVc. Italian, Florentine. (Met. Mus. of Art.)

Cassone panel: The War of Charles of Durazzo.
Left side: Charles enters Naples as Victor, 1381.

One episode in centuries of violent Neapolitan history and intrigue was Charles of Durazzo's capture of Naples and murder of its queen, Joanna I. She had named a distant cousin, Louis of Anjou, as her heir. René d'Anjou's claim on Naples, inherited by the French crown, together with the Orleans claim of Milan, were Charles VIII's excuse for the invasion of Italy in 1494, which revealed to the French masses a civilization beyond their dreams.

Durazzo's men are shown in the costume of the time of their invasion, more than a century before.

789-792. XIV-XVc. French Burgundian. (Dijon Museum.)

Claus Sluter. Four mourners.

To enrich the Carthusian monastery he had built at Champmol, Philip the Bold commissioned the Flemish sculptor, Sluter, to execute a magnificent altar tomb, with 40 alabaster figures representing mourners from all ranks of life.

Man: carrying large hat; wears small cowl over circular fur-lined cape, closed on right shoulder.

Bishop: the stole, which is worn, by a bishop, dependent from the shoulders, is here worn crossed, like that of a priest. There were many deviations of this sort during the Middle Ages; figure may be that of an honorary abbot, who is a simple priest permitted to wear pontificals; there are still honorary abbots in various parts of Europe. Mitre: rising and raking backward. Crozier; curve and tendrils becoming more elaborate.

Man: very new sleeve; full, gathered onto a long cuff of circular cut; buttoned tight at wrist; completely concealing hand of hanging arm; another expression of the idea manifested in prolonged sleeve of English bourgeois and ladies, and the shell-back gauntlet of English knights.

Carthusian monk: hooded scapular, held together by broad band, over fur-lined robe.

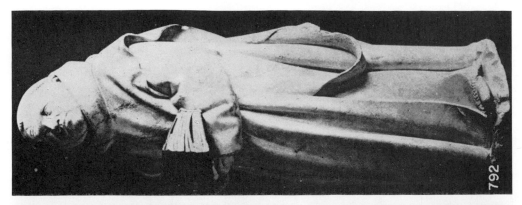

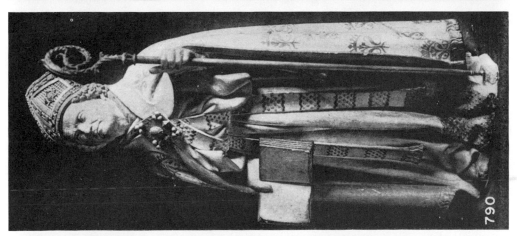

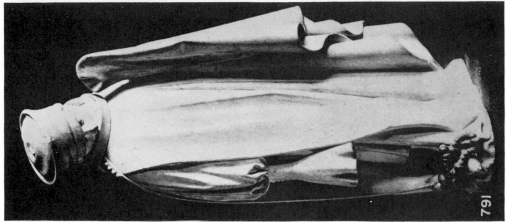

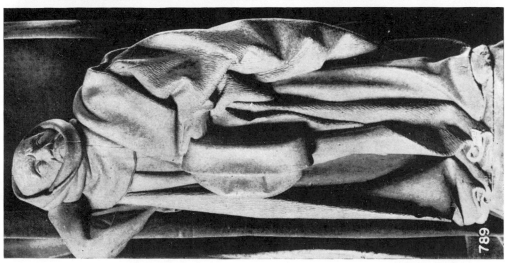

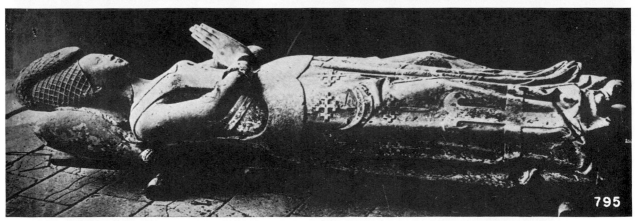

793. 1399-1401. French Burgundian. (Champmol Monastery.)

Claus Sluter. Isaiah: one of 6 prophets executed by Sluter for Philip the Bold, for the monastery where perpetual masses were to be said for the Duke's soul. Dressed in the costume of a rich gentleman of his period; tasseled pouches hang from handsome belt.

794. XVc. 1424-29. French.

Pierre de Theury. Tomb sculpture: Isabelle of Bavaria, wife of Charles VI.

The classic shape of the headdress of a great lady of the first-quarter of the XVc.; covered chin, of great lady or widow. Beneath the wimple and veil with fluted edge, the masses of netted hair, completely covering the ears, give the characteristic horizontal line to the top of the headdress, which, in full-face appears very wide; in profile narrow. The fact that Isabelle of Bavaria was completely bald and without eyebrows is supposed to have led, out of court snobbery, to the plucking of eyebrows and forehead, to give an exaggeratedly bald look to the unveiled head.

795. XVc. French. (Beuvil, Indre-et-Loire.)

Tomb sculpture. Jeanne de Montjean, d.1456.

796

797

798

By the third-quarter XVc. the netted headdress has become very high and narrow; ears, which have been covered for nearly half a century, are again beginning to be seen. The headdress is wired and padded to support the heavily jewelled netting and the horns formed by the stuffed roll. The skirt of her fur bordered cotte carries parted armorial bearings.

796-798. XVc. French. (Paris, Bibliotheque Nationale, ms. fr. 616.)

Livre de Chasse by Gaston-Phoebus.

One of the earliest books on hunting, the "Deduits de la chasse, des bestes sauvages et les oiseaux de proye," was translated into English in 1406-13 by Edward, Duke of York, under the title, "Master of Game." Of its author, Gaston III, Count of Foix (1331-91), called Gaston-Phoebus because of his beauty, Froissart, after his visit to the great court of Foix in 1389 says: "I never saw none like him of personage, nor of so fair form, nor so well made. . . . In everything he was so perfect, he cannot be praised too much."

It is probable that this copy belonged originally to Diane de Poitiers' father; he was reprieved as he stood on the scaffold, but his property was confiscated by Francis I. The book accompanied the king to the wars, and became part of the booty at Pavia. It was sold by a common soldier to the bishop of Trent. It was almost lost, and its binding badly charred in the 1848 fire in the Bibliothèque Nationale.

Start of the hunt (796): the Count's hooded robe, simple in cut, magnificent in its dragon-patterned brocade,* owes its dragging length to the influence of the houppelande. Its skirt, long in front, is necessarily slit partway above hem. The huntsmen wear high boots, laced up the outside of the leg, as well as the new bag sleeve. From the extraordinary collars of the houppelande, so much has been learned about cutting, that, by XVc., collars appear on garments worn by men of all classes. Horns slung by baldrics. Third man to right of count, and almost concealed, carries on his belt a wonderful pouch; a strap across its buckled flap holds a short hunting knife.

Tracking (797): huntsman in a broad brimmed straw hat, turned up in back.

Boar hunt (798): the mounted gentleman wears a short brocade gown of the houppelande type, collars on which are now becoming lower; bag sleeves, with a falling circular cuff, here thrown back. Precious collar of gold links is a new style. Hat, typical of the end of the XIVc., with Phrygian peak worn flopping forward. Strapped puttees. Dagging in leaf patterns has now invaded even the trappings of the horses.

---

* Gaston-Phoebus' personal emblem was a blazing sun; dragons, green with red and gold wings, were used as supporters by the Counts of Foix.

799-803. XVc. 1409-19. French. (Paris, Bib. de l'Arsenale. No. 5193.)

Boccaccio of Jean Sans Peur.

This *Boccaccio,* one of the many fine manuscripts which have come down to us in the libraries of the Dukes of Burgundy, belonged to John, the son of Philip the Bold.

799. Peasant: fur hat, worn over hood, but carried slung back by a cord; net pouch, fastened to belt, and slung above buttocks; socks with rolled top (cf. huntsmen, Livre de Chasse), but without feet. (Right panel) Banquet: oriental kings being served by man in tabard-like garment; cloth of diapered mediaeval pattern; flagon.

800. King: hood twisted and tied around brow; from such usages developed the cockscomb turbans worn with houppelandes, and later chaperons.

801. As the king hurdles the flames, his houppelande is presented almost in pattern form. It is of brocade, ermine-lined; it has, typically, an extremely high collar, flaring and trailing funnel sleeves, excessively dagged edges, and skirt slit high (in this case, at side, rather than at center front as was more common). His darker undertunic, also of brocade, has bag sleeves. The onlooker (extreme right), shows typical haircut of the first half of the XVc., cropped high above ears; he wears an interesting very short garment, in the nature of a jupon; it has, however a rather full, baggy sleeve, and, under the influence of the houppelande, a tiny slit in the front of its very short skirts. His companion wears the forward-flopping hat already seen on horsemen of Livre de Chasse illustrations; and pleated cote-hardi, the sleeves of which are also set on in pleats. Both wear parti-colored hose with sewn-on soles. Tapestry background and floor in typical diapered patterns.

802. On the little sailing ship, the king's two companions wear two typical forms of late XIV-e.XVc. headgear: one, often seen in a taller form, in which the crown resembles that of an opera hat, carries the now fashionable medallion; the other is draped, made from a hood, bound round by its liripipe into a turban, with the dagged hem of the hood falling in pleats over the rolled edge.

803. King, in robes with parted armorial bearings, being crowned by a bishop and two cardinals.

DOMESTIC ARCHITECTURE: MIDDLE AGES TO XVIII CENTURY

Until the invention of the wrought-iron I-beam in mid-XIXc., building height was limited to 5-6 floors. This was the first major advance over the techniques practiced more than 2000 years before by the Romans. Roman masonry was magnificent; they manufactured brick, tile and glass in the remotest outposts of Britain. Their villas, built around a court, which could be cooled by fountains and always provided a sunny or a shaded area, had running water and hot-air ducts under the floor which delivered heat in the "panel" form which is heating's newest refinement in the 1940's.

With the fall of their empire, Roman culture receded toward its Italian sources. Its techniques had only been imposed on Britain, and were largely forgotten there during the Dark Ages.

Concrete remained unused from Roman times until the rebuilding of the Eddystone Lighthouse in England in 1774.

Glass was used in English windows in VIIc.; but in 758 A.D. Cuthbert, abbot of Jarrow, asked the Bishop of Mainz to send workmen to supply "windows and vessels of glass because the English were so ignorant and helpless." The glass which Bishop Wilfruth installed at Worcester in the first-half of the VIIIc. was suspected of being of supernatural origin. A knowledge of glass-making was retained in Normandy, Lorraine and around Barcelona; colored glass, appearing in churches in late XIIc., was seen throughout Europe in XIII-XVc. From XIII-XVIIIc., the finest glass was that exported by Venice. Germany's ties with Italy were close; and in 1453 Philip the Good established Italian glass workers in Flanders, which became another center, exporting to England. Glass was in common domestic use in England by 1550; in e. XVIIc., as we will see, the dramatic entrance of coal as a fuel altered the entire industrial balance of Europe.

Knowledge of brick and tile making was retained in Germany and the Low Countries, which exported brick to the east coast of England. Manufacture was recommended in England in XIIIc.; use increased through XV-XVIc., and after the Fire of 1666 London was rebuilt largely in brick; by XVIIIc., it was the most common building material. Here, too, the Italians and Spanish were pre-eminent and earliest, with magnificent decorative glazed terra cottas in XIV-XVc.; cool floors of tile, and roof tiles which were not subject to shattering cold. From XIII-XVIc., floors were largely of tile: either the more durable red-brown and cream-white encaustic tiles of England, France, the Low Countries and Germany, or the more colorful but tenderly glazed majolica of Spain and Italy; or of marble. Where the floor did not remain beaten earth, it was of stone, so long as fires continued to be built upon it; then of tile or marble, lastly of wood.

In many places, stone is so good and plentiful that it has always remained cheaper than brick; as in N.E. England, up the Rhine, along the German seacoast and in parts of France. To Americans, brought up on weathered New England granite or New York gneiss, it is surprising to learn what a soft material newly quarried sand or limestone can be. In his specifications for St. Paul's Cathedral, Sir Christopher Wren required the stone to be seasoned for three years on a sea beach.

The most common building material in use through XVIc. was wood, which was becoming scarce in England and N.W. Europe. It was, in any case, so hard to fell, draw, adze and saw by primitive methods, and nails were so tedious to forge by hand, that timber was apt to be used only in the supporting frame. This was usually fitted together without nails, and the interstices filled in with interwoven wattles and mud (lathe and plaster), or later with brick. Diagonal bracing (as by projecting tree limbs) was often obtained by the actual use of trunks and limbs; with the increase of ship building the curved and seasoned timbers of old ships were worked into the framing. The patterns of the exposed dark wood frame and its light plastered stuffing were elaborated with infinite sophistication in the 4 to 5 story high, half-timbered houses of the Rhine Valley in XV-XVIc.; and with equal beauty in the lower, wider French and English forms of town or manor house or farm cottage. The upper stories were wider than the lower, to protect them from the elements, and to shelter passers-by and customers. A guild member's house was a combination of shop in front, opening out into the street, factory in back with a garden beyond, and living quarters above for the family and apprentices.

A wooden house in England before XVc. was about as weather-tight as grandfather's hayloft; its windows were glassless holes covered by batten shutters or wicker-work lattices which were hinged at the top and could be propped open in good weather. As in the castle, its fire was in the middle of the dirt or stone floor, and the smoke was supposed to go out of a hole in the roof. In Elizabeth's day a farmer's house is described as:

"Of one bay's* breadth, Got wot, a silly cote
Whose thatched spars are furred with sluttish soote
A whole inch thick, shining like a blackamoor's brows
Through smoke that down a headless barrel blows."

* Bay-16 feet, the module in multiplications of which a house was built, so many bays wide; during Tudor times, ranks of symmetrical bays were projected, stories high, from the face of the building, and were filled with windows in late XVIc.

Still, in 1628, "his habitation is some poore thatched roofe, distinguished from his Barne by the loopholes that let out Smoake, which the rain had long since washed thorow, but for the double seeling of Bacon on the inside." (John Earle: *Microcosmography*.)

Even in the bedrooms of mediaeval castles, smoke filtered out through slits high in the walls; the flue was a refinement, rare in Italy in XIIc., common in N. Italy by XVc. In cold N.W. Europe, the flue began to be common in XVc., and with the use of brick, late XVc., clusters of flues could be carried up in one chimney. The decorative value of tall chimneys was emphasized in French architecture in XV-XVIc. (See Ills. 807-810.)

The handsome house of Elizabeth's day was becoming well-lighted, comfortable and livable, and chimneys were making even unpretentious houses bearable. In 1577-89 Harrison says, "Old men yet dwelling in the village where I remain find things 'marvellously' altered within their sound remembrance . . . one is the multitude of chimneys lately erected in each village whereas in their young daies there were not above two or three but each made his fire against a reredos in the hall." (From: *Description of England in Shakespeare's Youth*.)

Roofs of cathedrals and palaces might be of lead or copper sheets; slate was used where found (see Ills. 807-810); tile, especially in milder southern Europe; wood shingles (East Anglia); and thatch.

In 1555, the Venetian Ambassador to England wrote, "In the North of England they find a certain sort of earth, well nigh mineral, which burns like charcoal and is extensively used, especially by blacksmiths, and but for a certain bad odour which it leaves would be yet more employed as it gives great heat and costs but little." Rising in veins to the surface, coal had been known in England since Roman days; by XIIIc. its use in the city of London had been forbidden, but as flues multiplied, it became practical, and early in XVIIc., the most important of all fuels. English patents for coal furnaces were granted in 1610; by 1616 no other fuel was permitted in English glass manufacture and the importation of glass was forbidden; by the third-quarter of the XVIIc. English glass was equal or superior to Venetian.

Now that the climate of N.W. Europe could be made comfortable all year round, Italy's Renaissance advantage of three good seasons to their one, was reduced to three against their present four; with a hot summer and inadequate fuel, Italy lost out in the new industrial age to England and the countries around the coal basins of Alsace and the Ruhr.

804-805. XVc. 1409. French.
(Paris. Bibliotheque Na-
tionale, ms. fr. 23279.)

*Demandes faites par le
Roi Charles VI,* by Pierre
le Fuitier, called Salmon.

804. Charles VI and Pi-
erre Salmon. 805. Salmon
presenting his work to
Charles VI in the presence
of Jean Sans Peur.

The basic plan of the
great mediaeval dwelling
provided a huge central
hall, from which doors led
at one end to the kitchens;
from the other end, to the
living quarters of the family. The size of the hall required the support of pillars and arches. Insufficient
heat with much smoke was
provided by a fire, often set
on a raised hearth in the
middle of the hall; in this
case, there was no flue, and
the smoke passed out
through an insufficient
hooded aperture in the high
ceiling. By XIVc., tall
screens blocked off
draughts as doors were
opened at the servants' end
of the hall. Above these
screens the musicians' gallery was placed.

At the master's end was
a raised dining platform
with long narrow tables, on
one side of which diners
sat in a row, and from the
other side of which they
were served. In great
houses the attendants on
the lord or lady were not
servants, but young people
of good family, sent there
as they would now be sent
to finishing school.* (See p.
298, footnote.)

The hall had a public
and civic character. It was
the law court, hotel, place
of business and entertainment of the lord's domain,
as the castle was the jail,
source of supplies and place

of retreat for the lord's people and their cattle in time
of danger. An overflow of guests was bedded down
in the hall, and their servants in the stables.

The private rooms were usually on a higher level
than the hall, set over the supply cellars; the "solar"
was a combination bed-sitting room, much less
draughty and smoky than the hall. Its fireplace was
set against the wall, the smoke leaving by slits high

in the masonry in the early days. It was the first fireplace in the building to be provided with a flue when
these began to be built. The bedroom was therefore
used as an audience chamber; Edward I and his
queen were struck by lightning and almost killed
in 1287, while sitting on their bed, surrounded by
members of their court. A small low window with
a wide sill served as a lectern (806).

The all-pervading chill of mediaeval court life is implicit in these illustrations: fur-lined gowns; tapestry-hung walls; curtained beds; double-hung windows; raised seats, draped with heavy fabrics and furnished with cushions under foot against the cold of the tile floors.

Pattern is now applied in a variety of ways. There are fewer borders and braids, except on conservative state robes (805). Floral and foliated asymmetric patterns, like those on the borders of illuminated manuscripts of the period, are variously used: diagonally (across bed-furnishings, 804, on certain portions [as sleeves alone] of houppelande). We see the familiar geometric designs in stained-glass windows, and diapered red and blue wall-hangings, but even the repeated patterns which we see on gowns and curtains begin to show increasing personal significance.

Typical of the XVc. is the increasing use of personal and identifying mottos, devices, badges and color. (See Ills. 807-810).

In the course of the hereditary enmity between the houses of Orleans and Burgundy, Louis, Duke of Orleans, served notice of his intentions by adopting as his badge a knotty stick which he distributed as a gilded New Year's gift, in 1406, together with the motto, "Je t' envy" (I defy you), a dice-player's term. As a counter-device, Jean Sans Peur assumed carpenter's planes and levels, and, as motto, another dicing term, in Flemish, "Hic houd" (I hold it). After the assassination of Orleans, the Parisians said, "Le bâton épineaux avait été raclé par le rabot!"† (The knotted stick was scraped by the plane.) These devices of Jean Sans Peur appear in the embroidery of his gown, and as pendants from a gold chain (806).

805. The canopies, fringed in red, black, and white (the colors of Charles VI), bear his motto: "Jamais." The hound with a crowned collar, which appears on his bed-hangings, and together with his motto, on the breast of his houppelande, was one of his emblems. The diagonal sprays shown on both are probably also significant.

---

* At the meeting of the Kings of France and England, Froissart tells us that "the Duke of Berry served the King of France with the comfit-box, and the Duke of Burgundy with the cup of wine; in like manner, the King of England was served by the Dukes of Lancaster and Gloucester. After the kings had been served, the knights of France and England took the wine and spices, and served the prelates, dukes, princes and counts; and after them, squires and other officers of the household did the same to all within the tent, until everyone had partaken."

The feudal period was extremely food-conscious: life was a feast or a famine, and when you had food, you gorged. A great lord assured himself of faithful followers by the profusion of his banquets; the sending of a dish from his own table was a mark of a king's favor; and it was a great compliment to send dinner ahead of you, and follow to help eat it.

† These symbols were used in place of actual names in political satires of the period, and were understood by everybody, just as "The Little Flower" meant Fiorello LaGuardia to the citizens of New York when he was Mayor. When an Englishman, in 1449, read a poem beginning: "The Root is dead, the Swan is gone, The fiery Cresset hath lost its light," he understood equally well that these were references to the Regent, Bedford: Humphrey, Duke of Gloucester; and the last Duke of Exeter.

Jean Sans Peur can also be recognized (extreme right) by his swan emblem, which is used all over his houppelande. The tapestries of the King's audience chamber are semé with the fleurs-de-lys of ancient France.

The houppelandes we see here are of various lengths, all fur-lined, with high funneling collars, elaborately dagged edges, and precious chains with pendants. The bag sleeve of the shorter garment shows under the long dragging sleeve of the houppelande; while the high houppelande collar has affected the collar of other male garments, designed to be worn without the houppelande. The headgear of the great gentlemen illustrate the late XIV-e.XVc. tendency to flop, either forward (turbans with Phrygian crown), or sidewise and back (those with hanging cockscomb, formed by dagged and pleated border of the hood, bound around the head).

806. XVc. 1409-15. French. (Paris, Bibliotheque Nationale, ms. fr. 2810.)

Merveilles du monde, by Jean Hayton, probably executed by *Jacques Coen* of Bruges.

Jean Hayton offering to Jean Sans Peur his story of travel, which was ordered by the Duke of Burgundy as a gift to his uncle.

807-810. XVc. 1409-16. French. (Chantilly, Conde Mus.)

Très riches heures du duc de Berri.‡ Executed by *Pol de Limbourg* and his brothers.

Jean de Berri, brother of the French king, and the greatest bibliophile of his time, maintained his own staff of artists and calligraphers. This book of hours was to have been the greatest treasure of his magnificent library; unfinished at his death in 1416, it was completed 65 years later by Jean Colombe. The occupations suitable to the 12 months of the year are shown against backgrounds of the chateaux he possessed or had built.

January: Banquet scene (807). The Duke sits at a banquet table, protected by a circular wicker screen from the excessive heat of the fire behind him. The decorations of the chimneypiece are all symbolic of his house or person: fleurs-de-luce of France; orange leaves; bears; wounded swans. The walls are hung with a tapestry of a battle scene, into which is woven an explanatory text. The floor is covered by a braided carpet. On the banquet table is set the great "salt cellar of the Pavillion," shaped like a ship,§ and surmounted by his bear and swan, which is recorded in the inventory of his estate. The sideboard bears a great deal of plate.

---

‡ Notes from M. le comte P. Durrieu's scholarly edition, with sumptuous color reproductions. LIFE magazine, Jan. 5, 1948, published all the plates in color.

§ Louis XIV's *nef* was a great gold salt-cellar in the shape of a ship, which all saluted in passing, as they did the king's bed; it held his salt, knives, and napkin between perfumed cushions and stood on the chimneypiece of the Cabinet of Medals when not in use.

Plate, in what seems to us like immense quantities, is meticulously described in XVc. inventories and wills. Sir John Fastolf's plate takes eight pages to enumerate, and that of Margaret Paston and Dame Elizabeth Browne is considerable. The most important pieces are named, like "his standing bowl called the Baron de St. Blankheare" (part of the loot of a naval engagement with the French), which Clement Paston bequeathed to his nephew. A lesser piece of Fastolf's is described as "a saltsaler like a bastell (bastile—small tower) alle gilt with roses weiying lxxvij unces."

From his bear (Fr. *ours*) badge, which surmounts this salt-cellar, Berri derived his pet-name for his wife, "Ursette."

Salt, indispensable and the symbol of hospitality, was a heavily taxed monopoly. The centrally placed salt-cellar was the most important piece of plate; the relative importance of the diners was indicated by their seating in relation to it.

Forks, though described in Miège's French-English dictionary of 1679, did not come into common use until the XVIIIc. Spoons were of wood or horn until XVc. A knife was the only common implement. Meat was at first laid in a slice (Fr. *tranche*) of bread, from which came the word "trencher," for the plates of wood (or for the rich, metal) which were the next refinement. Chinese porcelains had been seen in Europe in XIc., and fine ceramics had been produced in Moorish Spain since XIIc.; but the largely decorative ceramic wares of XV-XVIc. Europe were at least as costly as the finest plate, and were only for the very rich: armorial or portrait-decorated salvers, wine jugs, great vases, tankards, salt cellars, fruit bowls and floor tiles. Until the great English commercial china manufactures of the XVIIIc., wood, pewter, silver and gold utensils were usual.

The garments of Berri's chamberlain (behind him, with a staff, exhorting a reluctant man: "Approach, approach"), and those of the squires who serve, all bear his livery badge or colors, in some form; orange leaves; wreathed monograms; or the glowing crowns of the duke's own blue and gold robe appear on their gowns, hoods, or collars. Under the "ancien régime" it still took four people to serve a glass of water at court.

Parti-color and hoods are now used only on livery garments, such as these of green, red and white, or blue and white. Among the 15 robes in Fastolf's wardrobe is listed one, red, "of my Lord Cromwell his livery"; that is, Fastolf was the "man" of Ralph Cromwell, Lord Treasurer of England.

The scarlet-gowned cleric sitting beside the duke is the Bishop of Chartres, also a great bibliophile, and executor of the duke's will.

The houppelandes, typically fur-lined, slit, dagged, with wide sleeves, show a variety of collars: conveniently high (duke); high but turned back, as is the trend (chamberlain); low and standing; or with the V at the back completely unfilled by collar (squires with back to us, carrying scarves and nap-

kins). The squire at the end of the table has sleeves pinned back over shoulders while serving. High-cropped hair; fur hats; precious collars; belts and diagonally slung baldrics, all hung with bells or badges. Puppies wandering over the table; greyhound with characteristic collar of XV-XVIc., being fed slices from a leg of lamb, instead of scavenging bones cast on the floor, as was usual.

April: Engagement (808). In the first warm days of spring, mediaeval society is always glad to escape into the open from the damp, dark cold of the castle (Ill. 672: Italian Tirol frescos). Large entertainments tend to be held out of doors for this reason.

In the background, the Chateau of Dourdain, in which the Duke's most precious belongings were held, and its little attendant village; pond with fishermen seining; walled garden with lattice for training grapes.

Fiancé: Blue houppelande has sleeves of same blazing gold crowns worn by Duke. His companion; white, edged with yellow fur; high black hat; red tights. Fiancée: White-bordered gown of light and dark gray-blue brocade; dragging cape sleeves; black feathered hat with red, yellow and white ostrich plumes (feathers new, in XVc.). Her companion: black and gold; her red and gold brocade undersleeve is edged with gold fringe, also a new usage. Kneeling ladies: In back: black gown, white trim; deep blue undergrown, and blue and gold stuffed roundlet. In foreground: pink, lined with gray.

May: Riding party (809). Beyond the woods, the town of Riom, capitol of the ancient Duchy of Auvergne, one of the Duke's possessions. The riders, celebrating May Day, wear the traditional garlands of leaves, and the "Livery of May," green garments given by the Duke to his entourage. The festive, bell-hung baldrics they wear here on May Day, have left us the phrase, "with bells on." But their wear was not confined to May Day and their size was often enormous. (See Hero: Ill. 906).

John Stow describes the May Day amusements of England in late XVIc.

The servants with horns wear parti-colored livery, with badges on their left shoulders. Second gentleman in procession seems young for the King, but wears the livery colors of Charles VI: red, black and white. The first three ladies wear the Livery of May in various shades of green; flowing undersleeves with edges of fringe. Men's garments belted high, as were the houppelandes of women. Collars and baldrics; bell-trimmed; caparisons of horses.

June (810): Harvest on the Ile du Palais, with Paris as the Duke saw it from the windows of his Hotel de Nesles, on the left bank of the Seine. The Pont Neuf now stands at the point where the postern gate is shown opening on the Seine. Beyond the walls and garden, slate-roofed except for two red tiled towers (back left), are the Palace, the Tower of the Conciergerie, and the Ste-Chapelle. Women gleaners: in blue and white; kirtles laced over shirt, and tucked up; heads wrapped. Reapers: in rose, white and blue tunics.

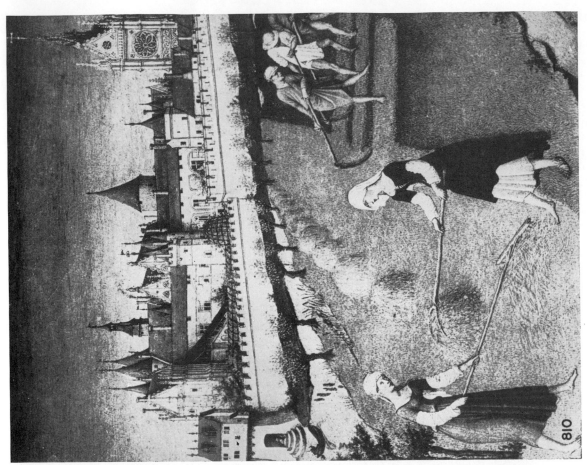

811. XVc. 1420-30. French. (Morgan Library, M. 453.)
Hours of the Virgin for Paris use.
Offices of the dead. Priests and acolytes; in center

a robed member of a confraternity, with the symbol
of the Virgin of the Ascension embroidered on the
front.

815   814

813   812

812-815. XVc. Flemish. (Amsterdam Museum.)
Figures from a chimneypiece: Counts of Holland, Countesses of Holland.
The only sleeve which does not appear to have been worn by both sexes is
the bag-sleeve shown on the count with the top hat (814); a simpler form is

worn on an embroidered garment in John Foxton's *Cosmography*, 1408. An
unusual form of turned-up, jewelled brim appears on the other count (812).
The countess in the round turban is a typical figure of c. 1410; her companion,
in the butterfly headdress, more nearly approaches mid-XVc.

816. XVc. 1432. Flemish. (National Gallery, London.)

Jan van Eyck. Giovanni and Giovanna Arnolfini.

Italian merchant and his wife, lived in Bruges from 1420-1472. Arnolfini wears a tabard-like cloak, sable-edged, over tunic and hose; hat of finely braided straw. Lower l. corner: pattens worn in mud.

His wife wears a trailing gown edged with fur; lower part of her long bag-sleeves decorated with double thicknesses of the material of the gown, cut into petals and appliquéd, loosely, in banked rows. Kirtle, furred at the hem. Belt gold, embroidered in red. Hair confined, above ears, by netted cauls. The veil, which they support in the horned effect of the headdresses of first third XVc., is edged by layers of fluting (German: *kruseler* headdress), seen in the Low Countries, Germany and England. Wedding ring worn on second joint of finger.

817

818

819

817-819. XVc. Flemish.

Roger van der Weyden: Three portraits.

817. Portrait of a young woman, c. 1435. (Kaiser Friedrich Museum.)

818. Bracque family altarpiece: St. Mary Magdalene, c. 1452 (Louvre.)

819. Portrait of a lady, c. 1455. (National Gallery, Washington.)

Domestic pins are new in early XVc. Their use, decoratively, is typical of the Low Countries. They fasten interchangeable sleeves to kirtle (818), veils to coifs (819), and supplement or replace tapes in the typically Flemish headdress of the "beguine" type (817). Decorative pins are used on the falls of hoods, as elsewhere, but in Flemish portraits, these are apt to be in the form of naturalistic insects, bees or flies, such as might have alighted, rather than brooches or pendants.

Buckles, belts and tabs are extremely rich here, as all over Europe except in Italy; rings, everywhere, are worn on thumb or middle joint. Headdresses are set far back on tightly drawn hair, but the forehead is not plucked bald as in France.

The Franco-Burgundian court styles are worn by the upper classes, but women's clothing in Flanders is higher necked, much more bourgeois than in France.

At the end XVc., when male costume is affected by Italian fashions, women's clothing will be greatly influenced by these middle-class Flemish garments, with their variety of enclosing hoods, coifs and wimples: they lead directly to the Tudor fashions of Anne Boleyn and Henry VIII.

820-822. XVc. c. 1438-40. Franco-Flemish. (Metropolitan Museum.)

Tapestry: Arras or Tournai. Courtiers with roses,

Arras was the first great tapestry weaving center; there had been wool weavers there for ten centuries, because of the plentiful growth of madder, one of the oldest red dye-stuffs. In England, the imports from Arras finally led to the generic name of "Arras" being used for tapestry of any provenance. By second half XVc. many other towns, among them Tournai, supplanted Arras in importance.

We have already seen the collar of the high-belted lady's houppelande turning downward (see Ills. 808, 809). It has now been lowered into a flat collar, frequently (as in Rose Tapestry), of fur; the front opening has necessarily deepened, and exposes a triangle of the material of the kirtle beneath. The present gown has discarded the dragging, funnel sleeve of the houppelande; the new sleeve of the gown is long and close; below the elbow it widens slightly toward the wrist, where it is turned back into a cuff, matching the collar.

High, padded, heart-shaped headdresses, with streaming scarves, still occur well into last quarter XVc., as do the towering wired forms of gauze veil. Jewelled pin on veil. As these headdresses mount,

ears will gradually become uncovered again; ladies' eyebrows and an artificial hairline will be carefully plucked.

Both men and women strive to appear bald under their elaborate headgear. Men's necks and heads are shaved to a point well above the ears. The cropped head is often covered by a cap, over which the hat is set; until, and even beyond second half XVc., no hair will show beneath the stuffed roundlet of the chaperon, although the cap may appear.

The chaperon is a more convenient, ready-made descendant of the headdress worn with the houppelande, which each arranged for himself by winding the liripipe of his hood, turban-wise, over the pleated folds of its dagged hem, the unopened hood having been laid, like a shawl, across the head.

Like the ladies' gowns, the short garments of the gentlemen display a reduced form of the houppelande collar; the cote-hardi has become a jacket. The row of buttons in front has been replaced by hooks at neck and waist. The fabric of the *jupon* shows through this front gap. The jupon will acquire padding on bosom and upper arm; it will become progressively shorter and will turn into the *doublet,* to which the lengthening hose will be trussed by *points* through eyelets, and which will carry a standing collar. The pleats of the jacket are so carefully fastened that a belt is not required to hold them in place (822, smallest man, right). The bag sleeve of first third

XVc. has passed out of use, but its effect lingers in the cut of the wide sleeves. These are now slit from the shoulder again, showing the color of the jupon-doublet and permitting its close sleeve to be thrust through the fur-trimmed outer sleeve.

Parti-colored hose are declining in favor: where we do see them worn by gentlemen on Rose Tapestry, they differ only very subtly in color from each other: a light with a darker brown; green-gray with warm gray. They continue to be worn in Italy, and reappear in general European use, in very elaborate forms, during the Italianate period around the turn of the century. Shoes have begun to assume a long point.

823. XVc. 1440. French. (Rouen, Church of St. Ouen.)

Incised slab: The architects of the Church of St. Ouen.

These worthy men, moving in more modest circles, wear houppelandes of easy length, with bag sleeves, modified collars and handsome belts, over doublets with high collars. Comfortable chaperons are carried slung over their shoulders, by long scarves.

824-825. XVc. c. 1445. Flemish. (Mansfield, Hardwick Hall. Coll. Duke of Devonshire.)

Tapestry: Hawking.

These costumes, of the class of society and period of the Rose Tapestries, are much more Flemish and German in detail.

The sexual differentiations of the houppelande developed most acutely in France. Worn by both sexes,

824.

the original difference was in the placing of the belt, always very high on women. In France, for the greater display of the belt, the bodice became close fitting, with a low V-opening which soon spread wide, uncovering the shoulders; it developed extremely narrow sleeves with a widening cuff, which might be turned down over the hand.

Here we see, instead, the old pleated fullness of the houppelande at the front of the bodice (see Ill. 817); the original funnel sleeve; or the bag sleeve which is worn by so many of the men on their short tunics; or the very wide sleeve, which we would expect to find on the robe of an elderly worthy. The front of the bodice fastens high, exposing none of the fabric of the kirtle beneath. The high collar has been turned back into the sailor collar, often so close around the throat that the necklace is displayed upon the fabric, rather than on the skin. The belt is handsome, but overpowered by the pattern and fabric around it.

Bag sleeves of both men and women have additional width gored in, halfway between shoulder and elbow (man, right of mill, 824; women lower r., 825).

The jackets of the men are bloused over the belt in a way which is much more German than French; as is also their dagging, which was a German origination. Dagging has gone far beyond mere snipped edges on hood and gown; it is now manifested in the appliquéing of petal-shaped pieces of material, as on Joan Arnolfini's dress (Ill. 816) and the Master of the Playing Cards, Ills. 976-79. (Cape at top left side of 825; sleeves of rider (824), lower left; hat brim on rider preceding him; roundlet of headdress, woman, upper left.)

826. c. 1447. Franco-Flemish. (Brussels, Bib. Roy. ms. 9242-4.)

Chronicles of Hainault, by Jean Wauquelin. Executed between 1447-50 by various artists in the studio of *Guillaume Vrelant* of Bruges. Jean Wauquelin presenting his work to Philip the Good.

It is thought that this frontispiece may be the work of *Roger van der Weyden*. It shows the great duke, patron of letters and founder of the "Bibliothèque de Bourgogne," the collection of fine manuscripts still preserved at Brussels. Like his courtiers, the duke wears the costume of the gentlemen of the Rose Tapestries, but with the additional finish and elegance which made his Burgundian court the arbiter of elegance for all Europe.

Nothing could better oppose and conquer the brocades of his entourage than the plain fabric and superb cut of Philip's garments.

He wears the collar and pendant of the Golden Fleece, the Order which he established in 1429, in honor of his marriage to Isabel of Portugal.

Chamberlayne says, "Then, for Raiment, England produceth generally very fine Wool, which makes our Cloth more lasting than other Country Cloth, and better conditioned against Wind and Weather; and in such Abundance, that not only all Sorts, from the highest to the lowest, are cloathed wherewith; but so much hath heretofore transported beyond the Seas, that, in Honour to the English Wool, which then brought Such Plenty of Gold into the Territories of Philip the Good, Duke of Burgundy (where the Staple for English Wool was in those days kept) he instituted that famous military Order of the Golden

Fleece, after the English Garter, the noblest Order of Knighthood in Europe."

The Toison d'Or was worn by 24 gentlemen, of whom his young son (later Charles the Bold), and

half a dozen others are shown, as well as by the Grand Master. In the duke's hand, what I had always supposed to be a walking stick, in the very latest fashion, proves actually to be a delicate hammer. In that day of emblems and badges, I suspect that it would be found to have some connection with the steels and flints of which the Collar is composed: it is possibly the baton of the Grand Master of the Order.

The shoulders of the duke's jacket show the padded *mahoîtres,* which become monstrously exaggerated during the next decade of doublet padding.

The front opening, no longer caught at the throat, spreads and is held at the neck by delicate lacings, exhibiting an embroidered shirt. To permit this, the doublet is also cut with a V-opening; only its standing collar shows above the fur which edges the neck of the jacket.

The roundlet of the duke's chaperon is padded into a spreading brim; its scarf is bound around it, under the chin.

All wear piked shoes. Stow writes to the "Cordwainers or Shoemakers Hall, which company were made a brotherhood or fraternity on the II of Henry IV. Of these cordwainers I read, that since the fifth of Richard II (1383) when he took to wife Anne, daughter to Vesalaus, King of Boheme [Wenceslaus was her brother; she was the eldest daughter of Charles IV, by his 4th wife, Elizabeth of Pomerania] by her example, the English people had used *peaked shoes,* tied to their knees with silken laces, or chains of silver or gilt, whereof in the 4th of Edward IV it was ordained and proclaimed that *beaks of shoon* and boots should not pass the length of 2 feet, upon pain of cursing by the clergy, and by parliament to pay 20 s. for every pair. And any cordwainer that shod any man or woman on the Sunday to pay 30 s."

To the duke's right is portrayed the Chancellor Rollin, in the outmoded gown of the conservative, now the characteristic dress of cleric or educator. It is slit for passage of the brocaded sleeve; hood thrown cape-wise over the shoulder. Rings on fore and middle fingers. Accompanying him, a learned worthy in a crimson gown, with a fine pouch at his girdle.

827-828. Same provenance as 826.

827. Carpenters and masons rebuilding town around a devastated castle.

Workmen in short doublets and jackets, slit at the side; skirts tucked up or protected by aprons. Man (second from left, hammering) and plasterer (extreme right) s h o w knots of the *"points"* by which tights are trussed to doublet.

Variety of sabre-like saws, adzes, hammers, trowels, and T-square. Woman (left, below ladder), shows back treatment of stuffed round turban; woman (extreme right) carries purse and knife on her low girdle.

828. Cardinal preaching in a courtyard.

To the familiar heart- and horn-shaped headdresses are added high hennins, gauzily veiled; high cylindrical hats, often, as here, with no veil; and also a great variety of the new hoods. These were often dark in color, and their draperies, of heavier materials, enclosed head and shoulders, falling in heavy folds behind. Meanwhile, we see the Burgundian fashions, worn by both sexes.

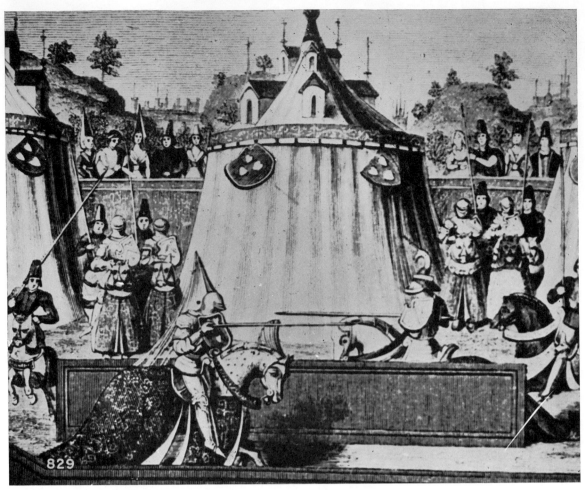

Ladies: bodices with very wide, low handsome buckles; narrowest possible sleeves, with turned-back cuffs of same color as collars.

Gentlemen: excessively short jackets, with padded shoulders and wide sleeves, too long for the arms; worn pushed up.

829. XVc. French. (British Museum, Harl. ms. 4379.)

Chronicles of England, France, and Spain, by Sir John Froissart.

A joust in the manner of one held at St. Inglevert in 1390, to fulfill a promise to the ladies of Montpelier. Each knight hung his shield before his tent. A shield blazoned with hearts hangs here on that pavilion; these are identical in form with the tents shown in Spanish manuscripts from XIIIc., and are brilliantly colored. In this picture they are white and blue, gold and green, and red and gold.* The helm of the French knight is topped by a hennin and veil, his lady's favors.

Stow describes the use of open spaces like bridges, or Smithfield (i.e. Smooth-field). In 1362, a joust was held during the first 5 days of May, before Edward III, his queen, and "the most part of the chivalry of England and of France, and of other nations, to which came Spaniards, Cyprians, and Armenians, knightly requesting the King of England against the pagans that invaded their confines." In 1374, Dame Alice Ferrers, Edward III's concubine, "as Lady of

* See It. End XVIc., *Assault on Empoli,* for origin of parti-color from these tents.

the Sun, rode from the Tower of London, through Cheap, accompanied of many lords and ladies, every lady leading a lord by his horsebridle, till they came into West Smithfield, and then began a great joust, which endured 7 days after."

In a tourney at Saumur in 1446, organized by René d'Anjou, Robert d'Estoutville, provost of Paris, conquered his wife, Ambroise de Loré, in sword battle.

In 1467 (Edward IV), "the Bastard of Burgoine challenged the Lord Scales, brother to the queen, to fight with him both on horseback and on foot. The King therefore caused lists to be prepared at Smithfield, 120 tailors yards and 10 feet long, 80 yards and 10 feet wide" (Stow) with galleries. The first day's combat was with spears; the second on horseback, during which the Bastard's horse fell on him. The third day's combat was with pole-axes, and when one entered his helmet the Bastard relinquished his challenge.

A "Round Table" had a more theatrical and social character than a tournament. The participants sometimes masqueraded as Arthurian characters; by Edward I's time, their parts were rehearsed in advance.

Round Tables were not confined to the nobility. The burghers of Tournai gave one in 1331, and challenged other cities—Paris, Bruges and Amiens. There were processions with banners, jousts in the public squares; and the sport of chivalry lapses into an amusement for civilians. (See Appendix.)

830-831. XVc. 1447. French. (Paris, Bibliotheque Nationale, ms. 2695.)

Traictié de la forme et devis comme on fait les Tournois, by René d'Anjou, executed by *Barthélemy de Clerk.*

René d'Anjou, king of Naples and Sicily, succeeded to the Duchy of Anjou, where he spent much time between 1443-70. His court wears the pointed toes and short tunics of France.

This manuscript, offered to Charles VIII by Louis de Bruges, Sieur de la Gruthyse, shows a tourney of the sort which Gruthyse had given, March 11, 1392, in which the colors of the Dukes of Brittany and Bourbon had been opposed.

It shows heralds and poursuivants in a variety of tabards, courtiers and attendants, with their masters' badges. Fringe-trimmed hat worn by René himself (see Ills. 985-86).

Commines (1475) tells how the King of France disguised one of his servants in a herald's coat and sent him with a message to the King of England, who gave him a favorable answer. "The king sent the Master of the Horse for the banner of a trumpeter to make his herald a coat of arms for the king was not so stately or vain as to have either herald or trumpeter in his train, as other princes have; therefore the master of the horse and one of my servants made up a coat of arms as well as they could; and having fetched a scutcheon from a little herald (called Plein Chemin, in the service of the Admiral of France), they fastened about him, sent for his boots and cloak privately, and his horse being got ready, he mounted, with a bag or budget at the bow of his saddle, in which his coat of arms was put."

830

831

832-835. XVc. 1448. Franco-Flemish. (Brussels, Bib. Roy.,
   ms. 9967.)

Ystoire de Helayne, by Jean Wauquelin, for Philip
the Good, executed by *Loyset Liedet* and *Guillaume
Vrelant.*

832. Dining end of hall: opposite sideboard set
with plate is a long canopied seat, in front of which
a trestle table would be set for dining.

The long sleeve of Philip's gown is worn pushed
up on left arm; close buttoned sleeve of doublet
passed through slit of right sleeve, the more conveniently to handle his walking stick, a new fashion.
Behind Philip, a shorter version of the same sleeve,
seamed to balloon at the top, in order to enclose the
padded upper sleeve of doublet (such as is shown on
right arm of gentleman in cape, directly above Philip's
right shoulder). Outer seam of doublet sleeve open
below elbow, and caught together over a display of
shirt sleeve.

Tall conical caps worn over new long bobbed hair.
Flopping Phrygian bonnet, now conservative, worn
with long gown. Medallions; collars with Golden
Fleece pendant; or fine strands of chain emphasize
horizontal line of shoulder; long pointed toes of
"poulaines." Fool in motley, with bells on skirt of
tunic, entering.

833. Henry, King of England, taking leave of his
wife and confiding her to the care of his mother and
the Duke of Gloucester.

Most of the costume elements are now familiar:
longer hose fasten to shorter doublet, of which only
the standing collar shows here, and permit extremely
short jackets, closed in front and with a bateau neckline and extremely wide shoulders, supported by the
padded doublet sleeve beneath. Carefully laid cartridge pleats, probably cut and seamed separately, on
gentlemen's gowns. Body and flaring skirts of the
jacket are separately cut and do not require a belt,
which often hangs loose (Henry and gentleman behind wife's attendants).

The headdress of the Queen Dowager clearly shows
the wire supports with hooked ends, which carry her
veil. Short veils over eyes, sometimes set inside crown
of headdress: high veiled hennins (attendant) have
a small loop at the forehead by which they might be
held steady. Cord necklace, falling between breasts
will increase in popularity into XVIc. Gowns extremely long all around, must be held up to allow
walking, in the typical female gesture of the century.

The preaching of the monk Thomas Conecte,
against hennins, to a crowd of 20,000 women in
1428, led the women to burn their hennins in public.
Conecte went on to Rome, attacked the dissolute
ways of the Papal court, and was burned for heresy
in 1434. After his disappearance, "the women that
like snails in a fright had drawn in their horns, shot
them out again as soon as the danger was over."
(Spectator, ii, p. 98.)

833.

834. Secret marriage of Ludie and Brisse, in the presence of the Archbishop of Tours and of Antoine.

In 1474, Philip de Commines tells us of the warlike bishops: "All the princes of Germany both spiritual and temporal, and all the bishops and free towns sent in their respective forces in great numbers. I was informed that the Bishop of Münster (who is none of the greatest), led into that army 6,000 foot and 1400 horse, all clothed in green uniforms, beside 1200 waggons; but his bishopric was hard by."

In England, until Henry I, bishops and abbots could make knights. William II was knighted by Archbishop Lanfranc. (Malmesbury.)

The first liveries seem to have been those of the chartered companies; guild members who had their own distinctive costumes, and were called "liveried companies," in the time of Edward III. The proliferating XVc. addiction to badges, mottos, scarves and liveries in the master's colors, led inevitably to the idea of uniforms.

But until the beginnings of a permanent army arose in the parish militia and cavalry established by Charles VII, the impulse toward uniformity could be shown only by small groups: followers of a feudal lord; members of a guild of craftsmen; or men of a certain town. Froissart describes Philip Von Arteveld's followers from Ghent, Alost, Grammont, Courtray and Bruges: "The greater part were armed

with bludgeons, iron caps, jerkins, and gloves of *fer de baleine,* and each man carried a staff bound and pointed with iron. The different townsmen wore liveries and arms, to distinguish them from one another. Some had jackets of blue and yellow, others wore a welt of black on a red jacket, others chevroned with white on a blue coat, others green and blue, others lozenged with black and white, others quartered red and white, others all blue."

835. Capture of Helayne, who is led to the palace.

Townswomen in kirtles, such as the ladies wear under fur-collared robes. Its neckline is becoming lower, squarer, and often shows a line of the skirt beneath. Skirt protected by an apron, or looped up when long. Between the two skirts hangs a belt carrying pouch, keys or tassel, a usage which will continue in the XVIc. Modest horned headdresses, or hood-like coifs, such as plain women have long worn; toward the end of the century, the heads of ladies will become enclosed in bourgeois hoods.

Gentleman (lower right, back view), shows that the padded shoulders of the doublet, and its high, stiff collar require that the collar of the outer garment be reduced to a line of fur, horizontal in front, and dipping in back. Gentleman receiving Helayne: tall, conical hat ending in a fruit-like stem, such as appears on the modern beret; on this cap, the stem is elaborated into a tiny plume.

836. XVc. Before 1450. French. (Berlin, Kaiser Friedrich Museum.)

Jean Fouquet. Etienne Chevalier and St. Stephen.

Etienne Chevalier was Treasurer of France, under two kings, Ambassador to England, executor of the will of Agnes Sorel, and patron of Fouquet, (who became court painter to Louis XI). He wears a crimson jacket, of which we clearly see the cut, padded shoulders, bag sleeve, and high set-in collar, cut like that of a doublet.

St. Stephen: brocade-trimmed amice, dalmatic and tiny cap, set over tonsure. Both are most explicit representations of the bowl-cropped male head of first half XVc.

837. Before 1450. French. (Antwerp Royal Museum.)

Virgin and Child. Diptych panel by *Jean Fouquet.*

The work of Fouquet and other XVc. miniaturists gave promise of an indigenous school of French painting which did not develop, probably due to the competition of Italian painters for French patronage, at the conclusion of the Italian wars.

The Virgin, on a fringed and tasselled throne, and wearing a royal crown and ermine mantle, probably represents the first of the politically influential royal mistresses, Agnes Sorel, d.1450, mistress of Charles VII.

The front of her very long, laced blue-gray kirtle (see Ills. 810, 818), is cut in three gored pieces, one of which takes a diagonal curve from armseye to breast, where it curves downward to waist. Here the excessive length of the garment is roached up, and held by a marvellous belt. Jewelled crown, set on plucked forehead, over oblong veil with a border.

838. XVc. 1450-60. French. (Louvre.)

Jean Fouquet. Charles VII.

Charles wears a great beaver hat, embroidered on crown and brim. Collar of doublet shows above low fur collar of jacket. The method of squaring off the shoulders by darts, accommodates the padded mahoitres, and fosters the wide horizontal shoulder-line.

839-46. XVc. c. 1450. French. (Paris, Bibliotheque Na-
            tionale, ms. 6465.)

Grandes Chroniques de France executed by *Jean Fouquet.*

839. Arnoul, Archbishop of Rheims, and his brother Charles, imprisoned at Orleans, by order of Hugh Capet; King Robert chanting the office in the church. Primitive boots of King and groom, soft, wrinkled, wide; front seams, side opening. Moat and drawbridge; caparison of horse.

840. Arrival of Emperor Charles IV at St. Denis.

Charles V's uncle fell ill and had to be carried in a litter. (see note on "whirlecote," Eng.XIVc., Luttrell Psalter.) As Dauphin of the Viennois, Charles V had done homage to his uncle, the Emperor.

841. Edward, son of the King of England (Edward I), gives homage to Philip the Fair, for the Duchy of Aquitaine and other French possessions. Philip, seated in chair of state, his robes, carpets and walls semé France. Two sceptres; topped by fleur-de-lys, and by the open "main de justice" of benediction.

Edward's robes red; golden lioncels. Entourage of parliamentary dignitaries and courtiers: at r., puffs of shirt show through slashed lower sleeve of doublet; 2nd from r., belt of cord, knotted in front.

842. Marriage at Paris of Charles IV the Fair and Marie of Luxembourg.

Ermine-bordered robes of state; sideless surcoat, worn over kirtle with tight buttoned sleeves, and belt at hips, of previous century.

Bishop: stole worn crossed, instead of hanging.

843. Queen Jeanne d'Evereux before the assembly of barons and nobles, after the death of Charles IV, the Fair.

Nobleman facing Queen: cap barely set on cropped hair; hat carried slung over shoulder by its scarf; thumbs caught in low belt: the very pattern of the costume and posture of his class and time.

844. Entry of John II, the Good, and Queen Jeanne de Boulogne into Paris, after the sacre at Rheims.

Trumpeters' banners, sash of preceding horseman, caparison of King's horse, (head armed), all fleur-de-lys sown. Colored sashes were an early manifestation of the impulse toward uniformity.

Queen: less ceremonial costume; ermine-trimmed fashionable gown, cuff turned down over hand.

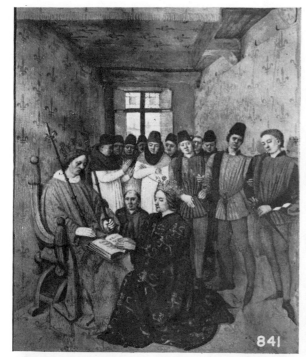

841

842

843

844

845

845. Entry of Charles V into Paris, preceded by the Constable Robert of Fiennes.

Another of the many gates in the walls of Paris. Fiennes wears the hat we associate particularly with Louis XI, scarf and drawn sword of office. He is preceded by identically dressed trumpeters, their hooded capes, almost vestigial, are decoratively slittered, a usage now confined to livery garments. Raised arms in doublet sleeve show jacket sleeve dependent from back of shoulder, and probably for decoration, rather than use. On unceremonious occasions, such sleeves were often knotted together in back, out of the way.

(The order in which these pictures are placed does not indicate the correct chronology of the events described. Ill. 840 falls, historically, between Ills. 854 and 846.)

846

846. Banquet offered Emperor Charles IV by King Charles V, in the Grand'Salle of the Palace, Paris.

Banquet table set on carpeted dais, up three steps, for greater ceremony. Walls specially hung; canopy for each personage.

Majordomo with staff and scarf; serving gentlemen with hanging jacket-sleeves; napkins over shoulders. Trumpeters: dagging persists on garments of servants.

From Fouquet: *Grandes Chroniques de France.* Paris, 1906. Berthaud freres.

847

847-48. XVc. French. (Chantilly, Musee Conde, ms. 187.)

Book of Hours executed by *Jean Fouquet* for Etienne Chevalier.

847. Fouquet's patron (see Ill. 836) k n e e l s, partly armed, before the Virgin. He was not a gentleman by b i r t h*, and did not have a coat-of-arms; the plumed hat beside him bears the M and the fleurs-de-lys of the house of the king he serves, (see Ill. 8 0 7, squire in front of sideboard). The quasi-biblical soldiers combine contemporary armor w i t h fancifully cut and studded brigandines, a n d feathered helmets.

In the background, a castle fights off an attack by dropping fire.

* Under Charles XII and Louis XI the services of bourgeois like Chevalier and poor gentlemen like Commines, rather than of peers of the realm, were being utilized in confidential positions.

848

848. Carpenters with auger and adze. Trunks are now high and well-fitting; but for strenuous work, the points which truss them to the doublet are loosed (see carpenters, Ill. 827), and the back part will often be seen, hanging free, with no false modesty hindering.

849

850

849. XVc. 1456. French. (Paris, Bibliotheque Nationale, ms. fr. 9087.)

Avis directif pour faire le passage d'outre-mer by Frère Brochard, translated and executed by *Jean Miélot,* for Philip the Good.

The concave scallops of cape and mantle, reminiscent of dagging and therefore reserved for ceremonial or livery use, have a XVc. addition of tassels. Frère Brochard, with another tonsured ecclesiastic, and a learned gentleman (not a monk, but possibly a cleric), in a suitable long gown with belt and pouch. Gentleman (extreme r.) in a chaperon the crown of which is now a circular piece of material, gathered into the roundlet; it is no longer the hanging pleated coxcomb of the old hood. Short circular cape (back in use, last half XVc.), of ermine-lined brocade, in the new, unsymmetrical diagonal patterns, like those of King and gentleman to l. Beside him, one of the brimmed "hats," in the modern sense, which appear in increasing numbers (see Color Plate, No. 3).

850. XVc. 1469. French. (Paris, Bibliotheque Nationale, ms. fr. 19819.)

Louis XI presiding at a chapter of the Order of Saint-Michel.

Founded in 1469, the order at first consisted of 15 knights or noblemen. Under Charles IX the number was so increased that its decoration was called the "collier à toutes bêtes."

In this meeting in the Salle des Chevaliers, at the Monastery of Saint-Michel, we see, at l., Charles of France, duke of Guyenne, brother of Louis XI and other known personages; and behind the King, a bishop, 4 officers of the order, chancellor, clerk, treasurer, and the herald-at-arms, Montjoy.

The robes and collar show the scallop shells of pilgrims, alternating with knots, a much-favored new motif, which appears on sleeves, girdles, and hose attachments (see Ill. 852); and on the armor of the angels, which had been adopted in XVc. as supporters of the shield of the French kings.

851. XVIc. French. (Paris, Bibliotheque Nationale.)

851. *Jean du Tillet.* Louis XI.

This portrait of King Louis XI is a reconstruction of a contemporary picture; the work of an artist who was familiar with the Grand'Salle of the Palace, and its collections of portraits, before their destruction by fire in 1618. Collar of St. Michel. 2 sceptres.

852. XVc. 1458. French. (Munich, Codex Gallicus 6.)

The Munich Boccaccio executed by *Jean Fouquet.*

In Nov. 1458, the Duke of Alençon was tried and convicted of treason in the provincial court of Vendôme. When Fouquet, in the same year, began his illustrations for Boccaccio's "Le cas des nobles malheureux,"* he used as a frontispiece this freshly dramatic case of an unfortunate nobleman.

A parliament at which the King presided in person was called a "Lit de Justice" (originally, the long bench on which he sat). We have the most exact accounts of this "Lit de Justice de Vendôme," which have been exhaustively studied, in conjunction with Fouquet's illustration, by the Count Durrieu.** They agree to the last detail, and the portraits of scores of known individuals have been identified.

The courtroom is in the colors of Charles VII, red, green and white, decorated with the rose-stalks which were his emblem; and winged stags with crown collars, (the emblem of the two preceding Charles, and adopted by Charles VII), support the royal shield.

The King, dressed in blue, with 3 white ostrich plumes in his hat, has his young son, Charles, sitting just below him on the dais. In front of the King are the Chamberlain (Dunois, the Bastard of Orleans, companion-at-arms of Jeanne d'Arc) in scarlet robe and gold baton of office; and the Chancellor of the Realm, in gold-barred scarlet robe. Facing the chancellor and reading sentence is the court clerk; seated below him are four special notaries in ermine hoods.

To the r. of the King and young prince is a top row of lay peers, Charles of France, Charles d'Orléans, Gaston de Foix, etc. To the r. of Dunois, the Chancellor, Guillaume Jouvenal des Ursins, in his white magistrate's hood and scarlet robe with 3 bars, sits beside the 1st President of the Parliament

(two bars), and high government officials. Below them, legal functionaries in white hoods.

To the l. of the King, the upper row consists of the ecclesiastical peers of France: the Archbishop-Duke of Rheims, Bishop Dukes of Laon, Langres, etc. Below them, a row of lay gentlemen officials. Below them, the ecclesiastical councillors of Paris, in ermine hoods. Seated on the floor, the "Gens du Parquet," Procurer General, advocates, and councillors of the King.

By the end XIVc. white coifs had passed out of general use, and were considered characteristic of lawyers. A wardrobe roll of Richard II, 1391, lists: "21 linen coifs for counterfeiting men of the law at the King's play at Christmas." By the last quarter XVc., they were worn only by clerics and lawyers; the outmoded capes and hoods, with conventionalized tippets, worn over scarlet or violet robes, have become specifically court or academic costume.

Guarding the enclosure, and controlling the crowd, are mace-bearing attendants; and men of the King's guard, carrying glaives, and wearing uniforms in his colors. Two of these (in crowd to l.) have striped sleeves. Attendant in c. with mace: typical swelling torso of padded doublet; padded upper sleeve, under jacket, would give broad humped *mahoître* shape. Guards to r. of corner: brocade-filled V-opening of jacket is much wider-spread than heretofore; points, like those which connect doublet and hose, are here knotted, to hold in place the padding of the upper sleeve. Knotted cords will be seen on several spectators, taking the place of the elaborate belts of earlier days. Rear view of man in crowd, (ext.r.), jacket has an inverted V of cartridge pleats; large flapped bag. To his l.: high, spurred boots, top of a different color; knife slung in back. To his l.: circular cape with hooded collar; not a hood closed all around in the old style, as worn by the lawyers. On the r. edge of the picture, a man facing away from the proceedings is easily recognizable as Fouquet himself (if compared to his self-portraits: 1456, Vienna, Liechtenstein Gall.; and 1470, enamel plaque, Paris, Bib. Nat.).

---

* Boccaccio: *De casibus virorum illustrum*, translated into English by Lydgate (1370-1451) as *The Fall of Princes.*
** P. Durrieu: *Boccace de Munich;* and *Oeuvres de Fouquet,* in which material given here will be found in greatly amplified form.

853-55. XVc. 1450-60. Franco-Burgundian. (Paris, Bibliotheque Nationale, ms. fr. 24378.)

The Romance of Gerard de Nevers, and of the beautiful Euriant, his love, executed by *Giot Dangerans.*

This manuscript, ordered by Philip the Good as a gift for Count Charles de Nevers, illustrates the life and fashions of his Burgundian court, which so influenced all Europe.

853. Gift of a hawk: One wall of the room has been eliminated, as was the convention among missal painters, to permit the showing of life, indoors and out.

Since the period of the Rose Tapestries, the V-collar of ladies' robes has spread wider; the increasingly visible placard is now made of brocade or embroidery; it is not merely the fabric of the under-gown. The lady carries what definitely appears to be a rather short, circular-cut, fur-edged overgarment, with sleeves; so narrow that it can only be for female wear. At this period, when the character of the costume lies in its short bodice and clutched-up skirt, ladies are never represented wearing an outdoor garment, which would obscure the line of the costume, but which obviously must have existed. This is the first female outer garment, with sleeves, which we have seen; the close sleeves and uncluttered bodice, for the first time make such a garment practical. The pleats of the gentleman's jacket, reduced in number, are becoming formalized; they are probably cut, independent of the body, and inserted, like the cartridge pleats in the back of the jacket of the spectator in Ill. 852. The series of chains fastened across shoulders adds to apparent width. He wears a "hat," and soft high boots with turned-down tops. The chaperon is beginning to pass. Timber construction of outbuildings.

854. The viol player: Arrangement of sideboard, trestle table, and long seat, set with its back to the fire (Ill. 807, Très riches heures). Heavily studded window shutters. The man, dressed for riding, wears hip-length circular cape, closing in front, and high, loose socks.

855. Round dance at court: The excessively short garments of the gentlemen of the Burgundian court do not cover the buttocks; their unbelted width will also be seen in the "Sieur de Gavres" (Ills. 873-76). Feathered hat, at c. front.

The back view of a lady shows the fur collar, the loose tab-end of the high, wide belt, which is jewel-studded. The widening V of the neck is now being filled in by necklaces, or, as in the case of the Queen, by a line of gauze, in the manner of a higher-necked undergarment. The new Burgundian headdress, the *hennin,* is shown at its highest.

From Count A. Bastard d'Estang: *Costumes, moeurs et usages de la cour de Bourgogne,* 1445-60. Paris, 1881.

856. XVc. 1450-60. Flemish. (Metropolitan Museum, Bache Collection.)

Roger van der Weyden. Man with a turban. Large, flattened red chaperon, without scarf, worn over skull-cap. Dark doublet with red collar; white shirt. Pink held in hand indicated prospective marriage.

857. XVc. c. 1476. Flemish. (Metropolitan Museum.)

Hans Memling. Marie, wife of Thomas Portinari. Compare with French costume, last half XVc.

Loops at forehead of steeple headdress were probably helpful in maintaining it in position.

858. XVc. 1473-5. Flemish-Italian. (Florence, Uffizi.)

Hugo van der Goes. The Portinari Altarpiece, right wing.

Tommaso Portinari, agent at Bruges for the Medici, was a lineal descendant of the father of Dante's Beatrice. The altarpiece was painted for the chapel of the hospital of S. Maria Novella in Florence, of which he was patron.

His family is dressed in the finest Franco-Flemish style. His wife has the M of her given name embroidered on her veiled hennin, and wears a jewelled collar painted by Memling. The daughter, whose laced bodice is seen on Memling's lady of quality, wears the band of a black hood, decorated with a brooch, over the flowing hair of a young girl.

859. XVc. Before 1480. Flemish. (Metropolitan Museum, Bache Collection.)

Hans Memling. Lady of quality.

Dark brown velvet hood; veiled gray hennin. Red velvet gown laced across a brown placard, and edged with white fur. The customary two necklaces, one thread-like, the other important, like that of Marie Portinari, or a flat braided gold chain with a fine pendant.

860-65. XVc. 1461. French. (Brussels, Bib. Roy., ms. 9392.)

Epitre d'Othea by Christine de Pisan (1364-1430), executed by *Jean Miélot.*

Christine de Pisan, of Italian extraction but reared at the court of Charles V, became a writer when left a widow with three children, at twenty-five. Her controversial feminist works brought her great fame, and tempting offers to live at foreign courts; adoring France, she remained there under the protection of Charles VI and the Dukes of Burgundy and Berri, by whom some of her books were commissioned. Her writings are filled with delightfully detailed pictures of the life of her times. The translation into English, by Stephen Scrope, was dedicated to Sir John Fastolf.

860. Diana with the young virgins: The high-waisted gown may be worn belted, or not; if it is, the belt is an important one. When worn low, the belt is a knotted cord, or slight chain.

861. Ceres sowing the earth: Shepherd with little house on wheels; farm horses with blinders and huge collars, hitched to a wheeled plough. Quasi-oriental touches are given to the headdresses of the mythological characters, who otherwise wear only their kirtles, which served as house and work clothes.

862. The rook advises the raven: The filling-in of the excessively wide V, which we have seen (see Ill. 855), is continued here, in the form of a bertha of gauze, reaching to the base of the throat. The V-line is reiterated by a cord, with heavy pendant, falling between the breasts, inside the tucker; as the neckline becomes squarer, at the end of the century, this cord will remain in use, in the XVIc.

Timber construction of thatched barn; wattle-fenced pastures.

863. Discord returning the golden apple to the table during the wedding feast of Peleus and Thetis: The now familiar dining pattern of sideboard, and fireplace warming the backs of diners, who sit beside, not opposite each other, at long narrow tables; dog underfoot, munching a bone cast from the table.

The squire serving at the l., wears the extremely short jacket, with his dagger slung in the new manner, over the buttocks. The sleeves of his doublet, almost entirely visible, as the jacket sleeve is slit through its length, are in their turn slashed along the entire length of the arm, and laced across the exposed shirt sleeve; the lacings are grouped. Thetis' crown follows the line of the roll of her high headdress. Cuffs spreading over knuckles; precious tab at free end of ladies' belt.

864. Atalanta's suitors vainly attempting to win the race from her: The neckline of her ermine-lined gown is now so low and wide that it cannot be held by fastening it to the exposed bit of the kirtle, alone. She wears an entire gauze bertha, with a standing collar, its transparency enhanced by the black cord necklace. Her buckled belt is as high, wide and stiff as possible, its tab finished with a stiff metal end, and decoratively large eyelets.

The suitor who is still on his feet shows to perfection the "points" which truss the long hose to the short doublet; which has the characteristic high collar, and the new open V, laced across the shirt bosom.

865. Ino sending cooked grain to be sowed: Dagged hoods, apron, pouch bag of workmen. The use of a high sock, on l. leg only, is undoubtedly connected with the specific job to be done.

From *Epitre d' Othea,* ed. by J. van den Gehyn. Bruxelles, Vromant, 1913.

866-67. XVc. c. 1477. Flemish. (Brussels, Bib. Roy., ms. 9231-32.)

La Fleur des Histoires by Jean Mansel, executed by *Simon Marmion*.

Useful rear views of costume are shown in this manuscript, executed for Jacques d'Armagnac, duke of Nemours (decapitated 1477).

866. Crowning of Charles V in chapel of castle. Towering veils of ladies of second quarter-second half XVc., supported by high horned headdresses or wire frames (see Ill. 883: Queen Mother). Jeanne de Bourbon, kneeling at prie-dieu, shows Queen's crown superimposed on folded veil of headdress; her sideless surcoat has the funnel sleeves of a houppelande; now so outmoded as to seem equally archaic, and equally suited for ceremonial wear. Ladies (3rd and 4th from l.), low V-neck, to girdle, finished with rolled edge. Charles V: coronation robes, and cape with conventionalized tippet.

867. Celebration of mass in church. Kneeling women at l. give rear views
of the new hood, with its back folds enclosing head and shoulders. Longer
and heavier head-draperies and cloaks are beginning to give to the costume
of ladies an enclosed look which, for some time, we have seen in the costume
of women of lower class. Rear view of horned headdress (women at front
of group); and of vestments of ecclesiastics and acolytes. Hats of very shaggy
beaver (on kneeling man, l. of ecclesiastics, and on standing gentleman with
cane, at r.)

868-70. XVc. French. (Paris, Bib. Nat., ms. fr. 2644.)

Sir John Froissart's *Chronicles of England, France, and Spain.*

Four volumes executed for Louis de Bruges, Seigneur de la Gruthuyse. These three illustrations, from one of many Froissart manuscripts, give a full picture of mediaeval life, indoors and out, in city and castle.

868. The decapitation of Guillaume, lord of Pommiers, and his secretary, Jean Coulon, at Bordeaux in 1375 on suspicion of treason by the English who still held that territory.

Blindfolded men: shirts of period; doublet, top of hose, and attaching knots.

Executioner: trunks have codpiece, which came into use, third quarter XVc., as hose lengthened and short doublets no longer masked the division; doublet has bolero. Gentleman, c.: long garment, slit up sides like a tabard, is new. Shirts have assumed a standing collar, which shows through the break in the high collar of the doublet; but with the V-openings of male garments, toward the end of the century, the shirt will become collarless and low-necked.

Man to l. of him: back view shows method of cutting and fitting high collar which is properly the collar of the doublet; we see it used here on a jacket. The elements of male costume are becoming unstable and interchangeable: almost anything can be expected. The small male fig. (3rd from r.), shows the orthodox sleeve of a doublet, such as is worn by the executioner (in two colors and slashed) used on a long gown, which is slit up the front and full below the belt, but as tightly fitted in the body as a doublet. This is about as far as a robe can get from the old-fashioned loose gown of the elderly man on the left.

In c. background, a hat shop exhibits its wares, its shuttered sides raised to form a roof over the counter.

869. Louis II, Count of Flanders, receiving the deputies of the burghers of Ghent, after their revolt in 1353.

The prosperity of Flanders, whose cloth trade was dependent on the free flow of wool from England, (see Ill. 826; also Appendix), had been endangered since the end XVc. by the quantities of cloth produced in England by immigrant Flemish weav-

869

* In late Sept., 1465, John Paston writes Margaret to find out where William bought his fine worsted: "which is almost like silk . . . thou it be dearer than viijs. . . . I wold make my doblet all worsted for worship of Norfolk." She answers: "I have do spoke for your worstede" (which got its name from the East Norfolk village where it was first produced), "but ye may not have it tylle Halowmesse and thane I am promysyd ye challe have as fyne as may be made."

ers,* and distributed by the Hanseatic League. After three quarters of a century of conflict, the burghers, harassed by floods and the Plague, were finally subdued by the pro-French nobility, and the XVc. decline of Flanders became inevitable. The hemp rope, which the magistrates and burghers henceforth wore about their necks on a certain-day of the year, in token of submission and penance, had been reduced to a blue ribbon by Evelyn's time (1641).

Louis stands on a dais, a rich brocade draped behind him, as protection against damp and draughts, and to heighten impressiveness. The sleeve of his jacket is slashed to show his doublet sleeve, slashed in its turn below its padded upper section, and strapped over the shirtsleeves. His sword, like that of the cupbearer, is slung in front.

Gentleman with a hawk: tall cap with a stem like a beret; brimmed hat (to be worn over it) slung over shoulder by its scarf, which he holds in his hand, in a gesture characteristic of the period.

Squires and pages carrying flagons, wear tabardlike garments, cut well above the buttocks; very high and well-cut boots with piked toes and turned-down colored cuffs; rows of fine chains; long bobbed hair.

The suppliants wear the new plebeian hood† with slittered border, and the longer, fur-edged garments of respectable, well-to-do bourgeois; bags hanging from the belt, which is wide; while the gentry carry a sword or dagger on a narrow belt.

† Nevertheless, the 15-page wardrobe inventory of a bluff, out-door character like Sir John Fastolf (Paston Letters) enumerates more than 20 hoods, beside his blue hood of the Garter. Many of these are parti-colored, or if of one color, are half velvet and half damask; and the edges are often described as jagged. He had, in addition, four red or black riding hoods, a "great rolled cap," two other caps, one of which was knit, an impressive beaver hat, and one "strawen hattis."

870. Richard II and Wat Tyler's rebellion. Froissart, Chap. IX: "The populace were everywhere rising against the nobility . . . On Corpus Christi day King Richard heard mass in the Tower of London, after which he entered his barge, attended by the Earls of Salisbury, Warwick, and Suffolk, and some other knights, and rowed down the Thames to Rotherhite, a royal manor, where upwards of 10,000 of the insurgents had assembled. As soon as the mob perceived the royal barge approaching, they began shouting and crying as if all the spirits in the nether world had been in the company." The king spoke to the people, but "the Earl of Salisbury cried out, 'Gentlemen, you are not properly dressed, nor are you in a fit condition for a king to talk with.'" The king was prevailed upon to return to the Tower, and the infuriated rebels marched to London, destroying "all the houses of lawyers and courtiers and all the monasteries they met with."

Richard's barge is hung with his arms as would have been the walls of his chamber, or the caparison of his horse. A lacy crown is set above the brim of his beaver hat. His brocade jacket is as short and loose as possible. He is accompanied by dignified men in long gowns and draped hats, younger gentlemen in garments as short as his own; soldiers in studded brigandines; rower in a short sleeved doublet.

On the stern, a lord in a sugarloaf cap carries his beaver hat slung over his shoulder. The neck-chains of his companion are tacked in place at the shoulders; they fall lower in back than in front, following the line which permits the emergence of the high collar of the doublet from the back of the jacket.

The embattled populace wear visored sallets, chapels, even old-fashioned closed helms; body armor, or studded gambesons over chain shirts; plate protection of most legs, and some arms; and carry swords, spears, or pole arms, in variety: their own, their fathers' or their grandfathers' left-overs.

871

871. Third quarter XVc. French. (Paris, Bib. Nat., ms. fr. 2646.)

Froissart's *Chronicles*.

This illustration, taken from another Froissart manuscript, shows the events described in Chap. XXII. A party was given in the ball room of the Hotel de St. Pol, at the king's expense, in honor of the wedding of two members of the royal household. A Norman squire, cousin of the bride, had provided disguises of linen, covered with flax, the color of hair; in which six members of the party had gone to disguise themselves. The Duke of Orleans, entering late, and not knowing of the king's orders that the torches should withdraw to one side, upon the entrance of the wild men, snatched a torch from one of his own bearers, to try to identfy the dancers. The hemp, and the pitch with which it was affixed, caught fire and the dancers, of whom the king was one, being chained together, could not be separated. The king's young aunt, the Duchess of Berri, saved his life by throwing her train over him. The Lord of Nantouillet broke loose and flung himself into a tub of dish-water in the pantry. Hugonin, the squire, and Sir Charles of Poitiers died on the spot; the Count de Joigny, and the Bastard of Foix, favorite son of Gaston-Phoébus, died at their own hôtels two days later. Queen: anachronistic robe and cape of royalty, belted low, but made of brocade; the cape carrying the contemporary wide, flat collar, and a standing sheer collar; gown with cuffs extended over the knuckles.

Ladies: widest necks and highest pointed hennins.

Orleans (under musician's gallery, with torch): wide opening of jacket shows doublet of brocade in a striped pattern, very different from the all-over patterns to which we are accustomed in France. (See striped Italian patterns of latter XVc.) Cuff spreading over knuckles, the effect of the fashions of one sex upon the clothing of the other.

Musicians in gallery: jacket sleeves slit lengthwise and slashed.

Photograph courtesy of Frick Art Reference Library

872. XVc. 1470. Franco-Flemish. (Louvre.)

Histoire de Charles Martel by *Jan van de Gheyn,* executed by *Loyset Liédet.*

Quarrel between Charles the Bald and Gerard de Rouissilon.

The photograph of this leaf, which shows wonderful exaggerations of the now familiar Burgundian costume was marked "Prayer Book, Louvre." Research shows it to be the missing leaf (in the Louvre) of Brussels ms.6-9.

Photograph courtesy of Metropolitan Museum of Art, Photograph Collection

873-76. XVc. (Franco-Burgundian. (Brussels, Bib. Roy., ms. 10238.)

Les Sires de Gavres.

In 1453, Philip the Good celebrated, at a great banquet, the battle of Gavres, in which the rebellious burghers of Ghent (see Froissart: Ill. 869) were finally defeated with huge losses. Laying his hand on a pheasant, brought in by heralds, he bound himself and his knights, by the "vow of the pheasant," to undertake a crusade. No attempt was made to carry out the project, but great sums were levied, and used for entertainments at court.

In contrast to the fine work of the Limbourgs and Fouquet, these are cheap, quick pen and wash illustrations, almost caricatures, but very spirited and informative.

When the Burgundian male costume had attained the limits of the idea of enormous width, squared and short, and the belts of the first half XVc. had been reduced to a cord, it was inevitable that it should occur to someone to loosen the tacking of the careful pleats, and let the jacket hang free, really square, really wide, as we see it in these illustrations.

873. Courtiers discussing the project with the Duke: back view of very short cape.

874. Disconsolate lady, bewailing her maidenhood and passing youth, by candlelight to her attendant; wears a hennin, veiled low over eyes; very wide belt and cuffs.

875. Marriage of the Duke's daughter: immensely wide fur borders of skirt which attendant holds up, over both concealed hands, in a characteristic female gesture of the period. Courtier: in fur-edged cape, open on r. shoulder.

876. The Sire de Gavres and his wife reunited: dagged hood indicates his journey. His companion holds one corner of his cape-like open jacket across his breast, after the manner of cloaks in Italy, toward the end of the century. Wife: hands characteristically concealed in fur cuffs.

877-78. XVc. c.1475. Flemish (Tournai). (Metropolitan Museum.)

Tapestry: presented by Pasquier Grenier, and wife, Marguerite de Lannoy, to Church of St. Quentin, Tours.

Priest: wedding; vested.

Woman receiving extreme unction: nightgowns not worn until end XVc.

Priest giving unction: every-day wear; long gown of any dignified gentleman.

Death-bed attendants, and kneeling donors: Flemish hoods, new (see Ill. 867).

879

879. XVc. Flemish. (Metropolitan Museum.)

Tapestry fragment: a noble company.

Details, extraordinarily fresh and bold, of the costume popularized by the Burgundian court, but with dramatically sloping shoulders, high-collared robes and jackets; doublets with still higher collars; and sophisticated combinations of solid color, pattern and texture, enhanced by the use of metal and jewels.

Lower row, l. to r. Truncated high cap, with tassel; jacket and doublet of different, equally bold brocades. Hennin and belt of brocade; wide neckline emphasized by flat, jewelled collar, two bias folds of sheer material, and elaborate wide necklace. Cape, closed on r. shoulder by four huge buttons; brocade collar and sleeves of doublet; towering, plain conical cap.

Upper row, l. to r. Brocade of the doublet and scarf, against plain masses of the gown; and of the soft, gathered shirt sleeves, unrestrained by lacings; necklace of twisted cord. Hat of brocade, with brocade scarf, and knot and plumes at sides; applied cartridge pleats on jacket. Brocade gown, with jewelled cuffs and mounting collar of plain material which serves to display necklace worn high upon it; scarved hat, softly pleated in at brow.

880. XVc. c. 1477. French. (Vienna, National Library.)

Book of Hours of Charles the Bold. Marie of Burgundy, at a shrine: depicting her marriage to Maximilian of Austria. Charles the Bold died in 1477, before the actual marriage of his daughter. Marie, seated in the shrine, before a picture of herself and her husband adoring the Virgin, is the quintessence of Burgundian elegance. Her hennin

880

is embroidered with her monogram. (See Marie Portinari: Ill. 858). Her precious belt is as wide, and is worn as high as possible. The extremity of width and slipping shoulder has been reached in this bodice; partly to support it, and partly in the reaction of a woman of great fashion-sense, her entire bosom is veiled by a bertha of gauze, into the high neckline to come from 1485. This conceals the precious wide collar (see Portinari, also), which will be replaced by chokers with a pendant.

Marie protects the precious binding of the missal, and the pattern of its gilded edges, by the cloth over her hand. Two red dianthus, signifying their marriage, lie near the vase of naturalistically painted fleurs-de-lys.

Flanders, in close relationship with Venice, imported glass, and then set up factories of her own, from which window glass was imported into England in second half XVc. Small bull's-eyes, rather easily blown, and showing a center lump where cut off the rod, were an early form of domestic window glass.

881. XVc. 1479. Flemish. (Bruges, Hospital of St. John.) *Hans Memling.* Mystic Marriage of St. Catherine. Sideless surcoat with brocade skirt and train. An approximation of the bald-looking head in a mounting, netted headdress is given by braids under a projecting veil and coronet.

882. XVc. 1481. Flemish. (Brussels, Bib. Roy., ms. 13073-74.)
Chronicles of Flanders.
Engagement of Maximilian I and Marie of Burgundy.

By this marriage, the daughter of Charles the Bold brought Burgundy and the Netherlands to the Hapsburgs. She wears the traditional ceremonious sideless surcoat and cloak, with the contemporary necklaces (see Ill. 857), and headdress over the flowing hair of a virgin bride.

The Emperor's ceremonial robe, fur-lined and slit up the sides, is collared in the new manner. He wears the plumes of third quarter XVc. in a twisted fillet.

883-86. XVc. Flemish. (Metropolitan Museum.)
Life of St. Godelième.
War-like bishops: (see Ill. 834).

887. XVc. c. 1480. French. (Morgan Library, M. 677.)
Hours of Anne de Beaujou (1460-1522).
Undershirt, laced kirtle and gown.

888. XVc. c. 1455. Flemish. (Penrhyn Castle.)
Dirk Bouts. St. Luke: self-portrait of the painter; glimpse of his studio. Cut of fur-lined gown clearly shown.

889. XVc. 1487. Flemish. (Bruges, Hospital of St. John.)
Hans Memling. Diptych of Martin Nieuwenhove: hair in transition from bowl crop to long bob; trimmed high up neck, but allowed to grow long. Thumb ring.

890. XVc. 1487. Flemish. (Hermanstadt Gymnasium.)
Hans Memling. Diptych of wife of Martin Nieuwenhove: Flemish hood; neckline rising and filled in with crimped gauze; important belt with tab of fine goldsmith's work; wedding ring on middle joint.

891. XVc. 1491. Flemish. (Metropolitan Mus.)
Master H. H.

Portrait of a gentleman: Italian influence
on male costume, end XVc.; wide V opening of doublet and jerkin, laced across fine
shirt; squaring of neckline; small cap and
long bobbed **hair**.

892

892. XVc. c. 1495. Flemish. (National Gallery, London.)
Master of St. Giles.

St. Giles protecting a wounded hind. During transition, end XVc., differentiation of garments becomes
difficult. Sleeves are transposed, and like plastron
fronts, are often interchangeable. Jackets have separate pleated skirts, *bases* (see mounted fig.) Cloaks:
collared, V-openings; or circular and thrown over
shoulder in the Italian manner. Small caps, or the new
bonnets with cut and turned-up brims, over bobbed
hair. Boots (archer): turned-down tops of another
color; soft and loose, clasped twice to fit below calf.

893

superbia

897

894

895   gula

898

896   Invidia

894. The Haywagon to Hell (detail)

895. The Table of the Seven Deadly Sins: detail, "Gula"

896. Seven Deadly Sins, "Invidia"

897. Seven Deadly Sins, "Superbia"

898. The Cutting of the Stone

H. van Acken (c.1460-1518), called Jerom or Hieronymus Bosch, from Hertogenbosch (Bois-le-duc), the strangely influential town of his birth (see Ills. 1101-02: Pilgrims) was Brueghel's spiritual master although he died before Brueghel's birth. Bosch greatly influenced Cranach, and worked for years at the Spanish court for Philip II; many of his teeming paintings are in Madrid.

No one ever painted everyday dress with more interest. Awls, needles, or arrows are stuck, usefully or decoratively, through hats as spoons and pipes are used in Brueghel's day. He delights in skates and pattens, pouches and wooden shoes (like those of the patient in the operation), hand-me-downs and wonderful glimpses of dress from unusual angles. The way a lady, kneeling at prayer, has knotted her hanging pink sleeves together at the back of the skirt, is the cause of the "Temptation of St. Anthony" (Lisbon). The "Charlatan" (probably a

893-98. XVc. Flemish. (Prado, Madrid.)
Hieronymus Bosch.
893. The Garden of Earth's Pleasures (detail)

copy, at St. Germain-en-Laye), shows a mixed group of bystanders and gullible ecclesiastics (one wearing blue spectacles).

Bosch started painting very early, between 1470-75. "The Cutting of the Stone" and "The Garden of Earth's Pleasures" are early works; "Adoration of the Magi," c.1490; "Haywagon to Hell," 1510. The "Table of the Seven Deadly Sins," also late, shows Superbia (Vanity) wearing a brown skirt, under a pink gown caught up to show its white fur lining (see Ill. 906), primping from a large box which shows coral beads and fine girdles.

TRANSITION IN DRESS BETWEEN MIDDLE AGES AND RENAISSANCE: 1485-1510

About half way through the fourth quarter XVc., the costume of women begins to lose its fantasy and extravagance. Whether worn by Anne of Brittany, twice Queen of France, or by the middle and lower class women of the "Dance of Death," the costume (of Franco-Flemish derivation) is becoming severe, sensible and bourgeois. It is familiar to us as the costume worn by nuns, and that of the Queens on a deck of cards.

FEMALE: Necklines are higher; the front closing often laps (see Ills. 899-902) in just the curving line which the old spread collar would have made, had the lady been caught in a storm, and tried to clutch the revers together over her chest. But in the main, the neckline of the gown takes over that of the kirtle, becoming squarer. The horizontal line of the top of the plastron rises convexly (see Ill. 905). The old V-neckline is often laced back and forth over the kirtle, or over a plastron of brocade; back closings are also frequently laced. Wide sailor collars appear.

The sleeve of the robe is often of elbow length; frequently cuffed, showing the forearm in the sleeve of the kirtle. Though the wide, funnel sleeve is usual, close-fitting separate sleeves, pinned or knotted on at the shoulder, will appear, as Flemish and Italian influences affect all European costume, from 1485-1510; after this, German-Swiss trends will overtake them. Italian influence is more noticeable in men's costume.

The overskirt, which was formerly so long that it had to be held up, is now as short (and frequently shorter) than the underskirt, though both may show trains in back. It is less often caught up by the hands, but is now apt to be pinned, hooked, tied or tucked into fixed position (see Ill. 906). As skirts grow narrower, the overskirt is slashed to permit this permanent drape. The skirts of both garments are cut separate from the bodice and gathered onto it, in back only. The train, when looped up to the waistline in back, emphasizes the bustled look.

The belt is now a cord or light chain, often with a dependent end at c. front. The turned-up overskirt often reveals several decorative objects hanging from the belt of the kirtle: pouch bags, rosaries, prayer books, etc.

The heads of the poorer women are, as we expect, bundled up, but in a way related to the hoods which the bourgeoises, even the Queen, now wear. In comparison with the flowing veils of the Middle Ages, these lappeted Renaissance hoods are of relatively heavy stuffs, and often of dark colors or black. They enclose the head increasingly, as new methods of fitting them are evolved. Like nuns' headdresses today, the heavy line of the edge of these dark hoods is usually softened by a fold or ruching of light, usually white, stuff beneath. After nearly a hundred years of apparent baldness, or carefully concealed hair, these hoods reveal the hair, simply parted in the center, or drawn back.

Women's shoes, which seldom show, follow the same changes as men's.

MALE: As Burgundian supremacy in fashion wanes, and that of Renaissance Italy grows, men's costume relinquishes its padded shoulder width. The doublet loses its standing collar and assumes a normal waist line. Its close sleeves are often tied on, and are thus interchangeable. It is becoming vest-like: it often has a full skirt, but like the sleeve, this may be separate and interchangeable, as in the case of the cartridge-pleated *bases,* (Ill. 450: Waffenrock) which we find listed independently in contemporary inventories of costumes. The neck of the doublet becomes progressively lower; as on women's gowns it is frequently square, laced across a shirt or plastron, or lapped over.

The jacket or jerkin, worn over the doublet, is, as before, fuller than the doublet, particularly in the skirts; has wider sleeves, and is apt to have a collar of the sailor variety also seen on women's costume. The sleeve of the jerkin is frequently slit, not only longitudinally, as earlier, but crosswise.

Jerkin and doublet take on each other's attributes, and are not always identifiable.

Gowns are long, wide, closed down the front, sometimes girdled; and as before, fur-lined. Their sleeves and collar are those of the jerkin. The comfort and dignity of long gowns continue to make them appropriate for older men and ceremonial occasions. The shorter, ungirded gowns with wide collars are coats in the modern sense.

Cloaks are much worn. They vary in cut and length and frequently carry large collars; they are often thrown or lapped in the new diagonal line.

Hose now reach the natural waistline, where they are trussed to the doublet, as before. The codpiece is increasingly evident; it will presently be featured. There is a re-birth of the idea of parti-colored hose, but in a greatly elaborated Italian form; the legs may differ completely; stripes may be countercharged; there is a great deal of embroidery, which is now more frequently used at the top, to give the appearance of trunks (see Ill. 906), than in boot-like forms at the bottom of the hose, as it had been used earlier (see Ill. 807). The same effect is obtained by the use of interwoven braids, with puffs and slashes.

Slashing in patterns, through which the fabric of the doublet or shirt was exhibited, was used, particularly on doublet sleeves, from fourth quarter XVc. The practice was elaborated, and used all over costume, both male and female, through first half XVIc., and continued for a century thereafter.

Shirts increase greatly in importance as low-necked overgarments, lacings and slashings make them visible. The neckline of the shirt, gathered and embroidered in black, red or gold, lowers in unison with the neck of the overgarment.

Shoe form changes rapidly during this period. While retaining the point, the toes spread progressively, until end XVc., when they lose the point. While still wide, they become round-toed low shoes with straps. Backless slippers, into which the toe was inserted, as in women's "mules" today, appear at beginning XVc. Boots with turned-down tops are less used after first quarter XVIc. Loose sock-hose, which had long been used by all classes to protect tights in bad weather, begin for the first time to be knitted, in a form without heel or toe, worn strapped under the instep, like Uncle Sam's trousers.

The tall Burgundian caps are supplanted by beret-like hats, often pinched into the form we still see on the ecclesiastical biretta. These hats usually have a brim, or a section of brim, turned up; cuts in the brim, laced across, the lacings often knotted; ends hanging, or serving to secure the hat under the chin; these *bonnets* usually carry medallions. There are also wide-brimmed hats, frequently of beaver, immensely plumed (see Ill. 906). As in Italy, the head was frequently covered by a small embroidered cap, which was retained under the hat.

Hair is worn in a long bob, often with bangs; typically of shoulder length and natural, but varying from lank and unkempt to exquisitely trimmed and tended, especially in Italy.

899-902. XV. 1486. French.

Danse macabre des femmes by *Pierre le Rouge;* pub. by Guy Marchant, Paris, 7 July, 1486.

899. The welcoming woman; the nurse.
900. The shepherdess; the woman with crutches.
901. The village woman; the old woman.
902. The second-hand clothes woman; the woman in love.

The allegory of the Dance of Death, in all its satiric bitterness, was repeated on thousands of wall paintings, woodcuts and engravings (one series by Holbein), and as a morality play, in France, Germany and England, from the days of the Black Death and the Hundred Years War.

903. End XVc. French. (Paris, Bib. Nat., ms. Lat. 1190.)

Anne of Brittany, wife of Charles VIII and of Louis XII.

904. XVc. c. 1494. French. (Paris, Beistegui Coll.)

Charles d'Orléans.

The little Dauphin, son of Charles VIII and Anne of Brittany, is shown in another portrait (Louvre) in brocade and the same sort of bib, with the brim of his cap turned down. Anne of Brittany's accounts have been preserved. She dressed the baby always in white and silver; we know how much she paid for silver cloth for his dresses, and that his caps were bought of Gorget of Tours for 50 *sols tournois*.

905. XVIc. 1509-13. Franco-Flemish. (Paris, Cluny.)

Tapestry: *The Allegory of Smell*.

Allegories of the five senses, together with the Lady of the Unicorn, make up the famous set of six tapestries from the Cluny, among the 200 tapestries lent in 1948 by the French government to the Metropolitan and other museums in the United States. Against a rosy background, set with flowering plants, these predominantly red and blue tapestries show the lion of valor and the unicorn of purity holding the arms of the Le Viste family; red with three crescents set on a diagonal blue band.

906. c. 1490. Flemish. (British Museum, Harl. M.S. 4425.)

Roman de la Rose.
Carole (dance) of *déduit* (mirth) in a garden.

This volume, which belonged to Count Henry of Nassau, contains some of the great fashion illustrations of all time.

Illuminated manuscripts were the fashion plates of their day. As long as they were executed by monks, who had forsworn women but were perfectly aware of the difference between male and female, those differences were explicitly expressed. No matter how sack-like her garments, the Scarlet Woman in a XIIc. Beatus is very much a woman; all the new knowledge of bias cutting is used in XIIIc. to outline the belly or emphasize the provocative hip of the Foolish Virgins.

Then the troubadours began to sing of a romantic love, serving without reward, perhaps at a distance and for a lifetime. This was a civilizing notion, which required the relinquishment of brute manhood. Secular artists began to represent knights in long gowns, mooning around castles after the ladies they adored. With the advent of the houppelande, a beard is about all that differentiates Richard II from a woman in a similar garment.

The continuing process of refinement imposed an ideal of adolescent charm on both sexes. The Burgundian courtiers are exquisite page-boys, and Marie of Burgundy (Ill. 880) is a breastless girl whose hennin would fall off in a tussle.

But people and their dreams of themselves grow up. We see it happening in costume, at the turn of XV-XVIc. as it does physically: the adolescent girl matures more rapidly than the adolescent boy. In the Roman de la Rose, the girls are just beginning to turn, as they do almost overnight, into the women and housewives of the XVIc. Their dress is becoming simple and severe: a black velvet hood and a plain golden-brown gown with its train fastened up out of the way in back. The boys with them seem reluctant to grow up; their dress takes a last wild fling, as though trying to outdo an extravagance, the limits of which have already been reached; immense white hats are bound on with lavender scarves, and trimmed with spangled feathers more than half as long as their bodies.

The Flemish hausfrau look, reinforced by rigid Spanish coat-dresses and men's felt hats which are not removed in the house, give a characteristically masculine look to the costume of Elizabethan women. The male adolescence of the XVc. becomes diluted in Elizabethan men to a dandified elegance which gives an effeminate look to some of the most completely masculine men in history. By XVIIc., females are women, without having to be aggressive about it, and men are men, going about their empire-building and business.

The new sobriety of women is not complete in the Roman de la Rose illustrations, but it is already in sharp contrast with the dress of the men.

1. *female*: gold turban; pink gown, with light gray-blue undersleeves; green plastron laced with red; pale gold chain-girdle with pomander. 2. *male*: tiny red cap with jewelled brooch, over long flowing hair; black beaver hat, slung over shoulder of golden-brown doublet, gathered at neckline over padded, swelling bosom; bolero; doublet sleeves losing their upper padding; hose tops white, striped in pink, lavender-gray, and green; lower part black, embroidered with gold; cream-colored sock-boots; black, wide-toed shoes; belt threaded through a tasseled pouch. 3.*f.*: black velvet hood with golden-brown crown, pinned with a brooch; golden-brown gown with convex neckline, turned-down cuff of XVc.; shirt puffings pulled through outseam of lower sleeve; permanently draped overskirt; caught by a brooch; black underskirt. 4.*m.*: white beaver hat with immense, color-spangled white feathers, bound by lavender scarf, worn over green cap; red and green jacket with wide lapels and borders, over a black doublet; dark gray hose; black shoes with thick, broad toes, dramatized by the reduction to a minimum of the leather around the heel; sole also narrowed at the heel; another fine belt and pouch. 5.*m.*: tiny red cap with turned-up brim; lavender-gray coat with grass-green lapels and slit pendant sleeves; gray beaver with white plumes under arm; black hose and shoes.

6.*f.*:black hood with green crown; girdle with immense red, blue, and green cabochon stones; gold gown, its black-banded hem, pinned up to show black lining, gives the characteristic bustled look. 7.*f.*: red and gold cap over flowing hair; pink gown with gray skirt, turned up to show its ermine lining. 8.*angel*: white beaver with cut and turned-up brim, bound with pink and lavender scarves; dark gold wings; white garment embroidered with red roses and green leaves; wide gold and white belt. 9.*f.*: black and golden brown hood; pink gown trimmed in black and gold. 10.*m.* red hat; cobalt blue jacket with hem and sleeve ends slittered and cut; wonderful tasselled pouch carried in back; yellow-green doublet sleeves; yellow hose; black shoes.

Musicians: cloaks open on right shoulder; slittered edges; parti-colored hose (now livery).

11. *harp*: black cap; wide-sleeved vermilion coat, lined with red; 1 green, 1 red doublet sleeve.

12. *pipe*: red cap; coat with 1 pink and 1 lavender-brown lapel; hanging pink sleeve, fringed in gold; black doublet with 1 green and 1 black sleeve; parti-colored shoes and hose, alternately black, gold, and gray.

13. *drum*: black cap and doublet; red coat with 1 green and 1 lavender lapel; pink doublet sleeve slit over black; parti-colored hose, alternately gray, gold, and black.

15. *hero*: with staff and anachronistic dress; old-fashioned short gown with bag-sleeves and a fringed hem; red hose and hat with fringe (see Ills. 985-986: Housebook); girdle pendants, which are probably the large bells worn on belts and baldrics from e.XV-e.XVIc. In 1415, Marie of Burgundy had a collar with these hanging, pear-shaped bells. (See the livery of May and the servants in the Très-riches heures: Ills. 807-810.)

The gold border is painted naturalistically with many of the favorite motifs of XVIc. embroidery: pea-flowers, vines, and pods; butterflies, insects, and snails; strawberries and a peacock; fleur-de-lys, rose, dianthus, forget-me-not, and pimpernel.

906

Ceste gent dont
le vue parole
Sestoient pue
a la carole

Et une dame leur chantoit
Qui liesse appellee estoit
Bien seut chanter et plaisamment
Plus que nulle et mignotement
Son bel refrain mlè bien lui fist
Car de chanter merueilles fist

Elle auoit la voir clere et saine
La quelle nestoit pas vulaine
Et tresbien se sauoit debriser
Ferir du pret et remuoiser
Les gens la tenoient mlt chiere
Pource quelle estoit la premiere
De belle face et plaisier
Courtoise estoit et non pasfiere
De loyeusete fut garnie
Et aussi de solas fournie

907-908. End XV-e.XVIc. c. 1502. French, Southern. (Issogne, Castello.)

Wall paintings. These Southern French wall paintings show costume of start of XVIc.; strongly influenced by Italian ways.

907. A mediaeval market place; draper's booth, with belts and caps hung on its open shutters. Traffic in strings of garlic and red onions, carrots, rutabagas; figs, plums and grapes; baskets of cabbage, melons and various squashes.

The simple roundlets and tiny caps favored by Italian women appear here, together with the new hoods. At l., the seated woman with spinning utensils at her belt, wears a horned roundlet; (braided hair was also brought together and bound into a similar point, second half XVc.). The new deep armseye of her sleeve is emphasized by the Italian differentiation **in color.**

The men wear the new bonnets with cut and laced-together brims. Padding is being removed from the tops of doublet sleeves; they remain full, but loose. This sleeve is also used on the jerkin. With the advent of pleated *bases,* separate and often interchangeable skirts to the jacket (Ill. 450) the doublet and jacket became less easy to differentiate. The gown of the man (c.), has the new broad, flat collar. Seams and edges are emphasized by lines of braid.

908. Tailor's shop: Parti-colored tights reappear, end XVc., in more elaborate forms than before (Ill. 906); in trunk-like patterns or multi-colored stripes, of Italian origin. Cut-out pieces of these tights, with codpieces, hang above the tailors. Their jerkins, in the new vertically striped materials, have **the square** neck of first quarter XVIc.

909

909. XIV-XVc. English. (Derby, Ashbourne Church.)

Tombs of John Cockayne (1404 A.D.) and civilian (1370 A.D.).

The knight: fringed surcoat bearing his canting arms of a cock. Aventail laced to bascinet through staples; cuff gauntlets; flowing moustache.

The prosperity of the XVIIc. cloth trade will be founded on the proposal of Sir William Cockayne, alderman and head of the Clothworkers' Company of London, that all cloth be dyed and finished in England before export.*

The civilian: cote-hardi, center-buttoned since mid-XIIIc.: precious belt, over the joining of the full skirt which gives sufficient solidity for attachment of hose; tasseled pouch; coif; hooded cloak caught on right shoulder.

910

910. XVc. 1400. English. (Nottinghamshire, Strelly Church.)

Sir Samson de Strelley, and wife Elizabeth.

The netted crespine has developed into jewelled boxes, surmounted by a coronet; from 1400 the boxes tend to descend and enclose the ears. Rising neckline filled in by a choker with pearl pendants, or by the SS collar, frequently seen on women.

---

* George Unwin: *Industrial Organization in the Sixteenth and Seventeenth Centuries*, Clarendon Press, Oxford, 1904.

911-12. XVc. 1400. English. (Gloucestershire, Deerhurst.)

Sir John and Lady Cassy.

The earliest remaining brass shows the Chief Baron of the Exchequer, in the linen coif which, by end first quarter XVc., is worn only by judges, lawyers and churchmen (Ill. 928). The Baron of the Exchequer, with judges and sergeants, made up the Order of the Coif. Fur-lined mantle with hood; under-tunic with sleeves extending over the knuckles, fastened by row of tiny buttons.

Lady Cassy, born Terri: reticulated headdress; long, loose gown, gored into a high buttoned neck; sleeves of kirtle extend over the knuckles.

913-14. XVc. c. 1410. English. (Lincolnshire, Spilsby Church.)

Knight and Lady (prob. 4th Baron, and 1st wife), of d'Eresby family.

Baron: armor of Transitional period, from mail to plate. Camail still worn under gorget and bascinet of plate. No jupon; breastplate, with mail gussets; and mail fringe below skirt of articulated plates, *fauld*, which supplants that of hawberk. Two belts; horizontal and diagonal. Orlé over bascinet; moustache.

Lady; houppelande (new gown, with high collar, flowing sleeves, belted high, fur-lined; largely replaces mantle). Inner sleeve, of length which heretofore covered knuckles, now falls back, as hand is passed through slit at wrist. Coronet over crespine headdress without veil; small net-covered bosses, above ears, until c. 1410.

915. XVc. 1401-1406. English. (Warwick, St. Margaret's Church.)

Thomas Beauchamp, Earl of Warwick, and Margaret, Countess of Warwick, born Ferrers.

One of the costliest monumental effigies ever ordered; made of latten.

Earl: armor of Camail period (see Ills. 591, 599) bearing Beauchamp arms. The ragged staff, which was a Beauchamp badge, is used on pommel and scabbard of sword, on roundlets at elbow, and on border of bascinet. The bear beneath his feet was another badge of his house. Moustache.

Countess: gown bears the arms of Ferrers; mantle Beauchamp. Nebulé headdress in late English form; sleeves extended over knuckles to end first quarter XVc.

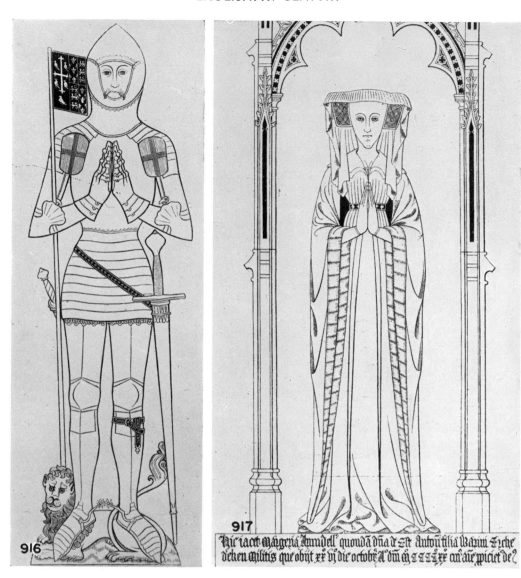

916. XVc. 1416. English. (Norfolk, Felbrigg Church.)

Sir Symon de Felbrigge, K. G.

Standard-bearer to Richard II, whose arms are shown on the banner he holds. Edward III was the first king to employ quartered arms (Azure, semé of fleurs-de-lys or, France, quartering gules, 3 lions passant gardant, England), which Richard II sometimes used (as here shown), impaled with the arms attributed to Edward the Confessor (azure a cross patée between 3 martlets or). He wears the Garter of the Order instituted in the middle of the XIVc.

Armor of Complete Plate period; bascinet, becoming more rounded; helm and gorget replace camail. Breastplate with oblong palettes (charged with a cross), protecting armpits. Skirt of taces, which increase in number; vestigial line of mail. Arms: articulated pauldrons, rerebraces, fan-shaped coutère, giving additional elbow protection, vembraces. Gauntlet: increasingly articulated but fingers not yet separated. Legs: cuishes, genoullières, jambes, sollerets, rowelled spurs. Belt: diagonal, holds sword, miséricorde at taces, right side; moustache; the Garter.

917. XVc. 1420. English. (Cornwall, East Anthony.)

Margery Arundell.

Houppelande: double collar, now worn flat (see Ill. 807). Headdress: netted cones of 2nd decade XVc. in England, wider, squarer, now covering ears; covered by shoulder-length square veil.

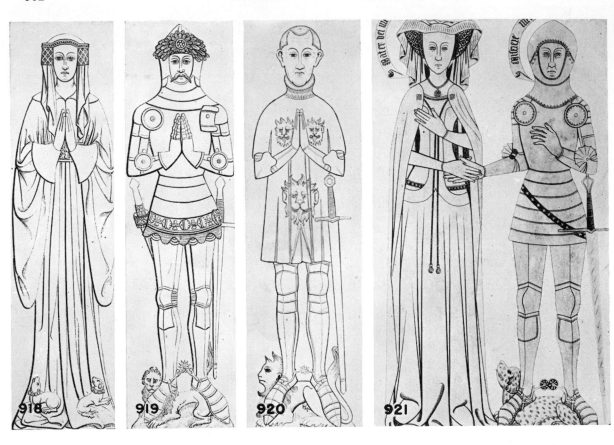

918-19. XVc. c. 1420. English. (Yorkshire, Harpham Church.)

Sir Thomas de Saint Quintin and wife Agnes.

Sir Thomas: Complete Mail period. Palettes of different shapes protect armpit; smaller, providing freedom of sword arm. Elaborate orlé on rounder bascinet. Belt: low, horizontal, and very elaborate, found till mid-XVc., though tendency is toward simpler, narrower, diagonal belts. Sword; handsome miséricorde. Below taces, elaborately scalloped mail edge. Moustache.

Agnes: collar of houppelande broader, flatter; belt lower, wider, more important; bag-sleeve of first quarter XVc. with gauntlet cuff. Bosses of reticulated headdress square, wide, cover ears; veil, shoulder-length, square.

920. XVc. 1492. English. (Sussex, Amberly Church.)

John Wantele.

Heraldic tabard, which appears c. 1425, in an early form; short sleeves cut in one with the garment; blazoned: vert 3 lions faces argent langued gules. Effigies are now frequently bare-headed and usually clean-shaven.

Stow, at the end XVIc., describes the tabard: "a jacket, or sleeveless coat, whole before, open on both sides, with a square collar, winged at the shoulders; a stately garment of old time, commonly worn of noblemen and others, both at home and abroad in the wars, but then, to wit, in the wars, their arms embroidered, or otherwise depict upon them, that every man by his coat-of-arms might be known from others. But now these tabards are worn only by the heralds, and be called their coats-of-arms in service."

921. XVc. c. 1420. English. (Kent, Herne Church.)

Peter Halle and wife.

Peter: Complete Mail period. Bascinet increasingly rounder; coutes fan-shaped. Sword-belt narrow, diagonal. No mail fringe below taces; no gauntlets; guarded rowel spurs. Clean-shaven.

Wife: classic sideless surcoat (persists nearly 150 years, from mid-XIVc.; its front placard being gradually reduced to a narrow strip); with accompanying cord-held cape. Pads of headdress beginning to assume heart shape, which will reach its culmination in third quarter XVc.

922-25. First quarter XVc. English. (London, Soc. of Antiquaries.)

Scenes from the life of St. Etheldreda.

St. Etheldreda, 660 A.D., was the daughter of the King of the East Angles. Twice married, but a perpetual virgin and an incorruptible corpse, she was the builder and abbess of the monastery of Ely. Bede tells us that "from the time of her entering into the monastery, she never wore any linen but only woolen garments and would rarely wash in a hot bath, unless just before any of the great festivals . . . and then she did it last of all . . . after having first washed the other servants of God there present. . . . She foretold the pestilence of which she was to die . . . (and) the number of those that should be then snatched away out of her monastery. . . . She was buried among them . . . in a wooden coffin."

Upper left to right: high horned headdress early form; headdresses, with round bosses, covering ears, surmounted by crowns (in other illus., by roundlets). Houppelandes; collars worn flat; variety of sleeves. Bishop, kings, ecclesiastics.

Lower left to right: masons wearing aprons; bowl crop of Englishmen's hair; Dead saint, with nuns, bishop, ecclesiastics, ladies and gentlemen.

926

927

926-27. XVc. c. 1427. French. (Paris, Bib. Nat., ms. lat. 1158.)

Book of Hours of Ralph Nevill, Earl of Westmorland (926), and Jeanne de Beaufort (927).

Ralph Nevill had 23 children; we are here shown 12 of his 14 children by Jeanne, his 2nd wife, together with 3 daughters-in-law. All wear houppelandes, or derivative garments, with flattened spreading collars

of end first quarter XVc. Sons wear bag sleeve (pokys—"pig in a poke"), which will soon be supplanted by the sleeve slit for the passage of the doublet-covered forearm. The women wear large heart-shaped French headdresses; the men show the English form of the bowl-cropped head; and wear the livery Collar of the White Hart. The blazoning of the coats of arms indicate the marriages, as: Nevill/Lancaster; England, York/Nevill; Mowbray, Plantagenet, Norfolk/Nevill.

928. XVc. 1430. English. (Essex, Gosfield Church.)

Thomas Rolf, Sergeant-at-law.

Not only the care of souls, but education, law, medicine, and charity had been administered solely by the Church. During XIVc., the separation of the professions began, at the time when long, loose, sober, hooded garments, currently worn by elderly men, were coming to be considered more suitable than others for clerical use. These garments, already antiquated, became fossilized in the dress of men (and women) of the Church, and of professional men, whose status remained semi-clerical although they might actually no longer be priests. The separation took place first in law, and last in education (within our grandparents' memory). The dress remains today in the robes of judges, monks, nuns, and hooded academic dress.

The coif and lappets of XIVc. are retained in legal dress in court or university in XVc. Sergeants are a privileged class, and wear a hooded cape of lamb's wool (budge) over a garment of the tabard-guarnache-scapular type, and a long gown.

A large colored plate (III) accompanying the informative explanatory text in the article on Robes in Enc. Britt., 11th ed., shows a law court, tempus Henry VI, and describes the difference between the different categories of legal dress shown there, and spectators and prisoners. Sergeants at law are more privileged than King's Counsel, and wear parti-colored robes (the "medlée cote" of Chaucer), in green and blue, diagonally or vertically striped in white. Judges, who belong to the same order, wear robes of the same form as sergeants but in scarlet, and their capes are furred with miniver; they wear XIVc. cloaks caught on the right shoulder, and coifs or furred hats. Variations in these colors, and the dress of King's Coroner, Attourney, Master of the Court, ushers, and tipstaff are discussed or shown. The whole set of 4 plates is reproduced from Archaeologica, Vol. XXXIX, 1863, p. 357-72.

929. XVc. English. (British Museum, Harl. ms. 4380.)

Mss. drawing: Treaty between the French and English.

930-31. XVc. 1458. English. (Leicestershire, Castle Donington Church.)

Sir Robert Staunton and lady.

Sir Robert wears a salade and Gothic armor showing increasing lamination for flexibility; and use of indenting, ridging and fluting of plates, calculatedly practical as well as decorative. Pointed, fluted tassets hang from the laminated fauld. Widely flanged guards at elbow; mitten gauntlets; English sollerets usually not piked, like ordinary footwear or armor of the continent.

Wife; heart-shaped headdress; less exaggerated than the French (see Jeanne de Beaufort, Ill. 927).

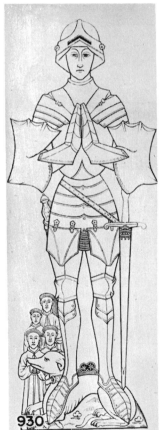

932-33. XVc. 1473. English. (Hertfordshire, Broxbourne Church.)

Sir John Say and Lady.

Sir John's tabard, like his lady's mantle, was enamelled to show armorial bearings; Say: party per pale azure and gules, 3 chevrons or, each charged with another humette countercharged of the field; and hers: Cheyny. Tassets increasingly fluted and indented; lengthening as fauld becomes shorter. He wears the Yorkist livery collar of Suns and Roses.

Wife: butterfly headdress of third quarter XVc. (see Ill. 833), short sideless surcoat, and heavy necklace characteristic of last half XVc. until superseded by fine knotted cords or bead chokers of XVIc.

934-38. XVc. c. 1485. English. (British Museum.)

Pageant of the Birth, Life and Death of Richard Beauchamp, Earl of Warwick (1382-1439), by *John Rows* of Warwick (1411-1491).

The illustrations for this life of the great warrior-Earl (son of Thomas B., 1400) furnish unique source material about military affairs of the period.

No. 934 shows the Earl in foot combat with Sir Pandolfo Malatesta at Verona. By casting down the baton which he holds, Sir Galaot of Mantua can end the combat, if he feels it necessary. The combat with battle-axes has been preceded by one with spears; the squires hold in readiness the swords for the encounter which will follow. Both were in complete armor, a rear view of which is given by Malatesta, whose crest is of plumes and jewels. The Earl's bascinet carries his bear and ragged staff, as crest. His sleeved tabard (see Ills. 830, 831). carries his bearings (see Ills. 532, 533).

935. The President of the "King's Court of France" receives three sealed letters from Warwick's herald, the letter he holds is sealed with a "maunche" (bag sleeve),* the feyld sylver a maunche gowlys. The secund Pavys (shown above arch) hadde a lady sittyng at a covered borde worchyng perles/and on her sleeve was tached a glove of plate/and her knyght was called Chevaler vert/and his letter was sealed wt the Armes, the felde sylver &ij barres of gowles/ And he must just xv courses & that shulde be ij sadilles of choyes/the iij de pavys a lady sittyng in a gardeeyn makyng a Chapellet/and on her sleeve, a poleyn wt a rivet/and her knyght was called Chivaler attendant/And he & his felowe must renne x cours wt sharpe speres & wt out sheldys/his letter was sealed wt golde & gowles quarte a bordour of vere/ thies lettres were sent to the Kynges coort of Fraunce

/And a noon other ijj Frenche knyghtes received them & graunted their felows to mete at day and place assigned."

Herald, in sleeved armorial tabard, riding boots, and spurs (length of which is increasing). Sword-bearer; long gown, handsome pouch. President and gentlemen; long gowns, jewelled collars and belts.

936. Richard, in armor and tabard, kneeling before Henry V, who wears parliamentary robes and crown, and is attended by sword-bearer and lords. To right, two Earls ride away, in full armor, wearing salades, one of which has a visor, the other a knob carrying a jewelled feather, both furnished with chin-pieces. They are preceded by Warwick's banner, borne by men-at-arms in studded brigandines, one over chain shirt, and with short sleeves of mail. All wear round salades, one over mail coif.

937. The Dauphin, and the Earls of Limoges and Vendôme defeated by the English. English archers, with bundles of arrows at their belts, in short brigandines over long mail shirts; protective cuff on left arm; barbutes on head. Behind them, spearmen, in visored salades. Warwick's banner borne by completely armed man in a closed helmet. Warwick in plumed helmet, mounted on plumed horse, which is given plate protection on head and neck. On right, crossbow men, with scimitar-like faulchions.

938. Richard kneeling before King on his return; followed by attendant wearing his ragged staff badge; on his doublet. Pennon with his bear and ragged staff. Horsemen with guisarmes and spears. King in trefoil crown, attended by hooded clerk and swordbearer.

The impulse toward uniformity is not new. The loyalty of feudal retainers had to be assured by food and clothing, which it was convenient to get in large batches, and so turned out alike.

Stow gives many lists of the expenses of Thomas of Lancaster for uniforms: in 1314, "1 cloth of russet for the bishop, 70 cloth of blue for the knights, 15 cloth of medley for the lord's clerks," and so on to a total of £460.15s, which dresses everybody down to the minstrels and carpenters. On other occasions, he got 65 cloths of saffron color for barons and knights in summer, or 100 pieces of green silk for the knights. This is uniformity, but of a sort, only.

Meanwhile, new loyalties besides the feudal arise. The solidarity of the city guilds sends 600 London citizens out to receive Edward I on his return from his wedding in 1300, dressed "in one livery of red and white, with cognizances of their mysteries embroidered upon their sleeves." The mayor, aldermen, and craftsmen of London met Henry V, on his return with French prisoners in 1415, in red, with red and white hoods; and. Henry VII was met by the usual London worthies, "all clothed in violet, as in a mourning color," after Richard III's death at Bosworth (Stow).

The united loyalties (now to the Crown, instead

---

* As on the arms of Hastings.

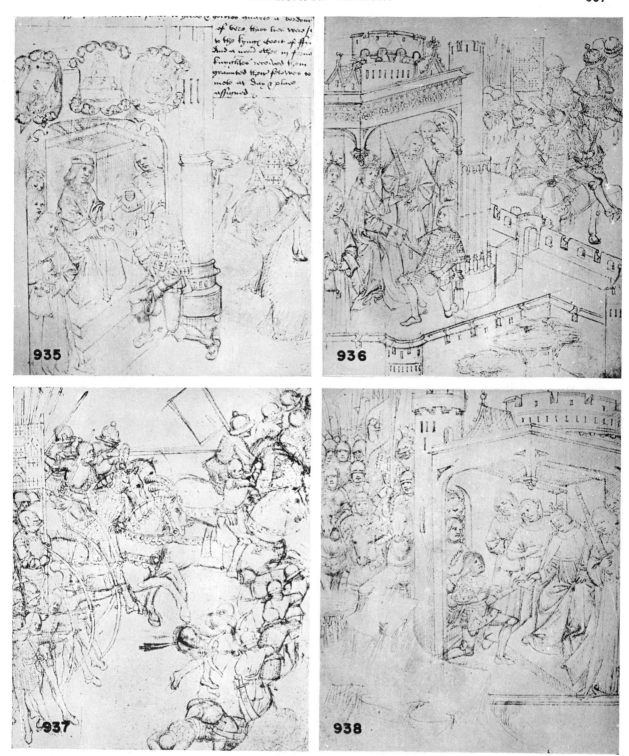

935

936

937

938

of a feudal lord) of both factions are rewarded by
Henry VII's Tudor collars of red and white roses
combined. But it is still in feudal use that the first
real uniforms appear. It is Stow again who tells us
that Richard Nevill, in 1458, had "600 men, all in
red jackets, embroidered with ragged staves before

and after" who were "lodged in Warwick Lane; in
whose house there was oftentimes 6 oxen eaten at a
breakfast, and every tavern was full of his meat; for
he that had any acquaintance in that house might
have there as much of sodden and roast meat as he
could prick and carry upon a long dagger."

939

940

941

939. XVc. English. (Eton College Chapel.)

Amoras sells his wife to the devil.

A great deal of English wall-painting was destroyed by the Parliamentary armies.

Anthony Wood of Oxford* said: "The pictures of prophets, apostles, saints, etc., that had been painted on the back-side of the stalls in Merton college choir, in various and antique shapes, about the beginning of the reign of King Henry VII were daubed over with paint, by the command of the usurpers, about 1651, to the sorrow of various men that were admirers of ancient painting." Brass plates with inscriptions were torn away from gravestones; Wood failed to shame the despoilers, but as he says with satisfaction, "A. W. had before this time transcribed them, which were afterwards printed."

Standard Italianate male costume of Europe at the turn of the century.

* Life and Times of Anthony Wood, Antiquary of Oxford, ed. A. Clark, Oxf. Hist. Soc. 1891-1900, 5 vols.; vol. I, p. 309.

940. XVc. 1488. English. (London, Nat. Port. Gall.)

Lady Margaret Beaufort (Tudor), Countess of Richmond and Derby.

Henry VII's pious and well-educated mother (1445-1509), founder of Christ's and St. John's Colleges at Cambridge, and of the Lady Margaret professorships of divinity at Oxford and Cambridge, took a vow of celibacy in 1504, after being three times widowed.

Her cream-colored French hood, embroidered in light brown, and veiled in black, is worn over a white cap; black wimple edged in white; dark red gown with gray fur cuffs.*

941. XVc. 1491. English. (Durham, Hexham Priory.) Freestone.

Rowland Leschman, Prior.

A prior was the head of a house of Canons Regular; they were secular clergy, attached to cathedrals and their colleges, and receiving a share of the funds of the institution, while retaining their own property. They lived a modified monastic life, but became increasingly non-resident; and might, especially among the lower orders marry.† Leschman was a "Black Canon." A contemporary XVIc. account says that an English Canon Regular "dressed in violet like the rest of the clergy." He wears a hooded, sleeveless, semi-circular cape and white, pleated rochet, over a cassock, probably fur-lined.

942-43. XVc. 1488. English. (Norfolk, Stokesby Church.) Brass.

Edmund Clere, knight, and Elizabeth his wife.

While many of the finest monumental brasses were of Flemish make, imported sheet-brass was used in local manufacture at Ipswich, Lincoln, and as in this brass, at Norwich.

The Cleres, who appear throughout the Paston letters, married many Elizabeths. Sir John Fastolf's sister, who married Sir Philip Braunch had a daughter, Elizabeth. She, by her 1st husband, John Clere, had 2 sons: Robert, who married the Paston's beloved cousin Elizabeth, and had a son, Sir Robert; and Edmund, the name of whose wife does not appear in the Paston letters.

This may well be that couple, though he died in 1463; since his mother survived to 1492 his wife may have outlived him, and the brass thus be of a later date.

Edmund wears a large visored salade with beaver (chin protection); convexly ridged armor with unusual shoulder, elbow and thigh plates; and a collar of roses.

Elizabeth's gown retains its XVc. length in front, but is assuming a XVIc. severity of line, as its neck

942   943

becomes squarer and shows the material of the kirtle in front. Her headdress is becoming a hood, the front band rising in a gabled peak at the forehead.

As early as 1449, Margaret Paston asks her husband that he "wyld bye a zerd (yard) of brode clothe of blac for an hood fore me of xliiijd or iiijs a zerd, for there is nether gode cloth ner gode fryse (frieze?) in this twn." In 1454, she prays that he "woll vowchesawf to remembr to purvey a thing for my nekke, and to do make my gyrdill." No necklace appears in her long will of 1482, but she leaves to her daughter-in-law "a purpill girdill harneised with silver and gilt"; to her daughter Anne, "my best corse girdill blewe harneised with silver and gilt"; and to Agnes Swan, her "servaunt, my muster develys (gray wool) gown, furred with blak, and a girdell of blak harneised with silver gilt and enamelled." In the inventory of Agnes Paston's plate, the girdles are identified by the name of the goldsmith from whom they were ordered.

The gowns which the ladies describe or ask for, are of "a goodly blue, or else a bright sanguine," murrey, black, green, violet or gray. The men mention murrey, blue, French russet, tawny, black and puce (furred with white lamb); one sends for a new vestment of white damask, from which he will make an arming doublet "thow I sholde an other time gyff a longe gown of velvett ffor another vestment." The men repeatedly send for hose-cloth, black, or of "holiday colors."

---

* Mrs. Reginald Lane Poole: *Catalogue of Oxford Portraits,* 3 vols., Clarendon Press, Oxford, 1925.

† "The Saxon priests had known no rule of celibacy. About the time of the Conquest, Hildebrand's dreaded decree began to find its way into England, and by the XIVc. it had been a long-established rule that no priest should marry. But the old custom never died out completely among the parish clergy, though their partners were now in the eye of the law mere concubines. . . . Priests brought up their children without fear, if not without reproach."—G. M. Trevelyan: *Eng. in the Age of Wycliffe.*

From Cotman: *Sepulchral Brasses of Norfolk* (942-43).

944

944. XVc. Spanish. (Solsona, Museo Diocesano.)
Last Supper.

The usual mediaeval seating along one side of a
long trestle table with one's back safe against a wall.
Knives and serving spoons are the only implements.
Wooden trenchers are used for cutting and eating
portions of meat, but food and drink are served in
superb Spanish pottery instead of the plate of the
rest of well-to-do Europe. Plates are scraped onto a
handsome tile floor for the dogs which lie waiting
beneath.

**945-46. Mid-XVc. Spanish, Catalonian. (Barcelona, Ca-
talonian Art Museum.)**
Father Garcia de Bernabarre (?) .
Banquet of Herodias (945); detail (946).

The costume of XVc. Spanish nobility was strongly influenced by French court fashions, and from
second third XVc., by Italian styles. A comparison
of these illustrations with the garments of Queen
Isabella and Joanne the Mad, will show regional
Spanish modes retained at the end XVc. in garments
which exhibit the XVIc. conventual trend. We will

see there these same extremely wide shirt sleeves, not
laced or strapped into puffs, but falling free through
the slit sleeve of the forearm; they will pass out of
use in the XVc. But in the bell-shaped, stiffened
underskirts (*farthingale, vertugale*) of these dresses,
and in the great importance of the long V-openings
of the bodice, with their display of the patterned
undershirt, and (in the case of ungirded gowns) in
the long, spreading V of the front openings, can be
discovered the genesis of the peculiarly Spanish fashions which will affect all European dress in another
century.

The padded edges of the bodice opening, to which
the sleeves are laced at the shoulders, will become the
characteristic roll, sewn into the armseye, between
shoulder and sleeve, of the following century.

In all these Spanish women's costumes, we notice
the complete absence of the extravagant outer-gown
sleeve; sleeves are largely of the close doublet type.
The extravagance of the Spanish sleeve is expressed
in the spill of the (frequently) patterned shirt from
some point in the lower arm.

945

946

The skirt, as in Italy, is rarely so long in front as to need holding up.

947-49. Mid-XVc. Spanish, Catalonian. (Barcelona, Catalonian Art Museum.)

Master of S. Quirse.

Retable of St. Clara and St. Marguerite; and detail.

Gentlemen and ladies, priests and pages, in these illustrations, wear costume of the French court type: padded shoulders; high doublet collars; and footwear. The wood-soled piked shoes of one page are identical with those shown in the Chronicles of Hainault; the other wears boots cut high at the knee and handsomely stitched.

The pages illustrate the difference in form between Spanish cropped hair and that of Italy and France.

The saint who kneels while she is being tonsured wears a short circular cape, which we see on other Spanish women of last half XVc. (see Ills. 951, 958).

950. XVc. Spanish, Catalonian. (Barcelona, Catalonian Art Museum.)

Master of St. George.

Retable of the Savior: detail.

951. XVc. Spanish, Catalonian. (Lerida Museum.)

Unknown Master.

Detail of retable.

952. Last quarter XVc. Spanish, Catalonian. (Madrid, Private Collection.)

Unknown master of the School of Lérida.

Detail of retable.

Spanish women's necklines though extremely varied in cut, remain comparatively high; but as necklines, all over Europe, become squarer, the top of the shirt becomes more important. Elsewhere the shirt is white and full, the rather horizontal neckline embroidered in color and metal. Only in Spain do we find these shirts made of stuffs in the bold striped patterns long characteristic of that country. The fullness of Spanish shirts is shown in the sleeves rather than in the body of the garment, and the shape of the shirt at the neck shows great variation, always in relation to that of the neckline of the gown with which it is specifically designed to be worn. The maid drawing water at the well wears the loose ends of her shirt-sleeves knotted.

Heads are covered more than in Italy, less extravagantly than in France. Close hood (central figure) is worn, also, by Mendoza's wife (954) under her huge crimped turban.

Cord and bead necklaces like these are seen in the last decades of XVc., particularly in Italy.

From Zervos: *Catalan Art* (947-49.)

953-54. XVc. 1455. Spanish. (Marquis of Santillana.)
Jorge Inglés, or his School. Iñigo Lopez de Mendoza and his wife.

955. XVc. Spanish. (Madrid, Nat. Gall.)
Letters of Ferdinand Bolea to the Kings of Aragon, Castile, and Portugal.

Don Carlos of Aragon, Prince of Viana (1421-61).
Viana was a charming and cultivated prince, who
lived much in Italy because of the enmity of the stepmother by whom he was poisoned upon his return
to Spain after the Catalan revolt.

956. XVc. 1455. Spanish. (Monastery, Sopetran.)
School of Jorge Inglés.
Panel: of Iñigo Lopez de Mendoza (Ills. 953-54).
His name implies that the painter of these pictures
was an **Englishman.**

From the five children of Iñigo Lopez de Mendoza,
Marquis of Santillana, d.1453, and his wife, daughter
of the Grand Master of Santiago, were descended
many of the greatest families in Spain: Velasco, Mendoza, Guzman, Medina Sidonia, and Olivares.

Mendoza and his attendant, like the prince of
Viana, wear typically French garments of mid-XVc.:
chaperon with streamer, or conical hat; padded
shoulders; high doublet collar; precious chains with
emblems; magnificent belts with pouches; and point-

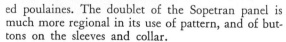

ed poulaines. The doublet of the Sopetran panel is much more regional in its use of pattern, and of buttons on the sleeves and collar.

It is interesting to compare the way in which the skirt of the Mendoza lady is set onto a low waistline, with the ribbed effect obtained in quite different ways, on the skirts of the attendants in the Ill. 951. Her full sleeve tightens toward the wrist, where it widens suddenly into a little circular, falling cuff.

All these illustrations show floors of decorated Spanish tiles; braziers and tables of wrought iron; and beds set on a raised platform, over which is

spread a specially woven thin carpet, the edges of which just reach the floor, such as are still used in Spain.

957. XVc. Spanish, Castilian. (Chicago, Deering Coll.)
Girard Master.
St. Sebastian.

The saint might be almost any youth of the late XVc., except for the narrowing cuff of his short sleeve, the hanging end of shirt sleeve, and his footwear. The shoes of Spanish men of this period show delightful variations and combinations of cut and color; I regret that we have not space to show more.

958. XVc. Spanish, Catalonian. (Barcelona Cathedral.) *M. Nadal.*

Retable of Saints Cosmas and Damian.

The lady wears the swelling turbans which we see in Italy and Germany, and upon the Lopez de Mendoza lady; skirt tucked, not held up, as in France, and with a square train; cape (see Ills. 947, 951); width of sleeve tucked into cuff.

959. XVc. 1460. Spanish. (Metropolitan Museum.) *Catalonian School.*

Salome with the Head of St. John.

With a French horned headdress, Salome wears

earrings (see XIVc. Sp.); sleeves of her gown are of the male doublet type, with a line of fur where the padding would end; train square. The tabard-like overgarment with tippets in front, worn by the queen, is often seen in Catalonian paintings.

Meat was brought to table on platters, but was still eaten from trenchers of bread (Fr. *tranche*—slice), with a knife as the only implement, even in a great Spanish household, hung with brocade and floored with beautifully painted tiles. These were originally used in wall decoration, but have descended to the floor.

960. XVc. Spanish. (Barcelona, Catalonian Art Museum.)
Unknown Master.
Retable of the Virgin and Child.

961-68. Last quarter XVc. Spanish. (Burgos, Brotherhood of the Knights of Santiago.)
Books of the Knights of Santiago.
Equestrian portraits of eight kings.

Three crusading military and religious orders were established in Spain during the XIIc. The Knights of St. James (Santiago) of Compostella wore red cloaks, bearing the lily-hilted sword of St. James; and those of Alcántara and Calatrava, the cross-fleury, in red and green, respectively.

The eight kings, wearing mail shirts with short sleeve characteristic of Spanish knights, may be compared with the knights in Ill. 984, in respect to the late XVc. use of plumes, and of words, decoratively.

969. XVc. Spanish, Catalonian. (Lerida Museum.)
Espalargues.
Retable, from Viella.

970. XVc. Spanish. (Madrid, Lestieri Coll.)
Alfajarin Master.
St. Vincent and St. Lawrence.
Large, heavy brocades and decoration of Spanish vestments (see Ills. 729, 751).

971. XVc. Spanish, (Madrid, Royal Palace.)
Att. to *Bermejo.*
Queen Isabella.
Isabella, "la Catolica," d.1504, the pious **Queen** who undertook personally to underwrite Columbus' explorations, and whose decisive intelligence was responsible for much of Spain's future greatness, wears a gauze hood over a small cap, its ends caught together and finished by a heavy Renaissance pendant,

in a manner which we shall see in later Spanish use, quite independent of headdress. The yoke which fills in the square neck of her severe dress is embroidered with the emblems of her personal inheritance of Leon.

972. End XVc. Spanish. (Chantilly, Conde Mus., ms. 1339.)
Devocionario de la Reyna Da. Juana, by *Marcuello.*
Ferdinand and Isabella, with their daughter, Joanne the Mad, mother of the Emperor Charles V, and Queen of Castile in her own right.

Mother and daughter wear gowns with the severe lines and square necks of the transition period, over the stiffened Spanish bell-skirt; and with the immense Spanish shirt sleeve pouring out of a close inner sleeve.

973. XV-XVIc. Spanish. (Madrid, Prado.)
Juan Flamenco; also att. to *Franc. Gallegos.*
Beheading of St. John.

To accommodate the bell shape of the stiffened underskirt, in Spain, the overskirt had either to be draped or slashed. In this center front line, its edge reinforced with embroidery, and showing the decoration which overlaid the horizontal stiffening beneath, we have the foundation of the Spanish skirt, and later Elizabethan costume.

The great bound pig-tail, falling from a tiny cap, appears in many Spanish pictures, and in Italian portraits as well, such as Botticelli's Port. of a Young Woman (K. F. Mus., Berlin), Piero della Francesca's Port. of a Young Woman (Pitti, Florence), and Sforza portraits (Ills. 783, 784).

Clogs, analogous to these very high, jewelled ones, will be seen on Carpaccio's Venetian **courtesans.**
The enormous shirt sleeve receives varied treatment

here: it even assumes the puff of an upper doublet sleeve, and pours out of a superimposed lower doublet sleeve.

974. XVc. 1420. German. (Frankfort-on-Main, Historical Museum.)

Middle Rhenish School.

Garden of Paradise.

Women in domestic dress: bareheaded; kirtle, often belted low and bloused.

Knight: new bag-sleeve; gambeson, growing shorter-waisted; V-back, vertically quilted, over chain shirt with dagged fringe of mail.

Man at tree: short circular capes and hoods, less worn elsewhere than in Germany, where interest in dagging persists. Huge circular cuffs (see Ill. 791), capable of concealing hand.

Compare these and Ills. 976-79 with Ills. 824-25 and Color Plate, No. 3, for application of leaves and petals, derived from dagging; usage which persists into last quarter XVc.

975. XVc. 1425. German. (Passau, Niedernburg Convent.)

Lower Bavarian School.

Queen Gisela of Hungary, as Abbess of the Convent.

Garments of an important, elderly lady of first half XVc.: crown over wimple and veil with the crimped, *kruseler,* edge characteristic of German costume to end first half XVc.

BEGINNINGS OF ENGRAVING, XVc.

With packs of cards begins a new era in illustration: engraving.

Wood engravers had worked in Germany since XIVc. During XVc. they provided block-letters and illustrations to be inserted into hand-written books, as the demand outstripped the productive capacity of the monasteries. In addition to "block-books," they produced illustrations of fables, biblical history, dances of death, to be given away by the rich or sold by the church.

Next came packs of cards for various games. 1460 is the first definite date which can be given to any known pack but there is reason to believe that the Master of the Playing Cards was producing before 1466; and the importation of playing cards into Venice had been prohibited in 1441.*

Many artists of XV-XVIc. had been trained as goldsmiths, and were expert engravers; Daniel Hopfer, Hans Burgkmair the elder, and Jörg Sorg worked for the Augsburg armorers, as engravers and designers, and like Dürer, produced plates showing armor. The Cranachs, the Behams, George Pencz in Germany, Lucas van Leyden in the Netherlands, and Marcantonio Raimondi in Italy made plates which are especially valuable for costume information.

976-79. XVc. c. 1446. German-Swiss. (Dresden Library.) *The Master of the Playing Cards.*

An Austrian writer of first half XVc. says: "Everyone dressed as he pleased. Some wore coats of two kinds of material. Some had left the sleeve much wider than the right, wider even than the length of the whole coat, while others wore sleeves of equal width. Some again embroidered the left sleeve in various ways, with ribbons of all colors or with silver bugles threaded on silk strings. Some wore on the breast a kerchief of various colors embroidered with letters in silver and silk. Still others wore pictures on the left breast. Some had their clothes made so long that they could not dress or undress without assistance, or without undoing a multitude of small buttons dispersed all over the sleeves, the breast and the abdomen. Some added to their clothes hems of a different color; others replaced hems by numerous points and scallops. Everyone wore hoods until the former headdress of men had disappeared. Cloaks were hardly long enough to reach the hips."

The large beaver hats, the largest of which carried clusters of plumes and a scarf for binding (see *Roman de la Rose,* Ill. 906, and Ills. 785-787) are new in Germany, and will travel over Europe during last half XVc.

* A. M. Hind: *A History of Engraving and Etching,* Houghton, Mifflin Co., Boston, 1923.

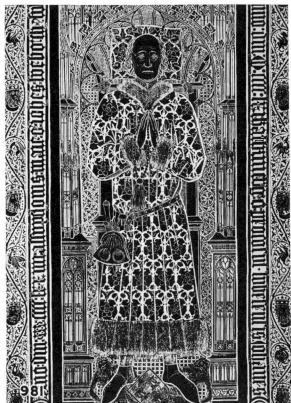

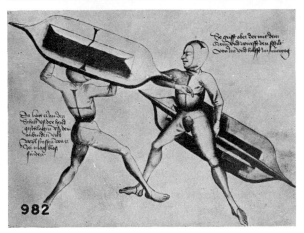

980. XVc. c. 1450. German-Swiss. (Metropolitan Museum, Print Room.)

Master E.S.

Sibyl and the Emperor Augustus.

This plate is the early work of a German, probably from Strassburg, who seems to have been trained in the Upper Rhine or Switzerland under the influence of the Master of the Playing Cards.

Immense white turbans, striped across the weft in metal, neutral colors and black, are seen on German-Swiss tapestries of mid-XVc., worn with brocade gowns in bold color.

The sleeveless *sorket* is not much worn after mid-XVc.; this example shows the wide, over-long sleeve which becomes attached to the closed surcoat of last half XVc. German-Swiss necklines of mid-XVc. are inclined to square in some way, without actually being square. Front fullness begins high; it is gathered or loosely pleated into the neckline, and the gown is immediately gored to great width. It may be belted high and bloused, full and loose, or it falls free in fantastic length and width. The front fullness tends to begin lower, as a panel of cartridge pleating, so that the upper bodice fits more closely. Meanwhile, the neck widens and rounds, exposing more shirt with its new embroidery; the skirt becomes more reasonable; but the sleeves grow longer and wider, and are often divorced from the material of the gown; they may be made of an entirely different material, or flow as a white shirt sleeve from a cap sleeve on the gown. (See Ills. 993, 994.)

Feet thrust into clogs, which are also worn by one of the men in the Master of the Playing Cards illustrations.

981. XVc. 1474. German. (Lubeck.)

Monumental brass:

John Luneborch, d.1474.

Lübeck, on the Baltic, one of the Free Cities and

head of the Hanseatic League, was governed by the aristocratic merchants who headed her great trading companies. Contact with Italy had spread over Europe such brocades as are used in this gown; typical of the fur-lined garments which developed out of the houppelande. Fine belt, with increasing numbers of handsome adjuncts.

982-83. XVc. 1467. Bohemian. (Duke of Saxe-Coburg-Gotha.)

Book of Fencing: Code de Gotha by *Hans Thalhofer.*

982. Fight with special shield, in the combat called "The Judgment of God."

983. Fight with pole-hammer.

These illustrations, from a book of instruction in all methods of single combat by the master-at-arms, Thalhofer (fl.1443-67)), clearly shows the attachment by *points* of the shortening doublet to the lengthening hose, with their early form of cod-piece; "dressing left" or "right" was a late refinement of tailoring. In the battle with war-hammers we see sleeves set into a deep armseye, and carried almost to the collarline, over the shoulder, after a German method of sleeve-cutting.

984-86. Last quarter XVc. German.

Housebook, by *The Master of the Housebook.*

No. 984 shows characteristically German form of women's dress of last quarter XVc.: very long and voluminous, fitting only around the shoulders; front fullness, loose or laid in cartridge pleats; sleeves tubular, but very wide and long, often gathered into armseye.

Increasing use of plumes: panache of horse, 984; male and female heads, 985-86.

Headdresses of wimple and coif are almost supplanted in Germany by last quarter XVc. by wound turban-like arrangements; often draped in spaghetti-like fringe (f. top, 985), which is also used on men's hats (bottom, 986); the ends of which are often individually knotted. A band under or around chin is often seen used by both men and women, particularly in German and Swiss examples: it is worn here (f. 986) and (984) by the man with cross-strapped pattens and short cape, the embroidered collar of which is set in (following the V-line which, in the jacket, used to permit the rise of the high doublet collar). Doublets are meanwhile becoming low-necked and laced across wide placards in the Italian

manner. The horn player (bottom, right) shows trunks strapped under instep, to be worn with shoes.

985. Costume of mounted men shows the influence of neighboring Italy, but the Burgundian fashions also persist in the enormously long pointed shoes and pattens, and in the short, wide loose jackets (lapped over, as seen in Ills. 785-787, 873-876). New are the capes and hoods of women (see Ill. 867), here seen in a German form: buttoned hood and cape, showing new interest in centrally massed pleats. Knight being armed for the tilt shows decorative use of letters and mottos (see text, Ills. 976-79), on caparison of horse, shield, and guard worn on left leg to prevent its being crushed at the barrier; tilting lance and German tilting helm of end XV-early XVIc.; arm guarded by gauntlet. Persistence in Germany of slittering (trappings of horse, whose rider wears a short coat with embroidered revers or scarf). Garlands in male hair. (See Ill. 994.)

986. Top row: women riding astride (until well into XVIc.), with *gebende* turbans, or plumes in the hair arrangement. Fool with fife and drum.

Second row: male hat bound under the chin; jacket closed by knotted points. Knight tilting shows leg on right side, not requiring a guard; deflecting flanges

987

988

989

990

991

of elbow pieces; poulaine sollerets. Male hats: fringed; set-in crown on puffed turban; horsetail plume.

987. XVc. 1491. German. (Metropolitan Museum, Print Room.)
Der Schrein od' Schatzbehalten, Nuremberg, 1491, illustrated by *Michael Wohlgemut.*

Wohlgemut's woodcut is the first engraved representation of a coach (see Ill. 574); it is still much easier to turn the three horses than the rigid wheels.

The large turbaned and fur-brimmed hats worn indoors by women and men are exchanged, in travelling, for small hoods or hats over bound chins.

988. e. XVIc. German. (Brussels.)
Germanic Customs, in German.

989-90. 1494-5. German. (Frankfort-on-Main, Art Institute.)
Albrecht Dürer. Costumes of Nuremberg and Venice.

Dürer made his first Italian trip at 22; in other drawings of Venetian costume made on this trip (especially a front and back view, in the Albertina, Vienna) Dürer shows similar little flat hats set on the crown of a veiled head, with flowing locks in front of the ears; the same wide-necked, short-waisted bodice; longer and more elaborately cut out and puffed sleeves; the same two immense buttons closing the skirt front; and great feet in the bundled-up form of patten.

To his own observations during 6 years of travel in Europe in the last decade of the XVIc., the Englishman Fynes Moryson added in his "Itinerary"* a compendium of "the opinions of old writers": "In apparrell the Italian women are said to be neate and grave (only the Venetians shew their necks and

_____
* Four vols., James MacLehose, for the Univ. of Glasgow, 1907.

breasts naked), the French light & variable, the Spaniards proud, the Germans foolish (perhaps because they weare extremely straight sleeves on their armes, and guard one and the same gowne with many and divers coloured guards), the Flemmings fine (no doubt they, and especially the Brabanders, excell for white and fine linnen, and for generall comliness of their garments). The Spanish women are said to be painted, the Italians lesse painted, the French seldome painted, and sometimes the Germaine Virgins never that I observed (except those of Prussen have perhaps borrowed this vice from the Muscovites their neighbors)."

991. XVc. 1495-1500. German. (Vienna, Albertina.)
A. Dürer. Knight in armor on horseback.

Partially armed, with leather jerkin, hose, and sock-boots. Late XVc. salade, very much extended in back; monogrammed (reaching end of its use). Large pauldrons of late German Gothic armor, ribbed in the

oncoming Maximilian style; plate protection of arms and of legs to knee only.

992. XVc. 1498. German. (Madrid, Prado.)

A. Dürer. Self-portrait at 26.

One of the handsomest of all pictures of the velvet-banded, German version of the Italian-inspired male dress of the turn of the century: gray, black, with gold-embroidered shirt.

More is shown, of a more beautifully pleated and embroidery-edged shirt, in Germany than anywhere else, whether its neckline rises into a standing collar of embroidery, or remains horizontal above a horizontal doublet neckline.

The extremely long hair which Dürer shows himself wearing for a decade or more is exceptional in Germany, and may be laid to the influence of his Italian trip.

993. Late XVc.-e. XVIc. German. (Dortmund, Propstei-Kirche.)

H. and V. Dunwege. Holy Kindred: altarpiece, wing.

Long, loose, full German gowns: variety of collars on rather high necklines; front fullness, from neck, or by inset cartridge pleats (in which case, belt hangs low, unrelated to the tacking which indicates natural waistline); long full sleeves. Headdresses of swathed turban type; or bound about, or falling over a swelling foundation.

994. End XVc. German. (Gotha Museum.)

Master of the Housebook, d.1505. Two Lovers.

Fine goldsmith's work fastens the rows of delicate chain, which maintain extremely wide neck-openings, and forms eyelets and tips for the cords at neck and sleeves lacings. These have replaced the important and precious belts of XIV-XVc.

Embroidery in red, black, gold or silver is used

on the bateau necks of exquisitely pleated full skirts, and ladies' headdresses.

Italianate male costume, with flowing garlanded hair. Lady's sleeves, spreading wider to the wrist, would hang below the knees, and conceal the hands if not pushed up. The pink she holds is the sign of an engagement; if red, of a newly performed marriage, a favorite time for having portraits painted.

995. End XVc. South German

Israhel van Meckenem, d.1503. The Feast of Herodias.

An immense mass of information about the transitional period in costume is given by this artist, who shows the influence of a stay in the Netherlands.

Arch, upper l.: Solider with pole-axe; doublet has appropriated the dependent sleeve of the jacket, in the form of completely unusable streamers, fastened beneath padded upper part of sleeve.

Gallery, l.: Men; buttoned hood; new slashed and laced bonnet.

Musicians, c.: All wear same livery badge; the new bonnets; new wide-toed shoes cut low around the heel; as well as old-fashioned poulaines. L.: interesting tight sleeve, of doublet-type, cut in one with dependent sleeve of jacket-type; slash exposing shirt at elbow. C.: horizontal slashes; long sleeve widening suddenly at cuff. R.: sleeve tight below elbow; full and slashed above, to show full puffed sleeve of shirt.

Balcony at r.: Man, new coat with lapels; long wrinkled tubular sleeves. M. (at r. edge) wears long coat, buttoned down back; separately cut skirt with clustered back-fullness; sleeve set in deep arms-eye.

Dancers, l. to r.: Ladies' gowns of 4 main types.

German: loose, with clustered cartridge pleats; long wide tubular sleeve on new coat with new lapelled fur collar; accompanied by turban.

Burgundian court: separate bodice and skirt; wide, low neck; important belt under breasts; accompanied by hennin.

German-Flemish: tight sleeves; long, wide opening laced across plastron; accompanied by a hennin, which is increasingly like a hood.

Flemish: separate bodice and skirt; relatively high necked; wide sleeves, showing undersleeves, and sometimes shirt-sleeves; belt not necessarily at waistline, and relatively less important than appended accessories.

Men, c. to r.: short Italianate jacket, sometimes with revers; laced or tied across plastron, which may be slashed. Shoes, pointed or with rounding toes.

Codpiece, fastened with knotted points. Long gored coat, with deeply set in, wide sleeves.

996. XVc. S. German. (Metropolitan Museum, Print Room.)

Israhel van Meckenem. The Lovers.

Woman in much more bourgeois costume than any shown in previous illustrations. Enclosing headdress and gown with the new-lapped-over closing caught together with the new and exciting common pin. Her separate outer sleeve, set very low, is probably pinned on, too. Overskirt pinned up in front, probably permanently. (See *Roman de la Rose*: Ill 906.) Girdle hung with knife, pouch, and housewife's keys. Piked shoes and pattens, but her bedroom slippers, under the platform, have the newer round toe. Door latch closed by a knife, which everyone carries, and uses at table.

Culture Moves North: XVI Century

XVI Century Background

The XVIc. was, like our own, a crucial century, during which the way of life of the next 350 years was established. It was a century of new freedoms, and of consolidation of power.

The discoveries of Africa, the New World, and ocean routes to the Far East coincided with the break-up of mediaeval restrictions. The religious and intellectual freedoms of the Reformation and increased literacy had been aided by the invention of printing.

The Black Death had doubled the wealth of the remaining population, and helped in the alteration of the old craft guilds into capitalist employers and traders belonging to the merchant livery companies, divided from the journeyman workers.

The increasing temporal power of the Papacy had a stabilizing effect. Rival city-states were welded into nations, with economies planned for commercial competition.

France, a howling wilderness at the end of the 100 Years War, recovered rapidly. An annual tax had been imposed by Jacques Coeur for the maintenance of Charles VII's standing army. The recalcitrant feudal nobility flocked to serve in the crown's cavalry, and were tied to the court for advancement. Henry IV used this regular income to improve internal communications, trade, industry and agriculture. The supremacy of the King was now well established, in a prosperous France.

The rulers of Spain, Portugal and the Empire made the mistake of deliberately hoarding, for their own aggrandizement, the riches brought by their explorations. While the condition of the lower classes was being improved elsewhere, their peoples were further repressed by inflation; the emigration of industry was not discouraged; and many valuable talents were lost, by persecution, to the Dutch. Repressive measures lost the Empire its possessions in the Low Countries, and its spectacular rise ended in failure.

The prosperity of Italy, South Germany and the Hanseatic cities was gone with the abandonment of the old Mediterranean trade routes from the Near East. Their bankers were weakened by their alliance, as money lenders, to the sterile financial policies of Spain and the Empire. The port of Antwerp took over the European distribution of goods brought from overseas by the Portuguese, until the calamities of 1585. By XVIIc. the Dutch, hospitable to refugees from Spanish persecution, controlled most of the profits of the Portuguese trade, and Amsterdam became a great industrial and commercial city.

The English, lacking the overseas riches of Spain, carefully developed their modest natural resources and their talents of seamanship, and encouraged the establishment of manufactures by refugee technicians, as the Dutch had done. Under the capitalism which Spain had rejected, her Protestant enemies throve and outdistanced her.

Development of Dress: German-Swiss Influence, 1510-1545

The Italian influences of end XVc. are superseded in e. XVIc. by German-Swiss fashions; these, in turn, give way to Spanish styles, toward mid-XVIc.

The slashed and puffed square width of German-Swiss costume influenced male garments, in particular, and invaded even gloves and shoes. English costume makes the least use of patterned materials, striped and slashed hose.

Men's Dress: The doublet and jerkin remain short-waisted, close-fitting, and difficult to differentiate. The low neck of the doublet rises and squares, finally assuming a collar. Sleeves are wide and slashed, but close at the wrist, and tend to separate into upper and lower divisions, analogous to those of the hose. *Picadils*: tabbed edge, below waist, or around armseye, last half XVIc. Jerkin, sleeved or not, assumes a square collar with notched lapels. *Bases* shorten and become less rigid. Gowns are of various lengths, with sleeves like those of jerkins; there are few cloaks.

The shirt's neckline rises, assumes a collar and delicate cord ties; the collar heightens, turns over, and takes on a gauffered edge, from which the Elizabethan ruff will develop.

Hose are divided into upper- and nether-stocks: i.e. breeches or *canions* (much slashed and puffed); and stockings (seldom so decorated, except among the Swiss soldiers); fastened together. Codpieces, *braguettes,* are increasingly evident. Garters appear; less practical than decorative.

Shoes: the short, wide, backless slippers become narrower, rounder and higher at the instep; slashed and jewelled.

The square-pinched, biretta-like bonnets, and caps, soon become relegated to the use of scholars and ecclesiastics and the elderly. They are supplanted by flat-brimmed, plumed bonnets; the plumes become reduced in number, and the nicked brim tends to droop, as it becomes narrower.

Bobbed hair commences to be cropped in the French manner, about 1520; and men, formerly clean-shaven, begin to wear moustaches and beards, which become square and wide; then lengthen.

With the increasing use of swords and daggers, diagonally slung, in the everyday dress of gentlemen, there is a decrease in the importance of chains, which tend to become cords or scarves, carrying a pendant. Increasing use of precious tags, *aiglettes;* rings.

Women's Dress: Women's gowns changed little until end first quarter XVc., and were less affected by German ways than men's clothing. Necklines arch and rise into yokes, and to high collars, c. 1540, when shoulder capes with collars appear, especially in Germany.

Outer sleeves widen into a great funnel, with a fur lining turned back into a cuff. Undersleeves are frequently interchangeable and have finished edges, instead of an outerseam, tied at intervals across puffs of shirtsleeves. The shirt collar rises, assuming a pleated edge; and shoes alter their form, paralleling male usages.

The skirt becomes of ground length, bell-shaped; and towards end first half XVIc. takes on an inverted-V front opening.

Hair retains its center front part, under regionally differentiated hoods, and the caps of Germany, Italy and Spain.

Goldsmiths' work appears in many, dependent forms: girdles, at hip line, with hanging pomanders; fur pieces with jewelled snouts and claws; aiglets.

Development of Dress: Spanish Influence, 1545-1610

The rigid and formal fashions of Spain begin to affect all European dress, after first third XVIc. The somber colors of the early part of the period become paler and brighter at the end. Lace is introduced into France from Italy in 1533 by Catherine de' Medici; its use increases enormously. Male costume seems effeminate, as women's clothing grows more masculine.

Male: Collars mount; waists lengthen, becoming corset-like with stiffenings. Padding, *bombast,* alters the form of the torso into the *peascod* belly of the last quarter XVIc., accepted by both doublet and jerkin.

Sleeves, with *picadills* or a roll at the armseye, remain close, may have a dependant sleeve, and are supplemented by swelling leg-o'-mutton forms in last quarter XVIc.

Skirts of body garments diminish to picadills, as the upper hose shorten and are hugely padded at the hips, with their outer fabric vertically slit into *panes.* There are also loose, unpadded forms of upper hose, usually longer (*slops, galligaskins*). Close-fitting knee-breeches, *canions,* which extend below trunk-hose (trunk slops, round hose, French hose) appear; as do other forms of breeches, caught at the knee (*venetians*); or cut off like our shorts. Codpiece disappears during last quarter XVIc.

Slashing appears in small formal patterns, or long slits, *panes.* It is much used on leather: buff military jerkins; long, close, laced or buckled boots, and shoes are cut in tiny punctured (*pinked*) patterns.

Many capes are used; long and short; with and without sleeves. Gowns of all lengths. A tabard-like jacket called *mandilion* is often worn slung across the body.

Knit stockings come into use and are clocked, by last quarter XVIc. Garters become more elaborate.

Shoes, natural in form, cover the instep; frequently light in color. In last quarter XVIc. a tongue develops, under straps from ankle, laced across instep through eyelets; from the bow develops a ribbon rosette, later made of lace. Slippers are worn indoors, and mules, *pantoufles,* protect the shoe outdoors. Cork platforms rise in thickness under the heel; in last quarter XVIc., heels appear on shoes for the first time, and toes begin to square.

The gathered or fluted edge of the turned-down collar (*falling band*), is elaborated into many forms of pleated, starched and wired ruffs, which tend to fall again in first quarter XVIIc.; matching bands or ruffles at wrist.

Hats vary enormously in form and by country. The gathered crown of the flat hat rises, often to great height, as its brim diminishes. Broad-brimmed felt hats appear, as well as the tiny turbans of the French court. Emphasis on hat band.

Cropped hair lengthens, end XVIc. Beards commonly worn; variety of forms in last quarter XVIc. Guarded rapier is slung from a narrow flexible belt. Gauntlet gloves common, last quarter XVIc.

Masks worn. Men's ears pierced for one or two earrings. Much jewelry.

Female: Women's costume, like men's, is characterized by higher necklines, longer and more rigid bodies, padded hips, and the use of picadills and rolls.

The bodice is increasingly pointed at the bottom, and corset-like. Arched square of bosom filled with high-necked tucker; finished by a ruff, last half XVIc. Bare bosom, without tucker, last half XVIc.

The turned-back funnel sleeve is discarded, last half XVIc. All varieties of male sleeves are worn by women. The close sleeve of last quarter XVIc. may have a high, wide top. The hanging sleeve of end XVI-e.XVIIc. is elaborately shaped, slashed and trimmed; the under sleeve, in this case, matches the underskirt.

One-piece gowns, open, coat-like, and masculine, worn by upper classes. Similarly cut short jackets for outdoor wear.

Skirts, funnel-shaped, frequently with inverted V-opening; supported by Spanish farthingale, *vertugale,* last half XVIc., which aids display of pattern of underskirt. French roll support at hips, last quarter XVIc. alters silhouette from cone to wide cylinder. Ankle-length skirt worn around turn of century.

The French hood flattens across the top, then dips in the center. Its fall, when gauzy, is seen elaborately wired to frame the face. Bonnets and hats, identical with men's, much favored; small caps on the back of the head, last half XVIc., as hair tends to be dressed over rolls.

The hair at first mounts on either side of the part. Then the part is abandoned, as padding increases to an extent requiring the aid of artificial hair, in e.XVIIc. Pearls, jewels and feathers decorate the front expanse of hair; the back is reduced to a knot covered by a caul, to avoid interference with the high ruffs. With XVIIc. the hair at the sides tends to fall in loose locks.

The high-collared tucker opens and begins to spread in last half XVIc. As the tucker is reduced or abolished, the collar increases in width and height, and is starched or wired into a fan framing the face, or is drawn close about the neck in a cartwheel ruff, often seen above a bare bosom.

In Italy, necklines are generally lower, outside regions dominated by Spain, and the bodice is often padded into the male *peascod* belly of late XVIc.

Shoes, slippers and pantoufles like male varieties, but seldom seen.

Increased use of cosmetics and lace; pearls and earrings, hanging pomanders and mirrors; lace-edged handkerchiefs, masks; gloves, muffs; fur skins and scarves.

DEVELOPMENT OF GERMAN REGIONAL DRESS: XVIc.

The crown of Germany had never been entirely hereditary. The emperor-king was also chosen by regional rulers: originally the Archbishops of Mainz, Trier, and Cologne, the King of Bohemia, the King of Bavaria who was also the Count Palatine of the Rhine, the Duke of Saxony, and the Margrave of Brandenburg. During the XIIIc. interregnum, the princely families tended to subdivide into endless small principalities, allotted at the will of the regional rulers. From the time of the Golden Bull of 1335, the power of the Electors increased, over both the Emperor, and the non-electoral cities and princes. Germany was thus prevented from being united, as France will be, with the waning of feudal power, by her kings from Louis XI to Louis XIV.

In the course of the XVIc., bourgeois costume, particularly that of women, becomes strongly differentiated by provinces, even by cities, forming the basis for later regional peasant costume. As everybody climbs the ladder socially, the bourgeoisie tend to become gentry, and their codified costume is taken over by the well-to-do peasantry. The regional styles of their people are worn by rulers, upon occasion or in partial form. (See Ill. 1003, and Spanish, end XVc.)

German regional dress is a very complicated subject, best covered by Hottenroth: *Handbuch der Deutchen Tracht,* Stuttgart, 1892-6. His material was taken principally from Jost Amman; D. Meisner's *Cosmographia,* 1606; Vecellio's *Hab. ant. & mod.,* 1590; and Winkler's *Stammbuch.*

Fynes Moryson's *Itinerary,* vol. IV, p. 204-18, describes the costume of Germany, Switzerland, the Low Countries, Bohemia, Poland and Denmark in 1591-5; and p. 217-38, the dress of Italy, France, Turkey, Scotland, Ireland and England.

The ways of regional costume are like the spot-patterns of insect species: they spread and alter gradually across plains and waterways, cross with new-met forms, and are stopped abruptly by natural barriers. A brief summary can only be rough and full of contradictions, as a century of time works its changes. But as a biologist's child, who was called upon to make a good many such charts during childhood, I have found it very interesting to spot each appearance of certain characteristics, in the illustrations of this century, on sheer tracings which could be set over a map, and to see how they filtered or stopped on the expected geographical basis.

Speaking, then, very roughly, we can say that fine pleating is seen in a great semi-circle running from Holland, through Lippe, Frankfort and Franconia, Bavaria (Nuremberg), and Saxony (Meissen), and into Silesia. In Nuremberg and Meissen it is used in the greatest quantities, on both capes and upper skirts of plain material, which at Nuremberg are often caught up in front. At the lower part of this swinging geographical line, pleating is often combined with headdresses bound around the chin.

Nuremberg shows wide, square necks, which tend to become filled in with gathered shirts and yokes; and, around first third XVIc., great cart-wheel hats, the brims of which are often edged with ostrich plumes. These hats, with segmented color, or regularly caught decoration around the brim, are worn later, in a somewhat smaller form, in the middle Rhine Valley, around Frankfort, Heidelberg, and the Palatine.

The *heuke,* a cape flowing from the crown of the head and covering the body, is characteristic of the Low Countries, and is worn east to Bremen (where it is seen in the greatest variety, both of cape and top). In its pleated form, it is seen from Antwerp, up the Rhine and Main to Frankfort, and at Bremen. Its plain form appears from Holland to Bremen, and up to Cleves and Cologne. Something usually projects from the top of the *heuke.* On the plain cape, in Holland, Cleves, and Bremen, it was a long duck-bill in front; at Bremen, a long horn, curving upward, is set at the forehead of a pleated cape. A plate with a standing, tufted knob is set over both plain and pleated capes at Bremen; this plate follows the westward bend of the Wesser, and goes on to Cologne. There are also forms like inverted bowls with spikes. The edges of the *heuke* are wired out, in Belgium and Cologne, during the last half XVIc.

At Lippe, Westphalia, Frankfort, and east into Silesia, aprons are often finely pleated; but the aprons of the Rhine Valley are narrow strips, partly tucked in at the belt, in such a way that the corners stick out free below the waistline. At Heidelberg, the apron is folded lengthwise, and then in four sections across, the ironed creases utilized as decoration, as is sometimes done on white Flemish hoods. Both aprons and skirts are embroidered, or made of brocade or velvet to match the bodice, as well as made of linen.

Around Frankfort and in Westphalia the shoulder capes of Holland are much seen; in the Palatinate and the Alsatian side of the Rhine, short flaring jackets are worn with tiny plumed male bonnets and bell-shaped skirts without waist-fullness, often of brocade; like the Spanish coat-dress, these come into more general use, last quarter XVIc.

The yoked and often laced bodice runs from the Low Countries up the Rhine to Switzerland; through Frankfort, where its front decoration stresses a vertical or cross, rather than a horizontal, line; up into Westphalia and across to Saxony.

The furred and collared garments of Slavic costume affect clothing in the Baltic, Silesia, Bohemia, Austria and Bavaria, particularly at Salzburg and Augsburg: V-necks with wide-spreading revers running into high collars; fur-lined capes and jackets with great wide collars; wide headwear, often of fur; chins, ears and foreheads banded against the cold; full skirts, and, since this is the outer edge of the area in which pleating is much used, we find pleated skirts, capes, and aprons. Sheer pleating seems to replace fur, where warmth is no longer an absolute necessity, but where fashions are influenced by full, warm garments and the bulk and shagginess of fur.

The most common sleeve has a mounting cap at the shoulder, usually cut in one with the sleeve. This cap sleeve is sometimes pendant, especially at Augsburg; it is often cut off just below the shoulder, the lower sleeve being extremely close and of another material. The high cap is not often seen, however, with the square-necked bodices, and is less frequent with the V-necked, high-collared varieties. These bodices of the southeast usually have a dropped shoulder-line, finished to match the collar edge; and an under-sleeve of a different material, which if white, often emerges, full, from beneath the cap, and is gathered in again below the elbow into a tight forearm; this, if close fitting, is apt to be ornamented from the cuff-line. The bell-sleeve of XV-e.XVIc., beloved of Flanders, persisted longest in the costume of Cologne.

Moryson, late in the XVIc., found the Germans "of all . . . Nations least expencefull in apparrell, whether a man consider the small prices of their garments, or their long lasting. . . . Citizens and men of inferior ranke, weare coarse cloth of Germany, and only the richer sort use English cloth; and this cloth is commonly of a blacke or darke colour, and they think themselves very fine, if their cloakes have a narrow facing of silk or velvet. . . . The Gentlemen delight in light colours . . . and Italian silkes and velvets, but most commonly English cloth, for the most part of yellow or green colour." Swords (worn by gentlemen and doctors of civil law) "have plaine pommels to them, never gilded; and the scabbards (not excepting the Emperour) are alwaies of leather. . . . The Saxons instead of Swords carry Hatchets in their hands . . . and weare hanging daggers with massy sheathes of silver or iron." German men wore "shirt bands of coarse linnen, short and thicke, onely in Prussia I observed them to weare long ruffs, with rebatoes of wire to bear them up . . . but seldom made of fine . . . cambrick or lawne, but of their owne coarse linnen, such as I have often seene the Spaniards to weare. . . ." German "handkerchers are very large, and wrought with silke of divers light colours, with great letters signifying words . . . so as they seem more like wrought saddle clothes, than handkerchers."

The richest apparel in Germany Moryson found in Danzig, where men and women "without any decent distinction of degrees" wore silk and velvet; "and the women seem much prouder of apparrell than the men. . . . Daughters of Citizens and Merchants, as well married as unmarried . . . did weare chains of Pearle, worth 300-500 gulden" and "short cloakes . . . of silke or satten . . . and that of changeable or light colours with Petticoats and Aprons of like colours, but not so frequently of silke; and I have seene Virgines of ordinary ranke . . . daily weare Silke stockings."

Moryson found that German matrons in general wore high-necked gowns, very short ruffs set with "poking sticks as small as reedes," and little hats.

Virgins wore close linen sleeves, "for they esteem it the greatest grace to have the smallest armes, and their petticoates are guarded with some ten or more fringes or laces of silk or velvet, each fringe being of a different colour one from the other . . . as variable . . . as the Raine-bow.

"Citizens' wives put off their ruffes when they goe out of the house, covering their neckes and mouthes with a linnen cloth for feare of cold, and they weare great heavy purses by their sides with great bunches of keyes hanging by chaines of brasse or silver; and all generally, as well married women as Virgines, goe with bare legges; and I have seene a Virgine in Saxony, refuse a paire of silke stockings offered her of gift; and the maide servants and married women of the inferior sort weare no shooes except they goe out of the house, and a great part goe also abroade bare footed.

"The married women hide their naked feete with long gownes, but the maide servants wear short gownes, and girding them up into a roule some handfull under the wast about their hippes (especially in the lower parts of Germany) many times offend chast eyes with shewing their nakednesse, especially when they stoope for anything . . . and in those parts of Germany, the Citizens' wives, like our little children, weare red and yellow shooes, and guilded at the toes.

"In generall, it is disgracefull to married women or Virgines (excepting at Augsburg, and some other few cities) to goe out of doores without a cloake, which commonly is of some light stuffe, as Grogram, or the like, faced with some furres, and at Heidelberg they never goe abroad without a little basket in their hands, as if they went to buy something, except they will be reputed dishonest."

Married women's heads are always covered, with a piece of velvet, hat or cap, "according to the use of the Countrey, and very many weare such crosse-clothes or forehead clothes as our women use when they are sicke.

"In many places the ordinary Citizens' wives have their gownes made with long traines, which are pinned up in the house, and borne up by maid servants when they goe abroad, which fashion of old onely great Noblemen used with us: And in many cities, aswel the married as unmarried Women, weare long fardingales, hanging about their feete like hoopes, which our Women used of olde, but have changed to short fardingales about their hippes."

Moryson remarks on the sober-colored or black garments of the Netherlands, and the extremely fine linen. "All women in generall, when they goe out of the house, put on a hoyke or vaile which covers their heads, and hangs down upon their backs to their legges. The vaile in Holland is of a light stuffe or Kersie, and hath a kind of horne rising over the forehead, not much unlike the old pommels of our Womens saddles, and they gather the Vaile with their hands to cover all their faces, but onely the eyes: but the women of Flanders and Brabant weare Vailes altogether of some light fine stuffe, and fasten them about the hinder part and sides of their cap, so as they hang loosely, not close to the body, and leave their faces open to view, and those Caps are round, large, and flat to the head, and are in forme like our potlids . . . used in the Kitchin; And these women, aswel for these Vailes, as their modest garments . . . and for their pure and fine linen, seemed to me more fair than any other Netherlanders, as indeed they are generally more beautiful."

Swiss citizens wear "large, round caps" like those of English 'prentices, together with cloaks, "whereas with us they are onely used with gownes, yea, and Swords also (which seemed strange to be worn with caps)." He describes their loose, vari-colored pluderhose. "The married Women cover their heads with a linnen coyfe, and upon it weare such caps as the men do (which are broader than we used in England) and commonly weare a linnen crossecloth upon the forehead. . . . The Virgins goe bareheaded with their haire woven up, and used short cloakes. . . . All . . . are apparrelled like the Germans, and affect nothing lesse then pride in their attire."

The Bohemians dress like the Germans, "and delight in greene, yellow, and light colours, but more frequently weare silkes and velvets than the Germans, and also false jewels of their owne." They also wear black cloth "with many laces and fringes of light colours, each fringe differing in colour." Prague draws so many foreign ambassadors and Italian merchants, that "the Bohemians are more infected with forraigne fashions, than the Germans. The married Gentlewomen attire their heads like our Virgines, and in like sort beare up their haire on the forehead with a wier." Like Germans, they wear short cloaks, long farthingales, and trains. "Citizens wives weare upon their heads large gray caps, rugged like gray Connie skinnes, and formed like the hives of Bees, or little caps of velvet close to the head, of a dunne colour, with the hinder skirt (or hinderpart) cut off and open. And upon their legges they weare white buskins, wrought with velvet at the toes; but upon their armes they wear large sleeves, and contrary to the Germans, thinke them to be most comely."

By late XVIc. few German men or women "weare gold rings, pearles, or Jewels: but Bohemia yields false stones like the oriental precious stones, vet of small or no value"; (garnets, and the glass which they had learned from Venice to manufacture in the XIIIc.; we get from them our stones for theatrical jewelry today). Moryson was shocked to find gentlemen wearing these false stones and rings of gold-washed brass. Women were seldom permitted chains, but "their Earles (vulgarly called Graves) and their Knights, sometimes weare gold chains, made of extraordinary great linkes, and not going more then once about the necke, nor hanging downe further then the middle button of the doublet."

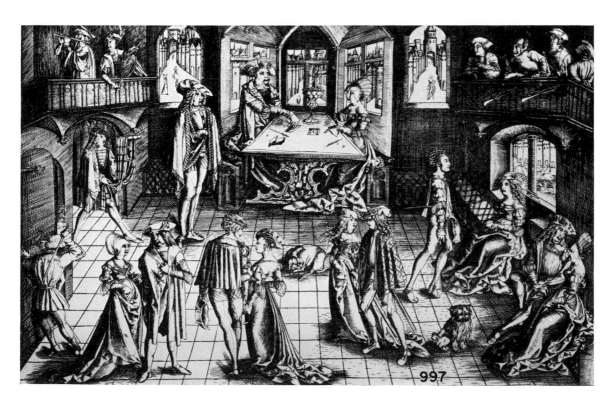

997. XVIc. German-Bavarian.

Master M. Z.

Dancing party.

This S. German engraving shows both types of male costume of the Transition period: newer, squarer, fur-collared garments; and the slender Italianate forms, with capes, circular or with dependent points, and trunk-like patterns differentiating top and leg of hose.

Elaborate puffing and slashing have invaded both m. and f. garments; but as yet, only on the exagger-atedly long, narrow sleeves. Both sexes wear the slashed bonnet, over hair done up in caul caps or flowing.

In Germany and the Netherlands, ladies' gowns will presently lose their trains, as they have already lost their loose fullness; they will retain their high-belted, widely cut bodice, though this will tend to be filled in with yokes (notice strap across back of shoulders, f., l. center); and the swelling headdresses worn well back on the head.

Shoes: round-toed, still ankle-high, slashed and tied. Beards.

998-99. First quarter XVIc. Alsatian.
(Morgan Lib., M. 399.)

Illuminated manuscript.
998. Gentry of Strassburg.
999. Peasants of Strassburg.

1000. XVIc. c. 1506. German.
(Brunswick, Ducal Mus.)

Lower Saxon School: altarpiece.
Mocking of Christ: detail of
center panel.

1001. XVIc. 1500-5. Dutch or Flemish. (Metropolitan
Museum.)

Unknown artist. Magdalena van Werdenberg, wife
of Jan, Count of Egmont.

Black and white costume of great distinction, in
velvet and the finest possible ermine. Simple Flemish
hood. The inner sleeve is rather loose and the shirt
sleeves are pushed up into transverse wrinkles; not
directed by the inner sleeve into becoming wrist
ruffles.

Balthazar Behem. The Behem Codex. XVIc. Polish.
(Cracow, Jagellonian Univ. Library.) Four plates from
the Behem Codex, the regulations of the guilds of Cracow,
were reproduced in color in "Vogue," for Dec. 1947;
therefore we merely indicate these easily available and
extremely valuable plates. They show the workrooms of
the artist's, shoemaker's, tailor's and cabinet maker's
guild members, with the tailors fitting customers, and the
shoemaker's wife taking the apprentice boys' mind off
their work.

1001

1002. First quarter XVIc. Flemish. (Metropolitan Museum, Bache Collection.)

Gerard David.

Nativity: side panel.

St. Vincent, in the robes of a deacon, stands behind the donatrice, whose coronet is set on her black Flemish hood. Orange-brown and silver brocade gown shows the convexly rising neckline, largely filled in, though not completely yoked in black velvet. The widening red inner sleeve, which funnels from the short sleeve-cap, originated from the white sleeve of the shirt.

1003. XVIc. 1502. German. (Meissen.) Monumental Brass.

Amelia, Duchess of Bavaria.

Costume of a widow of Meissen; bound head and chin; pleated cape with wide hanging bands.

1004. XVIc. 1517. German. (Meissen.) Monumental Brass.

Frederick, Duke of Saxony.

The breastplate of the bearded duke shows the fan-shaped flutings of the transitional period between Gothic and Maximilian armor; lengthening laminated tassets; broad toed sabatons; cross of Teutonic Knight on mantle.

1005-06. XVIc. 1504. German. (Frankfort-on-Main, Stadel Inst.)

J. Ratgeb. Claus and Margaret Stalburg.

1002   1003   1004

Claus' beaver is pinched into the angular shape seen in Flanders and W. Germany; it is worn at an angle, when set over a coif.

His rosary includes a pomander: *"pomme d'ambre"* (apple of ambergris)—a hinged, pierced ball, holding solidified perfume based on ambergris, civet or musk; used by both men and women, particularly in XV-XVIIc., to ward off infection or bad odors. In similar manner, Cardinal Wolsey held a clove-stuck orange during audiences.

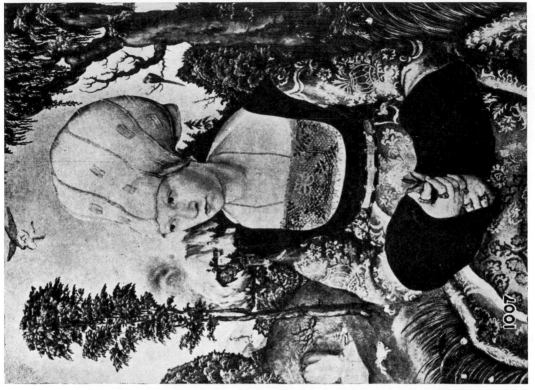

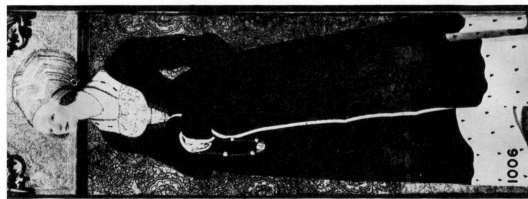

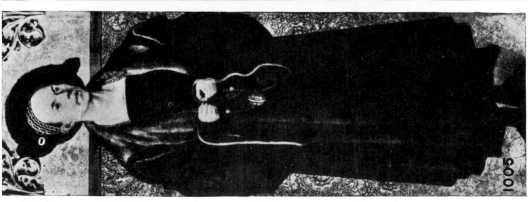

The gowns of the Cuspinian and Stalburg ladies are specifically German: extremely long, narrow sleeves; short-waisted, widely cut-out bodice, filled in by a plastron of magnificent and often jewelled embroidery, which is held in place by a scarf across the back of the neck; skirt of the new ground length. In the case of Margaret, this is extended into the bodice, the laced closing of which will be retained in the regional costume of German peasants to our day, though ousted by the Spanish styles of the gentry in third quarter XVIc.

The headdresses are also typical of Germany. Over jewelled cauls at the ears, embroidered gauze is drawn across the forehead and about the bulbous cap, set far back in the head.

1007. XVIc. 1502-3. German. (Winterthur, Coll. O. Reinhart.)
Lucas Cranach. Anna Cuspinian, née Putsch.

Anna was the wife of Dr. Johannes Cuspinian, physician, scholar and rector of the University of Vienna, of whom there is a companion picture in the same collection.

In the background are a fire, a falcon, heron and parrot, symbols of her birth under the zodiacal sign of Sol.

Her rings (now worn on thumb as well) are more elaborate than those shown in English portraits. German belts, worn high, have fine buckles and are without pendants.

1008. XVIc. c. 1508. Flemish. (The Louvre.)
Gerard David.
Marriage at Cana.
Picture packed with details of Flemish costume and Italianate influences during the first decade XVIc.

A. Male donor in the usual long, richly bordered or fur-lined gown.

B. Jewelled fillet over flowing hair of a maiden. Gown seen in so many Spanish-Italian portraits of late XV-e.XVIc.: brocade, with tied-on brocade sleeves, cut out and laced across a great spill of white, embroidered shirt sleeve.

C., H., M. Dark Franco-Flemish hoods in various stages of development. The raked-back curves (M) of the later French hood are being evolved here by turning back the top of a narrow, straight-falling hood (C) to show the rich materials of its lining, under-cap, and the pleated or quilted gold gauze of still another cap beneath. As the hood tends to become more enclosing, its skirts are slashed at the

shoulder (H) to form lappets (which will eventually come to be pinned up); brooch on falls.

D. Asymmetrical or lapped-over closings (see end XVc., Ill. 996: The Lovers) of jerkin; repeated lines of velvet trim, and shirt bosom smocked and embroidered into fine pleating (Ill. 992, Dürer: Self-portrait, 1498). Hair bound into a netted caul or turban.

E. Italianate garments; pleated shirt-front; hair cut in bangs across forehead.

F. Jerkin with carefully pleated skirts; shoe very much cut away, and strapped across instep.

G. Donor with rosary, in the white Flemish hood, which dips characteristically in the middle, and is folded and pinned or tied into shape at the nape, as the Franco-Flemish velvet hood will be. Wide-sleeved, fur-lined Flemish gown, with a convex neckline almost entirely filled in with black velvet.

I. Sheer gauze, treated like a white Flemish hood.

J. Lingering effects of the old horned and heart-shaped headdresses in veil drawn down to the forehead between knobs of hair (see Ill. 741: Barbara of Brandenburg; Gonzaga family). Alternative neckline, edged with embroidered bands, and filled with a fine white shirt (men D. and E.).

K. Bride with the ceremonious mediaeval cloak (see Ill. 529: Uta) caught by a cord between jewelled rosettes, over a contemporary Flemish fur-lined gown.

L. Turban, asymmetrically bound with narrow braid.

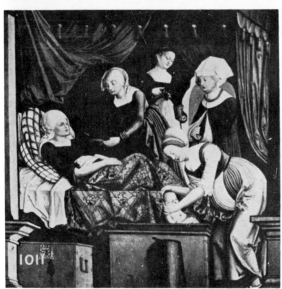

1009. XVIc. German. (Vienna, Coll. Baron van der Elst.)
Master of Frankfort, fl. 1490-15.

The Artist and his Wife.

The painter wears the beaver hat and flowing curls seen in Housebook illustrations (984-86), his wife a form of the béguine headdress. A rectangle of linen which has been folded is set so that the crease forms a dip over the forehead; the sides are crossed and pinned on either side; the back, which is often laid in careful folds, here falls free; and the hood is decorated with a pin in the form of an insect.

1010. XVIc. 1503, German. (Metropolitan Museum, Print Room.)
A. Dürer.

Coat of arms with skull.

The most wonderful of all flamboyant German crests and shields, using the wild man's staff as supporter. Gown and crown seen in the illustrations of wedding parties and festivities at Nuremberg. (See Appendix.)

1011. First quarter XVIc. German. (Nuremberg, Germanic Mus.)
H. S. von Kulmbach. The Birth of the Virgin (lower half of panel).

1012. XVIc. 1504-5. German.
Albrecht Dürer. Espousal of the Virgin.

As in Ill. 1011, an attendant wears the great banded coif and pleated, low-necked mantle of the church-going dress of Dürer's native Nuremberg.

By the technique of their manufacture, straw hats are, of all head-coverings, the most hat-like in the

modern sense (see Color Plate, No. 3). Felt hats of analogous form will appear, last quarter XVIc.

1013. First quarter XVIc. Flemish. (Minneapolis, Inst. of Arts.) Tapestry.

Prodigal Son.

Bonnets, slashed, bound and plumed more extravagantly in Flanders and Germany than elsewhere, are worn by the gentlemen; set or tied over other bonnets, caps, flowing hair, or swelling turbans of the f. type.

The ladies wear bonnets of the m. type, set on hoods or twisted turban. Hoods have side flaps pinned up, and the back curtain brought over the crown of the head in a stiffened brim.

The men's doublets and wide-collared cloaks are of the below-knee length of first quarter XVIc. Dependent lower sleeve almost severed (m. at ext. l.) .

Use of knots, cords and tassels on pouches, girdles, necklaces and bonnets. Dagger.

Shoes: squarer toes, lower cut, held in place by ties across instep.

1014-1018. XVIc. 1507-12. German. (Berlin, Kaiser Friedrich Museum.)

Hans Baldung.

Adoration of the Magi.

Baldung worked in the Upper Rhine, at Strassburg and Freiburg.

At end XVc. armor tends to lose its fine Gothic form; it swells and widens, and takes on some attributes of contemporary male costume. Its surface is richly decorated by fluting, engraving, and combinations of metal colors. The breastplate of Maximilian armor becomes globular and short-waisted. The pauldrons enlarge and sweep across the breast and shoulderblades; a high collar of plate is added. The skirt of tassets becomes hippy and short-waisted, as it lengthens and encloses the thigh. The great helm is supplanted by visored armets. Sabatons take the form of the broad-toed shoe. The knight's sword and its hilt lengthen; its quillens widen.

Over his breastplate, used as a placard, the knight (l.) wears a pourpoint cut in one with its circular skirts. Beards, moustaches; separately or together.

The small caps of German ladies, like the bonnets of the men, are sharply tilted over left ear when worn with a netted caul; set level when the natural hair is exposed.

Braid is used on the sleeves and yokes of these gowns, in the diagonal patterns which we have seen, since the late XVc., on cloaks with dependent points, like that of the Negro king in finely striped tights.

1019

1019. XVIc. 1511-15. Flemish.
(Berlin, Kaiser Friedrich Mus.)
G. van der Weyden.

Altarpiece; with donors: Arnold von Löwen and wife, Elizabeth von Breda.

The arms of the donors hang in the trees and appear on the sleeved surcoat of the knight (*Löwen*—lion), and on the mantle which his lady wears over her Flemish gown; identical, except for the lacings, with those of the XVc. R. van der Weyden portraits.

1020

1020. XVIc. Before 1511. German.
(Colmar Museum.)
Matthias Grünewald.

The Isenheim Altarpiece.

The garments shown on biblical characters in religious paintings are not always strictly contemporary. But the design which Grünewald, born in the Palatinate, gives to the mantle (which the f. ext. l. wears over her banded headdress) would seem to have been influenced, in its form, by the "heuke" of Holland and the Lower Rhine, and in its horizontal lines, by the banded fur cloaks of northern Germany.

1021-22. XVIc. Dutch. (Metropolitan Museum.)

Lucas van Leyden.

1021. The Milkmaid (1510).
1022. The Bagpiper (1520).

Barefoot women, with hose-like long drawers, beneath short, tucked-up kirtles. Loose hose of bagpiper, gartered, with sock-boots.

1023-26. XVIc. 1514. German. (Metropolitan Museum.)

Albrecht Dürer. Rustics.

Elastic as the hose of the standard-bearer appear, they are still cut from fabric. Knitting seems to have begun in late XVc., but the techniques of stocking knitting took about half a century to develop. Spanish or Italian stockings were occasionally seen in England before the mid-XVIc., but they remained a luxury until the invention of the stocking frame in 1589. Stubbes is indignant, in 1583, because "cloth (though neuer so fine) is thought too base," and people pay half a year's wages for a pair of stockings, "for how can they be lesse" (than a ryall, or 20 shillings) "when as the very knitting of them is worth a noble or a ryall."

The Swiss and German mercenary soldiers adopted and helped to spread the slashed and plumed style, of which we see the beginnings here.

Like the milkmaid and the bagpiper's wife (above), the dancing peasant woman wears a headdress of some pretensions; pleated apron, hung around the neck; pouch, knife, and keys at waist. Country men in hoods (which only they retain), pouches and knives, tattered hose and worn-soled boots.

1027. XVIc. c. 1515. German. Franconian. (Lichtenstein, Schloss Lichtenstein.)

Unknown artist.

Beheading of John the Baptist.

The soldier wears low-cut, square-toed black shoes and knotted garters; with yellow garments, diagonally slashed and puffed over black, and caught by black knots. White-plumed red hat slung over shoulders by knotted scarves. Short, square beard with moustache. Older man wears long rose gown, with brown fur collar and bonnet.

The lady holding the salver wears a brown skirt with a gold-embroidered, dark brown velvet bodice and sleeves, exposing much puffed shirt; slightly dependent belt, carrying a netted pouch and a case of toilet articles. White gauze drawn around white cap, embroidered in gold.

1028. XVIc. 1514. German. (Dresden, Picture Gallery.)

Lucas Cranach, elder.

Duke Henry the Pious.

Early in XVIc. Luther's friend, Cranach, became court painter to the Elector of Saxony. As perquisites, he was given a number of profitable monopolies. Painters were a variously gifted lot in those days; when an artist prepared his own colors, they were all chemists. Cranach was the proprietor of the only apothecary's shop allowed in Wittenburg; it remained in business until it burned in 1871. He was also given patents in printing, and sole rights to the sale of bibles.

The Lutheran duke, who succeeded his Catholic brother, and was the father of Maurice, the Elector of Saxony, wears a completely slashed costume: brocade-lined gown, doublet and upper hose, confined at the knee by embroidered, fringed garters, *krantz* wreath of dark and light carnations; heavy rope collar with pendant of clasped hands; continuously linked collar of ribbon gold; huge jewelled pomegranate pendants finish the short sleeve of his gown; seal and other important rings; shell-decorated sword hilt and dog collar.

Moryson says everyone but "Virgines of inferiour sort, or Gentlewomen" who "weare a border of pearle," from the highest to the lowest, commonly "wear garlands of roses (which they call Crantzes)," worn only by women in winter; "but in Summertime men of the better sort weare them within doores, and men of the common sort weare them going abroade."

He describes the method in which the rosebuds, damask for smell and others for color, are kept fresh all winter: laid in layers of rows on bay salt, sprinkled with Rhine wine, sealed with lead and kept in a cool, dark cellar; freshened with lukewarm water and Rhine wine for color, and rosewater for smell.

1029. XVIc. German. (Metropolitan Museum.)

Bartel Beham.

Leonardt von Eck.

The Bavarian Chancellor wears a scarlet judicial coif, pleated shirt with a ruffle-edged standing collar, and a full, low-necked beige gown, the cut of its sleeves providing fullness above the elbow, but on the outer part of the sleeve only.

1030. XVIc. German. (Munich, Alte Pinakothek.)

Hans Baldung.

Count Palatine Philip of Baden.

Nowhere is body-linen now more beautifully embroidered than in Germany; Philip's shirt shows the standing collar which will be common in another decade. Over the long, bobbed hair of first quarter XVIc., he wears a fine flat hat, with slashed and laced brim and pendant; a jeweled roll, run through a ring, is set on the crown.

1031. XVIc. German. (Munich, Alte Pinakothek.)

Bernard Strigel. Conrad Rehlinger, elder, at 47.

The founder of the important family of traders with Venice was a man of such standing in his

native Augsburg, that the Emperor Charles called on his services in a crucial new government, despite Rehlinger's Lutheran convictions and efforts to promote the Reformation.

Classic picture of a rich, middle-aged man of XVIc. Heads of elderly men and children, in cold climate, were protected by the mediaeval form of coif, or renaissance cap; hat was set over these for outdoor wear. In first half XVIc., combinations of hat and close-fitting cap, often decorated or netted, were fashionable, and not reserved for the old or bald.

The head must be uncovered before a sovereign, and the privilege of retaining a hat in his presence was an important reward. As new social classes rose and competed, the right to keep the head covered was jealously observed. Hats were generally worn indoors, by both men and women; men kept on their hats, for instance, in church and at table. Their removal was a real mark of respect.

1032. XVIc. German. (Sarasota, John and Mabel Ringling Museum.)

L. Cranach, e.

Cardinal Albrecht of Bavaria as St. Jerome.

After the manner of his times, the Elector-archbishop of Mainz (1490-1545), younger son of the Elector of Brandenburg, bought his cardinal's hat in 1518 with money borrowed from the Fuggers, and repaid by Papal arrangement out of the sale of indulgences.

Erasmus' friend, and munificent patron of the arts, he sits under a chandelier made from the actual horns which served as pattern for the branched Flemish brass chandelier; lumps of crystal are hung from it in a primitive attempt to intensify the candle light. Table built on a platform to keep the feet warm. Chests, which have stood on the floor, are beginning to be hung as cupboards.

1033. XVIc. 1514. Flemish. (The Louvre.)

Quentin Matsys.

The Banker and his Wife.

Flemish garments have changed little since the XVc., but the shirt sleeve of the banker's wife now has an embroidered cuff, and a flat hat is set on her folded and pinned headdress.

Many fine objects: the illuminated missal with its clasp, backing and beautifully decorated edge; covered standing cup; box of nested weights for the scale; repoussé bowl on the shelf; convex mirror in which we probably see the painter's self-portrait.

1034. XVIc. c. 1515. Flemish. (Metropolitan Museum.)
Bernhard Strigel.

Portrait of a German Lady.

Gold embroidered cap; gown of copper-brown brocade, edged with black velvet; shirt embroidered in gold, with colored motifs.

1035-36. XVI. 1516-18. German. (Metropolitan Museum, Print Room.)

Der Weisskunig, by Emperor Maximilian I.

1035. Illus. by *Hans Burgkmair.*

1036. Illus. by *Leonhard Beck.*

Der Weisskunig is Maximilian's autobiography, unfinished and finally printed in the XIXc.

The imperial regalia was kept at the favorite royal residence at Nuremberg. The city, not contained within walls like its rival, Augsburg, dominated a wide countryside, and was at the peak of its prosperity as the intermediary for the Oriental trade, between Italy and northern Europe. Watches were invented at Nuremberg; its artists were famous. A number of the Emperor's books were published there; he supervised their illustration by such Nuremberg artists as Dürer and Schäufelein; and the dress shown in them is that of Nuremberg. In the Burgkmair illustration, Mary of Burgundy, as a bride in Burgundian court dress, is teaching French to Maximilian, with courtiers in turn-of-the-century costume behind them.

In the Beck illustration we see the costume of Nuremberg (see Ill. 1010, coat of arms with skull); the characteristic crowns set over banded or netted hair, looped up at the ears, with an untidy loose lock in front. Wide, round-necked gown, its skirt fullness bunched together at the waist in front, where it is very short; trailing into a square train; long, pushed-up sleeves, the transverse folds of which become repeatedly bound and slashed.

The man at the left gives a classic picture of the gentleman of Nuremberg in first third XVIc.: wide, plumed hat, slashed and overlapping brim; square, jutting beard and curly, full hair; short chain of immense links (of which Moryson still speaks at the end of the century); knee-length coat, immensely full, in carefully laid pleats, under a wide, slashed and tied "sailor" collar; and huge full sleeves, which are often seen gathered together at the bottom into a hanging ruffle. Immense peaked, slashed, and tied-on, wide-toed protective overshoe for travel.

1037. XVIc. 1531. German. (Metropolitan Museum, Print Room.)

Cicero: "Officia." M.T.C., Augsburg, 1531.

1038 1039 1040 1041

Illus. by *Hans Weiditz*. Clerks writing. Fullness inserted in cartridge pleats.

1038, 1039. c. 1520. German. (Denmark, Odensee.)
Claus Berg.

Saints: painted wooden figures from altar.

Sculpture executed for a Danish church by a German artist from Lübeck shows what Moryson found later in the century. The Danes dressed like Germans, but particularly like Saxons; and the heads of gentlewomen, married or unmarried, were relatively uncovered, their hair "woven and adorned by rows of pearle . . . and borders of Gold." They also wore the standing Saxon collars.

The very low necks of e. XVIc. gowns tend to be-

come filled in by yokes, plastrons, and tuckers; but in Germany, where the décolletage was lowest, small capes, just covering the opening, began to be used at the end first quarter XVIc.; these came from the Low Countries, followed the Rhine and the North Sea and Baltic coasts, working their way inland.

1040. 1520. German. (Nuremberg, Germanic Museum.)
Master of the Mindelheim Kinship.

St. Zosimus and St. Barbara.

The decline in taste and beauty of ecclesiastical garments has begun; mitres mount and decoration becomes heavy and ostentatious.

St. Barbara wears the new shoulder cape, with the

characteristic German sleeve of the late XV-e.XVIc.: overlong and widening at the wrist.

1041. 1524. German. (Munich, Alte Pinakothek.)
Matthias Grünewald.

St. Maurice and St. Erasmus.

St. Maurice in swelling, fluted Maximilian armor; large shoulder pieces with standing *passe-gardes, ränder;* broad-toed sollerets, and a pair of gentlemen's gloves. Jewelled wreath, allied to the *krantz* of fresh flowers, which were often combined with gilded nutmegs.

St. Erasmus: wheel of his martyrdom and coats-of-arms on the apparel of his alb.

Steel cross-bow man: slashings of hat brim progressively diminishing in width; imperfectly fitting hose, gartered for practicality; wide-toed shoes, almost entirely cut away and strapped over the instep, with the leather carried unusually high around the heel, for the same reason.

1042. c. 1525. German. (Metropolitan Museum.)
L. Cranach, e.
Judith with the head of Holofernes.

1043-1045. 1525-30. German. (Vienna, Museum of Art.)
L. Cranach, e.
Three young women.

As the waistline becomes lower, the embroidered band of the plastron remains unchanged in width and position: the wide opening of the bodice is laced across the white shirt below. Belts, if worn, hang low over the pleated skirts, which like the laced bodices will persist in peasant costume. The massive and rigid Saxon collars are worn high on the neck, and here the largest chains appear. Rings of great beauty, in matched sets of 5, are worn on various joints.

The costumes favored by the wearers of these great plumed hats, set over pearl cauls, are a blaze of combinations of magenta, scarlet, orange, yellow with black and white. The plumed barett goes out of style, second third XVIc. and is supplanted by small flat hats, set level.

1046-47. XVIc. c. 1522. Hungarian.
Unknown artist.

Louis II, Jagellon, King of Hungary, and his wife, Marie of Austria.

Marie, who holds a pink, symbolic of her marriage at 17 to the 15-year-old king, was early left a widow, and succeeded her remarkable aunt, Margaret of Austria, as regent of the Netherlands. She wears a jewelled collar and pendant of Hungarian workmanship. Beneath her crown, her hair is in one of the braided arrangements over the ears, which reappeared on young women, first quarter XVIc.

Louis is always shown in the anachronistic Italianate high doublet collar and filleted, flowing locks, persistent in Hungary.

1048. XVIc. 1525. German. (Vienna, Art History Museum.)

Bernhard Strigel.

Emperor Maximilian I and his Family.

The Hapsburg emperor, "the last of the knights," founder of the standing army of *landesknechte,* brave, cultivated but unstable, is shown in a picture painted after his death by his court artist. With him are his first wife; their son, Philip the Fair; two of Philip's children by Joanne the Mad, who grew up to be Charles V and Ferdinand I; and Philip's son-in-law, the King of Hungary.

Mary of Burgundy, who had died in 1484, is shown in the headdress and jewels of the period in which the portrait was produced. The long-jawed Hapsburg males have the bobbed hair of their period, and Louis the long, flowing hair of Hungary.

The wide, flat hat, c. 1525, is often furnished with ties by means of which the side lappets can be held in place, if turned up. The neck of the doublet is still low, in these portraits, as is that of the one shirt which appears.

1049. XVIc. c. 1525. German.
Hans Holbein, y.
The Standard-bearer of the Vallée d'Urseren.

1049

In the Italian campaigns, the fashions of the Swiss mercenaries spread to the soldiers of the French and Imperial armies beside whom they served.

Holbein had lived in Basel from the age of 18, and maintained a house there for his family, although most of his work after 1527 was done in England. During a lean period at Basel, Holbein made this india ink and water color sketch for a stained-glass window.

As the use of slashing increases, there is a tendency to differentiate the legs by varying its direction, as was formerly done by the use of parti-color. Slashing was used on the front, rather than the back of garments, and is not often seen below the garter-line of the leg. This soldier wears gloves with a pendant at the cuff.

1050. XVIc. c. 1530. German.
Hans Sebald Beham.
Camp-followers.

One of Beham's many series of illustrations was of army life, soldiers of various ranks, provision and supply wagons. The commissary of a modern army did not exist; soldiers cooked and often had to forage for themselves; their women were permitted to tag along to do the K.P. and nursing, for which there was no other provision.

These Franconian costumes, with a fur collar from the district to the east, must have belonged to part of Nuremberg's large quota of 6,000 soldiers to the imperial army, seen by Beham before he moved to Frankfort. Fullness gored into the hem; wonderful pouches; knives from women's belts.

1050

1051. XVlc. German-Swiss. (Basel Museum.)
Hans Holbein, y.

Lady of Basel.

The back view of this Swiss lady, one of a series of drawings of the costume of Basel, shows the method of drawing gauze around the embroidered cap. The bodice is filled in with a shirt, the high collar of which is edged by ruching; long banded and puffed German sleeve; skirt caught up in front to show a horizontally striped underskirt. In place of the high Flemish-German belt, we see a loose girdle with a massive pendant; so long that it must be knotted, it hangs down the back, instead of the front of the gown.

1052. XVlc. 1525-26. German. (Darmstadt Ducal Museum.)
Hans Holbein, y.

The Meyer Madonna.

Painted for Holbein's patron, the burgomaster of Basel, Jacob Meyer, it shows him with his first and second wives, his daughter Anne, and two sons, kneeling on an Oriental rug. Other portraits show these to have been in wide use, but still a luxury to be shown off.

The elder son wears a full-skirted jacket, trimmed with plain velvet bands; its upper sleeve cut in two sections, and caught by ball fastenings and tipped laces. Tasseled pouch.

Meyer's wives wear the banded chins and full, pleated capes of matrons of Basel in their Sunday dress. Dürer's colored drawings of Nuremberg costume (Vienna, Albertina) show how different were the house, church, and dance dresses of Nuremberg.

Anne's exquisitely pleated gown, and shirt with high collar, are banded with lovely embroidery. Her braided buns of hair are dressed over a band of embroidery, topped by a flower-crowned cap to match.

1053. XVlc. 1525. Austrian. (Metropolitan Museum.)
Hans Maler zu Schwarz.

Ulrich Fugger.

The German equivalent of the Medici was the great trading and banking house of Fugger. Always devoutly Catholic, it began its rise in the late XIVc., bore arms by XVc., and was ennobled a century later at the peak of its powers as bankers to the Hapsburg emperors.

Like the Medici, the Fuggers were people of taste, liberality, and interest in the arts; a number of them had literary talent and they collected a great library. The "Fuggerei" at Augsburg still standing after 400 years was an early example of a housing development for low-income groups.

The Fuggers maintained agents in the Orient and the New World and their commercial establishments covered Europe. From these houses, reports were regularly sent to the Golden Counting House at Augsburg, where they were translated and copied by scribes for issue in five languages to a list of subscribers. Out of these "Fugger News Letters" (some of which, 1564-1605, were published in 1924, John Lane, London), grew our newspapers.

1053

1054

1055

1056

1054. XVIc. 1530. German. (New York, Coll. Dr. F. H. Hirschland.)
L. Cranach, e.
Portrait of a Man.

1055. XVIc. 1535. German. (Metropolitan Museum.)
School of Cranach.
Portrait of a Man.

1056. Second third XVIc. Flemish. (Metropolitan Mus.)
Conrad Faber. (C. von Creutzenach).
Portrait of a Man. (George von Rhein?)

Moustaches and short beards at their greatest square width; hair short; hats, caps and embroidered cauls of rich, dignified men.

Loose shirt-fullness is associated with slashing, as in Ills. 1054, 1056, where the short-waisted doublet of first half XVIc. is slit up from the waist for additional display of the shirt, puffed out above the breeches. All the shirts now have collars, three of which are richly embroidered and finished with a ruff. Collars begin to close with decoratively knotted cords, black against the white shirt; as the neckline rises, the ties will become white against a dark ground.

In periods of extravagance and luxury, the garments of the very great are often distinguished by extreme severity, as are those of Fugger (see Ill. 826).

1057. End first third XVIc. German.

Hans Sebald Beham. Banquet of Herodias.

The free-thinking cronies and engravers, the brothers Beham and George Pencz, all born around 1500, and all important sources of costume information, were banished from their native Nuremberg in 1525. From 1531 until his death in 1550, H. S. Beham worked in Frankfort.

It would be impossible to crowd into one picture more information about the life of Nuremberg.

The men's costumes show inordinately large, slashed, laced and plumed hats, worn over hair, clipped or enclosed in a caul; many beards and moustaches. Skirts are becoming fuller and looser. Slashed doublets and hose, gartered; often striped on one leg.

Doublets with ballooning upper sleeves and full skirts. Wide, bulky, knee-length gowns. Musicians in motley.

Women's skirts are predominantly of ground length, finely pleated and horizontally striped. The skirt, when long, is bunched up in front to show a bordered underskirt. As bodies take on a normal waistline, precious belts are omitted; with the long skirt, a loose belt may be worn low (see Ill. 1051). Bodices are excessively low, though the entire décolletage may be filled in with a yoke, collared to the ears. The women wear hats of the male type; caps of two sorts: set on the back of the head and veiled with gauze, or small pill-boxes with arrangements of braids; or netted hair.

1058

1058. XVIc. c. 1535. Flemish. (Frankfort-on-Main, Stadel Inst.)

J. van Hermessen. Riotous party in a brothel.

The women of this low-class establishment wear the particular white hood and narrow, yoke-like black velvet tippet, which appear to have indicated their trade; over gowns (mostly red) with separate black or white sleeves.

As the garments of the male patrons show, the use

of slashing was not much extended to the rear of the body. Foreground, male figs.: yellow doublet with full green sleeves; scarlet hose; low-cut, almost heelless slippers like those worn by c. fig. in scarlet cap; late version of the slashed, low-necked doublet without skirt, and hose in yellow. Man in yellow doublet and old-fashioned waist-length hose of blue wears a rapier with a guarded hilt, which is just coming into use.

1059

1060

1059. XVIc. 1535-40. Flemish. (Brussels, Count H. de Limburg-Stirum.)

Artist unknown.

Protestant Meeting in a Garden; also called Portrait of the Thiennes Family. Chateau de Rumbeke in the background.

The gown worn with the French hood in England, France and Flanders has a severe bodice, with a high, wide neckline; turned-back funnel sleeves, or one caught along the outer seam over puffs. Two older women wear white hoods of the earlier type.

Some of the men's jackets still carry pleated skirts, which, as they shorten, show the evolution of the slashed and gartered part of the hose into "paned" upper hose, slit into few divisions, and ending in a roll or slashed edge above knee. Collars with points, such as are shown on these jackets, will soon appear, heavily embroidered, on shirts. Slashed shoes of natural shape, covering the instep.

1060. XVIc. 1537. German. (Dresden, Picture Gallery.)

Lucas Cranach, elder. Duke Henry the Pious.

The Duke, whom we saw as a beautiful, cleanshaven and ringleted young man in 1514, is shown here with clipped hair and the widest, squarest and most elaborate of the beards now worn in Germany.

With his edged cape of mail he wears cuishes of moulded leather. The double-handed knight's sword has steadily increased in size; its quillons are wide, guarded only by a ring; it will go out of use altogether with the XVIIc. Swiss dagger in a magnificent sheath.

1061

1061. XVIc. After 1530. German.
Jörg Breu, elder. "Entry of of Charles V into Augsburg." Marshal.

A series of woodcuts shows the entire procession, which celebrated the Emperor's arrival for the Diet of Augsburg. During his stay, the Emperor was lodged at the house of Anton Fugger, who celebrated the event by lighting a fire of cinnamon bark with one of his guest's bonds of indebtedness.

With his elaborate jerkin and boots with turned-down cuffs and the long spurs of the period, the Marshal wears arm-guards and gauntlets; and an armet with mentonnière and vizor, surmounted by a female figure and an immense panache of ostrich plumes, which are repeated on the chamfron (which with the crinet or mane-guard arm the horse's head and neck), and on the poitrel and croupe, which protect its body, fore and aft. He wears a two-handed sword in a handsome scabbard, and carries his marshal's baton.

Courtesy of the Metropolitan Museum of Art, Print Room (1061)

1062-65. XVIc. 1538. German.
Heinrich Aldegraver.
Wedding Festivities.

Aldegraver was a Westphalian goldsmith-engraver who worked at Soest and Paderborn.

The male flat hat was worn by women, in Germany as elsewhere, first half XVIc. It is shown here surmounted by a circlet. The characteristic posture of a woman in the low-necked, short-waisted German gown is determined largely by the dragging weight of the skirt (see Ill. 1051).

Wide collared jackets, braid trimmed and with cartridge-pleated skirts, or a similar unbelted cloak, are German fashions which were successful elsewhere. In their earlier form they show great upper-sleeve fullness; later a sleeve of normal cut, often worn pendant, is seen on the cape form, particularly. Elaborately slashed and gartered slops worn with nether hose which are often striped on one leg. Wide-toed shoes; extravagant German beard and moustaches. Musicians: badges on tasseled cloaks. (See next page for 1062-1065.)

1066. XVIc. 1546. German. (Paris, Coll. I. Kleinberger.)
H. Mielich.
Pancratius von Freyberg zu Aschau.

The Bavarian nobleman wears one of the beautiful embroidered collars with long points, here ending in tassels, which appeared briefly in the forties.

It was in Germany that watches were first made, end XVc. They were at first globular, "Nuremberg eggs," and were necessarily carried or hung by a chain

1066

like a pomander. During XVIc. The mechanisms were refined until it was possible to make a watch small enough to be set on a bracelet or even a ring. The goldsmith's art was at its height; never had watch cases and faces been so beautiful. They were engraved, enamelled and jewelled in the form of crosses, octagons and hexagons, skulls, shells and animals. A

typically Renaissance pendant with a recumbent female figure hangs from his large-linked German chain.

The flat hat is losing its rigidity; as the crown is preparing for its rise, aiglettes are now set around the band of the hat.

1067. 1523-30. German. (Frankfort-on-Main, Stadel Inst.)

Bartholomaeus Bruyn, elder.

Portrait of a Patrician.

The Bruyns worked in the Lower Rhine valley, from Cologne to Amsterdam; the costume shows Flemish influences. Brocade hood over gauzy cap with pinned up lappets. Neckline filled in by a plastron of the "spangles" noticed by Moryson. Jewelled collar; shirt, the pleating of which is embroidered into a standing collar.

1068. XVIc. 1531. German. (Madrid, Prado.)

C. Amberger.

Frau Jörg Zörer.

Amberger worked around Augsburg. Bavarian costume south of the Danube has a special severity. Such headdresses and gowns as Frau Zörer's, with a yoke filled by a white shirt, still appear at the end XVIc. from Salzburg to Zurich, with the upper-sleeve fullness and tightening of the lower sleeve which we expect to find later in the century; around Salzburg the upper fullness is in a high cap, cut in one with the long, severe sleeve, while in Zurich this upper fullness is loose, like that of the son in Ill. 1052.

1069. XVIc. 1539. German. (Brunswick, Ducal Museum.)

B. Bruyn, elder.

Portrait of a Young Woman.

The Flemish-influenced costume of Cologne shows

the headdress specific to that city; its short-waisted gown of ground length, with the characteristically wide and magnificent belt and flowing bell sleeves of Cologne. Here the inner sleeve is of the male jacket type, especially beloved along the Rhine and into Switzerland.

1070. XVIc. German. (Munich Gallery.)

H. Mielich.

Frau Andreas Ligfalz.

Frau Ligfalz was the wife of an official in Munich where Mielich painted. Her logwood dyed blue-black gown, banded in velvet, with its tucker in the form of a *koller,* has the beautiful severity of south Bavarian costume. The bulbous cap, veiled over the forehead, the large amount of white at the top of the bodice, and the soft upper-sleeve fullness are seen particularly from the Nuremberg side of the Danube into Switzerland.

1071. XVIc. 1548. German. (Berlin, Kaiser Friedrich Museum.)

Unknown Saxon artist.

Portrait of a Woman.

The short, fitted shoulder capes which began to cover the low necks of German gowns c. 1525, were retained with later high-necked gowns, and into XVIIc. became part of the national dress of the Rhineland. Made of fur in the north, velvet-banded or embroidered, they are seldom as rich as that on this Saxon, whose headdress is typically based on a

wide band, and exposes more hair than in other provinces. Eighteen rings, pearl bracelet, looped and knotted chains, precious girdle clasped at the side, and tasseled and embroidered handkerchief.

Clocks and Watches

Herman Kirschner's oration in praise of travel in Germany, included by Coryat, says, "the art of making clocks that were in the time of Carolus Magnus brought into Germany by the munificence of the Persian Ambassador, which at that time were a great miracle to our people, the East and Persia her selfe that first gave them, having now received them againe from the hands and the wits of the Germans, doth greatly admire them, according as Augerius hath certified us."

Large clocks with bells, and often with elaborate mechanical figures of men, beasts and birds, which emerged to strike the hours, were set in cathedral and castle towers from Germany to England, during XIIIc. The first clock mentioned in England was set in a tower opposite the gate of Westminster Hall in 1288, and was paid for by a fine of 800 marks levied against a Chief Justice of the King's Bench.

The inaccuracy of the early mainspring was somewhat improved, second and third quarters XVIc., by the spirally wound fuzee; much greater refinements in the springs appeared, end XVIIc.

The first comparatively small clocks were made by Peter Henlein (1480-1542) of Nuremberg.

They had circular cases with hinged tops, and stood on a table, looking rather like a large inkwell. Louis XI (d. 1483) had one small enough to be pocketed by a courtier who was desperate from his losses at cards; however, it was apparently too large for the theft to pass undiscovered.

Henry VIII left seventeen standing clocks, with chimes and "Larums."

Watches were at first made of gilt bronze, probably because the early watchmakers were locksmiths. In Blois, in XVIIc., watchmakers had to buy their precious metals from guilds of goldsmiths and silversmiths. As in the weaving, dyeing, printing and engraving crafts, watchmaking families persisted for generations, and tended to marry within the guilds; there were women watchmakers, like Judith Lalement (whose name shows her German origin) owner of a factory in Autun in 1660. Many of the watchmakers were Protestants, who emigrated, bringing the trade to new countries, like England and Switzerland, which became pre-eminent in XVIII-XIXc. Rousseau came of a family of refugee watchmakers in Switzerland. Beaumarchais, author of "The Barber of Seville," son of the watchmaker Caron, first came to the notice of the French court when he published in the "Mercure" a protest against the piracy of his newly invented escapement; he made watches both for Mme. de Pompadour and the king, before purchasing a title.

Marvellously beautiful pendant watches began to be made in latter half XVIc., nowhere finer than in the French provincial towns; as at Autun by the Cusins (of whom Charles, who emigrated to Switzerland in 1585, was perhaps the greatest); at Lyons by the Combrets, from 1570; at Rouen, where in 1570, du Chemin made for Mary Queen of Scots two octagonal watches which were among the first to have rock crystal lids; as well as at Paris.

Elizabeth, who, like her sister Mary, loved watches, was served until 1590 by the refugee, Nicholas Urseau, and after 1580, by another, Bartholomew Nusam. Leicester's New Year's gift, 1571/2, to Elizabeth was a diamond-and-ruby-set watch, on a bracelet.

Great engravers like T. de Bry produced watch designs; the ring designs published in 1561 by Voerior of Lorraine show a ring set with a tiny watch, such as had already been worn in 1542 by Guidobaldo, Duke of Urbino.

Watches became the most luxurious of gifts, equalled only by snuff-boxes (from end XVII-XIXc.). They were worn in unnecessary multiplications; Marie de Medici unpinned a pair of watches from her gown and gave them to the Venetian Ambassador. In 1575, the Archbishop of Canterbury willed to the Bishop of Ely a watch set on a cane, as less reverend gentlemen had them set on daggers and rapiers. By 1622, watches small enough to serve as earrings were produced at Blois; and in late XVIIc., both Richelieu and Cagliostro wore a series of three-quarter inch watches as buttons.

This unnecessary display displeased the Puri-tans, who began to carry watches, for use only, concealed in pockets, as watches began commonly to be made small enough at the beginning of the XVIIc. As Puritan influence waned, watches continued to be carried in pockets; but by end XVIIIc., were commonly worn in pairs with two fobs, as was required in French court dress. Watches hung as part of ladies' chatelaines.

The beautiful rock crystal watches of XVIe.XVIIc., in octagonal and shell forms, or in crosses and skulls for the pious, were replaced in second half XVIIc. by charming enamelled forms. Multicolored golds began to be used in mid-XVIIIc.; and engine turnings, often covered by transparent enamel, in late XVIIIc.

The guild of English watchmakers was not founded until 1631. Many of its members were Quakers, like George Graham and Daniel Quare, inventor of the repeater watch. Alcock, Robert Smith, N. Vallin and the Jew, Isaac Symm, were among the great English watchmakers of the XVIIc. But it was the dead-beat escapement invented by Thomas Tompion (1639-1713) and improved by his pupil George Graham (1673-1751), which made possible the English watches of XVIIIc., the best in the world, until the magnificent plain, thin watches produced in Paris by A. Breguet (1780-1823). The firm of Breguet is still in existence; watches made by them soon after 1800 are perhaps superior to any produced since.

In late XVIIIc., Switzerland began to produce garish watches, especially for the Chinese trade, with engraved, jewelled and enamelled works visible through an inner cover of glass. France in XVIIIc. and Switzerland in early XIXc., provided charming ladies' enamelled watches in amusing shapes: banjos, lyres and flowers. The first good cheap watch was made in Switzerland, by Rosekopf, for 20 fr. in mid-XIXc.

1072

1073

1074

1075

1076

1077

1072. XVIc. 1560-90. French, Paris.

Watch by Nicolas Bernard: rock crystal case, bevelled in 8 panels; lid clear, lower part yellowish; metal hinge, finial, and snap.

1073. XVIc. 1580-1600. French, Autun.

Watch by Charles Cousin: case and cover of bevelled rock crystal, $1\frac{1}{2}''$ x $1\frac{1}{8}''$; gold and silver face.

1074. XVI-XVIIc. French, Paris.

Watch by Melchior Adan (m)?: shell-shaped rock crystal, mounted in engraved metal; silver hour band.

1075. c. 1592. French, Rouen.

Watch by F. Hubert: oval case, enamelled with

flowers and leaves in green, blue, and gold on white ground, spotted black; interior enamelled pale blue; crystal cover mounted in black and white enamel; hour hand only. F. Hubert's son, Etienne, made watches for Mary, Queen of Scots.

1076. XVI-XVIIc. 1590-1613. English, London.

Clock-watch by Michael Nouwer: engraved metal face; tangent wheel; screw adjustment.

1077. XVIc. 1610-30. French, Cartigny.

Watch by Denis Bordier: engraved silver dial, chain, and key. The Bordier dynasty of watchmakers had removed from Orleans to Cartigny, near Geneva.

1078. XVIIc. 1620-39. English.
Watch by Nicholas Walter: silver, enamelled face.
1079. c. 1630. English, London.
Watch by Robert Smith in Popesnose Alley: engraved silver, plain and dotted bands; dial silver, engraved with tulips and marigolds; floral balance cock, tangent wheel, screw adjustment.
1080. XVIIc. c. 1638. English, London.
Calendar watch by Thomas Alcock; polished silver with outer case of black leather, studded with silver; face, engraved silver; revolving center disk black, semé silver stars, shows moon's phases; revolving outer disk gives days of month; tangent wheel, screw adjustment.
1081, 1084. Second half XVIIIc. German, Augsburg.
The "Great Ruby Watch" by Nicolas Rugendas, y. (c. 1670-1730); case enamelled with flowers in relief and natural colors, set with rubies.
Inside lid enamelled pale blue, black scrolls; face with black numerals, enamelled with tulips and roses in natural colors, Time, a sundial, and death's-head.
1082. XVIIIc. c. 1695. English, London.
Traveling clock-watch with striking alarm by Thomas Tompion; silver; movement signed by Tompian, one of the greatest innovators in watch-making.
1083. XVIIIc. c. 1710. French, La Rochelle.
Watch by B. Hubert: gilt brass.

1085. XVIc. German.

Michael Ostendorfer. Landgraf Georg von Leuchtenberg (Upper Palatinate).

The pendant sleeve took new force from its use on these wide-shouldered cloaks (G. *Schaube*), and persisted after the simplification of the upper sleeve, becoming completely unusable and vestigial in late XVI-e.XVIIIc.

In Nuremberg c. 1530 the sleeve was often gathered, making the opening at the bottom unusable although the sleeve was slit elsewhere. The pendant sleeve was less used on women's garments; it appeared occasionally on the short, flaring jackets called *Schaubelein;* and an unused or unusable hanging sleeve was a feature of the severe coat-garments of Augsburg, fourth quarter XVIc.

XVI Century Engraving

The increased demand for engravings, midXV-midXVIc., was met by the great Flemish houses of commercial publisher-engravers: Hieronymus Cock, Brueghel's patron; Philippe Gall; and the family van der Passe (Crispin I, II, III, Simon, Madeleine and Willem) who spread from Flanders into England.

The XVIc. was the great era of exploration and interest in recording. Mercator and Hondius produced maps. Collections of costume plates of Europe, the New World and the Orient began to appear everywhere. (Queen Elizabeth will be painted standing on a colored map of Oxfordshire.) The trend began with the 2,000 plates of M. Wohlgemuth and G. Pleydenwurf: *Chroniques de Nuremberg,* 1493-1500. Weiditz' unique drawings of his travels, 1529-32, were not reproduced until our own time. But 17 editions of Sebastian Münster: *Cosmographie,* a sort of encyclopedia, were produced during XVIc., with translations into Bohemian, 1554, and French, 1562.

E. Vico of Parma (fl. 1541-67) produced about 100 plates of European costume which were the basis of the first great costume book, *Recueil de la diversité des habits,* published in France, 1562. This was followed by F. Bertelli: *Omnium feregentium nostrae aetatis habitus nunquam antehac aediti,* Venice, 1563; and the great works of Jost Amman from 1564-96.

Melchoir Lorch: *Turkische Tracht,* 1626, was a fascinating record of Turkish life by a man, who, like Weiditz, drew what he himself had seen in his travels during 1575 to 1581.

In the last quarter XVIc. there is a flood of such books; many artists producing several apiece, of which the most important is cited: J. J. Boissard: *Habitus variarum orbis gentium,* Malines, 1581;

the 500 plates of de Bruyn: *Omnis gentium habitus,* Antwerp, 1581, and his record of military costume; C. Vecellio's 600 plates, including Russia and Poland, in 1590, reproduced as "*Costumes anciens et modernes,*" Firmin Didot, Paris, 1859-60.

In 1590, the de Brys of Frankfort began their *Collectiones perigrinationem in Indiam Orientalem and Occidentalem,* with the purchase in England of drawings brought back from the first expeditions to Florida and Virginia; these were completed by Merian in 1634, and are reproduced in S. Lorant: *The New World,* Duell, Sloan & Pearce, N. Y., 1946.

At the end of the century came G. Franco: *Habiti delle donne Venetiane,* and his *Habiti d' Huomini et Donne venetiane, con la processione della serma. signoria et altri particulari Cioe Trionfi Feste et Ceremonie Publiche della noblissima città di Venezia,* 1610, reprinted by Ferdinando Organia, Venice, 1878; this shows meetings, councils, festivities, and home life of Venice. (At M.F.A. of Boston.) In 1601, J. de Gheyn: *Des habits,*

moeurs, ceremonies, façons de faire anciens et modernes. Meanwhile useful portraits were being produced by the Kilians of Augsburg (artists to the Fuggers); Goltzius; the brothers Wierix of Antwerp; and in England by Rogers, Peake, and Elstrack. They were followed by architectural and topographical plates, which include costumed figures, like John Speed: *Theatre of the Empire of Great Britain,* 1611, *Brittania Illustrata,* 1707-8, and Loggan's work.

In XVIIc. there are Crispin de Passe; Callot's Italian and gypsy plates; Bosse, Perelle, Aveline, Bérain, and the costume plates of Louis XIV's period, in France; R. de Hooge in Amsterdam; and the precious records of English and Central European costume made by the Bohemian, W. Hollar.

Reproductions of many of these will be found in the many volumes edited by G. Hirth: *Kulturgeschichtliches Bilderbuch aus vier Jahrhunderten,* Munich, 1923-5, and: *Les Grands Illustrateurs,* 1500-1800, Munich, 1888-91.

1086. XVIc. 1550. German. (Metropolitan Museum, Print Room.)

C. Amberger. Schlittenfahrt König Ferdinands.

Ferdinand, his grandparents' favorite, was brought up in Spain. But it was Charles V, despite all they could do, who inherited the Empire and his grandmother's Burgundian possessions. Ferdinand was made King of Austria, the Tyrol, the Hapsburg lands in S. Germany, and administered the Roman Empire ably for his older brother. Ferdinand married Anne of Hungary and Bohemia; when his childless brother-in-law Louis Jagellon was killed, he laid claim to both kingdoms, and succeeded in becoming king of Bohemia. On Charles's abdication, Ferdinand became emperor. Riding in this wonderful sleigh, which the Augsburg publisher attests to be accurately shown, must have been one of the real pleasures of his and his wife's transplanted life.

1087. XVIc. 1551. Flemish. (Brussels, Musee Communale.)

Peter Pourbus, e. Adrienne de Buuck, wife of Jan Farragant.

The approach of lace can be seen in the working of sheer fabric, in the wrist ruffles of the Slossgen lady, and of Adrienne de Buuck, as well as in the cuff of her glove. Shoulder cape lined with stiff, diaper-patterned silver and white brocade.

1088. XVIc. 1557. German. (Metropolitan Museum.)

B. Bruyn, y. Lady of the Schlossgen Family of Cologne.

The ermine sleeves show the bell form, at the end of its use elsewhere but persistent at Cologne. Patrician girls of adjacent Hainault wear ermine aprons to match these sleeves. The yoke of the gown of Cologne is still open, the opening filled with pearled plastron, pendant and embroidery; pear-shaped pomander.

1089-90. XVIc. 1550. German.. (Philadelphia, Courtesy of the John J. Johnson Art Coll.)

Barthel Bruyn, e.
1089. Donor, Son and St. Peter.
1090. Donor's Wife, St. Anne, Virgin and Child.

1086

The elaborate sleeves of the first half XVIc. are simplified in second half; show short Spanish caps or picadills in fourth quarter, when the hanging sleeve is largely unused and the short circular cloaks are worn as capes. The white cords which fasten the high shirt collars of the third quarter XVIc. often hang decoratively loose on the dark garments, the collar open.

The donor's wife wears the cap of Cologne with her Spanish coat-dress of velvet-edged brocade, fur-lined, over a satin underdress. This gown will be upper class wear during second half XVIc., particularly in Cologne, the Palatinate, Frankfort, Bavaria and Saxony, and will enter into the regional dress of Augsburg, as shown by J. Amman in 1586.

These gowns, moire-lined for summer wear, are often black. Black is much worn in XVIc. Germany in contrasting textures: velvet and cloth, moire, dull silk and brocade. Nothing could better set off the headdresses of sheer white or gold and pearled, the

1091

1092

1093

1094

is shown, with tactful touches of the costume of her province: the Saxon cap, its band set back of the ears, is worn with a garland (*krantz*); wide, precious Saxon collar at base of the throat; rounded line of underbodice; finely pleated apron.

1092. XVIc. 1556. German. (Vienna Art History Museum.)
H. Mielich.
Anna, Duchess of Bavaria.

The duchess holds a jewelled fur piece, chained to a girdle which is finished with a tassel in place of the older pomander. Portraits are apt to exhibit new and precious objects, such as the clock in front of her little dog. Castles are still cold; hot-water bottles have not yet been invented; and small spaniels, in addition to being amusing, stay 4 degrees warmer than a human being, and are happy to lie cozy on a lap or even tucked against a toothache.

1093. XVIc. 1558. German. (Vienna Art History Museum.)
J. Seisenegger.
Ferdinand, Archduke of the Tyrol.

The Spanish-German costume of the Archduke shows a brown velvet hat, white ostrich; gown of copper silk, guarded by bands of matching metal galoon; white and gold doublet, laced with gold, match the hose; natural-colored nether-hose and shoes; brown gloves.

1094. XVIc. 1555-9. Italian. (Metropolitan Museum.)
G. B. Moroni.
The German Warrior.

The German warrior, like the son of the Emperor Ferdinand I, shows standard European upper-class dress of the 50's: doublet with longer waistline, shorter skirts, dropped shoulderline, simplified sleeve, braiding in vertical lines; paned hose, with a little bambast set low.

wonderful goldsmith work, or the color used in bodice and apron embroidery.

1091. XVIc. 1551. German. (Dresden Gallery.)
H. Krell.
Anne of Denmark, Electress of Saxony.
The coat-dress now worn by great ladies

1095
1096

1097

1098

1095-96. c. 1560. German. (Berlin, formerly coll. R. von Kaufman.)

B. Bruyn, y.

Portrait of a Woman and her Daughter.

The mother wears the white béguine headdress of Flanders in its form specific to Cologne: excessively long falls looped and caught at the back of the headdress. The extremely wide and magnificent belt characteristic of this costume can be seen in the portrait of a mother and four daughters (companion picture of father and four sons), by an unknown painter of Cologne at this same period, in the Dresden Gallery.

The daughter wears the wide cap with looped braids of a young woman of Cologne, together with the characteristically belled sleeve; its bodice is more completely closed since first half XVIc.

1097-98. XVIc. 1564. Swiss. (Basel Museum.)]

Tobias Stimmer.

Jacob Schwitzer and his Wife Elizabeth.

Schwitzer was a leading citizen of Basel, head of the guild of wool carders. He wears black hat and shoes; red-brown brocade doublet; red upper-stocks with the cod-piece set in a diagonal, gored band; nether stocks and garters to match; black and gold dagger sheath with a silver cross.

Coryat found that the men of Basel and Zurich wore ruffs, never falling bands, and that the cod-piece remained in use, large and prominent; he and Moryson noticed the flat hats, like those worn by English 'prentices.

Elizabeth wears a wide coif, veiling the chin; brown, velvet-edged bodice, cream-colored apron, smocked and embroidered at the top, and tied on with knotted cord; ground-length skirt of natural colored satin (?), bordered in brown. Her fine belt, hanging by clasps over the pleated apron, carries the multitude of objects seen in Switzerland: a knife in its sheath, a "housewife" of sewing or toilet articles, as well as the usual fine pouch; gloves with an elaborate cuff.

1099

1100

1101

1102

1099-1100. XVIc. German. (Dresden.)

Att. to L. Cranach, e. (d.1553).

1099. Elector Augustus of Saxony, 1526-86 (1563).

1100. Anne of Denmark, Electress of Saxony (1564).

Tall embroidered hats with plumes, and short capes with high standing collars are a uniform of the Electors of Saxony in last third XVIc. The loose, *pluderhose* fullness between the panes of the upper hose is characteristic of Protestant German costume. Matching dagger and sword; embroidered gloves.

As in Ill. 1091, the Electress' Spanish gown is given regional touches: her underskirt has the Saxon cartridge pleating and an almost vestigial apron. Her sleeve, while much like that worn in Germany with this dress, has some regard for the Saxon regional dress in its third quarter XVIc. form. Its velvet bodice now has a puffed cap-sleeve like that of the Spanish gown, below which an extremely tight white sleeve has its forearm braceleted almost to the elbow with bands of embroidery; its hat is now a miniature flat hat, set horizontally over a pearled coif.

1101-02. XVIc. 1561. Flemish. (Budapest, Museum of Fine Arts.)

N. Neufchatel.

1101. Hans Heinrich, Pilgrim of Bois-le-Duc (Hertogenbosch).

1102. Mme. Hans Heinrich, Pilgrim of Bois-le-Duc.

It was not by chance that Bois-le-Duc produced Hieronymus Bosch, Brueghel's progenitor, this proud and somber man, and his pious Protestant-looking wife. Bois-le-Duc, a flourishing commercial town with the largest Gothic cathedral in Brabant, had begun to be attacked in XIVc. by the sort of conscience which led to the Reformation. The Confrèrie of Notre Dame, established there in 1318, in opposition to the corruption of the Church, admitted lay members, and came to be much concerned with charities. Its members believed that purity of soul and communion with God could be attained without the official intervention of the Church, and that theirs was the only true way.

Spanish influence is particularly strong in this immensely distinguished man's costume, simply guarded in velvet, with extremely high collar. The ruff, with hanging, decorative band-strings, is left open, as it is sometimes seen during third quarter XVIc. Poignard in superb sheath; rapier; fine pouch with a handkerchief; light gloves with a pinked cuff.

Women's hair in two braids was a Swiss usage which Coryat noticed in Basel, as in Zurich and Strassburg.

1103. XVIc. c. 1564. German. (Hamburg, Edouard F. Weber Coll.)

Ludger Tom Ring.

Lucia von Münchhausen.

The costume of Westphalia, where the Münchhausen family originated and Ring worked, is closely related to that of Cologne and of the triangle of Holland between Harlem, Leyden and the Rhine.

I have never seen the original of this picture, or been able to learn its colors. The headddess is worn with a garland (*krantz*). The high embroidered collar of the gown is clasped across the throat; the cape (*goller*) of velvet has a high collar and matches the deep cuffs. The top of the finely pleated apron is folded under and set beneath the woven belt. The front-laced bodice is of the same material as the finely pleated outer skirt. This, like the banded and pleated underskirt, is of ground length. Panelled room with surrounding bench.

1104-6. XVIc. c. 1575. German. (Metropolitan Museum.)

Ludger Tom Ring.

Christ Blessing the Donors.

These Westphalian costumes show the men in furred black.

The mother is in dark velvet with a close white hood. The daughter behind her, with looped braids under her simple cap, wears reddish brown. The elder daughter with the exquisitely pleated cap, clearly influenced by Holland, is in pinkish brown with the same deep cuffs and *goller,* woven braid belt and pleated skirt which we see on the others.

DRESS OF THE LOW COUNTRIES

The pictures of the elder Brueghel, of Antwerp, called "Peasant" Brueghel to distinguish him from his painter sons, "Hell" and "Velvet," show all the daily life of Flanders in third quarter XVIc.: carnival and Lent; illustrations of its proverbs, its children's games, the 7 Deadly Sins; soldiers, shepherds, peasants and beggars; weddings and dances, indoors and out. (See Color Plate, No. 6, Vol. II.)

It is hard to comment on the costumes in Brueghel. They are simple peasant clothes; the figures are too multitudinous to be indicated without a key drawing and numbers; new things can be found in them after years of familiarity.

Their peculiar richness comes out of the accidents and improvisations, even more than the intentions, of a thrift which borders on poverty. Worn garments are not thrown away; they are combined and supplemented: sock-boots over old hose; protective triangles tied above knees; a vest of one color over a shirt, over the tails of a still longer shirt; the color of an inner sleeve, rolled back or hanging below an upper.

These are hardworking, lusty people who like fun and color, must be comfortable and have no time or inclination for nonsense. The women's heads and chins are wrapped against the damp cold of their low land, which would take the starch out of anything they might be silly enough to pleat. They wear layers of skirts; the warm lining is one more color, when the skirt front is tucked up into the belt, and the darker underskirt bears the brunt of daily accidents. Skirts are short of the mud; aprons are never tokens of embroidered velvet here.

Except on soldiers, who have made the Swiss styles their own, there is no slashing, elaboration of upper hose, tailoring of cod-pieces: these latter necessities are reduced to tied-on triangles. Short breeches and sock-boots are added for warmth. Sleeves are comfortable; they neither constrict nor get in the way. The outermost of 3-4 body garments is apt to be practically sleeveless.

EUROPEAN DYESTUFFS

Dyestuffs are precious, local and hard come by, or imported and expensive. Garments are dipped, and lees of dyes combined, until the last bit of color is extracted; there is a serial richness of gradations of tones.

The Low Countries have always been the heart of the dye industry. Now the familiar mediaeval dyes are being supplemented by new dyestuffs, pouring in from the New World and the Orient, in XVIc.

The woad blues of Saxony are reinforced by the deeper blues of indigo. Until the invention of a fast green dye in 1811, green will be made by redyeing blue with yellow. (So be careful when you think of freshening your great-grandmother's patchwork. She would have washed it, since indigo is not water-soluble; but indigo is extracted by some dry-cleaning fluids, and the lovely greens may come back a nasty yellow, unless an expert is consulted. Even though the work dates from after 1811, the new dye did not immediately supplant old methods, and scraps from past generations were used.)

The madder of the Low Countries is the fast red of military and hunting coats until XIXc. The kermes of the cardinal's red gowns (used in Germany since XIIc.) is being replaced in XVIc. by cochineal imported by Antwerp from America.

Saffron yellow was the specialty of Basel; the safflower orange of Italy was part of the commerce of Frankfort.

There were the pale browns of German weld; Brazil wood red; the XVIc. purplish-blacks of the New World logwood; the orange-yellow series of fustic (combined with logwood for brownish-blacks); the lichen-purples of orchil and orseille, imported from Italy, but also locally present, to be scraped up patiently by sea-coast peasants, and still one of the beauties of the crofter-produced tweeds of the British Isles. There were other wood, bark and berry dyes, imported or collected, fast or fugitive; as well as all the rusty colors obtained from soaking iron scraps in acidified or chemically varied local waters.

With the great advances in chemistry of the XVIIIc. new dyes began to appear, but these XVIc. Flemings had at their command most of the dyes used until the invention of aniline dyes in second third XIXc. Everybody in Flanders knew something about dyeing, and their colors have a subtle, varied richness of which we have been deprived by standardization and fast colors, even though we have colors of which they could only dream.

1107. XVIc. 1566. Flemish. (Vienna, Art History Mus.)
Pieter Brueghel, e.
Murder of the Holy Innocents (left half).

The growing strength of the idea of uniformity is shown in the identical black-trimmed red jackets of the mounted Spanish soldiers. The manifest advantage of knowing your friends from your enemies was exploited in the garments of feudal retainers as it could not be with transient pressed soldiers or mercenaries. Colored scarves were a XVIc. attempt to consolidate these casuals, but lent themselves easily to trickery. There were few regular troops to be put into uniform before second half XVIIc.

The Print Room of the Metropolitan Museum treasures one of the invitations to the coronation of Matthias of Hungary. With it is included a woodcut of a black-clad rider, described as "a little pattern of a man," which the guests are asked to follow in outfitting their retainers, who will make the king's procession impressive. A lord now outfits his own men, at his own expense, not in his own colors, but for the aggrandizement of the growing central power of the king.

1108. XVIc. 1567. Flemish. (Munich Gallery.)
P. Brueghel, e.
Fool's Paradise.

An author, in a rose-colored doublet and hose with tied-on cod-piece, his writing implements hanging from his belt, sleeps on his fur-lined black gown; a peasant in dun hose lies on his flail; a soldier wears a dark gray doublet with red hose, seamed in black, in an elaboration of the Swiss style seen on Schwitzer.

1107

1109. XVIc. 1568. Flemish. (Louvre.)
P. Brueghel, e.
The Cripples.

Whether there is, or not, a punning relation in the fox-tails (emblem of the oppressive party of the Geuse) on the garments of the beggars (*gueux*), they help to make these some of the most loathsome creatures ever painted.

Europe was being ravaged by the new plague, syphilis, and fresh outbreaks of bubonic plague, the rat and louse-borne disease of poverty and filth. People turned scarlet or black and fell dead in the middle of a conversation on the street, and their better but infected clothing was snatched from their corpses by creatures like these.

1110. XVIc. 1569. Flemish. (Vienna, Art History Mus.)
P. Brueghel, e.
Peasant's Wedding.

There is evidence of Spanish oppression in many of Brueghel's paintings; the number of guests at such a Flemish wedding was limited to 20 by a decree of Charles V.

Bride with flowing hair in center, her wedding crown hung above. Women's simple béguine headdresses and velvet-yoked gowns with wide sleeves. Franciscan friar at the end of the table talking to an important townsman. Lappeted caps, retained in peasant use, could be tied under chin. Oblong wood trenchers instead of plates; no forks; everyone carries his or her own knife in a hanging sheath (even the aproned baby on the floor, wearing a too-large hat with a peacock feather); wooden spoon stuck in the hat of the farm boy who is carrying in tarts on an unhinged barn door. Buttoned closing along shoulder seam, best seen on green-lined black coat of man pouring wine. Bagpiper's hats, feather or medals sewn on edge. Hose are, plainly, still of seamed cloth; garters, *points* by which hose could be trussed hang in pairs; the other server has a bunch of shoe-string-like points knotted to his hat.

1111. XVIc. 1569. Flemish. (Vienna, Art History Mus.)
P. Brueghel, e.
Dance of the Peasants.

Bagpiper's doublet, untrussed for comfort like the dancer's, shows pairs of grommeted eyelets, through which the points tie. Cap with a hanging medal over a white coif.

Flemish aprons come well around the body, on strings tied at the back, but like the narrow aprons of the Rhine valley, the top corners of the apron hang free.

Male dancer with knife, and spoon in his hat. His companion's best headdress is folded with some care; pattern of the back of the square yoke, seaming of sleeve and bodice clearly shown; pouch and key from girdle.

Beyond her: untrussed hose, with a tied-on codpiece flap, are held up by a belt. In the group beyond the signboard of the inn, a fool in motley scarlet.

1112. XVIc. Flemish. (Vienna, Imperial Museum.)

Att. to *Pieter Brueghel, e.* The Shepherd.

This winning old wretch is delightfully dressed in a coat of many colors, stitched together with all his wife's left-over bits of wool.

His red cap is edged with blond fur. The jacket collar has the hooks and eyes, which we have suspected must be in use on the tight doublets of the gentry; it has a little bell as a top button. Great buttons covered with coiled cord fasten the jacket, which is of strips of natural, red, yellow, greenish putty, brown and blue, sewed with white, black, blue-black, red-brown and brown.

Diß ist ein Figur vnd eigentliche anzeygung eins gantzen Thurniers / wie der vor zeyten durch die Ritterschafft vnd vom Adel gehalten. Wie vnd was darinn / mit Seyl abhauwen durch die Grießwertel / Empfahung / Cleinoter abhauwung mit den Schwerdten / Straffung deß Schlagens / Schranckensetzens vnd außzihens / ꝛc. gehandelt worden.

1113. XVIc. 1566. German.

Thurnier Buch von Unsang Vrsachen Vrsprung, Frankfort-on-Main, 1566; illustrated by *Jost Amman.*

Fortunately for us, Jost Amman, a Swiss working in Nuremberg, was one of the most productive artists who ever lived. A pupil who worked with him for four years said that Amman produced enough during that period to fill a hay wagon. His woodcut books have been catalogued by C. Becker; *Jobst Amman,* Leipzig, 1851; and many have been reproduced, partly or entirely.

Among the most useful are the plates of this *Tournament Book,* 1566; *Trades and Workmen,* 1568 (all its 115 plates, as well as some from the *Tournament Book,* are reproduced by Hirth); military costume in the *Fronspergers Kriegsbuch,* 1577; *Costumes of the Catholic Church,* 1586 (of which the Print Room of the N. Y. Public Library has a copy, showing 102 plates of clerics, religious orders, lay members, and masked flagellants); the *Trachtenbuch,* published by Hans Weigel, Nuremberg, 1577; and the *Frauenzimmer Trachtenbuch,* published by S. Feuerabend, Frankfort, 1586 (reproduced in facsimile by the Holbein Society as *The Theatre of Women*), both of which show regional costume, particularly German. Amman illustrated books on everything from midwifery and cooking to tournaments; he also designed playing cards which are valuable for costume.

With the downfall of feudalism, the tournament had degenerated into an almost bloodless show. At the court of Henry VIII, it was intermixed with pageantry; under Elizabeth, it was reduced to a formula (see Ill. 1202: Queen's champion). The elements of pageantry were preeminent at the court of Catherine de' Medici's sons (see Medici Tap.). In France, and particularly in England the bourgeoise and yeomanry were advancing steadily into the gentry and nobility (see beginning of Eng. XIVc., Paston Family). Only in feudal Germany were generations of noble birth really important. The quarterings of 16 armigerous forebears were still necessary for entrance into German tournaments, where knights still solemnly sweated through the old knightly formulae. The inescapable element of pageantry was expressed, in Germany, in the panoply of the knight and his steed. Public squares, like bridges, were particularly suitable as tournament yards (see Appendix, Ill. 829: Stow).

Even in Germany, pageantry played an increasing part. In a celebration at the court of Dresden in 1591 (*Fugger News Letters*), for the christening of the child of the Elector of Saxony, the tilting ground was planted with 100 huge fir trees, decorated with oranges, pomegranates, pumpkins, live birds, and squirrels. The Elector led a procession of singing miners. Then 100 huntsmen brought in cages of bears, wild boars, wolves, lynxes, foxes, and small game. These were let loose and belonged to the person who caught them. Then larger animals were loosed to roam the tilting ground, guarded by dogs, who protected the populace when the wild boars charged. Four days of jousting, "run for money," then followed.

1114. XVIc. 1570. German. (Toronto Art Gallery.)

B. Bruyn, y.

Lady of the Vavasour Family.

Portrait by a German painter, of a Dutch lady, related by marriage to Sir William Vavasour.

With a white cap as fine and exquisitely embroidered as this one, the wide Dutch ruff is starkly plain. Spanish coat-dress with shoulder rolls patterned in the spirit of picadills. The separation of bodice from skirt is stressed by the picadill-edged point of the pinked satin doublet; the hips of the dark skirt are widened by the new bolster. The precious girdle tends to shorten. Gloves with a turned and slashed cuff.

1115. XVIc. 1577. Sweden.(Vastmanland, Ungso Church.)

Gravestone.

Elsa Trolle.

Flat hat set square on netted hair. Spanish coat with extremely high, wide collar. High-necked underdress with spreading collar and double ruff.

1116. XVIc. 1569. Dutch. (Metropolitan Museum.)

Dutch School.

Surgeon.

Quasi-ecclesiastical dress; surgeon's needle, other hand on a skull; hospitals and medicine are still administered by the Church.

1117-21. XVIc. 1581. Dutch. (Metropolitan Museum, Print Room.)

Omnium gentium habitus, or *Trachtenbuch,* Antwerp, 1581, engraved by *Abraham de Bruyn.*

Dutch, Belgian, and British sailors.

In first quarter XVIc., Weiditz shows Dutch seamen wearing these same clothes and the long wide breeches, which were commonly worn in Zeeland (where the sea was everyone's business), and which appear on Alsatian river boatmen. They were also a basic part of the dress of Basque men, who were the whale fishermen of mediaeval days, until Barents' discoveries led to Greenland whaling.

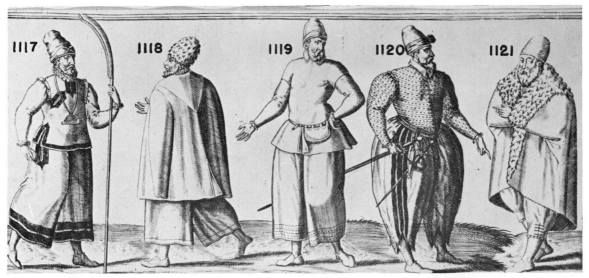

The Dutch sea-captain, holding an oar, and wearing around his neck the whistle which was his badge of office, shows braid trim and diagonal pockets; these will appear as a fashion at the turn of the next century, with loose breeches not unlike these, cut off above the knees like our "shorts." The similarity is so striking that the XVIIc. style, seen particularly in Spain and the Low Countries, must be an adaptation of this old-established seaman's style. In additional corroboration, the shorts show a useless but decorative buttoned side-slit, like those with which the long breeches of the Belgian and British sailors are provided for easy rolling.

Tall caps, bound close against the wind, are seen on all XVIc. seamen. The bare-backed galley slaves, chained together, which Evelyn observed at Marseilles in 1644, wore only these high bonnets, in red, and coarse canvas drawers.

1122. XVIc. 1577. German.

Trachtenbuch, Hans Weigel, Nuremberg, 1577; engraved by *Jost Amman*.

Burgher's daughter of Breslau, Silesia.

1123-24. XVIc. 1586. German.

Frauenzimmer Trachtenbuch, Frankfort, 1586; engraved by *Jost Amman*.

1123. Women's clothes are increasingly severe and masculine, and men's more blousy and effeminate, in Germany as elsewhere. With the apron, full, banded skirt, and rosary of the costume of Meissen, the high-born matron wears a circular cape and a hat with the heightening, pleated crown of the male variety. Moryson notes the short, jutting cloaks and hats in the form of an oyster-shell seen in Germany.

1124. The costume of a widow of Meissen, already seen on the Bavarian duchess, is one of the most striking of German mourning garments.

1125. XVIc. 1587. German.

Heindrik Goltzius.
The Standard Bearer.

No illustration shows better than this the artifically padded yet loosely effeminate male costume of the latter part of XVIc.: wreathed and plumed bonnet, worn with earrings (in male use, usually only one), and blowing curls; great loosely set ruff *à la confusion,* worn with the very pattern of the pinked peascod doublet at its most fantastic, its loose sleeves and galloon-guarded breeches laced and knotted along their open outer seams.

1126. XVI. c. 1585-1590. Dutch.

J. de Gheyn.
Mascarades.

Goltzius' pupil, who lived entirely in the Netherlands, did a series of 10 plates of carnival costumes in the spirit of the Italian comedy which was delighting Europe. (See XVIIc. Italian, Callot illustrations.)

With the high, puffed Italian bonnet, the musician wears loose Protestant *pluderhose,* with which the cod-piece survived longest; garters crossed behind and knotted above the knee.

The woman with her pouch, bunch of keys and aprons, show the pinned-on sleeve and shirt-puffs which have persisted in Flanders since early XVc.

Turkeys had been brought from the New World during this century. The wearer of the wattled turkey mask has the dashing new sombrero, embroidered as high felt hats often were, and with the very high crown of the last decade. Peascod doublet with overlapping skirts. Unpadded trunk-hose with cuffed canions and knotted garters. Shoes begin to show heels and mount over the instep into the tongue of the XVIIc.

1127. XVIc. 1594. German. (Metropolitan Museum, Print Room.)

P. Flindt. Woman.

Flindt was a native of Nuremberg. The border, brocade, embroidered apron, standing ruff, and pendant sleeve of Nuremberg's costume, at the end XVIc., are stylized here.

1128-29. XVIc. 1596. Flemish. (Metropolitan Museum, Print Room.)

Emblematica Secularis, 1st ed. 1596. Illustrated by *Theodore de Bry.*

With voyages of discovery and the new interest in strange and alien ways there comes a fanciful spirit of stylized exaggeration, which will be seen in Bérain's "inventions," in the potentates and American Indians of Louis XIV's pageants, and in Pillement's fantastic oriental flowers and chinoiserie in early XVIIIc.

The bell-like character of the skirts of the ladies of his city of Nuremberg at the end XVIc. occurs to a goldsmith like Flindt. De Gheyn's Dutch folk appear in grotesque carnival masks (see 1126).

A bizarre strain, seen in Flanders from Hieronymus Bosch in XVc. and in Brueghel, is combined with the stresses of years of existence under Spanish rule and religious differences, in the dichotomy of de Bry's symbolic Netherlands figures. The dress of a soldier at the turn of XV-XVIc. was indeed often divided down a center line, and striped and slashed into dissimilarity on either side. De Bry's soldier has an Italianate left side, after that manner; his right side has the newest collar, longer breeches, not packed with bombast, but with their padding and fabric quilted together. Adherents to Catholicism made these breeches their characteristic wear, as *pluderhose* were of Protestants. The ribbon tags at the elbow, fringed sash, garter-knots, and bows on the shoes are flowing. They differ from the former set rosettes as do the new sprays of hat feathers from the Elizabethan curled ostrich plume, both shown on the adjoining figure.

Outgoing and incoming fashions are set on opposing sides: the high-crowned Elizabethan hat, against the new, primarily military hat, the broad brim of which is cocked out of the way on one side; a small, formal multiple ruff against a wide loose one; a full sleeve with a wrist ruff, and a close, slashed sleeve with lace-edged cuff and braid-trimmed dependent sleeve; a doublet of normal waist length against its latest peascod form, prominently buttoned; loose *pluderhose,* crossed garters and rosettes, with higher trunk hose, canions, and a fringed knot; clocked hose with plain; pinked shoes with simpler ones which mount high on the instep. (See Appendix.)

1130. XVIc. 1597. Dutch. (New York, Cooper Union Museum.)

Hendrik Goltzius. The Dog of Goltzius.

Goltzius' dog is shown with the son of Thierry Frisius, the Flemish painter. Straw hat with wider brim and important hat band; ruff disintegrating into a collar, narrowly edged with lace and worked into open patterns, which are in themselves the origins of lace. Beautiful button and loop closing on jacket and on the bottom of the outseam of the new shorts, which have an embroidered edge. Pinking in small patterns. Rise of shoe into tongues.

1131-32. XVIc. 1524. French, Lorraine.

Gabriel Salmon (fl. 1504-42). Two Title Pages.

Salmon was court painter to Duke Anthony of Lorraine, whom Pierre Gringoire served as herald. Gringoire's *Blazon des Hérétiques* is a descriptive catalogue in verse of the heresies of Lutheranism.

The title page (1131) shows a figure, allied to the German-Swiss mercenary, dressed half as a peasant laborer, half as an armed nobleman. His costume is partly explained by a text in verse, which asserts that Lutheran heresy is discordant, contradictory, and makes itself ridiculous, like his dress. His body is tremendously elongated to signify the contempt and self-righteous pride which are the worst Lutheran vices. Their next worse sin is self-indulgence. They preach

"lubricité, erreur, et gourmandise," lure nuns from convents, urge priests to marry, and do not keep fast days; corrupt, venomous snakes writhe in his apron, and greedy rats gnaw the bag he carries.

Lance, spade, and book (nobles, commons, and clergy) signify the Lutheran destruction of authority, and of the existing social order; *"destruction de tous prelats, et diminution de la noblesse,"* while *"voullans commun* (i.e. the rabble) *vivre en auctorité."* The flames issuing from his body are another symbol of Lutheran destructiveness. The necklace may represent the vanity which Gringoire imputes to the Lutherans.

No. 1132 is the title page of de Seronville's *Victory over Lutherans.*

From George Clutton: *Two Early Representations of Lutheranism in France.* Journal of the Warburg Institute, I, 1937-38.

1133. Late XVI-e.XVIIc. Flemish. (Boston, Isabella Stewart Gardner Museum.)

Tapestries: Chateau and Garden Set.
Garden Scene.

Houses, affected by the architecture of Italy, have become lighter and airier, "fair houses so full of glass, that one cannot tell where to become to be out of the sun or cold," Bacon described them. Their gardens, with statuary, fountains, arches, and far-set pavilions, are enclosed with walls of espaliered fruit; vegetables are as decoratively used as flowers. The exotic turkey, with a crane, takes the place of the falcon in every mediaeval tapestry, but the collar of the hunting dog has not changed since the time of Gaston de Foix.

The costume is that of the turn of the century. The lady standing in the center wears the bolstered, drum-shaped skirt, with a number of objects, including a looking glass, hanging from her girdle. The girdle now finishes in an important jewel, just below the point of the bodice. The hair is now uncovered, studded with flowers, with a jewel at the center of the forehead.

Her suitor wears a felt hat of the new "derby" shape, plumed and banded; a low, open band collar; cape; padded venetians; and high boots with turned-down tops.

The seated man wears a short, skirtless jacket, braided in the new diagonal way, over a pinked doublet.

The couple walking off to the right show the simplified, caped, male outline with an important hat carrying a spray of feathers; and the female silhouette, with hanging sleeves, of the Medici tapestries.

1134. XVIc. English. (Windsor, H.M. the King.)
Unknown artist. Arthur, Prince of Wales.

1135. XVIc. English. (London, Soc. of Antiquaries.)
Unknown artist. Edward IV.

In the second of these two XVIc. portraits of XVc. personages, Edward IV, d.1483, wears Italianate brocade garments, the jerkin caught by horizontal strings of pearls, each carrying a fine, identical pendant.

Arthur, who died in 1502, at 15, wears the Tudor collar of the Red Rose of Lancaster and the White Rose of York which his father, Henry VII, had assumed upon his marriage to Elizabeth of York, to symbolize the reconciliation of their factions; the roses are linked with tasseled cords, their loops filled with pearls. His bonnet carries the medallion of a saint, and its slashings are caught by precious studs. Jewels worth £15,000 had been imported from France for Arthur in 1501, when he married Catherine of Aragon. His shirt is edged with fine Spanish embroidery.

1136. XVIc. c. 1518. English. (Oxford, Corpus Christi College.)
Corvus, Hans Johannus.
Richard Fox, Bishop of Winchester.

The bishop, whom we see in surplice, scarf and episcopal ring, painted by a Flemish artist, came of yeoman stock. During his youth, he had become intimate in Paris with "the great rebel, Henry *ap* Tudor," as Richard III called him, in opposing Fox's appointment to a vicarage. Immediately upon Henry VII's accession, Fox was called into his service, be-

coming confessor, as he eventually was executor, of the king's mother, the Countess of Richmond. Fox received increasingly important bishoprics as sinecures, and as Lord Privy Seal devoted himself to statesmanship. The marriage of Henry VII's daughter, Margaret, to the king of Scotland led to the union of the two crowns in 1603, and to the union of the kingdoms in 1707. Fox negotiated the marriage of Catherine of Aragon to Prince Arthur. Fox upheld the legality of Henry VIII's marriage to his brother's widow, and continued in power, though Henry called him "a fox indeed," until ousted by Wolsey.

After his retirement from government, Fox devoted himself to the conduct of the richest English bishopric, and founded (1515-6) Corpus Christi College, where the New Learning flourished under Italian teachers of Latin and Greek.

1137. XVIc. 1511. English. (London, College of Arms.)
Westminster Tournament Rolls.
The Answerers and Trumpeters.

The Westminster Tournament was held by Henry VIII in 1511, to celebrate the birth of his short-lived and only son by his first wife, the widow of his brother Arthur.

The Roll shows: 1. the procession to the lists; 2. the combat; and 3. the return to court. This is the right side of 2: it shows Les Venants, the 8 Answerers, the caparisons of whose horses, in courtesy to the Queen, bear the roses of Aragon, the castles of Castile, the cockleshells of St. James, and the pomegranate flow-

ers of Granada. Behind them, the return signal, *"A l'hostel,"* is blown by the trumpeters.

With the rounded forms of the XVIc. Maximilian armor, the Answerers wear armets—round-topped, beaked tilting helmets; mitons; sollerets of the sabot-shape which has superseded poulaines, in armor as in civil dress; and gored *bases* of alternating plain and brocade strips.

ENGLISH PAINTING, XVIc.

Aside from Nicholas Hilliard and Isaac Oliver(both influenced by Holbein), the most characteristically English painters of the Tudor period are foreign born like the German Holbein; the Flemish Ewarth, and the Gheeraerts and de Critz families, who worked entirely in their adopted countries; the Italian Zuccaro; and the Flemish Sir Anthony Moro, and Sir Anthony Van Dyke in Stuart times. It is hard to know what to call them when they *were* English painting, but unless they worked only in England, we credit them to the countries of their birth. In the case of Holbein and others, who painted the dress of so many countries, captions combine their nationality with that of the sitter whose national dress is shown, as: German-English, etc.

1138. XVIc. 1527. German-English. (Basel Museum.)
Hans Holbein, the younger.
Sir Thomas More and family.

Made by Holbein on his first English visit, and given in 1528 to their mutual friend Erasmus, this study for the painting shows the costume of the English upper middle-class household described by Erasmus. "More has built near London, upon the Thames, a modest yet commodious mansion. There he lives surrounded by his numerous family, including his wife, his son, and his son's wife, his three daughters and their husbands, with eleven grandchildren. There is not any man living so affectionate to his children as he, and he loveth his old wife as if she were a girl of fifteen."

The caps of the older men are of the square, biretta-like forms which by this time have been pretty well relegated to scholastic, legal and clerical wear. More's long gown has slit, dependent sleeves. He wears the

SS color with a Tudor rose pendant, and carries a muff, as does Johannes More, dressed in a judge's cloak. Young Johannes wears a short gown with a standing collar and braid-trimmed sleeves, puffed to the elbow. The bulky fullness of Henry's gown is gathered onto a yoke.

The ladies wear the English gable hood, one or both lappets of which had begun to be pinned up, towards end first quarter XVIc. Crossed bands of striped material conceal the hair. Over these is worn a white cap, often fastened under the chin and edged by a jewelled frontlet. The whole is surmounted by the wired or stiffened hood; this is usually of black velvet with a band of decoration covering the front section; with the fashion of upturned lappets, their plain dark lining conceals much of this decorative outer strip.

The 15- and 20-year-old girls wear rounder linen headdresses, over caps which fasten under the chin and show the parted hair.

The gowns, of floor length, have low, sash-like girdles with tassels and rosaries. Square-necked bodices, on some of which the front opening lingers, are filled with sheer yokes, *partlets* or *tuckers,* or with bands and necklaces in characteristic variety; they are laced or looped across with ties and chains, and carry funnel sleeves with fur linings, turned far back. Quilting gives body to the undersleeves, which are tied together at intervals along an open outseam, over the loose sleeve of the shirt.

1139. XVIc. 1524. English. (Norwich, St. John's Maddermarket Church.) Sepulchral Brass.
John and Lettys Terri.

This is a provincial family, no member of which is dressed in the latest fashion. In Terri's case, the archaic garments are the ceremonial dress of a mayor. The scarf of office hangs over the tabard-like XIVc. cloak, buttoned on the right shoulder, and showing the wide sleeves of an equally old-style undergarment.

The sons wear the square-necked, full skirted jacket of the Transition period, which is that of the mother and daughters.

Lettys' gown is that seen in Franco-Flemish tapes-

1140

1141

1142

1143

1144

1145

tries—end XVc.: high, square neck; train pinned up over the bustle of the back gathers of the skirt; and is worn with the specifically English form of hood, the pedimental (or gable or kennel) headdress, edged with a jewelled band. Her girdle, with its Tudor roses, is of the new, lower, wider sort, which has something sash-like, asymmetric and dependent about it—an effect given here by the hanging rosary; these will be seen until the religious disturbances begin. It might well have been a "muskeball" (pomander).

1140-42. XVIc. 1527. German-English. (Windsor Castle, the King of England.)
Holbein, y.
1140. Mrs. John Clement (Margaret Gigs), inscribed Mother Iak (nurse of the royal children).
1141. Lady. 1142. Queen Anne Boleyn.
The attributed names are doubtful, but all wear delightful and unusual forms of the current domestic cap, with fur or felt hats. Pins are still a novelty, and are as proudly displayed as in Flanders.

1143. XVIc. 1527. English. (Metropolitan Museum.)
British School: formerly att. to *Holbein.*
Lady Guildford, aged 27.

This portrait shows the hood with the back curtain long, full, and still undivided, but with one of the front lappets pinned up. On her plain dark gown, the emphasis on the small, neat shoulder is provided by continuing the chains which are looped across the bodice. Below the familiar pendant with pearls is pinned a delicate jewelled spray. The stiffening of her undersleeve is provided by external seaming, spaced like the bodice chains.

1144. XVIc. 1534. German-English. (Metropolitan Mus.)
Holbein. Margaret Wyatt, Lady Lee, at 34.
Lady Lee wears a variation of the French hood, which had reached England c. 1515, and which can be seen in its classic form on Catherine Howard. Lady Lee's béguine-like black hood is set before the light-colored, raked-back, crescent front of the French hood. Her red-brown brocade gown shows many new attributes: the high, standing collar line of gown and shirt; leg o'mutton sleeves caught by beautiful paired aiglettes across puffs of orange material, with white shirt sleeve showing only in the frill at the wrist; inverted V-opening of skirt, scarlet underskirt; oval pendants, increasingly massive.

1145. XVIc. 1536. German-English. (Vienna, Kunsthistorisches Museum.)
Holbein. Queen Jane Seymour.

The hood is seen here in its final development, with both red-and-gold lappets pinned up. Its back curtain has been slit; the r. section twisted up in back, and pinned into a "whelk-shell," and the l. carried around to the r. shoulder. Her red velvet gown, with pearl and ruby bands and magnificent pendant, has an all-over pattern in gold bugles on the turned-back sleeve. Over a shirt with black Spanish embroidery frill, the undersleeves of silver brocade are caught with ruby clasps. The V-opening of the skirt from a natural waistline shows the same brocade, and a jewelled girdle with double pendants.

1146

1147

1148

1146. XVIc. 1527. German-English. (Metropolitan Museum, Frick Coll.)
Holbein. Sir Thomas More.

The Chancellor wears the costume shown in the family group, including the XVc. bonnet, its brim cut away in front, and laced across the crown, which is characteristic of him.

The SS collar has been the official one of the house of Lancaster since last quarter XVc.; it is shown with the Lancastrian portcullis of Beaufort, which had become a Tudor badge in XVc., and a pendant Tudor rose.

1147. XVIc. 1532. German-English. (Berlin, Kaiser Friedrich Museum.)
Holbein. George Gisze.

This portrait is of a Danzig merchant, who lived in London as a member of the Hanseatic League's privileged "Merchants of the Steelyard"; so-called because, to the annoyance of the citizens, they were allowed to keep their own scales on the premises, instead of using the official scales of the City. They had been chartered by Henry III in 1259 to "bring hither as well wheat, rye, and other grains, as cables, ropes, masts, pitch, tar, flax, hemp, linen cloth, wainscots, wax, steel, and other profitable merchandise." (Stow.)

Gisze wears a form of the practical "flat caps, knit of woolen yarn black, but so light that they were obliged to tie them under their chins, for else the wind would be master over them. The use of these flat round caps so increased, being of less price than the French bonnet, that in short time young aldermen took the wearing of them" (Stow) and they were taken over by the London apprentices as their very own. His black gown is slit for the passage of the sleeves of the red satin doublet, their upper fullness pleated in at the elbow. Both jacket and doublet have the low, square neckline which begins to disappear at about this time. Shirt: gathered onto a cord at base of neck.

His table is covered by an Oriental carpet, such as the Venetian rivals of the Hanse distributed over Europe; carpet manufacture was not begun in England until later in XVIc. Accessories of trade: holder for a ball of cord, seal, inkwell and quills, shaker for blotting-sand, and scales.

1148. XVIc. 1526-28. German-English. (Washington, National Gallery of Art.)

1149

Holbein. Sir Brian Tuke.

The first British postmaster wears a flat cap over a black coif; chain with symbols of the Passion, over a fur-collared black gown. Through its slit sleeves we see gold and black checked sleeves of his doublet. A tiny frill finishes the shirred, embroidered collar of the shirt. He carries gloves.

1149. XVIc. 1536. German-English. (Florence, Uffizi.)
Holbein. Sir Richard Southwell.

Privy councillor and official of Henry VIII's court, Southwell played an important part in the confiscation of the monasteries, at the instigation of Thomas Cromwell.

Standard costume of the period, with the collar ties which will persist in use for another quarter century. In the 1560's, the high collar with ruff is often worn open, with the cords hanging.

1150. XVIc. 1533. German-English. (London, National Gallery.)

Holbein. The French Ambassadors to London, Jean de Dinteville and Georges de Selve.

Dinteville is dressed in black and rose, with a chain carrying a medallion of the Order of St. Michael, and a green and gold tassel hanging from his girdle. His flat hat bears a silver skull set in gold. Light, spotted lynx, with which his gown is collared and lined, has become a favorite fur; lines of fur were much used at the seams of the upper puffed sleeve, in both male and female costume.

Selve, later Bishop of Lavour, wears the 4-cornered mozetta like scholar's cap, and a fur-lined gown of brown brocade.

1151. XVIc. c. 1537. German-English (Chatsworth, Duke of Devonshire.)

School of Holbein. Henry VIII.

This portrait of Henry VIII is a copy of one portion of the Whitehall picture, later destroyed by fire, which the king ordered from Holbein in 1537; which showed him, his parents, Henry VII and Elizabeth of York, and Jane Seymour.

There are few pictures of the young Henry, attractive, athletic, learned and musical; but though puffy with disease, the sumptuously dressed 46-year old king is a figure of the most purposeful power and intelligence. Not only his resolution and competence, but a great interest in wardrobe, and the personal means to indulge it, were the king's legacy to his daughter, Elizabeth.

Henry's rivalry with the King of France was lifelong. He grew his great golden beard when he heard that Francis was bearded; he competed sartorially with Francis at the Field of the Cloth of Gold; and his death-bed message to Francis to "remember that he, too, was mortal" scared Francis into his own final illness.

Henry wears a high-collared doublet with white puffs drawn through the interstices of its embroidery; a vest, cut wide and low, and *bases* to match, of blue trimmed with silver braid and ruby-set gold clasps over white puffs. There are two white sashes, one of which carries the dagger with its red and gold mounts and tassels.

His gown is of red velvet, lined with sable and embroidered in gold. The upper part of its sleeve, which is usable, is gored and banded with gold embroidery done in cord; its unusable, hanging part is tubular, separately made and set on at the back. What would be the front (if worn) is vertically slit at the top, with the tabs turned back to show an embroidered lining. Elaborate cod-piece mounted on nether garments. White hose with the Garter; slashed white shoes, rising high over the instep, have short, laterally spread, square toes. Black bonnet with a white plume laid around the brim, the under side of which is sewed with gold tags.

Although the wall-hanging is probably of stamped leather, its pattern is a favorite for corded appliqué on costume.

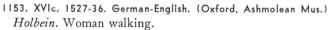

1152. XVIc. 1527-36. German-English. (British Museum.)
Holbein. English lady with rosary.

Back view shows the development of the pedimental hood. The back curtain has been supported, beneath, by a box-like extension of the gable-front. After the slitting of the curtain, the box had emerged, become independent, and the slit ends had been added to it. We see also the V-back of the square decolletage, and the pleats in the bodice, leading to the back fullness of the skirt.

1153. XVIc. 1527-36. German-English. (Oxford, Ashmolean Mus.)
Holbein. Woman walking.

She wears a gray dress with a black yoke; looped up by a catch slung over the shoulder, and by a tasseled yellow sash with rosary; beige underskirt; red petticoat; square-toed black shoes.

1154. XVIc. 1538. German-English. (National Gallery of Art, Washington.)
Holbein. Edward VI as Prince of Wales.

This portrait, presented to Henry VIII as a New Year's gift, 1539, shows the little son of Jane Seymour dressed in red and gold. Over a coif, he wears a flat hat with the single plume which had followed the profusion of feathers of the Transition period; its under-side is sewn with precious aiglettes, with which the gentry differentiated this enormously popular hat.

Lady Bryane, governess of the royal children, had great trouble getting clothes for them. This might be the very costume about which she wrote Lord Thomas Cromwell, just as Edward was getting his fourth tooth: "The best coat my lord prince's grace hath is tinsel, and that he shall have on at the time; he hath never a good jewel for his cap." As king, the boy Edward was left entirely without pocket-money, and as Mary and Elizabeth were alternately declared illegitimate they were badly neglected in childhood. Anne Boleyn's accounts show that despite the disappointment of Elizabeth's sex, she did once go to some pains to order a milliner to measure the baby for caps of purple and of white satin with a gold caul.

1155. XVIc. 1543. German-English. (Metropolitan Museum, Bache Collection.)
Holbein. Edward VI.

Side view of the flat hat, worn tilted in the Italian manner after 1520, over cropped hair. Collar line mounting.

1156. XVIc. 1538. German-English. (London, Nat. Gall.)

Holbein. Christina of Denmark.

Granddaughter of Joanne the Mad and widow of the Duke of Milan, the beautiful Christina repulsed Henry VIII, saying that she "had only one head," and was remarried in 1540 to the Duke of Bar and Lorraine.

This is one of the few full length female portraits of the period; it shows her in a one-piece gown of black velvet mourning, sable-trimmed, and with delicate stitching at the frill of her shirt sleeve. She carries buff gloves.

1157. XVIc. 1539. German-Flemish. (Louvre.)

Holbein. Anne of Cleves.

Holbein was sent to Flanders in 1539 by Henry VIII to paint the portrait of his bride, who in the flesh Henry found "no better than a Flemish mare," and soon divorced. Ample settlement was made on her and she remained in England, a good-natured person who appeared at court in her endless lovely dresses, each "more wonderful than the last," decorated with the fine needlework which was her only accomplishment.

English male clothing of this period is much more influenced than female by German fashions. Anne's completely Flemish costume, compared with the gar-

ments of Henry, shows the parallel developments which so often occur in male and female garments, in respect to the cut-out front of the bodice (Henry: doublet) over its partlet (Henry: vest); and the puffed upper sleeve with its band above the elbow. The lower sleeve is funnel-shaped, like her skirt which was described as "without a trayne after the Dutche fassyon," at a period when English ladies' gowns, almost alone, retain them.

The tucker or partlet and the cuff-bands of the shirt are not of the Spanish embroidery seen so far, but of cut-work; this antedates lace, which in fact grew out of cut-work; lace has been made since XVc. and will be common by XVIIc.

Her headdress is typically Flemish. Over a tiny, pearl-edged cap is laid an oblong of lawn; on this is set a swelling cap, gold and pearl embroidered, with the motto "*A bon fine,*" and a jewelled pendant pinned on the left side. Monograms and mottos continue to be used as they were in the XVc. Flemish hennins (see Marie Portinari, Ill. 858; Burgundy, Ill. 880): the wide belts of the hennin period have been much reduced, but Flemish belts continue to be precious and handsomely buckled, and in German and Flemish use, are worn high. Rings now appear in profusion; worn on the thumb as well as other fingers, they are small and simple in comparison with *carcanet* collars and pendants.

1158. First half XVIc. English. (Metropolitan Museum, Bache Collection.)

Master of Queen Mary Tudor. An English Princess.

The unnamed princess is dressed in brocade of a rosy red, much used at this time. Her shirt sleeves and yoke, which had gained a standing collar finished by a frill, are decorated in bands of Spanish embroidery. French hood over frizzed hair.

There are two portraits of Mary Tudor before 1533 by this painter.

1159. XVIc. 1540-41. German-English. (Toledo, Museum of Art.)

Holbein. Queen Catharine Howard.

Henry VIII's fifth wife wears a black satin gown; black velvet yoke with a standing collor; leg o'mutton sleeve (reputedly brought from Flanders by Anne of Cleves), its gold-embroidered black puffs caught by paired aiglettes; shirt ruffles of black Spanish embroidery.

She wears a brooch designed by Holbein, one of several for which his original drawings have been preserved. As was the case with the great salt-cellars and standing cups, important jewels were often given names. The stones from Mary, Queen of Scots' "Great Harry" were later set in James I's "Mirror of Great Britain."

On her slightly frizzed hair, she carries a classic example of the French hood; a white cap with a frill of gold tissue, under a raked-back crescent band, from which hangs a triangular tube of black velvet.

1160. XVIc. 1540-43. German-English. (Metropolitan Museum.)

Holbein. Lady Rich.

At about the end of its vogue, Lady Rich continues to wear the gable hood, but her high-collared bodice and standing shirt collar are both finished with the pleated ruffle, which foreshadows the Elizabethan ruff.

1161. XVIc. 1542. German-English. (London, St. Bartholomew's Hospital.)

Holbein. Henry VIII.

The aging king seems to have found this the costume most suitable to his infirmity and bulk. It appears in different colors, in various portraits, and was described in 1540 by Edward Hall: "His person was apparelled in a coate of purple velvet, somewhat made lyke a frocke, all over embrodered with flat gold of damaske with small lace mixed between of the same gold, and other laces of the same so goyng trauerse wyse, that the ground lytle appered: about whyche garment was a rych garde very curiously enbrodered, the sleves and brest were out lyned with cloth of golde, and tyed together with great buttons of Diamonds, Rubys, and Orient Perle, his swoorde and swoorde gyrdle adorned with stones and especiall Emerodes, his night cappe garnished with stone, but his bonet was so ryche of Iuels that few men could value them. Besyde all this he ware in baudricke wyse a collar of such Balystes (pink rubies) and Perle that few men ever saw the lyke."

In this case the coat is of dark gray, embroidered in gold, with ruby studs; the under-sleeve of snuff brown with emerald studs. It also appears in red and gold. Black hat with pearls, rubies and emeralds.

1162. XVIc. 1540. English. (Longford Castle, Earl of Radnor.)

Hans Eworth. Thomas Wyndham.

Eworth, whose name is variously spelled, was a Flemish painter who lived in England after 1543.

Wyndham, the navigator and explorer, who was drowned while returning from the Gold Coast, wears a spruce-green leather military jerkin, paned in the current small, massed patterns. The combed morion of the second half of XVIc. infantryman, richly decorated, shown above; headpieces are now seldom worn in portraits. Red scarf of an infantry leader; touch-box (powder flask) hung from neck; date of picture on gun muzzle.

1163. XVIc. 1540. German-English. (Frankfort-on-Main, Stadel Inst.)

Holbein, y. Simon George of Quocote, Cornwall.

"Sir George of Cornwall," as he is also called in some titlings of this picture, wears the flattest possible hat of black beaver, plumed on the right and tilted sharply to the left, over cropped hair. The brim, decreasing in size and no longer slashed, is decorated with an enamelled spray of violas, an enamelled medallion of a saint, and small gold ornaments: crossed fish, vases, and lozenge shapes. Natural beard and moustache of midXVIc.

Shirt collar of black Spanish embroidery shows cords for fastening; embroidered ruffles at wrists are full and gathered but not yet formalized. Interlaced cord decoration of black sleeve; gown edged in white; inner garment red and gold.

1164-66. XVIc. 1548. English. (Lancashire, Sefton Church.)

William Molyneux and his two wives.

The Molyneux had lived at Sefton since the Conquest; William, his wives, and the local monument maker all appear to have been country-living conservatives who clung to the old fashions.

The ladies show the pedimental headdress in one

of its last appearances, and William wears an antiquated mail coif, under the XIVc. Lancastrian SS
collar, which had been revived by Henry VII, late in
XVc.

1167. XVIc. 1546. English. (Knole, Lord Sackville.)
School of Holbein. Earl of Surrey.

Henry Howard, (1518?-1547), Earl of Surrey, eldest son of the third Duke of Norfolk, was brought
up "at proud Windsor, where I in lust and joy,
With a Kinge's son, my childish years did pass,"
as companion of Henry VIII's illegitimate son, the
Duke of Richmond. Surrey nearly married Princess
Mary, and Richmond eventually married Surrey's
sister.

Surrey's haughty, rash, intriguing temper took him
repeatedly from court favor to jail: for quarrels, for
eating meat in Lent, for breaking London windows
with Wyatt's son. He fought as one of the champions
at the jousts in 1540, was knighted in 1541, received
the Garter, and fought gallantly in many wars. But
he was tried and beheaded, on the accusation of
quartering his arms with those of Edward the Confessor (as his family continued to do after Mary's
accession); he was actually feared to be plotting,
with his father, against the king.

During four imprisonments, Surrey wrote his
tender love poems to Geraldine, and made a translation of the Aeneid which is the first English blank
verse. Of the transition between the Anglo-Saxon
Chaucerian poetry and the Elizabethan Renaissance,
Puttenham says: there "sprong up a new company
of courtly makers, of whom Sir Thomas Wyatt the
elder and Henry Earle of Surrey were the two chief-
taines, who having travailed into Italy, and there
tasted the sweete and stately measures and stile of the
Italian Poesie, as novices newly crept out of the
schooles of Dante, Arioste, and Petrarch, they greatly
polished our rude and homely maner of vulgar Poesie, from that it had bene before, and for that cause
may justly be sayd the first reformers of our English

meetre and stile." (From *The Arte of English Poesie*,
1589.)

Costume, with superb Renaissance appliqué and
embroidery, shows trunk hose very slightly padded;
slashed shoes still square-toed.

**1168. XVIc. c. 1548. English. (Hampton Court, H.M.
the King.)**
Gwillim Stretes. Gentleman in Red, called "Thomas Howard, Earl of Surrey."

Stretes, a Hollander, was painter at the English
court, c. 1546-1556, and completed some of Holbein's portraits. Entire costume is red, except for a
white plume in the velvet hat and the Spanish black
work of the white shirt; this has a high collar with
a ruffle at the top, and at the wrists. The short, wide
velvet gown has no dependent sleeve from the upper
puff; it is satin lined, and like the jacket beneath,
which is open to the waist, is trimmed with narrow
lines of gold; wide trunk-hose, without padding or
panes. A massive gold tassel hangs from the slung
dagger, and the cuts on the shoes are emphasized by
gold buttons.

**1169. XVIc. c. 1548. English. (Windsor Castle, H.M. the
King.)**
Att. to *G. Stretes* or *School of Holbein.* Edward VI.

The eleven-year-old king was painted several times
in this costume. In his hat, and that of the Gentleman
in Red (1168) the pleated crown is just beginning its
rise, which is indicated in the new diversion of interest from the underside of the brim toward what will
become the hat band.

His ermine-lined gown of bright red velvet is
guarded by gold bands; its collar is higher and narrower, the top of its sleeves less full than formerly
worn. His jerkin of silver brocade has the new high
collar, low waistline, slightly protruding belly, and
overlapping skirts. Horizontal cords, spaced like the
clasps on his father's 1544 coat, cross the corded bands
of decoration, and button. His trunk hose are padded;

1169

puffs are drawn through the cut-out pattern of their brocade and that of the jacket sleeves.

Black hat, shoes, dagger sheath and tassel; white hose. The first knitted silk stockings worn in England were given Edward by Sir Thomas Gresham, the merchant, whose trade with the Low Countries brought him into contact with such Spanish goods.

1170. XVIc. Before 1554. English. (Metropolitan Mus.)

British School. Lady Jane Grey.

Frances Brandon's accomplished and delightful daughter, who was for nine days Queen of England, and who was executed at seventeen, together with her father, Suffolk, and her husband, Dudley, wears her hair dressed over pads, under a ruche-lined cap, developed from the French hood; in other portraits, her cap shows a slight center dip.

The extremely high collar of her gown has a carefully goffered ruff, matching her wristbands; they are edged, though not yet with lace. Her gown shows the fur-slashed upper sleeve and fur collar of the coat-like, one-piece Spanish gown of mid-XVIc., which often has a high inner, as well as a low outer collar. Ropes of pearls will increase in use to the end of the century.

1170

1171

1171. XVIc. 1554 English. (Boston, Isabella Stewart Gardner Museum.)

Antonio Moro (*Sir Anthony More*). Queen Mary.

This portrait, by the Flemish artist who became an English knight, was sent to her prospective husband, Philip of Spain, and shows the daughter of King Henry VIII and Catharine of Aragon to have been "a little faded woman with a white face, no eyebrows, and russet hair. At thirty-seven, an old maid, disillusioned and wearied by years of cruel injustice." After his divorce from her mother, and Elizabeth's birth, Henry VIII had, for a long time, removed Mary from the succession. The diary of her extremely intelligent 11-year-old brother, Edward VI, relates that "The Lady Mary my sister . . . was called with my Council into a Chamber; where was declared how long I had suffered her Mass in hope of her reconciliation. . . . She answered That her Soul was God's and her Faith she would not change nor dissemble her Opinion with contrary doings. It was said I constrained not her Faith but willed her not as a King to Rule but as a subject to obey; and that her example might breed too much inconvenience." (See Appendix: Ponsonby.)

The restoration of the old religion, which cancelled the imputations of her illegitimacy, led to government persecutions for which she was not responsible, and her nickname of "Bloody Mary." She was actually a good and intelligent person, learned and a fine musician, who suffered from life-long ill health and extreme nearsightedness.

Mary, who wears a wide, flattened French hood over waved hair, and carries gloves with jewelled cuffs, is dressed in blue-gray velvet, with a characteristically plain bodice, and undersleeves and skirt of blue-gray brocade. Her standing collar has a frilled inner collar of Spanish embroidery, in addition to her shirt; the ruff is well on its way.

The queen loved jewels, as did her father and sister. By a ribbon from her short precious girdle, hangs the same reliquary which is also seen in a full-length portrait belonging to the Society of Antiquaries.

From her collar hangs one of Philip's many gifts, a diamond, with an historic pendant pearl "worth 25,000 ducats," called, from its travels "La Pelegrina." Found in 1517 by a slave to whom Balboa, in exchange, gave freedom, it became a prized jewel of the Spanish crown. After Mary's death it returned to Spain, was carried off by Joseph Bonaparte, and sold by Napoleon III to the Marquess of Abercorn. Because of its weight it was often lost; the pearl had been recovered from the upholstery of a settee in the English court, and from the folds of Queen Victoria's train, before Abercorn finally had a fastening bored into the end of the pearl. (See Appendix: Norris).

1172. XVIc. 1559. English. (Bettws-y-Coed, J. C. Wynne-Finch.)

Hans Eworth. Frances Brandon and Adrian Stoke.

Frances Brandon, mother of Lady Jane Grey, widowed by the execution of the Duke of Suffolk, was married the following year at 36 to the 21-year-old master of her horse, Adrian Stoke.

1172

We see her in the year of her death, dressed in a high-necked black gown with jewels and gold aiglettes. The neck ruffs and wrist bands, new at the time of her daughter's portrait, are now elaborately edged in gold. Black and gold French hood; slashed and jewelled gloves; fine rings.

Her young husband wears a lynx-lined black jacket with the standing collar of the 1560's and short sleeve, its slashings caught by gold tags; and an embroidered and slashed doublet, its ruffs edged with pink. The high male collar of the 1550-60's may be open or closed, and is often furnished with ties. It mounts straight up, and encompasses the ruff, which still appears to have some connection with the shirt; by the fourth quarter, the collar will be closely fitted and the formal band of the ruff will be fastened to its top.

1173. XVIc. 1567-8. English. (Metropolitan Museum.)

British School. Mary, Queen of Scots: the Duff-Ogilvy portrait.

The padded (*atifet*) arrangements of hair on either side of a c.part tended to be supplanted by unparted hair, drawn up over a pad, its height increasing into XVIIc. The feeling of a center part shows in the rolled edge of her tiny cap.

As the ruff (*band*) increased in size and became edged with lace, the fluted finish at the wrist of a close, or of a padded leg o'mutton sleeve, was usually replaced by a turned-back cuff, with lace. The closed circular ruff was commonly worn by married women.

Brantôme said that Mary looked like a goddess in everything, "even the barbarous costume of the savages of her country," that is, in Scot's dress.

Mary, who loved jewelry, especially pearls, wears only earrings and chains with this extremely simple costume. Through Mary's French marriage, some of Catherine de' Medici's best pearls passed into the English crown jewels.

Male infants, like this baby who became James I, wore women's gowns, in miniature, throughout the diaper period; then miniature male costume. Embroidered caps protected the heads of babies and elderly men; babies also wore every form of grown-up hat, in miniature.

1174. XVIc. 1566. Welsh. (Glamorganshire, Llanturt Major.)

Monumental effigy of a woman.

Nothing is known about the middle-class Welsh woman, whose memorial slab was found lying in a churchyard.

Women, as well as men, wore the plumed hat with a high pleated crown. The dress, with its wide ruff, shows the increase in padded rigidity of last half XVIc. The rectangular pattern, into which the covering of the leg o'mutton sleeve of a great lady would be puffed and jewelled, is achieved in this modest costume by a latticework of fabric bands. The outer

garment, tight in the waist, full in the skirt and sleeveless, except for the picadills around the arms-eye, is open in a V to the waist, with its flat collar spreading wide over the shoulders.

1175. XVIc. 1568-9. English. (Hatfield House, Marquess of Salisbury.)

Joris Hoefnagel. A Horsleydown Wedding.
(Bottom of page 438)

There are few more precious costume documents than this picture of a country wedding, where the gentry, bourgeoisie and country folk appear together. Women of all classes are seen to wear hats over hoods. The picture will repay much study.

1176. XVIc. 1573. English. (Nottingham, Wollaston Hall. Coll. Lord Middleton.)

Unknown artist. Lady Willoughby.

During the reign of Elizabeth, the character of jewelry alters: jewelled collars are replaced by draped strands of pearls; and oval medallions by more elaborate pendants, showing better cut stones, increasingly naturalistic enamel work in paler colors; miniatures; cameos; mirrors; and watches of all shapes, octagonal, fat and pomander-like, or flattened. (See Appendix.)

Both the form of the pendant and the spot at which it is placed are now less often symmetrical. Lady Willoughby wears her enamelled mermaid pendant at one side of her bodice, which is looped with strings of pearls combined with beads.

Interest in the hat now centers on its band. This carries the jewels formerly pinned to the under side of the brim; and from it, clusters of plumes emphasize the heightening crown. The male hat, much seen on women, is worn here, as was usual, with loose uncovered hair and a tiny reticulated cap, set on the back of the head. The hat, as well as the cap, is often worn indoors by women at this period, just as it is by men.

Lady Willoughby wears the one-piece open Spanish gown. Though it forms one garment with the gown beneath, its separate, coat-like look is emphasized by the flat, turned-down collar and cuffs, worn in conjunction with the 2 set ruffs at the neck, and those at the sleeves of the gown beneath.

Both forms of collars and cuffs are finished with a narrow purled edging of needlepoint lace. Brought from Italy in 1533 by Catherine de' Medici, lace-making received government encouragement in Flanders. Refugees from the religious persecutions by Spain in the Low Countries brought lace manufac-

ture to England in the last third of XVIc., and lace rapidly became the characteristic feature of late Elizabethan and XVIIc. costume.

The first laces were needlepoint, in the looped-cord patterns worn by Lady Willoughby, or in rectangular patterns based on the warp and weft of fabric; cut work; and the drawn, darned and whipped reticella laces.

Pattern books for lace and embroidery were widely published in second half XVIc. all over Europe. (Many are in the fine lace collection of Cooper Union Museum.) With the appearance of pillow lace, running patterns, analogous to those of the foliated appliqués of e.XVIc. become possible. These patterns, followed by embroidery in the freedom of its techniques, become the "crewel" embroideries of the turn of the century and XVIIc., asymmetrically patterned with birds, fantastic flowers, and scrolled leaves, under the added influence of printed India fabrics.

In costume, as we see by these sleeves, interest in cords and knots is being transformed into an interest in ribbons and bows.

1177. XVIc. c. 1560-70. English. (London, Nat. Port. Gall.)

Unknown Flemish artist; formerly att. to *Zuccaro.* Robert Dudley, Earl of Leicester.

Elizabeth's favorite, Amy Robsart's husband, brother-in-law of Lady Jane Grey, leader of the Protestant faction, and uncle of Sir Philip Sidney, who died under his command with the troops sent to the relief of the Low Countries, the Earl is the personification of the handsome, assured courtier. But his enemies unfairly said, "he was the son of a duke,

the brother of a king, the grandson of an esquire, and the great-grandson of a carpenter, and the carpenter was the only honest man in the family, and the only one who had died in his bed."

The Earl's court costume is advanced in style. The collar has reached the ultimate height, which "rose up so high and sharp as if it would have cut his throat by daylight." (Thomas Middleton: *The Ant and the Nightingale,* quoted in Morse: *Elizabethan Pageantry.*) The fluted edge of the shirt collar has become a developed ruff by the 60's, matching those at the wrists. Picadills at the top of the collar support the ruff; they also appear at armseye, cuff and bottom of the skirtless doublet. The doublet is now assuming the "peascod" belly form, is fastened by buttons in a close row (previously grouped), and is pinked in the new small punctures, combined with cuts. Sleeves, narrow in the 50's, widen during the 60's, when they begin to show padding. Incidentally, the word picadill is the diminutive of the Spanish *pica,* (spear); it was these cut edges, according to legend, which gave the name of Picadilly to the street leading to the house of the tailor who introduced the style in England.

Paned trunk-hose, whale-boned and padded, reach to mid-thigh and are squared off at the bottom; codpiece disappearing.

The Spanish-Italian bonnet, with higher, full crown, introduced in the 60's, surmounts a typically English head. The hair, not yet artificially waved, is brushed back, and down, in front of the ear in the beginning of the later love-lock. Although Stubbes

complained of the variety of the cuts of beard and moustache: "When you come to be trimmed they will ask you whether you will be cut to look terrible to your enemy or amiable to your friend," these long, sweeping moustaches and natural beard, with the jaw shaved above the line of the moustache, are specifically English.

From a precious chain hangs a medallion of the Garter, shown also above his right shoulder. The narrow belt follows, exactly, the waistline of the doublet: the belt is sometimes shaped, and is made flexible by metal swivel connections. Front and back attachments of the sword, with elaborately guarded grip, very wide quillons and anneau.

1178. XVIc. 1578. English. (Bisham Abbey. Lady Vansittart-Neale.)

Unknown artist. Sir Edward Hoby.

Hoby, whose uncle, Lord Burleigh, was the most important man in England, wears the high, stiffened hat of last third of XVIc., "standying a quarter of a yarde aboue the crowne of their heades," Stubbes complains.

It is often worn at a much more acute angle than Hoby, over his fluffed-out hair, wears this maroon-plumed black hat, with its band of gold ornaments and cluster of gold acorns toward the top.

Ruff embroidered in maroon, on high collar of slashed, cream-colored doublet, with buttons and embroidered edges of self-colored silk, and shoulder-line extended by a cap, instead of picadills or a roll. Maroon scarf.

1178

1179

1180

1181

1180. XVIc. 1577 English (Oxford Univ., Bodleian Lib.)
Christopher Ketel. Sir Martin Frobisher.

Explorer of the Northwest Passage, and with Drake and Hawkins, under Howard of Effingham, vanquisher of the Armada, the admiral wears a sleeveless leather jerkin, with picadill finish at arms-eye, waist and breeches. The high collar is cut in one with the body of the jerkin; the gores of the neck, like the front opening, are fastened by points which are left open below the throat, over padded, almost skirtless doublet, with rows of tiny buttons, and padded leg o'mutton sleeves of 1575-90, with pushed up length on lower arm.

These superimposed padded garments were terribly hot, and both men and women got relief by wearing them open to the waist. In the presence of the French ambassador, De Maisse, Elizabeth opened her gown to the navel.

Rapier on narrow sword-belt at waist of doublet; wheellock pistol of late XVIc. Light colored shoes, rising over the instep in what will become a tongue, when the strap closing of late XVIc. develops.

1181. XVIc. 1580. English. (Oxford, Ashmolean.)
Unknown artist. John Bull.

The English musician, organist to Elizabeth and James I, and probable composer of the national anthem, "God Save the King," was given permission to lecture at the university in English, instead of Latin, in which he was not proficient.

He wears an open cappa (which is now pretty well restricted to choral, ecclesiastic, legal and academic wear), with a fur-lined hood of brocade, and a superb "black work" collar.

Evelyn mentions the damask robes of the doctors of music in the procession into chapel of the companions of the Garter on St. George's day (23 April, 1667).

1179. XVIc. 1574. Flemish. (London, Nat. Port. Gall.)
Unknown Flemish artist. James I, aged 8.

Mary Stuart's suffering during her pregnancy produced a rachitic child, who could not stand till he was seven, and who always slobbered, with a tongue which seemed too big for his mouth. As Charles I also had weak legs and an impeded speech, these failures were more probably genetic.

Costume of various "natural" colors with olive-green velvet slops. Full, loose, breeches (venetians) never have cod-pieces and usually fasten below the knee, and are finished here by a picadill slashing.

High-necked, padded doublet of stitched chamois-colored leather, fastened at top only, by 3 gold buttons; has pointing front and short, overlapping skirts; sleeves quilted over some padding.

Belt, sword-belt, dagger and sword cases all of red velvet. Gauntlet and falcon. Flesh-colored hose, shoes of pale natural-colored leather.

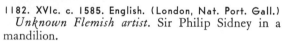

1182. XVIc. c. 1585. English. (London, Nat. Port. Gall.)
Unknown Flemish artist. Sir Philip Sidney in a mandilion.

The mandilion is a loose, tabard-like jacket, usually slit up the sides, and with sleeves pendant. It has the character of a cape, and is often rotated a quarter turn, and allowed to hang, as we see it worn here, "Collie-Weston-ward," as the Dean of Windsor described it. (Wm. Harrison: *Description of England,* 1577-8.)

The breeches, trimmed with braid to match the mandilion, have the diagonal pocket slits, often found on the variety of breeches which are cut off at the knee, like shorts.

1183. XVIc. 1588. English. (London, Nat. Port. Gall.)
Unknown artist: formerly att. to *Zuccaro.*
Sir Walter Raleigh.

The poet and historian, colonizer and explorer, who was for a decade a favorite of Elizabeth, and who after many misfortunes died on the scaffold by order of James I, introduced into European cultivation the tobacco and potato brought back by his captains.

He wears a costume of white, with black and silver. Soft, loose hair, continued into the beard; one earring only, as was worn by men. When Stubbes, in scolding women about fashions, comes to pierced ears he says: "Because this is not so much frequented amongst women as men, I will say no more. . . ."

Doublet of pinked white silk. Over the turned-down collar of the doublet is a sheer collar, matching the cuffs, shoulder cap, and band which extends beyond the edge of the doublet. The swordbelt below is trimmed in silver to match his paned velvet slops. His fur-collared black velvet cape is rayed with silver beads.

A full-length portrait by Gheeraerts, belonging to

Sir Stephen Lennart, shows Raleigh in 1602, dressed in brown, white, silver and beige, with his young son in dark blue and silver.

1184. XVIIc. c. 1610. Dutch.
Unknown engraver. Fleshly Disguises.

Although the funnel-shaped farthingale remained in use, another skirt was worn from c.1570-c.1615, which widened straight out from the waist, over a sausage-shaped bolster tied high about the hips.

In England, this French fashion was intensified into a drum-shaped silhouette, by a pleated ruffle going horizontally from the waist to, or beyond, the circumference of the skirt.

Since chairs could contain neither of these skirts, it became customary to sit on piled cushions on the floor, or on stools rather like a sawbuck with a stretcher top.

Restraining, fitted underbodices of heavy material (*vasquine, basquine,* from which our word *basque* comes) had been used in late XVc. The corsets of the first third XVIc. were rigid, hinged iron cages; these were replaced by flexible steel in Catherine de' Medici's time. In the latter part of XVIc., corsets were boned in patterns like those shown on these bodices, and were elongated and held firm by a center busk of metal, bone or wood. Below the waist, these corsets were finished with a roll and picadill, to support the skirt between the waist and bolster. The triangular front placard was often a superb example of embroidery.

This is perhaps a good place to explain the origin of the word "band-box." Neck ruffs (bands) were constructed by pleating immensely long strips of material onto a neckband. As ruffs grew wider and more elaborate, doubled and tripled, their laundering became the work of an expert. They were starched, often in color, set on a form, and gauffered

1184

with a sort of curling iron called a "setting" or "poking stick." The finished band was then set, for protection, into a low, wide "band-box." Ruffs eventually reached proportions which starch alone could not support; wire frames and stays, "underproppers" or "supportasses" had to be added. When these are withdrawn, in XVIIc., we see the wide bands falling limp.

Philip Stubbes has given us the most minute descriptions of ruffs, their starching and underpropping, as indeed he does of every other extravagant detail of Elizabethan dress; it is a temptation not to quote him by the page. The development of ruffs, Stow tells us dates from 1564 when "Mistris Dingen Van den Passe, born at Taenen in Flaunders, daughter to a worshipful knight of that province, with her husband came to London for their better safeties, and there professed herself a *starcher,* wherein she excelled, unto whom her own nation presently repaired, and payed her very liberally for her worke. Some very few of the best and most curious wives of that time, observing the *neatnesse and delicacy of the Dutch for whitenesse and fine wearing of linen,* made them *cambricke ruffs,* and sent them to Mistris Dinghen *to starch,* and after a while, they made them *ruffes of lawn,* which was at that time a stuff most strange, and wonderful, and thereupon

rose a *general scoffe* or *byword,* that shortly they would make ruffes of a *spider's web;* and then they began to send their daughters and nearest kinswomen to Mistris Dingen to *learne how to starche;* her usuall price was at that time, foure or five pounds, to teach them how *to starch,* and twenty shillings how to seeth starch. . . . Divers noble personages made them *ruffes, a full quarter of a yeard deepe,* and two lengthe in one ruffe. This fashion in London was called the *French fashion;* but when Englishmen came to *Paris,* the *French* knew it not, and in derision called it *the English monster."* (See sources on Tudor costume in appendix.)

Masks for outdoor wear came into use for both sexes during Elizabeth's time. Long masks were kept in place by a button, fixed on the back and held in the teeth. Masks of animals and grotesques were worn at carnival time, and by figures of Italian comedy.

Feather fans with a long stick remained in use in the second half of XVIc., even after the introduction of folding fans, on the Chinese model, by way of Italy in late XVIc.

The details of these gowns will be discussed, in their most exaggerated form, in the later gowns of Elizabeth.

QUEEN ELIZABETH

During her wretched childhood, Elizabeth was actually destitute of clothing. The royal governess wrote Lord Thomas Cromwell "beseeching .. that she may have some raiment, for she hath neither gown, nor kirtall, nor petticoat, nor no manner of linnen, nor foresmocks (pinafores), nor kerchief,

nor rails (nightgowns), nor mofelers (mobcaps), nor biggens (nightcaps). All these her grace must have. I have driven off as long as I can, that, to my troth I cannot drive it any longer." (E. Green: *Letters of Royal and Illustrious Ladies.*)

Elizabeth, in portraits of her as a princess, wears the classic Holbein costume; the gowns of the first years of her reign are rich but rather conventional. The tiny, slender queen, who never looked her age, was 50 before her vanity evolved the immensely personal style associated with her name.

Below a thickly painted face, great ruffs conceal an aging throat, though her bosom is often completely bare. Elizabeth, who seems to have had an over-active thyroid, complained of the heat while others felt chilly. Over her greying hair, curled auburn wigs mount, framed in wired-out gauze and dressed with the incredible jewels she loved, as all her family had loved jewels. Her fine hands are always on display, occupied with handsome accessories.

Elizabeth maintained a wardrobe of some 500 costumes: gowns prepared for the celebration of events which could be foreseen but were not certain; gowns to impress, startle, tell a story, or give warning.

Elizabeth's wardrobe was inherited by Anne, who had a parsimonious husband, and, we are told, had Elizabeth's gowns remade for her own use. This seems perfectly plausible (see Ill. 1362), until one looks at actual garments which belonged to Elizabeth (see Ills. 1187-89). They are so tiny that a good many 10-year-old American girls could not possibly get into them. Anne must also have been very small.

1185. XVIc. English. (Yale Univ., Elizabethan Club.)
Federigo Zuccaro. Queen Elizabeth.
Curled hair arranged within a jewelled wire frame, from which embroidered gauze falls, free and unwired. Ruff of reticella lace. French gown; moderate waistline; skirt with closed front; yoke and sleeves of jewel-studded embroidery; roll at armseye. Scarf and looped pearls lead to pendant with three nude figures. Ostrich fan with jewelled handle.

1186. XVIc. c. 1590. English. (Colonial Williamsburg, Va.)
Marcus Gheeraerts, e. Queen Elizabeth.
Gray tubular ruff and veil wired wide and caught to the sleeve of black gown, embroidered and jew-

elled in red, gold, black and pearl. Shoulders extended by roll and scalloped picadill. Gray undersleeve brocaded in Tudor roses and fleurs-de-luce in gold, rose and green.

Elizabeth appears to have liked a long line from neck to feet. We often find the centrally massed decorative bands of the Spanish gown used on the underskirt of her French dresses, where we would expect a pendant girdle; and this line is given unusual emphasis on some of her drum-shaped skirts with pleated cartwheel tops. When worn over hip bolsters, the inverted V-line of outer skirt of French gown must be cut in inverted U shape. Gloves with jewelled cuffs; feather fan caught on skirt.

Courtesy of the Elizabethan Club, Yale University (1185);
Frick Art Reference Library (1186)

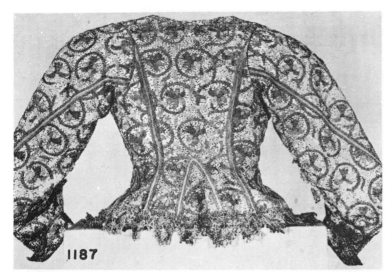

1187.

1187-89. XVIc. 1578. English. (Boston, Museum of Fine Arts.)

1187. Jacket.

1188. Stomacher.

1189. Embroidered coif in two parts.

These garments were left by Elizabeth as souvenirs after an overnight visit to Sir Roger Wodehouse, of Kimberly, Norfolk, August 21, 1578. They are done in gold, two shades of silver and gold sequins on natural colored linen, and show Elizabeth to have been a tiny creature.

1188.

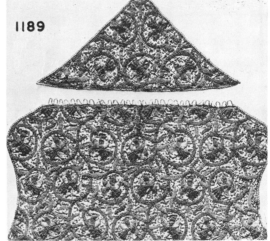

1189.

1190. XVIc. English.

Crispin van de Passe, after *Isaac Oliver*. Elizabeth of England. (Costume of 1588, engraved 1603.)

The earliest portrait of Elizabeth in the drum-shaped farthingale, open standing ruff and wired veil, which she made her own, is Isaac Oliver's little ink and water color drawing at Windsor; from it, Rogers and Passe drew the material for their later engravings.

This white and gold costume is supposed to be that worn by Elizabeth when giving solemn thanks at St. Paul's for the defeat of the Armada. Its bodice, oversleeve linings and overskirt are of white satin brocaded in gold. The undersleeves, stomacher and underskirt have puffs of white silk caught to cloth of gold by pearls and rubies, with emeralds used in addition on the borders.

She wears the ropes of pearls which will be standard at the turn of the century (see Ills. 1290-95), and her curled wig, surmounted by the crown, is pinned with pendant pearls. She carries the orb and sceptre.

1191. English XVIc. Sept. 20, 1592. (London, Nat. Port. Gall. Bequest of Viscount Dillon of Ditchley.)

Artist unknown. Queen Elizabeth: the Ditchley Portrait.

This portrait of Elizabeth, standing on a colored map of Oxfordshire, commemorates her visit to Sir Henry Lee, Viscount Dillon's ancestor, at Ditchley.

Her creamy white satin costume is accented with coral. Crown, necklace and pendant of pearls, rubies and coral. Wired veil of gold gauze, edged with pearl-sewn gold lace and jewels.

Her short skirt is much fuller than in the van de Passe engraving; the overskirt has been given up. The hexagonal pattern of the skirt puffs, and the edges of her trailing sleeves are sewn with gold studs of varying forms, set with rubies, pearls and sapphires, and fastened in opposing directions.

A rose is pinned to her white ruff; a folding fan is fastened to her girdle by a knotted, coral-colored ribbon; she carries brown gloves with slashed gold cuffs.

Color reproduction of Ill. 1191 may be found in Morse: *Elizabethan Pageantry*.

1192. XVIc. 1594. English. (Hatfield House, Marquess of Salisbury.)

Marcus Gheeraerts, e. Queen Elizabeth: the Rainbow Portrait.

In this portrait, full of symbolism, the words "Non sine sole iris" (No rainbow without the sun) appear above the hand which holds the rainbow; the sleeves of her orange, fawn and olive costume are embroidered with jewelled snakes; the lining of her outer garment, with eyes and ears; a mailed glove is fastened to her ruff: it warns that she is powerful and fortunate, wily and wise, that she sees and hears all.

Her crown is set over a brim shaped like the headdress of the previous century but many items of her costume are prophetic of the century to come.

The coat-like outer garment is becoming separated from the gown beneath, and is worn off one shoulder. In the manner of the XVIIc., the bodice is of linen, embroidered in colored sprigs, and the lace edging of its low, spreading bodice is assuming the scallops of XVIIc. lace, though it is still of reticella. She wears a tiny neck ruff, and a wider ruff on the bodice; behind this, the wired gold veil has been cut off, horizontally, in the manner of the next century, and is separated from the flowing ends which now start from the neck. We see the beginnings of another XVIIc. fashion in the way her hair is dressed, with trailing locks at the side. In addition to the familiar knotted ropes of pearls, she wears pearl strands as bracelets.

1193. XVIc. 1592-4. English. (Hardwick Hall, Duke of Devonshire.)

Unknown artist. Queen Elizabeth: the Hardwick Portrait.

English ecclesiastical embroidery, last third XIII to first third of XIVc. was the finest in Europe. With the introduction of Spanish work in first third XVIc. there was a revival, which lasted through the XVIIc. The Reformation ended ecclesiastical embroidery, dispersed fine church pieces into secular use as wall-hangings, and left great knowledge and energy to be channeled into the decoration of caps, gloves, shoes and bags, gowns and jackets, shirts, collars, scarves and handkerchiefs, pillows, chairs and hangings.

The first Spanish-inspired "black work," often relieved in gold, was followed by multicolored embroidery with gold and silver, of scrolls and naturalistic flowers and animals; and petit point. Turkey work, in imitation of Oriental carpets, began to appear in third quarter XVIc.; raised "stump work" decorated mirror frames and boxes in XVIIc.; samplers, mentioned in Shakespeare, are seen from XVIIc.; bed, window and wall hangings, embroidered in silk or wool, appear second half XVIIc., and yellow silk embroidery on white at the end XVIIc. (See Appendix.)

Elizabeth herself did fine work, but among the greatest embroiderers of their time were Mary, Queen of Scots and the Countess of Shrewsbury, with whom Mary spent fourteen years of her detention in England. This fabulous lady, known as "Bess of Hardwick," was by four marriages the richest woman in England; she thought that she would never die as long as she was building the great mansions she loved, like Hardwick and Chatsworth; and she did die during a hard frost which stopped construction when she was ninety.

Bess of Hardwick is supposed to have given the white satin stomacher and kirtle of this gown, which she had embroidered in all manner and color of exotic birds, beasts and flowers, as a Christmas present to Elizabeth, who sent in return this portrait of herself in the finished gown, with an overdress of gold-embroidered green velvet.

The wired veil is now fastened to the edge of the bodice, under the ruff. The gown is very short, its underskirt finished with a pearl fringe. Gloves, indispensable, and now a favorite gift; round feather fan; pendant fastened to side of skirt by ribbons attached to point of stomacher; slashed and embroidered white shoes.

European Textile Design

The inspiration of the design of European textiles had always been Oriental: Byzantine, Saracenic, Persian, and to some degree, Chinese. The XVIIc. trade with India and China brought fresh Oriental motifs, which became the rage of the XVIIIc.

Meanwhile, during XVIc., a European interest in realistically drawn natural flowers is shown in missal painting, in tapestries, in embroidery, and in costume. Of all Philip Stubbes' castigations of Elizabethan ways, none now seems so extreme as his hatred of sweet smelling flowers and of women who wear "nosegays and posies . . . sticked in their breastes before." Naturalistic sprigs of flowers replace the stylized Ottoman pomegranate, cone and leaf designs. Patterns mount and spread in the *candelabre* designs of Louis XIV brocade and lace. Formal interlaced patterns turn into loose, searching tendrils. Stylized and fabulous armorial birds and beasts, facing left and right, give way to animals in the pursuit of the chase (see Ills. 905, 1704), to exotic animals like the whale and camel, to butterflies in flight, beetles and worms.

Trained decorative artists appear in the XVIIIc., as did Watteau from the atelier of Charles Audran, keeper of the Luxembourg collection; and Pillement and Philippe de la Salle, who studied design at the Académie des Beaux Arts, founded by Mazarin in 1648. Their fanciful improvisations on Chinese and Indian motifs were immensely influential. Chippendale was inspired by Chinese furniture; little pagodas and peaked bridges appear in European gardens.

The old interest in naturalistic flower forms persists, meanwhile, and is reinforced by the romantic rocks, ruins and graves, cottages and farm animals, which came with J. J. Rousseau's influence in second half XVIIIc.

The amusements and games, the allegorical figures, favored at the turn of the XVIII-XIX centuries, and such literal scenes as that of the Jouy factory (Ill. 1894) tend to become imprisoned, during the Classic Revival, in repeated medallion patterns, often showing notable buildings. Historical scenes are popular, both in hangings and in printed handkerchiefs, as Steele had foreseen, when he asked in the Tatler, #3,1709: "Suppose an ingenious gentleman should write a poem of advice to a callico-printer; do you suppose there is a girl in England, that would wear anything but the taking of Lille, or the battle of Oudenarde?"

As the Jouy factory (see Ills. 1955-60) ran down between 1810-20, the Alsatian and English manufacturers came into their glory. But their great period of delightful sprigged dress fabrics, and bold chintzes with flowers, fruits and birds, declines with the general debasement of taste in second half of XIXc., as red, brown and black Paisley shawl motifs are combined with magenta and purple cabbage roses (see Ills. 2562-70, 2425-28). For bibliography, see Appendix.

1194. XVIc. English.

Elizabethan "black work."

1195. XVIc. English.

Embroidery: petit point on satin, appliquéd pansies and thistles.

1196. XVIIc. English.

Embroidery: polychrome silk and purl on white satin.

1197. XVIIc. 1672. English.

Mirror frame of stump work; story of Jael and Sisera, signed A.P.,1672. "Stump work," raised, padded, and often gathered, free of the background was used to decorate boxes, purses and mirrors in XVIIc. England.

"When my sister Jenny was in her sampler, I made her get the whole story without book, and tell it to me in needlework," Steele (as Sir Isaac Bickerstaff) says in the *Tatler*, # 84, Oct. 22, 1709.

1198. XVIIIc. 1715. English.

Embroidered apron: white linen thread on white muslin.

1199. Late XVIc. Italian.

Panel: Red cut velvet, brocaded in gold; compare with embroidery patterns.

450

1200. XVIc. English. (Windsor Castle, H.M. the King.)
Isaac Oliver. Sir Philip Sidney.

The miniaturist, Isaac Oliver (1566-1617), son of a Huguenot refugee, was the pupil of Nicholas Hilliard and teacher of a son Peter, who became court miniaturist to James I. Evelyn took some relatives to court in 1660 to show them the king's collection of Oliver's work. Another fine Oliver miniature shows the Three Brothers Brown and their Servant, in 1597, their hat-crown wreathed in twists of "cyprus" mourning crêpe.

Sidney's dearest friend, Fynes Moryson, said of the grave, radiant, and chivalrous Protestant poet, diplomat, and soldier: "Though I lived with him and knew him from a child, I never knew him other than a man." While serving in the army of his uncle, Robert Dudley, Earl of Leicester, he doffed his greaves because his companion had none, was wounded in the leg, and died at 32, at Reimagen, in 1586. All London, as well as the court, wore sober clothes in mourning for him. His funeral procession is shown in Laut: *Sequitur Celebritas Pompa Funeris,* 1587.

High, hard hat, over curled, lengthening locks. Lace band, low at throat; and cuffs. Jacket with shoulders widened by a roll; decoration in vertical lines, (analogous to *panes*); skirts, cut and overlapping in manner of XVIIc. Very short trunks, puffed but not stuffed, over canions finished with lace cuffs.

Soft, high boots with spurs, of which the Spanish ambassador told James I: "I shall amaze my countrymen by letting them know at my return that all London's booted and apparently ready to walk out of town." Gloves; long rapier.

Young Englishmen of fashion are now making the Grand Tour of Europe, as they will continue to do into the XIXc. Many, like Moryson and Coryat are publishing accounts of their travels; Sidney was much influenced by having been in Paris on St. Bartholomew's Eve.

1201. XVIc. 1589. English. (London, Victoria and Albert Museum.)
Nicholas Hilliard. Sir Christopher Hatton.

Nicholas Hilliard (1537-1619), was a goldsmith of good English family. Inspired by Holbein's miniatures, he became the first of the long line of English miniature painters. As court "painter in little" to Elizabeth, he executed her 1585 Ermine Portrait, at Hatfield House. In 1588 he painted Robert Dudley, Earl of Leicester (belonging to the Duke of Buccleugh and Queensbury), and a drawing, 1580 (belonging to Archibald G. Russel), showing the widest possible farthingale. His son and pupil, Lawrence, was an equally accomplished miniaturist.

The dancing of the attractive Hatton brought him into favor with Elizabeth, whose pet name for him was "mouton" (lamb). His solid ability carried him to the Lord Chancellorship in 1588.

At this time he was made a Knight of the Garter, the emblem of which he wears over one high, soft leather boot, pinked for flexibility. His feet are thrust into pantoufles, slippers with high cork platforms, covering only the instep, worn out of doors over the shod foot. His turned-down band is of cut work, lace edged. Tudor collar (see Ill. 1134).

Stubbes says: "They haue corked shoes, pisnets, and fine pantoffles, whiche beare them vppe a finger or two from the ground, whereof some be of white leather, some of blacke, and some of red; some of black veluet, some of white, some of red, some of greene, razed, caruet, cut, and stitched all over with silke, and layd on with gold, siluer, and such like: yet . . . to what good vses serue these pantoffles, except it be to weare in a priuate house, or in a man's chamber to keep him warme? . . . but to goe abroade in them as they are now vsed altogether, is rather a lett or hinderaunce to a man than otherwise, for shall hee not be fane to knock and spurne at euery wal, stone, or poste, to keepe them on his feete?" They are so hard to manage that some men's legs swell up with the effort, and Stubbes describes with his usual gusto the ways in which they kick up dust or accumulate filth.

1202. XVIc. c. 1590. English. (London, Duke of Buccleugh.)
Nicholas Hilliard. George Clifford, third Earl of Cumberland as the Queen's Champion.

The dissolute, freebooting earl who commanded the "Bonaventure" against the Armada, does not wear the Garter with which he was invested in 1592. This portrait probably represents him in the tournament of Nov. 17, 1590, when he jousted in place of Sir Henry Lee.

The very suit of colored Greenwich armor in which Hilliard painted Clifford, will be seen among the photographs of the Metropolitan Museum Armor Collection (see Ill. 461).

Photograph by gracious permission of H. M. The King of England

He wears the queen's jewelled glove pinned to his gold-trimmed, plumed white hat; blue steel armor with eight-pointed gold stars; pale blue tunic, lined in white, embroidered in gold and green roses and leaves, and bordered in jewelled gold.

1203. XVIc. c. 1590. English. (Earl of Chesterfield.)
Sir James Scudamore.

Some elements of this suit are also in the M.M.A. Armor Collection. The old sectional goring of the *waffenrock* skirt is commemorated in the way in which braid is laid on here.

1204. XVIc. 1591. English. (Cornwall, Fowey.)
Monumental effigy.
Alice, wife of John Rashleigh, and daughter of William Lanyon.

England in XIVc. had no fleet. The foundations of the naval power of the Devon privateers of Drake's day were laid by "The Gallants of Fowey," following the French sack of the little port, which became the most important in Cornwall until midXVIc. The largest of the prehistoric stone cromlechs of Cornwall stands at Lanyon.

This country gentlewoman wears a modest roll under her short gown. The V opening of her bodice is filled by a pleated shirt with high collar and plain ruff. Her shoes show the beginning of a real heel, and the extension of the top of the heel enclosure

into straps over the instep.

1205. XVIc. 1593. English. (Suffolk, Wrentham.)
Monumental effigy. Humphrey Brewster.

Complete armor of late XVIc. Ruff on high collared breastplate of peascod form; pauldrons spreading across chest; tassets, lengthening, like lobster tails, are buckled to skirt of breastplate. Scalloped finish used on costume also appears on armor. Gentlemen are now more often represented bareheaded, without hat or helm.

1206. XVIc. c. 1596. English. (Cleveland Mus. of Art.)
Isaac Oliver. Sir Anthony Mildmay.

Mildmay was Elizabeth's ambassador to the court of Henry IV of France, who "later complained of his coldness and ungenial manners."

The following description, signed W.M.M., is taken from the Bulletin of the Cleveland Museum of Art, Feb., 1927, no. 2.:

"This miniature must have been painted in or after the year 1596, for in it Sir Anthony is represented after knighthood had been conferred upon him. It is in all likelihood an official portrait, painted as a memorial of the signal honor of ambassadorship. Sir Anthony stands before his tent, which forms an elaborate baldaquin at the back of the picture. He wears parts of a parade suit of armor, beautifully decorated with engraved bands of gilded arabesques.

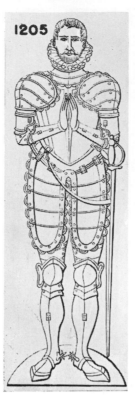

Across one shoulder, knotted beneath the gauntleted hand which grasps his court sword, is a blue sash edged with gold. His leg pieces have been removed and are shown on the floor near a cushion of crimson velvet. The right gauntlet lies on the table . . . cov-ered with a blue cloth fringed with gold. There is also a pistol inlaid with ivory, and his finely-shaped helmet, gorgeously bedecked with a blue plume of curling ostrich feathers. Beyond is a chair, late Renaissance in style, and to one side an iron-bound

1207

chest, upon which is carelessly thrown a garment, perhaps a brigandine, perhaps only a velvet doublet, gold and purple, lined with blue."

His Greenwich armor lacks tasses. The concave scalloping of the skirt of the peascod breastplate can be compared to that of Sir Philip Sidney's jacket. The very short trunk-hose of a man of fashion of the last quarter XVIc. (and Stubbes, of course, has a great deal to say about that subject), have a horizontal strap woven through the panes. The sword is occasionally thrust through the panes in just this way. Ivory hose and shoes with tongue, under straps tied with blue bows. Compare decorative seaming of blue and white tent with that used on Hoby's costume (Ill. 1178). Long hair, tiny beard and moustache, in one of extravagant variations of end XVIc.

1207. XVIc. 1596. English. (Penshurst, Lord de L'Isle and Dudley.)

Marcus Gheeraerts, e. Barbara Gamage, Lady Sidney, and her children.

The first wife of Sir Philip Sidney's brother Robert, who became Earl of Leicester in 1618, stands touching her sons: the year-old baby, who succeeded to title, and his elder brother, who died young.

The use of light colors in both men's and women's dress increased during last quarter XVIc., and the whole family is shown dressed in white.

Lady Sidney's short gown shows many characteristics of English XVIIc. style. Its closed ruff, graded in width, frillier and less rigid, is worn lower and looser on the throat. The bodice has a shorter waist which has almost lost its point, and is differentiated from the skirt by its embroidery. The ruffle at the top of the skirt is smaller, less rigidly pleated, and a

1209

1210

smaller bolster is used. The head is relatively uncovered; curled hair, loosely dressed, covers the ears.

Her older daughters wear miniature versions of the standard "Elizabethan" costume. Their petticoats show below their short skirts, as Elizabeth's often did. Twisted scarves outline the pointed waistlines, and a bow is tied around the arm of one. The elder son, still in skirts, wears a diminutive peascod doublet, with a low-necked lace collar, sash and swordbelt, and carries a plumed hat with a high crown.

The youngest children all wear aprons. Black cords replace the knotted pearls of the older sisters. The baby's bells and rattle hang from his belt, and are slung, baldric-wise, over the shoulder.

1208. XVIc. After 1596. English. (London Nat. Port. Gall.)

Unknown artist. Sir Henry Unton, with scenes in his career.

Unton (c.1557-96) whose mother was a daughter of the protector Somerset, was a member of parliament and a personal friend and companion at arms of Henry of Navarre.

In this picture, his portrait, flanked by Fame and a skeleton, stands above the pageant of his life, pictured from left to right, with the sun and moon in the upper corners indicating the beginning and end. His birth takes place at "Wadlie," his family home, with scenes from Oxford life above; his marriage feast with dancing, as an orchestra plays in the next room; travels to "Venis, Paddua, across ye Alpes to the Low Countries and Niminggan"; his meeting at **Cushia** (Coucy?) with Henry IV, to whom Unton became ambassador in 1591; and his death while on a second embassy to France; the return of his hearse

by land and sea; his funeral procession and sermon at Bolton Church; and his effigy.

The earliest English representation of an umbrella is supposed to be the white one which Unton holds over his head, as he rides from the Alps to Padua, in the upper right hand corner of the picture.

1209. Late XVI-e.XVIIc. English. (London, Victoria and Albert Museum.)

Nicholas Hilliard. Miniature of a gentleman.

Negligent curls. Ruff less studied, worn lower. Pale color; patterns of interwoven braid-like bands. The cape, apparently of the plush which came into use, together with beaver hats, during second half XVIc., is the short, full, circular one which commonly accompanies this costume, of extravagant leg o'mutton sleeves, peascod doublet, and the shortest possible upper hose (with or without canions).

Stubbes says: "Their dublets are no less monstrous the (sic) the rest; for now the fashion is to haue them hang downe to the middle of their theighes . being so hardquilted, stuffed, bombasted, and sewed, as they can neither worke, nor yet well play in them, through the excessive heate thereof; and therefore are forced to weare the (sic) lose about them for the most part, otherwise they could very hardly eyther stoupe or decline to the ground . . ."

1210. XVIc. English. (London, Nat. Port. Gall.)

Marcus Gheeraerts, e. Wm. Cecil, Barton Burghley.

The Lord Treasurer of England, who had served Edward VI, Mary and Elizabeth, wears under his hat the coif, and carries the staff, of his office. The collar of the Garter is worn over the red velvet robes of the order, made bulky by the padding of the trunk-hose beneath.

XVI CENTURY SPANISH COSTUME

The immense contributions of the Moriscos to Spanish art and costume were carried to the Spanish colonies of the New World, and can clearly be seen in present-day Guatemala and Mexico.

The characteristic parti-color of the mediaeval Morris (= Moorish) dancers is still in use at the time of the final expulsion of the Moriscos in e.XVIIc. Fringe is much used, in blocks of color as skirt sections are now joined in Guatemala (where striped and figured Moorish patterns [seen in Ills. 668-70] and the reds and purples which they loved to combine were incorporated into the already expert indigenous weaving.)

The Moors wore many short loose jackets, as well as the sleeveless surcoats of the XIVc. Alhambra paintings; these persisted in everyone's use in XVIc., especially around Barcelona. In their XVIc. form, they were often cut straight across the front below the knee, with the entire back section dragging in a square train.

The row of buttons down the front of this garment becomes one of the features of XVIc. Spanish woman's dress, instead of the swinging girdle chains and pomanders of the rest of Europe. This row of buttons is enriched with braid, the ends of which are often fringed. There is an element of fringe in the Spanish way of using aiglettes; and indeed the over-all stripings produced by rows of braid on all the doublets of Europe was a Spanish way of using the Morisco's striped patterns. The constantly covered head of the peasant woman of Guatemala is that of a Catholic whose head must not be bare in church, where she may go several times a day—a Catholic concept strengthened by Islamic tradition: a woman's face is theoretically not to be seen by men (see Appendix: R. M. Anderson article). The mediaeval mourning cloak, in black, with a hood or liripipe, is constantly seen in both male and female use in church-ridden, death-loving Spain. A hooded red or black cape is ladies' outer wear; a short form, usually with an extravagant liripipe, covers the face of a self-flagellating *penitente;* and the whole idea persists to this day in the black lace mantilla.

The traditionally veiled head of Moorish women had already been considerably altered in Moriscan use, and no longer covers everything but the eyes. It is now a very long piece of material, gathered as tightly as possible into a band which surrounds the head and is fastened under the chin; this very full mantle, which was usually but not necessarily white, might be short for riding on a donkey, or long and fringed for street wear. Its great width could be caught up over an arm which wished to make the effective gesture of covering the face, or it could be looped up at the sides and allowed to flow free in back, which was both practical and decorative. Variations of this

gathering around the face crept into use in Christian mourning cloaks.

There were also arrangements of diagonally folded kerchiefs over the head and shoulders; these stemmed from the Basque provinces and Navarre down into Castile. They were closed at the throat and down the front, with the points often tucked into the waistband, front and back. Over this, various headdresses were set; in Castile, this was often a small square. In the Basque country the top headdress was a fantastically tall horn, wound about with white, its point bent from the weight of a tufted end of binding or a mediaeval liripipe; there were constant strictures against the phallic indecency of these headdresses. In near-by Pampeluna (Navarre), the tall headdress was squared and often widened at the top; its white covering was drawn up over instead of twisted about it, and flowed down in back instead of being knotted at the top. The XXc. paintings of Miguel Viladrich Vilá (Hisp. Soc. of Amer.) show a forward-flopping Phrygian cap still a feature of Catalonian male costume.

A German scholar, in 1526, wrote: "In these mountains lies the land of the Basques, which has an impolite people and a peculiar language, which has nothing in common with the languages Italian, Latin, French, German and Spanish, and where the maidens are all completely shorn." The doctor was almost right. The nape of the Basque girl's neck was shaved like the bowl-crop of XVc. and the crown tonsured; from the remaining fringe all around the head two long, dank locks hung in front of each ear. These locks were also worn by young Basque men, and are seen on Moorish men and women, and ladies of Castile and Valencia in Weiditz' drawings (Ills. 1213-15). The looped hair of Isabella la Catolica (Ill. 971) shows this lock, beginning to break loose.

Basque skirts are short, full, and usually three in number, the outermost being turned up at the hips so that its hem makes a frill above the waistband of the apron; the bold horizontal or crossed patterns, characteristic of these aprons, are also used on the long, loose trousers of Basque men.

The old, old sleeve, prolonged and spreading over the knuckles, is worn all over Spain by both sexes, but it is now turned back to make a drooping cuff and show an additional color in its lining. The dropped shoulder-cap of Navarre is often elaborated with a frill, and shows an undersleeve which is full, if white, and of a different color than the bodice if close-fitting. In the Basque provinces and Navarre, bodices, undersleeves and layers of skirts are all of different colors: red, blue, green, yellow and purple; this varied use in color continued into XXc. as Viladrich's paintings show.

The dress of a Spanish lady developed a train, which had to be carried by an attendant as she walked to daily mass through mud or dust, on her high pattens. There were, classically, three skirts, definitely related by their hem decorations. The innermost was of ground length, fitting smoothly over a boned farthingale; this was sometimes worn alone, in house use, and is clearly shown in XVc. Catalonian wall-paintings. The second was only slightly shorter, its identical banding just clearing that of the underskirt. The outermost was short in front, dipping to meet the banding of the middle skirt in back, and was apt to show some fullness. The train, as it developed length and fullness, tended to become a square-ended extension of the back half of the upper skirt. The number of skirts was actually reduced to one, in grand wear, later in the century, but the appearance of superimposed skirts is always retained, in the way in which braid and puntas are applied; in a late effigy at the Hispanic Society museum, this impulse is reduced to a tuck above the trim of the hem.

Ladies of Catalonia, Valencia and Castile wear low-crowned, wide-brimmed hats, like a cardinal's or bullfighter's, trimmed with tufts or tassels on top of the crown, perhaps, and at each side certainly; under these, the brim is slit for the passage of a long cord, looped on the breast, which could be knotted tight under the chin. Great straw hats have long been worn by smocked Spanish peasants. Descerpz' "Recueil" (Fr., 1562) shows forms entirely different from the classic sombrero, worn by the Moor in the "Book of Chess" (Ill. 505). The long, bound tails of hair (Ill. 973), typical of Catalonia and Castile, also affected male costume (Ill. 1214).

We still see in Central America many other Hispano-Moresque details shown by Weiditz: poncho-like garments, sandals of many narrow leather thongs, and bound circlets to hold a shawl in place on the head. (See Ills. 1213-15.)

Weiditz travelled in a costume of a bloused smock and loose sailor trousers of yellow, diagonally striped in red, mittens, and a hood covering head and shoulders, under a feathered hat.

Weiditz shows a great deal of violet and olive green, or violet and red, used together in Spain; or a scarlet cape with a rosy-gray dress and dark red underskirt. Sleeveless surcoats were of brown, dark gray, or black striped with gold, and were worn over lighter or brighter gowns.

Lavender stockings are frequently seen with the red or yellow pattens, decorated in gold or silver. Leather shoes, usually black, often have the pointed, curled-up Moorish toe which we associate with a jester's costume, cut into points in back and at the instep (where bells would hang, in a fool's costume). Peasant men wear sandals which are handsome and imaginative, as footwear has long been in Spain, and still is in Latin America.

The marriage of uncloistered priests had become so common, even in Spain, that the costume of their wives was governed by decree; one of the "Recueil" illustrations is of a Spanish priest's wife, and very gay and unfettered she is.

SPANISH PORTRAIT PAINTERS: XVI CENTURY

Few of the great painters of XVIc. Spanish portraits were themselves Spanish. But the Empire, rich, widely connected and pious, was a great patron.

Titian (1477-1576), the Venetian who painted the greatest of all records of Spanish costume, was never in Spain; he was twice called to Augsburg, in 1547 and 1550, to paint the emperor and his family.

Antonio Moro (1512-76) was a Fleming who worked in Madrid from 1552, followed Philip (II) to England at his marriage to Queen Mary, and returned with him to Spain after her death in 1558.

A. Sanchez-Coello (1515-90) was of Portuguese extraction, Spanish-born, Italian trained. He returned to Spain in 1541, became court painter to Philip II, and had a daughter, Isabella Sanchez, also a portrait painter.

El Greco (c.1545-1614) was a native of Crete who studied in Venice, and by 1577 was working in Toledo, where he lived like a rich man and died in debt among his beautiful possessions.

Juan Pantoja de la Cruz (1551-1608), Coello's pupil, was Spanish and painted at the courts of Philip II and III.

Liano and Bartolome Gonzales were also Spaniards.

Rubens (1577-1640), a Fleming and Catholic, was closely allied with Spain, through his connection with the Archduchess-Infanta Isabella Clara Eugenia. He worked in Spain for Philip III in 1603; entered the archducal household as painter in ordinary and familiar in 1609. Accustomed to the greatest society, literate and polylingual, he was not only a painter but a diplomat, who served as ambassador in negotiations between England and Spain.

Velasquez (1599-1660), of noble Portuguese descent, became in 1624 court painter to Philip IV, of whom he painted forty portraits besides innumerable pictures of his family, dwarfs and courtiers. He was official host and guide to Rubens, and with financial aid from the king, spent 1629-31 in Italy as Rubens had advised. He was recalled from a second trip to Italy, 1650-1 by the king who too badly missed his daily companion.

1211. XVIc. First Quarter. Italian. (Morgan Library, M. 52.)

Breviary of Queen Eleanor of Portugal.
St. Barbara.

A border of the large, naturalistic flowers, often on a metal-colored ground, typical of XVIc. manuscripts, is seen on this breviary produced in Rome for a queen who died in 1525. St. Barbara wears the age-old ceremonial sideless surcoat of royal ladies, the skirt of which tends to be made in lighter colors.

1212. XVIc. 1526. Italian. (Madrid, Prado.)

Titian. Isabella of Portugal, wife of Emperor Charles V.

The least-covered hair of first third XVIc. is seen in Spain, Italy and parts of Germany. With these looped arrangements of braids, there are usually loose locks, or as in this and other Spanish examples, soft puffs of hair at the ears.

The focal point of interest of all Spanish female sleeves into the XVIIc. is the line of the seam below the shoulder; this will be at least partly open, and emphasized by braid. Where the bell sleeve is cut close to the upper arm in England, and its hem deeply turned back, the Spanish sleeve begins to widen from the armseye, and is not apt to be turned up; it is shortened on Isabella by being caught up at intervals to the upper part of the undersleeve.

From end XVc., the low square neck is, in Spain, filled by a shirt or partlet embroidered in a vertically striped design, which tends to become spoke-like from the base of the throat. As Spanish embroideries spread through Europe, the shirt tends to disappear in Spain, except as an important frill at the top of high collars on closed bodices. With embroidered shirts like Isabella's, puffed undersleeves appear; but the characteristic undersleeve of XVI-e.XVIIc. is a perfectly simple, close-fitting one of the male doublet type, horizontally ringed throughout its length in narrow braid.

Isabella wears pearl earrings and necklace with a fine pendant, and an ornament at the part in her hair.

1213-15. XVIc. 1529. German. (Heidelberg, Germ. Nat. Mus. Library.)

Trachtenbuch von seinen Reisen nach Spanien, 1529, und der Niederlanden, 1531-2, by Christoph Weiditz.

This collection of 154 drawings, never published until our time, was sketched by a young goldsmith and medallist who accompanied his townsman, D. Colman, (of the family surnamed "Helmschmied" from their profession), on his trip to Spain to deliver to Charles V the suit of armor "with the wild animals," (now in the Madrid Museum), from the famous Helmschmied shop in Augsburg.

Wieditz' drawings, from which he had probably intended to make one of the very new wood-cut costume books, gives irreplaceable information about the dress of different Spanish cities and provinces, the Indians brought back by Cortez, sailor's dress, methods of husbandry and transport, and regional dress of France and the Low Countries.

1213. Dress of a Spanish noblewoman: Characteristically Spanish pigtail, covered in white, bound in red; triangular earrings of three spraying drops in a form which was old at the time of the Alhambra paintings; fan of spider-web pattern. Her rose gown, trimmed in green, shows full shirt sleeves, multiple skirts of various lengths, square train projected from the back half of the skirt, high pattens decorated with the usual zig-zag designs; all equally Spanish.

1214. Castilian peasant going to market: As in Central America today, going to market, which is held once or twice a week, was the greatest of social events; people come from all directions, and a Guatemalan peasant woman may walk as much as three days to get to one of the great markets, sell as few as five eggs, then walk home, perhaps to pick up what eggs can be found and start back, if she still feels gregarious. Her man may carry nets of crockery or drag five pigs, but he wears his best clothes, and recognizes the inhabitants of the surrounding villages by their special costume, just as they can tell where he comes from by his dress.

This peasant's costume shows strong Morisco influence, if he is not one himself, as seems likely; except in predominantly Moorish Granada, Christian, Jewish, and Moorish blood was inextricably intermixed. His intricately wound turban is of Moorish inspiration; it ends in a tab of their red, blue and white fringe. His yellowish cloak is edged with their toothed appliqué in red, blue and white. Hoods of one color, often lavishly decorated, set into "sailor" collars of another are favorite wear of XVIc. Spanish shepherds. From this peasant's hood falls a tail, in Morisco sections of color, blue, red and white, wound with red and gold, and fringed in green at each division of color. His green undersleeves show the favorite Spanish finish: the old funnel-shaped prolongation over the knuckles, turned back to form a drooping cuff. With full trousers he shows an Hispano-Moresque form of footwear of interlaced thongs which tie above the ankle like modern *alpargatas*.

1215. House dress of a Morisco woman and child: The woman has a red and white striped headdress, held in place by a bound circlet of green, white and blue, like that of a modern Arab. With a parti-colored red and brown vest she wears a loose white jacket, full trousers, and footless stockings characteristic of Moorish women (see Ill. 505). She may go barefoot, wear platform sandals with a wide strap over the instep, or slippers with curled-up toes, like those the child wears with violet stockings, a parti-colored red dress, buttoned in gold, and a mantle of green, white and gold stripes.

1216. XVlc. 1532-3. Italian. (Madrid, Prado.)

Titian. Charles V and his Dog.

Few men have needed to be, more than Charles V was, able, p a t i e n t and adaptable. T h e w i d e l y spread Hapsburg empire, Spain and its Italian possessions, Burgundy and the Netherlands had to be kept in equilibrium, America conquered, France, Lutheranism and the Sultan combatted.

Charles was a great general, a capable rather than creative administrator, pious, but not bigoted, scrupulous, conventional a n d stubborn. He was ugly, but a fine figure of a man, with great dignity and taste, of personally decent and simple life except for gluttony; this led to agonizing gout, and in 1557 he retired from all his cares to a small house near a monastery, where he could enjoy country life, animals, children, reading and music.

Portraits by Titian, his favorite painter, show that Charles dressed wonderfully as a young man. He was accused of h a v i n g brought Burgundian luxury to Spain; but he was no more able than his mother had been to control by edict the lavish metallic decoration or silk brocades used at court; and in his own later days he dressed with simple sobriety.

With his black velvet bonnet, Charles wears a superb gold and white costume. His canions are of gold-striped white s a t i n, vertically paned and horizontally caught, to match the doublet which shows only at the lower sleeve, and through the slits of his cloth-of-gold doublet, corded in gold. As in the jerkins of Henry VIII and Francis I, the slits are part of its pattern; however, their small puffed cuts will pass out of use, while the slits seen here, low on the jerkin, will be extended to the breast, and will become an important fashion of the mid-century. Over these, Charles wears a cloak of white brocade, collared in sable, patterned with gold cord run through clusters of gold rings; white netherstocks and shoes; belt with sword, and dagger tasseled in white silk topped in gold; pendant of the Golden Fleece.

1216

1217. XVIc. Spanish. (London, Louis Raphael Coll.)

A. Sanchez-Coello. Queen Isabella, d.1539.

Hair is no longer looped about the ears; free locks persist at the sides but rise as the centrally parted hair begins to be brushed up from the temples.

In addition to the vertical cut, Spanish sleeves are subject to transverse cuts across the elbow-line; these may be in a horizontally set V from the inside of the elbow, in—and + forms, or in the inverted T form shown on these sleeves, one worn and one pendant.

The slashes of the bosom of the male jacket (1216) are lengthened on this very masculine jacket with its high collar and ruff, and close doublet; the horizontally banded doublet sleeve on women's garments shows a frequent subsidiary spiral effect, which will be influential into third quarter XVIc. Picadills at armseye and, in a scalloped form, at cuff.

Sheer scarf with pendant now separated from veil.

1218. Second quarter XVIc. Spanish. (Brussels Royal Gallery.

Copy of *A. Sanchez-Coello.* Margaret of Parma.

Charles V's able natural daughter, who followed her aunts as Regent of the Netherlands, holds a symbolic bridle in her hand.

Her clothing shows the startling and contagious masculinity of Spanish female dress of the XVIc.:

male bonnet with rising crown, over hair dressed high, but retaining bunched loose hair, ornamented; jacket with picadill finish at high collar and waist as well as armseye; flowing sleeve slit and caught along inner seam; close masculine doublet with high collar and elaborate shirt ruffle.

1219. XVIc. c. 1554. Flemish. (Madrid, Prado.)

Antonio Moro.

Catherine of Austria, Queen of Portugal.

Charles V's fanatically bigoted sister, under whom, as regent for her grandson, the Jesuits dominated Portugal, shows the veiled forehead of her grandmother with hair bunched over the ears as it so often is in the '50s, pendant earrings of the triangular, tasseled Spanish form, and fine jewelled collar. Severe coat-dress, embroidered fall at high collar; buttoned bosom-slits matching braiding of upper sleeve; brocade undergarment; wide belt, coat-of-arms buckle; Italian fan; lace inset handkerchief.

1220. XVIc. c. 1550. Flemish. (Prado, Madrid.)

Antonio Moro. Emperor Maximilian II.

The eldest son of the little boy in the Strigel portrait lived mostly in Spain until 1550. His portrait is by a Fleming, court painter to the Hapsburgs from 1549 to his death in 1575, often classed among the Spanish and English painters whom he influenced.

1220

1221

Maximilian's jerkin of pinked and slit white leather has the lowered waistline of second third XVIc. and the highest possible Spanish collar, finished with a scalloped picadill edge bound in gold to match its cap sleeves and double skirts. It is worn over a beautiful close doublet of white braided in gold.

Paned trunk-hose, in their early form shown here, have bombast (stuffing) used only below the line of the crotch, and match the doublet sleeves.

Beautiful classic pouch of the period; superb rapier with well developed knuckle-guard, and *pas d'ane* below straight quillons. Black bonnet with **tiny** plume; cord emphasizes the parting of crown from brim. Collar of the Golden Fleece. Gloves. Slit **shoes** of natural form.

On the fringed velvet cover of the table stands his closed armet, which has a considerably developed neck-guard and plumes set in its comb.

1221. XVIc. 1553. Italian. (Naples Museum.)
Titian. Philip II.

Isabella of Portugal was loved in Spain as her husband could never be, by a people who resented his necessary attentions to other parts of his wide-spread

possessions. Charles ingratiated himself with his Spanish subjects, at the time of the birth of his only son, by killing a bull in the public square of Valladolid in honor of the event.

Philip was a pleasant blond young man, rather defectively educated by a tutor during his father's absence; he was hardworking, over-meticulous and proud; attractive in his family life, as was his father, and like him, of relatively simple personal tastes. His marriage to Mary Tudor in 1554, however, required a magnificent wardrobe, of which his valet, Andreas Muñoz, left a descriptive inventory, and which introduced Spanish fashions to the English court. (It is given in detail in Norris: *Costume and Fashion: The Tudors*.) These costumes were largely in black, white, gold and silver combinations.

Here his padded doublet, jerkin, hose (still padded low), and shoes are of pale yellow, embroidered in silver: the gown, of brown satin and sable with paired aiglettes, has lost its pendant sleeve; below its top fullness it has assumed a lower sleeve, which used to be that of the garment beneath, and which is short enough to show the actual jerkin sleeve.

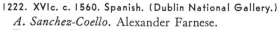

1222. XVIc. c. 1560. Spanish. (Dublin National Gallery.)

A. Sanchez-Coello. Alexander Farnese.

Farnese, who was Charles V's grandson by Margaret of Parma, followed Don Juan of Austria as governor of the Netherlands. As a successful general and diplomat, he consolidated the southern provinces into Catholic Belgium, loyal to Spain. During the struggle, however, Amsterdam acquired the trade of the port of Antwerp, as the more enter-prising Protestant part of the population took refuge in the Dutch Republic or England, enriching those countries and impoverishing Belgium.

Farnese wears the cloak with hanging sleeves slung like a cape across one shoulder, as it is usually carried; (see Sidney: Ill. 1182); it has a high collar and is notched into the beginning of our lapels. Increasing height of collar, and elaboration of collar edge into set ruff.

1223. XVIc. c.1565. Spanish. (Vienna Art History Mus.)

A. Sanchez-Coello. The Infante Don Carlos.

The wilful and disorderly lunatic son of Philip II died incarcerated about three years after this portrait was painted. The *Fugger News Letters* relate that he walked barefoot in the water with which he had caused his room to be deluged and had eaten nothing but ice-water and fruit for a week.

Like his cousin above, the Infante wears his sleeved and lapelled cloak as a cape. The panes of his shorter and wider hose show an effect of interlacing; this horizontal or diagonal interweaving was often actual, and the dagger is sometimes seen run through the panes like a darning needle. The shoe is becoming elaborated over the instep, where a tongue will develop at end XVIc.

1224. XVIc. 1569. Flemish. (Washington, Nat. Gall. of Art.)

Antonio Moro. Portrait of a Gentleman.

The gentleman, no longer considered to be the artist's self-portrait, wears a costume of black velvet and violet satin, with the highest of Spanish col-

lars, open in front in the manner of the 60's and after.

1225. XVIc. 1564. Spanish. (Vienna Imperial Museum.)

A. Sanchez-Coello. Portrait of a Woman.

The Hapsburgs tried to keep their great empire in equilibrium by a network of politically expedient engagements and marriages. In 1559, Philip II took as his third wife Catherine de' Medici's eldest daughter, Elizabeth of Valois; and in 1572, Elizabeth of Austria, daughter of Maximilian II, was married to Catherine's son, Charles IX.

It is therefore not surprising to find, in a Spanish portrait which must show one of the ladies of the new queen, French dress almost identical with that worn by Philip's niece as Queen of France. In the Coello portrait, the gown has the Spanish collar, so high that it must be worn open, elaborately edged; and in the Clouet, seven years later, a completely developed ruff. Glove with slashed finger; handkerchief.

1226. XVIc. c.1575. Spanish. (Madrid, Prado.)

J. Pantoja de la Cruz. Infanta Empress Maria.

The Emperor Maximilian II's cousin-wife wears

the scarf we have seen on Isabella la Catolica and others of her descendants: Christina of Denmark and Isabella of Portugal; here it is finely crimped and falls from the head.

Wrist ruffles remained inconspicuous in Spain until the complete development of the lace ruff which they now match.

The great *puntas* of Spain hang from ribbon or braid tabs, where the smaller paired *aiglettes* of the rest of Europe branch out from the fabric to which they are sewed.

The shape of the typical slit, pendant sleeve of Spain will show more clearly on examples at the end of the century.

1227. XVIc. 1577. Spanish. (London, Earl of Northbrook.)
A. Sanchez-Coello. Don Diego, son of Philip II.
For little boy's costume, see Ill. 1173.

1228. XVIc. 1575. Spanish. (Metropolitan Museum.)
El Greco. Cardinal Don Fernando Niño de Guevara.

With his red biretta, mozetta and cassock and lace-edged white surplice, the cardinal wears spectacles fastened around the ears by loops.

Spectacles were perhaps the invention of Roger Bacon; they are first mentioned in XIIIc., and their use was developed in Italy. In their earliest form, they are like two reading glasses pinned together through the handles so that they could be spread in a V and set or held on the bridge of the nose; glasses of this sort hang at the side of the desk of Ghirlandaio's St. Jerome, and are worn with Caligari-like effect in the Florentine engraving of the same period, purporting to show the ritual murder of St. Simon of Trent. (See Appendix.)

Dark rimmed spectacles, fashionable in Spain in XVIIc., were used on the mask of Zerbino, one of the Spanish characters of Italian comedy.

1229. XVIc. 1578. Spanish. (Toledo, Church of Santo Thome.)
El Greco. Burial of Count of Orgaz, detail.

The Count of Orgaz was a devout gentleman of the XIVc. who, according to legend, was about to be buried when St. Augustine and St. Stephen, to whom he had been very devoted, descended from heaven and laid him in his coffin.

1230

The priest of Santo Thomé and members of the Covarrubias family have been identified among the portraits of notables of Toledo, in their mourning cloaks with the cross of St. James, great ruffs and pointed Spanish beards.

The dalmatic of St. Stephen and the copes of St. Augustine and the priest show magnificent orphreys of Spanish embroidery.

1230. XVIc. 1579. Spanish. (Madrid, Prado.)

A. Sanchez-Coello. Infanta Isabella Clara Eugenia.

The Infanta, adored by her father, and the greatest matrimonial prize since Elizabeth, was thirty when Philip II realized that he was going to die. The Cardinal Archduke Albert of Austria, who succeeded his brother as ruler of the Netherlands, was freed of his vows by the Pope and married to his cousin, the Infanta. Their joint rule as "the Archdukes" was devoted and competent; they concluded a truce which renounced any authority over the United Provinces and tried to repair the economy of the Netherlands. But they died childless, and their country reverted to an impoverished Spain, which relied on her treasure ships, now being successfully raided by the Zeeland-ers and British. Meanwhile Spain expelled the Moriscos, her only good farmers and since centuries, her finest craftsmen, weavers and embroiderers, metal workers and pottery makers; these (since they alone prospered) must be the "sponges that soaked up all the Spanish wealth." Spain de-industrialized herself, as she had the Netherlands, and her glory decayed as the Dutch East India Company was being formed in 1600. (See Appendix: Trade.)

The girdle pendant is now becoming shorter, all over Europe; it has never been much used in Spain, where skirts have been massively decorated down the center-front for centuries; chains and pomanders would only tangle with studs and tags, braid and ribbon. The girdle is immensely rich in Spain, finished at the center by a pointing shield- or heart-shaped motif, matching the precious collar, and outlining the waistline as it lengthens and points.

The armseye roll is reinforced by tabbed picadills above and below; the sleeve of the gown is only an open strip behind the braided doublet sleeve.

She wears a high tilted bonnet, plumed on one side, over jewelled hair which is dressed in the unparted Spanish fashion, in a high padded pompadour.

1231. XVIc. c. 1571. Spanish. (Vienna Art History Mus.)

A. Sanchez-Coello. Queen Anne of Spain.

Philip married in 1570 his fourth wife, daughter of Maximilian 11, and mother of Philip III; she died before him in 1580, ill as he was.

She wears her parted hair rolled in the French way; chains of pearls; a tabbed picadill skirt on bodice, matching her shoulder-caps; dispensing with massive Spanish collar and girdle.

Ribbon loops (which will become extremely important in XVIIc.) have come into use on the jewelled puntas which catch her skirt and great sleeves.

She carries a handkerchief with lace insertion and edging in one gloved hand; gloves are beginning to be taken for granted; she wears only one, and its forefinger is slit to show a fine ring.

1232. XVIc. 1590? Spanish. (Metropolitan Museum.)

A. Sanchez-Coello. Infanta Isabella of Spain.

Hair and headdresses, in their most specifically Spanish forms,

mount to a point. Hats tend to disappear, in favor of jewels and rosettes set rather asymmetrically in the hair. Pearl earrings are worn in pairs; more elaborate earrings, often singly. Pearl ropes replace heavy jewelled collars. Folding fans are used. (See Ills. 1237-38 and 1290-95.)

Ruffs grow more enormous, and end in jagged points of lace. They tend to split and flatten, as on the Infanta (whose wire support with pendant fringe is clearly seen under the ruff-collar). Ruffs are frequently replaced by flat collars, wired high (1238). Reticella begins to be replaced by bone lace; and set ruffs at the wrists, by lace cuffs (which increase in width and importance); or, as in the case of the Spanish princess, by embroidered cuffs with lace-like notches.

Bodices also split and expose the bosom, though less so in Spain than elsewhere. Their points lengthen and the tabbed peplums deepen. Skirts become unified in cut and are gathered around the waist to accommodate hip bolsters; this forces the point of the bodice outward. The hip bolster has only the slightest effect on the cone-shaped Spanish farthingale at the end of the century; we never see the drum-shaped skirt with cart-wheel top used in Spain.

The sleeve we see here has been in long use in Spain. Tabbed wings now supplant the old roll at the shoulder; important jewels pinned on sleeve, just below shoulder.

The great era of braid has passed. Brocades in striped patterns are used in place of braid in tabs and on doublet sleeves, which are now braided only along their inner seam. Openwork galoon bands are now used, upon less austere brocades, lighter in color and delicately sprigged in smaller patterns. The somber stiffness of Spain is passing (see Ills. 1237-39).

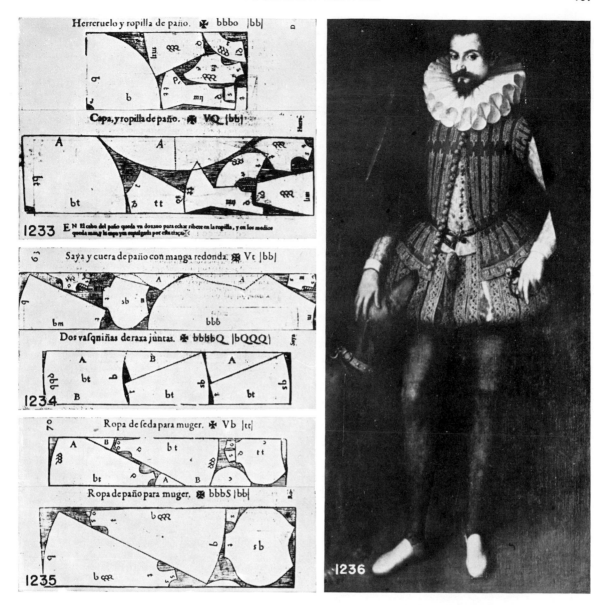

Herreruelo y ropilla de paño. ✠ bbbo |bb|

Capa, y ropilla de paño. ✠ VQ |bb|

1233 EN El cabo del paño queda vn dozauo para echar ribete en la ropilla, y en los medios queda mangas la capa y vn espaldarcillo por esta traça.

Saya y cuera de paño con manga redonda. ✠ Vt |bb|

Dos vasquiñas de raxa juntas. ✠ bbbbQ |bQQQ|

1234

Ropa de seda para muger. ✠ Vb |tt|

Ropa de paño para muger. ✠ bbbS |bb|

1235

1236

1233-35. XVIc. 1587. Spanish. (Metropolitan Museum, Print Room.)

Libro de geometria practica y traca, by Juan de Alcega, pub. by Guillermo Druoy, Madrid, 1587.

In the XVIc. flood of books on costume, it was inevitable that pattern books should appear. Alcega' is the first of these. (See Appendix.)

1233. A "wagtail" (which is certainly a wonderful name for a long-skirted jacket) and doublet of plush velvet; and a velvet cape and doublet.

1234. A skirt and bodice of velvet with round sleeves.

1235. A silk gown, and one of velvet.

1236. XVIc. (last decade). Spanish. London, Christie sale, June 27, 1924.)

Att. to *A. Sanchez-Coello.* Portrait of a Nobleman.

This gentleman's brown costume with mauve hose shows many new characteristics. He has the wide, boldly set ruff of the last decade; its shorter-waisted jacket with sleeve-wings, breast slits simulated by embroidery, longer skirts, and the XVIIc. impulse to be unbuttoned below the breast; short cape; very short, wide trunk-hose still carrying a cod-piece; shoes with soles but no heels, as yet.

1237. Last decade XVIc. Spanish. (Paris, Coll. Lazzaro.)
Att. to *A. Sanchez-Coello.* Portrait of a Lady.
1238. End XVIc. Spanish. (New York, George Mercer
Coll.)
Att. to *A. Sanchez-Coello.* Spanish Princess.
1239. XVIc. c. 1585. Spanish. (Madrid, Prado.)
Att to *T. F. Liaño.* Infanta Isabella Clara Eugenia
and the dwarf, Magdalena Ruiz.

Men's hats, whether worn by men or women, are growing higher and less gathered in the crown. The Infanta's plume, hair, and collar are higher, her ruff and skirt wider. The bell-sleeve, which never passed out of Spanish use, and is split along the inner seam

in the Spanish way, trails to the long train of her gown; this is characteristically developed out of the back section, alone, of what is made to look like a short skirt over a longer one, by the use of braid.

Her attendant, a dwarf, kneeling with the monkey, has the headdress of Northern Spain.

THE BOOK OF
COSTUME

VOLUME II

THE
BOOK
OF
COSTUME

BY
MILLIA DAVENPORT

VOLUME II

CROWN PUBLISHERS, INC.
NEW YORK

Eleventh Printing, November, 1976

PRINTED IN THE UNITED STATES OF AMERICA

CONTENTS

Volume II

1240. Late XV-e.XVIc. Franco-Flemish. (Metropolitan Museum.)

Tapestry. Country life: possibly scenes from a pastoral play or poem.

Straw hats, hoods, pouches, sock-boots and tucked-up gowns perennially seen in peasant costume; diagonal and laced closing of the transitional period.

1241, 1246. Late XV-e.XVIc. Franco-Flemish. (Metropolitan Museum.)

The Unicorn Tapestries.

Anne of Brittany, whom Maximilian I had attempted to marry, became the queen of Charles VIII; upon his death in 1498, she assumed black, instead of the customary white mourning of Queens Dowager, "reines blanches."

The research of James J. Rorimer has shown that these superb tapestries, from the chateau of Verteuil, celebrate Anne's marriage, in 1499, to Charles' successor, Louis XII. In the "Start of the Hunt," the first and last letters of her name appear, linked by the cordelière of the Order of St. Francis, which Anne had established in 1498 for widowed ladies; and on the collar of one of the greyhounds can be seen the words "FRNC REX."

Anne, whose motto was "Better die than be sullied" was intelligent, devout, narrow-minded and rather bourgeois. She was plain, and because she had a short leg, a slight limp became court fashion. She was the founder of the modern court with its many maids of honor. Brantôme, whose aunt was one of these, tells of Anne's constant efforts to augment their numbers from all parts of France, and her scrupulous supervision of their lives and training. She had, in addition, a guard of 100 gentlemen, largely Breton, and the terrace at Blois, where

they waited to attend her, was named by Anne herself, "The Breton's Perch."

1241. *The Start of the Hunt*: Beaver hats with clustered plumes bound across crown and under chin; sometimes worn over small felt bonnets; these, when worn alone, may also be plumed. The jerkins of the gentlemen have sleeves of another material; skirts plain or pleated. Tights with upper portions striped. Shoes, square toed, furlined and of ankle height.

1246. *The Unicorn is Killed and Brought to the Castle*: Variety and combination of male hats (one slung back by its ties), and small caps with turned-up brims, which are now being slashed, knotted and pinned: the cap is turning into a bonnet. Collarless jerkins and short sleeveless gowns. High boots, or leggings worn with ankle-high shoes, have turned-down cuffs of another color. Anne and her ladies wear severe high-necked gowns with lapped-over bodices. Hoods are simple, long, not yet slashed, and not very richly trimmed. General absence of precious accessories, rings, chains, and pendants; replaced here by cords and sashes. Rosaries, here as elsewhere,

until the Reformation.

1242-45. Early XVIc. French. (Paris, Bib. Nat.)
Hours of Anne of Brittany. Executed by *Jean Bourdichon.*

1242. Youths: in square-crowned bonnets, the brims of which are beginning to rake out from the perpendicular line shown in the Unicorn Tapestries.

Waist-high hose with wide cod-pieces, laced to brocade doublets with lowering neckline.

1243. Gleaners.

1244. St. Lifar as a bishop: his pleated rochet will be shortened to knee-length, during XVIc.

1245. St. Catherine: in ermine-trimmed, ceremonial sideless surcoat of a queen, its skirt of brocade.

1247. XVIc. 1503. French. (Paris, Bib. Nat., ms. fr. 225.)
Unknown artist: School of Rouen. Petrarch's *Les remèdes de l'une et l'autre fortune.*

Louis XII, Anne of Brittany, and Claude of France.

Louis wears his crown set around his bonnet, and the collar of the Order of St. Michael. He is followed by a cardinal and peers.

The jerkins of the two little pages have low, square necks and carefully seamed and gored *bases* of two

materials, countercharged at the border. Shoes are broad and strapped.

A center-front closing has superseded the lapped fronts of Anne's earlier gowns.

1248. Late XV-e.XVIc. French. (Paris, Bib. Nat., ms. fr. 143.)
Le Livre des Echecs Amoureux. Music.

This is the book of music lessons studied by the children who became Francis I and Marguerite of Navarre.

The Muse, seated between a harp and an organ, plays a zither-like psaltery. Fanciful touches, like the headdress and flowing German sleeves, make her otherwise standard gown of the transition period suitable for an allegorical personage. The lady in the background wears a hood which dips in the center in a Franco-Flemish way (as opposed to the gabled English form of hood).

Behind the carved linen-fold panelling are seen flute and hautboy players, a bagpiper, and a boy's choir, in skull-caps and surplices, supervised by an ecclesiastic wearing a four-cornered biretta.

1249. XVIc. 1507. French. (Paris, Bib. Nat., ms. fr. 5091.)
Story of the Conquest of Genoa, by Jean Marot.

Marot offering his work to Anne of Brittany. The square neck is rising convexly, and sleeves shorten as they become definitely funnel-shaped. Overskirt has inverted V-opening. Girdle, necklaces, and border of hood are becoming richer, as a shorter, more sophisticated hood is set farther back on the head, over a cap with an exquisitely gauffered edge, usually of gold gauze. This is the beginning of the *French hood,* which supplants every other form, in the wear of the upper classes toward the end of the XVIc.

spinning wife has a fine hanging pouch and ring of keys; 4th, nobility: braided carpet, cushions under foot, fine leaded windows, impressive show of plate; familiar garments; bead necklaces, used in Italy since late XVIc., are new in France.

1254. XVIc. c. 1520. French. (Paris, Bib. Nat., ms. fr. 1537.) *Unknown artist. Chants royaux du Puy de Rouen.*
Interior of a print shop.

Other illustrations in this ms. show masons, weavers, pottery-turners and armorers. The windows of a print shop now have leaded panes; marble paving slabs are increasing in size.

The scholars looking over proofs wear the expected rectangular cap, and a sleeveless closed gown with a collar and deeply curved front opening, for which the round-necked undergarment serves as placard: I believe this to be a specifically French form.

The foreman wears a jerkin with a standing collar, opening from the waist. The bearded printer's full shirt bulges between his short-sleeved doublet and slashed and gartered upper-hose; patterned caul-like cap; hair

1250-53. XVIc. 1510. French. (Amiens, coll. Jean Masson.)
The Four Estates of Society. Executed by *Jean Bourdichon.*

The 1st estate is savagery; 2nd, extreme poverty; 3rd, bourgeoisie: carpenter in his prosperous shop, its windows barred but without glass, wears cropped hair and a short-sleeved jerkin closed by knotted points; his

shorter; shoes broader, cut lower, with or without straps.

1255. XVIc. French. (Paris, Bib. Nat., ms. fr. 874.)

Unknown artist: *School of Rouen. Ovid's Heroides.*

The Red Chamber of the Danaïdes: Nightwear of both sexes; beds and hangings.

1256. XVIc. French. (Darmstadt Mus.)

Jean Clouet, d. c. 1541. Bath after Birth.

Many were bathed only at birth, as a preparation for marriage, and after their death; women bathed also after childbirth. To carry and heat enough water in a fireplace was difficult, and a bather had to be protected from the chill of a high-ceilinged, stone-walled room by a tent like enclosure.

1257. XVIc. 1515. French. (Louvre.)

Clouet, probably Jean. Francis I.

Jean Clouet, called Janet, and his son François were both painters at the courts of Francis I and Henry II. Jean, probably a Fleming, married a Frenchwoman c. 1520 and died c. 1541. François died in 1571. It is difficult to attribute definite works to Jean, but he is supposed to have drawn many of the chalk portraits of his school, some of which bear Francis I's own witty comments on the sitters.

Francis, though "he had the longest nose of any man in France except his jester," Triboulet, was a handsome man, witty, high-spirited, intelligent and amiable; personally courageous, selfish, capricious and unstable. He was passionately devoted to sports and amusements. Tennis, which had been played in some form since time immemorial, was a favorite game of both the French and English courts; Francis

loved it, and his son, Henry II, became the finest player in France.

The competitive magnificence of Francis and Henry VIII in their interview in 1520, at the "Field of the Cloth of Gold," made it one of the greatest costume parades of all time and bankrupted many of their courtiers. The "Chronicle" of the contemporary English lawyer-historian, Edward Hall, gives a detailed description of its costume and pageantry; two paintings at Hampton Court, att. to Vincent Volpe, show the embarcation and the meeting place; magnificent pavilions and tents, impressive temporary buildings, were shipped from England like stage scenery for erection near Calais.

Hall tells us that "The French King and his band were apparelled in purple satin, branched with gold and purple velvet, embroidered with [Franciscan] friars' knots, and in every knot were pansy flowers, which together, signified 'Think of Francis.' "

In the Clouet portrait, the puffs and slashes of Francis' black and white, gold and silver costume are subservient to its vertical bands of e. XVIc. embroidery, in which cord is used in interlaced patterns and to edge scrolled and foliated appliqué. His jacket, like that of Henry VIII, is cut away to expose the bosom of his doublet; this is still collarless and has the bateau neck which Francis favored.

His overgarment is made from a rectangle, slit up the front and across at the neck in a T, forming flaps which turn back as revers; the sides of the rectangle are folded up and caught on the shoulders, giving them additional square width and exposing the doublet sleeve.

Francis carries gloves; rapier with a well developed guard around the hand and the XVIc. "pas d'ane" guard below the quillons.

1258. XVIc. 1566. French. (Paris, Bib. Nat.)

Jean du Tillet. Francis I.

This portrait of the king in robes of state was painted several decades after his death by an artist who specialized in official portraits. The familiar symbols, cloak and gown are worn with contemporary slashed sleeves and wide-toed, low-cut shoes.

1259. Last third XVIc. French. (Chantilly, Conde Mus., ms. fr. 1672.)

History by Diodorus of Sicily, translated by Macault.

Macault is reading his work to Francis I, his three sons, and a group of courtiers which included the Chancellor Antoine du Prat, one of the favorites of the king's early years, and the later favorites, the Admiral de Brion and Anne de Montmorency, afterwards the mentor of Henry II. Behind the king's pet monkey stands a group of scholars in gowns and quadrangular hats.

We have no date for this illustration. But the king, by his marriage with Claude of France, who died in 1524, had 7 children; the third was the Dauphin, who died in 1536; the fourth, born in 1519, became Henry II; the sixth was the third son. We know that there was another edition of this work in 1535, which was also the year of du Prat's death. We may therefore judge the children's ages, and with the evidence of the costume, date the picture at the start of the 1530's. The neckline is still low, but rising and edged with a ruffle; hair not yet cropped; extreme square width of the shoes.

We see three views of a gown similar to that worn by Henry VIII both with and without dependent sleeve; in the latter case, the puffed upper sleeve is horizontally cut and caught with aiglettes. As on the costume of Henry VIII, tiny puffs are drawn through apertures in the embroidery. Netted hair under hat, as in German examples; dagger now carries a huge tassel.

1260. XVIc. 1543. French. (London, National Gallery.)
Corneille de Lyon. Portrait of a Man.

Jerkins with short sleeves, and decorated in grouped parallel lines are characteristic of mid-XVIc., but the high Spanish collar with a lace edged ruff would not yet have appeared on this garment in England. Many jackets retain a full upper sleeve, but the sleeve is tending to become simple and close, vertically slashed or corded, in mid-XVIc.

1261. XVIc. c. 1555. Italo-French. (Florence, Uffizi.)
Unknown artist. Catherine de' Medici, Queen of France.

The orphan who, at 11, cut off her hair and dared the Roman senators to be seen carrying her off forcibly (dressed as she was like a nun) from the Murate Convent she loved, needed all her amazing self-control and intelligence in her life as Queen of France. She was 14 when her uncle, Pope Clement, himself officiated at her marriage to the future Henry II. Her Medici energy, taste, intellect and love of sports endeared her to Francis I, but despite her great dowry, the French resented her "bourgeois" origin. The deaths of her uncle and father-in-law left her alone and slighted in a court whose calumnies have injured her reputation almost to this day.

Catherine, childless for a decade, loved the heavy youth who was her husband; while Henry II, resenting her superiority, neglected her mercilessly for Diane de Poitiers, 20 years his senior, who referred to her as "the shopkeeper's daughter." Eventually Catherine had 9 children, of whom 3 became kings of France. Henry's character developed slowly, and

1261

Many arts we now think of as French were actually brought from Italy by Catherine: fine cooking, lace making, fans and parasols, and the distillation of perfumes. Catherine, who carried parsley seed with her from Italy, imported her own chefs, skilled in the age-old variety of Mediterranean cooking and the iced sherbets of the Orient. Their arrival was coincident with the new foodstuffs and seasonings which adventurers were bringing back from the New World and the Orient.

Cane sugar began to supplement honey, which had been the universal sweetener; rum and molasses appeared. From America, too, came turkeys, potatoes, squash, maize (which travelled on to South Africa and India from the Mediterranean, just as Marco Polo had brought back spaghetti, or at least noodles, from China), chocolate, pineapples, and tomatoes ("love apples"), a decorative curiosity, but still considered poisonous in our great-grandmother's time. Tea and spices from the Orient, long known, became relatively available, and cooking became an art in which royalty itself dabbled from the time of Louis XV.

The 7 great pearls which were the Pope's wedding present to her, and hers to her daughter-in-law, Mary Queen of Scots, were appropriated by Elizabeth, and were use in the coronation crown of Edward VII.

As a young woman, Catherine was notable for fine eyes, hands and complexion, and her tiny 16-inch waist. Brantôme, who would never return to court after her death, says that she dressed superbly, was an excellent companion, had beautiful easy manners, loved dancing and sports, and made light of her later infirmities. She was not the inventor of the side-saddle, with which she is often credited, but was an indomitable horsewoman and hunter until the age of 60, despite a broken leg, fractured skull, and a fall " in which, thank God, I was not much hurt, and am only marked on my nose, like the sheep of Berri."

Catherine's standards of court dress and etiquette were rigid and high. Her children, the neurotically subservient boys and the rebellious Margot, all held her in great respect and longed for the good opinion of the mother who had disciplined herself in enduring dignity.

Catherine's gown is of black velvet, embroidered with gold and lines of pearls, set with sapphires at their intersections; the underdress of pink satin.

A gored underbodice of heavy material (*vasquine, basquine*) used from late XVc., had been followed by a rigid, hinged corset of iron bands. Another of Catherine's introductions from Italy was the corset of flexible steel, such as she wears with the vertugale under this gown.

The bodice carries the turned-back fur sleeve of the time of Holbein, but its waist is very pointed; and its crimpled and jewelled gauze partlet has the ruff, a decade or two ahead of the rest of Europe, which had also been brought from Italy by Catherine: a gauffered lace ruffle, set on a turned-up collar.

With this, Catherine wears a French hood, now without the fall, which would interfere with the ruff; fan of ostrich tips with a fine handle; magnificent cross and girdle pendant.

improved; Catherine's admirably decisive actions, during the king's absence at the disaster of Pavia, won her his respect in the last years of his life. Henry was fatally wounded in the eye by a lance, during a tournament in which the victorious king had sent Catherine word that he "would try one more lance for love of her." The queen, for the rest of her life, wore heavy mourning, which she barely lightened, on such occasions as the wedding of her son, by exchanging black velvet or satin for her usual dull materials.

As Regent for 2 of her sons, and during the last 30 years of her life, Catherine labored with all her Medici tolerance and statesmanship to reconcile France's religious differences, and to improve her courts of justice. At 68, immensely heavy, and no longer able to ride because of rheumatism, Catherine continued to travel about France in a litter on her "journeys of pacification." At 70, she crept from bed in her last illness to try to undo the mischief of the assassination of Guise, leader of the Catholic faction, which had been instigated by Henry III.

Modern historical research tends to absolve Catherine of cruelties beyond those characteristic of her times; and the duplicity of which she was accused appears to have arisen from her tolerance, far in advance of her times, of both religions, which infuriated both.

1262. XVIc. 1558. French. (Metropolitan Museum.)
François Clouet. Equestrian portrait of Henry II.
The king wears a black and gold embroidered
jacket with long skirts and pendant sleeves; doublet
sleeves and unpadded, paned trunk hose of white
and gold, pinked. Jack boots over embroidered boot-
hose. Gloves with a turned-back cuff.

The trappings of the horse show the linked letters
H and D, which Henry used on the façades of new
buildings or wherever else possible, to signify his
love for Diane de Poitiers.

1263-64. XVIc. 1562. French. (Metropolitan Museum,
         Print Room.)
Recueil de la diversité des habits, by François Des-
cerpz, Richard Breton, Paris, 1562.
These illustrations, showing the difference between
French and Flemish mourning, came from the first
real book on costumes published in France.

The unmarried French girl, in mourning for near
relatives, wears pleated cuffs to match her *barbe,* and
a hood with an extremely long narrow fall which she
carries over her arm. Gloves are now in common use.

In Flemish mourning, a very wide veil is wired
out to frame the head, and tucked up in back to give
a short, wide horizontal hemline.

Either black, white, or their combinations were
used in mourning, though white was more commonly
worn before Anne of Brittany's time. The pleated
barbe was worn by widows, with a beguine or other
hood, until the time of Catherine de' Medici, when
it was replaced by a wired-out hood, dipping low over
the forehead or carried out into a beak (Christine:
Ill. 1290). For the white mourning (*deuil blanc*) of
a young queen, a veiled hood over a tiny cap and a

pleated *barbe* under the chin, such as we associate
with Mary of Scotland. (See Ill. 1359.)

Pleating and mourning were associated in costume.
Francis I's widow wore a pleated white cambric
gown, embroidered in white, and the black mourning gowns of Catherine de' Medici are pleated, although the *barbe* has been given up.

Beside the deep mourning of *grand-deuil,* the half-
mourning of *petit-deuil* permitted the use of some
color, though its use was restricted to skirts, petticoats, the underparts of bodices, and hose. Violet was
often used; Brantôme says that beige and blue were
also permitted, and that this was sometimes stretched
to include flesh and chamois.

A girdle, rings and ropes of pearls were permissible,
but the use of cut stones was not.

Hooded mourning robes, completely covering the
garments, were worn in funeral processions. Margaret
Paston's will in 1482, directs that white mourning
robes with hoods be provided for her tenants, at her
funeral. With the advent of crepe in late XVIc., the
crowns of hats were wreathed in twists of black
mourning crepe. The dull textures of cotton and
velvet were considered appropriate for mourning;
silk was worn in Spain, and for a happy occasion like
a wedding, Catherine de' Medici permitted herself to
wear gleaming satin. (See Appendix.)

1265. Third quarter XVIc. French. (Metropolitan Mus.)
Corneille de Lyon. Portrait of a Widow.
Hood with a gold ridge, simple gold chains and
pearls only. Velvet yoke; standing collar lined with
white, informally pleated at top; puffed upper sleeve,
white puffs above wrist; wide vertugale and lengthening V waist.

La damoiselle en dueil.

Le dueil de flandre.

1266

1267

1268

1266. XVIc. 1548. French. (Chantilly, Conde Museum.)

François Clouet. Odet de Coligny, Cardinal de Chastillon.

The three Colignys, who played such important roles in the French wars of religion, were the Cardinal de Chastillon, and his Huguenot brothers: the Admiral Gaspard, assassinated on St. Bartholomew's Eve by the Guise, and Francis, known as the Sieur d' Andelot, who had led Gaspard into Protestantism.

Below his cardinal's hat, Odet wears the rich dress of a gentleman of the 1540's. His satin gown is lined and collared with lynx, which shows through slashes. His brocade jerkin shows a lengthening waistline and high collar, finished with a plain ruff, pleated but not rigidly set. He carries gloves with a slashed cuff.

Brocades of such large pattern have gone out of ordinary male use by end first third XVIc., and are retained here in ecclesiastical dignity. Plain materials pinked, braided, or embroidered in lineal or diapered designs replace brocade, in male use, until its reappearance in XVIIc.; and the brocades used in women's dress take on smaller, all-over and diapered patterns.

1267-68. XVIc. c.1560. French. (Paris, Bib. Nat.)

François Clouet. Admiral Gaspard de Coligny. François de Coligny, sieur d'Andelot.

The crown of the flat hat is rising and decoration is now set about the band. The high crowned Italian bonnet, which rises to such heights in English use, is less frequently seen in France than a small French form of toque, or a high felt hat (like that worn by the Puritans of New England).

These drawings show in detail the cut, fastenings and decoration of high collared garments and the ruffs which accompany them in France. The braid trim of d'Andelot's collar is repeated, in picadill form, as a ruff-like edge and a piping at the base.

The fine goldsmith's work shows another influence attributable to Catherine de' Medici. Court intrigue, which Cellini recounts in his autobiography, interrupted his work for Francis I, in the 1530's, but he returned to France to design much of the jewelry of Henry II, and French goldsmith's work of the time was greatly influenced by his style.

1269-74. XVIc. French.

Pierre Woeirot (c. 1531-89). Engraved designs for rings.

Most of the early engravers had received their training as goldsmiths, and could work interchangeably as executors or designers of jewelry, armor decoration, or book illustrations.

Woeirot, primarily an engraver of ornament, did a series of the kings of France, pubished at Cologne, 1591.

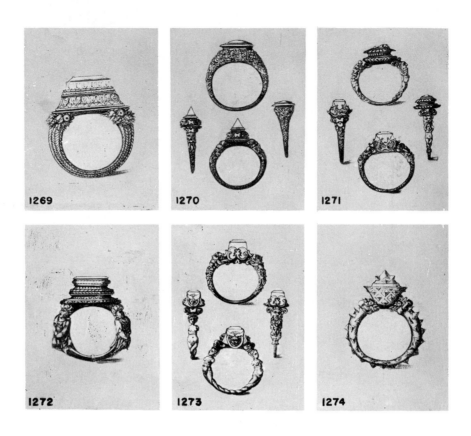

Courtesy of Metropolitan Museum of Art, Print Room

1275. XVIc. French. (Chantilly Museum.)

School of Clouet. Marguerite of Valois, Queen of Navarre, France, b. 1553.

Catherine de' Medici maintained high standards for the dress of her court. The lovely, learned willful child who became the fabled Reine Margot sought for her mother's approbation in all things, and became, as Brantôme never tires of telling, the most imaginatively dressed woman in France.

Henry of Navarre, her husband, dressed very carelessly, and once said about his habitually sober clothes: "I am grey without, but inside all gold." He attempted, in several sumptuary edicts, to forbid "any of the inhabitants of the kingdom to wear either gold or silver on their clothes, except the *filles de joie* and pickpockets, in whom we do not take sufficient interest to trouble ourselves about their conduct." Marguerite's lavishness clashed with Henry IV's parsimony, but they remained loyal friends after their divorce and his marriage to Marie de' Medici. Henry's second wife brought the greatest dowery of any queen of France, and probably spent more money on clothes than any woman who ever lived.

The French hood persists in England after its abandonment in the country of its origin. By the 1560's in France the favorite headwear is a small cap, worn on the back of the head, over parted hair, usually with earrings. Brantôme, who once saw Marguerite's natural hair, says it was black like her father's, but usually covered by wigs of varying colors.

The neck unfilled by partlet is a conventional usage for young girls in second half XVIc.; its off-the-shoulder width, emphasized by sheer puffs, is specifically French. The second half XVIc. emphasis on the top of the close sleeve is given here by petal forms; otherwise attained by the use of rolls, picadills, a sleeve cap, or by exaggerated cut.

1276. XVIc. c. 1571. French. (Louvre.)
Att. to *Clouet*. Elizabeth of Austria, Queen of France.

The wife of Catherine de' Medici's second son, Charles IX, wears a brocade gown; tucker crimped and jewelled in a diapered design; sleeves with a full cap are caught in a spiral design. Her jewelled collar matches her bodice top and the band in front of her tiny cap. Matching ruffs at wrists and high collar.

The silhouette of this gown can be seen on full-length figures on the Quesnel tapestries; in these, the waist is a little more pointed and the partlet, slit up the front, is turned back to form an open ruff.

1277. XVIc. 1560-70. French. (Paris, Bib. Nat.)
Jean Clouet. Rénée de Rieux, demoiselle de Chateauneuf.

As in England, the masculine hat is set over the little cap on the back of the head, in which the coiled hair is enclosed. But in France, the parted front hair is rolled in stylized arches, over pads. The slashed and braided gown has the open front and standing collar of the Spanish surcoat.

1278. XVIc. 1568. French. (Paris, Bib. Nat.)
Jean Clouet. Madeleine d'Aubespine, wife of Nicolas de Neufville, seigneur de Villeroi.

The partlet, slipping off the shoulders, is gathered into a standing collar, finished with a ruff. With the reappearance of the ruff in the 1820's, almost identical forms will be found in drawings by Ingres.

1279. XVIc. 1569. French. (Vienna, Art History Mus.)
François Clouet. Charles IX.

Gold-embroidered black velvet cape and jacket, with high collar and ruff, dipping waistline and the beginning of the peascod swelling above, but with the long skirts of his father's time. The cape lining is horizontally striped. Pinked white doublet sleeves and paned and padded trunk hose, nether-hose and slashed shoes. Hat crown rising and banded; moustache; sword belt with fine catches.

1280. XVIc. Dec. 31, 1578. French. (Chantilly, Musee Conde.)

Guillaume Richardière. Henry III presiding at the first ceremony of the Order of the Saint-Esprit, founded by him.

Tiny toque with a centrally mounting ornament, characteristic of Henry III and his court, as is the king's haircut, and the moustache and small pointed beard which accompanied it.

Robes embroidered with the monogram of the collar, and the badge of the Order: a white and gold Maltese cross bearing a white dove with outstretched wings, ordinarily carried on a blue ribbon, *cordon bleu.* Wide double ruffs; very short paned hose; padded sleeves, approaching leg of mutton form, elaborately pinked, carry only a small turned-back cuff. On kneeling figures: short French cape, ermine lining and collar; pinked shoes with cork lifts, but as yet no heel. Cardinal, other ecclesiastics, and officials of the order wear falling band collars.

1281. XVIc. 1570. French. (Metropolitan Museum.)
Corneille de Lyon. Portrait of a Gentleman.

Scarves and rosettes coming into use, seen here around a sugar-loaf hat of gored fabric. Small ruff on high collar cut in one with jerkin, which is vertically slit and buttoned only at the top; rolls at shoulder of widening, slightly padded sleeves.

1282. XVIc. 1574. French. (Metropolitan Museum.)
Etienne de Moustier. Man in a white doublet.

Hat crown higher; ruff larger; doublet with the sloping shoulder seen in France, slightly peascod, and with short skirts; sword belt with tassel; hose much bombasted.

1283. XVIc. Flemish. (Antwerp, Mayer van der Bergh Collection.)

Att. to *F. Pourbus, y.* Prodigal Son.

There are many prints and paintings of people playing musical instruments, of musical parties and weddings, during second half XVIc.; they are apt to be called the Prodigal Son. This picture, attributed to Pourbus, y., shows the costume we would expect to find in a Franco-Flemish picture of about the period of Pourbus' birth: diapered yokes, with standing collars beginning to open, their linen barely edged with pleating; loose jackets with high-capped sleeves; bell-shaped skirts; masculine hats worn by women; and the French hoods and multiple, heavy chains which persist from first half of the century.

Accompanying the lutes, wind-instruments and singers, the maid picks with a claw at a two-stringed instrument; it looks deceptively like the thermometer, which will not be invented for another half century. On the floor, in front of the maid, is a ewer, set in a basin which may also be hung on the wall, as we still see them used in country houses on the continent, in a dining room or passage-way. There are knives on the wooden trenchers; in XVIc. forks are used only in Italy; Coryat saw them nowhere else in 1608; a knife and fork in a case will become a luxurious wedding present in XVIIc., but forks will not begin to be considered a necessity, even among the upper classes, until XVIIIc. Jester with his bauble, and Negro page in attendance.

1284-87. XVIc. c. 1575. Franco-Flemish. (Florence Uffizi.)

The Catherine de' Medici Tapestries designed by *François Quesnel,* executed in Brussels.

About 1575, Catherine ordered a great series of tapestries, which were completed in about 5 years, as a gift to her native city of Florence. Henry II, had loved fêtes and pageants, such as those with which he had celebrated the marriage of Mary Stuart with his eldest son. Many of these took place at the chateau of Chenonceaux, which Henry had given to Diane de Poitiers, and Catherine had exchanged with her for Chaumont, after his death. Chenonceaux had been developed out of a mill on the river Cher; its waters were ideal for displays of fireworks and for naval pageants, and the forest of Amboise was a perfect setting for courtiers dressed as figures from classical mythology.

The tapestries celebrate marriages and other notable events at the French Court, at about the end of third quarter XVIc. One tapestry in this series (given in Piton, p. 168) shows carriages and riders approaching the chateau of Anet, where Catherine's own marriage contract had been signed. The only three coaches in France belonged to the queen, Diane de Poitiers, and to René de Laval, an enormously fat nobleman. Three other Flemish tapestries,

also in the Uffizi, showing her marriage festivities at Marseilles, were sent by Catherine as a wedding present to her cousin Cosimo I in 1539.

In 1573, ambassadors from Poland offered its throne to Catherine's third son, Henry of Anjou. Before he reluctantly left the woman he loved, the Princess of Condé, and accompanied them back to Poland, a fête was given in their honor in the gardens of the Tuileries. A ballet was performed by the queen's maids of honor; a description of it by the Italian ballet-master, Baltazarini, is preserved in the Bibliothèque Nationale, together with the ballet music, the words and airs of the songs, and a drawing of the movable "property" rock, on which the musicians are seated. Charles IX died in 1574, and Henry succeeded in eluding his Polish subjects and escaping to France to become Henry III. In 1575, Henry was married to Louise of Lorraine; many entertainments were given in their honor: tournaments, naval battles, displays of exotic animals.

1284. The Polish Ambassadors. The figure of Henry III in the l. foreground shows the characteristic beard and hair form adopted by the French court, in contrast to the clipped Polish heads, clean shaven, with handle-bar moustachios or long beards (standing beside Catherine). Except for one behind

Catherine, who wears a slashed costume with peascod doublet and ruff, the Polish entourage wears long, low-necked garments with sailor collars, and tasseled closings, in large-patterned brocades; feathered turbans, or hats turned up in back; chains and pendants.

Henry wears a high, puffed Italian bonnet with a curled brim; peascod doublet; venetians braided down side seams and finished with picadills; shoes strapped over instep, but without heels.

The male dancers wear short French hose, with canions to or below knee; peascod doublets; short, circular capes; guarded rapiers, characteristically slung; pattern on these male costumes is applied, not woven; hats, in the present sense, appear with crowns, brims and bands. The same garments are worn by the crowds in the background, often without canions.

The dancing maids of honor show pattern, woven or applied. Their high-necked bodices carry closed ruffs, alone or combined with open ruffs. Pendant outer sleeves have reappeared, and are combined with the close sleeves shown on the ladies in the background; finished with a roll or puff at the shoulder. Rear views show the tiny cap worn with heart-shaped, rolled hair.

Catherine, in the center, wears severe mourning, with her cap drawn down characteristically in a point on the forehead; veil wired into a heart-shape; light colored gloves; ruff.

Musicians, with lutes, viols, and harps are dressed in allegorical costume.

1285. Attack on an Island: Henry III was a cultivated and intelligent person, incapacitated by neurotic instability and effeminacy. His slender elegance was marred by a facial tic; he hid in the cellar during thunderstorms; collected tiny dogs which he carried in a basket slung around his neck. The crowd of favorites, *mignons,* with whom he surrounded himself, and on whom he spent immense sums, followed his lead. Their hair, beards, moustaches and eyebrows were dyed, curled, plucked and scented; their painted faces and their hands were covered at night by masks and gloves impregnated with skin creams. At court fêtes they sometimes appeared in women's clothes and wigs, while the ladies wore male costume, with feminine hair and ruffs.

Henry wears the small toque with front ornament, fluffed hair and one earring which is almost his uniform; braided and pinked peascod doublet; short trunk-hose with canions.

The bride, Louise of Lorraine, shows the meticulously rolled French headdress over pads, *arcelets;* this is much more studied and artificial than the curled or frizzed hair of England. Her cap has a gauffered edge; a jewel at the part gives the new triangular front effect, which began in the dip, characteristic of the Mary Stuart caps, and is further developed in the widow's hood worn by Catherine de' Medici.

Her gown and underskirt are of bordered brocades. The French vertugale has never reached the enormous hem circumference seen in some English gowns, and there has been a general European reduction in the spread of the farthingale and in the width of the V-front, since mid-XVIc. The new hippiness, shown in this skirt, will soon reach proportions equal to the drum-shaped English skirt of the 90's, with its cartwheel ruffle from the waist, where the French skirt will usually remain untrimmed. The sleeves are of plain material, their pattern applied; with their great shoulder rolls and smocked stiffening they foreshadow the immense padded leg-o'-mutton sleeves

to come with the wide-hipped skirt. Her wide decolletage carries an opening ruff of the Italian-French variety: a pleated edge on a standing collar, where the Elizabethan ruff is entirely pleated. The girdle is wider; its pendant reduced to a tab. She carries a marvelous example of the now indispensable feather fan.

Behind Henry III, Henry of Navarre, characteristically energetic, careless and comfortably dressed, wears loose venetians, smocked into diapered puffs, and a pinked doublet with a very plain band, instead of Henry III's high ruff.

The men-at-arms wear the German-Swiss unpadded *pluderhose,* which has the lining hanging full and loose between the panes, and bloused at waist.

1286. Combat at the Barrier: Henry of Navarre, on the l., and the king's younger brother, Alençon, at r., await their turn. Alençon was the suitor, 21 years her junior, whom Elizabeth called "Froggy," and for whom she and the English court wore mourning for a year after his death in 1584.

Both wear sumptuous armor, patterned in vari-colored metals, and worn with brocade venetians, closed below the knee.

1287. Attack on an Elephant: Marguerite of Valois stands with her brothers, the Duke of Alençon and Henry III. Her *arcelet* hair arrangement is elaborated by a border of tight curls. The neckline is opening and widening; the shoulder roll is incorporated, by cutting, into the upper sleeve. As with Louise of Lorraine, the girdle pendant has become a tab; both skirts have bordered hems. She carries a handkerchief instead of a fan.

Henry's peascod doublet is split, over brocade which matches his sleeves and canions.

In this period of travel and discovery there is a growing interest in exotic animals, and peoples ancient and contemporary. The hysterical Henry III had destroyed Louis XI's zoo, but Henry of Navarre's small menagerie contained an elephant. Here, the elephant is being attacked by Orientals and defended by Romans, while a crowd of mercenary soldiers in *pluderhose* watches the battle.

But the first elephant ever seen by so curious an Englishman as Evelyn was in Holland in 1641; in a backward country like Scotland, an elephant was first shown in 1680. (Law: *Memorable Things,* 1638-84.)

1288. XVIc. 1581. French. (Louvre.)

School of Clouet. Ball at the court of Henry III: called "the ball of the Duke of Joyeuse."

Henry III spent more than $2,500,000 on the wedding festivities of his *mignon,* Anne de Joyeuse, and the queen's sister, Marguerite of Lorraine. We see again, by these dancers at a court ball, that a gentleman of the XVIc., to first half XVIIc. is always cloaked in public and wears his hat at all times, even at home, replacing it with a cap for domestic comfort and bed.

The king sits under a red velvet canopy, with his mother in her familiar collar and widow's-peaked cap, and his wife in a flat, circular, open-front ruff and dramatically slashed sleeves. On the king's r. stands Henry, Duke of Guise, who will be assassinated in the king's own bedchamber seven years later.

The bride, in white and gold, with touches of red on her cap and under the lines of pearls which cross her inner sleeve, wears the French court version of the hip-bolstered skirt: circular, laid on in deep pleats and with a slight train. There is a new tendency, shown in the skirts of other ladies, to display the underskirt by catching up or turning back the outer skirt, which is no longer slit. The leg-o'-mutton sleeve is now elaborately decorated, in contrast to the plain fabric of the gown, and of the outer sleeve, where it is present. The bride's cap, analogous to the male hat of the court, has centrally placed, mounting decoration.

The groom has a white-plumed black hat; green cape, its rose lining to match the stockings, turned back to form revers and collar; green doublet, venetians and shoes.

There is great variety shown in the ruffs of both men and women.

François Roger de Gaignières, (1642-1715), squire in the household of the Duke of Guise, was already at 25 an art collector and man of erudition. He had to travel constantly in the provinces, and decided to keep a record of funerary and other monuments. As neither he, nor his valet-factotum (who was also a paleographer) could draw, an artist-engraver named Louis Boudeau was employed to accompany them from 1670-88. His talents were very modest, but his thousands of weak little drawings are all that remain to us of most of the material recorded.

Some of the drawings were given to Madame de Montespan, who loved antiques; eventually the entire collection, together with books and paintings was sold to Louis XIV for a small sum in cash and a pension and passed into government institutions.

French books on costume, with redrawn illustrations, like that by Quicherat, are greatly indebted to Gaignières. The Henry III balls, painted on copper, were part of Gaignières' personal collection. Some drawings by Boudeau are shown in Ills. 465, 658. The drawings, now in the Bibliothèque Nationale, Paris, have been listed: H. Buchot: *Inventaire des dessins exécutés pour Roger de Gaignières et conservés aux departements des estampes et manuscrits,* Paris, Plon Nourrit, 1891. Portfolios of loose plates have been published by the Bib. Nat.

Photograph courtesy of M. Jacques M. J. Manuel

1289. XVIc. 1581. French (Louvre.)

School of Clouet. Ball at the court of Henry III, called "the ball of the Duke of Alençon," d. 1584.

Henry, wearing the 8-pointed gold star of the Order of the Saint-Esprit on its blue sash (cordon bleu), stands at l. with his wife and mother. As in the other picture, the king's little dogs play in the foreground. Ladies sit on tabourets which accommodate their great skirts and have supplanted the cushions formerly used.

The bolstered skirt and leg-o'-mutton sleeve are at their most massive, now and at the French court. As the bodice has lengthened, the horizontal line of the yoke tends to disappear, under the influence of the collar-shaped ruff, which often begins its spread into revers upward from the point of the bodice.

With their peascod doublets, all the French courtiers now wear venetians; these usually have horizontal bands of narrow vertical slashing. The high-crowned hat, which we associate with the Puritans because it was commonly worn in their time, and was taken by them to America, appears, together with Henry's familiar bonnet.

Photograph courtesy of M. Jacques M. J. Manuel

1290-95. XVIc. c. 1595. Flemish. (Madrid, Prado.)

Unknown Flemish painter. Six princesses of Lorraine.

Christine of Denmark (1290), as a widow wears a veil wired in a peak, over a ruffled cap; the points of the veil caught together at the waist as a scarf. Gloves with slashed cuffs.

Claude of France (1291), Catherine de' Medici's daughter, is dressed in the costume of the period preceding her death in 1575.

Claude's daughter *Christine* (1292), brought up by Catherine, was her favorite grandchild; Catherine ceded her Florentine possessions and her claims to the duchy of Urbino to Christine, and provided a dowry of 600,000 crowns for her marriage in 1587 with the reigning Medici, Ferdinand I. Without special ability, Christine was a person of charm and utter goodness; she reformed the Florentine court; brought up well her son Cosimo II; was regent for her grandson, Ferdinand II; and had a great influence on Tuscany during the 50 years of her life there. Christine's brocade gown has the cut and pendant Spanish sleeve of the late XVI-e.XVIIc.; wired collar edged with magnificent reticella lace; hair worn in the mounting, unparted Spanish fashion; massive Spanish girdle; folding Italian fan.

The other princesses wear the French court dress and coiffure of the late XVIc. with beautiful and ever more elaborate ruffs.

1296

1296. XVIc. French. (Paris, Carnavalet Museum.)

Unknown artist. Dance around an elm in a village square.

This picture, given to the Carnavalet by the painter Ingres, probably shows the "Orme St. Gervais," the elm on the square of the nunnery-hospital of St. Gervais, under which the lord's justice had been meted since XIIc., and under which games are played and mummers and neighbors dance to the music of an orchestra perched in its branches. The costumes are even less pretentious than the simple dress shown in the "League" illustrations.

1297

1297. XVIc. May 14, 1590. French. (Paris, Carnavalet Museum.)

School of Pourbus. Procession of the League.

Paris, always a stronghold of the League and Catholicism, had held out for a year against the siege of Henry IV, whom the Sorbonne had declared a heretic, inadmissible as king even though his excommunication were revoked. The death of the old Cardinal of Bourbon, whom the League had recognized as Charles X, left little alternative to a belated recognition of Henry.

But on May 14, 1590, as a last effort, the League organized a procession of the strength available to the religious establishments of Paris: 1300 inflamed and militant Chartreux, Carmelites and Capuchins regular and secular, in all sorts of bits and pieces of armor and weapons, gathered in the Church of St. Jean-en-Grève. The Benedictines, Celestines and the Canons of St. Germain and St. Victoire refused to join them. Before Notre Dame, they were blessed by the Papal Legate, and in the excitement, a salute of

welcome let off by novices, killed two members of his entourage.

A most detailed contemporary account of the proceedings has been left in the "Satire Menipée," which purported to describe a procession three years in the future. Three paintings of the procession at different points in its passage, hang in the Carnavalet, and the Museum's "Guide explicatif" of 1903, (to which I am largely indebted) gives a full and fascinating account of the events, personages and localities.

In this picture we see the procession pouring from St. Jean-de-Grève (Gothic towers in the background, of a church which disappeared after the French Revolution) through one completed arch of the Hôtel de Ville (begun in 1532), where Parisian disorder traditionally begins, into the Place de Grève, where it so frequently also ended, since public hangings took place there from 1310-1832. The Grève (= river bank) had been a main port of Paris since Gallo-Roman days and remained much as we see it here, until it was first enlarged in 1673. At that time, the Gothic Cross, on the eight steps of which the unfortunate prayed, was set close to the bank. Between the first light building and those adjoining the Hôtel de Ville ran the narrow rue de la Mortellerie, where throats were cut nightly and dead bodies found every day. In front of it stood the Mast of St. Jean with its ladder-like cross pieces, before which (by a tradition antedating the Romans) a civic leader or the king himself appeared on June 23, in great state and wreathed with flowers, to burn a cask, a sack and a basket full of cats, while a salvo was fired; this was eliminated in the remodelling. Across the river we see the Ile de la Cité, with Notre Dame, the Hôtel des Ursins and the opening of the Port St. Landry, where a wooden bridge, built in 1623, brought the number of bridges up to eight. Far up the Seine we see the Convent and Quai of the Bernardins and in the mid-dle, the Ile St. Louis, which was not built upon until XVIIc., covered with lines of washing.

During the siege, food and drinking water were scarce; on the l. we see a water carrier and an outdoor kitchen, where a thin, salted oatmeal gruel was sold "as dearly as it had been milk." On the r. a butcher is selling the donkey and horse meat to which the city had been reduced.

The group of onlookers, to the r. in front of the inn, includes the dukes of Nemours and Mayenne, Governor of Paris and Lieutenant-Governor of the State respectively, with their wives and children and the duchesses of Guise and Montpensier. The costume of these French Catholic aristocrats shows us that what we think of as Puritan costume was simply the current dress of the middle and upper classes at the time of our ancestors' emigration to America: truncated conical hats, plain bands, easy knee-length breeches, plain capes, shoes with a tongue; women's small caps and arched hoods, plain bodices and sleeves, skirts of ground length with farthingale fullness. Complexions and hands are protected by masks and gloves. The soldier on guard wears a cabasset; one of the boys at play has the morion of another soldier on his head.

The procession of embattled churchmen is led by Dr. Rose, Bishop of Senlis and Rector of the Sorbonne, who has exchanged his ecclesiastical for his scholar's robes; and the Curé of St. Jacques in a violet gown and halberd, who tries to regulate the crowd; both we learn, freshly barbered for the occasion.

1298, 1299. XVIc. May 14, 1590. French. (Paris, Carnavalet Museum.)

French School. Procession of the League.

Also in the Place de Grève; standard of Saint-Michel in the background.

(The dual illustration above accounts for both 1298 and 1299.)

1300

1301

1300-01. XVIc. 1499-1503. Italian Umbrian. (Orvieto Cathedral.)

Luca Signorelli. The Fall of the Antichrist (1300) and The End of the World (1301).

Among the biblical personages, the youth in the r. foreground (Ill. 1300) wears the typical laced brocade doublet of the transition period.

In Italian male costume, both the use of brocade and these open-front garments will be supplanted by absolutely plain fabrics and austere cut. There will be an almost total avoidance, in Italy, of the rich embroidery used in England and France, and their cut-out jackets, exhibiting the bosom of the doublet. The extreme slashings and puffings of the German-Swiss styles will be avoided; hose will be notably unaffected, but will be more elaborately striped in Italy than anywhere else. Hair is enclosed in a netted caul in Italy, as in Germany and to some extent in France, but not in England.

The soldiers wear doublets striped in many

1302

colors, to match their hose, which are gartered and have prominent cod-pieces.

1302. XVIc. c. 1500. Italian-Venetian. (Venice, Academy.)

Gentile Bellini. Miracle of the True Cross: Catherine Cornaro, ex-Queen of Cyprus, Crowned.

Bellini, one of a dynasty of distinguished Venetian painters, shows Catherine in the last decade of her life, her crown set over one of the veiled headdresses which should be compared with those of XVc. Spain. We see small caps on the back of the head; loose hair at the sides, bound into a pigtail (in this case, wound around the head); a veil enclosing the face (here, bead-edged and caught together in back to fall as a replacement of the pigtail).

The laced bodice worn by G. Albizzi (Ill. 780) has become lower- and wider-necked, more cut out. The completely separated sleeves are knotted on, well below the shoulder, over draperies which go far beyond the original puffs of the shirt.

Earrings are worn which, like the necklaces, are related to the diapered patterns used in the plastrons and sleeves.

1303. XVIc. 1500-10. Italian-Venetian. (Venice Museum Civico.)

Vittore Carpaccio. Two Venetian Courtesans.

Carpaccio sees, understands, loves, and poetically transmutes all the life of Venice, even "the women whose faces are too heavily painted, with heavy mops of dyed hair" who "signal him from a balcony. He goes up. And here he is in the company of filthy little dogs, obscene monkeys, and cooing doves, and is confused by the thick perfume and the shining eyes." (Elie Faure: *Renaissance Art.*)

Near the peacock stands a pair of pattens with very high platforms, which remain characteristic of Venice through the XVIIc. Little caps set like topknots; interesting way in which sleeve puffings are tied at the back of the shoulder; ring worn on thumb.

The accounts given by the English travellers, Fynes Moryson (1566-1629) in his "Itinerary," and Thomas Coryat (1577-1617) in his "Crudities," describe the persistent differentiations of Venetian costume from the varied but always more modest styles of the rest of Italy.

Evelyn's diary notes the continuity, after a century and a half, of Venetian ways: chopines, and hair dyed in streaks and sunned on balconies. A print by Bertelli shows the *solana* sunshade brim used in this hair bleaching. (See Appendix.)

The Venetian gowns leave the heavily powdered neck and breast bare, sometimes exposed almost to the stomach. The coarse locally-produced linen of the shirts of Italy is stuffed about the body to make it desirably bulkier. The heavily rouged Venetian women, with their blonde hair (dyed if necessary), require assistance to walk on foot-high pattens in their gowns with trains. Moryson translates the proverb which describes them as "tall with wood, fat with ragges, red with painting, white with chalk."

From Christmas to Lent, Venetian courtesans might be seen on the street in men's doublets and breeches, light colored and carelessly buttoned. Italian ladies, as well as girls, continue to ride astride, dressed in men's clothing, but with women's headdress.

1304. XVIc. c. 1500. Italian Paduan. (Washington, Nat. Gall. of Art.)

School of Mantegna. Triumph of Chastity.

1305. Early XVIc. Italian-Venetian. (Carrara, Accademia.)

Vittore Carpaccio. The Birth of the Virgin.

Slight change, during a century, in simple domestic dress, often trussed up at hips.

Oriental carpets, imported and distributed by the Venetians, at first used as decorative furniture coverings rather than carpets; in Venice, hung over balconies during open air festivities. Patterned swaddling bands being prepared for baby. Platform footwear with folded and laced fabric tops, worn by old midwife.

1306. XVIc. c..1510. Italian-Sienese. (Washington, Nat. Gall. of Arts.)

Girolamo di Benvenuto. Portrait of a Young Woman.

Green, gold and white costume, with rubies and

pearls. Border of interlaced cord design, of the sort used on costume (see Ill. 1257).

1307-10. XVIc. 1505-7. Italian, Umbrian. (Siena, Cathedral Library.)

Bernardino Pintoricchio and assistants. Scenes in the Life of Aeneas Sylvius Piccolomini (Pius II).

In 1502, the excellent Cardinal Francesco Piccolomini (who became Pius III a month before his death) commissioned from Pintoricchio a series of ten wall paintings, representing episodes in the very full life of his uncle, Pius II, shown in the dress of 1490-1510.

Born in 1405 of an impoverished aristocratic family, Aeneas Sylvius became secretary to a series of bishops, papal secretary, and secretary and official poet to the Emperor Frederick III. He refused holy orders until 1446, then advanced rapidly from bishop to cardinal and in 1458, pope. He preached a crusade, and died on his way to the Orient in 1464.

1307. Aeneas on his way to the Council of Basel, a lay secretary in a group of cardinals and other ecclesiastics, wears a great beaver hat, bound across the crown and under the chin; gown with a handsome gored collar with braided seams. Another layman (background) shows front of similar garment.

Attendants wear plainly cut doublets; particolored and striped hose; shoes with the favorite Italian turned-down cuff. This is an era of cords and tassels, which appear on the handsome pouch and dagger, as well as on the bridle of the mule.

1308. Aeneas, Bishop of Siena, marries Eleanor of Portugal to his former patron, the Emperor Frederick III in Rome, in front of the column which was (later) erected to commemorate the marriage. To the l. of Aeneas stands Agnes Farnese, who married his brother.

Her costume, like that of the bride and the other attendants, should be compared to Sp.XVc. and It. XVIc., in respect to characteristics, some of which will have an immense influence on the costume of the second half XVIc.-e.XVIIc.

The veiled cap will alter, and the netted pigtail headdress with its fillet will pass with first third XVIc., as will the Spanish extravagance of looped shirtsleeve.

We have seen sleeves becoming independent of garments. In the Spanish sleeve of Eleanor's black and

and his assistants. They show doublets of the most austere cut; hose striped vertically, as well as horizontally in an effect of trunks; knotted cod-piece. Cloaks will disappear, and gowns shorten; brims of laced bonnets will become flatter. Hair is worn flowing or caught in a netted caul; cropped head is covered by an embroidered cap.

Behind them is a crowd of monks of various orders; above, the Pope, surrounded by cardinals; St. Catherine in her black and white Dominican habit.

Frederick, who was crowned Emperor by Pope Nicholas, three days after his marriage, wears the imperial crown, fringed tunic, mantle, and magnificent anachronistic shoes with poulaine pattens.

1309-10. Aeneas, as Pope Pius II, canonizing St. Catherine of Siena. It was stipulated that the designs, their laying out on the walls and all the heads were to be done by Pintorricchio himself. The paintings contain many portraits; those in the foreground of this portion are portraits of Raphael, Pintorricchio,

gold gown, there is a further independence of the lower from the upper section; they are separately cut on opposite grains of the fabric, and will develop into one of the most important features of the Spanish-inspired "Elizabethan" costume. So, also, will the skirt supported by the stiffened farthingale. The sleeveless, open overgarment which we have seen on Isabella, is worn by Eleanor and her ladies, slipped off one shoulder; from it will come the severe, masculine, coat-like garments of the late XVIc.-e.XVIIc.

1312. XVIc. 1514-15. Italian. (Metropolitan Mus., Bache Coll.)

Raphael. Giuliano de' Medici, Duke of Nemours.

Lorenzo's admirable son, at about the time of his marriage in France to Francis I's young Italian aunt, wears his black bonnet tilted, as is the rule when used over the netted gold caul which foreshadows cropped hair.

His gown of neutral greenish brocade with a line of gold along the sleeve seam, is heavily furred in dark brown. Black jacket with deep, square neck of first quarter XVIc; the scarlet doublet has the lapped closing, seen in various forms since 1500.

1313. XVIc. 1510-20. Italian (Louvre.)

Titian. Man with a Glove.

Shortening bobbed hair; extreme simplicity of line and fabric; finely pleated shirt, its neckline rising to a ruffle; fine chain and pendant, ring worn on forefinger; unostentatious use of jewelry in Italian male costume.

1314. XVIc. 1514-20. Italian-Venetian. (Lugano, Baron Heinrich Thyssen—Bornemisza.]

Vittore Carpaccio. St. Eustace.

1311. XVIc. 1512. Italian. (Siena.)

Baldassare Peruzzi. Alberto Pio di Carpi.

The learned ambassador, though bearded in the new fashion, wears his hair extremely long; this sort of protest is often seen at the start of a new trend. His hat is conservative in form; Italian caps and bonnets seldom show the excesses of slitting, binding and decoration seen elsewhere. His gown is lined with a variegated fur, which appears as a fringed edge, caught by loosely knotted, tasseled cords.

St. Eustace armor shows the rivets and fluting of the XVIc.; high collar; sabatons with moderate toes; sword without quillons has a double guard. The armet of the mounted knight gives good protection to the neck; shows no sign of the comb-like ridge which develops on most helmets during XVIc. Counter-charged striping of his costume.

1315. XVIc. 1520-30. N. Italian-Veronese. (Metropolitan Museum.)

Unknown artist. The Rape of Helen.

Striped doublets and hose, one leg and sleeve plain.

1316. XVIc. N. Italian-Veronese. (Florence, Uffizi.)

Giovanni Francesco Caroto (?) Elisabetta Gonzaga, duchess of Urbino (d. 1526).

Analogous countercharging in women's costume is shown by the daughter of Federigo I. Gonzaga; she married Guidobaldo, son of Battista Sforza and Federigo di Montefeltro, first duke of Urbino.

I give the genealogical information because her neck is edged in a pattern of letters, which may be a motto, and appears to have a device at the corners; gown, counter-charging and parti-color, and emblem on forehead are probably significant.

1317. XVIc. c. 1520. Italian, Lombard-Venetian. (Washington, Nat. Gall. of Art.)

Bartolommeo Veneto. Portrait of a Gentleman, called "Massimiliano Sforza."

Black and gold costume; doublet with c. front closing; medallion of St. Catherine. Gown similar to that of Francis I, slit and projecting, instead of tucked up at shoulders (see also Ill. 1257).

1318. XVIc. 1521. Italian. (Metropolitan Museum.)

Tommaso Fiorentino. Portrait of a Man.

Very large hats with upturned brims worn till c.1530; brim caught or tied at c. front, especially in Germany and Italy. Very plain black jacket with ballooning upper sleeve, gray lower sleeve; rising neckline, filled in by shirt with standing collar, common by 1525.

1319. XVIc. c. 1530. Swiss. (Metropolitan Museum.)

Unknown artist of Swiss School. Charles III, Duke of Savoy.

Nobleman in European dress. He wears the 15 gold love-knots and silver roses of the Order of the Collar, founded in 1362 by Amadeus VI of Savoy, for 15 companions. It is the principal Italian order. Its name was changed by Charles III to the Order of the *Annunziata;* its medallion represents the annunciation.

1320. XVIc. c. 1515. Italian-Milanese. (Washington, Nat. Gall. of Art.)

Bernardino Luini. Portrait of a Lady.

1321. XVIc. 1523. Italian-Venetian. (Madrid, Prado.)

Lorenzo Lotto. Portrait of a Bridal Couple.

1322. XVIc. Italian, Venetian. (Bergamo, Coll. Carrava-Morelli.)

Lorenzo Lotto. Portrait of a Lady.

The turbans which the Italians always loved, but had abandoned during the transition period for tiny caps covering only the back of the head, return in the e.XVIc. in huge round forms, ruffled, netted and knotted; very different in shape from the German headdress of equal size.

Instead of the funnel or close sleeve of English, French or German gowns, with their neat shoulder line, the sleeve of an Italian gown is apt to be voluminously gathered at the top, like the male jacket sleeve (Ill. 1052) of the boy in the Meyer Madonna.

In Italy, particularly in Venice, it is the female silhouette which is wide-shouldered and bulky; while that of the male is slenderer and more austere than in any other country.

Throughout XVIc. and in XVIIc., sable and marten skins are worn at the neck, or as in Ill. 1320, chained to hang from the girdle. We find them particularly in Italian and Spanish portraits, where they are frequently shown with jewelled muzzles and paws.

Italian men with cropped hair, like the bridegroom, often wear small turbans and caps, covered with pattern. The embroidered and ruffled high collar of the bridegroom's shirt is caught by a braided bar and loops, instead of the usual ties.

1323. XVIc. Italian, Venetian. (Florence, Pitti Palace.)

P. Bordoni. Portrait of a Woman.

1324. XVIc. 1523-7. Italian, Venetian. (Madrid, Prado.)

Parmigianino. Portrait of a Woman with Three Sons, called the wife of Lorenzo Cibo.

Milan and Naples, dependants of Spain, are more affected by the rigid, high-necked, large-ruffed Spanish garments, than is the rest of Italy, in which the breast often remains bare, the ruff small, and petticoats are used in place of the farthingale.

Moryson, who remarks on the simple unostentation of Italian male dress, notes that Italian linen is much coarser than that of Flanders, and that the Italians are not skillful at starching and gauffering the ruffs they do wear. Moryson describes the costume of Milan as decent; Naples, glittering and sumptuous; Genoa, neat and comely without laces or guards; Rome and Florence, modest: Ferrara and Mantua, proud of attire, wearing caps with gold buttons.

The characteristic Venetian bodice, long and pointed in front, pointed but short behind, is often cut extremely low and is fat-bodied. In the gown of this matron, the V is filled by a crimped and collared tucker.

Her netted headdress is drawn together in front; this spot is also the focus of interest in embroidered caps, such as that worn by the Lotto bridegroom (1321).

Delicacy of Italian chains; magnificent girdle with double pendants.

Knotted cord decoration of boy's high-collared jackets; cropped hair.

1325. XVIc. 1525-30. Italian, Florentine. (Washington, Nat. Gall. of Art.)

Bugiardini. Portrait of a Young Woman.

Gold fringed and embroidered white scarf used as a turban. Red gown, black velvet bands; full white shirt.

1326. Second quarter XVIc. Italian, Florentine. (Lucca Picture Gallery.)

Jacopo da Pontormo (1494-1557). Portrait of a Youth, wrongly called Giuliano de' Medici.

Italian version of the wide-shouldered gown with collar; complete absence of patterned fabric and jewels.

1327. Second quarter XVIc. Italian Venetian-Parmesan. (Naples National Museum.)

Parmigianino (1504-40). Portrait of a Man, wrongly called Amerigo Vespucci.

Embroidered collars with long points, finished with tassels, are seen in Italian and German portraits, first to second third XVIc.

1328. XVIc. c. 1553. Italian, Brescian. (Metropolitan Museum.)

G. B. Moroni. Bartolomeo Bongo.

This picture was probably painted c.1553 and the information and date of Bongo's death added after the death of both painter and subject.

Bongo was a doctor of both civil and canon law, apostolic pronotary, canon and dean of the Cathedral of Bergamo, rector of the University of Pavia, count and knight; his coat-of-arms is shown above.

He wears the square biretta and long, richly furred gown of an important ecclesiastic, academic or legal figure.

The Torre Communale of Bergamo is seen through the window.

France and England by jewels set at the intersections of the smocking; its ruff will become more dramatic and standardized in those countries, while in Italy it remains relatively modest and individually varied. The standard sleeve of second half XVIc. will become clarified out of this sleeve with its upper fullness.

In her lap, the duchess holds a fur-piece with an entire head of goldsmith's work, which is fastened to her girdle. Girdle in the form of a knotted and tasseled cord; gown sewn with motifs of knots, in place of points; wonderful pendant cross on a chain; pendant earrings.

Clocks have been set in towers since XIIIc.; during XVc., they become elaborately mechanical, with processions of comic figures appearing on the hour. By XVIc., handsome small clocks, like the duchess', begin to appear in portraits, and are followed by watches at midXVIc.

1329. First third XVIc. Italian, Florentine. (Frankfort-on-Main, Stadel Inst.)

Pontormo, or Bronzino. Portrait of a Young Woman with a Dog.

The common European male sleeve, puffed above, close and often of satin below, is little worn by Italian men but is characteristic of Italian female costume, and is often worn by German women.

Another of the imaginative Italian chains; knotted girdle with handsome netted tassel; center decoration of turban.

1330. XVIc. c. 1537. Italian-Venetian. (Florence, Uffizi.)

Titian. Eleonora di Gonzaga, Duchess of Urbino.

With her Italian turban, the duchess wears the Italian gown from which the rest of Europe, through Catherine de' Medici, will develop its standard costume of second half XVIc. Its characteristics will be exaggerated and elaborated elsewhere.

Its partlet is now less apt to be embroidered in vertical bands; its crimping will be emphasized in

1331. XVIc. c. 1540. Italian, Florentine. (Turin Picture Gallery.)

Bronzino. Portrait of a Lady.

Simple collar of cut-work, with long-waisted gown and loose, coatlike outer garment of Italian brocade, worn over petticoats instead of a farthingale, and fastened with horizontal cord catches (see Ill. 1161).

The jewels do not overwhelm the costume as they are apt to do in France and England, but are important in their freshness. The girdle has a reduced pendant, where the pomander of an English lady would bang her ankles if it were not for the protection of her farthingale; and in the unusual importance given to the c. front from which it hangs, can be foreseen the tab finish seen in the Catherine de' Medici tapestries. The pair of chain bracelets is also new.

1332. Second quarter XVIc. Italian, Florentine. (Milan, Prince Trivulzio.)

J. da Pontormo. Portrait of a Youth.

1333. Second quarter XVIc. Italian, Florentine. (Cambridge, Fogg Art Mus. Loan of Chauncey D. Stillman.)

J. da Pontormo. Halberdier.

1334. XVIc. 1535-40. Italian, Florentine. (Metropolitan Museum.)

Bronzino (1502-72). Portrait of a Young Man.

1335. XVIc. c. 1550. Italian, Florentine. (Washington Nat. Gall. of Art.)
Pontormo. Ugolino Martelli.

1336. Second half XVIc. Italian, Florentine. (Metropolitan Museum, Frick Collection.)

Att. to *Bronzino.* Portrait of a Young Man.

The slope-shouldered, narrow-hipped Florentine male silhouette; sleeve without rolls or picadills at shoulder, widest below elbow; low standing collar, easy and often open with little display of elaborate linen; almost no jewelry. Aiglettes sparsely but functionally used. Cod-piece differs from tailored and decorated English-French forms. Short hair; smooth-shaven face.

1337. XVIc. c. 1540. Italian, Parma. (Naples Nat. Mus.)
Parmigianino. Portrait of a Young Woman..

Towards end first half XVIc., narrow, pleated, decorative aprons began to appear in rich bourgeoise costume in N. Italy, Germany, Switzerland, Flanders and parts of France. During second half XVIc. these, and other contemporary details, became integrated into "regional" costume, which persisted in some cases to XXc. and are well covered by the illustrations in the small edition of Hottenroth. (See key titles in Appendix.)

The apron is worn with a short-waisted bodice and full skirt, which is usually banded horizontally; or it is the apron which is banded when the skirt is finely pleated.

Simple parted hair with the coronet braids of Italy, and a centrally placed jewel; pendant earrings. Animal skin, "flea fur," chained to waist. Tabbed picadill finish, seldom seen in Italy, at wide cuff, which is filled by embroidered edge of wide shirt sleeve. Gloves now part of the wardrobe of all well-to-do people.

1338. XVIc. c. 1540. Italian, Brescia. (Washington, Nat. Gall. of Art.)

Moretto da Brescia. Portrait of a Lady in White.

This is a splendid example of the absence of stereotype, the personal touches, and the persistent, centuries-old interest in rolled coronets and the hair itself, in Italy.

Puffs of hair are drawn through loops in the headdress, and tasseled ends of the parure are brought forward as pendant earrings: this is a stylization of the free tuft or lock which finished the twisted hair arrangements in XVc. Italy.

The gown has the full-bellied Venetian bodice, long in front, and cut straight across, at a point well below the separation of the breasts. During the next quarter century, the partlet will split and be turned back, exposing the breasts and serving only as a base for the ruff, in the ground-length costume with a slight train, shown in the early fashion books, such as *J. J. Boissard*: *Habitus variarum orbis gentium,* 1581.

The old horizontal or rayed shirt decoration has retired, here, under a sheer, smooth partlet, tied on the shoulders; the partlet actually exploits the bosomy fullness of the shirt, which shows also in puffs and ruffles at the cuff.

Below the enchanting, modest ruff, the breast-parting is emphasized by chains and heavy pendant. Her feather fan hangs from a chain caught to a bracelet. She carries gloves and her hand rests on a Persian rug; still precious, such rugs are hung over tables, chests and balconies.

1339   1340   1341   1342

1343

1339. XVIc. 1550-55. Italian, Venetian. (Washington, Nat. Gall. of Art.)

Titian. Portrait of a Lady, called Giulia di Gonzaga-Colonna.

With flowing hair and little wreath, the lady is informally dressed, as she might be at home. Under her green gown, with its slit and pendant Spanish sleeve, she wears only her wide-sleeved white shirt, edged with gold.

1340. XVIc. 1557. Italian, Brescia. (Metropolitan Museum.)

G. B. Moroni. Prioress.

The widow who became the prioress of the convent of the Nuns of St. Anna wears a cream colored headdress, horizontally pleated. A white kerchief is drawn about her goitre and tucked into the waist of her brown habit.

1341. XVIc. Italian, Parmesan. (Metropolitan Mus., Print Room.)

Enea Vico, fl.1541-67. Old Woman Spinning.

The need for getting their long skirts out of the way during active work is variously met in peasant costume. The classic plain Italian dress from Giotto's time has been short-waisted or belted just below breast, trussed up about the hips, and often has a fold above the hem. The apron covering this full-skirted garment cannot quite be deciphered: it surrounds the armseye, is included in the over- and underbelts of the dress, and is cut low or slit in front to permit passage of the distaff, which the over-belt helps to hold in position.

The most completely covered Italian head has always been that of an elderly woman of the lower classes: the cap and veil arrangement, in this case, seem to indicate widowhood.

Vico made a series of European costume plates, listed in Bartsch.

1342. XVIc. c. 1560. Italian, Brescia. (Washington, Nat. Gall. of Art.)

G. B. Moroni. Gentleman in Adoration before the Madonna (detail).

Around midXVIc., jackets were often short-sleeved, like this black one which shows the pinked sleeves of a red doublet, and a magnificently embroidered falling band. The second half XVIc. tendency toward beards is affecting the clean-shaven young Italian face.

1343. XVIc. 1553-5. Italian, Florentine. (Florence, Uffizi.)

Bronzino. Eleanora da Toledo, wife of Cosimo I, and her son Garcia or Ferdinand.

Cosimo I was the patron of Bronzino, whose companion portrait of Cosimo also hangs in the Uffizi.

Cosimo was fortunate in his marriage to the daughter of the Spanish Viceroy of Naples. She was rich, at a time when he needed money, was intelligent, and devoted to him and their eight children. While travelling with him for her health, the tubercular Eleanora and their favorite son,

Garcia, caught malaria and died within a few days of each other, in 1562.

The early Medici tradition of modest burial was completely altered by Cosimo; it would be interesting to know whether his great collection of Egyptian art influenced, as it might have warned him. Eleanora and the Medici after her were buried in their most magnificent clothes and wearing their jewels. A State commission, appointed in 1857 to examine the Medici tombs, which had been neglected and looted, was able to recognize Eleanora's body "with certainty by the rich dress of white satin embroidered with (black) 'galloon' trimming all over both the bodice and the skirt, exactly as she is depicted in the portrait painted by Bronzino which is in the Gallery of

the Statues (Uffizi), together with the same net of gold cord worn on the hair. Beneath this dress was an undergown of crimson velvet; and on the feet shoes similarly of crimson velvet." But the pearls and jewels had been looted.

Only the design into which partlets are smocked and jewelled, in continental Europe, is retained in the gold net yoke. There is no ruff or band; the low-necked Italian shirt barely shows as a line of embroidery beneath the yoke; its wide sleeves hang from the wrist in an unstudied ruffle.

The boy wears a beautifully embroidered shirt, its cuffs and falling band edged by a ruffle; long-bodied gown.

1344. XVIc. 1560. Italian, Venetian. (Vienna, Art History Museum.)

Copy of Titian by *Rubens*. Portrait of a Woman in White, formerly called the artist's daughter Lavinia.

The Venetian bodice, short in back, is beginning to be slit and laced over a decorative plastron, or voluminously gathered material; always thickened by shirt fullness or padding, it will be very susceptible to the influence of the male peascod doublet, in the last decades of the century. The very low decolletage is opening wider.

The fan is of a specifically Italian form, derived from Moslem lands, seen particularly in Venice: rigid and fixed to a stick. Used by all classes, it ranged from stark simplicity to elaborate decorativeness, but in either case was fringed and tasseled.

Coryat was much struck by the Italian fans: "Most of them are very elegant and pretty things. For whereas the frame consisteth of a painted piece of paper and a little wooden handle; the paper which is fastened into the top is on both sides most curiously adorned with excellent pictures, either of amorous things tending to dalliance, having some witty Italian verse or fine emblemes written under them; or of some notable Italian city with a brief description

thereof added thereunto. These fannes are of a meane price. For a man may buy one of the fairest of them for so much money as countervaileth with our English groat."

1345-46. XVIc. 1577. German.

Trachtenbuch illustrated by *Jost Amman*, publ. by Hans Weigel, Nuremberg, 1577.

1345. Woman of Verona or Dietterichbern: Theodoric the Great (Thiuda-reiks==Dietrich) was the hero of a confused German legend, of a Gothic king who emerged from Byzantium to conquer Italy and was dispossessed of his kingdom of Bern (==Verona), by his uncle.

The fashions of Southern Germany and Switzerland, passing through the Tyrol, affect N. Italian costume: high-crowned, white-covered headdress; severe lines of skirt and bodice, with completely closed high neck, globular and separated upper-sleeve fullness; apron with upper corners free of the waistband.

1346. Venetian noblewoman: Characteristic exposed breasts and rather blowzy, short-waisted fullness of Venice; with a great pleated and wired scarf, finished with tassels, used as a ruff.

1347. XVIc. c. 1580. Italian, Brescian. (London, National Gallery.)

G. B. Moroni. Portrait of a Lady of the Fenaroli Family.

Rose satin gown, short-sleeved like one form of male jacket; horizontally slashed, the edges whipped in gold thread. Underdress and sleeves gold. White standing collar, embroidered in rose. Fan is another of the rigid, tufted Italian forms.

1348. Last quarter XVIc. Italian, Florentine. (N. Y. Historical Society.)

Att. to *A. Allori* (*Bronzino*). Princess of Florence.

1349. XVIc. c. 1580. Italian, Roman. (Washington, Nat. Gall. of Art.)

F. Baroccio. Quintilia Fischieri.

In both Ills. 1348-49, we see severe, masculine Spanish styles; high collars; large formal ruffs; separation of bodice and skirt.

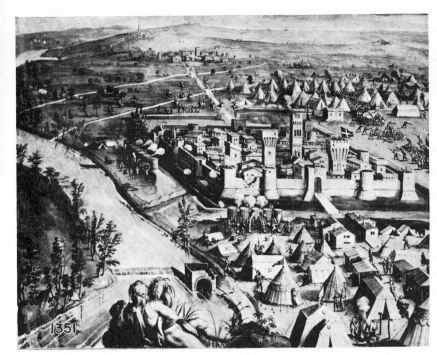

Quintilia's gold-embroidered bodice is green; her skirt blue. Fringed handkerchief.

The coat-like outer garment of the Florentine princess is of plum-red velvet brocaded on silver, its lapels and standing "Medici" collar faced with silver. Underskirt of shot silver, with red and gold. Handkerchief, lace edged, is an Italian usage, now spread through upper-class Europe.

1350. XVIc. c. 1580. Italian, Florentine. (Washington, Nat. Gall. of Art.)

A. Allori. Portrait of a Boy in Red.

Child's dress in Spanish fashion.

1351. Third quarter XVIc. Italian, Florentine. (Florence, Pal. Vecchio.)

G. Vasari. Scenes from the History of Florence: Assault of the Castle of Empoli.

Much of our information about Italian Mediaeval and Renaissance artists comes from Vasari's "Lives of the Painters." This wall-painting of the assault on a fortified castle gives us background material for military costume. The form and decoration of the tent has changed remarkably little from that shown in mss. illustrations of XIIc. Spain or XVc. France.

The tiny figures show halberdiers in *pluderhose,* and headgear of the morion and cabasset types.

After describing the costume of the Swiss guards at Fontainebleau, Coryat says: "The originall of their wearing of Codpieces and partie-coloured clothes grew from this; it is not found that they wore any until Anno 1476, at what time the Switzers tooke their revenge upon Charles Duke of Burgundie, for taking from them a Towne called Granson within the canton of Berne, whom after they had defeated, and shamefully put to flight, together with all his forces, they found there great spoyles that the Duke left behind, to the valew of three Millions, as it was said. (Commines lists the loot taken at Granson).

But the Switzers being ignorant of the valew of the richest things, tore in pieces the most sumptuous Pavilions in the world, to make themselves coates and breeches: some of them sold Silver dishes as cheape as Pewter, for two pence half-pennie a piece, and a great Pearle hanging in a Jewell of the Duke for twelve pence," (the Sancy diamond, 53½ grains, bought in 1835 by Prince Demidoff) "in memory of which insipid simplicity, Lewes the eleventh King of France, who the next year after entertained them into his Pension, caused them to bee uncased of their rich Clothes made of the Duke of Burgundies Pavillions, and ordained that they should ever after weare Suites and Codpieces of those varyegated colours of Red and Yellow. I observed that all these Switzers do wear Velvet Cappes with Feathers in them, and I noted many of them to be very cluster-fisted lubbers. As for their attire, it is made so phantastically, that a novice newly come to the Court, who never saw any of them before, would halfe imagine, if he should see one of them alone without his weapon, hee were the Kings fool."

1352. XVIc. 1570-75. Spanish. (Metropolitan Museum, Frick Collection.)

Doménikos Theotokópoulos, called El Greco. Vincente Anastagi.

The painter, whom we think of as Spanish, was a native of the island of Corfu, and was trained in Italy; in 1590 he became painter to the Spanish court.

Anastagi was a commander of both infantry and cavalry, and Governor of Malta during the siege. With armor bearing the white Maltese cross, Anastagi wears a high-collared Spanish ruff and the diagonal sash of a military commander, in green. Wide green velvet venetians of the 70's, galloned in gold; gartered white stockings; yellow shoes. On the floor, the combed morion of third quarter XVIc.

The World Widens: XVII Century

XVII Century Background

THE XVIIc. is a century of alteration, realignment, new strengths and energies, personal responsibility, and strain.

As royal prerogative gained over feudal power, the lord's responsibility for his own people was weakened.

The old, vertically-composed craft guilds, in which workmen, foremen, employers, merchants and shopkeepers shared (as crews, masters, and owners of fishing vessels still do in the proceeds of the catch), broke horizontally into commercial merchant-employers, and journeymen hired-help.

The new cleavage into capital and labor was strengthened by the rise of Protestantism.

The Catholic church, for all its rapacity, had never lost a real concern for the poor, and had never favored high interest rates. The Church completely controlled education, the law, medicine, and the administration of hospitals and all organized charity for the care of the poor, aged, and orphaned. These activities, which we now support by state and federal taxes, and the bequests of Rockefellers and Carnegies, were in those days paid for by the tithes of the church (one tenth of everyone's income, down to one out of a poor woman's ten eggs) as well as by additional funds from the rich and pious.

The dissolution of the monasteries was a redistribution of property as drastic as that being carried out in England today; the Church owned about one fifth of England's wealth, and administered it with the bureaucratic inefficiency of all over-large organizations. Protestants were enriched; and the charitable work of the Church, much of which had stemmed from the monasteries, was curtailed, while endless thousands of their former inhabitants were loosed into a world in which they were unfitted to compete; they starved, lawlessness increased, plague spread.

The invention of printing aided the rise of Protestantism. The Bible had been a possession of the higher levels of the Church alone; a monk or rich layman read his breviary; in order to read the Bible, he had to have permission of his religious superior. An unimportant layman could neither hope to own a manuscript Bible, nor be allowed to read it.

Printing provided cheap Bibles, which were critically read and pondered. People came to diverse conclusions: though disturbed, they might remain within the Church; but the tender, relaxed qualities of Catholicism were being impaired by the disunities, anxieties and struggles of the Counter-Reformation. Or they might join the Lutheran, Calvinist or other sects, which divided, competed and provided new tensions.

To forgive, or, worse, not to be able to forgive yourself is harder than to be periodically absolved of your burden by someone else. The ever-present Protestant concern with sin, and the austerity of a religion shorn of the Catholic graces and aesthetic satisfactions, drove the reformers, particularly the Calvinists, into industry for industry's sake. The rewarding money came to seem in itself good; God helped those who helped themselves. Calvin's ideals of service, more demanding than the tithes of the Church had been, were conveniently forgotten. The unfortunate and ineffectual tended to become objects of a determined, self-righteous charity, rather than part of the great body of the poor, weak, sinful children of God.

In the train of Reformation and Counter-Reformation went the devastation of the Wars of Religion. The states of present-day Europe were being formed, the limits of royal power defined, the part of the people in government explored, the courts freed of ecclesiastical rule.

The XVIIc. is France's century, as the XVIc. was Spain's. Least impaired by religious conflicts, she rises under the increasingly absolute rule of adroit Bourbon kings; her finances are established, agriculture and roads improved; industry, especially luxury industries, encouraged. She allies herself with the new power of the house of Vasa, under which the Swedes will go to the aid of Protestant Germany, and shoot to prominence and prosperity. France rivals a disunited Germany, of independent Protestant princes to the north (out of which Prussia will become preeminent in last third XVIIc.), and a weakened Empire, withdrawn around the Danube. But the end of the War of the Spanish Succession will see France's power suddenly controlled.

England, after nearly a century of internal preoccupations with Puritans and parliaments, Stuarts, revolutions and restorations, will emerge master of the Mediterranean and on her way to empire and world leadership, at the end of the century.

Spain has plummeted swiftly downward, her industrial potential self-destroyed, while she depends on her New World riches, her army and her proud tradition.

Italy is more disastrously disunited than ever, and Russia begins to emerge into Europe as Peter the Great combats Charles XII of Sweden successfully for the Baltic, and the Turks, unsuccessfully, for the Black Sea.

DEVELOPMENT OF DRESS: 1620-1655

Spain's influence on European fashion weakened in the second decade XVIIc., but she evolved for her own use the style of the Infantas, painted by Velasquez from 1645.

Clothes outside of Spain lost their farthingales and became easy and flowing. During the 30 Years War, the military styles of the Low Countries and Sweden affected male costume, particularly that of middle-class Germany. However, men of all ages, stations and callings, everywhere, went booted and spurred, with swords, leather military jerkins, cocked hats and carelessly slung cloaks. As in second half XVIc., it was ill-bred to appear in public without a cassock or cloak, and the hat was seldom removed, even within doors.

This, in Kelly's words, is the age of long locks, lace and leather. The military usage of leather does not affect women's increasingly feminine clothes. Otherwise, their development parallels that of men's to second half XVIIc. As bombasted breeches go out, so do hip bolsters and farthingales. So long as male breeches retain their quilted linings the materials of women's gowns keep a fat, padded look. Women's necklines become low, but alterations in the important collars and methods of decoration are analogous with men's. Almost the only hats worn by women are of the high-crowned masculine variety; caps remain very important only in Holland. Hair is combed back, hangs loose at the sides, and gains bangs and length as men's grows longer.

Regional costume was retained, particularly, by the North German seaports: Danzig, Lübeck, Hamburg and Bremen; up the Rhine, in those cities where it had become very distinctive: Cologne, Frankfort, Strassburg, to Basel; along the Danube, from Swabia, past Ulm, Augsburg and Nuremberg into Bohemia. Much of this costume is preserved in W. Hollar: *"Aula Veneris"* and *"Theatre of Women."* The courts of Germany west of the Rhine quickly succumbed to French fashion.

England develops her distinct van Dyck "Cavalier" styles in second quarter XVIIc., as Spanish influence wanes.

Italy shows Spanish influences long after they are supplanted elsewhere. In 1644, Evelyn notes the "Spanish mode and stately garb" of Genoa and the persistence in Venice of fashions which have endured for a century and a half.

France, which has gained over the rest of Europe during the 30 Years War, develops a civilization and a fashion-sense which overwhelms all others in second half XVIIc., a lead which she has always since retained.

MEN'S DRESS, 1620-1655

Doublets: As the peascod belly disappears, c.1600, the fitted doublet develops a shorter waist, longer point in front, wider shoulder caps, and longer skirts which are now apt to be slit and overlapping. The garment is often slit half a dozen times, vertically, across the breast and shoulder blades. In second quarter XVIIc. skirts grow longer, the body easier and shorter. The slitting is reduced to the center front and back seams, both of which are furnished with a row of buttons, but are usually left open.

By 1640 the belt has disappeared; the body and skirts are cut in one, and the garment is scarcely longer than a vest. A great deal of blousing shirt shows below its hem and through its open front. In first quarter XVIIc. the upper sleeve is also apt to be slit, like the breast and back of the doublet; close-fitting below the elbow.

As the doublet alters in second quarter, the sleeve becomes closer above, easier below, and unified. The slitting is reduced to the inseam; like the front and back openings of the doublet, it is edged with buttons, whether used or not.

With the vest-like doublet of 1640, the sleeves are closed, except for a buttoned wrist opening; this is turned back, forming, in embryo, the all-important cuff of second half XVIIc.; showing fullness of the shirt's sleeve, to match the shirt's bloused fullness above the breeches; the doublet is becoming a coat. On this garment, wide linen collars cover the shoulder, and the shoulder-cap disappears.

Jerkin: The sleeves of the collarless jerkin had become dependant and useless in late XVIc. Now they tend to disappear; but when no doublet is worn, sleeves of another material are added, braided like a doublet sleeve. These are seen particularly on the military jerkins of yellowish-colored natural leather which are fastened by lacings through eyelets, sometimes by clasps, never by buttons. Around 1640, the jerkin takes on the same short, unbelted form as the doublet.

Breeches and Decoration: Breeches continue to be fastened to doublets until the advent of the short jackets of the 40's. But instead of being tied together underneath, the lacings are now brought through paired eyelets along the waistline, and are tied outside in decorative bows.

The ribbons by which aiglettes were hung in Spain during second half XVIc. have now become more important than the points themselves; their use increases in loops, bows, rosettes and in spaghetti-like, uneven, uncut fringes, no thicker than a shoelace and as insignificantly tipped.

Breeches: The full knee-breeches of late XVIc. supplant trunk-hose during first quarter XVIIc. They lose their interior quilting and become narrower. There are also loose, ungartered breeches hanging below the knee; similar forms, cut off above the knee, like those worn around the turn of the century, reappear with vest-like doublets of the 40's. Until this time, breeches are high-waisted and caught to the doublet; but by midXVIIc. they slip low on the hips, unattached. As breeches become more like shorts or trousers, they develop a fly-closing.

The trim of breeches agrees with that of doublet; when it is split at c. front and back, showing shirt, they may also be split, similarly edged with buttons, and show an underwear-like white linen lining. They are gartered with the same loops, bows and rosettes used on the rest of the garment. With the wide collars of the 40's, the breeches may be cuffed with lace to match, or trimmed at outseam and bottom with wide, lace-like braids matching those used on the underarm seams and edges of the short doublets.

Footwear: Legwear is also closely related to the rest of the costume, in first half XVIIc. Silk stockings are generally worn by the middle and upper classes. Several pairs are worn over each other, pushed down to show their differing colors, and deliberately wrinkled. Since they are still precious, they are protected by a variety of gaiters and linen boot-linings, which are sometimes worn with shoes alone, as well as with most boots. (A frame for the mechanical knitting of silk stockings had been invented in England in 1621.)

Shoes now have heels and heavy soles (both red, in court wear), and a strap over the instep, decorated with a ribbon rosette or bows. Toward mid-century, the toes lengthen and are cut square across the tip.

But this is primarily the era of boots. With heel and sole support, these now fit well around the foot. Their extremely wide tops are worn folded down and then up again, tending to become wider and folded lower in second quarter of century. The cuff thus formed is a receptacle for elaborate garters, hem decorations of breeches, or the elaborately lace-trimmed inner boot-hose, folded in unison with the folds of the boot-top. In second quarter XVIIc. a great quatre-foiled plaque of leather is held in place over the instep by the straps of the ubiquitous spurs. Boots are now worn by everyone, and the spur is an adjunct, quite devoid of function. This leather plaque becomes enormous in the 30's, and is retained when boots return to riding use in last third XVIIc.

Linen is becoming increasingly visible and important; it must be treated as part of the body garments, as well as a frequent part of footwear.

The wired-out flat whisk, or Spanish *golilla* of 1610, and the full but unsupported *falling ruff*, begin to be supplanted, in second quarter century, by the *falling band* collar. Cuffs with scalloped edges have already appeared, worn with the falling ruff; they continue in use, growing fuller as the falling band collar (usually with a scalloped edge) spreads over the shoulders of the short-waisted, long-skirted doublet, and ousts the shoulder wings, at end first third XVIIc. With the vest-like doublet of the 40's, the collar is reduced

in size and loses its scalloped border; but now the fullness of the shirt appears between doublet and breeches, and below a sleeve, which is shortened by being turned back, later becoming a cuff.

Outer Garments: Cloaks and gowns are now indispensable outdoor wear. The slung mandilion fashions of second half XVIc. were developed in military use into longer, looser coats with easy, cuffed sleeves. The longer capes of the XVIIc. (often with pendant sleeves and square collars), are also worn slung about the body, and held in place by interior cords; these can sometimes be seen tied around the body, but are usually obscured by the great collar of the doublet, which is worn outside the cape or cassock.

For state and ceremonial wear, long gowns continued to be used as they are in England today. After 1620, trunk hose persisted only in livery or regalia wear.

Headwear: With the swashbuckling outer garments are worn dashing, plumed military hats, cocked at front, or on one or two sides for practicality; by last half XVIIc., they are often cocked into a tricorne. The other outstanding hat of the period is an essentially stiff one, with a narrower horizontal brim and a high, truncated cylindrical or conical crown. In last half of century there are low-crowned versions of this hat, typically trimmed with cord or loops, not feathers.

Hair: Hair has lengthened during the last decades of XVIc. Now all but the most dignified older men allow it to grow to natural length; at first c. parted; in second quarter of century, cut across the forehead in bangs; until parted hair reappears in the wig of the last half XVIIc.

Beards and moustaches are reduced in length as hair is allowed to grow. The upswept moustache of first third of century becomes smaller, as the beard changes to the Vandyke type and becomes very slight; in second quarter the beard disappears except on older men. Clean shaven faces are common from last half of the century, though tiny moustaches are worn till its final quarter; after that, hair disappears from faces until XIXc.

Accessories: The diagonal scarves worn by military commanders of second half XVIc. continue in use, and are now worn, as the beginnings of uniforms, by soldiers. Spurs and swords are seen on everybody; the slender rapier tends to be slung by a diagonal strap over the shoulder, in second quarter of century. Daggers pass out of ordinary wear. Umbrellas had appeared in late XVIc., but are still uncommon. Walking sticks come into fashion in first quarter XVIIc., and remain in use into XXc.

WOMEN'S DRESS, 1620-1655

The long-waisted, stomachered dresses of the turn of the century remain in use through first third XVIIc, with lowering necklines. However, the tendency is toward a shorter-waisted open gown or robe, for grander wear, worn over a cor-set-like bodice and skirt, supported by many pet-ticoats beneath. This is a development of the Spanish coat-dress (see Ill. 1114: Vavasour), spreading wide to show the underbodice and skirt. Skirt fullness is attained by goring in front and gathering in back, or by gathering all around.

Stiff, heavily patterned fabrics are much less used. Underskirts are of ground length, and are usually lighter in color than the skirt of the robe. The robe may have a train, and when its skirt is looped up at the hips to show the underskirt, end first third XVIIc., it is apt to be of thinner ma-terial than the underskirt, with bright lining.

The stomacher of the underbodice is some-times rounded, in first half of the century, but be-comes pointed again in the second half; in Hol-land it is apt to be richly decorated.

Jackets: With the short-waisted male doublets of the end of the first third of century, short-waisted bodices with tabbed skirts appear on women. When the jackets have full, paned or leg-o'-mutton sleeves, they are tied around, be-tween shoulder and elbow, with a rosetted ribbon. This matches a belt, fastened at side or c. front with a bow or rosette. Sleeves have a tall white cuff, which makes them seem shorter, and in sec-ond quarter century the sleeve does actually shrink toward the elbow, just as men take to turn-ing back the bottom of their sleeve. When these jackets do not meet in front, they are usually hooked fast along the stomacher. There is another form of jacket, which is often of quilted or flower-ed stuff. When it is thick, like the military leather jerkin, it is apt to be laced together at front or back. It usually shows a simple, easy sleeve, slit up along inseam and cut off near elbow.

In English inventories of 1600, the jacket or bodice with skirt attached is called a *kirtle;* the skirt alone, a *half-kirtle;* jacket alone, a *jump.*

Gown or Robe: The outer gown of first half XVIIc. has a sleeve slit down the inseam, and caught with a rosette, where it is cut off above the elbow. This is the split Spanish sleeve of the end of XVIc., the bottom section of which was al-ready almost truncated (Ill. 1238), and has now been dropped. During first third of century there are sometimes long strip sleeves, in addition, pen-dant from the armseye. With the short sleeve of the gown, the under sleeve of the bodice is cuffed, and tends to become fuller and shorter.

Necklines lower generally, into a rounded, then a squared form; this eventually widens and be-comes rounder, as the bodice slips off the shoul-ders in the latter half century. The neckline is at first much higher in back to support the con-tinuing ruff or wired-out collar; it becomes lower in back, though never so low as in front. Neck-lines alter as collars vary and combine.

The evolution of men's and women's linen and headgear in Holland (where it was most varied and influential) has been exhaustively charted by Fritjof van Thienen: *Das Kostum de Blütezeit Hollands,* 1600-60., Deutsche Kunstverlag, Berlin, 1930.

Linen: Ruffs at neck and wrists, and whisks persist through first third of century (the ruffs, particularly in conservative and bourgeois wear); both finish their careers, worn in conjunction with all sorts of falling collars and folded kerchiefs. These tend to spread, as shoulders are bared in latter half century, and kerchief becomes a drape around top of bodice, or disappears.

Hair is parted above the ears; the center section is drawn back and coiled into a bun above the nape, the curled sides hang loose and lengthen, as collars descend and widen. In first third of cen-tury there are clipped bangs; these tend to become curled locks and to rejoin the side hair in the '40's, while the bun becomes more conspicuous and is decoratively enclosed.

Head Coverings are always reduced or elimi-nated in proportion to elaborate attention given to the hair itself. This was as true of the XVIIc. as it has been of the 1940's. Caps almost disappeared, and were restricted to widows or conventional bourgeoises, except in Holland, their home, where they clung to the back of the head. Again as in our own time, kerchiefs and hoods covered the hair out of doors; the XVIIc. hoods are round in form, tied under the chin with ribbons, and are usually dark. At this time the black mantilla began to be worn in Spain. With these head coverings, and with the great hats which were worn for riding, ladies were now accustomed to wear masks.

Shoes followed male rules.

Accessories: With the increase in use of ribbons and lace, fine aprons come into style, and great pieces of jewelry go out. Pearls, modest in quan-tity, are retained in chains, bracelets, pendants, earrings and hair decorations.

As sleeves shorten, c. 1640, long gloves and muffs appear. Nightgowns begin to be used. Fans, hang-ing watches and mirrors continue in use.

"Women's Maskes, Buskes, Muffs, Fanns, Pere-wigs and Bodkins were first devised and used in Italy by Curtezans, and from thence brought to France and from thence they came into England about the time of the Massacres in Paris," accord-ing to Stow. In 1575, Van Meteren said that "Eng-lishwomen go about the streets without any cov-ering, either of heuk or mantle, hood, veil or the like. . . . Ladies of distinction have lately learned to cover their faces with silken masks or visards and feathers." Patches have now begun to accom-pany these headcoverings; but lowering necklines and loose curls brought with them a variety of outer garments: cloaks with collars, gored in front and full behind; ample "lap-mantles" which com-pletely covered the figure; many shoulder capes and kerchiefs; and little loose *casaques* or *sacques,* worn particularly in Holland and France.

1353. XVIIc. c. 1606. Flemish. (Florence, Uffizi.)

Att. to *F. Pourbus, y.* Henry IV.

Collars of Saint-Michel and Saint-Esprit worn with ermine-lined and collared robes, semé France modern; delicately pinked doublet sleeves; short wide hose, the loose lining of which scarcely shows between the paned straps. In XVIIIc. Mme. du Barry will demand that Louis XV reward her female chef for a magnificent dinner with the *cordon bleu* of the Saint-Esprit.

1354. XVIIc. 1602. French.

Léonard Gaultier. Henry IV, Gabrielle d'Estrées, César duc de Vendôme and Catherine Henriette de Bourbon.

Henry of Navarre needed nearly ten years to subdue and consolidate the France of which he became king following the assassination of Henry III in 1589. Opposed by the plots of Spain, the League, the Guises, Mayenne, Nemours and Joyeuse, the Protestant Henry IV fought for his great cities, one by one. In 1593 he was converted to Catholicism; the following year even Paris capitulated; but his Edict of Nantes assured security of worship and belief to the Calvinists.

In little more than a decade of peace (before he, too, was assassinated in 1610 by a Catholic fanatic whose act horrified all factions), Henry proved himself perhaps the greatest of French kings. He reorganized France and strengthened her alliances (as well as the position of his own Bourbon dynasty) with immensely resourceful and courageous energy, patient commonsense and a sympathetic interest in people of all sorts. His indulgent and astonishingly informal good-heartedness and gaiety and the quick audacious Gascon wit which colors his every word make him one of the most appealing of kings.

The government, finances and army were efficiently reorganized by Henry and his devoted min-ister, Sully. Great attention was given to communications: canals, roads and bridges, and to sanitation (which was particularly scandalous in Paris, with its celebrated mud which sticks like glue). He aided agriculture and established factories: Gobelins tapestry, silk, glass; protected and aided industry by laws and by commercial treaties with his many new allies, from Sweden to Italy. He built or completed important projects in Paris: the Hotel de Ville, Tuileries, Louvre, Palais-Royal and the Pont Neuf.

Lest he should marry his mistress, Gabrielle d'Estrées, Marguerite of Valois refused to divorce Henry IV during the many years of their amicable separation, but she did so in 1599, after Gabrielle's death, to enable Henry to marry Marie de' Medici and provide heirs to the throne.

Female: bangs frizzed at forehead, hair dressed high with jewelled ornament; fan collars; leg-o'-mutton sleeve reduced in size; drum-shaped skirt, with or without cartwheel top, supported by hip bolster; shoes with high cork lifts. Daughter: bonnet with c. massed decoration, like that worn by Henry III; lace-edged apron; seams closed by the favorite paired braid catches.

Male: hair fluffed and combed backward; ruffs and falling bands; doublets with short skirts, cut and overlapping, worn with diagonal blue sashes carrying the cross of the Order of the Saint-Esprit; short circular cloaks; short paned hose, padded into a horizontal bottom line; with canions and rosetted garters (boy); sword slung through a wide, decorated holster; high-crowned felt hats; with centrally placed decoration and cord hat-band; shoes with tongue tied over instep.

Until the large Dutch *kas* and French *armoires* begin to be incorporated into buildings, as closets, in XVIIIc., storage space is at a premium; trunks and chests are still convenient seats for the wearers of wide bolstered skirts.

1355. Beginning XVIIc. French. (Paris. Carnavalet Museum.)

Unknown artist. The Troupe of the Gelosi.

This troupe of Italian comedians, headed by the lovely, learned and virtuous Isabella Andreini, played several times in France between 1576-1604, under Henry III-IV. They were so popular that favorite preachers found themselves without congregations. After playing at Fontainebleau for Marie de' Medici in 1601, the Gelosi were pensioned by Henry IV.

The 7 characters, dressed in the costume of the turn of the century, are Oration and Isabella, la Pascalina, il Magnifico, Signor Pantalone, and a burlesque acolyte and valet.

The Italian comedy returned to Paris about 1622 with the company of Isabella's son, Giambattista Andreini.

Women had appeared in mediaeval miracle plays, but during Elizabeth's time, female parts were played by boys. Coryat had heard of women playing in public in London, but actually saw such a thing for the first time in Italy in 1611. The popularity of Italian comedy led to the general use of actresses on the English stage in second half XVIIc. Old women's parts were still sometimes played by actors in France in third quarter XVIIc., as occasionally happens in burlesque in our own time.

1356. XVIIc. After 1610. French.

Giles Rousselet, after *Grégoire Huret.* Gros-Guillaume.

1357. XVIIc. c. 1661. French.

Simonin. Molière as Sganarelle.

This engraving of Molière, acting the lead in his own play, is the only existing portrait of him made during his lifetime.

The great English theatre antedated the great French theatre by two generations. The first important theatre in Paris was the Hôtel de Bourgogne (1628), whose actors, trained in provincial fairs like the Foire Saint-Germain, became permanent members.

Gros-Guillaume (the fat Robert de Guérin) was one of the favorites of the *King's Company,* as the Italian troupe was called after 1610, in honor of Henry's inadequate subsidy, which was substantially increased by Louis XIII.

A rival troupe, Mondory's *Marais,* set up in 1629, took its name from one of a series of tennis courts*, successively burned down, on which they played.

* See Appendix.

1358

1359

1360

1361

Supported by Richelieu, they produced Corneille's plays until the
death of their leading actor;
eventually their remnant members were joined with the travelling company which Molière
brought to Paris in 1658. The
Petit-Bourbon Theatre, where they played his *Précieuses ridicules,* was to be demolished; they refurbished the marvellous private theatre which Richelieu
had built in his Palais-Royal, and as the *Troupe de
Monsieur,* under the patronage of Louis XIV's
brother, opened in 1661 with *Sganarelle, or the
Imaginary Invalid.*

Louis XIV made Molière one of his valets-de-
chambre; but the actor was snubbed by the officers
of the king's household because of his profession.
One morning the king invited Molière to eat his
"en cas" (the tray of food left by the bedside when
the king went to bed) with him. Each had a chicken
wing, served by the king, who announced to his following: "You see me engaged in entertaining Molière, whom my valets-de-chambre do not consider
sufficiently good company for them." (Mme. Campan).

1358. XVIIc. 1609-11. French, Nancy. (Met. Mus., Print
Room.)

Claude de la Ruelle. Engraved by F. Brentel.
*Pourtraict du convoy fait en pompe funèbre de
Charles III de Lorraine,* Part II.

Engravings of whole processions, coronations and
funerals, become common in e.XVIIc., conveniently
accompanied by text identifying the personages. The
funeral procession of Henry IV's brother-in-law, widower of Claude of France, shows the mourning robes
with liripipes which have been used in all countries
for many centuries (English: "doole" robes).

Herald's tabards worn with band collars over long
robes; Swiss guards in loose *pluderhose;* Charles' superbly caparisoned horse accompanied by 2 squires
and 4 footmen; the Rhinegrave Frederick with bare
sword; another Swiss; the Grand Master with baton;
the Grand Chamberlain with a gold key; another
lord.

1359. XVIIc. After 1610. French. (Turin, Pinacoteca.)
Att. to *F. Clouet.* Marguerite of Valois.
White mourning of queens.

1360. XVIIc. c. 1615. Flemish. (Florence, Uffizi.)
F. Pourbus, y. Isabelle of Bourbon, Queen of Spain.

1361. XVIIc. Flemish. (Florence, Uffizi.)
F. Pourbus, y. Isabelle of Bourbon, Queen of Spain.

Henry IV's daughter, the 13-year-old bride of Philip IV, in French and Spanish dress.

French: fan collar; low-bosomed gown of delicately sprigged brocade pinked in a diapered pattern; simple modified leg o'mutton sleeve; shorter-

waisted bodice necessitated by cart-wheel topped skirt, which is typically without train; frizzed hair dressed high with jewelled ornaments; looped pearls.

Spanish: closed ruff; flowing brocade-lined outer sleeve; segmented puffing of inner sleeve; stomacher with long point; funnel-shaped skirt of large-pattern brocade with train, inverted-V opening over elaborately trimmed underskirt. Lace-edged handkerchief; magnificent jewels (which, as Regent, she later pawned to aid the armies of Spain).

1362

1362. XVIIc. Flemish. (Versailles, Nat. Mus.)
Unknown artist. Anne of Austria.

Philip III's daughter, married in 1615 to Louis XIII, was insulted and neglected during 20 childless years by her husband, by Richelieu, and by many of the great families of France. As Regent for her late-born son, Louis XIV, she banished many of these enemies, and through the tact of Richelieu's most able and charming successor, Cardinal Mazarin, lived in secure importance.

Marie de' Medici had 3 favorite dresses (Young: *The Medici*); among these was one which she wears in her portrait in the Uffizi and the Rijksmuseum, and which, in a refurbished form, served her daughter-in-law, Queen Anne (just as Anne of Denmark made use of the dresses left over from Elizabeth's wardrobe).

It was a blue velvet gown sown with gold fleurs-de-luce; its fleur-de-luce-shaped stomacher of ermine was decorated with amethysts surrounded by 4 clustered pearls; its plastron was filled by an immense amethyst cross with 3 pearl drops. With this gown, Anne wears a contemporary ruff, very wide and shallow, adroitly pleated out of petal-pointed lace; hair combed back and frizzed low over the ears in the new fashion.

1363. XVIIc. 1610-17. Flemish. (Madrid, Prado.)
F. Pourbus, y. Marie de' Medici, widow of Henry IV.

The second Medici queen of France, brought up in the corrupt and murderous court of Francis of Tuscany and his unloved Austrian wife, carried an immense dowry to her marriage. She was a good-natured, stupid woman with a pink and blonde beauty (which Rubens admired) and beautiful taste in clothes. Regent 1610-1617 for her young son, Louis XIII, who was "as fit to reign as she," she was exiled by Richelieu in 1631. She escaped from Blois, fat as she had become, by being let down from a window; chose to live in poverty in Holland rather than to return to Florence; was chased out of Antwerp; and died in complete poverty in Cologne, a dependant of Rubens, whose patron she had been.

Widow's cap and veil in a reduced form of that worn by Catherine de' Medici, exquisitely pleated and wired out behind her petal-edged ruff, the same edging being used to border and fill in the decolletage of the bodice. The veil continues to be caught to the sleeve sections, as sleeves recede from the wrist and their paned fullness is formally caught about the arm. Skirt of delicately pinked satin shows the cartwheel top at about the end of its use. The ends of the veil, brought about the body from the elbow, are caught at the center of the skirt. Lace-edged handkerchief, and pearls.

1364   1365   1366

1364. XVIIc. c. 1622. Flemish. (Metropolitan Museum.)

Rubens. Anne of Austria.

In the 1620-30's, the great fan-shaped ruffs are combined with flat kerchief and collar arrangements; following the same impulse, cuffs of deeply pointed lace emerge from behind straight-edged cuffs, both of which are in visible retreat away from the wrist. Uncovered hair loosening at the sides; pearl choker and ear drops; ribbon rosette at bosom; fur muff on lap.

1365. XVIIc. 1627-32. Flemish. (Metropolitan Museum.)

A. Van Dyke. Mlle. de Gottignies.

Painting in cosmopolitan Antwerp and in France, 1627-32, Van Dyke (or Dyck) produced portraits of German, French, English, Spanish and Flemish subjects.

This is the standard upper-class European gown, c.1630: loosening hair; fan-shaped ruff in process of falling into a lace collar; composite cuffs, double or triple, reaching high on the arm to give the appearance of a shortening sleeve; sleeve and waist tied about with ribbons, knots and rosettes; brocade less used, its patterns more delicate.

1366. Second quarter XVIIc. French. (Chantilly, Musee Conde.)

Philippe de Champaigne. Armand Jean du Plessis, duke-cardinal of Richelieu.

The Cardinal wears the Order of the Saint-Esprit; red biretta, mozetta and cassock, and lace-edged surplice, the fullness of which is finely pleated.

1367. XVIIc. 1629. French. (Boston, Museum of Fine Arts.)
Bosse after *St. Igny.* Cavalier.

1368. XVIIc. French. (Boston, Museum of Fine Arts.)
Bosse. Lady.

1369. XVIIc. 1633. French.

Bosse. Cavalier following the latest Edict.

Abraham Bosse (1602-76), son of a tailor and author of one of the first treatises on engraving, produced innumerable sets of illustrations, which are the great documents of French costume in second quarter XVIIc.: the history of the *Prodigal Son,* and other Biblical parallels; *Marriage in City and Country;* the *Five Senses;* and all manner of occupation, showing school rooms, artist studios, shoemakers, engravers, workmen and soldiers. In addition both Bosse and Briot engraved a great series of French male costume after St. Igny in 1629. Callot did such plates in 1617 and in 1632, and there are similar plates of Dutch cavaliers by Nolpe, after Quast, in the 30's. In latter half XVIIc., the costume plates of Picart, St. Jean, the three Bonnarts, Valk, Trouvain, and Arnoult are supplemented by information, both on costume and outdoor life, provided by the small figures in topographical scenes, maps and panoramas, views of celebrated buildings and gardens, fêtes and processions, such as those of Rigaud, Mariette, and the Perelles in France.

1367. Though the lace collar of the jacket is worn over the coat, the collar of this cassock is edged with an allied lacy scallop, since it is worn slung over the shoulders like a cape. The coat sleeve is set into the armseye in back, but is free of the body of the coat in front for ease, in the manner of the old pinned-on sleeve. Fur-edged and embroidered gloves; boots becoming more delicate, their heels and toes fitted into matching pattens.

1368. All the knowledge of wiring gained in the flowing veils and standing collars of the turn of the century culminates in this stylized headdress combined with collar.

1369. Four of Bosse's invaluable engravings show ladies and gentlemen before and after Louis XIII's edict of Nov. 18, 1633. This forbade the wearing, on shirts, breeches, cuffs, headdresses or any other linen, of cut work or embroidery in gold or silver thread, passementerie or lace, whether manufactured in or out of the kingdom. The edict had little effect, as Bosse's later engravings show. (See Appendix: Blum.)

The courtier's valet is carrying off his doublet with paned sleeves, his fine belt and ribbon-knotted breeches. These have been replaced by a short-waisted open doublet with sleeves open along the inseam, showing a good deal of untrimmed shirt-fullness; plain band collar, wide over the shoulders, trimmed only by its tasselled ties. A tiny rosette hangs, not from the ear, but tied to the hair; this favorite usage of the 20's, developed out of the hanging threads of the end of Elizabeth's reign, is continued in the rosettes tied to hanging locks of ladies' hair, particularly in the Low Countries. His boots have small reversed cuffs and plain boot-hose, but enormous spur leathers over the instep. Hat with low crown, its brim wreathed about with comparatively flat plumes, in a way which will become extremely important in

the costume of Louis XIV.

1370. XVIIc. French. (Metropolitan Museum, Print Room.)

Bosse. "Marriage in the City": Return from the Christening.

1370. Fringed hair, combed back in the center into a bun at the back of the head, is much longer and beginning to cluster in curls at the sides. Lace nightcap and fur-collared dressing gown of the mother. Lady with muff (r.) clearly shows the remnant of the old pendant sleeve of the Spanish gown, slit up the inseam from elbow to shoulder (its lower half having been completely cut off), and its bottom corners caught together at the elbow by a bow, over the swollen inner sleeve; this gown has a wide lace-edged collar or kerchief, and is tied by a rosetted sash across a stomacher which matches the inner skirt. Woman with baby: lace-edged cloak with stiff collar must be worn back on the shoulders, since the kerchief or collar of the gown is always carried on top of the outer garment, by both men and women. Children: boy, still in diapers, wears skirts with a high-waisted doublet; his sister's hair and gown are miniature forms of adult wear.

1371

1371. XVIIc. 1637. French. (Metropolitan Museum, Print Room.)

A. Bosse. Galerie of the Palace.

The Palais Cardinal, built by Richelieu, became the residence of Anne of Austria and her children after his death, and was henceforth known as the Palais Royal. It is constructed around a garden surrounded by galleries of 186 tiny shops, where books, jewelry and trifles are still sold as they were at the height of the Galerie's fashion. This print was inspired by Corneille's comedy, *La Galerie du Palais.*

The shop to the l. is that of the king's bookseller, Augustin Courbé; the book being sold is Tristan l'Hermite's *Marianne,* which the Marais troupe had offered with great success in 1636, in competition with the Théatre de Bourgogne production of the *Cid;* with frontispiece by Bosse, it has lately been published by Courbé.

In the middle is a mercer's shop, out of which grew our department store. The chartered fairs, of which Saint-Denis in Paris was the oldest (dating from VIIc.) had periodically supplied needs of all sorts, as merchants brought in the goods of Europe and even of the Orient, and the local shops were kept closed. By XIVc. it was impractical to allow great fairs within Paris. Various categories of meticulously licensed and regulated shops were set up; the mercers were allowed to sell a curious mixture of jewelry, notions, metal goods of all sorts, including swords and daggers, boxes and containers. Centuries of attrition have reduced *mercerie* from its original significance of general merchandise to its present level of small dry-goods and notions.

This was an age of reckless expenditure. Shopping became a major amusement, best in Paris; and best

of all, in Paris, were the goods of these categories sold at the Galerie Mercière in the Palais. We see jewelry, fans, masks, gloves, muffs, caps, and the ribbon knots called *galants.* In the linen shop adjoining, are collars and cuffs and the band-boxes to hold them.

The edict of 1633 and that of 1634, which again forbade the use of satin and velvet, embroidery, and gold and silver stuffs, have obviously not been effective. But excess was beginning to bore the French. In 1645, the contrast between the Poles, at their embassy reception, and the simple ribbon-looped French costumes was noted by Mme. de Motteville.

1372-75. XVIIc. c. 1635. French. (Paris, Carnavalet Museum.)

Unknown artist. The Cries of Paris.

Permanent markets for all sorts of goods are being established, but the everyday needs of everyday people continue to be met by itinerant vendors, **crying** their wares, as only an occasional junk-man, or driver of an Easter flower wagon still does in New York. The Cries of cities like London and Paris will be popular subjects for prints for three centuries to come.

1372. 2: death to rats and mice. 3: cakes called *oubliés.* 4: hats. 5: hot pastries. 6: flints and steels. 8: handkerchiefs and collars. 9: sheet music.

1373. 1: Naples sand. 2: onions. 3: Holland cheese. 4. oranges and lemons. 5: hot chestnuts. 6: twig brooms. 7: vinegar.

1374. 1: stools. 2: iron utensils. 5: milk. 6: oysters. 7: grinder. 8: baskets.

1375. 7: *glands* tasselled band-strings for **collars.** 9: cherries. 10: broadsides.

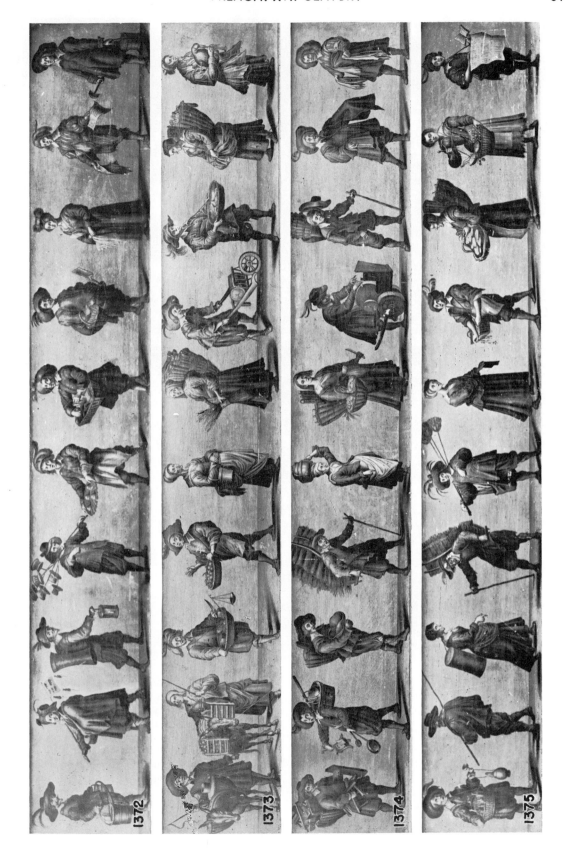

1376. XVIc. 1643. Flemish. (Madrid, Prado.)

F. Pourbus, y. Anne of Austria as a Widow.

The mourning cap and enclosing veil, which we have seen wired out and drawn about the body in various ways, since Catherine de' Medici, is here gathered into the edge of the plastron of the bodice.

The drum-shaped skirt with a pleated top is retained, as majesty has always tended to retain effective old-established usages long after they have been given up elsewhere; but it is fastened by the currently fasionable ribbon bows and rosettes. The wired collar, too, has largely passed out of use, but is too effective, framed by the wired veil, to be given up by a widowed queen; it is set low on the neck, however, depressed by a pearl choker.

1377. XVIIc. French. (Turin, Pinacoteca.)

French School. A Daughter of Amadeo I.

Victor-Amadeus of Savoy, who had married one of Louis XIII's sisters, had a number of daughters, the last of whom was born in 1636, and is probably the wearer of this gown, typical of the 1640-50's. Curls, massed at the sides, hanging low on the shoulders, are decorated like the gown with rosettes; neckline slipping low on the shoulders, horizontally banded bodice; sleeves short and cuffed; shirt sleeve caught with ribbon knot at wrist; as is often seen in male costume, ribbons of several widths are used, graduating down to the narrowest at the wrist; bodice point very long; skirts dragging in a train.

Loose bouquet of roses in a vase, at a time when paintings of flower and fruit arrangements begin to be seen.

PAINTERS OF MIDDLE AND LOWER CLASS DRESS, XVIIc.

Costume of the middle and lower classes is shown in the pictures prolifically produced by the brothers

Le Nain: Antoine, 1588?-1648; Louis, 1593?-1648; and Mathieu, 1607?-77; and by Michelin (1623-96). The French painter, Georges La Tour (1600-52), who worked in Holland as well, was chiefly preoccupied with the reflected glow of light, but his pictures show simple, middle-class French costume of great charm.

1378. XVIIc. French. (Paris, Pierre Landry.)
Georges La Tour. The Card Sharper.

The cut of costume is always explicit in La Tour's pictures, and even the simplest is apt to show a fine braid. These unusually elaborate Dutch costumes are full of rich, fresh detail: points hanging from the collar or as fringe from the armseye; beautifully embroidered shirts and collars; simple, wonderfully cut sleeves; unusual plumed turbans and hats. There is nothing quite like the clothing La Tour paints. I have always felt that, with the instincts of a great couturier, he eliminated a great deal of the clutter and impurity of line which actually existed.

1379. End of first half XVIIc. French. (Louvre.)
A. Le Nain. Family Reunion.

In these costumes, which show a strong Dutch influence, we see bows appearing, even on the instep of boots, toward the middle of the century. Both men and women show dangling side locks, which may be tied with bows, but women's hair is beginning to be wired out at the sides and hangs in corkscrew curls. Bands with tasseled strings no longer lie flat, but tend to rumple under the chin in the beginnings of the gathered cravat, as sleeves turn back into the beginnings of cuffs. The doublet grows shorter as the loose breeches of mid-XVIIc. are lavishly fringed with ribbon.

1380. XVIIc. French. (Paris, Paul Rosenberg.)
Mathieu Le Nain. The Feast of Wine.

1381. XVIIc. 1656. French. (Metropolitan Mus.)
J. Michelin. The Baker's Cart.

The costume of poor people is the least easy to date, based as it must be on comfortable garments of undramatic design, hand-me-downs from soldier days, and odd replacements, when it is not merely layers of rags.

Garments such as are shown in the Feast of Wine and in a companion picture (The Feast of the Bull), have been worn since the 30's, but the lacings around the breeches hem make it probable that they date from the end of the second third of the century.

1382. XVIIc. French. (Leningrad.)
Louis Le Nain. (Copy of The Bird Hunter.)

MEN'S DRESS, 1655-1715 (LOUIS XIV)

The doublet has only about another decade of life. It is now an open bolero-like garment, extremely short and with elbow-length cuffed sleeves. The shirt, full and soft, is bloused over the breeches (which now hang unsupported on the hips); below the short doublet sleeves, the shirt sleeve's fullness, pushed up and tied in puffs, is finished at the wrist by a ruffle. The collar hangs deep on the chest in an oblong which usually has rounded corners; it seldom lies quite flat and its tendency to buckle in the middle will become elaborated into gathered fullness; the collar turns into a cravat, *rabat,* by the 70's, worn with arrangements of ribbon bows above (later, underneath) or in the long negligent *steinkirk* form tucked into the vest in the 90's; *steinkirks* are worn also by women.

The breeches, already open, wide and decorated about the hem, are increased by gathering into several bulky forms of petticoat-breeches called *rhinegraves*: a petticoat, a divided skirt or full bloused pantaloons. These breeches are heavily decorated by ribbon loops, often hanging from the waistband below the bloused shirt, and characteristically massed at the hemline, particularly at the sides where the garter knot used to hang. There are elaborate combinations of these styles, as: a petticoat over longer pantaloons. The whole effect of multiplied horizontal ruffles is sometimes increased by another set called *cannons* (not the *canions* of XVIc.), fastened below the knee, reminiscent of the drooping boot-cuff and boot-hose, as boots are replaced by shoes with these garments. In the same spirit are stockings with very wide baggy tops, 1670-80.

Meanwhile the military cassock has been worn by almost everybody and has been found to be a most useful outer garment; about 1665 it begins to come into use as a collarless coat. The doublet, which has always been primarily an undergarment, now becomes a vest, at first sleeved; the sleeves may be long and tight, but are usually seen turned back in a cuff over the longer and wider cuff of the coat; as the vest tends to become sleeveless, its cuff effect may be retained as a piece of the vest material laid over that of the coat cuff.

With the new coats and vests of the 70's, narrower knee breeches, *culottes*, replace petticoat breeches; they become simple, closer fitting, closed by a few buttons or a buckled strap. Stockings are rolled to cover the knee strap or are drawn up smooth under it.

Coats, during their first decade of use, are cut rather straight like the cassock, reach to mid-thigh and are worn with waist-long vests; coat seams are unsewed below the waist though they may be closed by lines of buttons in the old ways. By the final quarter century, the coat is of knee length and increasingly shaped: a *justaucorps;* in the 90's its skirts are stiffened and widened by goring and by pleating at the seams.

The vest lengthens with the coat, though it is always a little shorter. While the coat stays open, the vest is closed throughout until the 90's when it opens to receive the ends of the steinkirk cravat; by mid-90's the vest is often buttoned only at the waist.

A vest, without the coat, is usual indoor wear; vests with sleeves are made especially for this purpose, and there are also dressing gowns. With all of these, the wig is apt to be doffed, and the clipped or shaved head protected by a *montero* or a nightcap.

The short coat sleeve of the 70's tends to lengthen, and to widen out below the shoulder, while its cuff grows wider, deeper and more important. Coat pockets originally followed the vertical or diagonal buttoned lines used on doublets; they come to be set horizontally, low on the skirts, and to climb higher, with heavy pocket-flaps, toward the end of the period.

Coats are of plain materials, increasingly edged and trimmed with metal galloon braids. Waistcoats and the turn-back to match them, which may appear on the coat cuff, are apt to be of brocaded material. Breeches are of the coat material or of black velvet.

With petticoat-breeches, boots are ousted by shoes, and rosettes by stiff bows. In final quarter of century, shoes close higher around the foot; round tongues become squared and very high during the 70's, tending to turn over and show another color. Square-cut toes, very long and narrow in the 70's, tend to shorten and the heavy red heels of the 70's to become higher and less clumping, as shoes become more delicate in the 80's and ribbon ties are replaced by small oval buckles, which in turn become squarer and larger in the XVIIIc.

Riding boots now have their cuffs turned up over the knee; the leg lengthens and becomes tubular; the tops tend to become smaller and to be cut away in back, and the quatrefoil stirrup-leather is replaced by a smaller rectangular one. The narrow *jack boots* are often closed by lines of buckles and there are similar *spatter-dash* leggings worn over shoes for riding. Cloaks go out of use, except for actual protection, as coats come into use.

Low-crowned, flat-brimmed hats begin to appear in latter half of century, growing wider-brimmed and more cocked in its final quarter; in the 90's, they become definitely tricornes, with an edge of metal galloon and an interior fringe of ostrich around the brim, replacing plumes. Caps continue to be worn in the home, and there are new fur-brimmed *montero* forms worn in the house or for riding.

Early in second half of century, parted wigs began to replace natural hair and are in universal use before the last quarter. These periwigs, at first imitating natural hair, become increasingly artificial; in the 70's their curls are carefully arranged; in the 90's they rise above the forehead in one or two peaks. During the century's final quarter they are sometimes seen tied out of the way in back, in the XVIIIc. fashion. Hair on the face disappears in last quarter of the century, not to be seen again until XIXc.

With the petticoat-breech costumes, ribbons are much used; in the final quarter century they still appear in a knot carried on the right shoulder. Wide sashes and baldrics continue in use to the XVIIIc., the baldrics becoming more elaborate.

Men's fashions are increasingly elegant, mannered and artificial. There is a great deal of what, on the stage, would be called "business," with wrist-ruffles and pockets, as hands manipulate handkerchiefs, snuff boxes, tall beribboned canes; men wear muffs hung by a scarf about the neck, and gloves become softer and simpler, carried as often as worn.

Women's Dress, 1655-1715 (Louis XIV)

The analogies between male and female costume are much less evident during second half XVIIc., except in women's riding costume which is masculine in everything but its skirt.

While men are still wearing short doublets and petticoat breeches, women (although the little tabbed jackets lacing down the back still exist) reappear in long-waisted bodices with a prolonged point in front.

Corsets are elaborately gored, and finished in a fringe of unboned tabs below the waistline: these are worn under the waistband of the underskirt, while the long-boned points of the front are carried out over the band.

Over these is worn a gown composed of a bodice and skirt. The neckline of the bodice becomes wider, more horizontal and tends to slip off the shoulders. Collars become a band of lace around the shoulders; and this formal band tends to become loose, draped and caught, scarf-like. Under the insistently moral influence of Mme. de Maintenon, shoulders become covered again, in the 80's, and the neckline approximately square. During the period of the beribboned male petticoat-breech, a ladder of ribbon knots, graduated in size, decorates the center line of women's long unified bodices. The bodice of the 80's is divided by its decoration into jacket and underbodice; the decoration, a collar or ruching, follows the front edges around the neck until they converge at a much shortened point a little below the normal waistline, and the V-opening thus outlined is filled by embroidery or brocade.

The full sleeves of the third quarter-century are often set on in careful pleats like those which join skirt to bodice; sleeves lose their inseam slit, tend to become shorter, showing more shirt puffs; but, again under the influence of Mme. de Maintenon, they become of elbow length, funneling from the shoulder and sometimes finished with a cuff, above increasingly lacy shirt frills.

The skirt of the third quarter-century, carefully pleated onto the bodice, has its center line marked by decoration, or open to allow the skirt to be looped up at the hips. Skirts had begun to trail in Van Dyke's portraits of the 90's; now both outer and inner skirts have trains, and these lengthen. The underskirt gains in importance and in flounced, petticoat-like decoration from the 80's. The caught-up overdress, heavier and more upholstered in the last decades, requires the support of whalebone, metal or basket-work *paniers* at the hips.

Women's shoes, with pointed toes and high, delicately shaped heels, are tied or buckled over the instep; they are often of embroidered or brocaded fabric.

As manners become freer, the "undress" worn at home receives more attention; loose uncorseted gowns, short fur-edged jackets and lacy capes are invented to be worn while receiving in boudoirs.

Loose hair at the ears tends to become bunched in curls in the 60's: these hang on the shoulders in the 70's and are heavily decorated with ribbon knots. There has always been a tendency to cover the bun of hair in back with some sort of cap; as the bunched ribbons now outgrow the hair in importance, they are combined with lace and fastened to the front of a sheer cap to form the fontange headdress of the 90's; the pleated height of this headdress increases so that it falls forward, in its late forms, to 1700. In e.XVIIIc., the cap, having lost its fontange front, becomes much smaller and concentrates on the ribbon lappets in back. Hair arrangement, at first wide, becomes higher and narrower as the fontange mounts, and like the periwig, is dressed in two horns in the 90's. In e.XVIIIc., hair arrangements are close and simple, and begin to be powdered.

Lacy hoods are worn in domestic undress, and hoods with shoulder-cape effects cover the elaborate fontange arrangements out-of-doors. Scarves, and shaped shoulder capes with long stole ends, are worn with the gowns of the last decades. Muffs continue in use. Aprons increase in importance and are worn through XVIIIc.; they may be white and lacy, but are often of colored silk or brocade, embroidered and trimmed with metal lace. Soft gloves of kid or silk in light colors become longer; mitts appear. Parasols are now common. Paint, patches, and perfume are used by both sexes. Elaborate jewels are largely supplanted by pearl chokers and eardrops; then, in French court use in the 90's, men's coats blaze with diamond buttons, and women's gowns are studded with immense diamonds.

The exquisitely put-together satin dresses of the third quarter-century are usually in pale colors: white, through ivory, to canary yellows. They are trimmed with white, gold, and a great deal of coral, in beads, gloves, and touches worked into gold bandings. These light colors were supplanted by darker, with the metal and fringe-trimmed, heavily upholstered brocade gowns of Mme. de Maintenon's time, which were, in turn, supplanted by light, pretty colors in XVIIIc.

The very large collections of Louis XIV costume plates in the Morgan Library and in the Museum of Fine Arts of Boston, include examples in which (thanks to an amusement of the Regency), the paper which represents fabric has been cut away, and the print backed by bits of contemporary brocades, of which we thus have many valuable samples.

1383. Second half XVIIc. French. (Paris, Carnavalet Mus.)

Fishermen's and Laundrywomen's Boats, Quai de la Mégisserie.

The Quai de la Mégisserie, built in 1369, got its name from the *mégisseurs* (lamb skin tanners) who then worked near-by. It is on the l. bank, above the Pont Notre Dame, with which Henry IV had bridged both branches of the river, across the upper end of the Ile de la Cité. In XVIIIc., water was still a commodity sold in the streets by 20,000 vendors, like the man we see, who will dip his buckets repeatedly in the river and dispose of 30-40 pails a day. (Saint-Evremond). Laundry was given out to be washed in the Seine and carried up the river to be dried on the Ile Notre-Dame, where it can be seen in Ill. 1297: the League procession. The sign on the fishermen's boat offers fat carp for 5 sols.

1384. Latter half XVIIc. French. (Paris, Carnavalet Mus.)

Fish sellers at the Halles.

The public markets had been removed from the Port de Grève, c.1135, to an open space; this became known as the Halles (halls) from 2 long sheds which were provided within a walled enclosure; and the fairs of St-Lazare and St-Germain were moved there by XIIIc. It had to be rebuilt in XIVc., when it changed from a market in which certain commodities were sold on given days, to the permanent market for all foodstuffs, which it still is.

1383

1384

1385

In order to emphasize the importance of Versailles, Louis XIV visited Paris as infrequently as three times a year. Monsieur, his brother, illiterate and friendly, loved the Foire Saint-Germain and was adored by the common people, particularly the fish-wives of the Halles. He used the Opera as an excuse to visit his town house, the Palais Royal; actually, he was mad about ringing church bells. After Monsieur's recovery from an apoplexy, Saint-Simon tells us, "the fish-fags of the Halles thought it would be proper to exhibit their affection, and deputed four stout gossips to wait upon him (at Versailles). They were admitted. One of them took him about the neck and kissed him on both cheeks; the others kissed his hand. They were all very well received. Bontemps (first valet of the king) showed them over the apartments, and treated them to a dinner. Monseigneur gave them some money, and the king did also. They determined not to remain in debt, and had a fine Te Deum sung at St.-Eustache, and then feasted."

At the christening festivities of Louis XVI's first child, the boxes of the king and queen, traditionally assigned to the charcoal vendors and the fish women of the Halles, were found to be filled already; the in-dignant worthies were mollified by being seated on the stage with the rulers to watch the French comedians in *Zaire* and *Le Florentin*. (Mme. Campan.)

These traditions lasted as long as the monarchy. At the birth of the Dauphin, Marie Antoinette received a delegation of *dames de Halles,* though these were not fish-wives, in black silk gowns (the established full dress of their order) and diamonds, one of whom read off from the inside of her fan a speech written by La Harpe; they were dined, as in Louis XIV's day, with the maitre d'hotel presiding, wearing the king's hat. (Campan).

1385. Latter half XVIIc. French. (Paris, Carnavalet Mus.)

Farces in the streets of Paris, rue Saint-Antoine.

The rue Saint-Antoine was formed from the latter part of the Roman road leading S.E. out of Paris. This went from the Ile, by the Notre-Dame bridge and the market-port of the Grève, turned through the marshlands of the frequently inundated r. bank, to the higher land about Saint-Gervais, and out the great gate guarded by the XIVc. Bastille, the fortress from which the Grande Mademoiselle had fired the cannon which saved Condé's army in the rebellion of the Fronde, and in which the Man in the Iron Mask died in 1703.

Parisians have always loved to walk, observe and listen. As long as man can recall, they have lived and amused themselves on their streets, as in no other city; whether to saunter, to bargain, to dance, to watch fire-works, a balloon ascension, a public execution in the Place de Grève, or to follow a flogging at the tail of a cart, which would end at the pillory in the Halles.

The rue Saint-Antoine was the longest and widest dry and open space within the fortifications; it was therefore the favorite gathering place for crowds at tournaments, carnivals and masquerades. Saint-Gervais, the earliest part of the r. bank to be inhabited, had been settled in XIIc. by weavers, dyers, tanners and an overflow of Jews from the ghetto on the Ile; it has always had a working class and commercial population.

But the Knights Templar had settled there, and it had always had a connection also with the aristocratic heart of Paris, from which the road started, as well as with the port on which its industry depended. The old palace on the Ile had been outgrown as a royal residence in Charles V's time. Three kings had already lived in the XIVc. hôtel des Tournelles; but when Henry II was killed, in one of the tournaments which were held in the near-by rue Saint-Antoine during XV-XVIc., Catherine de' Medici ordered the Tournelles demolished. The site of the hôtel and its gardens became the Place Royale. (P. des Vosges.) The turbulence of the university students led many aristocrats to move there from the Ile. As the chateaux of the Loire were built, many moved away, but during XVIIc. the promenade of elegant carriages at carnival time was called the "cours Saint-Antoine." In XVIIIc. the bourgeoisie still gathered there to see the young people off on the 9-10 mile trip to the Bezons fair. (For dress description, see Ill. 1387.)

Pictorial Fans: XVII Century

During second half XVIIc., fans painted with street scenes became fashionable. We reproduce 5 of 6 in the Carnavalet. Others, in the collection of Louis Serbat, are to be found in D'Allemagne (see Appendix). They show people in flight from a thunder storm at the chateau of Marly-le-Roi; the flower market on the quai near the Pont Neuf; and the bath-boats on the Seine, with the Louvre on the right.

The superiority of the standards of city life in mediaeval times, over those of the next three centuries, is not always realized. There was far more bathing in the Middle Ages than during XVIIc. Particularly in the German cities, there had been public bath houses since XIIIc.; these increased in number during XIVc., to 15 in Frankfort-on-Main, and 29 in Vienna, for instance. Coryat, in e.XVIIc., saw 13 inns in Lower Baden, with 300 hot baths, some of which had been in use since before the birth of Christ. The houses of the German bourgeoisie had bath rooms. In France, barber shops kept several tubs in the back room, and provided hot water, at least for male bathers.

Surgery became divorced from medicine in XIIc., when its practice was forbidden to the medical clergy. It was taken over by barbers, who also pulled teeth. The foundations of modern surgery and dentistry were the XVIIIc. schools of anatomy of the Drs. Hunter, who "helped to make" English surgeons "gentlemen," though Prussian officers of the XIXc. still expected to be shaved by the regimental surgeon.

Stow says soap was not made in London till about 1518, but there was imported Castile soap, or a "grey soap, speckled with white, very sweet and good, from Bristol, sold here for a penny the pound . . . and black soap for a halfpenny."

The mingling of sexes and ages at the public baths led to abuses, and they came to have a bad reputation, being attacked by both Protestants and Catholics during the religious fervors of XVIIc. As populations increased, supplies both of water and of the wood for heating it, became inadequate; syphilis was new and virulent; there were epidemics of plague and smallpox. Horror of the public baths became attached to the very act of bathing, and people lived in actual fear of water.

In third quarter XVII., tubs the size of a foot-bath began to be set in the small *entresols,* which made convenient dressing rooms. By second quarter XVIIIc., complete bath rooms began to be installed in chateaux, with tubs large enough for actual bathing, and comfortable arm-chairs with movable seats were set over chamber-pots. Water closets were a fascinating novelty to the provincial gentry, when the Cardinal-Archbishop de La Rochefoucauld, on a rare visit to his palace, had them installed at the end of a corridor.

Public hot baths began to be re-established in England in last quarter XVIIIc. (in England called *bagnios,* a word which, like the older word for hot baths, *stews,* came again to have disreputable connotations). But there had always been floating baths, wherever there were rivers, such as the curtained boats on the Seine (shown on a Serbat fan), or the baths established at the Porte Saint-Bernard.

1386. XVIIc. 1660. French. (Paris, Carnavalet Mus.)

Poultry and bread markets, Quai des Grands-Augustins.

The oldest of the Paris Quais was that of the Augustins, the "road on the Seine" of 1313.

1387. XVIIc. 1680. French. (Paris, Carnavalet Mus.)

Playing-card factory in a house on the Place Dauphine.

The Seine banks were constantly being restricted and raised, and the small islands consolidated. When the Pont Neuf was being thrown across the upper end of the Ile de la Cité, 2 small islands above it were filled in and incorporated with the Cité. In honor of the future Louis XIII, the new space was called the Place Dauphine; it is still lined with houses built in his time. The Ile Louviers, below the Ile Saint-Louis, was made part of the right bank in XIXc.

By 1698, the Place Dauphine teemed with itinerant quack doctors and dentists, and the pedlars and street musicians drawn by their customers.

In the factory, we see cards being glued and pressed, stencilled, dried, cut, packaged and sold. Through its open windows are the statue of Henry

IV and the Pont Neuf; the Louvre on the right; the College Mazarin (now the Institut) on the left, occupying a site for which the Tour de Nesles was demolished.

The costume of midXVIIc., as shown in Ills. 1383-87, was good-looking and practical; the working people shown on these fans wear it with little alteration from the time of the Cries of Paris (Ills. 1372-75) through the century, at the end of which the fontange headdress appears on women, as on court ladies. The women, working out of doors, have always liked covered heads, and find the loose hoods pretty and useful, though many still wear a kerchief; they have worn aprons and tucked up their skirts, long before these usages became fashionable. Male hair lengthens; becomes wig-like; and, as wigs come into universal use (even by monks and priests, with a false tonsure), the coarse goat or horsehair wigs of working men may even be powdered, as we see in the playing-card factory. Hat brims widen and become cocked; coats lengthen and become narrower; and cravats with ribbon bows beneath are worn by the workmen as well as by the elegant customer buying a pack of cards.

7   6   5   M A C L

1388. XVIIc. 1660. French. (Versailles, Nat. Mus.)
Designed by *C. Le Brun*. Gobelins Tapestry.

History of the King: Interview of Louis XIV and Philip IV of Spain at the Isle of Pheasants.

In 1660, despite Louis XIV's infatuation with Maria Mancini, niece of the cardinal, Anne of Austria was able to bring about her dream of the marriage of her son to the only daughter of her brother.

Philip IV, his court, and an immense procession escorted Maria Theresa to the frontier, where they were met by the French court on an island in the Bidassoa. The Spanish ladies travelled in 18 horse-drawn litters, the courtiers in 70 state carriages; there were 70 magnificently trapped horses, 900 saddle mules and 2000 other mules, 75 of which carried Spanish fabrics and luxury items belonging to the Infanta.

The dramatic contrast between the frizzed French courtiers in their lace cravats and gay, beribboned costumes and the dank-locked, somberly dressed Spaniards, brought to a sudden end the parochial development of Spanish costume; henceforward Spanish dress, like that of the rest of the world, will be basically French.

Wigs had been in use at the French court for 40 years. Louis XIII was bald, and adopted a wig after the Abbé de la Rivière appeared at court in a long blond one in 1620. A decade after his wedding, Louis XIV starts to go bald in his turn, and finally takes to the wigs he dislikes. Many of the courtiers wear unmistakable wigs, with their beribboned rhinegraves, so brilliant and unexpected in color that they may well be itemized; c. to l.:

Louis XIV: gold costume, banded in darker gold; cascades of cherry-colored ribbons; white shirt and cannons; flesh stockings; yellow shoes with high tongues, wide stiff pleated bows, soles and high heels of red; brown hat, cherry plumes.

Cardinal: red.

Anne of Austria: green gown, gold lace at shoulders; white above caught with green rosette.

Monsieur (Louis' brother Philip, duke of Orleans): gold cape; yellow costume; cherry ribbons; pink stockings; yellow shoes with red ribbons; hat and plumes of shaded pink.

5: Gold cape; light blue costume, banded in red-selvaged gold, and laced with blue-green ribbon; white shirt, gold lace wrist-ruffles; pink stockings; brown shoes and bows, red heels; hat of neutral felt with blue cock feathers.

6: White wig; blue coat laced with red-striped gold, short-sleeved, with gold cuffs and gold lace ruffles beneath; cherry-colored shoulder knots and other ribbons; red petticoat over white petticoat breeches; yellow stockings and shoes with blue pleated bows.

7: Dark greenish-gold cape and rhinegraves; brown ribbons; blue stockings; dark green shoes and bows.

On the Spanish side of the tapestry, Philip IV, blond and wigless, is dressed in gold-laced blue-gray, lined with deeper blue; wrist ribbons and stockings to match; heelless pink shoe with a cork lift and a tiny bow, such as is worn by all his courtiers. These are all cloaked, with the green cross of Alcántara or the red of Santiago, and wear natural hair, golillas or the old ruff; close doublets; narrow breeches gartered with small knots; some with wrinkled stockings and square-collared capes of Flanders.

The bride wears a quilted white or silver gown and coiffure familiar in so many Velasquez portraits.

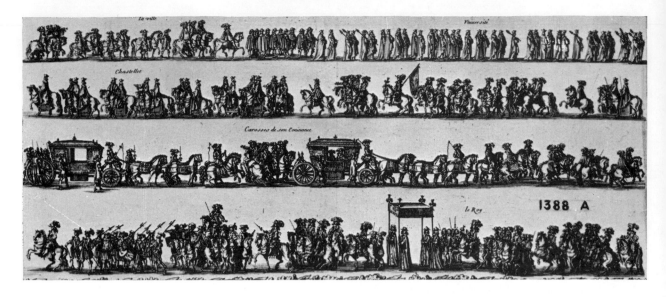

FRENCH ENGRAVERS: XVII CENTURY

As the fashions in portraits change, showing little more than hair and collars, a new source of information fortunately appears. Prints of views of gardens, fêtes, and architecture become extremely popular everywhere. They show in detail not only the costume but the means of transportation and the entire outdoor life of the various quarters. They often celebrate new buildings or important events; such things as the disappearance of former landmarks all help in dating the costumes of the small figures which fill the foreground. The name of the engraver, of the publisher, and the address from which they were sold may also be useful in dating costume.

However, there were whole dynasties of interrelated engravers, like the Perelles: Gabriel (1603?-77); Nicolas (1631-aft. 1678) and Adam (1640-95), and publisher-engravers like the Mariettes (four generations, among them Jean (1654/60-1742) and Pierre Jean (1694-1774), one of whom married the widow of the publisher Langlois, after his death in 1647, and continued business under Langlois' name at the same address. Luckily, the attendant text is often helpful.

1388A-1388B. XVIIc. c. 1660. French.

Jean Marot. Triumphal Entry of Their Majesties, Louis XIV and Marie-Thérèse.

Through XVIc., ladies and ecclesiastics might travel in carriages, but gentlemen rode on horseback; when too ill to ride, they stayed at home rather than be conveyed.

During the reign of Louis XIV, however, carriages began to be more comfortably suspended on straps, and in late XVIIc. on steel springs; male prejudice against them began to vanish. Public carriages grew rapidly in favor. London had them from 1625, and the 50 permitted in 1635 had grown to 700 by 1694, despite the competition of sedan-chairs. The French

"fiacre" got its name from the Sign of St. Fiacre, where carriages were first to be hired in midXVIIc. Paris. In last half XVIIc. stage-coaches began to make regular runs. By XVIIIc. carriages were becoming a luxurious necessity, and so personal, that one's empty carriage with its coach- and foot-men could be sent to funerals as a mark of esteem,

But into XIXc. some gentlemen always preferred to ride, as Louis does on his entry into Paris after his wedding.

1389. XVIIc. 1664. French.

Israel Silvestre. Les Plaisirs de l'Ile Enchantée, Versailles: entry of Louis XIV as Roger.

1390. XVIIc. 1670. French.

"Festival ad capita annulumque de cursio a rege Ludivico XIV:" armiger, Ephoebus, Americani.

Louis XIV and Versailles

Under Louis XIV, the woods in which his father loved to hunt were transformed by Mansart and the landscape architect Lenôtre into the great palace and gardens of Versailles, which became the official court in 1682.

$100,000,000 were spent on buildings, landscaping and water supply. The water-works were inspired by Fouquet's chateau at Vaux; but Versailles was so poor in water that new water works were built at Marly to collect water from as far away as Rambouillet (30 mi. from Paris) by 98 miles of aqueduct; even then, all 1400 fountains could be played only for the greatest fêtes. Fouquet was the minister under whom (as Colbert proved to Louis) only half the tax revenue reached the Crown. In the king's honor, in August 1661, Fouquet gave at his magnificent Chateau of Vaux one of the greatest entertainments in the history of France, at which Molière's *Les Facheux* was performed for the first time, and the banquet was supervised by the chef, Vatel. Three weeks later, Fouquet was in prison for life, Lenôtre was Louis' gardener, and Versailles was to come.

The Grand Canal, on which gondolas floated and fire-works were reflected, was a mile long and 200 feet wide; smaller basins had fountains with 50-70 foot jets. Along the canal ran the *Tapis Vert,* the endless lawn with its avenues of trees, off which were groves of clipped yew.

Versailles was not the wanton extravagance into which it deteriorated with Louis XV, but the perfectly executed expression of a profound philosophy. With the aid of Versailles, Louis detached his court from Paris and his nobility from their feudal, provincial roots. Here, each had his station below the princes of the blood (as they were below the king) but above someone else; constant effort was necessary to maintain and improve this position. Punctual daily attendance on the king was required, service in

his regiments, magnificent clothing and entertainment, gambling for high stakes. All this drained the resources of the nobles, who were then dependant on the king for preference, perquisites, pensions, advantageous marriages, and the advancement of their children. Almost total support of the largely tax-exempt feudal nobles was assumed by the king. Tax burdens of unimaginable weight and complication, in addition to their feudal dues, were laid on the common people. Much of France, owned by 25,000 noble families, mortgaged and bled by its absentee owners, returned to wilderness. For lack of seed and equipment, tenant farmers who looked more like lumps of dung than human beings, starved on buckwheat (or even hay) and water; any amelioration in their condition brought on fresh tax impositions. Even farmers who owned land abandoned it to beg in towns, or to emigrate, if they were not first caught and sent to the galleys. Hordes of state functionaries

took over the duties formerly performed by the feudal nobility, leaving them no occupation but daily hunting. Their exclusive hunting rights, originally ceded in return for their responsibility for the protection of their people from marauding animals, became fantastically distorted. Now, it is the animals who are protected and must be allowed to destroy crops, even kitchen gardens, without providing a mouthful of meat to the starving farmers.

Louis' policies gave France an efficient, centralized government, a uniformed and disciplined army, high standards of manners and elegance, and immense prestige abroad. The good and evil that grew out of these policies in the century which culminated in the Revolution are classically portrayed in Taine's "Ancien Régime," 1876.

"Who is he? He is a man that I never see," was a sentence which struck terror, as Louis intended. "The nobility has become another people with no choice left it but to crouch down in mortal ruinous indolence, which renders it a charge and contemptible, to go and be killed in warfare subject to the insults of clerks, secretaries of the state and the secretaries of intendants," said Saint-Simon.

To ameliorate the monotony of the rigidly disciplined court existence, Louis provided periodic shifts to other chauteaux, like Saint-Germain, and Marly (where one went only by invitation, and where etiquette was somewhat relaxed). There was much hunting, and all sorts of special entertainments in a court of which the manners and beauty were the wonder of the world. Since Marly was destroyed during the Revolution, Mme. Campan took pains to leave a description of its architecture, life and dress. Marly degenerated into an almost public gambling place. His hospitality, abused by all sorts of uninvited daily visitors, became an immense drain on the private purse of Louis XVI, who detested gambling. Marie Antoinette preferred the Trianon, and Marly was little used in last half decade of the reign.

Before Versailles was habitable, great fêtes began to be given there, in the finished portions of its gardens. One of the first was that of 1664, officially in honor of the king's mother and wife, but actually for the duchess of La Vallière, which was staged by Molière with music by Lully. In other pageants, the princes played Turkish and Persian potentates. In the 1670 illustration, we see the court version of another exotic, the American Indian (see Ills. 1389-90).

1391. XVIIc. French. (Met. Mus., Print Room.)

J. Bérain (1639-1711), engraved by Ia. le Pautre

(1618-82). *Ornaments inventez par J. Bérain.*

This strange procession of fanciful costumes "invented" by Bérain shows dress suitable for court masquerades. We learn from the "Mercure" which describes the costume worn at court events, of Berain's difficulties in producing at short notice the 8-10 different disguises into which the Dauphin changed during one masquerade in 1683.

These clothes show a mixture of styles, some of which date from late XVIc. Odd slashings and puffings occur, with breeches of all sorts: loose, close-fitting and petticoat forms. The current long coat appears with others whose divided and diagonally finished skirts stem from those like Sir Philip Sidneys in Oliver's XVIc. miniature (see Ill. 1200). There are fan collars from e.XVIIc., falling ruffs, band collars wide on the shoulders, and collars never seen on any man before. The women's gowns have the tasseled, upholstered look of Louis XIV dresses.

1392. Third quarter XVIIc. French. (Florence, Uffizi.) *Pierre Mignard.* La Marquise de Sévigné. For details of dress, see Ill. 1393.

Mme. de Sevigne and Her Times

The 1700 enchanting letters of Marie de Rabutin-Chantal, Marquise de Sévigné (1626-96), and the scandalous and witty *Histoire amoureuse des Gaulles,* of her cousin, Bussy-Rabutin, are among the greatest sources of information about French upper-class existence in latter half XVIIc.

The most accomplished letter-writer who ever lived (granddaughter of "Sainte" Chantal, the friend of St. Francis de Sales), the marquise was orphaned at 7. Fortunately, her guardian, an abbé-uncle, whom she called "Le Bien Bon," not only was an excellent business man who increased her fortune, but brought her up in a circle of important literary men. She was married at 18 to a Breton nobleman of no great fortune, whom she loved, and by whom she had two children; he spent her money, had many mistresses, but she never remarried after his death in a duel over one of them, "La Belle Lolo," when she was 25.

The marquise was affectionate towards her son, but doted almost insanely on her daughter, to whom she wrote daily letters whenever they were apart. The daughter married an elderly man who was for many years governor of Provence.

Madame de Sévigné's life was passed in the country at her husband's ancestral chateau, Les Rochers; after his death, much of her time was spent in the circle of the Hôtel de Rambouillet, and later in her own Hôtel Carnavalet, as the friend of Descartes, Pascal, La Rochefoucauld, Corneille, Saint-Evremond and of Mme. de La Fayette, whose *Princesse de Clèves* was the first great French novel.

Madame de Rambouillet, finding the life at court vulgar and dull, had begun, at 19, to gather around her the greatest literary men of Paris, mixed with the best of the aristocracy. She remodelled her hôtel for the purpose of holding great receptions, providing many smaller rooms for conversation, which she made the great art of the middle XVIIc. It was in satirizing her many and lesser imitators that Molière wrote his *Précieuses ridicules.*

Mme. de Sévigné, in those newspaperless days, recounts with the greatest gaiety, gusto, wit and detail, the occurrences, trivial or important, amongst servants, country neighbors, gossiping and intriguing courtiers, or the greatest philosophers; whether her transplanted Paris footman rebels at helping to get in the hay in the country; or Condé's chef, the great Vatel, commits suicide when the fish is late for dinner on Louis XIV's visit to Chantilly.

These were the days of great gardeners (like the English Tradescant) and chefs who were people of importance in their own right. Sauces were named after chefs, like Béchamel; dishes after great lords, who often collaborated in their invention: Soubise, or even the Earl of Sandwich, too busy as Lord of the Admiralty to eat more than meat between bread. With the Revolution, the gardens built for the aristocracy will become public parks, and the chefs whose masters have been guillotined, will work in inns or open restaurants, where any citizen with the price can and does, for the first time, eat like a lord.

Mauy important new usages date from Mme. de Sévigné's exact period. She was the first person to make coffee her beverage, although she underestimated its possibilities, since she indicated her preference for Corneille by saying, "Racine will pass, like coffee." The dramatic struggle of the forbidden painted India cotton fabrics was reinforced by her adoption of them.

In 1668, she bought her son Charles a commission in the Dauphin's Gendarmes, when service in Louis XIV's new companies of guards became an expensive fashion which it cost even more in royal favor to avoid.

Charles de Sévigné, like his father before him, and better men such as La Rochefoucauld and Saint-Evremond, had been the lover of the ageless and wonderful Ninon de l'Enclos, leader of fashion in her day, friend of Voltaire, Mme. de Maintenon and Mme. de La Fayette. After leaving the army, Charles and his childless wife became extremely religious, and both died cloistered. Mme. de Sévigné, the daughter who would not go to her mother for fear of infection, and the daughter's heir, all died of smallpox within a few years of each other.

1393. Third quarter XVIIc. French. (Metropolitan Mus.)
Unknown artist. Hortense Mancini, Duchess of Mazarin.

The gown of third quarter XVIIc. (seen in Ills. 1392-93) is still frequently of satin, but brocade is also used, and brocade-like designs sometimes scroll the bodice, which is simple in cut and smooth. The pleating which connects the skirts to the bodice is turning into gathers.

A deliberate negligence affects the neckline and sleeves. The bodice, cut to expose the shoulders and breasts, is finished with an informally gathered lace frill, or may expose that at the top of the chemise. The ropes of pearls or the scarves which edge it are caught with increasing asymmetry, and frequently trail from one side. Sleeves lose their formal cuff and set pleating at the armseye; they are loose, turned-back, pushed-up, or caught by small brooches above an increasing display of puffed and ruffled chemise sleeve.

Hair widens at the ears and is eventually held out by wiring; a love-lock hangs on the shoulder. Ropes of pearls are negligently wound through the hair, which is generally uncovered. In France as plumes abound on courtiers' hats, headdresses of ostrich tips are seen on great ladies.

The Mancinis

Cardinal Mazarin had 5 beautiful nieces and a nephew, the Duke de Nevers. Laura, the eldest (1636-57), married Henry IV's grandson César, Duke of Vendôme, who became a priest in despair at her premature death. Olympe became the countess de Soissons. Marie, with whom Louis XIV had been so much in love, married the jealous Prince Colonna.

Hortense, the loveliest of all, was proposed by Henrietta Maria as a wife for Charles II, because of her dowry of 4 million livres. Both Mazarin and Charles refused the match, which the king found beneath his dignity. In 1661, at 15, she was married to a duke who inherited Mazarin's fortune, after assuming his arms and name. He, too, was frantically jealous and travelled constantly

with his wife to keep her away from king and court. Leaving him, she continued to wander over Europe, travelling with her brother, with the Chevalier de Rohan, or with her sister Marie, in whose company she was arrested in Aix-en-Provence, both women dressed as men. Finally, she settled in England, where Charles wished to make her his official mistress, but she accepted a less royal lover.

For all her love of hunting, racing, cock-fights and gambling, Hortense Mancini was also the intelligent and witty friend of eminent philosophers. "Mme. de Mazarin is no sooner arrived in any place, when she sets up a house, and all the other houses are forsaken for hers. One finds there the greatest possible freedom; one lives there with like discretion" (Saint-Evremond). "She had, after all, balance and economy even in wasting her qualities and her gifts. . . . She lived and died a great lady" (Sainte-Beuve: *Causeries du lundi,* Oct. 28, 1849). French literature abounds in references to her, with "the longest, the finest, and the thickest hair in the world," attended by her little Negro page, Pompée, the thieving, drunken little rascal, pampered and torn by jealousy, who tried to keep everyone else away from her.

Hortense's fascination for Evelyn is visible through every disapproving entry in his diary, from his first dinner in the company of "the famous beauty and errant lady," at the Lord Chamberlain's in 1676, to her death in 1699.

Her youngest sister was Marie-Anne, the pet of the court of France, who married Turenne's nephew, the Duke de Bouillon. Her husband, too, had cause for jealousy, and she, too, travelled in Italy with her brother and visited her sister in England. Like Hortense, she was extremely intelligent and aided and encouraged literary men, notably La Fontaine.

Development of Military Uniforms

Kings and great feudal nobles had always been surrounded by bodyguards composed of gentlemen. During the XVc., these will be seen, increasingly, wearing the badges and colors of their lords. Stow says that William Paulet, Henry VIII's treasurer, who died Marquis of Winchester in 1572 (at the age of 100), "kept gentlemen and yeomen in a livery of Reading tawney"; and Thomas, Lord Cromwell, "a greater number in a livery of grey marble; the gentlemen garded with velvet, the yeomen with the same cloth, yet their skirts large enough for their friends to sit upon them." "The late (16th) Earl of Oxford . . . within these 40 years . . . hath . . . ridden into this city, and to his house by London Stone, with 80 gentlemen in a livery of Reading tawny, and chains of gold about their necks, before him, and 100 tall yeomen in the like livery, to follow him

without chains, but all having his cognizance of the blue boar embroidered on their left shoulder." By 1633, Evelyn's father, on becoming sheriff of Sussex and Surrey, will have his 116 servants and numerous gentlemen "every one liveried in the same garb" with green satin doublets, although this is a striking novelty, at that level.

The organization and subdivision of these bodyguards of the nobility began in XVc. Louis XI had married Mary of Scotland; Scottish archers, aiding France during the 100 Years War, were added to 2 companies of the *gardes du corps.* In England, Henry VII was establishing the Yeomen of the Guard about his person. In XVIc., Francis I increased his permanent guard to 8,000 and Henry VIII added the Gentlemen Pensioners (see Ill. 1467).

As the power of kings over feudal nobles increases, we see display, paid for by feudal lords, exploited for crown benefit. Matthias of Hungary's wedding invitation includes a "little pattern of a man" to be followed by the guests in outfitting their retainers, to give an impressive uniformity to the emperor's procession.

While Louis XIV sucks all France into Versailles and makes an army career almost a requirement for a young gentleman, troops are outfitted at the expense of their officers. In last quarter XVIIc., taxes begin to be levied to outfit and keep permanent standing armies at the expense of the population.

Coryat describes the various guards of the French king in 1609: 1600 foot-guards with musket, arquebus and pike, 200 of which are stationed at a time before the Louvre; 50 archers at the gate; a bodyguard of 400 archers and arquebusiers, of whom 100 are Scotch; 500 Swiss outside the gate and 100 with halberds and swords inside the hall. The archers of the bodyguard wore long-skirted, half-sleeved coats of white with skirts of mingled red and green, their bodies protected, fore and aft, by plain silver mail. The Swiss wore no coats, but paned doublets of red, yellow and blue, with puffs of yellow sarcenet between the panes, and colored cod-pieces.

The Scottish archers of the French crown were augmented in the 1630's by the *régiment d' Hébron,* raised by the Scotch Catholic soldier of fortune, Sir John Hepburn. Commanded by Ormond and other members of the Douglas family, these Scotch soldiers were returned to the British service in 1669, becoming the Royal Scots Fusiliers. Until disbanded in 1791, the Scotch guard in France was recruited, as far as possible, from Frenchmen of Scotch descent.

Aside from the *Suisses* in their traditional costume, Louis XIV's military establishment was dressed in the red, blue and white Bourbon colors: bodyguards in silver-laced blue coats, red breeches and black boots; blue companies of cavalry; red companies of light horse and gendarmes; mounted grenadiers; and the black and gray musketeers, who were named not from the colors of their uniforms but of their mounts. Officers, who had heretofore dressed pretty much after their own taste, began to wear scarlet uniforms with gold trim and silver scarves; color-bearers white; non-commissioned officers blue; soldiers gray trimmed with silver, with ribbon knots (differing in color by companies) on the shoulder—a usage out of which epaulettes developed. Hunting costume came under the influence of uniformity. Those who hunted the wolf with the Dauphin wore bright bright blue coats, laced with gold and silver, red waistcoats, blue breeches, boots, gold-fringed gloves and white-plumed hats.

Power had been consolidated in France while England was still recovering from civil war. The French army, both in the establishing of new units and forms and in their costuming, leads Europe by several years.

Red and blue, as common and fast colors, were most used in English uniforms. Anthony Wood noted quarrels between meanly dressed companies of russet and of blue-clad foot-soldiers at Oxford, October 2, 1642, and a reissue of smarter clothing in the next year.

The huge parliamentary army, though disbanded, was a constant worry to the restored Stuarts. They increased the number of troops they supported from 5,000 to 30,000, adding new regiments and categories of soldiers: Monk's Life Guards in scarlet tunics, blue collars and "bearskins," (later the Coldstream Guards); His Majesty's and the Duke of York's Guards, in red and blue respectively; the Queen's Own troop of cavalry; the Old Buffs (named from the buffalo leather of their accoutrements); the Scotch Fusiliers; the dragoons in "red coats and clokes" who, while in training at Oxford for service against the French, shot Dalby the tailor's wife through her privy door (Wood, January, 1679); and the "new sort of soldiers" described by Evelyn (June 29, 1678), destined to oppose those formed two years earlier in France, "called *Grenadiers,* who were dexterous in flinging hand grenades, everyone having a pouch full; they had furred caps with coped crowns like Janizaries, which made them look very fierce, and some had long hoods hanging down behind, as we picture fools. Their clothing being likewise piebald, yellow, and red."

Hitherto troops have lived off the land, been billeted on the populace, dressed by their officers, disciplined by and responsible to no one by law. The proliferation of these unsanctioned troops under James II caused Parliament, in 1688, to take over the control and support of the large army which was required overseas, and to formulate its discipline. Outside of this new militia, only the Yeomen of the Guard and the Gentlemen Pensioners remained as the king's bodyguard, unaffected by the new martial laws and Mutiny Act, which formed one of the basic changes in the British constitution.

DEVELOPMENT OF TEXTILE INDUSTRY IN FRANCE

Louis XIV's devoted minister, Colbert, envied the industrial development of England and Holland, and took the most energetic measures to encourage and improve French manufactures. Colbert listed the imported goods which could be made in France, encouraged foreign factories to move to France, and forbade French workmen to leave the country. About 100 establishments, including the Gobelins tapestry factory, were opened under the patronage of the crown. He set up rigid standards of quality, and punishments for failure to meet them. Duties on such goods as lace, fine materials, and knit stockings were doubled and tripled; eventually the import of Venetian lace and other goods which interfered (by being better) with the consumption of French manufactures, was completely prohibited. This enmeshed France in a governmental bureaucracy from which it has never escaped, but it did succeed in establishing France as a pre-eminent producer of textiles and of fine laces: needlepoints such as Point de France, d'Alençon, Argentan, Sedan, and pillow laces like Valenciennes.

Colbert also re-established in 1664 the *Compagnie des Indes,* which Richelieu had formed in 1642. It traded out of Pondicherry on the Coromandel coast, in amity with the nearby English, but hopelessly hampered by Colbert's endless regulations.

Its principal return cargoes were of India cottons, intended primarily for hangings and upholstery. These were a revelation to all Europe: so crisp and cool, easily cleaned, enchantingly pounced and painted, and in the early days so very cheap. Everyone fell in love with them, from their first appearance at the Foire Saint-Germain in 1658. The poor, in the hot port towns in the south of France where the *toiles* entered, wore nothing else. The aristocrats with a taste for the exotic (aped by Molière's *Bourgeois Gentilhomme* in 1670) had *Indiennes* made up into dressing gowns. Mme. de Sévigné brought some to her daughter from Marseilles in 1672. By the final quarter of the century they were universally worn by the bourgeoisie.

To protect the weaving industries, the importation or imitation of *toiles* was forbidden in 1681. They went temporarily out of fashion, as we learn from a poem in an almanac of 1861, in which a girl who has "retailed prints to small and great" laments that she must quickly find a place in the service of "the ladies created by her *toiles.*"

In 1685, however, the arrival of a shipload of India cottons ruined the woolen goods market, and sent the weavers out on strike. Except during 1695-8, when their import was allowed, by way of bolstering up the shaky *Compagnie des Indes,* the next seventy-five years provided 24 further prohibitions, with increasingly severe penalties of fines, jail sentences and confiscation. In 1736, in addition to the loss of the garment, there was a fine of 3,000 livres for wearing on the street a dress, coat, skirt, petticoat or apron of India fabric. The danger of losing their only dresses made it necessary for the townswomen of Southern France to do their marketing dressed in their husbands' clothes; people were even arrested for being seen through a window wearing *toiles.* As many convictions as possible had been urged by Colbert, for all crimes, or vagrancy, or merely for being a poor alien, in order to man the growing fleet of French ships with galley slaves.

Imitations of India fabrics had begun to be printed in France before 1685, and were as bitterly opposed by the weavers. With remarkable lack of vision, this new industrial possibility was suppressed. Reserve printing, alone, was allowed, since its technique offered a chance to quibble over the definition of printing. These prohibitions, together with the revocation of the Edict of Nantes, drove many of the best printers to England, Switzerland, Alsace and Holland, where cotton printing of superb quality soon flourished with a head start over what was finally to become one of the great industries of France.

Louis XV's court preferred *toile* to silk, and *toiles* remained for years the principal bootlegged, black-market commodity of France. The demand for them was too great to be controlled by the weavers; and the dishonesties of the system were so flagrant that in 1759 their manufacture was finally made legal. A government official, privy to the proposed change, set up the German brothers Oberkampf in a factory at Jouy, which was to become the greatest of all textile printing factories in late XVIII-e.XIXc. (See Appendix.)

French Fashion Plates, XVII Century

The fashion magazines of the XVIIIc. were preceded by series of single plates often purporting to show noble or newsworthy people, but always indicating the latest fashions. These were produced by I. Dieu de St. Jean during the 1670-80's; by members of the Bonnart family of engraver-printsellers: the brothers Nicolas (1636-1718), Henri (1642-1711), Robert (1652-1729) and Jean-Baptiste (1654-1686), and the sons J-B (1678-1726) and Henry. Also by J. Valk, the printseller, A. Trouvain (1656-1708), and N. Arnoult, who worked in Paris, c. 1680-1700.

The Morgan Library has one of the largest collections of these plates, some cut away contemporaneously, and backed by actual fabrics of the period. This collection, to which we are greatly indebted, is supplemented by the small but beautifully chosen collection in the Print Room of The Metropolitan Museum of Art.

The Elizabeth Day McCormick Collection of costume material in the Museum of Fine Arts of Boston includes a great mass of costume plates, much of it unique, from which the Museum has been good enough to make photographs for our use. Among their material can be found Trouvain's plates of Louis XIV's *appartements,* and their amusements; games of *trou-madame,* billiards and cards, dancing and refreshments; a collection of about 250 Bonnart plates bound together, and a large number of loose plates, among which are very early examples by St. Jean; late plates of Italian comedy by H. Bonnart and by Martin Engelbrecht; about 25 piracies (in reverse position) of Larmessin's plates of the trades; several of Pluvinel's *Manège royal;* original water-color plates of sets of theatrical costumes; and all manner of other material, such of which is still being catalogued (in 1947).

1394-97. Latter half XVIIc. French.

I. D. de St. Jean. Abbé in soutane (1394); Suit worn with a sword (1395); Suit worn with a sword (1396); *N. Bonnart.* King's page (1397).

In these transitional costumes of the 1670's, we see ribbon loops beginning to succumb to plumes, fine gathered lace, edgings of metal lace braids, and an increase in the use of fringes and fur.

Interest is drawing away from flat-brimmed hats with truncated crowns and ribbon trim, to hats with swinging brims, edged with metal lace and an interior fringe of ostrich, into which the crown disappears. The short wig, characteristic of an abbé, and that of No. 1395, are frizzed in the older way; those of No. 1396 and 1397 hang in corkscrew curls.

Coats have buttons down the entire front, although only the uppermost are closed, so that in No. 1394 and No. 1396, the old bloused shirt and ribbon loops at a low waistline, continue to be seen. Coats flare as they lengthen, with the open side seams in their skirts stressed, like the front opening, by braids. Pockets are horizontal but still set low. Short, narrow sleeves grow longer; the turned back cuff, still split, begins to flare into real importance. Fur-edged gauntlets have been worn for half a century, but their cuff increases in importance until the cuff of the coat flares sufficiently to replace them, as it is beginning to do in No. 1396.

Between petticoat or loose breeches and the important garters at the knee, we see cannons or the embroidered edge of a flaring stocking top, turned up and tacked, or falling free at the side. Clocked

stockings, with the characteristic shoe of the 1670's: heavy heels, long, narrow square toes; high, square tongue, which tends to turn downwards above small buckles. No. 1395 shows the old bows on the shoe, persistent, but set on the side of the shoe.

The costume of the king's page shows the newest trends. Lace is used, in profusion for these times: in the double rows of his cravat (the ribbon bows of which are on top, and appear to tie it, but will presently retreat and become merely a backing for the lace); in the ruffle (in memory of the bloused shirt) drawn through the bosom of his long coat (still without vest), and finished with the cross of the Saint-Esprit on a blue bow; in the ends and borders of the wide sash about his hips; in his shirt sleeves and the lingerie backing (developed from the wide stocking top seen on No. 1396) which backs the ribbon bunches at the side of his still baggy breeches. His shoes, too, have the new, more delicate heel, and high, glove-fitted look.

In Louis XIV's time, a coat profusely covered with braid about the upper arm and chest has a connotation of livery and service whether worn by the queen's groom, or by a page of the king, both nobly born.

Even a century later, D'Héziques, in *Souvenirs d'un page de Louis XVI,* says that on his arrival at Versailles in 1786, "there were 150 pages not including those of the princes of the blood who lived at Paris. A page's coat cost 1,500 livres" (crimson velvet embroidered with gold on all the seams, and a hat with a feather and Spanish point lace).

1398-99. Latter half XVIIc. French.

I. D. de St. Jean. Peasant from the Neighborhood of Paris (1398), Peasant Woman from the Neighborhood of Paris (1399).

The heavy, Italian-inspired laces, so suitable for high cuffs, and collars wired out or spread over the shoulders, are supplanted in third quarter XVIIc. by much more delicate needlepoint or bobbin laces, made of finer threads, in France and the Low Countries. Their designs flow in perpendicular candelbra or delicately scrolled and flowered patterns, attractive when gathered into cravats and ever deeper flounces. In late VII-XIXc., lace is furnished in large-shaped pieces, circular capes, triangular scarves, hoods with lappets, fans and round parasol covers. Italian lace, though always characteristic, is revolutionized by the filmy designs of the Northern lace makers.

The peasants have not yet been ruined by the court. Since it is they who make the lace as a part-time home industry, under the tutelage of the nunneries, the peasants can and do wear lace on their best clothes as beautiful as that of the greatest ladies. Women of all classes embroider; the bodice front and skirt borders of a peasant costume may be as fine as any other.

The woman's delightful lace hood is worn under a plain one of linen. A cape-like lace collar stresses the wide horizontal neckline, though the bodice, with its embroidered stomacher, has a square opening; its sleeves are short and wide, the cuff disappearing, with much display of chemise sleeve and its lace ruffle. Under a plain apron (for any other would detract from the lace and embroidery at the top and bottom of the costume), the outer skirt is tucked up and caught in back, over a skirt with an embroidered band. Women's slippers have high heels, much more delicate than men's, and toes barely, if at all, squared.

The wig of courtiers has not yet made its way down to peasants, even in their best clothes; the hair of this man is worn at its full natural length. His cravat is tied with ribbon loops, which also trim his wide-brimmed hat and petticoat breeches. His coat, while still buttoned only at the top, is longer, beginning to flare, while its pockets are rising; sleeve is longer; cuff united. Shoes with high tongues and heels and square toes are worn with clocked stockings.

Courtesy of the Morgan Library

1400. XVIIc. After 1674. (Morgan Library.)

N. Bonnart. Winter Coat, called a Brandenburg.

Modern Germany began with the union of Prussia and Hohenzollern Brandenburg, led by the Great Elector, Frederic William, and with his new standing army, nucleus of the Prussian army to come. They formed an important part of the coalition forces which defeated Louis XIV's plans for expansion. During France's invasion of the United Provinces in 1674, however, the Elector's army of 20,000 was defeated in Turenne's brilliant campaign to reconquer Alsace for France.

The greatcoats worn by the Brandenburgers made a deep impression on the French, who adopted them and called them by the invader's name. The writer of the appended verse admits that this is a funny looking coat, but argues that in addition to keeping the body warm, it protects the clothing. The Brandenburg is characteristically decorated by a braid trim, made into loops on one side and braided buttons on the other, for closing, used into latter half XIXc.

The cocking brim and its feather edging conceal the crown of the hat. Throughout the 1670's, wigs retain a natural look and are often finished with long, knotted lovelocks. The cravat is folded over, but now the ribbon knot, which used to be tied around it, is either eliminated or has become a stiff bow set beneath the fall.

1401. XVIIc. Jan. 1676. French. (Metropolitan Museum, Print Room.)

N. Bonnart. Man in a Dressing Gown.

A wig was hot and uncomfortable. The head beneath it was usually shaved, sometimes clipped, although as changes in wig form exposed the neck, hair was left at the nape to be mingled with that of the wig.

In the privacy of the home, the wig was not usually worn; the shaved head was covered, both for protection and looks, by an embroidered cap or fur *montero*. The coat, too, was usually removed; the sleeveless waistcoat and shirtsleeves sufficed, although a dressing gown was often worn over breeches, vest and shirt. Painted India cottons were favorite materials for these dressing gowns, *banyans,* and for a sleeved form of vest, especially made to be worn without a coat; these show a little decoration, in places which would be unseen and made of plain material in an ordinary waistcoat. Waistcoats of this sort were also made of embroidered linen, like many of the accompanying caps. Shoes were exchanged for *pantoufles* with equally high heels and long square toes, but no back; lace-bordered handkerchief and cravat.

Louis XIV, who had beautiful hair, would not

1400

1401

wear a wig until he began to grow bald at 35. Even then, he refused to have his hair shaved. Special wigs were made with holes through which his own hair could be drawn and mingled with that of the wig.

It was far from necessary to be dressed in order to receive, in second half XVII-XVIIIc. It was a mark of intimacy, and the *lever* or *coucher* of a king like Louis XIV was attended by any courtier who could contrive to get in. The king dressed by stages, first putting on a special short wig, and a dressing gown over his nightshirt, to breakfast among high ecclesiastics and peers. These gentlemen then removed their gloves and handed the king's garments and accessories, one by one, to his valet who warmed them if necessary. The king then exchanged his short wig for a long one, and was ready to go out.

The entire routine is described in minute detail by Saint-Simon. In order to occupy quantities of courtiers, the royal wardrobe was subdivided, to be handled by as many people as possible, and the royal body even apportioned for service into right and left sides. Mme. Campan, first lady of the bedchamber to Marie Antoinette, was about to hand the queen her chemise, when, one after another, there entered (removing gloves and in turn taking the chemise), a lady of honor, the duchess of Orleans and the countess d'Artois, while the queen sat up in bed, shivering, with her hands crossed over her breast, enraged at their insistence on their superior rights. (Mme. Campan: *Memoires.*) The *Enfants de France* fared worse. Their wet-nurse might suckle but not touch them. Specific persons performed certain functions at stated times. If the baby was stuck by a pin, or soiled its diapers immediately after being changed, it had to lie screaming for three or four hours, until the return of the person authorized to perform the proper service. (Barbier: *Journal,* Oct. 1670.)

1402. XVIIc. 1678. French. (Morgan Library.)

I. D. de St. Jean. Man of Quality in Winter Dress.

1403. XVIIc. French. (Morgan Library.)

N. Bonnart. Man in Winter Dress.

The verse below the Bonnart print says that the fur is attractive, and any man so well covered will not be taken by surprise, no matter how cold it may become. Men as well as women now wear black patches. The ribbon bow is now stiff and set beneath the fall of the cravat. His coat is completely closed down the front; its skirts have a definite flare. Breeches are becoming close-fitting and are rolled around the garter at the bottom. Knots decorate hat, sword and stick. His gloves have a fur border to match the costume; a tasseled handkerchief hangs from his pocket.

The neck of the collarless coat is usually covered by the wig. The man whom we see from the back wears an extremely simple wig, which will not interfere with the marvellous stole of fur and embroidery slung over his shoulder and held in place by a wide scarf about the hips. The split cuff of his sleeve has an interesting partial cuff of fur set into its upward fold. The split cuff of his gauntlet is also fur-edged; and it is possible that the fur we see below is that of a matching muff. The fine ribbons with a fancy colored border, used in his sword-knot, are probably a result of Colbert's concentration on French luxury trades. Today we still import such fine ribbons from France.

A fascinating plate by N. Bonnart, dated 1678, shows a man in heavy mourning, with a long veil trailing from his hat. (Museum of Fine Arts, Boston, not shown here.)

1404. XVIIc. Jan. 1678. French. (Boston, Mus. of Fine Arts, Print Room.)

J. J. Bérain, e. Interior of a Needlework Shop, from the *Mercure,* Jan. 1678.

All publication within the kingdom was regulated and supervised; not even the costume plates of Bonnart appear without *avec Privilège du Roy* (some-

times abbreviated to *A.P.D.R.*), just as the tasseled hat of a cardinal on the title-page of a Spanish book indicated the required sanction of the Church. The French genius for getting one's way within the law was formed by centuries of over-regulated existence; questionable material was apt to be sent to liberal countries like Holland or Switzerland to be printed.

The first French periodical was the weekly *Gazette,* started in 1631 under Richelieu's patronage. The *Gazette* of 1650-65 was in rhyme, much more informal and amusing. Colbert, who founded the Observatory and the Academy of Sciences (now the Institut de France) was also the patron of the learned *Journal des Savants,* which began in 1665 and is published still.

The *Mercure Galant,* founded in 1672, became the *Mercure de France* in 1728, and did not go out of existence until 1792. One of its editors was Thomas Corneille, the much younger brother of the playwright; many great literary men served and were served by it.

Like its predecessor, the *Mercure* published official bulletins of the court and state, foreign and local news. It also reported society news, reviewed openings, sermons and publications, printed the latest songs, showed the latest fashions and described the costumes worn at court functions by notable people. A lady of quality, seated on a canapé, reading the *Mercure Galant* in 1688, is shown in a plate by Bonnart in the Elizabeth Day McCormick Coll., Museum of Fine Arts, Boston.

On the men's side of the shop we see boots and shoes; wigs and cravats with their strings in ready-made bows; scarves, sashes and knots; petticoat breeches looped with ribbons; shallow crowned hats and gloves. On the women's side, slippers and gloves; ruchings and ribbons; caps and bows; bandings, laces; ready-made scarves such as the lady wears, and everywhere, bolts of patterned fabrics.

1405. XVIIc. India. (Metropolitan Museum.)

Tree of Life: Wall-hanging of Painted Polychrome Cotton.

India cottons were first used as wall and bed hangings, curtains and upholstery; then for dressing gowns, aprons and petticoats; and eventually for gowns of great pretensions.

Indian patterns were copied in Europe quite literally at the beginning, though the wood-blocks familiar to European printers were substituted for the Indian method of pouncing the outline and painting in the color. The Indians, in their turn, adopted this European invention, as the Europeans went on to the use of engraved copper plates and rollers.

"Inventions" on the motifs of classic Oriental themes, like this Tree of Life, such as the wonderful pattern books of *Baroque* and *Idéal* flowers and *Chinoiseries,* published in the 1770's by Jean Pillement, had an immense effect on the design of European fabrics (woven as well as printed, silk as well as cotton) and laces.

1406. Early XVIIIc. French. (Metropolitan Museum.)

Dressing gown of painted India cotton.

The early *Indiennes* were of such extraordinary quality in respect both to fabric and dye-stuffs, that many garments made of them have survived 250-300 years in exquisite condition, despite wear, washing and sunlight. This garment, although it actually dates from late in Louis XIV's reign, is characteristic of the fabric and cut of these first dressing gowns of cotton.

Borders of compound strips of running pattern, such as originally surrounded hangings like the Tree of Life, were cut up to make such edgings as we see on this garment; in Louis XV's time, gowns of *Indiennes* were additionally embroidered in metal thread.

1407. XVIIc. 1682. French.

Nicolas Bazin, after *J. B. Martin.* Queen Maria Theresa.

For riding and hunting in second half XVII-XVIIIc., court ladies wear a costume of male hat, wig, cravat and coat, with a trailing skirt. These are cut from small-patterned brocades instead of men's plain materials, or are laced with an extraordinary amount of metal braid; the hat is apt to be larger and more exaggeratedly plumed, and there is some exaggeration in the size of the masculine shoulder knot worn by the queen (from which the army epaulette developed). A superb example of such a riding costume (French, last quarter XVIIc., in gold-embroidered velvet) is 43. 1618 in Elizabeth Day McCormick Collection, Mus. of Fine Arts, Boston.

Umbrellas have been seen occasionally for a hundred years past but c. 1680, long-handled parasols begin to open over every woman of fashion. These are usually edged with fringe or tassels; in XIXc., great circles of lace will be especially made as parasol covers.

The queen's page wears his own long hair as he runs behind her; if his service were in the palace, he would doubtless wear a wig. "When the king goes to shoot, four pages of the Great Stables are sent to His Majesty, and they call them the four ordinaries. They follow the king and take charge of his dogs. Six pages from the Little Stables follow also. If any ladies go with the king, pages from the Great Stables accompany the ladies. The six pages from the Little Stables have the honor of carrying His Majesty's guns, and the game shot by the king is frequently distributed among them. In other hunts, when there are ladies mounted on horses from the Little Stables, a page of the Little Stables accompanies each lady." (*État de la France,* 1712; describes the different functions of the two stables, and the education given the young gentlemen serving there.)

The page's livery coat is distinguishable from that of an ordinary gentleman at court by its heavy braid stripings, covering the upper sleeve and chest, where the ordinary coat is untrimmed. If the tail of the horse did not interfere, we would probably see his forearm, below the wide cuff, encased in a close-fitting doublet sleeve, instead of full shirt sleeves. Such sleeves are sometimes seen in the costume of gentlemen around the '90's, but are common on musicians, hairdressers, valets, and others who would find the white fullness of a shirt sleeve difficult to manage, or keep clean while at work. This close sleeve is also apt to be heavily striped in braid, in lengthwise or chevron patterns. (See also Ills. 1424, 1417.)

1408. XVIIc. French. (Boston, Museum of Fine Arts, Elizabeth Day McCormick Coll.)

Boissevin. Lady Singing from a Book of Music.

1409. XVIIIc. French. (Met. Mus., Print Room.)

I. D. de St. Jean. Lady in Town Dress.

1410. XVIIc. French. (Morgan Library.)

I. D. de St. Jean. Lady Walking in the Country.

1411. XVIIc. 1683. French. (Morgan Library.)

I. D. de St. Jean. Lady in Morning Déshabille.

1412. XVIIc. 1683. French. (Met. Mus., Print Room.)

G. Valk. Lady in Summer Déshabille.

1413. XVIIc. 1683. French. (Met. Mus., Print Room.)

H. Bonnart. Young Lady of Quality.

In 6 of the most delightfully feminine informal dresses ever worn by women, we see ribbon loops (so consistently worn as long as hair is bunched at the sides) beginning to lose ground as hair arrangements mount. But ribbons are such a perfect trim for cotton and lace garments that their use is continued in informal summer dresses like that shown by Valk. Ribbons, however, are changing their manner. They are carried around a long boned bodice at the natural waistline, and finish with a freshly tied bow rather than the old *chou* of loops.

At Louis XIV's court, manners are being discovered, practiced and codified; style is all-important in conduct and costume, as in conversation and letters (see text, Ill. 1392). Saint-Simon says of Louis: "Never was a man so naturally polite, nor of such circumspect politeness, so nice in its shades, nor who better discriminated age, worth and rank, both in his replies and deportment. . . . His salutations, more or less marked, but always slight, were of incomparable grace and majesty. . . . But especially towards women, there was nothing like it. Never did he pass the most indifferent woman without taking off his hat

to her; and I mean chambermaids whom he knew to be such."

The old Marshal de Richelieu, who had lived under three courts, said to Louis XVI: "Sire, under Louis XIV no one dared utter a word; under Louis XV, people whispered; under your Majesty, they talk out loud." All will become studied and oppressive, by the end of Louis XIV's reign. During his and succeeding reigns, it is an actual ordeal to carry the weight of a dress suitable for appearance at court, and ladies will lie about their private apartments without "dressing," except for the few hours or even minutes of their official appearances. So regulated was court life under Louis XIV that everybody knew exactly where the king might be found at any hour of any given day. On his return, an apparently deserted court would suddenly be flooded with people who drained away, as suddenly, after his passage. Louis' own manners, dress and punctuality were flawless and he demanded no less of his court. Under Louis XV, we read of strange makeshift costumes, thrown on in unexpected crises: no such deviations would have occurred or been tolerated under his great-grandfather. With the much wider range of amusements in Louis XVI's reign, costumes will be changed four or five times a day, as ladies attend a *lever* at Versailles, play at milkmaid in muslin at the Petit Trianon, go to the Opera, and walk after it on the left side of the Palais-Royal.

In Ill. 1413, even the gown of the young lady of quality still keeps some of the charming freshness of the other informal dresses.

The legend under Bonnart's young lady stresses the protection of a fine skin against freckles, which is implicit in all the adjuncts of all these costumes: parasols; lacy hoods and sheer scarves, veiling the décolletage; long gloves of thin kid, or of elaborately knit silk, to the elbows; masks and fans.

There is lace everywhere. The singer practices in a hood of pleated black lace and the least utilitarian of lace aprons. The lady in town dress wears it, in the manner of the old horizontal collars, but it also edges her skirts and overlies the boning of her bodice. In the dress of beautifully mitred and arranged stripes, the entire shirt sleeve is of lace. In the morning undress, it borders the little combing jacket, apron and hood, and bracelets one arm, tied with a ribbon bow. The gown of Bonnart's young lady (which shows the beginnings of the stiffness of late Louis XIV styles) is based on the magnificent band of heavy point lace which finishes the under (and more important) skirt. Where there is already sufficient pattern in fabric or lace, fine net is used in scarf or hem flounce.

All accessories show great finish. Handkerchiefs have tiny acorns or lace bells at the corners; walking sticks, secured by a loop and bow, and parasol handles are as beautifully inlaid and engraved as busks; there are exquisite patch and snuff boxes; small mirrors; *chatelaine-nécessaires* full of tiny toilet and sewing and lace-making aids; *étuis* to hold sticks of wax which seal the letters everyone sends by someone's hand; and fans, which will be at their most elaborate in the XVIIIc.

1414. XVIIc. French. (Metropolitan Museum, Print Room.)

H. Bonnart. The Well-dressed Cavalier.

The coat, which began by being buttoned down the chest, is opening to expose the waistcoat. Both coat and vest are furnished with buttons and buttonholes throughout their length. The coat is now likely to be buttoned only at the waist and may even hang completely open; the vest is closed, as the coat used to be, but eventually it, too, may be fastened only at the waist.

The buttoned-back cuff, still split, is becoming much more important; here, it falls in circularly-cut extra fullness. The pockets, while vertical in the old fashion, are increasingly stressed by decoration, as are the seams of the armseye and sleeve. Breeches have lost most of their old fullness. Gauntlets are heavily edged with fringe.

1415. XVIIc. 1684. French. (Morgan Library.)

I. D. de St. Jean. Man of Quality in a Surtout.

There have been dictionaries and encyclopaedias since Greece and Rome but this is the century of the great dictionaries, as the XVIIIc. is of great encyclopaedias. The dictionary begun by the French Academy in 1639 took more than half a century to complete; meanwhile, many modest dictionaries are appearing. Guy Miege's I vol. French-English dictionary, published in London in 1679, can be immensely helpful to-day, as much for the words it does not contain as for its current, slang or obsolete words. (Chamberlayne. See Appendix.)

The *justaucorps* has been worn long enough for definition as a close-fitting coat, but such fashionable garments as the *Brandenburg* and *surtout* have not yet managed to enter a dictionary. The new surtout (literally *over-everything*) was, as it is today, an easy-fitting top-coat. We see it here, plainly trimmed, furnished with great patch pockets, buttoned down over everything, muffling the cravat; it is a real top-coat, and must have been a welcome garment in the bitter winter of 1683-4, which Evelyn tells us was felt "even as far as Spain and the most southern tracts."

Another top-coat with easy skirts and pockets, called a *pichena,* is shown in No. 7 of the bound volume of 250 Bonnart plates: Elizabeth Day McCormick Coll., Museum of Fine Arts, Boston. It is worn by a sea-captain, but the caption tells us that it is suitable for a rider, and for city and country wear, in rain or shine.

1416. XVIIc. 1684. French. (Morgan Library.)

A. Truvain. The Chevalier de Bouillon.

Research by the Morgan Library indicates that the Chevalier de Bouillon was a young adventurer at court. The Duke de Bouillon, father of the great Turenne (whose mother was William the Silent's daughter), had an illegitimate son whose descendants long contrived and eventually succeeded in being allowed to use the family name, de La Tour d'Auvergne. Possibly this young man is a left-handed nephew of Turenne, though he little resembles that modest Protestant Marshal of France, of whom Mme. de Sévigné said that he received congratulations on his victory at Turckheim, looking "a little more shamefaced than usual."

This is a young person of the most ostentatious and daring elegance, who may well be making his way on his looks and imagination.

Cleanliness is becoming a necessity, and the man who buttons himself up above the waistline is now accused of trying to conceal soiled linen. The chevalier, in the hot summer weather, dispenses with a waistcoat entirely, and transfers its attributes to his exposed breeches. These match the coat, instead of being the usual, barely-seen necessity; they carry the waistcoat's horizontal pockets, elaborately trimmed to match the side seams; the few buttons we would expect to see closed at the waistline of the vest are frankly set on the fly.

His light summer coat has a shawl collar, very startling in the day of collarless justaucorps. There is a great knot of fringed ribbon, matching his sword-knot, on the right shoulder of his completely new raglan sleeve, which is much less close-fitting in the arm, and has great, low-set, closed cuffs.

The expanse of sheer shirt front is partly filled by a very long, unusually pleated oval cravat, set on a soft band. Since he wishes to show off his coat collar, he dispenses with the customary stiff cravat strings and carries his

wig down his back, out of the way. His shoes have shorter toes, the new delicately fitted look, and tongues turned down over larger buckles. His hat, with an interior fringe of ostrich, is definitely cocked into a tricorne.

1417. XVIIc. 1687-8. French.

Nicolas Arnoult. The Family of Monseigneur the Dauphin.

Although Louis XIV had only one legitimate son, three grandsons seemed to assure the succession.

The Dauphin was a colorless person, "drowned in fat and sloth," and completely overshadowed by his father. He was distinguished only by his prowess as a boar-hunter, and by the exceptional taste with which he furnished his apartments, which were the show-place of Versailles. He lived on good terms with the Dauphine, a Bavarian princess, not at all beautiful but intelligent, charming and good, who spent as much time as possible with music and books, apart from the court she disliked. Their children, the *Enfants de France,* were Louis, duke of Bourgogne, b.1682; Philip, duke of Anjou (later Philip V of Spain), b.1683; and Charles, duke of Berry, b.1686. The Dauphine died in 1690; in 1711, the Dauphin died of smallpox; the extraordinarily promising duke of Burgundy and his duchess died within a few days of each other, in 1712, of measles; in 1714, the duke of Berry was killed in a hunting accident, leaving as the aged king's only heir the unpromising youth (born 1710) who became Louis XV.

Monseigneur, the dutiful son, sits with his family beneath a portrait of his father. Not until 1690 will the need to raise money for the wars force Louis to set an example to his lords by melting down 2,000 pieces of the carved and gilded solid silver furniture of Versailles, replacing it with carved wood, trimmed with copper-gilt. The silver furniture in the king's own quarters had diamond-studded drawer knobs. Most of Monseigneur's furniture was made by Boule, but there was a table of carved silver, made by Balin, which cost about $70,000; it may, for all I know, be the one seen here. The Dauphin and his wife sit, as is their right, in high-backed chairs; were his father in the room, the Dauphin would stand (see text, Ill. 1419).

All are clothed in metal-laced brocades. The coats are still rather straight-cut, capable of being buttoned down the front, and have vertical pocket slits. A wide, shallow cuff is buttoned to the narrow, short outer sleeve, and exhibits the lower arm in a close sleeve belonging to the waistcoat. The cravat is less important than the bows beneath. Shoes very high and close, with turned down tongue and jewelled buckle. All wear handsome sashes and the *cordon bleu.* The duke of Burgundy has fringed gloves, stick, miniature sword and a short wig. The babies, too young for wigs, wear beribboned and plumed turbans. The younger, dressed as a girl in boned bodice and lace apron; the elder, still in skirts, has the sleeves and neckwear of his father and big brother.

The Dauphine's dress is richly conservative, transitional between the standard low-necked dress of second half XVIIc. and the costume we associate with Louis XIV's court. Her hair, with long love-locks and small corkscrew curls at the temples, is begin-

1418

ning to be dressed higher, and its ribbon decoration is mounting. Lace handkerchief.

1418. XVIIc. c. 1689-90. French. (Morgan Library.)
N. Arnoult. Charles of France, Duke of Berry.

Berry himself said that his grandfather and the tutor of his eldest brother "thought only of making me stupid and stifling all my powers; I was a younger son; I coped with my brother. They feared the consequences; they annihilated me. I was taught only to play and to hunt and they have succeeded in making me a fool and an ass, incapable of anything, the laughing stock and disdain of everybody." He was, as a matter of fact, a pleasant, witty, and popular prince, who had the misfortune to marry the fifteen-year old eldest daughter of the Regent; she was intelligent and charming, vicious and reckless, drank herself into insensibility, and died young after childbirth.

The infant of No. 1417 is now in leading strings, but still in skirts, i.e. diapers.

At the age of seven, royal children were turned over to male tutors, usually a duke and a prelate. Until that time, the *Enfants de France* were in charge of a governess, at this time the Maréchale de la Mothe, herself a duchess. Like their elders, royal children were served only by gentlefolk.

When the king dined in public, *au grand couvert,* any well-dressed person in his kingdom might enter and watch. Ordinarily he dined alone (surrounded, as always, by a crowd of familiar courtiers) at a table in the room where he also slept; occasionally he invited another person, such as his brother, to sit down with him. His own old nurse and the governess of his grandchildren were among the few women who centered his chamber at this time; Saint-Simon says the Maréchale was the only woman he ever saw invited to sit with the king at the *petit couvert.* The king ate supper every night with his

family; about three times a week there was a court reception, *appartement,* with dancing, billiards, gambling for high stakes, other games very much like the pin-ball machine of today, and a buffet to be "pillaged" by the courtiers.

The nurse, however grand a lady, is dressed for the part in a silk apron, which has a sleeved top with diagonal trimming to match, related to the banding of her handsome gored underskirt. The new tendency of the bodice neckline to rise is indicated by the lingerie frills on her bow-trimmed bodice; ribbons tend to disappear from more formal dresses, except on headdresses and muffs. Sleeves are still short but their future length and funnel shape begin to show in the frills of the sleeve. The ruffles of her delightful bonnet are not yet formalized into the pleats of the fontange, universally worn in the 90's, with hair dressed high. Fan, patches and pearl choker, with a fine chain and jewelled pendant.

MME. DE MAINTENON AND THE LOUIS XIV COURT

We may well view the latter part of the 72 years of Louis XIV's reign through the life of Mme. de Maintenon, the most interesting woman involved in it.

Françoise d'Aubigné (1635-1719), granddaughter of the great Protestant leader, daughter of a trivial, improvident father (imprisoned for Protestant trouble-making) and a Catholic mother, was born in her father's jail. After his release, the family emigrated to Martinique, where he died penniless. Little Françoise was taken by her aunt, Mme. de Villette, whom she adored, and brought up as a Protestant. She was removed to the custody of her Catholic godmother to be reconverted: "I will believe anything, so long as you do not oblige me to believe my aunt is damned." In a family with a carriage and six horses, the girl went neglected, barefoot or in sabots, given shoes only when there were guests.

She was befriended by the comic dramatist, Scarron (whose name is commemorated in New York's Schroon Lake), a 42-year old invalid hunchback, who "has drawn many pleasantries from the irregularity of his shape, which he describes as very much resembling the letter Z. He diverts himself likewise by representing to his reader the make of an engine and pulley, with which he used to take off his hat" (*Spectator*, i, 17). Françoise chose, at sixteen and a half, to marry him. For a decade she lived in the most brilliant society, nursing him faithfully until his death in 1660.

To avoid scandal about the king's involvement with his new sister-in-law, soon after his own marriage, it had been arranged that he should court one of her maids-of-honor. The 17-year old Louise de La Vallière (1644-1710), whose name is preserved in that of a type of jewelled pendant, was exquisite and graceful despite a short leg, gentle, innocent and religious. She and the king both fell unexpectedly and deeply in love; they had a number of children, one of whom, Mlle. de Blois, be-came the princess de Conti.

At about the time when Mme. de Montespan was supplanting Mlle. de La Vallière as the king's official mistress, she met Mme. Scarron and had her installed at court as governess of the duke de Maine, Louis' beloved son by Montespan.

The *Mesdames* and *Mlles. de Blois* of these days can be very confusing. Louis XIV's son, the Dauphin, was *Monseigneur;* Louis' brother, Philip, duke of Orleans, was *Monsieur,* and the latter's second wife, the Princess Palatine, was *Madame,* to whom Mme. de Maintenon did not chose to be lady of honor. Louis' daughter by the duchess of La Vallière was *Mlle. de Blois,* until she married the prince de Conti; a younger daughter of Louis', by Mme. de Montespan, was then called *Mlle. de Blois,* until her marriage to her cousin, the duke of Chartres (later the regent Orleans), son of *Monsieur* and *Madame;* the young couple were called *Monsieur le duc* and *Madame la duchesse.*

There were three grades of palace service for noblewomen: *dame d'honneur; dame d'atours* (who took care of the wardrobe and knelt with a salver to receive the jewels removed at the *coucher*); and *dame du palais.* With her custo-mary self-effacement, Mme. de Maintenon refused the post of lady of honor to Madame, and sug-gested a suitable person to replace Mme. de Riche-lieu.

Meanwhile, another of Madame's ladies-of-honor, a person of completely different character, had determined to supplant La Vallière. Mme. de Montespan (1641-1707) was equally blonde and beautiful, but proud, vain and intriguing; witty and intelligent, although she resorted to witch-craft to gain and hold the king, and was supposed to have poisoned a temporary rival, Mlle. de Fontange (whose name lived after her death in 1681, in the headdress for which she was respon-sible). In 1667, Montespan became the *maîtresse tonnante et triumphante,* as Mme. de Maintenon described her, of the king. Her husband went about court wearing mourning for his lost honor, but accepted a pension and was sent off to distant service.

In late XVII-e.XVIIIc., we learn from d'Argen-son, only blue-eyed blondes were accounted beau-tiful. Black hair was disliked and red ridiculed. But its nearness to blonde gradually led to the acceptance of red hair; during last quarter XVIIIc., it even took the lead, and powders were used to redden hair.

La Vallière, who wished to become a nun, was forced to remain as official mistress for half-a-dozen hideous years. When she was finally al-lowed to enter the convent, she told Mme. Scar-ron: "When I am hurt by something at the Car-melites, I will always remember what those two people (Louis and Montespan) have made me

suffer." The queen's affection led her to visit Sis-ter Louise de la Miséricorde in the convent where, until her death, she washed the sisters' linen.

Everybody confided in the discreet, charming and dignified Mme. Scarron. Her high character at first alienated the king. When he was amusing himself tipping court ladies in their armchairs back to the ground, he passed by Mme. Scarron, saying: "Oh, with that one, I wouldn't dare," at which a courtier said he'd sooner try to pinch the queen's *derrière* than Mme. Scarron's.

Louis, however, came to respect her, making her Marquise de Maintenon. The queen, who eventu-ally died in her arms, said she had never before been so well treated by the king, and that she owed it all to Mme. de Maintenon.

During the eight years of her liaison with the king, Montespan had born him nine children, legitimized (as had been those of La Vallière) by Louis; among them the duc de Maine, Mlles. de Nantes, de Tours, de Blois, and the count of Toulouse.

Mme. de Maintenon's influence increased; Montespan failed to get rid of her by plotting her marriage to another hunchback, the elderly duke de Villars. The temper, scenes and activities of Montespan became increasingly distasteful to Louis. She was not invited to the court fête of 1679, but rather than shame their children, Louis allowed her to remain at court until 1691 when she, too, retired to a convent; at her death, he for-bade her children to wear mourning for her.

After the queen's death, Mme. de Maintenon and the king were secretly married by the Arch-bishop of Paris, in the presence of the king's con-fessor, the Jesuit Père La Chaise and a number of others. The tone of court life was raised and be-came much less amusing, its gowns less revealing. Louis had always had a very real religious feel-ing. Under his second wife's influence, this in-creased, although as she said, while he would never miss a sermon or a fast-day, no one could make him understand what was mean by hu-mility or repentance. Her own piety was true but not aggressive; and the greatest mistake of Louis' life, the Revocation of the Edict of Nantes, for which the Church had longed, was not due to her influence. The Protestants, who were among France's most worthy and industrious citizens, were driven to sympathetic neighboring countries; some of the most prosperous districts of France were depopulated and reduced to poverty, as weavers, and printers, watchmakers and gold-smiths set England, Switzerland, Alsace, Hol-land and Germany on the road to rivalry and su-premacy in these arts.

Mme. de Maintenon, who had always made her way discreetly and unostentatiously, devoted her-self to easing and simplifying the final thirty years of Louis' life. She spared him much routine business, sacrificed her own deep interests in other matters to the tedious restrictions of court and etiquette, and never let herself appear to the king otherwise than in good health and spirits, no matter what her real feelings.

She said he never saw her cry, even during his final illness, when he was 77 and she 81. Instead, they went through his papers, and the pockets of all his coats, laughing at their memories of what they found, and burning what might prove embarrassing. He said he regretted the wars he had waged, and that he had not made her happy. "It's true that he loved me more than anyone else, but even then he loved me only as much as he was capable of loving," she said, adding that without the aid of her religion, she could not have stayed on at court.

When the doctors told her that Louis, dying of gangrene, would never regain consciousness, she did not wait until his death, but drove off to St. Cyr, for fear of being molested and insulted on the way after the king's death. On a pension granted her by Orleans, she finished her life there in retirement.

———

1419. XVIIc. Before 1690. French. (Versailles, National Museum.)

Att. to *L. F. Elle.* Mme. de Maintenon and her Niece.

The wife of the king was a born teacher and social worker; the childless woman, whose own girlhood had been so insecure, loved children. One after another, she brought up young women like her cousin, who became Mme. de Caylus, and this namesake-

niece, the only child of her only brother. Little Françoise, b.1684, was married at 14 to an old friend of her aunt's, the Marshal de Noailles, and inherited the Chateau de Maintenon, which is still owned by the Noailles family.

With the first increase in her fortune, Mme. de Maintenon had founded a home of girls, which developed into the famous school of St. Cyr. She spent as much time there as the routines of court permitted. When the court was at Versailles, she could go each morning to St. Cyr; when it was at Marly, she could not get there at all. Her letters recount the constant frustrations of court life. "My little finger tells me that the news from England is good. One must console oneself by that for the other little contradictions one finds on the way. I was dining with my *cabale.*" (Her niece Noailles, cousin Caylus and five others, making a pleasant eight at table, joined twice a week, from five to ten, by the king, for supper). "The king prevented it; he should be coming here at 2 o'clock. Perhaps he will not come so early. He should be going out at four; perhaps he won't be going out. He is counting on a game at night. Perhaps we won't see him? I have absolutely no idea what I am doing tomorrow. All I know is that I am very trying to others and myself."

From the drive to St. Cyr, Mme. de Maintenon was apt to return without headdress or scarf, given to some poor woman picked up on the way in her carriage. Her taste in dress was very simple, and her bodice always cut so high that it was rumored to cover a defect. The duchess of Richelieu was astonished, one hot day, to find that her bosom was actually very handsome. Her linen was always exquisite and fresh. Her confessor at St. Cyr thought there was too much material in her dresses. When she protested, he said, well, it looked like too much when he saw it all spread about her as she knelt.

Her feelings about clothes are expressed in a letter of 1705, asking Mme. de Caylus to buy a short summer robe and petticoat to wear in getting out of bed when she was ill but still had to make a good appearance, since the king disliked the unadorned black costumes to which she inclined. She asks for a black and white petticoat of at least six widths of material, and a black and gold gown, neither of rich stuff. Violet and gold, or a "very Turkish blue" would do. "One must adorn the personage, while the person should only be thinking of the coffin."

Mme. de Maintenon's simple gown with train is collared to the throat with point lace. Her hair, which is beginning to be dressed high with a small curl on either side of the forehead, is covered with a scarf of sheer black bobbin lace, worn with a black *fontange.* This headdress, almost universal by 1690, came into being nearly a decade earlier when the hair of the girl for whom it was named fell down during the hunt and was put up with the help of her lace-edged garter. Though it reached almost unmanageable heights by 1700, it began as a standing ruffle of lace.

The little niece, though still in leading strings, wears the trained satin gown of a grown person, the bottom of the bodice finished with a line of stones; and her hair, though uncovered, is dressed on top of the head with a love-lock and tiny curls on the temples; by 1695, even children wear a fontange.

Through the window we see the buildings of Maintenon's beloved school, for which Racine wrote "Esther," first performed there in 1689 before the king; and where, in her old age, she deprived herself of her nightly cup of chocolate, fearing the effect of luxurious example on her 250 young gentlewomen.

The furniture is typically late Louis XIV. The chair with its curved, richly carved arm, is upholstered in velvet, bordered with metal galloon, fringed and tasseled, as is the cushion, set on a table with carved Baroque swags.

"The etiquette of seating is in this period the philosophy of royalty. Thus in order of importance range the arm chair, chairs with backs, joint stools, folding stools, hassocks with gold gimp, hassocks with silk edging. The Louis XIV throne chair was majestic—solid silver, draped with crimson velvet. The back was eight feet high, draped with gold embroidery carried by caryatids, fifteen feet high." (Aronson: *The Encyclopedia of Furniture.*)

Court life consisted of endless standing. Men almost never sat down, except at the card tables; women did so by permission. To sit on a seat not commensurate with one's rank, even though it were the only one available, led to "confusion," and was deplored (or worse) by the king, who noticed the least deviation from precedence.

The king, who had an extraordinary constitution, and could stand anything but tobacco and perfume, had no patience with human frailty. He endured the lack of all privacy, the three pairs of hands through which the least glass of water was handed him, the cold which froze the wine in its glass at dinner, or the heat engendered by crowds of candles and hundreds of courtiers. Ladies dared not faint in his presence. His coach never stopped on the road for the convenience of the queen, Mlle. de La Vallière, and Mme. de Montespan, as they rode together with him through Flanders, and the peasants thronged to get a look at the "three queens." Ladies who had lapsed from the king's standards of manners, withdrew from court, sometimes permanently to a nunnery.

French Court Life Behind the Scenes

Mlle. de Blois (b.1677, who became the duchess of Orleans), and Mlle. de Nantes (b.1673, later the duchess of Bourbon), two of the king's daughters by Mme. de Montespan, appear in "La Charmante Tabagie" (Ill 1422). The print represents an event described by St.-Simon, which took place at Marly, in the fall of 1695.

Everybody took snuff, and snuff boxes had become the conventional handsome present. Louis gave many of them, but detested tobacco personally; and smoking was considered extremely vulgar. The bored, spoiled girls teased the Swiss Guards into getting them pipes. They are shown in aproned magnificence and great fontanges, at a table under a grape arbor, playing cards, drinking and smoking amongst empty bottles and more cooling, smashed glasses and broken pipes. They were surprised by the Dauphin, punished next day by the king, and the story spread.

Of his half-sisters, the Dauphin much preferred the princess of Conti. She was even lovelier than the mother who had been named in her legitimatization; Montespan's daughters were at the disadvantage of having been merely declared legitimate. There was so much ill-feeling between the various half-sisters that Louis once threatened to have them locked up in their respective chateaux. The princess of Conti called the duchess of Orleans *sac-à-vin,* for she was always one to drown her annoyances. In return Mme. de Conti was called *sac-à-guenilles* (rag-bag). Montespan's high-spirited daughters felt that, as the king's daughters, they were condescending in marrying his mere nephew, and Condé's grandson.

Madame, the Princess Palatine, who had slapped her son's face in public in her rage at his marrying Mlle. de Blois, had a tongue as well as a temper beyond any other. She never forgave the gentle reprimand for some excessively indiscreet letters of hers, which had been put into Mme. de Maintenon's hands to deal with, by the secret police. She called her *"cette vieille ordure, ce méchant diable, cette ripopée* (mixture of all the leftover sauces dumped together, i.e. a mess), *cette ratatinée de Maintenon"* (meaning withered like an old apple). In fact, a great part of Mme. de Maintenon's reputation for hypocrisy comes from the hatred of the Princess Palatine and her competence at expressing it in the marvellous letters which were her constant occupation.

Name-calling increased at court with the XVIIIc. It might be in the form of nicknames as affectionate as Louis XV's *Coches, Loque, Graille,* and *Chiffe* for his daughters Victoire, Adelaide, Sophie and Louise; or as mocking as his courtiers' for his illegitimate son, the count de Luc, called the *demi-Louis.* It might be a "little language" of intimacy and affection, of discretion, of studied insult, or of simple vulgarity. Mme. de Lauraguais, herself known as *la rue des Mauvaises Paroles,* because of the names she made up for other people, called the Cardinal de Rohan the "broody hen," and d'Argenson, the "sucking calf." Mme. de Pompadour, in the circle of her *petits chats,* called the duke of Chaulnes "the pig," and called others the equivalent of "slut" and "pot-rag."

But *Madame* loathed the court as much as did Mme. de Maintenon when she wrote the princess des Ursins in 1707: "I find the women of today unbearable; their senseless and immodest clothing, their tobacco, their *gourmandise,* their coarseness, their laziness, all are so opposed to my taste, and it seems to me, to reason, that I cannot endure it."

the painter's daughter put the ermine-lined mantle over the marquise's shoulders, Mme. de Sévigné's letters tell us that Louis said: "Yes, Sainte-Françoise well deserves it."

1421. XVIIc. French. (Versailles, National Museum.)

Pierre Vignon. The Duchess of Orleans and the Duchess of Bourbon.

1422. XVIIc. 1698. French. (Boston, Museum of Fine Arts, Elizabeth Day McCormick Coll.)

N. Arnoult. La Charmante Tabagie.

These two smokers (Ill. 1422) are not the young women to be influenced by the example of a stepmother they find stuffy.

In Ill. 1421, bodices, in the spirit of allegorical portraits, slip off one shoulder and breast, and are negligently caught or garlanded by flowers (of the same natural sort which Mme. de Maintenon holds, in the portrait with her niece). The hems of their dresses, however, are finished with heavy fringes. With tassels, such as hang from the pillows, these fringes are handsomer and more elaborate at the turn of this century than ever before or since.

Their hair is dressed very high, in twin peaks, as men's wigs of the time are, with paired scallops, *favorites,* on the temples, repalcing the old corkscrew curls.

Jewelry is reduced to lacy, sprig-like brooches, allied to the small patterns of the brocade used in their gowns; small clasps and studs in the hair, chains of stones at the waistline or catching the bodice, or a line of pearls. Decorative and quite useless aprons are an indispensable part of negligée, and even of "dress" costume in late XVII-e.XVIIIc.

The little Negro page they are fondling wears pearl earrings and a slave's collar with his livery coat and loose, fringed cravat.

1420. XVIIc. c. 1694. French. (Louvre.)

Pierre Mignard. Françoise d'Aubigné, Marquise de Maintenon.

In these days of portraits of ladies as half-naked allegorical personages, like Diana with a bow and a leopard skin, the modestly covered Marquise, whom Louis often addressed as "your Solidity," was painted by Mignard rather as a sainted Roman lady. When

1423   1424   1425

1423. XVIIc. 1688. French. (Metropolitan Museum, Print Room.)

N. Arnoult. Lady of Quality at her Toilet.

1424. XVIIc. After 1692. French. (Metropolitan Museum, Print Room.)

R. Bonnart. Lady of Quality at her Toilet.

In its early form, the lace of the *fontange* is a mere ruffle, backed by ribbon loops, and subservient to a cap, also looped with ribbon, the lappets of which hang down the front of the shoulders.

As the hair mounts, the *fontange* or *commode* headdress becomes higher, stiffer, tiered, formally pleated and backed by wired ribbon loops. The cap and its trim are reduced to a crown and the ribbon tied around it; the lappets become two long strips falling down the back, which may be pinned up to the crown in various ways.

The Arnoult lady wears a little combing jacket of wide point lace and a petticoat which may well be of *Indiennes.* She sits on a fringe-trimmed stool, with late Renaissance turnings, at a dressing table which is still utilitarian.

Her maid wears an apron with a lace-trimmed pocket, and a belt full of dangling utensils, over a charming gored skirt. Great ladies are seen in such gored skirts when their clothes must be easily manageable, as in the shooting costume worn by the countess of Toulouse in Arnoult's print of 1678. (in the Print collection of the Bibliothèque Nationale, Paris.) Her lace is naturally less splendid than that of her mistress. But lace has become so completely a necessity that many inexpensive approximations were soon provided. There were drawn-work effects on thin muslin; in other cases, the muslin was starched to hold a lacy pricked design, and pointed up with white paint. Cooper Union Museum has several examples; two are reproduced in Miss Marian Hague's article on "Comparisons in Lace Design:" *Chronicle of the Museum,* Vol. I, No. II, Dec. 1945.

As a little page holds a silver basin and ewer, the hard-hearted Bonnart lady washes her hands—as she will of any evil passions her beauty may inspire, we are told by the accompanying verse.

Under her combing jacket, we see the handsome placard of her corset and her petticoat trimmed with bands of galloon and fringed gimp.

The page wears a braid-striped livery coat but no wig. Like the hairdresser, his undersleeve is close-fitting. They both wear the *Steinkirk* form of cravat. In the 1692 battle from which this took its name, William of Orange was defeated by the French under Luxembourg, although the French officers went into action without time to finish dressing. They knotted their cravats about the neck and tucked the long ends into a buttonhole. This fashion was adopted by women as well as men, and being very comfortable, had a long life; it is occasionally seen into the third quarter XVIIIc.

The dressing table is becoming more elaborate; lace-edged cover; larger and handsomer mirror; many charming boxes for patches, cosmetics and jewelry.

By 1687, merchants' daughters are also shown at their toilette.

1425. XVIIc. 1694. French. (Metropolitan Museum, Print Room.)

A. Trouvain. Duchess of Humières in a Ball Gown.

Great balls were given during marriage celebrations and many masked balls were held at carnival time. The *Mercure* of 1683 tells of five balls given that winter "in five different *appartements* at Versailles, all so grand that no other royal house in the world can show the like. Entrance was given to masks only, and no persons presented themselves without being disguised unless they were of very high rank. People invent grotesque disguises; they revive old fashions, they choose the most ridiculous things and seek to make them as amusing as possible . . . The Dauphin . . . sometimes had double masks, and under the first a mask of wax so well made that, when he took off his first mask, people fancied they saw his natural face and he deceived everybody."

The duke of Chartres' masquerade at Marly in 1700 "represented the Grand Turk and his menagerie. He was carried by slaves in a palanquin, and preceded by a great number of animals as natural as life. There were ostriches, cranes, apes, bears, parrots and butterflies. In his suite marched the officers and slaves of the seraglio, and the sultanas, who, together with the animals, danced an entrée pleasant and new." The *Mercure* lists the parts played by the various members of the nobility whose "costumes were magnificent. All the animals were as natural as possible. The apes, who were professional mountebanks, were wonderful."

The duchess, daughter-in-law of the not very effective Marshal who apparently remained in favor because of Turenne's affection for his rich and lovely wife, carries a mask and long gloves. She is dressed in a costume of Eastern inspiration, whether Polish or Turkish, with a high turban and cockade. Her loose gown is turned back with triple bars of galloon, each ending in a tassel, and is bordered with passementerie; it is worn with a vest-like corset, braided and tasseled.

All these forms of decoration are at a height which will not be approached again, even in the Victorian era. Passementerie is silk or metal lace, often spangled. Gimp, being braided, is more closely related to passementerie than to galloon, which is woven in ribbon-like bands. The various techniques are often combined, as when openwork gimps are woven into galloon; and all are combined with wonderful fringes and tassels.

Cooper Union has a rich collection of books of these trimmings, including livery galloons woven with the arms of a lord, a city, or the insignia of a cardinal. Some of these are shown in the article on trimmings in the *Chronicle of the Museum*: Vol. I, No. 7, Sept. 1942. The Museum's collection includes not only laces, woven and printed fabrics, buttons and trimmings, but a remarkable number of contemporary pattern books and artists' original designs for these, and such allied arts as jewelry, sedan chairs and coaches, furniture and wall decoration, architecture and gardens.

1426. XVIIc. 1694. French. (Morgan Library.)
A. Trouvain. Jean Bart, Ship's Captain.

This fisherman's son, a common sailor at 12, was prevented by his birth from making rank commensurate with his worth, until his audacity at blockade-running in the Channel brought him to the king's attention in 1679. From that time, his exploits in carrying war supplies, his speedy escape from English prison, his revengeful raids on English soil and shipping, the destruction of six enemy ships by his *Glorieux* alone, and his leadership of one hundred wheat-laden ships to famished France, caused Louis to ennoble him in 1694.

Trouvain's engraving commemorates his invitation to Versailles. Despite his magnificent clothes, his rough plebeian ways (indicated by pipe smoking) made the courtiers nickname him "the bear." In 1702, as a result of overwork and exposure, he died of pleurisy.

As the attributes of the waistcoat, when it is not worn, are transferred to the breeches (as in the case

of Bouillon, Ill. 1416), those of a coat, when it is worn widely opened, are assumed by the waistcoat. Here it carries the pockets, heavily trimmed by braid and fringe. The narrow coat sleeve is longer, widening below the elbow, its cuff set lower, so that little of the shirt sleeve is now seen except its wrist ruffle. His *steinkirk* is twisted before it is drawn through the buttonhole. Hat elaborately laced and plumed.

The table is of the new console variety, set on two (or sometimes one) front legs only, and braced against the wall.

1427. XVIIc. 1694. French. (Morgan Library.)

H. Bonnart. Madame la Duchesse.

The disparate views of the duke of Saint-Simon and the Princess Palatine focus to show the wife of the future regent as a big, dignified, lazy hypochondriac; lop-sided, long of tooth, over-painted but handsome enough, with her fine skin and chestnut hair; intelligent but with a slow, blurred speech, a great timidity towards her father, Louis XIV, and a fantastic arrogance toward the rest of the world, for which her husband nicknamed her "Madame Lucifer." She ate lying down, and "would like larks ready roasted to drop in her mouth. She is so vain that she thinks she has more sense than her husband, who has a great deal." (*Memoirs of the Duchess of Orleans*).

These are the words of Madame La Duchess' mother-in-law, Charlotte Elizabeth of Orleans, the Princess Palatine (on whose behalf, though without her desire, Louis' claims to the Palatinate led to the invasions of 1688). She was a violent and masculine German, a strange mixture of rusticity and stiff-necked pride of race. She despised the French court and everyone in it (with the definite exception of the king), beginning with his brother, her husband (a polite, painted little man who tottered on his high heels), and the king's daughter, her son's wife.

To the 800-odd, forthright, 20-30 page letters which the Princess Palatine wrote from 6 a.m. to 10 p.m., with time out only for dressing, prayers, mass, and a quick dinner, we owe much of our knowledge of her times. Other sources are the memoirs of Saint-Simon, d'Angeau, Mme. de Caylus, and the letters of Mme. de Sévigné.

The court preoccupation with style is manifested, not only in clothes and manners, but in speech and writing. It is possible for a noblewoman to be almost completely illiterate (like Mme. de Coislin, former mistress of Louis XV, in whose hôtel, in her great age, Chateaubriand and his wife rented a floor, and whose incomparable sense of form in speech is recorded in "Les Mémoires d'outre-tombe.") Madame's youngest granddaughter, for a brief time queen of Spain, was such an illiterate. But an excellent education is equally possible, in another sister of the same family; letter writing has become a great art; daily records are kept by people of both sexes, on which will be based the endless memoirs of the XVIIIc.

The letters of the visiting German baron de Pöllnitz in e.XVIIIc. describe a hurried call of the young duchess of Berry (eldest daughter of Mme. la Duchesse) on Madame, dressed in a scarf and constantly asking the time. Upon questioning, it turned out that she was not going for a walk by torchlight, but to visit the king. Louis XV was still a child; but Madame was outraged by the lack of respect shown by the duchess' costume. "Give the king the respects due him and you will have the right to exact from others those due you. You certainly can get yourself dressed, the few times that you go to see the king, since I, your grandmother, dress myself every day. A princess should be dressed like a princess, and a soubrette like a soubrette." The little duchess, furious but remembering her breeding, made a silent reverence and withdrew. (See Appendix.)

Under the influence of "Goody Scarron," as the Princess Palatine called Mme. de Maintenon, formal court dress became high-necked and rigid late in Louis XIV's reign.

The low neckline of the final quarter XVIIc. will continue to be seen through first half XVIIIc., as kings' daughters act or are painted as allegorical or mythological characters. This gown always displays a good deal of chemise top and sleeve, even a shoulder and breast. But in e.XVIIIc., even the Princess Palatine considers a decorous form of this gown suitable for herself, wearing it with just such an ermine-lined mantle. (See Appendix: von B.)

The very cold winters of 1683-4 and 1688-9, were followed by warm ones, ending with the extraordinarily mild winter of 1693-4.

The winter of '83 is illustrated by many plates in the bound Bonnart in the Museum, Boston. No. 40 shows a lady *en écharpe;* 58, a man carrying a muff and wearing an unusual cape with embroidered front edges longer than his coat; 59 has an overcoat hung, cape-wise, over his shoulders. There are several later plates of ladies huddled at fireplaces with their feet on the fender; No. 106, *December,* shows one shielding her face with a firescreen, held in a hand the back of which is protected by a sort of stiffened mitten, reaching only to the knuckles, leaving the fingers free.

In 1694-5, the Thames again froze solid (Evelyn), and the Princess Palatine tells us that the intense cold at Versailles froze water and wine in the glasses at table. 1696-7 was another bad year; but the worst within living memory, in France, was that of 1708-9. Mme. de Maintenon sat in an especially constructed chair, like a sentry-box, which protected her from draughts from all directions. It was impossible to heat the great, high-ceilinged rooms of Versailles during any winter; in these particular years we see court ladies draped in ermine-lined oblongs, as large as comforters.

Gowns are beginning to be impressively studded with jewels, but the costume worn by Madame la Duchesse, with its lappeted and shaped corset-edge, and her uncovered hair, has a Bérain-like theatricality, not far removed from the frankly professional costumes of Watteau's *French Comedians*. Madame la Duchesse had a stately bearing but an indistinct speech. This is probably a gown to be worn at a fête. The days of court ladies appearing in private theatrical performances have begun, but will not become notable until the advent of the spirited duchess of Bourgogne.

1428. XVIIc. 1694. French. (Morgan Library.)

N. Bonnart. Lady of the Court in an Ermine Skirt.

Another court lady attempts to outwit the cold of 1694 by a gored skirt of ermine, a muff trimmed with a fringed bow, gloves and a lace scarf long enough to be knotted at the throat, hanging from her increasingly high *fontange* or *commode,* with the curls called *favorites* at the temples. There are all manner of names for the components of the headdress. Regnard's comedy of 1694, "Wait for me beneath the elm," explains that the *mouse* was "a small bow of ribbon which is placed in the *wood.* I must tell you that a knot of frizzled hair which trims the lower part of the fontange is called the *little wood.*" (Lacroix: *Eighteenth Century*). Her cuffs are laced back by a cord, the tassels of which match those which fasten her bodice to the embroidered corset.

1429. XVIIc. 1695. French. (London, National Gallery.)

N. de Largillière. James Francis Edward Stuart and Princess Louisa Maria Theresa Stuart.

During his early exile, Charles II's brother James had proved himself a brave and brilliant military commander under Turenne and Condé. After his return, his honest and efficient administration of the Admiralty was admired by Pepys. In 1660, he secretly married Clarendon's daughter Anne, by whom he had eight children, two of whom, Mary and Anne, became Protestant queens of England. In 1662, he was converted to Catholicism; and the next year took as his wife a hated Catholic princess, Mary of Modena, vulgarly called "the Pope's eldest daughter." The Test Act, to prevent Catholics from holding office, was passed, and he lived on the Continent for some time, until restored to the succession.

James was a better man than his brother, but as a king, he was politically inept and blinded by the successful results of his early firmness. Neither the marriage of his daughter Mary to the Protestant prince William of Orange in 1677, nor Mary of Modena's apparent inability to have more children after a long series of miscarriages, dispelled fears of a Catholic succession. James' alliance with France; his approval of the Revocation of the Edict of Nantes; his persecution of dissenters while showering very high-church men with patronage, because he believed that such persons were already half Catholic; his punishment of the Tory opposition; and his setting aside of the Test Act, resulted (as Rome and even the most devoted English Catholics had forseen), in uniting factions which James believed to be safely at odds.

The son born to Mary of Modena in 1688 was supposed by many (including Bishop Burnet), to be an impostor planted to insure a Catholic succession. James' Protestant son-in-law was invited to succeed him as William III, and accepted in order to save England from being brought in on the French side in the wars which Louis was about to undertake. James fled to France, and after an inept Irish campaign in which he showed none of his old courage, crept back to die, broken and devout, at Saint-Germain under Louis XIV's protection.

"The Old Pretender," whom we see here with the sister born after him at the French court, was proclaimed king of England by Louis XIV after his father's death, and lived under Louis' protection. He failed in his attempt to regain the throne from the Hanoverian succession, by way of Scotland in 1715; was one of the possible kings of Poland by virtue of his romantic marriage with the daughter of John Sobieski; and died in 1766 in Rome where he and his wife lived as king and queen of England at the Pope's expense.

He wears his own hair; a series of bows behind his cravat; and a brocade waistcoat, the sleeve of which is seen in a turned-back band over the deep cuff of his wide-skirted coat. He wears the Garter and shoes with a high tongue turned down to show its red lining. His sister, still in leading strings, wears an apron of lace, matching that of her corset, pleated cuffs, and the *fontange* which her mother will be influential in bringing to its end.

1430. XVIIc. Nov. 4, 1696. French.

From an almanach of 1697. Reception of the Princess of Savoy at Montargis.

Louis XIII's sisters, Christina and Henriette, had married, respectively, Victor-Amadeus I of Savoy and Charles I of England. The latter's daughter, Henrietta Maria, was the first wife of *Monsieur;* their daughter had then been married to Victor-Amadeus II. His child, the 11-year old Marie Adelaide of Savoy, was found suitable as a wife for Louis, duke of Burgundy, eldest son of the Grand Dauphin. In 1696 she was sent to live at the French court, in preparation for marriage.

From Louis XIV's time to the Revolution, separate establishments were set up for each member of the royal family in childhood, as they were for husband and wife of the great nobility. The contempt in which the nobility held the bourgeois functionaries of the crown led any concern with expenditures to be considered, increasingly, ill-bred; until the wealth amassed by these busy servants led the ruined nobility to "manure their fields" by marrying their daughters. Everybody lived at the expense of someone else and intrigued for more money to throw away. The advice of an experienced courtier to a novice was, "Speak well of everybody, ask for every vacant place, and sit down when you can." For signing his name once a year, a great lord would receive a percentage of the duties of a seaport; at the king's death, the thousands of horses in the royal stables fell to the Royal Equerry; so, too, the house servants sold for their own benefit any candle which had been lighted, and any left-over food (for the purchase of which commissions had already been

paid). In 1780, by "great reformations of the table," the expenditure for the food of *Mesdames,* those three aged ladies, is brought down to 600,000 livres a year (Taine).

Louis XIV went in state to meet the Princess of Savoy at Montargis. The illustration shows the little princess with her fiancé (who was not actually present); the duchess de Lude, who had been selected as *dame du palais* of the Princess' establishment; the count de Brienne, the ambassador who had taken delivery of the princess; and the marquis and marquise d'Angeau, the gentleman and lady of honor of her household. The king has his brother on his right, the Dauphin on his left, and is followed by his sons, by Mme. de Montespan, the count of Toulouse and the duke du Maine; and his sons-in-law, the dukes of Chartres and Conti.

The little princess was not at all pretty and had bad teeth, but was graceful and had been carefully tutored by parents familiar with French ways. "She did not fail in anything," Louis said, in writing Mme. de Maintenon of his delight at her manners and spontaneous charm. She became the freest and happiest personal contact of the old king's entire life, Mme. de Maintenon's doll, and the pet of the court. "Everybody is now becoming a child again," the Princess Palatine wrote wryly, having found herself, with three of her ladies, playing *"colin-maillard"* (blind man's buff), with the little princess.

"In private, she clasped the king around the neck at all hours, jumped upon his knees, tormented him with all kinds of sportiveness, rummaged among his papers, opened his letters and read them in his presence, sometimes in spite of him; and acted in the same manner with Mme. de Maintenon," whom she called "aunt." "Despite this extreme liberty, she never spoke against anyone; gracious to all, she endeavored to ward off blows from all whenever she could; was attentive to all the private comforts of the king, even the humblest; kind to all who served, and living with her ladies, as with friends, in complete liberty, old and young; she was the darling of the court, adored by all; everybody missed her when she was away; when she reappeared the void was filled up; everybody, great and small, was anxious to please her; in a word, she had attached all hearts to herself . . . The king really could not do without her. Everything went wrong with him if she were not by. She had measured his disposition to an inch"; her tact and discretion were flawless. She never came or went without seeing the king, and after even the latest party, "nevertheless adjusted things so well that she went and embraced the king the moment he was up, and amused him with a description of the fête." (Saint-Simon)

Although the marriage was not allowed to be consummated for two more years, the twelve year old princess and 15½ year old duke were married December 7, 1697. She wore a costume of silver cloth, edged with precious stones: she could scarcely walk when she put it on a few days later to show her schoolmates at St. Cyr, which she had attended, under the name "Mlle. de Lastic," and where, in the January before, she had played in *Esther,* at its first performance. At the marriage the duke had worn a gold-embroidered black mantle, lined in rose, over a white costume with diamond buttons.

Her young husband did immense credit to the efforts of his tutors, Fénelon and the duke of Beauvilliers. They had transformed an adolescent of brilliant intelligence, who was also a monster of uncontrolled violence, cruelty, arrogance and stubbornness, into an almost unrecognizable 20-year-old model of goodness, courtesy, and devotion to deeply-felt responsibilities. "A king is made for his subjects, not the subjects for the king," he said at Marly within the hearing of Louis XIV, who felt it a criticism of his own life. His young wife helped to correct the rather excessive new austerity, which made him go without a desk, in a room which needed regilding, in order to spend the money on charity.

The death of his father, in 1711, gave France as the new Dauphin, a poised and friendly man, of quick, inquisitive, instructed intelligence. But a year later, within days, both he and his wife were dead, probably of measles, though poisoning was also suspected. A few weeks later, their oldest surviving son died, and the heartbroken king was left with no heir but the sickly child who was to become Louis XV.

Louis XIV had always insisted on perfect dress, but the brilliant costumes of his younger days were given up after his remarriage. "He was always clad in dresses more or less brown, lightly embroidered, but never at the edges, sometimes with nothing but a gold button, sometimes black velvet. He had always a vest of cloth, or of red, blue, or green satin, much embroidered. He wore no ring and no jewels, except in the buckles of his shoes, garters, and hat, the latter always trimmed with Spanish point, with a white feather. He had always the *cordon bleu* over his coat, except at fêtes, when he wore it under his coat, with precious stones, worth 8 or 10 million livres, attached." (Saint-Simon)

In this illustration, we see men's costume in all stages of transition, from coats of plain material patterned with braid, to those made of all-over patterned brocades, perhaps diamond-studded, but otherwise trimmed mainly along the seams and pocket edges. A coat of the plainest fabric now has cuffs of embroidery or brocade to match the elaborate vest.

Dress and masquerade costumes remained a passion with *Monsieur,* Louis' brother. We see him here, as Saint-Simon describes him: "A little round-bellied man, who wore such high-heeled shoes that he seemed mounted always upon stilts; always decked out like a woman, covered everywhere with rings, bracelets, jewels; with a long black wig powdered and curled in front; with ribbons everywhere he could put them; steeped in perfumes, and in fine a model of cleanliness. He was accused of putting on an imperceptible touch of rouge." *Monsieur's* one military command had been so successful that Louis took care he should never have another; according to his soldiers, he feared sunburn more than ball and powder.

His wife said, "As *Monsieur* loved to be covered with diamonds, it was fortunate that I did not regard them, for otherwise we should have quarrelled about who was to wear them." He danced well, she said, but not "like a man, because his shoes were too high-heeled." He is shown here in the longest wig and the highest heels of all, gloved, his coat sewn over with his diamonds.

Wigs are now universally worn, even by priests and monks, whose wigs have false tonsures. When they first came into use, under Louis XIII, their color was apt to be light or that of the natural hair. Darker perukes came into use; powder began to be used. Perukes are at their longest and fullest, now, at the turn of the century. As powder tended to litter the coat, wigs became smaller or were made of white hair, in a variety of subtle tints. There is already a good deal of variation in length, volume and form: in XVIIIc. wigs will become specialized by professions, and will last be worn by bishops in XIXc.; though they are still assumed in English official and legal wear. Diderot's *Encyclopédie* says that a wig might cost as much as 1,000 écus, but there were cheap wigs of goat's hair, and horsehair wigs which retained their curl. Wigs had to be dressed every two weeks, and preferably much more often; strenuous sports, like tennis, declined in popularity while wigs were in fashion.

Coat sleeves are longer and wider; skirts of coat full, with additional width pleated in at side-seam. Ambassador wears a shoulder knot of fringed ribbon.

The king had never liked the fontange headdress. On this state occasion the decorously gowned and gloved ladies wear it only as a backing for hair dressed in twin, diamond-studded peaks. In 1699, as fontanges two feet high seem to topple, d'Angeau's diary tells us that the king's distaste was so marked that the wife of the exiled English king, James II, gave up the fontange, and "in the twinkling of an eye, the ladies went from one extremity to the other." (Lacroix: *Eighteenth Century.*) Paris was less quick to follow Versailles, but the fontange was doomed.

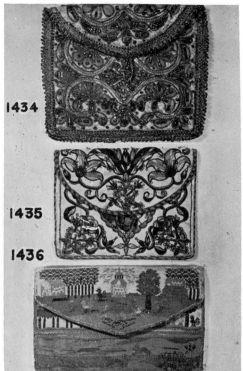

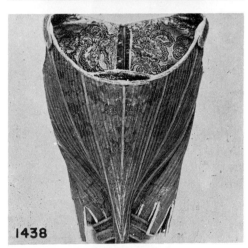

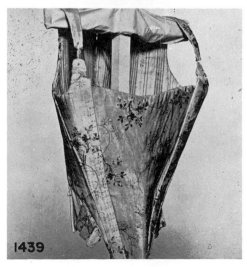

1431. XVI-XVIIc. English. (Boston, Museum of Fine Arts.) Needlepoint Bag:

Multicolor on Silver Ground.

1432. XVIIc. French. (Boston, Museum of Fine Arts, Elizabeth Day McCormick Coll.)

Brocade Pocket Book.

1433. XVIIc. French. (Boston, Museum of Fine Arts.)

Brocade Purse, showing the "Four Quarters of the Globe"; multicolored brocade with silver camel.

1434. XVII-XVIIIc. Spanish. (New York, Cooper Union Mus.)

Card Case.

1435. XVII-XVIIIc. Spanish. (New York, Cooper Union Mus.)

Card Case.

1436. XVIIc. English. (New York, Cooper Union Museum.)

Purse.

1437. XVIIc. American. (Brooklyn Mus.)

Corset of Natural Linen.

1438. XVIIc. c. 1620. French. (Boston, Museum of Fine Arts, Elizabeth Day McCormick Coll.)

Corset: blue silk damask, over wood; printed linen lining, brown on white. Built-in front pocket to hold a bottle of water to keep a bouquet fresh.

1439. XVIIIc. French. (Brooklyn Mus.)

Corset of Brocade. (See Appendix.)

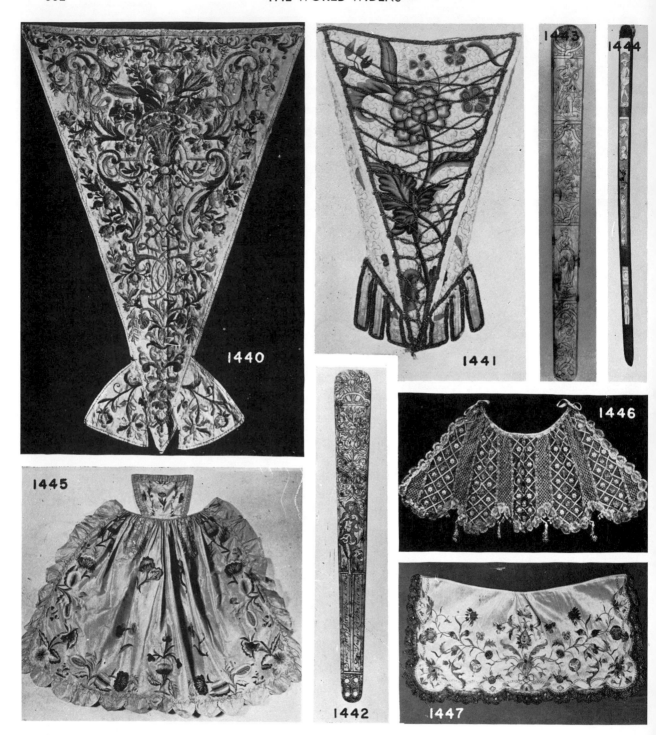

1440

1441

1443

1444

1445

1442

1446

1447

1440. Early XVIIIc. Italian. (Boston, Museum of Fine Arts.)

Embroidered Stomacher: white silk ground, polychrome silk embroidery.

1441. Early XVIIIc. English. (Metropolitan Museum.)

Embroidered Stomacher: silk embroidery on linen.

1442. XVIc. French. (Metropolitan Museum.)

Busk: steel with engraved inscription.

1443. XVIIc. French. (Metropolitan Museum.)

Busk: engraved ivory.

1444. XVIIIc. 1700-50. Italian? (Metropolitan Museum.)

Busk: wood inlaid with ivory, mother-of-pearl and tortoise shell.

1445. XVIIc. c. 1685. French. (Boston, Museum of Fine Arts, Elizabeth Day McCormick Coll.)

Embroidered Apron: yellow taffeta.

1446. XVIIIc. French. (Boston, Museum of Fine Arts, Elizabeth Day McCormick Coll.)

Gold Lace Apron (see Ill. 1455.)

1447. XVIIIc. French. (Boston, Museum of Fine Arts, Elizabeth Day McCormick Coll.)

1448

1449

1450

1451

1452

White Taffeta Apron: multicolor embroidery and gold bobbin lace edging.

In 1711, when Swift sent Stella silver lace for an under-petticoat, the entry of bullion lace had already been forbidden on pain of forfeiture and a £100 fine.

"Whereas two pieces of Silver Bone lace was brought to a shop in Winchester Street to be weighed, the Lace being suppos't to be stol'n, is stoped."† Mechlin and Brussels lace appeared in England under Anne.

1448. XVIIc. c. 1680. French. (Boston, Museum of Fine Arts, Elizabeth Day McCormick Coll.)

Woman's Shoe: light tan leather, dark olive green satin, and yellow straw appliqué simulating gold, seen also on bodice (Ill. 2084).

―――――――

† see Appendix.

1449. XVIIc. French. (Metropolitan Museum.)

Woman's Shoe: white kid and polychrome silk embroidery.

1450, 1452. First half XVIIIc. French. (Boston, Museum of Fine Arts, Elizabeth Day McCormick Coll.)

Woman's Brocade Shoe and Matching Clog: taupe satin ground, design white, yellowish green, pinkish red, pink, blue, and light tan; bound with dark brown.

1451. XVIIIc. c. 1750. English. (Metropolitan Museum.)

Woman's Shoes: these came to light during excavations in London, together with a quantity of men's knit hats and shoes. Heels covered with tan taffeta, narrowly edged with silver braid; vamps of leather and canvas, covered with green silk damask, and embroidered in silver. Similar pair dated c.1750, London Museum Catalogue of Costume, p.184,pl.LV.

1453. XVIIc. French. (Morgan
　　Library.)

J. Mariette. Mlle. de Pons.

In her difficult days as the
widow of Scarron, Mme. de
Maintenon was loyally ad-
mired by Bonne de Pons, who
became Marquise d'Heudi-
court, and her sister. With sufficient research, one could undoubtedly discover a good reason, and a date, for Mlle. de
Pons' appearance here; it
seems probable that she was a
relative of these old friends,
and sponsored at court, like so
many other girls, by Mme. de
Maintenon. She may have become the abbess, sister of
Prince Camille de Pons, who
as Mme. de Marsin was governess of Louis XV's children,
and like her father and brother received an income from
the king.

Whatever the date of the
plate, Mlle. de Pons' muff and
wrap indicate one of the very
cold winters, while the persistent bows on her corset, and
the unexaggerated fontange,
which are about all we can
see of her dress, suggest a date
not later than 1694.

1454. XVIIc. 1696. French.
　　(Morgan Library.)

A. Trouvain. Madame la
Princesse de Bade.

1455. XVIIc. French. (Morgan
　　Library.)

A. Trouvain. Madame la
Duchesse de Chartres.

1456. XVIIc. c. 1697. French.
　　(Morgan Library.)

A. Trouvain. Charlotte,
Landgrave of Hesse Cassel,
Queen of Denmark.

In the costumes of Mlle. de
Pons, the princess of Baden,
and Madame la Duchesse, we
see the steps by which line is
transformed into motion, like
that shown in the dress of the queen of Denmark.

Stiff brocaded fabrics, in large patterns, are giving
way to plain materials, gathered flounces and horizontal lines. The uncluttered gored skirt worn by the
first two ladies has been given additional fullness
(and motion), in the gown of the duchess by the
three great pleats set on either side. Mlle. de Pons'
skirt is of a large-patterned material, unadorned except for a hem binding, but the brocade of her very
new fringed wrap is lightly patterned. The princess'
skirt is of plain material; its bandings, wide but delicate in pattern, are set in predominantly vertical lines,
related to the goring. But there are underlying horizontal lines, and both are combined to form the
newly important wide band around the hem.

The duchess' costume is of delicately striped brocade. Its vertical lines are swamped, on the underskirt, by two wide horizontal bands, sparkling with
diamonds and shaking with fringe and tassels. A
third band is furnished by the metal lace apron; it is
only a step to the three gathered flounces of metal lace
worn by the queen. Purely decorative aprons, like the
metal lace one worn by the duchess, will be so universally worn that "low as a lady's apron strings"
will be the Tatler's description of a gallant bow in
society.

In its old form shown on the state ceremonial
dresses worn at Montargis (1430), the overskirt was
drawn back in a smooth flowing line and clasped at
intervals to the underskirt; now it is being bunched
up, in ways which culminate in the actual bustle
worn by the queen. On the princess, its corners stick

out; on the duchess, they are edged with passemen-terie; on the queen's gown, of perfectly plain material, they are edged with gathered lace. The skirt edges are now caught together at the center-back; and the frilled corners cascade below the bustle into which the top of the skirt is puffed.

1454. Prince Louis of Baden is actually in command of the Imperial forces opposing France in Italy, in 1696. But there are reasons for his wife's appearance here and now. Prince Louis, head of the Catholic branch of his house, is the hero who vanquished the Turks in 1689 and 1691. Louis XIV, not a bad Catholic, but a better Frenchman, had not entirely rejoiced with the rest of the Catholic world when a menace was removed from his enemy's back; and even Villars had opposed France's wanton devastation of Baden. John Sobieski III, who had saved Vienna from the Turks, has just died. There are eighteen candidates for the vacant throne of Poland; among them, Prince Louis vies with the duke of Lorraine, the prince of Conti, and Don Livio Odescalchi, nephew of Pope Innocent. In the end, the Elector of Saxony will win, by 8,000,000 florins and the renunciation of his Lutheranism, but at the moment it appears that the princess of Baden may well become the new queen of Poland. What the princess did become was an ancestor of Philippe-Egalité. Her daughter, not yet born, will be the adored wife of the Regent's scholar-naturalist son, for love of whom he will renounce the world, after her death in her second childbed.

1456. The court of the dissolute Danish king was a lavish imitation of Versailles; its amiable queen had the just sympathy and admiration of all Europe. Colored examples of this print show a fontange of red, blue, and gold; a red bodice with a gold *gourgandine,* a corset lacing over the fullness of the chemise (see Illus. 1465) like that of the duchess; a red overskirt, lined with blue, and flounced with white lace; an underskirt with alternating gold and silver *falabas,* the lace flounces which were introduced by Mme. de Maintenon.

Galloon is used on all these costumes; since metal galloon was wiry, it is pleated and bent, rather than cut, except where a band of fringe or another galloon would prevent fraying. It appears in the belt around the natural waistline of the queen; in bows on her muff and that of Mlle. de Pons; and hanging from the duchess' fan, always in combination with elaborately tasseled fringes.

Diamond earrings and a choker of huge pearls are standard with all who can afford them; obviously Mlle. de Pons cannot, and in any case she is unmarried. A cord, closed by a diamond slide, may be dropped into the corsage or display a diamond cross like that of the duchess. A profusion of immense diamonds is also sewn on the skirt bandings of the king's daughter; and the Danish queen has a huge brooch pinned on her muff.

Mlle. de Pons stands on rough ground in front of the walled garden of a very modest country house, although it probably passed muster as a chateau. The royal ladies appear on marble-paved terraces, against suitably formal gardens, complete with fountains and wrought balustrades.

1457. XVIIc. 1695. French. (Morgan Library.)

A. Trouvain. The Duke of Savoy.

The father of the proposed bride of the duke of Burgundy is shown in clothes which are handsome but not of the cut current at the French court. Unless we are being given the artist's idea of foreign styles, the sleeve would appear to have remained close in Italy, so that there is a marked difference between the width of the brocade cuff and the forearm of the sleeve. In France, the sleeve is easier at the top and increases in width to the cuff, which is scarcely wider than the bottom of the sleeve. The underarm seam has the old emphasis, and the skirts have little flare. He wears a *Steinkirk* and a magnificent scarf of fringe and passementerie; this holds in place the diagonal ribbon and its pendant ornament, which is probably that of a knightly order although it might just conceivably be a watch. Shoes have the old square toe and high tongue.

1458. XVIIc. French. (Boston, Museum of Fine Arts, Elizabeth Day McCormick Coll.)

N. Bonnart. Spanish Dress.

Bonnart's plate of Spanish dress no doubt antedates Trouvain's of Italian, but it is convenient to set them together as French pictures of foreign fashions.

The proud Castilian is somberly dressed as what may now be a sort of stage figure of a Spaniard: flat-crowned, wide-brimmed hat; his own lank hair, with a lock in front of the ear, specific form of moustachio and goatee; golilla and wrist ruffles on a jacket which retains the Spanish shoulder-cap; long cape; Spanish rapier; rosette-trimmed shoes of comparatively natural shape, without heels.

1459. XVIIc. 1696. French. (Morgan Library.)

A. Trouvain. Charles de Lorraine, Count de Marsin.

The house of Lorraine had long been alienated from France. Charles of Lorraine, who passed his life, Voltaire said, in losing his estates, had sold the succession of Lorraine and Bar to Louis XIV against a life income. His subjects would have none of this arrangement; Charles abdicated in favor of his brother, the cardinal-bishop of Toul, and fought against France in the army of his brother-in-law, the emperor Leopold. His brother, who had never taken orders, was enabled to marry his cousin, Claude of Lorraine. Their son, Charles, whose title was recognized everywhere but in France, helped to defeat the Turks and was one of the candidates for the Polish throne; he failed to seize Lorraine in 1676, and refused its restoration in partial form. It was finally returned to

his son, Leopold, who ruled it admirably. Upon the marriage of Maria Theresa to Leopold's heir, Francis of Lorraine, Louis XV arranged to keep prosperous Lorraine from being joined to the Empire, by exchanging it for the Grand Duchy of Tuscany, which the heirs of the Empire ruled well. From his genial and learned little court at Nancy, Louis XV's Polish father-in-law administered Lorraine and Bar, which prospered under the legendary "good king Stanislas," until it reverted to France on his death at 89. Nothing endeared Stanislas more to his people than his original method of taxation. He went to church, rose after the sermon, waved his hat for attention, and mentioned the sum he needed. Men would sneak the linen out of the house and sell it to augment their share, since the king returned any surplus. (Mme. Campan).

Marsin or Marchin, a property of the House of Lorraine, was a name used by its cadet branch, to which the Chevalier de Lorraine belonged; he was a dissolute crony of "Monsieur," and gossip credited him with having poisoned the latter's first wife, Henrietta Maria.

As we see in the garments of the count of Marsin, the coat which is intended to be worn open, displaying a handsomely laced waistcoat, is still of the older, straighter cut; its lining is important, its inner edge is braided, and its buttons remain small. The old running braids are largely replaced by scalloped, lace-like passementerie. His shoulder knot is of cord, finished with points. The influence of the *Steinkirk* is seen in the less formal cravats, the pointed or rounded ends of which are merely folded over.

1460. XVIIc. French. (Morgan Library.)

A. Trouvain. Monsieur le Duc de Chartres.

The eventual regent Orleans (nephew and son-in-law of Louis XIV), was a greatly gifted man with an extraordinary memory, and another victim of the conditions of court life. He had distinguished himself at Steinkirk, but was shunted off upon his return to Versailles. He combined a dissolute life in Paris with serious study of chemistry, painting and music.

Suspected of intriguing to replace Philip V as king of Spain, he was called back by Louis from brilliant military successes in Spain. Upon Louis' death he became regent by right of birth, succeeded in breaking Louis' will and attempted many liberal reforms. He gave back to Parliament rights which Louis had suppressed, attempted to enlist the services of the nobility which Louis had wasted, reduced taxes, liberated the Jansenists, and dreamed of revoking the

Revocation of the Edict of Nantes. But as an alternative to the bankruptcy of the state, which he had received in frightful financial condition, he became involved in the theories of the Scotch economist, John Law. Law's state banking system collapsed in 1719 after sensational beginnings and reckless speculation by all classes, who completely blocked traffic outside the offices of his Mississippi Company in Paris on the rue de Quincampoix. After this debacle and the suppression of the duke and duchess de Maine's conspiracy to replace him by Philip V, the Regent returned to the old governmental ways, serving as first minister from the majority of Louis XV, until his own death in 1723.

Chartres' costume, like that of the duke of Burgundy (1461), shows the increasing fullness of the skirts of the coat gored and pleated in at the hips. Coats are now, as often as not, made completely of brocade, which is more apt to be in a smaller repeated pattern than in the large, scrolled lace patterns used in the embroidery on the cuffs. When braid is used, its patterns are broken up, as in the zig-zag on Chartres' coat; the old block patterns in which braid was formerly applied are used by Burgundy in the placing of his sets of diamond buttons; these are now of immense size and Chartres uses scarcely smaller ones on his waistcoat as well.

Both wear hats cocked into definite tricornes. These have lost the lace edging which still appears on the hat of the prince of Savoy, and the plumes he shows have been reduced in France to a bare fringe of feathers, which will become a line of binding.

Burgundy's court costume, like those worn at Montargis (No. 1430), shows a square-edged cravat, but all are now folded over informally. Wrist ruffles are merely a fine finish to an unseen shirt sleeve. Shoulder-knots appear very generally; like sword-knots and the bows worn on muffs, they are finished by handsome, tassel-trimmed fringes. Shoes high, close, and delicate have a reduced tongue and a larger buckle than those worn by the duke of Savoy.

1461. XVIIc. 1697. French. (Morgan Library.)
Trouvain. Duke of Roquelaure.

Military life seems to have made Roquelaure, who became Marshal in 1724, extremely inventive about comfortable outer garments. This tasseled cape with a turned down collar is the forerunner of a loose, buttoned greatcoat with capes and pockets, which was still called a *Roquelaure* in midXIXc.

1462. XVIIc. 1695. French. (Morgan Library.)
Berey. Louis, Duke of Burgundy.

This engraving celebrates the marriage in December, 1697, of the Dauphin's eldest son to the little princess of Savoy (see Illus. 1430). He holds a portrait of her (wearing a *gourgandine*) propped on a carved table against a background of painted wall panels.

He is still the boy whose paroxysms of ungovernable rage, if crossed by no more than the weather, seemed to endanger his life and filled the court with apprehension at the prospect of his reign.

It is winter, although the fountains are still playing, as they do below the parterre on which Marsin walks in his summer clothes; Burgundy carries a muff suspended from his sash by the ribbon called a *passe-caille*. His breeches, like those of Chartres, are close and simple, without the obvious garter still worn by his father-in-law (1457).

DEVELOPMENT OF TRADES

The early craft guilds were composed of workmen, foremen, employers, merchants, and shopkeepers. In XIVc. the guilds began to split into trade and handicraft groups. Within these, major and minor guilds struggled for power. Should the blade- or the handle-maker control the knife trade? If weavers can dye, why cannot dyers weave?

The handicraft groups split into masters, and journeymen, many of whom could never hope to become masters. After an apprenticeship of 3-6 years, it was necessary to produce an expensive "master piece," pay a high entrance fee, and provide a banquet, even when guild membership was not limited to the children of masters.

Craftsmen within the livery companies were split into first and second class members: masters, and yeomen-bachelors, whose functions were defined. By end XIVc., shoemakers work with new leather; cobblers mend but do not make. Traders do not manufacture; masters do not do journeymen's work; journeymen are not supposed to do masters' work.

By 1405, the clothing trade had become divided into doublet-makers, who provided ready-made garments, and tailors who made to order. Fabrics were provided by the merchant guild of drapers; they considered the stock of trimmings kept by tailors as an infringement on their trade, and had them taxed.

Journeymen began to evade the control of the guilds by moving from their jurisdiction; great suburbs arose outside the city limits of London and Paris. In Germany, which was made up of small principalities, the journeymen were particularly hard to control, and took up the wandering careers which were still characteristic of itinerant German printers in America, into XXc.

Such conditions weakened the craft guilds by XVIc. The merchant-trader's guilds became richer and more powerful; they began to cut in on the trade guilds by their control of supplies; they brought in competing foreign goods. Guilds of merchants and artificers began to combine, always to the advantage of the merchant members.

The cap makers and hat merchants combined into the Merchant Haberdashers of 1500. The "linen armourers," tailors, and merchants were re-incorporated in 1503, as the Merchant Taylors, with Henry VII as an honorary member. The separately incorporated Fullers and Shearmen of 1507 were amalgamated in second quarter XVIIc. into the Clothworkers; they grew rich; many of their members became aldermen, and one, Lord Mayor; they rivalled the Drapers Company, one of the great original twelve.

The craftsmen of the early guilds, and the trading masters and yeomen of the XVc. were further split, in Elizabeth's time, into shipping merchants, merchant employers, small masters, and journeymen. The merchant employers became wholesale traders or large masters; the interests of small masters and journeymen began to coalesce in Stuart days.

The breeches-makers of Paris (equivalent to the Merchant Taylors of London) had acquired large interests in cloth production; in 1575 they combined with the drapers to control cloth (as the Merchant Taylors and Clothmakers did in London). The poorer masters were reduced to peddling breeches on the streets. Haberdashers and felt-makers combined in Paris in e.XVIIc.

In Paris in 1655, the *maîtres-marchands-tailleurs* (made-to-order) and the *marchands-pourpointiers* (ready-made) combined into the *maîtres-marchands tailleurs-pourpointiers* to control the clothing trade. By 1660, new statutes prevent *marchands, fripiers,* and *drapiers,* who are not members of the tailors' association, to make or sell any new garment.

A legacy from the old scramble to annex power can be seen in the variety of merchandise which may be sold in shops of a certain category. In the illustrations of Diderot's "Encyclopédie" we see that the XVIIIc. *boursier* manufactured not only purses, but certain sorts of caps, parasols, and Bavarian leather breeches. (See Appendix.)

1463-64. XVIIc. French. (Boston, Museum of Fine Arts, Elizabeth Day McCormick Coll.)

After *Nicolas de Larmessin, e.*
1463. Shoemaker.
1464. Tabletier.

Two of 25 hand colored plates which are contemporary piracies (in reversed position) of the enormously popular series of costume fantasies, based on occupations, by Larmessin, the elder, (1640-1725). The shoemaker exhibits among his footwear a man's shoe with a high platform sole and heel, clogs, *pantoufles,* boots, and shoes. A *tabletier* provides games, made from ivory, bone, horn, and ebony; and as the plates in the "Encyclopédie" show, makes other objects like combs and small boxes from the same materials. *Trou-madame* was one of the standard amusements at Louis XIV's *appartements;* unfamiliar game-accessories can be looked up in D'Allemagne. (See Appendix.)

1465. XVIIc. 1697. French. (Metropolitan Museum, Print Room.)

N. Arnoult. The French Tailor.

Since tailors had developed out of the *pourpointiers* and linen-armorers who provided padded and boned garments, corset-making was considered as part of tailoring; in any case, the corset was often a visible integral part of the gown.

Les Cris de Paris.

1466

Paris Chez F. Guerard vis a vis la fontaine St Severin a limage Notre Dame.

The five sets of plates of *Corps,* under *Tailleur* in Diderot's "Encyclopédie," show corsets for court and horseback, for pregnant women, boys and girls, as well as the difference between the long-bodied, straight-sided English corset, plain in front and laced down the back; and the curving lines of the French corset with its laced V-front.

1466. End XVIIc. or Early XVIIIc. French. (Morgan Library.)

F. Guérard. Cries of Paris.

As the easiest short-cut to an air of fashion, the *fontange* is quickly adopted by young women of the people. It is worn by the sellers of iced *tisane,* carp, tender root-vegetables, and by the girl with bouquets of jonquils, whose skirt hem is embroidered **and apron** edged with lace. The rather well-dressed young woman with the milk-jar on her head can only wear a cap with falls. The old women with baskets of artichokes and celery have bundled up their heads in the age-old kerchief.

The comfort of workingmen's clothes is slowly affected by fashion. Except for the young melon seller, they wear smocks; hand-me-down coats, long and straight; outmoded rabats, a knotted strip of something white, or no linen at all; comfortable full breeches; and flapping felt hats or cast-off *monteros.*

It seems to be a rule that for some time before privilege is about to be lost, those who enjoy it actually begin to lose their taste for it, whether or not they are conscious of the change, and whether or not they will fight to hold their privilege.

In XVIIIc., milkmaid styles begin to be worn as an alternative to oppressively panniered gowns. Style-consciousness increases among the lower classes. The pretty way in which the market women of Covent-garden manipulate a silk handkerchief as a head and neck covering will be copied by a famous procuress, adopted by her girls, carried by them to Ranelagh, and as the "Ranelagh Mob," will be worn by the aristocracy. (See Appendix.)

1467

From C. H. Collins Baker and W. G. Constable: *English Painting in 16th and 17th Centuries.*

1467. XVIIc. June 16, 1600. English. (Sherborne Castle, Lieut. Col. Wingfield-Digby.)

Marcus Gheeraerts, e. Visit of Queen Elizabeth to Blackfriars.

In describing the wedding of Lord Herbert and Lady Anne Russell, R. Whyte wrote Sir Robert Sidney: "The bride met the Queen at the waterside, where my Lord Cobham had provided a lectica made like a litter, whereon she was carried to my Lady Russell's by six knights." The last of these is the groom, dressed in white, as are his father (2nd from left), the Queen, and the bride who follows. The gentlemen preceding the Queen wear the Garter and its Collar, with pendant miniature of the Queen; black cloaks embroidered in gold; and costumes for the most part in combinations of pale shades of rose, gray and green; with ruffs of many layers worn high. Lord Cobham, sword in hand, precedes the litter, dressed in peacock blue.

Dark colors, preferred earlier in Elizabeth's reign, "only white excepted which was then much worn at court," are beginning to alter to the light colors preferred in "King James his Reigne" (Moryson). From late Elizabethan times, short velvet capes, in their grandest form are often made of beaver, like the costumes of the ambassadors sent to France to arrange Charles I's marriage: "cloak and hose of fine white beaver, richly embroidered with gold, particularly the cloak within and without, nearly to the cape. The doublet was of cloth of gold, embroidered so thick that it could not be discerned, and the whole beaver hat was full of embroidery both above and below."

The Virgin Queen and bride wear open ruffs, and have huge pendants pinned to their left sleeves. The attendant ladies wear the closed ruffs of married women, very wide, full, and lacy, but carried lower on the neck.

In the background are the Gentlemen Pensioners with their halberds; their rich costumes are uniform only in their black and gold color. They were established by Henry VIII at his accession as the second oldest English royal bodyguard, antedated only by Henry VII's Yeomen of the Guard, which stand behind the litter in this illustration, wearing the union rose (gold on silver) and skull-caps instead of bonnets. Norris suggests that this may be a concession to their age, in a bareheaded procession. (See Appendix.)

The Yeomen of the Guard "were wont to be 250 Men of best quality under the Gentry, and of larger Stature than ordinary (for every one of them was to be Six Feet high) . . . of later Times reduced to 170 . . . at present no more than 100. These wear Scarlet Coats down to the Knee, and Scarlet Breeches, both richly guarded with black Velvet, and rich badges upon their Coats, before and behind; moreover, black Velvet round broad-crown'd Caps (according to the Mode used in the Reign of Henry VIII), with Ribbands of the King's Colour: One Half of them formerly bore in their Hands Harquebuses (but ever since the Reign of King *William* the Harquebuses have been disused); and the other Half, Partizans, with large Swords by their sides." (Chamberlayne)

1468. XVIIc. c. 1600. English. (Metropolitan Mus.)
Unknown artist. Queen Elizabeth.

The new tendency of bodice and skirt to separate can be seen in the different materials used in this example of Elizabeth's standardized personal costume, towards the end of her reign. (See Appendix.)

Where her head is framed by the loops of her wired headdress, lesser ladies may show a quivering, aigrette-like hair decoration, allied to the spray at Elizabeth's breast.

She shows looped bracelets of pearls, caught to sleeve and little-finger ring, and the new naturalism and asymmetry in the rose buds fastened to her ruff.

1469. XVIIc. c. 1611. English.
Renold Elstrack. James I and Anne of Denmark.

A number of engravings show the new king and queen after his accession in 1604. In one by Wierix c. 1605, the king wears truncated conical hat, falling band, cuirasse and scarf, and short open breeches, from under which hang gathered garters. The queen is dressed with comparative simplicity; much less hair, combed up into a point, love-locks in front of each ear, skirt without cartwheel top, falling in gathers over a small bolster.

Theirs was not the elegant court of Elizabeth. James had grown into an ill-proportioned slovenly man, who, though an accomplished rider, had to be tied in the saddle. "He never washed his hands, only rubbed his fingers' ends slightly with the wet end of a napkin." (Sir Anthony Weldon)

The luxury, masques and amusements of the English court were a revelation to the king of poor Scotland and his provincial Danish queen. But James never cared about his own dress, except that the doublets be quilted against his fears of assassination; on his clumsy body nothing looked well. Though we see him here in rosetted shoes, he protested their making a "ruffe-footed dove" of him.

James poured out luxury, however, on his handsome favorite Buckingham whom he called "Steenie," while signing himself "the old purveyor." In the "little language" of the royal family we find James' detestation of pigs, and his characterization of Steenie as a dog preserved. Buckingham impudently calls James "His Sowship," and Anne of Denmark writes Steenie to "lug the sow by the ears." Buckingham writes from Spain (where he had accompanied Charles I on his fruitless, romantic quest for the Infanta) for more jewels: the king's best hat band, the Portugal diamond and the rest of the pendant diamonds, to make a necklace for the princess, and some rich chains for himself, else "your dog will want a collar."

"The wisest fool in Christendom," as Henry IV called James, had great pedantic learning, a quick coarse tongue, and a stubborn belief in absolutism, which embattled him with Parliaments and Puritans.

One of James' literary works was his "Counterblast to Tobacco," in 1610. Brought back, perhaps by Hawkins, in the third quarter XVIc., the use of the herb spread rapidly. Harrison in 1573 says: "In these daies, the taking-in of the smoke of the Indian herbe called 'tabaco' by an instrument formed like a litle ladell, whereby it passeth from the mouth into the hed and stomach, is gretlie taken-up and used in England, against Rewmes and some other diseases ingendred in the longes and inward parts, and not without effect."

The king and queen, standing below the arms of their countries, show the reduction in the use of braid and of all-over patterned brocades, which are being replaced by embroidered patterns running up from the hem.

The King's plumed bowler has a slightly cocked, wider brim; hair no longer cropped close; pleats shaping collar to neck show transition of open ruff into falling band collar; cape lengthening; pendant of the lesser George hanging by a scarf; doublet with slit, overlapping skirts; full breeches with padding and fabric cut and gathered as one; lace edged garter bow and the Garter on right leg; shoes with heels and rosettes.

The Queen's hair is padded very high and wide, with large, sparsely set decorations and a great brush-plume; frizzed curls along the hairline will soon become a straight fringe; slashing of sleeve just below the shoulder will be developed; pearls strung baldric-wise (like a military scarf); very wide drum skirt with elaborate cartwheel top; increasing importance of the skirt of the kirtle. Anne had inherited the 3,000 gowns in Elizabeth's wardrobe, many of them magnificently embroidered, and usable. (See Appendix).

1470. XVIIc. 1604. English. (London, Nat. Port. Gall.)
M. Gheeraerts. Somerset House Conference.

As King of Scotland, James had not been at war with Spain. The agreeable Juan de Tassis, sent by Lerma to congratulate James on his accession, had ingratiated himself and bested the French ambassador with many gifts of perfumed Spanish leather and gloves. Hostilities were suspended by James, who wished to see an end to the religious conflicts.

In 1604, after weeks of negotiations, during which the Spanish grandees were entertained by James at Somerset House at a cost of £300 a day, and after extensive bribing of the Howard faction by the duke of Frias, Constable of Castile, who headed the delegation, a peace was signed which left Holland alone, finally to conclude her struggles with the Archdukes in 1609.

Against tapestried walls, the Spanish plenipotentiaries on the left of the council table, which is covered with a fine rug, have the nearly identical somber costumes, neck and wrist ruffs, and beards as those painted by El Greco. There is more variety in the English negotiators: in the cut of their hair and beards, little caps on old bald heads near the open window, more complicated ruffs, braided and buttoned light doublets, short capes, and the preponderant absence of wrist ruffs.

1471. XVIIc. 1603. English. (Metropolitan Museum.)
Unknown artist (formerly att. to *Gheeraerts*). Henry Frederick, Prince of Wales, and Sir John Harington.

The lumpish, effeminate and timorous king, who had no taste at all, and his disdainful, masculine wife who had a great deal of taste, all of it bad, were the parents of two children in addition to Charles I, of the most luminous grace, dignity and taste. Henry, Prince of Wales and Elizabeth of Bohemia (who was called the "Queen of Hearts," because of her gallantry in exile) were, after all, grandchildren of Mary Queen of Scots.

From earliest childhood, Henry promised to become perhaps the greatest English king. He was already one of the four or five greatest book collectors of his time, and had formed an unsurpassed collection of coins and medals; he was a perfectionist as an athlete and horseman; he had his father's wit in a more attractive form; his was the most popular court, gay, intelligent and completely decorous. Young as he was, Henry championed Sir Walter Raleigh in the Tower, saying: "No King but his father would keep such a bird in such a cage;" and the realization of Henry's compassion, as Phineas Pett (Illus. 1485) knelt before the king during his entire trial for incompetence, led the old shipbuilder to name his next great 1400 ton warship "The Prince."

Henry's hunting companion is the son of Lord and Lady Harington, who had charge of his sister; their arms hang above them. Whether or not Henry was poisoned, before they were 19 both boys were dead. As he had for Elizabeth, James forbade the court to wear mourning for Henry.

Ruffs, originally of linen, were later made of lawn, and were sometimes dipped in colored starches. Ruffs of colored net, and collars of dyed batiste, edged with white lace (like the blue one the Prince wears here), are now occasionally seen. Yellow ruffs are constantly singled out for attack by writers and preachers in late XVI-e. XVIIc., and were forbidden in the Cathedral by the dean of Winchester. Their use came rather quickly to an end, when a physician's wife, Mrs. Turner (the leading yellow-starcher of her day, who was supposed to have brought the method from France), was condemned to be hung wearing one of her own abominable yellow ruffs; at the instigation of Lady Essex, she had poisoned Sir Thomas Overbury, while he was already imprisoned in the Tower for writing "The Wife," an attack on the liaison of his friend, the favorite Rochester, with the already infamous countess.

In latter half XVIc. lacy embroidery had begun to be used on high-crowned, plumed hats; replacing braid, it is now used only on edges and on the most important seams. The prince's doublet with overlapping skirts retains only a hint of the peascod belly.

He had been invested with the Garter in June and wears the pendant of the lesser George on its blue ribbon; his sword and hunting horn hang by two other crossed scarves. High boots with cuffs reversed. Cropped hair, with tiny lovelocks.

1472. Early XVIIc. German. (Hampton Court, H. M. the King.)

Unknown artist. Christian, Son of Henry, Duke of Brunswick.

Entire costume gored; seaming replacing braid decoration. Style comes as often out of limitations, as from any other factor: the cut of military leather garments was dependant on the size and imperfections of hides; new ways of cutting then affected non-military garments cut from cloth.

Around the turn of the century, there was a tendency to separate doublets and breeches completely, by color and decoration; the same impulse is followed in women's dress. During first half XVIIc., the costume will become completely unified. Both impulses are shown in this costume, in which the doublet of a dotted fabric, and breeches of plain, are both gored. The breeches, full, but gored and narrowed into the waist by additional interior gores, require a fly-closing; this is made of the dotted fabric of the doublet.

The collar, gored and standing like a ruff, is turning down into a band; it has the tasseled cords which have hung from band collars throughout second half XVIc., and which will continue to be used, but knotted, in XVIIc.

1473. XVIIc. 1608. English. (New York, Knoedler.)

M. Gheeraerts, y. Portrait of a Boy.

Embroidery began its rapid development in England during the latter part of Elizabeth's reign. The bold and fabulous growths, predominantly blue-green and rusty-red to yellow, familiar on the "crewel" embroidered white linen bed-hangings of second half XVIIc., stem from such work as Elizabeth's skirt in the Hardwick portrait, and the garments of this boy.

1474. XVIIc. 1611. English. (London, Christie sale, May 1, 1925.)

M. Gheeraerts, y. Frances Howard, Duchess of Richmond.

"Flowers and fanciful attire indicate festivities in connection with a wedding." (Morse: *Elizabethan Pageantry*.)

But, during the 100 years of her life, Frances Howard was always what in the U.S.A. today, would be called a "character." She gave supper parties with a great show of silver and plate, but no food, and ate alone later. She was immensely proud of the Dukes, her grandfathers, both dead on the scaffold; and lorded it over the Earl of Hertford, second of her three husbands, who used to take her down by asking: "Frank, Frank, how long is it since you were married to Prannell?" (Her first husband, a certain Prannell, had been, inexplicably, a London vintner of no pretensions whatever.) On the death of her third husband, Ludovic, Duke of Richmond, she announced that she would never again marry or eat at table with anyone less than a king.

Between 1610-20, necklines were occasionally cut much lower than on this bodice, even exposing the breasts entirely; male portraits in fancy dress show a doublet bosom cut almost away in the same manner.

With this neckline, a flat wired lace whisk is usually worn under the chin; its tasseled white ties hang down, over a black neck-cord falling between the breasts.

The lace-edge white bodice is scrolled with floral embroidery. The kirtle skirt, dark green, decorated in gold, is of the 1610-20 ankle length.

Her red cloak is worn in the currently beloved diagonal fashion; it is lined with white brocade; caught on one shoulder with a black bow; its embroidery is no longer in a band, but rises from the hem in patterns derived from reticella lace edgings.

White shoes with immense gold rosettes, airy decoration of the hair which is descending at the sides.

1475. XVIc. 1594. English. (Ditchley, Viscount Dillen.)

M. Gheeraerts. Capt. Thomas Lee.

This picture of male fancy dress is set, out of strict chronological order, as a parallel to Illus. 1474; the

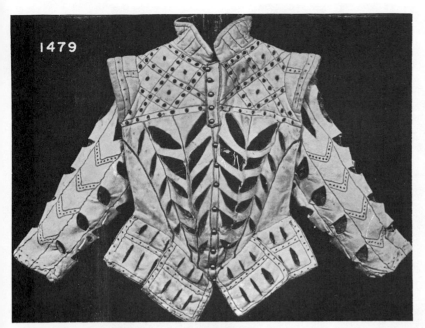

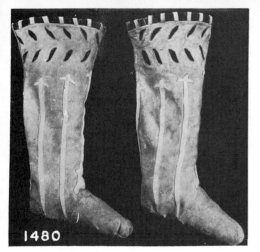

shirt open low on the bosom will also be seen in the Oliver miniature (Ill. 1491).

Capt. Lee wears a slightly peascod doublet open over a superbly embroidered shirt with a great lace collar; the length of the shirt is curiously rucked up and padded to simulate upper hose. With this vulnerable costume and bare legs and feet, he wears a pistol and dagger and carries a morion and shield.

1476. XVIc. English. (Boston, Museum of Fine Arts.)
Gloves with Embroidered Cuffs, said to have belonged to Queen Elizabeth.

1477. XVIIc. English. (Boston, Museum of Fine Arts.)
Gloves with Embroidered Cuffs.

1478. Early XVIIc. English. (Boston, Museum of Fine Arts.)
Embroidered Gloves.

1479. Late XVIc.-Early XVIIc. French. (Boston, Museum of Fine Arts, Elizabeth Day McCormick Coll.)
Man's Doublet: white leather, slashed and punched, trimmed with gold braid; olive green velvet (probably modern) under slashes; front padded in style known as *cosse des poies;* sleeves separate from rest

of doublet, but sewn to linen guimpe.

1480. Late XVIc.-Early XVIIc. French. (Boston, Museum of Fine Arts, Elizabeth Day McCormick Coll.)
Man's Leather Boots: light greyish white leather trimmed with appliqué of white leather; tops slashed with olive green velvet (possibly modern) under slashes.

1481. XVIIc. 1600. Bohemian. (Metropolitan Museum.)
Man's Pourpoint: cream satin, embroidered in colored silk.

1482. XVIIc. c. 1603-25. English. (Metropolitan Mus.)
Woman's Embroidered Jacket.

A guest at Elizabeth of Bohemia's wedding in 1613 wrote, "The Lady Wotton was reported to have a gown that cost 50 pound the yard for embroidery; and the Lord Montague bestowed 1500 pound in apparel upon his two daughters."

Photographs of a similar jacket, the actual garment painted in Ill. 1502, is reproduced with notes in A. F. Kendrick: *Book of Old Embroidery,* and *Embroidery,* part I, p. 17, fig. 10 and frontispiece.

1483. XVIIc. c. 1613. English. (Malmesbury, Charlton Park. Margaret, Countess of Suffolk and Berkshire.)

Daniel Mytens, e. Sir Edward Sackville, Fourth Earl of Dorset.

There is a companion portrait of his brother Richard, standing in the same setting; he wears one tasseled earring; his doublet, unbuttoned half way from the bottom, shows his full shirt, and has a baldric-like band disappearing into a slit in the bosom and crossing the shoulder underneath the garment; his lace-edged garters make a pattern against his stockings, and hang half way to the immense lace rosettes across on his shoes.

The Sackvilles were still children when Elizabeth died: Leicester and his elegance were gone before their birth. But their clothes are the last extravagant manifestation of the preceding period, and worn by no decadent courtiers, either. The Sackvilles, for all their personal beauty, were a family notable for wide interests, cultivation, courage, and competence. Edward was Bacon's defender, twice Ambassador to France, and privy-councillor to Charles I. It was he who retook the royal standard at Edgehill, after refusing Charles' order to conduct the young princes out of the battle, since "he would not be thought a coward for ever a King's son in Christendom." From Charles' execution until his own death, he never went out of Dorset House.

"The English," wrote Moryson at just about this time, "are more sumptuous than the Persians, because despising the golden meane, they affect all extremeties. For either they will be attired in plaine cloth and light stuffes (always provided that every day without difference their hats be of Bever, their shirts and bands of the finest linnen, their daggars and swords guilded, their garters and shooe roses of silke, with gold on silver laces, their stockings of silke wrought in the seames with silke or gold, and their cloakes in Summer of silke, in Winter at least all lined with velvet) or else they daily weare sumptuous doublets and breches of silke or velvet, or cloth of gold or silver, so laid over with lace of gold or silke, as the stuffes (though of themselves rich) can hardly be seen."

The brothers wear almost identical great lace-edged whisks; hair longer and fluffed; beards and moustaches reduced.

Edward's gloves deserve attention. They have the gauntlet cuff of the XVIIc.; but it is so related to the doublet in fabric, matching embroidery, and lace-edged scallops like those of the whisk, as to appear part of the doublet; a tiny wrist-ruff, set over the seam between leather hand and fabric gauntlet, adds to the illusion of a short glove worn with an extravagantly cuffed doublet. The ungloved hand shows the actual cuff to be a flat one of straight-edged lace.

"Milloners or haberdashers," Stow says in his varied spelling, "had not then any *gloves imbroidered,* or trimmed with gold or silke; neither gold nor imbroidered girdles and hangers, neither could they *make any costly wash* or *perfume,* until about the 15th yeere of the queane, the Right Honorable Edward de Vere, Earl of Oxford, came from *Italy,* and brought with him gloves, sweete bagges, a perfumed leather jerkin, and other *pleasant things*: and that yeere the queene had a *pair of perfumed gloves* trimmed only with four tuffes or *roses of coloured silke.* The queene tooke such pleasure in these gloves, that she was pictured with these gloves upon her handes, and for many years after it was called 'The Earl of Oxford' perfume."

Both brothers have heavily embroidered capes with wide collars slung over a shoulder; and wear immense, loose, embroidered slops. Edward is gartered below the knees; his silk stockings have embroidered clocks which almost surround the ankle; shoes with high heels and great choux on the strap are embroidered to match the doublet.

1484. Start of XVIIc. English. (London, Nat. Port. Gall.)

P. van Somer (copy of). Charles, tenth Earl of Nottingham.

The Lord High Admiral, Howard of Effingham, who vanquished the 149 great ships of the Armada with his 80 small ones, by "plucking their feathers one by one," was made Earl of Nottingham in 1596. He had advised Elizabeth to sign Mary Stuart's death warrant, and it was to him on her death bed that Elizabeth designated Mary's son as her successor. The Admiral retained his post under James I until charges of corruption, (in which the courteous and estimable old man of 82 had no part) brought about his resignation and the reorganization of the navy.

The admiral wears a cap indoors: quantities of these delightful caps, as well as the embroidered gloves of the period, are still in existence in our time. His hat stands on a table covered by a fine carpet; imported rugs are still luxury articles, although they have begun to be manufactured in England, in last quarter XVIc., and are the models for small pieces of tufted "Turkey work." Fringed velvet covers, often embroidered (Ill. 1486), tend to replace rugs as table coverings.

Scarlet peer's robes are worn with the Garter and its collar and blue sash. Doublet is slightly peascod; paned trunk hose will be retained with ceremonial robes. Shoes have high cork soles, raised in back, which preceded heels; ribbon ties over a tongue. Walking stick.

1485. XVIIc. 1613. English. (London, Nat. Port. Gall.)

Unknown painter. Phineas Pett, Master-builder of the Navy.

Ships had been built along the S.E. coast of Eng-

possible, so great and so casual were the movements of English armed shipping, whether independent or the Queen's own.

Despite the corrupt and lax administrations of the Admirals Effingham and Buckingham, and his own inadequate resources, James I showed great interest in maintaining his fleet.

Under his master-builder, Phineas Pett, naval construction advanced from a knack of science.

In 1641, Evelyn, saw the launching of Pett's "glorious vessel, the Royal Sovereign," (the first to be taxed and a contributing cause of the Great Rebellion). He banqueted with Pett at his country house, with its statues and gardens, and calls Pett "the most skillful shipbuilder in the world . . . the inventor of the frigate-fashion of building." By 1660, ships could be built of such size that an hereditary Royal Navy was no longer possible; Charles II had to levy taxes for their support. Evelyn had been impressed by the pleasure boats he saw in Holland; in 1661, the Dutch East India Company presented Charles I with the first yacht to be owned in England.

In his office above the shipyards (which we see through the window) Pett wears the embroidered cap which any man of the XVIIc. would have worn indoors in a less draughty place.

Pett's wired whisk shows a few of the pleats of its ancestor, the open ruff. Its dangling cords are now knotted.

The shorter-waisted pinked doublet shows sleeves

1485   1486

land, under expert Genoese supervision, since e.XIVc. Men-of-war were, however, a personal possession of the king, until second half XVIIc. No ruler before the Tudors had enough wealth for naval expansion. Henry VIII in his 5th year, "built a Ship, then accounted the biggest that ever had been seen in England, and named it Henry Grace de Dieu, or the Great Henry; it was 1000 tons." (Chamberlayne)

Until Henry VIII, privateers and merchant adventurers, exempt from admiralty control, had largely to look out for themselves and the defense of their own part of the coast. Under Elizabeth, incentives of piracy and trade expanded shipyards enormously. The Emperor's agent found effective espionage im-

caught along the inseam by bows; full baggy breeches, braided along the outer seam. Sword slung in the old manner. Rather full beard of a worthy man, neither young nor elegant.

1486. XVIIc. 1618-21. English. (London, Nat. Port. Gall.)

School of P. van Somer. Francis Bacon, Baron Verulam, Viscount St. Alban.

The impatient, ambitious intelligence of Burleigh's nephew, and his eloquence, of which Ben Jonson said "the fear of every man that heard him was lest he should make an end," alienated Elizabeth from utilizing Bacon's services. Under James I he rose quickly to the Lord Chancellorship, and aroused the fears of the favorite, Buckingham. Bacon was accused of corruption (of a sort generally accepted in his day), acknowledged his conviction to be "just, and for reformation's sake, fit," and retired from government to continue his philosophical and scientific writing. These works helped to free science from theology and laid the base for modern experimental investigation. Bacon's death resulted from an experiment; he took a fatal chill when he got out of his coach to pack a chicken carcass with snow, so that he might study the effect of refrigeration on putrefaction.

The hat with truncated cylindrical crown, seen last quarter XVIc., is wider brimmed, wreathed with a crepe twist. Hair longer; beard like that which Evelyn's father in 1620 "wore a little peaked as the mode was." The Chancellor's gown has a hanging sleeve strip and braid trim; he leans on a walking stick.

Braid is changing its character from flat, woven, running bands into rounded, braided open forms used with braided buttons, knotted, looped and fringed into frogged fastenings and patterns.

1487. XVIc. 1566 Dutch. (Metropolitan Museum.)

Quilted Cap of White Linen.

The parchment which was preserved with this cap is dated "Bruxelles, anno MDLXVI," and announces in Latin that it was made by Margaret of Parma's own hands, and is ordered by her to be given to Antonio du Granvelle, described as a most eminent and trusty servant of Philip, king of Spain. The Cardinal, her chief counsellor, seems to have revered it too much to wear it.

1488. Late XVIIc. Italian. (Metropolitan Museum.)

Man's cap: Knitted green and white silk.

1489. Early XVIIIc. English. (Metropolitan Museum.)

Man's Cap: White linen, embroidered in colored silk. Early XVIIc. versions of this embroidered cap have been seen in Ills. 1470, 1484, 1485.

When Miss Molly set out to marry old Isaac Bickerstaff, we are told (Tatler, #91, Nov. 8, 1709). "Things went so far that my mistress presented me with a wrought night-cap and a laced band of her own working."

The head of a well-born male is seldom seen uncovered. The hat is worn indoors as well as out, although it may be replaced by one of these caps. As heads are cropped for wigs, such caps, and heavier fur-edged monteros, become indispensable.

John More, the eccentric rector who turned Baptist in 1699 "went through Worcester with a handkerchief on my head, resolving never again to wear a wig . . . A neighbor objecting against my white cap I said the mountains and hills wear white caps, I am in the mode." (Ponsonby: *English Diaries*).

1490. XVIIc. English. (Dulwich College Gallery.)

Unknown artist. Nathaniel Field.

One of the three great acting troupes of the Elizabethan theatre was that of the Children of the Royal Chapel; its necessarily frequent replacements were made by the most brutal means. Field (1587-1633), who became the most brilliant young actor of his time, was the son of a Puritan preacher, violently opposed to the stage, who died shortly after Field's birth, and the brother of a later Bishop of Hereford. He was kidnapped into the company in early adolescence, in 1600. Field wrote two good plays, one with Massinger, with whom he was imprisoned for debt. He later became a member of the King's Players which had developed out of Burbage's troupe; Ben Jonson wrote "Which is your Burbage now? . . . . your best actor, your Field?" Before 1625, he had retired and died in 1633.

Shirts still are, as Stubbes wrote in 1583, "either of cambric, holland, lawn, or else of the finest cloth that may be got. And of these kind of shirts everyone doth now wear alike . . . wrought throughout with needlework of silk, and such like, and curiously stitched with open seam, and many other knacks beside. Shirts . . cost . . ten . . twenty . . forty shillings, some

five pounds, some twenty nobles . . and some ten pounds apiece."

This shirt with a falling band collar, and tie strings fluted to match the cuffs, is embroidered on the lines along which a doublet would be braided; earring cord; goatee and small moustache.

1491. XVIIc. Before 1617. English. (London, Victoria and Albert Museum.)
Isaac Oliver. Young Man.

Against a background of flames, the young man in this miniature wears a single earring, chain and pendant, with his beautiful shirt open almost to the waist. Women's bodices are seen, c.1615, cut out to below the midriff, barely containing the points of the breasts within the sides of the bodice. At the same period, this female U-opening is seen, with bare legs and feet, in male fancy dress; the same impulse is responsible for this open shirt. (See also Ill. 1475.)

1492. XVIIc. English. (Northampton, Ecton Hall.)
Isaac Oliver, d.1617. Anne of Denmark.

1493. XVIIc. English. (London, Victoria and Albert Museum.)
Isaac Oliver. Anne of Denmark.

1494. XVIIc. 1617 Flemish. (Hampton Court, H. M. the King.)
Paul van Somer. Anne of Denmark.

James thought armed hunting "a thievish kind of sport," but chased with a pack to the exhaustion of the court. The queen's hunting costume, worn with gauntlets and a male hat, is a severe version of ordinary dress. The hair and hip bolster are reduced to comfortable size; the low neck is filled with a lawn partlet; and a manageable wired whisk of bobbin lace, through which wind will pass easily, is buttoned together in front.

The note of dangling black is now often tied into the hair, on one or both sides; it is worn by both men and women, particularly on the Continent, and progresses from a thread-like cord to a ribbon ending in points, and, eventually, in tassel-like bows.

The miniatures by Oliver show two unusually interesting collars, above the low-cut bodice so characteristic of England, 1610-20; the frizzled hair and love-lock; and the clutter of ornaments, in which the costume of Elizabeth came to an end, as described in "Lingua, or the combat of the tongue," by Thomas Tomkis. (Quoted by Morse.) ". . . Five hours ago I set a dozen maids to attire a boy like a nice gentlewoman; but there is such doing with their looking glasses, pinning, unpinning, setting, unsetting, formings and conformings, painting blew veins and

cheeks; such stirr with sticks and combs, cascanets, dressings, purls, falls, squares, busks, bodies, scarfs, necklaces, carcanets, rebatoes, borders, tires, fans, palisadoes, puffs, ruffs, cuffs, muffs, pulses, fusles, partlets, frislets, bandlets, fillets, crosslets, pendulets, amulets, annulets, bracelets, and so many lets (hindrances) that yet she is scarce dressed to the girdle; and now there's such a calling for fardingales, kirtles, busk-points, shoe ties, etc., that seven peddlers' shops —nay all Stourbridge fair—will scarce furnish her: A ship is sooner rigged by far, than a gentlewoman made ready."

The androgynous character of Elizabethan costume is most striking in this moment of its decadence. Women's parts are acted on the stage by boys; women add to their more severe and rigid costume the hat which is the most masculine feature of male clothing; and men in long love-locks, wide loose breeches, and rosettes assume, on occasion, the extremely exposed breast which is the most feminine part of women's dress.

The two miniatures show Anne, "so low she went bare all the days I had the fortune to know her," as Osborne said, describing James' ostentatious farewell, "kissing her sufficiently to the middle of her shoulders," as he left her coach to hunt.

In her frizzed and love-locked hair, and over her gowns and the two interesting ruffs, Anne has pinned or hung a clutter of lockets and brooches, keepsakes, posies and animals. This is merely the tasteless cul-

mination of Elizabethan ways.

Burleigh's son, the Earl of Salisbury, though a cripple on crutches, was a delightful man. A letter written Sept. 18, 1592, by the Earl of Shrewsbury says: "Young Lady Derby, wearing about her neck in her bosom a picture which was in a dainty tablet, the Queen (Elizabeth) espying it, asked what fine jewel that was. The Lady Derby was curious to excuse the showing of it; but the Queen would have it; and opening it and finding it to be Mr. Secretary's (Salisbury's), snatched it away, and tied it upon her shoe, and walked long with it; then she took it thence and pinned it to her elbow, and wore it some time there also." Salisbury wrote verses about this, which Elizabeth heard of, and insisted should be sung to her.

(Intended Ills. 1495-97 did not arrive from European sources in time to be included in the book.)

1498. XVIIc. 1619. English. (Northampton, Lamport Hall, Gyles Isham.)

C. Janssens van Ceulen, e. Portrait of a Lady.

The excessively low-cut neckline is being filled in, and the ruff is declining. Attempts to give it fresh interest result in colored ruffs, of varying width, with contrasting edges, overlaid with points of bone lace. The Mary Stuart cap is also renewed by its covering of prickly points of lace.

1499. XVIIc. 1621. English. (London, Sir Osbert Sitwell.)

Cornelius Jansens (signed). Portrait of a Lady with her Daughter.

This portrait shows many specifically English characteristics in common with that of Margaret Laton's (No. 1502). Both women wear caps, of the Mary Stuart shape, which will recede and widen to frame the head, as hair becomes wider, longer and develops a fringe in the 1630-40's. On all three figures we see falling ruffs and whisks being transformed into the collars which will soon cover the shoulders. The child's whisk has developed long kerchief-like points; the neckline is set eccentrically in her mother's ruff; Margaret Laton's falling ruff is patterned along the sides of its central division.

Both ladies show the separation of skirt from bodice, the scalloped borders of which precede the long, tabbed skirts on the low-necked jackets of the 30's. The outer robe is reduced to a skeleton; sleeves shorten, cuffs become less close fitting; little scarves

and bracelets are clasped around the wrist. Earrings on cord.

The child in an apron has a scarf tied about the upper arm, prophetic of an important usage to come. From John Manningham's diary we learn that in 1601-2 "the play of shuttlecocke is become soe much in request at Court that the making of shuttlecockes is almost growne a trade in London."

1500. XVIIc. 1624. English. (London, Lord North.)

C. Janssens van Ceulen, e. Hon. Elizabeth North.

The steady rise of distinguished citizens into the nobility is well illustrated by the Norths. An eminent lawyer and clerk of Parliament became the first Lord North in 1554; the second was a soldier and courtier of Elizabeth; the third, father of the Hon. Elizabeth North, was a poet, an athlete, and friend of Prince Henry, an upholder of the Commons, and of Parliament in the Civil War.

The curative powers of the mineral springs at Tunbridge Wells were discovered by him in 1606, yet in 1630, Henrietta Maria and her suite had to live in tents while she took the waters after the birth of Charles II. A few houses and amusements were then provided, and with the visits of Charles and Catherine of Braganza, and of James with his family, Tunbridge became fashionable. It was favored by Puritans and has to this day an Evangelical flavor. Anne loved it, long before she was queen or it was paved, which was done in her honor; Tunbridge and Bath became the fashionable watering places of the XVIIIc. The springs at Epsom, also discovered by Lord North, were favored by people from East London, whom Pepys, on his visit, considered common.

The petal shapes, in which the lace of caps is finished, have been used in the metal leaves which replace lace on her headdress.

1501. XVIIc. English. (New York, Knoedler.)

M. Gheeraerts. Lady of the Lenox Family.

Characteristic of costume of the first quarter XVIIc., particularly in England, is the narrow bit of black cord, dangling somewhere. It may be caught under a finger and twisted about a wrist, as the Lenox lady wears it. One portrait of Elizabeth of Bohemia shows it trailing along a ruff, from a pierced ear. Small pieces of sentimental, keepsake jewelry are much seen now, like the pansies for

thought in the hair of the Lenox lady. In the same category are Elizabeth North's earrings, of hearts pierced by arrows. They might well hang by a black thread, like Margaret Laton's, except that the motif is used only once in each costume, and she already carries a keepsake ring hanging on a black thread, above her rose breast-pin enamelled in the combined colors of York and Lancaster.

1502. First third XVIIc. English. (London, Lord Harmsworth.)

Unknown artist. Margaret, wife of Francis Laton of Rawdon.

Sir Hugh Brawn's daughter, wife of the Yeoman of the Jewel House to James I, Charles I and II, is shown wearing a tunic which was bought, together with the portrait, from one of her descendants in 1929 for £4200; it is the best preserved and executed garment of the period remaining to us, and is reproduced with notes and photograph in Kendrick (see Ill. 1482).

The photograph shows the jacket to be of hip length, with shoulder wings, and a sleeve ending in a point which turns back to form a cuff, and is closed along the outer seam above the wrist. The jacket is of white linen, embroidered in gold, silver and colored silks, on a spangled ground, and edged with gold and silver lace. (See text, Ills. 1499, 1501.)

1503. XVIIc. Dutch-English. (Northampton, Lamport Hall. Gyles Isham.)

Mierevelt. George Villiers, First Duke of Buckingham.

James' favorite, "raised from a Knight's fourth son to that pitch of glory, and enjoying great possessions, acquired by the favour of the King upon no merit but his beauty and prostitution" (Lucy Hutchinson), was by 1616-18, the second richest nobleman in England. He eloped with the greatest heiress in England, the duke of Rutland's daughter, with whom he lived on the most affectionate terms, endowing her with his own immense estates.

Buckingham was a person of the most dazzling charm and beauty; intelligent, well-intentioned, pleasant to his inferiors, arrogant, reckless, no statesman, and unfitted for the power he wielded. Despite the opinions of Lucy Hutchinson, the Protestant Colonel's wife, Buckingham was liked and respected by far more estimable old gentlemen than Bishop Good-

man who insisted he was "inwardly beautiful as he was outwardly."

Twenty-six years younger than James, Buckingham was only eight year older than Charles, over whom he had great influence. After the favorite's assassination at thirty-six, Charles brought up Buckingham's children with his own; during his exile and for some time after the Restoration, Charles II, and the second duke of Buckingham, two years his senior, will be inseparable companions.

Lucy Hutchinson said: "It was common for him at any ordinary dancing to have his clothes trimmed with great diamond buttons, and to have diamond hat bands, cockades and earrings: to be yoked with great and manifold knots of pearl. . . . At his going over to Paris in 1625" (when Louis XIII called Buckingham one of the few English gentlemen he had ever seen), "he had twenty-seven suits of clothes made, the richest that embroidery, lace, silk, velvet, gold, and gems could contribute, one of which was a white, uncut velvet, set all over, both suit and cloak, with diamonds, valued at £14,000, besides a great feather, stuck all over with diamonds, as were also his sword, girdle, hatband and spurs."

The "knots of pearl," such as we are more accustomed to see, from the time of Elizabeth through first quarter XVIIc., worn by the greatest ladies, are tucked into the bosom of his jacket through slashes edged with small pearls, opposed to large ones as buttons. Trailing, thread-like lovelock on great whisk of bone lace.

1504. XVIIc. c. 1623. Dutch-English. (England, T. W. Fitzwilliam.)

D. Mytens, e. The First Duke of Buckingham as Lord High Admiral.

In official dress, he wears the otherwise outmoded trunk hose. As a gentleman of the period, he would have worn breeches gartered like those shown on Charles I. (Ill. 1505), midway in fullness between those of James I (Ill. 1469) and Charles, and probably boots.

His lace whisk is worn with the new jacket, slashed at the bosom, and carrying the breeches knotted through its pointed waistline; and the new sleeve, full and slashed above, close below the elbow. Garter and its insignia on a ribbon, cape, shoes with high heels and rosettes, walking stick.

1505. XVIIc. 1629. Dutch-English. (Metropolitan Museum.)

Daniel Mytens, e. Charles I.

In 1623, at Buckingham's instigation, "Baby Charles"—still Prince of Wales, and "Dog Steenie" set out secretly, as "Mr. John and Mr. Thomas Smith," on a fantastic quest for the Infanta of Spain whom Charles hoped to marry. Their small party dressed in "fine riding coats, all of one colour and fashion, in a kind of noble simplicity." (Howell's "Letters.") They spent one night in Paris, "disguised" in periwigs; Charles saw the French princess, Henrietta Maria, at a masked ball, and was recognized by a servant-girl from London. In Spain, magnificent entertainments were improvised; the Infanta was driven in a carriage, with a bow tied on her arm, so that she and Charles could look at each other from a safe Spanish distance. The people discovered that the English were not half-man, half-beast, as their priests had told them; presentation was made of the gifts James had provided: "a good looking glass, with my picture on it to be hung at her girdle, diamonds set like an anchor, three goodly peak pendants diamonds whereof the biggest to be worn at a needle on the middle of her forehead and one in every ear" (Hardwicke's "State Papers"); and more were sent home for. The decorum of the court was upset by Buckingham; Charles could not be converted to Rome; and after endless delays, the pair went home with a marriage contract which was never meant to be fulfilled.

In the couple of years which separate this portrait of Charles from another painted by Mytens in 1627, the king has grown a long lovelock; his doublet has developed bosom slashing, reduced shoulder caps; straight edged open cuffs have replaced pointed lace ones; and the boot, cuffed just below the knee in 1627, is now turned down much lower on the calf.

150o. XVIIc. c. 1628. Dutch-English. (London, Nat. Port. Gall.)

G. van Honthorst. Henrietta Maria, Queen of Charles I.

The year after his Spanish failure, Charles was married to the daughter of Henri IV and Marie de' Medici. Henrietta Maria, "a numble and quiet, black-eyed, brown-haired, and, in a word, a brave lady, though, perhaps, a little touched by the green-sickness" was taller than Charles had supposed. She lifted her foot to show: "Sir, I stand upon mine own feet. I have no helps of art. Thus high I am, and neither higher nor lower."

Priest-ridden and bitterly suspect because of her Catholicism and her Gallic gaiety, the queen had no one familiar with England to advise her; her own French entourage left her one dress and two undershirts, and a list of debts to them, padded to £19,000, on their flight back to France. She was a gay, brave, loyal and always beautifully dressed wife to the dignified, tasteful, well-intentioned, and calamitously unwise Charles. Yet she played a great part in the downfall of the king, who said he thought he could earn a living at any trade but tapestry-weaving, but who failed at the business to which he was born.

Satin is a favorite material in the new soft styles, increasingly untrimmed as it gains in popularity; here it is still embroidered in pearls. The neckline is wide and low, the remnants of the ruff appearing in the lace edge. A loose string of pearls is tied across the pearled outline of the old, long stomacher at a short waistline. Short, puffed sleeves finished with many ruffles, gathered together. Hair in tiny arranged curls against the cheeks and forehead. Pearl crown, earrings and choker; bracelets, folding fan.

1507. XVIIc. 1628. Dutch-English. (Chatsworth, Duke of Devonshire.)

G. van Honthorst. Elizabeth of Bohemia,* Countess of Devonshire, and her Children.

These are fashionable clothes, the daughter's showing later styles. But where Henrietta Maria's dress of the same year looks forward, these relate to old usages in many of their details.

The spray which the countess wears in her hair is the end of an Elizabethan fashion, done in newer pearls. Her ruff has the varied width seen in its widest, late forms; it is combined with the new spreading neckline of the short-waisted gown, emphasized by a kerchief-like collar, and jewels strung in an elaboration of a baldric. Across the tab of the stomacher, it is belted by a ribbon, to match the ribbon tie, called a *virago,* which catches the full paned sleeves between shoulder and elbow; these are short, finished with a ruff matching that at the throat. Her kirtle has the new all-over spot patterns, but a good deal of the old braiding is used on all the garments, though often in fresh ways. Fan tied to belt ribbon.

The boy at l., who grew up to be one of the original members of the Royal Society, wears his lace collar out, over the crimson cloak of a Knight of the Bath; jacket and breeches of a dot-patterned stuff.

The boy with the crossbow shows the doublet waist shortening; its overlapping skirts very long. Braid is used in patterns which emphasize goring and slashing. The continuation of sleeve slashings below elbow is unusual. Narrowing breeches, slit along outer seam and edged with buttons, show gartered underwear-like white beneath, as do the slashes of bosom and sleeves. Shoe toes squaring.

The daughter's flat collar is developing out of a fan-shaped ruff. Her sleeve finish, rows of ruffles gathered together, is newer than the pleated ruffs worn by her mother. Braid is used to give importance to the kirtle, and a diagonal border to the gown.

---

* There is a 1632 portrait (by Miereveld, in the National Portrait Gallery, London) of Elizabeth of Bohemia, with a black cord dangling from her earring over a similar ruff, graduated and very high in back of the head. It is, however, of a very different lady—the gay and gallant daughter of James the 1st—who bore thirteen children to Frederic, the Elector Palatine (among them Rupert and Sophia), and who lived on charity, sometimes a vagrant, after his death.

1508-09. XVIIc. Flemish-English.
Anthony Van Dyke.

1508. Henrietta Maria, Queen of England (1634). (Windsor Castle H. M. the King.)

1509. Henrietta Maria, Queen of England (1632-40). (Dresden Museum.)

Portraits by Rubens' pupil, Van Dyke, are wonderful costume documents. Beginning about 1618 in the Netherlands he painted the prelates and nobility of Italy from 1621-7; returned to Flanders where he and his master were court painters to the Infanta; went to England in 1629, returning to the Netherlands during 1634-5; thereafter, until his death in 1641, lived in London where he married an English noblewoman and was himself knighted. Differences in costume in the various countries, and their alterations in repeated portraits of the same personages, can be seen in the 537 chronologically arranged examples in the tremendously useful *Klassiker der Kunst* series; *Van Dyck,* Deutsche Verlags-Anstalt, Stuttgart, 1909.

"The portraits of this Fleming are so frequent in England that the generality of our people can scarce avoid thinking him their countryman, though he was born at Antwerp in 1598." (Horace Walpole: *Anecdotes of Painting in England,* 5 vols., 1782). Van Dyke painted so many pictures of Charles' family and court, that we call their styles by his name.

One of his pictures of Henrietta Maria with her dwarf, in 1633, shows her walking in a great, romantic plumed hat, and a braid-edged, high-necked masculine jacket, with a spreading collar. In 1634, her gown is of the plainest satin, low-necked, short-waisted, and laced with pearls across a stomacher, which is scalloped like the long skirts of the jacket; hems of skirts are also finished with such scalloped edges. Soft, full sleeves, finished with a ruffle at the elbow, show lace-edged undersleeves. Precious baldric; pearl choker, earrings, and strand around knot of hair. The little scallop of hair, of 1628, and the lovelock, are becoming corkscrew curls.

1510. XVIIc. 1632-40. Flemish. (Metropolitan Museum, Bache Coll.)

A. Van Dyke. Robert Rich, Earl of Warwick.

The son of Lady Penelope Rich, Sir Philip Sidney's lovely "Stella," wears a silver brocade doublet and crimson breeches, edged with gold braid; both are open and edged with buttons along the main seam. Crimson cloak, pink stockings, white shoes, black hat in hand.

1511. XVIIc. 1638. Flemish. (London, Lady Louis Mountbatten.)

A. Van Dyke. Lord John and Lord Bernard Stuart.

The younger sons of the king's cousin Esmé, Earl of Lennox, are shown here at 17 and 15; within half a dozen years both will be killed fighting for the Royalists.

Lord John, at left, wears a yellow doublet and crimson breeches; Bernard, a white satin doublet, blue cloak lined with white and blue breeches. Clogs protect toes of his boots, which have high red heels.

1512. XVIIc. 1632-41. Flemish. (Metropolitan Museum.)

A. Van Dyke. James Stuart, Duke of Richmond and Lennox.

John and Bernard's older brother, dressed in black, has the Star of the Garter on his cloak, and the lesser George on its blue ribbon.

1513. XVIIc. 1632-40. Flemish. (London, Duke of Grafton.)

A. Van Dyke. William Villiers, 2nd Viscount Grandison.

Grandison, who was killed in the civil wars in 1643, was the father of Barbara, Duchess of Cleveland; he wears gauntlets with embroidered cuffs; ribbon knots on immense leather plaques over the instep.

Red, blue, yellow, black, white and metallic colors are the favorites of this period, the reds running from pink, to deep crimson, to brightest scarlet.

"It is usual to turn back the cloak to display the rich lining, and where the doublet and breeches do not match it is common to find the lining of the

cloak matching the doublet and the cloak matching the breeches." (Kelly & Schwabe: *Historic Costume*).

In these pictures we see the collar (always worn over the cape or cassock) spreading until the shoulder cap disappears; doublet beoming shorter-waisted and more vest-like; decoration in openwork braids applied along the seams of underarm, sleeve and breeches; breeches narrowing and higher-waisted, often long, tubular and finished by gathered ruffles or spaghetti-like fringe. Lace-edged inner boot-hose of linen show in cupped cuff of boots, as the cuffs slip lower on the calf; heels become higher, and the leather plaques more enormous. Hair is lengthening, beards disappearing.

1514

1514. XVIIc. c. 1639. Flemish-English. (Metropolitan Museum.)

Van Dyke. **Earl of Arundel and his Grandson.**

Arundel, Earl Marshal and Constable of England, of whom Clarendon said there was "nothing martial about him but his presence and look," was the first great English antiquarian. He collected beautiful small objects and Greek and Roman sculpture; he was the patron of Van Dyke and Hollar, the friend of Evelyn and Sir Robert Cotton. He was responsible for the new use of brick in English building.

For a century, property had been changing hands and fine things in England destroyed or barely saved from destruction. Manuscripts acquired by Cotton, after the dissolution of the monasteries, were the foundation of the present Cottonian Library. Arundel's marbles went to Oxford; his library was dispersed between the College of Heralds and the British Museum, but his collections suffered during the civil wars.

There are many accounts, like Dowsing's, of destruction proudly performed under warrant; in 1643-4, at Clare: "We brake down 1000 pictures superstitious; I brake down 200; three of God the Father and two of Christ and the Holy Lamb, and three of the Holy Ghost like a Dove with Wings; and the twelve Apostles were carved in Wood on the top of the Roof which we gave orders to be taken down; and the Sun and the Moon in the East Windows, by the King's Arms, to be taken down." (Ponsonby: *English Diaries*). Evelyn says that at Lincoln in 1654, "the soldiers had lately knocked off most of the brasses from the gravestones . . . with axes and hammers . . . until they had rent and torn off some barge loads of metal, not sparing even the monuments of the dead, so hellish an avarice possessed them; beside which they exceedingly ruined the city."

Arundel was a general in the First Bishop's War, when the diary of Charles I's Privy Chamberlain, John Aston, tells us: "I had a cuirassier's armes for myselfe, close caske, gorget, back and breast culet, pauldrons, vambrance, left hand gauntlet, and cuisses and a case of pistolls and a great saddle." (Ponsonby: *Eng. Diaries*).

Falling band over gorget; baton of office. Grandson: doublet with small band, longer skirts; knee-breeches with garter bows; pearl baldric; shoe toes lengthening and squaring.

EFFECTS OF PURITANISM IN XVII-E.XVIII CENTURY

There were only two sorts of people in XVIIc. England: Dissenters and Royalists. The division, based on religion, was vertical, splitting families and comprising all classes. The excesses of each intensified the opposed feelings and behavior of the others, and there was much confusion of thought within each division. Under stress, Puritanism evolved from its Elizabethan reasonableness, and reached its most extreme form in the American colonies. But there were, within the party at any one time, persons of every degree of bigotry, often as opposed to the extremists in their own party as to people of the other persuasion.

There was much ambivalence in individuals, such as Cromwell's "overeager" General Harrison; who said that "gold and silver and worldly bravery did not become saints," when Colonel Hutchinson wore what his wife called "sad colored cloth, trimmed with gold and silver points and buttons . . . pretty rich, but grave, and no other than he usually wore"; but who, himself, waited upon the Spanish ambassador the next day "in a scarlet coat and cloak, both laden with gold and silver lace, and the coat so covered with clinquant (foil) that one scarcely could discern the grounds," while Hutchinson and others wore plain black. (Lucy Hutchinson: *Mem. of Col. Hutchinson*).

Puritans dressed and behaved like their contemporaries, but in a much toned-down way. The loyalist Anthony Wood said that at Oxford "they would avoid a tavern or alehouse, but yet send for their commodities to their respective chambers, and tiple and smoake till they were overtaken with the creature. And yet, of all men, none more than these were ready to censure the boone Royallist or any person they saw go in or out of a tavern or alehouse. Some, I confess, did venture, but then if overtaken would in their way home counterfeit a lameness, or that some suddaine paine came upon them." Generally speaking, their heads were cropped as though they were ready for the wigs they avoided; they wore dark clothes, with small plain bands instead of lace, and worsted stockings in place of silk. (A. Wood, *Life & Times.* Oxf. Hist. Soc. 1891.)

Wood, who had found the Presbyterians and Independents saucy, troublesome, conceited and rude to the "old stock," and their sermons interminable, attests, after the Restoration, to their diligence. He finds "nothing well done but by those who had their breeding during the intervall . . . The truth is they (i.e. the returning Cavaliers) have lost their learning," and have no aim but "to live like gent., keep dogs and horses, to turn their studies and coleholes into places to receive bottles, to swash it in apparell, to wear long periwigs." On Charles' visit to Oxford in 1666, Wood thought the courtiers "neat and gay in their apparell, yet very nasty and beastly . . . rough, rude, whoremongers, empty, careless"; not only were they insolent to great scholars "who had parted with their chambers and conveniences," but they had committed nuisances in their chimneys and studies (as, indeed, courtiers did in the great rooms of Versailles, for lack of accommodations).

Members of a dissenting minority are apt to be as contentious, but as thoughtful, earnest and literate as Wood found their Oxford students. Their numbers increased to a majority on a flood of leaflets, satires and periodicals. The Dissenters may be credited with much of the general improvement in education, which was particularly noticeable among middle and lower class townswomen, at a period when Royalist ladies were taught only graceful accomplishments, and were sometimes even more illiterate than the "beautiful and accomplished" widow of the sixth duke of Norfolk, who wished Pepys to accept delivery for her of "a parsell of Scottch plad of ten or a leven peses . . . I am encoreged to give you thes trubell . . . becaus now in my abcenc I have letell entreist in town." (Pepys).

The Puritan mistrust of art, music, the stage, and popular amusements impoverished English life, in which a good deal of taste had developed under Charles I. After the period of Rubens, Van Dyke, Honthorst, van Somer, Janssens, Mytens, and the English court miniaturist William Dobson, English painting consisted of such miniature painters as Samuel Cooper, and of the Dutch painter who became Sir Peter Lely, to whom Cromwell and a few other Puritans did sit. As Walpole said, "The restoration of royalty brought back art, not taste." Lely's even duller successor was the German, Godfrey Kneller. At propitious intervals, Flemish, Dutch, and French artists did make trips to England. But neither William nor Mary had taste, and Anne avoided court life as much as possible, leaving her ministers to preside at her drawing-rooms. Theirs is, on the whole, one of the most difficult periods in which to find illustrations of costume.

The Plague aided the Puritans in closing the theatres and public gathering places. Until the Restoration, the English theatre consisted of the private masques at court (in which Anne of Denmark and Henrietta Maria had delighted, for which Ben Jonson wrote, and the architect Inigo Jones provided the décor).

With the Restoration, comes brilliant, licentious comedy like that of Wycherly, heroic drama such as Dryden's "Conquest of Granada," and the first English opera, by the great Purcell. People flocked to the watering places like Tunbridge Wells and Bath, to the many pleasure gardens like Vauxhall and Ranelagh; to fashionable drives like the Ring in Hyde Park; and to the endless coffee houses which served as office and club, where for a fee a gentleman could read all of the new flood of periodicals and hear all the latest gossip.

The XVIIc. is that in which the King James translation made the Bible available, to become the keystone of the lives of millions. In another level of society, stage people begin to mingle on equal terms with the great world, noblewomen fight duels over actors, and Charles II, since he apparently must share Lady Castlemain's favors, advises her to let Harry Jermyn, the lady killer, go in favor of Jacob Hall, the wonderful rope dancer.

———

1515-17. XVIIc. 1638. English. (Kent, East Sutton Church.)

Monumental brass, signed Ed. Marshall. Sir Edward Filmer and his Wife, Elizabeth.

Sir Robert, eldest son of Filmer's eighteen children, became a political writer. His theory that government was, by God's decree to Adam, based on the authority of the father, naturally made him an ardent supporter of the king against Parliament; his house was despoiled ten times by his opponents. One wonders whether some of the younger sons may have reacted differently to authority, and profited by rebellion.

Sir Edward's short-waisted cuirasse has long skirts, as high boots with spur leathers replace plate protection of the legs. Frog fastenings of outer seam of loose knee breeches.

The elderly Lady Filmer also clings to a ruff, which widens in back; a wired-out veil and a long-waisted stomacher. Cuffs do not surround the wrist and are not scalloped.

Robert wears a cassock with cuffed sleeves over his armor, his widening falling band spread over the shoulders of the cassock. Other sons show a variety of jackets, garters, shoes and boots.

The daughters, all with caps, wear their hair loose at the sides and with a fringe. Collars lowering and spreading. Slashed sleeves, knotted around above the elbow, in the tie called a *virago*.

Under this rest in certaine hope of the resurection the bodies of Sᵗ Edward Filmer Knight and dame Elizabeth

together Fortefoure yeares and had issue Eighteene Children viz. nine sonnes and nine Davghters he depted this

1515

1516

1517

his wife Davghter of Richard Argall Esqʳ they lived

1518. XVIIc. 1641. Flemish-English. (Amsterdam, Rijksmuseum.)

Van Dyke. William of Orange and Mary Stuart.

The Dutch *stadholder,* whose son will become William III of England by virtue of his father's and his own marriages to English princesses named Mary, holds by the hand his little bride, dressed in greenish-gold brocade, in the exquisite taste of her mother.

The Rijksmuseum also owns a piece of the actual lace of the collar which spreads over the coppery satin of William's gold-embroidered costume. He wears stockings of a paler shade, which hang in deliberate wrinkles, and red-heeled shoes which are knotted, like his breeches, with loose gold, in scarf rather than ribbon form, as it will later be used. He carries a black hat, banded in jewels instead of the usual cord, in a buff-gloved hand, over the sword belt which passes underneath his jacket.

1519. XVIIc. c. 1642? English.

M. Gheeraerts, y. Beata, Countess of Downe and her Children.

This picture presents time-consuming complications, which often occur and which it may, for once, be interesting to outline.

It is one of four related pictures which had remained in the Pope family until it was sold at Christie's, July 11, 1930 (#63). It is accepted by Cust as the work of Gheeraerts, who died in 1636. According to Burke's Peerage, Beata Poole was married April 20, 1636 and Thomas, the heir, was baptised Sept. 20, 1640. The picture must therefore be c.1642-3, if the names shown are contemporaneous with the figures, as appears to be the case. In that case, the painting would seem to have been the work of another artist, who painted costume as beautifully and hands as badly as did Gheeraerts.

The Countess' costume is of white satin with multicolored silk and metal embroidery, and a blue scarf. Her short-waisted jacket has the widening

Photograph Courtesy of Frick Art Reference Lib. (1519)

1518

1519

neckline, gored peplum, short sleeves and wide cuffs of the 40's.

The children are dressed in olive green. The boy wears a masculine doublet, with skirts since he is still in diapers, and carries a plumed and tasseled hat. The diary of Sir Henry Slingsby (1601-50) relates that he got his son "the first breeches and doublet he ever had and made by my tailor Mr. Miller; it was too soon for him to wear them being but five years old, but that his mother had a desire to see him in them, how proper a man he could be—(Ponsonby: *English Diaries*). Lady Slingsby was an invalid and was dying.

1520-25. XVIIc. 1639-40. Bohemian-English. (Metropolitan Museum, Print Room and Boston Museum of Fine Arts, Elizabeth Day McCormick Coll.)

Wenzel Hollar. Ornatus muliebris.

Hollar is one of the world's great fashion artists. He was a Bohemian, born in 1607, driven from Prague and the profession of law by the Thirty Years War. He worked as an engraver under Merian in Frankfort in 1627-9, and in Strassburg and Cologne. There in 1636 he met the antiquarian, Arundel, who loved exquisite workmanship and the company of artists. He went with Arundel on his embassy to Vienna and Prague and returned to live with him in London. He passed into the service of the Duke of York when Arundel fled the Civil Wars, but eventually joined Arundel in Antwerp, where Hollar spent his most productive years, 1644-52. He returned to London, lived with the engraver Faithorne for a time, and died there in the greatest poverty in 1677.

Working by an hourglass at 4d. an hour, Hollar produced 2740 plates: architectural drawings, views of cities (particularly of London before and after the Great Fire of 1666), book illustrations, portraits, and his wonderful drawings of costume. These have been catalogued by Parthey, Berlin, 1853.

The *Ornatus muliebris* illustrations are of English costume c.1640. These are not great ladies in grand clothes, but the daily wear of the middle classes.

1520. Side locks and bun arrangement of the central portion of the hair, seen from the back. Collar edges cover the shoulders; waistline very short; skirt looped up over a handsome petticoat.

1521. Street costume of hood and mask, scarf, muff, and a chatelaine of some sort. French prints of Louis XIV's time often show ladies huddled over the fire, with their feet on the fender, partial mitts on their hands, screening their faces with long-handled fans. This fur-edged one, which may have had a

mirror center, must have been a comfortable accessory to hold on a visit in a chilly drawing room.

1522. Muffs occur in late inventories of Elizabeth's wardrobe and rapidly increase in use, being carried by men as well as women, even by army and naval officers during latter half XVII-e.XVIIIc. This wide-brimmed, truncated conical hat is almost the only one now worn by women; when a cap is worn, the hat is set over it. The ruff still persists in bourgeoise use, but is elliptical in shape, and, in this example, is reduced from a triple to a double ruff, and narrowed, over the bare breast of the laced bodice.

1523. Kerchief collar, over a dropped shoulder line, to avoid interference with the full, short sleeve; apron; skirt tucked up over a handsome short kirtle, showing handsome high-heeled slippers with rosettes.

1524. Simple home costume with a lovely cap and hanging embroidery scissors.

English embroidery has been notable since Tudor times and will remain so into the XIXc., although in the general dissolution of the XVIIIc., it begins to be neglected and we find the Spectator (#606, 1714) proposing:

I. That no young virgin whatsoever be allowed to receive the addresses of her first lover but in a suit of her own embroidering.

II. That before every fresh servant she be obliged to appear with a new stomacher at the least.

III. That no one be actually married till she hath the childbed pillows, &., ready stitched, as likewise the mantle for the boy quite finished.

But Sir Walter Calverly's diary, Nov. 27, 1716 says: "My wife finished the sewed work in the drawing room it having been three years and a half in doing. The greatest part of it has been done with her own hands. It consists of ten panels" (which still hang in Sir George Trevelyan's bedroom at Wallington). (Ponsonby: *English Diaries*).

1525. Marketing in pattens, with the embroidered hem of her jacket costume looped up out of the mud. The basket holds fine artichokes (cultivated in England for two and a quarter centuries), and some parsley and root vegetables for seasoning soup. Carrots and beets, as agreeable vegetables to eat, are the XIXc. creation of the French plant breeder, Vilmorin. Until his work, the carrot was a stringy, whitish-yellow root, unlike the wild parsnip (probably brought to England in Roman days), which Pliny knew could be transformed by several seasons of good tilth into a good vegetable.

1526

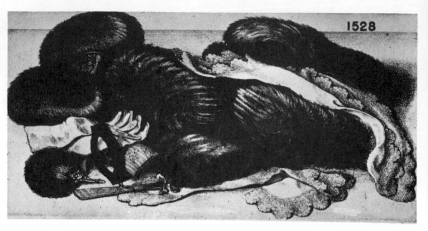

1528

1527

1526-27. XVIIc. 1643-4. Bohemian-English.

W. Hollar. The Four Seasons: Winter, and Autumn.

Scarcely a trace remains of the old rigidity of costume. There are black hoods and masks over loose curls; fichu-like collars; fur pieces and muffs; full, fashionable aprons; objects like fans, watches, mirrors or *nécessaires* of sewing or toilet articles hang from the waist; gloves lengthen as sleeves become short and wide. Background of the city views at which Hollar excelled.

Men, too, carry little kits of toilet articles, which it is gallant to use in public and in society. "Will you be combing your wig, playing with your box, or picking your teeth?" Steele asks in the Tatler, (#38,July7,1709). Before his execution, Charles I had given his gold toothpick case to Col. Tomlinson. Among the inventory of the effects of a fop (Tatler,#113,Dec.29,1709), appears "a very rich tweezer case, containing twelve instruments for the use of each hour in the day"; snuff, with three gilt boxes, one with a mirror in the lid, and "two more of ivory, with the portraitures on their lids of two ladies of the town."

1528. XVIIc. 1647. Bohemian. (Metropolitan Museum, Print Room.)

W. Hollar. Muffs.

While living in Antwerp, Hollar produced a wonderful series of etchings of muffs and accessories, of which this is one.

Masks are fast coming into fashion all over Europe. Pepys mentions them first, June 13, 1663, when he sees Cromwell's daughter, the Countess of Falconberg, "when the house began to fill . . . put on her vizard, and so kept it on all the play: which of late is become a great fashion among ladies, which hides their whole faces." He stops to get his own wife a mask, at a milliner's (Jan., 27, 1663-4). At the theatre again (Feb., 18, 1666-7), he scarcely sees the play for overhearing a charming, teasing, witty conversation between Sir Charles Sedley and two masked ladies obviously of quality and virtue, whom he did not recognize. One "did give him many pleasant hints of her knowledge of him, by that means setting his brains at work to find out who she was, and did give him leave to use all means to find out who she was, but pulling off her mask."

By 1712, masks have become the mark of prostitutes, and are worn by respectable women only at the first night of a play. However, the advertisement (in *Spectator* #546), of the opening of the "Blind Beggar of Bednal Green" at Punch's Theatre, says "No persons to be admitted with masks or riding hoods."

Muffs are coming into male use, also. On Nov., 30, 1662 Pepys "first did weare a muffe, being my wife's last year's muffe; and now that I have bought her a new one, this serves me very well . . . in this month . . . of great frost."

The fantastic Salter, "eminent barber and antiquary," as well as musician and inkeeper, ridiculed by Steele as "Don Saltero" (*Tatler,*#34, June 28, 1709), could be recognized a quarter of a mile away, as he held his horrible old grey muff to his nose, according to Babillard.

1529-30. XVIIc. 1645. English. (Oxford, Ashmolean Museum.)

De Critz. John Tradescant in his garden (1529), Hester and John Tradescant (1530).

In the age of discovery and colonization, and of quite general European travel by gentlemen imbued with the new spirit of inquiry, experiment and recording, begins the great interchange of plants between continents. About 1602, many new fruits and vegetables appeared in England from the Continent. They were taken to the New World, which had already given Europe the potato, tomato, tobacco, and pumpkin.

John Tradescant, jr., was the keeper of Charles I's Botanical Garden at Chelsea, in whose honor a three-petaled blue flower from America was named *Tradescantia virginica.* His father, a Dutchman living in England since 1600, had been gardener to the duke of Buckingham; he left a collection of North African curiosities, enlarged by the son with material from his own trip to America in 1637.

The will by which Tradescant's collections were left to his friend Elias Ashmole, was bitterly and fruitlessly contested by Mrs. Tradescant. Evelyn visited Ashmole at Lambeth on July 23, 1678, to see the collection which Ashmole had just given to Oxford. He noted particularly "a toad included in amber." Twelve wagons were required to remove the natural history specimens to the newly erected Ashmolean, the first great scientific museum, which had been completed from Sir Christopher Wren's design. On Feb. 17, 1683, Ashmole's diary says: "The last load of my rareties was sent to the barge, and this afternoon I relapsed into the gout." The Ashmolean is now an archaeological museum.

Tradescant gardens in an open shirt and easy, furlined coat. Mrs. Tradescant, sharing one of the botanical illustrations from the collection with her step-son, wears the high-crowned hat, familiar from the Hollar illustrations, set over her cap, and an enchanting embroidered petticoat, with a pendant watch at the waist. The interior of the cuff becomes important, as sleeves grow shorter and wider; the cuff is not folded, but is doubled back from a lace edge.

1531. XVIIc. English. (Oxford, Sir Kenneth Clark.)
Daniel Des Granges. The Saltonstall Family.

1532. XVIIc. 1648. English. (Northampton, Lamport Hall, Gyles Isham.)
C. Janssens van Ceulen, e. Mary, Daughter of Sir Eusebius Isham of Pytchley.

The lady, married first to Edward Reade and later to Sir Fleetwood Dormer, is shown as a widow; lace is replaced by composite collars of sheer-bound lawn; pearls are caught by black bows; heart-shaped chatelaine pinned at the waist.

1533. XVIIc. 1654. English. (Croome d'Abiot, Wostershire Parish Church.)
Tombstone by unknown artist. Second Wife of Lord Coventry.

The first nightshirts of the XVIc. did not differ much from day shirts; now they are coming to have a specific character and to be supplemented with dressing gowns and slippers. The bedroom has always been the most comfortable room; as houses are cut up into smaller, better heated rooms and large windows admit more sunlight, the bedroom increases in use for all but the most formal entertainment. Delightful caps (men's embroidered and women's lacy) and a dressing gown, over a corset and petticoats, or breeches and vest, tend to become informal wear in the morning hours, during which, regardless of sex, there is a great deal of visiting back and forth, during XVII-XVIIIc. In 1683, Evelyn sees the Duchess of Portsmouth "in her dressing room . . . in morning loose garments, her maids combing her, newly out of bed, His Majesty and the gallants standing about her."

Wood calls it, in 1663, "a strange effeminate age when men strive to imitate women in their apparell, viz. long periwigs, patches in their faces, painting,

short wide breeches like petticotes, muffs, and clothes highly sented, bedecked with ribbons of all colours. And this apparell was not only used by gentlemen and others of inferior quality, but by souldiers, especial those of the Life Gard to the King, who would have spanners hanging on one side and a muff on the other, and when dirty weather some of them would relieve their gards in pattens. On the other side, women would strive to be like men, viz., when they rode on horseback or in coaches weare plush caps like monteros, either full of ribbons or feathers, long periwigs which men use to weare, and riding coate of a red color all bedaubed with lace which they call vests, and this habit was cheifly used by the ladies and maids of honor belonging to the Queen, brought in fashion about anno 1662 . . . at their being in Oxon."

In Dec. 1674 Wood notes: "A great excess in apparel in men, women and children of the common sort: lace, fals hair, lace whisk, aprons, petticotes, lac'd shoes, fals towers of hair. This in Oxford . . . The decay of study, and consequently of learning, are coffy houses, to which most scholars retire and spend much of the day in hearing and speaking of news, in speaking vily of their superiors."

In the *Spectator's* time, 1711, young lawyers appear at coffee houses near the Temple in "nightgowns with our stockings about our heels, and sometimes but one on," to breakfast in dressing gown and slippers (#320). "Ladies likewise brought up the fashion of receiving visits in their beds. It was then looked upon as a piece of ill-breeding for a woman to refuse to see a man because she was not stirring; and a porter would have thought unfit for his place, that could have made so awkward an excuse." (#45).

On May 11, 1654, Evelyn says: "I now observe how the women began to paint themselves, formerly a most ignominious thing, and used only by prostitutes." By 1673, "the imprudence of both sexes (was) become so great and universal (that) persons of all ranks (keep) their courtesans publicly," and the increase of lawlessness is continually noted until a late entry in 1699, of "such horrible robberies and murders as had not been known in this nation, atheism, profaneness, blasphemy among all sorts," as well as insensate gambling, after a century of dissension and civil war, plague and fire.

Mrs. Saltonstall and Lady Coventry show delightful new forms of caps, night- and dressing-gowns. The babies, swaddled tight under their long gowns, wear caps which convert into bibs. The child whose hand Mr. Saltonstall holds shows the bows by which breeches would be tied to the short waist of his jacket, if he were out of diapers and skirts. The younger child in an apron is probably a sister.

Mr. Saltonstall's vest-like jacket, unfastened from the neck, has openwork braid along its seams. He wears the most wonderfully gauzy garter-ribbons, finished with tassel-dotted lace, and the highest heels on square-toed shoes. Light as all this is, we see a hint of the tasseled and fringed upholstery-like styles of Louis XIV, which are still with us today in hotel lobby decoration. His stocking wrinkles are akin to the flopping, turned-down cuffs and the folds of the inner hose, which are characteristic of the boots of the period.

Tobacco and Snuff

For a century after its introduction into England, tobacco was smoked in large clay pipes. Despite the "Counterblast" of James I, and Charles I and II's prohibition of tobacco-growing in England, smoking became habitual in XVIIc. Because of its supposed fumigant and medicinal properties, its use increased during the Plague of 1665. Jorevin says that in Worcestershire, during the reign of Charles II, children were sent to school with pipes, which they smoked at recess, while the teacher showed the novices how. A French traveller of 1671 noted Englishwomen smoking a great clay pipeful after dinner. At Garroway's Coffee House in Leeds, in 1702, a sickly child of three smoked three pipes, like the veteran he was, since he had been doing so for the year past.

In France and Spain, tobacco was used in the form of snuff, and carried in handsome boxes in Louis XIII's time. Louis XIV disliked most odors, and none more than tobacco. But snuff boxes had begun to rival (and eventually surpassed) watches as presents to mark appreciation or to honor visiting dignitaries. Louis XIV made many gifts of the beautiful snuff boxes of his period.

The English became snuff users in 1702, by an accident which is recounted by Charles Lillie, the perfumer and tobacco seller, whose name appears so frequently in the *Tatler* and *Spectator*. During the Spanish war, English ships commanded by Sir George Rooke raided Fort St. Mary, where among other great booty they took quantities of cochineal and some thousands of barrels of the finest Spanish snuff, each cask containing four tin canisters. On their return, in Vigo harbor they destroyed a fleet of galleons just in from Havana, loaded with rawhide bales of rough snuff to be manufactured in Spain. Officers and men received their shares of the fifty tons of snuff, as spoils of war; wagon loads of coarse "Vigo" snuff were sold in Portsmouth and Plymouth by the sailors for 3-4 d. a pound.

Snuff, "taken with pipes the size of quills out of small spring boxes" had been a luxury in England, known only to returned travellers and foreigners. Spanish Jews living in England recognized the quality of the Fort St. Mary snuff and bought it up. They, and the officers who kept their shares, eventually realized fortunes.

Snuff immediately became fashionable, and excise duties on it a rich source of government revenue as well as an incitation to smuggling. The tobacco was twisted into ropes. It was at first rasped with ivory graters, attached to a small box which was provided with a spoon; the name "rapee" (from *râper*) remained for coarse snuff. Graters were separated from boxes and snuff was taken with the fingers, as fine prepared snuffs were bought by connoisseurs with as much discrimination as vintage wines.

From Swift's *Journal to Stella* (whose companion, in his "little language," is M.D. or Dingly) we learn a great deal about the taking of snuff, 1710-11. In letter IV, he has "the finest piece of Brazil tobacco for Dingly that ever was born"; XXI: "I have left off altogether. I have a noble roll of tobacco for grating, very good. Shall I send it to M.D., if she likes that sort?"; XXIV: "Are you as vicious in snuff as ever? I believe, as you say, it does neither hurt nor good; but I have left it off, and when anybody offers me their box, I take about a tenth part of what I used to do, and then just smell to it, and privately fling the rest away"; XXXIII: "Then there's the *Miscellany*, an apron for Stella, a pound of chocolate, without sugar, for Stella, a fine snuff rasp of ivory, given me by Mrs. St. John for Dingly, and a large roll of tobacco, which she must hide or cut shorter out of modesty, and four pairs of spectacles for the Lord knows who"; LII: "You may keep the gold-studded snuff box now; for my brother Hill, Governor of Dunkirk, has sent me the finest that ever you saw. It is allowed at Court that none in England comes near it, though it did not cost above twenty pounds." To hold this, the Duchess of Hamilton made him a "pocket," like a woman's, "with a belt and buckle (for, you know, I wear no waistcoat in summer)."

An amusing bit of publicity by Steele in No. 138 of the *Spectator,* says: "The exercise of the Snuff Box, according to the most fashionable Airs and Motions, in opposition to the Exercises of the Fan, will be taught with the best plain or perfumed Snuff at Charles Lillie's, Perfumer, at the Corner of Beaufort Buildings in the Strand, and Attendance given for the benefit of young Merchants about the Exchange for two hours every day at Noon, except Sundays, at a Toy Shop near Garraway's Coffee House. There will likewise be Taught The Ceremony of the Snuff Box, or Rules for offering Snuff to a Stranger, a Friend, or a Mistress, according to the Degrees of Familiarity or Distance: with an Explanation of the Careless, the Scornful, the Politick, and the Surly Pinch, and the Gestures proper to each of them."

In No. 344 (1712), the affected "modesty" of snuff-taking women has been outgrown: "The Women, the fine Women (are) lately fallen into (the Custom) of taking Snuff. This silly Trick is attended with such a Coquet Air in some Ladies, and such a sedate Masculine one in others, that I cannot tell which most to complain of. . . . *Flavilla* is so far taken with her Behavior in this kind, that she pulls out her Box . . . in the middle of the Sermon, and to shew she has the Audacity of a well bred Woman, she offers it to the Men, as well as to the Women who sit near her."

By 1773, "smoking has gone out," Dr. Johnson says; he and his cronies, Garrick, Reynolds, and Goldsmith all take snuff. Eighty per cent of the trade of XVIIIc. tobacconists in London was in snuff. But in the first decades of the XIXc., cigars began to come in use; matches were invented; and by the middle XIXc., snuff formed only ten per cent of the tobacco business, and had become a plebeian habit.

The passion for giving, receiving, and collecting snuff boxes outlasted the habit of taking snuff. Boxes of Louis XV's period are less beautiful than those of Louis XIV, and less precious than the diamond-studded boxes of Louis XVI, which you

were supposed to give back. The necessity of luxury was becoming insupportable, and reduced to a gesture; Mirepoix paid a rental of £240 for a suit to be worn once at Court; dukes began to go spectacularly bankrupt.

Even the poorest had snuff boxes, whether of wood, horn or tortoise shell, pewter, brass or silver, lacquer, or the pretty, commercially produced Battersea enamels. French jewellers made a fortune at Maria Theresa's long-expected death by selling black shagreen snuff-boxes bearing a framed medallion of Marie Antoinette and the words *Consolation en chagrin.*

The finest snuff boxes were French. Like watches and engravings, they were produced by a relatively small number of dynastic and inter-related artists.

Frederick the Great loved tobacco in every form. He carried it in pockets especially lined with leather, and a receptacle to hold snuff stood in every room. These were often in the form of a "mull," a ram's horn with silver mountings. Thrifty though he was, Frederick left a collection of 1,500 snuff boxes; the prince of Conti had left 800, a decade before.

Napoleon took snuff habitually, and collected boxes. But the fashion was beginning to wear out. His brothers, the Kings of Westphalia and Holland, sometimes disappointed visiting dignitaries who expected a handsome snuff box.

Although George IV did not like snuff, he ordered it in 12 varieties for the snuff boxes he always carried; he paid £8205-15-1 for snuff boxes, as gifts to visiting ambassadors at his coronation.

Talleyrand said snuff was essential to diplomacy; it gave a man time to compose his features and collect his thoughts, while opening his box and taking a pinch.

The last of the great collectors was also one of the most impassioned. Lord Petersham (1780-1851), was a connoisseur of teas and snuffs. He dressed his household in snuff-colored liveries, and left a choice variety of snuffs which brought £ 3000 at auction, and a collection of snuff boxes for every day, and appropriate to every season of the year. (For sources of information, see Appendix.)

1534. XVIIc. French
Box: mother of pearl, tortoise shell, gilt metal.

1535. XVIIIc. 1740-50. French.
Box: agate and gold.

1536. XVIIIc. 1778-9. French.
Snuff box by Jean Joseph Barrière (app. 1750; master, 1763; still working, 1793): gold and enamel.

1537. Early XVIIIc. French or English.
Pendant: sardonyx cameo, set with smaller cameos in gold.

1538. XVIIIc. 17o7-8. French.
Snuff box: carved gold, encrusted with floral designs and enamel; portrait of Queen Anne on cover.

1539. XVIIIc. 1759-60. French.
Snuff box: by Mathieu Coiny (master, 1755-88): carved gold panels, reserved and painted with genre scenes, jewelled and enamelled.

1540. Late XVIc. c. 1600. German.
Pendant: ship; gold, enamel, pearls, and rubies.

1541. XVIc. Italian, Venetian. (Metropolitan Museum.)
Mirror Frame: wood inlaid with metal and ivory.

1542. XVIIc. French. (Metropolitan Museum.)
Mirror Frame: red leather, bead and passementerie, fake jewels.

1543. XVIIc. English? (Metropolitan Museum.)
Mirror Frame: champlevé enamel and coral.

1544. XVIIc. French? (Metropolitan Museum.)
Mirror: silver filigree.

1545. XVIIc. Italian. (Metropolitan Museum.)
Mirror: silver frame, partly gilt.

1546. XVIIc. English. (London, Victoria and Albert Museum.)

John Hoskins. Lady Catherine Howard.

Hoskins, called by Walpole, "a very eminent Limner in the reign of King Charles I, whom he drew with his queen and most of his court . . . was bred a face-painter in oil, but afterward taking to miniature, he far exceeded what he did before." (*Anecdotes of Painting.*) Hoskins, d.1664, was the uncle and teacher of Samuel Cooper (1609-72), the greatest English miniature painter. Other fine English miniaturists were Alexander Cooper, d.1660; David Des Granges (1611-75); Thomas Flatman, d.1688; and David Loggan, d.1692, the engraver of Oxford, who worked as a miniaturist in plumbago. While Elizabethan miniatures often show whole figures or even groups, like Oliver's Brothers Brown and their Servant, XVIIc. miniatures are unfortunately apt to be of bust length only. (For Miniature Painting sources, see Appendix.)

Lady Catherine, daughter of the Earl of Suffolk, led a blameless life as the wife of George Stuart, Seigneur d'Aubigny, who died in 1642, and of James, Viscount Newburg, who lived many years after her death in 1650.

Pale as death, she is the pattern of the new trends of mid-XVIIc.: curls wired out from the head, pearls, and a low, bright blue satin bodice, swathed and draped in scarves.

1547. XVIIc. c. 1660. Flemish. (Windsor Castle, H.M. The King.)

Hieronymus Janssens (1624-93). Charles II at a Ball at the Hague.

The romantic story of Charles II's flight, exile and return is largely spoiled by the Restoration, as "Bonnie Prince Charlie" tarnishes into "Old Rowley," nicknamed after a lecherous old goat in one of the palace enclosures.

After the defeat at Worcester, Charles and his lifelong crony, the second duke of Buckingham, became separated. Whether at White Ladies, or in the priest's hole at Boscobel, recognized by half a hundred people, but never betrayed for the £ 1000 reward, Charles went disguised as a woodsman, in the clothes of "trusty Dick," one of the children of Penderell, the miller; whose descendants, even in America, enjoy their shares of some £ 3000 a year, settled on them in perpetuity after the Restoration. Charles's costume consisted of a "leathern doublet with pewter buttons; a pair of old green breeches, and a coat of the same green; a pair of his own stockings, with the tops cut off, because embroidered, and a pair of stirrup stockings lent him at Madeley; a pair of old shoes, cut and slashed to give ease to his feet; an old gray greasy hat without a lining; a noggon shirt of the coarsest linen; his face and hands made of a reeky complexion by the help of the walnut tree leaves." Various such costumes, worn during the escape, are described in the king's own account, dictated to Pepys in 1680, and in the *Boscobel Tracts.* (See Appendix.)

The course followed by Buckingham (who had been Charles' sole companion during his jail-like existence as King of Scotland) had the audacity which was repeatedly shown in the life of:

"A MAN so various that he seemed to be
Not one, but all mankind's epitome.
Stiff in opinions, always in the wrong,
Was everything by starts, and nothing long;
But in the course of one revolving moon,
Was chemist, fiddler, statesman and buffoon.
Then all for women, painting, rhyming, drinking,
Besides ten thousand freaks that died in thinking.
Blest madman, who could every hour employ,
With something new to wish, or to enjoy.
Beggar'd by fools, whom still he found too late,
He had his jest, but they had his estate."

      Dryden: *Absalom and Architophel*

Buckingham actually made his way back to London, and set up on the street as a mountebank. "He caused himself to be made a Jack Pudding's coat, a little hat, with a fox's tail in it, and adorned with cock's feathers. Sometimes he appeared in a wizard's mask; sometimes he had his face bedaubed with flour, sometimes with lampblack, as the fancy took him. He had a stage erected at Charing Cross, where he was attended by violins and puppet-players. Every day he produced ballads of his own composition upon what passed in town, wherein he himself often had a share. These he sung before several thousands of spectators, who every day came to see and hear him. He also sold mithridate and his galbanum plaister in this great city, in the midst of his enemies, whilst we were obliged to fly, and to conceal ourselves in some hole or other." (Mme. Dunois.) Buckingham was an incomparable mimic; his waddling imitation of the progress of his enemy Clarendon, bellows swinging as purse, and preceded by a crony holding the fire-tongs as a mace, was as amusing as anything that had happened at court since the jester, Archie Armstrong's feud with the archbishop, and his grace at a dinner attended by his enemy: "Great praise be to God, and little LAUD to the devil."

There was a great deal of this sort of thing. Rochester, during his disfavor, performed as the famous German doctor, Alexander Bendo. The queen went to the fair at Audley-end with her ladies, disguised as country girls, to buy a pair "of yellow stockens for her sweet-hart." Two of her ladies, the Misses Price and Jennings, sold oranges in a play-house under the very eyes of the court, and ran into a great deal of trouble, returning in their coach.

During Charles' various exiles, spent wandering through France and the Low Countries, he lived at The Hague during 1648; after his exclusion from Holland, by the treaty of 1654, he made a secret visit to The Hague, which would not have been celebrated by a ball. It was, however, at The Hague that he received the commission from England, inviting his return as king.

We see the six-foot Charles with his shining black hair, as he was described by Mme. de Motteville, a year or so earlier, when his early good looks were already beginning to fail, "well-made, with a swarthy complexion agreeing well with his fine black eyes, a large ugly mouth, a graceful and dignified carriage, and a fine figure." He was always a fine dancer, rider, and tennis-player.

Full and difficult as the picture is, for comment, it shows the transitional costume of mid-XVIIc., with valuable rear views (l.) of a woman, and a man in a long military cassock (the garment from which the coat of latter half XVIIc. came), worn with the sword slung by a broad baldric. He wears the wide, tubular form of petticoat breeches, their hems laced with ribbon; wrinkled stockings; and cannons, gathered on a band below the knee.

Charles shows the new, wide hat; the standard costume of beribboned petticoat breeches and loose, vest-like jacket; worn with high-heeled shoes, the elongated toe of which spreads, c. 1650, just before it is cut square across. Bands have lost their irregular edges and are beginning to shrink back from the shoulders. Although periwigs had already appeared in Paris at the time of Charles' father's overnight stay there on his way to Spain, natural hair is worn here in the long form which preceded the general assumption of wigs.

The ladies' hair is lengthening, bunched at the sides in curls, the twist in back surrounded by a little Dutch cap. They carry gloves and fans, and show little bow-knots at the front or back of bodices, along the waistline (c., dancing), or on the outseam of long gloves (extreme l., and seated c.). They wear the dragging satin dress which tends to become looped in a bustle in second half XVIIc.; with long, corset-like bodices; horizontal necklines, deeply caped in lace and veiled in knotted scarves; and combinations of inner and outer sleeves of the utmost variety of finishes.

The room, with its heavily carved, gilded, and painted Dutch ceilings and walls, and high windows, is lighted by candles on the dividing pilasters, and by one of the great Dutch brass chandeliers, whose original form was that of clustered, pronged antlers.

1548-49. XVIIc. April 23, 1661. Bohemian-English. (Metropolitan Museum, Print Room.)

W. Hollar. Coronation Procession of Charles II.

This is a small section of Hollar's panorama of the whole procession. There is a 4-page account of it in Evelyn's diary; and the *Mercurius Publicus,* May 24, 1660 (q. by Malcolm, 1811, v. I, p. 295-304) describes the various groups and the colors of their costumes.

The high-crowned hats, which we are inclined to think of as Puritan because they were the hats worn to America by our ancestors, were worn by both factions alike, as these Royalist illustrations show; Puritans differed only in an avoidance of extravagances.

This hat, now ringed with feathers, will become low-crowned in a decade. Hair, parted and very long, now begins to be shaved off and replaced by periwigs which at first resemble natural hair.

The falling band will retain its oblong shape on the chest until final quarter XVIIc. It follows the old rule of appearing over the outermost garment: cape or the new coats which developed out of the cassock

and have as yet little shape.

Narrow knee-breeches and full Rhinegraves are shown, worn with ruffled cannons below the knee, or with sharp bows which have replaced soft bows, loops and rosettes at garter and shoe.

Kings of arms and heralds in armorial tabards. The formerly elaborate trappings of the horse are being reduced, even for parade use, to a saddle blanket. (Coronation procession of James II [1687] was similarly reproduced by Francis Sanford.)

ENGLAND AFTER THE RESTORATION

Fashions are now, and will remain, French.

The horse ridden by Charles at his coronation belonged to Fairfax (No. 1550), the Parliamentary general who had defeated his father.

The invention of gunpowder altered not only war and armor but horsebreeding. Armor disappeared and the heavy knight's charger with it. Speed became desirable. As carriage building became more expert in latter half XVIIc., four fast light horses could draw a coach, though a fine horse remained the quickest and the most elegant means of transport for anyone able to ride.

The best European stock had always been Spanish with some admixture with fast Arab horses during the Crusades; but heft was still necessary until XVIIc. Two Arab stallions had been imported under James I, and one under James II. Three more, brought back from the siege of Vienna, greatly impressed Evelyn (Dec. 7, 1684): "Such a head . . . in all regards beautiful, and proportioned to admiration; spirited, proud, nimble, making halt, turning with that swiftness, and in so small a compass, as was admirable." He is probably describing the Stradlington Lister Turk. Under William III were brought into England the three Arab stallions whose blood is in every race horse today: the Byerly Turk, and the Darley Arabian and Godolphin Barb.

Charles, his brother James, Duke of York, and the Earl of Oxford, gave the suits they had worn at the coronation as theatrical costumes for Betterton, Haines, and Price, who played Prince Alonzo, Prince Prospero, and Lionel, son of the Duke of Parma in "Love and Honour," by Shakespeare's reputed son, Sir William D'Avenant. Mrs. Barry received the wedding dress of her pupil, the Duchess of York, and her coronation robes after the Duchess became queen, to be used as theatrical costumes.

With the Restoration, Charles had licensed two acting companies, the actors of which, like himself, had had the opportunity to see the magnificently set theatrical productions of France. Killegrew, manager of the King's Men, and D'Avenant, of the Duke of York's company, became the most powerful theatrical producers of history, until our own days. Their respective theatres, the Drury Lane (after 1663); and the Lincoln's Inn Fields and later Dorset Gardens houses, rivalled

each other in the changes of movable scenery, which had been first instituted for D'Avenant by Inigo Jones' pupil, Webb. Killegrew's company was made up of Hart and Kynaston (originally actors of women's parts), Mohun, Lacy, and Mrs. Hughes, the sisters Marshall, Pepys' adored Mrs. Knep, and eventually Mrs. Boutell and Nell Gwynn. It was opposed by D'Avenant's Betterton (the greatest English actor of his age), and his brother, the two Noaks, Cave Underhill, Joseph Harris, and the Mrs. Davenport, Davies and Sanderson (the last of whom became Betterton's devoted wife), and later by Mrs. Barry and Mrs. Bracegirdle. Betterton, who managed the Dorset Gardens company after D'Avenant's death, was sent by James II to study stage productions in France. His lavish sets and costumes eventually forced the company to amalgamate with the King's Men in 1682, which remained the only company in London until 1695.

The Dorset Gardens, pleasantly set facing the river, was built from Wren's designs, with carvings by Grinling Gibbon. It deteriorated with the neighborhood until, in 1698, it was being used for lottery-drawings. Opera was briefly played there; then it was torn down and its second-hand building materials advertised in the Daily Courant in 1709.

The Queen's Theatre in the Haymarket was built by Killegrew in 1704 from Sir John Vanbrough's designs, specifically as an opera house; its acoustics were terrible and its roof had to be altered. There is a great new interest in music; silver tokens (designed by such artists as Hogarth) are issued to season subscribers to the concerts at pleasure gardens like Vauxhall; the tradition of concert and opera subscriptions begins. The £3000 required to build the Queen's was raised in £100 life memberships. So many of these were taken by members of the Kit-cat that Cibber says: "Of this Theatre I saw the first Stone laid, on which was inscrib'd *the little Whig*, in Honour to a Lady of extraordinary Beauty, then the celebrated Toast and Pride of that Party" (Lady Sunderland, Marlborough's daughter).

The institution of toasting arose in Anne's day, the Tatler (#24) says, from the ancient custom of dropping a roast apple or hot toast into mulled ale or wine. In Charles II's reign, when an admirer dipped and drank from the water in which a beauty stood at Bath, a fuddled bystander "offered to jump in, and swore, though he liked not the liquor, he would have the Toast." The Toast of a London club was elected by balloting. "When she is so chosen, she reigns indisputably for that ensuing year; but must be re-elected anew to prolong her empire a moment beyond it. When she is regularly chosen, her name is written with a diamond on a drinking glass. The hieroglyphic of the diamond is to shew her that her value is imaginary; and that of the glass to acquaint her, that her condition is frail, and depends on the hand which holds her."

During Anne's reign, some of the four theatres of London were open at the same time. There were not enough patrons to fill the cheaper seats, and servants were admitted free to the galleries. When Anne Barwick, "who was lately my servant . . . committed a Rudeness last night at the Play-house, by throwing of Oranges, and hissing when Mrs. l'Epine, the Italian Gentlewoman Sung," Mrs. Tofts apologised to Christopher Rich, manager of the Drury Lane, in a notice in the Daily Courant, Feb. 8, 1709.

The elaborate new scenery and mechanical efects at performances of "Dick Whittington and Cat" and the Opera, with Rinaldo, at the Haymarket are contrasted by the Spectator (14): "We had also but a very short allowance of thunder and lightening, though I cannot in this place omit doing justice to the boy who had the direction of the two painted dragons, and made them spit fire and smoke. He flashed out his rosin in such just proportion and in such due time . . . As to the mechanisms and scenery, everything indeed was uniform and of a piece, and the scenes were managed very dextrously. At the Haymarket, the undertakers forgetting to change their side scenes, we were presented with a prospect of the ocean in the midst of a delightful grove; and though the gentlemen on the stage had very much contributed to the beauty of the grove, by walking up and down between the trees, I must own I was not a little astonished to see a well-dressed young fellow, in a full-bottomed wig, appear in the midst of the sea, and without any visible concern taking snuff."

PURITAN AND CAVALIER

Fairfax, like his father, general of the Parliamentary forces, was succeeded on his resignation in 1650, by his lieutenant, Cromwell, and retired to Nun Appleton in Yorkshire on a £5,000 a year pension. Fairfax had pursued Charles I, to force on him a petition to listen to Parliament; had refused to sit as judge at his trial, since his fate was foreordained; and had led the commission to Holland, inviting Charles II's return.

Fairfax (1613-71) and his wife Anne, daughter of his superior officer, Lord Vere, at the time of their marriage in 1637, are a surprisingly youthful couple. Soest (1637-87) could scarcely have painted them before the Restoration, and they wear the costume of the 60's. Three generations later, the

Baron Fairfax descended from them will inherit great estates in Virginia from his Culpepper mother, will die there, a friend of Washington; and collateral descendants in Virginia will hold his title in XXc.

Another of their children will figure in the most fantastic exploit of the interregnum. George Villiers, the younger Buckingham, tired of exile in France on the proceeds of his father's pictures, conceived the idea of recovering some portion of his confiscated estates by marrying the only daughter of the man who had most benefited from his loss. Practically unconcealed, he arrived in England to court Mary Fairfax, whom he had never seen. Fairfax had no prejudice against an aristocracy to which he also belonged; he was an honorable man who felt bound to make such restitution, and a brave one, who must have been taken by Buckingham's sheer audacity. Cromwell, who had intended to marry one of his daughters to Buckingham, quarrelled with Fairfax; and Buckingham retired to Nun Appleton with the Fairfaxes, playing to perfection and enjoying the role of amiable country squire, until the Restoration brough him back to fortune.

The marriage was childless and the duchess dull. In a duel, in which two combatants died and the other four were wounded, Buckingham killed the Earl of Shrewsbury over the latter's wife (who is supposed to have dressed as a page and held his horse during the encounter). He then went to bed with the lady in his blood-stained shirt out of bravado—and because the demarcation between day and night shirts was not yet firmly fixed. Eventually he brought the "duchess dowager" to his own house. The outraged legal duchess found he had arranged in advance to have a coach waiting to take her back to her family.

The duke alternated brilliant speeches in the House with repeated imprisonments in the Tower, once for treason against Charles, who pardoned him. He wrote "The Rehearsal" a burlesque of the heroic drama which put the style of Dryden entirely out of fashion. "The Rehearsal" was imitated by Sheridan in "The Critic." The duke then tried to recoup his failing fortunes by founding the glass house at Lambeth, whose products Evelyn so much admired (Sept. 19, 1676). He wittily worsted the Jesuits sent for his conversion by James II; and finally retired, with £140,000 debts, to country life. The news of this Sir George Etheredge said he had heard "with no less astonishment than if I had been told the Pope had begun to wear a periwig, and had turned beau in the 74th year of his age." Buckingham died of a chill after hunting, but in circumstances far less squalid than recounted by Pope's poem.

The sober Fairfax, so dark that he was called "Black Tom," does not yet wear a wig, although under Cromwell, May Day, 1654 "was more observed . . . than for divers years past, and indeed much sin committed by wicked meetings, with fiddlers, drunkenness, ribaldry and the like. Great resort came to Hyde Park, many hundreds of rich coaches, and gallants in attire, but most shamefully powdered hair; men painted and spotted women." (*Cromwelliana*.)

Wood, who was no beau, but no Puritan either, paid "2s 6d for powder and mending of my periwige," when settling his quarterly accounts with his Oxford barber. He reports that Dr. John Owen, "the deane of Christ Church, had as much powder in his haire that would discharge eight

canons . . . and being a vaine person weared for the most part sweet powder in his haire," as well as lawn boot-hose tops, "in opposition to a prelaticall cut." Pepys, under less compulsion than the Oxford ecclesiastics to indicate his politics by his costume, first tries on wigs at Jervas, his barber's, May 9, 1663, balancing their trouble against their advantages; eventually buys two, at £3, and at 40s., and fails to make the stir he had expected when he appears at church in the better one, Nov. 8, 1663.

1550. XVIIc. German-English. (London, Nat. Port. Gall.)

Gerard von Soest. Thomas, Third Baron Fairfax and his wife.

Soest (1600-87), who came to London in 1656 and died there, was so ill-mannered and personally untidy that fewer women than men sat to him.

Fairfax, the humblest and most unpretentious of men, except in battle when "scarce anyone durst speak a word to him, and he would seem more like a man distracted and furious than of his ordinary mildness," wears a modest band, as befits a general of the rebellion; but as a rich gentleman, his band is fashionably cut and handsomely stringed, and worn with the satin-smooth, rather skimpy coat, usually quite untrimmed, which we see in so many Lely and Kneller portraits of Englishmen in latter half XVIIc.

His wife wears the beginnings of the studied satin negligence of the third quarter century, her ringlets now falling forward over the shoulders. The cut-and-fitted-together look has left the outermost garments; they appear to be rectangles, slung about the body, rather than gored capes. The cape-like lace about ladies' shoulders is disappearing in favor of an edge of shirt-frill, or scarves, knotted or caught with small brooches, and allowed to trail.

1551. XVIIc. 1660. Flemish-English. (Metropolitan Museum.)

Janssens van Ceulen. Dorothy Percy, Countess of Leicester.

Dorothy Percy, daughter of the ninth Earl of Northumberland, had fifteen remarkable children by her marriage in 1616 with Sir Philip Sidney's cousin. Of her daughter Dorothy, the Tatler (#61) says, "The fine women they shew me now-a-days are at

1551

best pretty girls to me who have seen "Sacharissa" when all the world repeated the poems (by Waller) which she inspired." One of her sons was Algernon Sidney, "that man of great courage, great sense, great parts," author of the "Discources concerning Government," which upheld resistance to oppression by the crown, and reaffirmed the importance of both Houses of Parliament in its restraint. He was executed on Dec. 7, 1683, on what Evelyn calls "the single witness of that monster of a man, Lord Howard of Escrick, and some sheets of paper taken in Mr. Sidney's study, pretended to be written by him, but not fully proved, nor the time when, but appearing to have been written before His Majesty's Restoration, and then pardoned by the Act of Oblivion." The Sidneys were handsome and cultivated anti-Tory aristocrats, too Protestant for Laud, too moderate for the Puritans. Their eldest son was another judge, who, like Fairfax, refused to take part in the farce of Charles I's trial, and was pardoned at the Restoration for the important part he had played, as Lord Lisle, in the Civil Wars.

Dorothy Percy is faultlessly dressed for the role of a handsome and high-minded, middle-aged Protestant of great position; everything is perfectly sober and suitable, rich and becoming. While the lovely Lady Isabella Thynne and Mrs. Fanshawe appear at chapel at Oxford during the interregnum "half-dressed, like angels," the countess is covered to the ears by exquisite sheer lawn and lace, the whole effect of which hangs by the thread of black below the sweep of her great hat, and leading to the bow on her bosom.

1552

1552. XVIIc. c. 1661. English. (Bratton Fleming, Basil Fanshaw.)

Sir Peter Lely. Sir Thomas and Lady Fanshawe.

The Fanshawes, for three generations remembrancers to the king's exchequer, were a family whose second and third generations were ruined by civil war.

Sir Thomas, the First Viscount; his brother Richard (the diplomat, translator of the *Lusiad,* and husband of the memoir-writing Lady Anne); and his son Thomas, the Second Viscount, were all in the loyalist army, and disabled to sit in parliament. The brothers "compounded" for the restitution of their estates, but were largely ruined. The second Thomas had to sell Ware, the family seat, for £26,000, after the death of his mother (daughter of Sir William Cokayne, Lord Mayor of London). One of his younger brothers, "a witty but rascally fellow, without a penny in his purse," was a great trial to Pepys (Feb. 23, 1667/8). He was asking "what places there were in the Navy fit for him, and Brisband tells me, in mirth, he told him the Clerke of the Acts, and I wish he had it, so I were well and quietly rid of it; for I am weary of this kind of trouble." Among James I's new devices for raising money had been his institution of baronetcies; first granted May 22, 1611 to seventy-five knights. Ninety receiving that honor, March 13, 1614, paid £1090 to maintain thirty foot-soldiers three years in Ireland at 8d a day. Powerful places in the government, with their valuable perquisites, were frankly sold. Now an English aristocracy pauperized by war (as that of France by the demands of court life under Louis XIV), was, like young Fanshawe, scrambling for places.

The younger Sir Thomas' first wife, Catherine Ferrers, "a very great fortune and a most excellent woman," had died in 1660. Since he had by his second wife (Sara Evelyn, widow of Sir John Wray) a daughter, who was herself married in 1675, Fanshawe must have remarried almost immediately. This portrait by Lely, (who also painted Sir Richard Fanshawe and his lady) probably celebrates the new marriage.

Like the miniature of Lady Catherine Howard, this shows the characteristic costume of the third quarter of the century, against which ministers were launching such attacks as Richard Baxter's "A just and seasonable reprehension of naked breasts and shoulders."

This loose informality also affects male costume; gentlemen begin to be painted in handsome shirts, barely showing under a great deal of slung drapery; then they will be painted in shirts and dressing gowns (see Ill. 1581); and by XVIIIc., in dressing gowns and caps.

1553. XVIIc. 1664. Flemish-English. (Windsor Castle, H. M. the King of England.)

Jacob Huysmans (1633-96). Frances Stuart, Duchess of Richmond.

Henrietta Maria's physician during her exile was one Walter Stewart. His daughter Frances came to England in 1662 as maid-of-honor to Charles' Portuguese queen, despite Louis XIV's promise to see her married "as well as any lady in France," if she remained at Versailles.

"It was hardly possible," Count Hamilton said, "for a woman to have less wit or more beauty. . . . She was very graceful . . . well bred, and possessed to perfection that art of dress . . . which is rarely attained unless acquired while young in France."

Charles made love to her for many years with little success, and even considered divorcing in order to marry her. Pepys' diary, 1663-7, is filled with entries about the king's infatuation, and comparisons of her beauty with that of the king's official mistress, the dazzling Lady Castlemain.

When the court went into mourning, April 23, 1666, "forcing all the ladies to go in black, with their hair plain, and without spots," Pepys finds Lady Castlemain "not so pretty as Mrs. Stewart"; on Oct. 30, he decides that "plain natural dress" becomes neither lady. But on Nov. 14, Mrs. Stewart is "a glorious sight . . . in black and white lace, and her head and shoulders dressed with diamonds," exceeding Lady Castlemain, "at least now." On Feb. 27, 1666/7, Pepys sees the King's "new medall," the copper penny, on the reverse of which Rotier had represented Mrs. Stewart as Brittania, as she appears to this day.

On April 26, 1667, "she was come to that pass as to

1553

1554

have resolved to have any gentleman of £1500 a year that would have had her in honour . . . for she could not longer continue at court without prostituting herself to the king, whom she has so long kept off."

Since the king opposed her marriage she eloped with the rich but dull Duke of Richmond. Charles expelled her from court; she sent back the jewels he had given her. But returning to court as the Queen's first lady of the bedchamber, she did eventually become Charles' mistress, retaining her influence despite a disfiguring attack of smallpox in 1668. Dying childless in 1704, she directed that an estate should be bought and called "Lennox-love to Blantyre," as a gift to her favorite nephew.

Frances Stewart was a superb horsewoman. Wood tells us that male red coats were worn as ladies' riding dress at Oxford, 1660-5. On Aug. 26, 1664, Pepys went "to see some pictures at one Huysman's, a picture-drawer, a Dutchman, which is said to exceed Lilly; and indeed there is both of the Queens and Maids of Honour, particularly Mrs. Stewart's, in a buff doublet like a soldier, as good pictures, I think, as ever I saw." On June 11, 1666, "walking in the galleries at White Hall, I find the Ladies of Honour dressed in their riding garb, with coats and doublets with deep skirts, just, for all the world, like mine; and buttoned their doublets up the breast, with periwigs and with hats, so that, only for a long petticoat dragging under their men's coats, nobody could take them for women at any point whatever: which was an odde sight, and a sight that did not please me."

Frances Stewart's "buff doublet," harking back to the cavalier styles of the civil wars, has the laced closing which has been characteristic of XVIIc. leather military garments. With her great sense of style, she uses the knot of ribbons which we would expect to find on the shoulder of a contemporary man's coat, as a more effective finish to the front lacing.

After a royal visit to Oxford, poor Mr. Fisher was never able to get back the lodgings in Merton from which he had been ousted for Mrs. Stewart's con-

venience. The scurrilous pages devoted by Wood (May 1, 1661) to the villainies of Tom Clayton, the new warden, (who had taken a fancy to the rooms while calling on the lady), can surprise no one who has ever lived through a row in a chaste institution like a college or museum. The heavy furniture which had been "well liked by Dr. Goddard, Brent, Savile &c., being disliked by that proud woman (Lady C.) because, forsooth, the said goods were out of fashion . . . all must be chang'd and alter'd to the great expence of the college . . . A very large looking glass, for her to see her ugly face, and body to the middle, and perhaps lower . . . and which cost, as the bursar told me, about £10," Wood accuses the Claytons of carrying off to their private country house, among other stylish new objects of which the college had kept no inventory.

1554. XVIIc. After 1660. Dutch. (London, Sir Philip Sassoon.)

H. Danckerts (1630-78). The Pineapple Picture.

This picture, by a Dutch painter who had studied in Italy, belonged to Horace Walpole. His notation on the back says that it shows Mr. Rose, the king's gardener, presenting to Charles the first pineapple grown in England. The scene is the landing from the Thames at Dawnay Court, Sussex, where the pits in which the palms were grown for protection still exist. (Sacheverell Sitwell: *English Conversation Pictures*.) Pineapples were still a rarity when the king gave Evelyn a slice of one from the Barbadoes from his own plate (Aug. 19, 1668); Evelyn was disappointed. "It has yet a graceful acidity, but tastes more like quince and melon" than any of the fruit to which it had been likened in Capt. Ligon's mouthwatering descriptions of travel.

Charles' "good-natured condescensions" were legendary. When the mayor, Sir Robert Viner, tried to drag the king back bodily for one more bottle at the Lord Mayor's banquet, Charles said, "He that's drunk is as great as a king" and returned. (*Spectator*, No. 462.) On a visit from America, Penn stood covered, after the Quaker fashion, in the king's presence. Charles took off his own hat. Penn asked, "Friend Charles, why dost thou not keep on thy hat?" and was told by the king, " 'Tis the custom of this place for only *one* person to remain covered at a time." (Gray's *Hudibras*.)

The amusing and quick-witted Charles had been defectively educated, but was an adroit politician of great natural gifts. "If this king loved business as well as he understood it, he would have been the greatest king in Europe," Sir Richard Bulstrode said. Bishop Burnet says Charles "told Lord Essex that he did not wish to be like a Grand Signor, with some mutes about him, and bags of bow-strings to strangle men; but he did not think he was a king so long as a company of fellows were looking into his actions, and examining his ministers as well as his accounts." After a life of poverty and exile, Charles wanted to stay at home, be king, and amuse himself. He had a considerable interest in science and the arts, and, Pepys, says, "a transcendant mastery of all maritime knowledge."

In this picture, Charles, who "delighted in a bewitching kind of pleasure called sauntering," and who walked every day in St. James' Park to feed the birds, is shown with the little spaniels which went everywhere with him. Their breed is still called by his name.

> "His very dog at Council Board
> Sits grave and wise as any Lord."

Both Charles and Mr. Rose wear wigs and long, easy-fitting coats with shoulder-knots, and sleeves caught back by bows. Charles' coat, with the Garter star on its breast, is still buttoned at the top, and has a pocket in its early form, barely above the hem; from it hangs a tasseled handkerchief. In 1667, when his mistress, Lady Castlemain, was losing £25,000 a night at the cards Charles himself disliked, Pepys says (Sept. 2), the king had "at this time no hand-kerchers, and but three bands to his neck," for lack of money to pay the linen-draper £5,000, "the grooms taking away the king's linen at the quarter's end as their fee . . . let the king get more as he can."

(For data on intended Ill. 1555, see Appendix.)

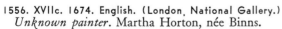

1556. XVIIc. 1674. English. (London, National Gallery.)
Unknown painter. Martha Horton, née Binns.
The widow of Joshua Horton of Sowerby was probably painted by a member of the de Critz family, in her weeds.

1557-58. XVIIc. 1670. U. S. A. (Charleston, W. Va., Mrs. Alexander Quarrier Smith.)
Unknown artist. Margaret Gibbs and Henry Gibbs.
Among the earliest American portraits of children are those of the Gibbs children, and of Madame Freake and Baby Mary, of Boston mercantile families. (See Appendix.)
All show the expected provincial time lag of several decades. Margaret Gibbs' gown is of red velvet, with red ribbons and fine lace; apron embroidered in blue-black; silver beads; wonderful square-toed white shoes with red soles and ribbons. Henry, who became the pastor of East Parish, Watertown, and married the daughter of the Rev. Nathan Appleton of Cambridge, wears a red cap banded in lace, a brown gown with red-brown cuffs, laced in gold and white galloon; plain white pinafore and band collar; and yellow shoes with red soles and bows.

1559

1559-78. XVIIc. 1675. English. (Metropolitan Museum, Print Room.)

David Loggan. "Oxonia Illustrata."

Sheldonian Theatre (1559), Academic Costume (1560-78).

The passion for recording which is characteristic of the XVIIc. led Oxford to make Loggan "public sculptor of the University," and to give Anthony Wood access to the records of the various colleges for his "Hist. & Ant. Univ. Oxon." Their books, with Hyde's catalog of the Bodleian, became Oxford's official presents to visiting dignitaries (with the addition of a pair of embroidered gloves on a visit from the king; festivities and processions attending such visits are minutely described by Wood: see Appendix.)

The new architectural and topographical plates of second half XVIIc.-first half XVIIIc. need figures and carriages in the foreground to give them scale. Useful costumed figures are found on such plates as Speed's *Map of the Kingdom of England,* 1646, Sanford's *Coronation Procession of James II,* in the various *Surveys, Annals, Almanachs* and *Cries of London* of the period, as well as in book illustration, which is becoming important. Loggan followed his *Oxonia* by *Cantabrigia Illustrata,* 1690, one plate of which shows country folk harvesting the surrounding fields.

The Sheldonian Theatre, designed by Sir Christopher Wren, was built and endowed by Gilbert Sheldon, Archbishop of Canterbury, and opened with the "great" Act of 1669. Its basement housed the university press, and the theatre with its painted ceiling was henceforth used for the degree-granting ceremonies of the Act, early in July. Throughout Act Saturday, Act Sunday and Act Monday, specific functions are held, while at the same time (and during this week alone), professional actors, rope-dancers, jugglers, and freaks were allowed to perform. Wood had paid 1s. 8d. for refreshments and to see the play given at the "Blewe Anchor," July 6, 1657, and went twice to see the "Turke" dance in 1658.

After the Restoration, "to spite the Presbyterians," both morning and afternoon performances were given at the "King's Armes in Halywell." Crowds thronged to Oxford to see one to three showings of ten different plays, "wherein women acted" (among whom was Roxilana, married to the Earl of Oxon) "making the scholars mad, run after them, take ill courses."

Elizabeth Davenport, called "Roxilana" after the part in the "Siege of Rhodes" in which Pepys found her incomparable, had indignantly refused to become the Earl of Oxford's mistress, but was tricked by him into a "marriage," performed by his herald, dressed as a priest. Wedding festivities have become so expensive that the fashionable trend is toward the smallest possible weddings, held in the country or at midnight. Children, wards, and their fortunes have been manipulated with so little heart or conscience, especially in England, that the era of clandestine, runaway, irregular marriages is beginning. Footmen, in their master's clothes and well-observed manners, court masked women who may be ladies or adventuresses; heiresses are abducted by fortune-hunters; marriages, legal or not, are performed in the "lawless" churches, or in prison chapels, which do not require banns, by equivocal ministers, often themselves prisoners, or by court clerks, impersonating their superiors, and giving forged certificates. Sion Chapel at Hampstead required a license, but advertised in the *Postboy* in 1710, that you could be married there free, if you had your wedding dinner in its gardens.

Wood's descriptions and Loggan's plates (which Wood often refers to as "the cuts" to his book), show academic costume at Oxford, just as the common, dignified dress of the Middle Ages, anachronistically retained in ecclesiastical wear, is becoming stylized and fixed into its modern form. (See Poole: Appendix.)

Wood mentions in 1649 the neglect of the old rules of academic dress under the "new comers," who "mostly were very meane and poor at their first comming" having gotten into good fellowships, "became wondrous malapert and saucy, especially to the old stock remaining. They went in half shirts, appearing at their brest and out at sleeves, great bands with tassel band-strings, and Spanish leather boots with lawne or holland tops," all avoiding "cassocks, or canonical gownes or coates, or curcingles, because they smelt too much of the prelaticall cut." Gowns with sleeves "as wide as those of surplices, a fashion brought into the Universitie by the Cantabrigians" were worn until 1666. Square or round academic caps, and hoods were not "woren in publick," and often not at Congregation and Convocation. Commoners often wore the gowns of gentlemen commoners, while the latter might appear in velvet faced gowns. The sleeves and facings of formal gowns of doctors of divinity were of velvet; of medicine, satin; of law, taffeta.

In 1660, "the next matter was to restore formalities and habits, totally in a manner neglected in the intervall, but sleeves and caps were not reformed to their exact size until Dr. Fell became vice-chancellor." Meanwhile (1663) "gentlemen commoners and other idle scollars" followed the courtiers' fashion of singing and whistling "in a careless way as they went too and fro . . . to the disgrace of the gown."

Dr. John Fell changed all that on Aug. 27, 1666. The new rules were printed in English as well as Latin "for the benefit of taylours:"

1. Servitours' gownes to have round capes and sleeves hanging behind the shoulder without any buttons.

2. The battelars' gowne altogeather the same with the servitours', excepting that the cape be square. [This is the type of gown now worn by commoners.]

1560. Undergraduate student of Civil Law, who has finished 4 academic years.

1561. Bachelor of Music.

1562. Bachelor of Arts.

1563. Bachelor of Arts, degree to be granted at Lent.

1564. Collector of Bachelor's degrees.

1565. Bachelor of Medicine.

1566. Proctor of the University.

1567. Proctor in an ermine hood (caputio ex minutio vario).

1568. Bachelor of Theology.

1569. Doctor of Medicine.

1570. Doctor of Sacred Theology.

1571. Doctor of Sacred Theology, in a scarlet cappa (capa coccinea).

1572. Doctor of Sacred Theology in a scarlet gown (toga coccinea).

1573. Members of the lesser nobility, Knights and Baronets.

1574. Sons of Viscounts, Marquises, Dukes and Earls.

1575. Superior bedells.

1576. Chancellor of the University.

1577-78. Attendants.

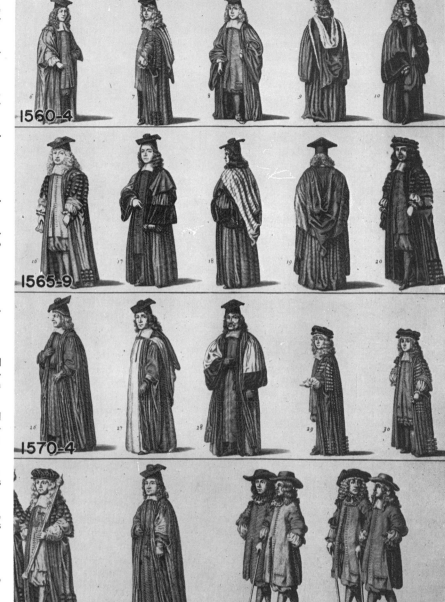

3. The commoners' gowne to be distinguished from the former by having half a dozen of buttons on each sleeve, not exceeding 5s the dozen nor the bigness in the public patternes.

4. The gent commoners' gowne to be half-sleeved, and, if they please, to have buttons not exceeding 4 dozen nor the rate of 5s the dozen nor the bigness in the public patternes.

5. A baronet's and knight's gowne, the same with the former, only distinguisht (if they please) with gold and silver buttons.

6. Noblemen to weare (if they please) coloured gownes, of the same form as the former.

7. Bachelaures of Arts and Foundation men that are undergraduats to weare wide-sleev'd gowns, the sleeves not reaching beyond the fingers' ends nor above an ell in compass. The Bachelaurs' sleeve to hang at length; the Foundation men turn'd up to the wrist.

8. None to weare mourning gownes, unless upon a cause approved by the head of the house and to be allowed by the vicechancellor and proctors. [The day before the burial of Dr. Oliver, president of Magdalene College, Oct. 27, 1661, "the university bellman went from college to college with the doctor's scarlet and square cap on, according to antient custome in these manners, to give notice when he should be buried." This custom had been prohibited by the Parliamentary Visitors, 1647-8. In 1675, "moorning gownes woren, as for thes 5 or 6 yeares past, by all sorts of scholars, and especially in the winter. Strange that no course is taken." In 1680, the vice-chancellor did not take the votes, at convocation, of

"those in mourning that would not vote for him; those that did, he took." Loggan's complete plates show these mourning gowns.]

9. Servitours, batlars, commoners, gentlemen-commoners of all conditions, being undergraduates, to weare round caps; gentlemen to have a hat-band upon them; knights, baronets, and noblemen being undergraduates to have velvet caps with silver or gold hatbands. [Our phrase "tuft-hunter" comes from the academic climbers who tried to become intimate with men of higher social rank, with gold tufts on their headgear.]

10. That persons studying the law being above 4 yeares standing in the University and being entred into the law-book be permitted to weare a half sleev'd gowne without buttons and a square cap.

"Which being published, all taylours, brokers, haberdashers and others whatsoever were warned not to make or sell any gowne or cap contrary to the patterne before mentioned next after S. Michael's day following. If any were found culpable then for the first offense, he was to pay 10s, halfe wherof was to goe to the University and tother half to the company of taylers. If the second time he offends, then 20s to be bestowed as aforesaid. If the third time, public discommoning, or dispriviledgd without hopes of restoration." (Wood)

Academic dress was formal, varying in color; or ordinary and black; with an intermediate form of convocation dress; red like the formal gown, worn by doctors.

The chancellor was an archbishop like Laud or Sheldon, or a great nobleman like Leicester, Pembroke, or Ormonde; his formal gown was of black silk laced with gold lace.

The vice-chancellor was the resident, acting head of the University, appointed for one year, but frequently reappointed. His power over Oxford was widespread. As an ecclesiastic, he controlled its pulpits and the conduct of heresy trials. His civil power gave him the discipline and jurisdiction over the night-watch and the streets, coffee, ale, and play-houses, markets and the prices of wine and ale, coaches and carriers, barber-shops, booksellers and censorship of the press. He supervised examinations, regulated academic dress, administered the finances of the University, and received the goods of felons and suicides.

The bedells were university officials, who did processional duty, and served as the vice-chancellor's messengers. They were six in number, an esquire and a yeoman bedell for each of the three faculties of theology, law, and arts and medicine. The esquire bedells wore gold chains and carried embossed silver-gilt maces or staffs, which they must surrender to the king when he visits Oxford; the yeomen bedells, plain silver-gilt maces. The vice-chancellor's accounts show that during XVIIc. there was also a "bedell of beggars," for whose gown £1 15s 9d was paid in 1693-4, and £2 in 1695-6. "Rebellious and seditious books," condemned by the convocation (including Thomas Hobbs' "Leviathan" and works by Thomas Cartwright), were thrown on a bonfire in the school quadrangle in 1683 by Gigur, the University bedell of beggars, before the vice-chancellor, bishop, and doctors in their "formalities."

Wood's diaries and compilations furnish an immense mass of information about such dress as is worn by the gentlemen in the lower corner of the sheet. Like Wood, they probably paid their barbers by the quarter; they might still wear their own hair, or wigs, costing at Oxford from 20 to 32s 6d. Their broad-brimmed castor (beaver) or demi-castor hats probably cost 11 to 24s; their bands, plain or laced, from 1s 5d to 13s 6d a pair. Their shirts were always made to order, probably by a woman. Wood once bought "3 ells and a quartern at 8 groats an ell" for a shirt which cost him altogether 8s 6d, and paid his sister Kit 7s 6d for another.

In the same way, the material for suits was never provided by the tailor who made up and kept the suit in repair. On April 24, 1665, Wood "bought a black shaloone suit (i.e. the material for it) of Mr. Fifeild and a studying gown of nectarello which cost me out of the shop £2 15s 9d.," and on May 4 paid "Mr. Hieron (Hearne) the taylor for making my suit 5s 6d; for making my studying gowne, 1s 6d." Wood's suits were apt to be black or sad colored. As his income increases, his costumes become more elegant and he rides a great deal more. On May 7, 1678, he puts on "a new riding camlet coat out of Mr. Fifeild's shop, £1 18s; making 4s; sising 1s; sum £2 3s," and on June 16, 1690 he has a new "white demity shuit; making 4s 9d."

In his least affluent days, gloves seem to have been a necessity; they were usually tan, wash leather or dog-skin and cost 1s to 1s 6d a pair. As cold weather set in, in Oct. 1661, Wood buys gloves to wear while writing. Wood's stockings were of black, pearl or sad-colored wool and cost from 3s to 5s 6d a pair; he is constantly paying "Bessie Creke for loyning and lengthening my new yarn stockings, 3d" or giving "Gooddy Gale" 6d for mending them. Shoes of russet or "liquored black Spanish leather" are made to order at Oxford for about 4s, and are kept in repair by their maker, or by the cobbler. With the growing interest in personal cleanliness, tooth brushes begin to appear in Wood's accounts about 1690.

In these straight, long-skirted coats we see the pockets in their early position, just above the hemline; the use of ribbon reduced to knots at shoulder, cuff, knee and shoe. The shirt, bloused above petti-coat breeches, is beginning to disappear, as vests lengthen and coat buttons are fastened lower.

1579

1579. Last quarter XVIIc. English. (Metropolitan Museum.)

School of Lely. Barbara Villiers, Duchess of Cleveland (Lady Castlemain).

The daughter of that "faultless person," Grandison, was, Burnet says, "a woman of great beauty, but enormously vicious and ravenous." She was married in 1658 to Roger Palmer, went with him to Charles' court in the Low Countries, and returned as Charles' mistress at the Restoration. She turned Catholic in 1663, and was treated with every consideration by Louis XIV's ambassadors, while she intrigued against the Chancellor, Clarendon, who would not permit any social relations between her and his wife. Her unpleasant husband was made Earl of Castlemain in 1662, and Duke of Cleveland in 1670. As James' ambassador to Rome he was the darling of the Jesuits, but was never allowed to complete his mission at the Vatican; at every audience, Innocent was siezed by a fit of coughing and had to withdraw, just as Castlemain began to speak; and, at his threat to leave Italy, Innocent said: "Only recommend him to rise early, that he may rest at noon; it is dangerous in this country to travel in the heat of the day."

Charles, childless by his Portuguese wife, had about 15 children by seven mistresses; six of Lady Castlemain's were perhaps his. She was "foolish but imperious, very uneasy to the king, and always carrying on intrigues with other men, while yet she pretended she was jealous of him. His passion for her, and her strange behavior towards him, did so disorder him, that often he was not master of himself, nor capable of minding business . . . in so critical a time," the bishop continues. Her lovers included leading actors, like Hart and Goodman; Jacob Hall the rope dancer; the playwright Wycherly; and the handsome duke of Marlborough.

Lady Castlemain lost immense sums at basset but could afford to gamble because of a large income: "£10,000 more a year to the Duchess of Cleveland; who has likewise near £10,000 a year more out of the new farm of the county excise of beer and ale;

£5,000 a year out of the Post Office; and, they say, the reversion of all the King's leases, the reversion of all the places in the Customhouse, the Green Wax, and indeed, what not! All promotions, spiritual and temporal, pass under her cognizance." (Andrew Marvell.) Clarendon, however, never allowed the Great Seal to be affixed to any paper on which her name appeared.

Her influence lasted about 10 years. She had always resented the superior beauty of Charles' son, born to Lucy Walters in exile, over her own children. Her position was weakened, after the marriage of "La Belle Stuart" who did not care to gamble, and laughed and built card-houses with Buckingham, while Lady Castlemain was losing her house and its contents at cards. It was further impaired by her behavior over her rivals. Nell Gwynn, the delightful actress, had refused a title and settlements. Charles, "so pleasant a man," even on his death-bed, asked the court to forgive him for being so long a-dying, and asked his heir, James, to "take care of Carewell (Querouaille, his last mistress), and let not poor Nelly starve," before he was hustled with horrifying lack of ceremony into his grave.

The duchess of Cleveland had gone to France in 1670; there in 1705, she married the beautiful but brutal "Beau" Feilding (whose footmen flaunted fantastic yellow liveries, slashed and plumed in black, and who turned out to have a wife already). In 1709, at 70, she died of dropsy.

Like the duchess of Mazarin, Lady Castlemain wears the simple, careless dress of the turn of the third to final quarter XVIIc., the underlinen of which overflows the neckline of the bodice, and forces its way out between the tiny jewelled clasps of the center-front, and is pushed up, with studied negligence, at the elbows. Her cloak is the new, informally draped and caught rectangle, unshaped by any bias cutting.

Walpole calls Lely's clothes "a sort of fantastic nightgowns, fastened with a pin." (*Anecdotes of Painting.*)

1580. XVIIc. German-English. (Marquis of Tweedale.)

Gerard von Soest. Lady Margaret Hay, Countess of Roxburgh.

"Lord Roxbrough . . . one of the flowers of this nobility," was one of the naval officers, whose loss, at the wreck of the Gloucester, is recorded by Pepys, May 8, 1682.

1581-82. XVIIc. 1687. English. (London, Messrs. Leygatt.)

J. M. Wright. Sir Willoughby Aston (1581), Lady Aston (1582).

The Astons were staunch Royalists, who had lived in Cheshire and served the Crown since the XIIc. Willoughby Aston was the only son of the heiress of Sir Henry Willoughby, Sheriff of Chester, and of that "stout and learned man," Sir Thomas Aston (a devout Churchman whose *Remonstrance against Presbytery, exhibited by divers of the nobilitie, gentrie, ministers, and inhabitants of the County Palatine of Chester,* was written in answer to "some brain-sick Anabaptist").

Wood records, with almost servile satisfaction, that Aston's cousin, Sir Henry Purefoy, had passed over an uncle to make Sir Willoughby heir to his estate of Wadley, the year before this picture was painted. Perhaps Purefoy appreciated fine manners more than did Sir Robert Newdegate, an extravagantly prodigal host, who mutters in his diary of "Sir W. A.'s ingenious but most abominable complimentall letter" of thanks for hospitality at Arbury. The bequest cannot have been unwelcome: Aston and his wife, Mary Offley, had eight sons and thirteen daughters to settle in life. (See Appendix, Newdegate.)

Sir Willoughby appears in the informal shirt and handsome dressing gown which is beginning to be fashionable indoor wear and which by XVIIIc. will appear on the streets, early in the morning.

Lady Roxburgh (Ill. 1580) and Lady Castlemain (Ill. 1579) wear approximately the same gown: its developing informality, as bunched-up and wired-out hair loses its artificial supports and begins to fall, is shown in the dress of Lady Aston. Its final form, the draperies of a goddess of antiquity, is worn by the Duchess of St. Albans.

1583. Late XVIIc.-Early XVIIIc. German-English. (Hampton Court, H. M. The King.)

Sir Godfrey Kneller. Lady Diana de Vere, Duchess of St. Albans.

The daughter and heir of Aubrey de Vere, the last Earl of Oxford, married Charles Beauclerk, Duke of St. Albans, son of Charles II and Nell Gwynn. He was a soldier, "a gentleman in every way de bon naturel, well-bred, doth not like business, is well affected to the constitution of his country" which he served under Charles, William and Anne. His wife was Lady of the Bedchamber and of the Stole to Queen Caroline, when she was Princess of Wales, while Charles was Grand Falconer.

There had been a decline of interest in falconry after James I's time. Its revival after the Restoration could not be maintained in face of the general use of firearms and the increase in agricultural enclosures. The "day" of falconry held on Oct. 1, 1828, by the Hereditary Grand Falconer of England, descendant of one of St. Albans' eight sons, was notably unsuccessful.

1584. Early XVIIc. (Boston, Museum of Fine Arts, Elizabeth Day McCormick Coll.)

Dress: grayish brown silk brocaded in gold; trimmed with gold and silver bobbin lace. Hem and back width are made of another (probably cheaper) material: brown ground, narrow stripes, warp figured, of minute geometric figures in blue, yellow and white; probably covered originally by some sort of loose panel or train.

1585-86. XVIIc. c. 1690. English. (Metropolitan Museum.)

Dress in Louis XIV style: gray wool, striped in indigo blue and henna, embroidered throughout in silver gilt in late XVIIc. conventionalized flower and scroll pattern done in satin and stem stitches. Belonged to the Wodehouse family, Kimberly House, Norfolk. (See Appendix.)

1587. XVIIIc. 1700-50. French. (Metropolitan Museum.)

Suit: mauve silk, all-over design of white flowers and green stems.

The "Corrupted Tottering Bishops"

Cartwright was the very pattern of Mrs. Hutchinson's "corrupted, tottering Bishops." He was the grandson of that Thomas Cartwright (1535-1603), "head and most learned of that sect of dissenters then called puritans," whose original distaste for vestments and ritual was extended by Cartwright into a concern for the entire originzation of the church. He was ousted from his Lady Margaret professorship, and served as Rector of the University of Geneva. Always impetuous, he declared, during his prosperous and respected old age, back in England, that he wished he could relive his life "to testify to the world the dislike he had of his former ways" which had caused so much trouble.

The grandson of the old Puritan had no difficulty in obtaining a vacant fellowship at Magdalen during the interval, but at the Restoration he turned ardently loyal and got the post of chaplain to the duke of Gloucester. He then began the collection of preferments and lucrative sinecures, which became one of the scandals of an age not easily disturbed by such things: Prebendary of St. Paul's, Vicar of St. Thomas', Prebendary of Wells and Durham, Dean of Ripon. When senility made two vacant bishoprics, "they resolved to fill them," Bishop Burnet says, "with the two worst men who could be found. Cartwright was promoted to Chester. He was a man of good capacity, and had made some progress in learning. He was ambitious and servile, cruel and boisterous, and, by the great liberties he allowed himself, he fell under great scandals of the worst sort. He had set himself long to raise the King's authority (which) . . . was from God, absolute and superior to law . . . So he was looked upon as a man that would more effectively advance the designs of popery, than if he should turn over to it. And indeed, bad as he was, he never made that step, even in the most desperate state of his affairs," when he fled with James on the arrival of William, followed him to Ireland, and there died. Cartwright's sycophancy is clearly shown in the 1686-7 fragment of his diary, published by the Camden Society, 1843.

Cartwright had thanked James for the Declaration of Liberty of Conscience in 1687, and in the next year, the Catholic James, who felt that the High Church was half Catholic anyhow, made his favorite, Cartwright, head of the Ecclesiastical Commission of 8 "to take cognizance of all defaults in both Universities," after Canterbury had refused to serve. "Everyone understood," Wood says, "that the design of the commission was to introduce a Roman hierarchy which assumes a power over the temporal, in order to the spiritual, good; yet here this commission grants the temporal power," to the Lord Chancellor and two others, such as the Lord Treasurer and Chief Justice with "power of excommunication, which is a purely spiritual act." The ecclesiastical visitors expelled 25 from their fellowships at Magdalene.

James, the bigoted Catholic, like many others, mistook the conscientiously tolerant William Penn for "a concealed Papist." "Penn is no more a Quaker than I am," the king declared of the Lord Admiral's son, who had returned from Louis XIV's court with what Pepys thought (Aug. 30, 1664) "a great deal, if not too much, of the vanity of the French garb and affected manner of speech and gait." Penn, imprisoned in the Tower and in Newgate as a Quaker preacher, was freed on the strength of his own speech in court. On the death of his father he came into a fortune, and was granted land in America against Charles II's debt of £16,000 to the admiral. Penn provided his American property with a remarkably liberal constitution which guaranteed complete religious freedom and, in 1682, made the first of a number of trips to Pennsylvania. While Penn was in England, he attempted to negotiate with William III in Holland, on James' behalf; there Penn met and was disliked by Burnet, as "a talking, vain man" who "had a tedious, luscious way, that was not apt to overcome a man's reason, though it might tire his patience." Dean Swift, on the contrary, thought Penn "spoke very agreeably and with much spirit."

1588. Last Quarter. XVIIc. German-English. (London Nat. Port. Gall.)

Gerard von Soest. Thomas Cartwright, Bishop of Chester.

In protest against the "prelaticall cut," during the interregnum, wigs, bands with tasseled strings (together with boots and lawn boot-hose), and refusal to wear the academic hat, had emerged as literally "protest-ant" wear. The arch-prelaticall Cartwright, therefore, wears the square hat without a wig, a small austere band, and the cassock, to which his grandfather had been so opposed, with ostentatiously full lawn sleeves.

The life of a clergyman, with a good living or two, was a cheerful and not at all onerous one, in the rollicking days of Charles' Restoration. On the road to his induction at Chester, Cartwright dined with the Marquess of Winchester at Bolton "from one at noon till one in the morning" (an invention of Winchester's to enable him to avoid matters he disliked). The journal of the Rev. Giles Moore, rector of Horsted Keynes, Sussex (Ponsonby: *English Diaries*) which he kept from 1655-79, lists purchases which, to our watered-down and perhaps canting sobriety nowadays, seem extraordinary every-day wear for a clergyman.

I bought two payre of gloves for which I payed 2s 3d the payer. I had them faced with my own fringe which cost me 1s 4d.

I bought a levitacal girdle containing 4 oz. of silke, 10s & ½ a yd of velvet; two worsted canonical girdles 5s.

I bought 2 yards and ½ of Devonshire red bazes to make me a waistcoat for which I paid 7s 4d and I bought a payre of silk stockings for which I paid £1:1; for silken tops 6s 6d and for a payer of black worsted stockings I gave 5s.

I bought of my countryman Mr. Cooke a shaggy demicastor hat of the fashion for which I payed 16s 6d.

I carried Mat (his god-daughter) up to London buying for her a new riding suite for which I payed 28s.

I gave Mat 1s to play withall and I gave her 2s towards a payr of stockings which she is to knit for herselfe. I also gave her 1s which she is to spend on dancings.

I sent for Mat's board for six weeks at Mistress Chalmers during which time shee made mee shirts and bands £1:10 and I gave her to buy a hood at the faire 5s.

The House of Commons Takes Control

Once rid of James, the House takes the bit in its teeth. It executes a series of moves more revolutionary than any until our own day. It establishes itself as the preeminent power in England, and the training ground for the brilliant political figures of the XVIII-XIXc. Taxes are elaborated, the coinage revised, and the ground work laid for the modern banking and financial systems of the country.

First, the Civil Lists are revised; the indignant William finds the Crown now less well off than at the time of his predecessor.

The army is removed from Crown control. It must now look to Parliament for pay and maintenance, and it is, for the first time, regulated and disciplined by the Mutiny Act, which, together with the Bill of Rights, the Toleration Act, and the Oath of Allegiance required by all office-holders, are passed by the 1690 Parliament.

The French wars require immense sums to be raised at a time when French privateers are destroying English trade. The happily tax-free England of Elizabeth, which so amazed the Venetian ambassador, will never again be seen.

The simple money-raising devices of James' baronage and Charles I's fines on all persons worth £40 a year who refuse knighthood, now seem childish. "Tunnage" and "poundage" excises on both imported and exported commodities had been levied in 1644. Under Charles II, there are many other devices, the most hated of which is probably the tax of 2s levied on each chimney in 1662. People had begun to be comfortable under Elizabeth; chimneys had multiplied. The rate of acceleration is now slowed. As an educational institution, Oxford feels it should be tax-exempt. Influential men are begged to lobby towards that end; but the Sheldonian continues to be taxed for three hearths in the theatre and seven in the basement print-shop.

In 1666 comes a 1% income tax, increased in 1694 to 4s on the £, and doubled for non-jurors (to the Act of Allegiance). A poll tax of 1s is levied on each subject, with an additional £1 for each gentleman, and £5 more for doctors of all university faculties. Poor prissy-genteel Wood, so proud of his cousins worth £2000 a year who have several times been offered a baronetcy, cannot forbear from declaring himself a gentleman, although he is outraged that an industrious person like himself should have to pay £1 more than the "idle scollars," amusing themselves at Oxford.

"Chimney money," repealed on William's promise as he came to the throne, was merely replaced by Halifax' window tax. There is none too much sun in England. Now houses are built with fewer windows; existing windows are blocked up; teeth, and the tuberculosis rate do not improve.

French wines and goods have been taxed off the market since 1668; customs and excise taxes are increased in 1670. By the final quarter century, smuggling, adulteration and substitution become common. Home-made gin replaces imported liquors; home-brewed beer follows beer taxes in e.XVIIIc.; and brews are fermented out of all sorts of strange substances after the malt tax which tries to control home brewing. Salt and sugar, tea, coffee, chocolate, tobacco and spices, soap and candles, paper, parchment and leather, textiles, glass, and hackney coaches are in turn taxed, and wine sellers and keepers of public houses are licensed. By 1695, there are taxes on birth, marriage, death and burial, and for widows and bachelors. To encourage its raising, wool is made tax-exempt, and an act for "burying in wool" is passed, while hemp and flax acreages are taxed. By 1701, all beasts of burden and peddlers are licensed.

Because tea is easy to smuggle, the English become a nation of tea-drinkers. To save a dying industry, the glass tax has to be repealed in 1697. The poll tax is replaced by a stamp tax. But stupid and venal tax collectors enable the rich to pay less than their share of this and of the new land and property taxes. It was even proposed to confiscate and melt all the silverware in England, at about the time that Louis XIV was melting up his silver furniture at Versailles.

English banking was far behind that of such early commercial civilizations as Italy and the Low Countries. Large sums were originally deposited for safety at the Mint, where they brought in no interest. After Charles I's requisitioning of this money, it became the custom to leave money with the goldsmiths, who advanced it at 8% to the government, against tax receipts, and paid their depositors 6%. Government obligations, backed by no current funds, had fallen to half their face value, so the government was actually paying 16% interest. In 1672, Charles II closed the Exchange without warning, confiscating the principal saved by some 10,000 people. This money, the foundation of the National Debt, did not begin to receive the promised 6% until five years later.

Montague was one of our preeminent Whigs forming the "Junto," which was the beginning of the modern cabinet. He became Chancellor of the Exchecquer after shares in the new Bank of England, which he had fostered, were quickly subscribed, and after the Bank provided funds with which to regularize the National Debt. The strength of the Bank of England was assured by provisions which, until 1826, prohibited the establishment of other banks owned by more than six people.

With the air of Sir Isaac Newton, now director of the Mint, Montague set about the long overdue revision of English currency. Confusing coins, dating from early English history, and later coins, halved, quartered or deliberately debased by clipping, and which caused England to pay a premium of 20-30% to get foreign exchange, were all called in. During May-June, 1696, Evelyn notes the disruption of trade caused by the lack of coins. "All was on trust . . . tumults are every day feared . . . for . . . want of current money to carry on the smallest concerns, even for daily provisions

in the market," until the Mint, working without closing, made up the deficiency by August.

Stow had devoted 6 pages to the complications of English coinage, up to 1598. Bad money had its uses. When Horace Walpole was escorting a lady from an evening party at Twickenham, they were held up and the lady gave the highwayman a purse of bad money, which she carried just for that purpose. A farmer in Yorkshire was afraid to receive 100 guineas in good coin, "lest he should be sent to prison as one of the gang of counterfeiters thereabouts." (Walpole: *Letters*.)

1589. Last quarter XVIIc. German-English. (London, Nat. Port. Gallery.)

Sir Godfrey Kneller. Charles Montague, Earl of Halifax.

Montague, one of the greatest figures in English finance, was a friend of Sir Isaac Newton since Cambridge days, and the patron of literature, "fed all day long with dedications" who, in his later arrogant vanity, was caricatured by Pope as "Bufo."

With the cravat worn after the battle of Steinkirk, 1692, and a mounting wig, Halifax wears a sleeved waistcoat, another form of the negligée attire favored at the turn of the century. Its slit sleeves are turned back, as in theory they always were, to form the trim of the coat sleeve, although the ordinary waistcoat was sleeveless. The waistcoat, skimpily cut, is caught together after the manner of women's bodices, but with braid frogs. This trim will be a favorite during the early decades of XVIIIc., and will reappear later in that century as well as in XIXc.

1590. XVIIc. 1605. German. (New York Public Library.)

T. De Bry. "Voyages to the East Indies," first published 1590. (1st Ser., Germ. ed., 1605.)

The King of Kandy and Admiral van Spilbergen.

Vasco da Gama brought back from his 1498 voyage to Calicut (from which is derived the word "calico") a letter from its ruler to the king of Portugal, which said that da Gama's visit had "given me great pleasure. In my kingdom there is abundance of cinnamon, cloves, ginger, pepper and precious stones. What I seek from thy country is gold, silver, coral and scarlet."

Trade with India was a Portuguese monopoly throughout the XVIc., but was lost to them by midXVIIc., as a result of Dutch and British pressure, combined with their own excesses of religion and arrogance.

Freed of Spanish rule, the Dutch embarked on the search for new passages to India. Barents attempted a Northwest passage to the Orient in his Arctic voyages, 1594-7. The way around Cape Horn was discovered in 1616 by the Dutch. And Dutch sea power enabled the Netherlands East Indies Co., founded 1602, to outstrip Elizabeth's English E. India Co. of 1600. The rivalry grew fiercer as the Dutch and English fought at home and England began to build her great ships, but it was resolved in 1689 under the rule of William of Orange.

1590   1592

1591

Spilbergen's alliance with the King of Kandy was concluded in 1602, but it was a third of a century before their joint efforts managed to displace the Portuguese by the tolerant Dutch regime.

The king's pleated costume shows the exquisitely patterned sheer cotton materials which will become an important part of India's trade with Europe: their importation in the XVIIc. and their production in Europe during the XVIIIc., will be bitterly opposed by the wool and silk industries, but much of French and English prosperity at the turn of XIXc. will be founded on cotton.

The admiral wears the standard costume of the turn of the century: beard and ruff; pinked doublet; full, rosetted breeches; shoes with ties and heels; a commander's baldric; sword slung from a narrow belt.

1591. Early XVIIc. Dutch.

Crispin de Passe. Prodigal Son.

In one of his series of illustrations of the story of the prodigal son, de Passe shows transitional forms of men's and women's clothes.

Ruffs are open, turning into falling bands, or wide and closed, sometimes still supported, but often worn low and flowing with the body lines around the neck.

Doublets are shorter waisted and easier; worn with long, full unpadded breeches, which often have the outer seam decorated, and fringed garters. Shoes are in transition; rosettes and heels appear as slashing goes out of use. Truncated high flat hats.

Women's hair is dressed high into a center point, studded with jewels and an aigrette; or little raked-back caps, pointed like the hair arrangements are worn, especially 1610-20. Gowns are of two types: the bolstered cartwheel skirt, which is seen to 1620, and the Spanish gown, the sleeve of which is cut across above the elbow.

Wall coverings are also transitional between tapestry and wall-paper. Paper is still made in sheets and will not become popular as a wall covering until it can be manufactured in rolls in XVIIIc. Meanwhile block printed linen is hung or stamped leather is glued to the walls. Raised plaster decoration of ceilings.

Chairs are now less severely rectangular; their arms had begun to be shaped in latter half XVIc. Spinets had developed a recessed keyboard, midXVIc.; originally box-like, they are now being mounted on legs. Typical hanging "goodly branches of brass for tapers" which Evelyn so admired in Holland in 1641.

1592. XVIIc. 1608. Flemish. (Metropolitan Museum.)
Unknown artist. The Dwarf, Hans Voorbrueg.

Household dwarfs retain their XVIc. popularity through XVIIc., and are frequently painted, with their owners or alone.

1593. XVIIc. c. 1609. Flemish. (Munich, Alte Pinakothek.)
Rubens. Self-portrait with Isabella Brant.

Rubens, shown with the beautiful bride of whom he painted so many portraits during the 17 years of their marriage, wears a black hat and cape, which is lined with wine-lees brown. His wide lace collar has the informality of an unsupported open fan collar. His beige doublet is corded in brown, with prominent shoulder caps and yellow sleeves, its lower buttons unfastened; "suntan" stockings.

With her Dutch costume, Isabella Brant wears a mannish hat of straw, faced with greenish-gold satin, set over a turned-back lace cap. Her blue-black braided jacket with revers is worn over a white and gold brocaded stomacher; wine colored skirt trimmed with gold; blue underskirt edged with gold. Bracelets on both wrists as sleeves prepare to retreat upwards.

1594. XVIIc. Dutch. (Berlin, Museum.)
Willem Buytewech. Bister drawing.

The Dutch etcher Buytewech (c.1590-c.1630) made a number of delightful drawings of Dutch costume of the first quarter century.

1595. XVIIc. 1608. Dutch.
Jacob de Gheyn (illustrator). "Maniement d'Armes," Amsterdam, 1608.

The musket was a heavier and more powerful development of the arquebuse which needed support for firing. "The armes of a Musquetier offensive are a Musquet . . . Bandoleer with 12 charges at the least, primer, bullet bag and pruning yron, with a rest of a length proportionable to his stature, and a sword. As for the defensive armes, he hath none,

1595

although in some parts I have seene them wear a Headpeace." A plumed hat was commonly worn, and a sword. (See Morse, Appendix.)

Earrings; falling band; trousers decorated across outer seam with parallel lines of fringed braid.

Changes in Armor, XVIIc.

The character of war changed during the Wars of Religion, when men fought less for glory than for personal conviction and survival; French and English fought against their brothers and the militia of the Low Countries staved off the superb Spanish professionals.

The invention of firearms had first made necessary the production of armor "proof" against them. Then soldiers became increasingly specialized and disciplined, as firearms improved and the use of each required training; armies moved faster, offense gained over defense, infantry over cavalry, and armor became a drawback.

The heavy cavalry alone wore the close helm; light cavalry wore burgonet, cuirasse, some plate protection of shoulder and upper arm, one gauntlet, and carried pistol and sword.

Rows of pikemen still preceded the increasingly important arquebusiers and musketeers; they carried ever-longer pikes, up to 18 ft., and wore morions, with upper bodies still completely armed.

They were followed by the more lightly armed and mobile arquebusiers, in morions and brigandines with mail sleeves, in front of musketeers with little plate protection.

The halberdiers, to mop up after the shooting, came last.

During XVIIc. armor became more disadvantageous, but was worn by the cavalry until it largely disappeared by XVIIIc.

The comb morion of the infantry was supplanted by the high Spanish morion-cabasset, and this, in XVIIIc. by round topped lobster-tail burgonet, iron hat and pikeman's pot.

With the invention of grenades, latter half XVIIc., groups of grenadiers were increased to companies in the Régiment du Roi by 1668, and on June 29, 1678, Evelyn says: "Now were brought into service a new sort of soldiers, called Grenadiers, who were dexterous in flinging hand grenados, everyone having a pouch full; they had furred caps with coped crowns like Janizaries, which made them look very fierce, and some had long hoods hanging down behind, as we picture fools. Their clothing being likewise piebald, yellow and red." These fur caps developed into the familiar Bearskin. By Dec. 5, 1683, "The King had now augmented his guards with a new sort of dragoon" (cavalry trained to fight on foot), "who also carried grenades, and were habited after the Polish manner, with long peaked caps, very fierce and fantastical."

1596

1596. XVIIc. 1613. Swiss-Papal.

Francisco Villamena. The Papal Officer, Jean Gros of Lucerne.

The Swiss Guard of the Pope was instituted in 1506 by Julius II. It consisted originally of 150 men, dressed at the Pope's expense, but not uniformly. Under Adrian VI, they dressed in white, green, and yellow, although these were not his colors. When 42 of its survivors capitulated in battle in 1527, they were all dressed alike in yellow, blue and red, the personal colors of Clement VII, which were retained. The red and yellow costumes of the Suisses appear in the description of Holy Week festivities, about which Pepys' nephew, John Jackson, wrote him from Rome, Dec. 25, 1699. (See Appendix.)

Another portrait of a Papal guard by Villamena actually shows the same person; during the ten year interval, Gros changed his name to Alto.

Gros was a non-commissioned officer. His halberdier's costume shows the beginning of the degradation of the Papal Guard uniform; but it is full of interesting detail of fullness, often inserted into gores, and of the removal of fullness, by goring at breast and sleeve. The full, long breeches are no longer paned, but a reminiscent effect is gained by the use of sections of pleating. His high-crowned hat carries the excess of plumes loved by Swiss soldiers since Holbein's time.

Gros stands by the base of a column, of the colonnade originally flanking Trajan's column, seen rising behind his right arm.

Courtesy of Metropolitan Museum of Art, Photograph Collection

1597. XVIIc. Flemish. (London, Nat. Gall.)

Hans Jordaens II (fl. 1620-43). Interior of an Art Gallery, detail.

Arundel was the greatest of innumerable amateurs of *articles de vertu* in his time. Evelyn's diary is a catalog of the great collectors of all Europe, their possessions, and the shops which catered to them. Evelyn was himself an incurable shopper, whether for maps and atlases at Hondius & Bleau's shop in Antwerp, or the wares of the gallery of the Palais-Royal. Nor was collecting any longer an interest confined to the nobility; in 1654, he went to see "one of the rarest collections of agates, onyxes and intaglios that I have ever seen either at home or abroad, collected by a conceited old hatmaker at Blackfriars, especially one agate vase, heretofore the great Earl of Leicester's." In 1661, he dined at Mr. Palmer's in Gray's Inn, "whose curiosity excelled in clocks and pendules . . . also good telescopes and mathematical instruments, choice pictures and other curiosities." Mr. Palmer would have been a good customer for the globes and chronometers, cameos and minatures, illustrated books, prints and paintings which these gentlemen are examining with the aid of spectacles, dividers, folding rule and magnifying glass.

The Royal Academies of Science, founded in Paris and London in the 60's, grew out of discussion groups of long standing. Tycho Brahe's and the other observatories of the XVIc. were privately supported, but Royal observatories were set up in Paris in 1667 and Greenwich in 1675; there is a print by Leclerc of Louis XIV's visit (in petticoat breeches) to the new Paris Observatoire.

Bouquets of natural flowers begin to replace the standing cups and jewelled objects which stood on tables in XVIc. portraits. Still lifes of fruit and game, and flower pieces, like that hanging high on the right, come into favor. An age which loved dwarfs and exotics was charmed by monkeys. A troupe of fashionably dressed monkey acrobats was one of the features of the Southwark Fair in 1660.

Standard costume of pinked satin; unrelated doublet and breeches, with seam and pocket decoration; garter bows; stockings tending to wrinkle; shoes with rosettes.

1598. XVIIc. 1615. Dutch. (Metropolitan Museum.)

J. A. van Ravesteyn. Arent Hermansz.

Costume of plain and pinked satin with brocade sleeves. Ruffs, even when pleated, take on an informal gathered look and may have irregular edges. Slit seam of sleeve edged with buttons and tiny loops. Gold trim of breeches-seam and garters. Cuff of gauntlet embroidered in a lace design. Plumed helmet and gauntlets.

COACHES AND CONVEYANCES

The word "coach" is derived from Kocs, the Hungarian town in which rude coaches were first built. Their use, at first by women only, spread to royalty, great ecclesiastics, and the infirm, in Germany and Italy. Sumptuary laws tried to control their use. Like all luxuries, they were then carried to the rich seaport cities of the Low Countries; by 1560, there were 500 coaches in Antwerp. Thence they were introduced into France and England.

The three coaches in Paris in 1550 belonged to the Queen, the King's mistress, and a nobleman too fat to ride; the queen's coach had leather curtains in place of the windows which did not appear until midXVIc.

About 1555, coaches began to be made in England. Elizabeth had a coach which could be opened to the air, built by Walter Rippon in 1564 for her state progresses about England. Her 2-horse coach, built in the eighth year of her reign by her Dutch coachman, William Booren, "was a strange monster in those days, and the sight of (a coach) put both horse and man into amazement." (*Harl. Misc.,*v.IV,p.218, and John Taylor, the Water Poet: *Works,* 1630.)

The first coach which we might recognize as such was brought to England by Fitzalan, Earl of Arundel, in 1580, Stow says. In 1611, the bride of Matthias of Hungary rode to her wedding in a coach of perfumed leather.

By midXVIIc., coaches "of the new fashion, with glasses, very stately; and . . . pages and lacquies . . . of the same livery" began to appear. Steel springs replaced leather straps c.1670. Grammont says ladies "were afraid of being shut up in (coaches): they greatly preferred the pleasure of shewing almost their whole persons, to the convenience of modern coaches." Between 1658 and 1758 the coaches of Paris had increased from 310 to over 14,000. (Saint Foix.)

Buckingham was the first person to be carried about London in a sedan chair, a conveyance just brought to England and patented by Sir Sanders Duncombe. This was bitterly resented, as his coach had been, by the common people. These new modes of travel threatened the monopoly of the Thames watermen. Coryat's enemy, the waterman-poet, John Taylor (1580-1653) wrote:

Carroaches, coaches, jades and Flemish mares
Doe rob us of our shares, our wares, our fares.
Against the ground we stand and knock our heels
Whilest all our profit runs away on wheels.

The Thames became a coach road during the great freeze of 1683-4 but in spite of the boatmen's fears, the river remained a favorite way of travel through the XVIIIc. Vauxhall Stairs, in 1750, was "a terrible confusion of wherries" as bawling watermen competed for fares.

Everyone is coach-conscious. There is rivalry in handsome equipages; citizens could identify coaches by their coach-work, the number and color of the horses, and the liveries of the men on the box, as readily as any small boy in the U.S.A. does his neighbor's green Plymouth sedan or black Buick convertible. Coaches become projections of and substitutes for their owners; they may be sent, quite

empty, to "swell a progress," or do honor at funerals.

1599. XVIIc. c. 1616. Dutch. (Metropolitan Museum, Print Room.)
J. van der Velde. May.

By the spring of 1616, a drive about the countryside is merely a pleasant pastime for Dutch ladies and gentlemen: the only excitement will be among the hounds as the coach clatters away; the swineherd goes about the business of getting his animals past the 2-horse carriages ahead with their coachmen on the box. The 4-horse coach is driven by a man riding postilion; glass windows have not yet replaced curtains, but there are doors, and the whole nail-studded leather body with its canopy and wheel guards has a certain elegance, far removed from the glorified farm-wagon of a half century before.

The two following engravings have been particularly chosen to show unaristocratic costume; but no dress of the first years of the XVIIc. has a longer, more stylized line than the Dutch cavaliers with their highest of hats, and their ladies whose lean, corseted waists are emphasized by looped-up skirts, immensely wide ruffs, and raking headdresses. These are best seen in the bistre drawings by William Buytewech (Berlin Museum) and in the engravings of the van der Veldes: Esias, c. 1590-1630; Jan, c. 1593 to after 1641; and Adriaen, 1635-72.

FOODSTUFFS, OLD AND NEW

Until Tudor times, the English appear to have lived on bread, meat, fish, honey and malt ale. Many of the vegetables and fruits introduced during the XVI-XVIIc. came to them from the Low Countries, which had either received them as a result of their trade with the Mediterranean and the East, or had long cultivated them. Cabbage varieties, including brussels sprouts, had been sold in Belgian markets in 1213, when the English had perhaps not yet discovered that their wild sea-cabbage was edible. Katherine of Aragon had to send to Flanders for the salads, turnips and carrots she was accustomed to eat at home.

The cherries planted by the Romans, 100 B.C. had been forgotten; cherries first reappeared in a Kentish orchard laid out in 1540. Pippins were planted in Sussex in 1525 by Leonard Mascall; grapes and currants arrived in mid-XVIc. Dr. Linacre, Henry VIII's physician, brought back musk and damask roses and Lord James Cromwell, musk roses and plums, from their travels. "Unknown" flowers were

planted in Norwich by the Flemish weavers who arrived in 1567: gillyflowers, carnations, and Provence roses. The first tulips came from Vienna in 1578.

Old herbals, like that of the surgeon, John Gerarde, gardener of William Cecil, Lord Burghley, in 1597, tell us what vegetables were known and what they looked like then.

Leeks had been a Welsh badge since 544 A.D.; Treveskis' herbal of 1526 recommends onions. Parsnips, brought to England from Germany by the Romans, had gone wild; no vegetable responds faster to simple good tilth, so parsnips were the standard root vegetable. Beets were pale and woody, and carrots a seasoning, scarcely edible. Spinach was grown in England in 1568; tomatoes from America were considered unwholesome. Gerarde's is the first English description of horseradish, and he was mad about parsley, which had come from Sardinia in 1548. Cucumbers arrived from N.W. India in 1573. Peas, wild and bitter, were eaten during the famine of 1555. Gerarde lists two varieties of potatoes, which Raleigh planted in Ireland in 1588, and which were grown in Wales and Scotland, where plots were fenced, before England, where land was held in common.

Asparagus and cauliflower arrived in the first decade XVIIc. and England played an important part in the improvement of the cauliflower. Gerarde tells how to boil and butter haricot beans, but scarlet runner beans received from S. America in 1633 were raised for their flowers. Watercress and 12 varieties of salad are shown in herbals of 1710-15, but watercress was first sold in London in 1808.

Flax and hops were imported from Artois in 1520, but hops were not grown in sufficient quantities in England for beer to become an important beverage until XVIIc. Bread was not made with yeast until 1650.

Melons, brought from Spain by Sir George Gardner, were a royal gift from James I to Buckingham; and then became a luxury costing 5 to 6s.

1600. XVIIc. c. 1616. Dutch. (Metropolitan Museum, Print Room.)

J. van der Velde. December.

The boats are almost frozen in the canal of this little Dutch town; beyond the bridge we see a farm wagon. A sailor in characteristic long trousers is walking from the left. The chimneys of the brick houses smoke, as women covered by long *"heuke"* buy the last vegetables. School is letting out. The children, well bundled up and shod, run past the inn with their lunch baskets and books, while the poor schoolmaster, who has had to keep his dog with him, walks almost barefoot, his legs and feet covered with a sort of combination legging and spat, which is buckled at the back of knee and ankle.

1601. XVIIc. Dutch. (Metropolitan Museum, Print Room.)
J. van der Velde, after *W. Buytewech.* Earth.

The characteristic *"heuke"* headdress of the Low Countries is seen in various beaked forms, or wired out like an Elizabethan veil, mounting the Rhine to Cologne. Its length varies; hanging to the ground in Holland, to half way below the knee at Antwerp, and to the elbow in Belgium. It is often worn with hats of an inverted-basket shape, as well as the

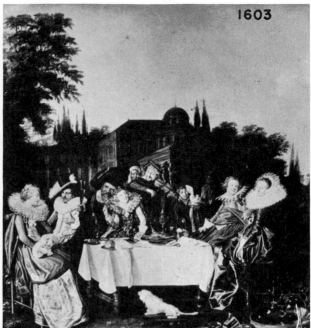

flat, knobbed plates shown here, and the tiny "tip-hoike" seen in Hollar's plates.

The dress beneath is apt to have a full skirt of ground length, worn with a close-fitting bodice beneath a short, fitted spencer.

The utilitarian apron may appear anywhere at any time; but the decorative apron which has been a feature of German-Swiss costume in final quarter XVIc., will not become an important part of European dress until final quarter XVIIc., when it will been made of gold lace or embroidered taffeta.

Until XIXc., long trousers such as we see on the figure to the r., will be worn only by farmers and sailors. The knee breeches derided by the class-conscious sans-culottes of the French Revolution will remain the mark of a gentleman, and a required part of formal court wear, down to our own time, more than a century after passing out of general use.

1602. XVIIc. c. 1615. Dutch. (Metropolitan Museum.)

Frans Hals. Merry Company.

The roistering, improvident Hals, who was given house, fuel and an annuity by the city in his bankrupt old age, was an enormously prolific painter of portraits and groups of all classes of society; and of banquets of military and governing associations, termagant fishwives and drunken gamesters.

The new impulse to portray natural, everyday objects is shown in the plate of pig's feet and sausages, the tankard and the bagpipe.

The loose lady's fan collar is not only double but has an interior edge of lace. It is worn with an embroidered doublet and skirt; satin inner sleeves and outer-sleeve lining; knots at throat and waist.

As in Brueghel's day, spoons and pipes are thrust through the cocked brim of the hat.

1603. XVIIc. Dutch. (Louvre.)

Dirk Hals. Rustic Feast.

The plagiarized central figures are not very successful, but in the full-length figures at the side, Hals' son shows some pleasant examples of the dress sketched by Buytewech.

1604. XVIIc. Flemish. (Metropolitan Museum.)

Adraen Nieulandt (1587-1658). Kitchen Interior.

The cook's little close cap and lace collared shirt might be worn at almost any time between 1620-50,

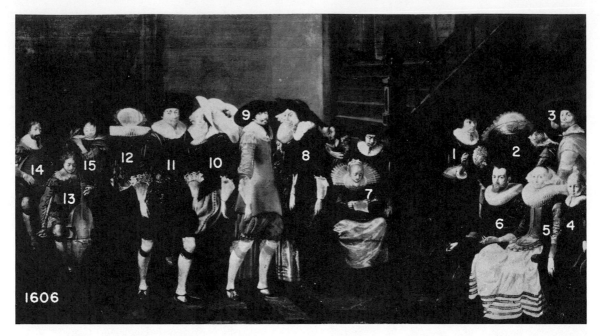

1606

but the flopping ruff of the delivery boy makes the late part of first quarter XVIIc. more probable.

Baskets of eggs, kitchen utensils, game and meat, now lovingly painted.

1605. XVIIc. 1619. Flemish. (Metropolitan Museum.)
P. Brueghel, the younger. Gamblers Quarreling.

Peasant costume changed little since the time of the elder Brueghel; tailored codpieces affixed to flap-codpieces. Separate sleeve persists in Flemish and Italian women's use.

1606. XVIIc. 1616?. Dutch. (Amsterdam, Rijksmuseum.)
W. C. Duyster. Fete in Honor of the Marriage of Adriaen Ploos van Amstel and Agnes van Byler.

Wonderful costumes (either very prophetic or questionably dated a decade too early), shown from all angles, and with every sort and combination of collars. The whorls of the wire support of a fan collar worn with another unsupported one (No. 2); unsupported collar worn with stiff ruff (No. 12); small round collar with stiffened fan in addition (No. 7); wide single ruffs; falling ruffs and bands. Cuffs

funneling to the elbow give an effect of shortening sleeves; this is actual on the scalloped sleeve of (No. 5); and on the turned back cuff of (No. 1). Turned-back caps, large on (No. 2, 5, 12).

The classic Dutch women's costume of first third XVIIc. is shown on (No. 5): jacket with stomacher emphasized by a scalloped border; underskirt patterned (also 8, 10); skeleton overdress with emphasis around the shoulder cap.

The gartered gentlemen in great hats so floppy that they will soon have to be cocked, show lengthening doublet skirts; slashed bosom and upper sleeve; watch at belt; breeches narrowing (11); and the long leather military jerkin, with lacings up the front and hanging from the tabbed shoulder caps; doublet sleeves barred across the open inseam with braid (as on musician, No. 13); outer seam of breeches open and edged with buttons (No. 9). Boy (No. 4) shows the increasingly fashionable wrinkled stockings, button trim on hat band to match shoulder caps, skirts and open front of doublet and studded belt.

Ladies, gentlemen and musicians alike wear curious cut-out heelless sandals.

1607. XVIIc. Dutch. (Metropolitan Museum.)
M. J. van Miereveld. Portrait of a Woman.

Wide cap of the early decades of the century worn over tiny close cap. Small interior collar of lace over a ruff with graduated pleats.

1608. XVIIc. 1618-21. Flemish. (Washington, Nat. Gall. of Art.)
Van Dyke or *Rubens.* Suzanna Fourment and her Daughter.

Four years after the death of Isabella Brant, Rubens married a lovely 16-year-old-girl named Helena Fourment, of whom he painted many portraits. This picture of her sister Suzanna, whether painted by Rubens, or more probably by his former pupil, Van Dyke, shows the same chain worn by Helena in the

portrait by Rubens.

Suzanna's pearl choker stresses the tendency of ruffs to sink lower on the neck. Stomachered jacket of small-patterned golden brown brocade; underskirt of rose and gold Italian brocade in the classic pineapple pattern, banded in rose-flecked gold; gold and white slippers; black overdress; white lace; tiny embroidered and jewelled dark cap of Flanders set over the bun of hair.

Her daughter wears a brown velvet hat, edged in white, set over a cap with rose and gold ties; little doublet with fan collar, picadill shoulder caps and tabbed border, of rose brocaded in white with gold lines; crossed by a baldric of purple; skirt of rosy-gold shot taffeta.

1607

1608

1610. XVIIc. 1628. Dutch. (Metropolitan Museum.)

M. J. van Miereveld. Dutch Lady.

The brim of the cap, seen on the older woman painted by the same artist, begins to be turned back in the first decade XVIIc., and to be worn farther back on the head as it tends to become smaller in the third decade. The ruff worn with this gown remains uncluttered, but the cuffs succumb to the general tendency to grow higher and to duplicate. The divisions of the peplum of the doublet become increasingly scalloped and foliated in lace-inspired patterns. The overgarment may be a jacket like that of Isabella Brant, or a long gown, cut straight with the torso to the waist and there gored wide over the hips; here it is loosely girded by a chain.

Gauntlets embroidered on the seam of fingers as well as on tasseled cuff.

1609

1610

1609. XVIIc. c. 1625. Flemish. (Munich, Alte Pinakothek.)

Cornelis de Vos. The von Hutton Family.

The parents are in standard Flemish black with cartwheel ruffs; the mother's is the somber Dutch gown which sets off a blazing gold stomacher, longer, rounder, more decorated and importantly edged than that of any other country. Elsewhere the stomacher will be a doublet with matching sleeves, which appear below the shoulder cap or truncated sleeve of the gown; but in Holland the stomacher is a vest, and the close sleeve agrees, not with it, but with the rest of the outermost garment. The ruff worn with these stomachers is always severe.

Boy by father: gray doublet and skirts, seamed in black and silver; petticoat with black embroidery.

Red-headed baby: cream dress and slippers; white cap and apron; coral necklaces, bracelets and shoe ribbons.

Oldest child, still wearing a baby cap, has her red hair drawn over it (as women's hair is drawn back) and a tiny gold headdress like her mother's set over hair and cap; the same impulse is shown in the center lock of the other children. She wears coral earrings and bracelets, flat wired ruff, brown bodice brocaded in silver, yellowish-green satin apron over a golden yellow skirt banded in blue-green.

1611. XVIIc. 1623. Dutch. (Metropolitan Museum.)

Frans Hals. Yonker Ramp and his Sweetheart.

The construction of military jerkins is dependent on the shape and imperfections of the skins used; they are usually cut in 2 to 4 front and 2 back sections. To avoid strain, seams are left open where possible. Horizontal seaming around the waist is avoided by goring the sections out into skirts which overlap to conceal weak spots in the leather; actual closing is by flexible leather laces. Reinforcement of edges and cuts is made decorative by embroidery, or, where no strain will be put upon them (as in this case), by buttons which fasten through scallops with pinked edges; their diagonal lines simulate a breast slit and the direction which the current waistline of the civilian doublet is taking, as it creeps up under the arms. The jerkin when not worn over a doublet has sleeves of the doublet type, made of a different material.

His companion has double collars and cuffs, of which the wide outer set is the sheerer.

1612. XVIIc. 1625-30. Flemish. (Florence, Pitti.)

Joost Sustermans. The General Leopold, Count of Tyrol.

1611

1612

1613

Leopold V, brother of Emperor Ferdinand II, married Christine of Lorraine's daughter Claudia, efficient Regent of the Tyrol after his death.

His lace-edged whisk is worn with a gorget which matches the blue and white plumed helmet beside him, and a magnificently embroidered jerkin of yellow leather. Boots wth square plaques of the same leather are drawn high over lace-edged boot-hose. Sword carried by a baldric-like band; baldrics are already very handsome and will become wider, more elaborate, often edged with fringe, into XVIIIc.; lace fringed sash. Goatee and moustache with lengthening hair.

1613. XVIIc. 1626. Dutch. (Budapest, Museum of Fine Arts.)

N. Eliasz. Portrait of a Man.

The pleating of ruffs is increasingly subtle; the effect of multiple horizontal rows is gained here by vertically set pleats.

This doublet, of the dotted stuff we have seen throughout first quarter XVIIc., owes much in cut to the military leather coats. But as it is a true doublet, its sleeves are of the same stuff. The lower buttons of the row on their outseam (which is becoming more important then the old braid-trimmed inseam) will soon begin to be left open and the cuff turned back. Full breeches with buttoned side slit. Chain worn baldric-wise with pendant medal; dagger now seldom carried except in military use. These are the days of the volunteer militia companies organized during the 30 Years War, such as the St. George and the St. Adrien Arquebusiers, very differently dressed from the other companies of governing burghers, to which the same men probably belonged, and whose banquets were also painted by Hals.

1614. XVIIc. c. 1630. Flemish. (Metropolitan Museum.)

Van Dyke. Portrait of a Lady.

This Flemish lady wears the characteristic dark caul cap and lace-edged double ruff (where the Dutch cap is white and the single ruff severe when worn with the important stomacher). Elaborate chains cross

the less conspicuous Flemish stomacher, with its braided doublet sleeves; these show below the pendant Spanish sleeve (cut in a + across the bend of the elbow) of the brocade overdress, which has simulated breast slits.

Deviations are the surprisingly long sleeves with ruffs instead of cuffs at the wrist, and the form of the handle of the fan.

1615. XVIIc. 1631. Dutch. (Amsterdam, Rijksmuseum.)

W. Geest, e., Portrait of a Little Boy.

Falling ruff, on the standard costume of a boy who is still in diapers: skirt fastened, as breeches would be on an older boy, by knots through the doublet waistline. Braid trim in random zigzags instead of the old parallel ways.

1616. First to second third XVIIc. Flemish. (Vienna, National Museum.)

Brussels Tapestry. Country Life series: Lute-playing Cavalier with Lady.

With the swashbuckling male cavalier styles, female costume begins to lose its rigidity. The romantic portraits of Helena Fourment painted by Rubens in the 30's are closely akin to this lady in her great plumed hat; soft, low-kerchiefed, high-waisted bodice with sleeves repeatedly tied about the arm.

Rugs and tapestries continue to be thrown over balconies on gala occasions. Architecture is approaching the XVIIIc. Baroque; but the "excess of superfluity" of this Flemish decoration lacks the delicate grace of Grinling Gibbons' carved garlands and fruit.

Exotic animals and fruits increase. Small monkeys and parrots are now fairly common; the first rhinoceros (unicorn) and W. Indian crocodile appeared in England in 1684.

1617. XVIIc. 1632. Dutch. (Metropolitan Museum.)

Rembrandt. Volkeravan Beresteijn.

Rembrandt van Rijn, b. 1606, son of a miller, studied painting in his native Leyden. In 1631 he moved to Amsterdam and immediate preeminence as a painter of group and single portraits during the next decade. In 1634 he married a beautiful blonde

and well-to-do Frisian girl called Saskia, whom he frequently painted until her death in 1642. The Portuguese Jews living on the same street with Rembrandt served as models for some of the paintings of his second period. In 1656 as times grew hard in the Netherlands, Rembrandt went bankrupt, but never ceased painting until his death in 1669.

Flat lace collar just showing under a ruff, slightly edged with lace, since it is not worn with the old sort of greatly exploited stomacher, but with the new short-waisted, belted gown with puffed sleeves. Stomacher subordinated to a belt finished with ribbon loops instead of the usual rosette. Jewelled stud in hair, behind which only the edge of the cap shows at the bottom.

1618. XVIIc. c. 1632. Dutch. (Berlin, Kaiser Friedrich Museum.)

N. Eliasz. Catarina Hoeft, wife of Cornelis de Graef, Bürgermeister of Amsterdam.

Few illustrations so clearly show the upper sleeve, completely truncated, and the widening inner sleeve (matching the underskirt and stomacher) showing below, but not yet tied in puffs around the arm. Very wide compound kerchief-collar and double cuffs; very short waist, belted with a side rosette matching those

which catch an asymmetric chain to the collar; fan chained to belt.

1619. XVIIc. 1635. Dutch. (Metropolitan Museum. Frick Coll.)

F. Hals. Portrait of a Woman.

1620. XVIIc. 1636. Dutch. (Metropolitan Museum.)

Isaac Luttichuijs. Portrait of a Young Woman.

One elaborate double form of cap of third decade XVIIc. does enclose the hair and ears; worn with wide shallow ruff and gown of black brocade and satin. The young woman has beautiful fringe-trimmed white gauntlets, and bag patterned with black lace; dark lace is similarly used on stomachers, boldly patterned in horizontal bands like that worn by Hals' Woman (Ill. 1642); "housewife" carried on a running chain from her belt.

1621. XVIIc. 1634. Dutch. (Paris, Gustave de Rothschild.)

Rembrandt. Martin Day.

Narrow braids used to give over-all pattern and gored effect, big beaver hat, lace collar spreading over shoulders and cape, waistline rising under armpits, knotted tags turning into formal rosettes, narrowing breeches, pleated garters, wrinkled stockings, largest possible rosettes on shoes cut out below strap.

1622. XVIIc. 1636. Flemish.

Van Dyke. Rupert, Prince Palatine.

This German prince, grandson of James I, was born in 1619, brought up in Holland, first visited England in 1636, but returned in 1642 to become the greatest cavalry commander of the first Civil War and to die in England, unmarried, in 1683. His sister Sophia or her issue, as the closest Protestant Stuarts, had been made heirs to the English throne, if previous rulers died childless; in 1714 her son, a far lesser man than his uncle, became king as George I.

Rupert's clear-sighted and inventive intelligence concerned itself with science, improvement of military equipment and techniques. He was, in addition, a fine engraver and the pioneer worker in mezzotint.

Van Dyke and Rupert were both in the Netherlands in 1634-5; but these are English clothes such as Van Dyke painted in 1632-9, and Rupert's only visit to England during Van Dyke's lifetime was in 1636.

Small lace collar worn over gorget; military jerkin over vest-like doublet with shortening sleeve, and increasingly full, puffed linen.

1623. XVIIc. c. 1638. Flemish. (Washington, National Gallery of Art.)

Van Dyke. William II of Nassau and Orange.

William the Silent's grandson was married in 1641 at 15 to Charles I's 10-year-old-daughter Mary. The very able Dutch Stadholder died of smallpox at 24, as his great son, William III, was born.

He wears a steel cuirasse over a yellow doublet; this has the short sleeve, full bloused shirt sleeve with wide informal wrist ruffles, and small, square tassel-tied collar of the 40's. Walking stick and riding crop.

1624. XVIIc. c. 1636. Flemish. (Metropolitan Museum.)
Adriaen Brower. The Smokers.

Tobacco was brought to Philip II from Mexico in 1558; the generic name of the plant, *Nicotiana,* commemorates the French ambassador Nicot, who sent its seeds to Catherine de' Medici. Pipes came to England about 1565. Harrison described its use in 1573 and despite the "Counterblast" of James, the use of tobacco increased greatly during the troubled XVIIc.

The smoker is the artist himself. His painter friend, de Heem, is the man with a small wind instrument stuck through his hat, as we have seen the spoon or pipe used in Brueghel and Hals pictures. Wide square collar with tasseled ties; sleeve unbuttoned and turned back at wrist; tasseled finish of loose breeches; wrinkled stockings worn with pantoufles.

1625. XVIIc. 1637-43. Dutch. (Amsterdam, R. Pelzer Coll.)

Albert Eeckhout. Portrait of a Negro Chief in the Dutch Service.

This picture formerly att. to van der Helst is by a painter from Amersford, Holland, who accompanied Prince Maurice of Orange to Brazil in 1637, and returned to Brazil in 1641 and in 1643 with the landscape painter, Franz Post. The date of Eeckhout's birth is not known, and he disappears with a painting dated 1664.

The Negro Chief wears rich clothing of the 30's: pink plumed hat, nasturtium-colored jerkin with hanging sleeves; and a doublet of brocaded white satin.

1626-27. XVIIc. 1637. Dutch. (Amsterdam, J. M. van Loon.)

J. M. Molenaer, Family Gathering, (2 details).

These details are from a very long painting which is one of Holland's greatest costume documents.

MALE: Hats: wide sombreros or cocked; great plumes reduced to a shaggy fringe around the band (I). Lace collars at their widest, fastened with tasseled ties; cuffs of high lace (A), loose ruffles (I), plain (E). Doublet: short-waisted, long-skirted, beltless; lacy braid along seams (A, I) and edges. Superimposed garments= jacket and vest (A). Military jerkin with sword belt (E). Sleeves short (A) or turned back (E). Breeches open (reappeared second third XVIIc.), or closed, with decorated outer seams and edges. Braid of seam beginning to disintegrate into fringe as it approaches fringed hem; visibly buttoned fly closing of breeches (E). Boots of polished leather with sock-boots (A, E); or wrinkled stockings, elaborate garters and hugely rosetted shoes (J, L). Hair on shoulders; moustaches; some chin tufts. Page boy's livery elaborately braided (F).

FEMALE: Short-waisted jackets with tabbed peplums worn over a single full skirt, which is decorated down center-front seam and around hem. Overgarment eliminated, but its old sleeve appears as the upper section, ending above the elbow and slit toward the shoulder; lower sleeve is increasingly full but not yet tied about the arm in puffed sections. Jacket, its belt finished at

the side by loops or rosette, is actually low-necked; but the neckline is completely filled by a yoke-like collar, covered by a folded kerchief, and worn with multiple choker collar of pearls. In latter half XVIIc., the inner collar will shrink and the kerchief side off the shoulders in a fichu. Hair, fringed at the forehead and loose at the sides, is drawn back and dressed with a pearl band across the crown. Child: cape with aigrette; gored seaming stressed by braid; lines of braid with fringed ends cross the center-front seam. Maid (G): white cap and gathered white shoulder cape with flat collar; brocade jacket with close fitting sleeves and short peplum, apron and full skirt.

ACCESSORIES: Glass manufacture had been established in Flanders by Philip the Good; by third quarter XVIc., heavier and less elegant versions of Venetian patterns began to be exported to England from Flanders; during XVIIc. Flemish glass began to be cut and engraved and was one of the familiar objects which Flemish artists loved to paint. In final quarter XVIIc. England began to produce better glass at Greenwich and Lambeth than was made at Murano.

Oranges are a treat but no longer a rarity. Evelyn saw orange trees 120 years old at Beddington in 1700 and one of the most magnificent of orange trees, the Grand Bourbon at Versailles, which still bears 200 fruit at a time, was transplanted there from Fontainebleau by Louis XIV. It had belonged to Francis I and was planted in 1421 by a princess of Navarre. But pineapples from the Barbados were still a novelty when the King cut off a slice for Evelyn in 1668.

A roast peacock in its plumage has been a great banquet dish since before mediaeval days; carried by manservant (deleted figure, ext. r.).

1628-32. XVIIc. Bohemian. (Metropolitan Museum, Print Room.)

W. Hollar. "Aula Veneris."

1628. Lady of Quality of Antwerp (1643).

1629. Leading Townswoman of Antwerp in House Dress (1648).

1630. Wife of a Merchant Citizen of Antwerp (1650).

The *hoike* mantle and *tiphoike* tufted forehead plate are typical outdoor wear of Antwerp, Cologne and Bremen; with a turned-back lace cap, long loose hair, and double skirts, the uppermost tucked up, and the underskirt heavily banded. Muffs for outdoor use; apron, fan, and plumed hat worn indoors over a cap in the late XVIc. way.

1631. Daughter of a Citizen of Prague (1636).

1632. Wife of a Merchant of Prague (1636).

In Bohemia a single skirt is worn with a fur cape, the broad revers of which turn into a square "sailor" collar. Over this is worn either a wide ruff or a collar characteristically squared off across the front. Locks in front of the ears are small and short; even into XVIIIc., little hair shows below the fur hats of Swabian, Bavarian and Bohemian regional costume, since these hats, in a sense, replace hair. The traditionally uncovered head of an unmarried woman has a little pill-box cap over the bun, while a married woman wears the characteristically conical fur hat of Prague. (No. 1633 is omitted.)

1634-37. XVIIc. 1643-45. Bohemian. (Metropolitan Museum, Print Room.)

W. Hollar. "Runde Frauentracht."

1634. The Hollar catalog identifies none of this set of costumes. We can see that the cap, and the needlepoint ending in a drop, are related to the *tip-hoike* which run north up the Rhine from Bremen and Antwerp to Cologne. It is worn with a sleeveless garment of which we unfortunately see little; it has one of the square fur collars which, originating in Bohemia, move west through Franconia and Frankfort-on-Main, to affect costume as far west of the Rhine as Luxemburg. These collars also appear along the coast of the North Sea, where it is probable that the wearer of this costume lived.

1635. In Bavaria the round fur hat is worn with one of the collars shown in the Prague illustrations above. Here it has moved west to meet the Dutch kerchief, come up the Rhine.

1636. Antwerp (1643).

1637. Augsburg or Nuremberg, worn with the square-cut Bohemian collar. The distribution of fur hats in Central Europe in XVIIc. may be thus roughly given:

Cap-shaped: Swabia, Basel, Strassburg, the Palatinate, Frankfort-on-Main, and Danzig.

Circular: Nuremberg and Augsburg, with a very wide form at Strassburg where hats have always been widest.

Square: Augsburg and Nuremberg, often with the squared-off collar which runs from Bohemia west to Hanau.

Conical: Augsburg, Nuremberg, from Bohemia. All these circular, square and conical fur hats have round headbands, rather than the curving bottom line of the Rhenish fur caps; and all are seen, simultaneously worn, in Bavaria.

High, spreading at top: Saxe-Altenburg.

1638. XVIIc. Dutch. (Amsterdam, Rijksmuseum.)

Frans Hals. Sara Wolphaerts van Diemen (1594-1667).

When the wide, plain ruff appears between 1620-30, it sways somewhat over the shoulder, and is apt to be elaborated, like other forms of collar, by notched lace. The cap slips back, until it merely frames the hair, by 1630.

1639. XVIIc. Dutch. (Metropolitan Museum.)

M. J. van Miereveld, d. 1641. Portrait of a Woman in a Lace Collar.

From 1620-30, the wide composite collars were still high in back; caps barely outlining hair, 1630-40.

1640. XVIIc. Flemish. (Metropolitan Museum.)

C. de Vos, e., d. 1651. Portrait of a Young Lady.

Hair with a fringe and longer, relatively uncovered; collars widest and flat on shoulders, c. 1635; wide, loose cuff with billowing ruffle.

1641. XVIIc. 1642. Dutch. (Metropolitan Museum.)

F. Bol. Portrait of a Dutch Lady.

Hair uncovered except the band around the bun; collar on sloping shoulder line; cuff shorter and wider; sleeve no longer tied around the arm at elbow.

1642. XVIIc. c. 1645. Dutch (Metropolitan Museum.)

F. Hals. Portrait of a Woman.

Black caps with a tongue running down the forehead, seen 1640-60. Shoulder more sloping, sleeve shorter, cuff wider; stomacher horizontally striped, with black predominating.

1643. XVIIc. 1655. Flemish. (Budapest, Museum of Fine Arts.)

A. Palmedesz. Portrait of a Woman.

Pointed black cap, combined with caul over the bun; bows on hanging side locks precede and foretell their turning into bunches of corkscrew curls.

The collar is slipping down shoulders, which are not yet ready to be bared completely; shirt as inner yoke. As the banding at the bottom of the collar becomes pre-eminent, the front closing is stressed in some way, often by an important pendant brooch. The sleeve itself is losing out to its cuff, which is in transition into ruffles. In bourgeoise use, especially, the skirt is often worn tucked up; in this case, the drape has been made an integral part of its construction.

1644. XVIIc. c. 1645. Flemish. (Metropolitan Museum.)

Unknown artist. Family Portrait.

Mother: kerchief closed high about the neck gives sloping shoulder line. Upper and lower sleeve unified, their former divisions and slits marked by braid, as is the center-front line of the closed skirt.

Boy with hawk on gauntlet: doublet open at bottom over puffed shirt; visibly buttoned fly of tubular breeches; band collars smaller, tending to lose scalloped edges.

All the seams of sleeve, trouser and skirt, formerly open, buttoned or trimmed, are closing and diminishing in importance. Cloaks grow longer and have square "sailor" collars.

1645. XVIIc. Flemish. (Metropolitan Museum.)

C. de Vos, e. (d. 1651). Mother and Children.

1644

1645

1646

1647

Hair bunched in curls at the ears. Kerchief collar, finished by a wide band of straight-edged lace, is softly gathered up in front; the stiff kerchief is turning into a soft fichu which will slip away from the throat and uncover the shoulders. Sleeves short and wide with full, puffed shirt-sleeves finished by a gathered ruffle.

The pin at her bosom shows the new trend toward faceted stones. Mediaeval jewels were polished round as star sapphires are today; Renaissance stones were carved and engraved; pearls followed in popularity. Jewel cutting had been established in Flanders by Charles the Bold in 1475; Antwerp and Amsterdam have remained the great diamond-cutting centers ever since. Diamonds had been mined in India since mid-XVIc.; they were brought back in quantity by the French jewel merchant, Jean Tavernier, from half a dozen trips to the East; his first trip to the great Golconda mines was in 1638-43. In 1725 the great

diamond mines of Brazil were discovered. The XVII-XVIIIc. are times of sparkling, cut stones.

1646. XVIIc. 1661. Dutch. (Metropolitan Museum.)

G. Metsu. Visit to the Nursery.

Hair and costume of both men and women, now flowing, full, and soft. Mother in red velvet sacque and white satin skirt; visitor in black, edged with red at cuff-tops.

Wicker crib, fur blanket, fur-edged velvet canopy; maid with warming box; Ispahan rug as table cover.

1647. XVIIc. 1647. Dutch. (Leningrad, Hermitage.)

Bartholomeus van der Helst. The Presentation of the Fiancée.

Bun covered by an important, projecting cap. Lengthening side locks, tied with bows analogous to tassels seen on Bosse's Cavalier after Edict of 1733, or Morin's engraving of Count d'Harcourt, "Cadet La Perle" (von Boehn: *Die Mode,* XVIIc., p. 61).

1648

The round line of the bottom of the collar, and its rows of lace at the edge, establish the point at which scarves will be drawn around decolletage, when collar begins (as it soon will) to recede from the neck.

The simplified sleeve is set into the armseye, and the skirt onto the bodice, by carefully laid pleats. As the gown becomes more unified and less decorated, it will rely for the character of its satin elegance mainly on these pleats, which become exquisitely fine.

1648. XVIIc. 1648. Dutch. (Amsterdam, Rijksmuseum.)

B. van der Helst. Banquet of the Civic Guards in Honor of the Peace of Munster, detail.

This company of cross-bow men is meeting in the great hall of the St. Jousdoeln, through the windows of which can be seen the brewery "het Lam": the early architecture of New York was of this type, brought to Nieuw Amsterdam by its Dutch settlers.

Great variety of military (C, D) and civilian costumes; very fashionable young man (E) and conservatively dressed old man (B); his pinked black satin costume of full breeches and doublet worn with yellow stockings still carries a ruff, but in concession to fashion the ruff is loose and the doublet short-waisted, beneath the scarf which each member wears as sash on baldric. (C) In cuirasse, has a lemon yellow doublet, gray breeches, red stockingsg. (D) The Color Bearer, Jacob Banning, is in black, with a blue sash

and black and white plumes. (E) In pearl gray, laced in gold.

Band collars are becoming smaller (A, C), their edges straighter (A. C, D), with a tendency to be cut longer, squarer and to buckle slightly under the chin (E, G).

Doublet sleeves are being turned back into cuffs (C, E), showing more shirt sleeve fullness, finished with loosely gathered ruffles (A). Military jerkins (C), like doublets (E), have shrunk into vest-like forms. (A) shows the old multiple slitting.

Short tubular breeches make much of their front closing (C) and are in process of drawing their decoration from side seam to hem (E) showing the new interest in horizontal lines, culminating in Ill. 1673.

Boot cuffs wider, cupped lower on the calf, worn with elaborate sock-boots and stockings in bright colors (C, E). Garters are now less often rosettes than ribbon loops; as tabs of decoration at the sides of open shorts (E), they are often quite without function.

The old romantic hat is still seen, but is being replaced by more austerely blocked shapes (G, F) with higher crowns (E, above him) and brims straight (E), or curling and soon to be cocked (G, F); plumed or not (G, F). Hair, worn short by staid men (B, G, F), may be very long and worn with bangs (A, C). (See Appendix.)

1649. XVIIc. 1652. Dutch. (The Hague, Mauritshuis.)

C. van Everdingen. Diogenes Seeking an Honest Man.

Blocked hats with square-cut tapering crowns have band of feather fringe replaced by ribbon loops (child I, and men behind woman C). Longest hair on most fashionable men (F, E, B, A); bangs (E).

Cloaks, slung or not, are longer (B, E, F) and grow "sailor" and other collars of their own, as the great lace collars (which were always brought out over the capes) shrink to small plain collars with importantly tasseled ties. Cuffs are replaced by soft

ruffles (F). Slitting of center-back of doublet (A).

Open breeches grow longer and much wider, and are heavily decorated with loops around the hems (E, F). As they descend, the boots are crushed lower, flaring very wide just above the ankle; boot hose are now multiple rather than lacy (E, F); these are also worn as gaiters, quite without boots (A). Shoe toes become long and narrow, cut square across the end (A, E, F).

Diogenes wears a hood, smock and bound leggings of a peasant (D). Hood of country woman (C), and regional costume and cap of woman (G) have scarcely altered since centuries.

1650. Third quarter XVIIc. Dutch. (Louvre.)

Karel Dujardin. Italian Charlatans.

Dujardin (1622-78) was a Dutchman, most of whose work was done between 1650-75. He made a great reputation in Rome, squandered his money and, returning to Amsterdam by way of Lyons, married an old heiress, whom he deserted after clearing up his debts. He died in Venice at 54.

Coryat explains that mountebank comes from *monta in banco*—to go up on a bench. He describes the 5 or 6 stages set up in St. Mark's Place, Venice, on which the mountebanks gave shows twice daily. Some wore vizards, or were disguised as fools, women, and characters in Italian comedy. While part of the troupe played and sang, others opened their trunks, took out drugs and cosmetics and with witty jests sold "oyles, soveraigne waters, amorous songs printed, Apothecary drugs, and a Commonweal of other trifles," at high prices which became lower by the end of the second show.

It was only a step from these "medicine shows" to the quack doctors who flourished all over Europe well into XVIIIc. The earliest quack doctors were apt to be Italian. Anthony Wood records the visits to Oxford of John Baptista de Succa in 1626-7, and

of Dr. Vincent Lancelles of Venice in 1661. But Dr. John Pundeen came 4 times to Oxford between those dates, "set up his stage first in St. Marie's Churchyard by the diall; from thence he was removed to the Saracen's Head." Wood quotes the handbill of Professor James Themut, a "High Dutch Physitian . . . of Vienna in Austria," advertising his ability to cure all sorts of diseases "through God's mercy. . . . Within a month after . . . he rann away and cozenned his patients of a great quantity of money." Swift tells Stella (Journal to Stella, XX) of avoiding an invitation to go with Steele to Sir William Read's: "Surely you have heard of him. He has been a mountebank, and is the Queen's oculist; he makes admirable punch, and treats you in gold vessels. But . . . I will not go, neither indeed am I fond of the jaunt." Read's handbill advertised his successes with everything from dropsy to cancer, but its woodcut illustration shows an eye operation.

As Chamberlayne will be able to boast, a century later, "the poorest People in *England* wear good shoes of Leather; whereas in . . . neighboring countries, the Poor generally wear either Shoes of Wood, or none at all." (*Present State of Great Britain,* 1755 ed.) But Italian donkeys are beautifully dressed.

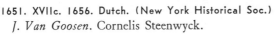

1651. XVIIc. 1656. Dutch. (New York Historical Soc.)
J. Van Goosen. Cornelis Steenwyck.

Above a view of Nieuw Amsterdam, the burgomaster of the Dutch colonial city which became New York, wears handsome garments which were in the latest mode at his last stay in Holland.

1652. XVIIc. 1655. Dutch. (New York, Cooper Union
    Museum.)

Cornelius Visscher. The Rat Catcher.

1653. XVIIc. 1656. Dutch. (New York, Cooper Union
    Museum.)

Cornelius Visscher. Gellius de Bouma.

Visscher's portrait of the noted ecclesiastic, and another of W. de Ryck, the opthalmist of Amsterdam, have always been known as "The Great Beards." "I find but few beards worth taking notice of in the reign of King James the First," wrote Eustace Budgell in Spectator, 331. But on these very old Dutch gentlemen in cap, gown, and the outmoded ruffs and beards of the days of their manhood, we see the beard at its greatest, just as it is disappearing until XIXc.

Photograph courtesy of the Metropolitan Museum of Art (1650)

1654. XVIIc. 1657. German.

Unknown artist. Procession of the Joiners and Cabinetmakers of Frankfort-on-Main.

A variety of doublets and coats worn with overflowing shirts and petticoat breeches; these are heavily beribboned below the bloused shirts and at the knees. Garters still appear with full breeches, but their knots are being transferred to the bottom of the outseam of the petticoat breeches; sometimes both forms are worn at the same time.

Baldrics are very wide and elaborate; hat crowns, squared off, are becoming lower; brims flat and wide, with plumes beginning to show a tendency to lie flat, surrounding the brim. Shoe rosettes supplanted by very wide stiff bows; square toes longer; heels higher.

Processions have an increasing quality of pageantry. Imaginatively costumed fabulous figures appear in the entertainments of Louis XIV, but the cabinetmakers of Frankfort stick to the old reliable fools and wild men; with a few American Indian headdresses added.

Tradesmen's houses, with shop or factory on the ground floor, and living quarters above. Guild members took great pride in beautifying their cities. Stow says, "The most beautiful frame of fair houses and shops that be within the walls of London, commonly called Goldsmiths Row . . . was built by Thomas Wood, goldsmith, one of the sheriffs of London in 1491. It containeth in number 10 fair dwelling houses and 14 shops, all in one frame, uniformly built 4 stories high, beautified towards the street with the Goldsmith's arms and the likeness of woodmen, in memory of his name, riding on monstrous beasts, all of which is cast in lead, richly painted over and gilt. This he gave to the goldsmiths, with stocks of money, to be lent to the young men having these shops, & . . . the front (was) again new painted and gilt over in the year 1594."

1655. XVIIc. c. 1660. Dutch. (Metropolitan Museum.)

Anton de Lorme, d. 1660. Figures painted by *G. Terborch.* Interior of a Church.

The male figures show the coat, at almost knee length, as well as the old circular cloak with square collar; breeches still loose but not full; lowered hat crown; one hat fringed with feathers and cocked into a tricorne.

Back view of hooded lady at l. shows looped and trailing skirts, tabbed jacket with short sleeves and much shirt sleeve, puffed above the elbow. The baby boy wears the new coat, very long, with very short sleeves and buttoned slits in its skirts; tiny sword slung by an important baldric.

Women and children of the people, in the garments shown by Brueghel.

1656. XVIIc. c. 1655. Dutch. (Metropolitan Museum.)
Gabriel Metsu. Artist and wife.

Ruffled boot socks, independent of boots, worn with shoes; knee-length coat has developed a closed cuff, buttoned back; horizontal pockets halfway up the skirts from the hemline.

Over her cap, his wife wears a hooded shoulder cape, pleated in around the neck, ingeniously folded up and carried in a semi-circle to cover the head.

Massive furniture of XVIIc. Netherlands, alternating square and turned forms; this is the type of furniture brought to New Amsterdam by the first Dutch settlers.

1657. XVIIc. c. 1660 Flemish. (Metropolitan Museum.)
Gilles van Tilborch. Visit of Landlord to Tenant.

Man, l.: rectangular collar hanging low on chest; jacket unbuttoned to show shirt; sleeves turned back in cuff: petticoat breeches with ribbon loops around waist; no boots, stockings beginning to be drawn up and rolled at knee. Musician, c.: hair of length immediately preceding the use of periwigs; voluminous shirt sleeve seen through and below short, slit doublet sleeve.

Women show headdresses and costume appropriate to their ages and positions. Young woman, l.: bunched curls falling on shoulders; fan. Necklines off shoulders, veiled in cape-like collars, combined with dark or light hoods, even on the baby; sleeves easy; short, puffed shirt sleeves tied with ribbons; aprons, light or dark, universally worn.

1658. XVIIc. Dutch. (Vienna, Czernin Gallery.)
Vermeer. The Artist in his Studio.

In his self-portrait, Vermeer shows one of the most extreme examples of slitting of the upper part of the doublet. Boots are being eliminated, but boot-hose are still seen, worn with shoes.

The beautiful maps, in the production of which the Dutch excelled, were favorite wall decorations in Holland. The cartouches of the borders contain panorama views, and often give important costume information as well.

1659. XVIIc. Dutch. (London, Earl of Northbrook.)
F. Bol. Married Pair at their Toilet.

During the 1650's and 1660's, painters like Rembrandt and Bol re-introduced late XV-XVIc. styles into their own costume, and that of their wives, particularly Rembrandt's Saskia; low-necked doublets, filled in with pleated shirts and band collars, which are often embroidered; soft beret-like hats, turbans and toques, quite unlike the current brimmed felts with blocked crowns. These romantic painters' usages had an effect on fashion.

Bol's wife wears the tongue-like headdress of the third quarter century, but some of the romantic style

1660

1661

1662

1663

is shown in the full shirt, and the embroidered band which finishes it, instead of the current collar or fichu-like band on the outside of the bodice, surrounding the shoulders. This show of pleated shirt coming up from under the bodice, and the baldric of pearls pinned from shoulder to sleeve across the bodices, are seen in Spanish costume.

1660. XVIIc. Dutch. (Metropolitan Museum.)

Terborch. The Toilet.

Little enclosed bun; hanging ends of hair tied with bows related to the tassels seen hanging from beneath male hair in the 30's. Back lacing of red corset bodice; sleeves of gown tied on by ribbon bows; yellow skirt.

1661. XVIIc. Dutch. (New York Metropolitan Museum, Frick Collection.)

Vermeer. Mistress and Maid Servant.

Little velvet jackets—yellow, red, blue, or green, edged with white fur, are characteristic domestic wear of the XVIIc. Netherlands. They appear repeatedly, outdoors and in, in pictures by contemporary Dutch artists: Gerard Terborch (1617-81) of Amsterdam and Haarlem, who traveled and painted all over Europe; Quieringh Gerritsz van Brekelenkam (1620-1680); Gabriel Metsu (c. 1629-1667) of Leyden and Amsterdam; and Jan Vermeer (1632-1675) of Delft, a much less prolific painter than the rest. Their pictures are seldom dated, and during this transitional

period show a mixture of old and new fashions at the same time.

Ermine-trimmed yellow velvet jacket; sleeve fullness carefully pleated in at top, gathered at bottom; white skirt, trimmed with coral. Fringe in little curls becoming stylized and consolidated at the ears; bun covered by tiny decorative cap. Maid in gray with dark blue apron.

1662. XVIIc. Dutch. (Metropolitan Museum.)

Q. G. van Brekelenkam. Mother Amusing Child.

Mother with kerchief-like hood, wide double collar, and apron over fur-edged jacket. Mules with heels stand by the embroidered hem of her skirt.

Baby in embroidered cap, kerchief and apron is set safe in an enclosed high chair; rings to play with strung on a fixed bar.

1663. XVIIc. Dutch. (Metropolitan Museum.)

Vermeer. Young Woman with a Water Jug.

The jacket with tabbed doublet skirts continues to be worn; here, a yellow jacket, banded with the dark blue-black of the skirt, shows a new hood and cape.

Holland is the rich crossroads of all commerce. These pictures are full of interesting and precious things: Oriental rugs, Spanish boxes and chests, Venetian mirrors, native silver, brass, and pewter, and the fine maps which were first produced commercially in the Netherlands.

1664. XVIIc. 1659. Dutch. (Metropolitan Museum.)

G. Metsu. The Music Lesson.

The man at the window shows the new coat, in red, heavily braided in brown and silver; worn with a neckcloth instead of a band collar; and one of the romantic velvet toques, trimmed with little tips (red), which appear in Dutch pictures of the 50-60's, and are repeatedly shown in self-portraits by Rembrandt and Bol. Red and gray cravat; longer cane.

The musician: a sash at the waist of his brown and red ribbon-fringed petticoat breeches; the lowest of flaring brown boots with red linings, white bootsocks, red hose; fringed sword-belt on floor.

The lady: a hood, locks tied with bows at the ends; blue scarf tied in a soft fichu around the shoulders of the corset-shaped bodice of her orange and silver costume, trimmed with red ribbons. Tiny pointed shoe on a warming box of coals.

1665. XVIIc. c. 1660. Dutch. (Metropolitan Museum.)

Q. G. van Brekelenkam. Sentimental Conversation.

Short open doublet; much shirt fullness; extremely wide square collar; petticoat breeches, ribbon trimmed at bottom of outseam; gartered stockings, still wrinkled, worn with square-toed shoes with bows; elaborate fringed sword belt on table.

Gauzy dark cap from the bun fastened to earrings. The high multiple windows of the Netherlands admit a great deal of light; lower rank has the early form of sliding interior shutter brought to America by the Dutch, of which there is an example in the Metropolitan Museum's American Wing.

1666. XVIIc. Dutch. (Amsterdam, Rijksmuseum.)

P. de Hooch. Linen Closet.

There is a great deal of creature comfort in the XVIIc. houses of the Netherlands. They are excellent houses by any standards, filled with light from ranks of high windows, arranged for good ventilation. Their shining tile floors are easy to clean, pick up the warmth of the house in winter, and retain its summer coolness. The houses open on brick-paved courts with gardens, where it is pleasant to do the dinner vegetables or drink with friends.

Getting at things which are packed in a chest is complicated, as anyone learns who has a lid rather than a door-type freezing locker today. The Dutch were the first to evolve from chests these immense "kas," the first adequate closets; closets will not begin to be built into houses for more than a century.

Satin sleeves set with fine cartridge pleating at back of armseye and cuff; fine banded petticoat. Handsomer and better made laundry hamper than can be found in New York in 1948. Little girl practicing golf shots perilously near the Delft tile of the stair riser.

1667. XVIIc. Flemish. (Carlsruhe, Picture Gallery.)

J. de Herdt. Woman Counting Money.

Spectacles, which were first scissored, and then tied in place, now pinch the nose. This Flemish equivalent of the Dutch velvet sacque is lined with fur and edged with embroidery; it is apparently part of a composed matching costume. Chain girdle with keys and pouch hangs on chair; many fine objects, including a standing piece of goldsmith's work.

1668. XVIIc. c. 1660. Dutch. (Washington, Nat. Gall. of Art.)

G. Metsu. The Intruder.

Seated lady reflected in Italian mirror with wings: gold and pearl decorated bun; green velvet jacket; lavender skirt trimmed in silver.

Lady arising: coral corset-bodice trimmed in silver; white satin petticoat; coral mules.

Maid: light brown dress; white cuffs; greenish-brown apron.

Intruder: gold-trimmed black coat; fawn hat.

On the Italian chair: the lady's coral velvet jacket and silver-trimmed matching satin overskirt.

Bed: still enclosed by curtains, has lost its wooden canopy as posts become more delicate.

1669. XVIIc. 1660-70. Dutch. (Washington, Nat. Gall. of Art.)

G. Terborch. The Suitor's Visit.

The suitor: black, white stockings, fawn hat; shoe toes square and spreading.

Lady: pearled cap and black bows; coral bodice; gold-trimmed white skirt.

Theorbo player: blue, silver hair bows.

Man behind: brownish gray.

1670. XVIIc. c. 1660-65. Dutch. (New York, Metropolitan Museum, Frick Collection.)

G. Terborch. Portrait of a Young Lady.

Black lace bands used on black satin, and as an edging over white satin banded in gold lace. Little ribbon knots at sleeves, bodice and in corkscrew curls.

1671. XVIIc. c. 1661. Dutch. (Berlin, Kaiser Friedrich Museum.)

A. van den Tempel. Nobleman and his Wife in their Park.

The nobleman's costume shows the favorite color combination of this period. His bronze satin doublet is worn with petticoat breeches lavishly looped below the belt and at the knee with variegated ribbons in reds, browns and beiges. The white shirt has green ribbons at the wrist and a wide green collar, edged with white lace. His baldric is black with an openwork emblem in silver; stockings sky blue. White boot-socks are worn, not with boots, but with black shoes, the red ribbons of which are halfway between rosettes and bows.

His wife wears the standard pale yellow satin gown, banded in gold lace, with a shaped white shoulder collar; black bows at the wrist.

Cattle (L. *capitale*=wealth, our "chattels") were

too valuable as draught oxen or milch cows to be lightly slaughtered, until a great deal of attention began to be given to cattle breeding in the XVII-XVIIIc. Venison was the predecessor of beef; the ownership of deer forests and parks and the right to hunt had been restricted to royalty and the great nobility. Limited park enclosures became naturally landscaped by the cropping and fertilization of generations of herds of deer and are now artfully planned; we are at the beginning of the great age of gardens and vistas. Property changes hands violently during the XVIIc. The old snob value of a deer park is reinforced by the increased demand for grazing land and a park, with or without deer, but certainly without cattle, is the desire of rich bourgeois or gentlemen of any pretentions.

1672. XVIIc. 1669. Dutch. (Carlsruhe, Art Gallery.)
B. van der Helst. Young Couple.

These are the classic costumes of c. 1670 at their most charming.

The man, whose hair is wig-like, wears the doublet in its last form, just before it is replaced for good by the coat and vest, and its rippling collar becomes gathered under the chin into a cravat.

The woman's gown leads directly into the satin-smooth low-necked dress of the early years of Louis XIV. Her hair hangs on the shoulders in ringlets clustered at the sides; even the fringe is in corkscrew curls. Her bodice has a row of graduated bows which will bring on the re-introduction of the V-front opening as necklines rise in Mme. de Maintenon's time.

1673

1674

1675

1673. XVIIc. Dutch. (London, National Gallery.)
G. Terborch. Portrait of a Gentleman.

There are German noblemen in rhinegraves more ruffled and beribboned but the culmination of elegance of this period is undoubtedly reached in the diamond-shaped silhouette of this gentleman. It is a triumph of diagonal and horizontal lines and of varied textures of black: polished leather, dull silk, and the deep richness of velvet.

The steeple-crowned hat and the circular cape are now almost old fashions, which are used with the utmost sophistication to reinforce the spread of the doublet opening, the petticoats, the flaring cannons. His hat is made new by the knot of ribbons on the crown; as the use of ribbons diminishes, such a knot will be retained on the shoulder of the coat. Here, ribbons of varied width are used at elbow and wrist; wide ribbons on the shoes, about the waist and massed at the sides of the petticoat breeches below the turn-back of the cape.

1674. XVIIc. Flemish. (Budapest, Museum of Fine Arts.)
P. van Lint (1609-1691). Portrait of a Man.

The coat, in its early form, worn with the old lace collar and without vest, over loose shirt and gathered breeches. It has pockets set low in the skirts; its cuffs are gaining in importance over those of the shirt, and the wrist ruffles of the shirt over the shirt's sleeves. Wig-like hair, hat brim rolling toward tricorne form, soft simple gloves, lace-edged handkerchief.

1675. XVIIc. c.1665-6. Dutch. (New York Historical Soc.)
G. Terborch. William, Prince of Orange (William III).

The posthumous son of the last great Stadholder and Charles I's daughter, married Mary, Protestant daughter of the Catholic James II. William and Mary were invited to replace James II in 1688, as Protestant discontent with the King was crystallized at the birth of a son to perpetuate the Catholic dynasty. William's precocious intelligence, chilled and sharpened by the difficulties of his childhood, endeared him less to the English during his lifetime than his noble plans and his diplomacy deserved.

William, born in 1650, appears to be about 15 or 16 in this portrait. His yellow and silver costume shows a laced leather coat, its sleeve finished with a ruffle of silver lace instead of a cuff; worn with a shoulder knot of silver and the new cravat into which the wide lace-edged collar has been gathered and reduced; full breeches; yellow stockings; brown shoes with a rounded tongue and small oval buckle; black and silver baldric; silver-fringed sash with tabs hanging at each side of waist. Hair is probably a wig. Black helmet with white plumes and red lining; breastplate; musket.

1676. XVIIc. Flemish. (Louvre.)
V. Boucquet (1619-1677). Standard Bearer.

An example of the combinations of two petticoats, the edges laced and the knees and sleeves looped with variegated ribbons. Baldric and sash wider and more fringed than ever; armor reduced to a cuirasse; stocking wrinkles carefully set around the calf; plumes laid around the brim of the hat will become a fringe of feathers as the hat becomes definitely cocked in the final quarter century.

1677. XVIIc. Dutch. (Metropolitan Museum.)
Pieter van Slingeland. Portrait of a Dutch Burgomaster.

1676

1677

1678

1679

1680

1681

1678. XVIIc. Dutch. (Minneapolis, Institute of Arts.)

B. van der Helst. Portrait of a Burgomaster.

The collar of van Slingeland's worthy, black-clad burgomaster, has been tied into a cravat by red ribbons on the lavishly gold-trimmed black costume of van der Helst's proudly pleased sitter.

1679. XVIIc. 1669. Dutch. (London, Wallace Coll.)

Caspar Netscher. Lace Maker.

The lace maker, socially intermediate between the ladies and their servants painted by Metsu and Terborch, wears a less pretentiously trimmed sacque with her lovely little cap.

1680. XVIIc. 1673. German. (Frankfort-on-Main, Stadel Inst.)

T. Roos. Portrait of a Woman.

German regional costume changes with French influence in latter half XVIIc. Ruffs tend to be replaced by other forms of collar, sleeves to be shortened and cuffed, with more show of ruffled shirt sleeve. South of Frankfort-on-Main bodices become much longer, particularly around Strassburg, Nuremberg and Augsburg. From Luxemburg through Mainz, Frankfort and Hanau to Nuremberg, and south along the Rhine to Strassburg, these long waists often develop into skirted jackets, like fitted masculine coats or riding costume of women.

The great fur hats, particularly those of Strassburg, which least enclose the face, are worn over lace caps; and as they approach the end of their use, degenerate, with the lace invading the fur of the hat. With the southwest German leaning toward masculine styles, male neckwear, such as this collar and the later steinkirk cravat, will be seen on women's costumes.

1681. XVIIc. c. 1680. German.

Princess Louisa Hollandina. The Electress Sophia and Her Daughter, Sophia Charlotte.

This portrait of George I's mother, with her daughter who became Queen of Prussia, was painted by her sister, the Abbess of Maubuisson. The great mezzotint engraver Rupert, was their brother.

This is the smooth-bodied simple satin gown of the '60-70's, its neck slipping off the shoulders, unadorned or caught about by a gauze scarf.

EUROPE GROWS COLDER

As I examined thousands of pictures for this book, I began to feel that a marked change in the climate of Europe must have begun by final quarter XVIc. Elizabeth's muffs, at the end of her reign, might be attributed to failing power in old age of a woman who had heretofore felt cold less than other people. But Englishwomen, notoriously uncovered out of doors in all seasons during most of the XVIc., take to muffs, hoods, and capes with everybody else, by XVIIc. It was obviously more than mere fashion; and all of the evidence pointed to continued low temperatures during XVII and XVIIIc. (See Appendix.)

Wretched as life must have been in barn-like buildings and wattle-and-daub huts, the winter temperature of Europe during the Middle Ages seems to have been substantially higher than after third quarter XVIc.; and there was still wood, to warm a smaller population.

The thermometer was not invented until late in Elizabeth's time, but when wine freezes in its casks, and is sawed up in chunks and sold by the pound, or slow-growing trees like olives, whose lives are measured by centuries, even millennia, split open, the facts are apt to be recorded.

C. Easton has arranged chronologically all the records of Western European climate since 396 A.D. (C. Easton: *Les Hivers dans l'Europe occidentale*, E. J. Brill, Leyden, 1928.) These bear out a dramatic series of events shown by the records of the church at Grindelwald, Switzerland. (H. Hildebrandsson, in *Monthly Weather Review*, June, 1916.)

There were a few bad winters during first half XVIc., but the over-all picture is of mildness so great that, during 1528-33, it seemed the climate must have changed for good: there was no snow, no ice, and flowers bloomed in mid-winter. Then came the "Great Winter" of 1565, which froze European rivers solid and split its trees. This was the beginning of a series of cold, snowy winters.

At Grindelwald, the receding lower glacier began to descend. It covered the heads of gold and silver mines which had been worked throughout the Middle Ages. By 1584, its ice had overturned the chapel of St. Petronelle, the bell of which was supposed to date from 1044 A.D. By 1593, it had reached the village, wrecking two chalets and many barns; it altered the beds of two rivers, and covered the road to Oberwallis. During the period of glacial retreat of 1860-80, the road and the buried houses reappeared. The glacier ice, 25 metres deep in 1570, increased to 100 metres during XVIIIc., and was reduced to 40 metres by 1880.

Easton's compilation shows that after 1565, when even the canals of Venice froze, winters became generally colder. One of the two or three worst of all recorded freezes was in 1607-8, the "Great Freeze in the reign of King James," when the Thames became a coach road, the walnut trees of Montargis died by the thousands, and the pines of Vicenza were blasted, as Coryat noted the following year.

Although there were at least six intervening winters worthy of being called rigorous or worse, the coldest weather in England in Evelyn's memory since 1620 was that of 1683-4, which froze Europe, even Spain. For months, the Thames was used as a street by coaches which ran from the Temple to Westminster for 6d. A "Frost Fair" of theaters, inns, and rows of shops, was set up on the ice, "even to a printing-press, where the ladies and people took a fancy to have their names printed and the day and year set down when printed on the Thames. Fowls, fish and birds, and all our exotic plants and greens universally perished. Many parks of deer were destroyed, and all sorts of fuel so dear that there were great contributions to keep the poor alive. No water could be had from the pipes—nor could brewers and divers other tradesmen work." (Evelyn.) Weakened by a 24-hour exposure of cold, people dropped dead on the streets of France and Flanders. In London, smallpox deaths rose to 200 a week, so that two thirds of the congregation were in black on Sunday, and a gaudy costume in a crowd caused general attention.

The winter of 1694-5, particularly terrible in France, is dramatically reflected in French fashion plates.

From Stockholm to Cadiz and Naples, the winter of 1709 surpassed everything recorded between 1608 and 1830; Louis XIV sold his gold plate for 400,000 francs to relieve his people. 1740 was a very long, cold winter; and cold-to-rigorous winters, especially in France and Italy, reappear frequently till 1763.

Then a reverse can be sensed. There is a run of normal winters, broken by rigorous cold in 1784 and 1789 (which froze the sea off Holland and split the olive trees of the Midi); warm and cold winters alternate; 1820 is bad; 1830 is one of Europe's recorded worst, especially in Spain and Portugal; 1845 is long and snowy from Sweden to Morocco. About 1860, the winters become generally soft and mild.

The prolonged cold, combined with a decreasing wood supply and a larger population, was an important cause of emigration to the New World; in Europe, it forced the use of coal for heating, which had been known since Roman times, but forbidden in English cities because of smell and smoke.

1682-83. XVIIc. Flemish. (Metropolitan Museum, Print Room.)

Romeyn de Hooghe. "Figures à la mode," Amsterdam.

The Dutch gentleman, followed by his Negro servant, shows the coat in its early long, unfitted form, its pockets rising, its corners caught together out of the way. This is necessary since he continues to wear a ribbon-fringed petticoat over full breeches; the old wide-brimmed boots are filled with boot-hose, but with their cuffs beginning to turn upward.

The turned-up coat corners are, as it happens, one of the most momentous ideas in the history of fashion. It is so useful that it is adopted by riders and military men all over Europe, by 1700.

Ingenious alterations in turned-back usages are characteristic of English costume in XVIIIc., and lead to lapels. In France, the turned-back corners are cut away, resulting in the tailored frock (Fr. *fraque, frac*) coat, from which come our formal and dress clothes for men.

The sleeves of his shorter, fringed vest appear as a matching ruffle below shortening and widening coat sleeves. His linen, as is usual, corresponds in fullness to the width of the cuff. Knots of ribbon on the slightly cocked hat, the shoulders, behind the cravat, at elbows, and at the wrists to which the whip is fastened by a loop. The tasseled canes of the next century will be hung from a button by this loop, when hands need to be free.

Fond as the Netherlands have always been of skating and sleighing, a good freeze is not common there, and when it comes, in our day, offices close. Dutch ladies in masks, kerchief-hoods, little fur capes or pockets, are otherwise dressed as they would be indoors. One holds her slipper while her cavalier, wearing a bunch of ribbons on the side of his hat, laces skates over a foot protected by nothing but a stocking.

Both Lipperheide and Colas date the 12 plates of the *Figures à la mode* at "about 1700," which seems to me to be nearly a quarter of a century too late.

1684. XVIIc. 1692. Dutch. (Metropolitan Museum, Print Room.)

R. de Hooghe, illustrator. "Relation de voyage de sa Majesté Brittanique en Hollande," by Tronchin du Breuil. The Hague, 1692.

Reception at the Westende Bridge to welcome William III. Europe now wears French costume, especially on ceremonious occasions and at court. Guardsmen; attendants in striped liveries.

1685. XVIIc. Dutch. (Detroit, Institute of Arts.)

G. Terborch. Young Man Reading.

The *montero* cap with a turned-up fur brim is worn as a riding hat, or within doors (where it is often worn in place of a wig) with a dressing gown. Hair is now replaced by an unnaturally woolly wig, separated over the shoulders.

The long coat of the 70's is frequently seen with a rather long, narrow sleeve, modestly cut and showing very little linen, with a small armseye and a tight-drawn look about the upper body.

Brown costume; *montero,* cherry and silver crown; yellow gloves.

1686. XVIIc. 1685. Dutch. (Budapest, Museum of Fine Arts.)

J. Weenix. Portrait of a Man.

Straight coat with narrow upper sleeve, worn with a long, closed brocade vest, which is probably sleeveless, although its material is used like a turned-back sleeve, to cover the wide coat cuff. No buttons on either garment, except at cuff. Knotted cravat with lace ends; full, unruffled shirt sleeve. Hair probably his own.

Negro servants replace dwarfs, except in Spain, and are frequently painted with their masters.

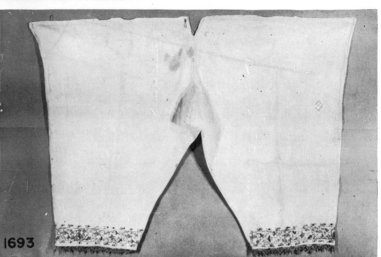

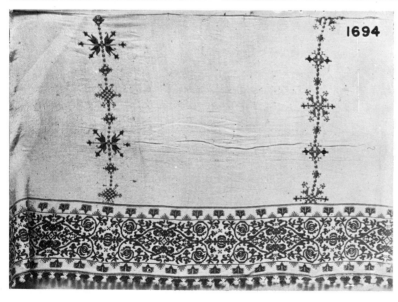

1687. Mid-XVIIIc. Flemish. (Cooper Union Mus.)

Rabat: bobbin lace; Brussels. Necktie end; one of pair; patterns opposed.

1688. XVIIc. Dutch. (Metropolitan Museum.)

Albert Cuyp (d. 1691). Cavalier and his Sons.

Long velvet riding coats, worn with turban or fur-trimmed *montero*; compare closing with gown of Electress Sophia (1681). Boots, now restricted to riding use, are long, softer, and have their tops turned up to cover the knee. Retention of braid in sleeves and chest, in livery use.

1689-93. XVIc. Italian, Sicilian.

5-piece Set of Linen Underwear, embroidered in

silk and metal threads: *camisa* (underdress), shirt, stockings (without foot), and 2 pairs of under-drawers. Underdrawers, like most refinements of dress, originated in Italy. Moryson mentions "silke or linnen breeches under their gownes" as being characteristic of Italian townswomen's dress. He says that they are not worn at all in Germany; they were obviously none too common in his native England at end XVIc.

1694. XVII-XVIIIc. Italian.
Apron : linen, embroidered in red silk.

1695. XVII-XVIIIc. Spanish, Salamanca.
Peasant Sleeve: embroidered in black and colored wools.

1696. XVIIc. Italian.
Knitted Mitts: probably ecclesiastical, in light and dark brick pink, lemon yellow, green, cobalt blue, and natural color.

1697. XVIIc. Italian.
Knitted Jacket.

1698-1700. Early XVIIc. Italian.
Knitted Stockings.

1701-03. XVII-XIXc.
Knitted and embroidered stockings.

KNITTING BY HAND AND MACHINE

Knitting in Great Britain apparently began in Scotland and filtered down into England. The earliest English mention is of knit wool caps in 1488. "Knitte hose, knitte peticotes, knitte sleeves" are mentioned in an Act of Edward VI in 1553, and the trade of hosier in 1563. The first worsted hose knit in England were supplied to Lord Pembroke (executor of Henry VIII's will) by Thomas Burdet, "an ingenious apprentice of St. Magnus' Church." (Wade: *British Chronology*.)

Stow says that Edward VI had a "payre of long Spanish silke stockings sent him for a great present," the first seen in England, and that Henry VIII had only cloth or taffeta hose "or that by great chance there came a payre of Spanish silke stockings from Spain."

"In the second yeere of Queen Elizabeth 1560, her silke woman, Mistris Montague, presented her majestie for a new yeere's gift a paire of black knit silk stockings, the which, after a few days wearing, pleased her highness so well, that she sent for Mistris Montague and asked her where she had them, and if she could help her to any more; who answered, saying: "I made them very carefully of purpose only for your

Majestie, and seeing these please you so well, I will presently set more in hand." "Do so (quoth the queene), for indeed, I like silke stockings so well, because they are pleasant, fine, and delicate, that henceforth I will wear no more cloth stockings."

Mary, Queen of Scots, at her execution wore "shoes of Spanish leather, the inside outward; green silk garters; watchet silk stockings, clocked and edged at the top with silver, and under them a pair of white Jersey hose." (Brummell, see Appendix.)

In Stubbes' time, cloth netherstocks were "thought too base" and were made of "jarnsey, worsted, crewell, silke, thred, and such like, or els . . . of the finest yearne that can be got, and so curiously knitte with open seame downe the legge, with quirks and clocks about the anckles, and sometime (haply) interlaced with golde or siluer threds, as is wonderfull to behold." They were still terribly expensive. "The time hath bene when one might have clothed all his body for lesse then a payre of these netherstocks will cost" People "will not sticke" at having 2 or 3 pairs, for which they have to spend their own earnings for a whole year.

A machine for knitting was invented in 1589 by the Rev. William Lee, a Cambridge graduate serving as a Nottinghamshire vicar. It was an excellent machine from the very start, and the entire stocking, jersey, and lace industry is founded upon Lee's machine, with refinements but no real alterations. He first made flat stockinet, but soon learned to "fashion" shaped garments. Nottingham was the heart of the later English machine lace industry, but since neither Elizabeth nor James showed interest in his invention, Lee took it to Rouen, under the patronage of Henry IV until that king's assassination.

There was no notable advance in knitting until 1758, when Jedediah Strutt of Belper attached a ribbing machine to Lee's frame. Ribbed stockings, often in blue and white, become common soon after, especially in France. Knitting was also enriched by the application of Jacquard techniques, in the beginning of the XIXc.

1704. Early XVIIc. Italian.
Border: cut-linen work: vine design in *punto reale* and *punto riccio* with figure motifs in *punto in aria;* edge of *reticella* lace of transitional type.

1705. Early XVIIc. Italian.
Alb: *punto in aria* on linen.

1706. XVIIc. Italian.
Handkerchief: reticella lace.

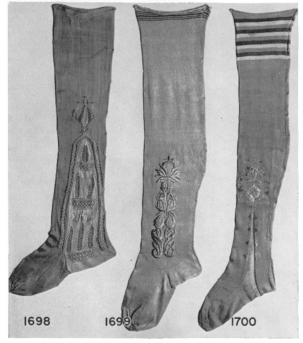

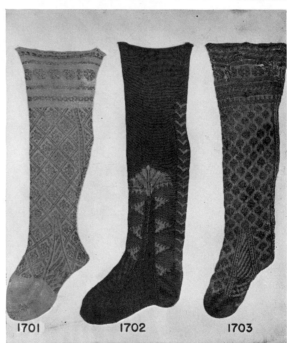

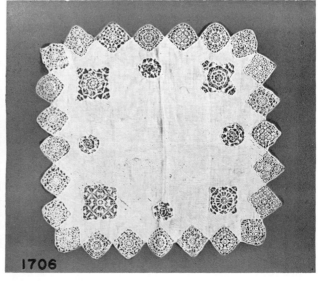

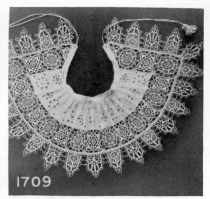

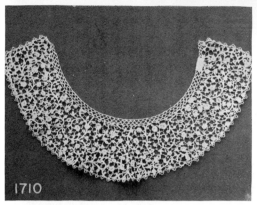

1707. XVIIc. Italian.

Handkerchief: bobbin lace.

Handkerchiefs were another refinement which originated in Italy, as did underdrawers. Unlike drawers, they became very popular in Germany.

The first laces were a sort of embroidery, based on the threads of fabric. The first *reticella* laces became less rectangular as workers gained skill. Their patterns had already begun to flow, even before the time when the basic threads of fabric had begun to be replaced by freely manipulated threads on bobbins.

1708. XVIIc. Italian, Genoese.

Collar: *reticella.*

1709. XVIIc. French?.

Collar: embroidered linen; border in *punto in aria* and reticella.

1710. XVIIc. c. 1650. Italian.

Collar: Venetian point.

1711. XVIIc. Italian.

Collar: rose point.

1712. XVIIc. Italian.

Tassels for band-strings: bobbin lace.

1713. XVIc. Spanish.

Woman's Leather Shoe: brown on white, red heel.

1714. Early XVIIc. French.

Patten: wooden sole, leather strap and heel, iron ring.

1715. XVIIc. c. 1620. Probably Italian.

Woman's Shoe: white leather; brown leather toe strap; pink silk floss tassels.

1716. XVIIc. 1610. Italian, Venetian. (Metropolitan Museum, Print Room.)

Giacomo Franco. "Habiti dell donne venetiane."

Franco's costume book shows XVIc. fashions persistent in Venice. The man wears the costume of Goltzius' Standard Bearer. The horned hair arrangements of the lady are specifically Venetian. She retains the bodice seen in Venice throughout the XVIc., high-waisted in back, low in front and padded across the belly, from which the idea of the male peascod doublet seems to have come. It is, as always, extremely low cut, with the great wired fan collar of latter half XVIc.; interesting use of lace at the armseye, where

Courtesy of Metropolitan Museum of Arts (1707-1712);
Museum of Fine Arts, Boston, Elizabeth Day McCormick Coll. (1713-1715)

the separate sleeves the Italians have long loved always
tend to show the linen of the undershirt. A single
skirt of brocade, undivided in the center and gathered
all around into the waistline, is a Venetian usage, as
is the fan chained to the girdle, which the rest of
Europe took from Italy.

In 1645, Evelyn found Venetian garb "odd, as
seeming always in masquerade." Some of their characteristic styles, like high chopines and hair deliberately streaked with dye, have persisted since Carpaccio's time. He describes their petticoats, "coming
from their very armpits"; the "knots of points richly
tagged about their shoulders," and their display of
"shift" at the shoulders; the general look of nakedness which they "usually cover with a kind of yellow
veil of lawn, very transparent"; and their enormous
pearls.

On their chopines he says the Venetian ladies are
"half-flesh, half-wood"; chopines are now forbidden
wear for plain citizens and for prostitutes. Ladies continued to wear *chopines,* to the time of the daughter
of the last Doge, Domenico Contarini. (Yriarte, see
Appendix.)

Prostitutes wear great veils of shot taffeta (with
broad, flat tassels of "curious Point de Venise" at the
corners) which cover the entire body. "Out of (these)
they now dart a glance of their eye, the whole face
being otherwise entirely hid with it, nor may the
common misses take this habit; but go abroad bare-
faced." Prostitutes are increasingly controlled: in
Florence, daily tribute is exacted from them by the
Medici duke, and though "not so much in value,"
by the Pope as well.

Gambling has become a passion with the Venetian
nobility; masked players, "without speaking one
word, come in, play, lose or gain, and go away as
they please."

The typical "clarissimoe" gown of the Venetian
citizen, with a flap over the shoulder which it had
inherited from the Roman toga, and the colors which
designated the wearer's status, are described in
Coryat's "Crudities."

TOM CORYAT'S CRUDITIES

Tom Coryat, a member of the household of Prince
Henry, set out in 1608 to make a tour of Europe on
foot and horseback. His account, published under the
patronage of the Prince of Wales in 1611, notes the
new and different things which struck an observant
young Englishman.

In France, the windows are filled with glass or
paper; there are wood shingles; parasols and fans are
used. He describes the corps of uniformed guards at
Fontainebleau, giving a plausible enough account of
the origin of parti-color.

He finds that he cannot enter Venice without a
bill of health from the preceding city. He describes
the costume of Venetian men, women, courtesans
and Jewesses; the superiority of their theater buildings
and the inferiority of their performances in comparison to those of England; the appearance of women
on the stage; "medicine shows" given by mountebanks; the use of forks, unknown elsewhere, umbrellas and lovely fans; the lace-canopied beds of
Italian inns; the walls hung with stamped leather and
windows filled with glass; the beautiful and costly
straw hats of Piedmont; the Spanish sleeve which has
reached female costume in Bergamo from Turin.

In N. Italy and Germany, the walls, even of inns,
are hung with armorial bearings; Zurich, Basel and
Strassburg have distinctive costumes; there are literally hundreds of public baths at Baden; stoves, and
clock-towers with mechanical figures in Germany;
the richest fair in Europe is held twice a year at
Frankfort.

1717. XVIIc. 1602. Spanish. (Madrid, Descalzas Reales.)

J. Pantoja de la Cruz. Royal Baby.

With his brocade doublet and skirts the baby has a flat wired collar which is in process of becoming a falling band, and matching bibbed apron. By a cord about the neck is fastened a bar hung with crosses and reliquaries. In his hand and from his bracelet and belt he has all sorts of delightful playthings: bell, rattle, hand, a branch of coral for teething and a horn.

1718. Second decade XVIIc. Flemish. (Florence, Corsini Palace.)

J. Sustermans. Maria Magdalena of Austria.

The Emperor Ferdinand II's sister was painted not long after her marriage in 1609 to Cosimo II de' Medici, of whom there is a companion portrait in the same collection. Her brother Leopold presently married Cosimo's sister. The endlessly interrelated Florentine court was large, delightful and cultivated. Cosimo brought to Florence Galileo, the inventor of the pendulum, thermometer and sector, who invented the telescope and produced his philosophical studies of gravitation and astronomy under Cosimo's patronage, until the Duke's death at 30. Maria Magdalena and Christine of Lorraine served as co-regents of Tuscany, both dressed magnificently to do honor to Ferdinand II de' Medici, whom they represented.

Under a pearl choker, she wears a great lace whisk, which in its *golilla* form appears in Spanish portraits by Velasquez in the 60's. The excessively cut and decorated edges of the stomachers worn in the Netherlands are latent in the embroidered sections of the skirts of her doublet.

1719. XVIIc. 1609. Spanish. (London, Christie Sale.)

J. Pantoja de la Cruz. Margaret of Austria.

Philip III's wife was the sister of Leopold of Tirol and Maria Magdalena.

She wears the standard Spanish gown, hair dressed higher, its decoration mounting, ever wider ruff, lengthening bodice and point, cone-shaped skirt relatively unaffected by hip padding.

1720. XVIIc. 1620. Flemish-Italian. (Metropolitan Museum.)

J. Sustermans. Cosimo II de' Medici, Grand Duke of Tuscany.

The Grand Duke wears the extremely conservative costume now seen only in Spain and Italy; paned trunk hose in their long, wide first decade XVIIc. form; long skirted doublet; ruff; old form of matching short circular cape, with Maltese cross; heelless shoes with small bows; magnificently damascened helmet with umbril (eye-shade) which is now in the Metropolitan Museum's Armor Collection.

1721. XVIIc. Spanish. (Nantez, Museum.)

P. de la Cruz, d. 1610. Portrait of a Lady.

When the lacy white ruff had been made as wide as possible it began to be boring; ruffs then began to be made of colored material, edged with metal lace. Or, as in this case, embroidery replaces lace in a ruff, set, however, on a lacy supporting frame of wire loops and lattice.

1722. XVIIc. c. 1620. Spanish. (Madrid, Prado.)

Unknown Madrid painter formerly att. to *Pantoja de la Cruz.* Isabella of Bourbon, Queen of Spain.

Isabella (or Elizabeth), first wife of Philip IV, beautiful and beloved by the Spaniards, was aunt and mother-in-law of Louis XIV.

She wears a gray ruff with a gown of gray brocade sprigged with green. The inner sleeve of her Spanish gown has felt the tendency of European sleeves to grow shorter and wider.

The influence of the hip bolster on European costume did not outlast first quarter XVIIc.; Spanish and Italian costume was late in accepting it but retained it longer; in Spain it was eventually transmuted into the enormously wide skirt of Velasquez' portraits.

The point and tabbed skirts of her bodice are developing into the form of the important stomachers of the gowns of the Netherlands.

1723. XVIIc. 1622-27. Flemish. (New York, Metropolitan Museum, Frick Collection.)

Van Dyke. Paola Adorna, Marchesa di Brignole-Sale. (*See also* Frontispiece; of the same period.)

The Marchesa's white and gold costume, with a brown scarf and tinted ruff, shows the importance of the stomacher to be growing in Italian as in Flemish costume.

The growing boredom of all Europe with the ruff in second decade XVIIc. is being shown in many ways. Its width from front to side may be increased; it may be colored, embroidered or edged with metal lace. There is a tendency to replace gauffered, pointed lace by ruchings of tulle. These impulses are shown in this ruff; its border looks less like the lace it still is than like a more delicately fluted edge, on a more largely and loosely pleated ruff, worn with wrist ruffles of the old form, differing also in color. White cuffs are sometimes enlivened by being worn over a bright-colored cuff. (See Appendix.)

With her simply dressed Italian hair, the Marchesa wears a tiny pearled cap with a brown aigrette (a form of the quivering spray set in the hair since late Elizabethan days); sash worn baldric-wise; longest form of Spanish sleeve flowing down the train of her gown.

1724. First quarter XVIIc. French.

Jacques Callot. Bohemiens: Le vant-garde.

Jacques Callot (1592-1635), the son of a herald-at-arms of Nancy, and destined for the Church, ran away at 12 with a band of gipsies to study art at Rome. He was recognized there and sent back forcibly to Nancy. At 14 he ran away and was again recaptured. He was finally allowed to go to Rome in 1608-9 to study engraving. He worked in Florence under the patronage of Cosimo II from 1612 until the Duke's death in 1627, and then returned to Nancy, which he had visited in 1621. His 1600 plates illustrate costume, the life of vagabonds and gipsies, the grotesque figures of Italian comedy, the miseries of war. Many of his plates appear in several forms, engraved originally in Italy and reworked at Nancy after his return to France.

These gipsies in their bedraggled, swashbuckling finery, must be very like the cavalcade with which Callot first traveled.

1725-30. Before 1627. French.

Jacques Callot. Bohemiens: L'avant-garde.

These costume plates, produced first in Florence, show: swashbuckling military figures in plumed hats, draped capes, loose gartered breeches and high, stiffened whisk collars; priests or scholar in long garments; town and country women, the former in a male hat, sleeves pinned on at the shoulders, showing puffs of shirt, embroidered apron over tucked-up skirt, and heelless shoes; the latter in straw hat, kerchief over shoulders and an apron full of faggots.

1731. Early XVIIc. French.

Jacques Bellange. La Seconde Jardinière.

Another etcher from Nancy, whose work shows strong Italian influence, is Bellange (1594-1638). With her uncovered, braided hair, fringed shawl, fine straw basket, narrow embroidered apron, and Roman sandals, the "second gardener" is obviously an Italian peasant girl.

1732. XVIIc. 1682. Italian, Bologna.

Giuseppe M. Mitelli (1634-1718). Alfabeto in Sogno: E.

This little figure, by one of the early caricaturists, though produced much later in the century, is set here with the Callots from which it stems; such fanciful composite costumes are shown elsewhere in latter half XVIIc. Other engravings by Mitelli show the costume of Italian comedy characters.

Guatsetto. 1733 Mestolino.

Riciulina. 1734 Metzetin

Pulliciniello 1735 Sig.ª Lucretia.

Cap. Spessa Monti. 1736 BaGattino.

Scaramucia 1737 Fricasso.

Scapino 1738 Cap. Zerbino

1733-38. XVIIc. French.

Jacques Callot. Italian Comedy Figures.

The figures of the *commedia dell'arte,* descended from established characters in Roman farce, began to be developed in Italy early in XVIc. and are with us still. The action, largely comic and frequently bawdy, was improvised upon the skeleton of a prearranged scenario by troupes of strolling players and acrobats: ladies, and their pert or ribald maids; lovers, and their elders, Pantaloon and the Doctor; the boastful Spanish Captain; and all manner of servants, resourceful, witty or dull: Harlequin, Scapin, Scaramouche, Mezzetino, Pierrot and Punch, as we call them now. The companies were imported to France by Catherine de' Medici. Italian comedy had become part of the life of all Europe by the XVIIc. (See Appendix.)

Lucrezia is one of the many elegant names borne by the innamorata; she is always played without a mask, as are her lover and her maid. Ricciolina is a witty form of her companion-servant, allied to the soubrette, Harlequin's Columbine.

Of the male servants shown, Guatsetto and Bagattino are related to Harlequin and his alert impudence. The first is a rollicking fun-maker, the second a teasing juggler. Mestolino and Mezzetino are almost identical: quick-witted but dumb in spots. Pulcinello is a dope; Scapin, a rogue; Scaramouche has some of the swagger of the Captains, of whom Zerbino is one of the more elegant: he wears dark-rimmed Spanish spectacles over his flashing eyes lest their glance shame the sun.

Many of the little porcelain figurines of the XVIIIc. produced at Nymphenburg, Meissen and Vienna show the personages of Italian comedy in their characteristic costume.

1739. XVIIc. 1616. French.

Jacques Callot. Intermezzo, after Guilio Parigi's Sketch in the Stanzoni de' Commedianti, Florence.

Plays, whether of the traveling carnival sorts, grown out of the jongleurs and minstrels of the Middle Ages; the miracle and morality plays performed by guilds or townspeople; or the great processions of the Church or of princes like the Medici, originally took place in the open air, in public squares or palace courts.

Stages with a backdrop were at first set up on wagons or platforms. The theaters of Shakespeare's time grew out of the use of cloistered palace courts, multiplied into tiers of seats protected by a roof. They were open to the weather in the center where the standees massed to watch a performance played on a permanent stage, which projected into the clearing and was roofed over only in the rear. Obviously the standees got the best view of the performance. In late XVIc. completely roofed theaters with seats in the middle and scenery in perspective, began to be built in Italy. One of the first and finest was the Teatro Olimpico at Vicenza, designed by Palladio, and standing today; Coryat described its superiority to English playhouses.

During XVII-XVIIIc. playhouses were built from the plans of the greatest architects, like Inigo Jones, who also designed the scenery for Ben Jonson's plays. Theaters were included in palaces and private houses, but the old tradition of being seated at the side and up, safe from the weather and the riff-raff, was responsible for the retention, to this day, of boxes at the side, from which the most costly seats give the worst view of the stage.

For the entertainment of Callot's patron, Cosimo II, Parigi, who belonged to a great family of designers of spectacles in second half XVI-first half XVIIc., provides a pastoral set with the Renaissance's beloved long vistas.

The first textbook of theatrical design and lighting, end first half XVIc., was Italian. It describes the correct scenery for the three types of performances: tragedy, performed on a street of palaces in perspective; comedy, in a public square; and a rustic setting for dancing pastoral or allegorical figures. (See Appendix.)

The reversed crescent silhouette of the female body in 1616 swings from a fan collar, wired high in back, past pendant Spanish sleeves, to trailing skirt-ends.

New fashions of Europe affect the dress of male spectators more than that of their ruler in his official portraits (Ill. 1720). But the ()-shaped silhouette is typically Florentine: the plumed hat is high rather than wide, the flaring collar wider than the hat brim, the square-collared cape is bundled about the torso, while the breeches, full at the waist, are reduced at the gartered knee, and the body tapers to an inconspicuous foot. Even the standing postures are studied to emphasize the bulging center. (Male figs.: Foreground).

1740. XVIIc. 1622-7. Flemish. (Washington, Nat. Gall. of Art.)
Van Dyke. Marchesa Balbi.

The Antwerp-born Marchesa, who may have launched her fellow-townsman, Van Dyke, on his career in Genoa, wears a gold brocaded dark green costume. Its silver ruff is embroidered in gold; wrist ruffles of gauze so sheer that they appear to be of a lighter green than the costume.

1743

1744

1745

1741. XVIIc. 1630. Spanish. (Paris, Gustave de Roths-child.)

Velasquez. Queen Maria Anne of Hungary.

With her black and gold costume, Philip III's daughter wears a sheer ruff of light brown tulle, gold-edged wrist ruffles, and a handkerchief of gold gauze.

1742. XVIIc. 1624. Spanish. (London, Cassell Coll.)

Velasquez. Gaspar de Guzman, Count of Olivares, Duke of St. Lucar.

Olivares, head of the household of the heir-apparent, became on his accession Philip IV's devoted minister, constant companion and alter ego, the most powerful man in Spain until his fall from favor in 1643. He was a man of immense pride, who refused to use the title of his acquired dukedom except in combination with that of his inherited rank; a man of bull-like power; a magnificent horseman. He shared none of Philip's love of art and the theater, but kept a great aviary, and carefully saw to the preservation of a mass of the Spanish state papers.

He wears the green cross of Alcántara on his black costume, together with symbols of his power, and the collar out of which Philip devised his *golilla*.

1743. XVIIc. c. 1630. Spanish. (London, formerly Dorchester House.)

Velasquez. Philip IV.

The King, of whom Velasquez painted so many portraits, was a well meaning man, somber, indolent and art loving, passionately devoted to the Spanish theater in the great period of Lope de Vega and Calderón. The Spain he had inherited from his far lesser father was already ruined; he left its government to Olivares, who was, for all his qualities, neither the economist Spain needed, nor any match for Richelieu.

The king dressed beautifully, wearing the *golilla* collar which was his own invention, and the moustaches which were carefully encased in a pomaded leather form at night. His most effective costumes were severe and dark. but their silhouette shows less clearly than in similarly cut, lighter examples such as those selected for reproduction.

Leather military jerkin with doublet sleeves matching the cuffs of his gauntlet and embroidered around the seam of the thumb. Baton and diagonal lace-edged sash of a military commander. Padded breeches worn with high, soft boots, their tops slashed to show a colored lining. Cocked hat with plumes and wide, crushed crepe scarf. The lock of hair in front of the ears is specifically Spanish. Spanish velvet table cover with fitted corners, caught with braided gold frogs.

1744. XVIIc. 1631. Spanish. (London, National Gallery.)

Velasquez. Philip IV.

Brocade doublet has short buttoned openings below throat and belt, outlined in heavy embroidery; matching diagonal pocket slits at its breasts and skirts. The breeches, with vertical pockets, are padded, reduced in width, buttoned along the outseam and gartered with rosettes. Dark gauntlets have slashed cuffs matching the doublet sleeves.

1745. XVIIc. c. 1633. Spanish (Madrid, Prado.)

Velasquez. Margaret of Austria on Horseback.

The queen wears a tall, plumed man's hat with her riding costume. Women's dress in l.XVI-e.XVIIc. has a severe masculinity. As it becomes more feminine in latter half XVIIc., women's riding costume will retain or exaggeratedly ape masculine styles.

Court Dwarfs

A dwarf, with the word written over his head, appears among the entourage of William the Conqueror in the Bayeux Tapestry. Dwarfs had been favorites in the noble houses of Europe since the Middle Ages. Nowhere were they more pampered, audacious, shameless, or ridiculous than in the somber, religious, severely formal Spanish courts of the late XVI-XVIIc.

Dwarfs might be witty, impudent and exaggerated, in the tradition of court jesters, like Charles V's Francesillo or Philip II's French buffoon, Brusquet. Others were little gamecocks, like the matador, Juan de Cazalla, who was accompanied by four scarlet-clad Negro giants; or like Henrietta Maria's Jeffrey Hud-

son (18 inches high when nine years old), a cavalry captain in the Civil Wars, who fought two duels, the first with a turkey-cock and another with an opponent who met him with a squirt and was later shot dead by Hudson from horseback.

Many were endearing little companions and confidants, to be indulged (and sometimes bribed), who could perform small services, or take charge of the more helpless dwarfs: the mad, deformed or idiotic. These last served as butts for teasing, or as contrast and relief from the almost unbearably tense grandeur of the court, as they stumbled, smashed and misbehaved.

The more intelligent dwarfs were carefully educated. The most winning although often the most hideous, were as beautifully dressed and shod as their masters. Elizabeth's Tomasina got 12 pairs of shoes at a time. Some had tiny weapons and saddles, like Philip III's Polish dwarf, Estanislao, a skillful hunter.

Maria Theresa's Moorish dwarf delighted the French court: thereafter little Negroes begin to replace dwarfs in late XVII-XVIIIc. portraits.

The common people who loved the "merry drolls," gave them the name of their favorite food: Holland, Pickled Herring: France, Jean Potages; Italy, Macaronis; Great Britain, Jack Pudding. So says the *Spectator,* in bringing the matter through April fool jokes, to the practical jokers of the e.XVIIIc. called Biters. (See Appendix.)

1746. XVIIc. c. 1633. Spanish. (Madrid, Prado.)

Velasquez. The buffoon, Pablo de Valladolid.

Pablillo wears a collar which, like that of Olivares, is not quite a *golilla;* the cape without which a man was not properly dressed in public; brocade doublet; rather full, gartered breeches; and the heelless shoes, the short hair and the locks before the ears, characteristic of Spain.

1747. XVIIc. 1631. Spanish. (Boston, Museum of Fine Arts.)

Velasquez. The Infante Baltasar Carlos and his Dwarf.

This is the first of nearly a dozen portraits of the extremely promising young prince, often painted by Velasquez before his death at 17. We can see him, still in skirts in 1631; by 1635, breeched, in hunting clothes and boots with a miniature gun, or in magnificent court costume, or riding a prancing horse with the most assured proud dignity of any six-year-old boy who ever lived; or in tiny armor in 1639. But never are we without feeling some part of Philip's pangs at his loss, 300 years ago.

The Infante at 2 wears dark olive green velvet, embroidered in gold. With his steel gorget he carries the scarf of a military commander, in warm red; red hat with gray-white plumes, trimmed in gold.

The dwarf, Francesco Lezcano's brown dress is braided and cuffed in dark red; gray collar, edged in red-brown, surmounted by a choker of dark red beads; apron edged in gray lace, embroidered in dark gray; he carries a rattle.

1748. XVIIc. c. 1628. Spanish. (Madrid, Prado.)

Velasquez and assistant. Doña Antonia de Ipeñarrieta y Galdós and Her Son, Luís.

The stiffened collar of Doña Antonia's severely cut gown supports a series of white collars, flat and fluted, variously edged with color and bobbin lace. The old scheme of braided doublet sleeve issuing through pendant gown-sleeve is nicely varied here. Both are of the same stuff; the inner sleeve is reduced to a deep cuff over which the upper sleeve is puffed, and to which it is caught so that they move together. The close sleeve, barely cuffed, is shortening as elsewhere in Europe, to show a pair of fine bracelets. The austerity of such gowns is lightened by a pearl baldric and fine buttons.

The picture of the child, whom she holds by his pendant sleeve as by a leading string (which developed out of this usage), was added later to her portrait by another artist. He had the Spanish lock in front of the ears, a falling collar of lace, apron with an openwork bib and bobbin lace edge, and a bell hanging from his belt.

1749. XVIIc. Spanish. (New York, J. P. Morgan.)

Spanish School. Portrait of a Child.

The loving care lavished on Spanish ecclesiastical garments had brought to perfection methods of patterned pleating. The technique commonly seen on albs is transferred here to a child's apron. It is worn with a headdress related to the *bourelet* seen on so many XVIIIc. French children in pictures by Chardin and Boucher.

1633. Similar visored caps, long-skirted jerkins with hanging sleeves and brocade doublet sleeves, gauntlets, easy breeches, rosetted at the knee, and soft high boots with a reversed top, are also worn by Philip and Baltasar Carlos in Velasquez portraits in the 30's, with snaphance rather than the wheellock hunting gun which the Cardinal appears to carry.

The dogs favored by male Hapsburgs since Charles V are always immense; Baltasar Carlos had a mastiff as large as himself; only dogs of the Queen and her daughter were tiny.

1751. XVIIc. After 1637. Spanish. (Madrid, Prado.)

Velasquez. Surrender at Breda.

On his first trip to Italy, Velasquez traveled in the company of the Marquis of Spinola, younger son of an old Genoese family of bankers. Years later, from his memory of Spinola's account, Velasquez painted this picture, which the Spaniards call "Las Lanzas," and which is one of the great documents of military costume, as it varies between nations.

This picture shows the *condottiere* commander Spinola receiving Breda's second capitulation to Spain in 1625, after its long dramatic siege.

The difference between the slender Spanish silhouette and the clumsier one of Flanders is shown in the groups at r. and l. Spanish hair is short, though it may show the ear lock, neckwear smaller, waist long, breeches narrow; boots high, soft and tubular, with no plaque over the instep and the slightest of heels. The curling Dutch hair is longer, the collar spreads over the shoulders of a short-waisted doublet with shortening sleeves; wide full breeches fall into the

1750. XVIIc. 1635-8. Spanish. (Madrid, Prado.)

Velasquez. Infante Ferdinand of Austria Hunting.

Philip's brother, the Cardinal Infante, succeeded their aunt as Regent of the Netherlands. He was an able and energetic administrator and a formidable general, whose victory over Gustavus Adolphus saved S. Germany for Catholicism.

This picture of the Cardinal Archbishop of Toledo in hunting clothes must have been painted after Ferdinand's departure in

spreading cuff of a boot with high heels and great
stirrup leathers; military leather jackets in l. foreground.

1752. XVIIc. 1640-2. Spanish. (Louvre.)
Velasquez. The Conversation.
1753. XVIIc. 1647. Spanish. (Madrid, Prado.)
Juan Bautista del Mazo (figures by *Velasquez*).
View of Saragossa, detail of foreground.

Spanish court costume continued to develop in almost parochial isolation until jolted by the impact
of French fashion in 1660, at the marriage of Philip's
daughter to Louis XIV.

But soldiering in Flanders affected the clothing of
the Spanish army and, through them, the costume of
Spain outside court circles.

The rapidity with which Flemish styles spread in
less than a decade is shown by illustrations 1752-53.

In the "Conversation," locks are long, collars
spread, waistlines short, and boots show reversed tops,
boot-hose, stirrup leathers and higher heels, although
the *golilla* and pendant sleeve persist and there is a
certain restraint in the adaptations.

By 1647, in the "Saragossa" picture painted by his
son-in-law, with figures by Velasquez, the men of
military age wear flopping boots filled with boot-
hose; short-waisted, mandilion-like jackets and military cassocks hung cape-wise on the shoulders; gold-
laced capes.

The clericals and civilians wear long, somber,
caped and collared cloaks, great rolled black hats
without plumes, and small *golillas* or tiny band
collars.

The women's back hair is caught up into a specifically Spanish cylinder instead of the little bun
seen elsewhere; hair is falling loose on either side of
the faces of all the women in Europe, but here it is
concentrated in front of the ear, after the manner of
the lock which began to separate from the rest of the
hair in Spain in XVc. The Spanish bodice has a
bateau or round neck banded with scalloped lace;
easy, untrimmed sleeves which are often those of the
shirt; and a peplum which covers the circumference
of the Spanish farthingale (seen in its most exaggerated form in the court examples which follow).

1754. XVIIc. 1640. Spanish. (Chatsworth, Duke of Devonshire.)
Velasquez. Portrait of a Lady.
There are very few Spanish portraits of ladies
who are not members of the royal family; theoretically they still lived in oriental seclusion, though a
starving and seething Spain was greatly affected by
the loose-living soldiers, returned from Flanders.
Workmen wore swords like gentlefolk and a masked
lady was not offended at being mistaken on the
streets for one of Madrid's 30,000 prostitutes.

This wonderful creature, of whom he painted two
portraits, may have been Velasquez' own daughter.
As "The Lady with the Fan" in the London Wallace
Collection, she is the timeless quintessence of our
dream of the black-eyed, black-clad Spanish lady:
mantilla and fan, bared bosom and rosary, as Goya,
or even Zuloaga in the XXc. would dress her.

In the Chatsworth portrait, the gown worn with her black lace mantilla is a domesticated version of the court gown. The decolletage is masked with lace below the choker collar. The bodice has the dropped shoulder and divisions of the easy sleeve of Ills. 1626-27, stressed by braids with an uneven edge. The skirts of the bodice, divided like those of a doublet, extend over the supporting frame of the skirt.

1755. XVIIc. Italian. (R. Smith Barry.)
Florentine School. Saint Elizabeth of Hungary.

1756. XVIIc. Spanish. (New York Hispanic Society of America.)
Unknown artist. Portrait of a Spanish Lady.

1757. End XVIIc. Spanish. (London, Sir Charles Robinson.)
Carreño de Miranda (1614-85). Spanish Lady.

Like illustration 1754, these are no official Hapsburg portraits in state costume, though none could be more magnificent than the greenish-silver brocade gown (1756) pointed up with coral bows and jewels.

From the 40's we see the natural hair of unmarried Spanish girls parted at the side, looped across the forehead, caught with a pleated decoration, and combed out to hang free. The hair of the smaller princesses continues to be dressed in this way throughout Velasquez' day; but the frizzed hair of queens and their adolescent daughters flattens at the crown and widens at the sides into a decoration-studded creation of the utmost artificiality.

The bateau neckline of the 40's proceeds to become rounder and to be elaborated, both above and below the line of pearls, until it reaches the throat and covers most of the shorter-waisted bodice.

The sleeves of this Spanish gown are influenced to an unusual degree by the bombasted, paned and tied sleeves seen elsewhere from the 30's. The wrist ruffles with their fan-like sections are an interesting compromise between the old idea of pleating and the new sheer, informally gathered finish (1756).

The triangular earrings, characteristic of Spain since Moorish days, are elaborated like the tasseled cord-ends of a Spanish Cardinal's hat. The line of pearls at the neck is characteristic of important Spanish gowns. Pearl decoration gives the necessary emphasis to a dropped shoulder-line, which has to carry the spectacular sleeves. The accent of the massive brooches is repeated in the watches at the waist. The handkerchief of a lady becomes enormous in Spain by 1660.

1758

1758. XVIIc. Spanish. (New York, Metropolitan Museum, Frick Collection.)

Velasquez. Philip IV.

In this scarlet military costume and baldric, blazing with metal, which he wears in three Velasquez portraits, Philip makes his first concession to European fashion, except for his hair which he has gradually allowed to lengthen: wide scalloped collar, open button-edged jacket and slightly widened boot-tops over which lace is turned down.

Although in 1655-69 his dwarf, Antonio el Inglés, wears flowing hair, wide collar, short-waisted jacket, wide-topped boots with great spur-leathers, and a hat smothered in ostrich, Philip himself, depressed by the death of his wife in 1644 and of his son in 1646, reverted to his *golilla* and somber Spanish dress, which continued to be that of his tactful courtiers.

1759

1759. XVIIc. Spanish. (Boston, Isabella Stewart Gardner Museum.)

Zurbarán (1598-1664). A Doctor of Law at the University of Salamanca.

Modern academic dress has been codified from the mediaeval scholar's gown: cap fringed in green; brown gown with scarlet hood.

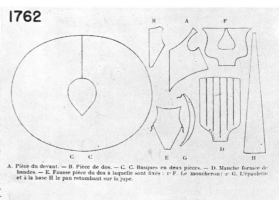

A. Pièce du devant. — B. Pièce de dos. — C. C. Basques en deux pièces. — D. Manche formée de bandes. — E. Fausse pièce du dos à laquelle sont fixés : 1° F. Le moucheron; 2° G. L'épaulette et à la base H le pan retombant sur la jupe.

1760-62. First quarter XVIIc. Spanish. (Paris, Worth Coll.)

Spanish court dress, and pattern.

1761. XVIIc. 1656. Spanish. (Madrid, Prado.)
Velasquez. Las Meniñas.

1763. XVIIc. c. 1652. Spanish. (Metropolitan Museum.)
Velasquez. Infanta Maria Theresa.

1764. XVIIc. Spanish. (Vienna, Art. Hist. Mus.)

Pupil of Velasquez. Mariana of Austria, Queen of Spain.

1765. XVIIc. 1664. Spanish. (Madrid, Prado.)
Velasquez. Infanta Margarita.

1766. XVIIc. c. 1680. Spanish. (Munich, Alt. Pinakothek.)
Juan Carreño de Miranda. Mariana of Austria as a Widow.

The death of Baltasar Carlos made it necessary to provide a new heir to the throne. In 1649, Philip married his niece, Mariana of Austria, a 15-year-old girl who had been intended for his son and was hardly older than his daughter, Maria Theresa.

Mariana, her German attendants and ways, were not beloved. When she shrieked with laughter at the antics of the dwarfs, her horrified Spanish Mistress of the Robes told her that etiquette did not allow sovereigns of Spain to laugh in public. Mariana and the King sat silent at the play, where he "did not move foot, hand or head, only casting his eyes about occasionally, nobody near him but a dwarf."

The Meniñas, whom we see with Velasquez, the German dwarf, María Bárbara Asquín and the Italian, Nicolasito Pertusato, were the Maids of Honor to whom was entrusted the care of the little Infanta Margarita, born in 1851. The king and queen are seen in the mirror, entering the room.

Margarita was followed by Philip-Prosper, twice painted by Velasquez, in skirts and in a miniature version of the latest European style to reach Spain, a decade or two late.

He lived only 4 years and was followed by Charles II, "the Bewitched," the calamitous end of too much Hapsburg inbreeding, who somehow contrived to exist for 40 years. Charles was so physically incapacitated that he had to be nursed until 6, could not be allowed to walk alone for years, and was always subject to fainting fits. He was too sickly to be educated, and it was impossible to keep him clean, but he was not actually unintelligent. When his illegitimate half-brother managed to have the Queen Regent banished to a convent and ordered the Infante's hair combed, Charles said, "Nothing is safe from Don Juan, not even vermin." It was during the Queen's two years out of power (during which she wore the nun-like mourning costume shown, c. 1680), that Spanish seamen in the Pacific, unaware of recent events at home, rechristened the Ladrone Islands as the Marianas in her honor.

The painter and male figures in the background of *Las Meniñas* wear the static costume of Philip's reign. Legend tells that Philip himself painted the red Cross of Santiago seen on Velasquez' breast; but the actual conferring of the decoration on the painter he faithfully loved for 36 years was delayed until 1659, while careful search discovered no Moor or Jew in the painter's ancestry and his position as royal painter was declared to be untainted by commercialism.

The development of the great Spanish gown from that of Isabel of Bourbon and Marie of Hungary, as the basque of its bodice spreads over the supporting frame of its skirts, can be seen in these examples and the Spanish ladies in Ills. 1754-57.

The ruff, which Isabel wore over an opened bodice in the 30's, disappears. The neck opening widens towards the shoulders, in a horizontal "bateau" neckline, seen particularly on young girls from the 40's. The neckline is stressed by a heavy edge of jewels or pearls above a deep hanging band of lace; a line of lingerie pleating (shirt) shows above the jewelled line. On women and adolescent girls, the neckline is apt to be more rounded, the inner pleating increased in width until it approaches the base of the throat; the lace band may be so deep as almost to cover the bodice.

The picadills at the shoulder become unified into a wing, which in turn is depressed into a dropped shoulder line.

The old +-slashed outer pendant sleeve is altered into a variety of vestigial pouch-like or strapped arrangements. The inner sleeve becomes fuller; its finish may be frilly, but in Spain it barely recedes from the wrist, although it is being shoved up toward the elbow elsewhere in Europe.

The cone-shaped Spanish farthingale becomes padded around the hips in the first quarter century to support the stiffened, shaped and extended skirts of the doublet. These are drawn out over an ever-widening frame, and the lines of the seams and divisions are dramatically stressed by asymmetrically edged galloon braids. On children's dresses, these braids are more apt to be tape-like, less differentiated from the gown material and applied in zigzag or diagonal patterns, or the gown may be cut on various grains of a striped fabric.

An appearance, at least, of superimposed skirts has always been favored in Spanish costume; this is still preserved as a fold or variation in direction of the pattern or trim at about knee height (1761-1765).

Below the accented line of the decolletage is set an immense jewelled medalion or brooch, often backed with ribbon or pleating. Caught diagonally across the bodice from sleeve to sleeve is a looped line of beads or pearls, related to the line on the decolletage, and often ending in another brooch caught on the sleeve. Folding fans, not gloves, are now indispensable.

The gowns of this period in Spain show a great deal of greenish silver with coral and darker greens, pointed up with black and gold. The *Meniñas,* for instance, are in silvery and darker green and in gray-green; the little Infanta in greenish silver; the female dwarf in blue-green; the male dwarf in red. In the 1664 portrait, Margarita wears a gown, the diagonal parts of which are of silver striped in coral, the horizontal parts in dark coral on light; the plume hanging down her hair at the right is coral; earrings, bows at neck and wrists and baldric of gold, with a line of black across the neckline. Other similar gowns are of silver and black, banded in gold at the neck, with a coral baldric and plum colored bows and plumes.

The Revolt of Minds and Men: XVIII Century

DEVELOPMENT OF DRESS: 1710-1795

EUROPEAN costume is henceforth French, except for a few years in the late XVIIIc. Even Spain succumbs, as the courts of Prussia and Saxony, Austria, Sweden and Russia slavishly copy France.

In England, characteristic and often very individual styles develop during XVIIIc. In the 1780's, possibly under the influence of great portrait painters, these styles take on a lovely simplicity which accords with contemporary French passion for Rousseau's naturalism. France is swept by a wave of Anglomania and English styles are supreme for the last two decades of the century. The differences between ceremonial or court dress, and ordinary wear, are defined. Our trousers, tailored cloth coats, and top-hats, make their appearance; elegance and good grooming actually go out of fashion among French and English men, as the Revolution approaches. Etruscan and Greek influences, felt in last quarter of century, will be reinforced by archaeological discoveries at Pompeii at the turn of the century, and by Napoleon's Egyptian campaigns in e. XIX.

The striking changes in costume during the XVIIIc. are seen in the heads of both men and women, and in the forms of women's skirts.

MALE DRESS

Hair. The full-bottomed wig, which dribbled powder over the chest of the coat and was a nuisance to active young men in the new military and naval services, is drawn back and got out of the way in a number of fashions. By the second third of the century, it is relegated to professional, or unfashionable elderly men. It continues to be worn by doctors, is last seen on bishops in mid-XIXc., although, like powder, it still appears in parliamentary and legal costume in England in XXc. But when, during a crisis in English affairs, Anne's brilliant young Secretary of State, St. John (Bolingbroke) appeared in a tie wig, the queen said he would probably come next to court in his nightcap.

Powder, used since Shakespeare's day, had begun to disappear long before it was taxed by Pitt, during the crucial flour shortage of 1795-1801. It last appears worn by an English eccentric of the 1840's.

Early in XVIIIc., the hair of the wig, which formerly stood in high points on either side of a part, begins to be brushed back from the forehead in a *toupet* (toupée), with "pigeon wings" from the temples: these develop into clusters of horizontal sausage-like curls by latter half century, the number of which is reduced to one by the final quarter. When the high padded and stiffened hair of women begins to collapse loosely, the hair of men's wigs (which have also grown high), loses its side rolls and turns into an analogous wide loose mass. Then, like women's hair, it is clipped into a combed out *hérisson* (hedge-hog) style.

The back locks of the lesser Ramilie wig are at first tied together at the nape of the neck by a black bow. Court style is always conservative. This fashion persists, as the successor of the full-bottomed wig, after the locks have become controlled in general wear.

Either they are enclosed in a black taffeta bag (*crapaud*) with a draw-string top; are braided or spirally wound about into 1-3 pigtails (which become very long c. 1740)—a favorite form in the army and navy; are clubbed into a *catogan,* at the end of third quarter; or fall into a couple of knotted locks.

Natural hair treated like a wig was not uncommon, and was often left unpowdered in everyday use; by 1765, this trend began to worry wigmakers.

Coats and waistcoats. The swelling which affects women's skirts, c. 1710, is accompanied by similar manifestations in men's costume during first half century.

Coats of knee-length, open or barely caught at the waist and worn with similarly cut, slightly shorter waistcoats, have already acquired a good deal of pleated side fullness in the skirts by the end of Louis XIV's reign. During first half XVIIIc., these skirts are held out by whalebone. horsehair, buckram or paper stiffenings.

In second half century, a profound change takes place in the cut of coats. It has been found convenient, at the very start of the century, to turn back and button up the corners of military and riding coats, after a XVIIc. Dutch fashion. This is exploited with great inventiveness in England, where coat fronts are affected and lapels also begin to develop.

In the final third of the century the skirts of all coats begin to be cut away in front, after this fashion, into a swallow-tailed frock coat (*frac*). The body of the coat hugs the torso; the side fullness of the skirts is reduced to a pleat or gore; the button, which has finished the top of the old fullness, retreats toward the back of the coat, as all the lines of the garment rake backwards.

Sleeves have grown longer in second half century. Their cuffs, large or small, open or closed, now become less conspicuous, as do the pocket flaps; and the neckline of the tail coat begins to rise into a standing collar. By 1778 the *frac* is adopted by Louis XVI, and persists far into XIXc. as official court dress, when it is otherwise quite outmoded by tailored cloth garments.

The waistcoat, following the lead of the coat, also becomes cutaway; but as the old correlation between coat and waistcoat lengths is abandoned, it is much shortened, into a vest.

Collars and lapels are emerging. In final quarter century, tailored cloth coats, often double-breasted, appear with lapels and turned-over standing collars. The waistcoat worn with these is a *gilet,* cut off square at the waist; it is also apt to be double-breasted and to carry lapels. The new short vests are sleeveless, their backs made of plain material, whereas the old long waistcoat, often sleeved and entirely embroidered, was worn at home as negligée with a nightcap, either alone or with a dressing gown.

The decoration of coat and waistcoat diminishes generally throughout the century, although the waistcoats of mid-XVIIIc. are often heavily trimmed with tassels and fringe. The long, back-slanting lines are particularly effective when completely untrimmed swallowtail coats are cut from narrowly striped satin. Plain cloths predominate from the 80's. Buttons increase in size and importance; earlier fabric-covered and embroidered forms are replaced by metal.

Overgarments. In addition to capes, there are many forms of loose buttoned topcoats and surtouts, such as the Roquelaure of the second quarter century. These tend to develop collars in second third of century, multiple capes during latter half, and to become fitted and double-breasted *redingotes* (i.e. riding-coats) in the period of English fashions, in final quarter.

The trend towards coachmen's clothes and ways in England is noted as early as Dec., 1738, when "Miss Townley" in the London Evening Post sees loose great-coats, called "wrap-rascals," dirty boots, and whips worn at the theater, not, as she had thought, by "a set of unmannerly, slovenly footmen sent to keep places," but by men she later saw paying for their box seats.

Breeches. The exposure of breeches as coats and waistcoats become shorter, and are cut away, requires a revolutionary method of cutting. Makeshift reductions of petticoat breeches had produced clumsily fitted, tubular breeches. These are now replaced by *culottes* cut on the bias, their legs springing apart like the open blades of a scissors. The diagonal cut is carried high in back for comfort. In front, the material which stretches across the thighs is sewed or buttoned onto a wide belt-piece, cut on the grain of the material to insure a trim waistline. The bottom of the breeches, which has been concealed by stockings rolled over the knee, is also made to fit; an outseam opening, buttoned like the front closing, or buckled by a band below the knee, allows the culotte to come down over the stocking, as it does almost universally in the latter half of century. As sleeves lengthen and cuffs become unimportant, similar buttoned slits will finish sleeve-bottoms, as they do today.

Smooth-fitting boots, reaching high on the calf, become an important component of English style in the 80's. Pantaloons of elastic materials, modelled on sailor's trousers, are drawn down to meet the boot-tops. It is difficult to tie them in place at the calf, and by 1793, they are extended to the ankle. On these pantaloons, a fly front or a pair of such openings replaces the buttoned closing of the culotte. A sharp division is being established between formal and informal garments. Boots and pantaloons were inadmissible at court. Their appearance at a coalition cabinet meeting in 1783 horrified Lord North, who was dressed in tail coat, culottes, and sword. The culotte, with its connotations of aristocracy, becomes a garment in which it is actually dangerous to appear among the pantalooned *sans-culottes* of the Revolution. It is retained as court wear in the XXc. Knee-breeches, instead of trousers, were still obligatory in small German courts, well into second half XIXc.

Footwear. The heavy jack-boot of XVIIc. goes out of use by second quarter XVIIIc., except on postilions who are constantly being called upon to help the coach out of the mire. They are replaced by closely fitted, delicate boots, and by many forms of fitted leather leggings, *spatterdashes,* and linen gaiters, buttoned up the outside of the calf. The old high tops, covering the knees, begin to be turned down, by the second third century, into an approximation of the boots worn by jockeys today.

The square toe of the Louis XIV shoe disappears by the first quarter century; its high tongue, during the second quarter, although red heels continue to be worn by the Macaronis of 1772. The shoe becomes a well-fitting pump of a natural shape. Its diamond, paste or silver buckles, larger in the third quarter, are retained in court wear, while what the manufacturers of Birmingham called "the unmanly shoe-string" began to replace buckles in everyday wear.

Hose. Stockings, with clocks embroidered in metal or silk, are commonly rolled over the knee of the culotte in the first half century and worn under the breeches in the second half. The mechanical stocking frame was modified, c. final quarter XVIIIc., to knit ribbed stockings, and striped hose, commonly in blue and white, begin to appear. The closing of the knee breeches over them may be laced, or finished with loops in the final quarter XVIIIc.

Hats. The hard, flat-crowned hat, cocked into a symmetrical tricorne, and commonly untrimmed except for a binding of metal braid, is carried in the hand or under the arm when the type of wig or toupet prevents its being worn. The Macaronis wore a minute tricorne slanting down their high-crowned wigs. The loops holding the cocks in place tend to relax, and the hard, flat hat to become much larger, higher and softer, degenerating into a bicorne in the final quarter, while one of the loops is elaborated into a pleated cockade. There have always been some round-brimmed, high-crowned hats: in final quarter XVIIIc., high-crowned hats, which develop into our top-hats, appear in England and are carried to France on the wave of Anglomania.

Linen. The Steinkirk has a long life in provincial wear, but is largely replaced, by the second quarter century, by a pleated muslin stock, fastened in back. The vertical gathers of the *rabat* are supplanted by the horizontally gathered *jabot* ruffles, matched by small wrist-ruffles. The waistcoat is open above the waistline, or only occasionally buttoned, in order to show the jabot ruffles. The *solitaire,* a black ribbon originating under the tie of the wig, is often folded about the neck, its ends crossed, pinned or knotted in front. The kerchiefs worn by women will be knotted about men's necks, late in the third quarter century, turning into *cravats.*

Accessories. Snuff boxes and toilet articles, muffs (enormous in final quarter century) and handkerchiefs, continue to be flourished and used in public. A gentleman still "pulls out his comb, curries his wig."

A sword is still a necessity in an inadequately policed and lighted world; it is commonly worn by gentlemen through the third quarter century; the shoulder-knot of ribbon which had helped to hold the XVIIc. sword-belt in place, disappears during first quarter XVIIIc. Gentlemen begin to tire of the sword in the third quarter, as legislation fails to prevent servants and workmen with egalitarian ideas from carrying swords. No longer worn in Parliament, swords went out of English use during the 80's except as part of court costume.

Canes, heavily knobbed with cloudy amber, become a mania c. 1710, and have a tasseled loop by which they can be hung from a coat button. Sword and cane are carried together, at first. Late in the century, quizzing glasses are often set in the head of a cane.

Utilitarian umbrellas of oiled fabric were used in bad weather in the Tatler's time; now they become fashionable. Appearing with the boots, great-coats, and top hats of the last decades they free gentlemen from dependence on coaches and sedan chairs.

Watches are still expensive, but in this era of conspicuous waste it becomes a fashionable necessity to carry them in pairs, or even as buttons, in series. Short vests allow pairs of fobs with dangling seals to be displayed against the long, pantalooned thigh; pantaloons begin to be held up with embroidered suspenders or braces.

Steel becomes more fashionable than precious metals during the 90's. It is used in buckles and fobs; it decorates buttons, in the fabrication of which all possible materials are exploited.

FEMALE DRESS

The extent to which the bondage of the *fontange* and the rigid gowns of late Louis XIV was resented can be seen in the rapidity with which they disappear c. 1710. This reaction is foretold by the flowing wraps of late XVIIc. The characteristic gown of the second and third decades XVIIIc. follows this impulse. It is a loose sacque (*contouche*) worn over a corseted bodice and underskirt; it is often open in front, sometimes sleeveless, and it flows behind in box-pleats from the shoulder. These pleats persist at the back of the bodice of the court *robe à la française,* and are even to be perceived in the back gorings of the bodice of the final quarter century's *polonaise,* two sections of which sometimes continue into the skirt.

But before discussing specific forms of XVIIIc. gowns, the outlines, determined by headdress and undergarments, must be defined.

Head. The death of the fontange was followed by nearly half a century of neat little heads, the hair cut 3-fingers long, powdered for ceremony, uncovered (especially in aristocratic use) or bearing tiny lappeted caps. Both cap and hair are surmounted, out of doors, by the pretty hoods so much admired by the *Spectator;* or from the 30's by pancake-like shepherdess hats.

Paniers and hair dressed low first appeared at Versailles in 1714, worn by two English ladies who were almost turned away from the king's supper because of their dress. Both styles appealed to the king; at mass the next day many headdresses had been reduced by three fourths in height. This amused uniformed persons, but upon the king's renewed compliments, was adopted by everyone at court.

In the 60's, both the hair mass and the caps covering it increase suddenly in size and elaboration. From 1740-85, *mob* and *fly* caps and the ruched *dormeuses,* enclose hair which, by the 70's, reaches a padded and powdered height, and an excess of decoration unheard of before or since. (See Appendix.)

The "head," pasted and pomaded over horsehair pads which may rise a yard high must be arranged by a professional. (An arrangement 72 inches from chin to top of hair, in 1772, is described by Lacroix.) As it remains untouched between the hairdresser's visits, one to three weeks apart, it usually becomes verminous.

The small shoulder curls previously seen in court wear now cover the shoulders. The back hair is clubbed into the Etruscan *catogan*. The crown of the head, feathered and looped with gauze, is topped by a fantastic clutter of decoration, which may include a sow with her litter, or a ship in full sail to celebrate the victory of *La Belle Poule* in 1778. These hair arrangements are protected out of doors by hoods like the *calash*, raised or lowered by fanwise supporting hoops, or by the gauzier *Thérèse*. In the daytime, equally ridiculous hats are worn, enormous or tiny and precariously tilted.

Differentiations are made between powdered formal or court coiffures, and the frequently unpowdered every-day arrangements; between the *bonnets* of ceremony, *chapeaux-bonnets* appropriate with both dress and walking costumes, and the equally elaborate but less formal hats, *chapeaux,* worn only in the daytime. An aristocrat of the second half XVIIIc. may find it necessary to change half a dozen times a day into costumes suitable for negligée at home, walking, riding, theater, supper, and the evening.

Large simple leghorn hats appear in England c. 1785, and largely replace caps. These wide straws arrive in France in the Anglomania of the last decades, together with beaver and other hats of masculine character. During the Revolution they are seen cocked, like men's, with the tricolor. Until the last decades, the tricorne is the hat commonly worn with riding habits.

In the 80's, the hair mass widens at the top and is squared off; then its support begins to be withdrawn. The hair, looser and wider in front, longer in back, may be a great mass of ringlets, in a *hérisson* (hedgehog), worn by men as well.

As powder reaches the end of its use, colored forms, blonde and red, appear briefly. By 1800, the head is again small, dressed in pseudo-Greek styles. Bonnets in poke shapes replace the great ruched hats which supplanted the all-enclosing ruched caps.

Skirt. The form of the skirt undergoes some five major changes during XVIIIc. The bustle and train of late Louis XIV are replaced, c. 1710, by a new form of the old farthingale. At first it is funnel-shaped and consists of a series of ever-wider hoops of wire, rattan, or whalebone, taped together from waist to hem, or run through slots in an ankle-length petticoat. Hoops come to be worn by women of every class, by working women, and even by nuns, of the more worldly sorts, such as canonesses of Remiremont and abbesses. (Mme. de Genlis). These hoops, covered by gathered ankle-length skirts, swell to the roundest possible form. It is almost impossible to gather up the hoops and skirts to pass through a door; stairs begin to be built wider to accommodate them. Around the middle of the century, hoops are often abandoned and replaced by stiff petticoats.

But mounting hair requires wide skirts for aesthetic balance. A new form of support is devised which gives an entirely different shape and motion to the skirt. It consists of narrow lateral wings, projecting over each hip. These *paniers,* made of several hoops, hinged and taped together, hang from the waist and do not fall much below the hipline. Seen from front or back, the skirts which fall vertically from this support are as wide as possible. From the side, the silhouette is very narrow. Pockets cut through the gathers of the skirts between the waist and the hips of the paniers, allow the wearer to slip in her hand, catch and raise the paniers. This method of support, seen early in Italy, is carried to its most extravagant six-foot width by Marie Antoinette from 1774. Its use in English court wear will be ended by George IV's command in the 1830's. All these supported over- and under-skirts are typically of ankle length; the split over-skirt of the *robe à la française,* worn with wide paniers, has a train. The short, gathered, white petticoat which serves as underwear is put on before the paniers and hangs close to the body.

The whole character of XVIIIc. dress comes from the limitations of motion imposed by wide paniers and top-heavy heads. The hooped petticoat gives a lovely, lilting movement to the skirts. The wide paniers give a more stately one, but the body must be swung to pass through a crowd or into the door of a coach. The roofs of sedans have to be hinged to enable the headdress to be got inside; the sedan can perhaps be closed again, if the angle at which the rigid lower bar of the panier can be tilted allows the lady to sink onto the seat instead of crouching. The head often had to be stuck out of the coach window, we learn from Mme. Campan. Even the motions of the arm are conditioned by problems of moving the elbows within the socket depression at the top of the skirt, between the waist and the rising tip of the paniers, and of removing them without clumsiness, when necessary. The most typical gesture of the XVIIIc. is the sweep of the bent arm in the carefully studied "exercise of the fan," while the elbows hug the body and appear to be supported by the paniers.

By 1780, the paniers grow smaller and c. 1785 are replaced, briefly, by hip-pads; then by the *tourneur,* a crinolined bustle, called the *cul de crin,* or, outside France, the *cul de Paris.* Although the *polonaise* worn with it is usually of ankle length, the bustle-supported skirts are, in general, longer and trailing.

Bodice. The bodice retains very much its XVIIc. form throughout XVIIIc. It usually has a stomacher, or an applied placard in that form, until the advent of the masculine coat styles of the last decades. The V may be filled, as in XVIIc., with a series of graduated bows; or be edged by a wide fold or ruching, running around the back of the high neck as a finish to the sides of the over-bodice, and continued down the front edges of the outer skirt, as it splits to accommodate ever-wider paniers. These bands, smoothly pleated *en platitude,* or shirred, may be laid on in straight or waving lines, on gowns which are apt to be of brocade or painted silk.

The bodice of the court *robe à la française* is actually fitted close to the body all around, but it appears to be corseted only in front. After the manner of the old *contouche* with its Watteau pleats, the fabric of the back of the bodice falls in pleats from the shoulder straight into the over-skirt. The short underskirt worn with this gown of the last half century is often quilted, or the petticoat has an embroidered border. The gathered lace *falabas* of late XVIIc. are a favorite trim of the first half XVIIIc., but the clutter of *pré-tentailles* tends to become *volants* of self material on the later petticoats.

The bodice is apt to fasten in front, under the fold which edges the outer bodice; but in latter half XVIIIc., back lacings in the manner of the English corset become common, and the lining of the bodice is apt to be boned along its gores, eliminating the corset. With the crinolined bustles, and multiple goring of *polonaise* bodices during the final quarter century, the waistline becomes shorter, aided by wide belts and fitted corselets.

Underwear has scarcely showed during XVIIIc. except as narrow ruffles. Tippets, scarves and fichus veil the bosom instead. This tendency increases during last half of century; great puffed and wired kerchiefs, *bouffantes,* appear with the short-waisted, trailing gowns inspired by English male styles. These are taken over by men, reduced to cravats, and in that form are returned to women's use.

By 1795, necklines are lower, shoulders more exposed, the waistline raised to a point just under the breasts; the sheer, naked gowns of the Classic Revival are beginning to be indicated.

Long, plain sleeves are seen at the beginning, and at the end, of the century; but the classic sleeve of the first half of century has an important cuff, pleated across the bend of the elbow or shaped; that of the second half replaces the cuff by ruffles, *engageantes.* In the final quarter century there are many deviations; puffed sections, *sabots,* appear which lead to the short, puffed cap-sleeve of the pseudo-classical gown.

Outer Garments. The hoods and scarves, tippets of sable or thin summer silk, capes, and long loose cloaks and coats like the *Joseph* of the first half century are apt to become elaborated during the latter half century. (See Appendix.)

There are elaborately gored short *caraco* jackets, pleated in back *à la polonaise;* fur tippets; *pelisses* edged with fur or eiderdown; and a great variety of greatcoats and *spencers,* based on riding or coachmen's coats in England, during the last two decades. These lead to coat-gowns of oriental inspiration: *lévites, circassiennes,* and to full, soft *chemises* of English muslin, which had been worn under them, but then appear alone. Combing jackets, short, completely enveloping, become a necessity and must also be charming; visitors of both sexes advise and admire, while the profes-sional hairdresser, on his regular visits, spends hours on his combined work of hair arrangement and millinery, during second half of XVIIIc.

Shoes and Stockings. Shoe and stocking colors tend to become lighter, until the last decades. Red stockings, common early in XVIIIc., become pale pink or green, and later white. High-heeled slip-pers and mules are of light colored silk, brocade, velvet or kid, embroidered in metal and colors. In the latter half of century, slippers, beautifully buckled or knotted, lose their high tongues. With the masculine styles for women, plain shoes of nat-ural shape, and even highlaced shoes with lower heels are worn, In the 90's, heelless satin ballet slippers with pseudo-Greek lacings appear; shoes are now apt to match the bright, light colors of yellow, blue or green gloves.

Accessories. Masks go out of English and French use during the first half of century, but con-tinue to be seen in Italy. Patches continue to be worn throughout first half century.

The most characteristic accessories of XVIIIc. are the beautiful painted folding fans; and bands around the throat (analogous to the *solitaire* of men) which requires ruffles, ruchings, and artifi-cial flowers when dresses become loaded with these decorations. Posies of real flowers, beloved since Elizabeth's day, are kept fresh at the corsage in a bottle of water, set in a pocket at the top of the corset.

The elaborate aprons of the late XVIIc. continue in use through first half of XVIIIc. For a brief period in the 1780's, while Marie Antoinette is playing milkmaid at the Petit Trianon, long, wide white aprons, with two big pockets and ruffles, are worn indoors and out.

Scarves, triangles and tippets, *palatines,* of lace or of very sheer gauze in dark colors, black, mul-berry or deep green, embroidered in metal and colored silk, preceded the great white muslin bouffant kerchiefs and fichus of final quarter.

Muffs, worn since XVIIc., are seen throughout XVIIIc., and increase, both in use and size, from the last decades into XIXc.

Silk gloves are supplemented by gloves and mitts of silk net, from about 1740. Short leather gloves appear with the redingote styles of the 80's. Long kid gloves increase in use during latter half century. In final quarter and early XIXc., their color tends to agree with that of the slippers.

Drawstring purses, in netted *babila* work, or decorated with needlepoint, appear in e. XVIIIc.; purses, often beaded, increase in use and variety into XIXc.

Thin canes, grasped in the middle, and the knobbed or gold-headed canes and crops which accompany the English-inspired styles of the last decades, are joined by long-handled parasols. These are often small, much trimmed with ruffles and fringe, but in final quarter, large, umbrella-like forms are fashionable.

Servants and working people strive throughout the century to emulate the rich in everything. So much imitation jewelry is sold that the names of leading manufacturers are still synonymous with the gold-washed brass jewelry produced by Pinchbeck, and the paste diamonds of Strass.

Such rivalry is never one-sided. Diamonds are more favored than pearls, but jewels decrease in importance as accessories grow more luxurious. The watch anyone can afford it still a dream, but it will be realized within the lifetime of many of the ladies and gentlemen who show off their affluence by wearing watches in fobbed pairs in the final quarter century. Watches and perfume flasks form part of the equipment of *châtelaines* and *nécessaires*. Charming boxes in opaque enamel on copper, or carrying pottery cameos, are available to anyone. But the snuff, patch and comfit boxes of the well-to-do, and the *carnets-de-bal* of final quarter-e.XIXc. are apt to be decorated with the newly invented machine-turnings, glazed with transparent enamels, and edged and monogrammed with diamonds.

Greek influence, felt during second half XVIIIc. and through the first quarter XIXc., brings cameos, seals and medallions. With miniatures, silhouettes and cyphers they are used on bracelets, fobs and necklaces.

Buckles and buttons become larger; buttons, though made of increasingly varied materials (see button plates) become, in general, more metallic. Crucible steel, a product of mid-XVIIIc., is still very expensive, and is a very fashionable metal at the turn of the century.

Fabrics and Decoration. Legislation instigated by the wool and silk industries during first quarter XVIIIc. tried to bar India cottons (worn at home and in the country by the aristocracy, and almost universally by everyone else) from both France and England. Acts half a century old had to be repealed to permit printing of fine domestic cottons, machine-produced by the new techniques of the third quarter XVIIIc.

The importation of fine linen from Holland and Germany was permitted, to support the export trade in English worsteds; and a great deal of this was worked by its wearers with embroidered sprigs inspired by the patterns of India painted cottons. But wool and silk were the chief wear of the second and third quarters of the century, with some striped, checked or plain domestic linen. English cottons combined a linen warp with a weak cotton weft until final quarter.

Gowns, at first relying mostly on line, become trimmed with fur, lace, ruffles and ribbons. The line in which decoration is applied tends to alter from straight, to serpentine, to draped. Satins are plain or striped. Silks are plain; changeable; striped (changing, roughly speaking, from narrow, to wide, to compounded and elaborated, then back to narrow); painted or brocaded in patterns, which loosen from heavy *candelabre* designs into sprawled and sprigged patterns of greater delicacy (sometimes between straight stripes or serpentine garlands and ribbons), much used in the *robes à la française.*

The petticoat shown under a split underskirt is apt to be embroidered in patterns which become diluted as they rise from a dense border, ruffled or quilted. The wide court gown of Marie Antoinette's time is more apt to be made of plain material, draped, ruched and pleated with gauzy decoration like that of the immense headdress.

In final quarter of century there is a flood of muslin and cotton fichus and gowns, plain or printed, produced by machine spinning and weaving, and either hand-blocked or roller printed, if patterned. Loops and drapes change into simple, gathered, flowing skirts of cotton or cloth.

Fashion Magazines. The magnificent *Monument de costume* of Moreau le jeune at the beginning of final quarter is followed by periodical publication of fashion plates, such as the French *Galerie des modes* and Heidelhoff's *Gallery of Fashion* in London, forerunners of the deluge of periodicals, filled with the latest styles, embroidery patterns and culture, for which the XIXc. is remarkable. Engravers exploit the new field of book illustration with careful attention to costume detail.

1767

1767. First Decade XVIIIc. French.
Claude Gillot. Italian Comedy.

Gillot, (1673-1722), painter-etcher-engraver-illustrator, was specializing in pictures of Italian comedy early in XVIIIc., when Watteau and Lancret became his pupils, and soon his rivals. Some of his costume plates were published as "Nouveaux dessins d'habillements á l'usage des Ballets, Opéras et Comédies."

This is Italian Comedy in its most sophisticated surroundings, at end XVIIc., with the gentry in stage boxes. Additional chairs were often set on the stage, but this usage became extremely unpopular; one intended for the duchess of Queensbury at Drury Lane in 1729 caused so much commotion that it had to be removed.

The Italian Comedy troupe in Paris, though more popular than the French company, was again banished by Louis XIV because *La fausse parade* appeared to be a satire on Mme. de Maintenon. "You have no reason to complain that Cardinal Mazarin tempted you from Italy. You came on foot, and you have made enough to return in your carriages." Under the Regent in 1718, the Italian players returned; playing in French, they were more popular than ever.

Italian comedy could be played anywhere, on a tennis court, in the courtyard of an inn, or from the tail of a cart in a public square. In London at Bartholomew's Fair, June 25, 1700, all "interludes, stage plays, comedies, gaming places, lotteries and music-meetings" were forbidden. But you could still "see a wonderful girl of ten years, who walks backward up the sloping rope drawing a wheelbarrow behind

her; also you will see the great Italian Master, who not only passes all that has yet been seen upon the low rope, but he dances without a pole upon the head of a mast as high as the booth will permit, and afterward stands upon his head on the same. You will also be entertained with the merry conceits of an Italian Scaramouch, who dances on the rope with two children and a dog in a wheelbarrow, and a duck on his head." (Malcolm: 1810.)

We see in the boxes a forest of fontanges and of high-peaked, full-bottomed wigs, only one of which is not powdered. To accommodate their height, cocked hats have deep crowns.

The three worldly abbés all wear short, powdered wigs, curled up at the nape and rolled back from the face in a toupet. Abbés are all very worldly now, and a great many are, in fact, not abbés at all.

Everyone is searching for a place; even starving peasants try to become begging townspeople. Position goes by rank and influence, except, to some extent, among the educated bourgeoisie. A member of the ruined provincial nobility is often indistinguishable from the local blacksmith with whom he gets drunk, except by his sword and his hunting rights. Everyone gambles and is in debt. "It is very vulgar to mind being in debt; debts are a proof and a confirmation of a man's greatness. It may be assumed that a nobleman who owes 2,000,000 is twice as great as a nobleman who owes only a million," as the Abbé Coyer said in his ironical "Bagatelles Morales." A nobleman seeks to "manure his fields" by marrying money; it is acceptable that he marry the widow of a rich tax contractor, but not that his daughter marry her son; a daughter for whom there is no dowry is shoved into a convent.

The eldest son of a noble family is destined for the army or navy; the services have three times too many officer applicants with the necessary four quarterings of nobility; no one can hope to rise from the ranks by merit.

The second son is sent into the Church, to capture as many livings, granted by court favor, as are needed to keep him in the best society.

The cadets scramble as best they can. "Whoever would, was a Chevalier, and whoever could, an Abbé—I mean a beneficed Abbé." They try to make themselves charming to useful people at court, who may help them to become what they pass for. Gramont was both the one and the other at the siege of Trino, when his brother let him loose upon the town

to shake off his rustic air. He so thoroughly gained the manners of the world that he says: "I could not be persuaded to lay them aside, when I was introduced at court in the character of an abbé. All that they could obtain of me was to put a cassock over my other clothes . . . I had the finest head of hair in the world, well curled and powdered (i.e. no wig as yet) above my cassock and below were white buskins and gold spurs. The Cardinal, who had a quick discernment, could not help laughing. Mother said, Well, my little parson, you have acted your part to admiration and your parti-colored dress of the ecclesiastic and the soldier has greatly diverted the court"; but she said that he must choose. He renounced the church "on condition that I keep my abbacy," and that his brother consent to keep him at school. (Gramont: Mémoires.)

1768. XVIIIc. French. (Metropolitan Museum, Print Room.)

P. I. Drevet, after *Hyacinthe Rigaud*. Bossuet.

Bossuet, a profoundly religious man, the greatest preacher in France until he became tutor to the Dauphin in 1660, was a moderate who dreamed of re-converting the Huguenots and Calvinists. He opposed the Jesuits who had done much to combat Protestantism, and who, with worldly expediency, were prepared to mitigate punishments after confession that might alienate the rich and important from the Church.

Non-resident higher clergy, fat with plural livings, left the care of their parishioners to parish priests so illiterate that one was found to be praying to St. Beelzebub. Mission priests and Sisters of Charity were established by St. Vincent de Paul to serve the poor in their world, not from the cloister.

The need for reform which had led to Protestanism was also felt by many Catholics, who found in Jansenism a way to be "Catholic but not Jesuit, evangelical but not Protestant"; religion was discussed with passion in drawing rooms; Catholics read the Bible like Protestants, encouraged by Bossuet.

Jansenism was declared heretical in 1653; the Edict of Nantes was revoked in 1681; Jansenist nuns of Port Royal were forbidden to admit new members

after the death of their patroness, Louis XIV's cousin, Mme. de Longueville. Bossuet, who had influenced Mme. de Maintenon, died in 1704 and the old king fell under the absolutist and reactionary influence of the Jesuits, La Chaise and Le Tellier. The latter had the Jansenist nuns of Port Royal expelled, their buildings razed, and the bodies in their cemetery thrown to the dogs. The Jesuits will give up their fine schools, use their missionary activities to become a rich trading company, and through abuse of power, will themselves be suppressed and expelled from France within a half-century.

Bossuet, for all his worth and goodness, was a much less interesting and successful tutor to the dull Dauphin, than his disciple, Fénelon, was to the Dauphin's brilliant, erratic son, Louis of Burgundy, for whose instruction the archbishop wrote the "Fables" and "Télémaque," and in whom he implanted many of the ideas with which Rousseau will alter world thinking in the XVIIIc.

We see Bossuet, as Bishop of Meaux, holding his scarlet biretta. He wears a plain band with his scarlet-lined ermine *cappa magna,* and shows the increasingly deep band of lace, sometimes forming half the garment, with which surplices and albs are bordered in late XVII-XVIIIc.

The princes of the Church, drawn from the aristocracy, live like princes. Some are men of real heart, like the Bishops of Auxerre and Boulogne, who sold their plate to feed their people during the famines of the first XVIIIc. decade; or the Curé of St. Sulpice, who kept only three dishes and slept on a borrowed bed. But the Cardinal de Rohan, the dupe of the Affair of the Diamond Necklace, born a prince and with preferments worth 2,000,000 livres a year, had his kitchen furnished with silver pots, and the point-lace border of his best alb cost 100,000 livres. He was sent to Vienna as ambassador to arrange Marie An toinette's marriage, but Maria Theresa was never able to have him recalled until after Louis XV's death. He spent immense sums, and dashed through Fête Dieu processions dressed in green and gold like the rest of his legation on the way to a hunt. The black market in smuggled silk stockings, operating from his secretary's office, sold more pairs in a year than Paris and Lyons together, Marie Antoinette told Mme. Campan.

1769. XVIIIc. 1708-9. French. (Metropolitan Museum, Print Room.)

Antoine Watteau. The Goddess Ki Mao Sao.

Watteau (1684-1721), son of a poor roofer of Flemish stock, came to Paris at 18. He was ill and poor from the start, never very well paid, and died early of tuberculosis. But he made fortunate contacts with painters and amateurs of broad knowledge, some of whom were very loyal; and the whole school of Louis XV painting: Lancret, Pater, Boucher and Fragonard, is based on his work.

After working with a scene painter who failed, and in a religious-picture factory, Watteau entered Gillot's studio during the latter's Italian comedy period. Forced out by Gillot's jealousy of his progress, Watteau began to study in 1708 with Audran, the curator of the Luxembourg Museum. Watteau's work was influenced by the architecture and gardens of the museum, and the Italian paintings in its collection, as well as by the graceful decorative *singeries* and *chinoiseries* in which Audran specialized.

The Goddess Ki Mao Sao is one of the characteristic products of this period in Watteau's work: its influence is felt by generations of designers, through Pillement to the textile printers of late XVIII-e.XIXc.

Watteau's pictures of camp life and soldiers, painted during a visit to his home at Valenciennes, also date from 1708-9.

1770. XVIIIc. French. (Metropolitan Museum, Print Room.)

N. H. Tardieu, after *Watteau.* Julienne and Watteau; cellist and painter.

Many of Watteau's paintings were preserved in the collection of the amateur, Jean de Julienne (c.1690-1766), and passed into the collection of the German emperor. Julienne is also responsible for the publication of Watteau's drawings, in the 4 vols. "Oeuvre," c. 1734, engraved by Cochin, J. & B. Audran II, Comte Caylus and Julienne himself.

The friends' wigs are reduced in size, less bushy, and end in curled locks. Coats tend to be plainer: in any case, these are specifically designed for work. The cuffs of the easy sleeves are closed except on Julienne's left arm. To eliminate friction as he plays, one sleeve is made without a buttoned cuff and is slit open.

1771, 1773-76. XVIIIc. French. (Metropolitan Museum, Print Room.)

Antoine Watteau. "Figures de différents caractères."

Two of the four volumes of Watteau's work published by Julienne are made up of 350 plates of the "Figures. . . ."

Watteau, better than anyone else, has preserved the spirit of the graceful, romantic, informal clothes worn between the periods of rigid formality of Louis XIV and the wired-out perkiness of Louis XV; the clothes shown in these engravings are, in any case, of the less formal type. These are young people at home, on a picnic in the country, walking or sauntering.

Hats are cocked, loosely and high, over deep crowns, because of wigs. But wigs flow in loose locks, ready to be tied back with a ribbon. Coats, with cuffs open or closed, hang loose and unbuttoned to display the waistcoat; this is still long, but grows disproportionately shorter as breeches are cut to fit. In some of the country scenes, amusingly gored and fitted short waistcoats with rippling short skirts, and long sleeves with slit ends, are worn with short capes, replacing coats: a sort of sports costume, worn with a short, almost bobbed wig.

In everyday use, the women's heads are covered by caps and turbans. There are little fur-bordered jackets. The material at the back of the bodice is laid on in characteristic "Watteau" pleats, flowing from the neckline into the skirt. In these flowing pleats, the informality of the loose sacques of the 1720's will remain, embalmed into XIXc., in the anachronistic formality of court gowns.

1772. XVIIIc. 1710. French. (London, Wallace Coll.)

Nicolas de Largillière. Louis XIV and family.

See also Color Plate on Box Label.

Nicolas de Largillière (1656-1746), though of French birth, lived with his merchant father in Antwerp and London during his childhood, and worked with Lely c.1674-8. He might have remained as court

painter to Charles II, but fled an anti-Catholic outburst in England to become an enormously successful painter of some 1500 fashionable portraits, male and female, in Paris. A predestined Academician, he eventually became its chancellor.

The ample succession, about which the king boasts, quickly vanishes. The Dauphin dies in 1711; both Louis of Burgundy and his eldest surviving son, the duke of Brittany, in 1712. A sickly baby, born during the year in which this picture was painted, is a last unpromising hope as the old king dies in 1715.

The king wears a richly laced suit with the old vertical pockets; the waistcoat completely closed; the coat buttoned at the waist. On him we see the full-buttoned court wig, hanging in front of the shoulders as well as behind, at about the zenith of peaked, woolly height.

Louis of Burgundy, in natural looking ringlets, dressed low and beginning to recede to the back of the body, wears a coat which also shows new trends in its velvet simplicity. It has heavy, horizontal pocket flaps and large buttoned-back cuffs, matching the waistcoat, which will tend to retain its richness although the coat becomes plainer. As wigs are bulky or high, the hat is apt to be carried rather than worn.

If he were not uncovered in the king's presence, the duke would probably still carry his cocked hat, edged with white plumes, under his arm.

All wear cravats. Young Louis' steinkirk is drawn through a buttonhole of his partly open waistcoat. The knotted ends of his father's cravat hang on his exposed shirt, as its waistcoat is open to the waist.

Stockings are drawn up and gathered to mask the bottom of breeches which are not yet well fitted. Shoes have high red heels and shaped tongues, turned down to show the colored linings.

The fontange is disappearing. The XVIIIc. is full of charming hoods, in endless variety of color and texture, which often cover the shoulders. Mme. de Maintenon, who is 75, has chosen a gauzy black one, gathered to enclose the face and veil the neck.

Before the rigid, bustled and furbelowed dress of the 90's is replaced by hoop skirts or loose sacques, it softens and becomes simplified, and is made of plain materials, often of velvet. The accent is on the front closing of the bodice rather than the V-shape of a plastron, although the V-closing is not lost sight of, and reappears. On Mme. de Maintenon's gown, this line is discreetly clasped together; on other gowns its delicately embroidered edges part, sometimes in

an informal diagonal or crossed-over line.

The child whose leading strings she holds is dressed almost exactly as his uncle had been.

1777. XVIIIc. French. (Former Coll. Sedelmayer.)
N. de Largillière. Lady and Child.
1778. XVIIIc. 1710-5. French. (Metropolitan Museum.)
N. de Largillière. Baronne de Prangins.

The Baroness and her husband were Swiss, who apparently lived for some time in Paris. A contemporary quatrain celebrates the luscious plumpness of the Baroness, amply demonstrated here in a white satin gown, with a gold-embroidered garnet girdle and red flowers. This is the large, serene, rather pop-eyed, goddess-like beauty of Louis XIV's period, soon to be supplanted by Dresden china delicacy and animation.

Hair continues to be dressed in high peaks with a curl at each temple for a time after the fontange is given up. It is dressed with jewelled clasps, a ribbon knot or flowers. Corsage bouquets are kept fresh by water bottles, in a pocket at the top of the corset.

Relatively undecorated gowns of plain fabric are caught about the body like dressing gowns, which that of the mother in Ill. 1777 may well be, as both sexes, all over Europe, spend much of their time, receive, and are painted, in negligée. The careless closing exposes the corset-lacings or a froth of lace on the chemise. The sleeves, too, are pushed up or clasped, almost at random.

1779. XVIIIc. c. 1715. French. (Versailles National Mus.)

R. Levrac Tournières. The House at Auteuil.

Levrac Tournières (1668-1752) was received into the Academy as a portrait painter in 1702, and an historical painter in 1716. He was an assistant professor in 1725; quarrelled with his colleagues, returned to his native Caen in 1750.

The cronies we see in this picture are (center) Prosper Crébillon (1674-1762), (right) Charles Du-fresny, Sieur de la Rivière (1648-1724), and (left) Bodin, the king's physician.

Dufresny, recipient of court sinecures from Louis XIV because of his illegitimate descent from Henri IV, collaborated with Regnard in a number of witty plays, and in 1705 wrote the "Amusements sérieux et comiques d'un Siamois," on which Montesquieu based his "Lettres persanes." Dufresny was uncontrollably extravagant, and instead of paying his washerwoman's bill, he eventually married her.

Crébillon père, son of a provincial notary-royal, had a period of great success at court as a tragic dramatist, followed by years of misfortune: the dowryless woman he had married died in 1707, leaving him with two children; his prosperous father died; his plays failed. He lived in bitter eccentricity, almost without food, endlessly smoking, in a filthy attic filled with animals and birds, until through the influence of Mme. de Pompadour, he was given various government posts (one of which was inherited by his novelist son) and a pension, and his later plays again became successful.

The full-bottomed wigs and clothes of Louis XIV's period are seen towards the end of their use. The crown of the full-bottomed wig is beginning to rake backward and flatten; its sides are breaking up into formal curls; it falls principally on the back of the coat. All three wigs are light brown.

The classic agreement in material of the waistcoat and the band trimming the coat cuff, arose from the usage displayed by Dufresny; his long gold waistcoat sleeve, slit at the bottom, is (or appears to be) turned back over the cuff of his gray coat. A red riding cloak is thrown over Crébillon's dark green coat. Bodin shows newer trends in his wig, and in his red-buttoned gray coat, the shaped fullness of which is massed farther toward the back. But all the breeches are cut in the clumsy old way. They agree in color with coats and stockings.

The serving woman, wearing a cap which is a modification of the old *fontange,* is dressed in red with dark green cuffs and a gray apron, in one of the simple wrapped-around gowns which preceded loose sacques; and a red and white petticoat of the stripes which are also much favored as overskirt linings in e.XVIIIc.

Green-painted walls with gilded mouldings; gilt chairs upholstered in darker greens.

ENGLISH COFFEE HOUSES AND FRENCH SALONS

Relationships between the sexes in society followed different courses in France and in England, during XVIIIc. The freedom of English women in Elizabeth's time had impressed foreign visitors; the implicit community of interest with men was not much affected by such tavern life as that of the "Mermaid" and Ben Jonson's club at the "Devil" where such women as appeared were of a different social level. But in last quarter XVIIc. Englishmen began to frequent the multiplying coffeehouses, which in the days of Queen Anne were largely monopolized by them. Coffee houses then became private clubs (some of which still exist), or remained as useful business adjuncts. Gentlemen go into politics, the military or naval service, or into business, and to the club and tavern, as never before. The segregation of the sexes increases; English women are left to the company of trivial men or of other women, as uneducated and without resources as they themselves usually are in XVIIIc. They pass the time with gossip and cards, tea and music, fashion and fine manners, shopping for clothes or china, and fall prey to the "vapors," an occupational disease of women who are bored and unoccupied to the point of hysteria. They have largely abandoned the fine sewing of their grandmothers but will be driven to other handiwork on the rather low level of *purfling* (unravelling), painting, cutting out, and pasting.

In France, increasingly repressive laws prevented any considerable unsupervised and unlicensed gathering of men, possible plotters against the monarchy. Large dinners could not be held, though small groups, like those led by Crébillon fils did meet at the *"Pelletier"* and the *"Caveau."* Cafés had begun to appear under the Regency but club life like that of England was never able to develop.

But a series of remarkable women appeared in France, after the death of the Regent, to carry on and perfect the salons which had begun in XVIIc. They were intelligent and competitive, witty or audacious, sometimes beautiful; many were born less to the aristocracy than connected with the higher administrative *gens de la robe,* the recently ennobled rich bourgeoisie.

There were completely aristocratic salons like the duke de Chartres' at the Palais-Royal, and the prince de Conti's at the Temple; salons of financiers like Grimaud de la Reynière, whose wife, nobly allied but not received at court, drew the court to her superb table. A salon filled with talent was presided over by a cook's beautiful daughter, Mme. Briffaud, whose husband was ennobled through the influence of Mme. du Barry.

The society which these women drew to their salons varied, but it was good of its kind, much of it risen by real capacity, and it was made up of both sexes. By the contrivance of women in salons, men became princes of the Church, ministers of state, members of the Academy, or were protected, as was Voltaire by Mme. de Richelieu to whom the Keeper of the Seals gave word of measures proposed against him.

One of the earliest XVIIIc. salons was that of Mme. de Tencin, d.1749, daughter of the president of the provincial parliament of Grenoble. She had been forced to take vows, but contrived to be released from them by 1714, and became a novelist. The suicide of one of her lovers in her own house broke up her earlier witty and dissolute salon. Literary men like Montesquieu, Marivaux and Fontenelle, whom she called "mes bêtes," and foreigners (like Chesterfield whom she was the first to entertain) enjoyed the good food and conversation of her later salon, in which she intrigued successfully to make her brother a cardinal.

Of Mme. de Geoffrin (1699-1777), who visited her death-bed, Mme. de Tencin said: "The cunning little woman has come to see whether she cannot inherit my property." In 1748 Mme. de Geoffrin, wife of a rich manufacturer, established a Monday dinner for artists and a Wednesday evening for literary men and the Encyclopedists at which the food was extremely simple; she entertained Walpole and Hume; the marvellous conversationalist, Mme. de Boufflers; and Mlle. de Lespinasse. Catherine of Russia tried to lure her to exhibit French intelligence and polish at St. Petersburg.

Her rival was the more aristocratic salon, from 1740, of the Marquise du Deffand (1697-1780), that intelligent "monster of wit," although her education had been "very irregular, very incomplete." Her original salon included Voltaire, Montesquieu, d'Alembert, the president Hénault, and the duchess of Choiseul. Becoming blind in 1754, she took Mlle. de Lespinasse as her companion, but broke with her on discovering that the companion was receiving her own friends at an earlier hour. The Encyclopedists

in a body followed Mlle. de Lespinasse. Whereupon Mme. du Deffand, bitter and spiteful, entertained no literary men until, at 68, she met Horace Walpole. It was to him, whom she loved with fantastic maternal tenderness, that she wrote her letters, in a prose that is "with Voltaire, the purest classic of its century, without even excepting any of the greatest writers." (Sainte-Beuve). To his care, she left her dog *Tonton,* who was "only vicious when beside his mistress."

There were others, like the overcrowded salon of Mme. Dupin de Forcalquier which Rousseau frequented; and that of old Mme. Doublet de Persan, who in 40 years never left her apartment in the wing of a convent, but learned everything, much of it "intolerably indiscreet," and sent it out over Europe in her "Nouvelles à la main," copied by her lackeys, despite the efforts of her nephew, the minister Choiseul.

1780. XVIIIc. 1718-9. French. (Metropolitan Museum.) *Antoine Watteau.* Le Mezzetin.

1781. XVIIIc. 1719-21. French. (Metropolitan Museum.) *Antoine Watteau.* The French Comedians.

Watteau's training with a theatrical scene painter and with Gillot gave him an abiding interest in the theater, dance and Italian comedy, which was perpetuated by his fellow-student Lancret, his pupil Pater, and the rest of his school.

Everyone is in love with the theater. From the court down, everybody acts. Every well-to-do merchant must have a private theater built into his house. Great ladies, who would not have spoken to an actor a century before, fight duels with each other over actor lovers, as ladies have already begun to do in England with the Restoration.

The Théatre Français is now installed in its own playhouse in the rue des Fossés; its sets and costumes in the style of Bérain with persistent and enormous court wigs and dramatic exaggeration. The wardrobe, as in England, is helped out by donations of royal robes of state.

In the center of the picture are the leading actors, Pierre Tronchin de Beaubourg (c. 1662-1725) and Mlle. Clairon (1670-1748), who still shout in the grandiloquent, posturing style detested by Voltaire, which will begin to disappear with Adrienne Lecouvreur and her successors.

To the left, the tragic figure of the Confidante weeps. Paul Poisson, as the comedy figure of Crispin, mounts the stairs to the right.

Mezzotino, one of the comedy servant-characters, whose costume is apt to be patterned, wears satin in the stripes which the e.XVIIIc. loved.

1782. XVIIIc. 1720. French. (Berlin, Charlottenburg Palace.)
A. Watteau. Gersaint's Signboard.

Gersaint was a picture dealer on the Pont Notre-Dame. It was in his arms that Watteau died, a year after painting him a signboard, of which we see both sides here.

It shows the costume of gentlefolk and of working people in all its grace and from many angles. Smooth little heads carry caps which are usually tiny. Flowing sacques, often sleeveless (4) hang in pleats or are bunched up in back (6). They are tied (9) or hang loose (13) in front. A low neck is apt to be filled in somewhat with a twisted cravat of the Steinkirk variety (9); the XVIIIc. is filled with scarves and tippets.

The locks of the gentlemen's wigs begin to be knotted at the bottom. Fullness in the coat-skirts is massed below a button at the waist of the side seam; an additional ripple between side seam and center back is provided by the cut (7). The skirts of both coat and waistcoat begin to flare (5). Pockets rise

1783

1784

1785

and are now always set horizontally.

The form of the shirt is shown on the workman (3). Coats worn by workmen are shorter and straighter, and their waistcoats almost vest-like (1). Béret-like striped caps, such as the one worn by (2) are seen on dancing gentlemen in the Lancret *fêtes champêtres* of the 30's.

1783. XVIIIc. 1722-4. French. (Madrid, Prado.)
   N. de Largillière. Infanta Anna Victoria.

1784. XVIIIc. c. 1724. French. (Versailles, National Museum.)

Att. to *A. S. Belle.* Anna Victoria, daughter of Philip V.

The bride intended for Louis XV was his cousin, the Infanta, b. 1718, who was sent to be brought up in France in 1722. She thought that the king was handsome, but that he talked no more than her doll. The young king's state was in every way so disquieting that it seemed advisable to marry him immediately to someone able to bear children; in 1725 the too-young infanta was returned to Spain.

We see her in a French gown of jewelled satin and lace, with her parted hair dressed high in points and *favorites* at each temple. The other dress is a modification of the heavily braid-trimmed basques of XVIIc. Spanish court costume.

1786

1787

The small uncovered head of the upper classes in e.XVIIIc. is trimmed with bouquets, delicate garlands and small bows; in court wear, a curl is usually brought over the shoulder.

1785. XVIIIc. French. (Versailles, National Museum.)

A. S. Belle. Catherine Elénore Eugénie de Béthisy and her brother, Eugene Elénore de Béthisy.

Mlle. de Béthisy wears a gauzy embroidered apron, its bib in the form of a stomacher, over a simply cut gown of brocade. Its heavy pattern shows an admixture of Far Eastern motifs. With hair dressed high and a fan, she is dressed like a grown woman.

Her brother, still in diapers, wears approximately the same braided gown we have seen on Louis XIV's grand and great-grandsons; the plumed turban has altered into a form of embroidered man's nightcap.

1786. XVIIIc. c. 1725. French. (Florence, Pitti Palace.)

J. F. de Troy. Louis XV and his sister.

Both *Vanloo* and *de Troy* belonged to dynasties of French painters.

Nicolas de Troy had sons, Jean and François; and the latter, a son, Jean-François (1679-1752), who studied in Italy and became an Academician on his return. The Cochins and other engravers have reproduced his paintings.

The Vanloos of Aix were Jacques; his son Louis; the latter's sons: Jean-Baptiste (1684-1745), and Carle-André (1705-65); and their nephews, Louis-Michel and François (the latter of whom died young while studying in Italy, together with his uncles). J-B. Vanloo painted important portraits in England, 1734-42.

Carle Vanloo, while at Turin, married the daughter of a musician named Sommis. Mme. Vanloo had an enchanting voice and did much to popularize Italian music in France; a picture by Vanloo at Versailles shows the family group exercising their various talents. Diderot says that Vanloo, an Academician in 1634: "could neither read nor write; he was born a painter as one is born an apostle."

Louis' full-skirted court costume, of plain material, with small buttons and deep, open cuffs, is more elaborately trimmed than ordinary dress. Braided seams have almost completely disappeared except in livery wear; delicate embroidery now follows edges and outlines pockets, as it will continue to do on coats as long as embroidery is used, and on waistcoats and occasionally on vests, into XIXc. With the conservatism of court wear, Louis is shown in a full-bottomed wig; handsomely clocked stockings; square-toed, red-heeled shoes, buckled high over a square tongue. The wig and shoes of everyday wear are shown on the suitor in illustration 1788.

The little princess wears an embroidered and lace-edged gauzy apron with a stomacher-shaped bib, over a trained dress of heavily patterned brocade; hair drawn high and dressed with small flowers (1786).

1787. XVIIIc. French. (Versailles, National Museum.)

J. B. Vanloo. Maria Leczynska, Queen of France.

The health of the five-year-old orphan who became Louis XV was so poor that it was not considered safe to subject him to much education. He became a neurotic child, silent and willful, badly brought up and malicious, who tortured his servants and threw messy food at people who bored him. His chief amusements were hunting, cooking and embroidery.

His health improved at adolescence, but it was thought advisable to have him marry immediately. A census was made of 100 suitable persons; nearly half were over 24; about a third were too young; 10 were too poor. The list was narrowed to 17, and eventually reduced to the Regent's sisters and the English princesses; but Anne of England refused to become Catholic, and one of the Bourbon princesses became a nun.

A princess who had been discarded as too poor was the eventual choice. The 21-year-old daughter of Stanislas Leczynska, exiled King of Poland, had been hidden in an oven, lost and found again in a stable, during her parents' flight. Going to her wedding she was almost drowned in the mud through which her coach drove.

The population was starving, but the courtiers wore stockings of pure gold thread, costing 200 livres, at the wedding, and the king was dressed in gold brocade with diamond buttons and a mantle of gold *point d'espagne*. The new queen gave away the contents of a velvet coffer of jewels she had received, saying that it was the first time in her life that she had ever been able to give presents. (Comte Fleury: *Louis XV et les petites maîtresses,* Plon, Nourrit, Paris, 1899.)

Louis, who had never shown any interest in women, was charmed with his wife. Unfortunately, she was very inhibited and in her own way as neurotic as he. She was afraid of ghosts, had to be read to sleep, slept under so many comforters that the king could not endure it, and got in and out of bed all night long to look after her dog.

She was a worthy and devout woman but, as her father said, she and her mother were the two most boring queens he had ever met. While her father reigned as Duke of Lorraine, his daughter bore Louis some nine children, and lived as much as possible in the three little rooms of her private apartment. The king, when he had to visit her, killed flies on the window pane. The burden of trying to amuse the newly awakened boy, who was never amused by anything, fell on a succession of mistresses: the whole series of the sisters de Nesle; Mme. de Pompadour who succeeded longest; and Mme. du Barry, as the king's taste descended the social scale.

The queen passed her time with a clavichord, music, and books; a little print shop; painting and drawing materials; a spinning wheel, loom and embroidery frame. She once decided to make four panels for a Chinese room. She actually filled in only some of the simpler parts of the background; her teacher stood at her elbow, directing every stroke, and repaired her work while she was at mass. As "her

own work," she bequeathed the panels to the Countess de Noailles, who built a new pavilion to house them, and had written over the door, "The innocent falsehood of a good princess." (Mme. Campan.)

The queen's gown also shows court conservatism. It is of brocade in a heavy *candelabre* pattern, but while it is worn with hoops, its overskirt is caught back, though only once, in a way reminiscent of the bustled dresses of Louis XIV's court. A trailing cloak, semé France and lined with ermine, is carried by a turbaned attendant; braid applied on sleeves of coat below shoulder indicate its livery character.

Like the lady in the following illustration, the queen's very short cap sleeve is pleated into the armseye, although in court wear the lingerie of the lower arm is formally pleated. The fitted bodice of this period is smooth and round, with the form of the old stomacher sketched upon it, by a series of graduated clasps or bows, or, particularly in the case of children, by the transparent V-shaped bib of the apron.

1788. XVIIIc. French. (Berlin, Kaiser Friedrich Museum.) *J. F. de Troy.* Déclaration. (1724)

The lady wears a sacque of wide-striped brocade, falling loose from the shoulders in front pleats, and unbuttoned low to show the bow-trimmed corset: short sleeves cartridge-pleated into the armseye; flower studded hair; bracelet of black ribbon with a medallion; mules.

The suitor shows an interesting, deep, open cuff on a stiffly flaring coat with high-set pockets. The large buttons of Louis XIV are replaced on the plain coat and brocade waistcoat by a multitude of much smaller ones. Breeches finished with a band fit smoothly over the stockings. Shoes have a much reduced tongue and heel, and small oval buckles. The wig is tied back with a bow, from which the ribbon of the *solitaire* surrounds the stock.

1789. XVIIIc. French. (Met. Mus., Print Room.) *Jean Pillement* (1727-1808). *Chinoiseries.*

1790. XVIIIc. French. (Metropolitan Mus., Print Room.) J. J. Avril, after *Pillement*. Baroque Flowers.

1791. XVIIIc. French. (New York, Cooper Union Mus.) *Pillement*. Fleurs Idéales.

1792. XIXc. 1830-70. English. (Metropolitan Mus.) Roller printed cotton: pheasants and palms.

1793. XIXc. 1837-51. English. (Metropolitan Mus.) Printed percale.

Persistence of the influence of Pillement, and of the motifs which inspired his delightful designs, of which the strange greens, brickish pinks, and yellows should be looked at in their original form of raised and colored engraving. Their effect, further debased, is still visible in XIXc. cottons.

1794. XVIIIc. 1728. French. (Metropolitan Mus.) *B. Picart*. "Enée et Lavinie," by de Fontenelle.

1795. XVIIIc. 1734. French. (Versailles National Mus.) *J. Raoux*. Marie Françoise Perdrigion (Mme. Etienne Paul Boucher d'Orsay) as a Vestal.

In the course of a quarrel with the chevalier de Rohan, Voltaire was imprisoned in the Bastille; on his release in 1726, he exiled himself for two years in England where he came to know all the important

literary and theatrical figures. The English stage of
the Restoration owed much to France; Voltaire returned with fresh ideas from England.

The tradition of boxes built and spectators seated
directly up on the stage as a part of the decor lost
force earlier in England than in France. A stage occupied only by actors was one of the English ideas
imposed on the French theatre by Voltaire; groups of
extras "dress" the sides of the stage in the tragic opera
by LeBovier de Fontenelle and Colasse, while the important action takes place in the center, against effects of belching smoke and fire, monsters and
emerging deities, which were a legacy from XVIIc.

But in the rivalry between Crébillon père, backed
by Mme. de Pompadour, and Voltaire, the exaggerated horrors of the former's tragedies were replaced
by the more reasonable stateliness of Voltaire's. A
whole generation of comparatively simple, natural
actors arose, and stage costume began to be affected
by the pretty simplicity of every-day dress. The stark
simplicity of Mlle. Perdrigion's satin gown is more
theatrically effective than plumes, scrolls, lace and
fringe inherited from Louis XIV.

1796. XVIIIc. French. (Metropolitan Mus.)
   J. B. J. Pater. Comical March.

1797. XVIIIc. French. (Paris, G. Petit Coll., formerly J.
   Fairfax Murray.)
   Nicolas Lancret. Danse champêtre.

1798. XVIIIc. c. 1730. French. (Washington Nat. Gall.
   of Art.)
   N. Lancret. La Camargo Dancing.

1799. XVIIIc. French. (Detroit Inst. of Arts.)
   N. Lancret. Breakfast of a Hunting Party.

Lancret (1690-1743) and Watteau were fellow students with Gillot. The enormously prolific lesser
painter outlived Watteau to become a successful
Academician.

Pater (1695-1736) was a pupil of Watteau, dismissed and then sent for again for a month's instruction when Watteau knew he was dying.

Marie Anne de Cupis (1710-70), who danced under the name of her Spanish grandmother, Camargo,
made a sensational debut at the Paris Opera at 16.
She had an enormous repertory and was the first
dancer to shorten the ballet skirt, to show her tiny
feet, which made the fortune of her shoemaker.
Everything she wore was copied; there was an epi-
demic of fashions *à la Camargo.*

The diagonal closing line, shown on the bodice of
Mlle. Perdrigion's bodice, is indicated on La Camargo's costume by a rope of its flowered trim.

Ladies' "sportswear" in the 30's is of three sorts:

Many wear jackets with slashed, flaring peplums
(1797,A; 1798,B). These usually have long, plain,
close-fitting sleeves; a wide, low neckline; and a bodice trimmed with a series of graduated bows. They
are worn with short, hooped skirts, which are usually striped in some way; woven stripes are used vertically (1797,A); braid stripes are applied horizontally at the hem or around edges (1798,B). When
two skirts appear, vertical stripes are used on the
underskirt (1797,E) or as a lining to the underskirt.

For riding, women wear men's coats and waistcoats, cut with an exaggerated flare, and men's tricornes.

Women also wear ordinary dress in the country: a

1800

smooth bodice, laced in back (1798,F); sleeves of elbow length, finished with ruffles (1798,F and K). A
ruche about the neck (1798,K) is often worn with
this dress. The hair is dressed up, formally, and may
even be powdered.

In "sportswear," men of the 30's often replace the
coat with a cloak (1798,A and G), worn over a but-
toned-up waistcoat with little skirts—almost a jerkin
(1798,E), often made of striped material (1798,G).

Or, coat and waistcoat are worn unbuttoned over
the full shirt, and easy breeches are actually laced
along the outer seams, with ribbons which are knotted above the knee (1797,C).

The hat most usually worn with these outdoor
country costumes is a sort of beret (1798,C), often
striped and finished with a rosette (1797,D; 1798,A
and G). Other hats are casually cocked (1798,E)
with a ribbon rosette, or trimmed with cock feathers
(1797,C; 1798,H). All forms are worn over short
wigs, usually not powdered, or over the bare, clipped head. In male riding dress, however, there is no
such informality; tricornes are worn with the wigs
and *solitaires* about the stock; fitted, flaring coats and
waistcoats.

1800. XVIIIc. 1731. French. (Louvre.)

J. Dumont. Mme. Mercier, nurse of Louis XV, and
her family.

A typical upper-class family in the XVIIIc. is fairly certain to have put some of its children into the
Church. The abbés and abbesses of Mme. de Genlis'
time mingle freely in society, keep carriages, entertain people of both sexes, and wear fashionable dress:
hoops, paniers, and powdered wigs, although usually
in a black-and-white, ermine-trimmed version. The
abbé is differentiated by his band collar and by his
comparatively short untied wig (E).

We see a variety of styles, appropriate to the ages
of the wearers.

The fashionable son (A) wears a wig with

pigeon's wings at the sides, and the long wound pigtail preferred by officers. His coat has the fullest possible stiffened skirts, their seam left open on the
right side to accommodate the sword, and caught together by occasional buttons (A,G). The edges of his
coat, and even its seams, are delicately embroidered.
But there is an unmistakable difference in the way
in which the XVIIc. braided style persists, almost as
a ghost, on the coat of this gentleman, while it is
heavily emphasized all over the livery coat of the
kneeling valet (K). Like his father (G), the young
man wears the muff of first half XVIIIc. slung from
his belt. His breeches close at the knee by tasseled
laces; handsomely clocked stockings are worn with
low-cut, low-heeled shoes of natural shape.

The youngest son (B) wears his *solitaire* tied under the chin in a bow, after a manner seen to 1750.
His waistcoat is stiffened, but as his coat is cut to
hang wide open in front, the sword does not have
to be stuck through its skirts. Pocket flaps have
mounted to the waistline.

The father carries both stick and sword, and
wears a dignified full-bottomed wig; but its top has
flattened, and its ends are knotted, whereas the wigs
of the younger men are drawn back and tied at the
nape.

Mme. Mercier (D), like her younger daughters
(F,I) wears a flowing sacque, open to the waist. The
sleeves of D and F have cuffs shaped at the bend of
the elbow by horizontal pleating; (I)'s sacque has
long, fitted sleeves.

The younger the woman, the more simple does the
treatment of her dress and head become. Mme. Mercier covers her hair with a cap; she wears a ruche
about her throat, and a fur tippet. The somewhat
younger woman (I) has a little frilled lappet hanging from hair dressed in curls at the side and a bun
in back. The ribbon with a jewel about her throat,
the embroidered scarf, the drawstring bag for her

1801

tatting, and her high-heeled, embroidered mules with peaked toes are characteristic of this period. Her gown is of a sprigged brocade; that of (H) is plain, but heavily trimmed with a garland. The hair of the youngest girl (F) is simply drawn up with a posy, and her completely plain sacque has a finished armseye. The sleeves we see are fastened to the undergarment.

1801. XVIIIc. French.

Nicolas de Larmessin, after *Lancret*. The Four Times of Day: Morning.

It is quite suitable to pour out the breakfast cup for a visiting abbé, in negligée: little cape or combing jacket, chemise, corset, brocade or embroidered petticoat and mules.

The maid brings a lace-lappeted cap. Servants, bourgeoises and older women now wear caps, but the cap is still primarily middle-class or domestic.

This is a well-to-do bourgeois household, but so young and pretty a mistress would wear a cap only with negligée. After she is dressed, her head will be bare, except for flowers.

The abbé, who keeps his hat under his arm, is almost certainly dressed in black, since he is probably making capital of his status. Except for his band collar and the comparative shortness of his toupeted wig he is dressed like any other man.

The floors are of inlaid woods; the walls hung with striped paper. The large sofa has the asymmetric back of Louis XV furniture. The dressing table, hung with sheer embroidery and littered with pretty toilet things, is here still essentially the table and mirror of Louis XIV. Inlaid tables with cabriole legs, drawers, and mirrors which fold down appear under Louis XV. Occasional tables appear with the advent of tea, coffee and chocolate, and pretty china cups, which do not yet have handles.

1802

1803

1804

1805

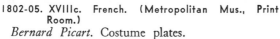

1802-05. XVIIIc. French. (Metropolitan Mus., Print Room.)
Bernard Picart. Costume plates.

1806-09. XVIIIc. 1735. French. (Metropolitan Mus., Print Room.)
Edmé Bouchardon. Cries of Paris.

Interest in exotic costume, aroused by explorations in late XVI-e.XVIIc., became extended to variations in costume in different parts of near-by countries, and by mid-XVIIc., to everyday life and common people near home.

Picart (1673-1733) was a Frenchman who worked in Amsterdam as well as Paris. He records such variations as the costume worn by pious girls under Jesuit supervision at Antwerp, who are dedicated to virginity until marriage and to the care of their parents during illness; a peasant girl in the costume of Brabant; a milk-seller on the outskirts of Paris; and a water-vendor of the city itself, in e-XVIIIc.

Nothing can equal the teeming life of London as Hogarth shows it, but at about the same time, Bouchardon's various series provide the best illustrations of the people of Paris streets.

The bewigged shoe mender is preparing to replace buttons on high spatterdashes which close by a series of pointed tabs.

The drink-vendor shows a diagonally closed coat. If left unbuttoned, its flaps would approximate lapels. These will not appear in France until late in the century, but the idea is germinating everywhere.

The poor Auvergnat knife-sharpener wears one old pair of thick stockings over another, thrust into backless slippers.

The hooded proprietress of the magic lantern carries a bodice, the boned goring of which is actually made decorative.

1810. XVIIIc. 1739. French. (Louvre.)
François Boucher. The Breakfast (detail).

1811. XVIIIc. 1743. French. (Metropolitan Mus., Frick Coll.)
F. Boucher. Portrait of his Wife (detail).

Boucher (1703-70), son of a designer of embroideries, was first trained as an etcher-engraver-illustrator, and executed some of the finest plates in Watteau's "Figures de différents caractères." His later studies in Italy affected not only his painting but the course of XVIIIc. book ornamentation. He became a successful painter on his return in 1731, was made Inspector of the Gobelins Factory, and in 1765, court painter. Besides portraits of Mme. de Pompadour, he executed large decorative projects to her order.

Both rooms show the charming interiors in which the well-to-do bourgeoisie live under Louis XV. The family breakfast takes place in front of a great mirror, panelled in blue-green and framed in gold, set over a pink marble mantle against coral-painted

1812

walls, and reflecting a blue-green door. The floors are inlaid parquet.

Furniture is light and comfortable, caned or upholstered; its lines are flowing and graceful; upholstery has lost the heavy brocaded patterns and colors of Louis XIV. Upholstered *bergère* armchairs or chaises longues with fat cushions and plump footstools have the same curved cabriole legs which are shown on an infinity of little night, tea, sewing and dressing tables, and on the chests of drawers, commodes, and consoles, which often have marble tops.

The breakfast chocolate is being drunk from a table in red and black lacquer. There are all sorts of standing and hanging shelves and cabinets to hold bits of oriental porcelain, trinkets and books. There are ormulu clocks and candles in scrolled gilt sconces.

Light screens fold in the old way, or are set on poles, particularly in England. They are papered, embroidered, painted or lacquered in bright colors and scenes, and are set against painted or papered walls.

A little girl plays with the toys which French middle-class children now enjoy, while the family breakfasts. Her beautifully dressed "baby" is propped against the cushioned footstool. The child wears a charming *bourrelet,* a padded cap, in lemon yellow, pink and white, and a bright, deep blue *robe à la française* with short cuffed sleeves (see Ill. 1810).

Watching her, a lady in white wears a short coral colored sacque and little black velvet hood over a lace cap set over a bunch of rosebuds. Baby in deep rose, sits on the lap of its mother in deep, rich blue; her

hair still cut rather short, and massed in rolled curls in back; black velvet bows at wrist and throat, tied with pink bow. Man with lightly powdered hair which appears to be his own, carefully dressed, wears a pistachio-green coat with an open cuffless sleeve, and a shirt in a greenish-yellow off-white.

Mme. Boucher lies in an enchanting white muslin negligée, with rose ribbons on cap and neck ruching, and a rose bodice trimmed with the shirred bands which are a characteristic decoration of second to final quarter century. A rose velvet workbag lies on the footstool, and her *chatelaine* watch is hung on the wall as a boudoir clock.

1812. XVIIIc. Before 1744. French. (Met. Mus., Print Room.)

P. L. Surugue, after *Chardin*. Card Tricks.

J. B. S. Chardin (1699-1779), son of a Paris woodworker, studied with Cazes, Coypel and J. B. Vanloo, and exhibited his wonderfully realistic still-lifes outdoors in the Place Dauphine. His first wife, who also came of working people, died in 1735, leaving him with two small children. In 1744, he married Marguerite Pouget, a well-to-do bourgeois widow, thrifty and intelligent. She took admirable care of his finances, and became like him, the intimate of Diderot, Rameau, Cochin and Aved. It was the latter fellow-artist who is supposed to have teased Chardin into portraiture, saying it was not so easy as painting sausages. Chardin became the most notable painter of the bourgeoisie in the intimacy of their homes; he became an Academician in 1728, and later its treasurer.

The bourgeoise will not join church and nobility in political power, as the Third Estate, until final quarter XVIIIc. It is now divided into three envious grades, many individuals of which are succeeding in rising above their original status.

The *gens de la robe,* judges and parliamentarians, administrators, tax-collectors and financiers, are rich and powerful. But even when recently ennobled or allied with the aristocracy by the marriage of their women, they are not received at court. Rather than risk rebuffs, they dine, discuss and play cards among themselves in a stiff, formal and rather heavy society. Their wives' imitations of Versailles fashions are apt to be tastelessly exaggerated. Because they are diligent, competent, respectable and home-loving, make money and pay bills, the thriftless and indebted aristocracy has mocked them from Molière's time: *Laissons les bons bourgeois se plaire en leur ménage.*

They are envied by the comfortable minor officials and tradesmen below them. These, in turn, are hated by the fermenting mass of workmen, servants, peasants and beggars.

In a household in the comfortable middle section of the bourgeoisie, we see the wig with pigeon's wings at the ears, tied high above the nape of the neck; that of the young man is encased in an oblong bag. His high tricorne has an irregular laced edge. The plain coat, trimmed only by buttons, has a standing collar, easy sleeves with large closed cuff, full skirts with the pocket flap set at the natural waistline. Breeches are closed both by buttons and by a buckled band with a long fringed end. The buckled closing is stressed on the shoe, its tongue and heel low.

The boy is just back from school, with drawstring bag and triangular striped apron tied about him, its bib-end caught in an upper coat button. His sister, in a ribbon-trimmed cap, shows the familiar reversed position in which the triangular bib is set on a girl's apron, following the line of a stomacher.

Typical light-weight, everyday chair of Louis XV, with decorative ladder-back slats and rush seat; tile floor; rug used as a table cover, in the manner of the past two centuries.

1813-14. XVIIIc. c. 1744. French. (Louvre.)

J. B. S. Chardin. Grace Before Meals (1813). The Industrious Mother (1814).

The typical bourgeoise head is always covered by some form of cap or hood. The child with folded hands wears the padded *bourrelet* (or *bourlet*), bound about the head by a protective sausage roll; it is usually brightly colored, and is worn over a close white cap.

Bourgeois women and children of both sexes wear aprons, often colored; those of women have a small square bib. White fichus cross at the bosom of plain

or striped dresses; cuffs are pleated across the inner elbow. While men's shoes are becoming plain, buckled black pumps, these housewives go about their work in pretty embroidered slippers and mules with pointed toes and the highest of heels.

The condition of children is greatly improved all over Europe, although the most fortunate probably belong to just such middle class French households as these. Children have many more toys. Dolls, called "babies" in the XVIIIc., drums, woolly animals to be dragged on a string, appear in almost every picture, and are as lovingly painted by Chardin as gleaming copper, pewter, silver and china, good furniture, and handsomely made odd pieces like the reel for the housewive's thread or the footstool she uses as a pincushion.

1815. XVIIIc. French. (Metropolitan Mus., Print Room.)

H. F. Gravelot. Pen drawing (detail).

The engravers of XVIIIc. find much employment in illustrations, vignettes and end pieces for the books which are seen lying open in so many French paintings. Everybody reads novels, which were first written in final quarter XVIIc. by Mme. de La Fayette and continued by Marivaux' "Marianne" and l'Abbé Prévost's "Manon Lescaut," and eventually by Rousseau's "Nouvelle Héloise" and "Emile"; Voltaire's satires, plays, moral tales, fables and chansons.

Gravelot (1699-1773), a French draftsman-engraver, lived mostly in England c.1734-54, and greatly influenced English book illustration by his work for editions of Dryden and Richardson.

This pen drawing is one of a preliminary series for book illustrations, belonging to the Metropolitan Museum. It shows the carved and gilded *boiseries* of a rich Louis XV bedroom, an *ormulu* clock, one of the delicate three-legged pedestal tea tables, set on a carpet made in France.

The nurse wears a little flat hat tied over a close cap, neck ruche and apron, with the plain bodice, pleated cuff, and swelling, round skirt of midXVIIIc. The mother lies in the cap appropriate to her lacy, beribboned negligée.

1816. XVIIIc. 1739. French. (Louvre.)

Louis Tocqué. Louis of France.

Louis Tocqué (1696-1772), son of an architectural painter, studied with Rigaud, and became, with Lar-

gillière, the most successful painter of the rich bourgeoisie. Unlike Nattier, whose eldest daughter he married, Tocqué managed his money very well. After painting the queen, the Dauphin and Dauphines, he made a triumphal tour of the courts of Northern Europe, painting the Russian Empress in 1757, and the Danish rulers in 1759 and 1769.

The wig of the Dauphin, father of Louis XVI, shows the necessary court compromise between the full-bottomed wig of Louis XIV and the neatly gotten-out-of-the-way wig of ordinary use. He wears the *cordon bleu* over a red coat, the open cuffs of which accord with the brocaded white satin waistcoat. The

heavy embroidery with which it is edged shows the midXVIIIc. tendency toward massive decoration, with edges of frogs and tassels. With the conservatism of court styles, his clocked white hose continue to be rolled and gartered over the knees, and his diamond-buckled shoes retain red heels, though they approach the every-day form.

The Dauphin, the most intelligent of Louis XV's children, encouraged his sisters to improve their defective convent educations. The globe indicates his interest in geography, an inherited passion of that adept map-maker, Louis XVI.

1817. XVIIIc. French. (New York, Mrs. George F. Baker.)
N. Lancret, d. 1743. Park of the Petit Trianon.

Even at Versailles there had to be certain informal spots. Louis XIV had transformed his father's hunting pavilion into a dairy-menagerie, where the little duchess of Burgundy loved to have supper. The Petit Trianon of Louis XV had a botanical garden; a little house of Sèvres porcelain was built there for Mme. de Pompadour; and eventually the Hamlet, in which Marie Antoinette played at farmer's wife.

Exotic modes of transport had always been provided at Versailles: gondolas; gilded barges; rolling chairs like those on the Atlantic City boardwalk today, in which Louis XV was pushed as a weak boy. Here we see ladies being drawn in a little gilded chariot by four mastiffs.

The costume suitable for strolling or picnicking in the woods remains substantially that shown in earlier Lancret pictures. The skirts have become fuller. The hair, formerly bare or dressed with flowers, now has a tiny cap or triangle of lingerie. Men wear wigs, powdered and tied, unpowdered and flowing, or the cropped head, in beret or high-crowned cap, without any wig.

1818-20. XVIIIc. French. (Metropolitan Mus., Print Room.)

Jean Rigaud. Diverses vues.

1818. Chapel of the chateau of Versailles.

Rigaud (1700-54) specialized in engravings of chateaux and parks.

The courtyard in front of the palace of Versailles had been railed in blue and gold in 1680. Its entrances from three roadways were guarded by soldiers. The main entrance from the avenue leading straight to Paris was used only by the royal family and princes of the blood. Carriages of the nobility who had been granted the "Privileges of the Louvre" were admitted by the side gates, where we see a two-horse carriage approaching. Everyone else alighted and walked, or was carried for 6 sous in one of the "blue chairs" with blue-liveried carriers which were provided by a concessionnaire. There was coach service twice a day between Paris and Versailles, and carriages and horses for hire. Any respectably dressed person was admitted to the palace.

1819. Basin of Neptune in the gardens of Versailles.

There has never been enough water at Versailles to keep the fountains playing continuously, and the Basin of Neptune is only one consumer, although one of the largest, with its allegorical figures spouting between six 60-foot jets and 22 smaller ones. People have always turned out for the spectacle; just as two-wheeled carts working on the estate found reason, in the middle of the XVIIIc., to cross beautiful coaches with an outrider and two men on the box, and a crowd which is not entirely made up of courtiers.

The rider near the coach wears a double-breasted coat, the breast flap of which, opened up, can be buttoned back and so become translated into lapels. Women's skirts have reached the limit of round size, and are beginning to be flattened into greater width.

1820. Wing of the chateau of Fontainebleau, from the Court of Fountains.

Francis I had poured his joyous vitality into the building and wonderful interior embellishments of his palace at Fontainebleau; Henry IV extended it. Lenôtre designed the parterre, beyond the pond, but under Louis XIV, so preoccupied with Versailles, the court merely moved to Fontainebleau in the autumn, to play tennis and *mail,* as it moved to Compiègne in the spring to review army manoeuvres. Christine of Sweden lived there after abdication, in 1656-7, and eventually it became a favorite residence again under Napoleon I.

Undisturbed by the painted, gilded and canopied pleasure boat, the carp of Fontainebleau were as huge, old, greedy, and fun to watch and feed as they are today.

1821. Mid-XVIIIc. French-Polish. (London, Victoria and Albert Mus.)

Moreau le jeune. Lady in a Sedan Chair (detail).

The frame of this picture is surmounted by the arms of the Leczynski family. Its background may show the palace of Willanow, near Warsaw. Its figures wear Polish and French dress of midXVIIIc.

Liveried servants and chairmen: striped red and white coats, edged with gold; legs protected by spatterdashes.

Lady: pale pink with pale green overdress.

Man bowing to kiss her hand: white coat, gold brocaded edge; blue hose; ribbon and medal of an order.

Bearded man with clipped head and beard, facing chair: gray cloak, blue and yellow sash, brown boots.

Man wearing the Golden Fleece and looking very like John Sobieski, the Polish king who has been dead for about half a century: gold armor and gray boots under a dark green frogged coat with a brown fur collar. These coats, brought to Western Europe by the Hungarian hussars, will become a striking fashion of e.XIXc.

Courtier in French dress, at ext.r.: white-figured red coat, Order of the St.-Esprit, white hose, black shoes.

Negro page with leashed and belled pugs: white turban, gold doublet, blue-green hose.

1822-23. XVIIIc. 1745. French. (Paris. Bibl. de l'Arsenal.)
C. N. Cochin. Jeu de Roi (1822). Bal paré (1823).

The intimate family groups of early XVIIIc., give way to great, gregarious entertainments in mid-XVIIIc.

At Versailles, gambling is still restricted to those who have the entrée; less formal courts like Marly are degenerating into gambling-houses, thronged by black-clad chevaliers of Louis XIV's military order of Saint-Louis, and other uninvited men who drive out from Paris.

Walpole writes from Paris, 1739, that it is dishonorable in France not to be in the army, but "no dishonor to keep public gaming houses. There are at least a hundred and fifty people of the first quality in Paris who live by it. You may go into their houses at all hours of the night, and find hazard, pharaoh, etc. The men who keep the hazard-table at the duke de Gesvre's pay him twelve guineas each night for the privilege. Even the princesses of the blood are dirty enough to have shares in the banks kept at their houses."

Walpole notes at the same time the excessive use of a very dark shade of rouge, and at a later time, 1763, the "dissonance of parade and poverty" among the French nobility even at Versailles. The duke of Praslin's footmen are "powdered from break of day," but wait behind him with red pocket handkerchiefs about their necks.

The smaller rooms of Versailles overheated quickly with crowds and candles, so that ladies are always afraid of committing the unforgivable fault of fainting. But the great hall of mirrors remains glacial. Men carrying muffs show decoration, which reinforces the vent of spreading coat-skirts, carried up the c. back seam. Court wigs are usually untied, and show two long and one short center lock.

The small, flower-dressed head of short hair is giving way in French court use to caps with lappets falling over massed, trailing curls. Enormously distended hoops, becoming flattened, display a petticoat scalloped with ruching; the overskirt is reduced to a train matching the darker bodice.

1824. XVIIIc. 1746. French. (New York, Cooper Union Mus.)

Surugue, after *Ch. Coypel*. Mme.** in a ball gown.

1825. XVIIIc. 1748. French. (Neuilly-sur-Seine, Weill Coll.)

J. B. Perroneau (1715-83). Duchesse d'Ayen.

Mme. de Maintenon arranged a marriage between her niece Françoise and the Marshal de Noailles, brother of her dear friend the Cardinal.

Two sons born of that marriage became Marshals of France; their lives and those of their descendants show the various fates of the aristocracy during the Revolution.

Louis, the witty elder son, duke d'Ayen until his father's death in 1766, refused to emigrate, and died of old age the year before his wife (nearly a half century older than we see her here), his daughter-in-law, and one of his granddaughters were executed in 1794. His son returned from Switzerland as a peer, on the Restoration.

The younger son and more distinguished general, Philippe, duke de Mouchy, and his wife, first lady of honor to Marie Antoinette, were both executed in 1792. Both their sons had been members of the States General in 1789; both emigrated. The elder, the prince de Poix, returned to France in 1800. The younger, viscount de Noailles, had served under Lafayette in America, and was one of the young aristocrats who had voted for the abolition of privilege in 1789. He returned to America, worked in a bank in Philadelphia, then served the English in San Domingo under Rochambeau, and died in a sea battle off Havana in 1804.

Lafayette had married a Noailles, granddaughter of the duchesse d'Ayen shown here. He had designed the tricolor cockade of the Republic, had been offered the command of the newly formed National Guard, and had ordered the capture of the fleeing royal family at Varenne on his personal responsibility. But because he was a moderate, he was declared a traitor by the Jacobins, and had to emigrate in 1792.

Mme.**, in Coypel's pastel, is supposed to be Mme. de Mouchy, "virtuous, pious, charitable, and irreproachable," who was so concerned with details of the correct wearing of capes and cap-lappets, that Marie Antoinette nicknamed her "Madame Etiquette." "Arrange all these matters, Madame, just as you please, but do not imagine that a queen born Archduchess of Austria can attach the importance to them which might be felt by a Polish princess who had become Queen of France." Mme. de Noailles decreed that lappets should hang; when Mme. Campan did not understand her signals, it was the Queen who whispered: "Let down your lappets or the countess will expire." Marie Antoinette was a child of the age to come, in her impatience with minutiae of etiquette, and her attempts to live as a human being among friends. This freedom was bitterly resented at court, and helped to bring down the regime.

Madame Campan, whose Memoirs tell us so much about court life under Louis XV-XVI, and who loyally loved and served Marie Antoinette, was condemned, but was saved by 9 Thermidor, to become head of two schools which Napoleon established for the education of the young womenfolk of his heroes. Her republican brother, Girondist ambassador to the U.S., was recalled by Robespierre, but stayed in America as Citizen Genêt and married the daughter of Gov. Clinton of New York.

Mme. de Mouchy's ball gown shows a modification of the long sleeve of the second quarter century, with the passementerie, fringe and tassels so much used during the next quarter, and the black ribbon about the neck, which tends to become a lacy ruching in the latter period.

The little lacy triangle, *cornette,* of Lancret's day is commemorated in the point of the cap which grew from it, shown in Mme. d'Ayen's pastel portrait. Her loose dress, pleated at shoulder and cuff, opens over a *corps* with stepped bows. The low neck is generally covered or filled; in this case, by a froth of lace and a neckband. Taffeta apron. Cane backed chair.

1826

1826. XVIIIc. c. 1755. French. (Versailles Nat. Mus.—
original at the Chateau d'Ew.)

L. M. Van Loo (copy). The Cup of Chocolate.

The Goncourts in "The Woman of the Eighteenth
Century" have pointed out the comparatively cozy,
homelike intimacy of group pictures of the nobility
in first half XVIIIc., in contrast to the gay, glittering,
cohesive conviviality of the third quarter century pictured by Saint-Aubin and Cochin, and the earnest,
apprehensive, decomposed groups spotted through
the same garlanded rooms, waiting for their fate, in
the final quarter.

The duke of Penthièvre, the richest man in France,
appears here with his son, the prince de Lamballe.
The latter's wife (who returned from safety in England to share Marie Antoinette's imprisonment in the
Temple, and whose head on a pike was paraded past
the queen on Sept. 3, 1792); his daughter, Mlle. de
Penthièvre, (later the duchess of Orleans, whose
pouf au sentiment is one of the most famous of all
extravagant coiffures); and his mother, the countess
of Toulouse, widow of a natural son of Louis XIV.

We see two typical coats of the beginning second
half century: Lamballe's of an all-over diapered pattern, relatively untrimmed, on which the emblem of
the Saint-Esprit is embroidered. Penthièvre's on
which hangs the Golden Fleece, has thick heavy em-

broidery massed in relation to buttons; this will soon
become frogs, braid loops and tassels.

The waistcoat is sleeveless. Its connection to the
coat, through the appearance of its fabric on the
coat cuff, is being lost, and it is beginning to be cut
away below the waist.

The "pigeon's wings" of the wig have become a
series of formal rolls. Diamond buckles cover the
shoe tongue and finish the knee closing.

The loose gown, with shirred or gathered edgings,
is opened wide (to accommodate hoops which are
approaching their limit of round width) over short
petticoats trimmed with *volants* of self material. A
bow, matching those on the ladder of the *corps,* is
added to a self-frill and three deep *engageantes* of
lace, as a sleeve finish, in place of the old pleated
cuff. Brocades, often striped, are sprigged; their
colors deep pinks and sharp light blues; the bows of
the *echelle* often lavender.

Hairdressing begins to show a slight elaboration
and height. That of an older woman of the aristocracy will now be covered by a pleated cap, dipping
in front like the Mary Queen of Scots headdress of
the XVIc., though the point is unrelated in its
origin.

Walls painted and carved with loves and garlands
of roses; parquet floors; graceful and comfortable
upholstered chairs.

1827. XVIIIc. 1754. French. (Versailles, Nat. Mus.)
J. M. Nattier. Mme. Henriette playing the cello.

1828. XVIIIc. 1756. French. (Versailles, Nat. Mus.)
J. M. Nattier. Mme. Adelaide tatting.

1829. XVIIIc. 1758. French. (Versailles, Nat. Mus.)
J. M. Nattier. Mme. Adelaide Music Lesson.

Jean-Marc Nattier (1685-1766), son of a portrait
painter and a miniaturist, and father-in-law of Tocqué, had none of the latter's astuteness in money

matters. He was ruined by Law's speculations in
1720, gave up historical painting which had admitted him to the Academy, and applied himself to
court portraits, which are the quintessence of Louis
XV's period rather than expositions of individual
character. His *Mesdames de France* are almost interchangeable. He died very old in miserable poverty.

Louis' first children were twin daughters, Elizabeth and Henriette, called "Madame Première" and
"Madame Seconde." Elizabeth, the only daughter

1827

1828

1829

who married at all, became the unhappy wife of Elizabeth Farnese's son, the duke of Parma, and died young of smallpox while on a visit to Versailles.

Henriette and Louis, the young duke of Chartres were in love; Argenson favored and Fleury opposed the match which would have strengthened the Orleans faction. After Louis' marriage to the princess of Bourbon-Conti, Henriette simply died of grief at 24.

Following the birth of the Dauphin and the duke d'Anjou, came a series of five daughters, born between 1732-7. Only Adelaide, the eldest, and her father's favorite, after Henriette's death, remained at court. Victoire, Sophie, Thérèse, Félicité (who died at 8), and Louise (Madame Septième, who Louis vowed was Madame Dernière), were all packed off to the abbey of Fontevrault until adolescence, to save expenses.

The king had a considerable domestic affection for his daughters, though the "thrust of the hog's snout," as the court called his habitually unkind and disturbing remarks can be seen in the nicknames he gave his daughters; which translate into something like "tatters," "sow," "rook" (which has also a connotation of raucous spitting) and "rags."

In the morning, Mme. Campan tells us, he climbed up to the apartment of Adelaide with a pot of coffee he had made himself. She rang to notify Victoire, Victoire rang Sophie, who in turn notified the lame Louise, who scurried from the farthest apartment of all, to be kissed.

At the débotter of the king on his return from hunting, Mesdames interrupted Mme. Campan's reading to throw on a strange, makeshift costume: hoop and gold-trimmed petticoat, and hooked-on train, with the upper undress concealed under a great black taffeta cloak. They were kissed, rushed back and untied their strings, and within 15 minutes altogether, were again at their embroidery, listening to Mme. Campan.

Adelaide, whose insatiable desire to learn was encouraged by her brother, was as industrious as her mother. She learned to play every musical instrument, even the horn and jew's harp, not very well, but she was once able to play for a country girls'

dance when the orchestra failed to show up. Beaumarchais' talent as a harpist helped him to entrench himself at court as her teacher. For a very short time, she was pretty. But she was brusque and harsh; it was she who first called Marie Antoinette "L'Autrichienne," which by the change of a vowel became the epithet of the populace for "the other, the alien bitch."

Victoire was pretty and kind, pious and stupid, greedy and fat. Marie Antoinette found her the kindest of the aunts. She had suffered horrors at Fontevrault, forced to say her prayers for penance in a vault in which her sister lay buried, while an insane gardener of the convent died screaming outside. On fast days she stayed up till midnight to stuff herself at 12:01 A.M. When her sister became a nun, she cried, saying, "I shall never have Louise's courage. I love the conveniences of life too well; this lounge is my destruction."

Sophie was incredibly ugly and odd, silent and shy. She tore past people, and to avoid looking at them "acquired the habit of leering on one side like a hare." She was terrified of storms and was affable and even demonstrative to the humblest person around when it thundered, although she was not even civil until the next storm.

Louise, short and deformed, was very nearly a saint. At 12, she told Mme. Campan, she was "not mistress of the whole alphabet," and learned to read with the Dauphin's help, after leaving the convent. She went out early in the morning, alone and on foot, through rain and cold in any weather, trudging from hospital to police station on her charitable errands. (The Goncourts). She kindly plied Mme. Campan with sugar water, while exhausting her with five daily sessions of reading. Then the secret came out: she was finally being allowed to become a Carmelite, and wanted to learn all the history she could before she retired to Saint-Denis. Marie Antoinette had a doll dressed as a Carmelite to prepare her daughter for the sight of her aunt's costume when the royal family went three times a year to visit Louise, and found ambitious princes of the Church thronging about what the queen called "the most intriguing little Carmelite in the kingdom." Louise told Mme.

de Genlis that the most difficult part of being a Carmelite was getting down a circular back stair alone. "I was obliged to seat myself on the steps and slide down." She had never descended even the wide stairs of Versailles without the arm of an attendant gentleman.

All the sisters loved flowers, but they had only window boxes in which to grow them, and no private place to walk, until Louis XVI settled their first incomes on his 40-year old aunts and bought them the chateau of Belville. That it cost $120,000 a year, after attempts at economy, to feed three old ladies and their households was the sort of thing that first became general knowledge with the publication of Necker's "Compte-rendu" in 1781, the first itemized statement of French government expenditures, and one of the causes of the Revolution.

Madame Adelaide tatting shows the pastime of the second and third quarter century. It preceded *purfling* (*parfiler*=unravel) of precious gold thread from brocade, epaulettes and lace, for which gentlemen provided the materials and helped in the destruction of something far more valuable than its gold-salvage worth.

Her small head, lightly powdered, is dressed with lace in a compromise between the old, uncovered head of a young aristocrat and the ubiquitous cap of the future. She carries a little lace-frilled tippet and a *ridicule* (reticule) for her handwork, with a deep rose gown, sewn with silver motifs and trimmed with lace backed with pink. At the music lesson, she wears the narrow fur trim which is also seen on men's coats in the 60's. The old round hoops have been replaced by laterally spreading supports.

THE CAREER OF POMPADOUR

Mme. de Pompadour (1721-64), born Jeanne Poisson, and her brother were baptized as the children of a tarnished court official; their actual father was probably the rich tax-farmer, Le Normant de Tournehem. The "king's morsel" of beauty was specifically educated at Le Normant's expense to become the king's mistress, as had been prophesied by a fortune teller. She was taught every accomplishment by the most eminent masters: music by the opera singer, Jéliotte; declamation by Crébillon; she became a dancer, a fine horsewoman, an amusing story teller, a more than good etcher and engraver, and a woman with wonderful taste in dress.

A husband was necessary to her plan; at 20 she was married to her protector's rich nephew, Le Normant d'Etiolles. She had a superb private theatre and became a leader in the society of the *haute bourgeoisie*. But that was far from court. She could only come to the king's attention by accident. As he hunted, his path was constantly crossed by a lovely horsewoman, or by a lady in pink in a blue carriage, or a lady in blue in a pink carriage, sometimes by a lady driving her own equipage. She finally met the king at a masked ball given by the city of Paris, separated from her heart-broken husband, and, as the Marquise de Pompadour, became the official successor of Mme. de Mailly in 1745.

In the year or two during which she actually was the king's mistress, and for the following two decades, she concerned herself in every detail of French politics, foreign and domestic. All state matters, all

preferment passed through her hands before reaching the king. Even her enemy d'Argenson (whose colloquial French was considered vulgar by a court used to Corneille and Racine), said it was better to have a straight and lovely nymph governing than an ugly, squatting monkey like the old Cardinal Fleury, even though pretty ladies, like white kittens, caressed you, and then bit and scratched. She aligned France with Austria, involving her in the Seven Years' War; helped in the expulsion of the Jesuits. She drew about her, protected, and subsidized men of letters of all sorts, including Voltaire and the Encyclopedists and their cronies, like her own republican physician, Quesnay, thereby playing a large part in bringing on the Revolution. She employed many artists in the embellishment of her chateaux, and was the patron of fellow-engravers; she encouraged manufactures like the porcelain of Sèvres; disposed of a great deal of France's money; and made herself indispensable to the "old paper-shuffler, who could hardly walk" (as Voltaire called Louis XV, finding it ridiculous that he should have lived and she, died.)

To keep the king amused she supervised and appeared in the performances of the palace theatre, and retained power many years after they ceased to be lovers. At 42, she was dying of tuberculosis, and trying to conceal the loss of her beauty, while abetting the transient mistresses of the Parc aux Cerfs. Louis XV was a person of habit, as Mme. de Mirepoix understood when she told the Marquise that it was her staircase the king loved; he was used to going up and down it; but if he found another woman with whom he could talk about hunting and his other concerns, it would be all the same to him in three or four days.

When Pompadour was dying (which only the royal family was allowed to do in a palace), with her extraordinary courage she had herself dressed in full court costume, and was driven off in the rain. The typically callous cruelty of the king is commemorated in the report (though it seems to be false), that he merely said: "The Marquise will not have good weather for her journey." The funeral oration of the queen's late *dame du palais* was turned, by a clever Capucin, into a eulogy of the queen herself. It was Maria Leczynska, to whom the marquise had always behaved correctly, who was most shocked by the immediate obliteration of her memory, as though she had never existed. That was the world, the queen said, and she found it scarcely worth the trouble to love it.

Diderot said that what remained of the Marquise's extravagant expenditures and meddling in government was "the Versailles treaty, which will last as it may" (it admitted English goods duty-free); "Bouchardon's Amour, which will be admired forever; a few of Guay's engraved gems, which will astonish antiquarians still unborn; a good little picture by Van Loo which will be looked at once in a while; and a pinch of ashes." With her passing there also evaporated a good deal of the resentment felt during her lifetime towards an immensely courageous and hard-working woman whose whole life, as she said, had been a combat. There were lesser women to follow her.

1831

1830. XVIIIc. 1755. French. (Louvre.)

M. Q. La Tour. Marquise de Pompadour.

Maurice Quentin La Tour (1704-88) studied with a non-Academic painter, and took up pastels which the Venetian Rosalba Carriera had made fashionable in 1720. Enormously prolific and successful, he endowed art scholarships and charitable institutions in Paris, and in his native Saint Quentin, where he retired at 80. A bachelor, he was the faithful lover for many years of an exquisite singer, Mlle. Marie Fels.

Character, of all things, interested the free-speaking, independent La Tour: "I plunge into their depths, and I bring them out whole," whether Rousseau and Voltaire from the salons of Mme. du Deffand and Mme. Geoffrin, lovely actresses, bourgeois financiers, the royal family, or Mme. de Pompadour. But he had the secret of pleasing his sitters while exhibiting their living souls.

The life-sized pastel portrait, which La Tour exhibited in the Salon of 1755, shows the Marquise as 1st minister; at her feet, the famous portfolio of state papers which Choiseul spirited away under a great red cloak on the very warm day of her death. Her elbow rests on the new Vol. IV of the Encyclopaedia. An engraving, a globe, and music indicate other interests.

Her hair is lightly powdered; lace under-petticoat and ladder of ribbon of bows on corset with matching gown and petticoat; sleeves with pleated self-ruffle and 3 tiers of lace, below a shirred band; mules.

1831. XVIIIc. 1755. French. (Metropolitan Mus., Frick Coll.)

François Boucher. Winter.

This is one of the four "Seasons" painted for Mme.

de Pompadour. The Frick Collection also includes a series of 8 panels which he provided for the octagonal boudoir of her chateau de Crécy, and armchairs of Beauvais tapestry, probably from his designs.

The sleigh is one of the fanciful means of transport constantly shown, and used, in pictures of the French court.

For winter, the shirred trim of summer gowns is replaced by ropes of fur, during the third quarter XVIIIc. Slippers, like the attendant's shoe to which curved skates are tied, are cut protectively high.

1830

1832. XVIIIc. 1761. French. (Versailles, National Mus.)

J. M. Frédon, copy of Van Loo.
Louis XV in robes of state.

The king wears his robes over the anachronistic XVIIc. costume of majesty, and carries a XVIIc. plumed hat. His wig is a modification of the full-bottomed court wig of Louis XIV; his shoes are contemporary, with diamond buckles.

1833. XVIIIc. French. (Aix, Museum.)

Q. La Tour. Duke de Villars.
Villars (1702-70) was little more than the son of the old Marshal, that "fanfaron plein d'honneur" at whose death in 1734 he inherited many honors, acquiring the Golden Fleece he wears here. Villars' homosexuality was so flagrant that he was nicknamed "the friend of man."

The two coldest winters of the XVIIIc. were those of 1741 and 1760. During the latter, Walpole wrote Montague, "Whether you have the constitution of a horse or a man," you were equally in danger. Soldiers froze to death, sitting on their horses, on the Continent. Walpole, for all "his immortality" had had a fever for seven weeks, and listed the noble ladies who had died of septic sore throat, including the duchess of Bolton, Lavinia Fenton, the original Polly Peachum of the "Beggar's Opera." 1766 was the other Siberian winter, though Walpole obstinately refused to add "a grain" to his clothing.

Fur-lined coats are seen throughout this long period of cold. A courtier's life consisted of endless waiting about in great cold rooms and draughty, inconvenient corridors. Walpole could keep comparatively cozy in his toy house at Strawberry Hill. But a fragile courtier like Hervey, or a self-indulgent one like Villars, found a fur-lined coat a necessity. For his embassy at the court of Tuscany, Stainville had a sable-lined silver coat, trimmed in gold, which cost $5,000. A coat magnificent enough for Marie Antoinette's wedding in 1770 cost so much that Mirepoix preferred to pay his tailor a rental of $1,200 for one day's use. (Lacroix: *Eighteenth Century*)

1834. Last quarter XVIIIc. French.

H. Chefer, after *Drouais.* Comte Philippe de Vaudreuil (1724-1802).

The naval officer, pointing out the scene of his triumphs against the English in 1777, shows a late appearance of the fur-lined and collared coat. The coat has lost fullness; its lengthening sides are cut away. The decoration of tassels and frogs on the coat has been very much reduced, and is assumed by the

exposed waistcoat. The curls of the wig are being reduced in number.

1835. XVIIIc. French. (New York, Albert Blum.)

J. B. Greuze. Comte d'Augievilliers.
Jean-Baptiste Greuze (1725-1805), a Burgundian who became a painter against his father's wishes, was brought to the Royal Academy in Paris as a boy, by a provincial artist who aided him. He was so precociously successful that he had to prove that his work was entirely his own. He married the daughter of the bookseller Rabute shortly after his return from studying in Italy, 1755-7, and was at the height of his success c. 1765 on the wave of sentimentality brought on by Rousseau. He was so infuriated by his admission to the Academy as a genre, not as an historical painter, as he had intended, that he refused to exhibit. Between his own stubborn carelessness and the extravagance of an unpleasant wife, he was always in difficulties, was ruined by the Revolution, and died in poverty.

Augievilliers was director of the Crown Buildings. His redecoration of an unused room in the king's apartment cost 30,000 fr. Louis XVI, very distressed, said: "With that sum I could have made thirty

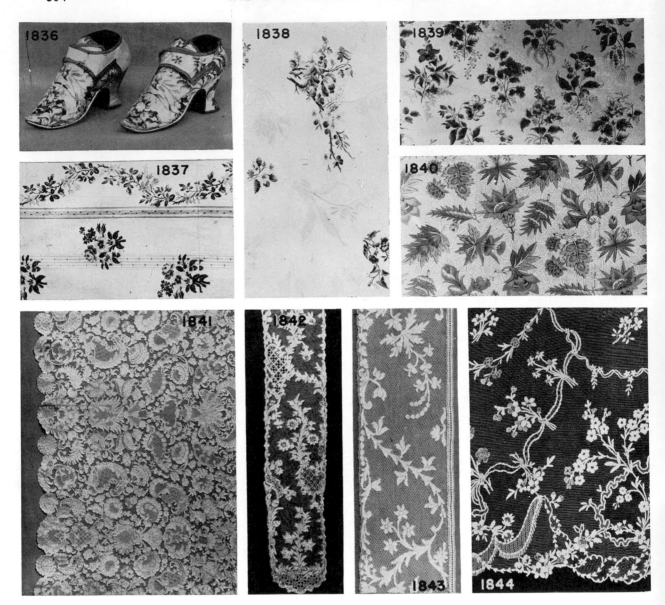

families happy." Mme. Marchais was called "Po-
mona" because of the beautiful fruit served at the
suppers of her salon; it was sent by d'Augievilliers
from the king's own gardens.

1836. XVIIIc. English.
Slippers: brocaded white silk.

1837. XVIIIc. Louis XVI. French.
Striped Floral Brocade.

1838. XVIIIc. French.
Floral Brocade.

1839. XIXc. 1837-51. English.
Printed Percale: floral motifs derived from XVIIIc.
brocades.

1840. XIXc. 1830-70. English.
Roller-Printed Cotton: degraded derivative of Pillement's designs and the patterns of floral brocades.

1841. First half XVIIIc. French.
Needlepoint Flounce: Point de France; *candelabre*
patterns.

1842. Mid-XVIIIc. French.
Needlepoint. Lappet: Point d'Alençon.

1843. XVIIIc. French.
Bobbin Lace Border: Valenciennes.

1844. Last half XVIIIc. French.
Point Lace: Argenta, worn by Queen Charlotte at
her wedding to George III in 1761.

1845. XVIIIc. 1757. French. (Metropolitan Mus.)

H. Drouais. Mme. Favart.

1846. XVIIIc. 1758. French. (London, Victoria and Albert Mus.)

F. Boucher. Mme. de Pompadour.

C. S. Favart, the dramatist, son of a pastry cook, became director of the Opéra Comique. With the assistance of the actress-singer-dancer-dramatist, "Mlle. Chantilly" (1727-72) whom he married in 1745, his productions became so successful that the rival Comédie Italienne contrived to have them closed. Favart was sent to the Low Countries with the army, by the Marshal de Saxe, to play impromptu comedy which was so brilliant that the enemy asked for an armistice in order to attend the performance. Saxe pursued Mme. Favart, whose recalcitrance, even after he had succeeded, led the Marshal to persecute both husband and wife until his death in 1750. From that time until her death, Mme. Favart was the leading actress of the Comédie Italienne. She altered its performances into the beginnings of true French comic opera, and was the first to play a peasant in an approximation of peasant costume, with bare arms and *sabots* instead of the customary gloves, jewels and paniers of a leading lady.

Mme. Favart's position allows us to see clearly the construction of the bodice of her turquoise-malachite green *robe à la française* and the pleats flowing from its shoulders; three lace ruffles below the self-ruffles of the sleeve. Hair powdered and lightly covered.

In many portraits (like one in Wallace Coll., London) Mme. de Pompadour is the epitome of the "Dresden china figurine" of the 50-60's, in pink, blue and lavender, ruching, ruffles and lace. Edges are now apt to be scalloped and shirred decoration to be laid on in serpentine lines.

Sitting in the woods with barely powdered hair, the marquise wears an absolutely simple, loosely fitted dress, laced at the throat, innocent of ruffles, and with pearl strands instead of her many bracelets.

1847-54. XVIIIc. French. (New York Public Library.)

Dictionnaire des Sciences. (Diderot's Encyclopédie).

A two-volume "Cyclopaedia" had been published in London in 1720 by Ephraim Chambers. While Zedler, the Leigzig bookseller, was producing his 64 vol. "Lexicon" in 1732-50, an Englishman and a professor from Danzig proposed a French translation of Chambers' work. There were heartbreaking complications with the king's printer and privileges; revision was necessary. Eventually Diderot and d'Alembert set out to provide a larger work, based on Chambers'. The first 2 volumes appeared in 1751-2; they were condemned as dangerous to church and state. Publication of the remaining 19 volumes was not completed until 1765. Society was split by its opinions of the anti-clerical Encyclopaedists. They were supported by the Minister, Choiseul, by Mme. de Pompadour, and by Malesherbes, director-general of the Librairie, who warned Diderot that the manuscripts were about to be confiscated and said: "Send them to me; they will not look for them here." Each volume was opposed, prohibited, and secretly circulated in France from abroad. "See how many philosophical writers there are at present," wrote d'Argenson (Dec. 20, 1750). "The wind from England blows over this stuff. It is combustible." This was even clearer to Voltaire by 1702: "All that I see is sowing the seeds of a revolution which will infallibly arrive, but which I shall not have the pleasure of witnessing. The light is spreading so from place to place, that it will burst out on the first occasion, and then there will be a fine row. The young men are very lucky: they will see many things!" (Letter to M. de Chauvelin, Apr. 2, 1762).

Louis XV's attitude toward the Encyclopédie vacillated with the various pressures brought upon him. He understood that it was dangerous, but had calculated that things would last out his time as they were. He seems not to have read it until a supper party at the Trianon. The duke de la Vallière suggested that Mme. de Pompadour's curiosity about how her rouge and stockings were made could have been answered by the confiscated Encyclopédie, and three servants brought in the 21 volumes.

The technical articles, as well as those on history, literature, grammar, and philosophy were written by Diderot, after painstaking study. The 10 volumes of the Encyclopédie published after 1765 were butchered by the printer, who took it upon himself to remove what he considered dangerous, after the last reading of the proofs. Diderot knew nothing about the deletions, until he consulted the books himself.

An extraordinarily complete picture of XVIIIc. life is provided by the Encyclopédie's 10 volumes of plates. They show us every industry, its men and women workers, its tools, and its products. We expect cheese-makers to wear smocks, but may not be prepared for the elegant attire of soap-makers. Pins are almost entirely the work of little boys. Goldsmiths sit on high stools, wearing gowns as long as a baby's christening clothes, perhaps to keep gold from slipping into pockets.

Do you need to know what an incubator for baby chicks, or a mechanical wheelchair looked like? How a ship of the line, or a royal galley differs from all the small sorts of boats in which the Dutch excel? The difference between a dozen sorts of carriages, like a *vis-à-vis, désobligeante, diable* or a *carrosse de jardin?*

You will find that *tabletiers* make not only chess

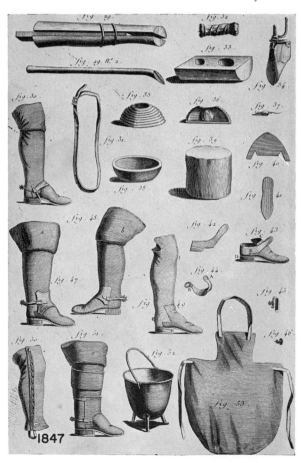

1847

and checkers sets, but combs, *carnets de bal* and card-cases of horn and tortoise shell, and that the women who make fans and feather-flower decorations for gowns are delightfully dressed themselves. You are shown how buildings are framed; how cotton and indigo are grown in the East, and stockings are knit in France. Soldiers in gaiters, with the skirts of their coats pinned together at the bottom, go through the manual of arms. Twenty-seven plates explain heraldry, blazonings and the orders of knighthood. You can even find the alphabets of all known languages, ancient and modern, from Abyssinia and Illyria, past the Malabar coast to Tibet—beautiful enough to be embroidered for their patterns alone.

1847. Cordonnier: Pl. II. Tome III, 1763.

Shoes, boots, leggings, and shoemaker's implements.

    30. boots
    43. shoes
    47. heavy bucket-top
        boots
    48. hunting boots
    49. hussar's boots
    50. dragoon's boots
    51. courrier's boots

1848-49. Gantier: Pls. II and IV. Tome IV. 1764.

Men's gloves and mittens.
Women's gloves and mittens.

1851. Tailleur d'Habits: Pl. V. Tome IX, 1771.

    1. coat
    2. vest
    3. breeches, *culotte*
    4. Bavarian breeches
    5. cassock, *soutane*
    6. abbé's long cloak
    7. abbé's short cloak
    8. redingote
    9. dressing gown
    10. court gown
    11. *gilet* short vest
        without skirts
    12. frock, *fracque,* a
        new sort of coat.

1852. Pl. VI, Tome IX. Detailed patterns of a coat.

    1-2 coat front
    3-4. crinoline stiffening at
        seam of skirts
    5-6. piecing of skirts (H)
    7-8. crinoline stiffening of
        front to support buttons and button-holes
    9-10. coat back
    11-12. crinoline stiffening
        to support seam of
        skirts in back
    13. collar
    14-15. pieces of sleeve
    16-17. pocket flaps
    18-21 crinoline stiffening
        pieces
    22-23. coat pockets
    24-25. cuffs

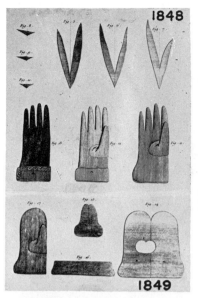

1848

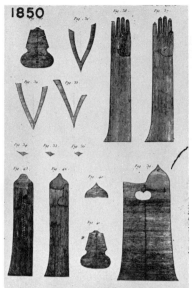

1850

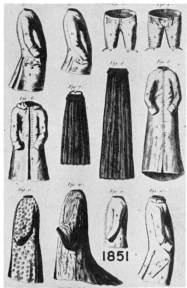

1849

1851

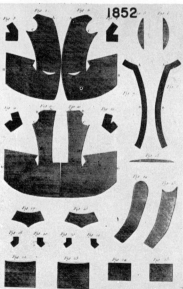

1852

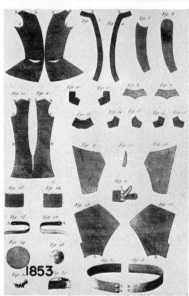

1853

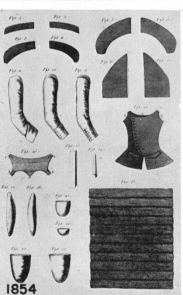

1854

1853. Pl. VII, Tome IX. Vest and breeches.

  1-2. front of vest
  3-4. crinoline stiffening of front
  5-6. pieces of sleeves
  7-8. pocket flaps
  9-10. crinoline stiffening
  11-12. back of vest
  13. crinoline at neck
  14-17. crinoline stiffening
  18-19. front of breeches
  20. front flap
  21. back buckle
  22-23. back of breeches
  24-25. pockets
  26-27. garter bands
  28. button mould
  29-31. method of making covered buttons
  32-33. belt of breeches

1854. Pl. VIII, Tome IX. Details.

  1-2. French collar
  3-4. German collar
  5-6. English collar
  7-8. pockets of a *fracque*
  9-11. different styles of cuffs for frock coats
  12. vest with crossed-over front
  14-15. tools used to burnish leather and flatten seams of leather breeches
  16. flap closing of leather breeches
  17-18. side pockets of breeches
  19-20. change pockets
  21-22. front pockets

1855. XVIIIc. 1768. French. (Metropolitan Mus., Print Room.)

"Supplément de l'art de la coiffure des dames françoises," by the Sieur Legros, Enclos des Quinze-vingts in Paris, Plate 48.

Legros is the author of the first manual of hairdressing. No. 48, from a supplementary edition published three years later, shows an arrangement formed of "un rang de coque de devant & le deuxième rang est en rosettes & boucles, faites en marron; le chignon natté en quatre cordons, moitié en parquet & l'autre moitié à jour & les bouchons faits avec le bout de la natté."

Women's hair began to be dressed by men about 1740, when peruke-makers were called in to arrange small rolled curls like those on men's wigs.

One of the first coiffeurs was Frison, made fashionable by Mme. de Prie. He refused to teach; he recognized Guigne, the king's barber, posing as the manservant of a customer, and outwitted him by doing an atrocious job.

Marie Antoinette's first hairdresser was Larseuer. She came to prefer the work of Léonard, but to spare Larseuer's feelings, she let him dress her hair, and then had it done over again by Léonard.

The great rival hairdressers of the 60's were Legros and Frédéric. Legros, originally a baker, opened an Academy of Hair, where ladies' maids and valets practiced on the hair of hired models. Dolls, dressed to show the latest Paris fashions, had been sent all over Europe from the beginning of the XVIIIc. Legros began to show hair fashions on these "babies" at the St. Ovide Fair, and in 1765, had 100 dolls on exhibition in his shop. Then he published his "Art of Hairdressing." Frédéric finally outstripped poor Legros, who was one of the vast crowds of unfortunates crushed to death in the Place Louis XV during Marie Antoinette's wedding celebration, to the relief of whose heirs the Dauphin and his new wife dedicated their entire income for the year.

In 1769 legal action was taken against the hairdressers, who now numbered 1200, by the Community of Master-Barbers, Wig-Makers, Bathers, and Washers. The victory was won by the *coiffeurs,* who argued that the *perruquiers* dealt with dead hair, on a block, but that the coiffeurs were artists, concerned with the embellishment of living hair, with the relationships of shape and color in hair, face, complexion, and with the millinery materials they used, which matched the gown.

The art of hairdressing reached its insane climax with Duppefort, Beaulard, Legard, and Léonard. It was to the last silly little man that Marie Antoinette entrusted her jewels, to be handed to her sister in Brussels, when Léonard emigrated with Choiseul. Léonard returned to France, and was listed among those guillotined and buried in a common grave with André Chénier, yet he turned up alive after a 20-year stay in Russia, and was Superintendent of Burials in Paris when he died in 1820.

Greatest of all hairdressing manuals was the French "Treatise of the Principles of Dressing the Hair of Women." Its 39 volumes showed 3,744 named fashions in use c. 1772.

As hair and its decoration mounted, Beaulard in-

1855

vented a push-button collapsible coiffure which enabled a woman to get into a carriage and sit upright.

Duppefort was playwright as well as hairdresser. His comedy "Les Panaches," describes a hair arrangement showing "the garden of the Palais-Royal with its fountain and the outline of its houses, without forgetting the great alley, the grille, and the café." (The Goncourts.)

The *pouf au sentiment* worn by the Duchess of Chartres in 1774 showed "in the rear, a woman seated in an armchair, holding a nurseling; this represented Monsieur le Duc le Valois and his nurse. At the right was a parrot pecking at a cherry, on the left a little Negro, the two pet beasts of Madame la Duchesse. And the whole was interwoven with locks of hair of all Madame de Chartres' relatives, her husband, her father, her father-in-law, the Duc de Chartres, the Duc de Penthièvre, and the Duc d'Orléans."

With the advent of professional hairdressers and the interrelationship of gown and hair trimming, the whole tradition of royalty being attended exclusively by gentlefolk, began to crumble. Marie Antoinette received her underwear from her ladies, and then withdrew to her closet to be finished by her dressmaker, the famous Rose Bertin, who could not be admitted to her chamber amongst her ladies. The Prince de Ligne says that reproaches against Marie Antoinette's luxurious dress were unfounded. Until the advent of Bertin, she was actually careless of dress, by court standards, and whenever possible, as at the Trianon, she wore the simplest muslins. The accusations seem to have arisen from the extravagant headdresses arranged by Léonard. The king detested them; the actor Carlin's daring burlesque with a peacock feather at a court performance was probably instigated by Louis XVI. Marie Thérèse returned a portrait sent by her daughter, saying: "It cannot be the likeness of a Queen of France, but that of an actress."

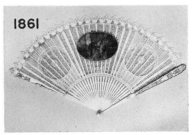

1856. XVIIIc. French. Regency.

Reverse: kid leaf, painted in gouache; landscape; infoliated medallions, surrounded by birds, flowers and fauns; sticks and guards: pearl matrix, carved and pierced; guards gilded.

1857. XVIIIc. French? (Late Louis XIV or Regency.)

Ivory; decorated with vernis martin; guards painted and gilded.

1858. XVIIIc. 1730-50. German.

Fan leaf: engraved, hand colored; by M. Engelbrecht of Augsburg.

1859. XVIIIc. 1757. English?

Park scene: painted kid mount; sticks and guards ivory, carved, painted with fruit and flowers.

1860. XVIIIc. French. Louis XVI.

Obverse: scenes from comedy; painted silk mount; ivory sticks and guards; medallions on sticks.

1861. XVIII-e.XIXc. English.

Carved ivory; medallion in vernis martin.

1862. XVIIIc. French. (Boston, Mus. of Fine Arts, Elizabeth Day McCormick Coll.)

Embroidered Collar: sheer yellow silk muslin ground embroidered with polychrome silks.

These collars were frequently worked on a very dark ground: plum, raisin brown, or laurel green. There are a number of them in the Museum of Fine Arts collection, but the light grounds photograph more satisfactorily. (See Appendix.)

1863. XVIIIc. French. (Boston, Mus. of Fine Arts, Elizabeth Day McCormick Coll.)

Embroidered Kerchief: sheer yellow silk embroidered in polychrome silks and silver. Square in shape, made to be worn folded, as shown, with silver and silk border worked only on the under part. (Ill. 1867).

1864. Early XVIIIc. English. (Boston, Mus. of Fine Arts, Elizabeth Day McCormick Coll.)

"Babila" Bag: lavender, green and white stripes. The Museum of Fine Arts has a number of examples of the exquisitely fine XVIIIc. netting technique called "babila work."

1865. XVIIIc. French. (Metropolitan Mus., Print Room.)

A. de Saint-Aubin. The Concert.

One of the large assemblies of the 60's, in the costume of Mme. de Pompadour's last years.

The skirts of the polonaise of the 70's will be looped, and in some cases actually drawn up by tasseled cords in a way derived from the form of curtain shown at windows of Mme. de Saint-Brisson's salon.

1866. XVIIIc. 1763. French. (London, Nat. Gall.)

L. C. Carmontelle. Leopold, Maria Anna, and Wolfgang Mozart.

L. C. Carmontelle (1717-1806), dramatic author and engraver, also made many completely delightful water colors of the rich in their most relaxed, informal moments: countesses sewing and talking together; Mlle. de Lespinasse with a book; Mme. d'Epinay's niece, Mme. d'Esclavelles, playing chess with M. de Linant while her old nurse looks on.

At 7, Mozart, the child prodigy, his older sister, and his violinist father made their second European tour. He charmed the French court as he had the Austrian, where the little boy had thanked Marie Antoinette in 1762 for picking him up when he fell, saying, "When I grow up I will marry you."

Wig tied in a bag; *solitaire;* coat longer and straighter in cut, but its skirts not yet cut away.

1867. XVIIIc. 1763. French. (Louvre.)

Olivier. Thé à l'Anglaise at the Prince de Conti's.

Mozart plays in the pink silk-hung white Gallery of the Four Mirrors, in the Temple; Jelyotte, the opera star, plays the guitar and sings. The host, who disliked being painted, is seen from the back talking to the finance minister, Troudaine. All the personages in the picture are known and are described by the Goncourts.

There are no servants. The ladies themselves serve tea and pass food kept warm in hot-water dishes.

Between Mlle. Bagarotti, in cerise and white stripes, and the Maréchal de Luxembourg in fur-trimmed white satin, are the Maréchale de Mirepoix in a fichu, her cap tied on by a black gauze kerchief, and Mme. de Virville in a sky-blue fur-lined pelisse. Behind their table stands Mlle. de Boufflers in pink, her bare head hardly powdered. The "delectable dowager," the elder Countess d'Egmont stands in a flowing red gown. The young countess d'Egmont, a "shepherdess on her way from the Opera to the Petit Trianon," wears a flat hat, lavender bows, and a lace apron. Behind her, Mme. de Boufflers, in rose, with a fichu and tulle-flounced apron plays maid. In the r. background the princess de Beauvau, in violet with a black scarf-collar serves a gentleman's glass.

1868. XVIIIc. 1766. Scotch-French. (Edinburgh, Nat. Gall.)

Alan Ramsay. Jean Jacques Rousseau.

Rousseau (1712-78) came of a family of French watchmakers who had emigrated to Geneva. The instability of his father left the child inadequately protected in France from the age of ten. His own "Confessions," begun during his English exile, tell the story of his life-long wanderings over Europe as a servant, secretary, musician of sorts and writer; of the mistresses and powerful friends who educated, supported, and protected him; of the endless quarrels of this man "born without a skin" (Hume); of his irresponsibility which sent his 5 children to the foundling hospital; and the madness of his last ten or fifteen years.

In 1761 appeared his novel, "La Nouvelle Héloïse"; in 1762, the "Contrat Social," which was anti-monarchical and had to be published abroad; and "Emile," a tract on education in the form of a novel. These revolutionized the life of the world.

The beauties of nature, simplicity, and feeling were discovered. Mothers began to nurse and educate their own children. Passionate friendships arose between women. Trustworthy middle-aged gentlemen trotted about, receiving confidences and furious if they found that something had been withheld. Everyone wrote diaries and confessions. Colloquial French words, such as d'Argenson had been ridiculed for using, replaced grandiloquent language. Powder seemed artificial; muslin and cloth replaced silk. Love became sentimental; keepsakes were exchanged, containing locks of hair and decorated with funeral urns, weeping willows and doves. Wild cliffs, ruined castles, broken statuary, were more beautiful than any cultivated parterre. Fashionable women's eyes were brimmed with tears, to indicate their agonizingly acute sensibilities. Rousseau did indeed "put the proud and weak on the wrong road." Whether in foolish innocence or bad conscience, aristocrats helped him to bring on their own downfall in the Revolution.

We see the professional child of nature in a sort of frontiersman's cap of shaggy fur like that of the collar of his cloak. Degrees of naturalness are being weighed in conversation; a cloak is "more natural" than a fitted coat, and such a rough fur would be called "more natural" than Villars' sables.

1869. XVIIIc. 1756. French. (Metropolitan Mus.)
Greuze. Broken Eggs.

1870. XVIIIc. French. (Metropolitan Mus.)
N. B. Lépicié (c. 1735-1834). Young Woman Knitting.
(For dress description of Ills. 1869, 1870, see "Cries of Paris," Ills. 1871-74.)

THE GREAT FASHION ARTISTS OF FRANCE

The greatest of the many great engravers of costume and manners in the latter half XVIIIc. was *Jean Michel Moreau* (1741-1814), called *"le jeune"* to distinguish him from his painter brother *Louis Gabriel*. His designs for the "Chansons" of Laborde, Marie Antoinette's valet de chambre, show court life, c. 1773. He illustrated the "Complete Works of Rousseau" in 12 vols. (1774-83). But his culminating work is the "Suite d'Estampes pour servir à l'Histoire des Modes et du Costume des Français dans le XVIIIe siécle," of 1776-83. They are the finest of all costume plates.

Augustin de Saint-Aubin (1736-1807) is only below Moreau in his portrayal of French life and costume. His brother *Gabriel* (1724-80) was a fine, less prolific artist.

Charles Nicolas Cochin, II (1715-90) came of a family of engravers, his mother, née *Hortmels*, being one also. His "Jeu du roi" and "Bal paré" are among the great records of court entertainments.

There were many others, some designers, some engravers after the work of other men; such as *Noël LeMire* (1724-1800); *Nicolas Delaunay* (1739-92); *F. M. I. Quéverdo* (1748-98); and the great German, *Daniel Chodowiecki* (1726-1801) who produced 2,000 book and almanach illustrations, among them Lessing's "Minna von Barnhelm" in 1770.

Coloring the sporadically produced costume plates of late XVIIc. by hand, or cutting out and backing them with fabric, was an amusement of the Regency, sometimes well and sometimes atrociously done.

Plate engraving in color did not begin until second half XVIIIc. Into XIXc. it was often cheaper and, as in the case of *Heideloff's Gallery of Fashion,* more luxurious, to color plates by hand. The plates of the *Galerie des Modes and Costumes Parisiens* are numbered or dated. At the turn of the century begins a flood of periodicals of fashion and culture, from which magazines like *Vogue* and the *Ladies' Home Journal* clearly descend. The long-lived *Ackermann's Repository* contains pasted-in samples of actual fabrics, produced in English mills, in addition to a color-illustration of a leading industry—say, the showrooms of the Etruria pottery works, fashion plates, embroidery patterns, articles on finance, music, new books, etc.

1871-74. Last quarter XVIIIc. French.

Cries of Paris.

The caps of the middle and lower classes begin to be prettily fluted like those of the aristocracy as competition drives towards the Revolution, and servants buy the old clothes of aristocrats from dealers like Joseph Longprix on the rue Saint-Honoré. France has become prosperous under Louis XVI; tax burdens are lightened; trade has doubled between 1758-88. "Revolutions are not always brought about by a gradual decline from bad to worse. Nations that have endured patiently and almost unconsciously the most overwhelming oppression, often burst into rebellion against the yoke the moment it begins to grow lighter. The regime which is destroyed by a revolution is almost always an improvement on its immediate predecessor, and the most critical moment for bad government is the one which witnesses their first steps toward reform. A sovereign who seeks to relieve his subjects after a long period of oppression is lost, unless he be a man of great genius." (A. de Tocqueville: *The Old Regime and the Revolution.* Harper, N. Y., 1856, p. 214.)

In all these illustrations the clothes are ample, comfortable and attractive. The shoes are good; even the man selling vinegar from a wheelbarrow (1871) wears clocked stockings. Vests are warm, often double-breasted, their colored linings turned back in revers. Twisted scarves help to hold up breeches or long trousers. The soap dealer and the hot-pastry boy (1871) wear hats as smartly cocked as the well dressed Turpin (1874), with a beribboned wig and a watch hanging from his buttonhole.

Girl (1869) whose eggs are broken wears a pretty dotted and ribbon-tied cap; her straw hat is imaginatively wreathed with ribbon; her great muslin sleeves, fichu, and apron are fresh; her skirt has a colored edge. The street women's skirts are striped like that of bourgeoise (1870) and they, too, have a lace fichu or an approximation of one for Sunday wear.

FRENCH COSTUME PLATES
of Moreau le jeune and others.

(Note key letters which are referred to in the
following discussion.)

1875. (A) *Moreau le jeune*: "L'aveu."

1876. (B) *Moreau le j.*: "*Coucher de la mariée.*"
1767.

1877. (C) Helman, after *Moreau le j.*: "*N'ayez pas peur, ma bonne amie,*" 1767.

1878. (D) *Moreau le j.*: "*C'est un fils, monsieur,*" 1767.

1879. (E) Helman, after *Moreau le j.*: "*Les délices de la maternité.*" 1777.

1880. (F) N. de Launay, after *N. Lavreince*: "*La toilette, 'qu'en dit l'abbé?'*"

1881. (G) P. A. Martini, after *Moreau le j.*: "*La petite toilette,*" 1777.

1882. (H) A. Romanet, after *Moreau le j.*: "*La grande toilette,*" 1777.

1883. (I) Carl Guttenberg, after *Moreau le j.*: "*Le rendez-vous pour Marly,*" 1777.

1884. (J) Heinrich Guttenberg, after *Moreau le j.*: "*La rencontre au Bois de Boulogne,*" 1772.

1885. (K) P. A. Martini, after *Moreau le j.*: "*Dame du palais de la Reine,*" 1777.

1886. (L) Launay le j., after *Moreau le j.*: "*Les adieux,*" 1776.

1887. (M) Patas, after *Moreau le j.*: "*La petite loge,*" 1776.

1888. (N) *Moreau le j.*: "*La fin du souper.*"

1889. (O) *Matthew Darly*: "Flower Garden," (English, May 1, 1777).

The ceremonious French gown is now worn with hair dressed high over pads, widened at the top by sausage curls, and surmounted by plumes, gauze and ribbons. (A, C, K, L, M, N, O.)

The smoothly rounded bodice follows the traditionally curved lines of the French corset. Its very low neckline (A), spreading wide at its base, exposes the breasts. It is edged with a little lace frill (L) which sometimes mounts into a standing Medici collar. By way of emphasis of the breasts, a bow is set at the top of the corset (the *parfait contentement*), and a ribbon about the neck, or a necklace disappears under it.

Sometimes (H, I) the Medici collar is transferred to a sheer tucker, in walking dress; its fluted edges run into the *parfait contentement*, after manner of the necklace.

The English bodice remains open, exposing a V; its edges are emphasized by pleats or shirred bands; its neckline is higher, and is veiled in scarves and handkerchiefs, which contribute to the V-appearance of the bodice front.

In French dress (B, C, E, F), V-fronts and kerchiefs tend to be relegated to negligée wear of ladies, and to the dresses of servants and housewives (D, E, F). Even these have lost the rigidity of the old placard-front with its busks. The bib of earlier aprons is the mark of servants' aprons by latter half XVIIIc.

The characteristic new bodice stresses breasts, small waists, and the roundness of the torso between them. Decoration is usually carried artfully down the center line of the bodice from the *parfait contentement*. But the fabric of the bodice tends to be rucked and wrinkled into horizontal fullness, so that the eye is carried around the body, below the springing breasts.

The ruffles at the elbows of close sleeves have a tendency to become gathered together at the bottom (E, I, N), and to turn into puffed bands, *sabots*.

The underskirt of negligée dress is usually flounced at the bottom; that of more ceremonious gowns may be trimmed with a flounce, with shirred bands, or with a combination of these, related to the trimming of the bodice and the sides of the overskirt.

As the paniers of court dresses are extended laterally to a great width (K), the underskirt becomes preeminent, and is garlanded with flowers, and looped gauze, while the overskirt disappears from view in front, and exists only as a long strip of train.

A series of new garments appears; *polonaises* (I), *caracos* (F) (and the more flowing *circassiennes*, *lévites* and *chemises* of the late XVIII.) for less ceremonious wear and for walking (to which all the French world had been set by Dr. Tronchin). These are coat-like, sometimes fitted in back *à la française* (F). They are caught together at the throat, or more usually at the *parfait contentement*, and are cut back, like a man's frock coat, and spread over the *paniers*.

The *caraco*, the first to appear, is a jacket, extended to cover the spread of the paniers. In a long form it was already worn by the bourgeoises of Nantes, when the duke d'Aiguillon passed through in 1768. Brought back in this way to Paris, it was cut short to the height of the pocket-slit of the skirt. It is edged with a ruffle, or in the perky bustled form *à la polonaise*, with puffed bands.

The back of the *polonaise* is gored and fitted; the gored sections may extend into the skirt, or a full skirt may be gathered onto a fitted bodice. In any case, the skirt is looped up on either side in back, in line with the two important gores, so that it is gathered up in three puffed sections. The trim at the bottom of the underskirt is often caught up in a series of smaller loops.

The *polonaise*, worn for walking, or in the country, was the forerunner of the tailored suit or sports dress. Hats, rather than caps or *poufs*, and watches with chains (later fobs) are worn with walking dress. For winter, there are *polonaises* with pockets, and fur-trimmed cloaks with collars, *pelisses*, which are accompanied by small muffs, as is the *polonaise*, but may be worn with ceremonious caps.

There is a tendency to loop up the skirts of all but the most formal garments (B, E, maid L). By the final quarter of century the skirts of walking dresses are often of less than ankle length.

Two impulses struggle for supremacy throughout the century: negligée, informal dress, cotton, against court paniers and silk.

Marie Antoinette's apologist, Mme. Campan, says that the queen preferred to wear white dresses of muslin, cambric, or Italian taffeta with muslin scarves, straw hats, and unsupported skirts in summer at Marly or the Trianon; until Rose Berlin's dressmaking was introduced at court by the duchess of Orleans in 1774, the queen wore diamonds only at court and

on fête days like Christmas and Easter. Her simplicity was censured. "What misconduct might not be expected of a princess who could absolutely go without a hoop," and who wanted people to sit down where they liked at the Trianon, without regard to old distinctions of chair and stool. This simplicity was first criticized, and then copied. It would have been in step with the times and better for the regime if Rose Bertin's influence had preceded the queen's taste for simplicity. But the Revolutionary guards looked everywhere at the Trianon for furniture set with rubies and diamonds, a legend which arose from stories of Louis XIV's solid silver furniture, combined with glass-studded theatrical scenery left over from his reign and stored at the Trianon.

The flounced blue, rose and violet gowns introduced by Mme. de Pompadour turn into white court dresses. Their borders and decoration develop from shirred fullness of self-material (A, C,) into *barrières* composed of puffings (L) of silver and gold, white and rose tulle and gauze, caught with perfumed flowers of silk, chenille, and of feathers. Straight lines of decoration become serpentine (K, L), then sprawl asymmetrically or are looped. The large, heavy brocade patterns of first half XVIIIc. become loosely sprawled or delicately sprigged across light grounds. There are many fine stripes (H,I) or stripes combined with bands of flowers (F and actual textile photos).

These blue stripes, and pink and white flowered patterns are reinforced c. 1775 by strangely-named new colors, striking rather than pretty: *puce* (the purplish-brown color of a blood-filled flea which a very great lady caught and found beautiful); *caca d'oie* (goose-dropping green); *boue de Paris* (that most clinging of all muds, with which everyone was splashed anyhow); *cheveux de la reine,* from Marie Antoinette's ash-blonde hair, which suffered so from the birth of her first child.

The allusive names which every color, hairdress and fashion received, often helps to date them. The paired half-paniers of 1750 were called *jansénistes* from the religious dissensions which were splitting society. Galloons *du système* alluded to Law's plans of financial reform. The pet word of 1730 is commemorated in fans *à l'allure*. The appearance of a comet in 1742; of the first rhinoceros; the place of an army victory; the name of a new ambassador; the birth of a dauphin; *à l'inoculation* of Louis XVI's brothers for smallpox by Dr. Joubert (a dangerous notion from the northern courts, which was blamed on the queen); *à la débacle* in 1768, when the bed of the Seine is cleaned; a new song like *Malbrouck* in 1786; the balloon ascensions of Montgolfier—all give names to fashions.

The negligees of white muslin and pink ribbons and the every-day dresses of India cottons, which the XVIIIc. adored, have been less readily available since Louis XIV's time. During most of the century the import of their fabric was forbidden, and it had to be smuggled. Mme. de Pompadour refused to have anything in her chateau of Belleville which was not contraband. (Goncourts). Lesser folk had to go without cotton or chance severe penalties, until France began to produce her own cottons. English muslins, ribbons and fashions, pottery and carriages (as well as such subversive notions as Magna Charta and habeas corpus) were admitted duty-free after the Versailles Treaty of 1783.

The ideas of Rousseau and Dr. Tronchin affect everybody: the beauties of nature, physical labor, walking and riding in comfortable clothing; nursing and educating your own baby, become fashionable (E, H, I, J).

The trend had begun earlier. Mme. de Pompadour is painted sitting in the woods, not walking on a parterre. Childless herself, and returning from the porcelain factory at Sèvres, she went out of her way to spy out the secluded spot in the Bois de Boulogne where Mlle. de Romans used to go, in a lace negligée, to nurse Louis XV's baby son (later the Abbé de Bourbon.)

The *lever* and *coucher* of the ladies and gentlemen who are being dressed and undressed in Moreau's plates (B, C, F, G, H,) do not differ in essentials from those of Marie Antoinette, of which Mme. Campan has left minute descriptions.

Like Moreau's bride, the queen went to bed under a great *baldequin* or *impérial* (B), which was also used to curtain off her small portable tub. (Only at St. Cloud was there a bathroom.) Her nightdress consisted of a nightcap, lace-trimmed chemise with sleeves, ribbon-trimmed corset, white taffeta dressing gown, and embroidered slippers.

On bath-day she washed wearing a wide gown of English flannel, lined with linen, and was dried under it, just as French girls were still taught to do during my school-days before World War I; more modesty, but the same notions of the essential dangers of bathing were involved in e. XXc. To avoid catching cold, she went back to bed on bath-day, and sewed or read until the public toilet at noon.

This was a prolonged ceremony which required many people besides her hairdresser and her ladies. The queen's clothes had already been selected, by an intricate ritual too long to explain, and more complicated than the choices we see being made. Her clothes were brought in, done up in green taffeta sheets, in wicker baskets. They were handed to her by her own ladies, but a tirewoman, two pressers and folders, two valets and a porter were also required. The four ells (4 yds. 6") of ribbon for her dressing gown, and two ells of taffeta which covered the basket of gloves and fans, were renewed daily, and must have kept the tirewoman's whole family in green taffeta aprons, capes and beribboned caps.

Lesser gentlefolk still required maids, valets and hair dressers, tailors and dressmakers, and most of these find it necessary to have assistants of their own.

Lavreince's (F) singer and musician try out a song while her hair is being dressed. Her doctor is concerned with her health; an abbé helps choose a length of striped floral brocade, brought in by a dressmaker and her assistant; two visitors chat.

The gentleman (G) holds an invitation which has just been brought by a liveried courier. He is swathed in night-shirt and dressing-gown, while a hairdresser takes a hot roller from an assistant, wearing an identical apron with a pointed bib buttoned to his coat. A tailor shows a new coat, held up by his assistant (whose striped stockings, like those of the abbé (F) were made on the new machine which knits ribs).

The nobleman (H), with the ribbon of his decoration across his chest, is now wearing his new frock coat. He pins on a nosegay; two fobs dangle from his breeches' pockets. With the sword and hat which wait on the chair, he will be ready to stroll with a friend, whose Order dangles on his breast, and the lady who waits in her walking costume of hat, fur-edged wrap, finely striped satin gown and rigid fan.

Gentleman in walking costume (I): a very cutaway frock coat, caught at the breast, just under the wide, rolling collar (male dress affected by female usages; the collar, equivalent to his companion's Medici collar, is caught at the point of her *parfait contentement;* the man's frock coat flows away from the button as her *polonaise* from its closing).

Lady's walking dress (I): parasol, plumed hat, braided hair clubbed up in back in a form of catogan; narrowly striped *polonaise* looped in gauze; petticoat shirred up in smaller sections; cord and tassel decoration of back gores. Another type of *polonaise,* even less formal, is very gauzy and summery.

Children with natural heads of hair play in the dirt, if they please, in pretty, comfortable wash dresses, with sashes about the waist. The waist and breasts have newly been discovered; the little girl has neither, so her sash is set high, in the trend towards the classic gowns of the turn of the century and Empire, which can already be discerned in the shorter waist and flowing outer garment of her mother's *polonaise.*

The groom wears a laced cocked hat; the gentleman, an informal riding hat cocked up softly into a shovel brim. Where a frock coat of ceremony would bare the breast, cutaway sports coats are closed for comfort at the throat.

Women's cutaway riding coats (J), almost indistinguishable from men's, closed with frogs, worn with sashes and skirts clear of the ground, plumed hats; one cocked behind by a button and loop, and worn with a long pigtail like a campaigner or sailor; the other, clubbed up behind.

A woman's riding costume, in the days when Tronchin set everybody to exercising, might have a gold-gallooned green satin coat and silver-trimmed pink skirt. A riding costume of 1786 is described as having triple collars on a coat of puce-colored shantung; ivory studs at front and pockets; a matching skirt with serpentine trimming in pink ribbon; pink doeskin boots; a canary yellow felt hat with green and white plumes; and hair clubbed into a *flambeau d'amour.*

Court costume (K): plumes, diamonds at the hair, ears, collar and necklace; overskirt reduced to a train, unseen from the front. A back view shows a method of attaching the train, drawn up with tasselled cords, after the manner of the *polonaise.* This court gown and the opera dress (L) show the elaborate *parement,* the demand for which can scarcely be met. Tulle, which got its name from the town where it was first made, appears during final quarter XVIIIc. Soldiers wove this net and worked on metallic trimmings in barracks and men-servants in livery embroidered while they waited in antechambers.

Courtiers and pages (K): In 1751 d'Argenson says: "The expense to courtiers of two new and magnificent coats, each for two fête days, ordered by the King, completely ruins them." Men's clothes are somewhat less elaborate now, but pages' coats cost 1,500 livres in 1786, and a lady's court gown like this might cost 10,000. (Taine: *Ancien Régime*)

Before and after the opera (L), ladies and gentlemen walked in full ceremonious dress in the Palais-Royal gardens and sat under the chestnut trees, until the galleries were built after the fire at l'Opéra in 1783.

The hair of the husband, who conducts the lady to her box, is dressed in a high *toupet* but falls loose behind in almost natural ringlets.

Her maid shows one of the inventive combinations of cap and kerchief from which great ladies begin to take suggestions.

Enrollment as a member of the companies of the Opéra or Comédie Française (M) was the dream of every little strolling player or pretty street girl. She became officially an *"artiste,"* was given independence from family control, and was spared from casual treatment by the police. She could make her way and marry into the highest circles, even after being kept. Upon marriage, she had to retire, but a royal order often allowed her to return to the stage.

A stage box had many uses. The occupant often paid no attention to the spectacle, but drew all the curtains and sat, unseen, comfortable in winter with fur wraps, feet on a charcoal warming box, in the company of visitors whom it might be difficult to receive publicly at home.

Dancer: last quarter XVIIIc. modifications of ballet costume established by La Camargo. Old woman: black and white cap and scarf; face enclosed by shell-shaped pleats of the cap.

Gentlemen: shorter double-breasted waistcoat forming sharp lapels; frock coat with deeply pointed collar and narrow inconspicuous cuff; wide curved shoebuckles covering entire instep.

People begin to tire of being waited on by a clutter of lackeys; they send them out and serve themselves at their ease (N). In Olivier's "Thé à l'Anglaise" (Ill. 1867) the countess de Boufflers, in an apron, replaces a servant while Mozart plays. Older ladies pour out tea. Chafing dishes and small stands make self-service comfortable. In France in XXc. that rare fruit, the pineapple, is still sliced from the bottom at table, and the remainder is set on a tall, handsome stand to await its next use.

Men's wigs are seen deteriorating toward natural hair; it may even be natural hair dressed as a wig in a careless style. Women's hair, clubbed up in back in braids, is set with the standard three plumes and gauze decorations of ceremony. *Polonaise* styles begin to affect more ceremonious dress, like this gown, banded with leopard between lines of plain fur (see also K).

All Europe is flooded with caricatures of extravagant fashions. This *pouf* (O), with its vegetable plots and gardener with a rake, is hardly more extravagant than many which were actually worn. Mme. de Matignon had her hair-dresser under contract at 24,000 livres a year, to supply her with a new headdress daily. (Taine: *Ancien Régime.*)

1890

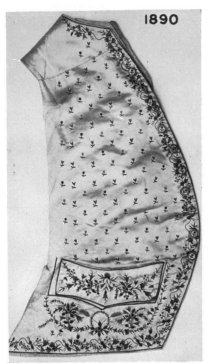

1891

1892

1893

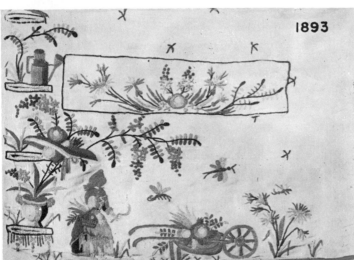

1895

1894

1890. XVIIIc. Louis XVI. French.
  Waistcoat: cream satin; chain-stitch embroidery in pastel colored silks.
1891. XVIIIc. French?
  Waistcoat: pounced and painted India cotton; part of male negligee.
1892. XVIIIc. French.
  Waistcoat.
1893. XVIIIc. French.
  Waistcoat: detail of embroidery.
1894. Early XIXc. French.
  Dress border: detail of embroidery.

Courtesy of Metropolitan Museum of Art

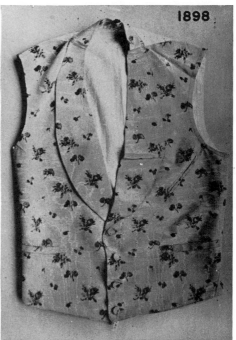

1895. XVIIIc. 1774-92. French.
   Waistcoat: embroidery detail.

1896. XVIII-XIXc. 1785-1805. Italian, Venice.
   Waistcoat: double-breasted.

1897. XIXc. c. 1800. French.
   Waistcoat: linen; double-breasted. Washable white dimities, twills, and corded cottons, embroidered in silver and sometimes a little black, were made especially for summer waistcoats in late XVIII-early XIXc. Museum of Fine Arts, Boston, has a number of examples.

1898. XIXc. c.1830. French?

Waistcoat: figured moiré.

1899. XIXc. English.
   Waistcoat: shawl collar; plum brocade, embroidered.

1900. XVIIIc. c. 1780. Italian, Venice.
   Coat and breeches: red grosgrain with satin stripe.

1901. XVIIIc. 1785-90. Italian, Venice.
   Coat: striped satin.

1902. Third quarter XVIIIc. French.
   Suit: black velvet coat, black satin waistcoat, blue glass ornaments; breeches modern.

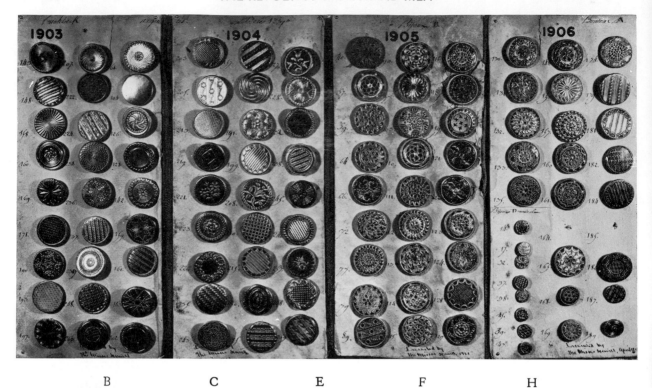

B   C   E   F   H

A   D   G

1903-06. XVIIIc. French. (New York, Cooper Union Mus.)

Sample card containing buttons of metal foil, metal thread and spangles. A contemporary note enclosed with this reads: "May, 1780, Notes of samples of buttons in gilding and silvering, sent to Messieurs Antoine Guillemot father and son of Thiers, and chez Garby, Manufactory of buttons at Clermont to be paid for with rebate for cash. From Nos. 1-30 all the buttons are (priced) at Ten livres the set of 30 large and 30 small."

Courtesy of Cooper Union Museum

1907. XVIII-XIXc. Various. (New York, Cooper Union Museum.) Buttons.

A. XVIIIc. French. Pearl, steel, glass, copper. B. XVIIIc. French. Pearl shell, metal foil, brass, rhinestones. C. XIXc. Dutch. Pearl shell, porcelain painted on blue, brass. D. XVIIIc. French. White paper, blue silk, glass, copper. E. Late XVIIIc. French. Insects, shells, sea-weed, tin, paper, copper, glass. F. Late XVIIIc. English. Stone ware mounted in copper. G. Late XVIIIc. Copper. H. XIXc. French. Steel, stained and cut out.

1908. XVIIIc. 1760-80. English, London.
Watch by John Witwer: gold, double case.

1909. XVIIIc. 1783-4. French, Paris.

Watch by Daniel Vauchez: back shows the Montgolfier balloon ascension, wreathed in wrought gold leaves, enamel and pearls; face black with white numerals, set around with diamonds; 2 hands; cylindrical escape movement. Only survivor of 12 balloon watches by Vauchez.

1910. XIXc. French, Paris. (Hearn Coll.)
Watch by Abraham Louis Breguet: gold with borders in champlevé enamel on front and back; painted pastoral scene.

1911. Early XIXc. Swiss.
Mourning watch and pin: gold and enamel, marked Tiffany for retailer.

1912. XIXc. Swiss.
Banjo watch.

1913. XVIIIc. c. 1790. French, Paris.
Watch by Vauchez.

1914. Late XVIIIc. French or Swiss. (Hearn Coll.)
Watch by Clary: gold face edged with pearls on blue enamel; back, enamelled portrait on white ground, studded with pearls.

1915. XVIIIc. French.
    Fob.
1916. Late XVIIIc. Swiss?
    Watch chatelaine; gold and enamelled steel.
1917. Late XVIIIc. English.
    Watch fob.

1918. Late XVIIIc. German.
    Fob, with seal and miniature.
1919. XVIII-XIX. German.
    Watch fob; silver and precious stones.
1920. XIXc. 1840-50. German.
    Watch fob; gold and enamel.

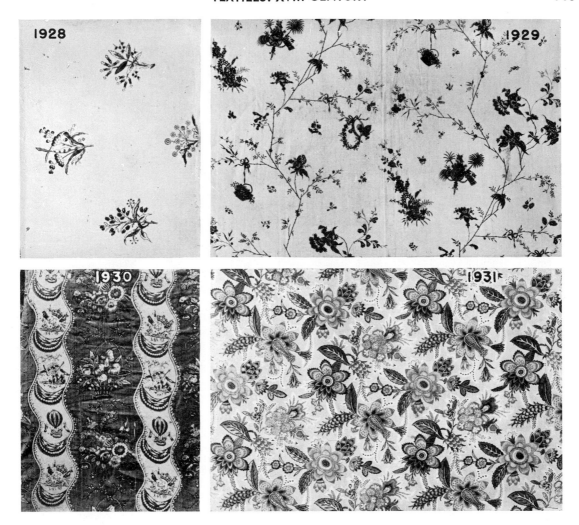

1921. First half XIXc. English.
Fob with seal.

1922. XVIIIc. 1777-8. French, Paris.
Carnet de bal: gold and enamel; *Souvenir* in brilliants.

1923. XVIIIc. French.
Etui for sealing wax, by Melchior René Barre (master, 1768-d.after 1791).

1924. XVIIIc. French.
Carnet de bal: Cotot enamel, *Je meurs ou je m'attache*.

1925. XVIIIc. English, Staffordshire.
Snuff box: Staffordshire enamel on copper; pastoral scene on white ground.

1926. Late XVIII-e.XIXc. French.
Bonbon box: Napoleonic symbols.

1927. Second third XIXc. English, London.
Snuff box: gold with cipher of William IV of England.

Containers are becoming increasingly specialized. Boxes to hold dance programs become a favorite in last quarter XVIIIc. Like everything else, they show the influence of Rousseau. Hard realism in love is turning to sentimentality, with weeping willows and funeral urns set on classic pillars.

The penny post is well established, with hourly

Courtesy of Metropolitan Museum of Art (1915-25, 1927-31); Museum of Fine Arts, Boston (1926)

collections from 500 London coffee shops. Everyone writes letters, however badly spelled. There are no envelopes; letters are often written on the back of the latest printed news-sheet, which the recipient will not have seen; it is folded and sealed with wax carried in an *étui;* seals dangle from every fob and chatelaine.

Charming, inexpensive enamelled boxes began to be mass-produced by an offset process at Battersea in 1750-60, and later at Staffordshire. They hold patches and pins as well as snuff, which is beginning to lose ground. Since Charlotte of Mecklenburg-Strelitz loved snuff and royalty is slow to change conventions, her sons, George IV and William IV, carried snuff boxes and went through the motions of taking it, without actually doing so. To offer and to accept snuff was a traditional mark of courtesy.

1928. XVIIIc. 1770-75. French.
Floral print: polychrome woodblock in linen.

1929. XVIIIc. c. 1785. French, Jouy?
Floral print: polychrome woodblock with black lines on linen.

1930. XVIIIc. 1790. French, Nantes? or Rouen?
Balloon print.

1931. Late XVIIIc. French, Jouy.
Floral block-printed cotton, from the Oberkampf factory at Jouy, with their mark; designed by *Dubuison*.

1932-38. XVIIIc. 1778. French.

"Galerie des Modes et Costumes Français" (1778-87).

The plates in this publication are in color. Quoted material, here given, has been translated from the original captions.

1932. *Le Clere.* "Young Woman."
"*Caraco à la Polonaise* of vermicelli-patterned cotton, edged with a narrow band; the petticoat edged with a wide band with garlands of flowers on a white ground."

1933. *Desraies.* "Young Lady Lying on a Couch."
"Hair dressed in a round bonnet of corded linen with a headband tied informally around it; fur lined pelisse over undress."

1934. *Desraies.* "Pretty Dancer."
"Pleated, low-necked caraco of golden brown Italian taffeta; flowered batiste apron, trimmed to match the caraco; rose colored bows."

Rosettes and ribbon; pair of fobs; increasing size of ruffled white hats; apron with large pocket reappeared briefly c.1780.

1935. *Le Clere.* "Dressmaker and Girl Delivering Work."
Fashionable dress, gloves and fan, but dark apron with bib.

1936. *Le Clere.* "Ladies' Tailor Trying on a Corset."
"Nut brown coat (lined with green); black velvet collar with two gold buttonholes; similar buttons and buttonholes on the suit; vest of cerise tricot with gold tassels; black velvet breeches (banded and buckled in gold); gray silk stockings. The young woman wears only a simple petticoat and white stockings; and her breast is covered [*sic*] with a yellow-tinted cambric."

White *pouf* with red ribbons, red and yellow flowers and green leaves; pink slippers ruched in green; pink and red striped dressing gown with a green lining and white *sabots* (on right, not shown).

Courtesy of Metropolitan Museum of Art, Print Room (1932-38)

1937. *Desraies.* "Young Woman on Her Morning Walk."

"*Polonaise* with tubular trimming; two watches; her hair dressed in a new *pouf* elegant."

Tall, tasseled walking stick; pair of fobs.

1938. *Le Clere.* "Bourgeoise."

"Striped satin dress; fur-trimmed *pelisse,* and white muff."

1939. XVIIIc. March 30, 1778. French.

Moreau le j. The Crowning of Voltaire.

The exiled Voltaire finally bought an estate at Ferney on Lake Geneva, to which pilgrimages were made from all over the world. After twenty-eight years he was able to return to Paris in 1778 for the opening of his last play "Irène," at the Théâtre Français. The old philosopher was acclaimed by the city; the other greatest citizen of the world, Benjamin Franklin, brought his nephew for Voltaire's blessing. The play was poor, but Voltaire was honored, a few weeks later, by a ceremony which was attended by most of the royal family—although not by the king.

Moreau shows Voltaire watching from a box. Actually, it was on Voltaire's own head, as he stood on the stage and the audience cried: "Let him be crowned!" that Mme. Vestris set the laurel wreath, while Voltaire's protégé, Lekain, declaimed, "'Tis the people of France that send it."

The Théâtre Français, run by its own members, the *sociétaires,* who paid for their own theatre, had become the most important in Europe. The first attempt to simplify the theatrical costume of Louis XIV, and relate dress to the play, was made in 1755 by the designer Leclere, and Sarrasin, the court costumer, for Voltaire's "Orphelin de la Chine." Lekain, whom we see on the stage in a long robe, gave up the tinsel cuirasse and plumes, and Mlle. Clairon played without paniers, for the first time on the stage since paniers were invented. Actors were dim figures on candle-lit stages; glittering sequins and waving plumes are not only a tradition, but will remain a necessity until theatres become well-lighted in XIXc. A personal pronunciation of Vestris' in declaiming words like *amour* as *amou—re,* still affects French dramatic acting. (Mme. de Genlis: *Mémoires.*)

1940. XVIIIc. 1778-85. French.

Paul Joilly. Franklin at the Court of France.

"Figure to yourself an Old Man, with grey Hair, Appearing under a Martin Cap, among the Powder'd Heads of Paris," Franklin said the year before his arrival as ambassador in 1778.

The king opposed French aid and recognition for America, even as he signed an alliance in 1778 after Burgoyne's defeat. But the wily old man in the brown coat of an "American agriculturalist," in his own unpowdered hair and his round Quaker hat, was already one of the world's most famous people. He was a member of all the important learned societies of Europe; his apparent modesty and mildness disarmed even anti-democratic courtiers; he was Catholic, Protestant or atheist, depending on the company in which he found himself; he ingratiated himself with every sort and condition of man and woman, young or old. "Such was the number of portraits, busts, and medallions of him in circulation before he left Paris that he would have been recognized from them by any adult citizen in any part of the civilized world." (F. C. Schlosser). (See Appendix).

At a reception for the democrat and Quaker, the court appears in simple, dark brocade gowns, not the pale, gauzy splendor of Moreau's *dame du palais* on a fête day; the headdress is also less extravagant, though it retains the three plumes required in court appearance. Men: muffs; widely ribbed stockings. Man (seen against arched doorway) shows the diagonally-set sprays of embroidery, which will develop into a massive gold form at Napoleon's court.

1941. XVIIIc. 1779. French. (Metropolitan Mus., Print Room.)

E. C. de Carmontelle. The Jeu de Bague.

In 1778, the duc de Chartres (later Philippe Egalité) bought a large property from Grimaud de la Reynière, seigneur de Monceau. Great gardens were designed by Carmontelle for the *Folies de Chartres,* as the park was then called. New city walls established by the Fermiers-généraux in 1784 reduced its size. It was nationalized in 1794 and rented as an amusement park where a chute-the-chutes was erected, and was variously disposed of by Napoleon and Louis XVIII. In 1852 it was reacquired by the city and redesigned by Alphand in 1861 into the present Parc Monceau.

The gregarious sparkle of the general assemblies of society of the 1760's at balls, gambling tables, or concerts, gave way to an era of waiting apprehension, aimless, witless gossip, relieved by bursts of mindless physical activity: games of hide and seek, and blind man's buff. (Campan).

The excavations of 1750 loosed a flood of styles *à la grecque.* Carmontelle had amused himself a decade before Hogarth's "Five Orders of Periwigs" (cf.) with the notion of constructing clothes composed

from the five orders of classical architecture.

The playful spirit of Carmontelle and of his era is expressed here in a merry-go-round with Chinese attendants, and grown women in *polonaises* and *caracos* snatching at brass rings—the intermediate step between puppet shows and mechanical toys beloved of the midXVIIIc., and the huge chute-the-chutes of the First Republic.

1942. XVIIIc. 1765. English, Woolmer. (Boston, Mus. of Fine Arts.)

Printed Cotton Bed Curtain: pastoral scene.

1943. XVIIIc. 1783. French, Jouy. (Metropolitan Mus.)

"Les travaux de la manufacture": showing the Oberkampf factory at Jouy, designed by J. B. Huot; red copperplate on linen.

1944. XVIIIc. c. 1790. French, Nantes. (Metropolitan Mus.)

"Tombeau de J. J. Rousseau": from Petitpierre et Cie., Nantes; copperplate in mulberry.

1945. XVIIIc. c. 1800. English (Metropolitan Mus.)

"Penn's Treaty with the Indians": historical cop-perplate in mulberry. Most of these copperplates were printed in a variety of colors; red, brown, blue and mulberry.

1946-63. XVIIIc. c. 1780. French. (New York, Cooper Union Mus.)

A. Brunias. Painted Ivory Buttons.

These buttons, which are supposed to have belonged to Toussaint l'Ouverture, the Negro ruler of Haiti, and a similar engraving in the Cooper Union collection, are the work of an Englishman, Abraham or Auguste Brunias (as the engraving is signed), or Brunais (as given by Thieme-Becker). He exhibited in the Free Society in London, 1763-4, Society of Artists, 1770, and contributed subjects from the West Indies from 1777-79. The print is dedicated to Sir Francis Blake, who had returned to England but came of a family which had been connected with the West Indies for generations.

The extremes of French costume and headdress are enchantingly modified and transmuted in this unique record of colonial Negro dress. Until the

French Revolution, the prosperous island of Saint-Dominique, as it was still called, had a large population of well-to-do free mulattoes and Negroes. The white population's antagonism to the granting of French citizenship to the Negroes in 1791, and the repressive measures they took, led to the Revolution of Toussaint and to brief, fantastic grandeur of Christophe's court, which ended with his suicide in 1820. Christophe's great peaked mountain-top fortress, built by man-power alone, is one of the world's most astonishing engineering feats.

Cotton began to be printed all over France, Al-

sace and Switzerland by 1760. Nantes, where the dynasty of the Petitpierres worked, 1760-1866, was the great pre-Revolutionary center of cotton printing for the export trade with Africa and the Antilles. By 1789, it had nine factories, employing 4,500 workers and producing 120,000 pieces.

1964. XVIIIc. 1780. French. (Met. Mus., Print Room.)

P. A. Wille. The Petit Waux-hall.

Jean Georges Wille (1715-1808) was a South German engraver established in Paris after 1736, who reproduced paintings by Rigaud, Tocqué and Pesne. His less talented son, *Pierre Alexandre Wille,* was an officer in the National Guard, and died in poverty in 1815.

The success of the English pleasure gardens led to their imitation in Paris. Two Vauxhalls were opened. The Waux-hall Torre (later the Summer Waux-hall) was opened by an Italian whose name it bore, in the mixed Saint-Laurent quarter of pleasure houses and aristocratic hôtels; it provided fireworks and pantomimes, and after 1768, great fêtes in a ball-room which became too crowded for dancing.

The end of the Champs Elysées was still dirty or muddy, but it had begun to be filled with places of amusements and cafés like the Ambassadeurs. The $450,000 Rotunda and gardens of the Waux-hall Colisée, opened there in 1770 for dancing, gambling and spectacles, had a comparatively short success of about a decade.

The showily overdressed young person wears one of the newest hats, which will surpass even the larg-

est *pouf* hair arrangement in size and elaboration. She combines a Medici ruff with a shoulder-cape, on a long-sleeved *polonaise,* looped up almost as short as a *caraco;* immense nosegay. Old companion-duenna in a round cap with semicircles of pleating over the ears; elaborate silk *palatine.* Tasseled cane and obvious wig; quizzing glass and head which may be own hair powdered. Concentration of any fullness of coat-skirts into pleats below a button, set farther back in cutaway frock coat.

1965. XVIIIc. 1783. French.

von Göz. Supplement to Faded Charms.

The lady's aids are as outmoded as her looks: patches went nearly out of style under Louis XV; blood is still let to insure a pale complexion, and rouge is worn only by actresses, though a natural, healthy look is beginning to be valued. Paired *jansénistes* have been superseded by crinoline petticoats; and the new corset of 1778 can be seen in *Galerie des Modes.* (No. 1936).

1966-67. XVIIIc. 1781. French.

"Galerie des Modes."

1966. *Le Clere.*

"Dress worn by a lady of quality during the mourning for Maria Theresa of Austria, mother of the Emperor and the Queen of France: *Pelisse-lévite* with ermine collar, belt and edges; petticoat of black-dotted white satin; matching muff banded in ermine; *pouf* surmounted by batiste flowers and plumes."

The *lévite,* a fitted gown based on the tabernacle robes of the priests of Jerusalem, continues the trend

Courtesy of Metropolitan Museum of Art, Print Room (1968-69)

towards flowing garments. The point of the bodice is beginning to be lost under belts and sashes.

1967. *Le Clere.* "Half Mourning."

"White silk vest embroidered in black; black silk or cloth coat; white silk stockings; narrow ruffles."

Hair loosens and roughens; vest shorter, its edges cut away sharply from lowest button.

There is a "recrudescence of noblomania" just before the Revolution. Interest is revived in genealogy and heraldry; coats of arms and coronets are imposed on personal belongings. Shopkeepers' wives, who probably used "l'Autrichienne" as a curse after Marie Antoinette's marriage, appear in mourning, and answer commiserations at their loss by explaining that it is for the queen's mother. During Marie-Thérèse's last year of ill health, Marie Antoinette had sewed grave clothes for her mother; black shagreen snuff boxes, marked with the queen's initials and the legend *consolation en chagrin* were profitably hawked about the streets immediately after Marie-Thérèse's death.

1968. XVIIIc. c. 1783. French

Fr. Dequevauviller, after *Lavreince.* L'assemblée au salon.

The Goncourts point out the strict lines of classic architecture, leading to a few forgotten cupids; the absence of effervescence, glitter and conviviality in these last salons where a few friends pass the time together in broken groups. A girl reads by a window; alone; an abbé and a woman holding an ear-trumpet play a game of tric-trac; the conversation in the background is an earnest dissertation; the card game is time won from boredom without the old excitement in gambling.

The *polonaise,* shirred trimmings and cap of the deaf woman are giving way to the plain, trailing belted English gowns, kerchiefs and hats of the callers. Locks begin to trail; even the hair which we see from behind is no longer turned up in firm arrangements of braids.

1969. XVIIIc. French.

Augustin Legrand, after *Lavreince.* Jamais d'accord.

Intimate friendship and confidences go on between women, even though their pets do not agree. Not until now does a cat begin to rival a dog as a pet. Chaste mirror; console table which is almost a Greek altar; vase of cottage flowers; late Louis XVI chairs with pads on arms.

Cap into bonnet; falling curls into uncurled locks; huge feathered hats. Kerchief puffed to chin, elaborated into a series of collars. Striped gown showing vestiges of the former *caraco* (reduced to a frill over the bustle), and the *polonaise* (in the way in which the white muslin overskirt, which is merely an extension of the apron, is looped up out of the mud).

1970-72. XVIIIc. 1785. French.

"Galerie des Modes."

A decade after *Watteau's* death, his younger brother *Noël,* had a son, *Louis-Joseph,* b. 1731, who married, and was living at Lille in 1755; he and his son, *François,* are both designated by the name *Watteau de Lille.* Many other useful fashion plates appear in the "Cabinet des Modes," 1785-9, Paris.

1970. *Watteau de Lille.*

"The gleaming Nymph of the Palais-Royal; offering to the public the charm of face and elegance of figure which bring her merited praises; her head is dressed *à la Suzanne* with a *juste à la Figaro.*"

One of the most eminent architects of the Revolution was the son of a watchmaker named Caron. A watch which the younger Caron made for Mme. de Pompadour first brought him to court attention; he married money and bought a title. After changing his name to Beaumarchais, he became involved in lawsuits and imprisonment; his own brilliant defense freed him; he found himself a popular hero. While working in England as a secret agent of France, Beaumarchais became a violent partisan of the American cause which he supplied with arms, personally and through the government.

Beaumarchais wrote two audacious plays about a character as subtle and witty as himself, named Figaro. "The Barber of Seville" was staged after some years of delay in 1775; the queen and the king's brothers acted in it at the Petit Trianon. "The Marriage of Figaro" was prevented from being shown for half a dozen years by the king. His brothers were part of the audience which, in 1784, received deliriously this mockery of the king and their own society. The old, old duke of Richelieu, who had lived under three French kings, told Louis XVI: "Sire, under Louis XIV, no one dared to utter a word; under Louis XV, they whispered; under your Majesty they talk out loud." A Frenchman, returning after long absence, found the chief change was that "people are now saying in the streets what used to be said in drawing rooms."

The names of characters in Beaumarchais' plays were applied to everything, as we see in the case of the Brilliant Nymph's headdress and close-fitting jacket.

Curls and chignon now tumble, loose and free. Caps return to domestic use, as informal hats and the great decorations imposed on ceremonious heads merge, indistinguishable and extravagant. Even the mob cap turns into a huge lingerie hat. The tailored English style is preeminent. The bosom is enormously emphasized, not by exposure in the earlier French manner, but by extravagant *bouffants*, English muslin kerchiefs. *Polonaise* and *caraco* have passed, but their influence is seen in the long point at the back of the bodice, in its frilled peplum, and in the concentration of interest and skirt fullness into a high, humped bustle on trailing skirts. The reappearance of muslin from England is so welcome that any garment not made entirely of muslin is apt to have an apron as well as a kerchief; many dotted muslins in use.

1971. *Le Clere*. "Suit for the Lieutenant of Police at Audiences."

Marc-René de Voyer, Marquis d'Argenson, was father both to the modern police force and to d'Argenson of the Memoirs, "the best citizen that ever tasted the ministry." The peculiar efficiency of the Paris police today is based on techniques established by d'Argenson during his twenty-one years, from 1697, as Lieutenant General of Police. He spread a finely-meshed net which caught information at every level. A report of every word, every occurrence at the palace, in the intimacy of every salon, as well as in every gathering of thieves reached him, not later than next day, from informants of every class, from members of the royal family down. The marquis had every necessary quality of decision and discrimina-

tion, but he was also a man of breeding, humor and even of surprising heart.

This official costume is, as we expect, conservative in cut, and anachronistic in detail, like the attached mantle of dignity, and in place of a stock and ruffles, the *rabat* worn at the time when the office was first established.

1972. *Le Clere*. "Negligée of a young lady of quality.

"The dress is a sort of *chemise* in thin silk; round gauze bonnet; frilled *fichu;* muslin apron. The child wears a frock coat with his sailor's trousers and hat."

Round cap elaborated into a bonnet; dresses of sheer materials, full and easy; pleated decorations have deteriorated into mere fullness. The *sans culotte* trousers of sailors and working men appear on the children of French gentlemen; full, ruffled collar.

1973-76. XVIIIc. 1784. French.

"Galerie des Modes."

1973. *Watteau de Lille*.

"Lovely Dorine, brilliant as Venus, occupied by thoughts of what she has read in a note dictated by the most acute love. Robe *à la Malbrouk* and hat *à la Charlotte*."

Proliferation of sentimentality—cottage nosegays, muslin, flounces and bustle. Anglomania: hat given the name of Queen Charlotte; everyone in France, including Marie Antoinette, sings "Malbrouk s'en va t'en-guerre." Shoe buckle turning into rosette.

1974. *Watteau de Lille*.

"Woman of quality lately risen from childbed walking at the hour of noon to take the air. The first fruit of a happy hymen is her sole occupation and augurs its durable happiness. She wears a large, lined satin *pelisse,* trimmed with two rows of martin, and her head is enveloped in a *Thérèse* of solid-color taffeta."

More hygiene, classical allusions, sentimentality and motherhood, together with warm cloak for the coldest winter since 1763, and an enveloping *calash* hood, which can be raised or lowered over the largest hat and headdress by the fanning hinged hoops which support it.

1975. *Watteau de Lille*.

"This English beauty, impressed by the rarities she has met with in Paris, but casting a proud air and in-

Courtesy of Metropolitan Museum of Art, Print Room (1970-76)

different glance at the beauties she sees crowding the Palais-Royal, walks with a majestic mien, dressed in a great winter *pelisse* made of satin trimmed with martin, and a long gown with double trimmings and a muff of shaggy fur."

The last of the *catogan* is seen here in her clubbed-up longest lock, under the wide, plumed English hat. Muffs increase in size and elaboration. In 1794, English costume is pale, worn with bright-colored beaver hats, and muffs of eiderdown or fur in striped combinations of white, beige or gray. By 1797, dresses are darker, maroon or puce. Muffs, greatly enlarged, are of darker furs, tan and brown, worked into elaborate check and diamond patterns.

1976. *Watteau de Lille.*

"Mincing Marinette with her darling pet poodle on a public promenade dressed in a light morning robe and hat *à la Zazara.*"

It was a similar small dog, escaped from its mistress, which jumped on Louis XVI as he walked in the Tuileries, and was killed by him with his stick.

Increased size of hat and plumes (black and white, with striped olive-green ribbons to match the dog's leash); elaboration of kerchief into puffed section enclosing chin, and cape of white pleating, over compound capes of the pink fabric of dress and petticoat. The vestige of the *polonaise* point in back is usually suppressed, as by this wide black belt. Trailing overskirt, lined with white to match the white ruffle and petticoat, is bustled up in back, in walking costume.

1977. XVIIIc. 1787. French. (Versailles, Nat. Mus.)

Copy of *A. Girous.* Mlle. d'Orléans Receiving a Harp Lesson from her Governess, Mme. de Genlis.

Mme. de Genlis (1740-1830), poor, noble, spirited, well-educated, and an accomplished harpist, was the niece of a clever writer, Mme. de Montesson, who became the secret second wife of the old duke of Orleans. In 1770, through this influence, Mme. de Genlis was made governess of the daughters of his son, the duke of Chartres (Philippe Egalité). In 1780, in an unprecedented move, she was also made tutor of the boys of the family.

Mme. de Genlis' educational methods were far in advance of her time. A botanist accompanied the children on their walks; lantern slides enlivened their history lessons, and Mme. de Genlis later published a series of educational plays which she had written for them to perform. The people who served them were chosen for special knowledge from different nationalities; each spoke his native language with them. Mme. de Genlis was an expert book-binder, and the children became almost professional leather-workers; they learned to marble paper, make artificial flowers, weave ribbons, carpenter—even to make wigs. Any technique about which they read in the Encyclopédie they were taken to see in the factory. They constructed miniature chemistry and physics laboratories complete with tiny implements and glassware; these were exhibited in the *Galeries* of the Palais-Royal, and during the Empire Mme. de Genlis saw them still on exhibition in the Louvre. Mlle. d'Orléans started harp lessons, twice daily, at five, and was so expert at seven years of age that she played with three other instruments at a regular weekly concert, before an audience.

Mme. de Genlis' "adopted" daughter, the delight-

ful Pamela, who was given in marriage by Philippe Egalité (Orléans) to the romantic, unfortunate Lord Edward Fitzgerald of the abortive Irish Rebellion, was probably Mme. de Genlis' own daughter by Orleans. Orleans represented a grave danger to the crown. He had married the greatest fortune in France; he associated with intellectuals; he was dissolute, but his manners were charming and very considerate. Court feeling against him became so intense and Marie Antoinette's enmity so particularly marked that Orleans spent a great deal of time in England between 1778-90. He became a crony of the sporting Prince of Wales, absorbed egalitarian ideas, and became the main channel through which Anglomania in ideas and clothes flooded France. He opened the gardens of his Palais-Royal to the public. Under his protection, orators inflamed its crowds; it was the incubation place and the heart of the Revolution. He renounced his title, became Citizen Egalité and a member of the Assembly, where he voted for Louis XVI's execution. He seems sincerely to have had no desire to be made king, but too many of his admirers wished it; his wealth and his popularity made him as great a danger to the Revolution as he had been to the Regime; in 1793 he too was executed.

Mme. de Genlis, like Orleans, suffered from the hatred of the royal family, and shared his republican sympathies, but not his fate. At the fall of the Girondist moderates, she fled to Switzerland with Mlle. d'Orléans and supported herself by her pen and brush until she was able to return to France on a pension from Napoleon. She wrote valuable ten-volume memoirs.

Soft, pseudo-classical *chemises,* hair-ribbons; striped, severe, long-sleeved costumes with jackets like a bob-tailed frock-coat, the backward flow of which is emphasized by large, plain *fichus* crossed over the breast and tied behind; hems and sashes edged with fringe; high-crowned leghorn hats.

The results of excavation of the cities buried by Vesuvius in 79 A.D. has been felt since c. 1760. Herculaneum was sporadically dug, 1748-80, and Pompeii systematically from 1763. Their bronze and marble statues, Roman wall-paintings and furniture have drawn many travellers, and affect European architec-

1977

ture, decoration and costume. Interest is particularly intense in fermenting France; it turns from its own traditions, court-supported, and therefore corrupted by the Regime, to what it feels is the uncontaminated art of the classic democracies. This will result in a period of great archaeological activity in Italy under Napoleon. His Egyptian Campaign of 1798-1801 will arouse interest in the art of another ancient civilization, as will Layard's expedition to Nineveh and Babylon, 1845-51.

Classic revival influence in architecture and furniture; Roman tripod music stand.

1978. XVIIIc. 1787. French. (Louvre.)

A. Vestier. Mme. Vestier and Child.

Antoine Vestier (1740-1824) began exhibiting late in 1782, and did a number of portraits and miniatures of National Guard officers, 1795-1801. His wife, daughter of the master-émailleur Révèrend, was also a portrait painter.

High-crowned Leghorn hats; striped ribbons and plumes set on loosely fluffed, unsupported hair. Simply cut, almost untrimmed gowns; embroidered muslin ruffles. Shoes trimmed with ribbon ruching in place of buckle. Children now wear short-waisted muslin dresses, the neck finished with simple ruffles.

1979. XVIIIc. 1787. French. (Versailles, Nat. Mus.)

Vigée-Lebrun. Marie Antoinette, Madame Royale, the Dauphin, and the Duc de Normandie.
1980. XVIIIc. 1789. French. (Louvre.)
Vigée-Lebrun. Mme. Molé-Raymond.
Elizabeth Louise Vigée-Lebrun (1775-1842), daughter of a professor of painting at Saint-Luc, was aided by Greuze and Joseph Vernet. She married a picture dealer-artist named Lebrun; became Marie Antoinette's favorite painter. She foresaw the Revolution and went to Italy in 1789; she painted her saccharine portraits in the German principalities and during six years in St. Petersburg. She returned to Paris in 1802, then worked three years in London.

Both the queen and the actress of the Comédie Française show hair only slightly powdered, falling wide and loose, under immense hats or *poufs;* gowns simple in cut, of unpatterned material, and fur-trimmed or with fur accessories. Children's clothes simpler.

Mme. Molé-Raymond has a blue satin hat, with a gray plume caught by a lavender-violet bow; gauze scarf crossed and tied in back, over a lavender-violet satin gown with a blue skirt. Beige-tan muff, in the terrible winter of which Mme. Campan tells, when the fish froze in the sea, and olive trees split in the Midi.

1981. XVIIIc. 1788. French. (Versailles, Nat. Mus.)
A. Labille-Guiard. Elizabeth of France.
Adelaide Labille-Guiard (1749-1803) studied miniature painting with E. Vincent and pastel with Latour, and did portraits of Mesdames, Louis XV's sisters. She was received into the Academy of Saint-Luc in 1774 and that of Paris, 1783, in both cases in the same years as was Vigée-Lebrun.

As the Revolution approaches, French costume loses its national assurance and homogeneity. It is affected by the classical democracies of the past; by the growing English democracy of the present; by exotic garments and turbans from the East; and by romantic XVIIc. styles which have shown an influence in England.

Louis XVI's loyal sister, the decent and kind Madame Elizabeth, who will lose her head in half a dozen years for no more than loyalty, wears a hat straight out of a Rembrandt or Bols portrait; it carries their favorite tall, uncurled ostrich plume, though the toque of velvet has been expanded into a brim with a cocking loop and button. Standing collar of lace; stomacher decoration; hem laced with XVIIc. guards. The same influence is seen on the baby's long-waisted, trailing dress with leading strings.

These "Van Dyke" styles with long, straight plumes, collars and cuffs, slashings and peplums affect dress through first half XIXc.

1982. XVIIIc. 1787. French.

P. L. Debucourt. Promenade of the Palais-Royal Gallery.

There are many colored engravings of the packed, mixed crowds of that hotbed of *égalitairisme,* the Palais Royal, in the years around the Revolution. Among the most valuable records of costume and manners are the aquatints of Philibert Louis Debucourt (1755-1832).

L. to r.:

Caricature of a man in tall coachman's hat with immense cockade, striped coat covered with square buttons painted with race horses, fobs dangling almost to knees, tasseled Hessian boots worn with knee breeches and stockings.

Man facing him: coachman's coat with tight body and long full skirts, controlled by a tab in back; immense buttons; braided whip.

Three daughters preceding mama and papa: caps set on powdered hair dressed in the old sausage rolls; *robes à la française* to the ground; watches swinging at the side on long chains, about as outmoded as a pomander in comparison to the paired fobs seen to the r. of them; mitts.

Two young women: immense hats, fancy ribbons, plumes; bosom exaggerated; waist infinitesimal; dangling fobs; dotted muslin; large shaggy muff of pale fur.

Children: girl in Van Dyke style; boy in sailor hat, triple collar like English redingote on jacket, breeches with knee-strings, boots with reversed tops.

Young woman: slightly powdered *hérisson* with falling *catogan,* satin pelisse, and large muff. Tiny cylindrical muff accompanying the dark bonnet to the r. Man in wig and *frac* carrying a huge beribboned muff. Man and woman at ext. r.: patterned cylindrical muffs.

1983. XVIIIc. 1788. French. (Met. Mus., Print Room.)

P. L. Debucourt. The Bouquets: Grandmother's fête-day.

Boy: high-crowned, wide-brimmed hat, striped frock coat and trousers; collar, tripled and wider.

Young mother: powdered *hérisson* with long straight lock; *bouffant* kerchief to the chin; dotted black lace cape; long-sleeved, untrimmed coat-dress and petticoat; dark sash-belt.

Little girl: shepherdess hat, short-waisted muslin dress, elaborate sash.

Grandmother: cap, *caraco,* flounced petticoat.

Young woman: hair dressed with a ribbon.

1984. XVIIIc. French. 1787-9. (Collection Chaux d'Est-Ange.)

Boilly. The jealous old man.

Louis-Léopold Boilly (1761-1845), self-taught son of a wood sculptor in Northern France, came to Paris in 1779. He saved himself, when denounced for his morals by another painter during the Terror, by a picture of Marat after his acquittal by the Revolutionary Tribunal. Boilly's crowds awaiting the arrival or departure of the diligence, playing billiards and smoking in cafes, are delightful documents of the costume and manners of the Empire.

The dress, with paired fobs, worn by the accused young woman is essentially that of Mme. de Genlis. The replacement of the muslin kerchief by crossed ropes of fur might indicate the extremely rigorous weather of 1789.

Fullness controlled by rows of shirring on the lower arm of older woman, and on short-waisted muslin gown of child; bordered ribbon sash.

1985. XVIIIc. 1790. French. (Florence, Uffizi.)

Vigée-Lebrun. Self-portrait.

1986. XVIIIc. French. (New York, Morgan Coll.)

Vigée-Lebrun. Marquise de Laborde.

The artist, and a member of the family of the count, Marie Antoinette's valet de chambre, who wrote the "Chansons de Laborde," illustrated by

Moreau le j., show romantic-exotic styles. Muslin turban, full neck ruffle like a child's, with a muslin puff beneath; metal-edged sash. Braids, used like a fillet across a turban of metal-edged gauze; long-sleeved *circassienne* over full *chemise* of plain and skirt of dotted, gauze; wide belt fastened with an enormous antique cameo.

1987. XVIIIc. July, 1789. French. (Met. Mus., Print Room.)

A. F. Sergent-Marceau. The People Running Through the Streets with Torches.

1988. XVIIIc. 1793-4. French. (Met. Mus., Print Room.)

R. Knotel. Uniforms of Officers and Troops of the National Guard.

The news of Necker's dismissal and retirement to Basle did not reach Paris until Sunday, July 12, 1789. The Palais-Royal crowds, led by Camille Desmoulins, feared that German mercenaries would be ordered to massacre patriots. Crowds surged through the streets all that night with torches, building barricades, burning customs houses and pillaging. The mercenaries were attacked, fled, and refused to return. The French guards stood between them and the people that night, but joined the people on the 13th when Lafayette established a citizens' guard. Ammunition had not arrived. The Arsenal and warehouse were sacked for arms and ammunition to supplement 50,000 pikes which blacksmiths had forged during thirty-six hours. Torches flared again all that night. On the 14th, the Invalides and the inadequately guarded Bastille and their supplies were taken. The king, who knew nothing of events in Paris, and who had had an unsuccessful day's hunting, wrote *"rien"* in his diary and went to bed, to be awakened in the middle of the night and told about the Revolution.

On the 15th Lafayette established the National Guard of Paris and was acclaimed its commander; he will refuse the supreme command of the National Guard of France in 1790. He designed for it a cockade of the white of the king with the red and blue of Paris, which, to the queen's indignation, Louis wore when he went before the Assembly on the 15th to promise cooperation, withdrawal of troops and recall of Necker. On June 12, 1792, Marie Antoinette will wear a tricolor and the King and Dauphin the Revolutionary red bonnet. The Assembly set to work on the Declaration of the Rights of Men and a Constitution, and the Revolution began to

spread through the provinces; chateaux and religious establishments were pillaged and burned; there were agrarian riots, and taxes could not be collected.

On the 17th the emigration of the nobility began, and grew to 6,000 a day.

Food did not reach Paris. On Oct. 5, a starving population marched to Versailles in a cold rain, inflamed by reports of the quite routine entertainment given a newly-arrived mercenary regiment which Lafayette had ordered to Versailles. The mob ordered "the baker, the baker's wife, and the baker's little boy" to leave Versailles and accompany them back to Paris, to take up the first period of their imprisonment as luxuriously maintained hostages in the Tuileries.

Make-shift citizen guards and weapons of July 12-15, with one grenadier (1987). National Guard uniforms during the Terror; shoes closed by laces.

1989. XVIIIc. 1774-93. French.

H. Robert. Allegory of the Decadence of the du Barry Family.

Marie-Jeanne Bécu (1746-93), illegitimate and uneducated, lively, warm-hearted, and very pretty, began life as a milliner's apprentice. She was discovered in a house of prostitution by Count Jean du Barry, who first used "Mlle. Lange" to draw trade to his gambling-house; he then married her to his brother Guillaume, as a necessary preliminary to her introduction to court in 1769, and her installation as Louis XV's mistress. She stayed with the King as he lay dying of smallpox, but before he could receive the last rites of the Church, he was forced to dismiss her. She lived in her chateau of Luciennes until 1792, on a pension finally granted by that "fat, ill-mannered boy," as she had described Louis XVI. She went to England to raise money on her jewels; at her return, on the testimony of former servants, like her Senegalese Zamar, she was convicted of selling state property and of having worn mourning for Louis XVI in London.

People of origins very like her own reviled du Barry during her lifetime, with a malevolence they had never shown toward Pompadour, and rejoiced at her fall. She was still contemptible to them in death, because she was the only person of consequence who went to the guillotine without dignity, weeping and pleading.

1990. XVIIIc. 1790. French. (Versailles, Nat. Mus.)
David. Bertrand Barère de Vieuzac.

Jacques Louis David (1748-1825), the most important painter of the classical revival, studied in Rome with Vien at the time of Winkelmann's excavations. He returned to Paris in 1780 as painter to Louis XVI. David became a leading Jacobin and voted for the death of the King, of Desmoulins, and of Danton, whose execution he sketched. He was the designer of the Revolutionary *Festival of the Supreme Being,* and painted large group pictures of Revolutionary and Napoleonic scenes. At the Restoration he was exiled to Belgium, and died there.

The clever, temporizing Barère (1755-1841), one of the most unprincipled and contemptible figures of the Revolution, was the journalist-orator who declared that "the tree of liberty could not grow were it not watered with the blood of kings." He began as an attractive provincial delegate and tutor of Orlean's daughter Pamela. He veered from Girondist to supporter of Robespierre; was influential in Robespierre's downfall, and was himself imprisoned. He served Napoleon, then played royalist and died a pensioner of Louis Philippe.

Wigs and powder were first renounced by the Jacobins; their absence becomes a trademark of the younger, more violent revolutionaries. Neck swathed high in a colored kerchief with knotted ends, over a high shirt collar. Narrow coat with standing, turned-over collar and notched lapels, open over short double-breasted vest with prominent lapels and paired pockets. Breeches with double-closing.

1991. XVIIIc. 1790. French. (Louvre.)
David. Marquise d'Orvillers.

Short natural curls bound by ribbon fillet. Gown: compromise between oriental and close-buttoned English coat styles; cut very low. Full chemise with spread collar, like those now worn by little boys, replaces kerchief; waistline shortened by sash. Oblong, ruffled-edged scarves.

1992. XVIIIc. French. (Metropolitan Mus.)
Leonard Defrance. The Rope.

In XVIIc. women rope-dancers wore skirts over their tights. Early in XVIIIc., they began to drop off their skirts during their act. "The Pleasantry of stripping almost Naked has since been practiced (where indeed it should have begun) at Bartholomew Fair," the Spectator said (No. 51).

Mixed company of spectators, the gentry in the middle. An abbé studies the performer through a spyglass. Woman and man in English styles: high-crowned hats and plain cloth garments; coat with long skirts, large buttons, short striped vest, riding boots. Townspeople and servants: caps, aprons and flounced petticoats. Boy in frock coat and breeches has frilled shirt collar opening out over the shoulders like our sailor collar.

1993. XVIIIc. c. 1791. French.

N. F. J. Masquelier, after *Moreau le jeune.* Arrival of Mirabeau at the Elysian Fields.

Gabriel-Honoré Riquetti, Count of Mirabeau (1749-91), was the son of a fantastic marquis and political writer of Marseilles, author of the "Friend of Man." The marquis detested his son, who had been hideously pock-marked at the age of three, and refused to let him bear the family name at school. The marquis, although his own life was as disor-

derly and turbulent as his son's, repeatedly got *lettres de cachet* issued against him for his conduct. After much time in jail, and revolutionary activities in Corsica, Mirabeau returned to Paris in 1771, and was readmitted to his family and society. He stumped the South of France and was elected to the Assembly in 1789. His brilliant, agile oratory, his logic and practical statesmanship, his culture and breadth of experience, made him its undisputed leader, until his constitution, weakened by excess, collapsed from overwork in 1791.

We see the fat, ugly, awkward, over-dressed and over-eager man described by his friend, the count de la Marck, arriving among the Immortals. The Spirit of Liberty floats over his head bearing the inscription, *Free France,* while Mirabeau hands a copy of one of his works to Rousseau from those which the other little spirits carry. Franklin, in his unpretentious dress, crowns him with oak leaves. Montesquieu, Voltaire, Mably and Fénelon approach to receive him, and Demosthenes and Cicero, in the background, watch and discuss the French orator.

1994-95. XVIIIc. 1792. French.

Debucourt. Promenade of the Palais-Royal Garden (1994). The Public Promenade (1995).

1994. Striped stockings are worn combined with culottes in the stripes which the Macaronis had loved, to give a premonitory effect of long trousers.

The accompanying frock coat is patterned (N, R), striped vertically (I), or horizontally. Its skirts are slender; their pleats have retreated to the back, below enormous buttons. Its sleeves are narrow, with an inconspicuous cuff. The collar is very high, often turned over; chest flaps are turned back into pointed lapels, exposing a short and usually double-breasted vest with lapels. A neckerchief mounts to the chin; shirt ruffles show only between the lapels of the vest. High-crowned, almost "top" hats (G, N), or bicornes (R), with a stressed cocarde, accompany these coats. English top hat, boots, sticks, and paired fobs (N).

Among the older men in the crowd we see every variation between this dress and the most conventional coat and wig, such as is worn by the gentleman in conversation with the nun.

Women's hats fall into four main categories. Very high-crowned, wide-brimmed Leghorn, trimmed with ribbon loops and bows which do not obscure the form of the hat-body (A, P, Q), are worn with the most dishevelled flowing locks and the most English garments. Hats with crowns concealed by masses of decoration are worn with more formally dressed hair (D, J), and English dress or a modification of it. Lingerie hats which developed out of caps (L) are worn with carefully dressed hair and frilly capes. Massed hair decoration of the *pouf* variety appears with the most conservatively French gowns. As *catogans* fall, the back hair is caught with a buckle.

Gowns of the English *redingote* style (A, J, P) have cape-like collars, wide lapels, long, tight sleeves, huge buttons, very wide belts which raise the waistline, fobs, crops, masculine neckwear (J), or puffed-out kerchiefs (Q). Fringe (A), enormous cameos (D), striped materials and crossed kerchief tied in back (M), dotted stuffs (Q), parasols (background, R. side). Child: sailor trousers and hat, frock coat with short sleeves and neck-ruffles.

1995. Where the catogan or falling hair, which is often topped only by ribbon loops (C, E), would be obscured by the brim of the hat, a scarf may flow from under the crown (A). Edges of kerchiefs (A and B), and the hem lines of short skirts (G), are becoming more insistently stressed. (A) is the perfect example of the type.

Multiple capes and collars, and buttoned tab fastenings (I). Male hair dressed like a wig, and falling into a collapsing *catogan* (I). Tricolor cocarde at knees (D, F).

Courtesy of Metropolitan Museum of Art, Print Room (1993-94);*Caisse Nationale des Monuments Historiques* (1995-96).

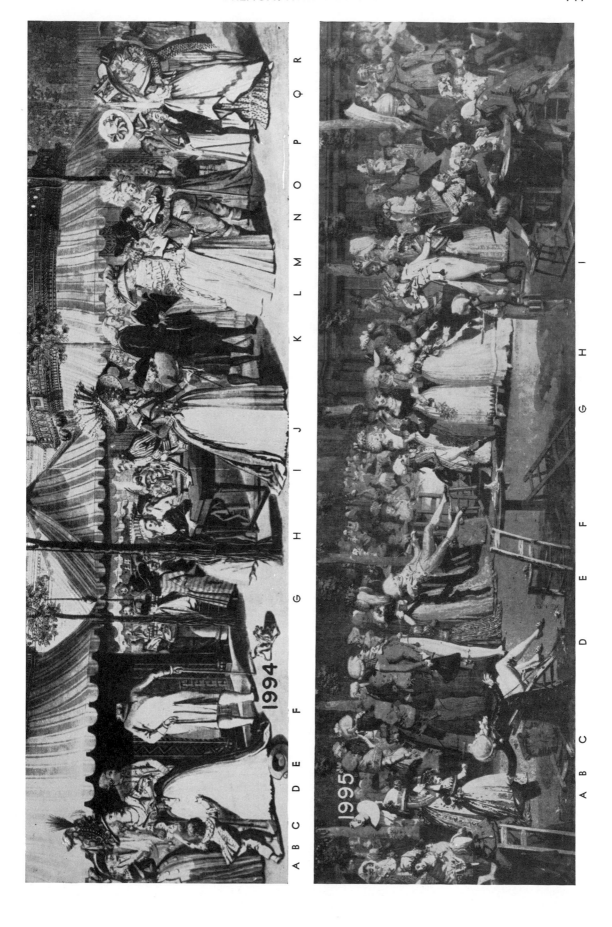

A B C D E F G H I J K L M N O P Q R

1994

1995

A B C D E F G H I

1996

1996. XVIIIc. 1794. French.
  Boilly. La Marche Incroyable.

The population which marched on Versailles in
sabots, and knitted while watching heads fall on the
guillotine, gets a first look at the fashions which begin about 1795 and culminate in the XIXc. Lanté-
Gatine plates of the Incroyables and Merveilleuses.

To our eyes, the costume seems much less likely to
scare a horse than anything seen within a horse's lifetime. Immense headgear turns into small, simple
bonnets with a scoop brim; hair has lost bulk and
length, although its locks are shaggy, after years of
careful dressing. The pouter pigeon bosom and crinolined *cul* are much reduced. As the back view of the
preceding lady shows, it is less the gown, than the
long narrow scarf drawn tight about the shoulders,
and the muff, which continue to give the new dress
some of the old aspect. Wide belts are completely
eliminated, but the new, very short waist has been
established at their top line.

Men's legs show a strong tendency to become covered. With fashionably delicate, pointed pumps without buckles, the man who is being driven wears
culottes which have descended to mid-calf. Those of
the driver are drawn down under his boot-tops, although they are still garnished with bunches of knee-
strings. The soldiers (l.) has low boots with long
hussar breeches; the shaggy mocker in striped stockings, high boots; the soldier-vendor, buttoned gaiters.

1997-98. XVIIIc. 1795. French. (Louvre.)
  David. M. Sériziat (1997), Mme. Sériziat (Emilie
Pécoul) and child (1998).

English fashions: Coachman's hat with buckled
band and cockade. Very high, turned-over collar and
prominent lapels on a coat which is becoming cut
away above the waistline into a tail-coat. High, muffling kerchief; short double-breasted vest with lapels.
The breeches are closed by a front flap. This was

sometimes shaped like an inverted square-bot-
tomed U, did not reach to the waist, and was ostentatiously decorated all around by braid, with tassel-
like elaborations in its pattern at the bottom. Paired
fobs tend to replace these, as the flap changes character, and is carried up under the vest, appearing as
two seams. Fobs lose ground, and are sometimes replaced by braided or quilted elaborations at the base
of the openings.

M. Sériziat's breeches are closed both by buttons
and knee strings, which have replaced uncomfortable
buckles, as the breeches and boots begin to meet.
Breeches are gradually drawn further down the leg,
by lacing the knee-strings around the calf, until
breeches of nearly ankle-length are attained. Then
boots are often abandoned; the wearer walks about
in stockings and low shoes with his ankles criss-
crossed by the ties which hold down his breeches,
while his lady's ankles are similarly criss-crossed by
the ribbons from her Greek sandals. Materials become more elastic; the breeches are buttoned above
the ankle, or they become wider and hang as trousers. (See Appendix.)

Leghorn hat trimmed with ribbon loops, and lined
with a cap-like *valance* of lace, tied over tumbling
locks, cut short over the head. Kerchief reduced to a
V-opening beneath the round-necked bodice of a
chemise dress. Waists are shortened and muslin fullness controlled between bands of shirring, or on the
mother by a ribbon sash and folded over neck-edge,
to stress vertical lines.

1999. XVIIIc. 1795-1800. French. (Louvre.)
  David. The Three Ladies of Ghent.

Madame Morel de Tangry's standing daughter
wears a *pelisse* over a very simple, classically-inspired
gown, belted directly under the breasts with antique
clasps. These pale gowns are worn with very elabor-

ate, brightly-colored hats, which are becoming bonnet-like, set back on the head, framing the face; their under-brims are elaborately decorated with shirred, crumpled or ruched silk and lace ruffles, in addition to piled flowers and silk on the crowns. Fluted neckruches, *fraises,* are seen throughout first third of XIXc. They tend to become attached to the dress as the neckline closes higher during the 20's; and to spread into wide collars, as shoulders widen in the 30's. They are often edged with ric-rac or other severe, narrow braids, or are rigidly gauffered. Scarves are oblong, often light-colored India shawls with fringed and patterned ends. Mme. Morel's *pelisse* has a typical cape-collar. Necklaces of graduated chains; watches on fine neck chains, tucked into belt.

2000. XVIIIc. 1797. French. (Versailles, Nat. Mus.)
Attributed to *A. Yon.* Napoleon I.

The Constitution of 1795 put the government in the confused control of a Directory of five presidents and two houses, and disqualified the main body of the proletariat. Monarchists and Churchmen fanned discontent. An uprising attacked the Tuileries where the Convention was sitting but was put down by an

obscure 25-year-old officer named Bonaparte, under command of Barras. In 1796, Barras married off his beautiful but troublesome mistress, Josephine Beauharnais, to the young officer, who left the same day for his Italian command.

After a brilliant success, he returned in 1797. He was young, ambitious and dangerous, and in 1798 was sent off on an Egyptian campaign. He came back from that to find a population which had been again disfranchised; corruption was rampant; a coalition of Europe was being formed against France. Napoleon staged the coup d'état of Brumaire by which the *Directoire* came to an end and, 1799, was replaced by a *Consulat* of three: Napoleon and two nonentities.

The shaggy man whom Aubrey, the military director in 1795 thought "the leanest and oddest object I ever cast my eyes upon," has gained assurance, but has not yet been polished by Josephine.

Extravagant collar on double-breasted coat which is being cut away into a knee length tail-coat. Its lines are accented by embroidery in a running Greek design, by which cuffs are given a new importance.

They have been buttoned close along the outseam; now they are turned back and open. Use of embroidery on dress garments will increase.

The wide-brimmed hat is cocked, square across the base, into a high-rounded bicorne. The cocking button is dropped to the forehead. The cocking loop, no longer attached to the crown, is drawn down decoratively to meet it, and encloses a huge cockade set high. Reappearance of gloves on men, with English styles.

Directoire chair, arm supported by a winged griffon. Fringe and gold embroidery in "classic" design on table cover.

2001-02. XVIIIc. 1799. French.
"Costumes Parisiens."

The periodical "Costumes Parisiens" was published from 1799-1831. Until about 1825 its plates were drawn by *Horace Vernet.*

2001. Man: high collar and wide trousers.

2002. Woman: veil in place of coiffure.

The "shaggy head" to which Walpole objected in the young English men of 1791, is worn in "dog's ears" with an English swallow-tail coat of cloth, the cuffs of which turn down to cover the knuckles (a usage which will reappear c. 1818), while the chin is buried in a knotted kerchief-cravat. English stick. High-crowned straw hat with a narrow rolled brim, is trimmed with a buckle, which has moved to the hat after leaving the shoe.

There are curious analogies between the rest of his costume and the current "classical" dress shown on the woman. In both, the waistline is raised high. His legs are draped in full, slit loose white cotton trousers (like his cuffs, this short, wide trouser will be seen c. 1818), as are her thighs in a muslin gown. He, too, wears heelless slippers, cut away to a minimum, which give the carriage and movement induced by the sandal of antiquity.

Her hair hangs in a shaggy fringe, her head is veiled like a Roman matron's, though in fashionable embroidered muslin. Whatever the climate of North Europe she continues to wear the thin draperies of Mediterranean antiquity into the first years of XIXc; and there were instances of women oiling their bodies to make their one thickness of draperies cling properly in the narrow dress of 1818-20.

Adaptation of Greco-Roman furniture; griffons as front legs of chair; severe rectangular pieces trimmed with wreaths and mouldings of gilt brass; Greek lyre.

2003. XVIIIc. English.
Racing scene: brown on white cotton.

2004. Late XVIIIc. French, Nantes?
"Diane chasseresse": brown copperplate on white cotton.

2005. XIXc. c. 1800. French, Nantes?
"Le Carrousel": red.

2006. XIXc. c. 1820. English.
Pictorial print: Hunting scene, mauve on white. Signed, *P. Pieter.*

2007. Early XIXc. French, Jouy.
"Monuments de Paris": designed by Hippolyte Lebas.

2008. XIXc. c. 1805. French, Jouy.
"Classic Medallions": mulberry copperplate, designed by Huot.

2009. XVIIIc. French. (Berlin, Kaiser Friedrich Mus.)
A. Pesne. G. F. Schmidt and Wife.

Antoine Pesne (1683-1757), a Frenchman, painted a good many portraits in Germany (1729-33), among them, this German engraver and pastellist (whose work was influenced by Pesne), and his wife.

Georg Friedrich Schmidt (1712-1775) wears a tasseled velvet turban, since he is without his wig, and a fur-lined velvet coat.

Women's costume in Germany and Flanders is more affected by French fashions than is English costume. Her short, unpowdered hair is dressed with flowers, without any sort of cap. She wears the new sort of bracelet, wide and set with medallions or cameos, and diamond earrings; a neck ruche, palatine of black lace; and a brocade gown, the sleeve ruffles of which are edged with ruching.

2010. XVIIIc. 1730. Flemish. (Metropolitan Mus.)
Peter Jacob Horemans (1714-90). Family Group.

A variety of nightcaps and turbans on men's clipped wigless heads; worn with unbuttoned garments, or rich dressing gown over a waistcoat. Older man—heavy wig with knotted locks; younger man—tie wig. The abbé on the balcony can be found living in every large Catholic household as secretary-companion-tutor, since there are not enough livings to go around and the best are plurally held by the aristocracy.

The elderly lady in the pleated, sheer black cap wears a brocade gown, apparently cut like that of Mme. Mercier (see Ill. 1800) but with a severely smooth stomacher in the Flemish tradition. The younger women are dressed in loosely and asymmetrically clasped plain satin gowns, with small powdered heads dressed with flowers.

The peasant costume of the woman servant was well established during XVIIc., but she wears slippers with tiny spike heels.

2011. Second quarter XVIIIc. German. (Vienna, Gall. Liechtenstein.)

H. Rigaud. Joseph Wenzel, Fürst von Liechtenstein.

Maria Theresa needed acknowledgment of her accession under the Pragmatic Sanction. Bavaria was hostile; England, the United Provinces, the Papacy and the Venetian Republic were friendly; Frederick II of Prussia falsely pretended to be.

Liechtenstein was sent as ambassador, c. 1740, to persuade France. He was reassured by the temporizing old Cardinal Fleury, but not until the Peace of Aix-la-Chapelle in 1748 did France finally acknowledge the Pragmatic Sanction.

Seven years after the end of the Seven Years War Maria Theresa's daughter, becoming the wife of the Dauphin, will experience the bitterness of France's continued hatred of Austria. But as the Revolution approaches there is a curious "recrudescence of *noblomania*"; at Maria Theresa's death mourning will be worn for the Queen's mother by French people far removed from court circles. (See Ills. 1966-67.)

Liechtenstein's ambassadorial robes show even more anachronistic characteristics than the French Royal Robes of State. He wears a modification of the XIVc.'s ceremonious dignified gown, and its chaperon with roundlet, together with a modified form of Louis XIV's full-bottomed court wig.

XVIII Century Venetian Dress

No costume is more dependent on the scale and perspective of its surroundings than that of XVIIIc. Venice. It is necessary to look at it in relationship with canals and squares, nearly empty or crowded with festival throngs, and with buildings and gondolas, as painted by Guardi and Canaletto; not only as it appears in the most detailed pictures by Longhi and Tiepolo.

Antonio Canale (1697-1768), called *Canaletto,* the son of a decorator, was a scene painter in his youth; studied in Rome for two years. Homesick for Venice, he returned in 1722 and never left his adored city for twenty-five years. He was hired by the year by the British consul, Joseph Smith, to produce a given number of pictures which Smith sold profitably to the English visitors who began to crowd Italy in XVIIIc. Meanwhile all the other artists of the last great resurgence of Venetian painting, including Canale's nephew, *Bernard Bellotto* (1724-80), (the other "Canaletto"), were travelling abroad, brilliantly rewarded. In 1746, Canale set off to London, which he revisited in 1751, after a meeting with his nephew at Dresden. His English perspectives of buildings and gardens (like Ranelagh and Vauxhall) and his nephew's of Vienna, Munich (where he was a court favorite) and Warsaw (where he died) are important for costume as well as for architectural panoramas.

Francesco Guardi (1712-93), Canale's pupil, was a rapid and prolific painter. His pictures show the

2012

great processions of Venice by water, the traffic of the Rialto, the crowds in piazzas and at theatres.

Giovanni Battista Tiepolo (1692-1769), a sumptuous fresco painter, has left precious costume documents on the walls of the Villa Valmarana (1737) and others.

Pietro Longhi (1702-85) painted in charming color with almost Hogarth-like fidelity many small pictures of the life of his contemporaries, rather than the glories of the city of Venice.

2012. XVIIIc. Italian, Venetian. (Toulouse, Mus.)

F. Guardi. The Departure of the Bucentaur.

By XVIIIc. the Doge had become a figurehead whose chief duty was to cast a precious ring from the State Galley, the Bucentaur, into the Adriatic at the yearly festival which symbolized the marriage of Venice and the sea.

As the Bucentaur leaves its moorings the shores are crowded with spectators and the basin of San Marco is filled with gondolas of every variety.

2013-16. XVIIIc. 1753. Italian, Venetian.

Gaetano Zompini: "Le arti che vanno per via della cittá di Venezia."

2013. Chair Maker. 2014. Old Clothes Vendor.

2015. Placing a Servant. 2016. Window Mender.

Short underskirts combined with even shorter overskirts are seen on young Venetian women of the people, and servants. Women's shoes are cut lower over the instep with lower heels and less exaggerated toes than in France.

Everywhere women's short hair began to be dressed like men's at the beginning of second third of century. "The Ladies of Norfolk universally wear periwigs and affirm that it is the fashion of London," Walpole writes Mann (Oct. 3, 1743). Wigs are not uncommon on women by midXVIIIc., and women's hair is usually dressed in this way with riding costume. Nowhere, however, does women's hair so completely imitate men's, with tie and pigtail, as with the masculine-influenced dress of Italian women of all classes. Their gowns are simple in cut, rela-

tively untrimmed, with longer sleeves, the cuffs of which remain shaped or buttoned back. There is relatively less show of linen and almost none of ruffles below the cuff.

The boy (No. 2014) shows the netted cap of XVIc. persistent in Italy.

2017. XVIIIc. Italian, Venetian. (Venice, Coll. Brass.)

P. Longhi. Lady in Riding Costume.

Masculine hat, with pigtail, *solitaire* and jabot, coat and waistcoat, worn with matching skirt, braided like a military uniform.

2018. XVIIIc. 1756. Swedish. (Stockholm, Nat Mus.)

A. Roslin. Baronne de Newborg-Cromière.

Alexander Roslin (1718-93), a Paris-trained Swedish painter, worked in France, Sweden and Russia among the highest society.

The Baroness is as covered with ruchings, ruffles, lace and fresh flowers as Mme. de Pompadour, but her gown shows an interesting close sleeve on the forearm below the elbow ruffles.

2019. XVIIIc. Swedish. (Stockholm, Hallwylska Coll.)

Bernhardine von Diesbach. Gräfin von Hallwül (1728-79).

In 1920 Walter and Wilhelmina von Hallwyl gave their home, its complete contents, and funds for its upkeep to the Swedish crown as a museum which is never to be altered. Its contents, reproduced in fifty-odd magnificent volumes, includes portraits of Hall-

wül ancestors from XVIc. The collection is extraordinary, primarily, as a record of every personal possession of the clothing and household effects inherited or acquired by a rich Swedish gentleman born in 1839. Not only art objects, porcelain and silver are reproduced, but shoes and socks, underwear and galoshes; court, hunting, and everyday clothes of the family; and their every possession down to the meanest utensils from the kitchen, the boot boy's cleaning equipment, the family mending kit, hardware and screws.

Everyone is playing at shepherdess in XVIIIc., even before Louis XVI's accession in 1774 when wheat and cornucopias, symbolic of hoped-for plenty, decorate everything.

2020. XVIIIc. 1758. German.

D. Chodowiecki. The Sisters Quantin.

Daniel Chodowiecki (1726-1801) was a German engraver who illustrated "Minna von Barnhelm" (1770), "Werther," and "Lotte" (1775), as well as many almanachs.

Simple domestic dress and caps.

2021-24. XVIIIc. 1760-1765. Austrian, Viennese. (Vienna, Karl Meyer Coll.)

Viennese Porcelain Figures.

2021. Pilgrim with Staff and Wallet; cockle shells on hat and cape (1765).

2022. Skate Seller with Fur Hat, Fur-trimmed

Coat and Muff (1760).

2023. Skate Seller with Ermine Muff (1760).

2024. Cavalier (1765).

Decorative figurines and groups are produced in the growing porcelain and pottery factories of Vienna, Germany, France and England in latter half XVIIIc. and first half XIXc. They are pastoral or genre, or pretty figures out of Italian comedy, like those dancing in Tiepolo frescos. (See Appendix.)

2025, 2027. XVIIIc. 1750. Italian, Viennese.

2025. Dress: green and white silk brocade.

2027. Matching stays and sleeves.

2026. XVIIIc. c. 1750. French.

Courtesy of Metropolitan Museum of Art (2025-27)

Bodice of Louis XV period.

2028. XVIIIc. French. (Boston, Mus. of Fine Arts.)

Headdress: quilted silk and brocade.

"The ladies have been for some time in a kind of moulting season with regard to (their heads) having cast great quantities of riband, lace and cambrick . . . What . . . would be substituted in place of those antiquated commodes. But (women) were all the last summer so taken up with the improvement of their petticoats, that they had not time to attend to anything else." (*Spectator*, 265, Jan. 3, 1711/12.) Now they begin to think of the other extremity. At the Opera, the Spectator notes the "prettiest coloured

hoods that ever I saw," in blue, yellow, "philomot," pink, and pale green, like a bed of tulips.

2029. XVIIIc. Italian, Venetian. (Venice, Coll. Countess Adele Salom di Corrobio.)

P. Longhi. Masquerade at the Club.

2030-31. XVIIIc. 1756. Italian, Venetian. (Venice, Palazzo Papadopoli.)

G. B. Tiepolo.
2030. The Mountebank.
2031. The Minuet.

2032. XVIIIc. Italian, Venetian.

G. B. Tiepolo. Punchinellos.

2033. XVIIIc. Italian, Venetian. (Boston, Mus. of Fine Arts, formerly Oppenheimer Coll.)

G. B. Tiepolo (drawing). Milliner's Shop.

People of every degree, even children, masked at carnival time. Variety of masks: beaked *bauta,* worn by gentlefolk (never without domino); round and half masks; masks of Italian comedy figures, worn alone, or with the appropriate comedy costume.

The trade and costume of the entire world came together at mediaeval Venice. In XVc., loose trousers entered popular dress. Many Venetians bore the name of their patron, Saint Pantaleon; the rest of Italy mocked Venice and its garb, in the comedy figure of an old Venetian called "Pantalone." Italian comedy became familiar to the rest of Europe, and "pantaloon" entered language as the name for trousers. With the decline of Venice and the rise of English sea-power, loose trousers became part of sailor's dress.

Gentlemen's clothes, though covered by dominos, can be seen to differ less than ladies' from current European styles. Long full wigs persist in Italy (mountebank, older gentleman to right at club masquerade). Buttoned cloaks with collars worn by men who are neither gentlemen nor liveried servants. Muffs, carried by men as well as women in Italy. Ladies' cloaks and characteristic short flaring coats with striped hems. Slippers with pointed toes but comparatively low heels. Very short skirts; long, plain, pointed bodices; pretty, clocked stockings on maid servants.

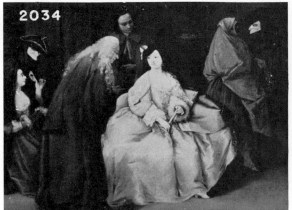

2034-35. XVIIIc. c. 1760. Italian, Venetian. (Metropolitan Mus.)

P. Longhi. 2034. The Meeting. 2035. The Temptation.

Italian costume continued its familiar course of independent development during XVIIIc. It reached its most delightful and most specifically Italian form in the costume of carnival time, particularly in Venice.

Carnival lasted ten frantic bacchanalian days before Ash Wednesday. Walpole wrote West from Florence (Feb. 27, 1740): "Masqued, too, I have done nothing but slip out of my domino into bed and out of bed into my domino; all the morn one makes parties in masque to the shops and coffee-houses, and all the evenings to the operas and balls. . . . What makes masquerading more agreeable here than in England is the great deference that is shown to the disguised." No advantage was taken to be ill-tempered, gross or bawdy, yet the freedom of carnival gave Walpole opportunity to make new acquaintances.

The masculine tinge, seen in the less pretentious Zompini illustrations, affect the costume of Venetian ladies as well. A black tricorne hat is always the apex of their characteristic pyramidal silhouette. This is built up through a series of horizontal truncations and spreading vertical cuts into an apparently simple triangular form of immense subtlety. The cocked hat; the *bauta* mask, with its spreading nose; the flow of the black domino (half opaque, half lace) over the specifically Venetian cape which in its turn spreads over the widest of half-paniers; even the accompanying fan—all are necessary parts of the total effect, built up of V's.

The cut of the costume is pure and austere, completely uncluttered by flounces on the skirt. In Venice, it is the cape which spreads open; the skirt is not slashed up the front. In maid-servants' costume a short underskirt is worn with an even shorter overskirt, which is often banded at the hem. This may be thrown up over the head, but it is never cut vertically in front.

There may be a line of decoration on the shaped cuff and on the cape front, to emphasize its spreading edges. There is no ladder of bows coming from a corset beneath, in Venetian costume. A flat embroidered placard gives the V-shape of a lady's bodice-front its necessary emphasis. Sometimes it is laced across; often it is severely plain. It may have the little peplum of the Columbine costume.

In France three graduated lace frills finish the sleeve. What appears below the shaped Italian cuff is frankly an undershirt; the ruffles which finish it are primarily of its fabric. On the lady in Longhi's "Meeting" the cut of the ruffles adds to the angular forms of the whole costume.

There are wonderful combinations of dilute color In Ill. 2034 the lady to the left wears a brick red bodice, tan skirt, green muff with blond fur and black. The man who bows wears a gray-blue domino; the man in back, a bricky-tan cloak. The lady is all in gold and silver, cream and lemon. Her maid (with pink and blue low-heeled slippers), has a green underskirt and throws her pink top-skirt over her head. The Metropolitan Museum has a collection of braided liveries such as that worn by the servant in "Temptation." His master wears negligée of yellow waistcoat, white dressing gown and blue and red embroidered slippers.

2036-37. XVIIIc. Flemish. (Metropolitan Mus.)

J. J. Horemans, y. 2036. Winter (1761).
2037. Autumn (1762).

Horemans the younger (1714-90), was one of a dynasty of prolific painters of Flemish genre scenes. Lower middle-class Protestant costume; men in unpowdered bob wigs; plain coats, vests of another fabric, trimmed only with ball buttons and buttonholes. Women in enclosing hoods with fluted edges, and fichus, are dressed in cotton prints. In "Autumn" the dress is of a large patterned scenic or floral print. The smooth-bibbed apron has an all-over motif; the petticoat is striped.

2038. XVIIIc. c. 1762. Flemish. (Metropolitan Mus.)

Raphael Mengs. Maria Louisa of Parma.

Raphael Mengs (1728-79) painted Charles III of Spain and his connections of Parma, Tuscany and Naples:

The wife of Charles IV of Spain wears a gown, the completely fitted bodice and skirt of which are cut in one piece. The construction of the skirt, to give fullness over the side wings, is made clear by the lines of the striped floral brocade. The pleats falling from the shoulders of the ordinary court gown are missing here. The lace sleeve ruffles, instead of falling over the forearm, are pleated and tacked back to the sleeve above the puffed finish. The bodice has no ladder of bows or embroidered plastron and carries no tippet scarf or palatine. They are replaced here by a bib of lace, as a background for the enamel and diamonds of the order pinned to her bosom.

2039. XVIIIc. 1770. French. (Metropolitan Mus.)

H. Drouais. Emperor Joseph II of Austria.

Marie Antoinette's brother was an enlightened despot, sensible, amusing, forthright and tactless, who was unable to force acceptance of his liberal plans. As Count Falkenstein, he visited his sister in France, scolded her for her giddiness and rouge, was horrified by the booths in the palace stairs and galleries where shopkeepers sold souvenirs almost at the doors of the private apartments. He insisted on sleeping at an inn with his servants.

Coat, losing fullness, grows longer and more cutaway, waistcoat shortens. Wig in a bag, its side curls multiple.

2040. XVIIIc. 1771. Swedish. (Stockholm, Nat. Mus.)

A. Roslin. Gustave III and His Brothers Discussing a Plan of Campaign.

2041. XVIIIc. Swedish. (Stockholm, Nat. Mus.)

P. Hilleström. Conversation at Drottingholm.

Per Hilleström (1732-1816) returned to Stockholm from Paris in 1750. He taught at the Academy in Stockholm of which he became director. His pictures also show the common people.

The King of Sweden and his brothers, whose mother was Frederick the Great's sister, were brilliant, learned and charming. Artists and people of distinction were beginning to make the tour of the new northern courts. They were both welcome, and delighted with the French atmosphere of the Swedish court.

Drottningholm, the Swedish summer court, was begun late in XVIIc. and finished in XVIIIc. by the son of the original architect. Its XVIIIc. theater had revolving scenery which is still of great interest to theatrical designers.

The life, interests and amusements of the court were thoroughly French, as are the metallically gleaming clothes of the King and his brothers. The costumes of the court ladies, however, are full of anachronisms dating from late XIVc. and XVIIc.: slashed and puffed sleeves and wired-out standing collars of lace are worn, without wide paniers, though they are accompanied by the high hair arrangement and the three plumes of latter half XVIIIc. court dress.

2042-49. XVIIc. 1780. German.

Daniel Chodowiecki. Figures From Almanachs and Book Illustrations.

Sword worn with more ceremonious clothes (2042); obligatory with court frock coat (2045); being given up in every-day wear (2043); or replaced by stick in clothes of English type.

Ceremonious snuff-taking; overcoat with wide collar, heavy top boots and pigtail; large muff and fur piece worn by gentleman (2042). The most ceremonious feather-topped "head" and gauze-draped court gown (2045). Umbrella and ermine cape carried by uniformed lackey; lady in negligée; gentlemen in Spanish *majo* costume; evangelical figure; business men with wide brims cocked high over deeper crown (2049).

English style: Round hat, own hair, wide collar, buttoned-back lapels, large plain buttons, stick, knee breeches and gaiters; short, square-cut vest, paired fobs (2043). English style with frock-coat and plain skirt (2044). "Head" dressed high (2044); plumes worn with *polonaise* as well as with *robe à la française, sabots* at elbow (2046). Raked-back *toupet* of Macoroni exaggeration; English garments: short vest, paired fobs with seals, breeches, soft high boots, stick (2047). Poor men in old-fashioned cast-offs; low-crowned cocked hats, long straight-cut coats and waistcoats (2048).

2050-52. XVIIIc. 1776-85. German. (Boston, Mus. of Fine Arts, Elizabeth Day McCormick Coll.)

Original Fashion Drawings.

2050. *Ein Kap*: gray-blue costume: a combination of *caraco* and officer's coat with buttoned-back edges, vest and wig, gray and white plumes, gold laced hat band, tasselled stick. 2051. *Herz Haube*: heart-shaped cap and matching kerchief; red gown; green apron, ribbons, and slippers. 2052. *Frisure à la Religieuse*: overhanging "Montgolfier" cap with green ribbon commemorates the first balloon ascension of the brothers Montgolfier in 1783. Pink cape-coat with gold buttons; collar, cuffs, and lapels of black fur, black slippers, white heels and stockings. Amazingly tasteless German version of the already fantastic French version of the long-waisted English style and cap.

2053. XVIIIc. 1776. German. (Frankfort-on-Main, Hauck Coll.)

Jean Noë Badger. Gogel Family.

2054. XVIIIc. c. 1780-5. Austrian. (Petraia, Villa Reale.)

Italian School. Family of Peter Leopold, Grand Duke of Tuscany.

When Maria Theresa married her cousin and friend Francis, duke of Lorraine, in 1736, his claims to Lorraine were exchanged for the Grand Duchy of Tuscany, whose last degenerate Medici ruler had died. Francis delegated Tuscan rule to Austrian regents until his son Leopold became eighteen.

Peter Leopold (1747-92) married Maria-Luisa of Spain and became one of the most progressive rulers of the XVIIIc. Until he became Emperor in 1790, the agreeable Tuscan court delighted the English visitors to Florence, although the natives resented its simplicity, after the Medici splendor which had ruined them. Leopold, enlightened but less aggressive than his brother Joseph, managed like him to alienate

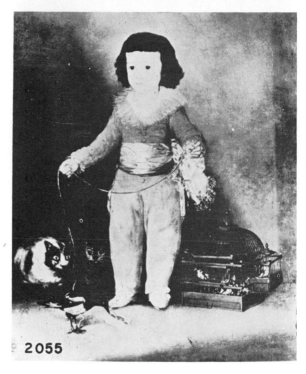

large blocks of his subjects: the nobility, by equalizing taxes and undermining feudalism; the church and its faithful, by attempts to control and rectify its faults, of which he had become aware during early studies for the priesthood; the people, by forcing a premature political maturity upon them. But he reformed government and law courts, and put them in Tuscan hands; replaced an expensive standing army by a citizens' militia; arranged free trade in food; drained swamps and improved agriculture for an underfed population.

German dress attempts to follow French fashions, but until the Congress of Vienna in 1815, Germany consists of many small, more or less provincial principalities, dependent on the taste of their courts and the physical difficulties of communication with Paris. Fashion plates begin to be sent out from Paris in final quarter century, and Bertuch of Weimar publishes the *Journal des Luxus und der Moden* in 1786, but intercourse is interrupted by the Revolution. Provincial England's notions of what was the current style of London, which had so amused the Spectator, are completely outdone throughout XVIIIc. by German fantasies about Paris fashions.

French style was most accurately followed at the court of Saxony; Frederick the Great was Francophile; the Austrian court was informed of French ways by its connection with Marie Antoinette.

The Tuscan court of her brother receives the world of Europe as it visits Italy; Leopold's thinking is affected by French philosophy, but the ceremonious dress of the court is a rigidly individual combination of Spanish, Austrian and French elements.

The Gogel family (2053) are in fairly good touch with France at Frankfort-on-Main, though the jackets and insistent trim of the three young females on the r., would not be seen in France in 1776.

The dress of the male figures of the Tuscan court (2054) is affected by that of Leopold's Spanish father-in-law, Charles IV. The younger boys wear the Spanish version of the open-collared, long-trousered costume: a closed tunic with a sash, *faja,* around the hips, rather than a coat open over a square-cut vest, as in England and France. The agreement of vest and breeches, and the insistent, repeated lines of heavy metal braid on the vests of the older males is a Spanish court fashion, repeatedly painted by Goya. The black stock, sometimes with a bow, is a lingering form of the *solitaire,* seen in Spanish and German dress of the final quarter century.

In this official group portrait hair is still powdered. That of the young girl (l.) is still dressed in a cere-

monious cap as the Princess Royal's was in 1778, a fashion which had been abandoned for children of the same family by 1785.

The application of a ruffle, like that of a petticoat, to the outermost of two skirts, is seen both on the girl (extreme r.) of the Gogel family, and on the Tuscan princess (extreme l.); it would not be seen in France. The two older ladies of the Tuscan court wear standard, slightly outmoded French dress.

2055. XVIIIc. 1784. Spanish. (Metropolitan Mus., Bache Coll.)

Goya. Don Manuel Osorio de Zuniga.

Francisco Goya y Lucientes (1746-1828), was born in Aragón, son of a master-gilder and his wife who came of aristocratic family. Their turbulent son, audacious and headstrong, found it advisable to leave one place after another in a hurry. From Aragón, he went to Madrid, but soon set off with a band of bullfighters to make his way along the Mediterranean to Rome as a musician and bullfighter. He left Rome suddenly for Madrid, where he married the sister of the court painter Bayeu, his former teacher; by her he had twenty children of which only one son lived.

Bayeu started Goya on a long career as a tapestry designer in 1776. Mengs influenced him to begin painting portraits in 1781. He made powerful friendships with the dukes of Osuna and Alba; was soon on familiar terms with the royal family, and became the lover of the duchess of Alba.

Many of his strange, satiric and terrible etched series were done after an illness which left him stone-deaf. His paintings, tapestry designs, drawings and etchings show the entire life of Spain: the courts of Bourbon and Bonaparte kings, officers and duennas, peasants and bullfighters, *majas* and *majos,* bullfighters, courts of inquisition, the horrors of war.

His brothers-in-law, the Bayeus, and his follower A. Esteve y Marqués show the same period in a good deal of variety; and Vincent López y Pontaña (1772-1850), the nobility of the following generation or two.

Spanish child's costume: scarlet tunic and trousers (see 2054): open collar with a gold and silver gauze *faja* and slippers with bowknots.

The ceremonious dress of little boys of the early XIXc. Bonaparte courts has a short jacket ending in two long tasseled points; long, high-waisted trousers,

heavily embroidered like the jacket along the outseam and hem and on the thighs. It can be seen in Victor Guye, page to King Joseph Bonaparte (Harding Coll., New York) and Pepite Corte (1813?-18?) (Mellon Coll., Pittsburgh).

2056. XVIIIc. 1786-7. Spanish. (Boston, Mus. of Fine Arts.)

Francisco Bayeu y Subias. Portrait of a Young Man.

Characteristic Spanish lapel, seen in a more exaggerated form on Bayeu's self portrait in 1769. The earliest square-cut vests were bordered along the bottom.

2057. XVIIIc. 1790. Spanish. (Washington, Nat. Gall. of Art.)

Goya. Marquesa de Pontejos.

The hair of lightly powdered heads is becoming lower all over Europe, and spreads wider with the lower locks falling, but the process is carried out with more formality in Spain.

This gauzy gray costume with touches of pink has long sleeves and a belted bodice with the round frilly neckline which is preferred to the kerchief in Spanish upper class dress. The round skirt is repeatedly caught

with the loose bows seen in Spain. Characteristic Spanish slipper and heel cut low over the instep, with a tiny pointed toe.

2058. XVIIIc. 1795. Spanish. (Madrid, Duke of Alba.)
Goya. Duchess of Alba.

The greatest beauties at the Spanish court were the wives of Goya's patrons, the dukes of Osuna and Alba. Even children on the streets stopped playing to watch the "utterly graceful and completely beautiful . . . prodigy"—the duchess of Alba with her cloud of wonderful black hair. Her plain, round-necked muslin dress has a hem of Spanish fringe, bow and sash of scarlet, long sleeves caught down over the hand, and a bracelet of medallions on the upper arm.

2059. XVIIIc. 1791. Spanish. (Madrid, Prado.)
Goya. Tapestry Cartoon: Blindman's Buff.

Goya dressed the figures of his Watteau-like pastorals in Spanish regional costume. The *majas* and *majos* he shows here were "gay members of Madrid's lower class who over-dressed in a fantastic manner." The tapestry weavers complained of "dandies and girls with so much decoration of coifs, fal-lals, gauzes, etc., that much time is wasted on them." (D. C. Rich: *Art of Goya.*)

1. Hat of blue ribbon, lightly powdered hair, pink dress, white lace, slippers and stockings. 2. Dark coif, blue gray bow; red jacket; black and yellow *faja;* golden yellow breeches trimmed in red; gray stockings, black shoes, silver buckles. 3. Blue gray net coif; coat and vest, dark and light brown; chestnut breeches; gray stockings. 4. Cream net coif, red jacket, brown-gold epaulettes, white skirt. 5. Dark greenish hat and cock feathers, brown gown, gold ruffles. 6. Gold coif; bluish jacket and breeches; greenish vest; gray stockings. 7. Gray net; yellow jacket trimmed in white puff; olive green breeches trimmed in silver. 8.

Dark greenish brown costume. 9. Black hat, gauze edged; powdered hair, white kerchief and apron; light yellow-green dress.

2060. XVIIIc. 1796-7. Spanish. (Metropolitan Mus., Print Room.)
Goya. San Lucar Sketch Book, India ink wash drawing: The Swing.

Goya spent six months in Andalusia with the duchess of Alba who had retired (or had been banished) to San Lucar at the beginning of her widowhood. This sketch book dates from that time.

2061. XVIIIc. Spanish. (Madrid, Prado.)
Goya. Wash drawing: Guitar Player and Dancer.

2062. XVIIIc. 1792. Spanish. (Metropolitan Mus.)
Goya. Don Sebastián Martínez.

Coats made of narrowly striped fabric are commonly seen in the last decade of XVIIIc. But the way in which these gay stripes are used to enhance the cutaway line and flapping lapel of a coat which remains open is characteristically Spanish. Large, ornate buttons, which preceded the large plain buttons of the English style of dress. Buttoned side pocket, partly seen on knee breeches.

2063. XVIIIc. 1796. Spanish. (Madrid, Prado.)
Goya. Francisco Bayeu y Subias.

A self-portrait by Goya's brother-in-law also shows this identical plain gray coat with characteristically cut and flapping Spanish lapels.

2064. XVIIIc. 1790. Spanish. (Washington, Nat. Gall. of Art, Mellon Coll.)

Goya. Carlos IV as a Huntsman.

Very wide-brimmed hat turning into a bicorne. Spanish cutaway coat. Blue and white Ribbon of the Order of Carlos III over a tunic-like vest, belted at the hips at the low line of the Spanish *faja*. Until breeches are successfully drawn down below boot-tops, boot hose of the XVIIc. sort are often worn in the last decades XVIIIc. The king's boot top is also of the XVIIc. shape, in a peak which could turn up to cover the knee. The characteristic boot of the turn of XVIII-XIXc. is either the English jockey boot with a turned-down band and boot-straps, or a low, rather spreading black Hessian boot, cut down in front (i.e., at the line described by the colored turn-down of the king's boots).

2065. XVIIIc. 1799. Spanish. (Washington, Nat. Gall. of Art, Mellon Coll.)
Goya. María Luisa of Spain.

The little princess whom we have seen in a Mengs portrait has turned into the revolting, raddled and dissolute Spanish Queen. She wears Spanish national costume in sheer dotted black with repeated horizontal trimming; black lace mantilla, great knot of ribbon, and fan.

2066. XVIIIc. 1790. Spanish. (Madrid, Prado.)
Goya. General José de Urrutia.

2067. XIXc. 1800. Spanish. (Madrid, Prado.)
Goya. Infante Don Luis María.
Son of Carlos III's brother, the Infante Luis, as a Cardinal.

2068. XIXc. 1800. Spanish. (Madrid, Prado.)
Goya. Family of Carlos IV.
Court dress: embroidered frock-coat and waistcoat; breeches, buckled shoes, tasseled sword. Spanish-Empire gowns with ceremonious tunic.

LIFE IN RESTORATION AND XVIIIc. ENGLAND

During years of poverty and exile, Charles I had ample opportunity to perfect the Continental pleasures of sauntering and looking on. This was one of many elements from which the subjects of "that pleasant man" constructed the new way of life peculiar to England in the XVIIIc.

"At this time," says Bishop Burnet, "the court fell into much extravagance in masquerading; both king and queen went about masked, and came into houses unknown, and danced there with a great deal of frolic . . . so disguised that none could distinguish them." The liberty afforded by masks was naturally abused and they began to fall into ill repute at the turn of the century.

Restless, pleasure-seeking and reckless, after years of war, people are constantly out of their own houses and about the streets, searching for amusements, which even courtiers fail to find in the stodgy, respectable courts of William and Mary and her sister Anne. Anne got out of attending her own receptions, leaving her ministers to do the honors; she sat silently gnawing her fan when she did appear. Swift went to court "to pick up a dinner" free. Anne's mourning for her consort was so prolonged that, after remonstrating, merchants managed to obtain a law limiting the duration of public mourning. Nor were the courts of the sensible Hanoverian Georges particularly amusing. George I arrived as a widower with a deplorable taste for undecorative German women; he spoke only German and cared nothing for dress. George II had some interest in fashion. Caroline of Anspach, his wife, was a tolerant woman of character and intellect, not without charm; she preferred the company of literary men, theologians and philosophers, and disconcerted the English court by the unseemly coarseness of her language. The English-born George III lived a happily domesticated life with the German Queen Charlotte, who bore him 15 children. He was an autocrat, long ill and for a time actually insane; neither of the couple had any taste or interest in art or literature. Their court was a stiff, uneasy horror, from which their sons revolted violently.

The luxury of transport by coach, sedan chair or barge has become a necessity. Licensed public conveyances, increasing in number each year, cater to those who do not keep liveried conveyances of their own.

Everyone goes by water or coach to Ranelagh, Vauxhall, or to innumerable other gardens, catering to all classes of society, as well as to take the waters at spas, like Bath, beloved by both Mary and Anne. Here they can gamble; listen to music and the new operatic performances; see spectacles like Mr. Winstanley's water works; watch exhibitions of horsemanship, gladiatorial combats, bull, bear, or dog-baiting, and cock fights; pick up new lovers; eat and drink in charmingly laid out gardens, while listening to nightingales. Coney Island is the debased end-form of this sort of amusement.

There is less and less real erudition. Men throng to coffee-houses and taverns to read the newspapers, gossip, meet their friends and do business. Newspapers have increased from the *Post Boy* of 1695 to 55 regular weeklies in 1709, usually issued to subscribers at 1d a sheet and printed on one side of the paper. Swift tells Stella that copies of the *Spectator* "never come my way; I go to no coffee-houses." The ½d Stamp Tax, which Swift predicts "will utterly ruin Grub Street," does kill the *Observator,* forces other papers to amalgamate, and while the *Spectator* has doubled its price and survives, it too will succumb late in 1712.

Most of the coffee we drink comes from Central and South America, to which the plant was brought in the e.XVIIIc., by way of Jamaica, from the Near East. A Greek scholar at Balliol had brewed his own coffee at Oxford as early as 1636, Wood tells us. But the first public coffee-houses in Oxford were those opened in Dec. 1650 by "Jacob, a Jew" and in 1654 by Cirques Jobson, a Syrian Christian. Coffee-houses immediately became enormously and time-wastingly popular. Their numbers multiplied and they took on club-like characteristics, as different houses served different colleges. Christopher Wren and the virtuosi and wits of All Souls', for instance, patronized the house opened in 1655 by the royalist apothecary, Arthur Tillyard.

The first coffee-house in London seems to have been the one established by a Greek in St. Michael's Alley, Cornhill, in 1652. The coffee-house serves as office, club, and post-office. Letters are left at coffee-houses for hourly collection, and many customers receive their mail at a coffee-house address; Swift's letters went to the St. James. Nearby inns are used as points of reference in addressing letters, since houses are not numbered. Men meet and entertain customers at coffee-houses, which usually cater to men of the same profession and political party, and become reduced to business use in the latter half of century. The different receptions with which the news of the death of the king of France would be accorded at 8 coffee-houses between the St. James and Garraway's is amusingly sketched in the *Spectator* (June 12, 1712).

Society is now aligned by political belief. Clubs, meeting at coffee-houses, are founded on eating or politics, usually both. The Beefsteak Club, of which the actress, Peg Woffington, was president and the only female member, was primarily an eating club. The October, which met at the Bell Tavern to drink "October Ale," was a Tory club. Kneller painted the portraits of the 40 Whig members of the Kit-Cat (named from Christopher Cat, who made their mutton pies), which met at the

Strand in winter and Hampstead Wells in summer.

Women are often downright illiterate, taught little but dancing, dress and manners. They, also, are so divided by politics that the *Spectator* (81) supposes that Whig and Tory ladies may come to indicate their politics by setting their patches on the right or left cheeks, and foresees difficulties with moles and pimples when "ladies patch out of principle." They visit constantly; send servants to inquire "Howdee" after each other's health—much as XIX-XXc. ladies leave cards. They have days at home; drink tea out of fine china, the collection of which becomes a mania. Tea and china are sold in the same shops, and are often bartered against used clothing, which brings good prices all over Europe.

Servants now dress with more luxury than their masters of the previous generation. Among their own class, they take rank from the rank of their masters, and dress as much like them as possible. They are accustomed to fine liveries, fresh gloves, and must meet a standard of cleanliness new even to those they serve. Gentlefolk who have eaten with their fingers all their lives are suddenly made ill by people too ill-bred to use forks; forks should not be wiped on a piece of bread but on a fringed napkin (furnished by Mr. Doiley, the linendraper, whose name they still bear), or they should be rinsed in a basin of water on the sideboard.

Ideas of politeness and cleanliness, though they had spread out over Europe from Louis XIV's court, become debased and diluted. Manners become gestures studied with French dancing masters. The middle half of XVIIIc. is, in actuality, one of the smelliest and dirtiest in modern history. Infrequently washed heads, caked with flour, housed vermin. The importation of the miraculously washable India cottons was prohibited in England and France.

Country people were crowding into towns, the old shallow wells of which were polluted and had lowered; they had not been adequate for a smaller earlier population. Improvement of the city's water supply had begun to concern public-spirited citizens in the XVIc.; Stow records sums given or willed by aldermen and good ladies towards this purpose, often requiring that an equal sum be laid out by the city. The earliest steam engines were those used to pump Thames water into the houses of the rich. Everybody else had less water than before, and perfume became almost a necessity.

Highwaymen, thugs and pickpockets infest the roads and cluster about fashionable meeting places. Bands of well-born young toughs called Mohocks, of which the *Spectator* and Swift's *Journal* complain constantly during 1711-1712, shove passersby into the gutter or "sweat" them in forced swordplay, roll old women down hill in barrels, but never take money. Dozens of such current names, signifying different categories of men—wasted or useless, dissolute or dangerous, rich, climbing, gambling, or desperately poor—are explained in *Proteus Redivivus, the Art of Wheedling,* published *tempus* Charles II, and in the *Complete Gamester,* 1674 (Malcolm, 1811.) The more important pleasure gardens advertise that they provide armed guards to conduct their patrons, street lighting is improved (though mostly from park to palace), and, through the efforts of the Society for the Reformation of Manners, young baronets who run chaises through with swords or cut off people's noses are apt to be arrested.

Roads are improved and rewards posted for the capture of highwaymen, as a network of flying coaches crosses England at regular intervals, carrying the post and meeting packet boats. English people not only travel but live abroad, and the Grand Tour of a young English gentleman now lasts three years. The first of four lighthouses at wave-swept Eddystone is built after the design of Mr. Winstanley, who was lost in its collapse during the great storm of Nov. 3, 1703.

As in France, wild gambling played a part in the necessary new stabilization of government finances, and led to the beginnings of insurance. Life insurance companies, like "The Lucky Seventy, or longest livers take all," of 1709, became a mania of the first decade.

Fire insurance was provided by three companies: the Phoenix of 1682; the Friendly Society of 1684; and the Amicable Distribution of 1695, which became the Hand in Hand. The insuring companies maintained liveried men to put out fires, and fastened their own leaden plaques of identification to insured houses. Shallowly buried water pipes often froze. The fire at the Middle Temple in 1677, when the Thames froze over, had to be put out with 100 kegs of beer from the Temple cellar and the Devil Tavern.

Windows in new houses are reduced in numbers, because of the new tax, but become larger and let in more light. Individual panes remain small until new techniques produce large sheets later in XVIIIc., but they are now hung sash instead of casements. An advertisement of 1710 describes the typical new house: "To be Let, a New Brick House, Built after the Newest Fashion, the Rooms wainscotted and Painted, Lofty Stories, Marble Foot paces to the Chimneys, Sash Windows glaised with fine Crown Glass, large half pace Stairs that 2 People may go up on a Breast, in a new pleasant Court, planted with Vines, Jesamin, and other Greens, next door to the Crown, near the Sarazen's Head Inn in Carter Lane, near St. Paul's Church Yard, London."

Wallpaper and paint reflect the light, which used to be absorbed by dark tapestries and stamped leather hangings. Furniture, now clearly seen against light colors, becomes more delicate and elegant, in mahogany and lacquer, with new forms of tea-tables. Large mirrors and chandelier crystals catch and reflect candle-light. Fireplaces in England burn coal, and better water is now piped into subscribers' houses from the Thames and other waterworks by steam pressure.

Gardens, beautifully planned and kept, are part of English life, both in country and city. While Louis XIV's court, and those of his successors, make country life in France equivalent to exile and bankruptcy, so that its great estates are falling into neglect and ruin, the dullness of the English court allows country life, which has always appealed to the English, to increase in importance. Changing agricultural methods, fencing and improved firearms make shooting on foot as pleasant a sport, in its way, as hunting on horseback. The owner of a property, walking over it for game, has its condition always under his eye, and ways of improving it constantly in mind.

Land tenure and agricultural methods, almost static since long before the Domesday Book, alter greatly during XVIIIc. The Industrial Revolution of the latter half century draws farmers from precariously held land which they have not the will, knowledge, nor means to improve. Fewer farmers must meet an increased demand for bread and meat. Leggy animals, descended by natural selection from those that survived drowning in English mud, begin to be bred into compact meat carcasses by Bakewell of Dishley. Turnips now provide winter feed. As Chamberlayne notes, all the English wear good leather shoes. New methods of tillage, introduced by Tull, Townshend, and Coke, are taken up by rich landlords who can afford to adopt them. Arthur Young transforms the whole English system of land tenure, to aid in this production.

Spinning and weaving were home industries, bringing in cash income to self-sufficient farm people, until Hargreave's spinning jenny, Arkwright's frame, and Crompton's mule upset the equilibrium of the industry in second half XVIIIc. There is, for the first time, an excess of thread and yarn, over workers to weave it. Weavers multiply in every vacant building. They prosper until a minister named Cartwright invents a power loom.

Nothing is more characteristic of XVIIIc. than the jealousy and competition to stifle rival trades. Now workers riot against machines, mills are burned, whole industries with their uprooted workers migrate north from river banks and depleted forests to coal-producing areas. Iron masters have learned to smelt with coke; blast furnaces, and the textile mills of Peel and Hargreaves, are worked by steam. In 1745, a druggist seeks and finds English clay to replace kaolin brought back from China as ballast; great potteries, like Wedgwood's, arise around Burslem. Steam navigation begins; bridges are rebuilt in iron; ships are plated with iron.

Country folk, unused to the sight of cash, go to work in factories and find themselves far worse off: uprooted, cramped in dark company houses, with no room to raise a pig and some cabbages, much less a cow. They are inadequately fed; fall prey to diseases to which isolated farm life has given no immunity; work 12 hours or more in factories, the air of which is filled with fine particles; they die of tuberculosis and silicosis. Drunkenness increases with misery, as gin and whiskey begin to be distilled in England. The good intentions back of the Poor Law and workhouse are horribly misused to insure a practically enslaved, immobilized labor supply. Economic pressure sends even children of five to tend machines.

The poor, orphaned, and unfortunate (whose numbers have immensely increased with war, plague, fire, and changing agricultural methods) have been neglected for the centuries since the abolition of the monasteries. Now the government, guilds and private individuals begin to be concerned with their welfare. Hospitals and asylums, free schools and workhouses begin to be built. They are still horribly inadequate, frequently heartless, and so clearly spread infection that small dispersed infirmaries are also established.

2069. XVIIIc. 1702-14. English. (New York, Knoedler.)
John Marcellus Laroon.

View of the Mall in the time of Queen Anne.

The two great parks of London in XVII-XVIIIc. are St. James' with its Mall, and Hyde Park with its Ring. Both were first enclosed by Henry VIII. While the Leper Hospital was being altered into St. James' Palace, the adjoining marshy meadows were drained and turned into a deer park with a riding path, and the 390 acres of the old Hyde Manor were turned into a deer and stag preserve.

Both were improved by Charles II. The 350 foot long Ring, first used for horse races, became the fashionable drive of the late XVIIc. An enlarged St. James' Park, laid out by Lenôtre with lines of lime trees, had a long canal for the water fowl which the king loved to feed, and which still exist there.

The Ring was enclosed by "a sorry Kind of Balustrade . . . but three Foot from the Ground, and the Coaches drive round and round this. When they have turned for some time round one Way, they face about and turn t'other; So rowls the World." (Mission). During the fashionable afternoon hours, after the theatre, 200-300 coaches might be seen driving at one time, their dust kept down by watering, for which a fee of 6d per coach had been imposed in 1664. Footmen and lackeys had to remain outside the guardhouse gate, where they played rough games, and where could be bought the usual refreshments of the period: ale, spirits and syllabub, tarts and cheese-cake. After 1695, masked women and hackney coaches were forbidden. By 1712, the sale of intoxicating liquors at the gate was stopped and no stage coach, hackney coach, chaise with one horse, cart, wagon, or funeral was allowed to enter the park.

The Mall, where smoking was banned, became the fashionable promenade. During the hours between 3 o'clock dinner and 8 o'clock supper (which were also the most correct hours for making calls), Swift made his daily turns around the Mall, greeting or walking with cabinet ministers, and writing Stella (XXIII): "It is prodigious to see the number of ladies walking there." The *Spectator* (437) notes the increase of bare shoulders as he watches Gatty walking in the park at "high Mall."

John Marcellus Laroon (1679-1774) was the son of Marcellus Lauron or Laroon (1635-1702), an engraver from the Hague who lived in England.

His picture shows women of all classes wearing the fontange, which the *Spectator* (#98, June 22, 1711) says "has risen and fallen above 30° within his own memory . . . About ten years ago the commode shot up into a very great height, insomuch that the female part of our own species were much taller than the men . . . We appeared as grasshoppers before them. At present, the whole sex is in a manner dwarfed and shrunk . . . I remember several ladies who were once very near seven feet high, that at present want some inches of five." Some of these tall ladies wore masks (which are now more apt to be worn by women of poor reputation) with mantles, horizontally decorated skirts and trailing overskirts draped into bustles. They carried fans.

Although the wigs shown on the men still hang on the chest in front, they have mounted into twin peaks and have begun to rake back from the forehead. Both the waistcoat (buttoned at the waist to catch the Steinkirk), and the coat are shorter, and flare as additional width is pleated into the skirts of the coat at the sides. Pocket slits are now finished with flaps. Frogs are used, as well as buttons, for closings. Hose are rolled or gartered at the knee over close breeches, *culottes.*

The fontange is a relatively easy way for women of the lower classes to attain a fashionable look, and it has been quickly adopted by younger women. It is worn by two, walking behind the water-carrier in utilitarian, rolled-up garments (l.). Behind them, riding parties precede and follow a coach with six horses. At the end of one row of lime trees a postilion in livery and sash wears the jack boots which begin to be worn by nobody else. To the r., a sedan chair waits, while a bearer reaches for one of the buckets belonging to a woman in a cap and dark, bibbed apron.

2070. XVIIIc. 1711. English. (London, Nat. Port. Gall.)
Sir Godfrey Kneller.

Sir Christopher Wren.

Wren, who "completed the work commenced by Jones, and established the present favorite fashion

of building" (Malcolm) was the most influential of the Italian-inspired English architects. Sir John Vanbrugh, the painter-architect who built the heavy, less well-scaled Blenheim and Castle Howard and the fantastic "Minced-pie" house at Greenwich, and whose theatre roof had to be rebuilt, was no such mathematician or artist as Wren, who rebuilt Jones' St. Paul's, altered Hampton Court, designed Trinity College Library at Cambridge and the brick buildings of Chelsea and Christ's Hospitals. The influence of Palladio, filtered through these three men, still influences the architecture of large public buildings. Its alternative influence in the XVIIIc. is the romantic Gothic style in which Horace Walpole rebuilt his fabulous Strawberry Hill at Twickenham and whose last remains are seen in Hudson River Gothic in America.

Wren, at 79, wears a dark wig. The first wigs in XVIIc. were of any color, often blond; now they are white or dark. Mr. Michon, a goldsmith, advertised in 1710, that he had "found out . . . a clear water" which would darken light hair. Wigs of human hair might cost 40 guineas, like Duumvir's (*Tatler*, #54); cheaper wigs had horsehair beneath, or were entirely made of horsehair. A country girl in 1700 sold her hair for £60 to get herself a dowry; a periwigmaker paid £50 for the long white hair of a woman who had died at 107. (Weekly Journal, c. 1720.)

Wren's clothing shows the trend away from Louis XIV richness, which is indicated in the garments worn at George II's birthday in 1735: "brown flowered velvets, or dark cloth Coats, laced with gold or silver, or plain velvets of various colors, and Breeches of the same." By then, "their waistcoats were either gold stuffs, or rich flowered silks of large pattern, with a white ground; the make much the same as has been worn some time, only many had open Sleeves to their Coats; their Tie Wigs were with large curls, setting forward and rising from the forehead, though not very high: the Ties were thick and longer than of late, and both behind; some few had

Bag Wigs." (Malcolm)

2071. XVIIIc. c. 1712. American. (Baltimore, Hist. Soc.)
Justus Engelhardt Kühn.
Eleanor Darnall.

Kühn was a German Protestant who painted in Maryland from his naturalization in 1708 till his death in 1717.

Although Maryland was established in 1633, primarily as a colony to which Roman Catholics might emigrate to escape increasing oppression and discrimination, religious toleration was practiced there. In 1715 the proprietor turned Protestant, Catholics were disfranchised, and an influx of German Protestants soon began.

The ancestor of this five or six year old girl is supposed to have come from England in 1672. She was married, c. 1728-9, to Daniel Carroll III of Upper Marlboro, Md., whose forbears had been immigrants from Ireland in 1688. Catholic families like the Carrolls were apt to send their sons to Jesuit schools in France; their cultural relationships were as often Continental as English.

Some trace of this may be felt in Eleanor's reddish brown dress, black train, lace apron and hair arrangement, as well as in the elaborate "stock" background of gardens and balustrades which the painter probably had on hand for rich patrons. "There were no estates resembling this scene at Maryland at that or any other time," reports James W. Foster, Director of the Maryland Historical Society.

One of the products which England hoped to get from her American colonies was silk. Silkworm culture was first established by James I, bounties were offered, and from Pennsylvania southward some little silk was produced. On George II's birthday in 1735, Queen Caroline "was in a beautiful suit made of silk of the produce of Georgia, and the same was universally acknowledged to excel that of any other country."

2072. XVIIIc. 1716-8. English. (Macpherson Coll.)

Capt. Edward Teach, known as "Blackbeard the Pirate."

Teach was one of many British privateers, operating under "letters of marque" during the Wars of the Spanish Succession, who turned to piracy on their own account after the peace.

In 1717 he captured a French merchantman which he converted into a 40-gun man-of-war and renamed *Queen Anne's Revenge*. In this he harried the West Indies and the Carolina and Virginia coasts.

Piracy was hard to suppress without the cooperation of authorities, and flourished because Spain preferred pirates, to traffic with her former enemy. It was unprofitable without a partner on shore, preferably a person of standing, to dispose of the loot. Pirates were often gentlemen, although Teach happened to be a ruffian; but his accomplice and protector was the Governor of South Carolina, whose administration led to rebellion and brought S. Carolina from control of the proprietors to that of the Crown.

Two sloops, dispatched by the Governor of Virginia in 1718, captured Teach's ship, and he was shot by their commander.

Teach wore his hair and beard, which were in themselves remarkable, tied at the ears by flowing ribbons. Otherwise, he and his men

2072

2073

2074

2075

2076

2077

2078

2074. XVIIIc. c. 1720. English.

Waistcoat: white brocade, embroidered in gold.

2075. XVIIIc. Italian.

Waistcoat: Sleeved waistcoats, with the hem patterned all around, are made for indoor wear without jacket.

2076. XVIIIc. Italian.

Waistcoat: quilted.

2077. First Half XVIIIc. French.

Waistcoat: green cut and uncut velvet, satin ground.

2078. XVIIIc. 1750-60. Italian, Venice.

Waistcoat: brocade. Brocades were especially woven for waistcoats. The Mus. of Fine Arts, Boston, has Ebenezer Storer's sleeved waistcoat, which is seen in the Metropolitan Museum's oval pastel by Copley.

wear the simple, utilitarian clothes with long trousers which for centuries we have seen on sailors and which, in less than a century, will be worn by most men.

2073. Early XVIIIc. English.

Waistcoat, negligée: linen, embroidered in pink, green, white and yellow silk, and silver gilt.

Courtesy of Metropolitan Museum (2073-78)

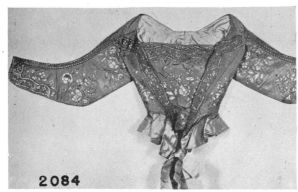

2079. Late XVII-Early XVIIIc. French. (Boston, Mus. of Fine Arts, Elizabeth Day McCormick Coll.)
Embroidered Muff: white woven-figured ground, embroidered with gold and polychrome silk.

2080. XVIIIc. American, Rhode Island. (Boston, Mus. of Fine Arts.)
Needlework Pocket Book with Silver Clasp, Hungarian point.

2081. Last Half XVIIIc. French. (Boston, Mus. of Fine Arts.)
Embroidered Pocket Book.

2082. XVIIIc. South German. (Boston, Mus. of Fine Arts.)
Sampler: patterns used in XVIIIc. purses.

2083. Early XVIIIc. English. (Boston, Mus. of Fine Arts, Elizabeth Day McCormick Coll.)
Quilted and Embroidered Sleeveless White Jacket.

2084. XVIIIc. French. (Boston, Mus. of Fine Arts, Elizabeth Day McCormick Coll.)
Bodice of Dress: pink taffeta embroidered in straw, giving an effect of gold embroidery.

2085. Late XVIIIc. American. (Boston, Mus. of Fine Arts.)
Strip of Crewel Work: valance or petticoat border.
A guest at the Princess Royal's wedding (1742) wrote: "The Duchess of Queensbury's clothes pleased me best; they were white satin embroidered, the bottom of the petticoat *brown hills,* covered with

2085

2086

all sorts of weeds, and *every breadth* had *an old stump of a tree* that ran up almost to the top of the petticoat, broken and ragged, and worked with brown chenille, round which twined nasturtiums, honeysuckles, periwinkles, convolvuluses, and all sorts of twining flowers which spread and covered the petticoat, vines with the leaves variegated as you have seen them by the sun, all rather smaller than nature, which made them look very bright; the robings and facings were little green banks with all sorts of weeds, and the sleeves and the rest of the gown loose twining branches of the same sort as those on the petticoat; many of the leaves were finished in gold, and part of the stumps of the trees looked like the gilding of the sun. I never saw a piece of work so prettily fancied, and am quite angry with myself for not having the same thought, for it is infinitely handsomer than mine, and could *not* cost *much more.*"

2086. Late XVIIIc. American. (Boston, Mus. of Fine Arts.)

Petit Point Picture: Boston Common with the old Hancock House.

When the *Spectator* (606 and 609) proposes a monumental inscription: "that she wrought out the whole Bible in tapestry, and died in a good old age, after having covered three hundred yards of wall in the mansion house," Cleora, who prefers real birds and flowers, says: "I hope to kill a hundred lovers before the best housewife in England can stitch out a battle."

2087. XVIIIc. English. (Chicago, Art Institute.)

Joseph Highmore. Pope at Twickenham.

Joseph Highmore (1692-1780), nephew of the sergeant-painter, studied art while apprenticed to the law, but became a professional painter in 1715. He was a pleasant, learned man, who painted many conversation pieces which are often mistaken for Hogarths; a number of portraits of royal or important people (including Harvard College's Hollis); and book illustrations like his twelve plates for Richardson's "Pamela" in 1744.

It was difficult for a Roman Catholic merchant's

2087

son like Pope to get a good classical education in England in late XVIIc. By rigid self-discipline, the brilliant seventeen-year-old prodigy was eventually fitted to produce translations of Homer, subscriptions to which brought in enough money to enable him to buy a house at Twickenham in 1719. Here he laid out his famous gardens and grotto and entertained the best company of his day: Swift and Gay, Bolingbroke and Bathurst.

An illness at twelve years had been too drastically treated. Pope (1688-1744) never grew beyond 4½ feet and became deformed. Eventually he had to be laced into "a bodice of stiff canvas," and could not put on without assistance the three pairs of stockings by which he tried to conceal the thinness of his legs.

He is in negligée: waistcoat, dressing gown and cap. A wig is uncomfortable, a shaven head cold, so we find XVIIIc. literary men, and painters like Hogarth, working in a night-cap or turban, even while otherwise completely dressed.

He is receiving a letter from John Searle, for many years his faithful body-servant and gardener, who has thrown an overcoat with a round collar over the waistcoat which was probably his working dress.

William Hogarth (1697-1764), son of a schoolmaster, was first apprenticed to a silverware engraver. Hogarth was an intensely alert and curious person who so trained his visual memory that he could reproduce whole theatrical performances at which he could not make sketches. In 1725 he engraved a shop bill advertising the removal of the linen-draper's or "slop shop" of his younger sisters, Mary and Anne, to "Ye King's Arms joyning to ye Little Britain Gate, near Long Walk," which "Sells ye best and most Fashionable Ready Made Frocks, Suites of Fustian, Ticken and Holland, Stript Dimmity and Flan'el Wast-Coats, blue and canvas Frocks, and blue-coat Boys Dra^{rs}," and similar materials "By Wholesale or Retail at Reasonable Rates."

His first great work was a series of twelve illustrations for Butler's "Hudibras," in 1726. It soon became his practice to paint a picture and then make an engraving from it. His "Harlot's Progress" (1731), published by subscription, was pirated. The "Rake's Progress" (1735) was protected by an Act of Parliament copyrighting an engraving, for the passing of which Hogarth was largely responsible.

In 1729, he was secretly married, though with the connivance of her mother, to the daughter of Sir James Thornhill, at whose art school he had studied.

His work for thirty-five years gives the most minutely complete picture of a life and a period which any artist has ever attempted. Every picture is a valuable document full of allusion and satire.

2088-89. XVIIIc. 1726. English. (Metropolitan Museum, Print Room.)

Hogarth. Samuel Butler's *Hudibras*: 2088. Hudibras in Tribulation. 2089. Hudibras at the Lawyer's.

Butler's satire of "The Presbyter Knight Going to the Wars," published between 1663-78, was founded on his own experience of life in the household of a former revolutionary general, and a brief period in a law office. Hogarth depended largely on Hollar's plates for his XVIIc. women's costume.

2090. XVIIIc. c. 1728. English. (Metropolitan Museum.)

Bartholomew Dandridge. The Price Family.

2091. XVIIIc. 1742. English. (Cambridge, Fitzwilliam Mus.)

Joseph Highmore. Mrs. Elizabeth Birch and Daughter. (Late appearance of dress of 2090.)

Satin gowns, with asymmetrically clasped bodice closings; slightly supported by hoops; short sleeves (still usually without cuffs), from beneath which the ruffled shirt sleeve emerges. Women's hair in transition: Mrs. Birch's hair has lost the Louis XIV look, but is still of natural length; that of the Price women has been cut to the new three-fingers' length, and is covered by caps with lace lappets or by smaller triangular caps. High-heeled slippers.

The form of the wigs of the Price men is determined by their ages; but the front locks of the full-bottomed wig on the oldest man are knotted and thrown back over the shoulders. Coat pockets high and horizontal. Deep closed cuff; two younger men wear coat sleeves entirely without cuffs, buttoned up the out-seam, to match the breeches. Shoe toes (square on the older man), are becoming more natural in shape, as feet of younger men show.

2092. XVIIIc. 1728-32. English. (London, Sir Charles Tennant.)

Joseph Highmore, sometimes att. to *Hogarth.* The Green Room at Drury Lane.

The Drury Lane Theatre of XVIIIc. was managed by Cibber from 1704, and by Garrick after 1747. The company before which Barry is rehearsing "Romeo" consists of Miss and Mrs. Prichard; Fielding; the generous and hasty Quin, who was afraid to appear in Gay's "Beggar's Opera"; and Lavinia Fenton, who became immortal as its Polly Peachum. It is as "Polly," the duchess of Boulton, that Walpole records her death. Satiric treatment of Sir Robert Walpole and bribery in the "Beggar's Opera" brought about censorship by licensing, under which the English Theatre still operates. It closed

all the theatres but the Drury Lane, Covent Garden, and Haymarket. Most of the almost numberless pleasure-gardens of XVIIIc. England flourished by evading censorship, calling performances "concerts."

An increase in the size of hoops is paralleled by greater flare in the skirts of men's coats. Coats are simple in fabric and trim, but lines of decoration, such as we see carried up the back vent of Barry's coat, reinforce its edges and prevent them from scissoring (see Ill. 2100). The long wigs of older men begin to have their front locks knotted up out of the way; in the wigs of younger men the long hair is drawn back and tied, often enclosed in a bag.

The English bodice has a long, straight, prim look, increased by the back lacing of its corset, in contrast to the more curved French *corps* which is commonly laced in front. English gowns are not much affected by the loose garments and flowing pleats of the *robe à la française* before midXVIIIc., and English gowns retain a comparatively uncluttered, circumspect look throughout XVIIIc. The edges of the bodice, finished with folds or shirred bands, scarcely emphasize the very discreet V-front.

There is no French *échelle* of laddered bows from the corset. The lace or plain kerchief over the shoulders is drawn under a bar of simple ribbon across the line of the corset-top. This may be trimmed with a bow, and another bow is sometimes seen at bottom of corset. These bars tend to multiply in number and become crossed lacings by mid-XVIIIc., but the closing does not lose characteristic simplicity.

The English skirt also remains plain, even after the round skirt changes to a laterally extended form. It is seldom split down the middle before this change makes it convenient; and when it is split, the revealed underskirt is plainer than that of France, although it is often handsomely quilted. Cuffs and the ruffles below them are also less elaborate than in France, although they become fussier by midXVIIIc.

But the English woman's head is covered long before the French. English caps are larger, more elaborate, and more enclosing. They may be tied under the chin; there are frilled mob-caps, large triangles and ovals (see Ills. 2093, 2099). Cap's long lappets hang or are pinned up, as Lavinia Fenton wears hers, to give a spreading roof-line above face.

2093. XVIIIc. 1729. English. (Metropolitan Museum.)

Hogarth. The Wedding of Stephen Beckingham and Mary Cox.

Weddings were often clandestine, usually private, and in any case small, during XVIIIc. The Marriage Act of 1753, which required public weddings to have repeated reading and publication of banns, was even considered by Fanny Burney an affront to the modesty of any women of sensibility.

The colors worn by this small wedding party in St. Martin's in the Fields are (l. to r.): f. in deep blue; m. dark gray; groom, pearl gray coat and hose, light blue vest, blue-gray breeches; bride, cream and gold; m. beige; clergyman, black, with white cassock and red hood; m. dark gray; f. shrimp pink; and f. pale yellow with blue bows.

2094. XVIIIc. 1740-50. French.

Chatelaine-nécessaire: gold and moss agate.

2095. XVIIIc. German, Regensburg.

Watch-chatelaine: gold, jewels, agate; key.

2096. Mid-XVIIIc. French.

Nécessaire: shagreen, mounted in gold.

2093

2094

2095

2096

2097

2098

2097. XVIIIc. 1740-50. French.

Contents of nécessaire shown in Ill. 2098.

2098. XVIIIc. French.

Nécessaire: gold and enamel egg.

Courtesy of Metropolitan Museum of Art

2099. XVIIIc. English. (Metropolitan Mus., Frick Coll.)

Hogarth. Miss Mary Edwards.

The eccentric Miss Edwards, daughter of Francis Edwards of Kibworth Harcourt, Leicestershire, was a great heiress. She was clandestinely married to Lord Anne Hamilton and was painted by Hogarth with her husband, but later repudiated the marriage and declared her son illegitimate, in order to protect her fortune. She is the central figure in Hogarth's *Taste in High Life* (see Ill. 2113).

Substantially the same English cap and dress worn by the bride, Mary Cox, are shown here in an extravagant, lacy form seldom seen in England. The open V of the corsage of her brocade gown is suppressed in favor of the hanging ends of her lace-trimmed scarf. The pleats which would ordinarily finish the edges of the bodice are pushed back toward the underarm. In addition to the conventional English choker of pearls, she wears an immense, diamond pendant. A watch-chatelaine with keys and accessories is pinned at her waistline.

2100. XVIIIc. 1731. English. (London, Countess of Leicester.)

Hogarth. Indian Emperor.

Dryden had followed a series of comedies by an heroic tragedy, "The Indian Queen," in 1663. This was immensely successful because of its wonderful settings and costumes. Mrs. Marshall played Queen Zempoalla in a real Indian gown, presented by Mrs. Aphra Behn. This was followed in 1665 by "The Indian Emperor; or, The Conquest of Mexico," in which Nell Gwynn made her debut. The play had a long life. George Farquhar, who had begun as an actor in a travelling company, was so unnerved by almost killing a fellow actor in its duelling scene that he turned playwright.

Hogarth's extraordinary visual memory reproduces a performance in the private theatre of Mr. Conduit, Master of the Mint, before the duke of Cumberland, the princesses Mary and Louise, the duke and duchess of Richmond, the duke of Montague, Earl of Pomfret and Captain Pointz. The children who play wear good standard French theatrical costumes with plumed turbans, instead of Mrs. Behn's actual Indian costumes. (Sitwell: *Conv. P.*)

Men's coats are of plain material, with flaring skirts and waist-high pocket flaps. Deep cuffs, open or closed, match the waistcoat; decoration is carried up the back vent of the coat. Wigs become strongly differentiated according to the age, situation and profession of their wearers—older men wear more conservative styles of heavily curled wigs; younger men tend toward the wig with toupet and bag (worn by the duke). Caps almost universally worn by English women and girls of the upper as well as other classes.

2099

2100

2101. XVIIIc. 1733. English.
Hogarth. Southwark Fair.

Southwark, where Shakespeare's Globe Theatre stood, is in the heart of London at the cross-roads from Southern England. A three-day fair in September, established there in 1492, was gradually extended to two weeks. Malefactors from the rest of London went into hiding among Southwark's poverty-stricken population. The reputation of the Fair became so bad that it was abolished in 1762.

The picture teems with allusion, and with information about poor people and their fun. In front of a booth where china is sold, a bag-piper with a walking dog operates a mechanical toy with his foot. A dice game goes on under a lantern advertising Cibber and Bullock's "Fall of Bajazet."

The great sign on the roof. carrying the legend "The Stage Mutiny" refers to the complications which followed Colley Cibber's sale of Drury Lane, the year before. Revolting actors, led by Cibber's worthless son Theophilus, are gathered in Covent Garden near the Rose Tavern. Cibber sits in the left corner with a sack of money. Highmore, who had "bought into" the theatre, holds a scroll marked "6,000 £." John Ellis, who has many pugilist friends, and is the scene painter of the company, brandishes a club.

2101

2102

Behind him, the widow of Robert Wilks, the actor, who holds a small share, carries a banner, "We'll starve them out." In the center are Mills in the plumed costume of "Bajazet," "Doll Tearsheet," Harper as "Falstaff," and Theophilus Cibber as "Pistol."

On the slack wires are acrobats, one of whom, Cadman, was killed later by a fall.

Lee and Harper's sign in the center advertises "The Siege of Troy." "Punch's Opera" is beyond. The Union Jack, as restored by Charles II, floats above.

In front, the actors drum up trade, as a circus parade still does today. An actor in plumes and scale armor is being arrested for debt by a sheriff. A fire-swallower performs on a platform.

In back of the peep-show the inevitable pickpocket operates on a country squire, with gloves and whip, his wife beside him. Mr. Fawkes juggles a bird. Above is the "Royal Wax Works" which shows "the whole Court of France." At the right, a broken-down horse carries a battered rider, the loose sleeve of whose sword-arm is held up by a ribbon elbow garter.

2102. XVIIIc. 1735. English.

Hogarth. Rake's Progress: plate 3.

The indispensable Hogarth plate is always an omitted one; how can one be satisfied with fewer than all eight illustrations of the "Harlot's Progress" (1731)? The eight plates of "The Rake's Progress" carry him down through Fleet Prison to Bedlam; and now one wishes one could have used the 1729 "Commissioners of the House of Commons examining the Warden of Fleet Prison" for mishandling his office.

The "leather-coat" of the Rose Tavern, Drury Lane, stands between a wench singing a bawdy ballad, *Black Joke,* and a trumpeter and blind harp-player. In back a neglected girl is setting fire to the map. All the Roman emperors on the wall have been smashed but Caesar, who is represented by a portrait of the cook—Pontiac. In front a "posture woman" is undressing for her act.

Pictures in which people are coming apart are very valuable. There is very little that we don't know about trouser buttons at fly and knee, after looking at "The Rake," or about wigs when we examine the standing man who is losing his. We see in the "posture woman's" discarded clothes the English corset, laced in back; the flaps at the bottom which hold it in place under the skirt-band; the simple laced-across placard on its front, and the ribbon bow which finishes the point as it is carried over the skirt. We understand the exact construction of her under-linen, the gores of her shoes, the clocked shaping of her torn stockings. As the curl comes out of drunken women's hair we see the three-fingers' length to which it is cut and the nasty old pad over which the hair is dressed. We see bonnet-like caps, mob-caps, and little caps dipping in the middle with their lappets pinned up. We see a girl with a narrow line of fur at the neck receiving the drunken rake's watch; (on the way he has vanquished a watchman and carried off his lantern and truncheon); a smiling Negro maid-servant; patched women in hoods and embroidered *palatines,* drunk, but still wearing their gloves.

2103. XVIIIc. 1737. American. (New York Hist. Soc.)

John Smibert. Johannes Schuyler and His Wife.

John Smibert (1688-1751), the first European

artist of importance to settle in America, was born in Edinburgh, the son of a dyer. He worked as a carriage painter in London where he also copied paintings, and as a portrait painter in Edinburgh, 1714-17. He then went to Florence where he copied Venetian paintings for the Grand Duke Cosimo III. About 1720, he met his life-long friend, Dean (later Bishop) Berkeley, through whose influence he was made professor of art and architecture in a "Universal College of Art and Architecture in Bermudas," for which funds never were appropriated. His wife and the rest of the proposed faculty sailed with him in 1728 and moved to Newport, Rhode Island, in 1729, where they waited in a body for two years. In 1730, Smibert married the daughter of a school-master-physician named Williams. She had a small fortune and some valuable property. At her well-located house in Queen Street, where Bishop Berkeley visited them, Smibert painted two hundred pictures of the austere provincial aristocracy, before his sight failed c.1748. He was the designer of Faneuil Hall in Boston, and also augmented his income by an art-supply and picture-frame business which his wife carried on after his death.

The names of two of the most conservative old Dutch families of America appear here. Schuyler (1688-1747) was the sixth son of Philip Schuyler who emigrated from Holland. His wife, Elizabeth Staats, widow of Johannes Wendell, wears a mourning costume which might have come out of a Dutch portrait of XVI-XVIIc., and which is considered suitable, in any case, for a Dutch matron of her age.

The body of Schuyler's bright butternut-brown velvet coat, with deep open cuffs, has the close, wrinkled look, tight at the underarm, of a Kneller portrait of the turn of XVII-XVIIIc. He wears a long cravat, rather than the current stock and jabot of Europe. His excellent wig also has the outmoded high backward rake from a flattened part, seen in Europe a decade or two earlier.

His costume shows the time-lag of provincialism. Hers is additionally retarded by age-old, static convention. A New Yorker will inevitably be reminded of the sisters, the last of the family, who lived unseen and finally died, barricaded in the great brownstone Wendell mansion on Fifth Avenue below the Public Library, to the delight of the Sunday supplements.

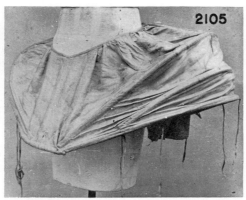

2104. XVIIIc. English. (Boston, Mus. of Fine Arts.)

Doll: dark green taffeta hoop.

This "baby," as dolls were called in XVIIIc., has a complete wardrobe of gown and hat, and a set of hanging pockets which hold her needlebook and handkerchief.

"Babies" also served as fashion models. Betty Crossstich's letter (*Spectator,* iii, 277) says she has received "a French baby for the year 1712. I have taken the utmost care to have her dressed by the most famous tire-women and mantua-makers in Paris . . . The puppet was dressed in a cherry-coloured gown and petticoat, with a short working apron over it, which discovered her shape to the greatest advantage." She describes its hair, patches on the breast, and its curious necklace.

2105. XVIIIc. c. 1750. Italian. Venetian. (Metropolitan Museum.)

Hoop: linen.

2106. XVIIIc. 1750-1800. Italian, Venetian. (Metropolitan Museum.)

Hoops: linen.

"Petticoats, which began to heave and swell before you left us (Sir Roger, *Spectator,* July 27, 1711) are now blown up into a most enormous concave, and rise every day more and more . . . (What ladies) have lost in height they make up in breadth. . . . A woman's honour cannot be better entrenched than . . . in a circle within circle." He supposed the first woman he saw "thus invested in whalebone" to be "near her time . . . but soon recovered myself out of my error, when I found all the modish part of the sex as 'far gone' as herself . . . The strutting petticoat smooths all distinctions, levels the mother with the daughter, and sets maids and matrons, wives and widows, upon the same bottom. . . . Should this fashion get among the ordinary people, our public ways would be so crowded that we would want street room." This is very much what did happen.

Skirts were supported in some way during most of XVIIIc. Louise de Bussy, at 111 years of age, died in 1737 from a fall while trying on paniers. In 1742, Harlequin, disguised as a saleswoman, says, "I have corfs, hoops, *paniers,* flounces, farthingales,

sacrissins, and *matelas piqués.* For prudes I have solid ones which cannot be raised; I have folding ones for gallants, and mixed ones for persons of the third estate . . . I have, by the grace of God, specimens of all sorts, English, French, Spanish and Italian. I make water carrier hoops for roundish waists, corfs for the thin-waisted and lanteras for the Venuses." (*Journal de Verdun.*)

The Goncourts list *paniers en gondole,* like water-carriers' yokes; *cadets* short above the knee; *à bourrelets,* which widened skirts by means of a padded band; *à guéridon,* which rested on a stand as the wearer sat; *à coudes* which were wide and supported the elbows, while describing a satisfactory oval, and were made with 5 rows of hoops (the first of which was called the *tracquenard* or trap)— 3 rows less than the English hoop; *criardes* of stiffened material which crackled, worn by great ladies and actresses; these went out of use with wickerwork *paniers* in midXVIIIc. and were replaced by whale-bone stiffened canvas skirts. In 1750, only the *janséniste* half-paniers remained, and these were ousted in 1760 by *considérations,* invented by Pamard the court dressmaker, which supported the dress without petticoat or *panier.* The idea of the hoopskirt as an "entrencher of honor" had a long life; Marie Antoinette was accused of immorality when she began to go without hoops.

2107. XVIIIc. 1738. English. (Met. Mus., Print Room.)

G. Bickham, Jr. The Minuet, No. 5: Letting Hands Go.

As soon as XVIIIc. girls were out of a nurse's care, they were handed over to a dancing master. He was probably much like the one recommended by Madam Prim, the Alderman's Lady (*Spectator,* 376), who "besides a very soft Air he has in Dancing . . . gives them a particular Behavior at Tea-Tables and how to place Patches to the best advantage, either for Fat or Lean, Long or Oval Faces."

Eustace Budgell's worthy citizen (*Spectator,* 67), who went with his wife to a ball at Monsieur Rigadoon's school, watched the French and Country (i.e. *contra*) dances with amazement at their famili-

arity. "They often made use of a most impudent and lascivious Step called *Setting,* which I know not how to describe to you, but by telling you that it is the very reverse of *Back to Back.*" When his daughter was "whisked round Cleverly above Ground in such a manner that I . . . saw further above her Shoe than I can think fit to acquaint you with," in a dance called "Moll Patley," he "seized on the Child and carried her home."

The first book which attempted to teach dancing by means of diagrams was published in 1588 by Thoinet Arbeau. New manuals with music and descriptions of as many as 358 figures appeared every two or three years during the first part of XVIIIc.

Typical entry in the secret diary of William Byrd of Virginia*: "I rose about 5, read Hebrew and Greek; I prayed and had coffee; I danced my dance." He must have been studying from diagrams, like the new lodger who shook the house so that the Tatler's Landlady thought he had gone mad. Addison (*Tatler,* 88) peeped in at the key-hole and saw a man "look with great attention on a book, and on a sudden jump into the air so high, that his head almost touched the ceiling. He came down safe on his right foot, and again flew up—alighting on his left; then looked again at his book, and holding out his right leg, put into it such a quivering motion, that I thought he would have shaken it off. He then used the left after the same manner, when on a sudden to my great surprise, he stooped himself incredibly low, and turned gently on his toes."

Both women's short, round skirts, and the skirts of men's coats have become very distended. The crinolined flare of the coat skirts would tend to force the sides of the vent to overlap in back; for this reason, they are reinforced by decorative bands or, as in this case, turned back double and trimmed with rows of button-holes. (See Barry, Ill. 2092.)

The knotted peruke has many forms; but when a knotted lock falls from either side of the toupet,

* Ed. Wright & Tingly, 2v. 1709-12, & 1739-41, Dietz Press, Inc. Richmond, Va.

there is always a lesser lock formed from the smooth hair in back.

2108. XVIIIc. 1738. English. (Metropolitan Museum. Print Room.)

Hogarth. Strolling Actresses in a Barn.

Through a hole in the roof of a barn belonging to the George Inn, a boy spies on the company as they prepare for the last performance of "The Devil to Pay." A handbill and list of the cast lies on the bed; a copy of the (proposed) Act against strolling players helps support a pan of too hot pap which is set on the crown, while mother, Jupiter's eagle, feeds her squalling baby.

The barn is filled with scenery, properties, and drying wash. Cupid climbs a ladder to fetch Jove's stockings off a stage cloud. An apron, cap, under-drawers and sleeve ruffles hang on the rope walker's line.

The weeping Ganymede, wearing only a shirt and a coat with deep open cuffs, is a girl who has to take the place of a missing actor and is going to be uncomfortable and ridiculous, even if she does succeed in getting into his breeches which lie on the bed. Aurora arranges the costume of the sympathetic Siren. Flora uses the basket in which stage jewels are carried (which is about to go up in flames from the candle) as a dressing table to hold her powder-shaker and oyster-shell of rouge, as she kneels in a torn hoop-petticoat to arrange her hair. Diana stands in her shirt, her taped-together hoops and skirt collapsed about her feet. Two little demons eat, drink and smoke from the altar. A female in tumbler's tights, and an old woman with a patch over her eye, The Tragic Muse and the Ghost, let blood out of a cat's tail (to make it fierce, we are told). Juno, in her diadem and jewelled stomacher runs over her part from the book. Her leg and pretty shoe are stretched out on the wheel-barrow. The Goddess of Night, played by a Negro woman, mends Juno's stocking. A monkey plays with Jove's helmet; kittens, with the orb and lyre; and a mitre is used to carry the company's volumes of farce and tragedy.

2109. XVIIIc. 1739. Scotch. (Edinburgh, Nat. Gallery.)

Allan Ramsay. The Painter's Wife.

Allan Ramsay (1713-84) was the son of the Scotch pastoral poet of the same name, whose bookshop and lending library (the first in Scotland) was the hotbed of Scotch literature.

The virile, attractive, and cultured son studied in London in 1733, Rome in 1736, and returned to immediate success in Edinburgh in 1739.

He was made king's painter in 1767, to Reynolds' disappointment—an establishment with a number of assistants was necessary in order to turn out the quantity of presentation portraits of the King for colonial gifts. Ramsay never recovered from an accident to his painting arm and died on one of his many trips abroad.

Soon after his return to Edinburgh from his studies, Ramsay married Anne, daughter of Alexander Bayne, first Professor of Scots Law in Edinburgh University, and painted her portrait the same year. She died in 1747, and Ramsay made one of the typical XVIIIc. clandestine marriages with a daughter of Sir Alexander Lindsay in 1752.

Anne Ramsay, in her lace *palatine,* is dressed in the French, not the English style. Jacobite Nationalists opposed Hanoverian Whigs in Scotland, and demanded the repeal of the 1707 Act of Union with England. Presumably the Baynes were ardent Jacobites; in any case, Scotch culture at this period was oriented toward France rather than England, through the sympathies of a large part of the population.

2110. XVIIIc. 1739-40. English. (London, Foundling Hospital.)

Hogarth. Capt. Coram.

Thomas Coram (1668-1751) rose from common sailor to ship's captain in the colonial trade, and lived for some years in Taunton, Mass., as a shipbuilder. On his return to London he was so moved by the condition of children around the docks of the East End that he worked 17 years and spent all his own fortune to get a royal charter granted in 1739 for establishment of a foundling hospital. To enter an institution, no matter how well-intentioned, during the epidemic-ridden XVIIIc., was practically a death sentence, and the privately supported Foundling Hospital was no exception. It finally received government funds and supervision. Coram was also interested in the education of Indian girls and the settlement of Nova Scotia and Georgia.

England leads in evolving many new forms of coat and topcoat with collars and double rows of buttons, by which the colored linings can be buttoned back and displayed. Coram wears shoes with the old-fashioned square toe, and his own gray hair, grown long.

2111. XVIIIc. 1741. English. (London, Nat. Port. Gall.)

J. B. van Loo. John, Lord Hervey.

Hervey had been intimate with the prince and princess of Wales and married the loveliest of the ladies in waiting. He quarrelled with George II and aligned himself with the chancellor, Walpole, whom he aided through the great influence he retained over Queen Caroline. The cushion he holds symbolizes his vice-chamberlainship of the royal household.

Hervey was involved in ugly recriminations with Pope, who was jealous of his friendship with Lady Mary Wortley Montague, and satirized him in the "Dunciad." Hervey left a valuable "Memoir of the Court of George II."

He was a fragile epileptic who died at forty-seven, two years after this picture was painted. The winter of 1741 was one of the coldest ever recorded. Hervey wears one of the first fur-lined coats, such as will be much more commonly seen after the bitter winter of 1760.

2112. XVIIIc. 1741. American. (Harvard University.), Robert Feke.

Isaac Royall and Family.

Robert Feke (c. 1705c.-1750), the best portrait painter of his time in America, was born at Oyster Bay, L. I., New York. The son of a Baptist minister, he was listed as a "mariner," and probably came in that way to Newport, where Smibert was already established. He married a Quaker whom he used to escort to meeting-house before going to his own church. He worked in Philadelphia in 1746-50, and painted twenty portraits in Boston on visits in 1741 and 1748-9. Ill health took him to Bermuda, where he died.

Royall (1719-81), a rich resident of Medford, was high in the court and council of Massachusetts, and became America's first Brigadier General during the French wars. He gave two thousand acres of land to endow a law professorship at Harvard. Sympathetic with the mother country, he went to England at the Revolution and died there, his American estates having been confiscated.

This provincial family is a decade or so behind English fashion. The women wear asymmetrically closed satin bodices (see Ills. 2090, 2091). Their capless heads show vestiges at the temples of the little scalloped *favorites* of Louis XIV's time. There is little fullness in the skirts of Royall's coat.

The time-lag betwen London and provincial fashion was not confined to the colonies. The *Spectator* (119-120) notes: "As I proceeded in my journey, I observed the petticoat grew scantier and scantier, and about three-score miles from London was so very unfashionable that a woman might walk in it without any manner of inconvenience. The Salisbury justice of the peace's lady was at least ten years behindhand in her dress, but at the same time as fine as hands could make her." As the *Spectator* went west to Cornwall he seemed to be back in Charles II's reign. The steinkirk of 1692 "arrived but two months ago at Newcastle, and there are several *commodes* in those parts which are worth taking a journey to see."

2113. XVIIIc. 1742. English. (Metropolitan Museum, Print Room.)

Hogarth. Taste in High Life.

The eccentric Miss Edwards commissioned a pic-ture from Hogarth for sixty guineas, as her revenge on those who had ridiculed her. The painting was never a favorite of Hogarth's, and the face he has used on the central figure, which satirizes the extremes of hoops, patches, and *robes à la française,* is astonishingly like Miss Edwards' own. (See Ill. 2099.)

The male figure is Lord Portmore, as he appeared at court on his return from France, encumbered by hat, muff, and hanging cane, and wearing a wig with a ridiculously long pigtail and a single skimpy curl before each ear. The two withered creatures express fashionable ecstasy over bits of porcelain; the great pot behind them is another expression of the craze for china.

The passion for French cooking is ridiculed by the monkey who reads a menu of absurd foods—cock's combs, duck tongues, rabbit ears, fricasseed snails and such—with a quizzing glass. His tail looks like Lord Portmore's wig; his own wig is in a square bag.

A bill for Lady Basto's gambling debt of £300 to John Pip lies on the floor by an immense stack of playing cards. A little Negro (the intelligent and beloved Ignacio Sanchez, who was painted by Gainsborough), holds one of the debased oriental figures which Hogarth ridicules without end. He is being chucked under the chin by the famous prostitute, Kitty Fisher. She lifts her hoops, since there is no space in one room for two such. A twisted scarf is buckled into place by straps at the top and bottom of her bodice; a watch and chatelaine hang from her belt.

All the pictures on the wall have significance. The dancing craze (see Ill. 2107) is noted in the figure of the French dancing master, Desnoyers, among butterflies. In the center, the Medici Venus (whose fig-leag is now half a loop); an amorino fans the flame of a burning hoop, before starting on a muff, cap and wigs; another massages a too-fat goddess. The same costume accessories are ridiculed in the adjoining picture. Below it, a girl in a pastoral hat and apron can scarcely make her way through clipped alleys in a garden; and on the fire-screen a woman in a sedan chair can hardly sit because of hoops.

2114-16. XVIIIc. 1745. English.
(Metropolitan Mus., Print Room.)
Hogarth. Marriage à la mode.

To settle gambling debts, a marriage has been arranged by their fathers between an easy-going young lord and the spoiled daughter of a rich alderman. Its course is shown by six plates: the marriage contract; breakfast; visit to the quack doctor; the toilette of the countess; the death of the earl; and the suicide of the countess.

2114. *Breakfast:* The viscount has returned to a disordered house from a night on the town; his wife's nasty little dog is much interested in a cap with ribbons which spills out of the pocket of his black and gold suit, worn with white stockings. A yawning, half-dressed man-servant in olive-green coat, brown breeches and black stockings, is just beginning to straighten out the disorder of last night's cards and music. A forgotten candle is about to set fire to a chair. The lady, in a lemony dressing cape, rosy white petticoat and blue ribbons has been looking at herself in a mirror, and drinking tea. The worthy steward is leaving in disgust, with his ledger and the bills, only one of which has been paid, and that a year ago.

The room is a satire on the architect, William Kent, and the tasteless decorations of the period. The "antique" bust is all

modern but the base; its nose has been chipped off deliberately. Debased oriental figurines crowd the mantel. The wall-fixture above the viscount's head is a nameless horror of clock and candles, fish, monkey, squatting eastern god, and foliage.

Hat, with wide, laced and feathered brim, cocked high; worn over a wig which has lost its curl. Coat with frog and braid trim which begins to supplant buttons. Little hood, short dressing gown; laced corset, brocade petticoat. The bald steward, with his pocket full of Methodist tracts, disdains a wig and lets what hair he has grow.

2115. *Visit to the Quack Doctor.* The viscount and a young girl have been taken to a quack doctor by an old procuress who wears black taffeta, a gold-edged red apron, flowered scarf and red ribbons. The viscount is indignant at the failure of the prescribed treatment. The quack, dressed in snuff brown with gold buttons and gray stockings, has risen from being a barber; a basin, notched to fit the neck, and a broken comb hang near a unicorn's horn, slung like a barber's pole among a collection of "rarities" and "curiosities" worthy of the would-be antiquarian, Don Saltero. Bits of clothing and armor ascribed to famous owners, a mummy,

a skeleton and a combination gallows and bottle opener "Seen and approved by the Royal Academy of Sciences at Paris."

Ruffled cap, tied about with blue ribbon; pretty, short blue and gold cape; lace trimmed apron, gold brocade petticoat, flowered in red and green, long kid gloves; enormous hoops, so large that there is a tendency to discard them altogether, around mid-XVIIIc.; watch chatelaines at waistline.

2116. *Toilette of the Countess.* The old earl is dead. The alderman's daughter is too wrapped up in the enjoyments of a fashionable countess (with coronets set on mirror and window frames) to concern herself with her baby, whose teething coral hangs forgotten on her chair. She is receiving a crowd of friends and hangers-on, while in white combing jacket, corset, yellow gown and pale brick-pink petticoat. A French hairdresser (whose coat is without cuffs, which might interfere with his work) curls her hair. A young advocate, with characteristic wig and gown, shows tickets, while pointing to a masquerade ball painted on the screen. This secret assignation, which the young earl will come upon, culminates in the earl's death in sword play and the subsequent suicide of the discredited and conscience-sticken countess, by laudanum. A fat, over-dressed Italian opera singer (dressed in putty color with dark gold brocade, flowered red and green, and a light putty-colored vest, black breeches, dark gray stock and stockings), laden with diamonds in earrings, *solitaire* pin and rings, sings to the interest of no one but a gushing lady in white with blue underskirt and ribbons. A mass of cards of invitation from such as she has spilled from his pockets. A mocking Negro servant offers her chocolate; a plain, hearty country squire plays by himself with his whip; a delicate young man, whose blue and gold coat has the new turned-over collar (in white, with a dark gray stock, brick breeches and light gray hose), sips chocolate with his hair in curl papers. A little blackamoor plays with odd lots of

fake antiques and oriental junk, which the countess has picked up at the auction of the effects of the late Timothy Babyhouse.

Wigs have entered upon the specialization, by profession and situation in life, which will eventually lead to their being given up, except by professional men. There is great variety in the form and decoration of coats worn by different sorts of people. The countess' woman friend wears the midXVIIIc. flat straw hat on top of a ruffled cap; kerchief tucked under a band across the top of the bodice, the long look of which is increased by double folds; skirt so distended by hoops that it must be slit up the front, but its edges and petticoat are untrimmed, in English use.

2117. Second quarter XVIIIc. English.
Spitalfields Silk Dress; quilted satin petticoat; cut paper lace fan.

Quilted petticoats (usually in satin, and in all colors but particularly in blue, white, greenish-white, green, and yellow) were a favorite handwork in the cold XVIIIc. An aunt in 1714 complains that her nieces, after gadding and tea-drinking, "go to bed as tired with doing nothing as I am after quilting a whole under-petticoat," and wishes they would work beds, chairs and hangings, instead of wasting their time with dress, play and visits.

2118. Third quarter XVIIIc. French.
Dress of Chinese Painted Silk. These hand-painted gowns are apt to have green, yellow, or white grounds. (M.F.A., Boston, has several.)

2119. Second quarter XVIIIc. English.
Dress of Spitalfields Brocade; in white, gold, henna and brown, worn by Lydia Catherine, duchess of Chandos.

A silk industry to rival Italy was the dream of most XVIIc. rulers. James I distributed 10,000 mulberry trees, for which the English climate was not really suited. In 1687, 13,500 Protestant refugee weavers settled at Spitalfields in N. London. When Sir Thomas Lombe set up silk spinning machines in England in 1718, (from drawings brought back

from Italy by his brother), the wool and cotton industries protested this threat to their prosperity, just as the growing Scotch linen-weaving trade had opposed the striped and checked patterns produced by the Spitalfields experts. Spitalfields silk weaving was repeatedly checked until it was moribund; then attempts were made to revive it by prohibiting any importation of silk, and exhorting everyone to wear Spitalfields out of patriotism. Queen Charlotte wore Spitalfields silk, or English calico, and embroidered her own gowns.

2120. Second quarter XVIIIc. English.
Green Damask Dress; quilted green taffeta petticoat; apron and matching hat, with polychrome and silver embroidery. Neckpiece of sheer drawn linen instead of lace.

2121. XVIIIc. French.
Hat with Appliqué Embroidery; shown with 2120.

2122. XVIIIc. c. 1785. French.
Printed Cotton Dress; straw hat.

2123. XVIIIc. 1762. (Boston, Mus. of Fine Arts.)
Sampler.
Lace developed out of fabric threads, punched or drawn, and worked. There is a return to these techniques in XVIIIc., either as an approximation of lace for those who cannot afford it, or out of the

boredom of those who have worn lace for a long time. (See Ill. 2120.)

2124-25. XVIIIc. c. 1745. English. (Cambridge, Fitzwilliam Mus.) J. Highmore. Illustrations for Richardson's *Pamela*.

2124. Pamela Shows Mr. Williams a Hiding Place for a Letter.

2125. Pamela Tells a Story.

Pancake-flat hats, with the lowest possible crowns, tied over ruffled caps. The English bodice has its kerchief tied in place across the top of the bodice, and drawn down to **intensify the long, lean line** of the bodice. The enormous hoops of mid-XVIIIc. occasionally force even English skirts to be slit up the middle, as is seen under Pamela's apron.

Severity of an Anglican clergyman in his cassock, band and solemn, deep-crowned hat, compared to the worldly dress of a French abbé; however, the typical ecclesiastical wig, in both countries, is of shoulder length, without knotted locks.

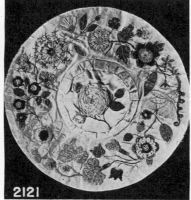

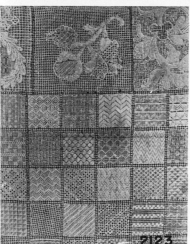

Courtesy of Museum of Fine Arts, Boston (2117-2123)

2126. XVIIIc. 1746. American. (Metropolitan Mus.)
Robert Feke. Tench Francis.

The Irish-born leader of the Pennsylvania bar wears a lawyer's wig with his brown coat and waistcoat.

2127. XVIIIc. Before 1750. Scotch. (Worcester, Severn, Stoke-Croome. Earl of Coventry.)

Allan Ramsay. George William Coventry.

A leader of the opposition, who became the 6th Earl in 1750.

2128. XVIIIc. English. (London, National Gallery.)

J. Highmore. Gentleman in Murrey-Brown Velvet.

Both 2127 and 2128 wear long, plain dark velvet coats, with very wide or deep cuffs; long, light-colored satin waistcoats. The heavily frogged and tasseled decoration of the Continent seldom appears on English coats, but the waistcoat is richly edged and may have a knotted fringe border below the last buttonhole. Wig with characteristic toupet of c. 1745.

2129. XVIIIc. Before 1748. English. (Greenwich National Maritime Mus.)

Hogarth. Lord George Graham in his Cabin.

The Navy captain, son of the duke of Montrose, who sits in his gilded mahogany cabin, was presumably painted before the establishment of uniforms in 1748.

He wears a brown velvet cap, gray-furred red gown, thrown over a turquoise-lined gray coat, white satin waistcoat, golden-brown breeches, white stockings, and red slippers. His friends are in green, with light green stockings; and in brown with gray breeches. They are attended by a cabin boy in a white apron and a Negro in a red-brown neckcloth, black coat and brown waistcoat. Graham's wig is set on the head of his dog.

The tradition of officers eating off handsome silver, even in the trenches, was established, Voltaire says, by the Marshal d'Humières in 1658, at the siege of Arras. In addition to unbreakable plate, Graham's cabin has a handsome china punch bowl.

Thomas Gainsborough (1727-88), son of a respected dissenting crêpe-maker of Sudbury, and his wife who did floral still-lifes, had painted all the scenery of Sudbury before he was ten. At fourteen he went to London, studied book-illustration with Gravelot, and returned to Sudbury for a couple of years. He removed to Ipswich in 1747, upon his marriage to Margaret Burr. Mrs. Gainsborough was charming and had a small private fortune; her real father seems to have been of very high birth. The couple were a great social success, and on the advice of Gov. Thicknesse, moved to Bath in 1759. The nobility, and the actors Gainsborough loved, like Garrick and Quin, crowded his studio and its musical parties. His fees of forty to one hundred guineas for half to full length portraits enabled him to rent Schomberg House in London in 1774. Gainsborough was one of the original members of the Royal Academy, but seldom attended its meetings after a quarrel over the hanging of his pictures in 1772, and had stopped exhibiting some years before his death from cancer. He was a handsome, gregarious, easily irritated man, who used to make up quarrels with his wife by sending his dog Fox with a charming note addressed to her spaniel Tristram. Gainsborough said that his brother Humphrey had anticipated Watts in inventing the steam-engine, and had been done out of a fortune.

Gainsborough's and Reynolds' portraits are the great English costume documents of their period.

2130. XVIIIc. 1749-50. English. (London, Sir Philip Sassoon.)
Gainsborough. The Artist, Wife and Child.

Dark coat and light waistcoat of mid-XVIIIc. The method of seaming and gathering the plain satin skirt over laterally extended hoops is clearly seen; long line of English bodice and kerchief is extended by plain narrow apron.

2131. XVIIIc. 1750-55. English. (England, Andrews Coll.)
Gainsborough. Mr. & Mrs. Robert Andrews.

Golden autumn in Suffolk when game birds are plenty and a squire carries a gun as he walks with his wife and keeps an eye on Auberies, his Sudbury estate. Mr. Andrews' buff coat, with dark velvet collar to match the breeches, is cut away and double-breasted, falling into exaggerated lapels when unfastened; the waistcoat is becoming cut away and shortened into a vest. The sparse, unpowdered wig on which a hat can be set and maintained while hunting, may even be his own hair. The hat crown is deeper, brim wider, with laced edges concavely cocked.

Over very wide hoops, the bodice of Mrs. Andrews' light, sharp blue gown is skirted like the coats of dancing girls painted by Lancret or Tiepolo. The English kerchief is usually caught across the line of the top of the corset by a ribbon, strap or pin. A wide, flopping hat is set over her cap.

2132. Mid-XVIIIc. English. (Kenilworth, Stoneleigh Abbey. Lord Leigh.)
Arthur Devis. James Brydges (1731-89), third Duke of Chandos, as a Youth.

The 1st duke of Chandos became immensely rich as paymaster of the forces abroad during the Wars of the Spanish Succession. He was Handel's and Pope's patron and lived in such style at "Canons," which cost £230,000, with his own Swiss guards lining his road to church, that he was known as "the grand duke" despite heavy losses in the African, Mississippi and South Sea crashes of 1718-20. Three

2135

2134

years after his death in 1744, "Canons" was sold for £11,000 and torn down for its materials, such as twenty-two steps each made of one piece of marble.

The 2nd duke bought Anne Wells from her drunken hostler husband, who was offering her for sale at Newbury as the duke passed through. Chandos had her educated into a charming person, and after her husband had drunk himself to death, and the duchess Mary had died, married her. When Chandos died "to the great joy of that noble family" the youth we see here became the 3rd duke. Anne Wells was not allowed burial in the family chapel where Handel had been organist.

The subject of an XVIIIc. English portrait is apt to be shown leaning against one of the classic urns, fountains or sundials with which private parks and public pleasure gardens are dotted. Great masquerades are being held, like the Venetian ridotto described by Walpole (Letter to Mann, May 3, 1749). A well known "conversation-piece" shows the con-

fusion of a couple who met at one of these balls, retired to a classic fountain in a remote part of the garden, and unmasked, only to find that they were husband and wife.

Brydges, mask in hand, cloak over shoulder, wears a waistcoat treated like a XVIIc. doublet, with lace cuffs, collar, band strings, rosettes at knees and shoes.
2133. XVIIIc. c. 1760. English. (Metropolitan Mus.)
Francis Cotes. Harry Paulet, Duke of Boulton.

Francis Cotes (1725?-70), a portrait painter in oils and crayon, and his brother Samuel (1734-1818), the greatest miniaturist of his day, were the children of an apothecary who, before censure by the Irish House, had been Mayor of Galway, and his wife, daughter of a high official in the Royal African Society. Francis seceded from the Society of Artists to become one of the original members of the Royal Academy; poor health sent him to Bath, where his patrons followed.

Lavinia Fenton's descendant, as an admiral, in the uniform established in 1748: blue breeches and coat with white facings and vest, laced in gold.
2134. XVIIIc. c. 1750. English. (London, A. Tooth & Sons.)
Hogarth. The Brothers Clarke of Swakeleys Round a Table Drinking Wine.

This picture of the brothers and their lawyers was probably painted to commemorate the purchase of their property at Ickenham, Middlesex. (Sitwell: *Conversation Pieces.*)
2135. XVIIIc. English. (London, Foundling Hospital.)
Hogarth. March to Finchley (1750).

Hogarth got from Hell Brueghel's *La grasse et la maigre cuisine* the idea for this canvas, which he dedicated to George III. The king, who "hated *bainting* and *boetry,* too," considered it an insult to his guards. Whereupon Hogarth ironically rededicated it to Frederick the Great.

It represents the moment in 1745 when the Young Pretender's army in Scotland seemed to threaten England; guards were marched to camp at Finchley to defend London.

With Highgate and Hampstead in the background, the crowd fills the Tottenham Court Road between the King's Head Tavern and the Adam and Eve, which at least until World War II still stood in the same place. An outdoor garden was an almost indispensable part of an XVIIIc. inn; Eden Street, to one side, now commemorates the Adam and Eve's *Paradise Gardens*.

A young guardsman starts off between sweethearts who are not only rivals for him, but represent the two political factions. The modest Protestant girl carries a picture of the duke of Cumberland and the words and music of *God Save the King* in her basket. The tough camp-follower, a cross on her cape, sells the *Jacobite Journal* and *London Evening Post,* and brandishes the *Remembrancer,* in which her banns have perhaps been printed.

From l. to r.: boy with fife; drummer; a Frenchman whispering to another, under whose overcoat shows a scrap of Highland plaid; an old woman with a baby on her back smokes a pipe; behind her, a boxing match with bare fists.

To the r. of the flag another officer kisses a milk girl in pancake hat with yoked buckets on her shoulders, from whom a boy steals milk, to the amusement of a pastry-seller, whose own wares are being stolen. In front of a very smug, proud officer, drunken soldiers fill their canteens from a keg of beer. In the r. foreground a drunken guardsman, who is losing his buttoned gaiters, reaches for a drink of gin being poured out by a woman; so does the baby on her back.

Ill. 2136 has been deleted.

2137. XVIIIc. 1754. Italian.

Canaletto. The Rotunda at Ranelagh.

The greatest of the London pleasure gardens were Vauxhall and Ranelagh.

Vauxhall in XVIIc. was called the New Spring Gardens, "a pretty contrived plantation," where one walked, picked flowers or cherries, and listened to the nightingales. Pepys ate lobster and syllabub there with his wife and Deb Mercer. Music, paintings,

statues and ruins were added to its twenty acres, to its alleys and wilderness, the windings and turnings of which were "so intricate that the most experienced mothers have often lost themselves here in looking for their daughters." Swift and Sir Roger de Coverley went there, but it had become rough and disreputable when a "Ridotto al fresco," by a new management in 1732 started it on a fresh triumphant career. Season admission to its concerts was by a silver token designed by Hogarth. Everyone went; Farmer Colin recounted its delights on his return. Walpole tells a story of a mad, show-off group of the aristocracy gone by water to Vauxhall, accompanied by barges of horns and carrying with them Betty the fruit-girl with hampers of strawberries, mincing chickens in butter and cooking them in a china dish over a lamp while all the people in the gardens tried to crowd around their booth. The refreshments to be had at Vauxhall were limited to wine, beer and syllabub, meat sliced so thin you could see through it, salad, cheese and such desserts as cheese-cake and tarts.

Walpole describes the difficulties of getting to the Ridotto of 1769 (in letter to Montague, May 10), but thought little of the entertainment and illuminations. With the aid of fire-works, balloon ascensions, parachute descents, side-shows, gas lighting and concerts, Vauxhall lasted halfway through XIXc.

By midXVIIIc., skirts, while they remain plain in England, are enormously extended laterally; bodices show the front lacings common all over Europe, and the back pleats of the *robe à la française* appear on many English gowns.

Ranelagh was built at end XVIIc. by the Viscount Ranelagh, another who had found the paymastership of the army profitable. Its gardens were the finest of their size in Europe. In 1741, Walpole wrote, "an immense amphitheatre, with balconies full of little alehouses was built in rivalry with Vauxhall, and cost about twelve thousand pounds. . . . Into which everybody that loves eating, drinking, staring, or crowding is admitted for twelve pence." By 1744, he says, "it has totally beaten Vauxhall. Lord Chesterfield is so fond of it that he says he has ordered all his letters directed thither. The floor is all of beaten princes. You can't set your foot without treading on a Prince or Duke."

The Jubilee Masquerade in the Venetian taste, which Walpole thought "far the best understood and prettiest spectacle" he ever saw, took place in 1749. But although everybody went there to be seen, it became a very boring place. Samuel Rogers said "all was so orderly and still that you could hear the whishing sound of the ladies' trains as the immense assembly walked round and round the room, and from time to time, as solemnly reversed."

The last superb spectacle at Ranelagh was the regatta and ball of June 23, 1775. Ranelagh finally closed in 1803.

2138. XVIIIc. 1756-61. English. (Althorp Park, Earl Spencer.)
Reynolds.

Margaret Georgiana, Countess Spencer and her daughter, later the Duchess of Devonshire.

Sir Joshua Reynolds (1723-92), with Gainsborough the greatest XVIIIc. English portrait painter, was apprenticed by his poor teacher-vicar father to a painter named Hudson, from whose stultifying influence he was rescued by a drunken artist named Gaudy, who said a picture should have rich texture "as if the colors were made of cream and cheese." He made useful friends in London in the 40's, painted in Italy, 1750-3, and was overwhelmed by society after his portrait of Admiral Keppel in 1755. His fees doubled between 1760-81, when he charged fifty to two hundred guineas for his wonderful portraits and £1500 for his dreadful historical pictures.

Reynolds was involved in the quarrels of Benjamin West and Hayman over the Society of Artists; withdrew, and was made the first president of the new Royal Academy founded 1768; his noble, detached tactfulness made him its greatest president. He was knighted and made George III's first painter after Allan Ramsay's death.

Experiments to attain a "cream and cheese" texture made many of his pictures impermanent, but they are wonderful records of costume worn by living persons, not fashion plates.

2139. XVIIIc. English. (Metropolitan Mus.)
British School (formerly attr. to Reynolds).
Portrait.

Olive costume and ribbons; tan brocade jacket.

2140. XVIIIc. English. (New York, Knoedler.)
Arthur Devis. The Putnam Family.

Arthur Devis (1711?-87) was a faithful exhibitor in the Free Society of Artists from 1762; he also repaired Sir John Thornhill's paintings at Greenwich and worked in India. His son, A. W. (1763-1822) painted a great many admirals and sea-battles.

During the 60's English upper-class dress (as seen in Ill. 2138-40) begins to show the effects of French

influences: lace ruffles, bows, shirred bands of decoration, and heads without caps on younger women. The newly-bared English head at first has a bleak, skinned-back look; then it loosens, or is studded with decoration (Putnam family) before becoming the higher, more ceremoniously dressed head shown on Queen Charlotte.

Bodices become shorter; the V-front widens into a U-shape. The kerchief is relegated to negligée, domestic dress or older women and is crossed, as though laced, by ribbons; these are sometimes caught at their intersections by flat, prim little bows (Putnam family) in place of the graduated ladder of perky bows seen on Mme. de Pompadour; the front lacing and bows come to be made of shirred bands rather than ribbon, in England, as shirred trimmings increase in use. Skirts have lost their round hoops and are unsupported; in England they are often bunched up asymmetrically, at the period when looped garlands are carried or worn (Putnam family).

Collarless coats, like Mr. Putnam's, are apt to rise high and wrinkle, as though begging for a collar.

2141. XVIIIc. 1759. English. (New York, J. P. Morgan.)
Hogarth. The Lady's Last Stake, or Virtue in Danger.

Lord Charlemont commissioned Hogarth to paint a picture on any subject he chose. The fourteen-year-old Hester Lynch Salisbury (later Mrs. Piozzi) served as the model for the young woman who, at five o'clock, as the candles burn low, has lost at piquet £500, her own jewels, and her husband's miniature and watch, to a young officer, in an unpowdered wig and uniform with cord fourragère.

English dress is becoming affected by French laciness, especially at the sleeve ruffles and neck ruche. The English bodice still retains its single bow at the top of a plain V—instead of a graduated ladder of bows. The skirt is slit over a plain petticoat, but is still untrimmed.

John Zoffany (1733-1810), a Bohemian Jew, fled his home young to study painting in Italy, and came to England c.1761. He painted dials for Rimbault's animated musical clocks, and backgrounds and draperies for portraits by Benjamin Wilson.

In Wilson's studio, the warm, gregarious, music-loving Zoffany made many friends, among them the painter Mortimer, whose acquaintanceship was wide and high, and Garrick, whose encouragement and introductions soon led Zoffany to great success as a painter of theatrical groups; he is the historian of the theatre in Garrick's time.

Zoffany's furniture, mirrors and silks had been

better than Wilson's portraits; and like Hogarth, Zoffany had the faculty of total recall, sharpened by painting seized moments in the theatre. His group portraits had such spontaneity (although the sitters might never meet in his studio), that Zoffany was soon painting "conversation pieces," as well as single portraits of the royal family and nobility. He already belonged to the Society of Artists; became one of the original members of the newly formed Royal Academy; and in 1772 showed a portrait of its members, painted, Walpole says, "by candlelight; he made no design for it, but clapped in the artists as they came to him, and yet all the attitudes are easy and natural, most of the likenesses strong."

Disappointed in his plan to make a voyage to the South Seas with Capt. Cook, the restless, extravagant Zoffany set off, c.1772, under George III's patronage, on a 2-year trip to Italy. His 2nd wife, an almost totally illiterate child of 14, was so enchantingly beautiful and sweet that she was received everywhere, and so naturally intelligent that she made up many deficiencies in her education while in Italy.

Zoffany painted everyone in the fashionable English colony in Florence, had his usual success at the Tuscan Grand Ducal court, and through its influence, went on to Vienna, where Maria Theresa created him a baron.

He returned to England, c.1774, to his intimacy with the royal family and Johann Christian Bach, to his musical parties on his barge on the Thames, served by lackeys with his new baronial crest on their magnificent liveries, and to endless portraits and conversation pieces. Among these, none is more valuable for costume than the delightful picture of the Hon. Charles Hope Vere, in the scarlet coat of the Archers, together with his two old sisters in enchanting home dress and aprons (property of Harry L. Verney).

Inspired by his friend Hodges, who did go with Cook, and who had painted successfully in India under Warren Hastings' patronage, Zoffany set off, in 1783, for a 14-year stay in India. As usual, he met, saw and painted everyone and everything: cock fights, tiger hunts, nabobs and their embassies, English governors and judges with their families, native servants and costumes, and their pets.

On the return journey, Zoffany suffered a stroke,

from which he and his painting never entirely recovered.

2142. XVIIIc. 1762. English. (Kenilworth, Stoneleigh Abbey, Lord Leigh.)

John Zoffany. The Farmer's Return.

This painting, the first theatrical group exhibited at the Society of Artists, belonged to Garrick. It shows him with Mrs. Cibber in the play of that name, recounting his week in London and his visit to Vauxhall.

As many theatrically effective details of a farmer's dress as possible have been incorporated in the lower part of Garrick's costume. Soft turned-down boots are supported by straps over the knees of breeches which close by buttons and ties. Stick and clay pipe for "business" with the hands. A knotted cravat and unpowdered wig distract no attention from the face.

Mrs. Cibber wears the enclosing hood-like cap of an older woman; the young mother a cap with pinned-up lappets. Kerchiefs pinned high at the throat, their points held down by apron strings going twice about the body.

THE DEVELOPMENT OF WIGS

A tendency toward baldness seems to have run through the ruling houses of Tudor, Valois and Bourbon.

As Elizabeth's red hair grew thin, it was covered by one of her eighty wigs, which ran from auburn through orange to gold, the colors which she made fashionable in her era.

Her cousin Mary Queen of Scots' own hair was black, her secretary, Nicholas White, said. In 1561 she had "perewykes," mostly red, for every day of the year, which were artfully arranged by Mary Seaton, her preferred lady-in-waiting.

It will be two centuries before the heads of royalty will be dressed by professionals. Mary's head was shaved for her flight in 1568, her French secretary, Claude Nau, said. She went to her execution "her borrowed hair a bourne (wig)." The executioner pulled it off, exposing her own hair, grown white in her forties. Women who did not have enough hair to cover high pads in late XVIc.–XVIIc. wore a "bourne."

Thomas Nash, in 1593, excoriated seekers after youth who wore periwigs, and Shakespeare mentions them in Hamlet (Act III, Scene ii).

Henry III of France began to lose his dyed hair while he was still Duke of Anjou. The fluffy hair combed up about his characteristic velvet toque was false.

His black-haired sister, Marguerite of Valois, also became bald. She selected her footmen for their beautiful blonde hair, which could be clipped when she needed a new wig.

Henry IV's hair had begun to recede long before he was murdered at fifty-three in 1610, but he was never a man who would bother with a wig.

The appearance of the Abbé de la Rivière in a long golden wig at the court in 1620, led to the use of periwigs by Louis XIII, who was growing bald, too.

Louis XIV hated wigs, but when he lost his hair in 1670, his wig-maker, Binette, provided them for him in every color and form, for negligée, walking, hunting and court wear. The most imposing wigs ever seen are the long ones, dressed high à la Fontange, in the later part of his reign.

Wigs arrived in England with Charles II, and came into general use during his reign. People had already begun to let their hair grow again during third quarter XVIIIc., though they powdered it for ceremony until the wheat famine and flour tax of 1795. The change and relaxation in fashion which began c.1784, was particularly noticeable among English men by 1790. The Crop Club, or Bedford Crops, young men of the Duke of Bedford's circle, formally gave up powder and had their hair washed and clipped in a ceremony at Woburn Abbey.

Wigs had become so specialized by professions that all but professional men, doctors, lawyers in court, clergymen and soldiers discarded them during George III's reign. As a badge of ecclesiastical dignity, they were longest worn by bishops; the summer of 1830 was so hot that bishops were excused from wearing wigs at William IV's coronation and looked to Greville very strange without them. The last appearance of the episcopal wig was on the Archbishop of Canterbury at Victoria's resplendent coronation, eight years later.

The first wigs, made on a net base, cost 50 to 80 livres and weighed as much as two pounds, before Ervais' improvements in techniques; and as much as 1,000 écus an ounce was paid for the preferred blonde hair.

Diderot's "Encyclopédie" discusses at great length the fabrication and dressing of wigs. We learn also that children's hair is too fragile. The best hair comes from beer and cider-drinking countries like Flanders, and from people between eighteen and sixty years old. Women's hair is better than men's; and that of country women (who cover it with caps and do not use powder) better than townswomen's. Goat's hair is used in cheap, provincial wigs; it has a lovely whiteness, but breaks off, as does horsehair. The paste used to set wig curls comes from the ginger-bread bakers in cities; in the country the wigmaker has to cook it up himself.

The most durable hair is chestnut; even children's brown hair can be used. Black is more desirable; *noir, petit noir,* and *noir jais,* a difficult color to find, but one which can be worn without powder. Gray tones are even better: *gris de maure,* which is *noir jais,* gone a quarter white; *gris salé,* brown hair gone a quarter white; and *blanc fond jaune,* blonde hair gone half white. Of white hair the most precious is *blanc agate,* dark hair which has turned completely white; *blanc perle* originally chestnut. *Blanc de lait,* originally blonde, or better still, red, is beyond price because of its texture and curling qualities.

The two sheets of plates under *Perruque* in the "Encyclopédie" show many forms of wig for both sexes. The ecclesiastical peruke is short and tonsured. The long, square *perruque quarrée* is, like the legal wig, persistent in English use today. It falls in two flaps with a tiny curl between them in back, exactly like a sheep's docked tail between woolly flanks. There are special pieces to extend the wigs of the legal *gens de la robe.* The *perruque à la naissance* has its back hair falling almost straight, and untied. The *perruque à la brigadière* is seen only on old-time military men by 1765. It covers the ears and has four sausage rolls carried completely around at the nape, with the back hair tied low beneath. There are wigs, both square and with knotted locks, which expose the ears. The "most modern" form is the *perruque à la régence,* the bag-wig which appeared "not forty years since" under Orleans. Wigs similarly cut to expose the ears, but without the bag, have their back hair drawn as much out of the way as possible, falling in two knotted locks, two spirally bound tails tied with small bows, or clubbed up and knotted into a *catogan.* The wig with two locks is more commonly worn at the German courts than elsewhere. "One cannot present one's self today before the King and Queen of Hungary without these two tails, young and old alike. They are also worn at great fêtes, at a *bal paré,* and by comedians in tragic roles."

There are women's wigs of two main sorts: The "modern" *chignon frisé* is a sort of cap of short curls "worn for the last twenty years, and perfected during the last ten." The fuller *chignon plein* has forms *en abbé, à la paresseuse,* and another with two curls at the ears. The *chignon relevé* has straight hair combed up high from the forehead, after the manner of Marie Antoinette's court headdresses; a sausage-like curl, *boudin,* runs vertically above each ear; for court and fête day use there are four to six extra curls which may be added, the two longest of which hang in back. The *cadinette* has a chignon of straight hair, but hangs long and square in back. There are demi-perruques to be combined with your own hair.

In England, wig-makers, few in number, worked outside the guilds until they became part of the Barbers, Bathers, Washers and Wig-makers, in 1634. Their number increased to two hundred by 1673, so that a new guild was established. Its statutes, in 1674, required that the basins which served peruke makers as signboards be white to distinguish them from the surgeon's yellow basins.

2143. XVIIIc. 1761. English.

Hogarth. The Five Orders of Perriwigs.

Hogarth's "Analysis of Beauty," 1753, was a confused treatise exposing his theories of aesthetics. In the "Five Orders of Perriwigs" he combines mockery of the as yet unpublished "Antiquities of Athens Measured and Delineated," by James Stuart and Nicholas Revett, with ridicule of a number of well-known people.

The Episcopal or Parsonic Order (equivalent to the "Encyclopédie's" abbé's wig, without a tonsure) is displayed on the Drs. Warburton and Squire, Bishops of Gloucester and of St. David's.

The Old Peerian, or Aldermanic is shown on the venial parliamentarian, Bubb Doddington, Lord Melcombe, and on the Lord Mayor, Sir Samuel Fludyer, whose full-bottomed peruke spreads over his entire back.

The Lexonic shows legal wigs, approximating the *perruque quarrée* of the "Encyclopédie."

The Composite, or Half Natural is a curlier English version of the French *perruque naissante.*

The Queerinthian, or Queue de Renard, is an exaggerated tie wig, with a distinct toupet and pigeon's wings (G.) developed into sausage-like rolls. These two last sorts have the ears exposed, like the French wigs of the same kind.

The bottom row shows Queen Charlotte with her ladies-in-waiting, their descending rank indicated by their coronets, wearing the necklock (d), which Hogarth calls the Triglyph Membretta.

In addition to the wind-blown toupet of the *Smart* (see Macaronis, 1773-4), the *London Chronicle* of 1762 describes the *"Prentice Minor-bob,* or *Hair-cap;* this is always short in the neck, to show the stone-buckle, and nicely stroked from the face to discover seven-eighths of the ears. Next, the *Citizens' Sunday Buckle,* or *Bob-major;* this is a first-rate, bearing several tiers of curls, disposed in upper, middle and lower order. Then the *Apothecaries' Bush,* on which the hat seems sinking like a stone in a snowheap. The *Physical* or *Chirurgical Ties* carry

much consequence in their foretops; and the depending ties fall fore and aft the shoulders with *secundum artem* dignity. The Scratch, or the *Blood's Skull-Covering* is combed over the forehead, untoupeted, to imitate a head of hair, because these gentlemen love to have everything natural about them. The *Jehu's Jemmy,* or *white and all white;* in little curls like a fine fleece on a lamb's back, we should say something upon, were it not for fear of offending some gentlemen of great riches, who love to look like coachmen."

The current hats of 1762 are described by the same writer. Six inch wide brims are "cocked between Quaker and Kevenhuller" (i.e in a bicorne running parallel with the shoulders). "Some have their Hats open before, like a church spout . . .; some wear them rather sharper, like the nose of a gray-hound; and we can distinguish by the taste of the Hat, the mode of the wearer's mind. There is the military cock, and the mercantile cock; and while the beaux of St. James' wear their Hats under their arms, the beaux of Moorsfield-mall wear theirs diagonally over their left or right eye. Sailors wear the sides of their Hats uniformly tacked down to the crown; and look as though they carried a triangular apple-pasty upon their heads.

"With the *Quakers,* it is a point of their faith not to wear a button, or loop tight up; their Hats spread over their heads like a pent-house; and darken the outward man, to signify they have the inner light.

"Some wear their Hats (with the corner that should come over their foreheads in a direct line) pointing into the air; these are the *Gawkies.* Others do not above half cover their heads, which is indeed owing to the shallowness of their crowns; but between beaver and eyebrows expose a piece of blank forehead, which looks like a sandy road in a surveyor's plan. . . . Hats edged around with gold binding belong to brothers of the *Turf."*

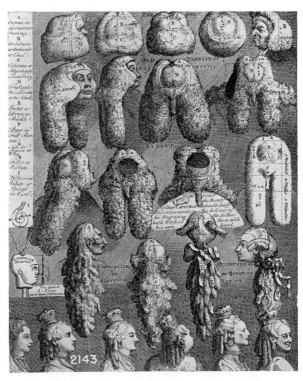

2143

2144. XVIIIc. 1754. American. (Metropolitan Museum.)
Joseph Blackburn. Margaret Sylvester Cheeseborough.

2145. XVIIIc. American. (N. Y., Mrs. James Gore King.)
Joseph Blackburn. Mrs. John Erving Jr. (1729-1816).

Joseph Blackburn (c. 1700-c. 1765) was a contemporary of Smibert and a competent English portrait painter in the manner of Highmore and Hudson. Few facts about him are known. He painted in Bermuda in 1753, and may have come from there to America. He was working in Portsmouth in 1762, and then is lost sight of; it is surmised that he may have accompanied his patron, Sir Robert Grant, who became governor of Jamaica shortly after that date.

Both illustrations show rich provincial versions of midXVIIIc. dress.

2146. XVIIIc. c. 1760. American. (Metropolitan Mus.)
John Woolaston, Alice Christie Colden.

Woolaston painted in America, 1751-69. His portrait of Mrs. William Allen (Detroit Inst. of Arts) shows almost identical costume.

2147. XVIIIc. 1760. American. (Metropolitan Mus.)
Joseph Badger. James Badger.

Joseph Badger (1708-65), son of a tailor in Charleston, Mass., was a glazier and house painter in 1739. He was never well paid and died penniless, although between 1748-60 (the period between Smibert's illness and Copley's rise) he was Boston's principal portrait painter. The most appealing of his earnest, rather wooden pictures are those of children.

Compromise between male and female styles used on boys who are not yet breeched: wig, cuffs, buttons on a gray coat which is prolonged into skirts, but has the low neck of woman's dress, without any linen; the *solitaire* is used in the manner of the analogous neckband of woman; (see Ill. 2148); black sash, embroidered in red and white.

2148. XVIIIc. 1761. American. (Baltimore, Gen. Lawson Riggs.)
John Hesselius. Charles Calvert of Maryland, and Negro.

Gustavus Hesselius (1682-1755) and his son John were the leading painters of portraits of the pre-Revolutionary southern aristocracy. Gustavus, born in Sweden in a learned family of clerics, was a cousin of Swedenborg. In 1711, he accompanied his brother to the Delaware parish to which he had been appointed by Charles XII. The first publicly commissioned work of art in America was probably the altar-piece he painted for a Maryland church, in 1721. As his son and pupil rose to eminence, Gustavus withdrew into his other profession of organ builder.

John Hesselius, (1728-78) "by whom the greater part of the family portraits in the old mansions of Maryland was painted, and that in respectable manner," (William Dunlop), was born in Maryland and returned there after his boyhood in Philadelphia.

By marriage with a rich young widow of an excellent Annapolis family, he was brought into the best society of Virginia and Maryland. Despite private means, he painted steadily throughout his life, producing c. 100 portraits, although his work became lifeless and stereotyped during his last fifteen years.

The charter of Maryland was issued in 1632 to George Calvert, the first Lord Baltimore, whose descendants remained the proprietors of Maryland until the death of the last Lord Baltimore in 1771.

This little Calvert boy is in his first breeches; but like other fanciful coatless costumes his waistcoat shows XVIIc. doublet details of picadills, slashing, lace cuffs and tiny ruff, worn with an untied *solitaire* which has the characteristics of little James **Badger's** sash (Ill. 2147). These waistcoat costumes are always accompanied by a formless cloak.

The slave's collared livery shows patterned braid, such as has become a livery characteristic.

2149. XVIIIc. 1764. English. (London, Nat. Port. Gall.)
T. Bardwell. Maurice Suckling.

Captain Suckling (1725-78), comptroller of the navy, was a son of Chancellor Walpole's sister. His niece, Catherine Suckling, married a vicar named Nelson. It was the efforts of his Suckling uncle, not the Walpoles, which launched the career of England's greatest naval hero, Horatio Nelson.

Uniform; wig reduced to one curl.

2150. XVIIIc. 1765. English. (Met. Mus., Print Room.)
Unknown Artist. A Perspective View of the Grand Walk in Vauxhall Gardens, and the Orchestra.

No. 36 in a scrap book, "A Sketch of the Spring Gardens, Vauxhall," recently acquired by the Metropolitan's Print Room, shows the "fine pavillions, shady groves, and most delightful walks, illuminated by above one thousand lamps, so disposed that they all take fire together, almost as quick as lightning, and dart such a sudden blaze as is perfectly surprising. Here are, among others, two curious statues of Apollo the god, and Mr. Handel, the master of musick as Orpheus, by Roubillac; and in the centre of the area, where the walks terminate, is erected the temple for the musicians, which is encompassed all around with handsome seats, decorated with pleasant paintings on subjects most happily adapted to the season, place and company." (From *England's Gazetteer,* 1751.) The paintings in the booths were by Hayman and Hogarth: sports, amusements and scenes from plays.

With the milkmaid styles which are becoming fashionable everywhere, elaborate aprons are worn; the overskirt begins to be looped up behind for comfort in the manner of the *polonaise.* Hats begin to be worn outdoors, differentiated from the caps of domesticity or of formal dress.

2151. XVIIIc. 1766. English. (Metropolitan Museum.)

Reynolds. Hon. Henry Fane and his Guardians—Inigo Jones and Charles Blair.

All wear their own unpowdered hair, slightly dressed. The young heir has a red coat lined with gray; its green collar matches the waistcoat. Tan breeches, lengthened to the boot-tops, retain the strap and gold buckle of knee breeches; black boots; black hat edged with gold.

The central figure wears a white coat, embroidered in gold and lined with green to match the waistcoat; white stockings and breeches with gold buttons; black shoes with gold buckles.

The seated figure to the left wears a green uniform coat and waistcoat, with red collar, gold trim and buttons.

Fane wears soft, glove-fitting high boots, supported by knee straps.

2152. XVIIIc. 1768. English. (Mourne Park, Earl of Kilmorey.)

Gainsborough. Viscount Kilmorey.

Capt. Jack Needham, of a family which had lived at Shavington Hall, Adderly, Shropshire, since 1438, became the 10th Viscount Kilmorey. His son, later the 1st Earl of Kilmorey, served with the forces in America and was taken prisoner at Yorktown.

As Ills. 2151-53 show, waistcoats are shorter; both waistcoats and coats, military and civil, are developing lapels as well as collars. Cuffs become reduced in size, tend to be stitched flat to the sleeve, and to become a mere buttoned slit. The cuff of Fane's guardian, wearing civilian dress, is not a rectangle, but a trapezoid, spiralled about the arm.

Wigs are frequently unpowdered; by 1765 the natural hair begins to be grown and treated like a wig, with or without powder.

2153. XVIIIc. 1766-8. English. (Blockley, Northwick Park, Capt. E. G. Spencer-Churchill.)

Reynolds. Warren Hastings (1732-1818).

Hastings, an orphaned child of good but impoverished family, was shunted about among distant relatives, one of whom was connected with the East India Co. This accident sent East an honorable administrator, the eventual governor-general of India, who with Gen. Clive, established England's supremacy in India. A newly arrived council in 1773 was outraged because "Hastings might have put on a ruffled shirt" to meet them. Ancient frictions of this sort, enmeshed in the struggle between Parliament and the East India Co. for control, led to Hastings' impeachment and trial in 1788. He had never drawn a nabob's exorbitant profits from his Indian connections; his vindication in 1795 left him ruined, dependent on pensions. This portrait was painted in England during the break between his two long periods of service in India.

2154. XVIIIc. 1766. American. (Metropolitan Museum.)
Copley. Mrs. Sylvanus Bourne.

With a provincial time-lag, Mrs. Bourne wears the dress of an elderly English woman of midXVIIIc. (a grander version of Zoffany's Farmer's Wife, see Ill. 2142): enclosing, ribbon-trimmed cap; kerchief closed high and caught with the English single bow; dress of plain satin, with unexaggerated wrist ruffles; mitts.

The parents of *John Singleton Copley* (1737-1815) arrived from Ireland just in time for him to be born in Boston. His father, a tobacconist, soon died; in 1745 his mother married Peter Pelham, an excellent painter-engraver, who also taught penmanship, arithmetic and dancing. Copley, who was producing good portraits and mezzotints at fifteen, wrote Lio-

tard (whose chocolate girl still adorns boxes of cocoa) asking for some good Swiss pastel crayons, which Liotard sent, astonished that anyone in America had even heard of such things.

A picture of his half-brother, Henry Pelham, with a squirrel, which Copley had sent to the Society of Arts, London, in 1766, was received by Benjamin West; he encouraged Copley to come to Europe.

Copley had married the gracious and lovely daughter of the agent of the East India Co., who was the consignee of the "Tea Party" tea. Copley lived in a fine Boston house and was very successful; but the riots in America shocked him; he embarked on a tour of Europe in 1774 and was joined by his family the next year.

He was equally successful in London, became an academician on the strength of one of his large historical pictures and never returned to America. "The first American flag hoisted in old England" was one he painted on a ship, in the background of a portrait in 1782.

Copley's daughter married a Boston man. His American-born son, educated in England, became the Lord Chancellor Lyndhurst, who worked for the liberalization of divorce for women, and the admission of Jews to Parliament; (his second wife was a Jewess).

2155. XVIIIc. 1766. American. (Metropolitan Museum.)
Copley. Joseph Sherburne.

Caps which protect the wigless head have changed during XVIIIc. from their gored and embroidered XVIc. form, into swathed turbans and gathered tam

o'shanters of velvet or satin. Waistcoat continues to be a necessary part of negligée, and is always worn under a dressing gown. Blue turban; red waistcoat; brown brocade dressing gown with mustard lining and edges.

2156. XVIIIc. 1766-7. English. (Windsor, H. M. the King.)
J. Zoffany. Queen Charlotte and Her Children.

The Queen, who will eventually have nine sons and six daughters, is shown with the eldest of her present family of six: the Prince of Wales (George IV) as a Roman soldier, and the Duke of York as a Turk. Boys have been "dressed up" in exotic turbans since XVIIc. and in anachronistic XVIIc. slashings and lace during XVIIIc., just as they will be put into sailor-suits at the end XVIIIc.

They are in Old Buckingham House at Windsor; the ormolu clock shown in the background has been set near Zoffany's picture, as it now hangs at Windsor Castle.

The silver mirror of the dressing table, hung in embroidered muslin, gives a profile view of the Queen's head, dressed and studded in a decorous form of the current French style. Her double neck-ruche matches the crossed bands which trim the U-shaped front of her bodice; the sleeves have three rows of lace ruffles below elaborate self-trimmings; the petticoat has a flounce of its own satin which has been snipped and pinked into a lace-like design —the forerunner of eyelet embroidery.

2157. XVIIIv. 1769. English. (Castle Howard, Hon. Geoffrey Howard.)
Reynolds. Frederick, fifth Earl of Carlisle.

The young earl, "fond of dress and gaming—not void of ambition," but who "had but moderate parts and less application," as Walpole said, wears the gold-tasseled green robes of the Order of the Thistle. Its collar is composed of the thistle which was the Stewart badge, and the sprigs of rue of the Pict kings: all this is XVIIc. court dress, in anachronistic ceremonial use with robes.

2158. XVIIIc. English. (Birmingham, English Mus. and Art. Gall.)
Reynolds. John Thomas, Bishop of Rochester.

John Thomas (1712-93), a vicar's son who became a school-master after Oxford, married the rich widowed aunt of one of his pupils. He entered the church and rose from a living of which his brother-in-law had the disposition, to chaplain-in-ordinary to George II and George III. He became Dean of Win-

chester and received the Order of the Bath in 1768; Bishop of Rochester in 1774. He married a second rich widow and founded four Queen's College scholarships for boys whose background resembled his own.

Reynolds painted him in the red robes of the Bath, with the gold civilian form of the Grand Cross over his lawn bands and the "comely surplice with sleeves" fixed in Anglican use by Archbishop Parker in 1566; the lawn sleeves had grown immense by XVIIIc. Short episcopal wig.

2159. XVIIIc. 1772-3. English. (London, Major A. W. Foster.)
Reynolds. David Garrick and Wife.

David Garrick (1717-79) came of French Protestants who had emigrated at the revocation of the Edict of Nantes. He came to London under the wing of Samuel Johnson, and set up as a wine merchant. He was completely stage-struck, wrote poor plays, hung about theatres and acted in place of sick friends. In 1741, he made his debut as a professional in Richard III; London went mad. "There was a dozen dukes a night at Goodman's Fields," said Walpole, who, however, disliked Garrick always. Society was completely won away from its former allegiance to the opera by Garrick's vivacious modern style. As we see the end of his tradition in elderly Shakespearean actors in XXc., it does not seem as natural as it did to audiences accustomed to Quin's pompous declamations.

The opera retaliated with various pressures. Garrick alternated between London and Dublin, until he bought the Drury Lane in 1747. He had been the lover of Peg Woffington, who so became the breeches of the male parts she played. Later Garrick married a central European dancer, Mlle. Violette, "the best of women and wives," of whom even Walpole had only good to say. Mrs. Siddons made her debut, not very successfully, at Drury Lane, just before Garrick sold it to Sheridan.

The English gown keeps its specific character during about the second third of XVIIIc. The *robe à la française* to which it finally succumbs is essentially that of the second half-century. England develops its own versions, while the same gown follows a somewhat different course in France.

The English bodice retains its straighter form; its top is never so wide open and revealing as in

France, and is veiled in all sorts of scarves and kerchiefs. English sleeves become more elaborate, with
much show of lace below a self-ruffle and decoration
at the elbow. The characteristic pleats from the
shoulder of the *robe à la française* usually flow into
the back of the skirt; the overskirt is not only slit to
show a triangle of underskirt, but its edges are
heavily bordered with puffings and pleatings, as is
the flounced petticoat.

The hair rises high over pads; the cap becomes less
a separate article of dress than an arrangement of
decoration related to a specific costume. England develops many forms of turban and cap of her own.

Mrs. Garrick wears a close undersleeve below the

flounces at her elbow. These were more commonly
seen in France in the first half of XVIIIc. than during the third quarter-century, when sleeves tend to
replace ruffles by puffs at the elbow. They will reappear in France with the English styles and bonnets
of c. 1784.

2160. XVIIIc. c. 1760. American. (Milton, Mass., the
      Misses Ware.)

Dress: of Mary Middleton Lovell, wife of James
Lovell, U. S. N., Collector of the Port of Boston.

2161. Second half XVIIIc. French.

Gown: linen, wool-embroidered in chain stitch;
yellow, pink, plum and green.

Courtesy of Metropolitan Museum of Art

2162. XVIIIc. 1774-93. French.
Gown: blue striped taffeta.

2163. XVIIIc. Late Louis XVI. French.
Robe *à la polonaise:* brocade of earlier date.

2164. XVIIIc. French.
Bodice and Skirt: block-printed cotton.

2165. XVIIIc. French, Marseilles.
Peasant Skirt: polychrome wood-block; possibly printed at Marseilles.

2166. XVIIIc. French.
Apron: white muslin, embroidered in gold thread, and edged with gold lace.

2167. XVIIIc. c. 1785. French, Marseilles.
Apron: polychrome wood-block print.

2168. XVIIIc. c. 1787. American. (Boston, Mrs. C. M. Stevens.)
Two dresses: yellow brocade; blue and yellow silk drouget.

2169. XVIIIc. English. (London, National Gallery.)
Francis Cotes. Mrs. Cadoux.
Mrs. Cadoux' white *robe à la française* with pink ribbons is worn over a pink petticoat. The English gown now shows flowing back pleats and is heavily trimmed with gathered serpentine bands of self material. The sleeves are finished with a pleated self-ruffle above the lace; the pink petticoat is trimmed with heavy serpentine ruffles of its own fabric.
Unpowdered hair with one of the English turbans of the 60's and 70's.

2170. XVIIIc. c. 1774-5. English. (London, Nat. Gall.)
Gainsborough. Mrs. Graham as a Housemaid.
Mary, daughter of the 3rd Lord Cathcart, was married in 1774 to Thomas Graham, later Lord Lynedock, one of Wellington's captains in the Peninsular War. This unfinished picture, painted after

the return from their honeymoon, was bought by the 5th Earl of Carlisle, who said it was perfect as it was, and must not be touched again by a brush.
A wonderful Gainsborough portrait of Mrs. Graham, now in the Edinburgh Nat. Gall., was discovered many years later, just as it had hung, at the end of their dining room, where her heartbroken husband had ordered it walled off when she died at thirty-five.
Ladies not only masquerade as housemaids and milkmaids, but styles originating at that level float up to the aristocracy. "The Ranelagh Mob, or the Hood from Low Life, a piece of gauze, clouted about the head, then crossed under the chin and brought back to fasten behind, the two ends hanging down like a pair of pigeon tails," was copied from the silk handkerchiefs which market-women tied over their ears, rolled about their throats, and then pinned up to the nape of their neck. "They were first worn in the Inner-Square of Covent Garden Market among the green-stalls. It was from there introduced into the Square or Piazzas among the stalls there. Mrs. Jane Douglas (of procuring memory) who was a very great market-woman in her way, was the first who made a Scotch lawn double neck handkerchief into the Mob above mentioned. Her females would do as the mistress did, to be sure; and after a little cut and contrivance, away they whisked them to Ranelagh. The ladies of fashion there, who sometimes dress almost like ladies of the town, immediately took the hint." (*London Chronicle,* 1762.)

2170A. XVIIIc. 1774. English.
Dickinson, after *Reynolds.* Mrs. Pelham.
English version of the loose jackets of the *caraco* sort, in a charming, completely embroidered costume.

2171. XVIIIc. 1773-1809. American. (New York Historical Soc.)
Charles Willson Peale. Peale Family Group.

The portraits for this picture, which was not finished until 1809, were painted in 1773. It shows a few members of a large and remarkably talented American family of naturalists and painters: C. W. Peale with his brothers, St. George and James; his sister Mrs. Ramsay, his first wife Rachael Brewer; his sons, Titian and Rembrandt; his cousin Margaret Durgan; his mother Margaret; the dog Argus.

Charles Peale (1709-50), of a family of English clergymen, came to Annapolis, where he taught school and married. Of his sons, Charles Willson Peale (1741-1827) and James were artists.

Charles Willson Peale married three times. By his first wife he had six children, all named after painters. Raphael and his more distinguished brother, Rembrandt (1774-1860), were artists; Rubens, a naturalist. Of his second wife's six children, Franklin was a naturalist, and his older brother Titian (named after a dead half-brother) was a naturalist-explorer, the illustrator of great ornithological and entomological works, and for many of his later years, examiner in the Patent Office.

James Peale, a miniaturist, married the sister of the painter Claypoole; he too had six children: Anna Claypoole and Sarah Miriam were well known, the one as a portrait painter, the other as a miniaturist. Margaretta painted still-lifes, and a banker son, seascapes.

C. W. Peale had a many-sided career. At thirteen he was apprenticed to a saddlemaker for seven years. He married and went into business for himself at twenty, with the backing of his employer and another Loyalist, who put him out of business when he joined the Sons of Freedom. With some instructions from Hesselius and Copley and two years study in London with West he returned to take Copley's place in Boston. Philadelphia was full of notables for the Continental Congress; he moved his family there in 1776. He painted Washington several times, and though deeply engrossed in military and patriotic activities until 1780, he managed, even while in camp at Trenton and Princeton, to record in miniature the faces of a large number of fellow officers. These he enlarged and exhibited in a gallery in Philadelphia after the war.

Then came the discovery of mastodon skeletons in Orange Co., N. Y. (still one of the richest sources). Two were excavated at his expense, and exhibited. One went to Europe in his son Rembrandt's care when he, too, studied with West. In 1802, West's gallery became the first important natural history museum in America, housed free in Independence Hall; later, it entered the Philadelphia Museum. Peale was also largely responsible for the foundation of the Philadelphia Academy of the Fine Arts in 1805.

Rembrandt Peale, born on a Bucks County farm to which his mother had fled from the British occupation of Philadelphia, was a talented child of wide interests. He made five European trips before 1835, the first for study with West. He was immediately successful in whatever city he found himself: New York, Boston, Philadelphia, London, or Paris, where in 1808 he painted celebrities and naturalists like Cuvier and Count Rumford (the American-born scientist) for his father's museum, and in 1810, Napoleon. He was a more accomplished, but a less endearing artist than his father.

The Peale men (in Ill. 2171) show simplification of the wig; the stock is increased by formal folds, the jabot is suppressed. The rise at the back of the coat's neck has now rolled over into a collar.

2172. XVIIIc. 1773. American. (Metropolitan Museum.)
Copley. Mrs. John Winthrop.

2173

Little boys show natural hair, free of cap, turban and wig.

Like the elaborately dressed Mrs. Winthrop, Mrs. Ramsay's and Rachel Peale's costume shows the gain of French influence; their hair and that of Margaret Durgan, and even of old Mrs. Peale is rising high and shows the cap in process of becoming a decoration of the hair rather than a separate object. Enclosing fichus and caps in the older, more sober English taste, on the older women.

2173. XVIIIc. 1772-75. English. (Panshanger, Lady Desborough.)

John Zoffany. The Cowper-Gore Family.

Goethe's travelled Englishman in *Wilhelm Meister* was patterned on the rich, eccentric 3rd Earl Cowper, godson of George III. He arrived in Florence on the Grand Tour, and went no further. Walpole commiserates in 1774 with Mann on the probable loss of a friend when Cowper is about to marry a Miss Gore, with whose family we see him at music. They lived in the greatest possible state, as favorites of the Tuscan Court.

Later, Cowper made one brief visit to England, and Walpole went to a concert of Italian music, not to hear the singer, but because he "was curious to see an English Earl who had passed thirty years in Florence, and is more proud of a pinchbeck Principality and a paltry Order from Wirtemberg, than he was of being a Peer of Great Britain, when Great Britain *was* something." They were introduced. "I should have taken his Highness for a Doge of Genoa: he has the awkward dignity of a temporal representative of nominal power. Peace be with him and his leaf-gold."

Lord Cowper stands in the center in a green frock-coat with small flat cuffs, white vest, breeches, and hose; and a wig with the high raked-back toupet of c. 1773. His fiancée, Miss Gore, in pink, stands before a picture which is still preserved at the Villa Palmieri. Her sister Emily, in blue, sits at the harpsichord with her father and his cello. Another sister and Mrs. Gore, in white, and in gray, listen. All show the French dress which is standard European wear.

2174. XVIIIc. English. (Parma Gallery.)

John Zoffany. Wandering Minstrels.

This picture, supposed to have been painted for Ferdinand of Bourbon-Parma, was given to the Academy of Parma by Zoffany when he became a member in 1773. A watch, probably stolen, is pinned to the vest of a dilapidated musician.

2175. XVIIIc. 1773. English. (London Museum.)

Unknown artist. A Macaroni: "Welladay, is this Son Tom?"

2176. XVIIIc. 1773. English. (New York, Mr. and Mrs. R. T. Halsey.)

John Raphael Smith. Miss Macaroni and her Gallant at a Print Shop.

2177. XVIIIc. 1774. English. (London, Duchess of Roxburghe.)

Thomas Patch. Group in Florence.

English winters were never so unpleasant, or its court life so dull as in XVIIIc. Colonial administrative posts take whole families halfway round the world. The wealth of the nabobs flows back to the mother country. Relatives remaining in England go at least for jaunts on the Continent, preferably to Italy. Art collecting is a mania. The English have money to buy Italian Renaissance paintings, or the

Canalettos supplied by Mr. Smith, the British Consul in Venice. Many return regularly to Italy. Some, like the Cowper-Gores (Ill. 2173) settle in the permanent English colony in Florence. They serve as a magnet to draw other English visitors, including painters like Tom Patch (1700-c.1774). Patch did this group picture after the manner of the caricatured Macaronis, shown in a print shop by another industrious print-maker, John Raphael Smith (1753-1812). Patch was also busy making engravings after Italian art, to be sold in such galleries.

Patch shows himself in conversation with the gesticulating Mr. Wilberforce, under a *View of the Arno* (now belonging to Mary, Countess of Ilchester). Sir Thomas Dick plays the harpsichord; Zoffany shows a drawing to Sir Henry Felton.

A picture by Zoffany of the Tribuna Gallery in Florence in 1779 shows not only Patch and his group and other regulars like Cowper and Sir Horace Mann, but more than a dozen other visiting earls, lords and notables, whom Zoffany painted in at twenty shillings a head, looking at an art collection. It includes Raphael's Madonna, unearthed by Zoffany, and sold to Cowper for a down payment and an annuity of £100 a year; and Titian's Venus, which the President of the Royal Academy, after his visit, persuaded Queen Charlotte to buy for 600 guineas.

THE MACARONIS

The "beaux" of George II's time are replaced c. 1749 by the "fribbles" of the early reign of George III. "Macaronis," extravagantly dressed, Italian-travelled young men, began to appear in the 1760's. Led by the dissolute and able Charles Fox (who will, in turn, lead the careless, neglected fashions of 1784-95), the Macaronis are at their apogee in 1772-3, when Walpole mentions them frequently: "Lord Chatham begat the East-India Co.; the East India Co. begat Lord Clive; Lord Clive begat the Macaronis, and they begat poverty." A year later, "The Macaronis, amongst whom exist the only symptoms of vivacity, are all undone, and cannot distinguish themselves by insensibility alone. They neither feel for families nor themselves."

A tendency toward extravagance in dress, already noted in the *London Chronicle* in 1762, culminates in a flood of caricatures, ridiculing the dress of the Macaronis, male and female. Their wigs, extravagantly clubbed behind, rise in a fantastically high toupet. "Every Smart . . . seems . . . to have been skating against the wind, and his hair, by the sharpness of the motion, shorn from his face." (*London Chronicle,* 1762.) A tiny Nivernois hat, tilted on the very top, is lifted, either by the point of the cutlass, or by the knob of the tall, tasseled stick, which are part of a Macaroni's equipment. Tom even carries a reticule at his wrist.

Their frock coats have small collars and are cut away to expose the whole chest. At first, they reach to mid-leg, and "are so much splashed sometimes behind," that the writer of the *London Chronicle* has "often been tempted to call out, 'Pray, dear Sir, pin up your petticoats.' " With these were worn "buttonless topcoats which only wrap over their breasts like a Morning Gown."

The linen of the Macaroni is extravagant; his very short vest is often without pockets. His skin-tight breeches finish with knee-strings. The whole costume drips with frayed-out ends of braid trimming, frogs and tassels; fobs and seals hang from pairs of watches. His shoes have high red heels and are often finished with ribbon bows and rosettes.

Miss Macaroni shows the matching height and extravagance of the headdress of the female type of Macaroni. She and her gallant wear the dotted and striped patterns to which the Macaronis were partial.

Tom's father wears the riding costume which is the uniform of a sensible old country squire.

2178. XVIIIc. Before 1775. English. (New York, Daniel H. Farr.)

John Zoffany. Dutton Family.

Mr. Dutton, who died in 1776, was born Napier, but had taken the name and coat-of-arms of his first father-in-law, Sir Ralph Dutton. He is shown in the drawing-room of Sherborne Park, Gloucestershire, with his second wife, her son James, the 1st Lord Sherborne, and fourth daughter Jane, who was married in 1775 to Thomas Coke of Holkham, later the earl of Leicester, the founder of modern agriculture and cattle-breeding in England.

Mrs. Dutton is protesting the card game which interferes with her Bible-reading. It is hot by the cannel-coal grate fire, and cold away from it. Her face is protected by a fire screen (decorated with a flower-filled urn) and she wears a long glove on her farther arm; elaborate closed cap, fichu, and black gown of an elderly Englishwoman.

Her son, dressed in grayish white with a yellow vest, wears a wig, sharply raked back in a high toupet, under "Macaroni" influence. Mr. Dutton is in purple with a conservative wig. Miss Dutton's hair is ceremoniously dressed high in the French fashion, with the ropes of pearls much used in England; black lace collar on pale green dress, worn with a quilted petticoat.

Card table of diagonally set veneer with a green

baize top; floor covered, as in Queen Caroline's room at Windsor, with large oriental rug; carved and gilded girandole, set with the oval mirror of third quarter XVIIIc., will develop into circular convex bull's-eye mirrors by end XVIIIc.

2179. XVIIIc. 1776. English. (Metropolitan Museum, Print Room.)

Robert Laurie (c. 1755-1836). Scene from "She Stoops to Conquer."

The manager of Covent Garden was reluctant to produce Goldsmith's second play in 1773. But unsentimental as it was, the hilariously farcical blunders in which Tony Lumpkin and the Hardcastles were involved during the five acts of "She Stoops to Conquer" made it a tremendous success.

Stage costume contrasting conservative and sporting dress: full-bottomed wig; old-fashioned neckcloth; stockings drawn up over breeches; square-toed shoes; cloak. Fitted jockey cap; riding coat; boots with long breeches; crop; and natural locks. Hood covering large coiffure and cap, will be given supporting hoops hinged into a *Thérèse* as the head increases in size; its cape is edged with cut "eyelet" embroidery. The *caraco* has the long inner sleeve seen in English use. (Ill. 2158.)

2180-81. XVIIIc. 1777. American. (Metropolitan Museum of Art.)

C. W. Peale. Samuel Mifflin, Rebecca Edgehill Mifflin, and granddaughter, Rebecca Mifflin Francis.

The first lace, reticella, developed out of fabric threads, drawn and worked; its rectangular patterns became rounded, and then freely worked on net. Now, as we see on the edge of Mrs. Mifflin's fichu, lace patterns are again being worked on the new, extremely sheer fabrics; punched with a coarse needle, drawn and embroidered in *point de Saxe* or *point de Dresde*. Her gray-brown satin wrap is either dotted, or possibly snipped into an all-over pattern, after the manner of XVIc. doublets. This impulse, similar to the new way of producing lace, can be seen in an unmistakable form on the hem of Queen Charlotte's satin petticoat (Ill. 2156). The lace of her wrap is worked on a wide, diamond-mesh net. Quilted blue satin petticoat.

Little Rebecca's front hair is clipped. She wears a gray-brown dress spotted with embroidery; *sabots* and sash of bordered light brown gauze.

Mr. Mifflin wears his own hair, clipped into a bang and curled at the nape. Unification of costume; plain gray-brown cloth with self-covered buttons and buckled knee strap; coat creeping high and beginning to buckle at the back of the neck. Plain shirt ruffles and stock; white stockings.

2182. XVIIIc. 1777. English. (Philadelphia, Joseph E. Widener.)
Romney. William Petrie.

George Romney (1734-1802), son of a Lancashire peasant, had been a carpenter and fiddle-maker, until he began to study at nineteen, and his work was noticed by the vicar, Rev. Laurence Sterne. At twenty-eight he gave the larger part of his savings to his wife, a servant-girl who had nursed him through a fever at 21, and went off to London.

Romney was uneducated, shy, and neurotic. He had no encouragement from the English court and was never admitted to the Royal Academy. His work became fashionable, but "so many of his sitters were killed off, so many favorite ladies dismissed, so many fond wives divorced before he could bestow half an hour's pains upon their petticoats, that his unsaleable stock was immense" (Richard Cumberland). Reynolds' most important rival went mad about Lady Hamilton in 1783, and painted her in every guise. In 1799, paralyzed and ill, he returned to his wife and family, whom he had supported but seen only twice in thirty-seven years. She nursed him until his death.

2183. XVIIIc. 1776-8. English. (London, Nat. Gall.).
Romney. Beaumont Family.

The coats of Mr. Petrie and the Beaumonts show the frogs of third quarter XVIIIc., which were often grouped, turning into paired buttons set on a braid trim. Waistcoats are shorter, light in color, matching

the breeches to which they are related—in Mr. Petrie's case by delicate matching embroidery on the buckled knee strap. Increased English use of one's own hair, unpowdered and informally dressed like a wig, sometimes clipped in a bang over the forehead (left).

With draped, untrimmed, informal gowns, which with English sporting dress will so affect French fashion from the 80's, English women wear their hair unpowdered in high, rather loose piles, asymmetrically dressed with twisted scarves.

2184. XVIIIc. 1774 or 1777-8. English. (Metropolitan Museum, Frick Coll.)
Gainsborough. The Hon. Frances Duncombe.

Women's and children's dress of second half

XVIIIc. sometimes show fanciful touches of XVIIc. style. Frances Duncombe's gown, looped up as English dresses are now apt to be in some way, is inspired by Henrietta Maria's pearled satin gowns, and accompanied by a plumed version of a XVIIc. Flemish hat. "Van Dyck" styles persist into XIXc.

2185. XVIIIc. 1778. English. (San Marino, California, H. E. Huntington Art Gallery.)

Gainsborough. Juliana Howard, Lady Petre.

The English style which overwhelmed France from the 80's is worn by this Catholic Howard married to a member of one of the other traditionally Catholic families of England. Huge, high-crowned black hat trimmed with ribbon loops, which never blot out its form, worn on loosely fluffed, lightly powdered curls; puffed *bouffant* kerchief; close-waisted, long-sleeved creamy muslin or gauze jacket (shown here in a short form which makes the line of the icy-blue satin bodice below it the equivalent of a very wide belt); untrimmed blue satin skirt, veiled in sheer creamy material. Gauzy black scarf, edged with lace.

2186. XVIIIc. c. 1778. English. (Washington, Nat. Gall. of Art.)

Reynolds. Lady Caroline Howard.

Children's dress will be revolutionized by simple English muslins like this tucked gown, worn with a blue sash of the wonderful ribbons England is now weaving and will export to France, pale yellow gloves, a lace-edged black cape, and a round cap, worn over hair cropped into bangs.

2187. XVIIIc. 1777-87. English. (Washington, Nat. Gall. of Art.)

Reynolds. Lady Elizabeth Delmé and Children.

Lady Elizabeth, born Howard, was the aunt of little Lady Caroline Howard. Unpowdered hair dressed high with characteristic English negligence, wound turban-wise with a metal-threaded scarf; softly draped muslin gown, rose cloak. Boy in red coat and breeches which reach half-way below knee; collar opening out over shoulders; vest of one of the piqué-like waled and corded materials, to which matelassé forms will be added at the turn of the century for vests.

2188. Late XVIIIc. English. (Metropolitan Museum.)

British School (formerly attr. to *Romney*). John Parker.

Large plumed beaver hat, as women's hats grow large and feathered.

2189. XVIIIc. 1778. American. (Hampton Court, H. M. the King.)

Benjamin West. Queen Charlotte and the Princess Royal.

Benjamin West (1738-1820) was born in Philadelphia of Quaker parents who opposed the interest in art which he showed at seven. At eighteen, however, he was painting portraits in Philadelphia; at twenty in New York. In 1760, he was helped to go to Italy for three years. He made a great reputation there and came to London in 1763. He became a familiar of the royal family and was one of the four artists who planned the Royal Academy. In 1772, he was made historical painter to the king. "We have an American, West, who deals in high history, and is vastly admired, but he is heavier than Guercino, and has still less grace, and is very inferior," Walpole wrote after seeing the Academy Show of 1775. West was a dignified, benevolent man and an excellent teacher; he succeeded Reynolds as president of the Royal Academy. In 1802 he went to Paris to study the art of Europe which Napoleon had massed in the Louvre.

The queen disliked the English court and avoided its life as much as possible, to live with her husband (who was already deranged, although not yet confined), in an oppressive domesticity which both enjoyed, but against which a number of the dozen children already born to them rebelled with violence. "The vivacity of the young queen of France has reached hither," Walpole wrote in 1775. "Our young ladies are covered with more plumes than any nation that has no other covering." Charlotte was unsuccessful in her opposition to plumes in a court which she did not dominate. But with her ruche-trimmed *caraco* and muslin apron (the frill of which is caught up into charming shells), she allows her hair to be dressed in a very high "head," with the scallops of a round cap appearing beneath its turbaned top.

The industrious little princess is conservatively dressed in silk with powdered hair high under a gauffered, beribboned English cap.

Greek column; helmeted antique bust.

2190. XVIIIc. c. 1779. English-American. (Washington, Nat. Gall. of Art.)

Benjamin West. Col. Guy Johnson and Capt. Joseph Brant.

Sir William Johnson (1715-74) came to America in 1738 to administer land in the Mohawk Valley belonging to his uncle, Sir Peter Warren. Johnson established remarkable relations with the Indians; he was adopted by the Mohawks, became superintendent of the affairs of the Six Nations, and eventually of all the Indians in the province. He fought in the French and Indian Wars and with Jeffrey Amherst, kept his tribes from joining Pontiac, and was rewarded with a baronetcy and an estate of 100,000 acres at what is now Johnstown, N. Y. He lived there in a great house like an English lord, a widower with an Indian mistress called Molly Brant. His son, Sir John, succeeded to the baronetcy and became an officer.

The trusteeship of Indian affairs passed to Sir William's nephew, Guy Johnson (1740-88), whose secretary and companion in the Cherry Valley massacres was the Mohawk Chief Thayendanega, otherwise known as Joseph Brant, Molly's brother. Brant was educated by Sir William at the Indian school in Connecticut from which Dartmouth College originated. He translated the Prayer Book and part of the New Testament into Mohawk, became a missionary after the war, and raised money to build the first Episcopal church in Northern Canada, during a trip to England in 1786.

Johnson wears a fur-lined cloak, Indian-made like his moccasins, leggings and cap, together with a red coat which has a low standing collar and flaps which button back into lapels.

2191. XVIIIc. 1780-88. English. (Washington, Nat. Gall. of Art.)

Gainsborough. George IV as Prince of Wales.

The handsome Prince of Wales, in his red coat, gold epaulettes and Star of the Garter, has become "the first gentleman of Europe," in revolt against his parents' dull parsimony. He will eventually become tainted with his father's instability, descend into incredibly undignified persecution of his hated queen after he fails to have her daughter declared illegitimate, and will earn the whole-hearted detestation of his people.

2192. XVIIIc. English. (Gloucestershire, Hardwick Court, Miss Olivia Lloyd-Baker.)

John Zoffany. The Sharp Family on a Yacht.

Many upper-class families of the XVIIIc. lived like

the Zoffanys and the Sharps. Both families loved music. Sharp was Handel's doctor; Zoffany, Bach's friend. Both had houses on the river, and yachts for musical outings. Zoffany had a summer house filled with musical instruments at his boat-landing. The servants on his pink, green and buff shallop wore liveries derived from his patent of nobility from Maria Theresa: scarlet and gold faced with blue, and shoulder-knots with his crest: a sprig of clover and buffalo horns rising from a baronet's coronet. The Sharp family lived in a house and a cottage at Fulham (seen in the background, to the right of the church), which were connected by an underground passage. They often entertained George III and Queen Charlotte at tea and music on the yacht. Zoffany connected his house and summerhouse on the Strand at Chiswick with an overhead passage, in expectation of a visit from the Prince of Wales, which never came off.

Musical parties on the Thames had been loved since Tudor days. In XVIIIc. they became a passion. Those who did not keep a liveried barge could rent a barge at any landing for a ride to one of the pleasure gardens; Walpole's letters are full of such parties, which were followed by a barge of horns or other music.

The people shown include: Dr. John Sharp (1793-1758), Archbishop of Northumberland; his wife,

daughter of the Dean of Ripon, and their only daughter, Anna Jemima, in pink and green. William Sharp, the surgeon, who paid Zoffany 800 guineas for this picture, steers. He wears the Windsor uniform (blue frock coat, scarlet collar) as a member of Princess Amelia's household. (He had refused a baronetcy.) His wife sits below in a blue riding habit, holding their only child, Mary (ancestress of the picture's present owner), and her kitten. James Sharp, the eminent engineer, holds a horn called a "serpent" and wears a hat. His wife sits above in lavender, black lace and a great cap. Their only surviving child stands beside him in white muslin, pink sash and plumed cap. Elizabeth Sharp Prowse sits at the harpsichord; her sister Judith, in a brown habit beside sister Jemima, holds a lute. Their youngest sister Judith sits in profile, wearing blue moiré and holding a sheet of music. Granville Sharp, the philanthropist, holds a double-flageolet and a sheet of music. An oboe lies on the harpsichord; a theorbo stands by the cabin boy (who still lived in 1848, and gave an account of the painting). Behind him is the yacht-master, and in front lies Zoffany's dog Roma. (Information from Sitwell: "Conversation Pieces.")

Clipped hair of boy, yacht-master, and girl; bushy short wig of archbishop; reduction of other wigs to one curl. Caps giving way to plumed hats; riding

costume from which walking dress of late XVIIIc. will develop.

2193. XVIIIc. 1783-90. English. (Trowbridge, Steeple Ashton, Edward Impey.)

Zoffany. Sir Elijah and Lady Impey with Indian Servants.

The Chief Justice of Bengal, Warren Hastings' friend since their school days; ayahs and servants wear Indian dress.

2194. XVIIIc. 1783-90. English. (London, Nat. Gall.)

Zoffany. Family Group.

This picture of a family with their favorite Indian servant probably came from the collection of Major-Gen. Martin, who founded a school in India, equivalent to Eton, for eighty boys.

The lady wears green and gold; her older sons, red suits with shirt collars opening wide; easy, square-cut vests, and loosening breeches, lengthening into trousers.

2195. XVIIIc. English. (Metropolitan Mus., Frick Coll.)

Gainsborough. The Mall in St. James's Park.

In one of Gainsborough's late pictures we see gauzy summer dresses, still short-waisted, frilly and looped up, under the influence of the *polonaise;* hair loosening and falling, but still powdered and caught together at the nape. Hats large, but still low and wreathed with decoration. The brim is sometimes convexly curved, intermediate between the elaborate English cap and the arrogant wide-brimmed, high-crowned hat which accompanied the pouter-pigeon kerchiefs, the long, lean waists and the plain, long skirts of the great English style.

2196. XVIIIc. 1782-4. English. (Washington, Nat. Gall. of Art.)

Romney. Mrs. Davenport.

The rigorous winter of 1784 brought large, shaggy muffs of pale furs like the white one which Mrs. Davenport wears with a fur-collared, caped *pelisse.* Such large muffs will have a life of a good quarter century, whatever the weather. Straw hat, trimmed with bows of plain over striped ribbon, is ruched about the top of the crown, and tied under the chin.

2197. XVIIIc. c. 1785. English. (London, Nat. Gallery.)

Gainsborough. Mrs. Siddons.

A provincial actor-manager, Roger Kemble, had twelve children, many of them distinguished actors, who have passed on to their descendants, the XXc. Kemble-Coopers, the majestic carriage and wonderful nose of the family. Sarah (1755-1831) became the greatest actress of the English stage; John Philip (1757-1823), manager of Drury Lane and Covent Garden and the leading actor between Garrick and Kean.

The carefully reared girl fell in love with an unimportant actor named Siddons, by whom she had a son. In a quite ineffectual attempt to break her spirit, she was put into service as maid to a provincial lady. In 1773, she married Siddons, and eventually made a most unsuccessful debut at Drury Lane. She played the provinces, and returned to triumphant success in London in Southerne's "Fatal Marriage" in 1782. Most awesome of all was her Lady Macbeth, 1785, which is said to have frightened people into fits. Only Rachel had more passion, and she lacked Mrs. Siddons' style and tenderness. On the hem of her costume, in Reynolds' portrait of her as the Tragic Muse, Dr. Johnson wrote his name, saying, "I would not lose the honor this opportunity afforded to me for my name going down to posterity on the hem of your garment."

The accord between English fashion of 1775 and the fire and dignity of Mrs. Siddons' personal style, make this the greatest picture of proud English beauty. Immense black velvet hat with bows and crown of plumes; narrow neck ribbon, disappearing *à la solitaire* into the long loose curls of the lightly powdered curled mass. Puffed kerchief over blue-striped gown, with crossed bodice-front and long sleeves. Muff and fur-edged *pelisse.*

2198. XVIIIc. 1785-7. English. (Metropolitan Museum, Frick Coll.)

Reynolds. Elizabeth, Lady Taylor.

2199. XVIIIc. c. 1788. English. (Metropolitan Museum.)
Reynolds. Lady Smith and Children.

The hats which accompany *bouffant* kerchiefs and long-waisted, severely simple, silk, satin and cloth gowns, have plumes set on top of the crowns; neither the plumes nor ribbon loops ever obscure the form of the hat body.

2200. XVIIIc. 1786. English. (Metropolitan Museum.)
Reynolds. Mrs. Baldwin.

Pink and white turban topped with pink flowers and green leaves. Braided locks are often combined in some way with exotic turbans. A dozen ropes of seed pearls, with one blue stone, are similarly looped in graduated lengths, from Mrs. Baldwin's black velvet neckband. The ermine-collared brocade garment, in mustard and green stripes and pink flowers, appears to be a *pelisse-lévite*. Jewelled pendant on a gold chain; mustard yellow scarf in lap.

2201. XVIIIc. 1783. American. (Metropolitan Museum.)
Ralph Earle. Lady Williams and Daughter.

Ralph Earle (1751-1801) and his artist brother, James, came of a family which had lived at Newport, R. I., for four generations. Earle's career was wandering, irresponsible and drunken; he twice married and deserted both families. In 1779 he went to England, where he was very successful. He returned to America in the late 80's, and worked in New York and New England. Alexander Hamilton persuaded his wife and other ladies to sit for Earle in his cell, where he was imprisoned for debt. His son, Ralph E. W. Earle, also a painter, married Mrs. Andrew Jackson's niece and lived at the White House throughout Jackson's entire administration.

2202. XVIIIc. 1784. English. (Metropolitan Museum.)
Reynolds. Georgiana Augusta Frederica Elliott.
2203. XVIII. 1784. American. (Worcester, Art Museum.)
Ralph Earle. Man with a Gun.

English costume shown in Ills. 2201-03: Woman: cap replaced by gauze scarves; loosening, unpowdered hair; severely simple, long-sleeved satin dress; *bouffant* kerchief.

Baby: cap, bangs, muslin and ribbons.

Hunting dress: breeches lengthened to meet boot-tops; coat with collar and lapels is being sharply cut away into tails at the line of the square-cut, double-breasted vest, which also opens into lapels. High stock; small, plain ruffles.

2204. XVIIIc. 1784. English. (Metropolitan Museum, Print Room.)

John Raphael Smith, after *Reynolds.* Joseph Deane Bourke, D.D.

The de Burghs, earls of Connaught from the XIIc., were descended from William the Conqueror's half-brother, Robert of Cornwall. After the murder of the XIVc. earl, the family split into factions: the "MacWilliam Eighters" of Connaught, and the "MacWilliam Oughters" of Mayo. The viscounts and earls of Mayo, of final quarter XVIIIc., were Mac-Oughters. Joseph Deane Bourke, Archbishop of Tuan, and eventually third duke of Mayo, took inordinate pride in this descent.

Episcopal wig, band, and immense lawn sleeves.

2205. XVIIIc. 1785. English. (Hampton Court, H. M. the King.)

Copley. Children of George III.

Fanny Burney (1752-1840), the author of "Evelina," became second mistress of the robes to Queen Charlotte in 1785. Her diary gives a wonderful picture of the intimate life of the royal family. Miss Burney's superior was Mrs. Schwellenberg, who had come with the queen from Mecklenburg-Strelitz; she never learned to speak coherent English, and was "swathed in the buckram of back-stairs etiquette." This "hateful old toad-eater, as illiterate as a chambermaid, as proud as a whole German Chapter, rude, peevish, unable to bear solitude, unable to conduct herself with common decency in society" (Macaulay) had charge of the queen's wardrobe and lace-buying. The royal family kept to itself, except for a drawing-room twice a week and a court ball twice a year. The clothing of George III's children (procured by aliens who had been trained, decades before, in the traditions of small, rigid courts) is slow to show the effects of the simplicity with which English upper-class children have long been dressed.

Nevertheless, though only the baby is dressed in muslin, there is a change since the Princess Royal's powdered and dressed "head" of 1778. A sister of about the same age now goes bareheaded with natural locks. Her yellow dress is silk, but it is tucked up for play over a white petticoat. The black bead trim of her dress anticipates narrow black velvet ribbon threaded through eyelet embroidery slots. The tendency toward open collars (so clear in preceding illustrations of boys' shirts) is noticed in the little extra collar set on her fichu.

The baby, and the sister in pink, who sits above the baby-carriage, (a new invention of English coachmakers, in which no one will ever surpass them for elegance), have huge blue ribbon sashes and great white or blue hats. The covering of the underside of hats is not laid on quite flat, and within a decade the hat brim will be covered by shirred and crumpled fabric, and will have a hanging valance of lace, foreseen in the ruched edging of the hat set over the baby's cap.

2206. XVIIIc. 1787. English. (Metropolitan Museum, Print Room.)

H. Ramberg. Exhibition of the Royal Academy.

The first regular art exhibits in London grew out of the success of a show of paintings in 1758 to raise money for the Foundling Hospital. The Free Society of Artists lasted only to 1774. The longer-lived Society of Artists was disturbed by quarrels. Benjamin West, who had great influence with George III, and three of its other members, submitted plans for a Royal Academy of thirty-six members, to teach art and to give annual exhibitions. This was chartered and at work in 1769. It outgrew quarters in Pall Mall, and the King, who paid its deficits until it became self-supporting in 1781, gave it exhibition rooms in the new Somerset House in 1780, where it remained until the National Gallery was built.

Reynolds, West, and Lawrence were its first three presidents. A picture by Zoffany, belonging to the King of England, shows its life class working by candle-light in 1772. Zoffany worked on the picture without plan, inserting new-comers as they entered the room, Walpole says.

The turn in fashion has been made, but older men still cling to conservative styles, and great variety is shown in the dress of the men.

In the r. foreground a tubby man with spectacles wears a shoulder-length wig ending in two heavy rolls of hair; his coat has ample skirts, large cuffs and no collar; it is completely open, wide and quite straight up-and-down, over a long waistcoat. To his left, a man with a quizzing-glass wears boots, long elastic breeches, paired fobs, a short, striped, double-breasted vest, an open coat, much cut away, with embroidered collars and cuffs, broad-brimmed round hat, and a crop. In the center, beyond the Catholic prelate, we see hair in a *hérisson,* a double-breasted tail-coat of cloth with a high collar and lapels, short breeches, a high-brimmed cocked hat, and a stick. At the door, on the left, a cutaway coat with one high closed button. Along the wall, a man in horizontally striped stockings points to a picture; behind him stands a clerical wig. In the extreme background, behind the prelate, is a high-crowned hat, heavily cockaded, almost into a bicorne.

There is much more unanimity in the women's dress. All the hair is loose; all the hats are enormous. Either they are high-crowned, wide-brimmed and laden with plumes, or they are of the lamp-shade shape, lingerie sorts which have grown out of the elaborate English cap and mob. The skirt is very full, very plain, though it may be caught up for convenience. The bosom is enormously puffed out with kerchiefs and the effect is stressed by scarves; the bodice, below, is typically close-waisted; it may have a sash or wide belt. Its most severe form is shown in the riding coat and huge plain hat (half way down l. wall). By the door on the l. is another form: a soft, muslin dress, its fullness repeated or stressed by flounces and bands. (Also child with dog, foreground r.).

XVIIc. "Vandyck" usages continue to affect costume, through latter half XVIIIc. into XIXc.; slashed sleeves and peplum (at r. wall exh., looking up, back view).

BATH AND THE "BEAUX"

Bath maintained its position as the center of the social life of England into the e.XIXc., but its greatest days were in the XVIIIc. Its baths had been used since Roman times; the Roman conduit is in use even today.

Royalty went there in XVIIc., but there were still no accommodations or roads in e.XVIIIc.; it was necessary to live in tents; Bath was full of thieves.

The supremacy of Bath can be laid to two architects, both named John Wood: father (d. 1754) and son (d. 1782); to their patron, Ralph Allen; and to the rule of "Beau" Nash.

The Woods' comprehensive plan gave Bath handsome crescents of identical, attached houses with paved roadways separating them from circles of lawn and park; and the N. and S. Parades with their shops.

Richard Nash (1674-1762) was a man of birth, taste, audacity, organizing ability, and no fortune. He managed a pageant at the Inns of Court so well that he was offered a knighthood which he refused unless a pension went with it. He lived by gambling, and was suspected of being a highwayman. He collected 50 guineas on a wager that he would not stand at the door of the York Cathedral as the congregation was leaving, dressed only in a blanket. His gambling took him to Bath, and in 1705 he became master of ceremonies of its assembly rooms, after his predecessor was killed in a duel. He became the virtual ruler of Bath and of English society. He set rules of dress and behavior at the balls and assemblies in Bath's gaming house and pump-room (from which Ernie Byfield's Chicago establishment got its name). He forbade the wearing of boots and swords and reduced dueling. Once he took a white apron off the duchess of Queensbury, as "proper only for Abigails"; watched over young women and warned them against adventurers like himself; eliminated smoking in the presence of ladies. He cleared out the robbers, paved the roads, mended the chairmen's manners, provided lodgings, and fixed a scale of prices.

Queen Anne had loved Bath; with visits from George II and Caroline in the 30's, it was established as the most fashionable spot in England. The Germanized court offered no competition; all the painters, actors, writers, all the nobility, wealth and gaiety of England, and anyone else who could cram in, were concentrated at Bath.

Nash, in his famous great cream-colored beaver hat (which no one would dare to steal, he said), his liveried lackeys, and coach drawn by six grays, was supreme. When gambling was abolished at Bath in 1745, the town gave Nash a pension, a concession for the sale of souvenirs and snuffboxes, and eventually, a magnificent funeral.

Nash's successor as the ruler of English fashion was George Bryan Brummell (1778-1840). His grandfather was a shop-lodginghouse-keeper; his father became Lord North's secretary. The boy was known as "Buck" Brummell at Eton, where his taste in dress was already notable. He made a great reputation for wit and fashion at Oxford, became "Beau" Brummell, crony of the Prince (the Prince Regent, later George IV), came into a fortune and lost it, retired to the Continent to escape his creditors and died in a charity hospital at Caen, dirty and paralyzed. "Beau" Brummell's complete sway over society came from his sharp, amusing self-possession, and his dress, which was spectacular only in its flawless perfection and taste. The Prince of Wales "began to blubber when told that Brummell did not like the cut of his coat." (Moore: *Memoirs*.)

2207. XVIIIc. English.
Anonymous Print. A View of the Parade at Bath.
2208-11. XVIIIc. 1785-8. English Fashion Plates.
There is still a wide admixture of old and new styles in men's clothing, hair and hats. Hat brims are wider, often round. The way in which brims are cocked is turning *tricornes* into *bicornes;* the tassels which hang from either side of the hat of the wheel-chair attendant stresses this two-horned appearance, and draws the corners down in the now convex line over the forehead. These bicornes, heavily laced and cockaded, are a feature of the massively decorated court dress of Napoleon and his generals which remains embalmed in XXc. official dress of French Academicians.

Skirts become very full, bunched up into bustles, into which the waistline sinks, and becomes shorter.

Wide, plumed hats accompany tailored walking dress; hats like inverted lamp-shades, derived from caps and made of pleated and puffed fabric, are characteristically worn with muslin dresses, flounces and aprons. *Caraco* (l. side, back view); puffed *cul de Paris* (fat woman, center).

In the Parade at Bath, petticoat flounces hang free, below a projecting heading; No. 2211 shows the heading expanded and sewed down at the top into a band of shirring. The trend of the treatment of muslin is away from free-floating ruffles, in the direction of repeated, controlled bands of shirring: petticoats, No. 2208; sleeves, No. 2209; sleeves, bodice, petticoat, No. 2211. The utilitarian umbrella appears: Nos. 2208, 2210; gloves are worn or carried.

2212. XVIIIc. 1781. English.

Paul Sandby, after *Nicholas Dance.* Aquatint: "Jason and Medea," Tragic Ballet.

Even in private theatricals, English heads have become so covered with plumes by 1775 that "comedians, singers, dancers, figurantes, might all walk at a coronation." (Walpole.) European ballet costume continues to be simply a modification of the dress established by La Camargo.

2213. XVIIIc. 1787. English.

John Jones, after *Downman.* Thomas King and Elizabeth Farren.

Elizabeth Farren (c. 1759-1829) was the daughter of an apothecary turned strolling player. In 1797 she became the wife of the 12th earl of Derby. Thomas King (1730-1805) was a strolling player, picked out of a booth at Windsor, and taken to Drury Lane by Garrick; he was also a theatrical manager, wrote farces and gambled himself into poverty.

King's and Miss Farren's greatest roles were Sir Peter Teazel and Miss Hardcastle in a brilliant performance of the "School for Scandal" in 1777. It is probably as Sir Clement and Emily in Burgoyne's "Heiress" that we see them here in the exaggeration of stage costume.

Between the ruffles at the bosom, and the fullness of the skirt, rising into a bustle, the torso almost disappears, and the waistline grows shorter.

2214. XVIIIc. 1789. English.

Peter Simon, after *Downman.* Scene from "Tom Jones."

Even in the beautiful new houses at Bath, servants' quarters are in the attic, as hot and cramped as this maid's old attic is cold and bare.

The kerchief is less puffed, its ends crossed around the body, sometimes tied in back; here they are tucked into a sash which also holds the muslin apron. Figured bodice, quilted skirt; slippers with ribbon strings. Hat and striped scarf hang on a nail.

Tom, with his sleeve slit and tied over his broken arm, wears his own hair, a knotted kerchief, and a great bunch of seals. His rival shows the construction of shirt and under-drawers, and a head clipped for a wig, under his woman's disguise.

George Stubbs (1724-1806), son of a leather-dresser of Liverpool, studied and taught anatomy at York Hospital in 1746. He kept a private menagerie of animals, wild and tame, and in 1758 began eighteen months of dissection of horses, before making the illustrations for his classic "Anatomy of the Horse," first published in 1766. He began to work in enamel in 1771. Available copper plates were too small so he persuaded the Wedgwood potteries to make large plaques, thus becoming a friend of the Wedgwood family, whom he has painted riding and driving (1780). Stubbs painted such themes as the Prince of Wales' Phaeton with Thomas, the state coachman, in scarlet and gold livery (1793), and the officers, trumpeter and troopers of the 10th Light Dragoons (1793).

Stubbs is the ancestor of the English sporting print; he had worked for a year and a half at Goodwood for the duke of Richmond, painting horses and hunts. In 1790, the *Turf Review* put £9000 to the credit of the hard-working and reliable Stubbs, to enable him to record all the great racehorses; but because of the war only sixteen were finished. This is the time when the blood of three great horses, the Darley Arabian, the Byerly Turk, and the Godolphin Barb, was being fused to produce the modern race horse, which the Stud Book will begin to record in 1806. One of Stubbs' pictures is of the Godolphin Barb, a small horse which had drawn a cart in Paris, and was imported by Coke of Holkham. The blood of this great sire combined with

Courtesy of Metropolitan Museum of Art, Print Room (2207, 2208-11)

that of the Darley Arabian in a grandson, Eclipse, one of the great racers and great studs of all time.

There is much fascinating information about the completely different horse breeds seen through the millennia in our illustrations: mean, weedy horses of little stamina in Egypt, the Italian peninsula and Rome; fast, wiry little horses of Greece, and big-boned Scythian and Manchu horses which are combined in the polo pony of India. Arabs and Barbs, combined with fine, native cart-mares, the "mad horses" of Spain, and the massive Percherons of the French Knights, into the Spanish Barb which we see rearing under Spanish royalty from XIIIc. Stallions of this breed, sent as royal gifts, improved the horse of the European knight, and were the progenitors of the coach horse. Then fleet Arab, Turkish and Barb, painstakingly bred for centuries in their native lands, arrived in XVIIc.-XVIIIc. to father the modern race-horse (James Reynolds: *A World of Horses,* Creative Age, 1947.)

Courtesy of Metropolitan Museum, Print Room (2212-14)

2215. XVIIIc. 1787. English. (London, National Gall.)
George Stubbs. Phaeton and Pair.

Under George III, English carriage-building surpassed all others. Everyone now wants to go to the new pavilion which the Prince of Wales started to build at Brighton in 1786. McAdam is repairing old roads and Telford will soon begin to build new. The Society of Arts has offered prizes for carriage-design, one of which Elliot will win in 1804 for his elliptical springs. These will allow the airiest of carriages to be drawn by the most sprightly of horses. In 1787, the single horse of a cabriolet must still be a powerful animal; the two horses of a phaeton can be a great deal lighter. These equipages and their riders have already evolved an immense style in England, which no one shows better than Stubbs.

This is the English costume for riding and driving which swept over France in the 1780's and brought English carriages of equal simplicity and dash with it: immense plumed hat, puffed kerchief, long fitted cloth coat-dress; men's long breeches and boots, short vests, and round hats.

2216. XVIIIc. 1787. English. (Kenilworth, Sir Osbert Sitwell.)
Copley. The Sitwell Family.

Left to right: Boy in blue-green coat with brass buttons, half-long yellow-green trousers; mother wearing muslin with green and white striped sash; boy in red with a white sash; father in dark green coat, scarlet lining, fawn breeches and black boots.

2217. XVIIIc. 1787-9. English. (Arlesford, Hants, Lord Northbrook.)
Reynolds. Sir Francis Baring and Political Associates.

Baring (1740-1810), grandson of a Lutheran minister of Bremen, founded the great English house of Baring Bros. and became Europe's greatest merchant. We see him, wearing his own undressed hair, with two associates at the end of the first of his twenty-two years as a Whig in Parliament: peer in robes, wearing the George and collar; anachronistic wig and rabat which accompany robes of the Chancellor of the Exchequer, a post which will be held by Baring's grandson.

2218

2218. XVIIIc. 1789-96. American. (Washington, Nat. Gall. of Art.)

Edward Savage. The Washington Family.

Edward Savage (1761-1817) was a Massachusetts goldsmith who began to paint portraits about 1789. He studied in London with West in 1791, and in Italy. He was connected with the New York and Boston Museums, which opened after Peale's in Philadelphia. He painted this portrait, finished in 1796, from sketches made in 1789.

George Washington Parke Custis, Martha Washington's grandson, born 1781, shows a boy's shirt collar opened wide over the coat, in an equivalent of the kerchief of women; women's usages often influence the necklines of boys' clothes.

The knee-breeches, which the President wears with his uniform coat and boots, have not been extended below the boot-top as in Europe.

Elinor Parke Custis' dotted muslin gown shows the way in which a wide belt or sash is raised to cover the entire torso between waistline and breasts, in the transition period from puffed kerchiefs. When the sash is eliminated, the short-waisted Directoire-Empire dress has been brought about.

Mrs. Washington, like a European woman of her age and station, continues to wear a black lace scarf, fichu, and a cap which has grown fashionably high. Her greatest conservatism, or provincialism, is shown in the pleated finish of her skirt edges.

Billy Lee, the Washingtons' favorite servant, has hair dressed in an approximation of a wig.

2219. XVIIIc. c. 1790. English. (Metropolitan Museum.)

Romney. Mrs. George Horsley.

2220. XVIIIc. English. (San Marino, California, H. E. Huntington Art Gallery.)

Rev. M. W. Peters (1742-1814). Flageolet Players.

2221. XVIIIc. 1791. English. (Hellingly, Sussex, Jack Herbert Michenham.)

Romney. Lady Hamilton as Ambassadress.

2219

2220

2221

2222   2223   2224

Straw and fabric-covered hats, often decorated on the underside, are being tied down into bonnets. A favorite line, as of a crossed fichu tied about the body, is followed in the cut of Lady Hamilton's *caraco* jacket. Its edge is cut away, then the corners are tacked back; it ends in miniature tails. This bob-tailed coat can be seen in the Parade at Bath, Ill. 2207. Left side, back view, woman: laced jacket with little tails (Flageolet Players).

2222. XVIIIc. 1792. English. (New York, Edward S. Hark-ness.)

Sir Thomas Lawrence. Miss Farren.

The cloud of the actress Elizabeth Farren's powdered hair is almost indistinguishable from the fur of her *pelisse* and great muff; gloves are now indispensable.

2223. XVIIIc. 1790. English. (New York, Racquet and Tennis Club.)

Valentine Green, after *Lemuel F. Abbott.* Mezzo-tint: Goffers at Blackheath. (Port. of William Innes.)

A putting-match between three players, shown in the tail-piece of an e.XVIc. Flemish *Book of Hours* (British Museum) is the earliest picture of a golf game. XVIIc. Flemish pictures continually show golf games, often played on ice, and one is shown in a Rembrandt etching of 1654. Golf had been imported to Scotland from the Low Countries long before; by the midXVc. there was legislation against it as a useless sport which was hurting archery practice. "The Royal and Ancient Game of Goff" was a favorite of many Scottish kings, before Mary Stuart was criticized for playing it soon after Darn-ley's murder. James II, as duke of York, was challenged to play it by two English noblemen for high stakes. He chose as his partner Johne Patersone, a shoemaker, who built a house, still standing at 77 Canongate, with his half of their winnings. Until golf clubs were formed in England in XIXc., Scotch-men living in London played, like the officer in the picture, at Blackheath.

The practical double-breastedness of early military and sporting coats has been lost; the lapels are permanently and decoratively buttoned back, and the coat is held together by concealed link buttons.

2224. XVIIIc. 1790. English.

George Morland. The Squire's Door.

This is the classic example of the English riding hat and coat, with lapels, multiple capes, large but-tons, and kerchief, which made costume history in the mid-80's and 90's. Postilion's hat replaces the traditional tricorne; it is dark brown with great brown bows, crown wreathed in orange scarlet to match gloves; coat slightly less brilliant scarlet, gray-ish skirt, white kerchief.

2225-26. XVIIIc. 1790. U.S.A. (Litchfield, Hist. Soc.)

Ralph Earle. Col. Benjamin Tallmadge and Son William, Mrs. Benjamin Tallmadge and Children.

Tallmadge (1754-1835), leading citizen of Litch-field, Conn., was a Revolutionary officer and member of Congress from Connecticut.

2227. XVIIIc. 1792. U.S.A. (Hartford, Wadsworth Athe-neum.)

Ralph Earle. Chief Justice Oliver Ellsworth and Wife.

Oliver Ellsworth (1745-1807) was a rich lawyer who had studied theology, a member of the Continental Congress and of the Constitutional Convention. It was the "Connecticut Compromise," offered by him and Roger Sherman, which established representation by two houses of Congress. Our present Federal Court system was another of his many services, and he was the first Chief Justice. He was largely responsible for Jay's treaty with England. In 1800, Ellsworth went to France where he negotiated a treaty of free commerce with Napoleon.

2228. XVIIIc. 1793. U.S.A. (Wash., Nat. Gall. of Art.)

Gilbert Stuart. Mrs. Richard Yates.

Gilbert Stuart (1755-1828) went to Scotland with his teacher in 1772, returned in 1773 to his native Rhode Island; then went to London in 1775 to work with West. He painted royalty, but in 1787 fled to Dublin from his extravagant debts. He returned to America about 1792, worked with great success in New York and Philadelphia, and before his death in 1828 he painted the first half-dozen presidents, and many notables. From 1805 until his death Stuart lived in Boston.

The War of Independence changed America's traditional cultural allegiance to England. French fashions continue in sympathetic use in America long after they have been supplanted by English styles in France. The familiar time-lag between the continents is stretched by difficulties of communication at the turbulent end of XVIIIc.

American women of Revolutionary families, like Mrs. Washington and Mrs. Tallmadge, cling persistently to French ways of the 70's. The wife of conciliatory Chief Justice Ellsworth, and Mrs. Yates —depicted a year or two later, show more nearly current European styles in their long-sleeved, untrimmed satin dress, crossed fichus, and high caps.

Turkey carpets or hooked rugs, Ill. 2227, cover floors.

2229. 1785-90. U.S.A. (Providence, R.I., School of Design, Museum of Art.)

James Earle. Elizabeth and Martha Paine.

James Earle (1761-96) studied with his brother Ralph. In London he married the widow of a Loyalist who had returned to England. James Earle painted the notables of Charleston, S. C. and of London. He died of yellow fever in Charleston, on a return to America for a visit.

Short-sleeved muslin dresses are apt to be worn with long taffeta gloves which have a drawstring to tighten them about the upper arm or to have a long, taffeta sleeve set into the armseye under the short muslin sleeve. Since Elizabeth Fales Paine's taffeta sleeve is white, she has replaced the upper sleeve with a froth of ruffles, reminiscent of the edge of a frilled kerchief; blue black beads and a narrow pink ribbon at the waist. As an elderly woman, her Aunt Martha has retained the kerchief, which is tucked under the low neckline of her Directoire gown. The contrast between her long brown taffeta sleeve and her muslin sleeve is set off by a white satin ribbon tied about the upper arm.

2230. XVIIIc. 1797-1801. English. (London, Nat. Gall.)

James Downman (1750-1824). Sir Ralph Abercrombie with his son or secretary.

Abercrombie was an exceptionally enlightened and capable general who had served in Ireland and Holland and was killed in Egypt in 1801. The maps of the West Indies refer to his notable services at Sta. Lucia, St. Vincent and Trinidad, from which he returned in 1797.

At the turn of the century, there were a great many sprigged white vests, with washable forms, in heavy corded and patterned cotton, figured in silver, of which the Museum of Fine Arts, Boston, has a collection.

Hepplewhite shield-back chair of late XVIIIc.

2231-32. XVIIIc. 1794. U.S.A. (Metropolitan Mus.)

Gilbert Stuart. Josef de Jaudenes y Nebot; Martha Stoughton de Jaudenes.

The *chargé d'affaires* of Spain in the United States from 1791-96, wears Spanish official costume: dark blue velvet, with scarlet lining, waistcoat and breeches, massively embroidered in silver; white stockings; black hat with red ribbon.

His wife's froth of hair, powdered gray, is dressed with white, gray and blue-edged feathers, and the beloved pair of tall, uncurled ostrich plumes of the turn of the century; white taffeta dress, brocaded in gold, with white and gray gauze at the neck, a white corselet embroidered in gold, white and gold jewelry, chatelaine, round enamelled pendant watch and blue medallion bracelet.

ENGLISH FASHION MAGAZINES: LATE XVIII—EARLY XIX CENTURY

Nicholas Heideloff, a young German from Stuttgart, was working in Paris; at the Revolution, he fled to London where he published *Heideloff's Gallery of Fashion,* monthly from 1794-1803. It is probably the most luxurious of all fashion magazines. The copy at Museum of Fine Arts, Boston, belonged to Queen Charlotte. The plates, colored by hand, with touches of metal, show a great deal of the new outdoor life. Ladies read poetry on a stone bench by moored ships, 1795; stand in poke bonnets and wind-blown morning dress at the edge of a cliff, overlooking a beach and bath wagons, 1797. We see the blue beaver hats of 1794, the great parti-colored muffs of pale fur or eiderdown of 1794-7; the prodigiously trimmed scarves of 1795-7; the ribbon-laced sandals, high on the calf, of 1797.

Magazines of fashion, culture and information arrive in a flood with the XIXc.

Ackermann's Repository, published 1809-28, is particularly valuable for its pasted-in clippings of actual fabrics, newly produced by English and foreign firms. Its colored frontispiece is usually of the showroom of an important firm: e.g., Mr. Ackermann's art supply shop; Harding, Howell & Co., the drapers; Wedgwood's pottery. It tells of the gifts prepared for the British Embassy to the Chinese Emperor, displayed at Mr. Ross's Rooms, and shows fitted boxes and work tables, toilet sets, scent bottles

of cut and milk glass. Other articles deal with culture, science, current events, the stock market, the theatre, and show new fashions in furniture and decoration, as well as dress.

The Journal of Design, published by Chapman & Hall for a few years after 1849, continues to use actual samples, and shows swatches from the first American factories, like Dunnell in Providence. During 1850, it published serially a most valuable history of the textile industry, written by the head of the Broad Oaks firm. Such a chronology of new techniques is priceless in dating textiles and costumes. The old method of overprinting or pencilling blue on yellow to give green continued to be used long after fast green was produced in 1811. Turkey red discharge was a monopoly of Koechlin of Mulhouse until Broad Oaks got British patent rights. Machine printing of borders did not begin until 1825; color printing was slowly increased from two to six rollers by 1850. Manganese oxides date from 1827 and provide a series from yellow through orange to brown. "Fondu" and "rainbow" patterns begin in 1823-4. The ability to print on thin wool "delaines" as well as cotton coincides with the blue and brown cobalt styles of 1836. There are infinite combinations of wool with cotton and silk; "challis" becomes a favorite fabric. "Glenyou plaids" commemorate Victoria's visit to the Highlands, and are followed by "graduated rainbows" and the epoch-making "dahlia" colors which bathe everything in magenta and purple in 1844.

2233. XVIIIc. 1794. English. (Port Sunlight, The Lady Lever Art Gallery.)
George Stubbs. Wedgwood plaque: The Haycart.
One of a series of pottery plaques, c. 30″ x ″40, of outdoor scenes, executed by Stubbs.
2234-35. XVIIIc. English.
Heideloff's Gallery of Fashion.
2234. (Aug., 1794.) Two Ladies, *en neglige,* Taking the Air in a Phaeton.
"Headdress: white stamp-paper hat, trimmed with a green riband and tied down with the same. One green and one yellow feather placed on the left side. Green gauze veil. The hair in small curls; plain chignon. Plain calico morning dress with long sleeves; the petticoat trimmed with a narrow flounce. Plain lawn handkerchief, green sash, lawn cloak trimmed with lace and tied behind, york tan gloves, yellow shoes."

"Headdress: straw colored hat, trimmed with orange and purple ribands, and a white lawn handkerchief, embroidered in lilac, tied down with a white riband. One lilac and white cross-striped large ostrich feather on the left side, the hair in light curls and hanging down in ringlets behind, bound with a half-handkerchief tied into a large bow in the front. Chemise of spotted muslin, trimmed with a double plaiting of broad lace about the waist, tied in front by a lilac riband, short loose sleeves, tied in the middle with the same riband. Lilac-colored sash tied behind, jonquille coloured gloves and shoes." (Text accompanying the original illustrations.)

The parasol is green, which is the usual color. The three mounting plumes, which were set in front in April (when publication began) remained there until they were moved to the l. side in August.

White horses, with black harness, yellow rosettes, and orange and yellow bands on the bridle, draw a yellow, phaeton, striped in orange.

2235. (Jan., 1799.) (Child). "The hair combed into natural curls; half-handkerchief of pink and white striped muslin, tied around the head with a bow in the front. Gray Spencer, trimmed around the waist with black velvet; muslin frock.

The hair cut short in the front, and combed straight; the hind hair in short ringlets. Bonnet of scarlet cloth, trimmed with velvet, and fur bands, bouquet of flowers of *leather* in the front. Round dress of Scotch cambric, long sleeves with Vandyke cuffs; the whole trimmed with lace, tied upon the breast with a purple satin riband. Fur belt. Mamelouc cape. Purple jean shoes, trimmed with scarlet. Gray gloves.

The toupee cut short, and combed into feather curls; the hind hair cropped. Bonnet of white satin, trimmed with purple velvet bands and cross bands, finished at the top of the crown with a small *rosette* of the same. Round satin cloak trimmed with point lace. Full muslin stock. Large gold hoop earrings. Purple Spanish leather shoes."

Muffs have grown larger, darker, more elaborate and more indispensable.

2236. XVIIIc. 1799. English. (New York, Mr. & Mrs. G. B. Wagstaff.)

Richard Westall, eng. by *C. Knight.* Fishing party.

At the Revolution and during the two following decades, "Reform" clothes for men are seen, based on workingmen's smocks, late Greek fitted tunics, and on XVIIc. doublets; they are often affected by XVIIc. slashing, especially at an upper-sleeve puff, and by "Vandyked" collars of toothed lace. This tunic and tights sports costume is its typical form, usually worn with a full beret or loose turban.

Elizabethan or "Vandyke" standing ruffs of notched lace also appear on women's low-necked dresses. These wired collars, and the *fraise* neck ruche are two opposed influences by which the composite neckline of 1820-40 will be formed. The low neck will slip to the shoulders and become horizontal. The standing and often notched collar will col-

2236

lapse into laterally jutting wings, often toothed, over leg-o'-mutton sleeves, while an inner bodice like a bertha will rise smoothly over the shoulders to the base of the throat. Then the horizontal shoulder line will weaken, leaving a high-necked gown.

2237. Late XVIIIc. French.
Bobbin lace: application d'Angleterre
2238. Early XIXc. English.
Lappets: appliqué lace
2239. XIXc. English.
Bobbin lace edgings: Bedfordshire, Buckinghamshire, Honiton, English Mechlin, Northamptonshire.

Lace-making began in England in 1567, when Flemish refugees from Alva's persecutions settled in the Midlands. Pillow lace was made in Buckinghamshire to the West of London, Bedfordshire and Northamptonshire to the N.W. Settlers from Ipswich and Suffolk, to the N.E., brought lace making to Ipswich, Mass., in 1630—41,975 yards a year were produced there by 1790. Honiton lace-making was brought to Devonshire by Dutch refugees.

Courtesy of Metropolitan Museum of Art

2237

2238

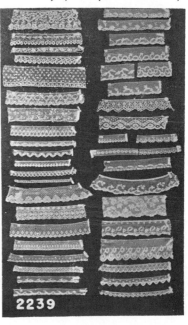

2239

The Mills Rise: XIX Century

XIX CENTURY DRESS: WOMEN

THE changes in this century have been usefully charted by Cecil Willett Cunnington (*English Women's Clothing in the Nineteenth Century.* Faber and Faber. London, 1937) whose collection of 1100 costumes, 2000 accessories, fashion plates and books covering 200 years of English Women's dress has been bought by the Manchester Museum for £7000.

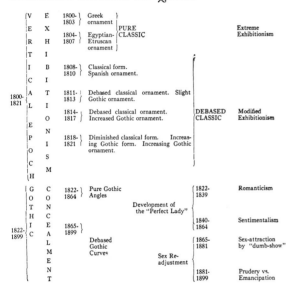

FRENCH REVOLUTION TO 1820.

The English muslin *chemise,* the basis of "classical" dress, was essentially a tube with one drawstring at a round neck, and another at a high waistline.

During the Directoire, the neck became lower, sleeves shorter, waistline higher, and the back of the skirt lengthened into a train. Tunics and slit over-dresses were added, 1803-1810; made obligatory in court use under Napoleon; and were turned into coat-dresses, *douillettes,* for domestic wear, fitted *pelisse-robes* and *redingotes* of the following periods. There are also apron-like *tablier* overdresses, open down the back.

About 1803, the full, gathered top of the *chemise* began to be covered and replaced by a tiny fitted bodice, which reached only to the armpits and the base of the breast. The front breadth of the skirt remained straight; the back breadth began to be gored and to lengthen, with its fullness massed at the center-back. The skirt of this *robe en caleçons* (to 1820) was so narrow that walking was difficult; only one petticoat was worn under it, and excessively fashionable women wore only tights; stockings were often omitted with the naked classical styles. People became so used to seeing women outdoors, dressed in muslin, during a decade of fairly warm winters, that it was feared they would ruin their health when they began to wear warm clothes indoors during the generally cold winters of 1810–1820.

About 1810–14, the neckline for daytime became higher; long sleeves were added below a puffed cap-sleeve; the skirt began to be gored wider to the hem, and to be shortened in daytime use; decoration of cord, braid, and bands of self-material replaced Greek, Etruscan and Egyptian motifs, and Hungarian, Polish and Russian frogged decoration, used on men's coats, appeared on women's riding habits, and on boys' clothing.

The favorite wraps of the Directoire and Empire were large square or oblong shawls, of the size and proportions of the Greek *chlamys* and *himation,* draped in Greek ways.

The *Spencer* (see male style) which appeared c. 1804, was a long-sleeved, short-waisted, fitted jacket, an outer garment equivalent to a bodice but differing from it in color. The Spencer, together with long scarfs and *pelisses,* remained in use through first third XIXc.

Hair was at first caught up in Greek knots, held by fillets and combs, with a hanging fringe of locks at forehead and ears. Wigs were provided in every color, quite unrelated to the wearer's natural hair and dramatic changes were made several times a day. Towards the end of the period, hair tended to be parted, drawn smoothly, and bunched into locks at the ears.

Headwear was modelled on classic helmets, oriental turbans with cock feathers, and single tall uncurled ostrich plumes. Hats with fabric tops and straw brims decorated on the underside and veiled in lace (see Ill. 1800 Ladies of Ghent) tend to become tied down into plainer bonnets: there are also hats of male top-hat shapes, and of beaver.

The classical white muslin dresses, embroidered in silver, gold or white, were worn with brightly colored long gloves and mitts; low satin or kid slippers tied with crossed ribbons; plumes, turbans and ribbons. Scarfs were often of poppy red or violet; muffs, *pelisse* edgings and neckpieces, and tippets of pale furs and eiderdown; reticules and purses of beads, straw, steel and fabric; combs, necklaces, corals, bracelets.

1821 TO 1840.

Dramatic changes take place in the form of the body and of its clothing in the first years of the 20's. The waistline, which has been tucked under the breasts, drops to its normal position on a pointed or belted bodice. The gored skirt flares toward the hem and is supported by quilting or starched embroidered petticoat ruffles; it shortens, from shoe to ankle length; then it becomes fuller, first pleated at the waist; then gathered with a boned petticoat and hip and bustle pads, *tourneurs*. At the end of the period, it barely shows the point of the shoe and has reached a width of 7 or 8 breadths.

The spread at the top of the bodice is even more dramatic.

The bodice of the daytime *pelisse* is closed to the base of the throat, but it is widened by collars spread out over an immense fullness at the top of the sleeve, which assumes a leg-o'-mutton form. The round or square neck becomes horizontally cut across the shoulderline, which is further extended by wings projecting beyond the full sleeves. The fullness at the top of the leg-o'mutton sleeve slips down toward the elbow in the 30's; the wings above them droop into a dropped shoulderline, onto which are set sleeves, which are puffed at intervals around the elbow, and close-fitting below it, at the end of this period.

On the wide-winged bodice, pleated or draped decoration is laid on in a V, from points far out on the shoulder to the center of the waist belt. These decorations, like the dress itself, have dramatic form. They are made of fabric, piped, banded, folded into notched or zigzag patterns, looped into scrolls and shells, or cut into tabs, and applied, often diagonally, on repeated bands which rise horizontally on the skirt from the hem towards the knee.

Puffed flowers and leaves of gauze are also used. They tend to become flattened into spots of appliqué, as the fuller skirt loses decoration, becoming plain, slightly flounced, or edged with fringe, and often slit up the middle, at the end of the period.

The *pelisse* turns into a warm, high-necked dress, closed down the front; in its later form by bows. The neckline of the "round" dress is often raised by lingerie *chemisettes*, tuckers, widespread *pèlerines* and fichu-like *canezous*, the points of which are caught by the belt. They turn into white shirtwaists. These too, droop and become reduced as the shoulderline drops, the bodice becomes more pointed, and the longer, fuller skirt splits in the middle.

With the sloping shoulderline, cashmere shawls increase in importance. The old fitted *pelisse* goes out of style; but mantles become increasingly shaped, fitted, and hooked together into *pelisse-mantles* with long tab points and fringe trim.

The wide-shouldered dresses of the early part of the period are accompanied by enormous hats of leghorn or fabric on wire frames, laden with masses of feathers and 10–12 yards of looped ribbon, in brilliant colors. With these, the bunches of curls rise to the temples; and hair begins to stand (end first quarter XIXc.) dressed into 1 to 3 tall loops on the crown of the head supported by high ribbon loops, flowers and tortoise shell combs. About 1827, curls are often massed on left side, but less jewelry is worn. As shoulders narrow, hats are reduced into smaller, more enclosing bonnets. In evening dress, flowers are tucked at right ear.

As the shoulderline droops, the parted hair is combed in loops covering the ears; lappeted caps appear; hats of the 30's turn into bonnets and *capotes,* which surround the face and conceal it entirely from profile view.

When form and trimming become less acute, the thin merino and challis wools, muslin and silk in plain, sharp lavenders, greens and geranium pinks, become patterned into chintzes, ginghams, brocades, foulards, shot broché or striped silks and velvets of darker, heavier colors and textures; brown, violet, blues, black in violent tasteless combinations.

Fine batiste underwear was a XIXc. invention of the Empress Josephine, who changed three times a day. Underdrawers are not commonly worn by women until end first third XIXc. Then they are so long that their lace edge shows when the skirt is raised; they consist of two unconnected tubes, tied on at the waist by strings, one of which frequently becomes undone, so that one leg is occasionally dropped on the street; pantalettes had been made part of dress of English girls early in XIXc. and are worn through the 50's.

The corsets of XIXc. were long, becoming shorter by 1810; they were padded to improve the form of the 20's, and tightly laced to conform to the increasingly exuberant, plump ideal of the 30's.

All the tight bodices had to be lined; the short early forms closed by lacings, ties and buttons; the later ones principally by hooks and eyes.

Sleeves, collars and skirts require support, at first by starching, quilting and padding; then by boning and horsehair crinoline.

The earlier dress is still white with touches of brilliant color. There is a great increase in the use of silk in England—as its importation is allowed from 1824 and duties are reduced from 30% to 15%. There is even some increase in the use of Spitalfields silk. Silk lace, *blonde,* becomes immensely popular at about the time of Victoria's accession, and has its longest life in Spanish use.

Black slippers, slippers matching the costume, or white for evening, tend to replace bright-colored ones with ribbon ties around the leg. Shoes, laced up inside or front, appear, often with lighter colored silk fabric or kid tops, or buttoned gray or buff gaiters, which almost obliterate the toe. In the 30's shoes themselves are often made of fabrics, and become square-toed by 1827. Stockings are occasionally black or flesh, but are usually white.

Narrow cashmere scarfs with light grounds are replaced by darker square cashmere or paisley shawls. Gloves and mitts of kid, suede and net become shorter, embroidered and trimmed. White hats are large. Parasols are tiny, embroidered or fringed. Handkerchiefs. Hair looped or braided over the ears. Earrings hang and necklaces and paired bracelets appear; brooches at collars of day dresses.

THE 1840's.

Romanticism influenced by Scott, Victor Hugo and Dumas, fils.

The body and spirit become immobilized, sheathed and protected, drooping, helpless and meek; colors muted.

Smooth, parted hair is looped down over the ears in bands, braids or spaniels' ears of corkscrew curls, flattened with bandoline.

Large oval bonnets and *capotes,* still rather ornate and tied under the chin, prevent side glances or views; caps in daytime and evening.

Arms are imprisoned by dropped shoulders; sleeves set from that line become long and plain, then bell out; the ruffles which used to be set at the junction are reduced to folds on a cap.

Torsos are enclosed in long severe, smoothly-boned bodices over tightly laced corsets; their long points emphasized by V decorations from the wide shoulderline. Necklines do not hug the throat, at the beginning of the period, even when the bodice is cut high; and are often open a third to halfway down in a V which tends to close and rise. Evening bodices are cut straight across the shoulderline, which is surrounded by a flat valance of wide lace.

Layers of long full petticoats, banded with horsehair, support even fuller skirts, which make exercise difficult. Women drink vinegar to keep thin; good health is no longer well bred. Women do not exercise. They pile on flannel and merino underwear in the terrible cold of 1845.

At the beginning of the period there are skirts, slit in front and vertically patterned or made of vertically striped fabric, but as skirts widen their trim becomes horizontal. Borders *en disposition* are worn or printed on dress lengths and are accompanied by fashion plates, showing how to use the borders in making 3-flounced skirts and

in trimming the V of the bodice (see 2552-55). In the mid-40's the fullness of the skirt is not gathered into the waistline but pleated and gaged on.

A new impulse which will lead to the bustled dresses of the 70's is shown in the flounces of evening dresses, which are scalloped or draped up and caught with bows and flowers.

The long *pelisses* and mantles of the 30's become shorter *pardessus,* knee length, more closely fitted, with the corners of their skirts rounded off.

Both colors and patterns of fabrics are subdued and wavering. Striped and plaids are often *chiné* (the pattern, tied and dyed onto the warp, has an indistinct, irregular edge), *fondu* or blended in rainbows. There are shot taffetas, watered, *broché* and corded silks; gauzy *barèges* and *mousselines de laine* (delaines), and their various combinations with cashmere, merino and alpaca. (See Journal of Design, p. 791.)

Elaborate silk aprons, worn indoors, handkerchiefs; bouquets and lace; buttons, brooches, bracelets, and drop earrings; flower-wreaths on hair in the evening.

1850–1864: SENTIMENTALISM.

Talleyrand, who died in 1839, said, "He who has not lived in the years just preceding 1789 cannot know the pleasures of living."

The exhilaration of revolution was followed by a period of unprincipled venality, conscienceless acquisition, and exploitation, insistent luxury and search for distraction. Against this was set melancholy regret for grace that was gone, boredom and disgust with the crass materialism, the increased standardization and the industrialization of the present, and the future.

The Goncourt *Journals* record it: (translated by Louis Galantière, Doubleday, Doran, Garden City, 1937)

1857: "Who does not keep a carriage these days? What a society! Everybody is determined to bankrupt himself. Never have appearances been so despotic, so imperious, and so demoralizing—the thing has come to such a point that many shops now open credit in favor of their clientele, who pay only the interest on their debts."

When the first auction sale of photographs is held at the Hotel Druot in 1857: "Everything is turning black in this century, and is not photography the black vestment of the visible world?" (See Appendix).

The first commercial photography was by Daguerre's 1839 method, on silvered plates which were permanent but could not be reproduced. Daguerrotypes continued to be made long after plate photography began in the 40's. *Cartes de visite* mounted with portrait photographs first became fashionable in the 50's.

On Nov. 1, 1860, the Goncourts say, social life

is in evolution; even wives and children appear in cafés; home life is dying; the upper classes go to clubs; the lower classes to cafés. The "Universal Exposition" of 1867 is "the final blow levelled at the past, the Americanization of France, industry lording it over art, the steam thresher displacing the painting, in brief, the Federalization of Matter."

The first great International Exhibition was opened in London in 1851. It was housed in the epoch-making brilliance of the 20 acre Crystal Palace, six stories of iron-supported glass, with a swelling, vaulted glass roof, designed by the greenhouse builder, Sir Joseph Paxton. Backed by the Society of Artists which offered prizes, it drew 6,000,000 and was followed by exhibitions in other countries. The most notable were in Paris in 1855 and in 1867, which had exhibitions of machinery, the architecture of all nations, and a series of restaurants serving national foods; the Philadelphia Centennial of 1876; and the great Paris Exhibition of 1878.

The Crystal Palace was not only light and airy; its seats were comfortable. Comfortable, handsome, functional furniture and architecture could be provided by any country carpenter, after the publication of Sheraton's volumes of furniture design in late XVIIIc.-e.XIXc., and the handbooks of architecture in the early XIXc.

Against this standardization, the clear light, the bare space of the classical revival, and ingenious factory-produced cheap American furniture, was set the Romantic Gothic Revolt, from Horace Walpole's time into XIXc. XVIIIc. furniture was put into the servants' rooms. After his marriage in 1859, William Morris built his "Red House"—all brick, narrow mullioned windows and gloom. With his pre-Raphaelite artist friends, he started a firm which produced the "Beautiful" furniture, stained glass, wall-paper, and clutter of decorative objects which crammed Victorian homes; he also made a good, comfortable, functional new chair.

The sewing machine had been invented by 1830 but it became practical in 1843 with Howe's lock-stitch machine; almost simultaneous improvements were made by Wilson, Grover, Singer and Gibbs. The machine was first used in shoemaking. By the 50's, it was producing cheap, ready-to-wear men's clothing. In 1858, the great couturiers of Paris used it; and in the 60's, almost all clothing was machine-sewed and on its way to standardization.

Mass production needed mass outlets. A department store with 150 employes, the Ville de France, had been started in Paris in 1844; the Grands Halles in 1853; the Bon Marche in 1876. In the U.S.A., Oak Hall opened in Boston in 1851, and a department store at Broome St. and Broadway in 1851; A. T. Stewart's in 1863, and

the Grand Depot, in remodelled carbarns in Philadelphia, in 1876. (S. Giedion: *Space, Time and Architecture.*)

A midwestern American, Mrs. Amelia Jenks Bloomer, brought to London in 1851 her reform dress of a jacket, knee-length skirt, and Turkish trousers. In a new impatience with restraint, women begin to take over simple, masculine garments, hats, jackets, vests and boots, and invent comfortable walking and bathing costumes.

The Empress Eugenie replaces piled petticoats, c.1855, with a round crinoline skirt threaded with parallel hoops of whalebone or wire, a revival of the farthingale. With it, hoops reach their ultimate rounded width by the end of the 50's. If steps are not mincing, the hoop bounces up and the foot is seen; soon hands will catch up the skirt, exposing petticoats and shoes, boldly.

The great dressmaker of XIXc., the founder of the *haute couture* of Paris, was Worth, an Englishman who had worked in the silk-trade in Paris, before setting up a dress making establishment in 1858. He came almost immediately to the attention of the Empress Eugenie. His career as dressmaker to her white-clad court, and to the actresses and *cocottes* who have become more important than courts in launching styles, is recorded in many entries in Mme. Octave Feuillet's 4 volumes; his 30-year rule of fashion was carried on by his two sons.

During the 50's, parted hair, smooth or waved, tends to be drawn backwards and massed at the nape in curls or braids, which are often netted.

Hats appear; bonnets become smaller, made of fancy straws; caps with lappets are worn indoors by all English married women; wreaths, with evening dress.

Corsets are more elastic, and long bodices shorten as skirts become much rounder and fuller and give the waist a narrow look by contrast, not by tight lacing. Skirt ruffles multiply in number, become much narrower and project from the plane of the skirt. The hem of the skirt takes on more importance in the late 50's, and gains a wide, pleated flounce. There are also plain, full skirts, banded with zigzags in lines of velvet or braid.

Sleeves spread into wide pagoda forms, which show more of the full white sleeve of the chemisette, gathered into a tight waistband. Necklines rise to the base of the throat, and white collars become smaller.

Mantles grow shorter, in jacket or shawl-like shapes which fall into points, front and back, and are fringed.

With the invention of aniline dyes, lurid fuchsias, magentas and violets appear which appeal to the new adventuresomeness in women. Color contrasts are stronger, materials more varied: velvet, moiré, satin, and brocade are woven or used in combination with plain fabrics; there are grenadines, barèges and gauze, and new fabrics like challis and nainsook. Trimmings are made of chenille and jet, ball fringe and tassels, buttons, Honiton and Brussels lace. There are aprons, short embroidered gloves; tiny muffs; reticules of jet beads and embroidery mounted in steel, silver and gold; fans, bouquets and small parasols; gold combs, knobbed hairpins, dotted hair nets, pendant earrings; jewelry of coral, jet and hair; many bracelets. Shoes with elastic side and heels, striped stockings.

THE 1860's.

During the 60's, ears reappear; parted hair is massed at the nape of the neck in chignons, curls and braids; masses of false hair are added and enclosed in spangled or chenille-dotted nets, and small hats tip forward to display the chignon's mass.

Hats tend to replace bonnets and caps, and are more laden with trimming in England than in France. Men's styles are daringly taken over by women. Ladies' tailors make jacket and skirt costumes, under the lead of the new Princess Alexandra.

The belted *canezou* grows into the white shirt-waist, worn with a separate skirt, as are red Garibaldi blouses, braided Zouave jackets and boleros.

Mid-Victorian ladies escape from enormous skirts and crinolines. Crinolines are reduced to frames of diagonally set wire, which thrust skirt fullness backwards into the bustles of the 70's. Skirts are cut in gores, and become completely smooth around the hips by last third of the decade. Princess garments appear and waistlines are lengthened by long laced corsets which, with high heels, induce the "Grecian Bend." Skirts shorten in front and drag backwards into the trains of the 70's.

Women lift skirts to show brilliant contrasting petticoats, bright colored shoes trimmed with tassels and plaid or striped stockings. English fashion, usually a year or so behind French, leads in these daring "fast" masculine and petticoat styles, which the Empress Eugenie met with on her visit to London in 1862.

The line of small ruffles on the skirt sinks toward the growingly important, pleated, petticoat-like flounces on the braided hem. Unruffled skirts have tabbed or asymmetrically shaped panels falling from the waist. Trimming is in Greek key designs, elaborate fringe, upholstery-like pleatings, lace, or even leather. On evening skirts, decoration is asymmetrically cut or looped, and puffed into bustles and polonaises.

Pagoda sleeves become plainer, showing more of the sleeve of the chemisette; then are slit and begin to enclose the wrist, making the chemisette sleeve less important. The simple closed sleeve of the tailored costume of the 60's becomes the common sleeve of the bustled 70's.

Cloaks become larger, more flowing, and cape-or-coat-like, with wide pagoda sleeves. Like everything else, they are laden with gimp, tassels, fringes, of jet, beads, bugles, and chenille. There are cashmere and yak lace shawls, elaborate filigree buttons, and a profusion of jewelry; cameos and jet medallions, chains and dog collars, earrings, brooches and many bracelets. Parasols grow larger as hats diminish in size.

Costumes continue to be made in two colors but the brilliant combinations of the beginning of the decade grow sober. With bustled dresses there is a revival of French fashions, from Watteau to Louis XV. The tailored costumes are usually cut to the base of the throat, with a small white collar. Evening necklines, slipping off the shoulders, often rise and become squares with the end of the decade. A great deal of attention begins to be given to underwear and its embellishment by embroidery.

XIX CENTURY MEN'S CLOTHING

FRENCH REVOLUTION TO 1820.

The Revolution brought plainer cloth coats in a variety almost impossible to separate as they overlap and merge with top coats, which are turning into forms of regular coat.

There were three basic coats. The new English double-breasted, with high turn-over collar and important lapels, tended to become squarely cutaway across the waistline, while its tails retreated to the back and fell straight. Worn with knee-breeches, or more customarily with pantaloons, it becomes everyone's ordinary dress.

The single-breasted cutaway coat, with a high standing or turned-over collar, was worn with knee breeches or pantaloons, and was eventually reduced to a riding-coat (an exchange in position with the double-breasted coat, which had originated as a riding and military garment).

The court *frac,* which went out of use during the Revolution, is revived by Napoleon in court and uniform use. Its coat and waistcoat, which are sometimes related, are heavily embroidered, according to the rank of the wearer, and are usually of velvet (often violet); worn with satin knee-breeches and the *chapeau bras*—the flat hat grown out of the *chapeau à l'androsmane,* which can be carried under the arm.

During the Revolution French gentlemen are seen in the Jacobin red stocking-cap of the galley-slave, the sleeveless *carmagnole* jacket, and working men's loose blue linen trousers. From 1800–1885, there are smocks and classical tunics (see Ill. 2236) worn with long tights and loose berets.

There is an even larger number of new overgarments, some of which turn from overcoats into suit coats. The "poor devil" was a flopping plebeian coat. The *Jean de Bry* coat of 1799-1800 had a standing collar of velvet, small lapels, padded shoulders. It closed high on the breast with three large buttons and was then so sharply cutaway into short, narrow tails with pockets massed at the back, that the space between its very high waistline and the top of the breeches was filled by the vest. The ankle-length, multiple caped "Garrick" is seen throughout first quarter XIXc. There are *surtout, capote* and *redingote* overcoats which come to be worn with vests and pantaloons as forms of warm, skirted coats. They hang at levels between knee-length and half-way between knee and ankle. The "Spencer" jacket resulted from a hunting accident in 1792 in which most of the tails and sleeves of Earl Spencer's coat were torn off, and he bet that he could make his present ridiculous state a fashion. By 1804-5 it had become a very important article of women's dress; on men it was seen as a sort of extra chest-protection: a tailless or tabbed, short-waisted coat with sleeve-caps, worn over another coat. About 1807 appear braided and frogged Polish, Hungarian and Russian overcoats, the braided trim of which can be seen affecting men's, women's and children's clothes to the 50's.

Coat collars, standing or turned-over, are at first high about the ears, supported by boning; lapels are very important; and sleeves close-fitting. During the first decade, the armseye enlarges; the top of the sleeve becomes full and gathered; the cuff is often turned down or prolonged over the knuckles; the shoulder seam is drawn far down on the back of the coat; the waistline is tightened, so that the coat rolls into wrinkles around the waist in back, and tends to close higher in front. As the 20's approach, the collar, which has grown more rounded and rolling, arches away from the neck in back; the shoulder widens, the waist tightens and the chest puffs out.

The early tail coat, with collar to the ears, chin muffled in an immense cravat, enormous lapels and very long tails, in its *incroyable* form is often made of striped satin. Coat tails are customarily of knee-length or shorter to 1815; then lengthen, to the knees or longer as the 20's approach.

Throughout this period the *gilet* is cut square across the bottom; it is plain, embroidered or striped; single- or double-breasted. Two vests of different lengths and colors are often worn together, until the 30's, and one of them is apt to be vertically striped. *Gilets* are of waist length or very short at the turn of the century, lengthen to the hips, c.1812, then shorten again as bosoms puff out. While coat collars remain high the collar of the *gilet* is high, whether it is a standing or a turned over form; the *gilet* follows the lead of the coat lapels and collars as these change. Single- and double-breasted vests are interchangeably worn with either single or double-breasted coats,

but the standing collar is particularly the attribute of the single-breasted garment. Only with court costume does a waistcoat have a cut-away bottom, until the 1820's.

Breeches have a broad, front-flap opening from c.1780–1840. As they lengthen into pantaloons at the turn of the century, and grow high waisted, they come to be supported by braces or suspenders over the shoulders.

Knee breeches are worn with both single and double-breasted coats until about 1815, although they have become generally superseded by longer forms during the first decade. Elderly English country gentlemen occasionally wore them into 1870's. They are required in court costume until 1830, then become optional. Pantaloons were introduced into English army use by Wellington, c.1806, during Peninsular war, but opposition to them was still so strong in 1812 that English university students wearing them in chapel were marked as absent.

As boots appear, breeches lose their buckled band and are fastened by knee-strings below a line of buttons. By 1790 many breeches have been drawn down under the boot-top to the calf. By 1800 they are commonly of ankle length and begin to be held down by a strap under the sole of the shoe. As boots begin to be less worn, c.1815, breeches become shorter, full at the waist, wide in the leg and are generally strapless, until c.1820, when they become close fitting and strapped again until about 1840. All these tight pantaloons are made of knit stockinet or pliable doeskin, usually in lighter colors than the coat: greys, beiges, and yellows, black occasionally used with black coats; and yellowish cotton nankeen or white in summer. There are also striped forms, vertically patterned like the favorite blue and white stockings of 1770–1805, or horizontally (as seen on Goya, working in his studio, in a self-portrait). Long breeches buttoned down the entire outseam (such as we show in Alken's 1819 "Real Meltonian" series) are seen a decade earlier and are carried spatlike, over low shoes. With the appearance of Polish styles, informal pantaloons often have corded, braided or quilted patterns on the upper thigh around the flap-closings, where paired fobs used to dangle.

Either shoes or boots are worn with knee breeches. The tendency toward boots, growing throughout the final quarter century, becomes a mania from 1790–1815. There are English jockey boots with reversed tops and boot straps; Hessian, and Suvaroff boots, which have their tops scalloped into two arcs, from the joining of which hangs a tassel. There are soft boots in great variety: high and close-fitting; or short with tops flaring between ankle and calf-height, spats and gaiters in all lengths. About 1813–15 spurs are seen.

The first strapped pantaloons are worn either with boots, or with dark low shoes and light stockings. Both this type, and the shorter, wider trousers of c.1815–25 are commonly worn over soft black boots which begin to turn into shoes in the second third XIXc.

Until c.1825 collars are soft, attached to the shirt and turned up to the ears. They surround the jaw from 1800–30, and then tend to be turned down over the cravat. The kerchief which goes twice about the neck to be knotted in front is worn 1790–1830; then begins to be turned into a bow tie. It is typically white, though there are striped forms from the Revolution to 1815. Collars become detached from shirts, and starched c.1825. Ruffled shirt fronts are seen through the openings of single-breasted waistcoats until the 30's and later still in court costume. But from the 20's the frill falls at one side of a buttoned closing.

At the Revolution, hair loses its powder and is dressed in two principal fashions: the short-combed-out hedgehog, *hérisson;* its longer form *à la Titus;* or in shaggy "dog's-ear" locks, combed forward over the forehead and ears. This form developed into curly sideburns which continued to be worn when the shaggy locks become full and curlier about the ears, after 1815.

The tricorne had been pretty well replaced late in XVIIIc. by the hat turned up front and back *à l'androsmane.* The most exaggerated form of this was worn with the striped coat of the *Incroyable;* it became the hat of Napoleon's army and court. As the flat *"chapeau bras"* which could be carried tucked under the arm, or worn, but which it was never permissible to lay down, it continues in ceremonial dress use today in the costume of French academicians.

The plain English "round" hat had early Revolutionary connotations, but it was so practical that it made great strides. By 1812 it was universally worn, with conical, sugar-loaf, or spreading top-hat crown; its brim was apt to be rolled up slightly on the sides with a dip over the forehead.

Paired fobs continue to be worn, but by 1810, interest in them is transferred to the paired closing of the front flap; even this diminishes when trouser-tops become fuller, c.1815. The watch is then worn singly with a black ribbon fob, as a convenience, or with a bunch of seals.

Snuff continues to be taken; cigar smoking begins, but will not become common until practical wooden matches are invented in England in 1827. The French match of 1805 was an amusing curiosity which was ignited by dipping it into a bottle of sulphuric acid.

Sticks and quizzing glasses continue to be carried; gloves, usually yellow, are worn, especially after the bright mixed colors and patterns of the early period tend to become browns, grays, blacks, and blues, worn with lighter trousers, black hat and boots. Buttons (made of steel or pearl at the turn of the century) turn to brass or gilt.

Blue was especially fashionable and was used both in day and evening dress. The best tailor of 1816 was Weston of Old Bond Street, whose light *bleu céleste* was famous. Brummell, the arbiter of the period in England, wore carefully folded starched white cravats and perfectly tailored plain clothing. In the daytime, his brass-buttoned blue coat was worn with a buff or light colored waistcoat, buckskin breeches or pantaloons, over Hessian boots. At night, his blue coat was accompanied by a white waistcoat, pantaloons of blue stockinet, strapped over varnished black shoes worn with striped stockings. Court dress was worn at the opera and Almack's Assembly Rooms in London.

1820-40.

The corseted look for which the coat has been straining is now attained by cutting the tails separate from the body of the coat. The bosom springs open and is rounded. There are rolling shawl collars, sometimes slightly notched, which are no longer dragged away from the back of the neck. The shoulder seam moves back up into position and the shoulder line is widened with padding; sleeves become plain and close.

Coats are single or double-breasted, but are so shaped that they hold their form without being closed; double-breastedness is becoming a matter of lines of decorative buttons, as useless as the vestigial buttons on an evening tailcoat today. By 1835 the collar becomes longer, more acutely notched into prominent stitched lapels. Tailcoats are less squarely cutaway across the front and their tails hang below the knee. Blue and black continue to be dress-coat colors. In ordinary wear bottle green, mulberry and warm browns are added to black and blue coats.

But among the wonderfully individual forms of coat and topcoat, which are developing toward their culmination in the 40's and 50's, are knee-length, skirted coats with shoulder capes and sharp wide lapels, for informal wear instead of the tail coat.

Macintosh had invented waterproof cloth c. 1825; by 1830 it is used in all sorts of deeply caped travelling coats and ulsters with half-belts in back which could be buttoned to make them fit more closely. There are many very long overcoats, fitted, loose, or even full and cape-like. Until the 30's they often close by tabs. There are forms with one to four capes; fur-lined and collared *pelisses* with braid trim and frogged closings. Coats begin to be made of textured and patterned tweeds; pockets are often set in a diagonal line. Fur and long, full outer garments are usually related to the weather; they are sometimes hold-overs from the previous bad year, anticipations of another such, or mere swank like a mink-coat in Indian Summer in New York. 1820 and 1823 were rigorous winters; fur-lined Polish coats and four-collared ankle-length capes are common. The intervening years were mild, but 1830 was one of the four worst winters ever recorded. From 1830 to 1871 the weather was relatively mild, with the exception of 1838, a long winter in 1845, cold winters in 1854 and in England 1855. The short loose sports coats of the 40's and 50's could only have developed during a long run of good seasons.

Vests follow the lead of coats, and become single-breasted, or are double-breasted merely by virtue of two rows of buttons. Like coats, vests curve open, round and low, with shawl collars, the notching of which turns them into sharp lapels at the end of the period. They then begin to dip slightly at the bottom or to spring apart into points below the last button. Into the 30's two vests of different lengths are often worn together, plain over striped, or dark over light. The general trend toward variety and pattern in men's clothing is particularly shown in vests. They are made of embroidered velvet or sprigged brocade, and there are white vests which are striking with darker coats and trousers, and black neckcloths.

The pantaloon of 1820 is full about the waist even when its bottom has again become narrow and strapped under the boot. It now becomes as long as possible and narrow, following the dimensions of the limbs and narrowing at the ankle. The characteristic look of the pantaloon of the 30's comes from its tautness between braces and sole, so that the line of the thigh strains through in front, and the calf in back. About 1835 the pantaloon begins to change into trousers; it exchanges a fly-opening for the flap. Its cut becomes a little easier, so that it can be made of cloth, and the familiar grays, greens and black are enlivened by corduroy and twilled textures and small patterns.

Collars become detached from shirts and begin to be starched c. 1825. The frilled shirt continues to be worn, and is required at court, but a tucked and buttoned front closing becomes more interesting.

The neckcloth becomes reduced. About 1830 it is replaced by stiffened cravats of serge, camlet, or satin, usually black, occasionally purple, and in evening dress of white satin. These buckle in back and have a bow in front. There are also "dickies" of dark stuff which are crossed and pinned and replace the shirt entirely.

Count D'Orsay, a Frenchman, who was the English arbiter of fashion in the 30's and 40's, is to be seen on the "New Yorker" magazine's

original cover and in the little cut on their masthead. His fitted neckcloth of 1834 is continued into an artfully crumpled mass of satin which covers the entire breast above the rolled collar of the waistcoat. His watch chain is worn around the neck, is looped before its passes through the top button hole, and then continues into the watch pocket on the right side of the vest.

The rather full head of the 20's is cut shorter in back by 1830 and is combed up into a quiff above the forehead. About 1835, it begins to be given a part on the left side, which is continued down the back of the head. Hair is combed away from this part into locks over the ears, or bunches of curls around them. As the collar and stock come to outline the chin, rather than to muffle it, in the 20's, the sideburns are continued in a fringe of artificially curled beard, running along the jawbone and under the chin of a clean-shaven face. Moustaches, which have been reserved for the cavalry, begin to be worn by civilians in the 30's.

Soft black Wellington boots, long, narrow and square-toed, are worn under strapped trousers. Gloves remain yellowish; sticks are carried; wide-brimmed top hats of smooth black beaver with tall crowns. Caps have been worn since 1800 in peaked Orleans and Russian, Austrian and Hungarian forms of army forage cap. With the increasing individuality of men's costume during the 30's and 40's caps multiply in forms and in use with the new waterproof travelling and hunting coats.

1840-1850.

During the 40's and 50's many varieties of new coats for morning and sports wear appear, and there is an increase in the use of bold patterns, stripes, checks and plaids. There are formal tail coats, many skirted coats, developed out of overcoats, and new morning jackets in loud patterns.

The shoulder seam drops down in back; sleeves become a little fuller and longer so that they wrinkle across the bend of the elbow. The curved waist lengthens into a long torso by 1850. While this process is taking place, skirts are set on a low line, between the normal waist and the hips, in cutting the loud single-breasted morning coats, which have their front corners rounded off. Buttons are large, and button holes are sometimes set diagonally to accentuate the swing of these coats. Coat collars become wider. Lapels (which had become acute in the late 30's) are prominent, but more rounded, rolling from a lowered waistline. Coat skirts and tails fall short of knee-length; a facing of dull silk is often carried well out on their lapels; the coat tends to be buttoned higher in the 50's and 60's.

There are still many fancy silk and embroidered velvet vests as well as wash vests for summer. But the parallel between vest and coat begins to disappear in the 40's, although the **vest** becomes longer waisted and is then buttoned higher, as the coat makes these changes. It may now have a rolled shawl collar, while the coat collar is deeply notched; its bottom is usually spread in points below the last button.

Trousers lose their shoe-straps during the 40's. They are still very long and close-cut at the bottom, but their fit becomes much easier. During the 40's they are often made of striking plaids and of stripes used horizontally as well as vertically; the most unusual patterns are worn with the new short outercoats which are made of plain materials. Fawn and gray trousers (rather than the earlier buff or white trousers) are worn with patterned coats and with the tailed and skirted coats. In the 50's the outseam is often braided and most trousers have hip pockets in the seam.

With the 50's there is a tendency to make coats, vests and trousers match. There are plaid and fancy tweed suits with more squarely cut skirts from 1855. Many completely black costumes of cloak, coat and vest and trousers appear in the 60's.

The 40's and 50's are filled with a wonderful variety of coats and top-coats, especially for day, travel and sports. There are formal overcoats with cape and small velvet collar; fitted coats; catalonian and hooded burnoose cloaks, and heavily braided short overcoats with hoods; short, double-breasted box-coats with big buttons; tiers of pocket flaps with another on the cuff; bell-shaped and raglan-sleeved loose coats falling to mid-thigh. Coats are of black, lined with sky-blue; dark blue, green and brown; coffee, leather color, gray, and tweed mixtures; in single or double-breasted or cape forms.

The top hat changes, c.1855, from the English beaver to the silk hat which the French have learned to waterproof. Its crown takes on a cylindrical stovepipe form with a narrow brim.

Informal felt and straw hats with low crowns and wide brims appear in the 50's, together with a wonderful assortment of visored caps for sports wear: jockey caps, caps with earflaps, caps shaped like those worn today by locomotive engineers, made of striped and plaid materials and tweed and trimmed with fur in cold winters.

Hair is still parted, but the part is often on the right side and approaches the center by 1850. The artificially curled ends of the hair of the mid-30's loosen into waves by the late 40's. In the 50's the hair is cut shorter and plastered down with Macassar oil, against which ladies pin anti-macassars on the backs of chairs.

There were a good many clean-shaven faces during the 40's; the fringe of beard below the jawbone, so characteristic of the 30's, is not continued under the entire chin, by the late 40's. Moustaches ceased to be the exclusive attribute of the English military after the Crimean War; they are seen alone on a clean-shaven face, or with the imperial worn by loyal Bonapartists in imitation of Napoleon III, whose perfect dress is even more influential than that of Victoria's consort Albert.

The new interest in the chin is related to changes in the shirt and collar. Shirts have lost their frill, and have ousted the dickey. They now have an inset bosom of tucked linen.

Made-up cravats go out of fashion before 1850. Their place is taken by a necktie, which is at first rather soft and full, becoming flatter and narrower by the 60's. Four-in-hand ties, and stocks like the Ascot worn by ushers at a wedding today appear by the 60's, worn with a stickpin. The old black stock continues in use by elderly men to 1870, with the collar turned down over it.

The choker collar of 1840 had a shaped top sewed onto a band, so that the collar curved away from the face. The edge begins to turn down; then the choker is largely superseded by a stiff standing collar. In 1848 the collar is very low, uncovering the column of the neck; it becomes higher by 1860; by the 70's the front is tabbed back or cut away to spare the adam's apple, and low, striped, turned-down collars appear.

Laced boots began to replace soft, low Wellington boots in the 50's; buttoned boots appear during the 60's; both begin to have colored uppers. Men change into wool-embroidered slippers in the house.

The use of tobacco is increasing. Cigars are elegant. Snuff loses ground; the low habit of pipe smoking gains during the 60's. Cigarettes had been brought back from the Crimean war and become as socially acceptable as the cigars; in the emancipating years of the 60's women begin to try them. But from the 50's, men retire to another room to smoke, and change there into smoking jacket and cap, which they remove before joining the ladies.

Gold watch chains, from the buttonhole to the watch pocket replace the looped neck-chain of the 40's.

THE 1860's.

During the 60's men's garments lose their shapely elegance. They are less close-waisted, more sack-like and baggy, and are made of thicker, clumsier materials.

The Empress Eugenie continued to exert an influence on costume for a longer time after her marriage in 1853 than did Napoleon III, who was ill for some years before his empire ended in 1870. Alexandra and the Prince of Wales affect fashions after their marriage in 1863; the tailored suit for women was fostered by her, and the eventual King Edward VII was always superbly turned out. But photographs of men of the 60's show a majority looking like seedy old-time American congressmen and Shakespearean actors, in battered stovepipe hats, rather wrinkled coats, and loose, flopping trousers, far removed from the fashion-plate ideal of the period.

Coats, vests, and trousers are now apt to match. Checked trousers and colored odd vests may be worn with sack coats, and striped or light-colored summer trousers with dark, matching frock coats and vests.

Single-breasted sack coats grow longer and more shapeless. Their collars and lapels are small, as coats come to be buttoned high on the chest; the lower buttons are unfastened and the edges of the coat spread or are cut away, often rounded at the corners.

Sleeves widen around the upper and middle arm and narrow toward the wrist, in fashion plates; in actuality, they are apt to appear as rather wide tubes, characterless except for wrinkles.

Frock coats are single or double-breasted, and close high. Their lapels are sometimes faced with dull silk; their tails usually fall very short of the knee.

Evening coats are cut square across the front; their tails are now more sharply cutaway and shorter.

Trousers grow wide and baggy in the middle; the fashionable trouser of the mid-60's remains wide above, but is made very tight about the calf, and there is often a line of braiding along the outseam. In actuality, trousers, especially light summer ones, appear in most photographs as flopping, shapeless and tubular. Knickerbockers appear, worn with sack shooting coats.

The most interesting men's garments of the 60's are the caped cloaks and the overcoats. Cloaks are full, and fall one third to one half way between knee and sole. They are slit at the side for the arms to pass, have a deep cape to the waist or hip line, and often a small velvet collar which hooks together at the neck. Velvet collars are no longer used on suit-coats, but are often seen on long, rather fitted overcoats which have a real elegance, and are sometimes edged with braid.

Waistcoats, fancy or matching the coat and trousers, lose shape as coats do. Double-breasted vests are seen with open frockcoats, but the usual vest is single-breasted, buttoned high like the coat but throughout its length, and is much exposed by the spreading edges of the coat.

Narrow-brimmed silk stovepipe hats, black, white or gray for the races, continue to be worn; crush opera hats appear in the 60's. But wide-brimmed, low-crowned felt hats of the "porkpie" sort become common from the 50's; round bowlers appear with the 70's. These new alternatives to the top-hat's formality reduce the popularity of the cap in the late 60's and the 70's, although there are "deerstalkers" for hunting.

Hair styles of 1860 are extremely varied. The center part of the 50's tends to become a side part from which the hair is combed away flat; however, hair is also seen combed back. The head of hair is full at the ends, which are sometimes waved; the ears come into sight in the 60's. In the beginning of the decade, hair is also rather full in back, although it does not reach the collar, and tends to spring out below the pressure line of the hard hat. But the back of the head is often trimmed as short as it is today.

There are fewer clean-shaven men during the 60's and 70's but there is great latitude in styles and combinations of face hair. Whiskers grow longer and are combed out into mutton chops and "Dundrearys"; full beards appear. Moustaches and beards may be worn alone or in any combination. With the fall of the second Bonaparte Empire, the dashing Imperial is less seen. The long reign of the yellow glove is over; now they run from grays to lavender.

2239A. French XIXc. c. 1800. (Met. Mus. of Art, Print Room.)

Gabriel à Coblentz. Conversation piece: silhouettes on verre églomisé.

Max von Boehn's *Miniatures and Silhouettes** reproduces German cut-out pictures in white set on colored paper, made in 1631; and English examples from 1699. These cut, outline pictures were popular, even before they acquired the name under which they became a mania between 1768-80.

Through Mme. de Pompadour's influence, the post of comptroller-general of French finance was held through seven and a half months of the year 1759 by Etienne de Silhouette (1709-67), who loved cut-out pictures so much that they had been used to decorate a room in his chateau de Brie. Silhouette's popularity was destroyed by his new program of taxes on land and pensions; the nobility found themselves about to be reduced to bare essentials, and among other forms of protest and ridicule, Silhouette's name was given to these pictures of outlines.

---

* E. P. Dutton, N. Y., 1928, 40 col. and 200 black and white illustrations; the source of much of this information.

Their popularity was increased by the excavations of black-figured Greek pottery, and profile busts on ancient coins and cameos, and by the publication of handsomely illustrated works on *Physiognomy* by a German named Lavater, between 1775-8. The long-familiar silhouettes had occurred to Lavater as a way to collect illustrations of his theories; Mme. de Genlis did not believe in them, but interest in them was general and fashionable. Everybody was sentimental, sorrowing with *"Werther"*; Lavater was Goethe's dear friend, so they were eager to send him their silhouette, and perhaps find it used.

The most expertly cut and purest silhouettes are of last third XVIIIc. Then, they begin to be debased and set against shaded backgrounds, often less attractive than Gabriel à Coblentz' method of backing glass with drawn lines and crackled gold.

Graeco-Roman effect on form: chocolate pot and furniture; hair dressed in classical knot with classical comb, necklace and earrings set with cameos; high-waisted, short-sleeved Empire gowns. Man: long tail-coat and boots. Sentimentality: kitten playing with wool.

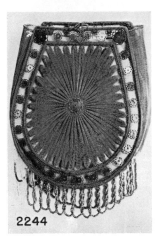

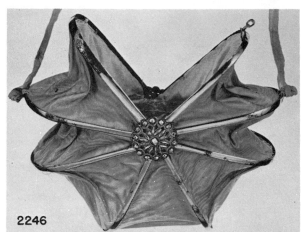

2244

2245

2246

2240. XIXc. 1810-15. French. (Boston, Museum of Fine Arts.)

Printed cotton dress; green, yellow, and red. Plaited straw bonnet. Multicolored straw bag, woven and glued. Handkerchief, dilute brick color and yellow plaid. Gold necklace.

2241. XIXc. c.1800. French. (Boston, Museum of Fine Arts.)

Dress of India gauze shot with silver. Bead "bird cage" bag; greenish-blue and white beads; floral border, and *Ces fleurs vous parlent de moi,* worked in beads.

2242. XIXc. 1810-15. French. (Metropolitan Museum.)

Ball gown; white gauze, silk appliqué.

2243. XIXc. 1825-30. French. (Boston, Museum of Fine Arts.)

Dress of pink and silver shot India gauze; white mull skirt embroidered in pink, dull orange, and black with orange leaves. Netted "miser's" purse in

2247

silk, henna, yellow-green and steel beads, in paisley and cone pattern, with a steel ring. Fan of pierced horn leaves. Necklace and earring set, medallions and chains.

2244. XIXc. c. 1800. French. (Boston, Museum of Fine Arts, Elizabeth Day McCormick Coll.)
Spun steel bag.

2245. Early XIXc. French. (Boston, Museum of Fine Arts.)
Spun steel bag.

2246. XIXc. c. 1800-15. French. (Boston, Museum of Fine Arts.)
Folding bag of beige moiré, with steel frame and cut steel button.

New steel-making techniques in late XVIIIc. made steel jewelry possible. It provided a discreet replacement for the twinkle of diamonds, which had become dangerous in Revolutionary times, and was in any case becoming a little boring to those who could afford diamonds. Cut-steel, often combined with paste and mother-of-pearl, made handsome buttons and buckles, and catered to the desire for luxury of those who had longed for diamonds.

2247. Early XIXc. French. (Boston, Museum of Fine Arts.)
Six beaded and netted "miser's" purses.

2248. Empire Dresses: Left to Right:

French, 1805-10. Cream colored muslin dress embroidered with silver metal thread in all-over floral repeat pattern.

European, 1804-14. Spencer of light brown satin with a self-pattern.

French, 1804-10. Cap of embroidered mull trimmed with tucks and lace.

Italian(?), 1805-10. Dress of gold raw silk.

French(?), 1804-14. Turban of white satin with yellow French knots. Scarf of cream-colored sheer muslin embroidered with drawn work and gold metal thread.

Viennese, 1804-15. Dress of white muslin with vari-colored bead embroidery. Scarf of white muslin with embroidered leaf border.

Spanish(?), 1810-15. Dress of white piña-cloth with multi-colored silk embroidery and sequins.

Viennese, 1804-14. Spencer of green and pink striped satin.

French, 1804-14. Cap of embroidered mull with lace.

2248

2249. XIXc. 1810-30. French.

Man's court coat: Light brown uncut velvet, embroidered in chenille.

2250-51. XIXc. 1804-14. French.

Man's court costume: Coat and vest of purple brocaded velvet, embroidered in silk.

2252. Early XIXc. Italian, Venetian.

Livery coat: Olive green flannel (see Italian, 1750, Longhi).

2253. XIXc. 1810. French.

Woman's court mantle: Red velvet, embroidered in gold; worn by the Princess of Leon at the marriage of Napoleon and Marie Louise.

"Costumes Parisiens"

Dated and numbered plates marked "Costumes Parisiens" come from the *Journal des dames et des modes,* founded in late XVIIIc. by the abbé de la Mésangère. Its plates were re-issued in annual volumes as *Costumes parisiens de la fin du* 18e *siècle et du commencement du* 19e. During more than four decades of life, it absorbed eight other fashion magazines. It is listed in the *Union Catalog of Periodicals* as *Gazette des Salons,* one of the names it bore in its later, weekly, form. Its long life, beautiful plates (of men's as well as women's fashions), and its excellent text make it one of the most important and influential of all fashion magazines.

Descriptive captions on the plates are given in translation.

2254-58. XIXc. French. (Metropolitan Museum, Print Room.)

2254. "Round embroidered *toquet,* cloth Spencer." (1800)

This *toquet* (see No. 2258) is of eyelet embroidered muslin. The combed-down fringe of hair becomes bunched in curls, high on the temples, c. 1820. Muslin dress; cloth Spencer, with sleeves extending over the hand, opens in two long points: the "Chinese" Spencer. Low-cut, heel-less slippers.

2255. "Young man's careless dress." (1802)

Top hat of beaver; wide brim curled at the sides; no hat band. Shaggy head becoming curly; hair extended down the jaw. High, turned-up collar; cravat; *jabot* ruffles are added to the shirt, as the vest opens; low striped vest with standing collar, cut square across the bottom.

The "Jean de Bry" coat, in its later exaggerations of short waist, puffed sleeve-top, and collar climbing up the back of the head, became a favorite butt of caricaturists. This is approximately its original form: a double-breasted cloth coat with three sets of buttons, cut square to show the vest hanging below; tails gradually cut away, falling short of the knee; long, notched lapels, collar climbing high in back; sleeves gathered full at the armseye, and prolonged over the knuckles. Breeches cut full into trousers, but are still very short; they have just been released from being drawn down under the boots by strings, and still have a slit for closing; stockings, low-cut heelless slippers; fob; stick.

2256. "Lace veil. Tunic. Cashmere shawl." (1803)

Indecision of the fringe of hair, which is no longer willing simply to be combed forward and down; locks oiled; veiled in a long, narrow lace scarf. Necklines are still very low, but there is a

strong alternative interest in the base of the throat; a *fraise* or necklace is apt to be worn. Tunics begin to be added to classical gowns, c. 1800. As skirts shorten, the tunic is lost, but decoration is carried up from skirt hems, c. 1815, toward the point at which the tunic used to end. Cashmere shawl, patterned at the ends, with a great deal of white in its border.

2257. "Cloth redingote, trimmed with velvet." (1803)

Cloth redingote with two velvet capes and the tabbed closing taken from men's cloaks. As the warm weather of the first decade XIXc. passes, the redingote is turned into a warm, lined indoor garment, the *douillette,* which has long sleeves and is tied together at intervals by ribbon bows, or hooked together under a line of ruching. The garment and its vertical front line disappear c. 1840 as the new fullness of skirts is emphasized by horizontal trim-

mings. Taffeta hats (see No. 2258); gloves; long embroidered gauze scarf.

2258. "Trimmed hat *(chapeau),* Lingerie bonnets, *Capote* of taffeta with straw lace, *Capote* of taffeta, *Capote* of *Sparterie* and taffeta, Crepe bonnet, Hat of taffeta and straw." (1804)

The categories of e. XIXc. headcoverings overlap and merge in confusion.

Ceremonious headcoverings derive from the *pouf* arranged by the hairdresser on the ceremonious "head" of Marie Antoinette's time, although they are now usually bought ready-made: turbans, *toques, cornettes,* and triangular pinned or tied handkerchief-like arrangements.

Outdoor head coverings fall into the main headings of *chapeau, capote,* and *bonnet.*

The *chapeau* is a hat: it has a crown and a brim, as in Ill. 2257.

The *bonnet* always has a connotation of softness and of ribbon ties under the chin. It has a brim in front, and a rather important crown; it is shirred, corded and gathered into form, rather than stiffened.

The *capote* is a bonnet which consists mostly of its rigid brim, made of straw or boned into shape; it has a soft, gathered crown, and it, too, is tied under the chin. It is the ancestor of grandmother's sun bonnet.

The *toquet* of eyelet embroidery in Ill. 2254 is an intermediate: in the softness of its brim, ruffled edge, prominent crown, and its ties coming from the crown of the head, it is bonnet-like; but its brim is shaped like that of a *capote.*

majas, the girls in the drawings, Doña Teresa and Doña Narcisa, show the entirely different torso which is the foundation of Spanish costume: high-bosomed, with a longer, neat waist, and a swaying back line. It is this body and posture that make Doña Narcisa so triumphantly Spanish, in comparison to the Queen in not dissimilar dress in 1799. Doña Teresa's coat dress is based on the Spanish coat of Bayeu and Martinez.

2261. XIXc. 1806. Spanish. (Brooklyn Museum.)
Goya. Tadeo Bravo de Rivério.
Spanish lapels, collar and cut of shorter-waisted, double-breasted European coat; sword and traditional hat.

2262. XIXc. c. 1800. Scotch. (New York, Duveen.)
Sir Henry Raeburn. Mrs. John Hutcheson Ferguson.

2263. XIXc. 1801-2. Scotch. (New York, J. P. Morgan.)
Raeburn. Miss Rose (Mrs. Bell.)
Triangular scarves, like those which tie on caps in Olivier's *Thé à l'Anglaise* and "half-handkerchiefs" mentioned by Heideloff were the ancestors of the *cornette* headdresses, which were worn throughout the first third XIXc. and affected bonnets into the 1860's. By the 1820's *cornettes* develop into lingerie caps, in which the point has almost disappeared,

2259. XIXc. c. 1801-4. Spanish. (Washington, Nat. Gall. of Art.)
Goya. Doña Teresa Sureda.
2260. XIXc. 1805. Spanish. (Metropolitan Museum.)
Goya. Doña Narcisa Barañana de Goicoechea.
Spanish court dress, and even the Queen's version of national costume in 1799, is influenced by the short-waisted Empire fashions of Europe. All the other Goya women: the duchess of Alba in 1795, the

2266

but they are differentiated from all other caps by being carried under the chin, framing the whole face in a ruffled edge. In the 30's the *cornette* may have become a mere lingerie band with a gauffered edge, tied under the chin, and is sometimes seen as a ruffle under a hat, enclosing the face.

Mrs. Ferguson's *cornette,* midway in development between the tied triangle and the made-up cap, is worn with a Van-Dyked neckline and a narrow India shawl.

Miss Rose: long black lace scarf with inner edge ruffled.

2264. XIXc. c. 1800. U.S.A. (Metropolitan Museum.)
Ezra Ames (1768-1836). Philip van Cortlandt (1749-1831).

The American patriot and statesman of the great New York family shows characteristics of first decade XIXc.: method of notching the longer, rolled collar of a plain dark cloth coat with covered buttons; striped vest with covered buttons, opened to show the sheer jabot. In this case, while the vest has a standing collar, the shirt collar has not risen above the stock. Uneven locks of hair combed forward.

2265. XIXc. c. 1802. U.S.A. (New York Historical Soc.)
C. W. Peale. Mrs. James Madison.

The fragile and scholarly Madison was married in 1794 to Dolly Todd, a plump and charming Philadelphia widow of great social aptitude.

Gauze and metal turban; uneven locks of hair combed forward; *fraise* at throat; short but not close gold chain; narrow lace-edged sheer scarf; pale satin Empire gown, as short-waisted as possible; puffed sleeves to which long sleeves are now often added, unless extremely long gloves are worn.

2266. XIXc. 1803. French. (The Louvre.)
Boilly. The Arrival of the Diligence.

A network of diligence routes now covers Europe. People begin to travel for other reasons than bare necessity. Novels are filled with details of journeys,

since all novel readers have taken or hope to take just such trips as Jorrocks and the Yorkshireman set off on by "the nine o'clock Dover heavy" from the Bricklayer's Arms. Boilly's picture might serve as an illustration for Surtees: "Jorrock's Jaunts and Jollities." Only the pickpocket (who has already been seen in Boilly's *Marche incroyable*) is missing from the crowd of beggars, pedlers, cloaked and top-hatted coachmen, porters, and the soldiers who always appear among the passengers. Since luggage has to be carried on the roof of the coach or in the passenger's hands, it consists of luggage rolls, light *portemanteaux* and boxes, oddments stuffed into pillow cases or tied up in tablecloths, luncheon baskets, and umbrellas.

At the far left, an elderly man of the people wears the double-breasted, sleeveless vest which was brought to Marseilles by workers from Carmagnola in the Piedmont, got to Paris, and as the *carmagnole,* entered the dress of the people and the professional revolutionaries; it can also be seen in the *Marche incroyable.*

The hat *à l'androsmane* is turning into the rigid, flat *chapeau bras.* The officer also shows the braided openings of the front flap of long elastic breeches, through which his sash is run; the way in which these breeches are held in place at the waist when the flap is down is shown by the man who is relieving himself at the coach-wheel. The porter kneeling beside the officer's tasselled Hessian boots wears long trousers, buttoned in gaiter-fashion down the out-seam.

Social differentiations are shown by the heads of women. The elderly woman of the people, and the pretty young fruit vendor with the officers, the nursemaid who kneels to blow the child's nose in the center, and the seated woman who adjusts her little girl's cap, all have their heads covered in ways appropriate to their ages. The mother and older daughter of the middle class family which clamors for

father's notice are above wearing caps; their uncovered hair is twisted in Greek knots.

The most fashionably dressed people stand apart at the right. The lady is dressed with formality: long orange gloves, a pink and white *capote,* a bow of deeper pink on her white dress, which has a knot of pink ribbon appliquéd on the trailing end of the skirt she holds up, showing blue stockings and brown shoes. The early XIXc. is filled with amusing bags; hers is of a pink so deep that it is red, and consists of no more than some tassels sewn around the center of a square which has its corners knotted together. Child in peacock blue. The man, whose hair is extended well down the jowls, carries a crook-headed cane, with yellow-green coat, buff breeches, and black boots with mahogany tops.

2267. XIXc. 1804. English.

Thomas Ryder, after *Sir Thomas Beechey.* Queen Charlotte.

An elderly lady, dressed with complete suitability and complete awareness of the latest style, but no undue regard for what she finds inappropriate in it, has an aura of the 90's. She belongs to a time when short sleeves were ceremonious; neither the current very short or very long tight sleeve suits her so well as the caught and puffed sleeve of the 80's-90's. She has shortened her underskirt very slightly, and tucked up its embroidered overskirt in recognition of the draped overskirts of the first five years of XIXc., but she has retained the waistline, skirt fullness, kerchief and reinforcing long scarf knotted at the waist, trailing overdress skirt, and high-crowned cap of the 90's. She veils her cap with the current lace scarf of an imitation Roman matron.

2268. XIXc. 1804. U.S.A.

Pavel P. Svinin (1787-1839). Sunday morning in front of the Arch Street Meeting House in Philadelphia.

One of several water colors by a Russian who visited Philadelphia shows the costume of Quaker women at a time when its severity blended successfully with classical styles, and even gave their dress

a startling air of advanced fashion. For all its severity, the Quaker bonnet has an exaggerated scoop which the European *capote* will not achieve for several years, and the Friends' skirts are as short as European women's are on their way to becoming in another decade.

Father with his wide-brimmed hat, long hair and XVIIIc. dress is Benjamin Franklin at Louis XVI's court, almost to the life.

2269. XIXc. 1805. French. (Boston, Museum of Fine Arts.) *Debucourt.* Les courses du matin.

The passers-by and waiting crowd, making its morning round of rich patrons' houses, give a clear picture of dress suitable to many occupations.

A coachman waits for the elegant young couple which is being admitted by a servant in a powdered livery-wig. The young gentleman wears a beaver with extravagantly curled brim, cape with two cloaks, light pantaloons buttoned tight at their bottoms, some four inches above the ankle; white stockings, and slippers reduced to a minimum.

His companion shows the disintegration of classical costume. The original tubular, gathered muslin dress has been cut into a fitted bodice with the skirt fullness concentrated under it at the center back. Braids of artificial hair are worked into such an elaboration of "classical" knots and fillets that a bonnet has been achieved; it has a completely unclassical bouquet stuck in the front, and lacks only bonnet-strings; it is undoubtedly a wig.

Five categories of women's wigs are advertised *(Morning Post,* March 18, 1800) by Mr. T. Bowman's remodelled establishment in the West End: the "Tresse à la Grecque, when put over a short headdress, is a complete full dress. Price half-a-guinea, 1, 1½, 2, 3, 4, and 5 guineas." Plate 2 in Gillray's *Progress of the Toilet,* dated 1810, shows a maid about to set a wig on her mistress' clipped head.

In front of the coachman, the driver of a smart equipage decorated with Napoleonic laurel, delivers

boxes for a peruke-maker. There is practically no business left in men's wigs, but women order them in all colors, and change, from red, to black, to blonde, within a matter of hours. All the boxes he carries are addressed to women; one is for Napoleon's mother, Madame Mère. At the left, two delivery-men accept snuff. One carries a magnificent pair of lacquered boots; he wears a bicorne; coat with high collar and large lapels, cut short to show the vest; long striped pantaloons; and English top boots. The other has a striped neckcloth, hoop earrings and a cropped head; he has the look of a convict, freed after long service on the galleys. He carries a bundle of new garments, tied up in the square of cloth which preceded cardboard boxes, and which is still the method by which theatrical costumes are carried.

The man from whom they accept snuff shows the plight in which the hairdressers, as well as the wigmakers, now find themselves. He clings to a powdered, tied wig; wears a striped coat and stockings, with knee-breeches, gaiters, and the apron of his trade. The box which he carries advertises the many other services by which he contrives to live, now that neither ladies nor gentlemen need the services of *Furet, artiste:*—he is also a chemist and cosmetician; he provides elastic corsets, suspenders, stockings, and is a costumer for both sexes.

Behind Furet, a dancing master, in a *hérisson*-cut tie wig, carries a rolled waltz and stands in a carefully arranged position. His collar mounts excessively high in back; his shirt ruffles reach to the bottom of his vest, which has only a button closed; his breeches are cut as high as possible, though they end with knee-strings to show his white-stockinged leg to its full advantage. Beyond him is one of the round felt hats which began to be worn in France at the turn of the century.

A tail-coat and an XVIIIc. coat, worn with knee breeches, are shown on the symphonic composer (5) and the painter (7); long stockinette pantaloons on

the bespectacled architect who carries plans and elevations for doing over an alcove in the currently fashionable Etruscan taste. Beside him, a smart bicorne is set, back to front, in the current fashion, over combed-forward locks.

During the last quarter XVIIIc., after centuries of being dressed like their parents in miniature, children finally achieved clothes designed especially for children. That independence is not maintained in early XIXc. We seldom see such literal carbon copies of grown people as are shown in this picture. Little boys of first half XIXc. do wear sailor suits, little bell-boy jackets, and plaid tam-o'-shanters. But until Dickens' day, children's dress, especially that of girls and of the littlest boys, is strongly affected by adult, especially female styles.

The mother wears an Empire gown with standing ruff and pleated hem, taffeta gloves so long that they have to be tied about the upper arm, and a turban.

The little girl's hair is fileted by a braid, and tied up in a Grecian knot; she has laced sandals, and an Etruscan scarf, sewed part way to her hem and then drawn up over the shoulder.

Her brother's costume is strongly affected by the uniform of the Empire infantryman; his beaver hat with beaked brim lacks only the brush of the Hungarian shako; his vest approximates the light-colored chest piece buttoned onto the uniform, and he wears its high-waisted breeches and boots.

The nursemaid wears the stylized cap of the region of her origin.

The extravagantly artistic amateur of antiquities, carrying a portfolio of sketches, is wrapped in a toga-like cape, and shows the sleeves prolonged over the knuckles, in its most excessive form.

The old author, with the manuscript of a new novel in his pocket, is dressed in seedy XVIIIc. wig, clothes and hat. The ordinary dress of little boys is seen on the pair building card houses, instead of peddling their papers, which are carried in a wicker-work basket, shaped like a Dutch boat.

2270. XIXc. 1807. U.S.A. (Metropolitan Museum.)
Gilbert Stuart. Commodore Isaac Hall.

2271. XIXc. English. (Metropolitan Museum.)
Charles Lucy. Lord Nelson in the cabin of the
"Victory."

This picture, painted in 1853, shows Nelson in
his admiral's uniform in the cabin of the ship on
which he died at Trafalgar in 1805.

2272. XIXc. French (Metropolitan Museum.)
Ingres. Portrait of a Gentleman.

Light gray-brown overcoat; chocolate brown coat;
black beaver bicorne, with white and gold decoration, carried flat under the arm.

**2273. XIXc. 1805-10. French. (Philadelphia, John G.
Johnson Collection.)**
Ingres. Louis Charles Mercier Dupaty.

Very dark green coat; white vest and stockings,
pearl gray breeches, decoration with red ribbon.

In both 2272 and 2273, we see collars to the ears;
immense white knotted cravats; wide ruffles, flattened to one side, show through low opening of
white vests with enormous standing collar and self-
buttons. Their coats have the very high, characteristically notched lapel of c. 1810-15; full upper sleeve,
forced or gathered into armseye. Locks at ears grow
down the face; as the collar recedes, the line of
beard will move down and follow the jawbone.

**2274. XIXc. 1806. French. (New York, Cooper Union
Museum.)**
Debucourt, after *C. Vernet.* Aquatint: Miss Fran-
coni performing at the Cirque Olympique, Paris.

Rosalie was the granddaughter of Antonio Franconi, the founder of the Paris hippodrome.

Sea-bathing became immensely popular by the
beginning of XIXc. Theatrical people made the resort of Cabourg their own. The Goncourts, who
visited it in 1863, found it a "singular place—like a
fairy show," where La Franconi had a "chocolate
colored chateau flanked by four towers like English
privies."

Rosalie is, naturally, costumed as an amazon. Her
assistants wear either a semi-military uniform with
a forage cap; or a version of the poetic Reform costume seen in the *Fishing Party,* Ill. 2236.

The lady in the taffeta gloves and *capote* carries a
cashmere shawl with the white ground which was at
first preferred. Her muslin dress is less developed
than that of the caller in Ill. 2269; its bodice and
skirt are separately cut, but the goring of the back
of the bodice has not eliminated all fullness.

2275. XIXc. French. (Metropolitan Museum.)
Aubrey-Lecomte, H., after *Juinne.* Mme. Récamier
in her apartment.

Although this print was produced in 1827, it
shows Madame Récamier in the style she made her
own in first decade XIXc. Empire room with a rose-
bush growing in a newly excavated antique urn.

**2276-79. XIXc. 1806. French. (Metropolitan Museum,
Print Room.)**
"Costumes Parisiens," (periodical).

2276. "Flower decorated comb; ball dress; *palatine*
edged with martin."

2277. "Straw *capote;* little Scotch plaid fichu;
walking dress."

2278. *"Capote* with a crown of puffs; Bagnières shawl."

2279. "Yellow straw hat, tied with an organdie fichu; dress trimmed with little tongues of cotton material."

In these four fashion plates, the new trends announce themselves. Hem trimmings have been used on gowns throughout the Classical Revival. Although any of the forms is likely to be seen at any part of the period, the trend of trimming has been a deterioration of fringe into pleating, and of pleating into gathered ruffles.

The Classical gown first lost its repetition of vertical lines in its front fullness. Pleats were massed in back and kept vertical by the weight of dragging trains; this is the time at which hems were least decorated (2266, 2280). By a new impulse, trains begin to be cut off; skirts are shortened, and pressure from the back fullness makes hems flare at the side. This new horizontal line is emphasized by ruffles and lines of notched Gothic decoration at the hem. There is a sash around the waist; the round neckline begins to turn square. More lines are cut across the body by the new short capes. The ubiquitous narrow scarf becomes squarer, and is often carried for its color, rather than worn. The bosom is still exposed, but a handkerchief is knotted about the throat or a sheer cape falls in tiers from a *fraise.*

Classical purity begins to degenerate; combs are decorated with the little bouquets which are carried or fastened onto every costume. Curls fall down the jaw, like the sideburns of men; braids which used to filet the head slip to the forehead in an approximation of the coronet of the Napoleonic court. The classical sandal turns into a laced shoe. Greek and Etruscan patterns give way to Scotch plaids, and locally made shawls (2278) compete with oriental.

2280. XIXc. 1807. French. (Yousoupoff Coll.)
Boilly. Billiard Game.

Billiards is one of the oldest games, but it was for centuries restricted to the very rich. Public billiard halls had been licensed since mid-XVIIc, but the Revolution gave an impetus to life outside the home, and billiards, "which gives at once activity to the limbs and grace to the person" (*Morning Post,* 1809), became very fashionable at the beginning of the XIXc. both with men and women. In an age of wagers on competitions of all sorts: cocking, bull-baiting, prize fights and horse races, billiards became the favorite betting game.

Beautifully established women were another aristocratic luxury, like fine food, which the Revolution made available upon occasion, to anyone who had the price. A series of extremely elegant and business-like prostitutes help to take men away from home in XIXc. Women, curious rather than jealous about these superbly dressed and emancipated legendary creatures, also go to public places, hoping to catch a glimpse of them. (See Appendix.)

A delightful early photograph shows a gentleman of the 50's playing billiards with four cocottes who are inmates of a very grand establishment.

The whole family, including the children and dogs, goes to the billiard parlor. Mothers and grandmothers keep on the mob caps and fichus of middle age and domesticity. The gowns worn by the young girls have reached their highest point of arrogant, completely untrimmed nakedness. They are worn with a minimum of underwear; trains drag out the lines of the longest young bodies ever exhibited. But the costume, though provocative, is still dewy-fresh, uncontaminated by the shame which is about to emerge and alter it.

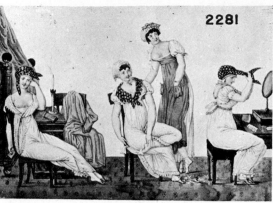

Hair has grown prettier; it is twisted, rather than braided and bound, into Greek knots which end in loose curls; the hair about the forehead, which was at first jaggedly fringed, then frizzed, now falls in pretty corkscrew curls.

2280A-2281. XIXc. French. (Met. Mus., Print Room.)
Print Room.)
"Le Bon Genre," (periodical).
The "Bon Genre's" first edition, 104 plates, appeared in 1817. The 1822 edition included eleven additional plates; a third edition was published in 1827. Its illustrations are lively and witty statements of the life of Paris since the beginning of XIXc., with a text of explanatory paragraphs, rather than fashion plates.
   2280A. Lingerie bonnet-makers (1807).
   2281. Grisettes getting ready for bed (1807).

These sewing girls in workshop and dormitory have learned to make clothes for themselves, as charming as the quilted capotes they turn out for the customers (2364-68). The folded scarves, colored and fringed, which they wear about their shoulders, have become the uniform of working women. They are warm and gay, and are tied around the cap to protect it in bed or out of doors, where the lower bourgeoisie (into the XXc.) do not wear hats. The deviations from the persistent cap of working women, shown in Lanté-Gatine plates of 1825, advertise wares which the hat-seller and artificial hair worker provide for their customers. Aprons, worn by working women with simple dresses of plain or printed cotton, begin to be carried up onto the bodice in bibs; but working women long retain the high waistline because of the convenience of the bibless apron set under the armpits. Hems are trimmed with narrow lines of embroidery, or braided, corded, scalloped or ruched.

The necklines of these working girls, like those of the upper classes, tend to be filled in or covered by *fraises,* multiple capes or standing ruffs. One works in long taffeta gloves, the fingers cut away to make mitts. Front laced shoes, strapped and tied slippers, heelless mules at bedtime.

2282. XIXc. Aug. 22, 1807. French. (Versailles National Museum.)
J. B. Régnault. Marriage of Jerome Bonaparte and Catherine of Württemberg.

2283. XIXc. c. 1807. French. (Versailles National Mus.)
A. J. Gros. Catherine, Queen of Westphalia.

2284. XIXc. French. (Rome, Prince Scipione Borghese.)
F. P. S. Gérard. Prince Camille Borghese.

Some of Napoleon's siblings had married as they wished, before he was in a position to control their choice. He arranged marriages for the rest, and a magnificent one for himself, and set his family on the thrones of Holland, Naples, Westphalia, Spain and Tuscany between 1806-8. The costume of these courts was that of Napoleon's.

His gay and beautiful sister Pauline, widow of Gen. Leclerc, was married in 1803 to Prince Borghese. She soon left him and Rome, but friction with the new Empress sent her from the Paris court in 1810.

Jerome Bonaparte, returning from the West Indies by way of the United States, fell in love with a Miss Patterson of Baltimore and married her in 1803, when he was nineteen. Their marriage was legal in the U. S. A., and the Pope refused to dissolve it. Napoleon excluded his brother's wife from his empire; she went to London where she bore the son from whom the Bonapartes of Baltimore are descended. The marriage was annulled by imperial decree and Jerome was made King of Westphalia on his marriage to the Princess of Württemberg. Their daughter was the Goncourts' adored Princess Matilda, the center of a circle of the greatest literary men in Paris from 1850. Marcel Proust offered to act as her secretary for the memoir he could never persuade her to write, before she died, very old, in 1904.

In England, where court life had not been interrupted by Revolution, the hoop continued to be required in women's official dress. The attempt to combine contemporary fashions with hoops, and to drape an Empire dress, somehow, over a hoop that now had to start at the armpits, became so ridiculous that the use of hoops was abandoned in 1820. (See Appendix.)

The traditional cutaway frock coat continued to be worn at the English court, together with waistcoat, knee breeches, buckled shoes and sword. The coat was simple and untrimmed and followed contemporary fashions with proper dignity.

Napoleon needed for his Empire a gorgeous court costume which should be totally divorced from that of the previous regime.

2282

2283

2284

He borrowed some usages from the great days of the XVIIc.; the ruff, *rabat,* rosetted shoe and plumed hat, for men. Rank was rigidly indicated by neck-wear and by the amount of massive embroidery. The Emperor's costume was set apart from that of his gorgeous court by its ostentatious simplicity. His brothers' and brothers-in-law's garments are stiff with embroidery; Napoleon's coat has only the simple laced seams of the XVIIc.; he wears a plain, sheer cravat, negligently knotted, in place of their lace ruffs and *rabats.*

The men wear a slender velvet tunic or cutaway coat, reaching almost to the knee, blazing with metal in oak, laurel or palm leaves, and sun rays. It has a high standing collar, close sleeves and a sash about the waist, from which the sword hangs; a matching circular cape with an important collar; knee breeches, silk stockings and rosette-trimmed pumps.

A collar of toothed lace, like that of the XVIIc. wired ruff, is added to the contemporary white classical gown of women. Its neckline is cut square across the front; it has short puffed sleeves. The Empress' arms are bare; her ladies wear long gloves or have an additional close sleeve to the waist. The whiteness of the dress is made impressive by elaborate silver embroidery about the hem and narrow lines of vertical embroidery running up to the waistline. A narrow court train of brilliant velvet (flame, green, purple), lined with white and blazing with a border of silver embroidery, is fastened around the high waist, with a medallion closing at the center front in Napoleonic leaves, Etruscan and Egyptian patterns, (see Ill. 2253.) A glittering diadem, matching comb, earrings, and necklace accompanies the court gowns. A great many of these complete *parures* of diamonds, amethysts and other cut stones, are still to be seen, in the case specifically made to hold and display them. French court costume retained this whiteness through the last court of Eugenie, although the gown altered with the fashions.

The Queen of Westphalia's riding dress shows a combination of Napoleonic embroidery at its hem; a XVIIc. bonnet with the brush decoration which the wars of XVIIc. introduced from eastern Europe; together with lines of ermine which on the sleeve approximate XVIIc. slashings, and on the chest the horizontal braided decorations of the uniforms of XIXc. Hungarian mercenaries (which affect men's, women's and boys' coats in first half XXc.).

2285. XIXc. 1808. French. (Metropolitan Mus.)
Ingres. Lady and boy.

Drawn in Rome, with the Villa Medici and the Trinitá del Monte in the background (detail).

2286. XIXc. 1809-10. French. (Met. Mus., Frick Coll.)
David. Comtesse Daru.

2287. XIXc. 1812. French. (Germantown, Henry P. Mc-Ilhenny.)
Ingres. Comtesse de Tournon.

2288-92. XIXc. 1808-9. French. (Met. Mus., Print Room.)
"Costumes Parisiens" (periodical).

2288. *"Cornette* of embroidered muslin. Robe of *toile de Jouy."* The *cornette,* worn for day or evening, is a cap derived from a triangle. It is tied under the chin, and, in this case, also has "horns" fastened back over the crown. More figured materials, now in darker colors.

2289. "Glossy hair dressed with flowers. Decorated tulle robe."

2290. "Cossack attire."

Classical overdress turning into a long, coat-like overgarment, in which vertical lines and front closing are maintained, as in redingotes; these dresses are usually called "Circassian" or "Russian."

2291. "Coat with a single row of buttons. Leather breeches." Men's coats and women's gowns follow the same impulse toward lowered waistlines. Black hat; beige-gray coat; hose and white striped vest; white breeches; black boots with tan tops.

2292. "Hair dressed in braids. Corset *à la Ninon."* Gillray's *Progress of the Toilet,* Plate 1 (2295) shows the English corset of 1810 to be long and lank, extended below the buttocks. The French corsets define the new, longer, but much more closely laced waist; and are cut shorter, since skirts begin to spread into gores.

In 1802, "the celebrated Madame Récamier . . . created a sensation, partly by her beauty, but still more by her dress, which was vastly unlike the unsophisticated style, and *poke* bonnets, of the English women. She appeared in Kensington Gardens, *à l'antique,* a muslin dress clinging to her form like the folds of drapery on a statue; her hair in a plait at the back, and falling in small ringlets around her face, and greasy with *huile antique;* a large veil thrown over her head, completed attire, that not unnaturally caused her to be followed and stared at."

(Countess of Brownlow: *Slight Reminiscences of a Septuagenarian,* London, 1867.)

Under the influence of *huile antique,* the hair on the crown of the head becomes smooth, and is parted rather than drawn back. The fringe at the forehead is artfully arranged in little scallops and curls, which are glossy with oil. The fringe is becoming massed at the forehead in a bunch (2289), which follows the crown's tendency to become parted (2286, 2287). Little clipped tabs of hair (2290) commemorate the loose locks which used to fall at the ears (2279). Ears become uncovered, and the old dangling lock is commemorated by drop earrings (2286). Braided wigs (2292) and flowers (2286), arranged around the low line at which the court diadem had been set, begin to be abandoned; hair arrangements become more stylized, less decorated; and bunches of curls again begin to obscure the ears (2287).

The supremacy of unadorned, white, vertical dress is ended.

The skirt continues its transition into a ∧-shape, as its hem-line is reinforced by more ruffles, bands, zig-zag decorations and ruchings. The front panel of (2289) has taken its outline from the vertical lines of embroidery on the court skirt, but its net trim carries the eye from center front towards the shoulders and the side seams of the hem. The vertical lines of embroidery have begun to disintegrate in other ways. The motifs which composed the lines separate and move to right and left; all-over patterns result (2294); these become common on the new colored cottons (2288, 2290). Dark satin and velvet are used for ceremonious dresses (2287). The neckline is still wide and horizontal, but the low V-opening (2287) announces itself in the triangular *pelerine* collar of (2288); and in the diagonally folded square scarf, and the chain ending in a pendant just at the center-front of the belt of the plump Roman lady (2285).

This line will become extended into the widest shoulders ever seen, in the 30's, over leg-o'-mutton sleeves. The Countess Daru's bodice is short and square-necked; horizontal folds are already forming above the belt; and the eye is drawn to the shoulders by the crumpled subdivisions of her puffed sleeve; other short sleeves are finished with bows (2288, 2289). Then we see the waistline lengthening, and the fabric above it rucked up into deliberate folds, which are extended into the fullness of subdivided sleeves. In the gown of Madame Le Blanc (Ill. 2342) the fullness is drawn up under a corded center line which stresses the new impulse to separate the breasts.

There is an impulse to raise necklines and lengthen sleeves (2287, 2288, 2290). The standing ruff of lace on the court gown plays a part in forming both the new V-neck and the notched, toothed, or zig-zag lines of Gothic decoration (collar and cuffs in 2290; *palatine,* 2288). The "Stuart" or "Vandyke" ruffs are moved to the new, high-necked, long-sleeved dresses (2288, 2290). To some extent, the ruff replaces the *fraise,* and the long sleeve takes the place of gloves; it is trimmed at the wrist with lingerie **cuffs** (2290) or ribbon bows and ruching (2287).

The transition of lace, back into the fabric from which it originated, continues, largely in the form of eyelet embroidery.

Necklaces change character, become more massive and drop lower. The old multiple fine chains, looped to a few medallions, turn into a series of linked flat ovals of decreasing size (2282, 2286), classical medallions are replaced by cut, colored stones, often amethyst or topaz, surrounded by pearls; these in turn become outmoded as necklines rise. The old bead choker or chain grows longer and indicates the centre-front of the belt by its cross or enamelled pendant (2289). Chains increase in length and are looped up again to the watch pinned to the belt (2342).

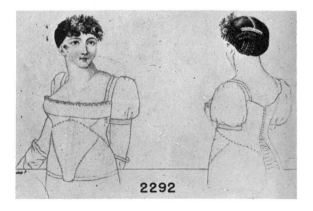

2293. XIXc. 1809. French. (Metropolitan Museum, Print Room.)

P. Debucourt. The Dance Mania.

The belt has momentarily become interesting; it is elaborated into corselets, which push up the breasts, define their separation, make them interesting in a fresh way. Then the corselets are forgotten. Necklines are cut excessively low to exhibit the pair of breasts; shirred up to stress their separateness. On high-necked daytime dresses, scarves are crossed to emphasize the breasts individually (see Ills. 2296, 2300-01).

Very short dancing skirts, garlanded around the hem with flowers in high relief, are much used, 1810-15 (2294). Women's hair sometimes clipped like a man's during first decade. Hair dressed with artificial braids, bouquets, close interlaced caps; bonnets; *capotes* and a hat with a crown of hinged pleats, made of diagonally striped taffeta (seated, doorway). Infantryman and man with immense decorated *chapeau bras*. Folding *lorgnon* used by man in checked vest (background, l.). Exaggerated Jean de Bry coat, with striped breeches (ext. r., foreground).

2294. XIXc. March 13, 1810. French. (Versailles, National Mus.)

Mme. P. Auzou. Marie Louise of Austria taking leave of her family.

Hair dressed *à la grecque* with braids and coronets; or parted into ringlets with flowers.

Ceremonious dress: wired XVIIc. ruff; embroidered all-over patterns; slightly gored skirts; hems edged with lace ruffle, large projecting flowers, or beaded decorations; long gold chains, looped up to a pendant or watch at belt.

Officer in court dress; tasselled Hessian or Suvaroff boots.

2295. XIXc. 1810. English. (New York Public Library, Print Room.)

James Gillray, after an amateur. Progress of the Toilet: Series of three plates. 1. *The Stays.*

2296   2297   2298

2299

The long English corset, which the French ridicule for decades to come, in the "Bon Genre."

2296-98. XIXc. 1811-12. French.

"Costumes Parisiens" (periodical).

2296. "Virginia hat. *Douillette* of Florentine taffeta." Hat crowns rise to accommodate the hair. Trimmings are bold and imaginative; here ribbon is made of strips of the bonnet's straw bound in taffeta. The second decade of XIXc. is rather consecutively cold. The *douillette* is a soft "cuddly" interlined dress, with long sleeves and a high neck; it retains the long front closing and untrimmed hemline of the whole *redingote-douillette* series of garments. Its sleeves show sectioning and puffing, which will be released to form full leg-o'-mutton sleeves. Standing collar of embroidered muslin which has completely replaced lace.

2297. *"Bandeau* of diamonds; robe of Lyons silk." Increased use of cut precious stones. Hair massed on the top of the head with tall combs. "Vandyke"

collar now two wired sections, prepared to be bent over in the fantastically projecting wings of the 20's. The looms which Jacquard introduced at Lyons in e.XIX are producing corded and textured fabrics with a minimum of the hand labor which used to be required. The classical-Napoleonic laurel leaves have now become puffed decorations; naturalistic nosegays stuck at intersections of puffing.

2298. Man: plaid cravat; striped vest; coat collar lower, thrusting out from the neck in back; waist longer; skirts less cutaway, fall rather full and short. Breeches, now recognizably trousers, still keep side-closing slit, though it cannot be closed; trousers are not yet strapped under the shoesole. Hair extended along jaw.

Woman: the sleeve seen on the *douillette* (2296) done in corded cotton on a summer dress. Scalloped standing collar and trim of eyelet embroidery which divides the breasts and is set (prophetically, see Ill. 2297) around the armseye. Tucked hem. Eyelet embroidery sash and handkerchief. When flowers are used to trim summer hats, they are like these sprays of lilac, as bold as the straw braid or feather trimmings; the character of flowers on gauzy evening garments is entirely different (2297).

2299. XIXc. 1811. French.

"Le Bon Genre" (periodical). Guessing the Kiss.

The neat braid-trimmed wigs, which came to be set over women's clipped heads and hanging locks of the first five years of the XIXc., result in natural hair, neatly and carefully dressed, smoothed and coiled. Pretty domestic dresses with necklines widened by crossed scarf and sleeves given new importance by cap or ruching around armseye.

Familiar man's dress with velvet collars.

2300-01A. XIXc. French. (Metropolitan Museum, Print Room.)

"Costumes Parisiens" (periodical).

2300. "Open-work straw hat. Percale dress." (1812)

2301. "Hat of *gros de Naples*. Dress and pantalettes of percale." (1813)

"Women's drawers in e.XIXc. (as shown in Gillray's *Progress of the Toilet,* Ill. 2295) were knit knickers of cotton or wool. Ankle-length lingerie pantalettes came to Paris with the English fashions for active little girls, c. 1807. Their embroidered ruffles were sometimes also seen under women's short dresses, c. 1809-17. Drawers do not appear to have become an established part of women's dress until late first third XIXc. (P. Dufay: *Le Pantalon Féminin,* 1906.) Little girls wore pantalettes for about the first two-thirds of XIXc., but by 1860 they had grown shorter and plainer.

Both the girl and woman show standard summer dress: brightly colored hat of straw or taffeta; the bold outline of its high crown and curved bonnet-like brim is never confused by the imaginative trimmings, which usually give it emphasis. *Gros de Naples* is a corded silk. Lace, when made out of straw, has a character which accords well with the eyelet embroidery with which dress hems are trimmed. Colored scarf, crossed to emphasize breasts individually, and knotted in back.

2301A. "Hat of uncut velvet. Merino *redingote.*" (1813)

Textured materials (gros de Naples, lace straw, seen above) are preferred for simply trimmed, boldly designed hats, like this exaggeration of the plumed uniform hat of the infantryman, done in uncut velvet which has the texture of Turkish towel-

2301A

ling. The triply collared English coat which has been in use for thirty years, is shorter and has a standing collar and ruff, and a greatly enlarged upper sleeve.

2302. XIXc. 1814. French.

Ingres. Seated Lady.

High smooth hair arrangements in braids and loops at the crown force the high crowns of the hats seen in the fashion plates above. Increasing importance, elaboration, and height of the collar; diagonal closing of bodice, influenced by crossed scarves (above). Sleeve much wider and fuller at shoulder.

2303. XIXc. 1812. French. (Versailles, National Mus.)

F. P. S. Gérard. Joachim Murat, King of Naples.

The arrogant male beauty and magnificent uniforms of one of the most brilliant of all cavalry leaders, Napoleon's companion-at-arms and brother-in-law, helped to establish his popularity as King of Naples in 1808, succeeding Joseph Bonaparte. In 1812, he is the commander of the Grand Army and is not yet quite involved in the network of treachery— his own, Austria's, and England's, which will bring him to his death in 1815. His sons lived and married in the U. S. A.; one was postmaster of Tallahassee, Florida; the other returned to France and recognition by Napoleon III during the Second Empire.

The incomparable cavalry, which Matthias of Hungary had established in XVc. to fight the Turks, spread as mercenaries and made their own hussar uniform the cavalry uniform of all European armies: a fur busby with a high brush; braided jacket; loose fur dolman hung on the left shoulder; hussar boots with tassels.

Men, women and children borrow from this idea-filled costume during first half XIXc. Especially during the period of the Napoleonic cavalry's most brilliant achievement, 1806-15, civilians wear fur-lined coats with frogged and braided chests; fur hats; breeches decorated on the thighs along the front flap opening by hussar patterns in braid, or in quilting which was very effective on leather. The braided outseam of today's dress trouser is a remnant of the hussar uniform.

2303

2305

2304

2306

2304. XIXc. 1814. French. (Versailles, National Mus.)

A. J. Gros. Duchesse d'Angoulême.

Louis XVI's daughter, the most important woman at court after her uncle's accession, shows the court costume of Louis XVIII to be simply a development of that established by Napoleon.

The ruff has been flattened into a wide collar; sleeves are enlarged and elaborated; fabric of the bodice gathered up above the belt; increase of all-over embroidery; ermine-lined train.

2305. XIXc. 1815. French. (Versailles, National Mus.)

French School. Lazare Carnot.

The great military engineer who had voted for Louis XVI's death, offered his services to Napoleon during the Hundred Days (Spring of 1815). He defended Antwerp and was made a peer (as we see him in Napoleonic court costume) just before Louis XVIII's second restoration, upon which he emigrated to Germany. His son was an eminent French statesman; his grandson a president of the Third Republic.

2306. XIXc. 1818. French. (Versailles, National Mus.)
Théodore Géricault. Louis, King of Holland, and his son, Napoleon III.

First Empire dragoon uniform, so short-waisted that a vest must be worn with it. Hussar's uniform with braided pattern on the thighs, which are appropriated to civilian use.

2307. XIXc. 1812. Scottish. (Edinburgh, National Gallery.)
Raeburn. Col. Alastair Macdonel of Glengarry.

Fashion felt the impact of Scottish national dress when it began to appear among the frock coats of the English court. Reforms in Scottish representation increased the number of tartans seen in England and their influence on fashion, after 1833.

Clan costume was a relatively late development, scarcely known before the XVIIc. Before 1600, the Gaels of Scotland "wear, like the Irish, a large and full shirt, coloured with saffron, and over this a garment hanging to the knee, of thick wool, after the manner of a cassock." (N. d'Arfeville, cosmographer to Francis I, after visiting Scotland in late XVIc.)

Moryson, who gives a great deal of information about the dress of both sexes and all classes in city and country, in both Ireland and Scotland, found the Irish in the "remote parts," c. 1600, going naked except for a cloak; the shirts of the rest of Ireland were "coloured with saffron to avoid lowziness, incident to the wearing of fowle linen." Standards of cleanliness were notoriously low in Scotland as well, but by Moryson's time, country men and "inferiour citizens" in Scotland wear "cloakes made of a course stuffe of two or three colours, in Checker worke, vulgarly called Plodan. Husbandmen" wear "gray or 'skie' homespun and blew caps very broad," he says, apparently trying to make the necessary differentiation between the dress of Highland and Lowland Scots.

The clan badge, which long antedated the tartan, was a sprig of some common plant, usually evergreen, like the oldest badge—the boxwood of the MacPhersons, holly, hawthorne, broom, yew, myrtle, club-moss; or a common flower like sunflower or foxglove.

The tartan, peculiar to the Highlands, seems to have begun as a regional distinction, and to have become differentiated between clans—men of the same name and blood, from the patriarchal chief down to his least vassal, using the same tartan, badge, and war-cry. Tartans became elaborated among clans: the chief's tartan, worn by him and his heir; the common tartan; and dress and hunting tartans.

The first clear reference to Highland tartans occurs in the bills for James V's hunting costume in 1538 for *"variant cullorit* velvet to be the Kingis Grace ane *schort Heland coit"* and some *"Heland tertane."* In 1587, Hector MacLean, heir of Duart, paid rent for the island of Islay with 60 ells of cloth in the colors of the Duart hunting tartan.

By e.XVIIc., the saffron shirt was replaced by the *breacan-féile* or belted plaid, and the *féile-beg,* or little kilt. The former was a twelve-ell length of tartan, partly pleated and belted into a kilt, with the remainder carefuly draped up over the shoulder, pinned in place there, and allowed to hang down in back. The kilt was six ells long, pleated and crossed over in front; it remains in modern Highland dress, while the long belted plaid has been replaced by a coat and scarf.

Every detail of Highland costume, for all occasions, its accessories and the methods of wearing them, has become rigidly established by convention, and can only be summarized briefly: Blue bonnet, with clan badge and other decorations; scarlet garters, correctly knotted. Doublet with characteristic diamond or lozenge-shaped buttons, made of cloth, velvet, or tartan cut on the bias; kilt; shawl or long shoulder plaid (the latter always removed before entering a ballroom); plain or tartan hose (the pattern again on the bias here). All tartans used in a costume must belong to one clan. In dress use, the dress tartan must be used throughout. Low buckled black shoes; goatskin sporran; claymore and dirk. All belt and shoe buckles, all metal ornaments and mountings, must show identical Gaelic patterns, and belong to a set. Antique muzzle-loading pistol; powder-horn, carried on the right side, mouthpiece forward. (See Appendix.)

2308-09. XIXc. 1814. French. (Metropolitan Museum, Print Room.)
Vernet-Gatine. "Incroyables" (periodical plates).

Horace Vernet's "Incroyables" and "Merveilleuses," engraved by G. J. Gatine, are as good fashion plates as ever were made; the only difficulty is in deciding what to omit. Original captions are quoted in translation.

2308. "Hat with narrow, flat brim. Cravat with colored border. Gilet of matelassé piqué. Short coat with square tails set low. Boots with steel-shod heels."

The black hat now has a narrow ribbon, finished in back by a buckled bow. Red bordered cravat. Yellowish-brown vest of one of the new *matelassé* fabrics. Slate gray coat has a collar, stitched into standing (instead of boned), and therefore able to roll away from the neck, in the new impulse; shoulder seam drawn far down the back; waistline tightened and then prolonged so unnaturally low, with pockets set on the buttocks, that the coat rides up into wrinkles around the waist; cuffs with buttoned closing. Blue-gray breeches; black Hessian boots with small, high, clicking heels (after years of gliding in heelless pumps).

2309. "Breeches and gaiters of natural colored leathers. Cane-umbrella."

Green umbrella, lined with yellow-green. Yellow vest striped in green; highest possible standing collar, self-covered buttons. Vest has grown longer and more tightly fitted at the waist, so that it, too, rides up in wrinkles. Gray coat, matching buttons. Collar rolling back from the neck begins to show the rounded bosomy curve of the coming era

low pocket-flap, spyglass. The dangling fob has grown uninteresting; seals hang at a buttonhole, through which a heavy link chain runs to the watch pocket. Leather breeches with buttoned side pocket; leather gaiters strapped to breeches.

2310-14. XIXc. 1814. French. (Met. Mus., Print Room.)
Vernet-Gatine. "Merveilleuses" (periodical plates).

2310. *"Capote* of écru percale. Scotch plaid fichu and boots. Percale umbrella."

The light brown *capote* has a brim hinged like a *calash,* in an impulse which we have already seen expressed in the crown of a hat. The *fraise* has been expanded into a flat triple ruff, since the daytime neckline must now be high; the elaboration of the lingerie collar has been moved to the sleeve-cap as its importance grows. The X-sash has grown so wide that it composes the entire red, yellow and green tartan bodice, the closing of which becomes diagonal. Yellow-green gloves; red-edged handkerchief. Notched and tucked lines of decoration mount higher as the skirt is shortened to show red, blue and yellow tartan boot, finished with red and yellow ruffles.

2311. "Velvet hat. Merino *Redingote* lined with astrakhan."

Increasing dominance of the hat; black velvet. Collar of poison-green redingote quilted, in a zigzag pattern, into standing and rolling; lined with lemon yellow. Enlargement of sleeve toward leg-o'-mutton shape.

2312. "Percale *capote* surmounted by a gauze fichu. Percale dress. Lace stockings."

The clean, severe lines of hats and bonnets deteriorate; this shirred crown is tied with a twisted pink and white fichu; the ruffle at the back of the *capote* replaces an important collar. Growing importance of the sash, especially in back, and elaboration of its pink and white ribbon. Increased use of tucks. Pink slipper with white lace stockings.

2313. "Hat *à l'Anglaise.* Spencer *à l'Anglaise.*"

Plain English style. Hat with straw lace edge shows the increased mass of the ringlets on either side of the forehead. Pink-on-pink fichu tied around a sort of *fraise.* Long-waisted pink spencer with very long but comparatively narrow sleeves. Green gloves; gray parasol with white fringe; lemon yellow laced boots.

2314. "English hat. Ninon robe."

Wonderful black and white costume. Puffed bodice stresses separation of the breasts and spreads the neckline wide at the shoulders. Fullness is maintained by twisting the sheer crisp ninon of the very long, wide sleeve, and tying it at the wrist.

2315-17. XIXc. 1815-16. French.

"Le Bon Genre" (periodical).

2315. English and French Costumes.

2316. English dress.

A number of "Bon Genre" plates of 1814 and 1815 make fun of English dress. The "disgrace of English women's little flat hats, long lank corsets, and badly cut skirts" can be seen throughout the unsophisticated, dowdy illustrations of *Ackermann's Repository.* The "Bon Genre" (with No. 2315) says it is only necessary to set them beside the contrast of "our Parisiennes" to have a caricature ready-made. The text of Ill. 2316 remarks that a visit to Paris has somewhat improved the appearance of one Englishwoman (r). Her tasselled hat will appear in Ackermann in March, 1816.

The "Bon Genre" delights in caricaturing Englishmen: their long jaws; protruding rumps; uniforms; and extravagantly cut coats—too long, too short, too narrow, or too tight; and their heavily strapped squire's boots, which the French are abandoning after taking them from the English in the first place. The English now offend by a new style, shown on the officer (Ill. 2316, r.): "If one saw only *one* of these Englishmen with pantaloons over boots, one would be tempted to think he had lost his mind or memory, but among these gentlemen it is a general fashion." Within a couple of years, the French and everyone else will wear pantaloons over boots, and continue for decades to do so. It is entertaining to notice how many Paris shops will soon be run by "Mr." or "Mrs.", or be called "La Belle Anglaise."

2317. The beautiful café-keeper.

The Revolution tossed a great many chefs out to fend for themselves. They set up in whatever cellars they could afford at the only trade they knew. Aristocratic food became available, for the first time, to any passerby with the price of a meal. Such food was one of the factors which drew people from home into public places in XIXc.; fine cooking soon became generally assimilated into French existence, and the tradition of wonderful food to be found in unexpected holes-in-the-wall has never quite died out after a hundred and fifty years. But the ex-chef of a prince, prospering as a restaurant-keeper, could soon offer luxurious surroundings as well, which were as great a revelation as his food to the man-in-the-street. The throne on which the café-keeper sits dispensing lemonade had cost 12,000 francs and "passed" from an Italian palace to restaurant use after a bribe of 4,000 francs.

The seated gentleman shows the style which will be current in the 20's: hair combed forward from the crown, and up into a quiff; line of hair continued down the jaw as the collar grows lower to expose it. White collar replaced by a black satin dickey which rises into a rather high fitted collar,

all cut from one bias piece or two strips folded over and pinned. Rolling collar, arched wide around the bosom. Wide, sloping shoulders, close-fitting sleeve set on a low armseye. Shaped torso with skirts separately cut, swinging in a curve over the rump, and cut away with a curve at the sides. Long glove-fitting trousers, which will soon be strapped under the elegant black boots, have a braided outseam. Top hat with slender conical crown, and narrow brim which tends to grow wider during the 30's and 40's. Boots show the new, shaped high heel.

Café-keeper's parted hair, sleek against the head, is piled in tall loops, supported by combs, on the crown of the head. Her other customer wears the high-crowned hat required by this hairdress; knotted plaid scarf between *fraise* and multiple cape-like sleeve caps of her *redingote*.

2318-20. XIXc. 1816-17. French. Metropolitan Museum, Print Room.)

"Costumes Parisiens" (periodical).

2318. "Embroidered muslin *cornette*. Morning dress."

The *cornette's* closing under the chin has been elaborated into a *fraise,* since the neck must not be uncovered; and the collar of the dress has been spread wide over the shoulders into a yoke. Shoe toes become long and square as skirts grow longer.

2319. "Hat of silk plush. *Redingote* of *levantine.*"

Women have grown so used to keeping cozy during a long series of cold winters, that fashion plates load a large muff and fur-trimmed slippers on a fur-trimmed redingote of the new, twilled sarcenet called *levantine,* during what turned out to be an unusually warm winter.

2320. "*Spencer* of *levantine.* Percale dress."

The Spencer, with its buttoned sleeves, prophesies the wider shoulder-line and longer waist. Skirt is more gored; its hem decoration tends to become less rigidly horizontal, scalloped or edged with soft flounces; patterns turn from repeated embroidery eyelets to swinging sprays.

Courtesy of Mus. of Fine Arts, Boston, McCormick Coll.
(2316) ; Metropolitan Mus., Print Room (2315, 2317)

2318

2319

2320

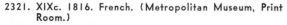

2321. XIXc. 1816. French. (Metropolitan Museum, Print Room.)

Ingres. Gabriel Cortois de Pressigny.

Shoulder-length powdered wig retained in ecclesiastical use, but much reduced in front, exposing the ears.

2322. XIXc. 1815. French. (Metropolitan Museum, Print Room.)

Ingres. Hon. Frederic Sylvester Douglas.

2323. XIXc. 1816. French. (London, British Museum.)

Ingres. Sir John Hay and his Sister.

2324. XIXc. 1816. French.

Ingres. Mrs. Vesey and her Daughter.

Ingres' exquisite drawings of these five members of the English colony in Rome were made possible by Conté's wonderful new crayons. In the 30's "black-lead pencils" will sell at 12 a shilling.

Pencils had been made in Nuremberg by Gesner in last quarter XVIc. from the newly discovered English plumbago. XVII-XVIIIc. artists—Simon van der Passe, Faithorne, Loggan, and the miniature painters beginning with Hilliard and the Olivers, had worked with exquisitely sharpened bits of the graphite. The pencil business of the Fabers of Nuremberg was set up in 1760.

But like so many superior things, really good lead pencils were the result of deprivation and improvisation. When the wars cut off the supply of graphite, Conté of Paris (an artist, chemist, and inventor of the most brilliant virtuosity, who "had every science in his head and every art in his hand") combined clay and graphite in 1795.

Shoulder seams of men's coats are carried far down the back to draw the collar away from the neck. Overlong waistline and sleeves force the material to ride up in horizontal folds (Ill. 2308). Braided and frogged topcoats, inspired by Hussar uniforms.

The extremely high waistlines of 1813-8 are often dramatised, not by a Spencer, but by colored skirts worn with long-sleeved, high-necked white muslin bodices, gathered and shirred on cords like the longer-waisted *canezous* of the 40's.

The English have been twisting India scarves into turbans, as Miss Hay does, for nearly half a century. During XIXc., turbans tend to become made-up headdresses for evening wear. By the 30's they are almost the uniform of matronly mothers, massed along the sidelines at balls, and are scarcely worn by anyone else.

Reasonably plumed bonnets like Miss Vesey's are seen throughout the second decade; as hat brims flatten and spread, at the beginning of the second quarter-century, ostrich is joined by paradise, and both are prolonged and worked into fantastic swooping and swirling twisted forms. Mrs. Vesey wears a veiled *cornette*.

2325. XIXc. 1817. French. (Boston, Museum of Fine Arts, Elizabeth Day McCormick Coll.)

"Le Bon Genre" (periodical). Promenades Aériennes.

Chute-the-chutes have just been built at ruinous expense at the *barrière du Roule* (now the Parc Monceau). One rides three times around two 400-foot chutes, and then comes down a last steep fall from its 63-foot platform. A café spreads through twelve arcades and all the attendants are in uniform.

Men: the newer, narrow-brimmed, straight-crowned hat. Rounded lapels and bosom of frock-coat, now buttoned close at the normal waistline, and again cut away into slender, longer tails. These double-breasted coats, often blue with brass buttons, have extremely long sleeves covering the knuckles (c. 1815-21). The trousers which accompany them are nankeen, or other light yellowish or grayish

color, expertly cut, not yet strapped under black boots. Spurs on boots, c. 1815-20.

Women: apron-like *robes en tablier* are seen during the first two decades of XIXc. Spencer with triple rows of buttons, borrowed (without braid, in this case) from the hussar uniform; the same arrangement is common on little boys' short jackets c. 1825.

2326. XIXc. c. 1817. French. (New York, J. P. Morgan.)
Sir Henry Raeburn. Lady Maitland.

Simple, unsophisticated British hair and plain long-sleeved muslin dress; wide, open collar; crossed closing; no color except square scarf.

2327. XIXc. c. 1817. French. (Metropolitan Museum.)
T. Géricault. Alfred Dedrieux.

Children have been dressed in the English way for three decades. Little boys' dress is affected by that of both women and men: parted hair, longer ringlets, very wide-open muslin collar; ankle-length trousers, slit at the bottom, buttoned high (at the line of a woman's bodice, since there is no vest; and laced fabric boots, like a woman's).

2328. XIXc. 1818. English. (Whitemarsh, Pa., George Widener.)
Ben Marshall. Weston Family.

Country clothing: soft, low-crowned felt hats; single or double-breasted coats, loose and comfortable; single-breasted vests; leather breeches and gaiters. Riding habit with cape-collar and plumed bonnet.

The Weston squires dress very much like Surtees' description of Michael Hardey, master of the farmers' hunt, at forty. "Handley Cross" was published in 1843; Hardey had died at eighty, before Mr. Jorrocks was invited to take over the pack; so the clothes described are of e.XIXc. "His hunting costume consisted of a good nut-brown coat, almost matching his complexion, a scrupulously clean white neckcloth, with a large flat-pocketed red waistcoat, patent cord breeches, and mahogany colored top-boots. His undress, or home costume was the same with drab gaiters, instead of boots; and his full, or evening costume, ditto, without the gaiters." Well brushed, broad-brimmed hat. Peter, his huntsman, dressed like his master. Other members of the hunt in that day were James Fairlamb, in "a single-breasted plum-coloured coat, with large silver buttons, black boots, and white lambswool stockings drawn over his knees." Stephen Dumpling, the doctor, "dressed in orthodox black, with powder, and a pig-tail, drab shorts and top-boots."

2329-30. XIXc. 1819. English. (Gen. Cowie Coll.)
Henry Alken. "The Real M." series: *How to Qualify for a Meltonian.*

2329. *How to go to cover.*

2330. *How to take the lead.*

Those who hunted with the Meltonian were astonished to learn that "Ben Tally Ho," whose prints they admired, was the pseudonym of one of their youngest members, Henry Alken. Alken was challenged to a duel of prints by Sir Robert Frankland, which led eventually to the six plates of "The Real M." for which Alken also wrote the text, which we quote.

2329. "Be careful, even in your ride to cover, to sit with great apparent ease and grace, however uncomfortable it may be in reality. Let your horse be thoroughbred, and never ride at a less rate than 16 miles an hour. With regard to dress, I shall say but little as I have given the costume as nearly as possible in the following plates, but I must observe that Real Meltonians either are, or affect to be, a very hardy race; they disdain the frock coat used by their forefathers and appear as here represented. I shall not be surprised in the course of another season to see them (if they are not extinct) dressed in silk caps and jackets." The "Lead" shows a rider with his left hand thrust nonchalantly in his breeches pocket. "Let your attitude be extremely careless, but at the same time determinedly singular. However extraordinary the leap may be, never appear to think it of consequence."

2330. The bad sportsmanship of the Meltonian, which led Osbaldiston to withdraw his hounds from the field in protest, is mocked in the "Lead" caption. "Few sporting men arrive at this elevated situation. If, by being well laid in, you have an opportunity of taking the lead, do it at all risks. You must have no more fellow-feeling in fox-hunting than you have in your political career. . . . Should you be called upon to make your appearance before a coroner's jury, you may calculate on the pleasure you will afterwards receive . . . to hear—in an undertone— . . . *That is one of the most desperate riders in the world,* etc. . . . Do something like all this, and you may at last be taken for a *Real* M."

Top hat crowns spread as the body begins to change form. The over-long, straight coat-body had forced the bosom of the coat upward. Douglas (No. 2322) thrusts his hand into this fullness. As the 20's approach, the torso shortens and becomes rounded. The waist is nipped in, forcing the body into hips and swelling bosom which fills out the loose fabric. The back is curved; the notched collar also becomes rounded and starts to climb back to the neck. Changes show clearly in Alken's profile views, in which the coat keeps the narrow, well-fitted sleeve (often seen 1815-18) instead of approaching the over-long, pushed-up sleeve of the 20's.

The coat is not the only practical feature of English riding dress to be taken over in France; analogous breeches buttoned along the outseam also were borrowed; and protective panels can be seen on the street-sweeper (Ill. 2331).

2331. XIX. 1818. French. (Boston, Museum of Fine Arts, Elizabeth Day McCormick Coll.)

Debucourt, after *C. Vernet*. Passez-payez.

Getting around the muddy streets of Paris in the rain was a centuries-old problem. With the Revolution and the disappearance of sedan-chairmen, there begin to be prints showing ladies of the 90's being carried pic-a-back over rushing gutters by bare-legged men, for a fee. By 1810, skirts grow shorter, long *pelisse-redingotes* cover muslin dresses, bonnet-like hats protect heads, women wear boots and carry umbrellas. A plank and the steadying hand and wooden shoe of a street sweeper are enough, but he still collects a fee.

A decade before MacIntosh's first waterproof cloth, a street sweeper's neck is protected by a wide hat of beaver felt, his back by a deep "sailor" collar; short loose jacket; scarf wound around the waist as a French workman still wears it; trousers with heavy extra panels set along each leg and tied together in back; sabots.

2332. XIXc. 1818. French. (The Louvre.)

Ingres. Stamaty Family.

Bonnets smaller, brim arched around the face; taffeta folded over the crown; fussier trim of flowers and veils. Smoother hair, parted and braided and looped high on the crown. Neckline and collars spread wide on shoulders; crossed-over collars or ruffles; bare neck emerging; shortest possible waistline. Sleeves long and full, wide at shoulders; ruffle-trimmed around the armseye, or covered by projecting collar; tied at the wrist, and elaborated over the hand. Hem decorations narrower and less insistent, corded lines or soft ruffles.

Young boy: collar cuts a wide horizontal line across the shoulders; breeches buttoned to a high waistline; top of costume influenced by women's.

Father and son: double-breasted garments; high notched collars; straight, rugged masculine lines of 1810 rather than the new curves of the 20's. Characteristic trouser of 1818, full and spreading wide below the knees (in fashion plates, this funnelling-out trouser leg of 1818 is often much shorter than that worn by the Stamaty boy).

2333. XIXc. c. 1820. French. (Chantilly, Conde Museum.)
Boilly. Checker game at the Café Lamblin.

Male costume is becoming softer, longer, and more curved; as it loses masculinity, moustaches appear to assert maleness. Lapels roll and are rounder; coat fronts and tails are cut with swinging curves, and are longer, with tails falling to the knee or below. Sleeves have a soft, graceful leg-o'-mutton shape, and narrow toward the wrist, from which they spring wide again over the knuckles.

Mixed company and styles: old gaffers in breeches and buckled shoes, with a nightcap to keep draughts off a bald head. Man with huge umbrella wears a hat left over from the Revolution. Workmen in the identical cap, loose short jacket and neckcloth which French workmen wear today.

Pretty girl at the counter makes change by the light of a shaded oil lamp. These became practical when chimneys were added in XVIIIc., and are now common; a hanging lamp is being lit above the company by a match. Gas lamps were first used in street lighting in the 1790's. The smell was so bad and the method considered so dangerous that the use of gas, even for outdoor lighting, was ridiculed and opposed by Sir Humphrey Davy. Lamps using animal or vegetable oil were preferred for indoors, long after gas had come into use in large buildings like foundries and breweries. The gas lamp installed in Ackermann's Fine Arts Repository in the Strand in 1810 (when the Gaslight and Coke Company finally succeeded in getting a charter) made a sensation. There is a legend that "a titled lady was so pleased with the light at Ackermann's that she wanted to take it home with her in the carriage." (Ashton.)

2334. XIXc. 1818. English. (Metropolitan Museum, Print Room.)
Rowlandson. The Last Jig, or Adieu to Old England.

English sailor costume: round, low-crowned hat; short, straight, square-cut jacket, with double rows of buttons, and small lapels; knotted cravat; loose short breeches over another pair of close knee-breeches; buckled shoes. Low companions smoking the vulgar pipe.

XIX CENTURY ENGLISH CARICATURISTS AND ILLUSTRATORS

With Thomas Rowlandson (1756-1827) begins the great line of English caricaturists and illustrators of the XIXc. Rowlandson worked for Ackermann, both as a magazine and book illustrator: *Microcosm of London,* (1810); *Dr. Syntax* series (1812-22); *Vicar of Wakefield* (1817); *World in Miniature* (1821-27).

James Gillray (1757-1815), unbridled satiric plates.

Robert Dighton (1752-1812), an excellent caricaturist, (and a discriminating print collector who stole regularly from the British Museum for a dozen years before he was caught) and his son Richard (fl. 1800-27).

Henry Alken (1784-1851), described by Christopher North as "a gentleman, who has lived with gentlemen . . . feels the line that separates the true old *domini terrarum* from the *nouveau riche,* (and) not only can do what Cruikshank cannot, but he can also do almost anything that Cruikshank can." Principally, between 1813-44, he produced series of hunting and sporting prints, sketch books, sporting scrapbooks, illustrations for the *National Sports of Great Britain,* which were sold by subscription to the country gentry by travelling book agents; and Nimrod's *Life of a Sportsman,* 1842.

Isaac Cruikshank (1756?-1811?), and his sons, Robert (1789-1856) and the great George (1792-1878 often worked together. The sons together illustrated Pierce Egan's *Life in London,* and George, Dicken's *Boz.*

"Phiz" (H. K. Browne, 1815-82) was Dickens' illustrator from *Pickwick* (1837) onwards. John Leech (1817-64) worked for *Punch;* illustrated Surtees: *Handley Cross* (1854). C. S. Keene (1823-91) was the other leading illustrator for *Punch.*

2335. XIXc. 1818. French. (Metropolitan Museum, Print Room.)
Horace Vernet. Stage Coach.

"Many alterations have lately taken place in the building of carriages. The roofs are not so round. . . . The circular springs have given way to whip springs. . . . No boots are now used, but plain coachboxes, with open fore ends. . . . During the last summer ladies were much oftener seen travelling seated on the box than in the carriage." (*The Times,* London, 1803.) On this pleasant day the stuffy interior is used for the dogs.

Young bloods, sitting on the box, began to tip the coachman into letting them handle the reins. Many became as skillful as professionals, and "Tommy Onslow," later Lord Cranford, used to wear the hayband leggings with which coachmen kept their legs warm. The Whip Club (which became The Four in Hand), Barouche Club, Tandem Club, and others, were formed, each with its distinctive uniform.

At the meet of the Four in Hand Club in Cavendish Square in 1809 (*Morning Post*) the members wore a blue (single-breast) coat, with a long waist and brass buttons, on which were engraved the words: "Four in Hand Club." Their waistcoat was of Kerseymere (a twilled fine woolen cloth of a peculiar texture) ornamented with alternate stripes of blue and yellow; small clothes of white corduroy, made moderately high, and very long over the knee, buttoning in front over the shin bone. Boots very short, with long tops, only one outside strap to each, and one to the back; the latter were employed to keep the breeches in their proper longitudinal shape. Hat with a conical crown, and the Allen brim (which even Ashton, in his *Nineteenth Century,* could not identify); box or driving coat, of white drab cloth, with fifteen capes, two tiers of pockets and an inside one for the Belcher handkerchief; cravat of white muslin spotted with black. Bouquets of myrtle, pink and yellow geraniums were worn. In May of the same year, the club buttons had already gone out of fashion, and, "Lord Hawke sported yesterday, *as buttons,* Queen Anne shillings; Mr. Ashurst displayed crown pieces."

2336. XIXc. 1818. French. (Metropolitan Museum, Print Room.)
Géricault. Boxers.

Boxing was an XVIIIc. sport which grew in popularity as swords ceased to be worn.

Two men are mainly responsible for its rise to favor with the aristocracy. Jack Boughton (1705-89) who invented the boxing glove (for use in practice only), formulated the rules of the ring, and ran the amphitheatre in the Tottenham Court Road until 1750; and John, "Gentleman Jackson" (1769-1845) who made boxing agile and scientific. His pupil, Lord Byron, said Jackson had better manners than those of "the fellows of the College whom I meet at the high table." Both were on intimate terms with the most distinguished men of their time. John Gully, the prizefighter, was George IV's page, and became M.P. for Pontefract.

Prize fights were always fought with bare fists, pickled into toughness; fighters wore their hair long, until Jackson caught Daniel Mendoza, the Jewish fighter who owned the Lyceum, by his hair in 1790. Boxing was still a combination of wrestling and other methods; a round lasted till a man was knocked down. The fight ended when one man was unable to come to the middle of the ring when called.

The decline of boxing socially has already begun by 1818, but Géricault shows two immortals: Tom Cribb and his Negro opponent, Thomas Molyneux. Cribb wears high, loose gaiters and Molyneux, half-long breeches buttoned over striped stockings. As the coat begins to be curved in, the shape of the top hat develops swinging lines also.

2337. XIXc. c. 1820. U. S. A. (Washington, Nat. Gall. of Art, Mellon Coll.)

John Lewis Krimmel (1787-1821). Artist and family.

It would be hard to find more touchingly simple, pretty, appropriate clothes than are worn by the Krimmel family and doll.

The dressing of the little girls' parted hair with ribbons and braids is differentiated with as much loving taste as are their plain little dresses by a colored piping or yoke, bias band or scalloped hem. The women have made trimmings for their dresses from the fabric of the gown, shirred, or corded and braided; each *cornette* cap is exquisitely right.

The skirts of men's coats are only just beginning to be cut separately from the body. When, as in the case of the Krimmel men, this has not yet been done, the long, enclosing skirts of the single-breasted coat of 1818-20 fall rather straight and plain; the collar rolls; the sleeve is easy but not full at the armseye.

Mrs. Krimmel may have tailored the men's coats herself, as many a wife did in America in 1820. I think she did. It is quite impossible for any two people to put in a row of pins in the same way; anyone who has worked in a big dressmaker's or theatrical costume shop can recognize the work of different fitters. Every garment in this picture has the look of being very carefully made by a woman: one woman, or perhaps the accustomed joint work of two.

Mr. Krimmel: olive green coat. Son: gray-blue coat, black vest, fawn breeches. Mrs. Krimmel: red dress, with rose belt and bow under chin.

L. to r.: Girl in yellow dress, piped in red. Grandmother: *cornette* with striped rose and silver ribbon, brown dress, black apron. Girls: lavender hair ribbon, blue dress; black; cream dress with rose yoke; girl between her and mother: olive green dress, rose hair ribbon.

2338. XIXc. c. 1821. French.

Trade Card of *Mme. Lenormand.*

2339-41. XIXc. French.

"Costumes Parisiens" (periodical).

2339. "Chemise pleated in back, the invention of M. Styndyk; boneless corset, laced in front. Boots laced on the inside." (1822).

2340. "Gauze hat. Percale dress, corsage *à la Sévigné,* bouilloned sleeves, the hem ornamented with a lace ruffle, *entre deux,* and a band of embroidery." (1824). "Bouilloned" refers to puffing which ripples like the surface of a simmering pot.

2341. "Crepe hat banded in satin folds, ornamented with tufts of lilac. *Redingote* of *gros de Naples* trimmed with braided satin." (1821).

2342. XIXc. 1823. French.

Ingres. Mme. Le Blanc.

The trend turns from pattern towards rounded form. We have watched the appearance of the rounded breasts. Now other body curves begin to be exploited; trimmings no longer lie flat; hair becomes sculptured.

Everything is done to enhance the long plain curve of a sloping shoulder line, as it drops to a lowered armseye. In Ill. 2337, Mrs. Krimmel's shoulder seam is merely corded; in these fashion plates, we see yokes or little shoulder capes and their horizontal trimmings carry the eye towards the enlarged cap of the sleeve.

Wide shoulders help to make the longer, belted waist look small and round. The corset is gored and laced to shape the waist, but is not yet long enough to round off the hips and buttocks. These are indicated, rather than defined, by contrast with a small waist, by more definite goring of skirt seams, and by the aid of M. Styndyk's new chemise, the fullness of which helps to round out the skirt in back.

Hem decorations become much reduced and are set lower, especially on cloth and coat dresses. Trim-

mings stand out from the fabric, as roses have done, for some time on dance dresses.

The fabric itself "simmers" (see note about Ill. 2340), and boils up into puffs. Cloth dresses are trimmed with rows and braids of cord covered with fabric. The trim of lingerie dresses becomes frillier and more puffed; in addition to raised flowers and horizontal lines of puffs and ruffles, we see separate motifs applied; these sometimes reach as high as horizontal trimmings used to be carried. Mme. Lenormand's figure on the left shows a motif taken from a cashmere shawl, carried out in a froth of ruffles. The upper line in which ruffles are applied is often waved (Lenormand. l. figure); toothed edges are being rounded in scallops; color helps eyelet embroidery to rise above the fabric on which it is worked.

Hair no longer falls. It is parted, rolled, braided, and worked into standing loops.

Bonnet-like hats are a little larger; their enclosing round brims become flattened across the top as the shoulders grow wider (No. 2341). Brims are made entirely of pleating (No. 2340); or pleating is set as a lining inside straw brims; it, too, changes character, becomes softer, is gauffered into roundness, or gathered.

2343-59. XIXc. 1821. English. (New York Public Library.) *I., R.* & *G. Cruikshank.* Illustrations for the 1821 Edition of Pierce Egan's *"Life in London: or the Day and Night Scenes of Jerry Hawthorne, Esq. and his elegant Friend Corinthian Tom, accompanied by Bob Logic, the Oxonian, in their Rambles and Sprees through the Metropolis."* (Written in 1812.)

B. Yellow paradise in a red hat, green-blue coat with yellow collar lining, over light green dress.

C. Black hat (like all), white linen and vest, dark blue coat, white pantaloons striped in red, lemon yellow gloves.

Recumbent Man. Malachite green coat, greenish yellow waistcoat, white pantaloons.

D. Blue coat, greenish yellow vest and pantaloons.

E. Yellow straw with red-tipped white ostrich, purple coat and gown, cherry scarf, brown handbag, white gloves.

F. All black.

G. Reddish plum coat with black Hussar braiding, white pantaloons.

H. White plumes, garnet bodice, pale pink dress.

I. Bright blue coat, white linen and vest, pink breeches and stockings.

J. Dark plum coat, dark gray trousers.

K. Green coat, white breeches and stockings.

L. Deep purplish-rose gown.

M. White plumes, pink gown.

N. Yellow-brown bonnet and costume, deep blue scarf.

O. Dark.

P. Dark blue coat, black pantaloons, yellow gloves.

Q. Red and yellow turban, cherry bodice and cloak trimmed with ermine, white skirt.

2360. XIXc. 1821. English. (New York, Harry Peters.)
Henry Alken. "Sports of Great Britain": Fishing in a Punt.

2361. XIXc. 1823. French. (Metropolitan Museum, Print Room.)
"Costumes Parisiens" (periodical).
"Straw hat. Silk cravat. Cashmere *redingote*. Vest and trousers of piqué."
Light brown straw hat; blue gray coat; red, yellow and green plaid scarf; white vest; blue gray and white striped trousers; blue belt; violet fob and gold seals; black boots.
Male and female outlines alter sympathetically. Men's waistlines curve, and shoulders slope and widen. The sleeve is set farther out and lower; its top, which had become rather smooth, c.1818, is now eased in with more fullness over padding (2361). The lapels are rounded, even on a double-breasted coat (2360). Coat skirts tend to enclose the thighs from c.1818; *redingotes* are worn with vests and trousers as suit coats (2361). Garters are buttoned up to short sporting breeches (2360). Long trousers

have now acquired a buttoned front closing, are strapped under the boot, and probably have side pockets.

2362. XIXc. 1824. French. (Paris, Carnavalet Mus.)
Boilly. "A la santé du roi!"
Boilly's lithograph appears in colored and uncolored forms, under two titles. The version which was published, probably for political reasons, as "A la santé des lurons!" is identical except for inscriptions on door frame and shutter.
Shirts continued to be cut full, with a dropped shoulder and full sleeve, into second half XIXc.

2363. XIXc. 1824. U. S. A. (Philadelphia, Academy of Fine Arts.)
C. W. Peale. The Artist in his Museum.
The skeleton of one of Peale's mastodons shows below the curtain, and part of a lower jaw lies at his feet. Peale himself shows the persistence of the old knee breeches and buckled shoes, worn with a frock coat with velvet collar, on an elderly, conservative American gentleman.

2364-68. XIXc. 1824. French. (Metropolitan Museum, Print Room.)
Lanté-Gatine. Working Women of Paris.

2364. Straw hat seller: Black and green spencer bodice; shoes of light and dark blue; natural color straw hat.

2365. Cook: Red and white striped kerchief head-dress, mustard yellow dress.

2366. Woman of the petite bourgeoisie: Red, green and white scarf, light pumpkin yellow redingote, green gloves, blue reticule and umbrella (edged with red and yellow), black slippers.

2367. Artificial hair worker: Black apron, yellow dress.

2368. Lady's maid: Red dress, yellow and green plaid scarf, pale blue shoes.

Superb dressmaking and millinery are becoming

save work, but makes it possible to do more, in the same amount of time. They changed the bottom sheet and moved the top sheet down every two weeks, where we change both once or twice a week, and do six times as much laundry. Few of us have got around to realizing that wonderful as an electric mixer is for big jobs, about half the work we do with it can be done as fast with a fork or wooden spoon, which is a lot easier to wash up. It has interested me to realize how insidiously the process has worked during the last twenty-five years of my own life-time. Handkerchief linen, batiste and good crêpe used to be bought by the piece, and kept in a bottom drawer with carefully evolved basic patterns. It seemed perfectly reasonable to have shoes and gloves made to order, together with one perfect tailored suit. Almost everything else was made by hand at one's leisure. Suit blouses had seams hemstitched or faggoted together, cuffs and jabots of exquisitely tucked and pleated linen; they would cost perhaps

2364 2365 2366 2367 2368

the great industry of Paris in 1824. The taste and skill with which thousands of little *grisettes* have become endowed, are reflected in their own dress and in the clothes which their mothers and sisters wear at work and at marketing, twenty-five years before the sewing machine comes into use.

We look the way we do, shopping at the supermarket today, because Seventh Avenue's mass-production of clothing is New York's great industry. Our most eminent dress-making houses are infected by it; their made-to-order departments grow smaller each year. No one today can possibly afford to pay for handwork as fine as these women of a hundred and twenty-five years ago display, and no one thinks she has the time to do it herself. Women, a hundred and twenty-five years ago, were not yet the victims of labor-saving machinery, which at best does not

$125 apiece today, and one had them by the dozens in those days.

The dresses are made of the fashionable mustard and pumpkin yellows; the shoulders are widened by a gay square folded on the bias, the ghost of a Spencer, or bands of color. Their *cornettes* are delightful; and are protected at work with kerchiefs knotted high with all the art in the world. The uncovered head of the little hair worker displays the braids and curls she makes; the others can afford only an artificial curl or two at the edge of the bonnet.

There has seldom been a more comfortable, practical or attractive dress than that of c.1815. These working women have retained its plain, easy sleeve; its high waistline and its hem with low-set horizontal trim, to accommodate the aprons they must wear.

2369. XIXc. c. 1825-6. English. (Metropolitan Museum, Frick Coll.)

Thomas Lawrence. Juliana, Lady Peel.

2370. XIXc. 1826. French. (Metropolitan Museum, Print Room.)

"Costumes Parisiens" (periodical).

"Hats of Italian straw, trimmed with satin ribbon and flowers, organdy *canezous* trimmed with embroidery. One skirt of taffeta, the other of *cotepalis*."

2371. XIXc. 1826. French. (Metropolitan Museum, Print Room.)

"Petit Courrier des Dames" (periodical).

"*Redingote* of *gros de Naples* with bias-cut toothed and bow-knot trimmings. Crêpe hat with flowered gauze ribbons and *blonde*. From the shop of Mme. Mare."

Standing: lavender and black; yellow hat trimmed in black.

Seated: blue and black; rose and black hat, both trimmed with silk lace and with gauze ribbons which were either woven or painted.

2372. XIXc. 1827. French. (Metropolitan Museum, Print Room.)

"Petit Courrier des Dames" (periodical).

"*Longchamps Fashions. Gros de Naples* robe trimmed with a flounce and two rows of *chicorée*. Grenadine scarf. Rice straw hat trimmed with marabou."

Standing: lemon yellow with white sleeves and hat, marabou trimming, yellow shading to orange tips. Red, green and yellow scarf of a sheer open mesh material, usually woven of silk against wool.

Seated: white and blue.

Hat crowns have grown high to accommodate braids and loops of hair on top of the head. As shoulder lines widen, the rounded, enclosing brims of bonnets have been flattened on top. By c.1823, the round bonnet has largely been replaced by a hat with a very wide brim, made of black or violet velvet in winter, or of natural-colored straw or colored crêpe, trimmed with feathers, ribbon loops, and a few flowers. The ribbon stands in knotted loops, allied to the way in which the hair is dressed on the crown of the head. The form and trim of the straw bonnet is commemorated in the way silk lace is carried under the chin (Ill. 2371) and in the trimming on the under side of brims. A great deal of paradise like Lady Peel's is seen during the 20's and 30's. There are also flat velvet berets for day wear, and turbans (often decorated with paradise) for evening.

The *pelisse* is now either gored and fitted to a longer waistline like the *redingote* (2371), or becomes a mantle with arm slits (2369). In either case, its collar (often of white fur) has widened with the shoulder-line of dresses, and is apt to be prolonged into tippet ends in front. As skirts grow wider in the 50's, the skirts of coat and cloak have to be given up; this cape-collar with tippet ends becomes the basis for the typical outer garments of the next period.

The neckline has become established at a horizontal line across the shoulders. The space above is bare, in carriage, dress, or evening gowns; on a *redingote* or *canezou,* it is filled in by a bertha and elaborate, spreading collars.

Horizontal folds across the bodice (No. 2342) have succeeded in forming the horizontal neckline; now they turn diagonal or vertical (2370) to enhance the longer line of the torso. Sleeves are gored or gathered into rounded leg-o'-mutton tops, and now end at the wrists in small neat cuffs, or pairs of important wide bracelets (2369).

The *canezou* collar has been developed into a white shirtwaist with sleeves of its own, worn with a buckled belt over the characteristic checked or plaid skirt. Skirts are sharply gored into a smooth, tight waist in front, and are gathered into great back fullness, supported by pads.

Colors become striking and are used in combination (trim 2371, feathers 2372, skirts 2370). Brilliant checks and plaids are woven (2370) or applied (scarf 2372). Notched decorations and bows become rounder; feathers curl into fat little tips (2372); bias cutting allows toothed decorations to be puffed out (2371), and flounces to be set on in rounded rather than gathered fullness. The edges of scallops are pinked; they have the quality of the marabou trim on 2372; ruchings are frilled like the salad called *chicorée frisée* (2372).

Shoes have long narrow toes, slightly squared and gaiters or gaiter tops of fabric laced on the inside of the foot.

Short gloves are worn with long sleeves and paired bracelets.

2373-79. XIXc. 1825-8. English. (New York Pub. Lib., Print Room.)

Geo. Hunt after *Theodore Lane* (1800-28). The Rival Whiskers.

To the gentleman with the spy-glass (A), the dragoon (B), the short man (C), and the Horse Artilleryman (D), with their jowls and chins surrounded by lush curls, as well as to the chimney sweep (E) and the old girl in bonnet and shawl, the wearers of the straight flowing whiskers (F and G) "look not like the Inhabitants o'the Earth and yet are on 't."

Boots are beginning to disappear, strapped under breeches. The short man wears the full hippy breeches of the 20's, loose about the leg. The taller bewhiskered man shows breeches of the earlier form closer at the knee than below; they retain a buttoned side seam although they are strapped over boots, since such tight breeches could not be got over boots in any other way. Coat skirts are cut separately to allow a fitted waist, and pockets with flaps are set in the seam to emphasize the jut of the skirts at the hip. The square-cut *gilet* is pointing downward into a vest. Eyeglasses swing from chains around the neck; watches are worn on similar chains, which are run through the top buttonhole of the vest, then to a right hand pocket.

2380-82. XIXc. 1827-29. French. (Metropolitan Museum, Print Room.)

"Petit Courrier des Dames" (periodical).

2380. "Straw hat with knotted plumes. Moiré dress embroidered in silk. From the shop of Mrs. Guay et [*sic*] Paris, Rue de Richelieu No. 55."

2381. "Italian straw hat ornamented with birds of paradise. Robe of embroidered Palmyrienne. Pèlerine

2383

THE BUSTLE !!!

and boa of tulle. From the shop of la Belle Anglaise, Rue de la Paix No. 20."

2382. "Robe of *gros de Naples* cut in three directions, trimmed by a deep flounce with points. From Mr. Burty's shop, Rue de Richelieu No. 89. Straw hat from the shop of Mme. Mure."

With these plates (2380-82) we reach nearly the limit of brilliant color and Gothic trimming, although not quite the limit of distortion of body form.

Shaded orange and yellow plumes are knotted into fringe. A white fabric which is already heavily patterned, like moiré, is embroidered with monstrous blue, yellow-green and purple strawberries, laid on in a serpentine line, and disappearing into full scalloped flounces.

Yellow birds of paradise, knotted with blue and yellow ribbons and long streamers of fancy gauze accompany a gown of a new shot silk and wool fabric, in what Americans would call "Alice" blue, embroidered in white, with huge puffed white sleeves. The beloved streamers of 1825-35 are further carried out in the completely absurd tulle boa. Its alternate, white embroidered in white, has pink and yellow ribbons and belt.

Flowers undreamed of in nature are wired high and veiled in lace, with yards of streaming gauze. Stripes are cut and laid over each other, every which way, in folds and tongues.

Shoes, definitely square-toed, have gaiter-like fabric tops, or cross lacings; they become increasingly

low cut by 1833. Short kid gloves disappearing under the cuff or paired wide bracelets, set with medallions. Small drop earrings.

2383. XIXc. c. 1827-9. English. (New York Public Library, Print Room.)
William Heath. The Bustle.

The *cornette* which she wears while dressing has been as wildly elaborated by bows and wired flowers as the great hat she will wear with her plaid gown; it has the bias-cut hem and skirt decoration set on in overlapping diagonal curves, which is seen in England c.1828-29.

This is probably the most informative picture in existence of the long narrow-waisted corset, and the bustle required by these gowns.

2384. XIXc. 1828. U. S. A. (New York, Harry Peters.)
John A. Woodside (1817-50). Country Fair.

Male dress in rural Maryland; Quaker in round hat and knee breeches (r.).

2385. XIXc. Published in 1844. U. S. A. (Metropolitan Museum, Print Room.)
William Henry Brown (1808-1883). John Randolph (1773-1833).

The old Republican leader, Pocahontas' descendant, who freed his own slaves, had died of tuberculosis more than a decade before this combination of silhouette and lithograph was published. He wears clothing of the 20's, with knee-breeches, stockings and boots, and keeps his handkerchief in the pocket provided in the coat tails, before the days of side pockets in trousers.

2384

2385   2386

2386. XIXc. 1825-30. English. (Metropolitan Museum, Print Room.)

Augustin Edouart (1788-1861). Cut-paper silhouettes, painted ground: The Magic Lantern.

The silhouettes suggest a date c.1826. The elderly gentleman seated with his peg-leg stuck out, still wears a wig; short wide pantaloons, and low shoes with a bow. So does the operator of the magic lantern, whose shirt collar still stands, but is not excessively high. The gentleman to the right has a full, rounded head of hair and coat with a high collar, but the tendencies of the 30's appear in his sloping shoulder, smooth sleeve, long swinging lines and long fitted trousers. The lady has the mounting hair of 1825-30, and the short waist and bell-shaped flounced skirt of England c. 1826.

2387. XIXc. c. 1825. U. S. A. (Metropolitan Museum.)
Chester Harding (1792-1866). Mrs. Thomas Brewster Coolidge.

Mrs. Coolidge wears a favorite English hat of e. 1825, which has a swinging black velvet brim, many plumes, and is worn over a lacy *cornette* which frames the face. Grey *pelisse*-mantle with a small ermine collar, and lemon yellow gloves, all of which appear to be of about the same date.

2388. XIXc. c. 1830. Spanish. (Madrid, Prado.)
V. Lopez y Pontaña. Queen Marie-Christine de Bourbon.

Spanish court costume, after Goya, is accurately painted by Lopez y Pontaña (1772-1850). He shows the wife of Ferdinand VII in a wonderful jewelled *parure:* hair ornament worn with bunches of diagonally-set sausage curls (1825-30's), earrings, necklace, and wide belt; embroidered gown with horizontally pleated bodice-top (1825-30's).

2389-90. XIXc. 1829. French. (New York Public Library.)
"Costumes Parisiens" (periodical).

"Polish *redingote* with interlaced embroidery. Pantaloons of Balkan earth color. Cloth coat with velvet collar. Silk gilet over gilet of piqué. Cashmere pantaloons."

There are excellent plates of men, especially of their outer garments, in the "Costumes Parisiens" of 1828-31.

The Polish redingote, of military inspiration, has a standing military collar; standing collars become a feature of the dress of the 30's. Coat collars and lapels are at their most prominent and rolling, 1825-30; during the 30's, coats tend to close high, often by two rows of buttons, and lapels either jut wide, high on the chest or are suppressed altogether. The jut of the hip, 1825-35, is apt to be stressed by a pocket flap set in the waistline.

Trousers worn over boots are longer and wider than those worn with striped stockings and pumps. The latter type, which has a rather persistently stressed outseam, will prevail; cutting becomes more expert, and the trouser which follows the proportions of the limb (though it may be a great deal wider in actual use than in fashion plates) becomes longer in the 30's, and is usually strapped under the boot.

2391-92. XIXc. e.1830's. German. (Metropolitan Museum, Print Room.)

William Alexander Wolfgang von Kobell (1766-1853).

Pencil and white chalk on blue paper. Sketches of horsewomen:

Classic riding dress of 1830-3; collar grows higher; sleeve tops have reached their ultimate balloon-fullness; skirts begin to be pleated and gathered onto the bodice.

2393. XIXc. c. 1830. French. (Met. Mus., Print Room.)
Achille Devéria. Dumas, père.

The elder Dumas was the son of a Napoleonic general who was himself the offspring of a Santo Dominican Negro woman and a French marquis. When the Goncourts met him at the Princess Matilda's in 1865 his negroid hair had turned pepper and salt, and he had grown enormous, with a moon-like face and the "tiny eye of a hippopotamus, bright, cunning and watchful, even when veiled; his voice was hoarse, his facts flabbergasting, his memory immense"; the "sober athlete of the *feuilleton* and of copy," had no wit, color or nuance, and never touched wine, coffee or tobacco.

In one of Devéria's many lithograph portraits Dumas wears boots with long squared toes and small, low heels, and one of the alternative trousers of the period: tight, widening toward the bottom, and ending well above the ankle. By 1833-4 this trouser will become longer and very wide, shrinking again by 1835. Another pantaloon of the period is so long, that it breaks across the instep as it is strapped down under the boot.

The standing collar of the shirt barely shows above fitted cravat, which is becoming tied with a flat bow. Dumas' vest has the high, standing collar which has reappeared with the 30's, together with a coat collar, which is again carried high in back. This is a preliminary to the wide, very sloping shoulder-line of the mid30's, which will slide into a close, narrow sleeve finished with a small turned cuff. Dumas' shoulder is still narrow; his sleeve still puffed at the top and extended over the hand. Watch on chain around the neck.

The variety of cut and fabric in men's clothes during the 30's defies any brief summary. The *Journal des Tailleurs,* (at Metropolitan Museum Print Room), published from the office of the *Petit Courrier des Dames,* 1830-40, provides not only hand-colored plates of monthly new fashions, but exact patterns, and pages of explanatory text about coats, redingotes, pantaloons, vests, mantles, uniforms, women's riding habits, boys' and girls' clothing, dressing gowns, masquerade costumes, and men-servants' liveries.

Similar information, for the mid-40's, may be found in Joseph Conts: "A Practical Guide for the Tailor's Cutting-Room," Blackie & Son, London (after 1844), which also contains "clerical and forensic" dress, military, naval, and Highland costume, directions for cutting for "disproportioned persons," and liveries for page, footman, postillion, tiger, groom, coachman, and jockey. (M.M.A., Print Room.)

2394-95. XIXc. 1830. French. (New York Public Library.)
"Costumes Parisiens" (periodical).
"Cloth *pelisse* with a shawl collar of velvet, closed by bordered tabs. Coat with velvet collar. Cashmere pantaloon."
The pelisse is brown with a gray collar and brilliant blue-green lining. The coat beneath is bright blue; vest gold and white. The immense white cravat forces the shirt ruffles to lie flat as they are pinned by a brooch. Black pantaloons and pumps; white stockings dotted in black.

2396-98. XIXc. 1834. French. (Paris, Bibliotheque Nationale.)
H. Daumier.
2396-97. "Un rentier des bons royaux, un rentier des Cortes."
2398. Cartoon from *L'Association mensuelle.* "Ne vous y frottez pas."
Fashion plates and fashionable portraits have a wonderful antidote in Daumier: haranguing parliamentarians, bored judges, suspect lawyers with widowed clients, people who live well or badly off their dividends, kings, generals or class-conscious young printers.

Hat crowns are straighter, the brims less curved. Collars, often of velvet, mount high in back and are more important than lapels, as many coats and overcoats close higher, often by two rows of rather closely set buttons. The small figure with outstretched arms shows the velvet-collared, double-breasted tail coat of the 30's, cut across at a line somewhat lower than the fitted waist.

2399. XIXc. c. 1830. French. (Metropolitan Museum.)

Wedding dress: embroidered India muslin.

2400-03. XIXc. c. 1830-35. U. S. A. (Metropolitan Museum, Costume Institute.)

2400. Child's rose and tan changeable silk dress. (c.1830)

2401. White silk wedding dress in fancy weave with moiré stripe (1831-34). Cream-colored blonde lace veil (c.1830).

2402. Hanging on stand: a printed cotton dress with floral pattern on a cream ground (c.1835), found in Maine. Cream-colored silk dress (Viennese 1833-34) of fancy twill with an all-over self-pattern in leaf design.

2403. Tan silk taffeta dress with self-trimming (c.1830), found in Connecticut. Natural leghorn hat.

2404. XIXc. c. 1830. English.
  Pelisse of quilted striped silk.

2405. XIXc. c. 1833. U. S. A.
  Wedding dress: white satin embroidered in white
silk.

2406. XIXc. c. 1836-7. English.
  Visiting dress: dark red moiré.

2407. XIXc. c. 1845. U. S. A.
  Brocade dress.

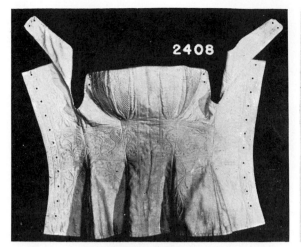

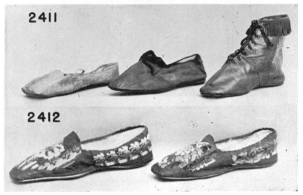

2408. XIXc. Probably English.
    Corset: quilted white sateen.

2409 Mid-XIXc. French.
    Man's straw hat.

2410. XIXc. (early) English?
    Buskins: elastic sided blue kid.

2411-12. XIXc. U. S. A.
    Shoes and slippers.

Courtesy of Museum of Fine Arts, Boston (2408-09);
Metropolitan Museum (2410-12)

2413

2414

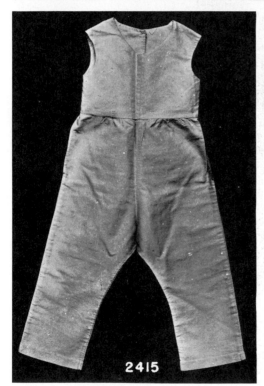

2415

2416

2417

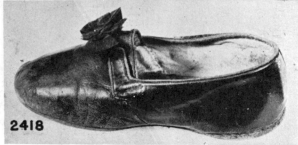

2418

2415. Breeches: white cotton sateen; waist buttoned down center back; drop seat fastened to waist.
2416. Sock: knitted cotton.
2417. Linen shirt.
2418. Shoes: black leather.

2413-18. XIXc. 1837. U. S. A. (Boston, Mus. of Fine Arts.)

Boys' clothing: worn at the age of 5 by Henry Augustus Thompson of Charlestown, Mass. (b.1832-d.1837), cousin of Benjamin Thompson, Count Rumford.

2413-14. Coat: front and back. Black wool broadcloth, black velvet collar, tan cotton fancy piqué attached waistcoat front.

2419. e.XIXc. French or Spanish. (New York, Cooper Union Mus.)

Gloves: white kid, printed and painted in wavy green lines; medallions of Liberty on back, crossing bands with flowers on wrist.

2420. XIXc. c. 1840. Spanish.

Gloves: yellow kid, printed in black; design of ovals; scene of gentleman giving a present to lady seated under a tree (back); chain with links of lozenge shapes and floral forms (wrist); tops scalloped.

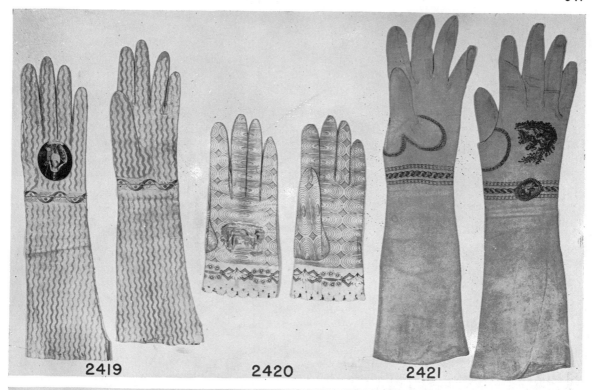

2419   2420   2421

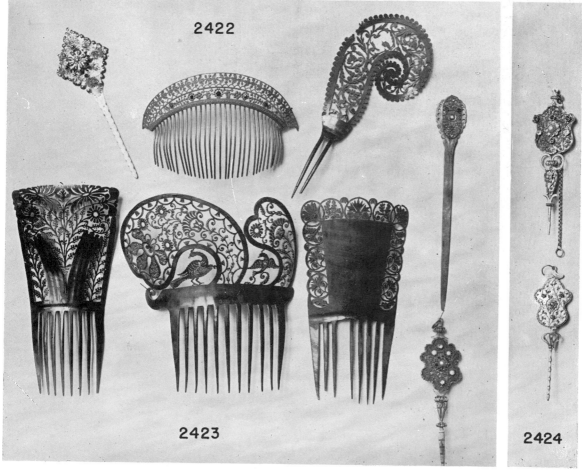

2422

2423

2424

2421. XIXc. c. 1820. English?
   Gloves: suede, printed in black; leaf design at thumb piece; country scene with boy and girl (back); three bands with medallions of boys' heads (wrist); inside mark undecipherable. "Patent," with crown and shield supported by lion and unicorn.

2422-24. XIXc. German and Austrian. (Metropolitan Museum.)

2422. French comb, gilt brass and ruby glass beads.

2423. Three German tortoise shell combs.

2424. Sides. Austrian, Salzburg, silver hair ornaments.

2425. XIXc. English.
Floral polychrome: roller printed cotton.

2426. XIXc. after 1837. English.
Simulated patchwork: printed cotton: medallions from scenes in "Pickwick Papers."

2427. XIXc. 1830. Alsatian Mulhouse.
Wool challis.

2428. First half XIXc. U. S. A. (Metropolitan Museum.)
Patchwork quilt. Calico, and later, silk, from used garments, make quilts invaluable costume documents. A quilt in the Philadelphia Museum, made by daughters who used to work in the shop of John Hewson, the first calico printer to work in America, undoubtedly contains samples of his work; it would be interesting to eliminate as many of its recognizable imported pieces as possible. Another important quilt in the Staten Island Museum (gift of Miss Yetman) is made up of homespun, obviously locally printed, and undoubtedly the work of the Old Staten Island Print Works, which opened early in second decade, XIXc.

2429. Mid-XIXc. English.
"Giroflé-girofla": roller-printed cotton, purple and mauve on buff.

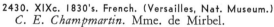

2430. XIXc. 1830's. French. (Versailles, Nat. Museum.)
C. E. Champmartin. Mme. de Mirbel.

Portrait of a fashionable portrait miniaturist, (wife of a distinguished botanist) who enjoyed the patronage of Louis XVIII in his old age.

2431. XIXc. c. 1835. U. S. A.
J. J. Audubon (1780-1851). Mrs. Anna Cora (Ogden) Mowatt.

Mrs. Mowatt (1819-70) married at fifteen, and three years later went to Europe for some time. In 1845 she wrote a play, *Fashion* (which was delightfully revived in the 1920's by the Provincetown-Greenwich Village Theatre). She then turned

actress, toured America and Europe with E. L. Davenport as her leading man. Her blameless life, charm and intelligence did a great deal to improve the social standing of the profession. The artist is the great ornithologist.

2432-33. XIXc. 1830's. French.
Paul Gavarni. "Les Français peints par eux-mêmes": 2432. *Woman sketching,* 2433. *Chasing butterflies* (detail).

Sulpice-Guillaume Chevalier (1804-66) who signed himself "Gavarni," the brilliant and cultivated satirist of Louis-Philippe's epoch, was born poor,

and began as a fashion artist for *La Mode;* the success of *Charivari* was due to his caricatures, and he became the most prolific and sought-after book illustrator of his day. In addition to those for Sue and Balzac, he made many of the illustrations for "Les Français peints par eux-mêmes." He did a score of series of pictures of *lorettes,* students, and young people's gaiety; then turned to bitter, grotesque denunciations of humanity in general, and family life in particular.

"Les Français peints par eux-mêmes," L. Curmer, Paris, 1840-43, consists of five volumes about Paris, and four on the Provinces. Gavarni, H. Monnier, Gagniet, Cousin and others illustrate articles of hundreds of authors, who describe people of every category; duchesses, sisters-of-charity, actresses, mothers, boarding school girls, midwives; the army, national guard, and even the camp followers; jails and their inmates; occupations as varied as cemetery gardener, sailor, phrenologist, and travelling salesman; the different provinces, with their customs and dress.

As dress in 2430 to 2433 indicates, angularity can no longer be maintained. The width of the costume begins to slip and soften. The wide, level hat brim again begins to curve around the face into a bonnet. The sharp projections of the collar, below a deep yokes, are softened into yoke-shaped cape collars (2433), or are given up altogether (2431, 2432). The sleeve cannot be made any larger, and its decline is foretold. Its fullness begins to slip down the shoulder, as the disappearance of wings brings the armseye into sight; the first inches of the sleeve top are pleated or shirred into the equivalent of the

dropped shoulder into which the bodice of the 40's will be cut. There is a further tendency to reduce the sleeve by tightening the lower arm (2431). By 1836 the *gigot* sleeve will have been demolished.

Mrs. Mowatt shows the transitional skirt, between the gored form, smooth at the hips and full behind and the full round skirt, made of straight lengths sewed together (2430).

As jutting wings, made of the same fabric as the dress, tend to disappear, the lingerie collar on the yoke grows more important; it is sheer and soft, set well down to show the column of the neck (2432).

Mme. de Mirbel's costume shows the simultaneous softening of color and line. The variation which we have seen in the orange-to-yellow feathers (2372) is commemorated in her warm purplish-pink bonnet tied with yellow-pink ribbons. Her short-sleeved white dress is finished with wide, gold-buckled black bracelets. Its tab ends are crossed under a white belt, narrowly lined with orange and blue. Black slippers laced over white stockings.

During the 30's, the hair is often parted on either side, the center section combed back, the sides combed down smooth, turning into locks or ringlets in front of the ears, and the long hair braided, coiled, or built up into loops on the crown (2431, 2432).

The imaginative colored aprons of working girls have begun to be incorporated into dress (2280A-2281). This practical fashion has been taken over in the delaine sketching costume; pretty silk aprons are on their way to becoming fixed in the domestic dress of gentlewomen in the 40's.

2434. XIXc. 1831. French.

"Costumes Parisiens" (periodical).

"Cashmere turban executed by Mr. Alexander. Robe with flat embroidery in silk. Cashmere mantle edged with crushed astrakhan."

2435, 2437. XIXc. 1833. French-English.

"Le Follet Courrier des Salons" (periodical).

This periodical, subtitled "Ladies' Magazine," had both French and English offices. The introductory words of the captions (which we italicize) are in English of a sort. In translating the balance of the text, we have followed the orthography of the period, rather than make it conform to modern usages.

2435. *"Morning-dress:* coiffure executed by Mr. Mariton, Rue St. Honore, 244. Robe of chiné gros de Naples, with a lace guimpe and trimming, from the workship of Mme. Neuette-Larcher, dressmaker to H.M. the Queen (Rue Vivienne, 4)."

2437. *"Valking dress:* straw hat, crown of gros de Naples, from the workshop of Mlle. Bonté, Rue des fossés Montmartre. Pelerine-mantelet of plain mousseline lined with gauze, from the shop of Mme. Chaigneau-Popelard, Boulevart Bonne-Nouvelle, No. 4."

2436. XIXc. c. 1835. French.

A. Devéria. Mlle. Amigo of the Théâtre Italien.

The smooth sloping shoulder, bare or covered with a guimpe, has become paramount. Peaks over sleeves have turned into widespread smooth collars, which either stress the dropped armseye, or are eliminated altogether.

As outlines soften, so do fabrics and trimmings. Eyelet embroidery and projecting ruffles give way to flat embroideries of silk (2380) which are now applied on the skirt itself (2434). Fabrics are patterned all over in small printed and often indistinctly woven patterns in moiré and chiné silks (2434-35). Lace returns in small patterns; net gloves.

The fullness of the sleeve is being crushed down from the shoulder, and up from the wrist, into a puff set on a dropped armseye.

Elaborately dressed hair, which in 1833 requires the services of Mr. Mariton, becomes smoothed down to the ears and simplified by 1835 (2436). Hat brims become smaller and more enclosing; crowns and trimming are reduced in unison with hair.

2438. XIXc. 1833. English. (New York Public Library, Rare Book Room.)

Henry Alken. "Jorrocks' Jaunts and Jollities" by Surtees: Mr. Jorrocks Renounces the Acquaintance-ship of the Yorkshireman.

Robert S. Surtees (1803-64) came of an old Durham family. He helped found, and was the first editor of, the "New Sporting Magazine." In 1833 he wrote for it a series of stories about a sporting cockney grocer, and his adventures with the Surrey Hunt and Stag Hounds, shooting, betting at the Newmarket races, aquatics at Margate, his trip to Paris, and a dinner party at home. It was from these stories that Dickens got the idea for "Pickwick Papers." The collected stories were published in 1838 as "Jorrocks' Jaunts and Jollities," with pictures by *Phiz;* Ackermann republished it in 1843 with fifteen colored plates by Alken. In "Handley Cross," 1843, illustrated by John Leech, we have a continuation of Jorrocks who has now become a M. F. H.

"Jorrocks" is a mine of information about English sporting life and dress, which Surtees differentiates in detail by age and position in life. His trip to France with Stubbs is equally full of fascinating stuff about manners and clothing.

Jorrocks and the Yorkshireman have started on their autumn trip to Paris. We ride with them toward the Channel, learning the colors of all sorts of smart new turnouts, their horses and accompanying liveries. We see how people dress, and pack in hat-boxes, carpet-bags, with the last-minute left-overs done up in a red handkerchief.

The captain of the French mail packet is "dressed much like a new policeman, with an embroidered collar to his coat, and a broad red band around a forage-cap."

Men travellers wear a "sable-collared frockcoat," or "a blue camlet cloak, green travelling cap, with a large patent-leather peak."

Customs-house officials in France are dressed in green coat, white trousers, black sugar-loaf "caps," and have swords by their sides.

Jorrocks runs into Thompson, with "mustachios, in a hussar foraging cap stuck on the side of his head, dressed in a black-velvet shooting jacket, and with half a jeweller's shop about him in the way of chains, brooches, rings, and buttons." The traveller is offered a cigar from a box of "beautiful Havannahs," and promised a clean towel every third day, at the inn favored by the British colony of Boulogne. He flips his Hessian boots clean with his handkerchief, combs out his whiskers, calls on the British consul, who wears green spectacles. (Astigmatism began to be corrected with cylindrical lenses c.1827. Book illustrations are increasingly filled with spectacle-wearers.)

The travellers take a diligence for Paris. The conductor wears "the usual frogged, tagged, and embroidered jacket and fur-bound cap." Among the other passengers are an Englishman in "a dark blue camlet cloak, fastened with bronze lion-head clasps, a red neckcloth, and a shabby, napless, broad-brimmed brown hat"; a "red-trousered dragoon, in a frock-coat and flat foraging cap with a flying tassel";

an Englishwoman "either an upper nursery-maid or lower governess," old and ugly enough to travel alone, dressed in "a black beaver bonnet lined with scarlet silk, a nankeen pelisse with a blue ribbon, and pea-green boots"; and a very well "got-up" Frenchwoman. "Her bonnet was a pink satin, with a white blonde *ruche* surmounted by a rich blonde veil, with a white rose placed elegantly on one side, and her glossy auburn hair pressed down the sides of a milk-white forehead, in the Madonna style. Her pelisse was of 'violet-de-bois' figured silk, worn with a black velvet pèlerine and a handsomely embroidered collar. Her boots were of a color to match the pelisse; and a massive gold chain around her neck, and a solitary pearl on a middle finger, were all the jewellery she displayed."

Mr. Jorrocks, who had "caught a glimpse of her foot and ankle as she mounted," opens up his English-French phrase-book, Mme. de Genlis' "Manuel du Voyageur," and goes to work to pick up the Countess.

She has hung her bonnet from the roof of the diligence and tied a "broad-brimmed cambric kerchief over her handsome lace cap"; she falls asleep on Mr. Jorrocks' shoulder, and the Madonna *front* slips to show her own graying hair. We learn, incidentally, during this part of the trip, that gloves, handkerchiefs, gowns and reticules in Paris have lately been affected by the "giraffe mania."

Alken's illustration above shows a Sunday afternoon in the Tuileries gardens, which is filled with "emigrating English" and "Parisians returned from their chateaux." Mr. Stubbs has "indulged in six sous worth of chairs—one to sit upon and one for each leg—and, John Bull-like, stretched himself out in the shade below the lofty trees, to view the gay groups who promenaded the alleys before him."

"First, there came a helmeted cuirassier, with his wife in blue satin, and a little boy in his hand in uniform, with a wooden sword, a perfect miniature of the father. Then a group of short-petticoated, shuffling French women, each with a greyhound in slips, followed by an awkward Englishman with a sister on each arm, all stepping out like grenadiers. Then came a ribbon'd chevalier of the Legion of Honour, whose hat was oftener in his hand than on his head, followed by a nondescript-looking militaire with fierce mustachios, in shining jack-boots, white leathers, and a sort of Italian military cloak, with one side thrown over the shoulder, to exhibit the wearer's leg, and the bright scabbard of a large sword, while on the hero's left arm hung a splendidly-dressed woman." It is "Monsieur le *Colonel Jorrockes,*" done up in a great pair of false mustachios, accompanied by the Countess, with whom he is now living.

The Yorkshireman calls on them at one o'clock. He is admitted by a half-dressed Negro serving man, into a messy room full of red velvet chairs. The Countess is "of course . . . still *en déshabille,* with her nightcap on, a loose robe de chambre of flannel, and a flaming broad-striped red-and-black Scotch shawl thrown over her shoulders, and swan's-down-

2438

lined slippers on her feet. Mr. Jorrocks had his leather pantaloons on, with a rich blue and yellow brocade dressing-gown and blue morocco slippers to match."

Mr. Jorrocks goes to dress and returns "en grand costume—finely cleaned leathers, jack-boots and brass spurs, with a spic and span new blue military frock-coat, hooking and eyeing up to the chin, all covered with braid, frogs, tags, and buttons." Jorrocks complains that "it is rather tight—partiklarly around the waist," but thinks the Yorkshireman should have one too. The Countess suggests that he also get "some of those things—not pantaloons—not those sacks of things called trousers" (which the Yorkshireman is wearing). It turns out that she means black satin breeches.

It is arranged that Mr. Stubbs will accompany them to a *soirée-dansante* given by the Countess de Jackson, a *marchande de modes,* married to an English horse dealer. At nine o'clock that night, he toils back up the dirty stairway to the Countess' apartment on the third landing (see Paris apartment house: Ill. 2489), and is received by the Negro Agamemnon, who has now got into "a roomy uniform of a chasseur—dark green and tarnished gold, with a cocked hat and black feather, and a couteau de chasse, slung by a shining patent-leather belt, over his shoulder. The "Colonel" is "extremely smart: thin black gauze-silk stockings, black satin breeches; well-washed, well-starched white waistcoat with a rolling collar, showing an amplitude of frill; a blue coat with yellow buttons and a velvet collar, while his pumps shone as bright as polished steel." . . . "Rouge and the milliner had effectually reduced (the Countess') age from five-and-forty down to five-and-twenty. She wore a dress of the palest pink satin, with lilies of the valley in her hair, and an ex-

quisitely wrought gold armlet, with a most Lilliputian watch in the centre." Off they go to waltz. This is the sort of invaluable information with which Victorian novels are packed.

2439. XIXc. 1834. French.
"La Revue des Modes de Paris" (periodical).
"Ladies' riding habit in zephyr cloth with a velvet collar. Merino pantaloons, morocco boots. *Panne* coat, velvet collar, corded gray-white velours pantaloon."
Dark blue habit; pale lavender hat, with pale gray-green scarf and matching green gloves; yellow boots.
Bottle-green coat, black collar, yellow gloves.
The riding habit has developed extremely sloping shoulders and a longer waist. It is worn with long breeches strapped under the boot, like men's pantaloons. The small figure shows the lapels of the habit, three rows of buttons, standing collar and stock tied in a bow, and a pleated and ruffled shirt.
The man is a typical figure of the 30's: tall, slender silk hat; bunched curls at male as at female temples; jaw framed by sideburns and standing collar. What is essentially a double-breasted overgarment has been turned into a tail coat with a smooth, close sleeve. Its double row of buttons is set in a V to stress its narrow-waisted torso; the skirts are cut away at a point below the exaggeratedly fitted waist, and are rounded off to outline the hips' roundness before falling in long, straight square tails. Striped pantaloons strapped over boots with long, narrow, square toes and spurs. Tasselled stick.

2440. XIXc. 1837. French.
Gavarni. Court dress.
The court coat has had a standing collar throughout the century. It is roundly cutaway, tight-waisted,

and rounded over hips and buttocks like coats in general; worn with knee breeches and *chapeau bras*.

Ladies' hair in spaniels' ears at the side, with the knot on the crown slipping lower down during the 30's. The customarily rather plain skirt of the 30's is looped up over flounces of the lace which is used in court dress. Long kid gloves, since the arm and hand are pretty consistently covered during the 30's.

2441. XIXc. 1835. French.

Henri Monnier. The composer Zérézo.

The composer shows the vast difference between the fashion-plate ideal and the pantaloon under the actual stresses of thigh, knee and buttocks.

2442. XIXc. 1835. French.

Town dress: The wide, flat, deliriously trimmed hats of 1827 turn into bonnets with strings coming from far back on the neck, a bow set on the under side of the brim, and paradise or ostrich trimming. By mid-30's the bonnet starts to enclose the face and

for a year or so scoops high in front. By 1840 it becomes smaller and more rounded—a frame for the face. Its brim drips with lace which is carried under the chin like a *cornette;* or a lingerie frill like that of a cap is set around the crown opening under the brim. Short kid gloves, disappearing into long sleeves; lace handkerchiefs.

Mantles have bow-tied *pèlerine* collars and huge open sleeves which are given form by several tucks across the elbow.

Men's collars large, high in back, often of velvet; coat with reduced lapels buttoned high on chest; tall, rather straight-crowned top hat; fringe of beard outlining chin.

2443. XIXc. 1836. English. (New York, F. Ambrose Clark.)

James Pollard. Manchester-Liverpool Mailcoach.

Courtesy of Metropolitan Museum, Print Room (2439)

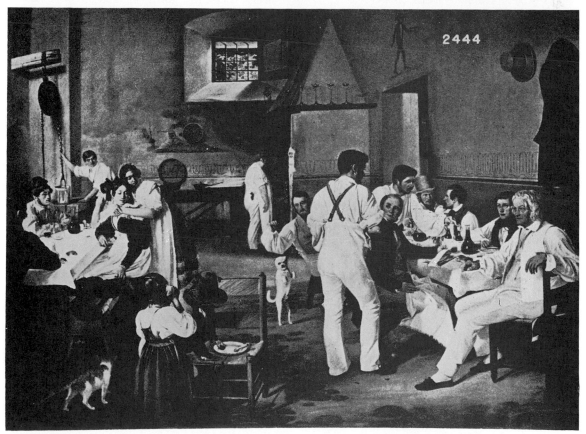

Floating veils on enclosing bonnets as well as top-hat of riding habit (2439).

Dark dickey and coat, separated by a line of white vest, worn with a forage cap and light-colored (probably waterproofed) topcoat. Colored cravats; light and dark toppers.

2444. XIXc. 1836. Danish. (Frederiksborg Museum.)
Conrad Blunck. Danish Artists in a Roman Inn. The seated figure in the foreground is the sculp-tor Thorwaldsen. Dark cravats; shirts with full sleeves; vests have a skeleton back of plain fabric; trousers require suspenders, and have side pockets into which the handkerchief can be stuck. The fashion plate figure of the mid1830's seems rather remote, and there is little difference between the comfortable clothes shown here and those which a similar group would be wearing a century later, with the exception of hats.

2445-46. XIXc. 1838-39. French-English.

"La Mode" (periodical).

2445. Hair parted, waved and curled. Moustache with beard or hair surrounding chin. Collar turned down over a crumpled dickey of dark satin; separated by line of white vest, which parallels the coat collar; wide jutting lapels, set rather high, on short, double-breasted coat. Characteristic short, fitted topcoat of 30's; narrow, glove-fitting trousers strapped over delicate boots.

Standing stock and cravat, with ruffled shirt, the cuffs turned back over the shallow coat cuff; fitted frock coat; fancy brocade vest; trousers strapped but cutaway over instep to show striped stockings and low bow-trimmed shoes.

Coat collars are set low on the neck and lie flat. Single-breasted coats are worn open; their fronts cannot be closed, and the roll of the lapel is carried down almost their entire length. Top hat crowns taller and heavier.

2446. "Dressing gown in Persian taste from Doucet. Little lappeted bonnet from Mme. LaSalle. Redingote with pelerine of Tulasne Ledoux. Divan from Maigret. Embroidery frame, canvas and wools from Serré Delisle."

Victorian domesticity rampant. When her husband has worn out his complete Persian outfit from Doucet, which is the favorite gift of the 30's and 40's, the lady (who wears kid gloves even while embroidering), will undoubtedly make him a pair of wool-embroidered slippers. Hair, smooth to the ears, then falling in long bunched curls, is covered at home by a cap with long lappets. The skirt front has begun to be split and its edges decorated, in e. 30's. In late 30's the hem of the underskirt is trimmed; by the 40's, the slit overskirt disappears, and the remaining skirt may have several rows of ruffles. At the turn of 30's-40's, cartridge pleating is a favorite method, both of trimming and attaching the skirt to the waistband.

2447-48. XIXc. 1838. English. (New York Public Lib.).
"Court Magazine," Vol. 2 (periodical).

Descriptions which accompany plates are quoted, without modernization of orthography.

2447. *"Toilette d'Intérieur*: Fashionable morning costume. Redingote of pearl grey silk. Corsage half high, made tight to fit the bust, and crossing in front. The skirt is likewise made to cross, and is rounded at the lower corners. The trimming consists of a single *bouillon* round the corsage, and a double round the skirt, with a tolerably deep lace at the edge. The sleeves are quite plain at the shoulder, the remainder full, and the wrist plain and deep. At top are two *bouillons* and a lace frill. Blonde cap, ornamented with flowers and ribbons. The border is deep; it is quite plain across the brow and full at each side of the face; bows of pink ribbon are placed underneath the border at the right side, and a full-blown rose at the left. Hair in bands; white kid gloves; black shoes."

2448. Sitting figure: "The dress is made in a similar fashion to the one just described. The cap is also like the other, with the difference of two half-wreaths being put at the back of the border instead of the trimming underneath."

2449-50. XIXc. 1839. English. (New York Public Library.)
"Court Magazine," Vol. 4.

2449. Seated figure: *"Toilette d'Intérieur. Home Morning Dress.* Dress of white muslin: corsage *demi-décolletée* (half high); the back has a few gathers at the waist; the fronts cross and are in large set folds on plaits; round the neck is a narrow lace. The sleeves are short and do not even cover the elbow. They are quite tight and have double tucks (which are cut the cross way) put on as plain as possible and close together so that the upper tuck covers the putting on of the one below it, and so on. The skirt has rather a deep flounce, at the very bottom. Aprons of *broché* silk with a flounce of the same all round and a double one at the bottom; the pockets are on the outside, rather pointed at bottom; they are put on with a narrow flounce all round except at top. The cap consists of a mere *cornet à la paysanne;* the crown is like a half handkerchief plaited into form at the back; the lappets in front descend below the ears and are turned up again and fastened amidst the plaits at the back of the cap; they are considerably stiffened and in three or four deep plaits on folds. A coloured ribbon, after forming a rosette-bow in front, encircles the cap and finishes in a bow with long ends at back; a small bouquet of rose is placed at the left side. Hair in smooth bands, the ends braided and turned up at each side of the face. Bow of coloured ribbon fastening the corsage in front. Hair chain. Half-length black netting mittens."

2450. "Redingote of *poux de soie, couleur cendre.* The corsage is made to fit perfectly tight to the bust, and without a waistband. The back is plain, the fronts *en chale,* like a gentleman's waistcoat, with collar turned over and lapels turned back; it merely meets at the waist in front. It will be perceived that the collar and fronts are lined with buckram or some other stiffening to make them sit as in the plate. The sleeves are tight at top, confined in plaits toward the wrist, the remainder full. The skirt, which is very long and very ample has five *rouleaux* down each side of the front, which are continued round the bottom of the skirt. These *rouleaux* are put in a bunch close together at the waist, but occupy a wider space as they go down. The chemisette is of cambric, the front in set plaits, and *à sabot,* or small plaited frills down the front; round the neck is a lace or cambric frill. The ruffles are cambric trimmed with lace. Hat of *paille de riz* lined and trimmed with delicate pink *crepe lisse.* A bunch of roses is placed as low as possible at the right side, and a light wreath of the same crosses the brow and descends a little at each side under the front of the hat. Hair in bands. Pale yellow gloves. Black varnished leather shoes."

2451. XIXc. 1830-40. French. (Boston, Museum of Fine Arts, Elizabeth Day McCormick Coll.)

Silk apron: embroidered in "ribbon work" in brilliant colors; one apron on plum, another on brown ground, in same collection.

Aprons reappeared in the latter half of the 30's, and increased in use. "Never was there a greater rage for aprons," of satin or shot silk for morning or afternoon, than in 1847.

2452. XIXc. c. 1842. French. (Metropolitan Museum, Print Room.)

La Sylphide Corset.

From which of the magazines published by the *Société des Modes Réunies* this loose plate comes has not yet been determined. Hottenroth dates a redrawing of it as 1850, which is so nearly a decade too late that it may be a misprint. We are not much helped by its name; the incomparable grace of La Taglioni in *La Sylphide* (Thackeray: "The New-

combs") had caused costume accessories to be called by that name long before and after she chose that ballet from her repertoire for her New York début in 1838. There is a *La Sylphide* parasol in England in 1846.

Sleeve puffs on a dropped shoulder-line (which the little boned shoulder caps would support) were passing fast by the 40's. Dark bows at the collar are seen throughout the 30's and most of the 40's. But the collars of these chemisettes have lost all lateral spread; they are small and round, and the chemisette is designed to fill in the deep V-opening of the early 40's. Hair has the coronet braid of end 30's. As curls grow longer and looser at the beginning of the 40's, their earlier bunched form is commemorated in the ribbons at the ears of small caps. The museum sets a tentative date of c. 1842.

2453. XIXc. 1839-40. French. (Versailles, Nat. Mus.)

F. X. Winterhalter. Marie of Orleans, wife of

Prince Alexander of Würtemberg, and their son, Philip.

Louis-Philippe's daughter, who died at about this time, holds the son born in July 1838.

Until 1840, a full sleeve is still occasionally seen; it is finished by a turned-back, ruffled cuff, and has a deep, shirred upper section, which is concealed here by the spreading, ruffled, crossed and pinned collars, into which the old shoulder caps have sunk. Hair is looped smoothly at the ears; the cap again begins to cover the daytime head, and its lappets or trim replace bunches of falling curls.

2454-55. XIXc. 1840. U.S.A. (Metropolitan Museum.)

Nelson Cook. James Merrill Cook, Anne Cady Cook.

Slight provincial time-lag, more apparent in Mrs. Cook's dress: see neck and sleeves (2431) and coarse mesh net and lace morning dress (2435). Hair looped above the line of the ears in the simplest way of the 30's. Good band of deep lace, which she has no intention of ruining by cutting, has been pleated together in a fan to give it play.

2454. Black satin stock; rounded opening, tight, high waist and enclosing skirts of 30's; velvet lapels have the more rounded form, and the sleeves the buttoned seam opening of the late 30's-40's; braid-covered buttons, white cuff emerges as sleeve shortens.

2456. XIXc. 1840. U.S.A. (Charleston, S. C., Coll. of City.)

C. Meyr. Firemasters and officers of the Volunteer Fire Company.

Much less distortion of male body form and cut of clothes in U.S.A. Strapped pantaloons, longer and easier in the lower leg; many long tubular trousers. The new jacket of the 40's, buttoned above the waistline, cut away below; diagonal pocket with flaps (2 from r.).

High silk toppers and lower-crowned light-colored hats.

2457. XIXc. 1841. U.S.A. (Washington, Mellon Coll.)

Henry Inman (1801-46). Charles Fenno Hoffman (1806-84).

The author, editor and lawyer shows hair parted at the side, waved and curled, as is the longer fringe

of hair along the jowls. Fitted stock and tied cravat. Shoulders wider and sloping; sleeve plain, shorter, shows a line of shirt cuff; lapels wider, their edges stitched and often (from c. 1835) faced with velvet. Coats, which have largely been worn closed during the daytime in the 30's, open to show vests; these are noticeable in satin, brocade or embroidery (c. 1835-60). Pantaloons (pleated fullness at waistline c. 1838) are also covered with pattern; diamonds, checks, loud stripes, even embroidered sprigs on light summer pantaloons when worn with plain coats (c. 1835-60). Coat, vest, pantaloons and cravat are usually of different color and fabric during the 40's; all are capable of being loudly patterned, but only one patterned garment appears in each outfit, as: a dark brown coat and white vest with yellowish striped trousers, or white pantaloons and a leather vest with a checked coat. The exception is the pat-

terned cravat, but this is separated from a fancy coat by a plain vest.

The watch-chain, which in D'Orsay's time was worn around the neck, has now dropped into the opening of the vest; it will grow shorter and be carried from a lower buttonhole to the vest pocket.

2458-59. XIXc. 1841. French. (Met. Mus. of Art.)
Gavarni. "Les Lorettes."

2458. *Mon petit homme, faut être raisonnable . . . c'est mon parrain qui veut absolument me faire un sort, dans son bien des Bouches-du-Rhône pour l'éducation de sa petite . . . je vais te laisser la mienne.*

2459. *Mon adoré . . . dis-moi ton petit nom.*

The *lorettes,* shown in a wonderful series of color plates, were the little lights o'love who practically filled the new apartment building near the church of Notre-Dame de Lorette in 1840.

Men: top hat wider brimmed and curving; parted and curled hair; beards; collar turned down over cravat; rounded male shoulder, torso and hips; tight-waisted patterned pantaloons, full at hips, pleated into waistband, narrow below, strapped under boots and cut away over instep.

Women: wide shoulder abandoned for wide hips; an enormous amount of ungored width was gathered into fashionable skirts. Gloved hand and long sleeve connected by pairs of wide bracelets; plaid umbrellas.

2460. XIXc. April 1842. U.S.A. (New York Public Lib.)
"Godey's Lady's Book" (periodical).

Godey's, the most influential American fashion magazine, was published from 1830-98. Its plates are both in color or black and white, like this one. The chief defect of *Godey's* is that plates seldom have an explanatory text, at this period, and that the quality of the plates, during its long life, is variable.

These ladies, wearing short gloves under all circumstances show (l. to r.) the mitred folds seen in 2449-50 becoming simplified and drawn down a lengthening bodice, while the V-neck begins its rise to a high, closed line by the addition of embroidered collars.

Bonnets close by knotted, scarf-like ties, often patterned, rather than ribbon bows and streamers. (See plaid cravat, like those of the men in 2474, knotted like these bonnet-ties, at the throat of lady in 2475.)

Frogged and corded trimmings increase in use on women's clothes, and on men's top-coats and dressing gowns during the 40's.

Curls become fewer in number, longer and more spiral (like shavings) during the 40's; the sides of evening caps lengthen with them. Curls and evenings caps tend to become eliminated; the evening head of the 50's may show a curl or two, but is decorated with flowers, rather than a cap.

Black net and lace scarves with long, knotted fringe ends. Cords threaded with small bead-like ornaments are seen across foreheads in afternoon and evening dress during latter half of 30's and first half of 40's (third from left).

Skirts continue to show inverted V openings to mid-40's; are edged with puffed cordings (Ills. 2447-48) or unhemmed ruchings with pinked or frayed edges and are frequently caught together down the front with knots or frogged ornaments.

Fabrics in combinations of heavy and light stripes are used especially in 1841-2 in combinations of diagonal against vertical. Sleeves becoming plainer and closer during first half of 40's, and are finished by a small tight cuff.

There is a great deal of lace during the 40's, but

it tends to be superseded by fringes and frogs, running designs in cordlike braids, and by rosettes and appliquéd roses, on bonnets and evening dresses; all in very much debased taste, according to general midXXc. opinion.

2461. XIXc. 1843. French. (New York Public Library.)
Grandville. "Les petites misères de la vie humaine," by E. Forgues:

"Je traverse le boulevard, où vingt fumeurs effrontés m'obsèdent de leur attention quêteuse."

"Grandville" was the pseudonym of a strangely talented artist named Jean Ignace Isidore Gérard (1803-47).

His illustrations for "Les petites misères de la vie humaine," which follows the trend set by "Les Français peints par eux-mêmes" are straightforward enough. His really astonishing surrealistic productions show the metamorphosis of women into bright flowers ("Les fleurs animées," 1847), and of people

into frightful animals ("Scènes de la vie privée et publique des animaux," 1843).

Top hat crowns and brims are more insistent; great variety in hair: cut full all around, or combed down and under smoothly—in a way related to women's oiled loops of hair; or clipped short; moustaches, beards or mutton chops, alone or combined. Great variety of topcoats, sometimes caped or hooded in latter half of the 40's, with larger buttons than in the 30's; single-breasted topcoats often closed by tabs or frogs; diagonally set pockets in the skirts of topcoats. Many men carry sticks during the late 30's and the 40's. The unaccompanied lady is bothered by a score of men puffing on cigars and urchins smoking the still vulgar pipe.

2462. XIXc. 1844. French. (Hendecourt Coll., Southeby Sale 1925.)

Ingres. Mme. and Mlle. Reiset.

The descent of the *canezou* blouse from the sleeveless *fichu-canezou* is clear in this illustration. The points of the corded and gathered fichu hang over the belt.

The *canezou* was, strictly, a white blouse, but its corded and puffed treatment affected other pale colored garments (2468-9). V-necklines are filled in with chemisettes, collars and cravats, the ends of which are shaped like rabbit ears, rather than flat ribbons. Curls, longer and lanker, start higher on the head.

2463. XIXc. 1842. French. (Metropolitan Museum, Print Room.)

Grandville. Poster: "Fables of Florian."

Women's hair has been looped madonna-fashion during 30's to cover the ears. The natural tendency of the ears to break through is especially exploited in the 40's. A loose tress separates from the rest of the hair, and is worked around the ears, as a frame, or in a loop above the ear. The rest of the hair is braided. On girls it falls in two ribbon-tied pigtails, which are sometimes wound spirally over the ears. But ribbon knots decorate women's coiled braids also, and they wear necklaces, lace collars, brooches, and scarves similar to the girl on the poster (who undoubtedly wears pantalettes and a rather long skirt.) The bonnet brim surrounds the head so closely, that the back must be cut away. Coiled hair may fit into the tiny crown, or is concealed by the ruffle which covers the back of the neck.

Everybody can now have imitation paradise feathers made in Paris from cock feathers, and very durable. Miss Jelly, the dressmaker, took hers off her Sunday bonnet, in costuming her lodger, Capt. Doleful, as the Great Mogul, for the Handley Cross fancy dress ball.

Long hanging ends are loved in the mid40's; they become shawl-like and pointed, in the 50's, but they are now still band-like in France—long narrow scarves which are held tight around the shoulders; scarves and ribbons on hair, hats, and hanging sashes (2458).

2464. XIXc. 1845. Swedish. (Stockholm, Hallwylska Collection.)

Unknown painter. Brothers Hans and Walter J. Hallwyl.

Boys' clothes have been apt to show the influence of sailors' or soldiers' uniforms from final quarter of XVIIIc. The chests of fitted jackets or full blouses are decorated with two or three rows of buttons, which draw together towards the waist; or the same pattern is braided or laced across the chest. Long trousers. Low laced shoes.

2465. XIXc. 1844. English-French. (New York, Daniel H. Farr.)

E. H. T. Pingret (1788-1875). Arrival of Louis-Philippe at Windsor.

Mme. de Genlis' pupil, Philippe-Egalité's son, earned his living as a teacher in Switzerland, after the Revolution, with which he had been in complete sympathy. He travelled with his brothers in America for three years, and then settled in England at Twickenham. When a brother became tubercular, Louis-Philippe went with him to Italy. There he married a granddaughter of Marie Thérèse and Charles IV in 1809, and lived until Louis XVIII's accession brought them back to immense estates in France. He sent his eight children to public school, and because of liberal leanings was forced to live in England again in 1815-17. At the Revolution of 1830, he walked through the streets to the Hôtel de Ville, and was proclaimed king. Victoria and Albert visited him in France in 1843, and in 1844 he returned their visit. With age, he became more Bourbon and reactionary; in 1848, he and Queen Marie Amélie found it advisable to slip away, as "Mr. and Mrs. Smith," to England, where he died.

Small round bonnets; flowing veils; *pèlerine-mantelets* with long tab ends, shawls, shorter *pelisses,* over long, full, round skirts, some with the vertical front trimming, which appeared briefly, mostly plain, tending towards horizontal flounces.

Girls in pantalettes under seven-eighths-long dresses, pair of long braids; tiny boy in rather long dress with pantaloons.

2466-71. XIXc. March 1843. U.S.A. (New York Public Library.)

"Godey's Lady's Book" (periodical).

This plate, in soft, pale colors, shows l. to r.:

2472

2466. Boy: black top hat, bright blue blouse, and trousers with some of the fullness of a woman's skirts.

2467. Boy: because younger, shows even more female influence, combined with a man's tasselled green forage cap; green dress over white, lace-edged pantalettes.

2468. Lady: pink and blue flower-trimmed bonnet; gray gown with the shirring seen on so many *canezou* blouses of the 40's. Gloves and embroidered handkerchief.

2469. Lady: scarf-tied pale blue bonnet and gown. Her yellow *palatine* or *pèlerine-mantelet* shows the roses which are embroidered or applied on many evening dresses of latter half of the 40's; combined with foliated embroidery, lace, and tabbed rosettes.

2470. Girl: white bonnet, lined with dark and light rose shirrings; brown cloak; white dress and pantalettes.

2471. Girl: rosette-trimmed pink bonnet tied like a cravat; blue-green pardessus. The borders of outer garments are increasingly edged with running corded patterns, which will become fancy braids and fringes by the 50's.

2472. XIXc. 1843. French. (New York Public Library.)

E. L. Lami. "The American in Paris in Summer." Lami's illustrations for Jules Janin's two books, translated as "Summer in Paris" and "Winter in Paris," give enchanting pictures of Paris existence in home, street and park.

The dry comment of a very old man in the country a quarter of a century ago, when a guest of mine set off for a sun bath, was: "There used to be a style if a sun-ray hit you, it'd kill you." His provincial childhood had been lived under the tradition, at least, of tightly constricted Victorian ladies, doing a little needlework in a dark-papered room behind heavily curtained windows, and drinking vinegar against the "green sickness" or living on toast and tea to enhance a white skin. It was protected out of doors by a completely concealing bonnet, long sleeves and wide bracelet to insure no dark line above the short glove. The glove protected the whiteness of a hand which was (ideally at least) never seen, because it was never ungloved.

Between the hysteria and tuberculosis induced by this sort of life, we see a great many convalescing ladies, slightly propped up, surrounded by rewarding solicitude.

Men's hair was parted on the side and cut full all around. Shaped collar, set on a curved band, arches around the face or begins to turn down over the dark cravat or dickey fastened with a brooch. Soft, curved shirt cuff turned back over cuff of dark suits, with matching coats and trousers. These are cut with great elegance in long, less closely fitted lines, and are worn with white vests of piqué or corded cotton. Flower in lapel; rings, gloves. Top hat of the visitor is carried after the tradition of the court *chapeau bras* which is never set down.

It is after ten by candlelight. The ladies wear simple home evening dress, with uncluttered skirts, masses of lace at the elbows, in the sleeve elaboration seen especially in France; and lace scarves or collars at comparatively high necks. The visiting lady wears more ceremonious evening dress, with a valance of lace around a low neckline and no sleeve trimming below it. She wears a cap, but caps are beginning to lose ground already.

The invalid wears an informal cap, but like the other ladies at home here, bare heads are often trimmed instead with twists and loops of ribbon or cord.

2473. XIXc. 1843-4. English.

"Phiz" (*H. K. Browne*). Dickens' "Martin Chuzzlewit." Pleasant Little Family Party at Mr. Pecksniff's.

The strong-minded widow of a deceased brother of Mr. Martin Chuzzlewit, and "her spinster daughters, three in number, and of gentlemanly deportment . . . so mortified . . . with tight stays . . . that . . . sharp lacing was expressed in their very noses," show skirts slightly less developed than those in Louis-Philippe's 1844 visit, still full in back only. But the pelisse is already having difficulty in covering them, and is being shortened; veiled bonnets; V-necked, long-waisted bodices, rather large collars.

Sitting by Mr. Pecksniff (is it Mrs. Spottletoe?): bows in hair and chain with pendant.

Mr. Spottletoe: beard without moustache; black dickey-cravat; watch chain around neck, velvet collared coat, differing in color and fabric from vest and breeches.

George Chuzzlewit, the "gay bachelor cousin" . . . so overfed "that the bright spots on his cravat, and the rich pattern on his waistcoat, and even his glittering trinkets, seemed to have broken out upon him," shows another version of the quiff of hair beside Mr. Pecksniff's. Mr. Chuzzlewit's "very dark and very hairy" grand nephew sits with a bell-shaped top hat on the knee of his horizontally striped pantaloons, with one of the light-colored short topcoats hanging on his shoulders: all pantaloons still strapped under boots.

2474. XIXc. Early 1840's. Scotch.

David Octavius Hill. Chalmers Family at Merchiston.

Wedgwood, the potter, had produced fugitive silhouette images on sensitized paper by the turn of the century. Research from 1814 enabled Nicéphore de Niepce to make fixed pictures on silvered plates. His process was refined after his death in 1833 by his son Isidore, in partnership with Daguerre, and published in 1839. Photography began to be practiced, almost immediately, all over the world.

David Octavius Hill (1802-70), a Scottish portrait painter, was the first great photographer, and remains one of the greatest.

The dresses are made from a fabric which was extremely fashionable in England in 1841. Solid stripes are crossed by almost invisible lines, between which blocks of chiné pattern or flower motifs form a broken stripe. The stripes are effectively used here with the spreading collars of the late 30's to exploit construction shown in the 1839 plates. They replace mitred folds in cutting the bodice; they form diagonal closings and panels under the split skirt front, and are used in sleeves which become increasingly plain and close-fittting—1840-45.

Men's top hats grow more massive and belled. Parted hair grows longer in back. Cravats are colored, or patterned in stripes or plaids, and almost conceal the collar, which begins during the 40's to turn down over the cravat. Coats and topcoats are worn open and have grown longer, ending below rather than above the knee.

Vests end in points, are often made of brocade, and are usually lighter or darker than the rest of the costume.

Trousers are lighter in color than coats, have become more tubular, and have lost the strap under the boot.

2475. XIXc. Mid-1840's. Scotch.

David Octavius Hill. Lady in a Flowered Dress.

In England, in first half of the 1840's, the sleeve is apt to be simple, close and finished with a cuff. During the latter 40's, it shortens, and begins to bell out over a shirred and puffed white inner sleeve. Necklines grow higher and collars closer in latter half of 40's. The bonnet of first half of the decade is roundly enclosing and is fastened under the chin in knotted ties (like the plaid cravat worn by the lady), rather than by a bow of flat ribbon.

Hair has been worn smoothly looped (as an alternative to ringlets), sometimes exposing the ear, from the early 30's.

Hill's photograph of Margaret Fuller in 1846 shows an almost identical hair-do, worn by the American feminist who was drowned on her return trip when her ship went down off Fire Island.

Watch on cord around neck, pinned at waist. Cashmere shawl with long, knotted fringe.

2476. XIXc. Mid-1840's. Scotch.

David Octavius Hill. Lady Ruthven.

The close bonnet of first half of 40's becomes wider spread at the bottom in 1845-6. Horizontal lines have been used in opposition to vertical since the late 30's, but do not begin to prevail until second half of 40's. After the wide embroidered collars of the 30's, lace and net reappeared and were used for a decade or two in pèlerines and flounces; a great deal of it was black like Lady Ruthven's folded shawl.

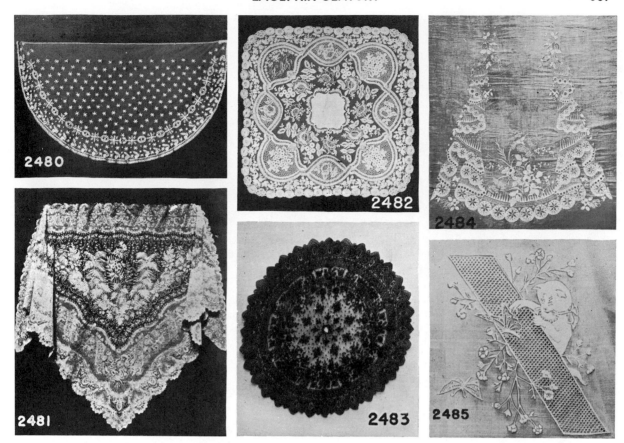

2480

2482

2484

2481

2483

2485

2477-79. XIXc. 1840-48. U.S.A. (Metropolitan Museum, Print Room.)

Southworth and Hawes (fl. 1840-62).
2477. John Quincy Adams (1767-1848).
2478. Harriet Beecher Stowe (1811-96).
2479. Emerson School.

Southworth and Hawes were in partnership from 1840-62. These photographs are difficult to date accurately because they show, seated, people who are not concerned with the latest fashion.

Mr. Adams wears clothes one would expect to find on an elderly man at any time between the beginning of the photographers' partnership and the subject's death: a double-breasted tailcoat with velvet collar; unstrapped trousers; laced shoes instead of boots.

Fringed black lace and net scarves and high-necked bodices, shirred horizontally like Mrs. Stowe's, are seen throughout the 40's, but the high mounting of her corkscrew curls makes mid-decade to second half decade seem probable, despite her apparent youth.

The Emerson School for young ladies in Boston was run by the son of the minister of the Uni-tarian church; Ralph Waldo Emerson, another of his sons, taught there for several years after his graduation from Harvard. There were decades during which schoolteachers could look like this one, but his laced low shoes and collar, full back hair, combined with the small collars on his pupils' high-necked bodices, the shirred band attaching sleeves to a dropped shoulder, and the increasing width of the bottom of sleeve of the dotted dress, the spiraling of braids around the ears, make a guess of 1846 reasonable.

2480. Early XIXc. French.
Bobbin lace veil: sprays of bobbin lace appliquéd on machine net.
2481. XIXc. French.
Shawl: needlepoint and point de gaze.
2482. Mid-XIXc. Flemish, Brussels.
Handkerchief: Brussels lace.
2483. XIXc. French.
Parasol cover: black Chantilly.
2484. Mid-XIXc. French.
Embroidered panel: part of 4-piece muslin dress.
2485. XIXc. German.
Square of embroidered china silk.

2486. XIXc. 1844. Spanish. (Madrid, Museo Romantico.)
Vincent Lopez. Marquis de Remisa.

Lapels roll back throughout the length of an open coat and become wider. They are connected to a wider collar at a deep notch, from which a seam runs down, piecing the lapel with a strip of even width. This is the vestige of the center seam which was necessary to make coats which overlapped fit

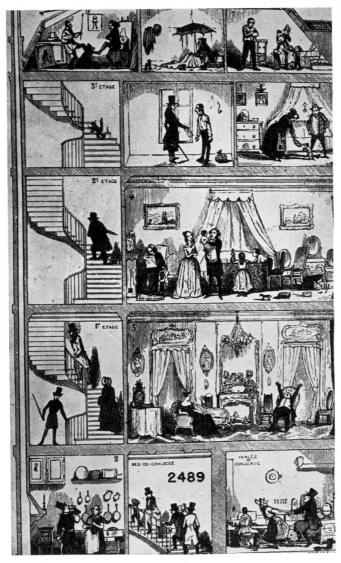

over a globular chest. Sleeves slightly longer. Tied cravat, important shirt and vest buttons; chain from second buttonhole to watch pocket. The Marquis' trousers are still strapped under patent leather boots.

2487. XIXc. 1845. French. (New York, Frick Coll.)

Ingres. Countess d'Haussonville.

Hair looped above the ears and drawn back into a braided bun, dressed with ribbon loops.

Neckline rising on all dresses, day or evening. Interest is being transferred, in evening dresses, from a horizontal neckline with a lace valance or rigidly pleated band, to a V-line leading from the point of a shorter-waisted bodice to the sleeve. Sleeves, which have scarcely been seen, are elaborated in the new way—by manipulation of fabric into gathered and corded puffings. Skirt fullness is increased by gathered flounces, which begin as one flounce at bottom, increase to three in the 50's.

2488. XIXc. Mid-1840's. French. (New York, Cooper Union Museum.)

Constantin Guys (1805-92). The New Fashion.

Guys, son of the chief commander of the French Navy, was born c. 1805 in Flushing where his uncle was the French plenipotentiary. He was in Greece with Byron in 1824, and travelled all over Europe, the Near East and North Africa. He served in the Dragoons and lived the life of a dandy, until indignation at his father's remarriage to a sixteen-year-old girl sent him to London to "live by his wits." Nobody quite knows when he began to draw his better-known pictures; there is little information about their dates. By 1848, he was a staff artist for the *Illustrated London News* and covered the Crimean War for them. He fell on ill days, and consorted with the Baudelaire coterie and with gutter characters whom he drew wonderfully as he had done blooded horses, elegant carriages and fashionable women. In 1885, he was run over and was taken to a hospital where he died seven years later.

Shop girl peers out to look at fashions seen c. 1845; long, loose *pelisse-mantles* with fur edging and long cylindrical muffs; bonnets with veils and wide loops and strings hanging down in back.

2489. XIXc. 1845. French.

Bertail (pseudonym). "Le Diable à Paris": Cross-Section of a House in Paris, Jan. 1, 1845.

2490. XIXc. French.

Constantin Guys. Sketch: Pen ink, and water color.

Hair longer, waved rather than curled (second half of 40's) moustache; very full hair on jaws, with moustache. Evening dress: white bow tie; pleated shirt front, now without ruffle, exposed by low-cut white vest, the skirts of which spring apart below the last closing (lapped over, as are some bodice-closings); wide trousers, no longer strapped over boots; long narrow squared toes; straighter stove-pipe hats.

Coronet braid high on head (late 40's); the slit-skirt line of e. 40's persists to 50's in hanging sash ends in front; long lace scarf; short gloves; fan.

2491. XIXc. 1849. German.

August von Kreling (1819-76). "Alte und neue Kinderlieder": Christmas Eve.

Husbands now change into dressing gown, cap and slippers at home; pipe smoking is rising socially.

Small loop of hair at ears; braids set as a coronet in the Guys illustration tend to slip lower into a coiled bun, c. 1850.

Wonderful German toys at the holiday, which was especially developed in Germany.

2492. XIXc. 1843. French. (The Louvre.)

Théodore Chassériau. The Artist's Sisters, Adèle and Aline.

Bodices partly or entirely corded in this way are

2492

2493

seen from the late 30's through the 40's and are the basis of the shape of the *canezou* into the 60's. Hair is often waved and drawn back, dressed with small, gold-edged combs and coiled in back, rather than looped or with bunched curls.

2493. XIXc. 1845. French. (Versailles, Nat. Mus.)
  F. X. Winterhalter. Marie Caroline Auguste de Bourbon, duchesse d'Aumale.

2494. XIXc. 1845. French. (Versailles, Nat. Mus.)
  F. X. Winterhalter. Marie Clémentine d' Orléans, princesse de Saxe-Coburg-Gotha.

2495. XIXc. c. 1850. French. (Metropolitan Museum, Print Room.)
  Achille Lefèvre, after *Winterhalter.* Marie-Amélie, wife of Louis-Philippe.

Winterhalter's portraits, which royalty loved, are scarcely portraits at all, but the period of the lovely lace-flounced gowns painted by this German has come to be called by his name.

The duchesse d'Aumale's ceremonial gown is veiled in black lace. Its bodice is drawn down into a long point, but its waist is actually shortened in the way of the 50's. Its neckline combines and elaborates the two favorite finishes of evening gowns: a wide band of pleated fabric, mitred at center-front like picture-frame moulding; and a lace valance. Here the lace bands are doubled, and finished with a pleated heading which may be said to sketch the third flounce of the 50's (Marie-Amélie). The gown also shows the new interest in manipulated self-fabric in the deep pleats by which the skirt fullness is obtained.

With these new trends, the gown also shows the persistence of shaded color. It allies a rosy pink with a yellower pink, used under the lower flounces of lace on the skirt, down the point of the bodice, and on the folds under the first lace valance. The favorite roses of the mid40's and 50's help to alter the horizontal line of the valance in the direction of the bodice cut *en coeur* of the 50's. Ubiquitous trailing black lace scarf of mid40's.

The princess of Saxe-Coburg-Gotha's less formal summer muslin evening gown, its shirred heading threaded with ribbon, shows the formal folds deteriorating into gathers, laid across the bodice in a diagonal closing line.

Elaborated puffings are seen, particularly in France, on evening gowns which do not carry a lace valance.

When curls are worn, they are larger, longer and more spiral, and start higher on the temples. The back hair is set in a braided coronet which tends to slip into a bun at the nape.

The cap loses favor with younger women, who now dress their hair with flowers, loops and puffs of ribbon, and feathers.

With her long, aging face, Marie-Amélie retains the diagonally set sausage curls of the 30's.

Caps have for a long time been worn by any woman who has been married long enough to have a baby, and the queen is the mother of eight.

The buckled belt of the 30's continues to be worn in the 40's on bodices which do not finish in a point. Elaborate French sleeve. Bracelets increase in im-

2496

portance—not the pairs of wide band bracelets at the wrist of long-sleeved gowns, but elaborate single bracelets worn higher on the arm; gloves slightly higher, with XVIIc. slashed cuffs.

2496. XIXc. Jan. 15, 1848. English. (New York Public Library.)

"The Ladies' Newspaper" (periodical, later called "The Queen"). Quotations are from original text accompanying the picture.

"Costume for a little boy between six and seven years of age. Hat of black felt, the crown round and the brim turned up on each side. Instead of a band, a cord passed twice around the hat, and tied in the back, where it is finished with two tassels. Paletot of gray cloth, edged all around with embroidery in gray soutache. Trousers of blue cloth, gathered on a band at the waist. Black glazed leather shoes and garters of chamois leather.

"Carriage dress. Bonnet of pink therry velvet, trimmed with white lace, and a white voilette attached to the edge of the bonnet. Dress of Pekin with satin stripes, green and rose color. The skirt with three flounces, each edged with green silk fringe, headed by two rows of green velvet. The corsage is high and plain, and the sleeves tight to the arm and fastening closely to the wrist, where they are finished by turn-up cuffs. Gloves of pale yellow kid.

"Walking dress. Bonnet of embroidered velvet, with pale green satin, and a demi-wreath of velvet flowers on the outside. Strings of green satin ribbon, the same colour as the lining and undertrimming of bows of ribbon and velvet flowers in variegated hues. A pardessus of rich brown satin, of the paletot form, and thickly wadded, so that, with an appearance of lightness, it combines a sufficient degree of warmth for the promenade, even on the coldest day. The pardessus is finished at the bottom, up the two fronts, and at the ends of the sleeves, by a deep row of quilting. The dress, which is of the same material as the pardessus, is also quilted up the front. Slate-coloured kid gloves."

2497. XIXc. 1848. U.S.A. (Baltimore, Walters Art Gall.)

R. C. Woodville. Sailor's Wedding.

Bride: *canezou* with shirred sleeves and shoulder worn with round skirt trimmed with three rows of tucks.

Sailor: after the quiffs of the 30's and the curls of the 40's, hair grew longer. It was sometimes set carefully around the ears in what we would call a "page-boy bob." Shiny patent-leather sailor's hat, low-crowned, wide-brimmed; "sailor" collar, worn with neckerchief, open over short jacket; wide trousers.

Best man: collar turned down over knotted, fringed kerchief-tie first worn, knotted like bonnet-strings, by women (2475); pleated shirt front; horizontally striped vest.

Older men: stock or standing collar; double-breasted vest; felt or stovepipe hats in light colors.

Mother: standard bonnet-and-cashmere-shawl costume.

2498. XIXc. 1848. U.S.A. (Baltimore, C. Morgan Marshall.)

R. C. Woodville. Politics in an Oyster House.

Booth in oyster house: jet for gas light. Beards begin to appear. Man, with crêpe mourning-band on tall, cylindrical top hat, wears shoes with light-colored buttoned uppers. Side pockets in trousers.

2499. XIXc. 1849. English.

"Phiz." Dickens: "David Copperfield": After Mr. Waterbrook's Dinner-Party.

There are still many variations of excessive collars (like the host's), stocks and ties, and comic heads of hair (like Tommy Tucker's, in the back-ground) for Dickens to make fun of, among Mr. Waterbrook's refined guests of Bank and Treasury, all "iced for the occasion . . . like the wine." Pantaloons have lost their straps. Some have grown long and wide, into trousers; others, like those of the bespectacled man, are extremely short and tight, to exhibit his shoes with the fashionable light-colored tops.

2500. XIXc. July 1850. French. (Metropolitan Museum, Print Room.)

Lacouchie. "Le Parisien" (periodical).

The 50's bring an extraordinary and inventive assortment of short coats, designed for specific purposes and times of day; the first real "three-piece suits;" and breast pockets on coats.

Low-crowned, wide-brimmed hats, in light colors, edged with braid, appear in informal use. There are light-colored silk toppers, tall and cylindrical, as well as the more formal black.

Hair had been comparatively flat in back, though long and curled at the ears during the 40's. It turned smoother and longer in back in the late 40's. With the 50's, it fluffs out full all around. The hair along the jowls also fluffs out into mutton chops.

The newest collar is turned down very low over a loose bow tie, exposing a bare column of the male throat for the first time in three centuries. Shirt fronts are pleated and obviously buttoned. Loose

bows are tied around standing collars in more formal dress.

The new complete, matching suit, worn by the fisherman, has a longer waist and lapel, and rounds off into cutaway skirts over a rounded rump. Although it has not been found necessary in this case, these bob-tailed skirts are often cut separately and seamed on to a waistline, which is cut on a diagonal line to correspond with the slanting breast pocket.

The most characteristic thing about all these new garments is an interest in parallels. This line is most carefully maintained in the relationship between the line of vest and coat openings; the white piping on the vest of the stage or movie banker is a last vestige of this elegance. Edges are stitched, piped or faced, and the silk lining of topcoats begins to be displayed.

Vests lengthen with coats, and are prolonged and spread apart below their last button, from which a short chain is carried to the watch pocket.

When striped fabric is used in vests, it is cut on a diagonal to enhance the new piped and diagonal lines of the rest of the garments.

Trousers are much easier in cut. The more ceremonious pantaloons are pleated into the waistband, braided along the outseam, and inconspicuously held down by a wide band under the boot. The trousers worn by the fisherman have matching spats, which mask all but the tips of shoes. His companion's frankly short, unstrapped trousers are worn with bow-trimmed pumps. The shoes of the young fisherman have buttoned, light-colored tops.

The young servant with clipped hair who carries the fish, shows livery anachronisms in stock and knee breeches (worn with gaiters), together with a smart new coat with flap pockets, a line of striped vest, and a forage cap.

Pince-nez glasses on a cord around neck as women carry watches (Ill. 2475).

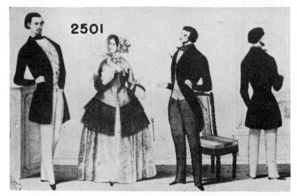

2501-03. XIXc. Spring and Summer 1850. U.S.A. (New York, Harry T. Peters.)

T. S. Sinclair. Fashion Plate for S. A. and A. F. Ward of Philadelphia.

Most men's fashion plates seen in the U.S.A. before the end of the Civil War are frankly French. This is one of the early American-made ones. No doubt it is based on French sources, just as the identical French gown turns up in English, German and French magazines, as fast as it can be copied.

The elegant European silhouette loses some of its ease in crossing the Atlantic.

The Marquis de Remisa (2486), the men in Lami's illustrations (2472) are European gentlemen; The *Parisien* fashion plate (2500) shows mannequins of gentlemen. Sinclair's plate is charming, but there is something provincial, self-conscious and sententious about it. The men in the top row all look as though they had just been elected to their first term in the House of Representatives, and were taking a deep breath in their new outfits, to say a few words at a farewell reception.

They show, however, the same new sloping shoulder, longer waistline and shorter skirts, on clothes which have under consideration the idea of closing again across the chest, and of becoming unified suits of one material. This is least obvious in summer fashion plates which show trousers in light colors and stripes. Hair is not curled artificially, but is full at the sides and nape. Collars turn down over dark or fancy tied cravats. Fancy vests, very chesty and full of buttons and watch chains. Sports clothes are shown on men's fashion plates everywhere, with low-crowned sports hats, in straw, for summer, and light-colored toppers for riding and the races. The American frontiersman's outfit for hunting is seen in European fashion plates.

Flat-crowned, wide-brimmed hats, like the Amazon's (2545), appear in the 50's and will be common by the 60's.

Caps are retained by ladies, but they are small, set on the back of plain hair which is parted and drawn up; they are trimmed with flowers and streamers of fancy ribbon falling down behind.

Bonnets, as in Europe in 1850, jut far out in back, and are rose-trimmed; their brims are drawn around the chin and are tied with small bows and streamers of ribbon with a fancy edge.

The bodice shown in *Godey's,* April, 1842, was cut in a few large sections, with gored panels set over. The 1850 bodice takes over the gores while getting rid of the decoration. It is shorter, carefully curved and fitted, and is trimmed with narrow bands of ruched, quilted and shirred fabric along a V-opening. The shoulder is smoothly rounded; the sleeve is easier and shorter, and flows wider at the bottom. The bare lower arm is loaded with bracelets in the evening. A full sheer white chemisette sleeve, gathered onto a close band at the wrist, flows from the short bell sleeve in daytime. Skirts are wide and become increasingly gored as their size increases.

Pardessus are smoothly fitted and untrimmed around neck, shoulders and waist. Their short sleeves and skirts both bell out and are heavily edged with flounces, lace or fringe.

Gowns, like that worn under this pardessus begin to be made of brocades and flowered stuffs, reputed to be in the style of one of one or another of the Louis' of France, between Louis XIII-XVI.

Riding habit with rather long basque worn with a full, round skirt and wide-brimmed, low-crowned hat.

2504-21. XIXc. 1851. English.

"Townsend's Magazine" (periodical).

Plates in color, with little or no explanatory text.

Nothing is more characteristic of the late 40's and the 50's than the variety of short outdoor coats for both sexes. There are short, loose sacque-like jackets, shaped *visites,* paletots and pardessus; and cloaks, mantelets and *sorties de bal,* which are usually founded on shawl and scarf shapes and increase in use as skirts spread too wide for the straighter forms of jacket.

Another fashion magazine of the period says: "How we contrived to exist before the pardessus was invented seems now a difficult problem to solve; a lady of fashion needs at least five: (1) of cashmere or merino for the morning; (2) of velvet for calls; (3) of silk or satin trimmed with lace for dinners; (4) of lace, for full dress; (5) one lined with fur for going to a ball. For (1) the "Louis XV," stiff with rich facings; for (2) the "Mousquetaire," coquettish; (3) the "Duchess," magnificent in ornament; (4) the "Puritan," elegantly simple; (5) the "Hungarian casaweck," richly trimmed with fur.

("Townsend Magazine" description of Ills. 2504-21:)

"Pardessus of the Pompadour style, of coloured silk heavily fringed; demi-long sleeves; some open, over the chest and fastening with two buttons, others hanging loose and only closed at the neck."

"Louis" styles are potent influences; the belling *pagoda* sleeve of Louis XIV with its rows of lace flounces (2508, 2511) as the entire silhouette becomes pagoda-like (lower center); Louis XV brocades and flowered cottons (lower, c.); which will be followed by Louis XVI *caracos* and *polonaises.*

Bonnets have round brims which tend to spread wider; they are shaped like a present-day peach basket, and are set well back on the head, projecting behind and exposing the face completely. There are bonnets of straw, velvet, silk, or lingerie capotes; the inner brim usually lined with color or shirring; trimmed according to the season with flowers, fancy ribbon, or winter feathers.

With the bloomer begins the whole series of "fast" styles, masculine adaptations which accompanied the "women's rights" movement, and the beginning of cigarette smoking by women.

The waistcoat (2510) was the fashionable sensation of 1851. It was often elaborately embroidered or brocaded, but we see it here in its most audacious plain form, complete with little watch pockets, and accompanied by a pair of pockets in the skirt, analogous to the new side pockets in trousers. Another such style is the plain little jacket (2506) with buttoned tab closings and pocket flaps.

The Scotsman represented in Cruikshank's "Bloomer" (2531) is an allusion to the popularity of plaids which are seen in fabrics and ribbons in women's and boys' clothing (2505) and (2520).

Pantalettes grow shorter, and like everything else white, are covered with embroidery, eyelets and notched edges. They are not only worn by girls, but by boys of astonishingly large size.

2504. Pink bonnet, violet gown.

2505. Blue and green bonnet, brown and black dress.

2506. Tan bonnet, dull lavender jacket and skirt.

2507. Pink bonnet, blue jacket braided in black.

2508. Yellow-green bonnet, rose mantle, braided in black, over a white skirt.

2509. Lavender bonnet, green mantle with wide collar.

2510. White bonnet, yellow ribbons, braid patterned white skirt, white vest, dull brick pink jacket and skirt.

2511. Black bonnet with pink flowers, leaves and ribbons, with the last remnants of the cornette tied under the chin; gray-blue patterned dress.

2512. Girl: flat yellow straw hat, pink ribbons and dress with horizontal lines of flounces, blue buttoned shoes.

2513. Little girl with pink parachute: flounced white raised embroidery, blue fringed sash, and blue shoes with a pleated cuff.

2514. Little boy: tabbed blue jacket and dress; striped stockings and green shoes.

2515. Girl: white bonnet, pale salmon-tan dress, white boots with black toes.

2516. Mamma: pink straw bonnet, green and black "Persian" percale redingote; matching mantelet with a capuchon hood (seen also on men's short sports coats).

2517. Big boy: tan tie, black coat; brown and black plaid trousers, striped stockings and black shoes.

2518. Swinging girl: wide yellow straw, pink ribbons, white blouse made like a man's shirt, pink skirt, black shoes.

2519. Boy: straw hat with streamers; short-sleeved tan blouse, white shirt and trousers, brown shoes.

2520. Boy: white cap—black and white plaid band; blue and black plaid dress, gray and black buttoned shoes.

2521. Boy: cocoa brown, embroidered in white roses and leaves; long pantalettes, and high brown gaiters.

2522. XIXc. 1851. French. (London, Nat. Gallery.)
Ingres. Mme. Moitessier.

Women break out of rigid, concealing clothes in the 50's, as out of constricting convention. In another year, bloomers will appear in Hyde Park, and women will speak publicly on female rights.

Mme. Moitessier shows luscious bare shoulders, arms covered by handsome bracelets, and hands without gloves holding a fan (in which the renewed interest of the late 40's continues). Hair is no longer curled, or dankly looped; it looks very clean and well brushed, and is drawn back, under the scrap of lace which the evening cap has become.

There are a great many wide triangles in the costume of the 50's, especially on the outer garments, like the *mantillas* and *sorties de bal* which grew out of folded shawls. The fringed corner which finishes the bodice of her brocade gown is of that nature, and is combined with the wonderful, flowered and bordered fancy ribbons of the 50's.

Tiny cords are worn about both men's and women's necks (2475, 2500).

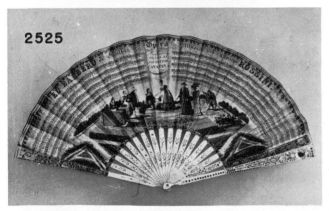

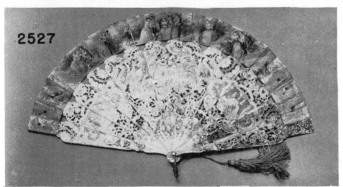

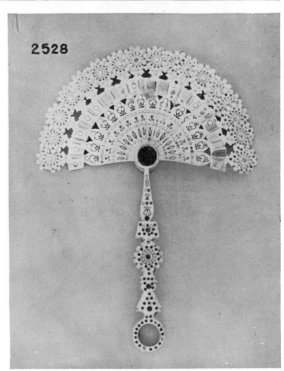

Courtesy of Metropolitan Museum of Art

2523. XVIIIc. (end Directoire.) French.

Fan: paper and wood; 5 groups representing *les jarretières, la danse, la folie, le colin maillard, la main chaude;* French verses at top of leaf.

2524. e.XIX. Empire. French.

Fan: brisé; horn engraved with floral design, embossed with gold, and spangled.

2525-26. XIXc. c. 1835. French.

Paris fan: probably made for the Spanish trade; by Coustellier; carved ivory stick, leaf, engraved and painted with episodes from Rossini's *Barber of Seville,* and part of score.

2527. XIXc. 1840-50. French.

Fan: sticks of pearl matrix, silver gilt; painted mount.

2528. Late XVIII-e.XIX. French.

Fan-lorgnette: brisé; ivory, carved and inlaid with mica.

2529. XIXc. c. 1850. Spanish?

Fan: Chantilly lace, 2 colors, mounted on pearl matrix sticks. (See Appendix.)

2530-31. XIXc. 1852-53. English. (New York Public Library, Print Room.)

George Cruikshank. "Comic Almanack" (periodical).

2530. "The Rights of Women, or the Effects of Female Enfranchisement."

2531. "The Bloomers in Hyde Park, or an Extraordinary Exhibition for 1852."

Cruikshank was a most vital and prolific illustrator and cartoonist. Born into a family of artists in 1792, he was at work by 1811. He and his brother Isaac illustrated in color the invaluable compendium which Pierce Egan had written in 1812 as *Life in London.*

Cruikshank lived to 1878, but his period of extraordinary usefulness for costume ends at about the time when the *Comic Almanack* (begun in 1835) ceased publication in 1853. For all their interest, the two frontispieces we reproduce are inferior to hundreds of black and white vignettes of the earlier decades.

"THE RIGHTS of WOMEN" or the EFFECTS of FEMALE ENFRANCHISEMENT

The "Bloomers" in Hyde Park, or an Extraordinary Exhibition for 1852

2532. XIXc. 1854. English. (New York Public Library.)

John Leech. "Handley Cross": Sir Thomas Trout and the Bloomer.

The influence of the sensational garment brought from the U.S.A. by Mrs. Amelia Bloomer spread to the provinces and caused Surtees to write a supplementary chapter for the 1854 edition of "Handley Cross." In Leech's colored plate, Constantia, lovely daughter of Mrs. Mendlove, hostess of the Turtle Doves Hotel, is shown in the entrance hall, in 1854, in "the full-blown costume of a Bloomer."

Constantia, very much the blonde soubrette, lets her curls flow over a fitted gray jacket with short perky skirts, a tiny white collar and a large, deep rose bow at the throat, a short but very wide hoop skirt, with three tiers of rose-bound flounces, and white muslin pantalettes gathered around the ankles.

In the five-fold colored frontispieces to the later *Almanacks,* Cruikshank amuses himself with the bell crowns and exaggeratedly curved brims seen in the Gavarni and Grandville illustrations, and the extraordinary variety of new hat shapes in the fre-

quently battered condition never seen in fashion plates and portraits, and seldom even in photographs.

Odd trousers, and men's suits with bob-tailed jackets and large pocket flaps are now seen in the loudest patterns ever known. "William the Conqueror" (right) wears a short cocoa brown jacket with huge buttons, patterned in a dark brown plaid, four units of which cover his back, plain cocoa brown trousers, a brown hat of a low-crowned bowler shape, a shirt collar dotted in red spots nearly as large as a dime, and a red cravat. Its ends are so widespread that in our back view of William we see their ends projecting on either side of his luxuriant brown beard, almost as Cruikshank caricatures them in the "Bloomer."

Versions of the wide flat hat seen on the Sinclair Amazon appear in Hyde Park on every age and sex, and on a woman riding sidesaddle in bloomers.

Small parasols, canes with horn handles, fringed shawls patterned in garlands of flowers; a Scotsman (in reference to Highland fashions), and every sort of bloomer Cruikshank could think of.

2533. XIXc. 1852. U.S.A. (Metropolitan Museum.

Samuel Waldo and *William Jewett*. Portrait of an old lady.

Samuel L. Waldo (1783-1861), son of a Connecticut farmer, painted either signs or portraits until he was taken to South Carolina by the Hon. John Rutledge. Money he made there enabled him to study in England with West and Copley in 1806. He returned to New York, where he painted "scores of heads . . . of dignified, benevolent gentlemen, with white hair and white chokers, or of ladies in wonderful caps and shawls."

William Jewett (1792-1874) was grinding colors for a Connecticut carriage maker when Waldo finally succeeded in releasing him from his apprenticeship. He lived with the Jewetts for nearly two decades, and from preparing Waldo's paints, became his co-worker. He lived in New Jersey after 1842.

Elderly provincial lady—under less compulsion than Queen Marie-Amélie (Ill. 2495) to make any concessions at all to new fashions—retains the comfortable dress of the 30's which she knows to be extremely becoming and suitable. Her wonderful cap and *fraise* are, however, edged with the new padded and raised embroidery.

2534. XIXc. 1853. U.S.A.-French. (New York Public Library, Art Room.)

Jules David and *Compte-Calix*. "Monitor of Fashion," No. 1 (periodical).

"The Monitor of Fashion," with plates by two French dress designers, Compte-Calix and Jules David, was published from Sept. 1853 to 1854 in New York by Genio G. Scott. It has lovely delicate plates of extremely elegant gowns, and of embroidery patterns. The colors in which it was printed have sometimes altered, and often stain the opposite pages.

The fastidiously gloved visitors show embroidered white costumes which have grown entirely high-necked.

L. to r.: Deeply notched eyelet and raised embroidery flounces *à disposition*, like the ready-made dress lengths of printed or brocaded materials especially produced to be made up into flounced dresses, and sold with accompanying plates to show how the patterns may be utilized; tiny cap with a long fall of crisp, sheer ruffles and blue ribbons.

Cord-embroidered jacket-like bodice; pink ribbons at small collar and volants of raised and eyelet embroidery on the pagoda sleeve.

Green bodice, edged with embroidery.

Cap with lavender and brown ribbons, gray Louis XIV coat, laced in gold, worn with an embroidered white vest and lingerie sleeves, and a lavender and white skirt in a fragmentary plaid pattern.

2535

2535. XIXc. 1854. French. (Montpellier, Musee Fabre.)
Gustave Courbet. "Bon jour, M. Courbet . . ."

The fine provincial museum at Montpellier had been founded in 1837 with the collection of a M. Fabre. Another local art-lover, who intended to leave his pictures to the museum was a M. Bruyas, who got every artist he knew to paint his portrait.

Bruyas and his servant have gone out to meet Courbet, who is arriving on foot for a four months visit.

All show the wonderful beards which have reappeared for the first time in over two hundred years.

Courbet wears the shirt of his period, still wide and shapeless, with a small turned-back cuff. His trousers are tucked into the cloth tops of buttoned boots, after the manner of infantrymen's gaiters.

With a soft cap, Bruyas wears one of the wonderful new short country coats, lined throughout with a striped material which is rolled over the edge as a binding. Similar coats can be found through the 60's, with contrasting piped or braided edges. Their influence could still be seen in smoking jackets and dressing gowns in e. XXc., which were often made of reversible material, one side chocolate brown, perhaps, and the other a light snuff, finished with an edge of twisted silk cord.

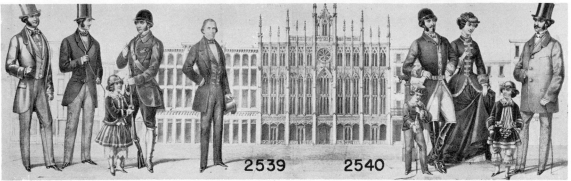

2536-40. XIXc. 1854. U.S.A., Philadelphia.

F. Mahan. Paris, New York and Philadelphia fashions for Spring and Summer, 1854.

The fertility of invention shown in dress, particularly men's dress, during the 50's, was only one expression of the ferment and excitement of a tense decade.

Authors, artists, workers and women are all stirring in revolt. Formal religion is losing its hold, but the effort to synthesize a variety of new ideas and feelings has the force of a religious revival.

The aristocracy is being supplanted by the rich. Wives with money arrive in England from America and the outposts of Empire. Industrialization is shifting populations as never before in England; new inventions are constantly being made, especially in America, which has small manpower for the utilization of great resources.

Wide casting about for bases can be seen in the clothes and backgrounds of these fashion plates.

After a return to the Gothic, style has marched ahead chronologically, Louis by Louis, through the XVIIc. and XVIIIc.; in details of men's clothing shown here, it has arrived at a period scarcely more than a generation before its own time.

The New Gothic Masonic Temple is flanked by traditional XVIIIc. brick houses with small-paned windows, on one side; on the other, by office buildings of the new sort. The cotton goods district in downtown New York is still largely housed in buildings of this type built just before and after the Civil War. Castiron allows buildings like A. T.

Stewart's store of 1863 (now Wanamaker's), which was based on an Italian model, to provide more air and light than most offices built between the 70's and the most recent decades.

The lacings and hanging ends of ribbon on the jacket of the lady (2537) are of XVIIc. inspiration. The braided riding habit with wide cuffs and plumed hat (2540) is Louis XIV; the parlor furniture and hangings, Louis XV and XVI. An attempt is being made to reintroduce lace at the wrist of a gentleman (2539); his shirt has the ruffles and brooch, and another man (2536) the notched lapels of e. XIXc.

A great effort was made in mid-50's to popularize elaborately embroidered trousers (2536-2538); it was not very successful, although trousers did become loudly and enormously crossed with plaids. There are also a great many fancy vests, which will go out of use rather abruptly in first half of the 1860's.

Shirt bosoms are pleated; curved collars, set on a straight band, can stand or be turned down; with patterned vests and trousers, cravats are of plain satin, tied in thick wadded bows.

Shoulders are sloped by drawn-back seams; waists are long; skirts separately cut; sleeves usually have button-trimmed cuffs. Pockets, finished in many ways, are set in all sorts of new positions. One man (2539) has a diagonal pocket on the left chest; a tiny change pocket above the waist on the right; and a flap pocket set in the waist seam. Corduroy hunting outfit with jockey cap and gaiters (2539).

2541. XIXc. 1854. French. (Metropolitan Museum, Print Room.)

A. L. Noël, after *Winterhalter*. Empress Eugénie.

The Napoleonic tradition of white gowns with colored velvet trains is continued in the gowns of the court of Napoleon III.

The lovely evening gowns which Worth made for the Empress remain one of the classic forms of evening dress in our own XXc.—probably the most graceful in movement and the most universally becoming that has ever been contrived.

Gowns made of lace flounces are almost entirely a court fashion, but designs of white lace edgings on colored silk grounds are provided in the dress lengths *à disposition*.

Soft, natural parted hair is drawn back into a coil (which swells in size, so that the shape of head coverings will have to be changed to accommodate the mass). Quantities of important bracelets.

2542-44. XIXc. 1855-56. French.

E. Guérard.

2542. The Tuileries Gardens.
2543. The Boulevard des Italiens.
2544. The Palais d'Industrie.

2542. Nursemaids in trim uniform or the dress of their native province. Children in variations of the clothes seen in Ill. 2512-21: skirts with many ruffles, belted blouses, open jackets, trimmed with scallops, braid, buttons and Scotch tartan; worn with pantalettes or trousers; folding Scotch caps with streamers, forage caps, soft round hats, or in the case of girls, very small caps or mere hair ribbons.

2543. Smartly turned out equipages stop at the curb of Tortoni's establishment for a word with a gentleman who has been having one of its celebrated ices.

2544. Mixed crowds, drawn by the great Industrial Exposition of 1855.

The skirt of 1850 might have three gathered flounces of approximately the same depth worn over horsehair-stiffened petticoats. By latter half of the 50's, the flounces have multiplied in number, and are often of varying depth. Each flounce is now backed by stiffening and is ruffled on, so that it stands out from the body of the skirt. Its edge is scalloped, sprigged or edged to enhance the irregular protruding look. The increased size and weight of the skirt has been made possible by the new artificial crinoline petticoat, stiffened by whalebone, wire or watch-spring steel.

The body now appears triangular (2542). The tiny head has, paradoxically, been brought about by the increased bulk of the hair at the back of the

head (2541). Peach-basket-shaped bonnets cannot be set over it, and are replaced by little tied-on triangles, the old cornette come back (2544). Smooth shoulders spread into pagoda sleeves, and skirts below them become so distended that it is increasingly difficult to cut a fitted outer garment to cover them (2544). Shawls, or flowing mantles based on the triangular form of a shawl, also try to avoid crushing down skirts which it is hard enough to hold out; their use increases.

Tiny parasols; flat hats with streamers (like that on little girl, in 2544), which, it is felt, still give the complexion some protection, now that women are unwilling to be caged in a bonnet.

Wonderful details of omnibuses; flower seller and tied apron (2543, ext. right).

2545. XIXc. 1856. French. (Metropolitan Museum.)

G. Courbet. Amazon.

Habits of dark cloth are high necked, with narrow mannish sleeves, short basques tabbed in back, and scantier gored skirts, with most of the fullness drawn toward the back. Ribbon-trimmed black silk hat. The sleeve of the habit has been shortened to show a shirt sleeve and cuff, as in the current gown. The cuff-button is set low, although the turn-back of the cuff has deepened.

2546. XIXc. 1857-62. French.

Pierre Petit. Delacroix.

This photograph, taken in Paris in 1862, shows the painter with the same beard and hair, collar and stock, and the identical trousers and topcoat he wears in an 1857 photograph. The exception is the suit coat, which in 1857 has a velvet collar and braid-edged lapel. The trouser pocket, more clearly seen in the 1857 photograph, is not a straight slash, but is pointed like an envelope flap; fly closing now well established.

2547. XIXc. 1858. English.

John Leech. Illustration for "Ask Mamma."

There are not many surviving examples of the orange paper covers in which Victorian novels, like Surtees' "Ask Mamma" were published serially, in parts, at 1s. each.

Leech gives us a rare opportunity to see a Victorian gentleman in embroidered suspenders and flaring, turned back cuffs, tying a stock, while a maid gets her mistress into a ball gown. Women's hair, massed lower in back, is now apt to be waved.

The trim of an evening bodice is set on the line of the old lace valance, but in the general tendency toward scalloped edges, the material is apt to be caught up in front and at the shoulders. Skirts are apt to be trimmed by similar swags of material caught by flowers, bows, or both. A tendency towards asymmetry is shown early in the 50's in the placing of garlands of flowers across the bodice, running down the upper section of the skirt of an evening gown. Hair dressed with trailing flowers at the ears; many bracelets.

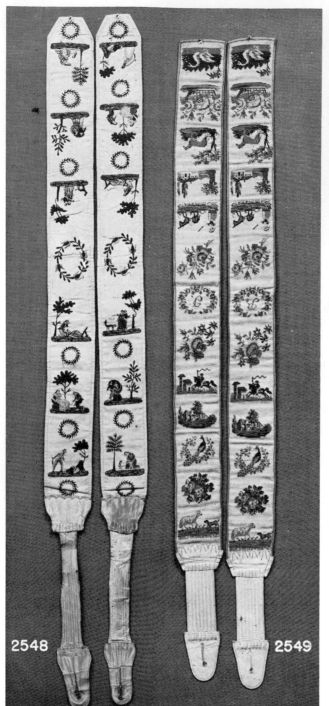

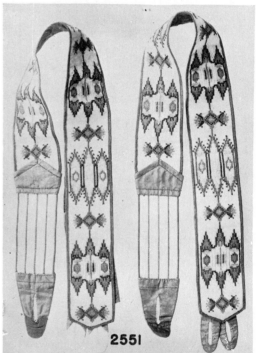

2548-49. Early XIXc. French. (Boston, Mus. of Fine Arts.)
     Two pairs of embroidered suspenders.
2550. XIXc. English? (Metropolitan Museum.)
     Man's silk handkerchief: red and yellow.

2551. Early XIXc. French or German? (Metropolitan
     Museum.)

     Pair of braces.

2552. XIXc. 1852-9. French.
Lithographed fashion plate.

2553. XIXc. 1858. French.
Calling costume; fawn taffeta brocaded in brown velvet in a lace design.

The elaborately bordered fabrics of the 50's and 60's were woven in special dress lengths, à *disposition*. They were accompanied by fashion plates showing how dresses might be cut from the available pattern, and the proportions to be used. Here we see the identical fabric, in suggested use as an evening dress, and made up into an actual visiting costume.

2554-55. XIXc. 1858. French.
"Nouveautés de Paris" (periodical fashion plate).
2554. Robe de mousseline à volants de coté.
2555. Robe d'organdi à deux volants doubles.

Materials were also printed in different patterns in allied colors (like the brown, beige, dull yellow and white seen here), so that they could be used together in alternating flounces of the newer sort: larger in number, and apt not to be identical in depth or pattern. The rise, multiplication and increased fullness of the skirt are paralleled by the sleeve; both its pagoda shape and the skirt outline become formless. With the approach of the 60's, the clutter begins to be cleared away. Sleeves are less

trimmed, or are close in toward the wrist, or made plain and close, or so shortened that the shirt sleeve takes over. Horizontal decoration is pushed down toward the hem in small ruffles, velvet bands or braid. The front of the crinoline flattens and the skirt is often panelled with a ruched or pleated edging. In this muslin robe, panels are cut from a pattern which at least recalls rows of small ruffles.

Materials, we find from reading such advertisements as those in the "Illustrated London News" in 1858, are sold by the dress length. King's of Regent St. lists "the new autumn silks: striped and checked £1 2s 6d the Full Dress, Shepherd's Plaid Silks, Gros de Afriques & Gros Royals, Brocaded Poult de Soies; three-flounced silks: £2 2s 6d, two-flounced silks £2 18s 6d, velvet flounced silks £5 10s 0d, Moirés antiques £2 18s 6d, and Lyons silk velvets 7s 6d per yard" (for the favorite trimming).

Dresses can be bought partly finished: "Shepherd's-check flounced dress, made up in all colours, (the skirt) lined and richly trimmed with velvet with materials for Bodice, price 14s 9d; with our new Paris Jacket made and trimmed to correspond, 18s 6d the Dress complete. Drawings and patterns free. For country orders, size around the shoulders and waist, with the length of the skirt."

Courtesy of Metropolitan Museum of Art (2553); *Print Room* (2552, 2554-55)

2556-57. XIXc. 1857. German. (New York Public Lib.)

"Der Bazar" (periodical). Nov. 15. Parisian Modes.

Left. Robe of violet grenadine with three volants checked in darker color and trimmed with narrow silk fringe. Smooth bodice with *bretelles* and collar of notched lace; full mousseline sleeves with double cuffs of valenciennes.

Right. Robe of green rep with a double skirt, trimmed with matching tassels and braid. "Medici" sleeves with five puffs; ruffs at wrist and throat. Grenadine velvet hat trimmed with black lace.

2558-61. XIXc. 1857. German.

"Der Bazar," Dec. 1. Parisian Modes.

These French plates are found recopied in English and American magazines at about the same time.

The new long cloaks with oriental names, resulting from the Crimean War, have open sleeves, pèlerines and capuchon hoods, tassel and braid trim.

Flounced skirts are being replaced by plainer skirts, often *à tablier,* with apron-shaped panels in front, patterned in small squares or diamonds, narrowly cross-hatched in lines of self-colored velvet or satin, and dotted with vertical lines of buttons or passementerie.

2558. Gray taffeta dress: apron-shaped panel in velvet linen edged in buttons. Mantle of blue and black *drap mousaya* with blue wool trimming and tassels. Hat of field-gray taffeta and velvet, trimmed with a tuft of lace on one side, grape tendrils on the other, tulle ruche under brim and band of velvet in back.

2559. Gown of fancy material. Dark brown *Caid* mantle trimmed with galloon Brandenbourgs; the burnous has a capuchon hood. Red velvet bonnet, trimmed with three rolls of velvet, curled plume, tulle or blonde.

2560. Steel gray cashmere dress. Mantle *à l'hongroise.* Corded green silk hat with velvet leaves and flowers under the brim. Compromise between triangular, flattened bonnet and the oncoming hats; curtain of bonnet turning into a rumpled brim in back.

2561. Wool dress; apron panel diapered in narrow satin bands trimmed with lines of passementerie. *Pultava* mantle in brown plush, striped in white. White satin hat with a lace ruffle and garnet lining.

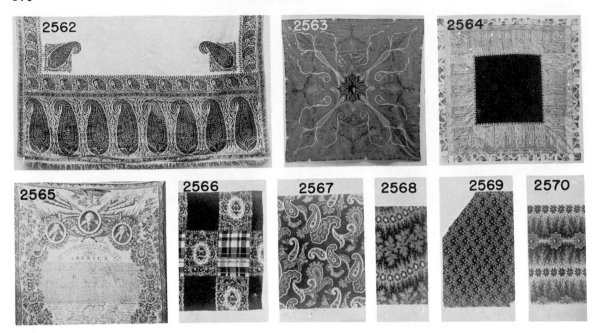

2562. XVIII-XIXc. India.
Cashmere shawl.

2563. Early XIXc. India.
Cashmere shawl: brick red ground, embroidered border.

2564. XIXc. India.
"Paisley" shawl: black center; palm leaf border in red, blue and green.

2565. Early XIXc. English.
Printed handkerchief: *Declaration of Independence.*

2566-67. XIXc. c. 1840. Alsatian, Mulhouse.
Two cotton calicos: "paisley" shawl designs and colorings; impure, degraded derivatives.

2568-70. First half XIXc. Alsatian, Mulhouse.
Three cotton calicos: designs particularly popular in black, gray, lavender and purples.

2571-74. XIXc. French.
"Le Moniteur des Dames et Demoiselles" (periodical). 2571-72. Plate by *Jules David:* Church (1857); 2573-74. Plate by *F. C. Compte-Calix:* Country (1858).

Hats and coats are reestablished in everyday use but, as in late XVIIIc., they are informal. Church and calling costumes still require bonnet and shawl.

Jules David shows children dressed for first communion:

2571. Mother: small white bonnet over a tumbling chignon. Hair is frequently clubbed into a net in the late 50's. The usage will increase and the nets become dotted with chenille. Chocolate-brown and black plaid gown, and India shawl. As both women show, shawls or shawl-like coverings have largely replaced fitted overgarments: the shawl adds to the triangular body outline, protects the chest and shoulders without deforming the distended skirt, which offers plenty of problems as it is. A fine India shawl was light but extremely warm; it was also a luxury comparable to mink or sable today; its cost could rise into the thousands.

2572. Daughter: increasingly fussy lower sleeve of late 50's, often in repeated puffs, with the new interest in panels expressed in wide ribbon tabs.

2573. The hunter wears a wide-brimmed brown hat, green corduroy coat and white trousers.

2574. His lady: wide flat brown hat with red flowers, green leaves, and black streamers; black and white shawl, with a capuchon hood bordered in plaid, tasseled and fringed in red, blue, green, black and white; gown with white ground, bands of blue plaid and beige flowers.

2575. XIXc. 1858. U.S.A. (New York Public Library.)

"Graham's Magazine" (May), Philadelphia.

Calling costumes follow the trend already set by walking dress. Skirt flounces are less rumpled; their numbers are reduced, and the outline of the costume becomes more clearly defined than in Ills. 2556-57. The division by plain and checked material combined on one flounce in 1857, is now made on alternating flounces. The flounces are laid on flatter; a scalloped edge commemorates the actual projection of the 1857 flounces.

Apron-shaped panels, cross-hatched and studded into diaper-cloth patterns, are characteristic of the late 50's (2558-61).

The apron is used here on a coat-costume allied to that worn by the Empress Eugenie. This fashion plate shows the new smoothness of the bodice and shoulder-line, which is emphasized in the captions of fashion plates, as bretelles are eliminated. Sleeves of dresses and chemisettes also become less complicated.

Hats worn with walking dress are still apt to carry the flowers, lace and strings of the bonnet from which they are just becoming differentiated. By the 60's they will become plainer and their brims smaller. White walking dress; brown hat and strings, with trimming of white lace and pink and white flowers.

Casaque for visiting, heavily trimmed with black lace, worn with the required bonnet, over a blue and black gown; small parasol of white lace.

Boy in white dress, magenta jacket and gaiters, plaid stockings.

2576-77. XIXc. 1858. German. (New York Public Lib.)

"Der Bazar," Aug. 8.

Clearer bell-shaped outlines and reduction of clutter; fewer horizontal lines; projecting flounces replaced by bands of pleating.

2576. Dress of horizontally striped gray taffeta, trimmed in gray taffeta with puffings of violet taffeta. "Horn of plenty"-shaped sleeves with shoulder caps and a "jockey" of violet puffing. Sleeves of embroidered mull. Rice straw bonnet trimmed with white tulle and violets.

2577. Black barège gown, with two skirts; pleated trim à la vielle, like the edgings of XVIIIc. skirts. Ruched bretelles; sleeves a yard wide at the bottom. Black crêpe bonnet trimmed with black taffeta braids, black dahlias with salmon-colored glass centers, and black silk lace (blonde). The inevitable lace parasol of ceremonious dress. This French design appears in fashion magazines in England and U. S. A. as well.

2578-80. XIXc. 1858. English. (New York Public Library.)
"Illustrated London News," Oct. 2.

Original text quoted.

2578. "A dress in the new style called *à six lis*. It has a double skirt—the upper one consisting of six breadths of silk of two different kinds; the one being plain rose colour and the other having a light gray chequered with rose.

"The breadths of these two different silks are disposed alternately, and the upper skirt is edged with white and rose-colored fringe, having a head of passementerie. The corsage is three-quarters high, and over it is worn a small fichu Antoinette made of white tulle, disposed in flat plaits, each one headed by a plisse of narrow, rose-colored ribbon. The sleeves, which, like the upper skirt of the dress, are made of two different silks, are wide and do not descend lower than the elbow. They are trimmed with fringe like that which edges the skirt, under-sleeves of plain tulle in three puffs, between each of which there is a ruche of rose-colored ribbon with a small bow in front of the arm. The lower skirt is composed of chequered silk, edged by a broad band of rose colour. Bonnet of paille-de-riz, with crown of rose-colored tulle, encircled by a wreath of small roses and foliage. Undertrimming, a cordon of the same."

2579. "Dress with double skirt of green silk, of that bright marine hue to which the French have given the name of vert d'Azof. The corsage is plain, high to the throat, and pointed at the waist both in front and at the back. The sleeves are slit open in front of the arm, and edged round with tassel fringe. The same trimming edges the upper skirt of the dress.

The scarf mantelet of black silk is trimmed with very rich chenille fringe. Bonnet of white silk, trimmed with mauve color. The bavolet (or curtain) is made of mauve-colored ribbon, and the wide strings are edged with a narrow plisse of mauve color. The undertrimming consists of a demi-wreath of white daisies, placed on the upper part of the forehead, under-sleeves of plain muslin, confined at the wrists by coral bracelets."

2580. "Evening Costume. Dress of white muslin with three flounces, simply edged with broad hems. The low corsage has a berthe of maltese lace, and the sleeves are trimmed with the same. Sash of tartan ribbon, fastened in front of the waist in a bow, and long flowing ends. Bows of the same ribbon on the shoulders. Collarette of black velvet, fastened in front of the throat by a pearl brooch. Headdress: bows of black velvet fixed in pearl-headed Italian pins. Black velvet bracelets with pearl snaps."

2581-87. XIXc. 1858. French-U.S.A.

"Le Progrès: Bulletin of Fashion," No. 98, New York (Feb.).

An American publication shows the fashions of Paris hat, shoe and shirt makers.

There is still great variety in hat crowns and brims; they will become much less romantic with the 60's, and turn into plain stovepipe hats, most resembling the central example shown here.

Hair is still full, but there is a tendency (shown by the same man) for the back of a gentleman's head to be trimmed short, as only servants' hair has been cut in the fashion plates of the last decades. Beards, dundrearies, mutton chops and moustaches

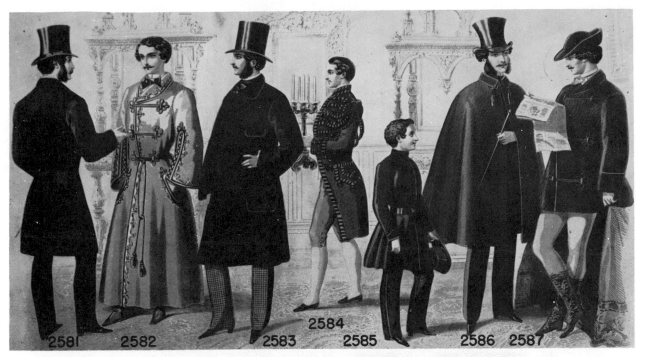

continue, but more clean shaven faces appear in the 60's. Shoe heels become much higher, and heels begin to appear on women's shoes as well.

The cut of clothes still has a romantic elegance, but the approach of the long, heavy, shapeless clothes of the 60's can be sensed, except in the trousers. These are still made from checked cloth and show no signs of baggy knees, whereas the shapeless trousers of the 60's are plainer, sometimes braided down the outseam, striped rather widely, or patterned in small checks.

Vests decline in importance, as coat fronts begin to button, or, in the case of frock and tail coats, are cut to meet. The waistline slips lower; coat skirts are longer and straighter; sleeves widen throughout; overcoats for city wear are much longer and straighter, with breast pocket flaps, smaller buttons, and edges "enhanced by the application of a peculiar

and neatly stitched binding." (Adv. in *Illus. London News,* Oct. 23, 1858.) Capes have been worn through the romantic period; the 50's are full of cape-like coats and coat-like capes. There is, if anything, an increase in frogged and tasseled closings on short, informal topcoats, and on smoking jackets and dressing gowns, all of which have shawl collars.

Footmen in XVIIIc. court livery and fourragères, heavily braided. The young son of the house in a military looking belted blouse and braided kepi.

Interest is working back through the Renaissance to the Gothic; massive carved furniture with coats of arms.

2588. XIXc. 1858. U.S.A. (Boston, Mus. of Fine Arts.)
Winslow Homer. Boston Common.

Round crinolines and hoops were hard enough to manage without wind. Feet and legs inevitably begin to show just before the crinoline starts to be

Courtesy of Metropolitan Museum, Print Room (2581-87)

flattened in front into greater manageability. The struggle to conceal the feet is admitted to be a lost cause. Shoes come to have heels and decoration and stockings are made in colors, stripes and plaids. In Boston in 1858, there are heels on shoes, but the only plaid legs are the gaiters of the little boy who has lost his plumed straw hat.

Top hat with straight brim and crown; long, less fitted coat; cuffs a little longer over the hand; checked trousers. Canes have horn or metal heads bent at a right angle.

2589-95. XIXc. 1859. U.S.A.-French.

"Le Progrès: Bulletin of Fashion," No. 110, New York (Feb.).

Increase of costumes for sports, indoors and out, and for comfortable leisure at home. A great deal of pattern is still used, but it tends to become smaller and to be used on all three pieces of the suit. Trousers and sleeves are wider; coats straighter, longer, buttoned higher, with great attention to edges; these are stitched, piped or braided. Bows and four-in-hands better tied; cravats crossed and stuck with a gold pin. Watch chains with massive links. Back hair trimmed shorter.

The Gothic revival brings a renewed interest in fencing; suits of armor stand about and crossed swords decorate dark, gold-scrolled wallpapers. There are half a dozen advertisements weekly in the *Illus. London News* of Heraldic Offices where family arms, crests and pedigrees can be obtained. Coats of arms begin to be seen again.

Heavy velvet curtains, divans and comfortably upholstered chairs, button-tufted and fringed. Anything for which a beadwork, crochet or cross-stitch cover can be made now has one, and the band about the upholstered chair was undoubtedly some of the hostess' woolwork. All the weeklies and fashion magazines now publish fancy-work patterns, but they are probably seen at their most wonderful in the huge plates (of tea-cosies, netted bottle cases, paper flowers, and every article of wearing apparel of the whole family) found in "Der Bazar, Illustrirte Damen-Zeitung," published in Berlin from about 1854 (New York Public Library).

Black enamel and gold decorated furniture, some inlaid with mother-of-pearl. Machine-produced ingrain carpets in quantity in the latter half 50's cover the floor from wall to wall.

2596. XIXc. 1859. French. (London, Nat. Port. Gall.)
Winterhalter. Albert, Consort of Victoria.

2597. XIXc. 1859-60. French. (Vevay, Musee des Beaux-Arts.)
Courbet. Dr. Max Bouchon.

A good deal of slope-shouldered elegance is retained, but trousers are more tubular. Albert's head is conventionally fluffy, but Dr. Bouchon's hair, beard and moustache are uncurled and smoothed down in the new way. Heavier, wider-toed shoes.

2598. XIXc. c. 1859. U.S.A.
Thomas Read. The Children of Marcus Ward.

Boy's hair slicked down. Baby boys in the U. S. A. appear in underwear-like outfits, completely white and much tucked and embroidered. They are bow-tied at each shoulder of a low slipping neckline like that of a woman's evening dress. A very amusing American primitive in the New York Hist. Soc. shows a boy with a small dog and a huge drum, similarly dressed with knee-length drawers and no petticoat. Victorian Gothic furniture. Round tables with circular velvet or broadcloth covers to the floor, edged with fringe and embroidered in colors on gold.

2599. XIXc. 1859. French. (Delphine Ramel Coll.)
Ingres. Mme. Ingres.

Mme. Ingres' bodice elaborates the use of fringed shawl borders and corners seen on Mme. Moitessier (Ill. 2522). The flowered brocades of the periods of the various Louis' are passing, and the ribbon streamers at Mme. Moitessier's shoulders have be-

come complicated by the 60's into dipping caps, set over puffs. In evening gowns, a line of lingerie rises from under the neckline of the shorter-waisted bodice. Hair returns to smooth loops over the ears. Lappets with rounded ends hang from caps and bonnets, and are tied under the chin. The rounded and trimmed ends of bonnet strings may spread over most of the bosom of a cloak in the 60's.

2600. XIXc. 1858-60. English. (London, South Kensington Museum.)

D. G. Rossetti. Elizabeth Eleanor Siddal.

The beautiful Miss Siddal, who married Rossetti in 1860 and committed suicide in 1862, had been a milliner's assistant and a model for the Pre-Raphaelites. She is shown here in the sort of esthetic garment with which they attempted to reform women's crinolined and corseted dress. Rossetti, a friend of William Morris since Oxford, joined with him, Burne-Jones, and others in founding the firm of Morris, Marshall & Faulkner in 1862, for the reform of architecture and interior decoration as well.

2601

2601. XIXc. 1860. English.

John Leech. Surtees: "Plain or Ringlets." The Gipsy's Prophecy.

Little round hats with a feather are worn over hair caught in chenille-dotted nets. Older women wear small triangular bonnets fastened with long, wide bonnet strings tied in a substantial bow. Tiny frilled parasols. Man (background, l.) in a white summer suit and round-crowned hat; low-crowned bowlers are common by mid60's. Riding habit (backgr. r.) short basques; gored skirt cut longer and fuller in back than in 1850.

2602. XIXc. c. 1860. English. (Metropolitan Museum, Print Room.)

W. M. Thackeray. Mr. T. Visiting Mrs. W. H. Brookfield.

This very amusing combination of silhouette and water color, supposed to be by the novelist's own hand, is so full of contradictions that it may very well be a forgery. Mrs. B. was married in 1841; the little girl of perhaps six might be well along in a series; Mrs. B.'s three skirt flounces could scarcely lie so flat after the mid50's, nor her skirt have become so distended much before that time; it is probably a rather uninspired cutting of the dress of the turn of the 50's and 60's. Thackeray died late in 1863, but the firm of *Morris, Marshall, Faulkner & Co.* founded in January, 1862, had scarcely had time to become an extremely potent influence or to have developed its own style to this extent. In any case, the architecture and decoration shown here are pure "artistic" 1870's:

Small-paned windows set over narrow, herringbone panelling; dado, lined with china; lamp set on a bracket; Eastlake furniture; bric-a-brac filling a what-not; photographs and pictures in easel frames; Chinese jardinières and umbrella-stands filled with cactus, dried pampas grass, and palm leaf fans. Similar panelling in my grandfather's very "elegant mansion" of the period, in U. S. A., was done in strips stained alternately light and dark, which gleamed, cherry and lemon-colored, under mirror-like varnish; the window was in red, blue, green, yellow and purple glass.

2602

2603. XIXc. c. 1847. English. (Metropolitan Museum.)
Victorian wedding dress: pale gray satin with moiré stripes.

2604. XIXc. c. 1854. U.S.A. (Museum of the City of New York.)
Wedding dress: cream taffeta.

2605. XIXc. 1860. U.S.A. (Metropolitan Museum.)
Dress for a 13-year-old girl: Alsatian-made challis.

2606. XIXc. c. 1860. U.S.A. (Brooklyn Museum.)
Walking dress: apple green and white figured silk.

2607. XIXc. 1860. U.S.A. (Museum of the City of New York.)

Ball dress: lavender silk, brocaded in gray velvet. Worn at the 1860 ball for the Prince of Wales.

2608. XIXc. 1861. U.S.A. (Museum of the City of New York.)

Victorian ball dress: white moiré and turquoise blue velvet.

2609. XIXc. c. 1863. U.S.A. (Metropolitan Museum.)

Victorian ball dress: blue taffeta, brocaded in black velvet.

2610. XIXc. 1863. English-Scottish. (Toronto, Capt. James W. Flanagan.)

Ball dress: Stuart tartan; made by Elise of London for Alexandra, Princess of Wales, for a ball at Balmoral Castle.

2611. XIXc. c. 1860. French.

Pink taffeta ball gown, trimmed with ruching of self material, and frills of cream-colored lace.

2612. XIXc. 1860-64. English.

Ball dress of lilac ribbed silk trimmed with ruching of lilac taffeta and black and cream lace. Black lace mitts and shawl.

"What-not" with shells and china souvenirs; artificial flowers under a glass bell.

2613. XIXc. c. 1864. Viennese.

Purple faille silk visiting dress trimmed with applied feather motive done in black chenille and velvet ribbon.

Cap of black and white net trimmed with purple ribbon bows.

2614. XIXc. 1865. English.

Cherry red satin visiting dress trimmed with red velvet and black lace. Black lace coat (American c.1865). Hat of natural colored straw trimmed with black lace and red flowers (European c.1865).

Courtesy of Metropolitan Museum, Costume Institute

2615

2615. XIXc. U.S.A.

"Illustrated London News," Nov. 24, 1860. Grand Ball given at the Academy of Music, N. Y., in honor of His Royal Highness, the Prince of Wales.

The greatest social event which had ever taken place in the United States was the ball for the Prince of Wales. He arrived as "Lord Renfrew" and is the slender young man in the middle, the Ribbon of the Garter with which he had been invested in 1858 across his chest. It took the democratic United States more than half a century to recover from its interest in nobility, which got worse before it got better.

Women's clothes are still influenced by XVIIIc. court styles. The photograph of gown (2607) worn at this ball shows a bordered silk à disposition in a French lace pattern. The girl with whom the Prince dances has an XVIIIc. overskirt over a common form of underskirt made of narrow rows of puffings. Necklines dip toward the parting of the breasts. The decoration of the top of the bodice, usually puffed, is elaborated at the shoulders, sometimes over a puffed sleeve.

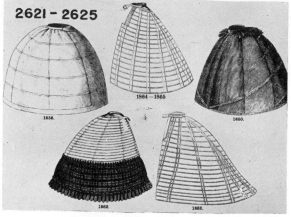

2616-20. XIXc. 1862. French. (Metropolitan Museum, Print Room.)
"Les Modes parisiennes" (periodical). Petticoats, corsets, and skirt-lifter.

2621-25. XIXc. German. (New York Public Library.)
"Der Bazar," Oct. 1, 1864. Crinolines from 1858-1865.

2626. XIXc. French.
Photograph of street. Shops exhibiting crinolines.

Crinolines, when they appeared in mid50's, were a great improvement over piled-on petticoats. But they had many disadvantages. They were inflammable. "Not a year passes but in this country alone hundreds suffer death by burning through crinoline." Eventually, women of all classes wore crinolines, and could burn up while cooking dinner in a sweeping skirt, as well as while waltzing in a skirt puffed with tulle.

"Eugénie hoop skeleton skirts" and "Vigoria crinoline petticoats," advertised in "The Queen," 1858, were largely replaced by cages of hoops made of watch-spring steel "so flexible that they can be wound around the finger," covered with "lace yarn." (Advertisement. Godey's, 1858.)

Douglas and Sherwood's "new expansion skirt" was an improvement for flexibility and support over their patent adjustable bustle and skirt of fine cloth, whalebone, and eyelets; its expansion adjustments and slides are silvered against sticking, as the rubber-

covered ones do. Gutta-percha covered hoops, on the other hand, were washable. All forms of uncased metal hoops were likely to catch in the shoe.

Every month in every magazine read by women for nearly two decades, new patents are advertised which positively obviate some complication attendant on hoops. A unique method, in each case, keeps them from being heavy, weak, inflammable, dirty, rusty, menacing traps, or causes of embarrassment. One does "not cause accidents"; another "allows a lady (to) ascend a steep stair, throw herself into an armchair, etc., without inconvenience to herself, or provoking the rude remarks of the observers." (Quoted by Cunnington.)

Mme. Demorest, who published the "Mirror of Fashion" in New York in 1862, also had an emporium which sold sewing machines (with extra self-tucking and quilting attachments at $5), eagle talon hooks and eyes, and her "Prize Medal Skirt," which "Godey's" speaks of as superior:

"These graceful, durable and economical skirts possess and combine every desirable quality. The standards are very numerous, and being passed through the covering, prevents the possibility of their slipping on the springs or GETTING OUT OF ORDER, and as their peculiarity has been patented, they cannot be sold by other parties generally. The size is very moderate, and the shape that which is best adapted for giving a graceful and undulating flow to the fullness of the dress. The materials of which the springs are composed has been wrought and tempered to an exquisite nicety. The strength is equal to any emergency to which it is likely to be subjected." You also got twice as many springs for half the price of former wire supports, in Mme. Demorest's wire skirt.

By 1850, little whalebone was used in corsets. They were elaborately gored, with set-in gussets of elastic. Front closings with spring latches were first shown at the 1851 exhibition. George Roberts' showrooms had "500 real linsey-woolsey and patent steel petticoats and 5000 pairs of stays to choose from" in 1858. (Ill. London News.)

Corsets become shorter-waisted with the approach of the 60's; they close in front or back, with a steel busk in front, few bones, and many elastic gussets. As the crinoline diminishes, the corset becomes more tightly laced.

The round crinoline of 1858 becomes flattened in front by 1862, and has been made much smaller above. From then until the return of the bustle in the 70's, the crinoline is progressively skeletonized. By latter half 60's, it has usually returned to the form of a gored petticoat of fabric with a flat panel in front and a few steels threaded through slots in the bottom; or it may be held out by rows of horsehair-filled puffings. It may simply be a steel-threaded hem hung on tapes from the waist.

With summer dresses, two white petticoats were worn over a crinoline, or one white petticoat over a "steel petticoat." With other dresses, the crinoline was covered by one colored petticoat of silk or wool.

English women are becoming physically active by the 60's. They walk and participate in sports for which special clothing will have to be provided.

Crinolines bounce; English women become less perturbed by what is revealed, and early in the 60's, begin instead to exploit it. Petticoat hems become as elaborately trimmed as the hems of dresses, and are made in brilliant colors: red, plaids, or stripes, as are stockings. English walking boots are trimmed and made in bright, eye-catching colors. Methods of hitching up the skirt mechanically are contrived, by which the petticoat is permanently displayed.

England, usually a year behind France, leads France by a year in these matters of striking shoes, stockings and petticoats; English colors are more violent and English hats and bonnets are overtrimmed by French standards.

The English petticoat with hitched-up skirts was notice by Eugénie on a visit to England; by the summer of 1862 French fashion plates show skirts which exploit what is underneath. Skirts hitched up by mechanical devices come quickly into general French use, and can be seen on Manet's *Street Singer* (1862, Ill. 2736).

During the 60's, hips are made increasingly slender; skirts are gored and petticoat fullness is set further down on deeper yokes. By 1865, the prob-

lem of keeping the hem of the skirt hitched up for active wear is solved by making the skirts of walking dresses shorter than the petticoat.

Mechanical lifting devices had begun to be advertised in second half of the 50's. "Nicolls' Patent Highland Cloak for ladies," says the Illus. London News in 1858, "somewhat resembles the old Spanish Roquelaire and has an elastic Capucine Hood. It is not cumbersome or heavy and measures 12 to 16 yards around the outer edge, falling in graceful folds from the shoulder, but by a mechanical contrivance (such being a part of the patent) the wearer can instantly form semi-sleeves, and thus leave the arms at liberty; at the same time the cloak can be made as quickly to resume its original shape. . . . The price will be two guineas and a half for each cloak, but with the Mecanique and a lined Hood, a few shillings more is charged."

Mme. de Plument's method (2616-20) of catching up her handsome petticoats is no doubt a specialty of her corset shop.

This interest in conversion and mechanical devices is not restricted to clothing. "Der Bazar," that catch-all of the latest gadgets, shows patent folding bent-wood chairs in 1864. America, with her great resources and small population, had been forced to invent labor-saving devices during the 50's. "The only substructure capable of supporting the drawn-up skirt gracefully" in 1863, is the *"cage Americaine."*

The American sewing machine, with special attachments (like Mme. Demorest's) is used to finish the already partly-made women's dress. Men's and boys' clothing becomes almost entirely factory-made during the 60's.

American folding beds, mechanical devices and wonderful tools, shown at the Philadelphia Centennial Fair in 1876, will fascinate English people, who have relegated to the attic or servants' rooms, and long ago forgotten, the ingenious convertible furniture invented by Sheraton (*Designs for Hunting Furniture,* 3rd edition, 1812).

Women's clothing, sold ready-made or semi-finished in the 50's, becomes almost entirely machine-sewed by the 60's. During this decade, women's clothing becomes subdivided into more special categories than had ever been known before, or seen since the 70's. There are clothes for the house alone, for walking on the street, for walking at the beach at Brighton; for playing tennis or bathing; clothes for church, for making calls; for different sorts of evening wear. Some are made by tailors, others by dressmakers. Hats may be worn with some; others require the more formal bonnet; all take different shoes, coats and wraps.

This makes it possible for a large part of women's clothing to be factory-made, as boots and shoes, and men's and children's clothes already are. By the final quarter-century practically all inexpensive everyday and work clothes of both sexes will be factory produced.

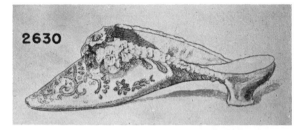

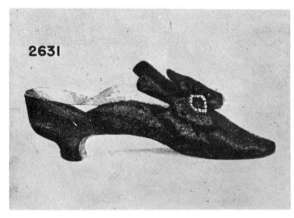

2627-32. XIXc. 1860. French-English.

"L'Illustrateur des Dames" (periodical). Plates of fashions shown at the London Exposition.

Crinolines bounce; feet show; shoes acquire heels and are made well worth looking at.

2627. Bottine de Dames (Angleterre): black with green uppers.

2628. Bottine-Eugénie (Angleterre): copper brown.

2629. Soulier de Boudoir (France): white, lined with blue; blue and white trimming.

2630. Descente de lit (France): white, lined with a light sharp blue to match heel, and touches in its white trim.

2631. Mule, Louis XIV (France): cerise.

2632. Bottine de Bal (France): black boot with a silvery-gold heel and appliquéd stars and moon; gold, silver and white fringe.

2633-41. XIXc. 1864. German.

"Der Bazar," Dec. 1.

Higher and more elaborate boots, which, the cap-

tion explains, follow the trend toward masculine styles.

2633. High boot of Russia leather; Cossack embroidery in black and white silk; black ball fringe, buttons and velvet bow.

2634. Boot checkered in black and gray leather lozenges; toe of patent leather; closed by gray cord and large white mother-of-pearl buttons; notched top finished with black lace.

2635. High boot of brown morocco, edged with black patent leather; dark brown taffeta laces and three brown chenille tassels.

2636. Pansy purple velvet shoe, gray border, flower appliqué in gold satin, purple cord and tassel.

2637. Young girl's half high boot of brown rep, trimmed with a bunch of flowers made of black lace or passementerie.

2638. Black patent leather shoe, lined with red morocco, red cord edge and tassel.

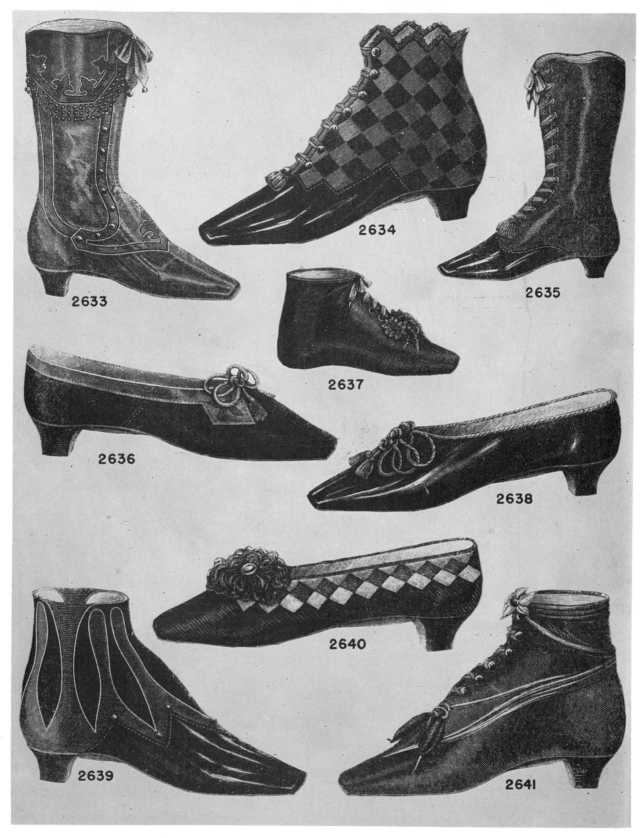

2633

2634

2635

2637

2636

2638

2639

2640

2641

2639. Boot of Romany leather and elastic, trimmed in patent leather with jet ball buttons.

2640. Black grosgrain shoe, checkered appliqué in white and purple; rosette of black chenille with a white mother-of-pearl center.

2641. Black satin boot. Three rolls of gray plush at the top represent the stalk, and gray leather trim on the boot, the leaves, seed pods, and flower of a reed-plant; gray pearl buttons.

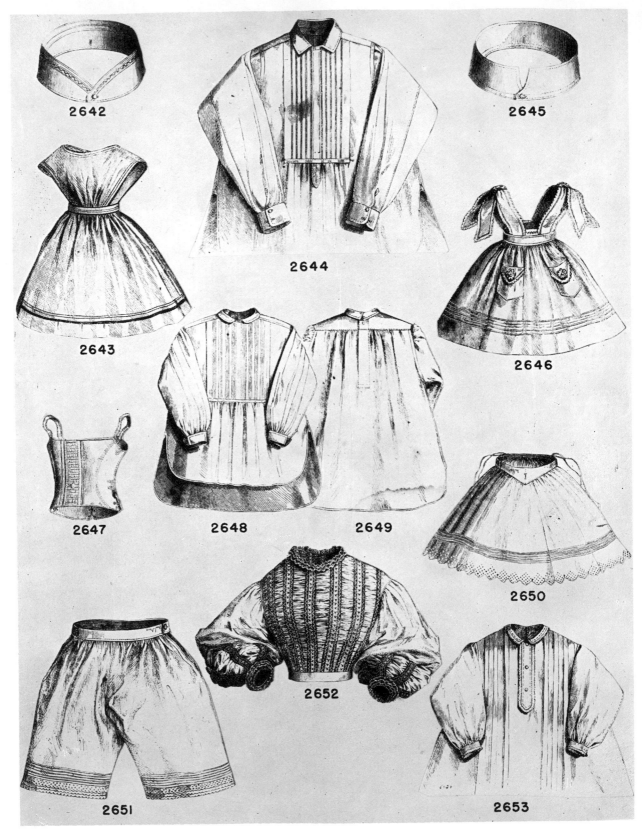

2642-63. XIXc. 1862. German. (New York Public Lib.)
  "Der Bazar," April 1.
2642, 2645. Collars: man.
2643, 46. Pinafores: girl, 3-5 years; girl, 5-7 years.
2644. Shirt: man.
2647. Corset: girl, 4-6 years.

2648-49. Shirt: boy.
2650. Petticoat: girl, 3-5 years.
2651. Drawers: girl, 6-8 years.
2652. White blouse: girl, 9-11 years; blouses of
the elaborate *canezou* type are extremely popular
with women as well.

2653. Nightgown: girl, 10-14 years.
2654, 55. Nightcap; Zouave chemisette: lady.
2656. Shoes: baby, 6-12 mos.
2657. Embroidered bee (actual size), for cashmere shawl.

2658. Embroidered cashmere scarf.
2659. Bed jacket: lady.
2660. Collar and chemisette: lady, negligée dress.
2661. Sleeve with cuff: lady, negligée dress.
2662, 63. Chemise, gauffered trim; nightshirt: lady.

2664-69. XIXc. First half 1860's.

Cartes de Visite.

2664. George Becks (New York c.1860)

2665. Man and 2 women (unknown).

2666. Husband and wife (St. Johns, New Brunswick).

2667. Man in checked suit and leggings (Provenance unknown, April 8, 1862).

2668. William Byron (Provenance unknown, April 16, 1863).

2669. Photographed by Southwell Bros., London, Photographers Royal.

2670-75. XIXc. French.
Cartes de Visite.

2670. Empress Eugenie (French, latter half of 50's).

2671. H. R. H. the Princess Alice, Mother of the Czarina (English, 1862).

2672. The future Edward VII and Alexandra, about the time of their marriage (English c.1863).

2673. Black pillbox hat with feathers (Provenance unknown, 1862).

2674. Ermine trimmed jacket (unknown).

2675. Embroidered tabs on chest (unknown).

The passion of the 1850's for Louis XIII-XVI dress and furniture is most familiar to us now in the horsehair-covered rosewood or mahogany chairs which the Victorians evolved out of Louis XVI forms, and which we see in so many of these *cartes de visite.*

Women began to assume men's coats and vests by 1850. Jackets, such as the Empress wears, based on French court coats, with basques equivalent to one of the standard three skirt flounces, are typical of the 50's. The Empress appears to have liked this coat-style very much; she is shown in photographs of the 60's wearing it, with cuffs and a much reduced peplum edged with long fringe.

The Empress, who led in replacing layers of flounced petticoat by the crinoline in 1856, was beautifully dressed by Worth in perfect rather than extreme taste, but is apt to be years in advance of the usual photograph.

Other elements of her dress are seen in French fashion plates of latter half of the 50's. These plates are first redrawn in English magazines; a few weeks later they appear in *Der Bazar,* and the month after that in *Godey's.* By the time an American girl has been photographed in a dilution of the style, in her best, but not absolutely new dress, several years have passed. The English time lag is about one year.

With the crinoline, skirts can afford to lose their puckered flounces and turn full, round, simpler and more becoming. Trimmings alter in the same way; puffed bands become formalized into cartridge or flat pleated self-trimmings—which will become standard in the 60's. The Empress wears this sort of trimming at a time when the partly made up dresses advertised in English newspapers are all banded in velvet, and many are still cluttered with flounces. Sleeves also become simplified, together with their undersleeves; the Empress wears high close cuffs, just before the close sleeve begins to reappear as an alternative to pagoda and bishop sleeves, in the last years of the 50's; white undersleeves also become simplified, and high cuffs appear on plain sleeves. Instead of bretelles, a slight fullness is carried down her bodice from each shoulder.

Square India shawls, folded into a triangle, are supplanted by long, scarf-like shapes (2671) before they (and similar lace shawls) disappear altogether with the advent of the bustled dress.

The reduction of the crinoline begins first at its top by the beginning of the 60's. English girls who, in 1865, are "brave enough to be seen without crinolines" are "remarked for their extremely forlorn appearance." There is only a band of bottom support on the skirt of (2675). The young girl of Nancy in 1865 (2679) is lank indeed.

At the turn of the 50's-60's, in France, and in 1860 in England and America, begins a series of bolero-like jackets: gold braided red Garibaldi jackets, zouave jackets, the Spanish braided velvet jackets, Figaros and the "Alexandra" which appears at the time of her marriage (2672). White blouses of the lingerie canezou type, or scrolled in corded patterns, and loose red Garibaldi shirts trimmed in black soutache, are worn with colored skirts, belts and fitted corselets, throughout first half of 60's. Large buttons run up dress fronts from late 50's through the first years of the 60's. Black velvet ribbon with pendant at throat (2671, 2672) and Manet, 1866, *Woman with Parrot* (2739).

Round skirts of even length tend to become flattened in front, and to drag out in back, with the front and sides gored, and fullness massed toward the back. By mid60's crinolines are worn by women of all ages and classes. Active young women appear in skirts well off the ground, during the daytime. Skirts are no longer drawn up mechanically for walking, but are made in distinct categories of short skirts and bustled trained skirts for calling and evening. London tailors and habit makers begin to make women's daytime clothes of the sort in which Alexandra looked particularly well.

Curls were worn bunched behind the ears *à l'hongroise* for a couple of brief years at the end of the 50's, and began to be seen again in daytime use at mid60's. As the head becomes squarer bonnets are largely replaced by hats, but their bows and wide strings are continued in round embroidered tabs at the throat (2675). Designs for their decoration appear in pattern books for several years before 1865.

Edward (2672), one of the best dressed of kings, wears a standing wing collar, dotted tie, run (like Dickens', 1857) through a ring, matching vest and coat with braided edges, and gray trousers.

2676-81. XIXc. 1860-67. French.

2676. Woman seated among fuchsia plants.

This dress, which shows analogies with Ill. 2670 in its cartridge-pleated trim and fullness of the bodice from the shoulders, is set, by a fascinating chance, against a background of fuchsia plants. The beloved colors combined in fuchsia flowers were among the first coal-tar dyes to be produced: mauve, 1856, followed at the end of the 50's by magenta and solferino (fuchsia), Hoffmann's Violet, Iodine Green, Bismarck Brown, and Aniline Blue and Black. We see costumes carried out largely in these new aniline colors, by 1863-4, in the strongly contrasted costumes characteristic of the 60's.

2677. Rigolboche, Queen of the Can-Can.

Rigolboche was not one of the elegant cocottes like Cora Pearl or the prodigal Anna Deslions, although she had diamonds and carriages to match theirs. She danced at the Mabille Gardens in the 60's, where the Prince of Wales and the greatest figures in French society and the arts could be found on Tuesdays and Saturdays. Rigolboche was ugly as a death's head, smoked like a chimney, and yelled out anything that came into her head, in rough, audacious slang and a voice like broken glass. She danced with a uninhibited frenzy which nearly dislocated her wonderful legs. Instead of

dying bankrupt at forty-four like Cora Pearl, she retired early to the Côte d'Azur where she finished her days running a most respectable boarding-house for ladies.

2678. Cape and lace scarf (1863).

2679. Young girl from Nancy (1865). Skirt without crinoline.

2680. Veiled head (1865).

2681. Plumed hat, lace scarf (1867). Black lace and tulle squares and triangles reduced from shawls to scarves and veils. Hat brim rolled up at sides; pendant earrings, as hair is drawn up; masses of artificial hair in chignon.

2682-83. XIXc. 1860-65. Italian. (New York Public Library, Picture Coll.)
Garibaldi.

The triumphs of the Italian liberator in the summer of 1860 and the enthusiasm with which he was received in London in 1864 gave a long life to fashions inspired by his pill-box cap and blazing shirt.

Young women were adopting men's styles, from jockey cap to boots, and taking pleasure in violent contrasts. Nothing pleased them more, for half a decade, than these Garibaldi styles. They wore the pill box, scrolled with braid, exactly like the versions in which he was photographed; it also affected the shape of other hats. His bloused red shirt is always full and buttoned down the front, with a loose sleeve and tight cuff; it is often plain, but in its character-

2682

istic form has a tucked bosom and is more elaborately decorated with gold or black soutache than
the shirt he wears here. "Garibaldi striped silks" appeared in 1860 in England.

**2684. XIXc. 1863. English. (New York Public Library,
Picture Coll.)**
Edward VII as Prince of Wales.

2685. XIXc. 1867. English. (Culver Service.)
Charles Dickens.

On his second American lecture tour, the English
author is dressed to knock his provincial audience
cold in admiration of his elegance. It still has a
certain force.

The degradation of the patchwork quilt had begun by the 50's, but quilting was still a technique
in which many women were proficient, despite
Mme. Demorest's sewing machine attachment. *Der
Bazar* in the latter half of the 50's shows the first
turned down shirt collars for men, elaborately patterned in quilting over cord; very attractive they
are, too.

During, and for a few years after each excessively
cold winter: 1830, 1845, quilting reappears. There
was a series of rigorous winters in the mid50's. By
their end, the emancipation of women had begun;
they start to walk instead of being driven in a
closed carriage. Until quilting is ousted by sealskin
in the 70's, it makes comfortable muffs and linings
for short walking coats. Quilting was taken over
by men in the cold winters of 1860-61-65. The vest
worn by T. M. Fay, Union College Class of '60, is
handsomely quilted in a basket-weave pattern. The
shift to plain or braid-edged vests has already begun
in 1860; quilting moves to the handsome linings of
men's loose coats and capes, which wearers have
been holding back and displaying since the latter
half of the 50's.

For all the velvet and quilting shown by Dickens,
men's clothing is turning fast, from 1860, into forms
familiar to us now. Dickens wears a plain turned-
down collar, pleated shirt front, and straight cuffs.
Like the Prince of Wales (Ill. 2672) he wears his
necktie hanging like a modern four-in-hand; it is
not yet knotted, but is drawn through a seal ring,
as fussy gentlemen still wore theirs in e.XXc. His
waistcoat is of velvet, but is plain; by 1860 the
watch chain of large links is commonly caught by
a bar through one of the buttonholes between the
middle and the bottom of the vest, and dangles a
bunch of seals and trinkets.

In the engraving of the Prince of Wales (after a
photograph of 1863), we see the formal afternoon
dress of the next half century established in essentials.

2683

2684

2685

Men's Dress: As Shown in College Photographs of Early 1860's

The early 1860's is the turning point in men's dress.

Until you have examined photographs of the graduating class of—say Union College, Schenectady, N. Y., in 1860, it is difficult to believe how much variation will be found in head and facial hair, collar and tie, vest and coat details. Culver Service has a number of war-time sets from Amherst, Hamilton, etc., which usually include favorite professors and the college janitor. Their examples from Union have been used because they show the widest range, and are accurately dated.

Some of the best-dressed young men appear in clothes such as their fathers have worn through the 50's; others, in buying their first suit of "store clothes," have happened to hit on new trends which lead to the 70's. The direction in which styles move are seen on the handsome, fashionably dressed Hamilton boy (2694), on Prof. Root, in his matching coat and vest of textured material, and on the Union class of 1868, in their freshman year.

Hair may be as short as Ingham's, rather like a farm hand's today, or fall in locks like Custer's scouts (Pitt, Fargo); there is a good deal of involved work with a comb about the ears (Campbell).

The long-haired Fargo and short-haired Ingham are completely shaved; moustaches are combed down like Gleason's, or twisted wide like Pitt's. Green has a complete beard. A fellow who looks like Gen. Grant has hair on the jowls and a shaved chin; McElroy has the same pattern, long and fluffed; Flick and Morrison (who also has an imperial) have their jowls shaved.

Collars stand, high and overlapping (Van Winkle), or low and flat as a choir boy's, exposing the neck (Fargo), or are turned over and stiffly starched (Green); there is often a three-inch gap in front, to show off an enormous tie, like Pitt's soft, thick bow, or "Grant's" fringed satin.

Bow ties of whatever form in 1860 have a common characteristic: they are tied with affected negligence, with an end and loop under the vest and coat collar, and the other side out and over. The most characteristic tie of 1860 is a narrow ribbon, striped across the end, often in red or black. Gleason's, striped lengthwise in velvet, merely dangles from a knot. Morrison's is patterned diagonally. $\Sigma \Phi$'s wear their pins in huge cravats, like Campbell's plaid, tied and twisted over to cover the shirt front. Other shirt fronts are closed by large, dark pearl studs (Gleason, Van Winkle).

There are many fancy, brocaded vests with long lapels, opening low (Flick, Green, Campbell, and Fay's handsome quilted vest), in the manner of the 50's. These are worn with coats with long lapels, worn open, with fronts parallel. There are other vests which compromise between the old open front and the new impulse to button up high, shown by Gleason and McElroy. Fargo's checked vest, which would choke him if closed, has in fact a loop from the fourth buttonhole for catching it together. Over it appears the diagonal strap which is seen on many young men in the early 60's (2694); its use is not confined to America, but where it goes and what it carries I do not know. Gleason's coat, without lapels, follows this same open and closed bulge, into which the hand is sometimes thrust as in a sling.

McElroy's suit is actually the latest thing. Its bound edge is buttoned high, once, and then spreads open; small lapels expose the chest on which a breast pocket is set on the level of the button. Campbell's suit, though it still carries a velvet collar and is worn with a waffle-patterned vest, also shows new trends: a rough textured and patterned fabric (Prof. Root), in place of broadcloth; small, short lapel with its buttonhole set diagonally; piped pocket edge. Gleason's coat may be compared to Ill. 2706; and the clothing of the handsome Hamilton boy, with Ill. 2712.

2686

2687

2686-2700. XIXc. 1860. U.S.A. (Culver Service.)
2686. Alburn I. Fargo, Monterey, Mass.
2687. Unknown.
2688. Edgar B. Van Winkle, N. Y.
2689. Unknown.
2690. W. H. McElroy, Albany.
2691. E. C. Morrison, Modena, N. Y.

2692. W. H. Pitt, Granger, N. Y.
2693. Douglas Campbell.
2694. Edgar W. Crowell (Hamilton College, 1865-68).
2695. Weston Flick, Great Valley, N. Y.
2696. Prof. E. W. Root, brother of Elihu (Hamilton College).

2697. T. M. Fay, Pavilion, N. Y.
2698. William Green.

2699. George T. Ingham, Salem, N. J.
2700. A. Will Gleason.

2701. XIXc. Mid-50's. Provenance unknown.

Seated Woman with Fur Stole.

Hair form, wide collar, large brooch, and short, wide, lace-flounced bell sleeve of mid50's. Sealskin, which everyone will wear in the 70's, begins to be advertised in the 50's, and is proudly shown off here in an interesting form. The stole, related in shape to the many fichu collars with tab ends, is accompanied by a pair of cuffs which have no connection with the dress. They are obviously intended to be worn, out of doors, in reversed position, over the conventionally clasped hands of the period to form a cylindrical muff.

2702. XIXc. Mid-60's. U.S.A.

Stereopticon View at Saratoga Springs.

Happy middle class crowd at Saratoga at about the end of Civil War. Crinolines are still wide at the bottom, but the cylindrical form of the 1858 crinoline has become pyramidal. Decoration sinks toward the hem which begins to drag out in back. Loose paletots and mantles. There are still wide-brimmed hats plumed around the brim, and plain small banded hats. But brims are rolling up at the sides, and begin to dip forward, with decoration massed on top.

Light-colored top hats are more sporting than black; many pork pie, boater and incipient low-crowned bowler shapes. The young man (l. of c.) shows the characteristic light trousers of the 60's, often with matching vest (Ill. 2712), worn with knee-length topcoats; sleeve characteristically clumsy and over long. Behind him, l., a widely-spaced turned-down collar.

2703. XIXc. c. 1860. U.S.A.

Niagara Falls.

Summer dresses of the small shepherds' checks and dots of the late 50's. Plumed hat, with swinging brim; bodices, losing crossed fichus, have in their place a shoulder cap, often fringed, or a sleeve gathered full onto a dropped shoulder-line; fringed shepherds' check shawl; smaller white collars. Men's coats long; sleeves wider, baggy, sagging at elbow. Pork pie hats.

Courtesy of Culver Service

2704

2704. XIXc. 1865. U.S.A., Schenectady.

Freshman Class of 1868, Union College.

The Union College class of 1860 showed all sorts of extravagantly long or roached-out hair, beards, mutton chops and moustaches.

In 1865, the freshmen are uniformly clean shaven. Their hair has none of the wild tumbled look of Flick (2695) and Fargo (2686). It is slicked down, much closer to the head in oiled waves. The roached-out hair back of McElroy's (2690) and Campbell's (2693) ears is reduced to a turn-up like a drake's tail, and the part moves a little closer to the center.

Turn-over collars no longer show the wide gap seen on Flick, or on the very "hick" character in the Saratoga stereopticon picture. String ties, bows, and ascots are all less noticeable. The only patterned tie shown here is seen on the boy (back, 5 from l.) who wears the only silk vest; his coat most nearly resembles the 1860 form, with its longer lapels, worn open, with more nearly parallel edges (although the edges are somewhat cutaway here).

The 1865 coat follows the trend indicated by McElroy in 1860: short lapels, buttoned high on the chest, with edges sloping away below. The thick clumsy sleeve of e.60's (in Saratoga photograph) remains wide at the elbow but narrows toward the hand and is shorter. As on McElroy's suit and in Ill. 2712 there are many contrasting bindings and buttons, but the high pocket, which was set at the level of the first button on McElroy's suit, has dropped toward the second, or (in the case of the double-breasted suit), as low as the breast pocket of Ill. 2712.

Matching vest and trousers in plaid (instead of light color, as in Saratoga photo) on seated figure, r. Fancy vests have been almost entirely replaced by plain tailored vests, with no decoration except the fashionable contrasting bindings and buttons; watch chains from a bar in a middle buttonhole to vest pocket. Trousers are wide and tubular. There are many round-crowned hats with slightly curling brims, the binding of which is often contrasting. One cap.

The seniors, in 1865, do show more fantasy in facial hair, with which they have more to experiment than the freshmen. But they are notably less lush than the class of '60.

2705-16. XIXc. 1860-62. Portuguese. (New York Public Library.)

"O Mensageiro das Damas" (periodical).

It is during the 60's that the present-day dress of men becomes universally established. Clothing, for both men and women, is being subdivided into categories suitable for one occasion and inappropriate for another. Fancy vests and light trousers agreeing with neither coat nor vest pass out of fashion rapidly after 1860 (compare Union College and photos of 1860 with group of 1865). There are widely striped trousers; but the strongest tendency is towards agreement of at least two pieces of the suit, and the matching three-piece suit for morning wear comes into use (2716). The new trend of 1861 is for vests and trousers to match, as we see they do commonly by 1865 (Ill. 2712 and group photo, Union College). The bound edge, which is seen from the late 50's is particularly noticeable on vests (Ill. 2712, and 1865 group Union Coll.).

Suits and loose finger-length topcoats have plenty of pockets and all trousers have fly closing. Straw hats, shaped much like modern panamas (2706) and boaters (2716) are worn with informal clothes, together with turn-down collars. These have grown high (2706, 2716) and are accompanied by well-tied bows, or long ties in the nature of four-in-hands, although they are still apt to be folded over or passed through a ring, rather than knotted.

The tendency of the 50's to show off handsome coat linings increases with the quilted linings of the 60's (2713 and 2685).

The more enclosing brims of women's bonnets are trimmed on the under side with a row of flowers above the hair; ruches of tulle at the cheeks; full projecting curtain of lace, straw or fabric behind; bonnet strings still important.

Women's dresses are usually machine-sewed. The boned bodices, smooth and slope-shouldered, are often without shoulder caps; bretelles are barely recalled in occasional ruched decoration down the front of the bodice; the wide bottom of the sleeve tends to close in, altering the bell into a bishop sleeve, as wide or wider at the elbow than at the bottom.

The skirt, gored into a more slender hipline, remains very wide below. It is much plainer, with its trimming (when horizontal) concentrated on the hemline or lower third of the skirt. When flounces are used they are narrow, repeated, frilly, (often with a pinked edge) and are made of plain-color materials; though on an 1860 skirt (2705), two colors continue to be alternated.

Borders *à disposition* pass with the beginning of the 60's. Cartridge pleated and ruched trimmings often agree in fabric and color with the body of the gown. But in the main, decoration is now contrasting, both in color and texture (fur, 2708; lace, 2715; velvet bands, 2723-24). It often has an irregular edge (2708, 2711). A tendency of the skirt to be notched, cut or drawn up to show the petticoat (2711) will increase.

2705. White bonnet with a scarlet edge, scarlet flowers set under brim, white ruching below the hair-line, black lace curtain and cream-colored ribbon. Lavender dress patterned in black; alternate black and lavender ruffled trim.

2706. (June, 1860) Straw hat, black band. Turned-down collar with stitched decoration, garnet tie, gray coat, white trousers, black shoes, blue-gray gloves.

2707. (March, 1861) Dark gray topcoat; cool gray vest; standing collar with black tie; blue gray breeches and boot tops; yellow gloves.

2708. White bonnet and plume, purple edge and curtain in back, cerise bows. Gray gown, appliqué of brown fur; lemon yellow gloves.

2709. Bonnet of yellow straw, violets and leaves, with violet ruching and bonnet strings. Light cocoa-colored gown.

2710. (July, 1861) Gray top hat, vest, and breeches. Black stock, gold pin and heavy watch chain. Brown coat with stitched collar, lemon yellow gloves.

2711. White bonnet and strings and black lace

fall, lined with cerise and trimmed with grapes and roses. Malachite green dress.

2712. (Sept., 1861) Blue tie with striped ends. Off-white vest and trousers, bound and banded in black; black coat displaying satin lining and binding. Black top hat.

2713. (Nov., 1861) Black top hat. Turned-over collar, purple tie. Brown cape with velvet collar, and quilted light gray lining. Striped gray trousers; lemon gloves.

2714. White bonnet, strings and fall, trimmed with lavender and white flowers. Greenish-gray dress, lavender ruchings.

2716. (Aug., 1862) Yellow straw hat, black binding and band. Turned down collar, scarlet tie. Gray mixture three-piece suit, lavender gloves, black patent leather pumps; gold watch chain. Cigarette, coming into more common use with the Crimean War.

2717-22. XIXc.

Cartes de Visite, 1860-65.

2717. San Francisco?

2718. Bridgeport, Conn.

2719. Bridgeport, Conn.

2720. Liverpool.

2721. Pittsfield, Mass.

2722. France: Empress Eugenie.

Hair, which has been brushed down from a part for decades, begins in the 60's to be brushed sideways from it, squaring the crown of the head and the forehead. The old crescent of braided back hair, which had helped to form the oval head (2718) falls or is netted into a chignon of more oblong shape, parallel with the neck (2719, 2722). Details of every step in hairdressing (as well as in every branch of sewing and fancy work) between mid-50's to mid80's, can be studied in the huge plates of "Der Bazar, Illustrirte Damen Zeitung" of Berlin.

One of the sleeves to appear in the late 50's, as fichu-like bretelles lose ground, is basically close fitted, but covered with a series of puffs. Mrs. James Gordon Bennett wears the *canezou*-like sleeve as she welcomes the Japanese envoys in 1860 (Frank Leslie's *Illustrated Newspaper*). Flowing sleeves continue to be seen on summer dresses and bolero jackets. On heavy silk dresses this sleeve, set under an epaulette at a dropped shoulder-line, tends to close in toward the wrist (2718-19). This sleeve form is exactly paralleled by the shape of men's sleeves, sagging toward a baggy elbow (Ill. 2669).

By mid60's, there are many completely smooth, untrimmed bodices and sleeves (2722). Braided zouave jackets and Spanish bolero styles affect the bodices of dresses with which they are not worn. Their outlines are sketched in braid or buttons (2719, 2721), on bodices which are rising into little standing collars. The points of vests are elaborated into tabs and trimmed with upholstery-like pleatings (2719).

Emphasis is shifting from sleeves. The skirt will become looped up to show the petticoat, on its way to becoming bustled in late 60's. The line of the bodice, down the front or across at the height of the epaulettes, will become stressed by pleating. In second half of the 60's these trimmings outline a round or square yoke; it may be filled in by lingerie chemisettes, or be continued in the fabric of the dress, to a standing collar.

2723-26. XIXc. 1861. French. (New York Public Lib.)
"Moniteur de la Mode," January.

2723. Hair dressed with pink and blue morning glories and green leaves, and ostrich tips in two shades of pink. Pink bodice, banded in deeper pink with bouquets matching hair decoration. Skirt of pink puffs, edged in black and white lace. White scarf, fan, gloves, and single but important bracelet on each arm.

2724. Cerise bonnet, strings, and puffs under the brim; white ruching at the cheeks; black lace at back of crown, and curtain. Tan gown trimmed in black velvet.

Many diagonal lines and diamond patterns, which tends to become less geometric and regular within a couple of years. The double skirts of the late 50's have become united; what was the lower skirt is trimmed, and its pattern is carried up at the sides in a line established by decoration or long tabs in the late 50's. This placing of decoration had given

the outline of the skirt à tablier. The diamond patterns with which the apron front had been crosshatched continue in favor, but are more broadly executed in velvet straps. Zigzag, notched and diamond effects seen everywhere cause the ends of the straps to be cut in points.

2725. Straw hat trimmed with a rose and white ostrich plume. Shirt with mannish standing collar and tie, and deep, turned-back cuffs. Severe walking costume in yellowish-fawn (with matching gloves); black trim in bolder lines; bolero jacket (favored through first half of the 60's) with notched sleeves; row of buttons up front (late 50's-e. 60's).

2726. White bonnet and strings; roses under brim, and rose plumes. Mole brown gown edged in garnet. Bell sleeves gathered into bishop sleeves; tabs replaced by sash ends, cut off diagonally. Saw-toothed hem of the upper skirt has the bold contrasting edge used also in men's dress. The small crisp ruffles of the petticoat-like underskirt are set on with an upholstered finish. (July, plates by *Jules David*.)

2727. XIXc. 1861. U.S.A.
"Godey's Lady's Book," March.
The diagonal line of 1861 is applied with the new bold simplicity on a dress prophetically cut on princess lines.

2728-35. XIXc. 1862. French.
"Moniteur de la Mode" (periodical). Plates by *Jules David*.

2728. (March.) Evening costume in two shades of yellow: light combined with pumpkin, worn with a white ostrich plume, and trimmed with white lace. The skirts of evening and calling gowns all tend to be shortened and cut up in some way to display the underskirt.

2729. Costume of Diana for one of the many costume balls of the 60's. Red crescent and flowers; red and yellow bow and quiver. White gauze shirt and harem trousers. Leopard skin; skirt of shaded green leaves over pink. Gold shoes (see 2632).

2730. (March.) Diagonal lines becoming spiral as they lose force. Red and white flowers, green leaves, with a taffeta dress of a sharp aniline green, between jade and malachite, trimmed with white lace.

2731. Quilted bonnet, white lined with rose; blue-black bows set under and on top of brim; black fall with a white line and white lace border; white bonnet strings with black lines. Purple gown, boldly patterned in black squares set on their points; bodice springs apart below the last button into the tabs of a vest.

2732. (June.) Gauzy summer bonnet: the old line of flowers under the brim has been forced out by the rise of ruching (which used to be set at the cheeks), and flowers are reduced to a red, yellow and green posy, with daisies scattered over the crown; white bonnet strings. The favorites among all the aniline colors appear in the lavender gown, the skirts of which are deeply cut up and turned back to show narrow violet ruffles.

2733. Like her companion's, the under brim of the yellow and white bonnet is entirely filled with ruching, and merely set with a small green and white bouquet; white strings. Full white shirt with scarlet collar and cuffs. Princess gown of brilliant blue-green trimmed with bright, deep blue; skirt permanently drawn up under its braid and tassel decoration, to show the white skirt beneath.

2734. (July.) The straw hat which accompanied walking dress in 1861 had acquired an ostrich plume, but was narrower-brimmed than the hat of 1858. By 1862, the brim has become much smaller and the plume (here shaded in deep rose) is accompanied by ribbon bows (dark blue) rather than flowers.

The costume shown here is composed of all the favorite items of informal dress of first half of the 60's. When not so insistently braid trimmed, it is apt to be accompanied by Garibaldi's little braid-patterned pill-box hat.

In this case, the costume is of greenish putty color, with the ubiquitous soutache braid trim of the period, in black. The shirt, with its little mannish collar, and full sleeve gathered into a tight cuff, is white. The enormously popular red Garibaldi shirt is made in the same way, and is usually braided on the bosom. Zouave and bolero jackets with simple funneled sleeves are enormously popular; so is the "Swiss corselet" or belt seen here, which is often notched, above and below, into two points instead of one. The same is true of loose paletots and capes, reaching a little below the hips, which are seen on many cartes de visite of first half 60's.

2735. Bonnet (filled with ruching), plume, and fall are white; crown and strings, arsenic green; white shirt with a magenta bow tie. Gray gown with a waistcoat-like bodice and lapels; strap trim in arsenic-green.

2736. XIXc. 1862. French. (Boston, Mrs. Montgomery Sears.)

Manet. Street Singer.

Pill-box hat; loose paletot with bound edges **taken**

over from men's dress. Skirt hem caught up mechanically.

2737. XIXc. 1862-3. French. (Louvre.),
Manet. Luncheon on the Grass.

2738. XIXc. c. 1864. French.
Photograph of Gustave Courbet.

2739. XIXc. 1866. French. (Metropolitan Museum.)
Manet. Woman with Parrot.
Dressing gown; medallion on black ribbon at throat.

2740. XIXc. 1863. German.
"Der Bazar," May 8.
Mantles and mantillas for summer. The loose jackets, hanging to just below the hips, become longer and more closely fitted. The gowns beneath them are laced in through the torso, gored into smoother hips, and are often cut in a princess line. There are "fast" little mannish topcoats (upper left) worn with severe hats. Collars, cuffs and lapels increase in importance; sleeves are more tubular. Trim more resembling that used on dresses; running "Greek" key designs replace the familiar soutache braiding. Burnous and Talma cloaks continue; cloaks are caught together in back, rather than actually hooded.

Plain little bowlers, taken over from men, and high-crowned hats with ostrich and a ribbon band,

2740

2741
2742

supplement the familiar wider forms, which are trimmed with plumes or a nosegay, and often have a valance of lace all around the brim.

Bonnet brims stand high and squarer, behind hair dressed high above the temples; back hair falls low, clubbed into a *catogan,* often supplemented with false hair, and set with elaborate combs. Lower left: skirts and cloaks made of material in small repeated patterns.

Plaid stockings and brightly colored boots worn by women, as well as children.

2741-42. XIXc. 1863. German. (New York Public Lib.) "Der Bazar," May 15.

Acute patterns of squares and diamonds are becoming curved, or are mitred into running band and Greek designs.

The trim of boned and fitted bodices outlines a yoke or bertha. Necklines are higher, with standing collars, ruches and bow ties. Sleeves either return to a long, simple form of the bell sleeve, which preceded the bishop sleeve, or become tubular. White undersleeves are reduced. Buckled belts.

Der Bazar gives illustrations in actual size for setting on these decorations and for laying out the pleating, which is done by the methods of an upholsterer of our day.

The wide-sleeved dress is in the fashionable new "tourterelle," a turtle-dove gray, tinged with brown; pleated hem of black taffeta; trim of white lace and

black velvet. The curled hair is more elaborately dressed with black lace and a hanging veil.

The other dress, of violet poplin, is trimmed with violet taffeta and black velvet. Cap of mousseline, black velvet ribbon and rosettes of violet ribbon. Hair rolled back from the temples, full, square and high.

2743-49. XIXc. 1863. U.S.A.

"Godey's Lady's Book," September.

Women have a great deal more hair, elaborately arranged in a multitude of ways: coronet braids, combs, flowers and ribbons, caps and catogans; but always rolled or drawn away from the face, higher and squarer at the crown, and massed longer and fuller in back. A center part is far from absolute now, and the hair is often waved or curled.

The variety which had been instituted by skirts, is now surpassed by bodices. They are elaborated by both cut and trim. It is no longer inevitable that they button up the front, and it may be difficult to decide just where they do close. Most of these gowns have been so affected by the Zouave jackets of the e. 60's, that they give at least the appearance of a skimpy fitted jacket (cut well away from the neck) worn over a plain, high-necked bodice. The return of the pagoda sleeve (in a longer, more tubular form) is also an effect of the jackets, on which wide, simple sleeves appeared, while dress sleeves inclined toward elaborate bishop shapes.

2743. Brown dress, on which a long, fitted, open-front coat has been sketched in black lace; large elaborate bow at throat.

2744. Mother exhibiting puppet show: blue gown, trimmed in black, with dark blue ribbons. Wide, low neckline; shoulders covered by a white bertha finished by a ruche at the throat.

2745. Child on lap: white bertha; low-necked white dress embroidered in red.

2746. Girl on hassock: dark gray, trimmed in dark red with ball fringe.

2747. Flowers in hair. Dress in two shades of gray, trimmed with black lace; its bodice juggles the themes of bolero and the Swiss belt so often worn with it.

2748. Green, braided by black soutache into a coat-dress with important cuffs. Return of cap; white with green trim. Chairs (often folding), made of bentwood or reed in rounded form, are advertised by 1861.

2749. Pink jacket dress, with pink frogged and buttoned lapels and collar.

2750-54. XIXc. June, 1864. U.S.A.
"Godey's Lady's Book," June.

Return of the lace cap; bonnets; informal hats, trimmed with plumes and ribbon, rather than flowers; brims dip forward, in the line on which hats will come to be tilted. Gloves white to pale lemon yellow.

The amount of applied trimming is being reduced as more patterned materials, in relatively modest, inconspicuous patterns, are used.

Scale patterns and careful instructions have to be given in all the fashion magazines for laying out and constructing the decorations which are used. Interlaced diamond patterns in simple velvet bands have become short tabbed straps, elaborately bordered and braided (2754). The small ruffles and banded cartridge pleatings of e. 60's have been combined into ruffles cut on the bias, and laid on with upholstery-like regularity. Even these tend to be replaced by deep scallops and fringes.

2750. Small ruffled and tasseled parasols. Rosered bonnet; white mantilla caught with tassels at a bertha top. Magenta gown with small dark figures.

2751. White hat and plume, red bow. Dark gray dress with self-color fringe and tassels, lighter gray pipings and carved pearl buttons; corselet front and apron give princess form to gown; underskirt in narrow, lighter gray stripes, with piped scallops.

2752. White hat with bright cobalt-blue bow. Black and white costume of patterned and plain fabric. Round corselet (another step in the transition to the princess cut); skirt slashed to show small frill of the underskirt.

2753. White hat, red trim and strings. Buff coatcostume, strap decoration done in black braid.

2754. Black lace Figaro jacket with epaulettes cut with a bertha top. Cobalt blue gown with elaborate black-braided tabs; ruching with a pinked edge set over a carefully pleated bias-cut flounce at the hem.

2755-56. XIXc. 1864. German.
"Der Bazar," July 15.

2755. Swimming suit for ladies. The long, loose, ambiguous chemise in which women have bathed, is replaced during first half 60's by bathing suits in which it is possible to swim.

2756. Gymnastic dress for young girls. Pantalettes have practically disappeared, but their advantages are retained in loose trousers in dresses specifically designed for athletics.

2757. XIXc. 1863. Swedish. (Stockholm, Hallwyl Coll.)
Agnes von Hallwyl, age 7.

2758. XIXc. 1866-7. French. (Louvre.)
Edgar Degas. Portrait of his cousin's family.

High boots and pinafores. Pantalettes coming to the end of their use during first half 60's.

2758

2759-64. XIXc. 1864. U.S.A.
"Godey's Lady's Book," November.

The earlier two-skirted or coat-skirted effects (2743-49) are being broken up and shortened, especially in front.

Bodices are no longer bolero jackets, but are carried down, in a fitted princess line, into postilion's tabs and tails. Interest is being focused on the back of the skirt over the buttocks, where skirts will soon be caught up into polonaises and the bustles of the 70's. There are points, jagged tabs, heavy mixed and ball fringes. The scrawlings of soutache (hem, 2759) are being supplanted by more parallel patterns in wide braid or cord elaborated into Hungarian loops and frogs, and trimmed with braid-covered wooden moulds, hanging like tassels (2764; sleeves and waistline of coat, c. figure).

Bonnet brims rise high in front and are trimmed with jutting quills (2763); the curtain in back edged with ball-fringe or jet pendants.

Back hair clubbed into coarse-meshed chenille nets or ribbons, when not covered by bonnet curtains.

2759. Red and green hair decoration. White jacket and black skirt, both banded in ruby red, scrolled in black soutache.

2760. Gray hat, malachite green and white ribbons, white bouquet; black hair net. Black jacket, jet studded. Dulled malachite green tabs, edged with black lace, over a plain skirt of a dirty pink.

2761. White bonnet with strings and fall narrowly striped in black and white. Gray coat and skirt; self colored frogs; ruby red vest.

2762. White bonnet and falls; lavender crown and puffed brim, trimmed with red roses and pointed green leaves. Salmon-buff gown, trimmed with black lace; hem of skirt caught up to show petticoat, tabbed alternately in white and cobalt blue, both with a line of black braid. Pocket in skirt front.

2763. White bonnet, jet trimming, black feather and green spray. Light violet gown, trimmed in black and violet.

2764. Kneeling girl: red-purple hair ribbons and white chenille net. Shirred white blouse with Medici sleeves; pinafore dress of stone-gray trimmed with red-purple velvet in a Hussar pattern.

2765-69. XIXc. June, 1865. U.S.A.

"Godey's Lady's Book," June.

Narrow stripes, small all-over repeats, more "made" trimmings, scalloped, folded over, and set with tassels and pendants. Closer sleeves. The long, clear princess line is disturbed, as waistlines shorten under Empire influences in France, and hips spread. Skirts are much narrower and rounder at the hem, fuller and less gored at the waist, and begin to be caught up about the hips (2769) as well as in front to show petticoat flounces (2767). Forward rake of hats continues.

2765. Hair trimmed with violets and white lace. White gown, banded in light violet with white tassels.

2766. Black and white fabric, trimmed with black lace, and cobalt blue bands and tassels; red fan.

2767. Light brown straw with white plumes. White blouse, black embroidered. Cocoa brown costume, Figaro jacket and Swiss belt, trimmed with black braid and pendants; white petticoat flounces, banded in red.

2768. Black lace cap; light violet overdress, edged with buff braid, patterned in red and green, and skirt-pockets; white underdress.

2769. White straw hat with red and white plumes. Black and white striped dress; sash ends and scallops in dull cherry red.

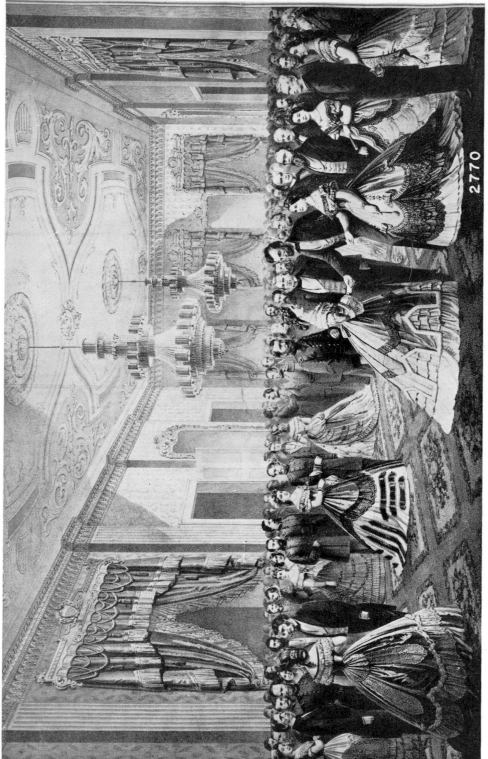

2770

2770. XIXc. 1865. U.S.A.

"Frank Leslie's Chimney Corner" (periodical). Grand Reception of the Notables of the Nation at the White House.

Hair dressed with elaborate combs of gold filigree and jet, chains and ornaments, flowers and ribbon. Bead necklaces, earring, important gold bracelets, fans, lace handkerchiefs.

Shorter-waisted evening dresses with trains, showing Empire and "Pompadour" influences. Double skirts, the uppermost with battle-mented or scalloped edges; increased interest in the back of the skirt—basques, tabs, sashes, the ends of which sometimes catch up the overskirt.

The familiar small flounces and strap decorations are used below tabbed and scalloped overskirts. Newer gowns have underskirts which might have been executed by an upholsterer: draped and caught in a scale pattern, with an overskirt inspired by XVIIIc. French court styles (2 from r.); button tufted with train and sash knotted over buttocks (background, l. of center).

2771   2772   2773   2774   2776

2775

2771-76. XIXc. Nov., 1865. U.S.A.
"Godey's Lady's Book," November.

2771. White hat, violet quills and streamers; violet paletot and skirt with matching cord trim.

2772. Hair banded in tan. Black coat trimmed with braid and jet. Tan striped skirt.

2773. Tan bonnet with lavender tassels and lining, white ruche, green and lavender trim; stone gray bonnet strings with border in lavender, green and white. Greenish-blue dress with wide buckled belt, skirt pockets and a yoke banded in stone gray.

2774. Pale gray hat and costume, trimmed in dull malachite green.

2775. Seated girl: black hair ribbons with long streamers; black boots. Dull red-violet costume edged with black and white braid and white cord fringe.

2776. White blouse; warm blue violet jacket and taffeta skirt, trimmed with jet.

2777. XIXc. 1865. French.

Dollfus Mieg & Cie. Robe trianon.

Fashion plate published by the great Alsatian firm of cotton printers to show the use of one of their bordered fabrics.

Flounces patterned *à disposition* in 50's were followed by half a decade in which plain colored fabrics predominated, and decoration and edgings were largely made of fabric and applied: cartridge pleating and ruchings; or bands of color laid on in straps, or outlining invected and tabbed borders of upholstery-like skirt hems.

Now there is a return to small overall patterns; as in this gown in the lavender and black combination which becomes popular with the advent of aniline dyes. A tabbed, strap-like, repeated belt-closing is used on the border of a plain morning dress, which is cut with the new (and transient) simplicity which preceded the bustle. Parasol. Hair rolled high and square at the temples, with a large chignon, curls behind the ears. Long dangling earrings. The neckline is raised by a ruche which replaces the small collar. More pattern is used on bodice, the bosom of which rounds as the waistline is tightened; sleeves plainer and closer; skirt fullness drawn toward the back and lengthened, soon to be caught up in a bustle.

2778. XIXc. 1867. French. (Paris, Luxembourg.)

J. F. Bazille. Family Reunion.

Appendix

The way in which this book has been put together, the sort of material to be found in this Appendix, and its organization, have been discussed in the Introduction.

No bibliography of costume books is attempted here. Any Library equipped for costume research will have such comprehensive works as:

Hilaire and Meyer Hiler: *Bibliography of Costume*, H. W. Wilson Co., 1939.

Isabel Munro and Dorothy E. Cook: *Costume Index*, H. W. Wilson Co., 1937.

These supplement older works like:

René Colas: *Bibliographie générale du costume et de la mode*, 2 vols., Librairie René Colas, Paris, 1933.

Katalog der Freiherrlich von Lipperheide'schen Kostümbibliothek, 2 vols., Lipperheide, Berlin, 1896-1905.

The standard dictionaries of costume words are:

Victor Gay: *Glossaire archéologique du moyen-âge et de la renaissance*, 2 vols., Paris, Société bibl., 1887-1928.

Camille Enlart: *Manuel d'archéologie française*, III, *Le costume*, Auguste Picard, Paris, 1916.

Guidance, and leads to source material and to the most important books on every aspect of life in all periods of history, can be found in publications of the Clarendon Press, Oxford, and of the Cambridge University Press. For instance, the Cambridge Ancient (6 vols), Mediaeval (8 vols), and Modern (13 vols. and Atlas) Histories; J. E. Sandys: *Companion to Latin Studies*; Barnard's *Companion to English History (Middle Ages)*; *Shakspere's England*, 2 vols., Clarendon Press, Oxford, 1916; and so on, to and beyond the 2 vols. of *Early Victorian England*.

Wonderful bibliographical material on the whole mediaeval period will be found in:

Louis Jean Paetow: *A Guide to the Study of Mediaeval History*, F. S. Crofts & Co., N. Y., 1933, prepared under the auspices of the Mediaeval Academy of America.

There are, however, some books which are cited because their illustrations are entirely documentary. Others are so useful that reference is frequently made to them in our text or appendix. If they are not found below, look for them under the Chapter Headings to which they relate, in the Appendix. They have been given key abbreviations for the sake of brevity.

[Leloir] Maurice Leloir: *Histoire du costume, de l'antiquité à 1914*, H. Ernst, Paris, is the most sumptuous and ambitious of modern books on costume. Its illustrations are frequently in colored facsimile, always documents or photographs of actual garments. Its publication, interrupted by World War I, was never completed. Few libraries have its 5 volumes, but it is worth communicating with the Union Catalog of the Library of Congress, to find whether it is available in your city, and where. Many patterns and outline drawings of details.

[von Boehn] Max von Boehn: *Die Mode, La Mode*, or *Modes and Manners*. I do not suppose that there has ever been anything to compare, in quantity, quality and modest price, with these 8 little volumes. The text is good in all languages. The quality of reproduction is best in the German edition. The chronological arrangement is good, from the first Christian centuries through the XVIIIc. Wonderfully chosen pictures are jumbled with infuriating carelessness in the 4 volumes which cover 1790-1914.

[Hottenroth] Frédéric Hottenroth: *Le Costume chez les peuples anciens et modernes*, Armand Guérinet, Paris, gives outline drawings of European dress, armor and jewelry, and some patterns, from IVc. B.C. to 1870, with special emphasis on German peasant dress, to which Hottenroth devotes another classic work in German.

Despite my distaste for books illustrated by line drawings, I cannot deny that the "little" Hottenroth is part of the foundation of a costume library. You could no more design imaginative costumes from it than you

could create a very spirited fish from inspecting a plate of its boiled bones, but it is a valuable skeleton on which to hang accumulated information.

[Köhler] Carl Köhler and Emma von Sichart: *A History of Costume*, David McKay, Philadelphia, gives patterns and photographs, together with some outline drawings, of costume from the Ancient Orient to 1870.

[K. & S.: Short Hist.] Frances M. Kelly and Randolph Schwabe: *A Short History of Costume and Armour, chiefly in England, 1066-1800*, Scribners, N. Y., 1931.

[K. & S.: Hist. C.] F. M. Kelly and R. Schwabe: *Historic Costume, a Chronicle of Fashion in Western Europe, 1490-1790*, Scribners, N. Y., 1931.

The exceptions to my feelings about line drawings are found in these two admirable books, covering all too limited a field, in which documentary illustrations in color and half-tone are supplemented by unimpeachable line drawings by Mr. Schwabe, Slade Professor of Art at University College, London. They provide good glossaries of the most important words relating to costume and armor. I consider them the best one-vol. books ever published on costume.

[Norris] Herbert Norris: *Costume and Fashion*. Vol. I, *The Evolution of European Dress Through the Earlier Ages*, 1924. Vol. II, *Senlac to Bosworth, 1066-1485*, 1927. Vol. III, parts 1 & 2: *The Tudors, 1485-1603*, E. P. Dutton, N. Y. Vols. IV: *The Stuarts* and V: *The Hanoverians*, are to come. Vol. VI: *The Nineteenth Century*, written with Oswald Curtis, was published by J. M. Dent, London, 1933.

A great deal of research went into these volumes, to which I am indebted for facts, quotations and color notes. His illustrations are entirely redrawn.

[Piton] Camille Piton: *Le costume civil en France, du XIIIe au XIXe siècle*, E. Flammarion, Paris, has wonderful illustrations and a very poor text.

[Hirth's Form.] Georg *Hirth's Formenschatz*, 35 vols., Munich, 1877-1911, is a wonderful photographic compendium of the art of all ages. His other great compilations of engravings are listed under *Culture Moves North: XVIc.*

[Leggett] William F. Leggett: *Ancient and Mediaeval Dyes*, Chemical Pub. Co., N. Y., 1944, is a very useful small book.

[D'All. Acc.] Henri D'Allemagne: *Les accessoires du costume et du mobilier*, 3 vols. Schemit, Paris, 1928, gives photographs of XII-midXIXc. objects: jewelry, purses, fans, combs, buttons, snuff boxes, etc. Like all his books, it is invaluable, of impeccable scholarship, and superbly illustrated.

[Forrer] R. Forrer: *Die Kunst des Zugdrucks*, Schlesier & Schweikhardt, Strassburg, 1898, has fine reproductions of textiles of XII-XIVc.

[Lacroix, A. M. A.] Paul Lacroix: *The Arts in the Middle Ages, and at the period of the Renaissance*, Chapman & Hall, London, 1870.

[Lacroix, M. C. D.] —: *Manners, Customs and Dress during Middle Ages and during the Renaissance period*, 1874.

[Lacroix, M. R. L.] —: *Military and Religious Life in the Middle Ages and at the period of the Renaissance*, 1874.

[Lacroix, S. L.] —: *Science and Literature in the Middle Ages and in the period of the Renaissance*, Bickers & Son, London, 1878.

Dorothy Hartley and Margaret M. Elliot: *Life and Work of the People of England*, a pictorial record from contemporary sources, G. P. Putnam, N. Y., is an admirable series of books. Volumes on the XIV, XV, XVI, XVIIc. have been published. Conquest to 1300, and XVIIIc. were in preparation, and have probably been published.

The Ancient Orient

[Heuzey] L. A. and J. Heuzey: *Histoire du costume dans l'antiquité classique, l'Orient, Egypte, Mesopotamie, Syrie, Phoenicie,* ed. "Les Belles-Lettres," Paris, 1935. is the most scholarly work on the costume of this period.

[H. & H.] Mary G. Houston and Florence S. Hornblower: *Ancient Egyptian, Assyrian and Persian Costume,* London, 1920.
Köhler also gives patterns for this period.

[Pope] Arthur Upham Pope: *Survey of Persian Art, from Prehistoric Times to the Present,* 6 vols., Oxford University Press, London, 1938-9. We are much obliged to text and illustrations of these sumptuous volumes.

[Enc. ph.] *Encyclopédie photographique de l'art: Musée du Louvre,* 3 vols., ed. Tel, Paris, 1935-38; Parts 1-5, Egypt; 6-12, *Ancient Mesopotamia (Sumer, Babylonia, Elam)* ; 13, *Seals and Cylinders;* 14, *Canaan (Phoenicia, Judea, Arabia)* , is the source of many fine illustrations.

[Louvre] Louvre. *Antiquités orientales; Sumer, Babylonia, Elam.*

[Hall] H. R. H. Hall: *Babylonian and Assyrian Sculpture in the British Museum,* 1928.

[Sarre-Herzfeld] F. Sarre and Ernst Herzfeld: *Iranische Felsreliefe,* 3 vols., Berlin, 1912.
Among other useful books are:
Albert Neuberger: *The Technical Arts and Sciences of the Ancients,* tr. by Henry L. Brose ,Macmillan, N. Y., 1930: antiquity through the Roman period.
G. Rawlinson: *The Five Great Monarchies of the Ancient Eastern World,* 3 vols.ᵧ 1871. (Re-issued, 190-? by Dodd, Mead & Co.)
G. Maspéro: *Life in Ancient Egypt and Assyria,* 1892.
O. M. Dalton: *The Treasure of the Oxus,* London, 1926, and E. Herzfeld: *Am Tor von Asien,* Berlin, 1926.

SOURCES OF OUR ILLUSTRATIONS:
1. (Louvre) .
5, 6, 7, 9, 11, 12, 33. (Enc. ph.) .
18, 19, 26. (Hall) .
29-33, 35-37. (Pope) .
34. (Sarre-Herzfeld) .

The Nile

Egyptian costume is treated by Heuzey, Houston and Hornblower, and by Köhler.

[Riefstahl] Elizabeth Riefstahl: *Patterned Textiles in Pharaonic Egypt,* Brooklyn Museum, 1944, 56 p. and 56 photographs.
Pagan and Christian Egypt, 1-10 Century A.D.—the catalog of the Brooklyn Museum's great exhibition in 1941. It has notes by John D. Cooney and Elizabeth Riefstahl, an excellent bibliography, 86 p. of text and 105 more pages consisting of about 170 large photographs. We are largely indebted to these two volumes for our information about Coptic dress. Cooper Union, Victoria and Albert, and Berlin Museums also have rich Coptic collections.
Etoffes byzantines, coptes, romaines, du IVe au Xe siècle, A. Guérinet, Paris, 16 pl., partly col.

[Ency. ph.] The Louvre's *Encyclopédie photographique de l'art,* and

[A. A. E.] *The Art of Ancient Egypt,* Phaidon Press, 1933, are rich sources of photographs.

[N. deG. D.] Wall paintings in Egyptian tombs have been reproduced in sumptuous color facsimile in N. de Garis Davis' *Ancient Egyptian Painting,* 2 volumes, and others devoted to specific tombs, published by the Metropolitan Museum of Art.
Cairo Museum: *Catalogue générale des antiquités égyptiennes,* and publications like those of Chicago University's Oriental Institute, and Berlin Museum, are useful.
General works like Sir W. M. Flinders Petrie: *Arts and Crafts of Ancient Egypt,* and his *History of Egypt;* A. Erman: *Life in Ancient Egypt,* Macmillan, 1894; G. Maspero: *Life in Ancient Egypt and Assyria,* Appleton, 1892; and Sir J. Gardner Wilkinson: *Manners and Customs of the Ancient Egyptians,* Dodd, Mead, 1879, are full of costume information.

SOURCES OF OUR ILLUSTRATIONS:
55-72, 92-94. (N. deG. D.) .
73, 74. Schiaparelli: *La Tomba dell' Architetto Cha.*
79-87, 95-98. (A. A. E.) .

The Greek Sphere

[Bieber] M. Bieber: *Entwicklungsgeschichte der Griechischen Tracht,* Berlin, 1934: scholarly text, illustrated by photographs.

[Repond) Jules Repond: *Secrets de la draperie antique,* Les Belles-lettres, Paris, 1931: photographed reconstructions of Greek dress; as well in Heuzey, Houston and Hornblower and Köhler.
Schuchardt: *Studien zur Altgriechischen Tracht.*
Studniezka: *Beitrage zur Geschichte der Altgriechischen Tracht,* Abh. des Arch. Epigr. Seminares der U. Wien, Vienna, 1886.
Sir William Ridgeway: *The Early Age of Greece,* 2 vols., Cambridge, 1901-03.
T. D. Seymour: *Life in the Homeric Age,* 1908.
Chadwick: *Heroic Age,* 1911.

[Zervos] C. Zervos: *Art en Grèce,* Cahiers d'Art, Paris, 1936, and Enc. ph. provide beautiful photographs.

SOURCES OF OUR ILLUSTRATIONS:
130-31. Matz: in "Antike," XI, pl. 179, 14.
132, 136. Also information about 138: Arthur J. Evans: *Palace of Minos,* 4 vols., 1921-35: a rich source of information about Aegean dress and decorative motifs. architecture and life.
135. Enc. ph.
139. Zervos.

ETRUSCAN

[Marthe] J. E. Marthe: *L'Art Etrusque,* Firmin-Didot, Paris, 1889: deals with Etruscan dress.
The best way to learn about Etruscan costume is to look at pictures. Since Celtic, Phoenician, Greek and many other cultures met in rich Etruria, there are quantities of well illustrated works which deal with her art, from the Early Iron Age down. Among them are:
Della Seta: *Italia Antica.*

[R. MacI.] D. Randall-MacIvor: *Early Iron Age in Italy,* 1927, and *Villanovans and Early Etruscans,* 1924, both pub. by Clarendon Press, Oxford.
C. Q. Giglioni: *L'Arte Etrusca.*
P. Ducati: *Storia dell'Arte Etrusca.*

[Weege] F. Weege: *Etruskische Malerei,* which reproduces the tomb paintings from Corneto.
Loukomski: *L'art étrusque.*

For Etruscan helmets and the transition into European helmets see:
Léon Coutil: *Les Casques Proto-Etrusques, Etrusques, et Gaulois,* W. Sifter, Gand, 1914.
Sir Guy Francis Laking: *A Record of European Arms and Armour through Seven Centuries,* 5 vols., London, G. Bell & Sons, 1920-22.

For Greek armor see:
Franz, Freiherr von Lipperheide: *Antike Helme.*
Reichel: *Homerische Waffen.*
R. Burton: *The Book of the Sword.*

SOURCES OF OUR ILLUSTRATIONS:
148. Also information: R. Maci I. He gives a line drawing of the entire pattern of the Certosa situla, and descriptions of the other situlae mentioned.
149. *Notizie degli Scavi,* 1938, p. 240, fig. 10.
145-46, 151-53, 203, 214-16. Enc. ph.
161. Hinks: *Catalogue of Greek, Etruscan and Roman Paintings and Mosaics in the British Museum,* 1933.
170, A, B. British Museum: *Guide to the Early Iron Age.*
195-97, 229-31, 233. Scheffer: *Die Kultur der Griechen.*
204-06. Picard: *La vie privée dans la Grèce classique.*

SCYTHIAN

SOURCES OF OUR ILLUSTRATIONS:
250. Bulletin, Russian Archaeol. Commission (in Russian) , 49, pl. 2, fig. 3.
252. M. Rostovtzeff: *Animal Style in S. Russia and China.*
254. M. Rostovtzeff: *Iranians and Greeks in S. Russia.*
256-57. "Revue archéologique," 4th series.
259. Dimitrescu: *L'art préhistorique en Roumanie.*

Romans and Barbarians

[Wilson] L. M. Wilson: *Clothing of the Ancient Romans*, Johns Hopkins Univ. Studies in Archaeology, No. 24, Johns Hopkins Press, Baltimore, 1938. Also see Heuzey, and Repond.

SOURCES OF OUR ILLUSTRATIONS NOT ACKNOWLEDGED IN TEXT:

273, 274, 278. Enc. ph., and text.

276. *Dura: Preliminary Report, 1933-5*, Yale University.

277. M. Rostovtzeff: *Dura-Europos and its Art*, Clarendon Press, Oxford, 1938. [Rachel Wischnitzer: *The Messianistic Theme in the Paintings of the Dura Synagogue* (rep. of the 30 panels), Univ. of Chicago Press, 1948].

279-87. Hayford Peirce and Royall Tyler: *L'Art Byzantin*, 2 vols., Librairie de France, Paris, 1932-34. [Peirce-Tyler.]

288. A. Kingsley Porter: *Spanish Romanesque Sculpture*, 2 vols., Florence, Pantheon, 1928. [Porter: *Sp. Rom. Sc.*]

289-90. Hans Achelis: *Die Katakomben von Neapel*, Leipzig, Hiersemann, 1935-36.

291-92. Hartel and Wickoff: *Wiener Genesis*.

293. Testo: *Il Rotolo di Giosue*. (Latter 2 are in Morgan Library.)

297, 298, 302. Photos by Prof. Karl Lehmann-Hartleben.

307, 308. W. A. Ritter von Jenny: *Germanischer Schmuck des Frühen Mittelalters*.

Barbarian Dress

Köhler; Norris, vol. I; and such volumes as the book and museum reports on Jutland finds, mentioned in footnotes, our p. 89. I am indebted to Mr. William H. Forsyth, Assistant Curator of Mediaeval Art at the Metropolitan Museum of Art for information on jewelry of the Migration periods, shown on our pp. 71, 72, 91 and 92.

The Roman Catholic Church

Father Joseph Braun: *Die Liturgische Gewandung*, Freiburg-in-Breisgau, 1907 is the greatest authority.

Catholic Encyclopaedia, N. Y., 1907 on.

English and Protestant vestments can be seen in works by Druitt; Bloxam; H. J. Clayton: *Cassock and Gown*, Oxford, 1929; P. Dearmer: *Linen Ornaments of the Church*, Oxford, 1929.

I am obliged to the Very Rev. Msgr. Thomas J. McMahon for the chart of ecclesiastical vestments and colors on our p. 94, drawn from C. F. Du Cange: *Glossarium ad Scriptores Mediae et Infimae Latinitatis*. To it should be added colors of the "church cassock" for choir wear: priest, black; bishop and archbishop, purple; cardinal, scarlet; pope, white; deacon and sub-deacon, black; monks, color of order.

The dalmatic and tunicle distinctive of deacons and sub-deacons are never worn by priests, unless officiating as deacons or by papal privilege; worn under the chasuble, never under the cope; and over the stole. The Pope's tiara is the symbol of his office and jurisdiction; his ordinary head covering is the *pileus*, skull cap.

Ills. 327-30 are taken from A. W. Pugin: *Glossary of Ecclesiastical Ornament and Costume*, 1868.

The Dark Ages, VII-XIc.

[Barnard] Barnard's *Companion to English History: Middle Ages*, Clarendon Press, Oxford, is an excellent one-vol. guide to English life and dress, of and after the Conquest.

[Bede-A-S Chron.] *The Ecclesiastical History of England* by the Venerable Bede, b.673, and the *Anglo-Saxon Chronicle* (Caesar to midXIIc), are the source books of the period preceding the Conquest; published together in I vol., George Bell & Sons, London, 1903.

[Malmesbury] The *Chronicle of the Kings of England* by William of Malmesbury, b.1095/6, same publisher, 1895, is a fine costume source for the years 449-1142, especially for the Conquest which had taken place during his parents' time. Anglo-Norman warfare is discussed in Chap. III of

[Round] J. Horace Round: *The Commune of London*, Archibald Constable & Co., Westminster, 1899, which is a miscellany of fascinating scholarly information about the early Mediaeval period in England.

[Wright] Thomas Wright: *The Celt, the Roman, and the Saxon*, a history of the early inhabitants of Britain, down to the conversion of the Anglo-Saxons to Christianity, Arthur Hall, Virtue, & Co., London, 1852, with some engraved illustrations by Fairholt, is obviously not the latest work on the subject, but I have found its one vol. useful, ever since it was given me in my childhood, together with most of the books mentioned above, by my aunt, Frances G. Davenport, the historian.

Eric Millar: *La miniature anglaise du Xe au XIIIe siècle*.

SOURCES OF OUR ILLUSTRATIONS:

331-33, 337, 351-354. Westwood: *Miniatures and Ornaments of Anglo-Saxon and Irish Manuscripts*.

334. H. F. Blunck: *Die nordische Welt*.

335. G. Hirth's *Formenschatz*.

336. Raimond van Marle: *La peinture romane au moyen-âge*.

From bound volumes of photographs, belonging to the Pierpont Morgan Library:

338-39. Valenciennes Ms. 99, 38 photos.

340. Gerona Ms. 60, 173 photos.

341. Codex Aemilianensis, 42 photos.

344. Trier Stadtbib. Ms. 31, 76 photos.

360. Burgo de Osma 2, 2 vols. photos. Also in T. Rojo Otcajo: *El "Beato" de la catedral de Osma*, ed. de Cluny, Paris, 1942, 29 col. plates.

361-363. Bib. nat., lat. 8878, photos, but endlessly reproduced.

342, 347, 349, 350. Adolph Goldschmidt: *German Illumination*: Harcourt Brace, N. Y., 1928: vol. 1. Ottonian [Goldschmidt: Ott.]. 343. vol. 2. Carolingian Period. [Goldschmidt: Carol].

345, 348. Merton: *Buchmalerei in St. Gallen, IX-XIc.* Columban's hermit followers had an immense but short lived prestige. The Benedictines, the only other monastic order existing in Europe, entirely supplanted them by VIIIc. and were the only religious order until the great Xc. rise of Cluny. St. Gall, taken over by the Benedictines, remained for three centuries one of the greatest monasteries in Europe.

355, 366. Bastard: *Portraits de Nicéphore Botaniate, empereur d'Orient et de l'impératrice Marie sa femme*.

357, 358. Max Hauttmann: *Die Kunst des Frühen Mittelalters*, Berlin, Prophyläen, 1929.

359. Porter: *Sp. Rom. Sc.*

364-365. Basserman-Jordan: *Bamberger Domschatz*.

366-369. *Miniature sacre e profane del anno 1023 illustr. l'Enciclopedia medioevale di Rabano Mauro*, Monte Cassino, 1896, 133 col. pl.

372-374. *The Tapestry of Bayeux*, Society of Antiquaries, London, 1819-23.

375-78. Swarzenski: *Salzburger Malerei*.

Knighthood in Flower, XIIc.

Heraldry

Arthur Charles Fox-Davies: *A Complete Guide to Heraldry*, Dodge Pub. Co., N. Y.

Woodward: *Treatise on Heraldry, British and Foreign*, 1896.

Joseph Edmonson: *Complete Body of Heraldry*, 1780.

Mrs. Bury Palliser: *Historic Devices, Badges, and War Cries*, S. Low Son and Marston, London, 1870.

In blazoning, color is never applied on color, nor metal on metal. The fur *vair* is *argent* and *azur* unless specifically blazoned. *Gules* (red) and *azure* (blue) come from the Persian *gúl* and *làzurd* (lapis-lazuli), and show Arab influence from the Crusades. The *field* (background) may be *semé* (sown or powdered) with fleurs-de-lys, as in the old arms of France, crosslets, lozenges, etc.

Establishment of bearings:

In 1047, Geoffrey Plantagenet, grandfather of Geoffrey II of Anjou, "Martel," described in a rage "the color of his horse and the arms he meant to use" in a specific combat. (Malmesbury.) In 1160, Matthieu I de Montmorency bore no arms on his shield; the shield of Matthieu II de Montmorency, in 1177 bore the early Montmorency arms.

In XIVc., when the arms of France changed from the small fleurs-de-lys semé, of *France ancient* to the 3 large ones of *France modern*, the led coursers of the French Lord de Coucy were richly caparisoned with housings which mixed the ancient arms of Coucy with those he now bore. Froissart records the rage of Sir John Chandos at finding his arms borne by the Marshal of the French, Lord John de Clermont. Because of the truce they had to wait until the next day's battle to settle the matter by arms. By 1386, Sir Richard le Scrope sued, rather than fought Sir Robert Grosvenor concerning the right to use a certain coat of arms. (Rickert: *Chaucer's World* gives excerpts of the testimony.)

SOURCES OF OUR ILLUSTRATIONS:

386. *Canterbury Psalter,* introduction by M. R. James, Humphries & Co., London, 1935.
387. Tancred Borenius and E. W. Tristram: *English Mediaeval Painting,* Pegasus Press, Paris, 1927, 101 pl. [Borenius-Tristram.]
396. *Congrès archéologique de France,* Angers & Saumur.
402. Oskar Wulff: *Altchristliche u. mittelalterliche Byzantin. u. Italien. Bildwerke,* 2 vol. Berlin, 1909-11.
403. *Miniature del Registro di S. Angelo in Formis.*
405-408. Albert Boeckler: *Das Stuttgart Passionale,* Augsburg, 1903.
409. *Miniaturen des Kupferstichkabinetts der Staatlichen Museum,* Berlin.
410. Gantner: *Kunstgeschichte der Schweiz.*
411, 420, 421. H. F. Blunck: *Die nordische Welt.*
412, 413. *Die Regensburg Prüfeniger Buchmalerei des XII-XIIIJ.*
414-417. *Hortus Deliciarum,* Schlesier & Schweikhardt, Strassburg, 1901.
422-425. Brit. Mus. Add. 11695, from 2 bound volumes of photographs in the Morgan Library.
426. J. Dominguez Bordona: *Spanish Illumination,* 2 vols., Harcourt Brace, N. Y., 1930. [Bordona]
4313-434. Porter: *Sp. Rom. Sc.*

Feudal Lords and Kings, XIIIc.

Sources of information: Arms and Armor, 650-1650 A.D.:
The preeminent collections and catalogs of armor are those of the *Vienna Historical Museum;* of the *Armory of the Castle of Churburg,* the personal collection of the armor of generations of the ancestors of Oswald Graf Trapp (trans. with notes by Sir James G. Mann) ; the *Metropolitan Museum of Art.* The armor of the *Wallace Collection* has been catalogued by S. J. Camp; that of Madrid's *Armeria Real,* by Count Valencia de Don Juan; that of various Swiss collections, by Charles Buttin.
I have relied mainly on publications by the Curators of the Metropolitan Museum of Art (listed below), and on the following:
Germain Demay: *Le costume d'après les sceaux,* Paris, 1880.
Auguste Demmin: *Arms and Armour,* London, Geo. Bell & Sons, 1877.
C. C. ffoulkes: *The Armourer and his Craft* (from XI to XVIc), 1912.
J. H. von Hefner-Alteneck: *Waffen* (from beginning of Middle Ages to end of XVIIc.), 1903.
F. M. Kelly & R. Schwabe: *A Short History of Costume and Armour, chiefly in England,* 1066-1800.
Sir Guy Francis Laking: *A Record of European Arms and Armour through Seven Centuries,* 5 vols., London, Geo. Bell & Sons, 1920-22.
Sir James G. Mann: *Notes on Armour of the Maximilian Period and the Italian Wars,* "Archaeologica," LXXIX, 1929.
Viollet-le-Duc: *Dictionnaire raisonné du mobilier français.*
In describing illustrations of armor in the Metropolitan Museum of Art, I have drawn heavily, by quotation or abstract, from Bashford Dean: *Catalog of Arms and Armor,* M.M.A., 1930; Stephen V. Grancsay: *Historical Armor,* a picture book, M.M.A., 1946; ibid: *Mutual Influences of Costume and Armor,* a study of specimens in the M.M.A., Bulletin, vol. III, 1930-31.
Ills. 435-436 are charts prepared under the direction of Bashford Dean, former Curator of the Arms and Armor Collection of the M.M.A., and of Stephen V. Grancsay, the present Curator. We are greatly indebted to Mr. Grancsay for permission to use them. They were executed by Stanley J. Rowland, Hashima Murayama, and Randolph Bullock, the Assistant Curator.
We reproduce photographs and drawings after rubbings of monumental effigies and brasses (referred to under chapter headings, XIVc. on, by key names), taken from:

[Boutell] Charles Boutell: *Monumental Brasses and Slabs,* London, Cogswell, 1847.
[Cotman] J. S. Cotman: *Engravings of Sepulchral Brasses of Norfolk and Suffolk,* 2 vols., 1839.
[Creeny: I. S.] Rev. W. F. Creeny: *Incised Slabs on the Continent of Europe.*
[Creeny: M. B.] —: *Monumental Brasses on the Continent of Europe.*
[Crossley] F. H. Crossley: *English Church Monuments,* London, 1921.
[Dunkin] Edward E. H. W. Dunkin: *Monumental Brasses of Cornwall,* London, 1882.
[Haines] Rev. H. Haines: *A Manual for the Study of Monumental Brasses,* Oxford, 1848.
[Photol.] *Photolithographs of Monumental Brasses.*
[Stothard] C. A. Stothard: *The Monumental Effigies of Great Britain.*
[V. & A. R. of B.] *Victoria and Albert Museum: Catalogue of Rubbings of Brasses.*
[Waller] J. G. Waller: *Monumental Brasses.*
There are many others such as:
Frederick Chancellor: *Ancient Sepulchral Monuments of Essex.*
A. Hartshorne: *Recumbent Monumental Effigies of Northamptonshire.*
T. and G. Hollis: *Monumental Effigies.*
E. S. Prior and Arthur Gardiner: *An Account of Mediaeval Figure Sculpture in England.*
An excellent picture of XIIIc. life, amply backed by research, can be found in William Stearns Davis: *Life on a Mediaeval Barony, a Picture of a Typical Feudal Community in the Thirteenth Century,* Harper & Bros., N. Y., 1923.

SOURCES OF OUR ILLUSTRATIONS:

465. (Piton).
466. (Hirth).
467. Henri Focillon: *Peintures Romanes des églises de France,* Paul Hartmann, Paris, 1938.
438-86. M. R. James: *Drawings by Matthew Paris.*
487. O. E. Saunders: *English Illuminations,* 2 vols. Firenze, Pantheon, 1927. [Saunders]
488-90. *Rutland Psalter:* int. by Eric George Millar, Roxburghe Club, Oxford, 1937.
491. *La Estoire de Seint Aedward le Rei,* ed. by Montague Rhodes James, Roxburghe Club, Oxford, 1920.
492. Saunders: v. II.
493. Victoria and Albert Museum: *Catalogue of Rubbings of Brasses.*
494. Antonio Morassi: *Storia della Pittura nella Venezia Tridentina,* Rome, Libreria dello Stato, 1934.
499. C. Zervos: *Catalan Art,* from the 9th to the 15th century, W. Heinemann, London, 1937. [Zervos, C. A...
501-06. Bound vol. of photos at Morgan Library: *Book of Chess.*
Page 181, top col. 2. *The Disk of Theodosius* can be seen in Peirce and Tyler.
The many *Book of Chess* mss. show Negroes, Jews, monks, pharmacists, and the identical tents used throughout all the wars of Mediaeval Europe.
507-12. Bordona: shows many other mss. of the *Cantigas* and *Book of Chess.*
Page 184. Glove as gage: When Maurice de Prendergast is accused of treason, in the XIIIc. Anglo-Norman *Book of Howth:*
"E Morice a sun guant plie
A son seignur lad baille" and in XIVc., "He shall wage his law with his folded glove (de son guant plyee), and shall deliver it into the hand of the other, and then take it back and find pledge for his law" (Round: *Commune of London.*)
513-15, 522-23, 525-26, 529. Hauttmann; Patterns in Hottenroth and Köhler.
517-20. Bound vol. photos in Morgan Lib., but beautifully reproduced in *Heinrich von Veldeke: Eneide,* ed. Albert Boecklin, Otto Harrasowitz, Leipzig, 1939, 91 pl., part col.
524. Georg Swarzenski: *Die lateinischen illuminierten Handschriften des XIII J., in den Ländern am Rhein, Main, Donau,* Berlin, 1936.
527, 530-31. Erwin Panofsky: *Die Deutsche Plastik des XI bis XIII j.,* Munich, K. Wolf, 1924.
528. *Deutsche Kunst,* Bremen, Angelsachsen Verlag, vol. 8, No. II.

The Rising Bourgeoisie, XIVc.

Sir John Froissart (1337/8-1410/20): *Chronicle of England, France and Spain,* is of course the greatest XIVc. European source. Unlike Chaucer, who must have talked to everybody, his French contemporary and acquaintance, Froissart, spoke only to gentlefolk. But no man in his time even approximated Froissart's acquaintanceship among all the nobility and gentry between Scotland and Venice, nor his charm and gusto.

Other rich English sources, in addition to those given on our p. 196, are:

Geoffrey Chaucer: *Canterbury Tales.*

Ralph Holinshed: *Chronicles of England, Scotland and Ireland,* 1578, from which Shakespeare drew his material for Macbeth, Lear, and the historical plays.

John Stow: *Survey of London,* 1598: ed. Henry Morley, George Rutledge & Sons, London, 1890: full of information about earlier days and ways.

Joseph Strutt: *Sports and Pastimes of the People of England,* London, Methuen, 1903.

Eric G. Millar: *English Illuminated Mss. of the XIVth and XVth Centuries,* Paris & Brussels, G. van Oest, 1928.

Sources of monumental brasses and effigies are listed in appendix of chapter: *Feudal Lords and Kings.*

SOURCES OF OUR ILLUSTRATIONS:

Full titles of Brass sources are with Armor in appendix of previous chapter.

532-33. *Rows* Roll by John *Rous;* in the *Paston Letters* we find this name variously spelled, even in the same letter, as: Rowse, Rouse, Rows, Rus, Russe. The *Rows Roll* has disappeared; copy in College of Arms, London.

534, 536. *Two East Anglian Psalters at Bodleian, Oxford,* described by Sidney C. Cockerell and Montague Rhodes James, Roxburghe Club, Oxford, 1926. (*Ormesby Psalter,* 34 pl., 3 col.; *Bromholme Psalter,* II pl., I col.).

535. *Gorleston Psalter; library of C. W. Dyson Perrins,* described by S. C. Cockerell, Bernard Quaritch, London.

537-38. *The Antiquities of Westminster Abbey.*

439-52. *Tickhill Psalter,* D. D. Egbert, N. Y. 1940, 111 pl.

553. Boutell.

554-55. Waller.

556, 557-58. V. &. A., R. of B.

560. The *Ellesmere Chaucer,* reprod. in facsimile, Manchester, the Univ. Press, 1911. Some in color.

561. *The Treatise of Walter de Milamete,* Oxford, Roxburghe Club, 1913.

562. Crossley: *Eng. Ch. Mon.*

563. Boutell: *Mon. Br. and Slabs.*

564-74. *Luttrell Psalter;* int. by E. G. Millar, London, British Museum, 1932, 183 monochromes and 2 col. pl.

575-84. *Romance of Alexander;* int. by M. R. James, Oxford, Clarendon Press, 1933.

585. *Photolith. of Mon. Brasses.*

586. Cotman: *Sepul. Br. of Norfolk and Suffolk.*

When Jeanne de Navarre (d.1304) travelled to Bruges and Ghent with Philip the Fair, she was astonished at the wealth she saw: "I thought I was the only queen there, but I saw more than 600." A rich trader of Valenciennes, at the French court, end XIIIc., was offered no cushion. He sat on his pearl and gold embroidered cloak, lined with fur, and left it, saying to the servant who reminded him of it, that it was not the custom in his country for people to carry their cushions away with them. (Lacroix: Middle Ages.)

588-89, 590. Borenius and Tristram: *E.M.P.* The sculptured effigies of the 2 daughters and 3 sons (Ills. 588-89) in ordinary dress, c.1380, from Edward III's tomb in Westminster Abbey, are shown in K.&S.: *Sh.Hist.,* Pl. XII.

591. V.&A.: *R. of B.*

592-93. Boutell.

594. Cotman.

595-96. *Photolith. Mon.* Most of the names on these Norfolk brasses appear in the *Paston Letters;* Stapleton helps John Paston settle a lawsuit between their cousins, Brian Stapleton and Elizabeth Clere.

597.] Boutell.

598-99. V.&A.: *R. of B.*

600-01. Boutell.

602. Color repr. of "Wilton House Diptych," in K.&S.:

S. H. "Sion Cope" rep. in *Enc. Brit.,* 11th ed., Embroidery, pl. II, fig. 9. Effigies of Edward III's sons, York Minster and Anne of Bohemia; rep. in line drawings, S. R. Gardiner: *Student's Hist. of Eng.* p. 237, and 267. "Atchievements" of Edward, the Black Prince, photos in *Vetusta Monumenta,* vol. VI., embroidered robes of Richard II, vol. I.

603. The Rev. Thomas J. McMahon, as a professor at Dunwoodie, had been kind enough to help in ecclesiastical research. As the Very Rev. Msgr. McMahon, he told me about the tiaras, but lacking the facilities of the college library, was unable to give a final answer on the other Papal vestments, nor have I found anyone else willing to commit himself.

627. Chantilly, Musée Condé:*Cabinet des Mss.,* vol. I.

628. H. M. R. Martin: *Les Joyaux de l'enluminure à la Bibl. Nat.,* Paris et Bruxelles, G. van Oest, 1928.

637-41. *Manessa Codex,* Leipzig, 1925-27, 320 col. facs.

642-47. *Rohmfahrt Kaiser Heinrichs VII* ed. Georg Irmer, Weidmannsche Buchhandlung, Berlin, 1881, 39 pl., part col.

648. *Das Soester Nequambuch, das buch der Freuler Stadtbuch,* pub. by Hist. Comm., Prov. Westphalen.

649. Photos in Morgan Lib., of Ms., which in 1933 was in hands of the dealer Weiss of Munich.

650-52. Creeny: *Mon. Br. of Eur.*

653. Floerke: *Das Weib in der Renaissance.*

654. Boutell.

657. [Vitry-Brière] P. G. Vitry-Brière: *Documents de sculpture française,* 3 vols., D. A. Longuet, Paris, 1906-11.

658. Gaignières Coll. Many rep. in Piton.

660-61. *Les principaux mss. à peintures de la Bib. Roy. de Belgique,* ed. Father J. van den Gheyn.

662. Couderc: *Album de Portraits,* enluminures des mss. du moyen-âge, VI-XVc., Bib. Nat., Paris, ed. Gazette de beaux-arts, 1927.

668-70. Goury and Jones: *Plans, Elevations, Sections and Details of the Alhambra,* 2 vols., London, 1842-45.

The Renaissance Begins, XVc.

G. F. Young: *The Medici,* Modern Library, N. Y., 1930.

Jacob Burckhardt: *The Civilization of the Renaissance in Italy,* Oxford Univ. Press, N. Y., 1945.

J. A. Crowe and G. B. Cavalcasse: *History of Painting in Italy, Umbria, Florence and Siena from the second to the sixteenth century,* J. Murray, London, 1903-14, among innumerable works on Italian painting.

Much material in Vasari's delightful yet reliable biographies of artists refers to XVc. although written in XVIc.

Eric Millar: *English Illuminated Mss. of the XIVth and XVth Centuries.*

Paul Durrieu: *La miniature flamande au temps de la cour de Bourgogne,* Bruxelles et Paris, G. van Oest, 1921.

Religiöse Kunst aus Hessen und Nassau: Verlag des Kunstgeschichtlichen Seminars, Lahn, Marburg, 1932, 2 vols. of pl., I of text. Is invaluable for illustrations, not only of pictures and sculpture, but of embroideries, tapestries, printed textiles, and many other articles in secular use.

G. J. Demotte: *Tapisserie Gothique,* Paris & N. Y., Demotte, 1924.

Philippe de Commines (c.1445-c.1511): *Memoirs,* by the father of modern history, who served Charles the Bold and Louis XI, is valuable for the years 1464-1495.

SOURCES OF OUR ILLUSTRATIONS:

674-77. Photographs in Frick Art Reference Lib.

678. Ignaz Seelos: *Fresken-Cyclus des Schlosses Runkelstein bei Bozen,* Plan 29, Tafel XIX, col. rep.

705. *Die Tarocchi.*

708-10. A. M. Hind: *Early Italian Engraving,* vol. II. In 4 vols. (vol. 2-4 are plates). Quaritch, London, 1938.

711: Schubring: *Cassoni,* vol. I.

717-18. Musée Condé, Chantilly, has many Pisanello sketches. Shoulder plates like those of St. George: Boccacino's "Procession to Calvary," rep. in J. Starkie Gardner: *Armour in England,* part 2 (Foreign Armour), p. 32, Macmillan, N. Y., 1892.

720-23. Pietro Toesca: *La pittura e la miniatura nella Lombardia,* U. Hoepli, Milan, 1912.

741-42. I am much indebted to research by the Art Division

of the N. Y. Public Lib. for information about these two pictures.

753, 756, 757, 759. Photographs courtesy of Henry Varnum Poor.

784. I am grateful to Fern Rusk Shapely, Research Division of the National Gallery of Art, Washington, for this information. In Mrs. Shapley's *A Portrait of Francesco Sforza*, (15 p., 13 ills.) "Arts Quarterly," Winter, 1945, the *spazzola* is seen in relief on Sforza coats-of-arms, and on the lance rest of the interesting armor worn by Francesco in the N.G.A. portrait.

789-92. Liebreich: *Claus Sluter*. Information on Ill. 790 from Rev. T. J. McMahon.

793. Troescher: *Claus Sluter*.

795. Vitry-Brière.

796-98. Camille Couderc: *Livre de Chasse par Gaston-Phoebus, Comte de Foix*, imp. Berthaud frères, Paris, 1909, 87 pl.

799-803. Henri Martin: *Boccace de Jean sans Peur*.

Page 295. Domestic Architecture:

S. F. Markham: *Climate and the Energy of Nations*, Oxford University Press, London, 1924.

S. Giedion: *Space, Time and Architecture*, Harvard University Press, Cambridge, 1943, a book of major importance—a history of architecture, its materials, and its underlying philosophy, since the Middle Ages, with excellent photographs.

Louis Mumford: *The Culture of Cities*, Harcourt Brace, 1938, and *Techniques and Civilizations*, 1934, both well-illustrated, outline the changes in cities: mediaeval, baroque and industrial.

A. Newberger (see app., *The Ancient Orient*) reveals the extent of the degradation of techniques in Europe, after Roman times.

Cooper Union, started in 1854-5, and eventually raised to 7½ stories, would have been the first steel-skeleton building, had Peter Cooper not decided that he could improve on the beams he had already prepared and sold them to Harper Bros. The first iron bridge was that over the Severn in 1775-9, and at about the same time, iron was used in factory roof construction in England.

804-06. Camille Couderc: *Album de portraits*.

807-10. *Très-riches heures*, ed. Durrieu, Plon Nourrit, Paris, 1904.

812-15. The figure from Foxton, Trinity College, Cambridge, is reproduced in K.&S.: *Short Hist.*, as are more figures of the counts and countesses than the Victoria and Albert Museum was able to supply, immediately after the war.

823. Boutell.

826. Quotations from Chamberlayne: *The Present State of England*, 38th ed., 1755, and Stow: *Survey of London*, 1598.

827-28. Frick Art Reference Library photographs.

829. Information about this illustration is largely taken from Margaret Scherer: *About the Round Table*, Metropolitan Museum of Art Bulletin, 1945.

There was very little open space in a mediaeval walled town. In 1395, London Bridge was the scene of the joust between David, the Scots Earl of Crawford, and the English Lord Wells. At that time the bridge was coped and "was not replenished with houses built thereupon, as it hath since been, and now is," Stow tells us (1598). He describes the bridge of his day as "having with the drawbridge 20 arches made of squared stone, of height 60 feet and in breadth 30, distant from one another 20 feet, compact and jointed together with vaults and cellars; upon both sides be houses built, so that it seemeth rather a continual street than a bridge." The early bridge, without houses, therefore offered a long, wide space and sound foundation for a joust.

830-31. Reproduced under same title; at Morgan Library.

832-35. *Ystoire de Helayne*, ed. J. van den Gheyn, Vromant et cie., Bruxelles, 1913, 26 pl.

839-46. Fouquet. *Grandes chroniques de France*, imp. Berthaud frères, Paris, 1906, 51 pl.

847-48. *Oeuvre de Fouquet: Heures de Maistre Etienne Chevalier*, ed. M. l'Abbé Delaunay, L. Curmer, Paris, 1866-7, 2 vols., col. pl.

849-50. Couderc: *Album de portraits*.

851. Bib. Nat.; *Portraits des Rois de France*.

873-76. *Les Sieurs de Gavres*, Van Dale, Bruxelles, 1845.

880. Metropolitan Museum of Art photograph.

893-98. Good color reproductions of the "Charlatan" and others in Jacques Combe: *Jerome Bosch*, ed. Pierre Tisne, Paris, 1946.

899-902. François Courboin: *Histoire illustrée de la gravure en France*, vol. 2; 4 vols. Paris, Le Garrec, 1923-28.

904. Courboin: *Album de portraits*.

906. In such matters as the bells worn by the Hero, garters, gloves, and accessories, as well as civil, military, and ecclesiastical costume, Enlart: *Manuel d'archéologie française*, vol. 3, *Costume*, is invaluable.

907-8. Frick Art Reference Library photographs.

911-12, 915, 918-20, 932-33. Waller.

913-14, 916, 921, 928, 930-31. Boutell.

917. Dunkin: *Mon. Br. of Cornwall*.

922-25, 939. *Catalogue of an Exhibition of British Mediaeval Art*, Burlington Fine Arts Club, London, 1939.

934-38. *The Pageants of Richard Beauchamp, Earl of Warwick*, in facsimile, Roxburghe Club, Oxford, 1908.

940. Mrs. Poole's *Catalogue* is an extremely valuable work which gives color and biographical notes.

941. Creeny.

942-43. Cotman: *Sep. Br. of Norfolk*.

945-52, 960. C. Zervos: *Catalan Art from 9th to 15th Centuries*, W. Heinemann, London, 1937; superbly illustrated like all Zervos' books.

953-54. See Ill. 922.

955, 961-68. Bordona: *Sp. Ill.*, vol. II.

972. *Chantilly: Cabinet de mss.*, vol. I.

975. *Hirth's Formenschatz*.

976-79. Max Lehrs: *Katalog der im Germ. Mus. befind. Deutschen Kupferstiche d. XVj.*, Nuremberg, 1887.

981. Creeny: *Mon. Br. of Cont. Eur.*

982-83. Hans Thalhofer: *Livre d'Escrime*, ed. Gustav Hagsell, Prague, 1901.

984-86. H. T. Bossert and W. F. Storck (publishers): *Mittelalteres Hausbuch*, by Master of the Amsterdam Cabinet, Leipzig, 1912.

995. Lippmann facsimiles, Metrop. Mus. Lending Coll.

Culture Moves North, XVIc.

Sources of information about Tudor costume:

Edward Hall (c.1498-1547): *Chronical*, 1542; complete ed., 1809; *Henry VIII*, 1904. Hall was a lawyer and member of Parliament. His eyewitness accounts of the reigns of Henry VII-VIII are rich in glamorous detail.

William Harrison (1534-93): *Description of England*, published in 1578, together with:

Ralph Holinshed (d.c.1580): *Chronicles of England, Scotland, and Ireland;* 6 vols., 1808. Harrison's work is the basis for *Shakespeare's England*, 2 vols., Clarendon Press, Oxford, 1916; Shakespeare got the material for his historical plays, Macbeth, and Lear from Holinshed; Sir Walter Scott is another debtor to Holinshed.

Philip Stubbes (c.1555-c.1610): *Anatomy of Abuses*, 1583. Absolutely nothing is more informative, nor more wonderful reading, than the revilings, item by item, of every excess of Elizabethan fashion by a very eloquent Puritan of whom Nash said: "It is a great pity for him, that, being such a good fellow as he is, he should speak against dice as he doth." The 3rd ed. of 1585 was reprinted by W. Pickering, London, 1835.

John Stow or Stowe (1525-1605): *Survey of London*, 1598; amended in 1603, 1618, 1633, 1720 and 1754; reprints of 1598 ed. in 1842, 1846, 1876. Any page references I may have given are from the H. Morley ed., George Routledge & Sons, London, 1890, which has no index.

Stow was a tailor's son turned antiquarian; the facts he amasses were fascinating in themselves, and his expression of them quaint and appealing. The number of editions gives some indication of the book's importance, but it was also the begetter of many similar and invaluable books in XVIIc., such as *L'état de France*, and Chamberlayne's *Present State of England*.

John Speed (1552-1629): maps, particularly the *Theatre of the Empire of Great Britain*, 1611, contain delightful costumed figures in the cartouches and borders.

William Camden (1557-1623): *Brittanica*, written in Latin, trans. in 1610, and *Annals of the Reign of Elizabeth*, trans. 1635. He was the antiquarian after whom the Camden Society, publishers of so many important books, was named.

Thomas Coryat (1577-1617): *Crudities,* 1611; 2 vols., James MacLehose, Univ. of Glasgow, 1905, and

Fynes Moryson (1566-1630): *Itinerary,* 1617; 4 vols., same pub., 1907, were two observant young Englishmen's records of what they saw during years of travel in Europe and the Orient, at the turn of the century.

Arthur Ponsonby: *English Diaries,* Methuen, London, 1922, provides excerpts from diaries, and a bibliography of those available in reprint.

Pictures of Tudor dress:

The best portraits of Elizabeth are by the Flemings, Marc Gheeraerts, the elder, b.1525, and his son Marc, the younger, b.1561, who came to England with his father in 1568. He married into the family of another dynasty of Flemish painters domiciled in England, the de Critz, and died in England in 1636. Federigo Zuccaro (1542-1609) was an Italian who worked in England from 1574-82. Indigenous English painting begins at the end of the XVIc. with Isaac Oliver and Nicholas Hilliard.

Good reproductions are to be found in:

Walpole Society publications, especially the article on *Gheeraerts,* vol. 3, 1913-4.

Collins Baker and Constable: *English Painting, 16th and 17th Centuries,* Harcourt Brace, N. Y., 1930.

Miniature Painting: see list in appendix ref. to Ill. 1546.

Sir Lionel Cust (editor): *Catalogue of the Pictures, etc. in the National Portrait Gallery,* London, 14th ed., 1909.

H. K. Morse: *Elizabethan Pageantry,* Studio, London, 1934, is based on beautifully chosen illustrations, accompanied by text taken from contemporary authors.

Kelly and Schwabe: both volumes, and Norris, vol. III, Books 1 and 2, are particularly useful at this period, together with the old and always good F. W. Fairholt: *Costume in England,* 1896 ed., and John Hewitt: *Ancient Armour and Weapons,* 1859-61.

London Museum: The Cheapside Horde of Elizabethan and Jacobean Jewelry, Cat. 2, 1928, illustrates and describes what was probably the stock of a XVIIc. jeweller, dug up in 1912 at the corner of Friday St. and Cheapside: XV-XVIIc. jewelry and Roman cameos and intaglios.

Information: Horace Walpole: *Anecdotes of Painting in England,* 6 vols., 1782.

European sources:

Benvenuto Cellini (1500-71): *Autobiography,* of the Florentine goldsmith, soldier, and adventurer, who spent much time in France in the service of Francis I.

Giorgio Vasari (1511-71): *Lives of the Painters* (1550), himself a painter, studied the painters of Italy under Medici patronage, and is our principal source of information about them.

Pierre de Bourdielle, Seigneur and Abbé de Brantôme (c.1540-1614): *Memoirs* (12 vols., ed. Lalanne, Soc. de l'Hist. de Fr., 1864-96). Brantôme was familiar with the court of Marguerite of Valois, in which his mother and grandmother had served, travelled in Scotland with Mary Stuart, knew Elizabeth, and Charles IX, journeyed in Italy, Spain, Morocco, and wrote his memoirs at the end of his life.

Fugger News Letters; 1568-1605, John Lane, London, 1924; see Ill. 1053.

Christopher Weiditz: *Trachtenbuch von seinen Reisen nach Spanien,* 1529, *und den Niederlanden,* 1531-2, ed. Dr. T. Hampe, Museum, Nuremberg, 1927; rep. partly in color, text in English, Spanish and German. (N. Y. Pub. Lib., Art Room.)

Dimier: *Histoire de la peinture de portraits en France au XVIe siècle,* 2 vols. Paris et Bruxelles, G. van Oest, 1924-26.

Georg Hirth: *Les grands Illustrateurs,* 1500-1800, 6 vols., Munich, 1888-91.

Hirth & R. Muther: *Kulturgeschichtliches Bilderbuch aus drei Jahrhunderten,* XVI-XIX. G. Hirth's Verlag, Munich, 1923-5: the greatest collection of woodcuts and engravings of Europe. Vol. III: Costumes.

SOURCES OF OUR ILLUSTRATIONS:

1003-04. Creeny: *Mon. Br. of Cont. Eur.*

1010. Costume of Nuremberg: shown in plates by Hans Scheuffelein, 1530, available in reproduction; in Holbein's colored drawings of day, church, and dance dress (Vienna, Albertina); and in the *Weisskunig.* (Ills. 1035-36)

1023-26. Lippmann facsimiles, Met. Mus. Lending Coll.

1035-36. Emperor Maximilian I: *Der Weisskunig,* ed. by Marx Treitzsaurwein, Vienna, 1775.

1038. Oskar Fischel: *Chronisten der Mode,* Muller, Potsdam, 1923; an assortment of fresh, finely selected and reproduced documentary illustrations, carried into the XXc.

1046-47. Roblot-Delondre: *Portraits d'Infantes,* XVI siècle, Paris: G. van Oest, 1913.

1049. *Les dessins de Hans Holbein,* le jeune. Publ. par Paul Ganz, Genève, Ed. d'art et de science, 1939.

1050. *Bilder-katalog zu Max Geisberg, Der Deutsche Einblatt-holzschnitt,* (first half XVIc.), Munich, H. Schmidt, 1930.

1058. Color rep. in K.&S.: *Hist. Cost.,* p. 49.

Page 403. Clocks and Watches: Sources of Information:

G. C. Williamson: *Catalogue of the Collection of Watches, the property of J. Pierpont Morgan,* Cheapside Press, London, 1912.

G. H. Baillie: *Watches,* their history, decoration and mechanism, Methuen, London, 1927 (many color pl.).

Collection of Watches loaned to the Metropolitan Museum of Art by Mrs. George A. Hearn, privately pr., 1907.

Wade: *British Chronology,* Bohn, London, 1847; this is, by the way, a very useful book, which lists new usages and laws, many relating to dress; statement about 1288 clock. Coryat gives much information about clocks. Norris, vol. 3, gives the inventory of Henry VIII's clocks.

Page 414, and Ills. 1107-11. G. Glück: *Pieter Brueghel the Elder,* Hyperion Press, Paris, 1937. Reproduces his paintings in color with enlargements in offset.

1115. Blunck: *Nordische Welt.*

1122, 1126. Hirth: *Kult. Bild.*

1123-24. (at N. Y. Pub. Lib., see Ill. 1113).

1125. Lippman facsimile.

1128-29, 1131-32. My embarrassment at my ignorance of these Netherlands symbols has been considerably relieved by a very kind letter from Mr. Edgar Wind of Smith College, who says there is little he can tell me. The figure 1128 is a bird-catcher, as the inscription says, but he seems to have been generalized into a catcher of animals of all kinds—a pied piper. The monkeys and rabbits probably have their usual connotations of sensuality and fertility. In connection with 1129, he indicated the Clutton article, p. 287 ff, from which Ills. 1131-32 and their text were drawn. Lorraine is, of course, adjacent to Flanders.

1135, 1137. Exh. Br. Med. Art.

1138. *Handzeichnungen Schweizerischer Meister,* (XV-XVIII Centuries).

1139. Cotman.

1152-53. *Les dessins de Hans Holbein.* (See Appendix on Ill. 1049.)

1161-62, 1172. Collins Baker and Constable: *Eng. P.,* 16-*17th c.*

1164-66. Waller.

1171. Quotation from the *Literary Remains of Edward VI,* Clarendon Historical Reprints, 1884, which ends after "I fell sick of the measles and small-pox," of which he died at 16. I am obliged to Norris for the information about "La Pelegrina."

1172, 1178, 1207. Collins Baker and Constable.

1176. See London Museum: Cheapside Horde.

1184. Hirth: *Kult. Bild., vol.* 3.

1190. Lippmann facs.

1193. For more information, see A. W. Kendrick: *English Embroidery,* and *Book of Old Embroidery.*

Page 448. European Textile Design, see Henri Cluzot and Francis Morris: *Painted and Printed Fabrics,* a history of the manufacture at Jouy and other ateliers in France, 1760-1815, Met. Mus., N. Y., 1927. Has a good bibliography. The finest book on Jouy toiles, with notes by Cluzot, appeared later: Henri D'Allemagne, *La Toile imprimée, les indiennes de trait,* Gründ, Paris, 1942, 2 vols., 1 of text, 1 loose plates, many col.

Page 455. Covered faces, Moorish women: earlier instances shown in Ruth M. Anderson: *Pleated Headdresses of Castile and Leon, XII-XIII c.,* "Notes Hispanic," Hisp. Soc. of N. Y., 1942.

1213-15. Full title of rep. given in XVIc. Eur. sources.

1228. Engraving with spectacles, rep. in Hind: *Early Italian Engs.,* pl. 74.

1230. *The Hispanic-American Review,* Duke Univ. Press, Nov., 1943, has culled from ships' registers of the

House of Trade in Seville an extremely informative list of the merchandise carried by Spain to America, 1534-87, and the provenance, by countries and cities, of many articles. Dolls came from Flanders, chessmen from France. The largest proportion of goods from outside Spain was clothing from France and Holland, then Portugal, England, Italy and Germany, in order. Certain Spanish cities specialized in clothing production.

1233-35. Tailor shop of 1588, master and 2 assistants, and all equipment, shown in James P. R. Lyell: *Early Book Illustration in Spain*, Grafton House, London, 1926, fig. 140. Lyell gives 1 page of each of the most important books published in XV-XVIc. Early Spanish engraving was largely in German hands; and tends to show standard European dress of the period before their migration to Spain. Striking Spanish dress is shown in the 1502 ed. of *La Celestina*, Seville, 1502, by Jacob Cronberger (Lyell, fig. 120). All publication was censored in advance by the Church. Wonderful tasselled Cardinal hats, significant of patronage, appear on title pages (into XVIIIc. in Manila); shown in Fr. Vindel: *Manual gráfico-descriptivo del Bibliofilio Hispano-Americano*, 1475-1850, Madrid, 1930.

1247, 1249. Couderc: *Album de portraits*.

1248, 1254. Martin: *Joyaux d'enluminure*.

1258. Bib. Nat.: *Port. des Rois de France*.

1259. Meurgey: *Principaux mss. à peintures du Musée Condé, Chantilly*.

1263-64. Crêpe: excellent example in the hats of Isaac Oliver's *Three Brothers Brown and their Servant*, 1597 (Earl Spencer Coll.); see *Burlington Mag.*, Feb. 1917, vol. 30, p. 57c; *Connoisseur*, July, 1937, vol. 100, p. 28; and K.&S.: *Sh. Hist.*, pl. XVIII.

1280. *Chantilly: Cabinet des mss.*, vol. I.

1296-99. Mediaeval Paris, before alteration by Louis XIV, can be seen in the enchanting bird's-eye map in an extremely useful book, *Cosmographie universelle*, Nicolas Chesneau, Paris, 1575 (Met. Mus., Print Room). Much help in early history, vanished or altered locales, can be had from it. Also from the Marquis de Rochegude: *Guide pratique à travers le vieux Paris*, Champion, Paris, 1923; and Henri Sauval (1620-70): *Histoire et recherches des antiquité de la ville de Paris*, 3 vols., Paris, 1724.

1303. Bertelli's *solana* brim, shown in C. Yriarte: *Venice*, Geo. Bell, London, 1880, p. 242.

1311. *Illustrated Catalog of Pictures of Siena*.

SOURCES OF INFORMATION ON COSTUME:

Stubbes, Coryat and Moryson are useful for the early part of the century in England.

The greatest sources of the Restoration are, of course, the diaries kept by the dignified John Evelyn (1620-1703), which covers his life span; and that by the contemporary whom he characterizes as a "worthy, industrious and curious person": Samuel Pepys (1633-1703), who kept his indiscreet diary, in shorthand, from 1660-69.

Evelyn, a well-born, cultivated, and much traveled courtier, sought and was sought by most of the persons of the artistic, architectural, scientific, and literary worlds of his age. He visited great houses, and gardens (of which he was himself a notable designer), was the intimate of the greatest virtuosi and antiquarians of Europe, particularly Arundel, Cotton, founder of the Cottonian Library, and Ashmole. Evelyn established Grinling Gibbons' career by his introductions to Charles II and Sir Christopher Wren; consulted the great engravers: Bosse, Perelle, Hollar, Nanteuil and Prince Rupert, and published a *History of Chalcography*. He investigated new scientific discoveries, as well as every sort of amusing curiosity.

Pepys, of yeoman stock become gentry with good connections, rose high in the Admiralty service by his industry. He willed his fine library to his college of Magdalen at Oxford. His secret diary is full of wonderful gossip and the most minute, shameless and vital accounts of daily life, with details on his wife and servants, meals and hangovers, clothes and amusements, his contemporaries and their manners. There is nothing dull about Evelyn's diary, but that of Pepys is certainly one of the most honest and entertaining ever written.

Other valuable sources are:

Jonathan Swift: *Journal to Stella*, (1710-13), Methuen,

London, 1901. *The Life and Times of Anthony Wood*, antiquary of Oxford, described by Himself, 5 vols., Oxford Historical Soc., 1891-1900, is a masterpiece of editing on the part of Andrew Clark. Its 5th vol. is made up of 6 separate and incomparable indexes. Anthony à Wood (1632-95), whose diary and recordings of Oxford life are the best and often the only information we have, kept daily accounts of his expenditures. [Mrs. Reginald Lane Poole: *Catalogue of Portraits in the possession of the University, Colleges, City and County of Oxford*, 3 vols. Clarendon Press, Oxford, 1925].

Thomas Fuller (1608-61): *History of Cambridge*, pub. 1655; and *Worthies of England*, 1662.

Lucy Hutchinson: *Memoirs of the Life of Colonel Hutchinson*, (1615-64); and the various satires of William Prynne (1600-69), give the Puritan side.

Gramont's *Memoirs of the Court of Charles II*, ed. Sir Walter Scott, Bohn, London, 1864, includes in the same volume Charles II's own account of his escape, as dictated to Pepys, and the *Boscobel Tracts*. Gramont (1621-1707) was a French nobleman who served under Condé, was an intimate of Louis XIV, was temporarily exiled to London, where he married the beauty Elizabeth Hamilton, and lived at intervals during Charles II's restoration. From information given by Gramont at 80, his brother-in-law, Anthony Hamilton, wrote one of the most frank and vivid of memoirs.

Bishop Gilbert Burnet (1643-1715): *History of His Own Time*, pub. 6 years after his death. Burnet was an intimate of William and Mary. Chamberlayne's *Present State of England* (see app., Ill. 1415). *Memoirs of the Verneys: Hatton Family Correspondence*. Account books kept by the thrifty Quakeress, Sarah Fell (pub. 1920). And the *Household Book* (1663-66) of the Scots Archbishop Charp.

English Diaries, ed. Arthur Ponsonby, Methuen, London, c.1922, gives a chronological list of English diaries, XVI-XIXc., and excerpts.

Horace Walpole: *Anecdotes of Painting in England*, 5 vols., 1782. Splendid examples of e. XVIIc. portraits will be found in Morse: *Elizabethan Pageantry;* and of whole century, in Collins Baker and Constable: *English Painting in the Sixteenth and Seventeenth Centuries*, Harcourt Brace, N. Y., 1917; and the same authors' *Lely and the Stuart Portrait Painters*.

For books on miniature painting, see Appendix on Ill. 1546.

Works devoted to *English Conversation Pieces*, such as those by Sacheverell Sitwell, or G. C. Williamson, are excellently illustrated and informative.

Of later books, see:

John Heneage Jesse: *England Under the Stuarts*, 3 vols., Geo. Bell & Sons, London, 1893. It is rich in well documented quotations, and illustrated by engravings from original documents; much costume information, and leads to other sources.

John Ashton: *Social Life in the Reign of Queen Anne*, taken from Original Sources, Scribner & Welford, N. Y., 1883, is extremely valuable.

Some French sources are listed in text of Ills. 1427, p. 547, or like Saint-Simon and Mme. de Sévigné, are described in detail under other captions. *Memoirs of the Duchess of Orleans*, Chatto & Windus, London, 1904; Barbier: *Journal;* Saint-Evremond; and some information about this period in later memoirs, like those of d'Argenson and d'Heziques. *L'Etat nouveau de la France* (see App., Ill. 1415). Sainte-Beuve: *Causeries du lundi* is full of precious information about XVII-XVIIIc., as are Racinet, Lacroix, and D'Allemagne, and Hippolyte Roy: *La vie, la mode et le costume au XVIIe siècle, époque Louis XIII*.

J. E. Farmer: *Versailles and the Court under Louis XIV*, Century, N. Y., 1906, is a useful book to which I am much indebted.

Moreau-Nélation: *Les Clouet et leurs émules*, 3 vols., and Hirth's vols. of prints.

SOURCES OF OUR ILLUSTRATIONS:

1354, 1356, 1357, 1407, 1417, 1430. Bouvy: *Gravure de portraits et d'allégories*.

1355-57. The movements of the early theatres from one to another *jeu de paume* can be followed in Rochegude (see Ills. 1296-99).

1369. André Blum: *A. Bosse et la Société française au XVIIe siècle*, Morance, Paris, shows all the plates.

1388. Color rep. in Piton.

1389-90. *Chalcographie du Mus. Imp., vol. 32, Ch. XII: fêtes et cérémonies*, (Met. Mus., Print Room). *Courses de Testes et de Bague faites par le Roy*. Denkmäler des Theatres, Nat. Theatre, Wien, pub. by R. Piper, Munich, is also good.

1415. Edward Chamberlayne (1616-1703), later secretary to the first Earl of Carlisle, while travelling on the Continent during the civil wars, came upon *L'Estat nouveau de la France*, published in Paris in 1661. On it he modelled his equally valuable *Present State of England*, first published anonymously in 1669, of which there were 3 editions in the next year, and 36 by 1755. They are mines of information.

Guy Miege (1644-1718?), a scholarly Swiss who came to England at Charles II's coronation, was Carlisle's secretary during his 1663-5 embassy to Russia, Sweden, and Denmark, and published his *Relation of Three Embassies* in 1669. Miege later taught geography and French, published a number of grammars and dictionaries, and in 1691, a *New State of England*, which Chamberlayne resented as a plagiarism. It was inferior, except in geography, but went through 18 editions by 1748. With the uniting of England and Scotland, the editions of both men's works, after 1707-8, were called *The Present State of Great Britain*.

Page 547. A. Savine: *Un séjour en France sous Louis XV, Lettres du baron de Pöllnitz*, Louis-Michaud, Paris, 1909. Princess Palatine by Rigaud, rep. in von Boehn: *Die Mode*, XVIIIc., p. 7.

1437-39. F. Libron and H. Clouzot: *Le Corset dans l'art et les moeurs du XIII-XXs.*, Paris, 1933.

1447. Quotation from Ashton: see above.

Page 558. Information on trades from George Unwin: *Industrial Organization in the 16th and 17th Centuries*, Clarendon Press, Oxford, 1904; Stow: *Survey of London*, 1598; Anthony Wood: *Life and Times*; and Diderot's *Encyclopédie*: *Tailleurs*.

1463-65. *Trou-madame* plates in Museum of Fine Arts, Boston, Elizabeth Day McCormick Coll. See Henri D'Allemagne: *Histoire des jouets*, 1902; *Récréations et passe-temps*, 1905; *Les Cartes à jouer du XIV-XXe siècle*, 1906, all pub. by Hachette, Paris (Cooper Union Museum).

1466. "Ranelagh Mob," *London Chronicle*, v.XI, p. 167 seq., 1762; long quotation by Malcolm: *Manners and Customs of London*, 1810, v.2,p.338, a very useful source.

1467. R. Whyte quotation from Morse; white beaver inf. from Beau Brummell: *Male and Female Costume*. Norris, vol. III, lists the personages in this picture, and describes alterations in costume, under different sovereigns, of these bodyguards. Quotations from Chamberlayne, 1755 ed., p. 107. Various editions list officers of the government and all Crown establishments, give incumbents by name, down to the lowest ranks, giving duty, pay and dress.

1468. A series of contemporary engravings of the funeral procession of Queen Elizabeth in 1603, showing people of every degree in mourning costume, is reproduced in "Vetusta Monumenta," Vol. III. The diary of the undertaker, Henry Machin, from 1550-63 (pub. by the Camden Society, 1848), describes funerals, ceremonies, revels, pageants, trials and executions under Edw. VI, Mary and Elizabeth.

1469. Colvin: *Engraving and Engravers in England*. Anne's use of Elizabeth's wardrobe, from Kendrick: *English Embroidery*.

1467, 1475, 1529-30. Collins Baker and Constable: *Eng. Painting, 1500-1700*.

1515-17. Waller.

Page 583-4. Tobacco and Snuff information from: John Ashton: *Social Life in the Reign of Queen Anne*, taken from original sources, Chatto and Windus, London, 1904.

Jonathan Swift: *The Journal to Stella*, Methuen, London, 1901.

Max von Boehn: *Miniatures and Silhouettes*, E. P. Dutton, N. Y., 1928 (40 col., halftone pl.)

Richard and Martin Norton: *History of Gold Snuff Boxes*, Phillips, London, 1938.

Henry Nocq: *Tabatières, boites, étuis, XVIII-XIXe s.*, de la collection du Musée du Louvre, van Oest, Paris, 1930.

H. D'Allemagne: *Les accessoires du costume*, Schemit, Paris, 1928.

1546. Miniature Painting sources:

Charles Holme (ed.) and H. A. Kennedy (text): *Early English Portrait Miniatures in the collection of the Duke of Buccleugh*, Studio, London, 1917.

G. C. Williamson: *History of Portrait Miniatures*, 1531-1860, George Bell, London, 1904, 2 magnificent vols., largely English.

Ernst Lemberger: *Portrait Miniatures of five centuries*, Hodder and Staughton, N. Y., no date; 75 col. pl.

A Collection of English Miniatures by Hilliard, Oliver, Cooper, Cosway, Smart, Plimner, and other artists of the 16th, 17th, and 18th centuries; plates and text, no author, date or publisher (Frick Art Reference Library).

Max von Boehn: *Miniatures and Silhouettes*, E. P. Dutton, N. Y., 1928, 40 col., 200 halftone.

The Morgan Collection.

1547. Charles' own account, and the *Boscobel Tracts* are included in Gramont's *Memoirs of the Court of Charles II*, ed. by Sir Walter Scott, Bohn, London, 1864.

1555. (omitted, because permission for its use had not been received by our deadline) should have been *Gilles van Terborch*, The Tichborne Dole, 1671, belonging to Sir Anthony Doughty-Tichborne, Alresford, Hants, England. It can be seen at the Frick Art Reference Library. It is one of the most important costume documents of Restoration England. In 1150, the tender-hearted lady of Alresford, lying on her death-bed, renewed her pleas to her husband to give part of his rich wheat lands to the hungry villagers. Lord Tichborne said grimly that she might give away as much of his property as she herself could walk around. She contrived to get out of bed; on her hands and knees, she encircled in one day a 23 acre plot which is still called "The Crawls," and laid a dying curse on the Tichbornes. The manor house would crumble; there would be seven generations of sons, and seven of daughters; then the name would end, unless the family gave a gallon of flour to every grown person and half a gallon to every child in the village of Alresford on every Lady Day. The dole was given, until the family left England 600 years later. The curse was then fulfilled in every detail, the lordship finally failing on a Tichborne who had changed his name to Doughty. In 1947, the current master of Alresford got permission from his government to buy flour, with ration points given up by the villagers, in order to fend off the Tichborne curse. ("Time," March 17, 1947).

1557-58. These, and many other fine early portraits appear in the Worcester Art Museum: *XVIIc. Painting in New England*, 1935. Permission to use the Freake portrait has been refused by the new owners to James Thomas Flexner: *First Flowers of Our Wilderness*, Houghton, Mifflin & Co., Boston, 1947 (an admirable book), and to us. Fortunately the former owners allowed it to be reproduced, and its delightful vermillion, lemon yellow, and sage green costumes can be seen in a fine color reproduction by Max Jaffe.

1559-78. Anthony Wood: full title in sources, above.

Mrs. Poole's *Cat. of Oxford Port.* (full title above) supplies information, including color notes, about portraits of every sort of person connected with Oxford, from the earliest times to 1925, including such characters as Mother George, an old female servant of Wadham College in XVIIc. Unfortunately, another Oxford character is missing: "Mother Louse," the innkeeper mentioned by Wood, "probably the last woman in England that wore a ruff." An engraving of her does, however, exist; as I remember, by Faithorne.

1581-82. Lady Newdegate: *Cavalier and Puritan*, diaries and newsletters of Sir Robert Newdegate (1644-1710), Longmans Green, N. Y., 1901, gives an idea of XVIIc. prodigality. He lists the foodstuffs used during the 12 days of Christmas, 1668; equivalent amounts were given away:

By the Cook.		Dairymaid
2	Beefes	140 pounds of
6	Muttons	butter
6	Veales	
18	Turkeys	
50	Geese	Beer
16	Ducks	17 Hogsheads
42	Capons	of Beer
2	Pullets	3 Hogsheads
3	Chickin	of Ale
3	Pigs	1 Barrel of
1	Swan	March Beer
1	pay Bird	
	(peacock?)	
100	Rabbits	
100	strikes	
	of Wheat	

1585-86. Details photos in Preston Remington: *English Domestic Needlework of the XVI-XVII-XVIIIc.,* Metropolitan Museum of Art, N. Y., 1945.

1591. Hirth: *Kult. Bild.*

1595. Thomas Kellie: *Military Instructions for the Learned,* q. by Morse.

1596. Hirth: *Kult. Bild.* For its history and alterations in costume, see Col. Repond: *Le costume de la garde suisse pontificale et la renaissance italienne,* Rome, 1917. The origin of their parti-color uniforms is given under the Ill. by Vasari, end Italian XVIc.

1624. Tobacco: a Presbyterian minister like Henry Newcombe continually tells his diary, 1661-3: "How tobacco doth too much fill my thoughts and selfe denial about such a stinking thing might do well . . . I doe see my slavery with . . . this base tobacco." (Ponsonby: *Eng. Diaries*).

1648. Holland, in the second half of the XVIIc., abounds in group portraits of volunteer militia companies, men and women board members of guilds and hospitals, and other civic associations. Hals, from 1615, and Rembrandt during the 30's painted dozens of them, as did other artists like the Dutch Jan de Bray (1607-97), and the Flemish G. Flinck.

1654. Hirth: *Kult. Bild.*

1681. Ward: *The Electress Sophia and the Hanoverian Succession.*

Page 630. Europe Grows Colder: Mr. Benjamin Parry, Chief of the U. S. Weather Bureau in New York, became interested in my intuitions about the change in climate, and was good enough to help me substantiate them by indicating the Hildebrandsson article.

The "Frost Fair" is mentioned in *A Young Squire of the Seventeenth Century,* from the papers (1676-86) of Christopher Jeaffreason, 2 vols., Hurst and Blackett, London, 1878.

Page 634. Knitting by Hand and Machine: quotation from George Bryan Brummell: *Male and Female Costume,* Doubleday, Doran, N. Y., 1933. "Beau" Brummell's book was pieced together verbatim, from other writers, without acknowledgements. Mary's entire costume is described with obvious accuracy by a contemporary, but in this case, I do not happen to recognize the source.

1716. G. Yriarte: *Venice,* George Bell & Sons, London, 1880; he also wrote a useful *Vie d'un Patricien de Venise au XVIe siècle,* illustrated by unusual woodcuts by Bertelli and Franco. Coryat; full title given in XVIc. sources.

1723. Colored cuffs: *Peter Candid's* Countess Palatine Magdalena von Neuburg (Schleissheim Gallery), with a silver doublet sleeve, has lace cuffs worn over a flaring cuff of the scarlet of her overdress (in color in von Boehn: *Die Mode, XVIIc.,* opp. 14).

1733-38. See Lucien Duchartre: *Italian Comedy,* John Day, N. Y., 1928; Allardyce Nicoll: *Masks, Mimes and Miracles,* Harcourt Brace, N. Y., 1931; and George Freedley and John Reeves: *A History of the Theatre,* Crown, N. Y., 1941, with an excellent bibliography.

1739. For information on methods of staging, consult Lee Simonson: *The Stage Is Set,* Harcourt Brace, N. Y., 1946, which carries the history of theatrical design to our own times; and Allardyce Nicoll: *Development of the Theatre,* Harcourt Brace, N. Y., 1927, both beautifully illustrated.

Page 644. Court Dwarfs: see Alice Jane McVan: *Spanish Dwarfs,* "Notes Hispanic," Hisp. Soc., N. Y., 1942, p. 97-129. Ciba Simposia: *Dwarfs,* is one of that wonderful series of monthly pamphlets, issued and sent to physicians by the Ciba Pharmaceutical Products, Inc., Summit, N. J. They are illustrated by beautifully chosen documentary pictures or by photographs, and cover such a range of subjects as Twins, Shoes, Clothing and Hygiene, Cities and Houses.

1760, 1762. *Société de l'histoire du costume,* Bulletin.

The Revolt of Minds and Men, XVIIIc.

From the beginning of the XVIIIc., we are almost overwhelmed by the rich flood of primary source material.

In England, the *Spectator, Tatler* and their many imitators, and half a hundred newspapers at a time could be read free in the coffee houses. Information can be had from the *Gentleman's Magazine;* from plays, poems and novels by Gay, Pope, Swift, Defoe, Fielding, Goldsmith, Boswell and Johnson. Defoe's *Tour* tells much about all classes in the provinces in 1724; there are Arthur Young's *Tours* (1768-80) and his *Travels in the Kingdom of France,* 2 vols., published in Dublin in 1793. Swift's *Journal to Stella* is precious, as are the *Journals* and *Letters* of Walpole. There is no end to the memoirs, letters and journals: Lord Hervey's *Memoirs of the Court of George II,* Lady Mary Lepel Hervey's, Lord Chesterfield's, John Wesley's; those of Mrs. Delaney, Maria Edgeworth, Fanny Burney (Mme. D'Arblay), and endless others.

In France there are fewer periodicals or great writers but quantities of wonderful memoirs: d'Argenson's (1694-1757) which cover 1725 and 1756; those of dukes like Luynes and Lazun; of Mme. Campan who is painstaking and reliable in matters of court routine and dress, if nothing else; of Mme. de Genlis, etc., never forgetting the usefulness of Voltaire. This would be beyond our powers of assimiliation. Fortunately there arises, especially in France, a series of great writers, all stemming from the period they describe, who have done it for us. These secondary source books, well documented and reliable, include Taine's *Ancien Régime;* Sainte-Beuve's *Causeries du Lundi;* the Goncourts' *Woman of the 18th Century;* Chateaubriand's *Mémoires d'outre-tombe.* Even Michelet is invaluable, as is Lacroix: *Eighteenth Century.*

In the XIX and XX centuries all the XVIIIc. courts and kings and mistresses will be described in quantities of books by later writers such as Pierre de Nolhac: *Le château de Versailles sous Louis XV:* Count Fleury: *Louis XV et les petites maîtresses;* and a great series by the industrious Imbert de Saint-Amand on courts and court ladies.

In England we have precious source material in such books as later editions of Chamberlayne; in James P. Malcolm: *Manners and Customs of London during the Eighteenth Century,* 2 vols., Longmans, Hurst, Rees and Orme, London, 2nd ed., 1810 (book written in 1807); and John Ashton: *Social Life in the Reign of Queen Anne,* Taken from Original Sources, Scribner and Wellford, New York, 1883. All give a wonderful mass of information from contemporary sources about dress, manners and amusements.

Sacheverell Sitwell: *Conversation Pieces* and C. G. Williamson: *English Conversation Pieces,* reproduce beautifully (often in color) and describe the less formal group pictures by Copley, Cotes, Davis, Gainsborough, Hayman, Highmore, Morland, Patch, Stubbs, Zoffany and many others of XVIII and XIXc. I am greatly indebted to both books. Lady Victoria Manners and C. G. Williamson: *John Zoffany,* John Lane, London, 1920; magnificent book. Warwick Wroth: *London Pleasure Gardens of the Eighteenth Century,* Macmillan, London, 1896.

The best biographies of American painters are to be found in the *Dictionary of American Biography,* Scribners, 1931, published under the auspices of the American Council of Learned Societies; from it I have drawn most of my material on Smibert and his successors.

Page. 654. Women's heads and caps: The French Night Cap; Ranelagh Mob, or the Hood from Low Life; Mary Queen of Scots Cap; and the Turban Roll worn around Mecklenburgh Caps, are described in the "History of Costume," *London Chronicle,* 1762, v. X, p. 167 seq. quoted by Malcolm, v. 2, p. 338.

Page 656. "Joseph": Advertisements of stolen goods (liberally quoted by Malcolm, v. 2, Chap. VIII) give names, descriptions and colors of articles of male and female dress of XVIIIc. England.

SOURCES OF OUR ILLUSTRATIONS:

1770. "Oeuvre de Watteau."

1816, 1818-20 Another equipage was a *brouette*, a sedan chair on two wheels, drawn by one chairman: Gillot's *Vinaigrettes ou Brouettes* (Louvre), is produced in Hilaire Belloc: *The Highway and its Vehicles,* Studio, London, 1925.

1862-63. Mme. d'Epinay wears a dark collar of this sort in her portrait by Léotard (Louvre), reproduced in Helen Clergue: *The Salon,* G. P. Putnam's Sons, N. Y., 1907, opp. p. 120. I think I remember one on Julie de Lespinasse, in one of Carmontelle's many drawings at Chantilly.

1871-74. The yellow coats worn by Fersen and his colleagues masquerading as coachmen, at the flight of the royal family, were part of the Condé liveries for which Longprix was highest bidder, at the suppression of privilege in 1789 (G. Lenotre: *The Flight of Marie Antoinette*).

1940. These Sèvres medallions were sold in the booths which cluttered staircases and corridors of Versailles, to the disgust of Marie Antoinette's brother, on his visit. *Benjamin Franklin and His Circle,* Metropolitan Museum of Art, N. Y., 1936, reproduces a great many medallions, designed by Flaxman for Wedgwood, which are invaluable for the information they give on wigs, neckwear and all the new collars appropriate to men of different professions, like Sir Hans Sloane, Dr. Henry Pemberton, the physicist, William Penn, or the elder and younger Pitt.

1997. Breeches held down by criss-cross ties are shown in a caricature of Col. Duff, afterwards Lord Fyfe, rep. in John Ashton: *The Dawn of the XIXth Century in England,* T. Fisher Unwin, London, 1906, p. 252. (This contains many excellent contemporary quotations, though it is not so good as his enchanting *Social Life in the Reign of Queen Anne*).

2021. Karl Mayer Sammlung: *Wiener Porzellan.* This famous collection (illus. cat. in M.M.A.Lib.) belonged to the father of Francis G. Mayer, the photographer of so many museum collections, who made the Kodachromes of the Brunias buttons (Ill. 1946-63), despite their fixed bull's-eye covering of glass.

Page 744. Of many studies on the content of Hogarth's work, I am perhaps most indebted to *The Works of William Hogarth,* 10 vols., George Barrie & Sons, Philadelphia, 1900.

Pages 761-63. Wigs: Kelly and Schwabe: *Hist. Cost.,* p. 201, shows 4 wigs from the *Encyclopédie.* Fig. 89-A, B, *perruque à noeuds;* C, D, the soldier's *perruque à la brigadière;* fig. 90 A, B, the *catogan; C, perruque à deux queues.*

2223. *Sporting Prints and Paintings,* Metropolitan Museum of Art, N. Y., 1937.

The Mills Rise, XIXc.

Source material is too plentiful and too easily available for listing.

Page 796. Claude Blanchard: *Dames du coeur,* éd. du Pré aux clercs, Paris, 1946, shows 17 of the first photographs ever made. Some are of great cocottes like Cora Pearl, and the Goncourts' neighbor and friend, Anna Deslions, who dressed with great elegance and launched styles. There are also actresses and dancers in costume, among them Mogador in male dress; Rigolboche, queen of the can-can; and Alice la Provençale, high-kicking and showing her long white drawers.

Early photographs form only part of the superb illustrations in color, and black and white, of *Un siècle d'Elégance française,* éd. du Chêne, Paris, 1943.

Page 806. *Costumes Parisiens.* The life histories of these early XIXc. fashion magazines can be traced with the help of G. Vicaire: *Manuel de l'amateur des livres du XIXc.* 1801-93; Paris, 1900.

2280. See Appendix reference for page 796. *Dames du coeur.*

2283. Empire dress with hoops: A drawing of an English court dress of 1810 will be found in Norris and Curtis: *Cost. and Fashion,* vol. VI, pl. 31, Dent, London, 1933.

2307. d'Arfeville quotation, from a most useful small book on Scottish dress, badges and war-cries, illustrated by many colored plates of tartans. All editions of *The Scottish Clans and Their Tartans,* W. and A. K. Johnston, Edinburgh, are not as good as the 11th, of 1913, to which I am indebted.

2329-30. Walter Shaw Sparrow: *Henry Alken,* Scribners, N. Y., 1927, is full of useful things like the front and back views of lines of spectators at the finish of Squire Osbaldiston's legendary wager of 200 miles against time, mounted on Tranby.

2440-42, 2627-32, 2676, 2678-81. *Siècle d'Elégance française.*

2444. Blunck: *Nordische Welt.*

2474. Not many of the Metropolitan Museum's wonderful collection of photographs by Hill have as yet been photographed. The Print Room was kind enough to select the Chalmers Family as the next to be done, because of its varied costume. The male portraits show many wonderful cravats, vests and coats. Brady's Civil War photographs are also in the Print Room. As we go to press, I have just discovered that one of their newly acquired early photographs by Braun, shows the Countess of Castiglione holding the identical black and white lace fan in the Museum's collection, shown in our Ill. 2529.

2488. Cooper Union has many of his pen, ink and water color studies of ladies and gentlemen, walking and driving, at balls and operas, in the 40's and 50's. Others are reproduced in *Constantin Guys, The Painter of Victorian Life,* ed. Geoffrey Holme, Studio, London, 1930.

2501-03. From Harry T. Peters: *America on Stone,* Doubleday Doran, 1931. Valuable illustrations of American lithographs.

2589-95. Gothic Revival handiwork: In *Der Bazar, Illustrierte Damen-Zeitung,* on top of my favorite tea-cozy sits a stuffed dog, carrying in his mouth a miniature of his mistress' bead bag. I once had to sit for some time on a green velvet couch-cover, the work of a Victorian needlewoman who was so in love with her really superb technical capacities that she had carried life-size acorns (in full relief, done in real gold thread) from the border onto the top, in lieu of tuft-buttons. One of the most amusing by-products of research for this book was to come across what must have been the source of her design: the set of jewels, furnished by Ball, Black & Co. for Mme. Oviedo's diamond wedding, shown in *Frank Leslie's Illustrated Newspaper,* vol. 8, 1859, p. 363.

2677. Claude Blanchard: *Dames du coeur.*

INDEX

The Index is meant to guide the reader to the elements of costume. To have entered every possible reference to each item would have resulted in an unwieldy, impractical mass. Therefore, an attempt was made to select representative examples of each of the elements. Roman numbers refer to page entries in the text; italic numbers refer to illustrations.